PHILIP'S

STREET ATLAS

West Yorks

Bradford, Halifax, Huddersfield, Keighley, Leeds, Wakefield

First published in 1996 by

Philip's, a division of
Octopus Publishing Group Ltd
2–4 Heron Quays, London E14 4JP
An Hachette Livre UK Company

Fourth edition 2007
First impression 2007
YODA

ISBN-10   0-540-08990-7 (spiral)
ISBN-13   978-0-540-08990-1 (spiral)

© Philip's 2007

Ordnance Survey®

This product includes mapping data licensed
from Ordnance Survey® with the permission of
the Controller of Her Majesty's Stationery Office.
© Crown copyright 2007. All rights reserved.
Licence number 100011710.

Printed and bound in Spain
by Cayfosa-Quebecor

Contents

III   **Key to map symbols**

IV   **Key to map pages**

VI   **Route planning**

VIII   **Administrative and Postcode boundaries**

1   **Street maps** at 3½ inches to 1 mile

201   **Street maps of centres of Bradford, Halifax, Leeds and Wakefield** at 7 inches to 1 mile

217   **Index** of towns and villages

220   **Index** of streets, hospitals, industrial estates, railway stations, schools, shopping centres, universities and places of interest

Digital Data

The exceptionally high-quality mapping found in this atlas is available as digital data in TIFF format, which is easily convertible to other bitmapped (raster) image formats.

The index is also available in digital form as a standard database table. It contains all the details found in the printed index together with the National Grid reference for the map square in which each entry is named.

For further information and to discuss your requirements, please contact james.mann@philips-maps.co.uk

Symbol	Description
22a	**Motorway** with junction number
	Primary route – dual/single carriageway
	A road – dual/single carriageway
	B road – dual/single carriageway
	Minor road – dual/single carriageway
	Other minor road – dual/single carriageway
	Road under construction
	Tunnel, covered road
	Rural track, private road or narrow road in urban area
	Gate or obstruction to traffic (restrictions may not apply at all times or to all vehicles)
	Path, bridleway, byway open to all traffic, road used as a public path
	Pedestrianised area
DY7	**Postcode boundaries**
	County and unitary authority boundaries
	Railway, tunnel, railway under construction
	Tramway, tramway under construction
	Miniature railway
Walsall	**Railway station**
	Private railway station
South Shields	**Metro station**
	Tram stop, tram stop under construction
	Bus, coach station

Symbol	Description
♦	**Ambulance station**
♦	**Coastguard station**
♦	**Fire station**
♦	**Police station**
+	**Accident and Emergency entrance to hospital**
H	**Hospital**
+	**Place of worship**
i	**Information Centre** (open all year)
	Shopping Centre
P P&R	**Parking, Park and Ride**
PO	**Post Office**
	Camping site, caravan site
	Golf course, picnic site
Prim Sch	**Important buildings, schools, colleges, universities and hospitals**
	Built up area
	Woods
River Medway	**Water name**
	River, weir, stream
	Canal, lock, tunnel
	Water
	Tidal water
Church	**Non-Roman antiquity**
ROMAN FORT	**Roman antiquity**
87 237	**Adjoining page indicators and overlap bands** The colour of the arrow and the band indicates the scale of the adjoining or overlapping page (see scales below)

Abbr	Full	Abbr	Full	Abbr	Full
Acad	**Academy**	Inst	**Institute**	Recn Gd	**Recreation Ground**
Allot Gdns	**Allotments**	Ct	**Law Court**		
Cemy	**Cemetery**	L Ctr	**Leisure Centre**	Resr	**Reservoir**
C Ctr	**Civic Centre**	LC	**Level Crossing**	Ret Pk	**Retail Park**
CH	**Club House**	Liby	**Library**	Sch	**School**
Coll	**College**	Mkt	**Market**	Sh Ctr	**Shopping Centre**
Crem	**Crematorium**	Meml	**Memorial**	TH	**Town Hall/House**
Ent	**Enterprise**	Mon	**Monument**	Trad Est	**Trading Estate**
Ex H	**Exhibition Hall**	Mus	**Museum**	Univ	**University**
Ind Est	**Industrial Estate**	Obsy	**Observatory**	W Twr	**Water Tower**
IRB Sta	**Inshore Rescue Boat Station**	Pal	**Royal Palace**	Wks	**Works**
		PH	**Public House**	YH	**Youth Hostel**

The small numbers around the edges of the maps identify the 1 kilometre National Grid lines

The dark grey border on the inside edge of some pages indicates that the mapping does not continue onto the adjacent page

Enlarged mapping only

Symbol	Description
	Railway or bus station building
	Place of interest
	Parkland

The scale of the maps on the pages numbered in blue is 5.52 cm to 1 km • 3½ inches to 1 mile • 1: 18103

0	¼	½	¾	1 mile
0	250m	500m	750m 1 kilometre	

The scale of the maps on pages numbered in red is 11.04 cm to 1 km • 7 inches to 1 mile • 1: 9051

0	220 yards	440 yards	660 yards	½ mile
0	125m	250m	375m ½ kilometre	

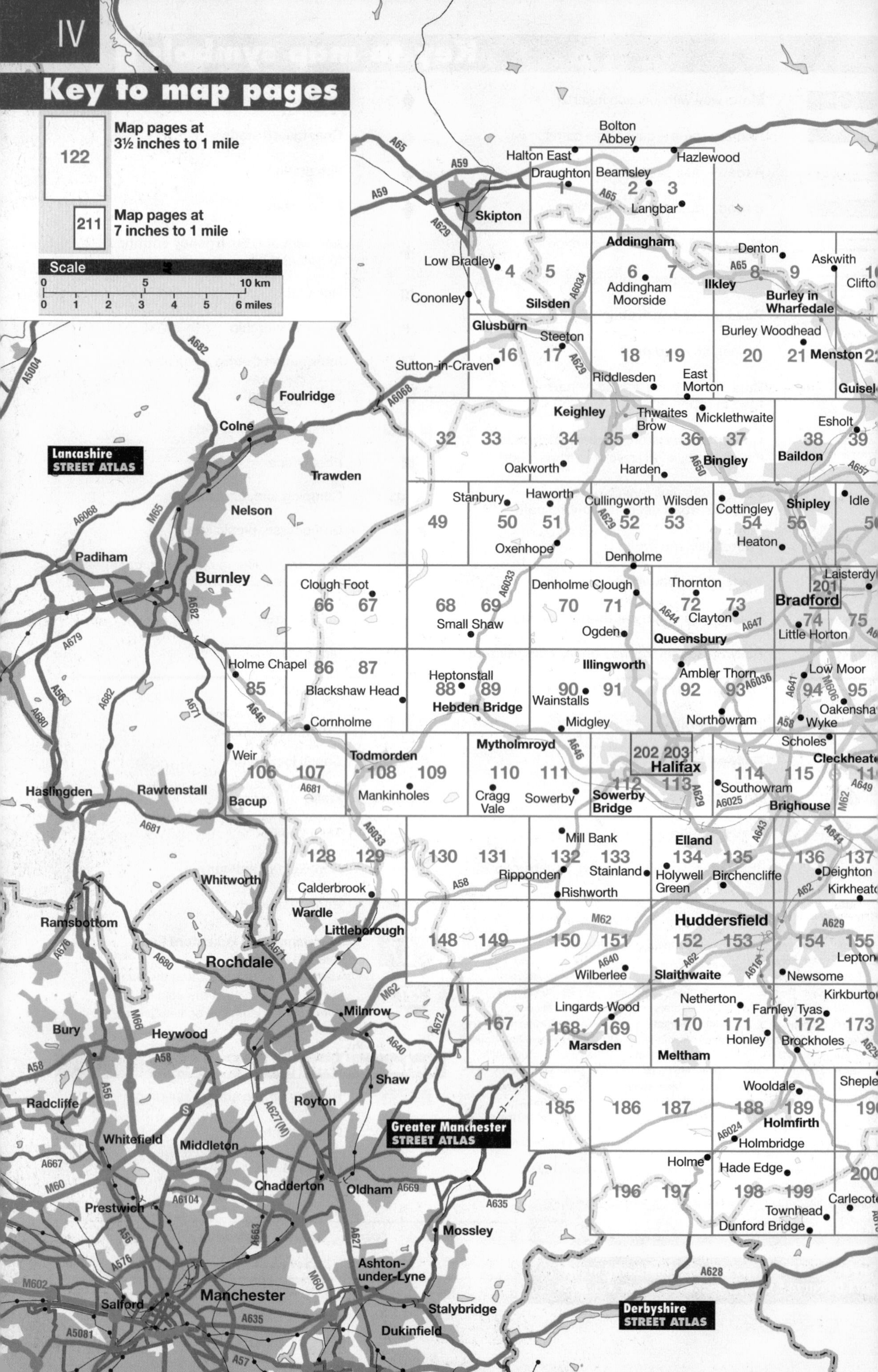

Key to map pages

Map pages at
3½ inches to 1 mile

122

Map pages at
7 inches to 1 mile

211

Scale

0 _____ 5 _____ 10 km

0 — 1 — 2 — 3 — 4 — 5 — 6 miles

Bolton Abbey

Halton East
Draughton
Beamsley
Hazlewood

Skipton

Langbar

1 **2** **3**

Addingham

Denton
Askwith

Low Bradley
Ilkley
Clifto

4 **5** **6** **7** **8** **9** **10**

Cononley
Addingham Moorside
Burley in Wharfedale

Silsden

Glusburn
Steeton
Burley Woodhead

Sutton-in-Craven
16 **17** **18** **19** **20** **21** Menston

Riddlesden
East Morton
Guisel

Foulridge

Colne
Keighley
Thwaites Brow
Micklethwaite
Esholt

32 **33** **34** **35** **36** **37** **38** **39**

Trawden
Oakworth
Harden
Bingley
Baildon

Lancashire
STREET ATLAS

Nelson
Stanbury
Haworth
Cullingworth
Wilsden
Cottingley
Shipley
Idle

Padiham
49 **50** **51** **52** **53** **54** **55** **5**

Oxenhope
Denholme
Heaton

Burnley
Clough Foot
Denholme Clough
Thornton
Laisterdy

201

66 **67** **68** **69** **70** **71** **72** **73** Bradford

Small Shaw
Ogden
Clayton
74 **75**

Queensbury
Little Horton

Holme Chapel
86 **87**
Illingworth
Ambler Thorn
Low Moor

Heptonstall
85
88 **89** **90** **91** **92** **93** **94** **95**

Blackshaw Head
Wainstalls
Northowram
Oakensha

Cornholme
Hebden Bridge
Midgley
Wyke

Scholes

Weir
Mytholmroyd
202 203
Cleckheate

Todmorden
112 Halifax
114 **115** **11**

106 **107** **108** **109** **110** **111** **113**
Southowram

Bacup
Mankinholes
Cragg Vale
Sowerby
Sowerby Bridge
Brighouse

Haslingden
Rawtenstall
Mill Bank
Elland

Whitworth
128 **129** **130** **131** **132** **133** **134** **135** **136** **137**

Calderbrook
Ripponden
Stainland
Holywell Green
Birchencliffe
Deighton

Rishworth
Kirkheato

Wardle
Ramsbottom
Huddersfield

Littleborough
148 **149** **150** **151** **152** **153** **154** **155**

Rochdale
Wilberlee
Slaithwaite
Lepton

Milnrow
Newsome

Bury
Heywood
Lingards Wood
Netherton
Kirkburto

167 **168** **169** **170** **171** **172** **173**
Farnley Tyas

Marsden
Honley
Brockholes

Shaw
Meltham

Radcliffe
Royton
Wooldale
Sheple

185 **186** **187** **188** **189** **19**

Whitefield
Middleton
Holmfirth

Greater Manchester
STREET ATLAS
Holmbridge

Prestwich
Chadderton
Oldham
Holme
Hade Edge
200

196 **197** **198** **199** Carlecote

Mossley
Townhead

Dunford Bridge

Salford
Manchester

Ashton-under-Lyne

Stalybridge
Derbyshire
STREET ATLAS

Dukinfield

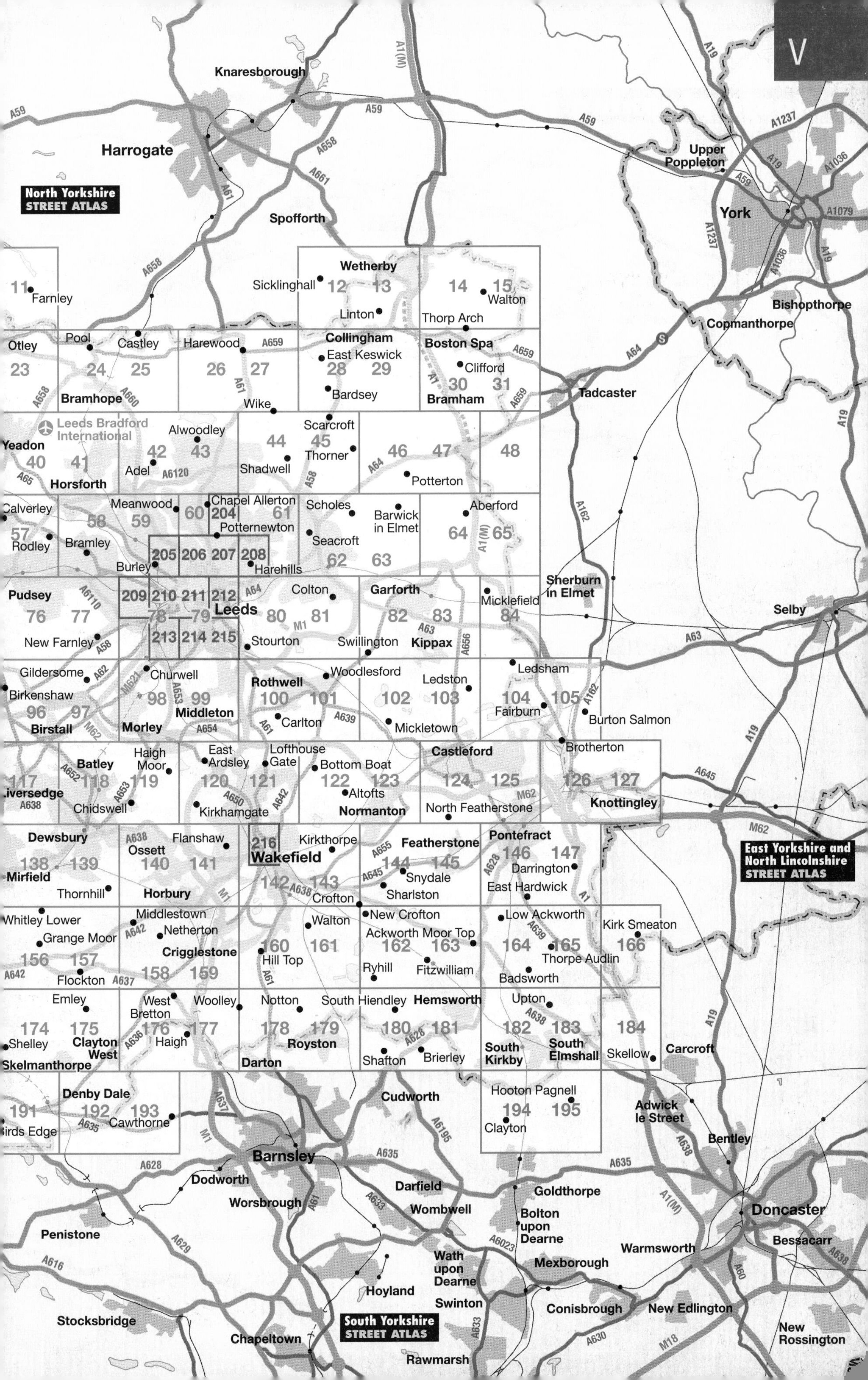
V
Knaresborough
Harrogate
North Yorkshire STREET ATLAS
Spofforth
Upper Poppleton
York
Bishopthorpe
Copmanthorpe
Tadcaster
Wetherby
Sicklinghall
Linton
Walton
Thorp Arch
Boston Spa
Clifford
Bramham
Collingham
East Keswick
Bardsey
Harewood
Wike
Otley
Pool
Castley
Bramhope
Farnley
Leeds Bradford International
Yeadon
Horsforth
Adel
Alwoodley
Shadwell
Scarcroft
Thorner
Potterton
Calverley
Rodley
Bramley
Meanwood
Chapel Allerton
Potternewton
Scholes
Seacroft
Barwick in Elmet
Aberford
Burley
Harehills
Pudsey
New Farnley
Leeds
Colton
Stourton
Garforth
Swillington
Kippax
Micklefield
Sherburn in Elmet
Selby
Gildersome
Birkenshaw
Birstall
Churwell
Morley
Middleton
Rothwell
Carlton
Woodlesford
Mickletown
Ledston
Ledsham
Fairburn
Burton Salmon
Brotherton
Batley
Haigh Moor
East Ardsley
Lofthouse Gate
Bottom Boat
Altofts
Normanton
Castleford
North Featherstone
Knottingley
Liversedge
Chidswell
Kirkhamgate
Dewsbury
Ossett
Flanshaw
Wakefield
Kirkthorpe
Featherstone
Pontefract
Darrington
East Hardwick
Mirfield
Thornhill
Horbury
Crofton
Snydale
Sharlston
East Yorkshire and North Lincolnshire STREET ATLAS
Whitley Lower
Grange Moor
Middlestown
Netherton
Crigglestone
Walton
New Crofton
Ackworth Moor Top
Low Ackworth
Kirk Smeaton
Hill Top
Ryhill
Fitzwilliam
Thorpe Audlin
Badsworth
Flockton
Emley
West Bretton
Woolley
Notton
South Hiendley
Hemsworth
Upton
Shelley
Clayton West
Skelmanthorpe
Haigh
Royston
Darton
Shafton
Brierley
South Kirkby
South Elmshall
Skellow
Carcroft
Denby Dale
Cawthorne
Birds Edge
Cudworth
Hooton Pagnell
Clayton
Adwick le Street
Bentley
Barnsley
Dodworth
Worsbrough
Darfield
Wombwell
Goldthorpe
Bolton upon Dearne
Doncaster
Bessacarr
Warmsworth
Penistone
Wath upon Dearne
Mexborough
Hoyland
Swinton
Conisbrough
New Edlington
Stocksbridge
South Yorkshire STREET ATLAS
Chapeltown
Rawmarsh
New Rossington

Route planning

Scale
0
5
10 km
0
1
2
3
4
5
6 miles
Skipton
Keighley
Burnley
Bradford
Halifax
Rochdale
Bury
Oldham
Huddersfield
Ashton-under-Lyne
MANCHESTER
Trafford Park
COLNE
NELSON
ACCRINGTON
RAWTENSTALL
HEYWOOD
ROYTON
PRESTWICH
SALFORD
STALYBRIDGE
BRIGHOUSE
HOLMFIRTH
ILKLEY
BINGLEY
SHIPLEY
Gargrave
Barnoldswick
Earby
Glusburn
Silsden
Addingham
Burley in Wharfedale
Menston
Baildon
Foulridge
Barrowford
Trawden
Brierfield
Padiham
Haworth
Oxenhope
Queensbury
Illingworth
Hebden Bridge
Mytholmroyd
Todmorden
Bacup
Whitworth
Littleborough
Wardle
Milnrow
Sowerby Bridge
Elland
Slaithwaite
Marsden
Meltham
Shaw
Middleton
Chadderton
Whitefield
Radcliffe
Mossley
Dukinfield
Droylsden
Failsworth
Eccles
Tintwistle
Crowden
Hadfield
Upper Barden Res.
Lower Barden Res.
Walshaw Dean Res.
Widdop Res.
Hollingworth Lake
Dove Stone Res.
PENDLE HILL
BOULSWORTH HILL
THIEVELEY PIKE
BLACK HILL
BLEAKLOW HILL
Y
o
r
k
W
e

VII
Burnt Yates
Ripley
Brearton
Nidd
Ferrensby
Farnham
Arkendale
Little Ouseburn
Great Ouseburn
on-Ouse
Birstwith
Clint
Scotton
Coneythorpe
Allerton Mauleverer
Thorpe Underwood
Newton on Ouse
Shipton
Wigginton
Haxby
Darley
Hampsthwaite
Killinghall
Scriven
Flaxby
Whixley
Nun Monkton
Green Hammerton
Beningbrough
Earswick
Kettlesing Bottom
New Park
Starbeck
Knaresborough
Hopperton
Moor Monkton
Overton
Skelton
Kettlesing Head
Harrogate
Forest Lane Head
Woodlands
Goldsborough
Kirk Hammerton
Nether Poppleton
Upper Poppleton
Huntington
New Earswick
Rawcliffe
Cattal
Bland Hill
Beckwithshaw
Harlow Hill
Oatlands
Walshford
Hunsingore
Hessay
Clifton
Rossett Green
Little Ribston
Tockwith
Knapton
York
Heworth
Osbaldwick
Brackenthwaite
Pannal
Follifoot
North Deighton
Cowthorpe
Long Marston
Rufforth
Holgate
Acomb
Spacey Houses
Spofforth
Bickerton
Hutton Wandesley
Nunthorpe
Lindley Green
North Rigton
Kirk Deighton
Bilton in Ainsty
Woodthorpe
Braythorn
Kirkby Overflow
Sicklinghall
Askham Bryan
Fulford
Farnley
Stainburn
Wetherby
Walton
Angram
Askham Richard
Huby
Weeton
Linton
Wighill
Healaugh
Bishopthorpe
Leathley
Netherby
Chapel Hill
Collingham
Bilbrough
Copmanthorpe
Dunkeswick
Thorp Arch
Catterton
York West Services
Otley
Pool
Castley
Harewood
Boston Spa
Acaster Malbis
Naburn
Arthington
Weardley
East Keswick
Clifford
Newton Kyme
Colton
Deighton
Bramhope
Old Bramhope
Bardsey
East Rigton
Bramham
Tadcaster
Appleton Roebuck
Escrick
Eccup
Leeds Bradford International
Cookridge
Wike
Scarcroft
Bolton Percy
Acaster Selby
Rawdon
Alwoodley
Scarcroft Hill
Stutton
Kirkby Wharfe
Holme Green
Tinshill
Holt Park
Adel
Moor Allerton
Shadwell
Thorner
Ulleskelf
Stillingfleet
Horsforth
Roundhay
Potterton
Towton
Ryther
Kelfield
Meanwood
Chapel Allerton
Wellington Hill
Barwick in Elmet
Church Fenton
Cawood
Riccall
Rodley
Hawksworth
Headingley
Potternewton
Scholes
Aberford
Saxton
Farsley
Bramley
Kirkstall
Woodhouse
Seacroft
Barkston
Biggin
Wistow
Stanningley
Burley
Harehills
Whitkirk
Manston
Sherburn in Elmet
Little Fenton
Barlby
Swinnow Moor
Armley
Sheepscar
Garforth
Old Micklefield
Micklefield Garden Village
Pudsey
Leeds
Halton
Colton
Newthorpe
Selby
Wortley
Holbeck
New Micklefield
Thorpe Willoughby
Farnley
Hunslet
South Milford
Hambleton
Wood
New Farnley
Beeston
Ledston Luck
Monk Fryston
Brayton
Tong
Swillington
Kippax
Lumby
Drighlington
Churwell
Rothwell
Woodlesford
Great Preston
Ledsham
Adwalton
Gildersome
Rothwell Haigh
Ledston
Hillam
Gateforth
Burn
Bruntcliffe
Rothwell
Robin Hood
Oulton
Allerton Bywater
Fairburn
Burton Salmon
West Haddlesey
Birstall
Morley
Middleton
Carlton
Mickletown
New Fryston
Birkin
Chapel Haddlesey
Tingley
East Ardsley
Methley
Brotherton
Batley
Woodkirk
Lofthouse
Castleford
Ferrybridge
Beal
Kellington
Temple Hirst
Hirst Courtney
Heaton
Haigh Moor
Stanley
Bottom Boat
Sutton
Mount Pleasant
Chidswell
Kirkhamgate
Outwood
Altofts
Whitwood
Kellingley
Eggborough
Hensall
Heckmondwike
Gawthorpe
Wrenthorpe
Normanton
North Featherstone
Knottingley
Dewsbury
Dewsbury Moor
Earlsheaton
Flanshaw
Wakefield
Ackton
Woodhouse
Pontefract
Ferrybridge Services
High Eggborough
Cridling Stubbs
Gowdall
Snaith
Ossett
Lupset
Warmfield
Featherstone
Chequerfield
Whitley
Great Heck
Pollington
Thornhill
Sharlston Common
Snydale
Darrington
Womersley
Balne
Thornhill Lees
Horbury
Sandal Magna
Sharlston
West Hardwick
Purston Jaglin
East Hardwick
Aire and Calder Navigation
Thornhill Edge
Middlestown
Crofton
Foulby
High Ackworth
Wentbridge
Little Smeaton
Walden Stubbs
Sykehouse
Grange Moor
Overton
Netherton
Durkar
Crigglestone
Walton
Wragby
Low Ackworth
Kirk Smeaton
Fenwick
Midgley
Great Cliff
Hall Green
Hill Top
Wintersett
Ryhill
Fitzwilliam
Ackworth Moor Top
Thorpe Audlin
Barnsdale Bar Services
Norton
Fosterhouses
Flockton
West Bretton
Woolley Edge Services
Kinsley
Havercroft
Badsworth
Upton
Wrangbrook
Campsall
Moss
Emley
Woolley
South Hiendley
Istoneville
Askern
Sutton
Fishlake
Roydhouse
Notton
Felkirk
Hemsworth
North Elmsall
Skelbrooke
Burghwallis
Haywood
Braithwaite
Shelley
Clayton West
Royston
Moorthorpe
South Elmsall
Owston
Thorpe in Balne
Kirk Bramwith
High Hoyland
Haigh
Shafton
Brierley
South Kirkby
Carcroft
Skelmanthorpe
Lower Cumberworth
Kexbrough
Darton
Staincross
Carlton
Grimethorpe
Hooton Pagnell
Hampole
Skellow
Adwick le Street
Barnby Dun
Denby Dale
Upper Cumberworth
Cawthorne
Barugh
Monk Bretton
Cudworth
Clayton
Almholme
Kirk Sandall
Tivy Dale
Gawber
Barnsley
Great Houghton
Brodsworth
Woodlands
Toll Bar
Upper Denby
Silkstone
Ardsley
Thurnscoe
Thurnscoe East
Arksey
Edenthorpe
Noblethorpe
Little Houghton
Bentley
Armthorpe
Hoylandswaine
Dodworth
Kendray
Hickleton
Marr
Scawsby
Wheatley
Nutwell
Worsbrough Common
Darfield
Billingley
Goldthorpe
Barnburgh
Newton
Intake
Doncaster
Thurlstone
Silkstone Common
Wombwell
Bolton upon Dearne
Sprotbrough
Hyde Park
Cantley
Penistone
Spring Vale
Hood Green
Worsbrough
Broomhill
Harlington
High Melton
Bessacarr
Cubley
Oxspring
Crane Moor
Platts Common
Birdwell
Brampton
Adwick upon Dearne
Cadeby
Balby
Thurgoland
Jump
Hoyland
Wath upon Dearne
Mexborough
Snowden Hill
Pilley
Tankersley
Elsecar
Dearne
Warmsworth
Wortley
Swinton
Old Denaby
Denaby Main
New Edlington
Loversall
Rossington
Midhopestones
Harley
Conisbrough
Stocksbridge
Howbrook
Deepcar
High Green
Wentworth
Upper Haugh
Kilnhurst
Old Edlington
New Rossington
Bolsterstone
Ewden Village
Chapeltown
Nether Haugh
Rawmarsh
Hooton Roberts
Clifton
Wadworth
Wigtwizzle
Wharncliffe Wood
Burncross
Thorpe Hesley
Thrybergh
Ravenfield

Major administrative and Postcode boundaries

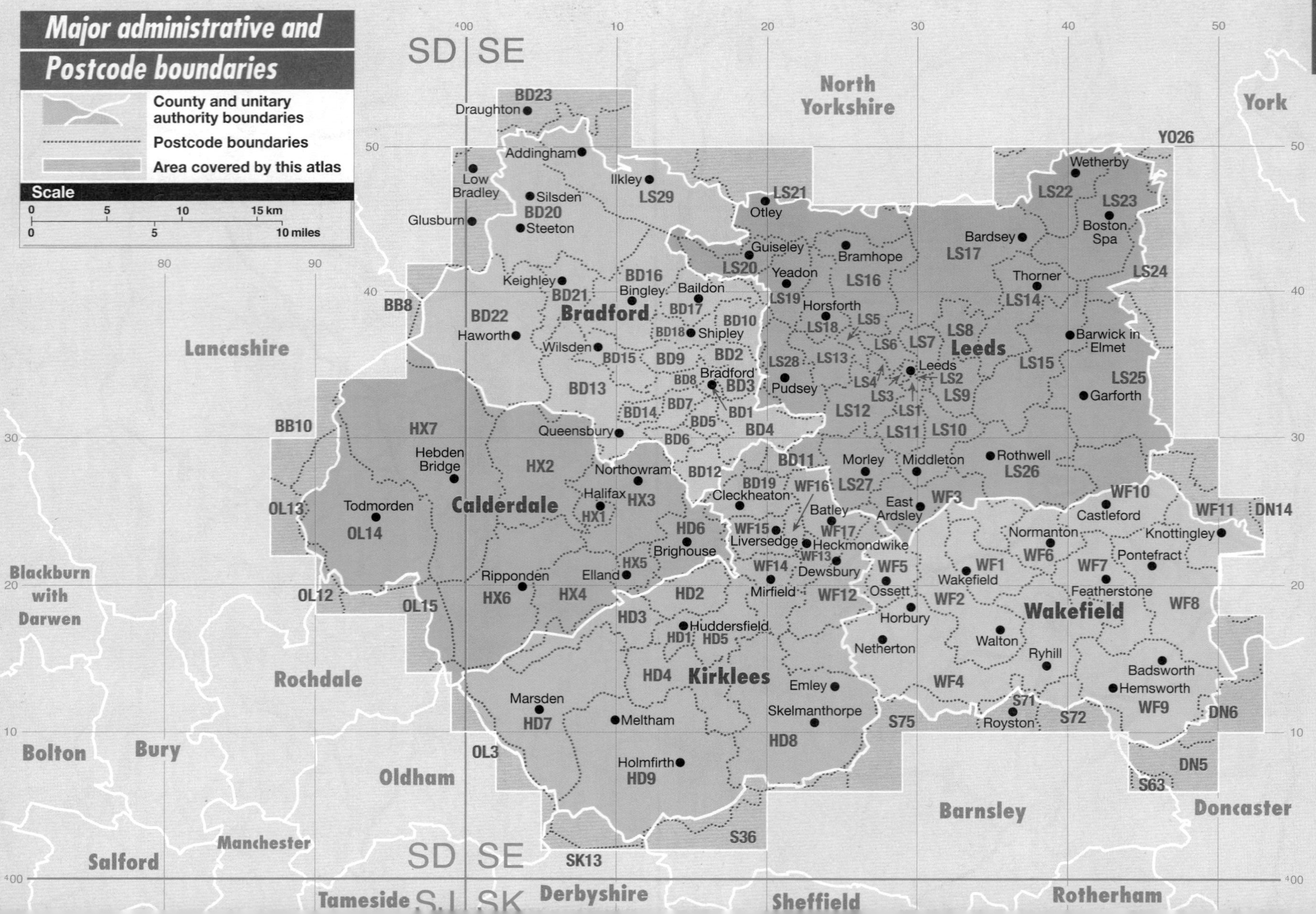
County and unitary authority boundaries
Postcode boundaries
Area covered by this atlas
Scale
0 5 10 15 km
0 5 10 miles
SD | SE
SD SE
SJ SK
North Yorkshire
York
Lancashire
Blackburn with Darwen
Rochdale
Bolton
Bury
Oldham
Salford
Manchester
Tameside
Derbyshire
Sheffield
Barnsley
Rotherham
Doncaster
Bradford
Leeds
Calderdale
Kirklees
Wakefield
Draughton
Addingham
Low Bradley
Glusburn
Silsden
Steeton
Ilkley
Otley
Guiseley
Yeadon
Bramhope
Keighley
Bingley
Baildon
Shipley
Haworth
Wilsden
Queensbury
Bradford
Horsforth
Pudsey
Leeds
Bardsey
Wetherby
Boston Spa
Thorner
Barwick in Elmet
Garforth
Morley
Middleton
Rothwell
East Ardsley
Hebden Bridge
Todmorden
Northowram
Halifax
Cleckheaton
Batley
Liversedge
Heckmondwike
Dewsbury
Brighouse
Elland
Ripponden
Mirfield
Ossett
Horbury
Wakefield
Normanton
Castleford
Knottingley
Pontefract
Featherstone
Huddersfield
Netherton
Walton
Ryhill
Badsworth
Hemsworth
Emley
Skelmanthorpe
Royston
Marsden
Meltham
Holmfirth
BD23
BD20
LS29
LS21
LS20
LS19
BD16
BD21
BD22
BD17
BD10
BD18
BD15
BD9
BD2
BD13
BD8
BD3
BD7
BD14
BD1
BD5
BD6
BD4
BD12
BD11
BD19
BB8
BB10
LS22
LS23
LS24
LS17
LS16
LS14
LS15
LS25
LS18
LS5
LS6
LS7
LS8
LS28
LS13
LS4
LS3
LS2
LS1
LS9
LS12
LS11
LS10
LS26
LS27
YO26
HX7
HX2
HX3
HX1
HX5
HX6
HX4
HD6
HD2
HD3
HD1
HD5
HD4
HD7
HD8
HD9
OL13
OL14
OL12
OL15
OL3
WF16
WF15
WF17
WF13
WF14
WF12
WF5
WF3
WF10
WF11
WF1
WF6
WF7
WF2
WF8
WF4
WF9
DN14
DN6
DN5
S63
S71
S72
S75
S36
SK13

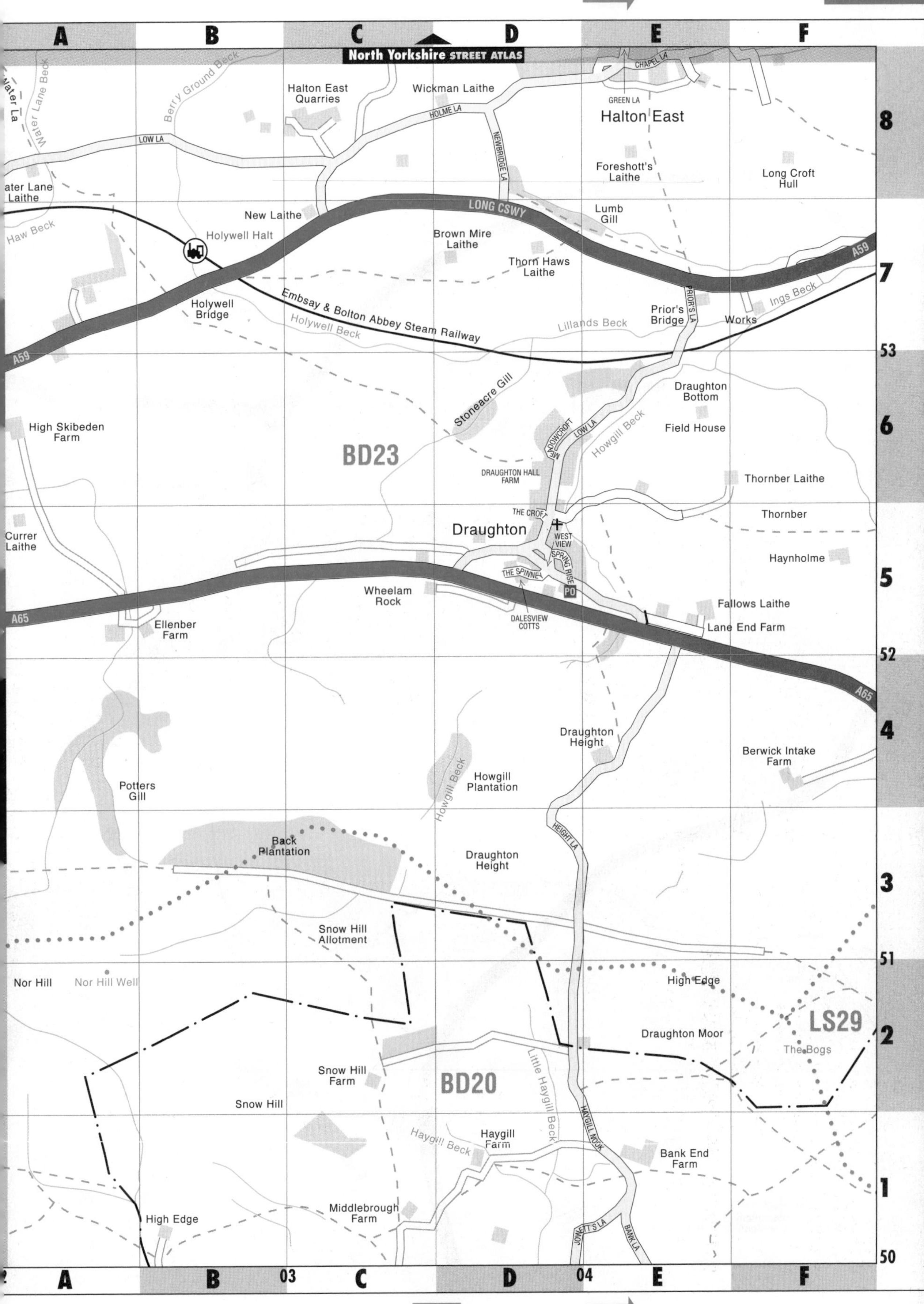

North Yorkshire STREET ATLAS

A B C D E F

Water La

Water Lane Laithe

Berry Ground Beck

Halton East Quarries

HOLME LA

Wickman Laithe

CHAPEL LA

GREEN LA

Halton East

Foreshott's Laithe

Long Croft Hull

8

LOW LA

New Laithe

NEWBRIDGE LA

LONG CSWY

Lumb Gill

Holywell Halt

Brown Mire Laithe

Thorn Haws Laithe

A59

7

Holywell Bridge

Haw Beck

Embsay & Bolton Abbey Steam Railway

Holywell Beck

Lillands Beck

PRIOR'S LA

Prior's Bridge

Works

Ings Beck

53

A59

Stoneacre Gill

BD23

MKT.WINDCROFT

LOW LA

Howgill Beck

Draughton Bottom

Field House

6

High Skibeden Farm

DRAUGHTON HALL FARM

THE CROFT

Thornber Laithe

Thornber

Currer Laithe

Draughton

WEST VIEW

SPRING RISE

Haynholme

5

THE SPINNEL

PO

Wheelam Rock

DALESVIEW COTTS

Fallows Laithe

A65

Ellenber Farm

Lane End Farm

52

Draughton Height

Berwick Intake Farm

A65

4

Potters Gill

Howgill Beck

Howgill Plantation

HEIGHT LA

Back Plantation

Draughton Height

3

Nor Hill

Nor Hill Well

Snow Hill Allotment

High Edge

51

LS29

Draughton Moor

The Bogs

2

Snow Hill Farm

BD20

Little Haygill Beck

HAYGILL NECK

Snow Hill

Haygill Beck

Haygill Farm

Bank End Farm

1

High Edge

Middlebrough Farm

JOWETT'S LA

BANK LA

50

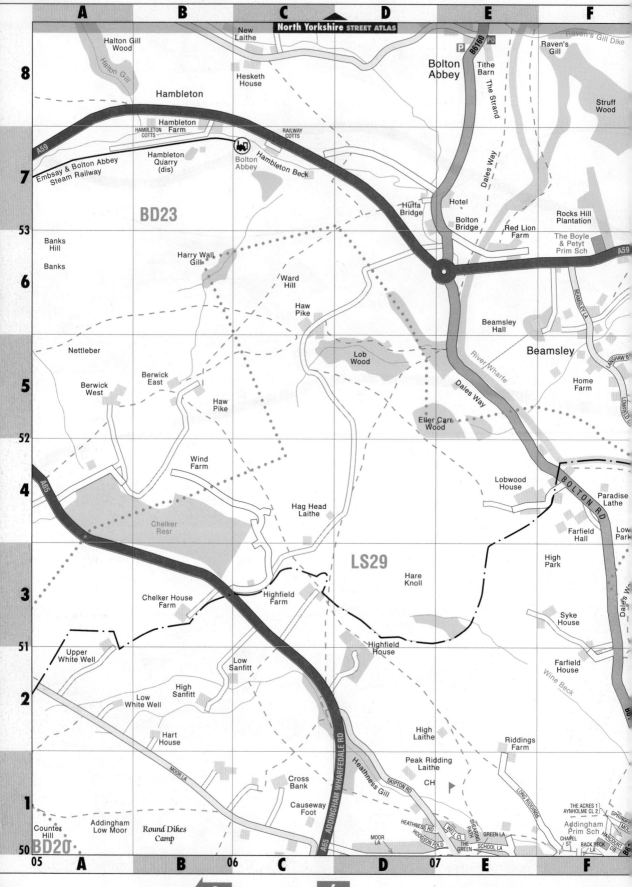

North Yorkshire STREET ATLAS
A B C D E F
8 7 53 6 5 52 4 3 51 2 1 50
05 06 07
Halton Gill Wood
Halton Gill
New Laithe
Hesketh House
Bolton Abbey
Tithe Barn
The Strand
Raven's Gill Dike
Raven's Gill
Struff Wood
Hambleton
Hambleton Farm
HAMBLETON COTTS
RAILWAY COTTS
A59
Hambleton Quarry (dis)
Bolton Abbey
Hambleton Beck
Embsay & Bolton Abbey Steam Railway
B6160
Dales Way
Hotel
Huffa Bridge
Bolton Bridge
Red Lion Farm
Rocks Hill Plantation
The Boyle & Petyt Prim Sch
BD23
Banks Hill
Banks
Harry Wall Gill
Ward Hill
Haw Pike
Beamsley Hall
BEAMSLEY LA
Beamsley
Nettleber
Lob Wood
River Wharfe
Berwick West
Berwick East
Haw Pike
Home Farm
Eller Carr Wood
Wind Farm
Lobwood House
BOLTON RD
Paradise Lathe
Chelker Resr
Hag Head Laithe
Farfield Hall
A65
LS29
High Park
Hare Knoll
Chelker House Farm
Highfield Farm
Syke House
Upper White Well
Highfield House
Farfield House
Wine Beck
Low Sanfitt
High Sanfitt
Low White Well
Hart House
High Laithe
Riddings Farm
ADDINGHAM WHARFEDALE RD
Heathness Gill
Peak Ridding Laithe
MOOR LA
Cross Bank
SKIPTON RD
CH
LONG RIDDINGS
Causeway Foot
THE ACRES 1
AYNHOLME CL 2
Counter Hill
Addingham Low Moor
Round Dikes Camp
HEATHNESS RD
HODGSON FOLD
WELL CL
SHEARING PATH
GREEN LA
THE GREEN
SCHOOL LA
Addingham Prim Sch
CHAPEL ST
BACK BECK LA
HARCOURT DR
BD20

1

6

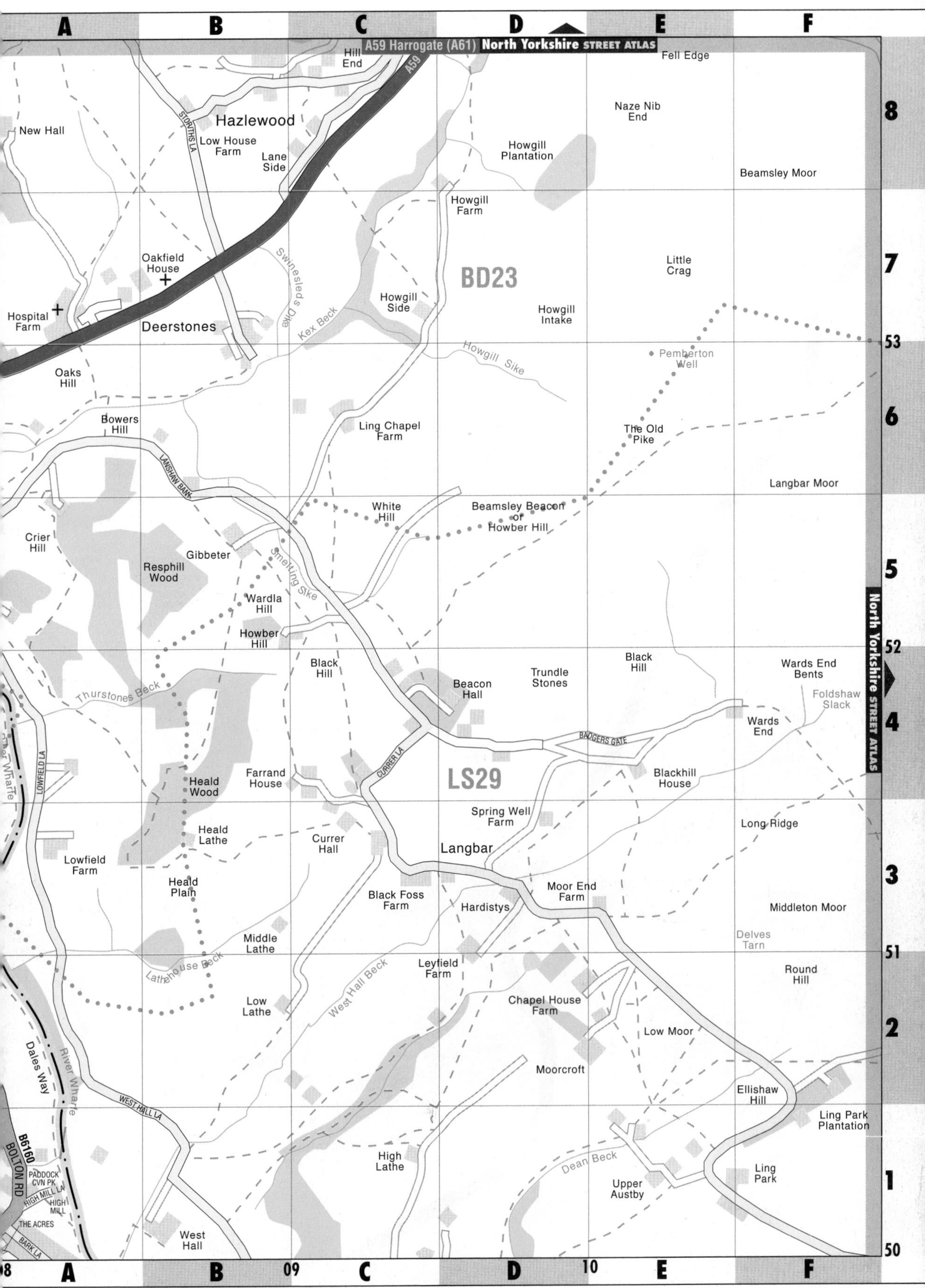

A59 Harrogate (A61) **North Yorkshire** STREET ATLAS

New Hall

Hazlewood

Low House Farm

Lane Side

Hill End

Howgill Plantation

Fell Edge

Naze Nib End

Beamsley Moor

Howgill Farm

BD23

Oakfield House

Little Crag

Hospital Farm

Deerstones

Howgill Side

Howgill Intake

Howgill Sike

Pemberton Well

53

Oaks Hill

Bowers Hill

Ling Chapel Farm

The Old Pike

6

Langbar Moor

Crier Hill

Gibbeter

White Hill

Beamsley Beacon or Howber Hill

Resphill Wood

Wardla Hill

5

Howber Hill

Black Hill

52

Black Hill

Wards End Bents

Foldshaw Slack

Farrand House

Currer La

Beacon Hall

Trundle Stones

Wards End

4

Heald Wood

LS29

Blackhill House

Long Ridge

Heald Lathe

Currer Hall

Spring Well Farm

Lowfield Farm

Langbar

Moor End Farm

Middleton Moor

Heald Plain

Black Foss Farm

Hardistys

Delves Tarn

51

Middle Lathe

Leyfield Farm

Round Hill

Low Lathe

West Hall Beck

Chapel House Farm

Low Moor

2

Dales Way

Moorcroft

Ellishaw Hill

Ling Park Plantation

B6160 BOLTON RD

WEST MILL LA

High Lathe

Dean Beck

Upper Austby

Ling Park

1

PADDOCK CVN PK

HIGH MILL LA HIGH MILL

THE ACRES

BARK LA

West Hall

50

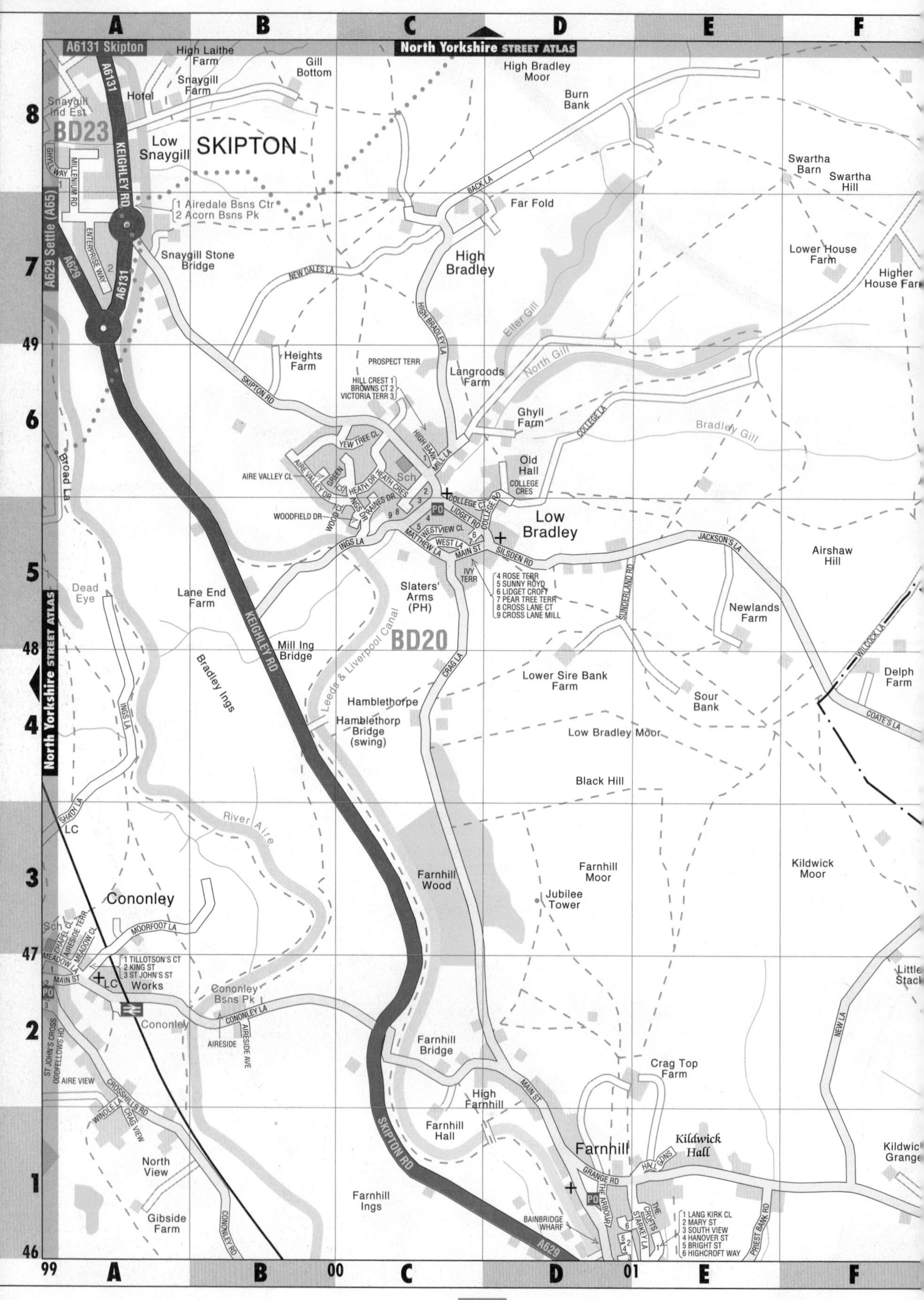

A   B   C   D   E   F

8

BD23

A6131 Skipton

High Laithe Farm

Gill Bottom

High Bradley Moor

Burn Bank

Swartha Barn

Swartha Hill

Hotel

Snaygill Farm

Low Snaygill

SKIPTON

Snaygill Ind Est

Far Fold

Back La

Lower House Farm

Higher House Farm

1 Airedale Bsns Ctr
2 Acorn Bsns Pk

Snaygill Stone Bridge

New Dales La

High Bradley

7

49

A629 Settle (A65)

Enterprise Way

Millennium Way

Ghyll Way

Keighley Rd

A6131

A629

Heights Farm

Prospect Terr

Hill Crest 1
Browns Ct 2
Victoria Terr 3

Langroods Farm

Ghyll Farm

Elter Gill

North Gill

College La

Bradley Gill

6

Skipton Rd

Yew Tree Cl

Aire Valley Cl

Aire Valley Dr

Heath Dr

Sch

High Bank

Mill La

Old Hall

College Cres

5

Dead Eye

Broad La

Lane End Farm

Bradley Ings

Woodfield Dr

Wood St

Symnes Dr

Green

Ings La

Matthew La

West La

Westview Cl

Main St

Ivy Terr

College Cl

College Rd

PO

Silsden Rd

Low Bradley

Jackson's La

Sunderland Rd

Airshaw Hill

Newlands Farm

48

BD20

Slaters' Arms (PH)

4 ROSE TERR
5 SUNNY ROYD
6 LIDGET CROFT
7 PEAR TREE TERR
8 CROSS LANE CT
9 CROSS LANE MILL

Crag La

4

North Yorkshire STREET ATLAS

Ings La

Shdt La

LC

Mill Ing Bridge

Leeds & Liverpool Canal

Hamblethorpe

Hamblethorp Bridge (swing)

Lower Sire Bank Farm

Sour Bank

Low Bradley Moor

Black Hill

Coate's La

Wilcock La

Delph Farm

3

Cononley

Sch

Chapel Cl

Aireside Terr

Meadow Cl

Moorfoot La

River Aire

Farnhill Wood

Jubilee Tower

Farnhill Moor

Kildwick Moor

47

Meadow Cl

Main St

PO

1 TILLOTSON'S CT
2 KING ST
3 ST JOHN'S ST

LC

Works

Cononley Bsns Pk

2

Cononley La

Aireside Ave

Aireside

Cononley

Farnhill Bridge

Main St

Crag Top Farm

New La

Little Stack

1

St John's Cross

Oddfellows Ho

PO

Aire View

Crosshills Rd

Crag View

Windle La

Cononley Rd

North View

Skipton Rd

High Farnhill

Farnhill Hall

Grange Rd

Hall Gdns

Farnhill

Kildwick Hall

Kildwick Grange

46

Gibside Farm

Farnhill Ings

Bainbridge Wharf

A629

The Abbotts

The Crofts

Starkey La

1 LANG KIRK CL
2 MARY ST
3 SOUTH VIEW
4 HANOVER ST
5 BRIGHT ST
6 HIGHCROFT WAY

Priest Bank Rd

99   A   B   00   C   D   01   E   F

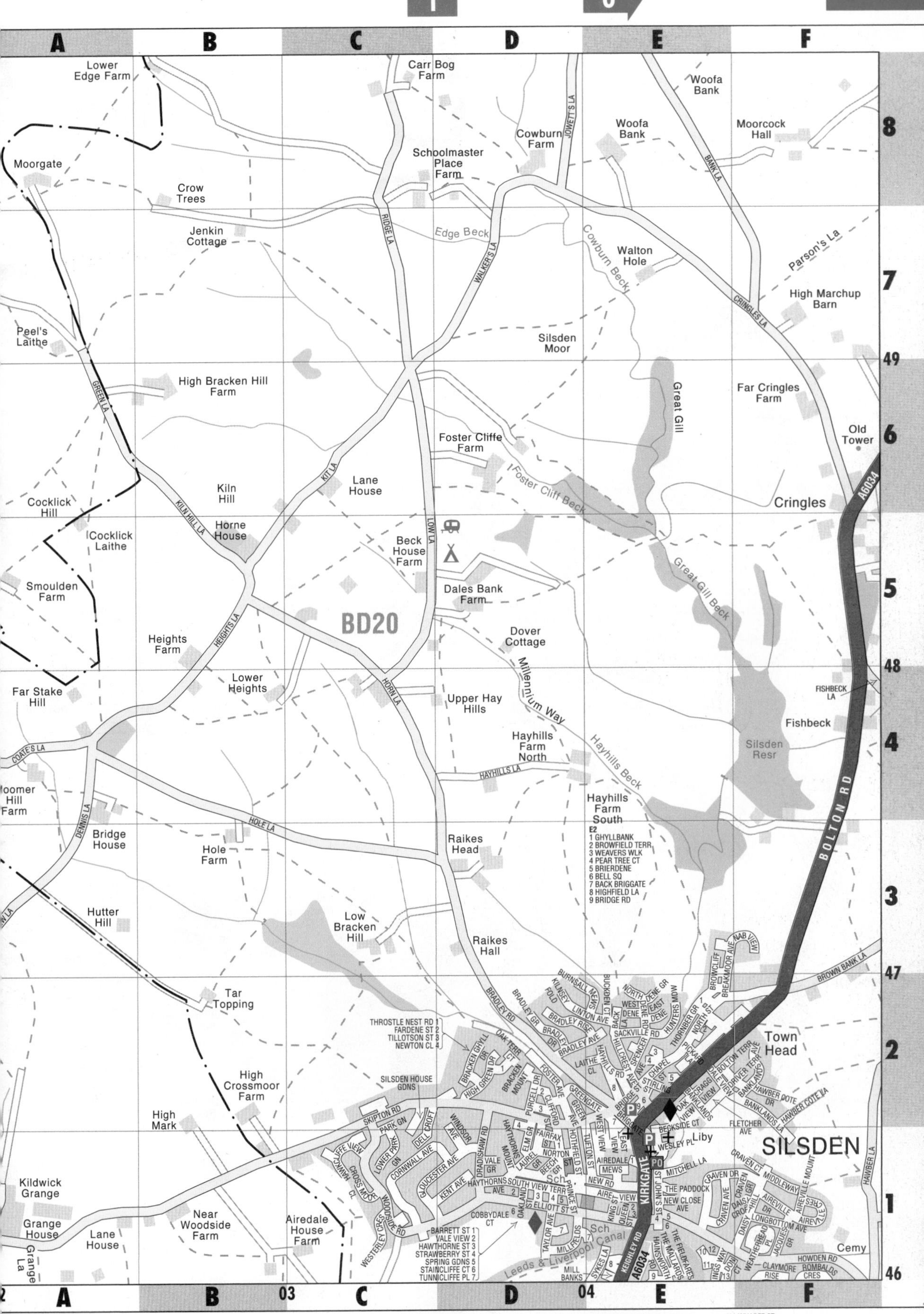

A B C D E F

Lower Edge Farm

Woofa Bank

Moorgate

Carr Bog Farm

Cowburn Farm

Woofa Bank

Moorcock Hall

Crow Trees

Schoolmaster Place Farm

Jenkin Cottage

Edge Beck

Walton Hole

Parson's La

Peel's Laithe

High Bracken Hill Farm

Silsden Moor

High Marchup Barn

High Bracken Hill Farm

Foster Cliffe Farm

Great Gill

Far Cringles Farm

Cocklick Hill

Kiln Hill

Lane House

Old Tower

Cocklick Laithe

Horne House

Cringles

Smoulden Farm

Beck House Farm

Dales Bank Farm

Great Gill Beck

Far Stake Hill

BD20

Heights Farm

Dover Cottage

FISHBECK LA

Lower Heights

Upper Hay Hills

Fishbeck

Bridge House

Hayhills Farm North

Silsden Resr

Hole Farm

Millennium Way

Hayhills Beck

Hutter Hill

HOLE LA

HAYHILLS LA

Hayhills Farm South

E2
1 GHYLLBANK
2 BROWFIELD TERR
3 WEAVERS WLK
4 PEAR TREE CT
5 BRIERDENE
6 BELL SQ
7 BACK BRIGGATE
8 HIGHFIELD LA
9 BRIDGE RD

Raikes Head

Tar Topping

Low Bracken Hill

Raikes Hall

Town Head

High Crossmoor Farm

THROSTLE NEST RD 1
FARDENE ST 2
TILLOTSON ST 3
NEWTON CL 4

High Mark

SILSDEN HOUSE GDNS

SILSDEN

Kildwick Grange

Grange House

Lane House

Near Woodside Farm

Airedale House Farm

BARRETT ST 1
VALE VIEW 2
HAWTHORNE ST 3
STRAWBERRY ST 4
SPRING GDNS 5
STAINCLIFFE CT 6
TUNNICLIFFE PL 7

Cemy

Leeds & Liverpool Canal

MILL BANKS

8
7
49
6
5
48
4
3
47
2
1
46

A B C D E F

E1
1 NICOLSONS PL
2 MILL FIELD CT
3 MITCHELL SQ
4 CLOG BRIDGE
5 HAINSWORTH ST
6 WATERLOO MILLS
7 MONKMANS WHARFE
8 ALBERT SQ
9 THE KINGFISHERS

11 WHARFE CT
10 WASHBURN CT
12 RIBBLE CT
13 NIDD CT

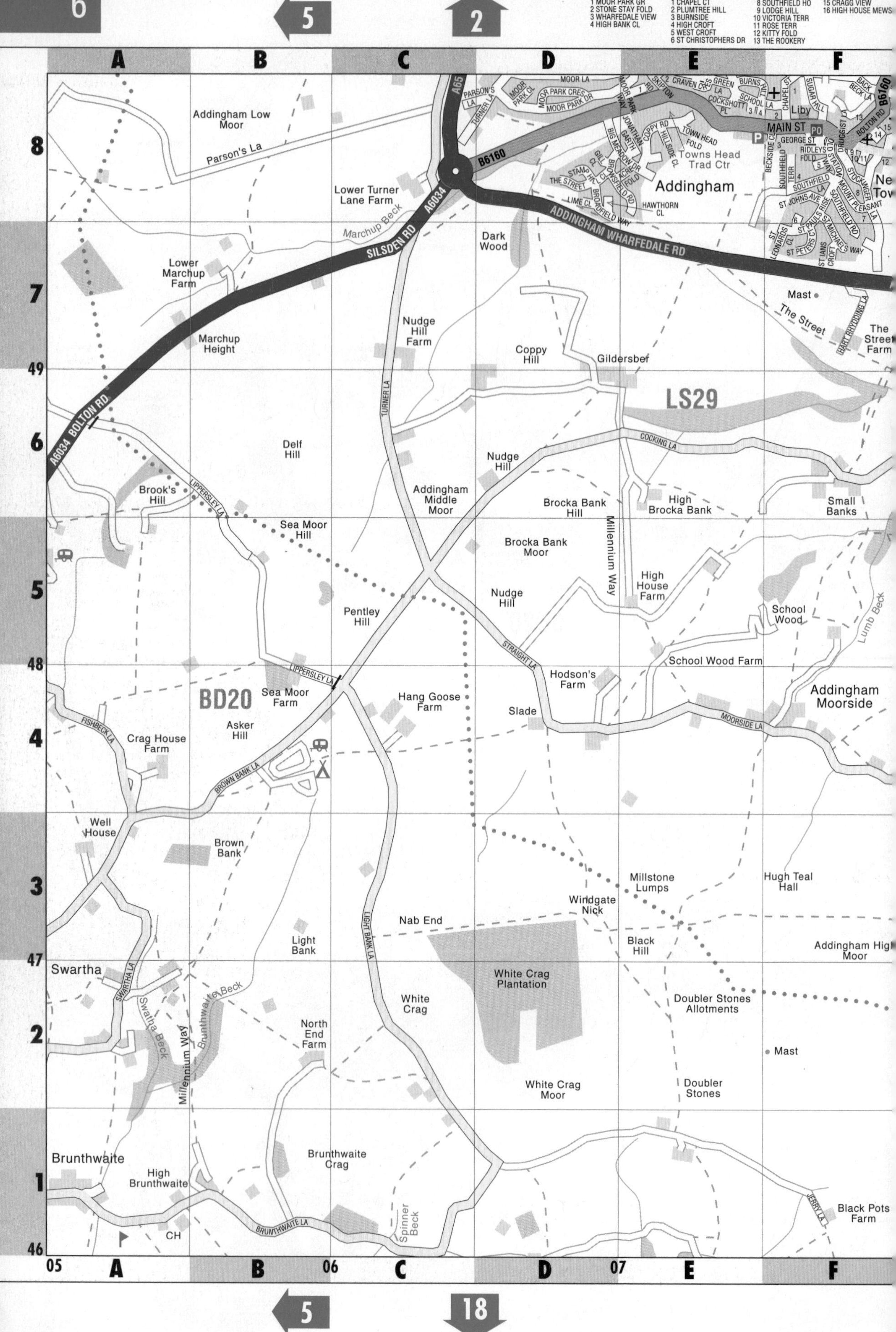
5
2
E8
1 MOOR PARK GR
2 STONE STAY FOLD
3 WHARFEDALE VIEW
4 HIGH BANK CL
F8
1 CHAPEL CT
2 PLUMTREE HILL
3 BURNSIDE
4 HIGH CROFT
5 WEST CROFT
6 ST CHRISTOPHERS DR
7 STORITHS CT
8 SOUTHFIELD HO
9 LODGE HILL
10 VICTORIA TERR
11 ROSE TERR
12 KITTY FOLD
13 THE ROOKERY
14 KILNERS CROFT
15 CRAGG VIEW
16 HIGH HOUSE MEWS
A
B
C
D
E
F
8
7
49
6
5
48
4
3
47
2
1
46
05
06
07
Addingham Low Moor
Parson's La
Lower Turner Lane Farm
Marchup Beck
SILSDEN RD
A6034
A65
B6160
MOOR LA
Addingham
Towns Head Trad Ctr
ADDINGHAM WHARFEDALE RD
MAIN ST
Dark Wood
Lower Marchup Farm
Marchup Height
Nudge Hill Farm
Coppy Hill
Gildersber
LS29
Mast
The Street
The Street Farm
A6034 BOLTON RD
TURNER LA
COCKING LA
Delf Hill
Brook's Hill
LIPPERSLEY LA
Nudge Hill
Addingham Middle Moor
Brocka Bank Hill
High Brocka Bank
Small Banks
Sea Moor Hill
Brocka Bank Moor
Millennium Way
High House Farm
School Wood
Lumb Beck
Nudge Hill
Pentley Hill
STRAIGHT LA
School Wood Farm
Hodson's Farm
Addingham Moorside
BD20
Sea Moor Farm
Hang Goose Farm
Slade
MOORSIDE LA
FISHBECK LA
Crag House Farm
Asker Hill
BROWN BANK LA
Well House
Brown Bank
Millstone Lumps
Hugh Teal Hall
Windgate Nick
Nab End
LIGHT BANK LA
Light Bank
Black Hill
Addingham High Moor
Swartha
SWARTHA LA
White Crag Plantation
Bunthwaite Beck
Doubler Stones Allotments
Swatha Beck
White Crag
North End Farm
Mast
White Crag Moor
Doubler Stones
Brunthwaite
Brunthwaite Crag
High Brunthwaite
JERRY LA
Black Pots Farm
Spinner Beck
CH
BRUNTHWAITE LA
5
18

3
8

A
B
C
D
E
F
Nessfield Court
Dean
Nesfield La
Dean Beck
Raw Riddings
HARDINGS LA
Hallcroft Hall
Town Beck
LOW MILL LA
Nesfield
High Austby Farm
Sion Hill
Castleberg Scar
HOLME INGS
SMITHY GREAVES
Sewage Works
Low Mills
GILL LA
ADDINGHAM WHARFEDALE RD
Tivoli
Low Austby
Austby
Myddelton Lodge
OLD LA
ILKLEY RD
Lumb Ghyll Farm
LUMB GHYLL LA
BRANT BANK LA
Wharfedale
Owler Park
Terrace Gill
OWLER PARK RD
River Wharfe
COCKING LA
COMMON HOLME LA
CH
GOODWOOD
Riddings Lathe
NESFIELD RD
OLD LODGE HILL OR HARDINGS LA
Gate Croft
Dales Way
Sports Ctr
The Hollins
Low Lathe
Hadfield Farm
RIVERSIDE WLK
Over Gate Croft
Hollin Hall
APPLE TREE GDNS
A65
SKIPTON RD
LS29
THE BRAMBLES
DALE VIEW
EASBY CL
VICTORIA GR
WOODLANDS
VICTORIA DR
Addingham Moorside
CURLEW CL
BRIERY CL
KINGS RD
Cragg House
Netherwood House
Briery Wood
WOODLANDS CL
NORWOOD PK
MOORSIDE LA
Rams Gill
Briery Wood Farm
GROVE RD
HEBER'S GR
HEBER'S MOUNT
WHINFIELD
Hardwick House Farm
PARISH GHYLL DR
PINES GDNS
HEBER'S GHYLL DR
PREMIERE PK
PARISH GHYLL LA
Addingham Crag
Addingham High Moor
Hardwick Holes
Brackenwood
HOLLIN HALL DR
UPPER PARISH GHYLL LA
QUEEN'S DR
Heber's Ghyll
Woodhouse Crag
ILKLEY
HILLBROOK RISE
QUEEN'S DRIVE LA
oon Stone
Piper's Crag
Millennium Way
Panorama Reservoir
PANORAMA DR
OAKLANDS
WESTWOOD DR
WESTWOOD RISE
Swastika Stone
Black Beck
Intake Heads
Silver Well Cottage
KEIGHLEY RD
Long Ridge End
Long Ridge
Black Beck Hole
Coarse Stone Edge
Keighley Rd
BD20
Crawshaw Moss
Bare Hill
Hollin Hall Peat Pits (dis)
Shepherd's Hill
Heber Moss
Grainings Head
8
7
49
6
5
48
4
3
47
2
1
46
09
10

19
8

A B C D E F

8

7

49

6

5

48

4

3

47

2

46

Primrose
Hill

Hill Top
Farm

Lane
End
Farm

Bore Hill

Stubbs Wood

Westville House
Prep Sch

Middleton

The Hollies

Old Lodge Hill or
Hardings La

Coppy Wood

Middleton
Woods

Grange
Farm

Bow Beck

Skirfa Beck

West Park
Wood

THE COPPICE

DUKES
HILL

THE ARBOUR

GILL BANK

WOODSIDE
CT

LOW CL

Stubham
Wood

Hudson
Wood

Nell Bank
Centre

Hudson's
Wood

Beck Foot
Farm

RUPERT RD

Dales Way

River Wharfe

Cemy

1 LEAMINGTON RD
2 LEAMINGTON TERR

Sewage Works

Riverside
Bsns Pk

DENTON RD

LS29

Denton
Bridge

NESFIELD
RD

CLIFFORD AVE

STUBHAM RISE

SYCAMORE
CT

ST NICHOLAS RD

OLICANA PK

LAKESIDE
CT

DENTON RD

MIDDLETON AVE

GILSTEAD WAY

Beanlands Par

ASH GR

2

ASH GR

1

RUVARDLE
VIEW

NORTH PK RD

WHARFEDALE RD

ASHLANDS RD

Kimberley

DANSK WAY

LOW BECK

RIVER VIEW

ROMBALD'S

SUNSET

WYVIL CRES

COLLYER VIEW

Wheatley
Grange

WHEATLEY LA

B6382

A65

COUTANCES WA

All Saints
CE Prim
Sch

SKIPTON RD

A65

STOCKELD
WAY

RIVERSIDE
WLK

OLD LANE RISE

BRIDGE LA

LEEDS RD

Drill
Hall

THWAITES

Ashlands
Prim Sch

Mus

CHURCH ST

Castle
Hill

WHARFE VIEW

NELSON RD

EAST

WEST PARK

MARY'S CV

Sch

WOODLANDS

MAYFIELD GR

HAMPSHIRE RD

VALLEY DR

BLACKTHORN
RD

BYRON
HO

Ben Rhydding

4

ILKLEY

Railway Sta

WILMOT RD

GOLDEN BUTTS RD

LITTLE LA

ST HELEN'S WAY

WOODS
MEWS

ST PAUL'S RD

Sch

ST JOHN'S
RD

CHELTENHAM AVE

MOORFIELD
WAY

MOORFIELD
RD

ILKLEY

TH Liby

SPRINGS LA

STEPHENSONS WAY

CARNEGIE

SPRINGFIELD AVE

WHARFEDALE DR

PARKLANDS

BOLLING RD

PO

DENTON

WHEATLEY AVE

BRIGHTON

BEN RHYDDING DR

ROWLEY CT

WELLS CT

RICHMOND

Coronation

Ilkley
Gram
Sch

BACKSTONE
LA

SOUTHWAY

MANLEY RISE

MANOR
RISE

WOODROYD
GDNS

HIGH
CLARE CT

LONGCROFT

WHEATLEY
GDNS

Ben Rhydding

ALBANY
WLK

SKEDDA
RISE

SEDBERGH
DR

COMPASTURE RD

CLIFTON RD

Moorfield
Sch

Greystones

RYEDALE
PK

THE HAY
MAIN ST

LOWER
WHEATLEY

CHESTNUT CL

WHEATLEY GR

HYDROLE CT

HIGH WHEATLEY

HIGH WOOD

PARISH GHYLL DR

PINEWOOD
CL

QUEEN'S DR

QUEEN'S DRIVE

WESTWOOD DR

HILL TOP

BRODRICK DR

1 CHANTRY CL
2 ANNANDALE CT
3 GROVE HO
4 ST MARGARET'S TERR
5 DEACONESS CT

CROSSBECK RD

CROSSBECK

MOUNT
PLEASANT

TARN CT 1
MOORSIDE CT 2

CRAIGLANDS RD

MAXWELL RD

Ben Rhydding Rd

CONSTABLE RD

HANGINGSTONE RD

UNDERCLIFFE RISE

CH

Gib Field

The
Tarn

The
Tarn

White Walls
Visitor Ctr

Cow
& Calf

P

Cow & Calf
Hotel

Barmishaw

Millennium Way

Backstone Beck

Rocky Valley

West Rock

Ebor Way
Dales Way

Ilkley Crags

Ilkley Moor

Cranshaw Thorn
Hill

Dales Way Link

Pancake Stone

Badger Stone

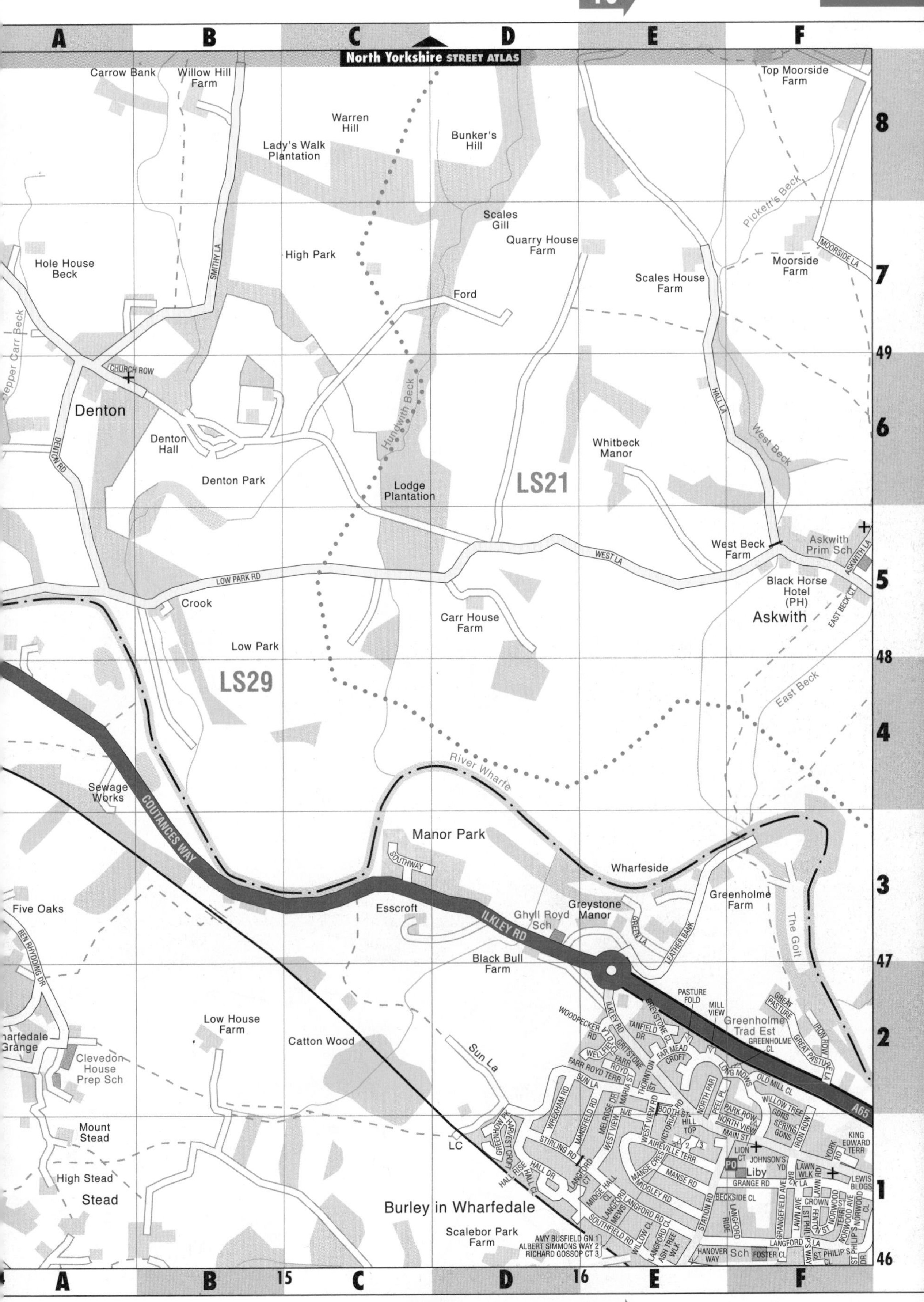

A B C **North Yorkshire** STREET ATLAS D E F

8

Carrow Bank Willow Hill Farm Top Moorside Farm

Warren Hill Bunker's Hill

Lady's Walk Plantation

Scales Gill Quarry House Farm Moorside Farm

7

Hole House Beck High Park Ford Scales House Farm

49

CHURCH ROW

Denton West Beck

6

Denton Hall Whitbeck Manor Askwith Prim Sch

LS21

Denton Park Lodge Plantation

West Beck Farm West La Askwith La

West La Black Horse Hotel (PH) **Askwith**

5

Low Park Rd Crook Carr House Farm East Beck Cl

Low Park **LS29**

48

Sewage Works River Wharfe East Beck

4

COUTRANCES WAY

Five Oaks Manor Park Wharfeside Greenholme Farm

Esscroft Southway Ghyll Royd Sch Greystone Manor The Golf

3

Ben Rhydding Dr Ilkley Rd Green La Leather Bank

Black Bull Farm Greenholme Trad Est

47

Pasture Fold Mill View Great Pasture

Iharfedale Grange Low House Farm Catton Wood Sun La Woodpecker Rd Tanfield Dr Far Mead Croft Greenholme Cl Great Pasture La

2

Clevedon House Prep Sch Old Mill Cl Willow Tree Gdns A65

Spring Gdns Iron Row King Edward Terr

Mount Stead Sun La LC Wrexham Rd Mansfield Rd Melrose Pl West View Ave North Par North View Main St Lion Ct Johnson's Yd PO Liby York Lawn Wlk Lewis Bldgs

High Stead **Stead** Hall Dr Stirling Rd Langford Booth St Hill Top Victoria Terr Aireville Terr Manse Rd Station Rd Grange Rd Beckside Cl Crown St

1

Burley in Wharfedale Scalebor Park Farm Southfield Rd Langford Cl Willow Cl Langford Foster Cl St Philip's Sch St Philip's La

AMY BUSFIELD GN 1 ALBERT SIMMONS WAY 2 RICHARD GOSSOP CT 3 Hanover Way

46

A B 15 C D 16 E F

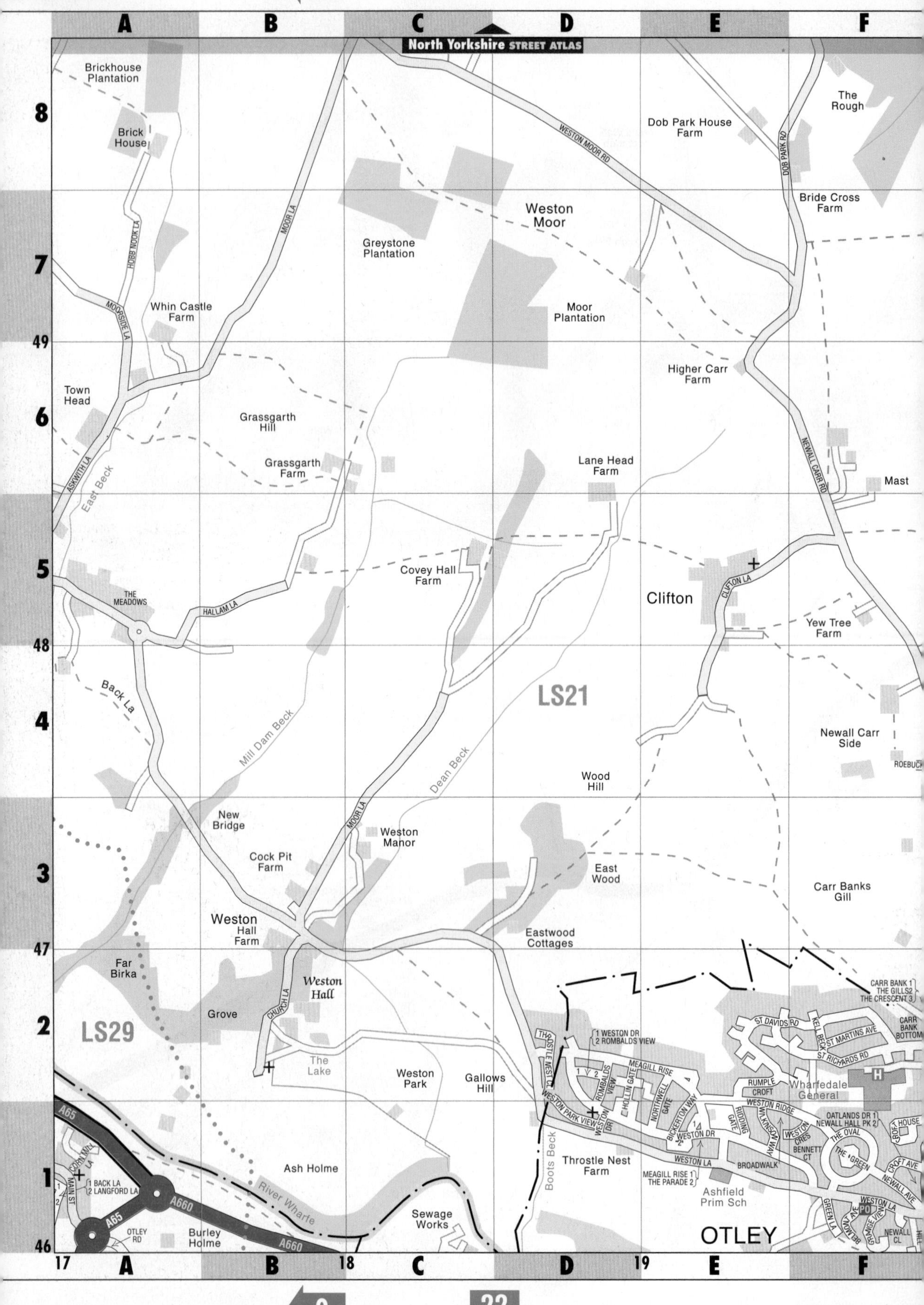

North Yorkshire STREET ATLAS

A **B** **C** **D** **E** **F**

Brickhouse
Plantation

8

Brick
House

Dob Park House
Farm

The
Rough

Weston Moor Rd

Dob Park Rd

Bride Cross
Farm

Weston
Moor

Greystone
Plantation

7

Moorside La

Moor La

Whin Castle
Farm

Moor
Plantation

Higher Carr
Farm

49

Town
Head

Grassgarth
Hill

Lane Head
Farm

Newall Carr Rd

Mast

6

Askwith La

East Beck

Grassgarth
Farm

Covey Hall
Farm

Clifton

Clifton La

5

The
Meadows

Hallam La

Yew Tree
Farm

48

Back La

LS21

4

Mill Dam Beck

Dean Beck

Wood
Hill

Newall Carr
Side

ROEBUCK

New
Bridge

Cock Pit
Farm

Moor La

Weston
Manor

East
Wood

Carr Banks
Gill

3

Weston
Hall
Farm

Eastwood
Cottages

47

Far
Birka

Church La

Weston
Hall

CARR BANK 1
THE GILLS 2
THE CRESCENT 3

CARR
BANK
BOTTOM

2

LS29

Grove

The
Lake

Weston
Park

Gallows
Hill

ST DAVIDS RD

NEIL BECK

ST MARTINS AVE

ST RICHARDS RD

Weston Park View

THE CASTLE NEST

Rombalds View

1 WESTON DR
2 ROMBALDS VIEW

MEAGILL RISE

Weston Ridge

RUMPLE
CROFT

Wharfedale
General

H

OATLANDS DR 1
NEWALL HALL PK 2

NEWALL AVE

A65

JOHN ST MILL

MAIN ST

1 BACK LA
2 LANGFORD LA

Ash Holme

River Wharfe

Boots Beck

Throstle Nest
Farm

MEAGILL RISE 1
THE PARADE 2

Ashfield
Prim Sch

BROADWALK

THE 'GREEN

THE OVAL

Bennett
CT

Weston Cres

WAINS WAY

Riding Gate 7

Weston Dr

BACKSTONE WAY

NORTHWELL
GATE

Meagill
Gate

1

OTLEY
RD

A65

A660

Burley
Holme

Sewage
Works

OTLEY

CROFT AVE

GREEN LA

MAIN ST

WESTON LA

NEWALL
CL

46

17 **A** **B** **18** **C** **D** **19** **E** **F**

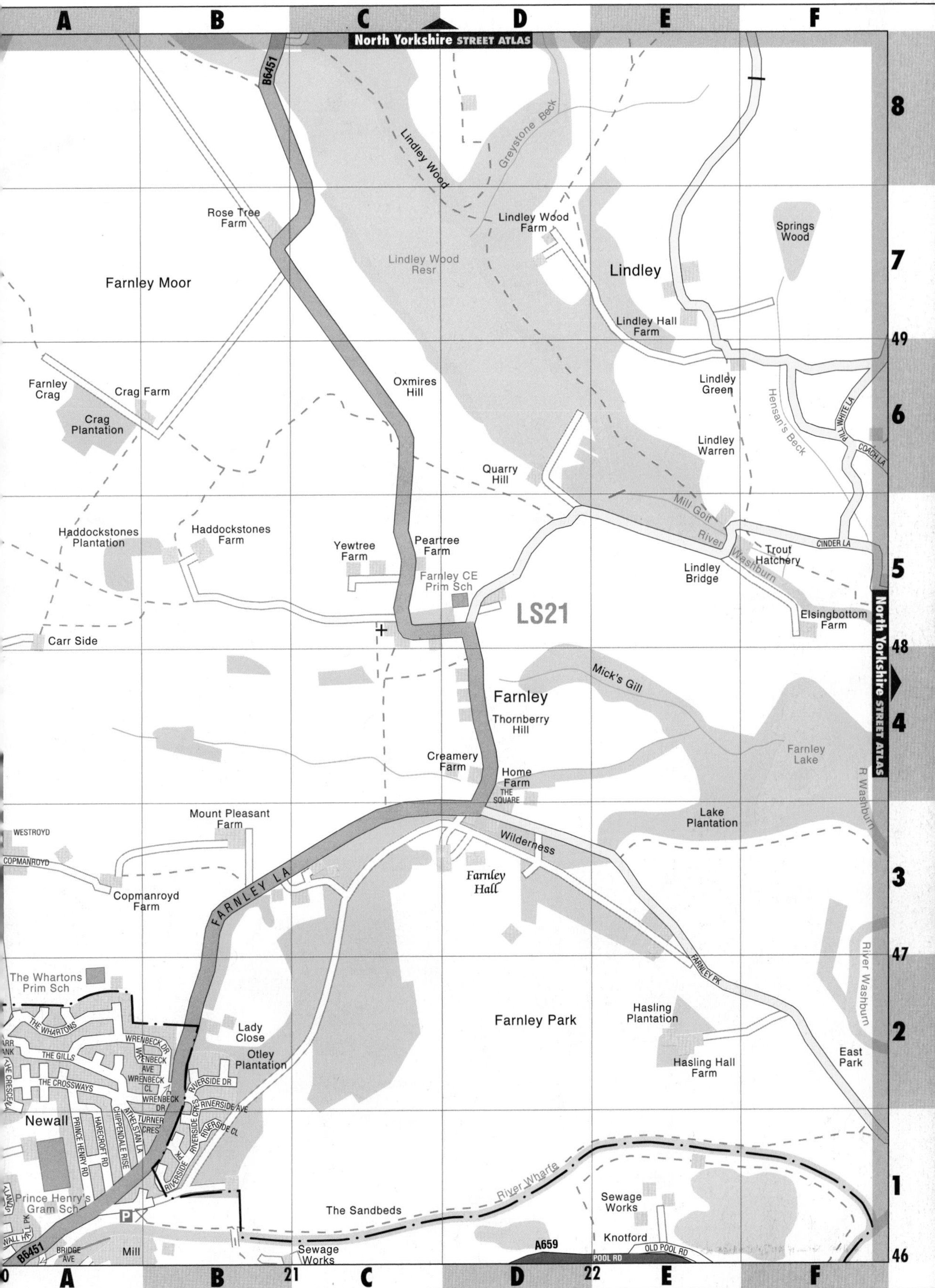

A B C D E F

8
7
49
6
5
48
4
47
3
2
1
46

Farnley Moor

Rose Tree Farm

B6451

Lindley Wood

Greystone Beck

Lindley Wood Farm

Lindley

Springs Wood

Lindley Wood Resr

Lindley Hall Farm

Farnley Crag
Crag Farm
Crag Plantation

Oxmires Hill

Lindley Green

Lindley Warren

Hensan's Beck

PUL WHITE LA

COACH LA

Quarry Hill

Mill Goit

River Washburn

Trout Hatchery

CINDER LA

Haddockstones Plantation

Haddockstones Farm

Yewtree Farm

Peartree Farm

Farnley CE Prim Sch

LS21

Lindley Bridge

Elsingbottom Farm

Carr Side

Mick's Gill

Farnley

Thornberry Hill

Farnley Lake

Creamery Farm

Home Farm
THE SQUARE

Lake Plantation

Westroyd
Copmanroyd

Mount Pleasant Farm

Wilderness

Farnley Hall

Copmanroyd Farm

FARNLEY LA

Farnley PK

R Washburn

Farnley Park

Hasling Plantation

East Park

The Whartons Prim Sch

Lady Close

Otley Plantation

Hasling Hall Farm

THE WHARTONS
WRENBECK DR
WRENBECK AVE
WRENBECK CL
WRENBECK DR
THE GILLS
THE CROSSWAYS
TURNER CRES
RIVERSIDE DR
RIVERSIDE AVE
RIVERSIDE CL
CHRISTIAN LA
CHIPPENDALE RISE
HARECROFT RD
PRINCE HENRY'S RD

Newall

Prince Henry's Gram Sch

River Wharfe

Sewage Works

Knotford

BRIDGE AVE

Mill

The Sandbeds

Sewage Works

A659
POOL RD

OLD POOL RD

B6451

A B C D E F

A | B | C | D | E | F

8

Fox Heads Farm

HG3

Royal Oak Plantation

A661 Harrogate

Crag Plantation

Home Farm

Stockeld Grange

Spofforth Park

Fox Heads Wood

HIGH LA

WHINS LA

FOX HEADS LA

A661

HARROGATE RD

A66

7

Whin Lane Farm

Toad Hole Beck

Stockeld Park

49

Bowrake Farm

STOCKELD LA

Sicklinghall Wood

Spring Wood

6

PARK LA

Scott's Arms (PH)

Dairy Farm

Skerry Grange

Sheep Field House

SICKLINGHALL RD

5

ADDLETHORPE LA

KIRKBY LA

Crackhills La

Sicklinghall Com Prim Sch

MAIN ST

BACK LA

CHAPEL CT

THE CRESCENT

PO

HAZELDENE COTTS

WETHERBY RD

Linton Spring (Hotel)

North Yorkshire STREET ATLAS

Poplar House

Sicklinghall

Sicklinghall Grange

48

GEECROFT LA

LONGLANDS LA

Linton Spring Farm

4

Hill Croft Farm

LS22

Devonshire Whin

Devonshire Wood

3

Paddock House Farm

PADDOCK HOUSE LA

Paddock House

West Plantation

Sicklinghall House

Ebor Way

47

Old Wives' Wood

Lime Kiln Wood

2

Carlshead House

Wood Hall Hotel

TRIP LA

Ebor Way

Lawn Rein

River Wharfe

1

River Wharfe

Carlston Hill

Carlstonhill Farm

Spring Wood

Ox Close

Cow Wood

LINTON COMM

Whitewe House Farm

46

Woodhall Bridge

LS17

A | B | C | D | E | F

35 | 36 | 37

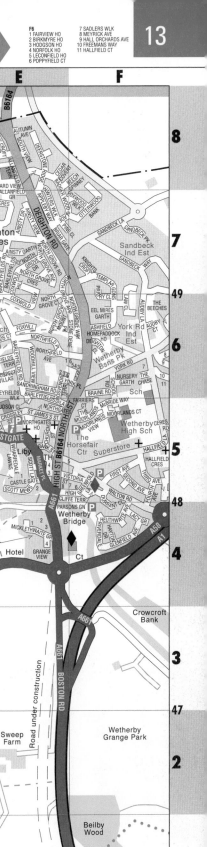

E6
1 NORTHFIELD MEWS
2 RHODES HO
3 LEATHAM HO
4 GRAY HO
5 BARLEYFIELDS MEWS

F6
1 FAIRVIEW HO
2 BIRKMYRE HO
3 HODGSON HO
4 NORFOLK HO
5 LECONFIELD HO
6 POPPYFIELD CT

7 SADLERS WLK
8 MEYRICK AVE
9 HALL ORCHARDS AVE
10 FREEMANS WAY
11 HALLFIELD CT

North Yorkshire STREET ATLAS

A1(M) Scotch Corner (A1)

B1224

46

Broad Walk

A1

Sandbeck House

Sandbeck Wood

Cockshot Wood

Sand Beck

SANDBECK LA

RACECOURSE APP

Ingmanthorpe Park

Swinnow Hill

Swinnow Park

YORK RD

B1224

Moss Carrs Farm

Sandbeck Ind Est

HM Young Offender Inst

Sand Bridge

Champagne Whin

Works

SANDBECK WAY

CARR LA

THE ROWANS

THE BEECHES

NETHERDALE

CITHEROLE

MEYRICK AVE

HALL ORCHARDS AVE

FREEMANS WAY

MONTAGU RD

SYKE RD

GUNTER RD

CERES RD

Hallfield Cemy

THIRD AVE

HALLFIELD CRES

BORREL CL

LS22

Wetherby Race Course

Springs LA

P

Stables

Springs Wood

MOOR LA

Sykes House Farm

The Rampart

SPRINGS LA

WALTON RD

A1

Park Hill Farm

Heuthwaite La

WATERSDALE LA

Ebor Way

Crowcroft Bank

Sewage Works

WETHERBY GRANGE

Wray Wood

Flint Mill Grange

West Field

LS23

FLINTMILL LA

WOODLA LA

WETHERBY RD

WOODLAND CT

WOODLAN

WATSON CH

Wetherby Grange Park

LEYS LA

River Wharfe

Whin Covert

New Springs

Middle Field

The Leys

DEEP DALE

Cave

Hall Farm

Hall Wood

Thorparch Hall

Thorparch Park

PEAR TREE ACRE

THE VILLAGE

Lady Elizabeth Hastings CE Prim Sch

The Pax Inn (PH)

DOWKELL LA

Thorp Arch

MULBERRY GARTH

WHINS LA

CHURCH LA

Gunter Wood

LEYS LA

DEEPDALE LA

WEST AVE

WEST LA

WEST END

WEST DALE

West Park

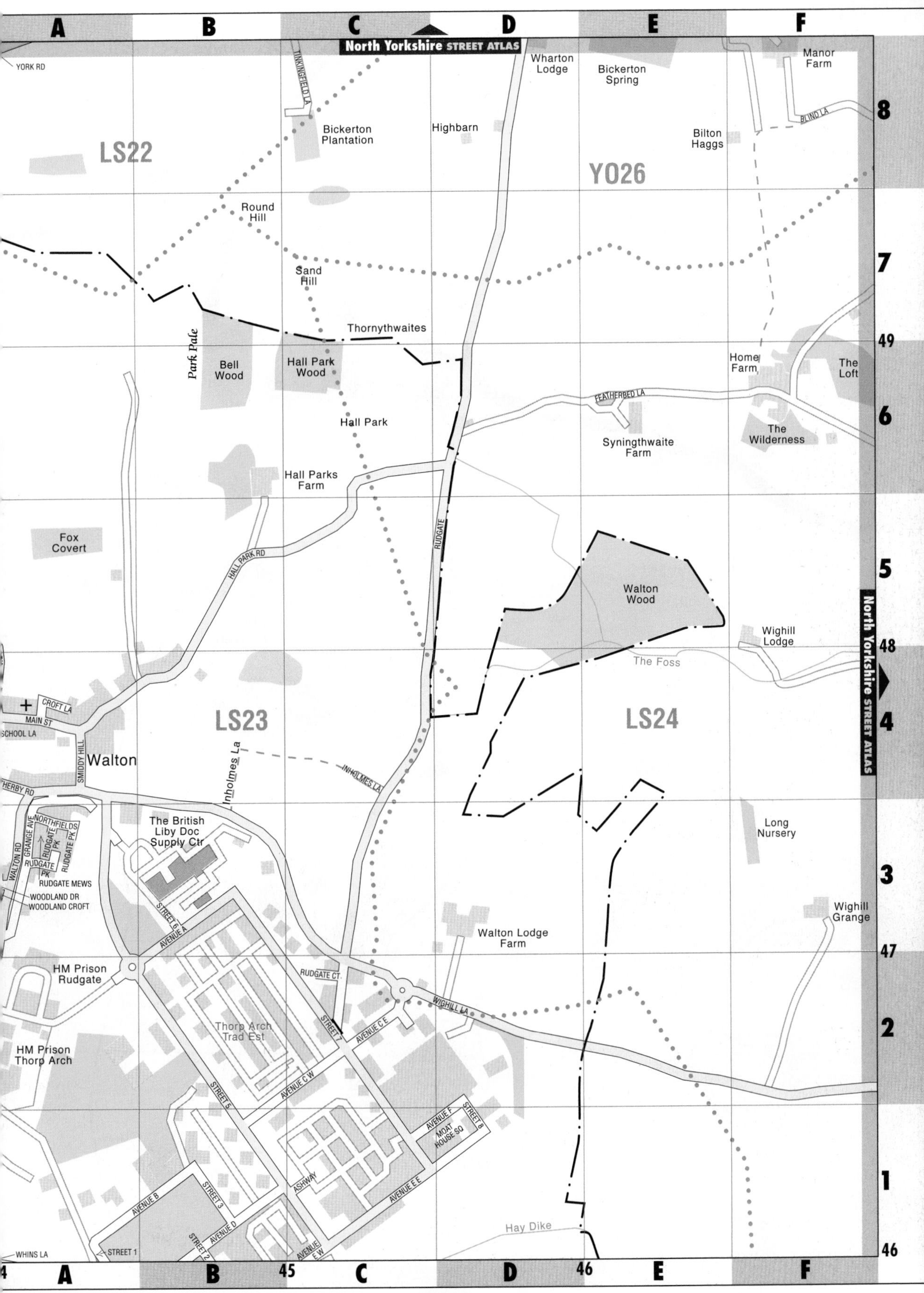

North Yorkshire STREET ATLAS

LS22

YO26

LS23

LS24

Walton

North Yorkshire STREET ATLAS

York Rd
Wharton Lodge
Bickerton Spring
Manor Farm
Bickerton Plantation
Highbarn
Bilton Haggs
Blind La
Round Hill
Sand Hill
Thornythwaites
Home Farm
The Loft
Park Pale
Bell Wood
Hall Park Wood
Featherbed La
The Wilderness
Hall Park
Syningthwaite Farm
Hall Parks Farm
Rudgate
Fox Covert
Walton Wood
Wighill Lodge
Hall Park Rd
The Foss
Croft La
Main St
School La
Smiddy Hill
Herby Rd
Inholmes La
Inholmes La
Long Nursery
Northfields
Grange Ave
Walton Rd
Rudgate Pk
Rudgate Pk
Rudgate Pk
The British Liby Doc Supply Ctr
Wighill Grange
Rudgate Mews
Woodland Dr
Woodland Croft
Street 6
Avenue A
Rudgate Ct.
Walton Lodge Farm
HM Prison Rudgate
Thorp Arch Trad Est
Street 7
Avenue C E
Wighill La
HM Prison Thorp Arch
Avenue C W
Avenue E
Street 8
Moat House Sq
Street 5
Avenue F E W
Avenue E E
Avenue B
Street 3
Street 4
Ashway
Avenue E E
Hay Dike
Whins La
Street 1
Street 2
Avenue E W

8
7
49
6
5
48
4
3
47
2
1
46

A
B
C
D
E
F

4

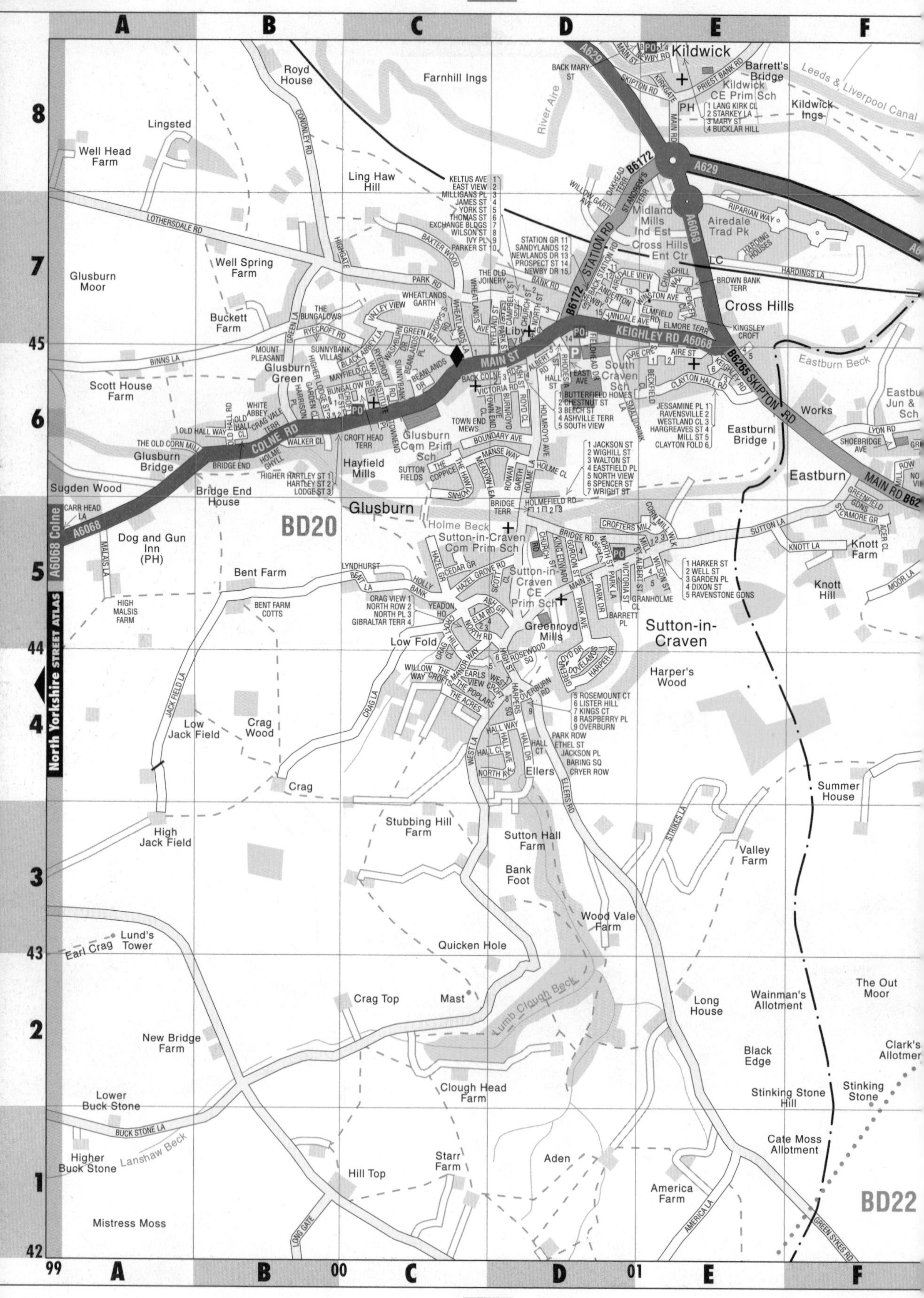

A B C D E F
Kildwick
Barrett's Bridge
Kildwick CE Prim Sch
Kildwick Ings
Leeds & Liverpool Canal
Royd House
Farnhill Ings
River Aire
Lingsted
Well Head Farm
Ling Haw Hill
Midland Mills Ind Est
Airedale Trad Pk
Cross Hills Ent Ctr
Glusburn Moor
Well Spring Farm
Buckett Farm
Cross Hills
Scott House Farm
Glusburn Green
South Craven Sch
Eastburn Beck
Works
Eastburn Bridge
Glusburn Com Prim Sch
Hayfield Mills
Glusburn Bridge
Sugden Wood
Bridge End House
Glusburn
Eastburn
BD20
Holme Beck
Sutton-in-Craven Com Prim Sch
Dog and Gun Inn (PH)
Bent Farm
Sutton-in-Craven CE Prim Sch
Knott Farm
Knott Hill
Greenroyd Mills
Sutton-in-Craven
Low Fold
Harper's Wood
Low Jack Field
Crag Wood
Crag
Ellers
Summer House
High Jack Field
Stubbing Hill Farm
Sutton Hall Farm
Valley Farm
Bank Foot
Wood Vale Farm
Lund's Tower
Earl Crag
Quicken Hole
Crag Top
Mast
Lumb Clough Beck
Long House
Wainman's Allotment
The Out Moor
New Bridge Farm
Black Edge
Clark's Allotmer
Clough Head Farm
Lower Buck Stone
Stinking Stone Hill
Stinking Stone
Lanshaw Beck
Higher Buck Stone
Starr Farm
Aden
Cate Moss Allotment
Hill Top
America Farm
BD22
Mistress Moss
A629
A6068
B6172
B6265
KEIGHLEY RD A6068
SKIPTON RD
MAIN ST
COLNE RD
LOTHERSDALE RD
BINNS LA
SUTTON LA
A6068 Colne
North Yorkshire STREET ATLAS
1 LANG KIRK CL
2 STARKEY LA
3 MARY ST
4 BUCKLAR HILL
KELTUS AVE 1
EAST VIEW 2
MILLIGANS PL 3
JAMES ST 4
YORK ST 5
THOMAS ST 6
EXCHANGE BLDGS 7
WILSON ST 8
IVY PL 9
PARKER ST 10
STATION GR 11
SANDYLANDS 12
NEWLANDS DR 13
PROSPECT ST 14
NEWBY DR 15
1 BUTTERFIELD HOMES
2 CHESTNUT ST
3 BEECH ST
4 ASHVILLE TERR
5 SOUTH VIEW
JESSAMINE PL 1
RAVENSVILLE 2
WESTLAND CL 3
HARGREAVES ST 4
MILL ST 5
CLAYTON FOLD 6
1 JACKSON ST
2 WIGHILL ST
3 WALTON ST
4 EASTFIELD PL
5 NORTH VIEW
6 SPENCER ST
7 WRIGHT ST
HIGHER HARTLEY ST 1
HARTLEY ST 2
LODGE ST 3
1 HARKER ST
2 WELL ST
3 GARDEN PL
4 DIXON ST
5 RAVENSTONE GDNS
CRAG VIEW 1
NORTH ROW 2
NORTH PL 3
GIBRALTAR TERR 4
5 ROSEMOUNT CT
6 LISTER HILL
7 KINGS CT
8 RASPBERRY PL
9 OVERBURN
PARK ROW
ETHEL ST
JACKSON PL
BARING SQ
CRYER ROW
8
7
45
6
5
44
4
3
43
2
1
42
99
00
01

33

5
18
E8
1 NIDD CT
2 THANET GARTH
3 DOBSONS WHARF
4 SWALE CT
5 AIRE CT
6 LOW HOUSE FARM CT
7 MALHAM CT
8 THE KINGFISHERS
A
B
C
D
E
F
Grange La
Leeds & Liverpool Canal
Grange Bridge
Lane House Bridge
Woodside Bridge
Cowling Bridge
WALKER'S PL
SYKES LA
A6034
LOW HOUSE DR
GLAISDALE CL
CROFT FIELD
CALDER WAY
DERWENT CT
CLAYMORE RISE
CHARLTON GR
INGS WAY
JENNINGS CL
ROMBALDS CRES
WINDGATE
HEBER CL
HOLDEN LA
BRINDLEY RD
TELFORD CL
WATERSIDE
LONGFIELD CRES
HAWBER LA
RIVERSIDE COTTS
BELTON RD
RYEFIELD WAY
Marrtree Bsns Pk
HAINSWORTH RD
KEIGHLEY RD
Silsden Beck
HEN HOLME LA
BRUNTHWAITE BRIDGE LA
LOW LA
Silsden Bridge
Silsden Ings
Millennium Way
River Aire
Steeton Ings
INGS RD
TEWITT CL
WILSON AVE
TEAL CT
CURLEW CT
HERON CL
GAMEL VIEW
CURRER WLK
ROBIN DR
THORNHILL RD
STEETON GR
Steeton & Silsden
Hotel
Millennium Bsns Pk
STATION RD
RIVOCK AVE
LOW LA
COURTYARD MEWS
Howden House Farm
ST STEPHEN'S CT
SUMMERHILL LA
SUMMERHILL DR
SUMMERHILL AVE
STEETON HALL GDNS
ELM VIEW
STYVETON WAY
PARK HO
GARFORTH AVE
PARKWAY
CLOUGH AVE
ELMSLEY ST
CHURCH CL
Airedale General
TEAL HO
TEAL MEWS
HAREWOOD DR
HALSTEADS WAY
THORNHILL GR
PARKWAY
POT LA
STONE GR
EAST PAR
STATION VIEW
CRICKETERS WLK
MAIN RD
HAREFIELD CL
SKIPTON RD
GRANGE RD
GRANGE TERR
VINCENT AVE
HAREWOOD AVE
MOORSIDE AVE
BRACKEN RD
WILLIAMS RD
COPPY RD
BURLEY CT
CHAPEL RD
THE SHROGGS
DALE CRES
QUEEN ST
FORGE
VIEW
MILL LA
UPPER SCHOOL
SCHOOL ST
MARKET ST
HIGH ST
FALCON CLIFFE
1 ASHGROVE
2 MURTON GR
AIREBURN AVE
Steeton Manor
Coppy Farm
Steeton Prim Sch
Steeton
Hawkcliffe House
DALE VIEW
CARTMEL
BOBBIN
MILL CT
WOOD ST
SEED HILL TERR
QUARRY COTTS
Hollins Bank
1 CROFT ST
2 BEECH ST
3 DIXON CL
4 BOBBIN MILL CL
5 HILL TOP
Bank House Farm
Twr
Hawkcliffe Farm
Currer Wood
GHYLL CL
Moor La
BARROWS LA
Steeton Beck
BD20
HOLLINS BANK LA
A629
Whitley Head
INTAKE LA
Little Snowden
Meadow Field Farm
Brighton Wood
Great Snowden
The Hollins
Gilvatt's Allotment
SKIPTON RD
B6265
BAR HOUSE LA
RIVOCK AVE
RIVOCK GR
White Field Farm
Hunters' Hill
FERNCLIFFE DR
Steeton Moor
Millennium Way
REDCAR LA
WESTY BANK CROFT
Moorhouse Allotment
HOLLINS LA
HOLLINS CL
Middle Redcar Farm
Bairstow's Allotment
Whinburn Farm
Dam Green Top
Cockshot Dam Green
Tarn Hill
Tarn House Farm
Four Oaks Lodge
BD22
Cutshaw Moor
Higher Redcar House
Redcar Tarn
GREENACRES DR
SHANN LA
Tarn Laddy
Prospect House
BRAITHWAITE EDGE RD
TARN LA
BLACK HILL LA
Cutshaw Farm
BD22
WESTWAY
8
7
45
6
5
44
4
3
43
2
1
42
03
04
34
18

A B C D E F

8

Brunthwaite Beck

Tomling Cote Farm

Ghyll Grange

Far Ghyll Grange Farm

Brunthwaite Bridge (Swing)

Holden Beck

Out Laith

Dirk Hill Sike

7

Holden Bridge

Howden Park Farm

Rough Holden

45

Holden Bridge (Swing)

LOW LA

Spring Crag Wood

Robin Hood Wood

Rivock Oven

6

Rivock Edge

Pinfold Hill

Mast

Low Holden Farm

Alder Carr Wood

Holden Gate

BD20

Heater

5

Lodge Hill

Jaytail Farm

44

High Carr

Clough Beck

Holden Park

CH

Carr Delph

Marsh Farm

Larkfield Farm

4

CH

High Wood Head

Heights Farm

SILSDEN RD

Low Wood Head

The Height

3

A629

7 CROFT HOUSE LA
8 BACK CROFT HOUSE LA
9 SYKE SIDE
10 BIRCHWOOD AVE

Elam Grange

WESTERN AVE

BANKS LA

Leeds & Liverpool Canal

ELAM WOOD RD

River Aire

MALVERN CRES

TURNBERRY CT 1
NURSERY CL 2
AIREVILLE ST 3
BACK AIREVILLE ST 4
ST JOHN'S CT 5
HANOVER CT 6

Low Utley

Cemy

Low Wood CT

THE RIDINGS

COLES WAY

DUNKIRK RISE

SCHOOL HOUSE FOLD 1
SOUTHFIELD MOUNT 2

B6265

CEMETERY LA

LC

High Cote

WEST BANK RD

SCOTT LA W

BYLANDS

SLADE LA

RIDGEMOUNT RD

PROSPECT TERR

2

SKIPTON RD

Cemy

KEIGHLEY

LEACH RD

LEACH WAY

SCOTT LA

Low Banks

SCHOLARS WAY

WESTFIELD CRES

1 LEACH CRES
2 WEST BANK GR

High Utley

Greenhead High Sch

Stoneycroft LA

BACK BLOCK VIEW

BD21

Leache's Bridge (Swing)

Riddlesden St Mary's CE Prim Sch

GRANGE CRES

GRANGE GR

SILVERDALE AVE

CANAL RD

AIRESIDE AVE

GRANBY DR

Beechcliffe

PATTIE ST 1
DUKE ST 2
AGNES ST 3
RAILWAY ST 4

Keighley Ind Pk

1 ANNIE ST
2 BACK BYRL ST
3 BYRL ST
4 BACK CALEDONIA RD
5 CALEDONIA RD

Stockbridge

SMITHVILLE

Hospital

1

B6285

Holy Family RC Sch

GREENTHWAITE CL

Cliffe Castle (Mus)

A629

A629

FLASBY ST

ASHLEIGH

A650

ROYD WAY

Keighley Ret Pk

HARD INGS RD

Works

ROYD INGS AVE

Coronation Bsns Ctr

KIRKBY ST

Alston Ret Pk

ALSTON RD

THE COURTYARD

BRADFORD RD

HAZELWOOD AVE

BEECHWOOD AVE

B6265

42

SPRINGFIELD RD

LIME CL

LC

BARDEN

06

A650

East Riddlesden Ha

05

A B 06 C D 07 E F

E1
1 LAKE ST
2 VALE ST
3 FORD ST
4 POOL ST
5 RIVER ST
6 CROSS RIVER ST
7 DALE ST
8 BACK FLORIST ST
9 BACK COLENSO RD

10 COLENSO GR
11 AIREWORTH CL
12 CORNWALL RD
13 COLENSO WAY
14 COLENSO WLK
15 ATHOL ST

F1
1 MATTHEW CL
2 BACK RIPLEY ST
3 RIDDLESDEN ST
4 RIVER MOUNT

A   B   C   D   E   F

8

Sike Head

East Buck Stones

West Buck Stones

LS29

Cowper's Cross

Keighley Rd

Dirk Hill Sike

Bucking Hill

Whetstone Gate

7

Whetstone Allotment

Masts

Thimble Stones

45

Brown Seaves

High Moor

6

Morton Moor

High Bradup

Low Bradup

ILKLEY RD

Lay Thorn Hill

Rivock

5

Bradup

BD20

Brass Castle

Bradup Beck

Low Moor

44

Sweet Well Dike

Fenny Shaw Allotment

Upwood Hall Farm

4

Upwood Hall

The Glen

Fenny Shaw Beck

Moorcock Farm

SILSDEN RD

Glen Farm

Stanbury Hill

3

HIGHBECK PK

Sunny Dale

MOORSIDE FARM

MOOR SIDE COTTS

Morton Dam

43

BARLEY COTE COTTS

UPPER MILL ROW

2

How Beck

BURY LA

West Morton

STREET LA

Moorlands Farm

Ousel Hole

Botany

LAKESIDE

Providence Row

BARLEY COTE

1 SOUTHFIELD MOUNT
2 BARLEY COTE GR
3 SOUTHFIELD WAY
4 SOUTHLANDS GR W
5 SOUTHLANDS DR
6 SOUTHLANDS AVE

Dene Hole

BOTANY RD

GREEN END RD

UPWOOD LA

Sunnydale Pk

ALMA TERR

FIELDEDGE LA

SOUTHLANDS RD

HERDWICK VIEW

ALLEY WAY

Bury La

HARTLEY'S SQ 1
THE SQUARE 2
BACK LA 3
CROFT RD 4
HIGH FOLD 5

SUN ST

OLD SIDE CT

OTLEY RD

BD16

1

CARR LA

HOSPITAL RD

NEWLYN RD

CALESIDE RD

WESLEY RD

BROAD DALE CL

CARR BANK

SOUTH VIEW

East Morton

STOCKSHILL LA

STUDLEY CL

SILK MILL STEPPING

CARR LA

Green End

Belle Vue Farm

BRADFORD RD B6265

Riddlesden

Leeds & Liverpool Canal

MILLSTREAM RD

THORNEYCROFT RD

ELDERBERRY CL

BROCKLEBANK RD

MIDDLEFIELD

SWINE LA

CARR LA

HIGHFIELD MEWS

HIGHFIELD CL

BADGERSTONE CL

BUCKSTONE GARTH

LAYTHORP TERR

Otley Mount

ASHWOOD DR

A   B   09   C   D   10   E   F

42

19
8

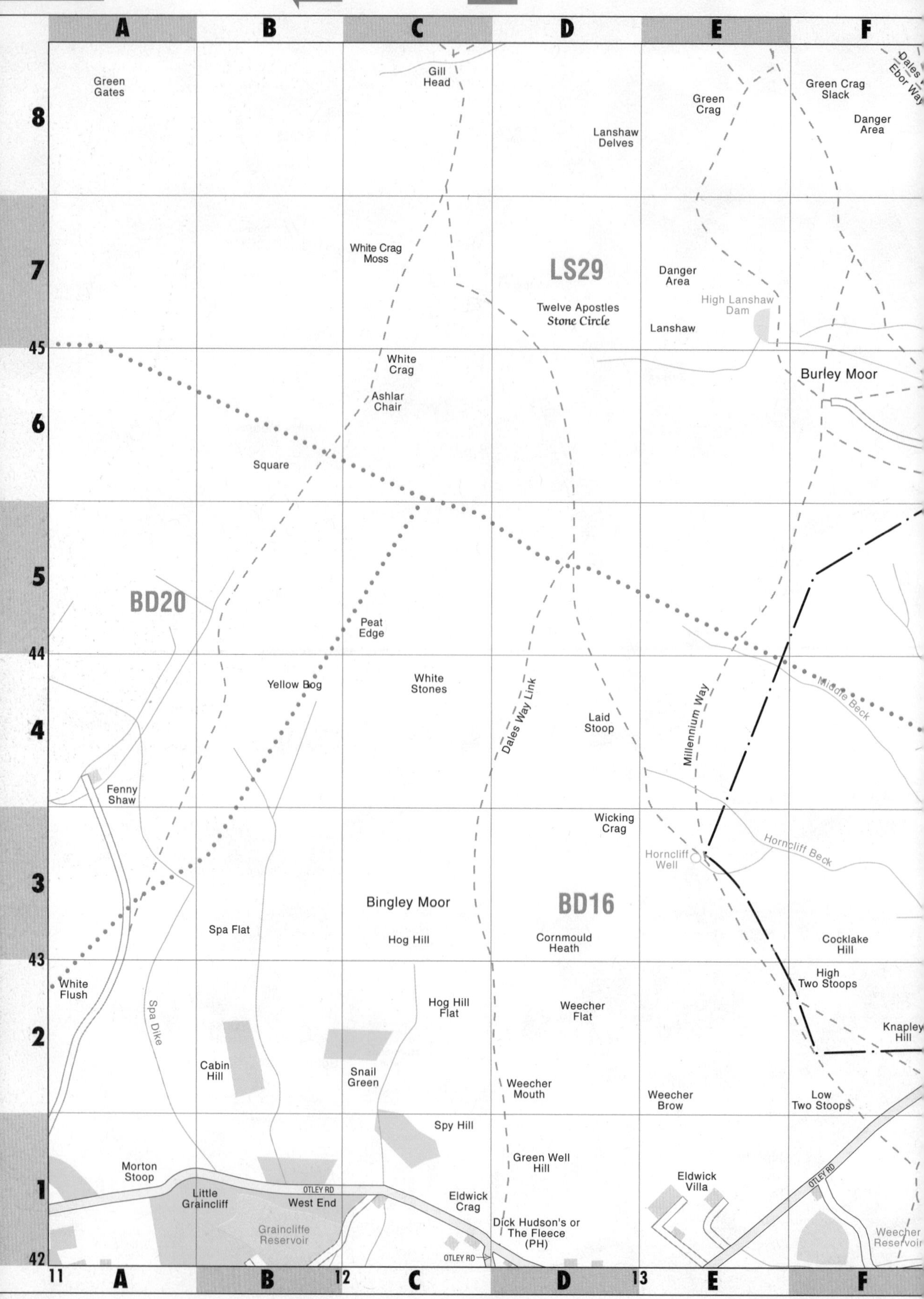
A
B
C
D
E
F
8
7
6
5
4
3
2
1
45
44
43
42
11
12
13
Green Gates
Gill Head
Green Crag
Green Crag Slack
Dales Ebor Way
Danger Area
Lanshaw Delves
White Crag Moss
LS29
Danger Area
High Lanshaw Dam
Twelve Apostles
Stone Circle
Lanshaw
White Crag
Burley Moor
Ashlar Chair
Square
BD20
Peat Edge
Yellow Bog
White Stones
Dales Way Link
Laid Stoop
Millennium Way
Middle Beck
Fenny Shaw
Wicking Crag
Horncliff Well
Horncliff Beck
Bingley Moor
BD16
Spa Flat
Hog Hill
Cornmould Heath
Cocklake Hill
White Flush
High Two Stoops
Hog Hill Flat
Weecher Flat
Spa Dike
Knapley Hill
Cabin Hill
Snail Green
Weecher Mouth
Weecher Brow
Low Two Stoops
Spy Hill
Morton Stoop
Green Well Hill
Eldwick Villa
OTLEY RD
Little Graincliff
West End
Eldwick Crag
Graincliffe Reservoir
Dick Hudson's or The Fleece (PH)
Weecher Reservoir

19
37

9

22

Stead Crag
Woofa Bank
Moor House
Burley in Wharfedale
West Lodge
Barks Crags
The Hermit (PH)
Spring Bank Farm
Crag Top
Lower Lanshaw Dam
Carr Bottom Resr
Burley Woodhead
Hag Farm
Reevadale
York View Farm
Bleach Mill
Southpiece Cottage
Whiddon
Danger Area
Stocks Hill
Craven Hall Hill
LS29
Heather Bank
Gynest
Menston
Rifle Range
Hill Top
Hawksworth Shaw
Hawksworth Moor
Reva Hill
Derry Hill Farm
Derry Hill
White Flush
Intake Gate Farm
BD16
Whin Hills
High Royds Hall
Reva Resr
Leedale Farm
Knapley-Ing Farm
Old Wood Farm
LS20
Old Wood
West Wood
Storth House
Jum Bridge
New Dam
Odda Hill
Rushy Beck
Coldstone Beck
Millennium Way
Carr Beck
Ebor Way
Dales Way
Matthew Dike
Black Beck
Middle Beck
Horncliff Beck
Jum Beck
STEAD LA
MOOR RD
MOOR LA
COLSTON DR
JUBILEE TREES
ROSE GARTH
PROSPECT ROW
STONEY LA
GREEN LA
HAG FARM RD
BLEACH MILL LA
MOOR LA
WEST WINDS
MOUNT PLEASANT
HILLINGS LA
BINGLEY RD
OLD WOOD LA
GOOSE LA
ODDA LA
OLD LA 1
MILL LA 2
CLARENCE DR
MENSTON OLD LA
A65
BRADFORD RD
WILLIAM FOSTER WAY 1
SCALEBOR SQ 2
CONISBOROUGH CL 3
RON LAWTON CRES 4
JOHN GILMOUR WAY 5
JILL KILNER DR 6
GREEN ACRES
DONALD ALDRED DR
SOUTHFIELD RD
SMITHY LA
STATION RD
STATION APP
THE ROBINS
HANOVER GDNS
HANOVER WAY
THE COPSE
ST PHILIP'S CL
PROSPECT RD
ST MICHAEL'S
OAK WAY
OAK AVE
PEASBOROUGH VIEW
GREENFIELDS WAY
GREENFIELD CL
HOLME GR
HILL CRES
ENDOR GR
ENDOR CRES
CHERINGTON CT
WESTBOURNE DR
VICTORIA AVE
WHIDDON CROFT
CRAVEN PK
FAIRFAX RD
CROFT CL
CROFT PK
MAIN ST
STOCKSHILL GARTH
HILLSIDE CT
DERRY HILL
DERRY LA
BARN CL 1
CROFT CT 2
HARGRAVE CRES
HAWKSWORTH DR
ST PETER'S WAY
Sch
PO
A
B
C
D
E
F
8
7
45
6
5
44
4
3
43
2
1
42
15
16

38
22

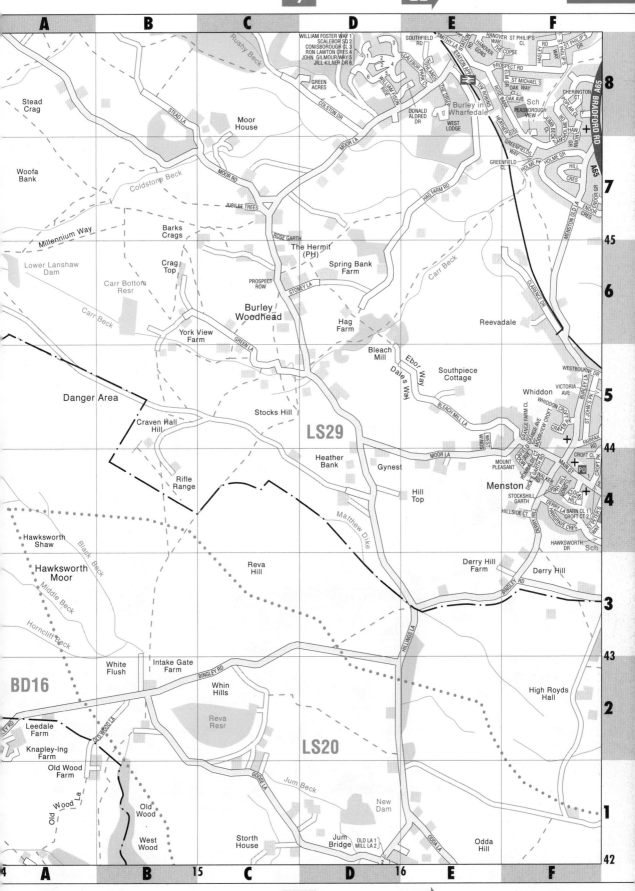

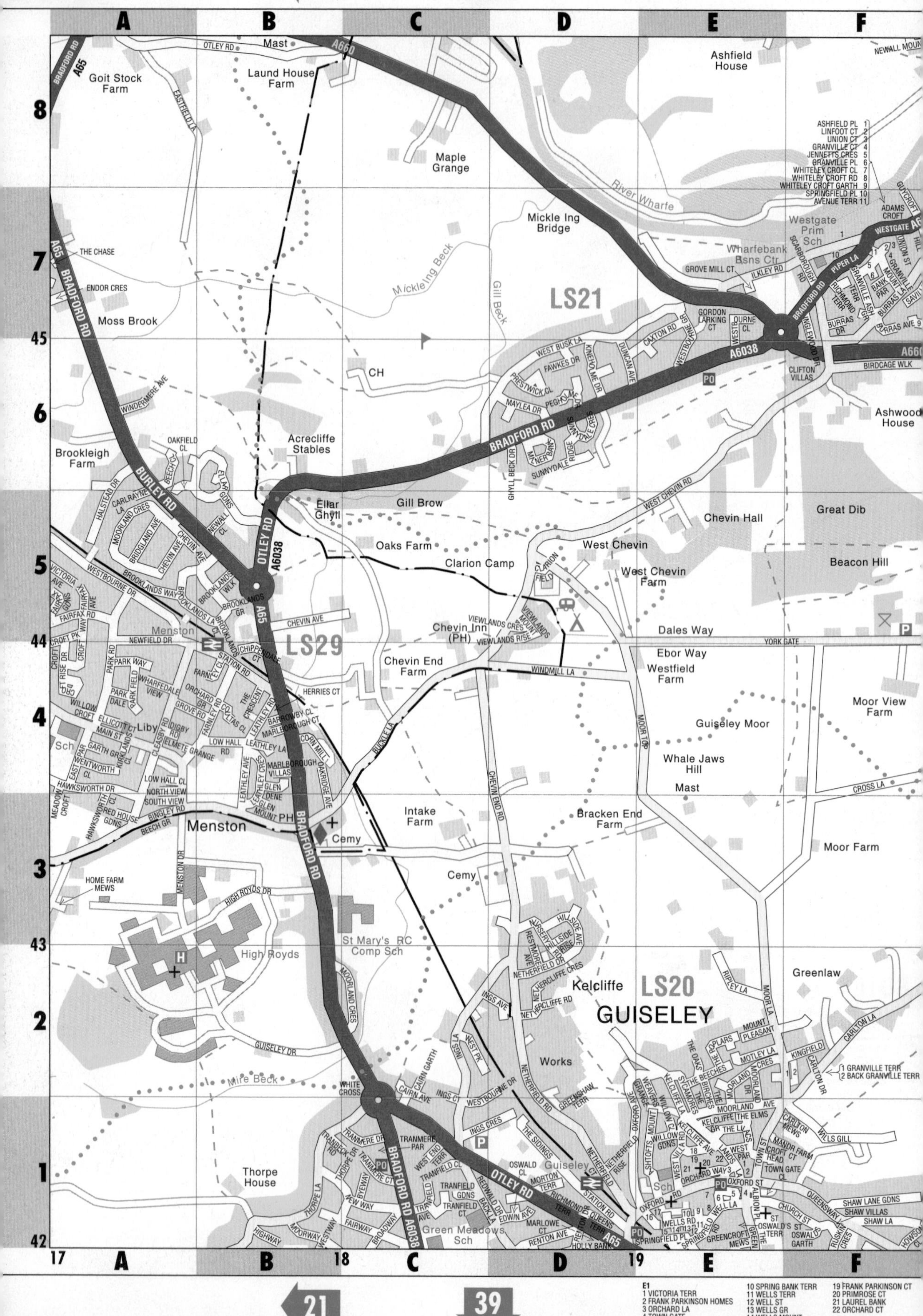

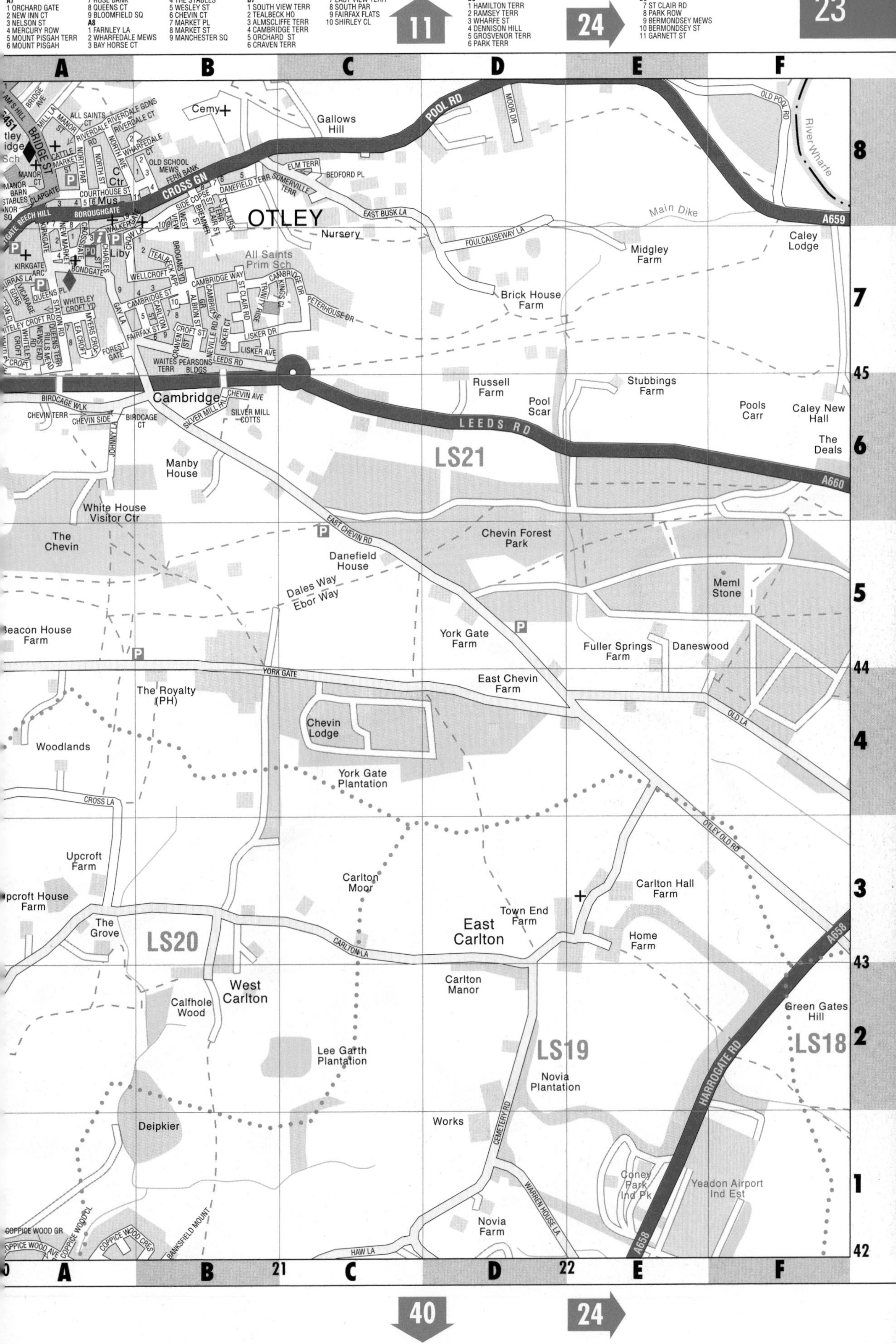
A7
1 ORCHARD GATE
2 NEW INN CT
3 NELSON ST
4 MERCURY ROW
5 MOUNT PISGAH TERR
6 MOUNT PISGAH
7 ROSE BANK
8 QUEENS CT
9 BLOOMFIELD SQ
A8
1 FARNLEY LA
2 WHARFEDALE MEWS
3 BAY HORSE CT
4 THE STABLES
5 WESLEY ST
6 CHEVIN CT
7 MARKET PL
8 MARKET ST
9 MANCHESTER SQ
B7
1 SOUTH VIEW TERR
2 TEALBECK HO
3 ALMSCLIFFE TERR
4 CAMBRIDGE TERR
5 ORCHARD ST
6 CRAVEN TERR
7 EAST VIEW TERR
8 SOUTH PAR
9 FAIRFAX FLATS
10 SHIRLEY CL
11
B8
1 HAMILTON TERR
2 RAMSEY TERR
3 WHARFE ST
4 DENNISON HILL
5 GROSVENOR TERR
6 PARK TERR
24
B8
7 ST CLAIR RD
8 PARK ROW
9 BERMONDSEY MEWS
10 BERMONDSEY ST
11 GARNETT ST
A
B
C
D
E
F
8
7
45
6
5
44
4
3
43
2
1
42
OTLEY
POOL RD
Cemy
Gallows Hill
BRIDGE ST
CROSS GN
BOROUGHGATE
ELM TERR
BEDFORD PL
EAST BUSK LA
Nursery
FOULCAUSEWAY LA
Midgley Farm
Main Dike
A659
Caley Lodge
OLD POOL RD
River Wharfe
All Saints Prim Sch
Brick House Farm
PETERHOUSE DR
LISKER DR
LISKER AVE
LEEDS RD
Cambridge
CHEVIN AVE
BIRDCAGE WLK
CHEVIN TERR
CHEVIN SIDE
BIRDCAGE CT
SILVER MILL HILL
SILVER MILL COTTS
Russell Farm
Pool Scar
Stubbings Farm
Pools Carr
Caley New Hall
The Deals
LEEDS RD
LS21
A660
Manby House
White House Visitor Ctr
The Chevin
EAST CHEVIN RD
Chevin Forest Park
Danefield House
Dales Way
Ebor Way
Meml Stone
Beacon House Farm
York Gate Farm
Fuller Springs Farm
Daneswood
YORK GATE
East Chevin Farm
The Royalty (PH)
Chevin Lodge
OLD LA
Woodlands
York Gate Plantation
CROSS LA
OTLEY OLD RD
Upcroft Farm
Carlton Moor
Carlton Hall Farm
Upcroft House Farm
Town End Farm
The Grove
LS20
East Carlton
CARLTON LA
Home Farm
A658
West Carlton
Carlton Manor
Green Gates Hill
Calfhole Wood
LS19
LS18
Lee Garth Plantation
Novia Plantation
HARROGATE RD
Deipkier
Works
CEMETERY RD
Coney Park Ind Pk
Yeadon Airport Ind Est
WARREN HOUSE LA
Novia Farm
COPPICE WOOD GR
COPPICE WOOD AVE
COPPICE WOOD CL
COPPICE WOOD CRES
BANKSFIELD MOUNT
HAW LA
21
22
40
24

23

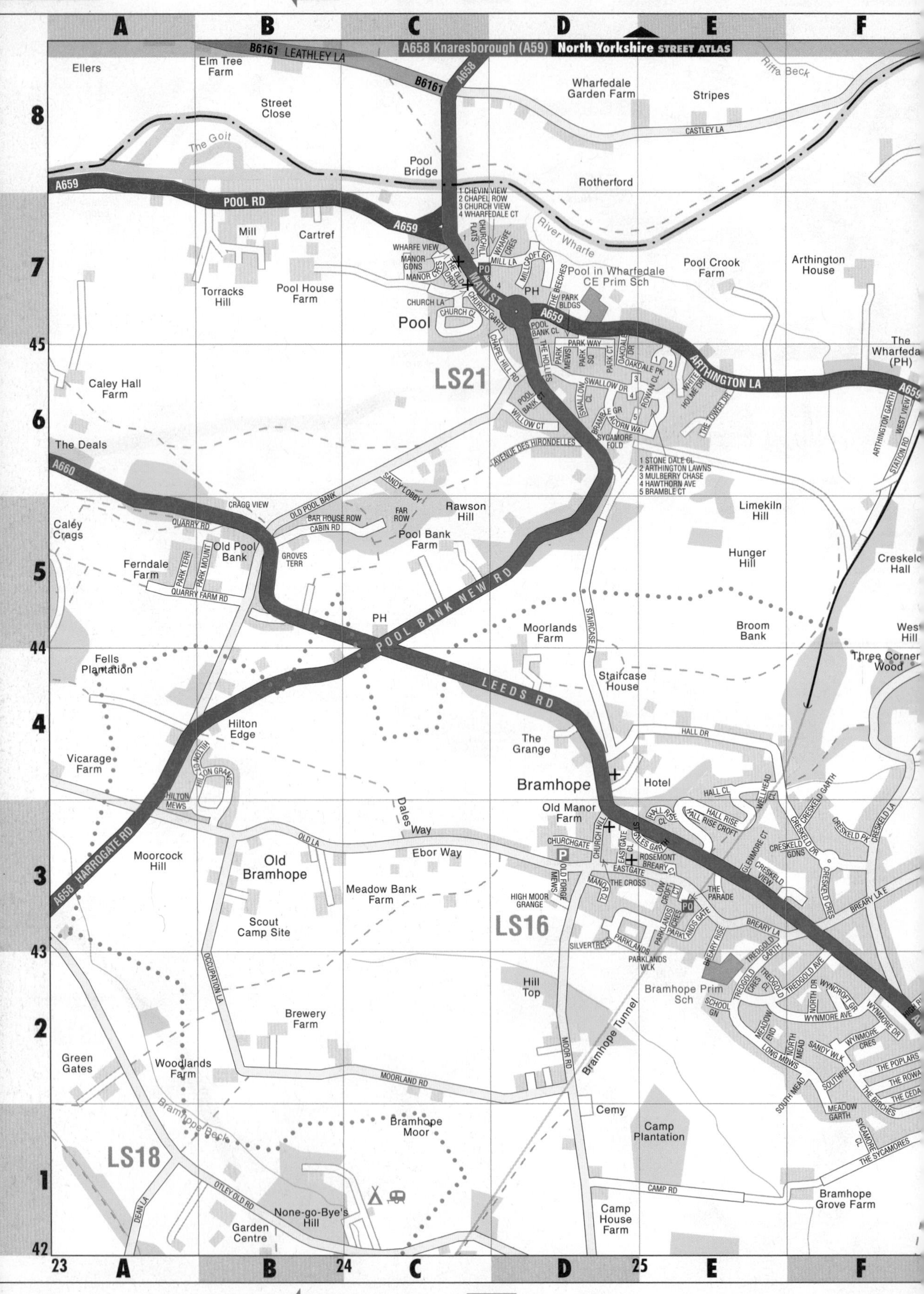

A
B
C
D
E
F
A658 Knaresborough (A59)
North Yorkshire STREET ATLAS
B6161 LEATHLEY LA
Ellers
Elm Tree Farm
Street Close
Wharfedale Garden Farm
Stripes
Riffa Beck
CASTLEY LA
The Goit
Pool Bridge
A659
POOL RD
Rotherford
1 CHEVIN VIEW
2 CHAPEL ROW
3 CHURCH VIEW
4 WHARFEDALE CT
River Wharfe
Mill
Cartref
Torracks Hill
Pool House Farm
Pool
Pool in Wharfedale CE Prim Sch
Pool Crook Farm
Arthington House
MAIN ST
CHURCH LA
CHURCH CL
CHURCH GARTH
CHAPEL HILL RD
PARK BLDGS
THE BEECHES
MILLCROFT EST
MILL LA
WHARFE CRES
WHARFE VIEW
MANOR GDNS
MANOR CRES
PH
LS21
ARTHINGTON LA
The Wharfedale (PH)
Caley Hall Farm
The Deals
POOL BANK CL
THE HOLLIES
PARK MEWS
PARK SQ
PARK WAY
PARK CT
OAKDALE DR
OAKDALE PK
SWALLOW DR
SWALLOW CL
ROWAN CT
BRAMBLE GR
ACORN WAY
SYCAMORE FOLD
WHITE HOLME DR
THE TOWER DR
WILLOW CT
POOL BANK CT
AVENUE DES HIRONDELLES
ARTHINGTON GARTH
WEST VIEW
STATION RD
1 STONE DALE CL
2 ARTHINGTON LAWNS
3 MULBERRY CHASE
4 HAWTHORN AVE
5 BRAMBLE CT
A660
CRAGG VIEW
OLD POOL BANK
SANDY LOBBY
FAR ROW
BAR HOUSE ROW
CABIN RD
QUARRY RD
Rawson Hill
Limekiln Hill
Caley Crags
Old Pool Bank
Pool Bank Farm
Hunger Hill
Creskeld Hall
Ferndale Farm
PARK TERR
PARK MOUNT
GROVES TERR
QUARRY FARM RD
POOL BANK NEW RD
PH
Moorlands Farm
Broom Bank
West Hill
Three Corner Wood
Fells Plantation
STAIRCASE LA
LEEDS RD
Staircase House
Hilton Edge
HALL DR
The Grange
Vicarage Farm
HILTON CT
HILTON GRANGE
HILTON MEWS
Bramhope
Hotel
Old Manor Farm
HALL CL
HALL RISE
HALL RISE CROFT
WELLHEAD CL
CRESKELD GARTH
CRESKELD PK
CRESKELD LA
CRESKELD DR
CRESKELD GDNS
CRESKELD CRES
CRESKELD VIEW
GLENMORE CT
Dales Way
Ebor Way
OLD LA
Moorcock Hill
Old Bramhope
A658 HARROGATE RD
CHURCHGATE
CHURCH HILL
EASTGATE
ST GILES GARTH
ROSEMONT
BREARY CT
THE CROSS
Meadow Bank Farm
HIGH MOOR GRANGE
OLD FORGE MEWS
MANOR CL
LOW CROFT CT
THE PARADE
BREARY LA
BREARY LA E
Scout Camp Site
LS16
SILVERTREES
PARKLANDS
PARKLANDS CRES
PARKLANDS GATE
PARKLANDS WLK
BREARY RISE
TREDGOLD CRES
TREDGOLD CL
TREDGOLD GARTH
TREDGOLD AVE
OCCUPATION LA
Hill Top
Bramhope Prim Sch
SCHOOL GN
NORTH DR
WYNCROFT GR
WYNMORE AVE
WYNMORE DR
WYNMORE CRES
Brewery Farm
MOOR RD
Bramhope Tunnel
MEADOW END
NORTH MEAD
LONG MDWS
SANDY WLK
THE POPLARS
SOUTH MEAD
SOUTHFIELD
THE ROWAN
THE CEDA
THE BIRCHES
MEADOW GARTH
Green Gates
Woodlands Farm
MOORLAND RD
Cemy
Bramhope Beck
Bramhope Moor
Camp Plantation
SYCAMORE CL
THE SYCAMORES
LS18
CAMP RD
Bramhope Grove Farm
OTLEY OLD RD
DEAN LA
None-go-Bye's Hill
Garden Centre
Camp House Farm
8
7
45
6
5
44
4
3
43
2
1
42
23
24
25

23

41

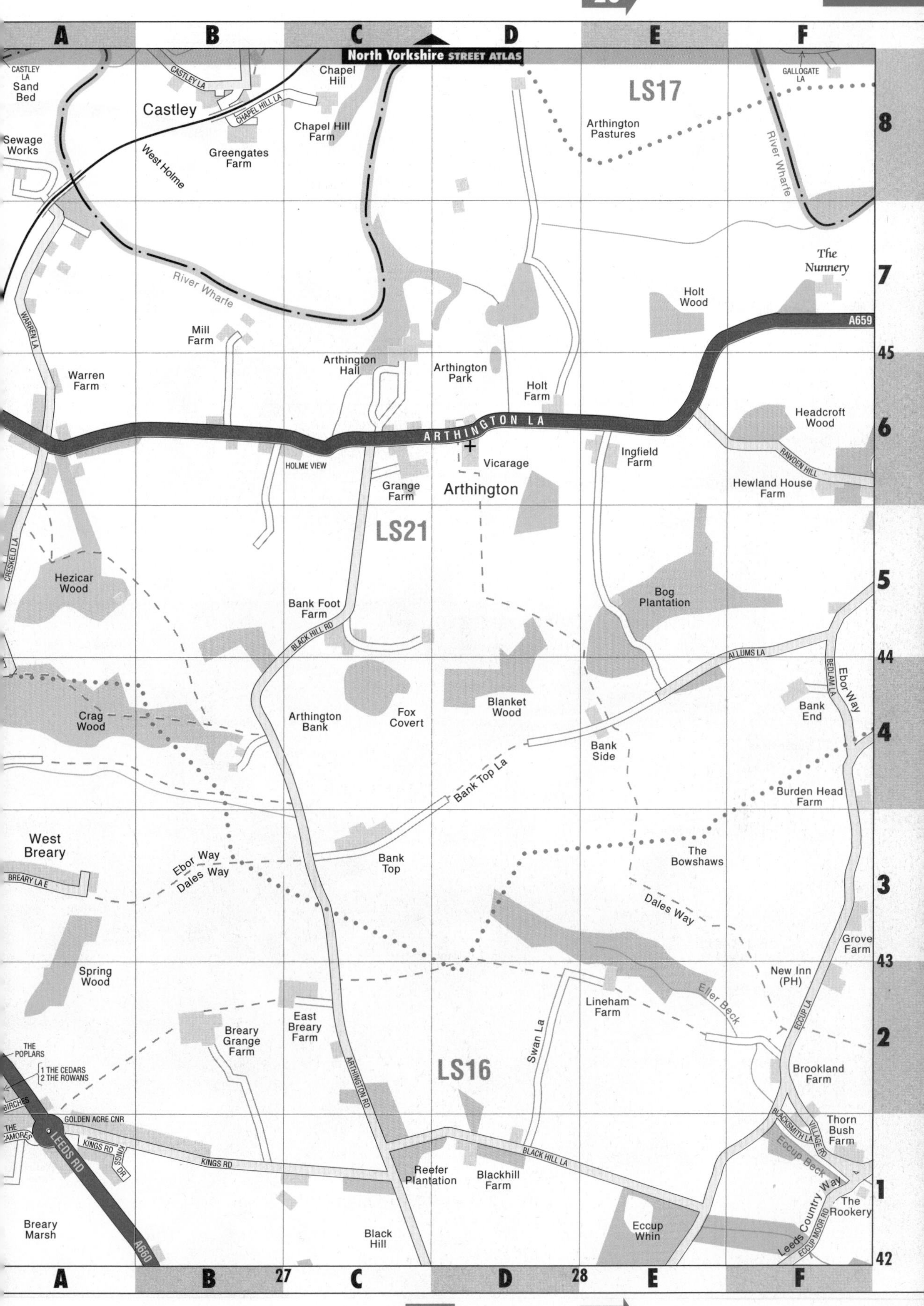

LS17

GALLOGATE LA

CASTLEY LA
Sand Bed

Sewage Works

CASTLEY LA

Castley

Chapel Hill

Chapel Hill Farm

Arthington Pastures

River Wharfe

8

West Holme

Greengates Farm

CHAPEL HILL LA

The Nunnery

7

River Wharfe

Mill Farm

Warren Farm

WARREN LA

Holt Wood

A659

45

Arthington Hall

Arthington Park

Holt Farm

Headcroft Wood

6

ARTHINGTON LA

HOLME VIEW

Vicarage

Arthington

Ingfield Farm

RAWDEN HILL

Hewland House Farm

Grange Farm

LS21

ORESKELD LA

Hezicar Wood

Bank Foot Farm

Bog Plantation

5

BLACK HILL RD

ALLUMS LA

44

EBOR WAY

Crag Wood

Arthington Bank

Fox Covert

Blanket Wood

Bank Side

BEDLAM LA

Bank End

4

Bank Top La

Burden Head Farm

West Breary

BREARY LA E

Ebor Way
Dales Way

Bank Top

The Bowshaws

Dales Way

3

Grove Farm

43

Spring Wood

Eller Beck

New Inn (PH)

ECCUP LA

THE POPLARS

1 THE CEDARS
2 THE ROWANS

East Breary Farm

ARTHINGTON RD

Lineham Farm

Brookland Farm

2

Breary Grange Farm

LS16

SWAN LA

GOLDEN ACRE CNR

THE SYCAMORES

BIRCHES

LEEDS RD

KINGS RD

KINGS RD

KINGS DR

Reefer Plantation

Blackhill Farm

BLACK HILL LA

BLACKSMITH LA

VILLAGE RD

Eccup Beck

Thorn Bush Farm

ECCUP MOOR RD

Leeds Country Way

The Rookery

1

Breary Marsh

A660

Black Hill

Eccup Whin

42

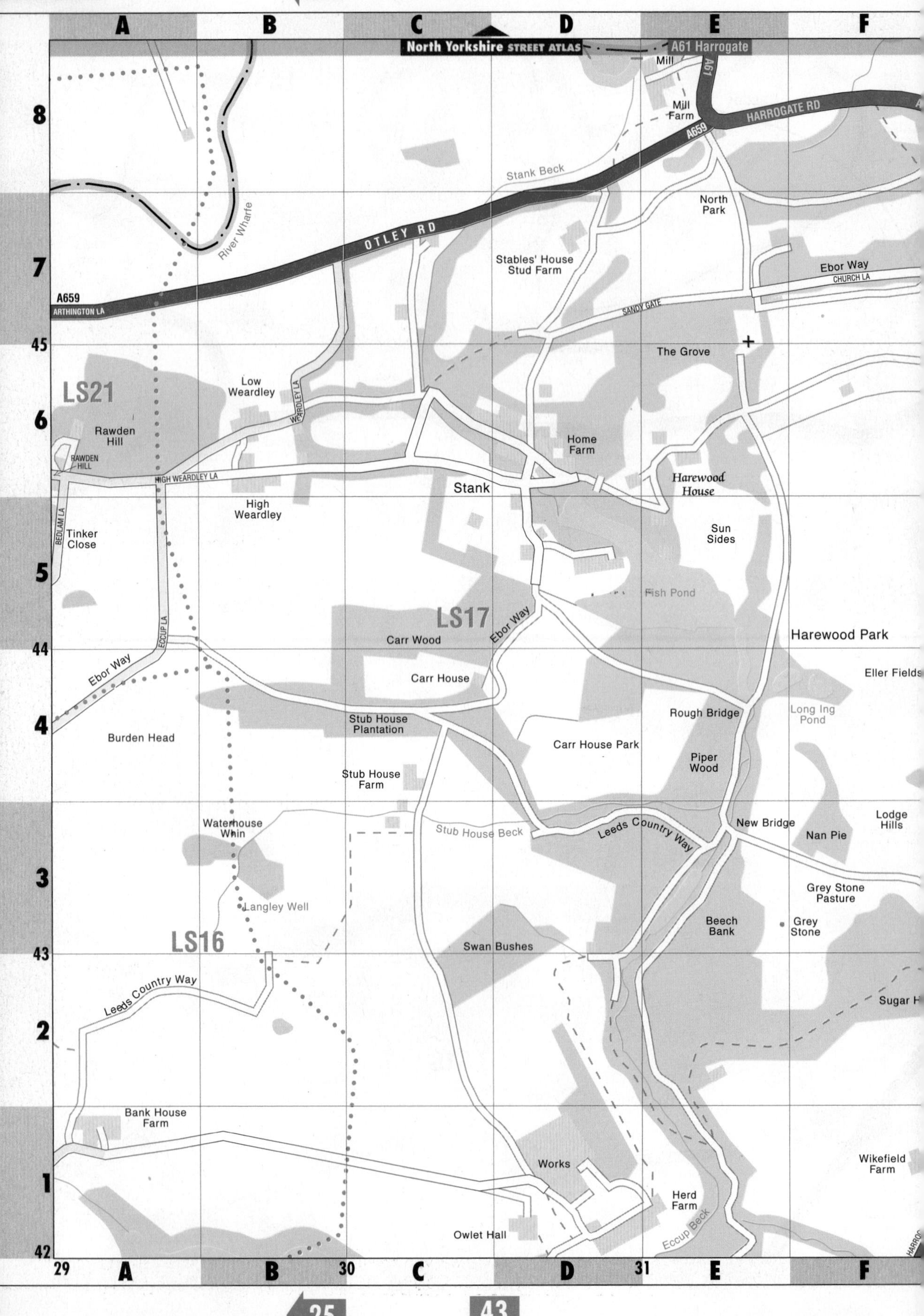

North Yorkshire STREET ATLAS

A61 Harrogate

A B C D E F

Mill

HARROGATE RD

Mill Farm

A659

A61

Stank Beck

North Park

OTLEY RD

Ebor Way

CHURCH LA

8

Stables' House Stud Farm

7

A659
ARTHINGTON LA

SANDY GATE

45

The Grove

+

LS21

Low Weardley

6

Rawden Hill

WEARDLEY LA

Home Farm

Harewood House

Stank

RAWDEN HILL

HIGH WEARDLEY LA

High Weardley

Sun Sides

BEDLAM LA

Tinker Close

Fish Pond

5

Ebor Way

LS17

Harewood Park

44

Carr Wood

Ebor Way

Eller Fields

ECCUP LA

Ebor Way

Carr House

Long Ing Pond

4

Burden Head

Stub House Plantation

Carr House Park

Rough Bridge

Piper Wood

Lodge Hills

Stub House Farm

Waterhouse Whin

Stub House Beck

Leeds Country Way

New Bridge

Nan Pie

3

Langley Well

LS16

Swan Bushes

Beech Bank

Grey Stone

Grey Stone Pasture

43

Leeds Country Way

2

Sugar H

Bank House Farm

1

Works

Herd Farm

Wikefield Farm

Owlet Hall

Eccup Beck

HARRO

42

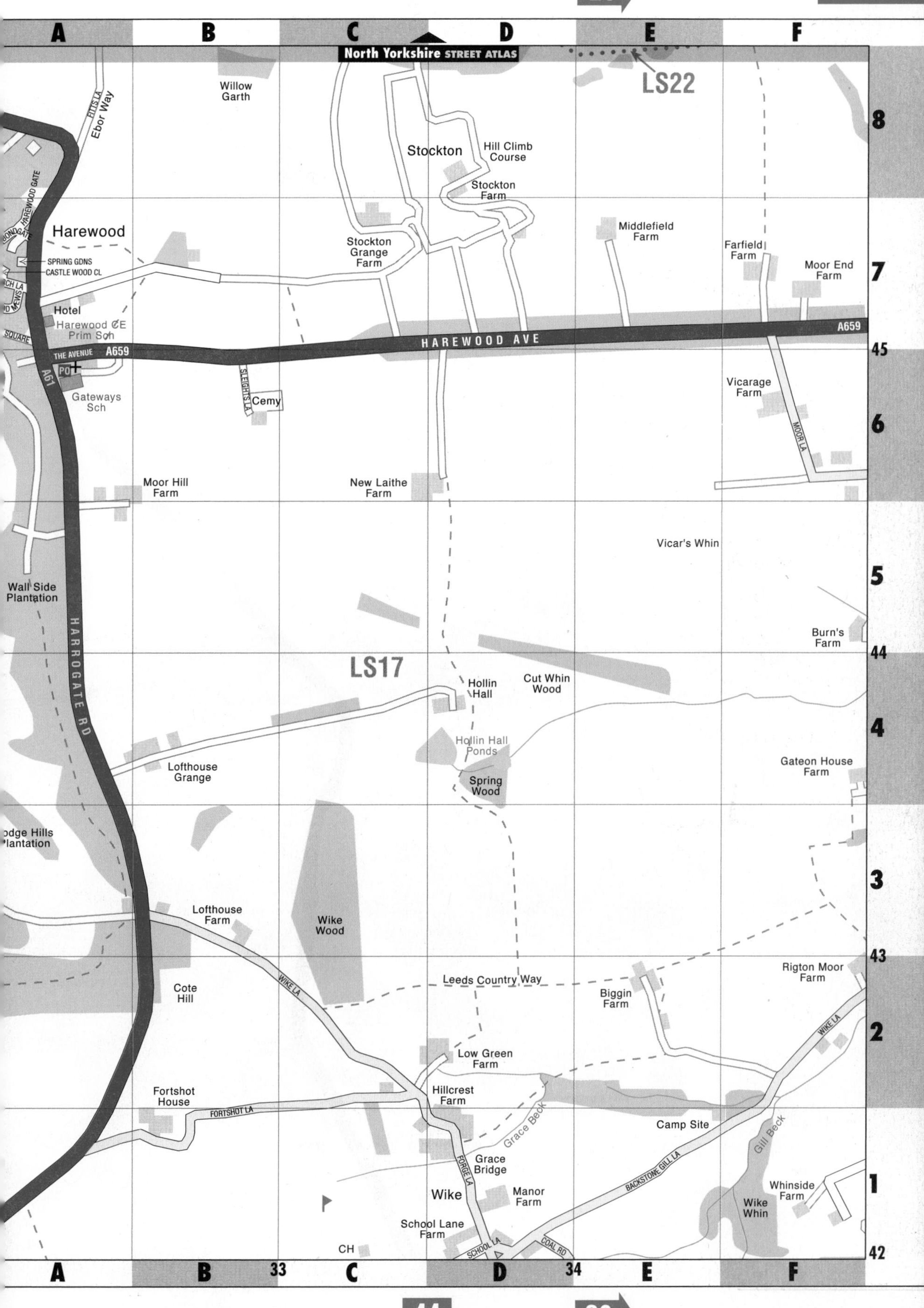

A   B   C   D   E   F

8

North Yorkshire STREET ATLAS

LS22

Willow Garth

Stockton

Hill Climb Course

Stockton Farm

Middlefield Farm

Farfield Farm

Moor End Farm

7

Harewood

SPRING GDNS
CASTLE WOOD CL

Stockton Grange Farm

Hotel
Harewood CE
Prim Sch

HAREWOOD AVE

A659

45

THE AVENUE   A659

PO+

Gateways Sch

SLEIGHTS LA

Cemy

Vicarage Farm

MOOR LA

6

A61

HARROGATE RD

Moor Hill Farm

New Laithe Farm

Vicar's Whin

5

Wall Side Plantation

Burn's Farm

44

LS17

Hollin Hall

Cut Whin Wood

Gateon House Farm

4

Hollin Hall Ponds

Lofthouse Grange

Spring Wood

odge Hills Plantation

3

Lofthouse Farm

Wike Wood

WIKE LA

Rigton Moor Farm

43

Cote Hill

Leeds Country Way

Biggin Farm

WIKE LA

2

Low Green Farm

Fortshot House

Hillcrest Farm

Grace Beck

Camp Site

Gill Beck

1

FORTSHOT LA

FORGE LA

Grace Bridge

BACKSTONE GILL LA

Whinside Farm

Wike

Manor Farm

Wike Whin

School Lane Farm

SCHOOL LA

COAL RD

CH

42

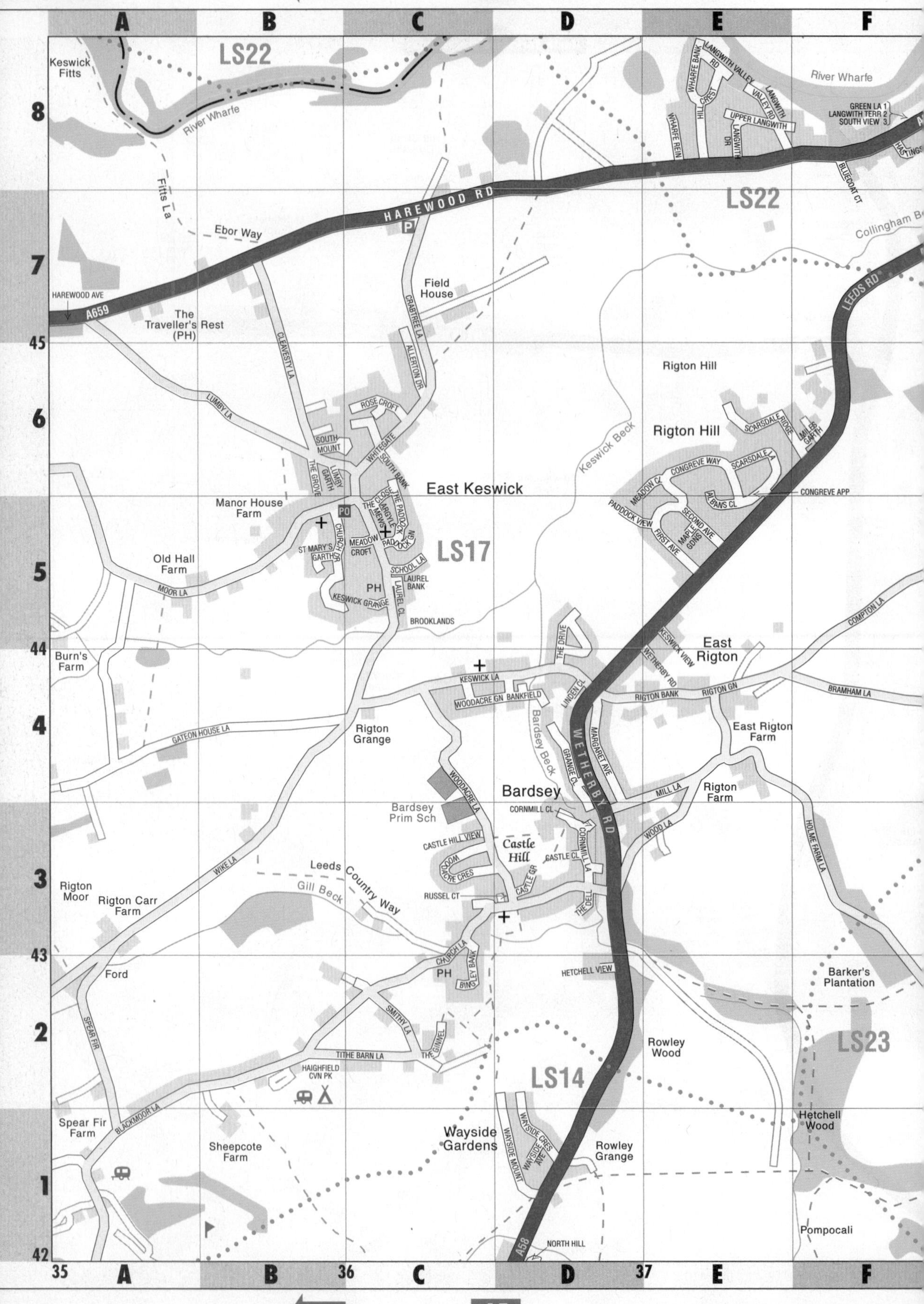

LS22

Keswick Fitts

River Wharfe

LS22

River Wharfe

GREEN LA 1
LANGWITH TERR 2
SOUTH VIEW 3

WHARFE BANK
WHARFE VALLEY RD
LANGWITH VALLEY RD
LANGWITH
CREST
HILL
UPPER LANGWITH
WHARFE REIN
VALLEY DR

HASTINGS

BLUECOAT CT

HAREWOOD RD

Collingham B

LEEDS RD

Ebor Way

Fitts La

Field House

8

7

45

HAREWOOD AVE

A659

The Traveller's Rest (PH)

Rigton Hill

Rigton Hill

SCARSDALE RISE

Keswick Beck

Rigton Hill

CONGREVE WAY

SCARSDALE
UPPER GARTH

6

LUMBY LA

ROSE CROFT

WHITEGATE
SOUTH BANK

SOUTH MOUNT

THE GROVE
LUMBY GARTH

East Keswick

LS17

MEADOW CL
PADDOCK VIEW

ALBANS CL
SECOND AVE
FIRST AVE
MAFT GONG

CONGREVE APP

Manor House Farm

CHURCH LA

THE PADDOCK
THE CLOSE
THE MEWS
KIRK LA
PADD

PO

St Mary's Garth

MEADOW CROFT

SCHOOL LA
LAUREL CL

PH

Old Hall Farm

MOOR LA

KESWICK GRANGE

LAUREL BANK

BROOKLANDS

East Rigton

5

44

Burn's Farm

THE DRIVE

Keswick Beck

WETHERBY RD

East Rigton

COMPTON LA

KESWICK LA

WOODACRE GN
BANKFIELD

LINDEN CL

RIGTON VIEW

Rigton Bank

RIGTON GN

BRAMHAM LA

4

GATEON HOUSE LA

Rigton Grange

Bardsey Beck

MARGARET AVE

East Rigton Farm

MILL LA

Rigton Farm

3

WIKE LA

Leeds Country Way

Gill Beck

WOODACRE LA

Bardsey Prim Sch

CASTLE HILL VIEW

Bardsey

CORNMILL CL

WETHERBY RD

CORNMILL LA

WOOD LA

HOLME FARM LA

Rigton Moor

Rigton Carr Farm

CHURCH LA
RILEY BANK

SCOM
CACHE CRES

Castle Hill

CASTLE GR
CASTLE CL

CORNMILL LA

THE TERR

RUSSEL CT

HETCHELL VIEW

Barker's Plantation

43

Ford

PH

BYNS

SMITHY LA

THE GINNEL

Rowley Wood

LS23

2

SPEAR FIR

TITHE BARN LA

HAIGHFIELD CVN PK

LS14

WAYSIDE CRES
WAYSIDE MOUNT
WAYSIDE AVE

Hetchell Wood

1

BLACKMOOR LA

Spear Fir Farm

Sheepcote Farm

Wayside Gardens

Rowley Grange

Pompocali

42

A58

NORTH HILL

Collingham

LS22

LS17

LS23

Cow Moor

Collingham
Fields

Howcroft
Wood

Collingham
Moor

Mast

Compton Grove

Compton La

Compton

Dalton
Parlours

Waver Spring
Pond

West
Woods

Lady
Wood

Lund
Wood

Dalton
Hill

Spring
Wood

Old Pickhill
Rash

Hope
Hall

Holme
Farm

Wothersome

Stubbing
Moor

Ragdale
Plantation

Stubbing Moor
Plantation

Bramham
Park

Lendrick
Hills

Terry Lug
Farm

Terry Lug
Cotts

HAREWOOD RD

LEEDS RD

A659

MAIN ST

A58

WATTLESYKE

A659

A1

Road under construction

JEWITT LA

COMPTON LA

COMPTON LA

BRAMHAM LA

MOOR LA

BIRDALE FIELD LA

DALTON LA

HOLME FARM LA

THORNER LA

THORNER RD

Bramham Beck

Milner Beck

KENNELS LA

THE VALE

CRABTREE HILL

CRABTREE GN

MILLBECK GN

29
14

A
B
C
D
E
F
8
7
6
5
4
3
2
1
45
44
43
42
41
42
43
Moor End Farm
Moor End
LEYS LA
DEEPDALE LA
WEST AVE
WEST END
THE MOORLANDS
THORP ARCH PK
Weir
THORP ARCH MILL
THE VILLAGE
CHURCH CSWY
WHINS LA
THE GREEN
HIGH ST
A659
MOOR END
A1
Grove Farm
NURSERY WAY
HOLLY RD
WICKHAM CL
PARKFIELD DR
HAYFIELD AVE
MEADOW CL
BOWNAS RD
CHESTNUT AVE
SPRINGFIELD
Holgate Lane
LYNTON AVE
LEE ORCHARDS
BRIDGE CL
MILL LA
BRIDGE FOOT
1 THE CLOSE
2 SHIRES CT
3 HIGHFIELD
4 PINE TREE AVE
River Wharfe
Ebor Way
Church Field
LING CROFT
CHESTNUT GR
PARK RD
JACKDAW LA
OAKS LA
THE ORCHARD
WOODLEA
CHURCH MEWS
ST MARY'S ST
PADMANS LA
ROYAL TERR
BRIDGE RD
Libys
HEATHFIELD LA
CARLETON CL
WICKHAM AVE
BEECH RD
CLARENDON RD
FIELDHEAD PADDOCK
RC Prim Sch
WHITHAM CL
WESTWOOD CROFT
CHURCH ST
LIME TREE AVE
SPA TERRACE
SPA LA
Saline Baths
MOOR SIDE
BRAMBLE AVE
CARLETON DR
QUEEN'S RD
HELMSLEY RD
ST JOHN'S VIEW
JERVAULX CL
IVY LA
FIELDHEAD CT
Sch
Prim Sch
STABLES LA
SPA MEWS
THE TERRACE
RIVERDALE GDNS
HEATH DR
WOODSIDE RD
EGGLESTONE SQ
BOLTON WAY
BYLAND CL
FOUNTAINS AVE
RIEVAULX CL
CHALY FIELDS
APPLE TREE CL
ASHERTON GR
HALL CL
HALL MEWS
BEECHES END
HUDSON MEWS
GROVE PK
ROSEDALE RISE
St Mary's CE Prim Sch
PRIMROSE LA
LIME TREE GDNS
CHESTNUT END
THE SQ
RIVER VIEW
GAS WORKS LA
WINNOW LA
CLIFFORD RD
CLIFFORD MOOR RD
Helmsley Farm
Boston Spa
LONSDALE MEWS
DE CL
GROVE RD
GREEN LEA CL
GROVE GDNS
GROVE CRES
GROVE CRES S
ASHFIELD PADDOCK
Boston Spa Sch
St John's Residential Sch for the Deaf
BOSTON RD
ST JOHN'S RD
Martin House Hospice
GREYSTONE CL 1
HOLLY BUSH CT 2
BOSTON MEWS 3
GROVE TERR 4
GREEN LA
Clifford Moor
CINDER LA
The Albion (PH)
Firgreen Beck
Clifford Moor Farm
RHODES LA
BRIDGE GARTH
WILLOW CRES
WILLOW AVE
MOOR AVE
BELLWOOD AVE
CHAPEL MEWS
BAR LA
WILLOW GR
LOW WAY
BURNS WAY
CHAPEL LA
Firgreen Bridge
LAIRUM RISE
SOUTH VIEW
ALBION ST
ALBION TERR
NURSERY WAY
ASHMEAD 1
WILLOW GLADE 2
ALBION CL 3
ST EDWARD'S TERR 4
CHURCH VIEW MEWS 5
WILLOW LA
ST LUKE'S CL
WESTWOOD COTTS
HIGH ST
CLIFFORD CT
NEW MILL LA
CLIFFORD MILL
Road under construction
NUNNERY WAY
PH
LEA CROFT
SPRINGFIELD
MILL DAM
OLD MILL LA
Clifford
LS23
Wilks Wood
Victoria Farm
VICTORIA PL
BRAMHAM RD
West Woods Farm
Bramham Prim Sch
Carr Beck
WINDMILL RD
HEYGATE LA
THE KNOLL
LYNDON WAY
LYNDON RD
LYNDON CL
LYNDON SQ
LYNDON AVE
LYNDON CRES
CROFT DR
CLIFFORD RD
FIRBECK RD
Windmill
The Mill House
Bramham
MILNTHORPE LA 1
MILNTHORPE GDNS 2
MILNTHORPE CL 3
MILNTHORPE GARTH 4
WETHERBY RD
CROFT RD
BRADFORDS CL
NEW RD
FIVE GARTH CL
CHURCH MDWS
PROSPECT BANK
BACK LA
VICARAGE LA
RHODE'S HILL LA
MILNTHORPE WAY
BACK ST
FRONT ST
LOW WAY
TOWN HILL
HIGH ST
1 BAY HO
2 FREELY FIELDS
3 FOSSARDS CL
4 CROPSTONES
5 CHURCH HILL
TOULSTON LA
TENTER HILL
ALMSHOUSE HILL
CRAG GDNS
THE CRAG
FOLLY LA
FOLLY VIEW
ORCHARD CT
THORNER RD
New York Farm
BOWCLIFFE RD
FREELY LA
ABERFORD RD
Biggin Park
Bramham House
Bramham Lodge
Bramham Moor
Bramham Beck
Bramham Biggin
HEADLEY LA
Bramham Park
Openrakes Beck
Well Hill
Bowcliffe Hall
Road under construction
Wellhill Farm
LS2

29
47

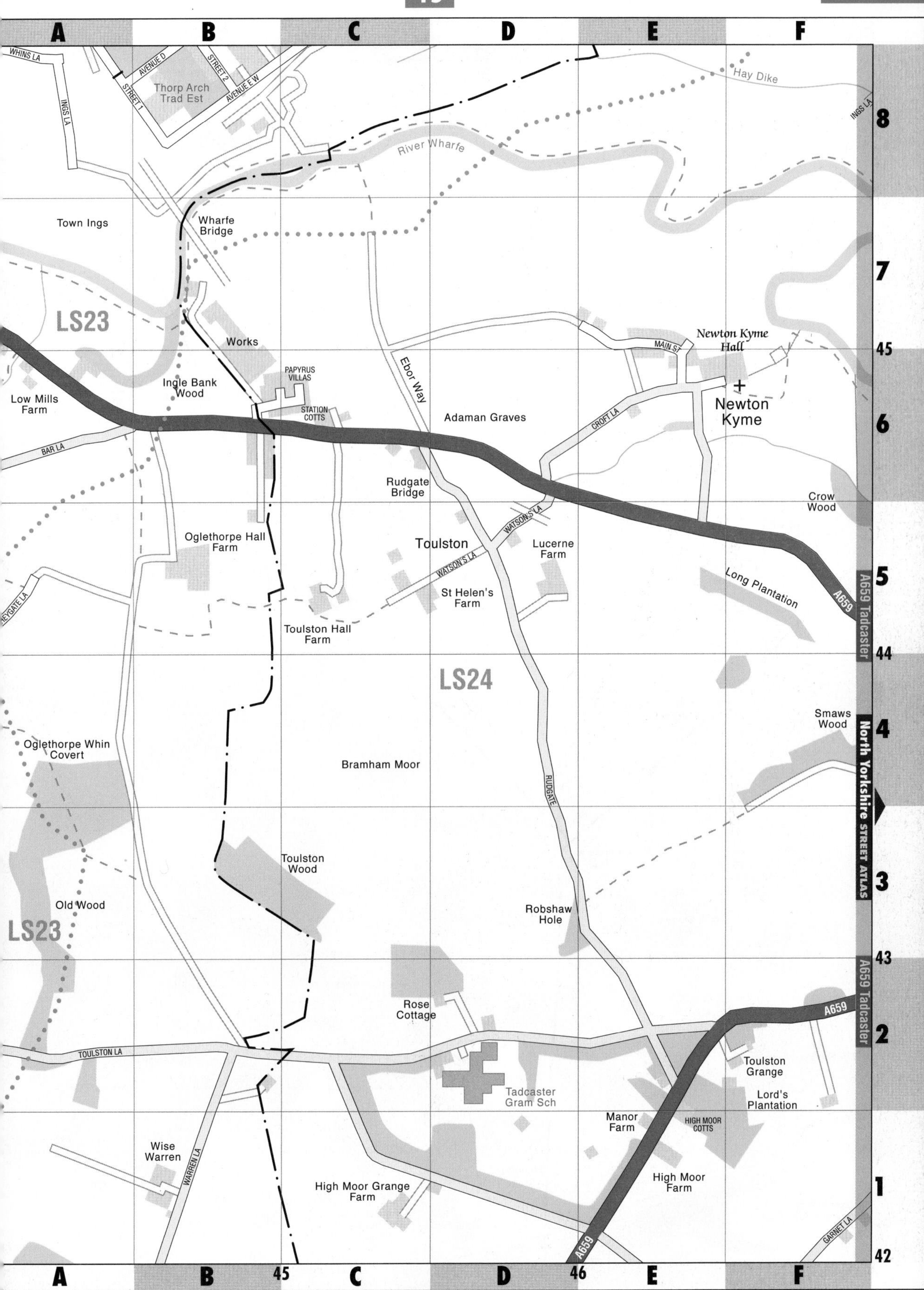

A B C D E F

8

WHINS LA

INGS LA

AVENUE D

STREET 2

STREET 1

Thorp Arch Trad Est

AVENUE E W

Hay Dike

INGS LA

River Wharfe

Town Ings

Wharfe Bridge

7

LS23

Works

45

Low Mills Farm

Ingle Bank Wood

PAPYRUS VILLAS

Ebor Way

Adaman Graves

Main St

Newton Kyme Hall

Newton Kyme

6

BAR LA

STATION COTTS

Croft La

Rudgate Bridge

Crow Wood

Oglethorpe Hall Farm

Watson's La

Toulston

Watson's La

Lucerne Farm

Long Plantation

A659 Tadcaster

5

HEYGATE LA

Toulston Hall Farm

St Helen's Farm

44

LS24

Smaws Wood

4

Oglethorpe Whin Covert

Bramham Moor

RUDGATE

North Yorkshire STREET ATLAS

3

Old Wood

Toulston Wood

Robshaw Hole

LS23

43

Rose Cottage

A659 Tadcaster

A659

2

TOULSTON LA

Tadcaster Gram Sch

Toulston Grange

Lord's Plantation

Manor Farm

HIGH MOOR COTTS

Wise Warren

WARREN LA

High Moor Grange Farm

High Moor Farm

1

A659

GARNETT LA

42

A B C **45** C D **46** E F

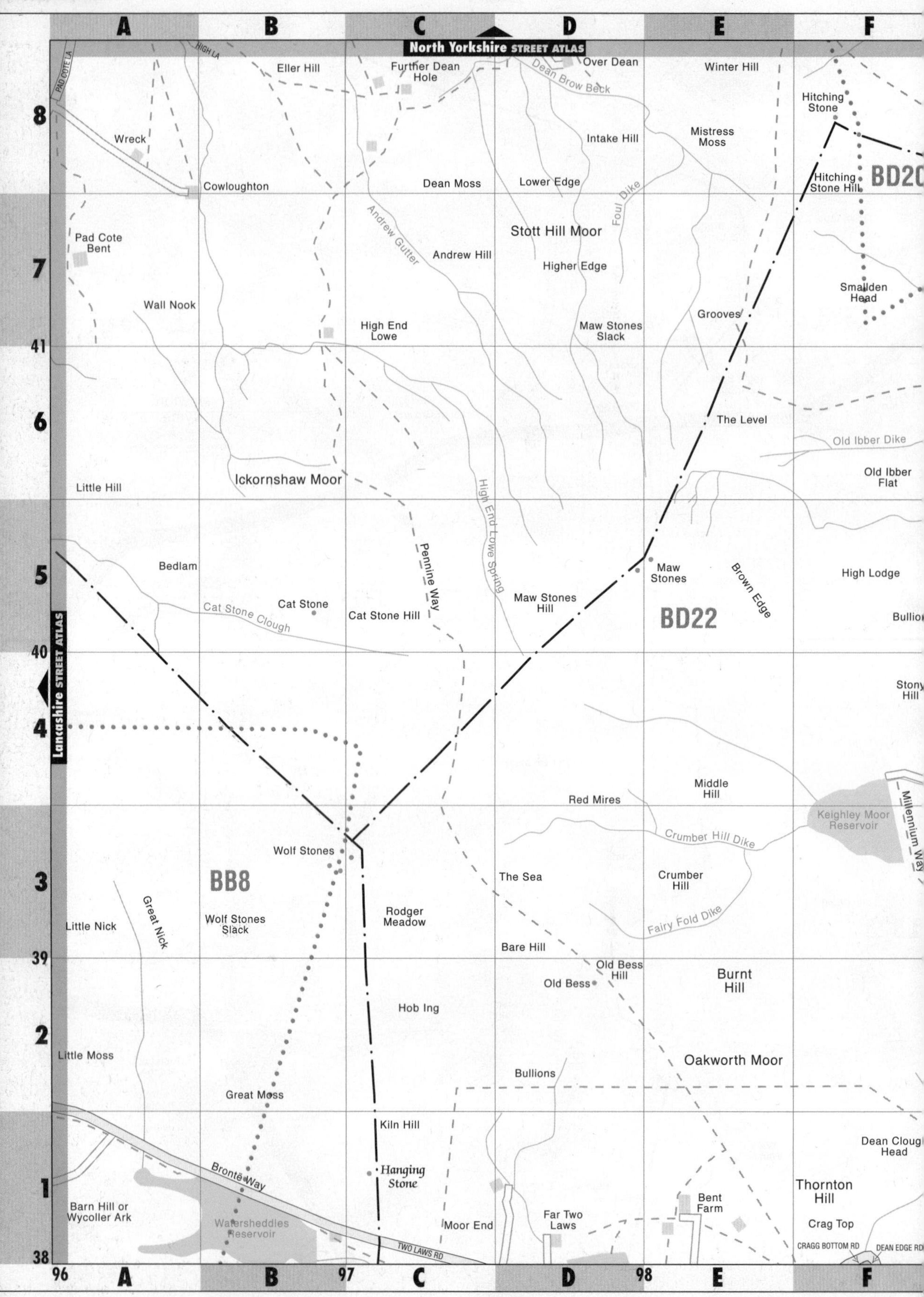

A **B** **C** **D** **E** **F**

PAD COTE LA

HIGH LA

8

Eller Hill

Further Dean Hole

Over Dean

Dean Brow Beck

Winter Hill

Hitching Stone

Wreck

Intake Hill

Mistress Moss

BD2O

Cowloughton

Dean Moss

Lower Edge

Foul Dike

Hitching Stone Hill

Pad Cote Bent

Andrew Gutter

Stott Hill Moor

7

Andrew Hill

Higher Edge

Smallden Head

Wall Nook

High End Lowe

Maw Stones Slack

Grooves

41

Little Hill

Ickornshaw Moor

High End Lowe Spring

The Level

Old Ibber Dike

6

Old Ibber Flat

Bedlam

Pennine Way

Maw Stones Hill

Maw Stones

High Lodge

5

Cat Stone

Cat Stone Clough

Cat Stone Hill

Brown Edge

BD22

Bullion

40

Stony Hill

4

Middle Hill

Red Mires

Keighley Moor Reservoir

Millennium Way

Crumber Hill Dike

Wolf Stones

BB8

The Sea

Crumber Hill

Fairy Fold Dike

3

Little Nick

Great Nick

Wolf Stones Slack

Rodger Meadow

Bare Hill

39

Old Bess Hill

Old Bess

Burnt Hill

2

Hob Ing

Little Moss

Bullions

Oakworth Moor

Great Moss

Kiln Hill

Dean Clough Head

1

Bronte Way

Hanging Stone

Thornton Hill

Barn Hill or Wycoller Ark

Watersheddles Reservoir

Moor End

Far Two Laws

Bent Farm

Crag Top

CRAGG BOTTOM RD

DEAN EDGE RD

TWO LAWS RD

38

96 **A** **B** **97** **C** **D** **98** **E** **F**

Lancashire STREET ATLAS

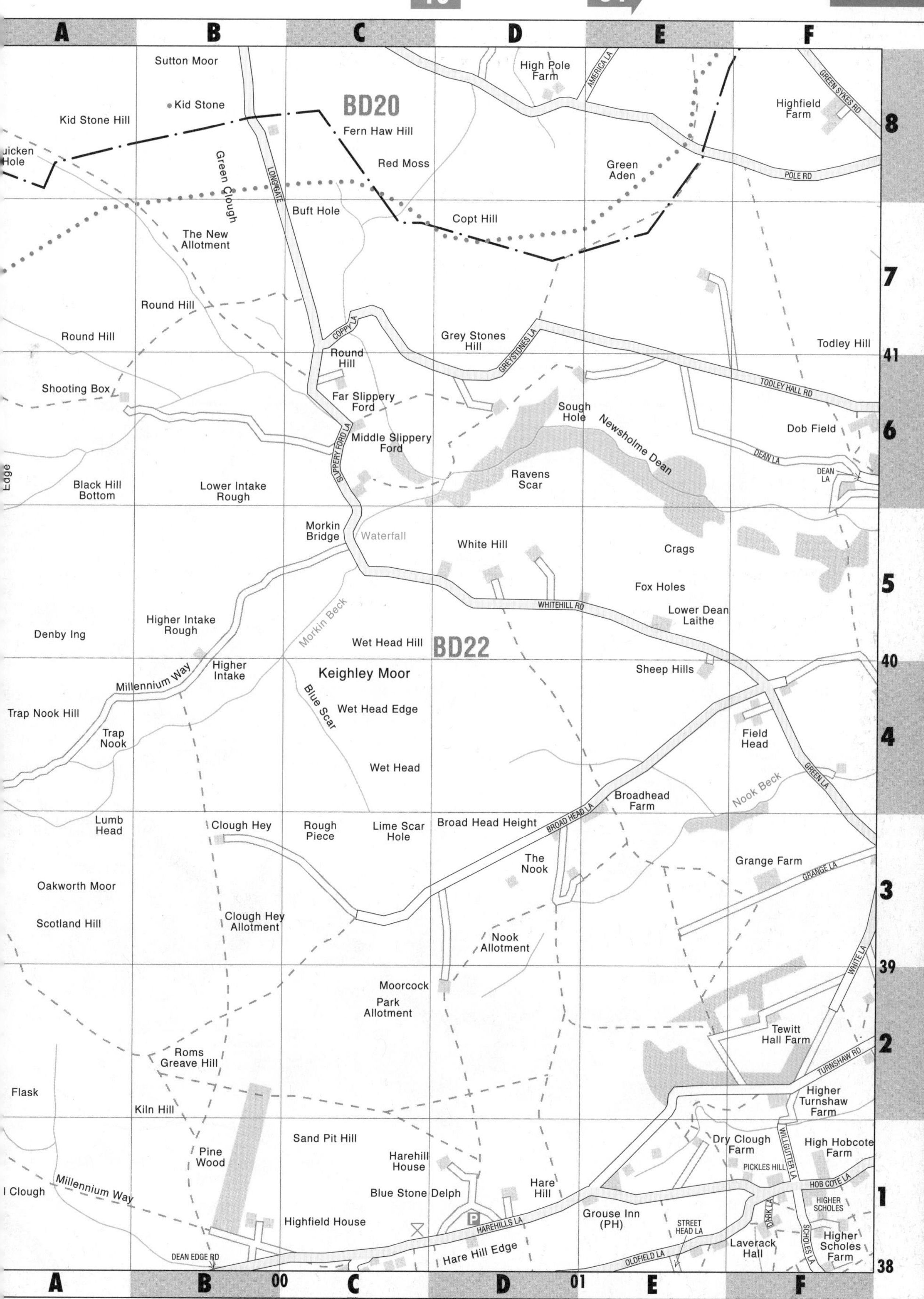

	A	B	C	D	E	F

Sutton Moor

High Pole Farm

AMERICA LA

Highfield Farm

GREEN STOKES RD

Kid Stone

BD20

8

Kid Stone Hill

Fern Haw Hill

Quicken Hole

Red Moss

Green Aden

POLE RD

LONGGATE

Green Clough

Buft Hole

Copt Hill

The New Allotment

7

Round Hill

41

Round Hill

Round Hill

Grey Stones Hill

GREYSTONES LA

Todley Hill

COPPY LA

TODLEY HALL RD

Shooting Box

Far Slippery Ford

Sough Hole

Newsholme Dean

DEAN LA

Dob Field

6

Edge

Black Hill Bottom

Lower Intake Rough

SLIPPERY FORD LA

Middle Slippery Ford

Ravens Scar

DEAN LA

Morkin Bridge

Waterfall

White Hill

Crags

5

Morkin Beck

Fox Holes

Higher Intake Rough

BD22

Wet Head Hill

WHITEHILL RD

Lower Dean Laithe

Denby Ing

Higher Intake

Keighley Moor

40

Sheep Hills

Millennium Way

Blue Scar

Wet Head Edge

Field Head

4

Trap Nook Hill

Trap Nook

Wet Head

GREEN LA

Nook Beck

Lumb Head

Clough Hey

Rough Piece

Lime Scar Hole

Broad Head Height

BROAD HEAD LA

Broadhead Farm

Grange Farm

GRANGE LA

Oakworth Moor

The Nook

3

Scotland Hill

Clough Hey Allotment

Nook Allotment

39

WHITE LA

Moorcock Park Allotment

Tewitt Hall Farm

2

TURNSHAW RD

Roms Greave Hill

Higher Turnshaw Farm

Flask

Kiln Hill

Dry Clough Farm

High Hobcote Farm

Sand Pit Hill

Pine Wood

Harehill House

PICKLES HILL LA

WHILGUTTER LA

HOB COTE LA

I Clough

Millennium Way

Highfield House

Blue Stone Delph

P

Hare Hill

Grouse Inn (PH)

STREET HEAD LA

HIGHER SCHOLES

1

Laverack Hall

Higher Scholes Farm

DEAN EDGE RD

HAREHILLS LA

Hare Hill Edge

OLDFIELD LA

SCHOLES LA

38

	A	B	C	D	E	F
		00		01		

33 17

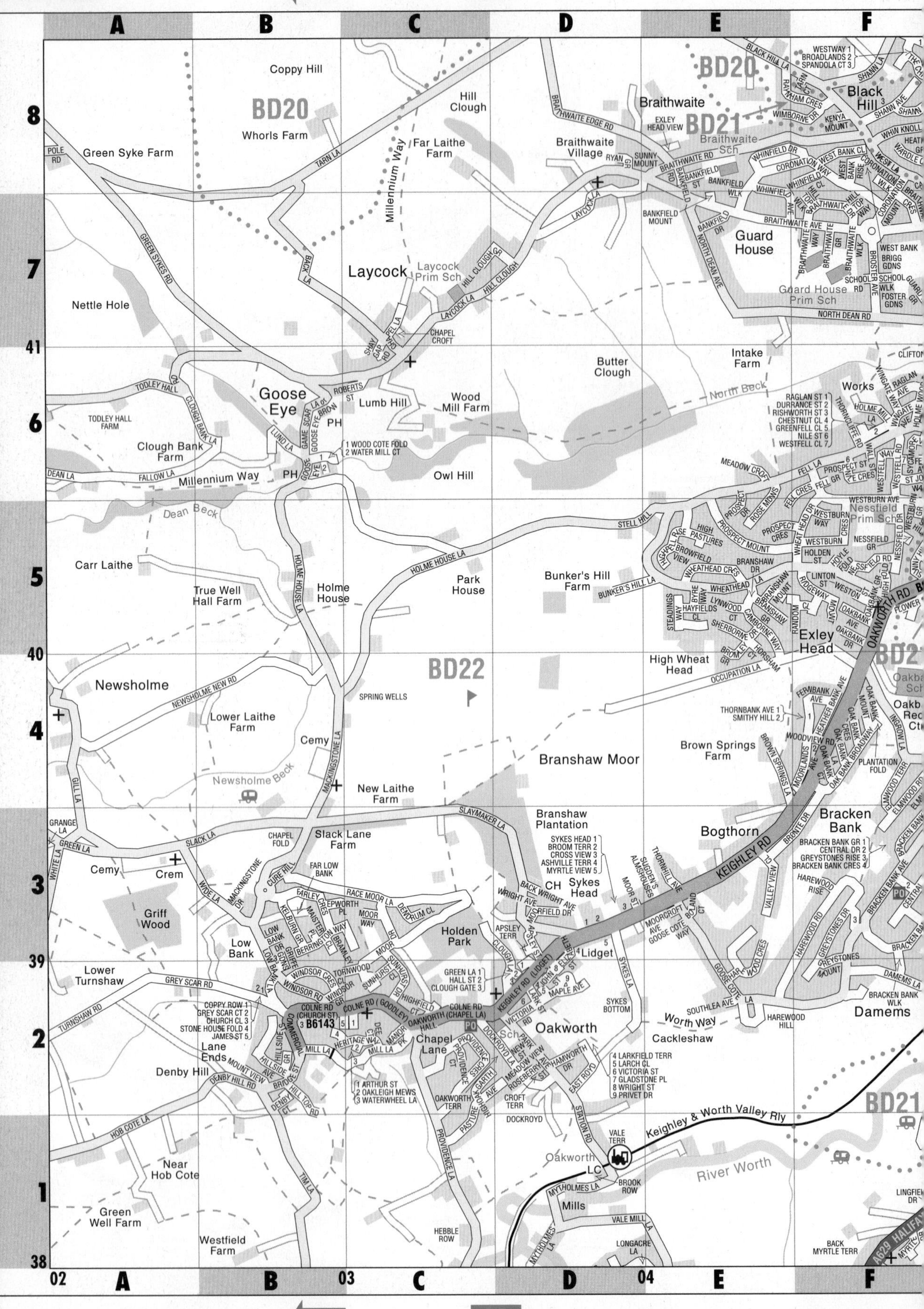
A
B
C
D
E
F
8
7
41
6
5
40
4
3
39
2
1
38
02
03
04
Coppy Hill
BD20
Whorls Farm
Hill Clough
Far Laithe Farm
Millennium Way
Braithwaite
BD21
Braithwaite Village
Braithwaite Sch
Black Hill
Green Syke Farm
Pole Rd
Tarn La
Green Sykes Rd
Back La
Laycock
Laycock Prim Sch
Laycock La
Hill Clough
Hill Clough Gr
Guard House
Guard House Prim Sch
North Dean Rd
North Dean Ave
Nettle Hole
Chapel Croft
Intake Farm
Butter Clough
North Beck
Works
Todley Hall Rd
Todley Hall Farm
Goose Eye
Lumb Hill
Wood Mill Farm
Roberts St
PH
Clough Bank Farm
Clough Bank La
Fallow La
Dean La
Millennium Way
Owl Hill
1 Wood Cote Fold
2 Water Mill Ct
Meadow Croft
Dean Beck
Stell Hill
Carr Laithe
True Well Hall Farm
Holme House
Holme House La
Park House
Bunker's Hill Farm
Bunker's Hill La
Nessfield Prim Sch
Exley Head
Oakworth Rd
High Wheat Head
Occupation La
Newsholme
Newsholme New Rd
Lower Laithe Farm
BD22
Spring Wells
Cemy
Branshaw Moor
Brown Springs Farm
Mackingstone La
New Laithe Farm
Newsholme Beck
Gill La
Grange La
Green La
White La
Slack La
Chapel Fold
Slack Lane Farm
Slaymaker La
Branshaw Plantation
Bogthorn
Keighley Rd
Bracken Bank
Cemy
Crem
Griff Wood
Sykes Head
CH
Low Bank
Holden Park
Lidget
Lower Turnshaw
Grey Scar Rd
Turnshaw Rd
B6143
Colne Rd
Oakworth
Chapel Lane
Sykes Bottom
Worth Way
Cackleshaw
Damems
Lane Ends
Denby Hill
Denby Hill Rd
Mount View
Hob Cote La
Providence La
Dockroyd
Station Rd
Vale Terr
Keighley & Worth Valley Rly
River Worth
BD21
Oakworth
LC
Brook Row
Mytholmes La
Mills
Vale Mill La
Near Hob Cote
Tim La
Green Well Farm
Westfield Farm
Hebble Row
Longacre La
Back Myrtle Terr
A629 Halifax

33 51

A6
1 Nashville Terr
2 Nashville St
3 Carlby Gr
4 Nashville Rd
5 BK Rydal St
6 Cross Rydal Rd

7 Back Oxford St
8 Hardwick St
9 Fourth Ave
10 Cross Lister St
11 BK Mannville Rd
12 Cheyne Wlk
13 Mannville Way

14 Mannville Wlk
15 Mannville Pl
16 Arncliffe Gr
17 Arncliffe Pl
18 Queen Elizabeth Ct
A7
1 BK Simpson St

2 Spencer St
3 Waterhouse St
4 Talbot St
5 BK Sladen St
6 Sladen St
7 BK Paget St
8 Paget St

9 BK Edensor Rd
10 BK Ada St
11 Ada St
12 BK Cartmel Rd
13 The Gables
14 Poplar Terr
15 New Town Ct

B6
1 Third Ave
2 Second Ave
3 First Ave
4 Ward St
5 BK Balfour St
6 Balfour St

B6
7 BK Hird St
8 BK Acres St
9 Ashfield St
10 Back Minnie St
11 Calton St
12 Kensington St

B6
13 North Beck Ho
14 Ebor Ct
15 Quebec Ho
16 George's Sq
17 Mantra Ho Bsns Ctr
18 St Peter's Ct

E8
1 Rylstone St
2 BK Rylstone St
3 Grape St
4 Timber St
5 Airedale Rd

18 **36** **35**

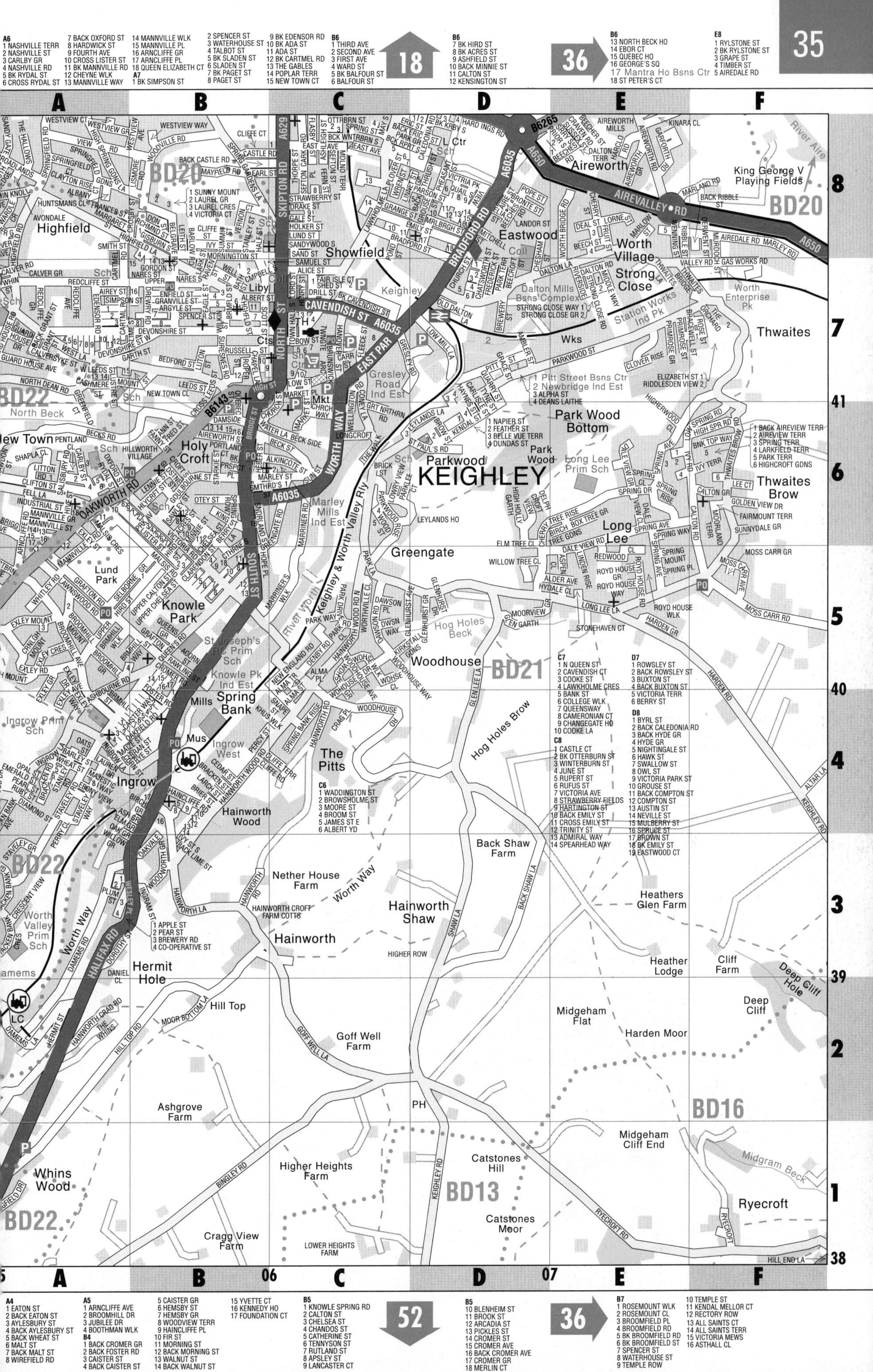

C7
1 N Queen St
2 Cavendish St
3 Cooke St
4 Bank St
5 College Wlk
6 Queensway
7 Changegate
8 Changegate Ho
9 Cooke La

C8
1 Castle Ct
2 BK Otterburn St
3 Winterburn St
4 June St
5 Rupert St
6 Rufus St
7 Victoria Ave
8 Strawberry Fields
9 Hartington St
10 Back Emily St
11 Cross Emily St
12 Trinity St
13 Admiral Way
14 Spearhead Way

C6
1 Waddington St
2 Browsholme St
3 Moore St
4 Broom St
5 James St E
6 Albert Yd

D7
1 Rowsley St
2 Back Rowsley St
3 Buxton St
4 Back Buxton St
5 Victoria Terr
6 Berry St

D8
1 Byrl St
2 Back Caledonia Rd
3 Back Hyde Gr
4 Hyde Gr
5 Nightingale St
6 Hawk St
7 Swallow St
8 Owl St
9 Victoria Park St
10 Grouse St
11 Back Compton St
12 Compton St
13 Austin St
14 Neville St
15 Mulberry St
16 Spruce St
17 Brown St
18 BK Emily St
19 Eastwood Ct

A4
1 Eaton St
2 Back Eaton St
3 Aylesbury St
4 Back Aylesbury St
5 Back Wheat St
6 Back Malt St
7 Wirefield Rd

A5
1 Arncliffe Ave
2 Broomhill Dr
3 Jubilee Dr
4 Boothman Wlk
B4
1 Back Cromer Gr
2 Back Foster Rd
3 Caister St
4 Back Caister St

5 Caister Gr
6 Hemsby Gr
7 Hemsby Pl
8 Woodview Terr
9 Haincliffe Pl
10 Rift St
11 Morning St
12 Back Morning St
13 Walnut St
14 Back Walnut St

15 Yvette Ct
16 Kennedy Ho
17 Foundation Ct

B5
1 Knowle Spring Rd
2 Calton St
3 Chelsea St
4 Chandos St
5 Catherine St
6 Tennyson St
7 Rutland St
8 Apsley St
9 Lancaster St

B5
10 Blenheim St
11 Brook St
12 Arcadia St
13 Pickles St
14 Cromer St
15 Cromer Ave
16 Back Cromer Ave
17 Cromer St
18 Merlin St

B7
1 Rosemount Wlk
2 Rosemount Cl
3 Broomfield Pl
4 Broomfield Rd
5 BK Broomfield St
6 BK Broomfield St
7 Spencer St
8 Waterhouse St
9 Sherborne Rd

10 Temple St
11 Kendal Mellor Ct
12 Rectory Row
13 All Saints St
14 All Saints Terr
15 Victoria Mews
16 Asthall Cl

52 **36**

35
19

East Morton
Micklethwaite
Crossflatts
Harden
Cemy
Swine Lane Bridge
Nursery Farm
Hebble Bridge
Carr House Farm
Hill Top Farm
Sewage Works
Cliff Farm
Morton Bridge (Swing)
Crossflatts Prim Sch
Leeds & Liverpool Canal
Deer Park
Laythorpe
Greenhill Farm
Works
Round Hill
Currer Laithe Farm
Marley
Marley Brow
Hutler Hill
Upper Transfield Farm
Castlefields Ind Est
River Aire
Transfield Top
Raven Royd Farm
Druid's Altar
Hollin Plantation
Bingley Grammar Sch
Swing Bridge
Bingley Five Rise Locks
Bailey Hills
Race Course Plantation
Cross Gates
Heather Park
Lady Blantyre's Rock
Home Farm
Coppice Pond
St Ives Est
Moor Edge
Low Park
Cuckoo Nest
Myrtle Park
Myrtle Park Prim Sch
Ford
Beck Foot
Woodbank
Harden Grange
Harden Beck
Millennium Way
BD20
BD21
BD16
AIREVALLEY RD
BRADFORD RD
HARDEN RD
KEIGHLEY RD
MAIN ST
LONG LA
ALTAR LA
B6265
B6429
A650

35
53

A1
1 HAZELHURST AVE
2 HAZEL BECK
3 HAZELMERE AVE
A2
1 CRANBROOK HO
2 EMSLEY HO
3 BENTINCK HO
4 PORTLAND PL
5 YORK CRES

6 CANNON ST
7 ROBERTSHAW HO
8 CALVERT HO
9 WEST VIEW HO
10 HEALEY LA
11 HARRIS ST
12 LEONARD'S PL
13 MERCHANTS CT
14 ASHFIELD CT
15 BACK UNITY ST S

16 OAK BANK
17 HARRISON ST
A3
1 CROSS LA
2 CHARLES ST
3 LYNDON TERR
4 NORFOLK ST
5 RUTLAND HO
6 KELL ST
7 WHITLEY ST

8 BARRAN ST
9 AMY ST
10 JARDINE RD
11 PREACHERS MEWS
12 MYRTLE ST
13 SYDNEY ST
14 BELMONT MEWS
15 HOLMCARR CT
16 ELLEN ST
17 FERNBANK AVE

18 ELIZABETH ST
19 NETHER MOOR VIEW
20 EBRIDGE CT
21 AYRTON CRES
22 FALKLAND CT
23 FERNBANK RD
24 DUBB LA
25 OLIVE TERR
26 FERRAND ST
27 ST JOHN'S HO

A3
28 RICHMOND HO
29 OXFORD HO
30 ELDON HO

A4
1 MONK BARN CL
2 LEYBURN GR
3 WESTLEIGH
4 STAVELEY RD
5 STAVELEY MEWS
6 SHELLEY CT
7 FOULDS' TERR
8 PRIORY CL
9 SCARWOOD CL

F1
1 ALBERT RD
2 HERBERT ST
3 FANNY ST
4 EDWARD ST
5 AMELIA ST
6 GEORGE ST
7 WILLIAM HENRY ST

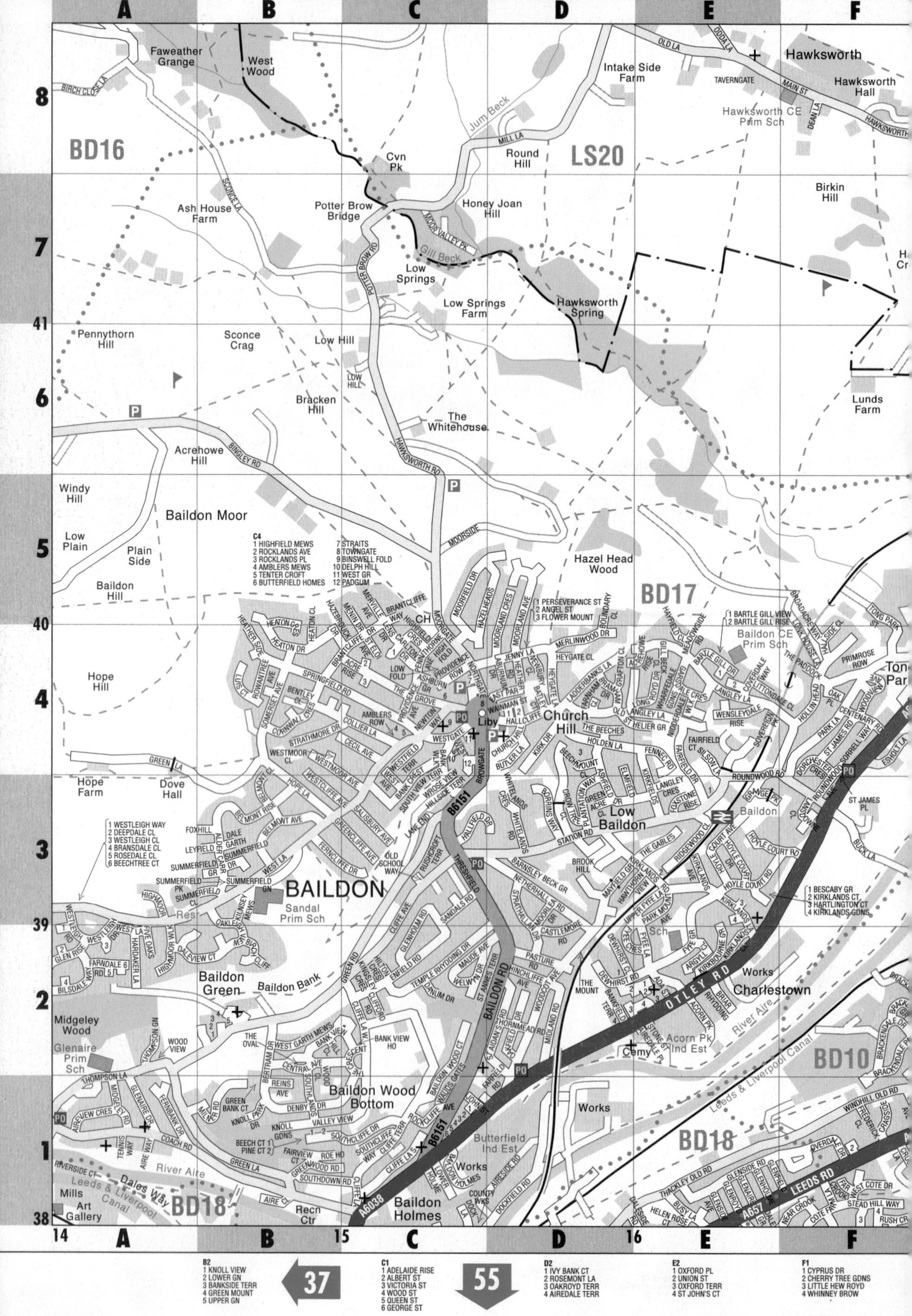

C4
1 HIGHFIELD MEWS
2 ROCKLANDS AVE
3 ROCKLANDS PL
4 AMBLERS MEWS
5 TENTER CROFT
6 BUTTERFIELD HOMES
7 STRAITS
8 TOWNGATE
9 BINSWELL FOLD
10 DELPH RISE
11 WEST GR
12 PADGUM

1 WESTLEIGH WAY
2 DEEPDALE CL
3 WESTLEIGH CL
4 BRANSDALE CL
5 ROSEDALE CL
6 BEECHTREE CT

1 PERSEVERANCE ST
2 ANGEL ST
3 FLOWER MOUNT

1 BARTLE GILL VIEW
2 BARTLE GILL RISE

1 BESCABY GR
2 KIRKLANDS CT
3 HARTLINGTON CT
4 KIRKLANDS GDNS

B2
1 KNOLL VIEW
2 LOWER GN
3 BANKSIDE TERR
4 GREEN MOUNT
5 UPPER GN

C1
1 ADELAIDE RISE
2 ALBERT ST
3 VICTORIA ST
4 WOOD ST
5 QUEEN ST
6 GEORGE ST

D2
1 IVY BANK CT
2 ROSEMONT LA
3 OAKROYD TERR
4 AIREDALE TERR

E2
1 OXFORD PL
2 UNION ST
3 OXFORD ST
4 ST JOHN'S CT

F1
1 CYPRUS DR
2 CHERRY TREE GDNS
3 LITTLE HEW ROYD
4 WHINNEY BROW

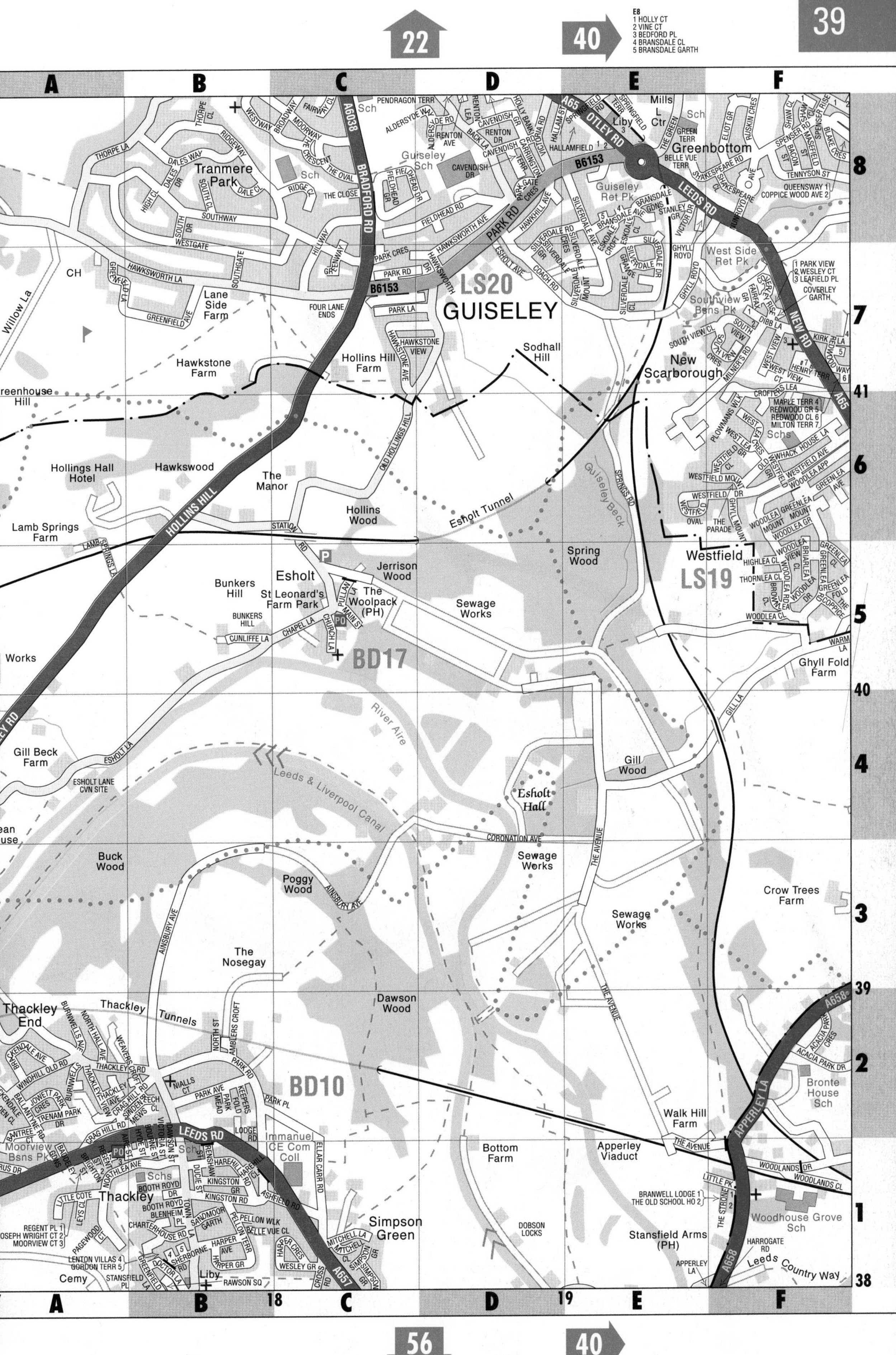

B7
1 HAWORTH CT
2 CHAPEL HILL
3 DEVONSHIRE PL
4 TOWN HALL SQ
5 MANOR SQ
6 OLD HAWORTH LA
7 LANE FOX CT
8 HARPER TERR
9 SOUTH VIEW RD
10 SANDY WAY
11 THE GREEN
12 MANOR TERR
13 NETHERFIELD TERR

39

B7
14 BANKSFIELD TERR
15 MARSHALL CT

C7
1 ST ANDREWS CL
2 GRANVILLE TERR
3 CAVENDISH ST

23

C7
4 HUDSON'S TERR
5 CARLTON TERR
6 BACK ALMA ST
7 ALEXANDRA TERR
8 QUARRY MT
9 FLOWER MT
10 ROCKFIELD TERR
11 ALBERT TERR
12 ALBERT SQ

A B C D E F

8 7 41 6 5 40 4 3 39 2 1 38

Yeadon Banks
Yeadon Haw
Cemy
Yeadon Moor
Coney Lodge Farm
Harrogate Rd
Carlton Beck
Hotel
Shaw Lane
Damfield Farm
LS20
Yeadon Tarn
Nunroyd Park
1 SUNNYBANK CRES
2 SUNNYBANK CT
Leeds Bradford International Airport
Sports Ctr
Liby
World's End
Kirk Lane Mills
Westfield Ind Est
TH
Bsns Pk
Sch
Motel
Plane Tree Hill
Henshaw
Rufford Park
Cold Harbour Farm
DINSDALE'S BLDGS
PENNYTHORNE CT
Low Hall
GREENACRE PARK MEWS 1
BENTON PARK AVE 2
Greenside Farm
YEADON
Nether Yeadon
LS19
Larkfield
Billing Hill
Rawdon Littlemoor Prim Sch
Larkfield Dam
LONDON ST 1
PRINCESS ST 2
BACK LOMBARD ST 3
GROSVENOR MEWS 4
UPPER LOMBARD ST 5
THE ROW 6
1 LAKESIDE WLK
2 LAKESIDE VIEW
3 LAKESIDE TERR
4 MOUNT VERNON RD
5 LAKESIDE GDNS
6 LAKESIDE CHASE
7 KEELHAM DR
LS18
Whetstone Farm
Rawdon
1 WENTWORTH TERR
2 BILLINGWOOD DR
3 EGERTON TERR
4 AIREDALE VIEW
Bayton House
Little London
Rawdon St Peter's CE Prim Sch
CH
Lane Ends
Rawdon Hall
HENLEY HILL 1
HIGHFIELD TERR 2
HENLEY VIEW 3
Low Green
Beechwood
Horn Hill
Gill Beck
Acacia Farm
Cragg Wood
Rawdon Carrs
Works
BD10
River Aire
Leeds Country Way
West End
Woodhouse Bridge
LS28
Cragg Wood
Crem
Woodleigh Hall Farm
Well Royd
Leeds & Liverpool Canal

20 A B 21 C D 22 E F

39

C6
1 WINDMILL FOLD
2 WINDMILL PL
3 SPRINGWELL TERR
4 SPRINGWELL CL
5 GRANGE TERR

57

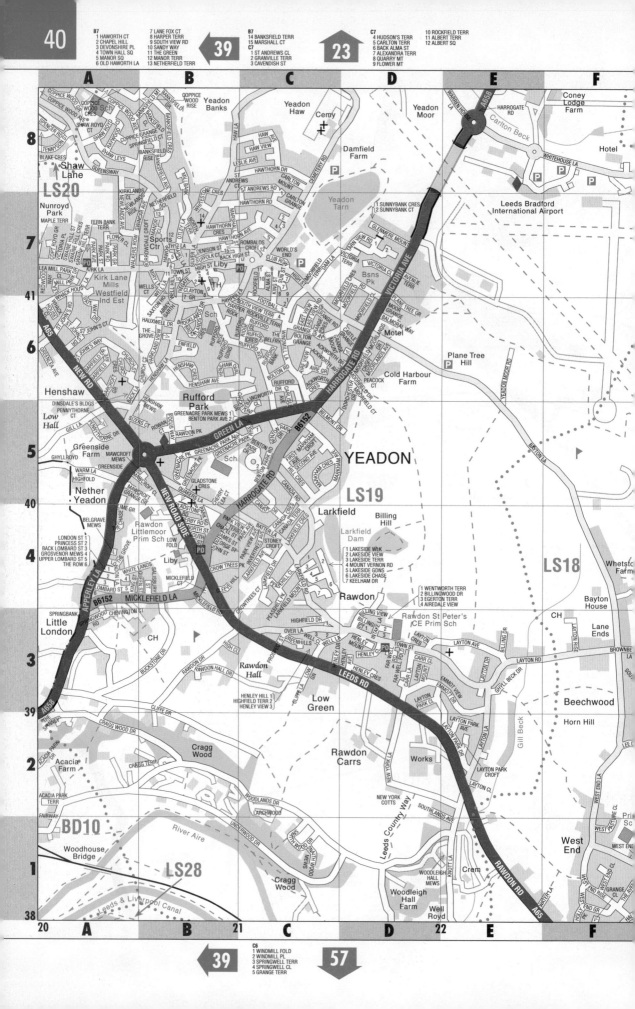

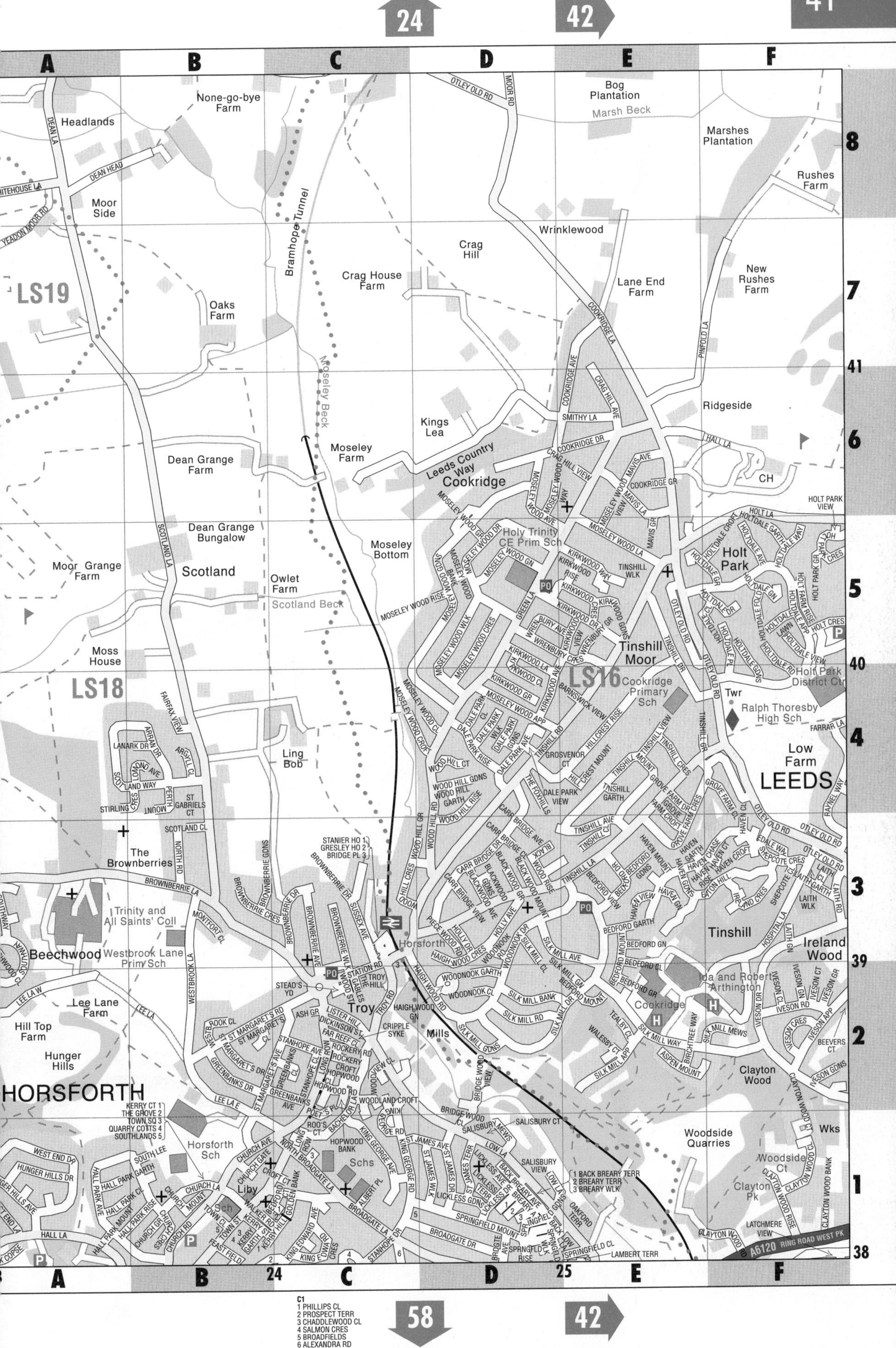

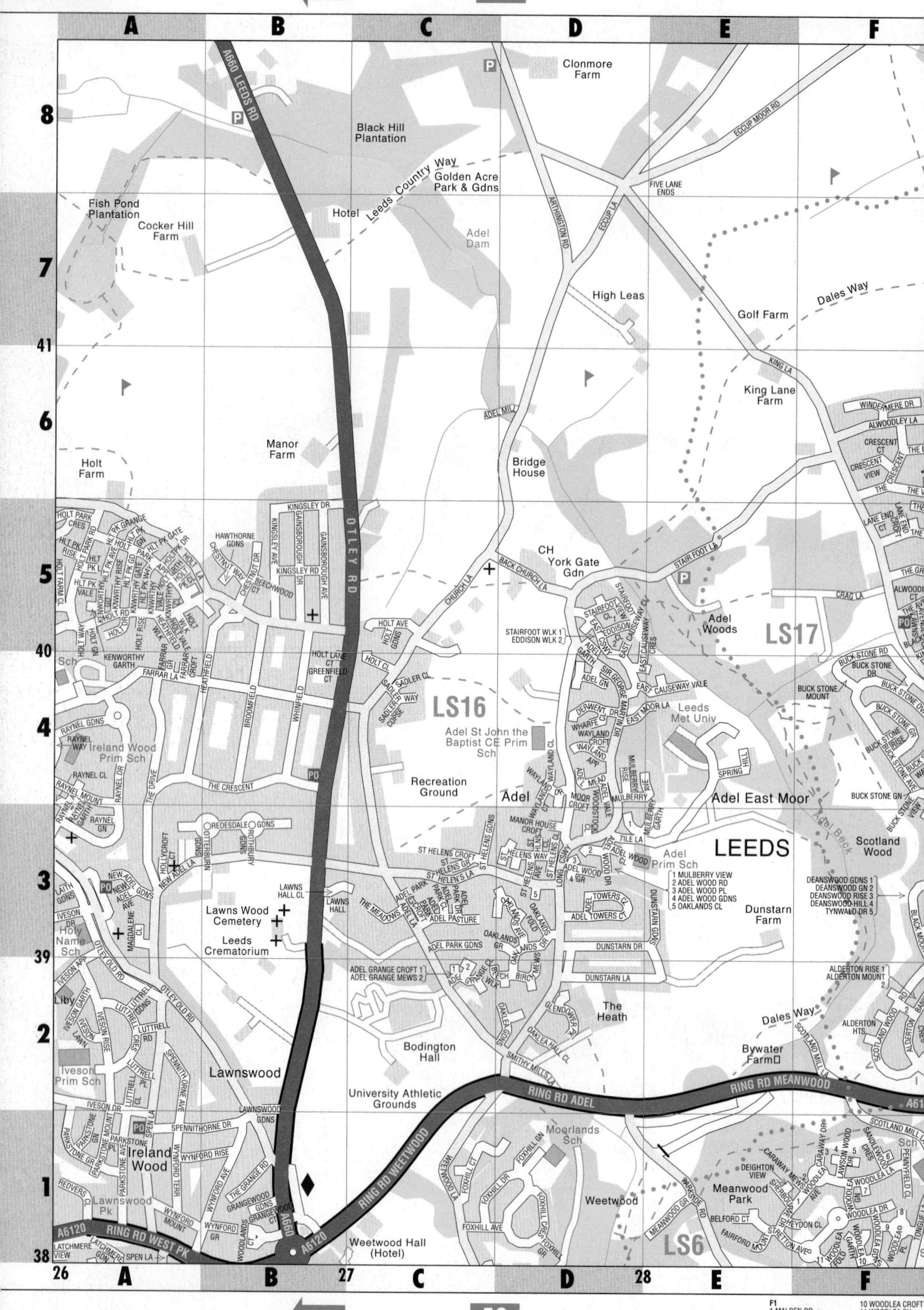

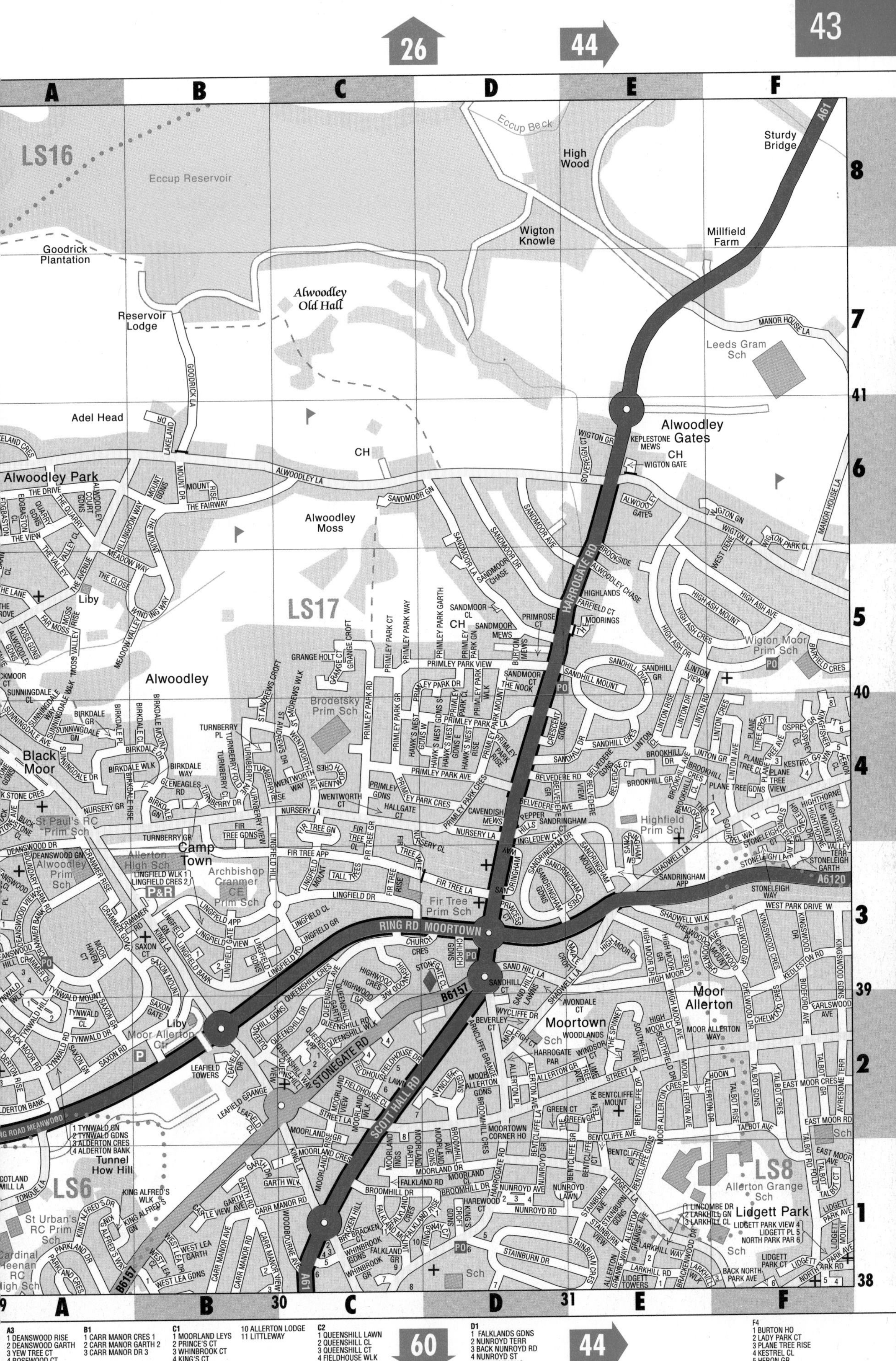

43
27

Wigton Heath Farm
Wigton Moor Whin
Wigton Moor
Wike Ridge
Wike Ridge Farm
Sturdy Beck
Shaw Hill
Brandon La
Collier Beck
CH
Blackmoor Farm
Brandon Hall
Hall Farm
Brandon Ings
Nursery
Brandon Grange Farm
Brandon Drain
Brandon
Low Brandon Farm
Brandon Royd
Slaid Hill
Shadwell
Liby
LS17
Shadwell Grange Farm
Blackwood
Oakhill
Manor Farm
Shadwell Prim Sch
Ferndale
Woodhouse Farm
RING RD MOORTOWN
A6120
RING RD SHADWELL
LS8
Great Heads Beck
Hobberley House
Ram Wood
Upper Lake
Castle
Cobble Hall
Redhall House
Wellington Hill
Tropical World
Mansion Hotel
Roundhay Park
Waterloo Lake
Cobble Hall Farm
Park Villas
A58 WETHERBY RD

43
61

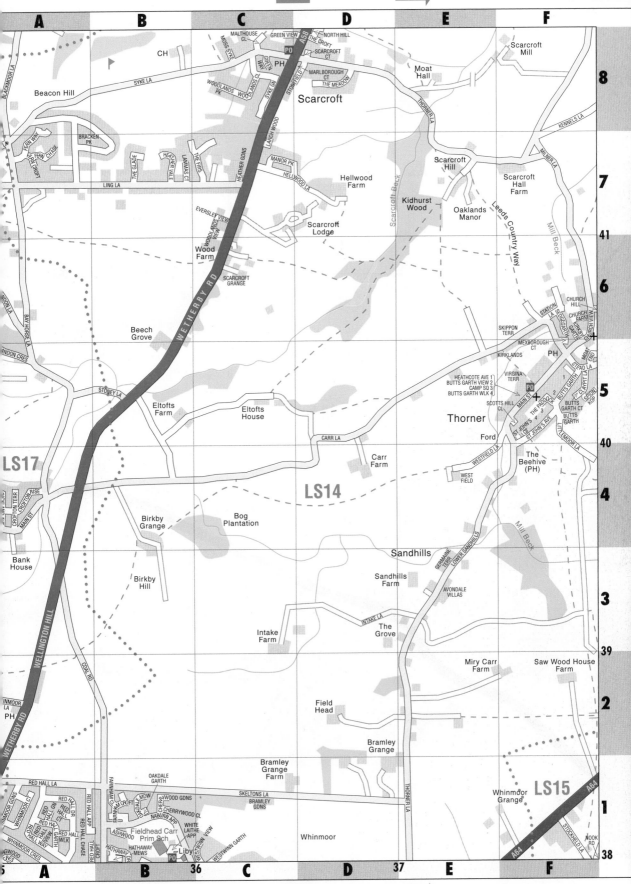

A B C D E F

8
7
41
6
5
40
4
3
39
2
1
38

Scarcroft Mill

Moat Hall

Scarcroft

Scarcroft Hill

Scarcroft Hall Farm

Kennels La

Milner La

Mill Beck

Beacon Hill

Syke La

Woodlands Pk

Ling La

Bracken Pk

Fern Way

Fern Croft

Blackmoor La

The Glade

Heather Vale

Lammas Ct

The Firs

Heather Gdns

Manor Pk

Larch Wood

Hellwood La

Hellwood Farm

Scarcroft Beck

Kidhurst Wood

Oaklands Manor

Leeds Country Way

Eversley View

Woodlands View

Scarcroft Lodge

Wood Farm

Scarcroft Grange

WETHERBY RD

Beech Grove

Bay Horse La

Moor La

Brandon Cres

Stoney La

Eltofts Farm

Eltofts House

Carr La

Station La

Selege Garth

Church Hill

Church Farm

Kings Garth

Church View

Skippon Terr

Mexborough Ct

Kirklands

PH

Virginia Terr

Main St

Stead La

Scott Kop

Claypit La

Butts Garth

Butts Garth Ct

Butts Garth

Littlemoor La

Heathcote Ave 1
Butts Garth View 2
Camp Sq 3
Butts Garth Wlk 4

PO

Scotts Hill Cl

St John's Ter

The Paddock

St John's Ave

Thorner

Ford

LS17

LS14

Carr Farm

Westfield La

West Field

The Beehive (PH)

Birkby Grange

Bog Plantation

Birkby Hill

Bank House

Wellington Hill

WETHERBY RD

Coal Rd

Inmoor La

PH

Sandhills

Germane Terr

Lower Sandhills

Mill Beck

Sandhills Farm

Avondale Villas

Intake Farm

Intake La

The Grove

Miry Carr Farm

Saw Wood House Farm

Field Head

Bramley Grange

Bramley Grange Farm

Skeltons La

Bramley Gdns

Cherrywood Cl

Thorner La

Whinmoor

Whinmoor Grange

LS15

A64

Stockheld La

Nook Rd

Red Hall La

Oakdale Garth

Ashwood Gdns

Farnham Cl

Naburn App

White Laithe App

Westwinn View

Westwinn Garth

Fieldhead Carr Prim Sch

Liby

PO

Red Hall Ct

Red Hall Wlk

Red Hall Chase

Whinmoor Cres

Ringwood Cres

45
29

A B C D E F

8 7 41 6 5 40 4 3 39 2 1 38

The Shambles
Privet Plantation
Bramham Park House & Gardens
The Garden
Bramham Park
LS23
KENNELS LA
Milner Beck
Milner Wood
Norwood Bottoms
Thorner Beck
THORNER RD
Norwood House Farm
BRAMHAM RD
Whittle Car
Bramham Moor
Nova Scotia
Kellfield Grange
KENSINGTON AVE
MANOR GDNS
KIRKFIELD CRES
CHURCH HILL
KIRKFIELD LA
KIRKFIELD AVE
ELLERKER RD
ST PETER'S GARTH
THE CLOSE
KIRK HILLS
KIRKFIELD
MANGRILL LA
Jenny Sober Plantation
Thorner CE Prim Sch
STEAD LA
Thorner
Leeds Country Way
ELLERKER LA
Thorner Moor
LS14
Potterton Mo
Park House Farm
Kiddal Lane End
The Fox and Grapes (PH)
Woodlar Farm
Kiddal Wood
Kiddal Hall
Redhills Plantation
Saw Wood
Kiddal Bridge
KIDDAL LA
Old Plantation
Potterton
POTTERTON LA
Potterton Hall
Morgan Cross
Flying Horse Farm
Potterton Beck
Leeds Country Way
Potterton Park
LS15
A64
MIRY LA
Woodhouse Farm
Whinmoor Nook Farm
NOOK RD
Arthursdale
DARK LA
Rake Beck
Potterton Bridge
Limekiln Hill

38 A B 39 C D 40 E F

45
63

30
48

A
B
C
D
E
F
A1
Road under construction
HEADLEY LA
Paradise Farm
LS23
Dawsonfield Plantation
Rakes Wood
Bramham Park
Camp Hill
Spen Common
Open Rakes
SPEN COMMON LA
Quarry Farm
Spen Farm
Openrakes Beck
SOUTH APP
Bramham Moor
Obelisk
Black Fen
Beccamoor Wood
New Black Fen
LS24
Whitewells Bottom
Crossroads Farm
CROSSROADS COTTS
A1 (M)
A64
NORTH APP
Blackfen Plantation
Becca Moor
45
Windsor Farm
OCCUPATION LA
Whitewell Farm
Becca Lodge
Becca Moor
Cowthwaite Plain
Beccamoor Plantation
Graystone Plain
LS15
Hazel Wood
Nut Hill Farm
Nut Hill
Cowthwaite Plantation
Hick Wood
Little Moor
SOUTH APP
Mast
Birch Spring
Black Horse Farm
Becca Home Farm
Becca Hall
LS25
South Plantation
Becca Park
ABERFORD BY-PASS
Strawberry Hill
HAVERTHWAITES DR
GREYSTONE PK
Becca Low Wood
MAIN ST
St John's
Becca Banks
Cufforth House
GREYSTONES CL
ST JOHN'S CL
THE DALE
FIELD LA
Ridge Plantation
The Ridge
Cock Beck
8
7
41
6
5
40
4
3
39
2
1
38
42
43

64
48

A **B** **C** **D** **E** **F**

8

Headley
Plantation

Mast

WARREN LA

HEADLEY
COTTS

University of Leeds
(Headley Hall Farm)

Bramham Moor

A659

Hill of
Comfort

A659

A64

Brick House
Farm

GARNET LA

MOOR LA

A64

Jackdaw Crag
Quarries

Crag
Wood

7

SPEN COMMON LA

Spen Common

41

6

Headley Bar

Warren House
Farm

A64

White
Smithy
Farm

Beck House
Farm

PARADISE LA

5

Mast

NORTH APP

LS24

CHANTRY LA

White Quarry
Farm

40

Castle
Farm

Hazelwood
Castle

Peggy
Ellerton
Farm

Lowpark
Farm

4

Hazel Wood

South App

Hazelwood
Park

3

SOUTH APP

Lodge
Farm

Harper Rash

39

LS25

2

Mawfield
Spring

Hayton Wood

1

Bullen Wood

Newstead
Farm

Cock Beck

38

Hayton
House

Castle Hi
Wood

44 **A** 45 **B** **C** 46 **D** **E** **F**

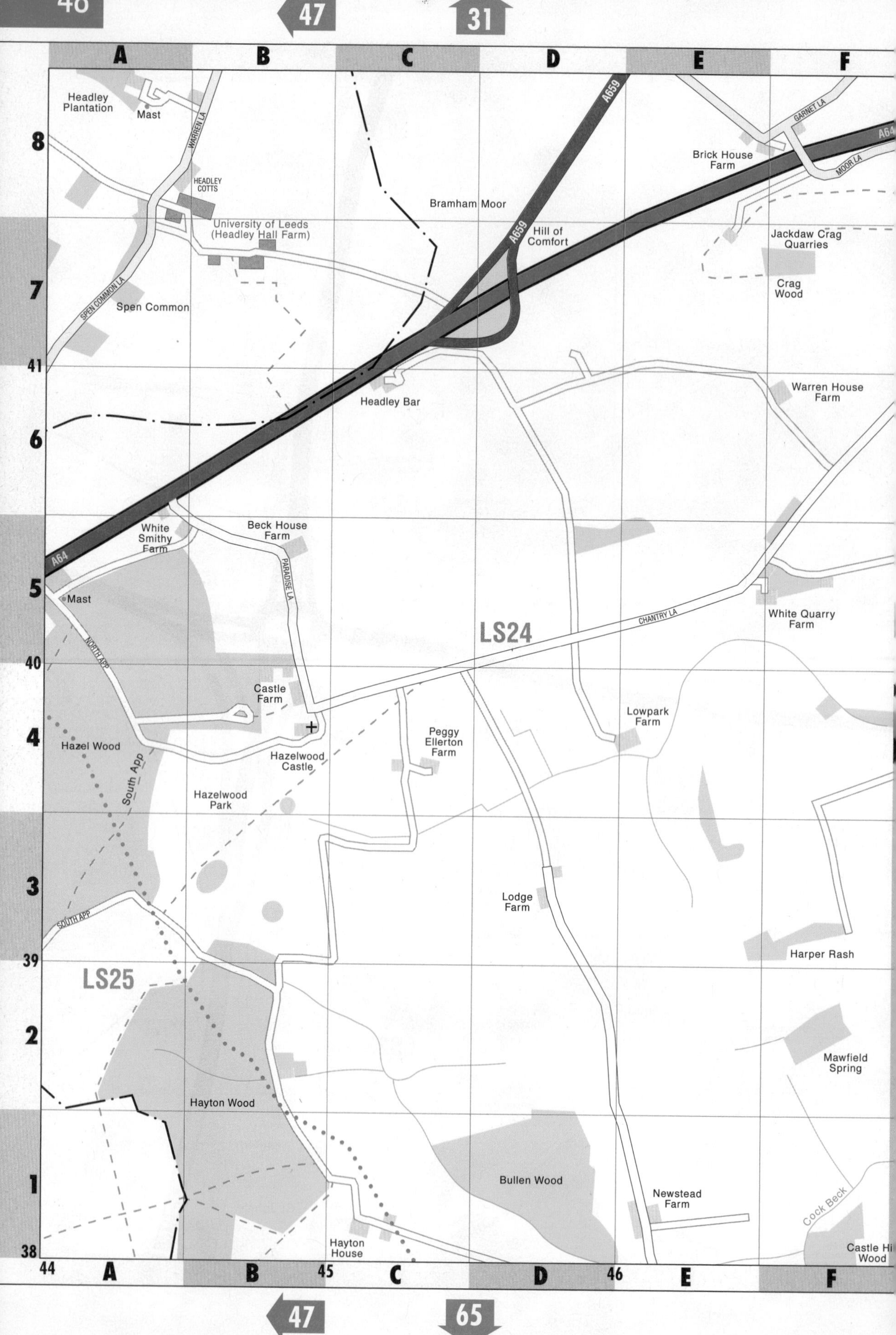

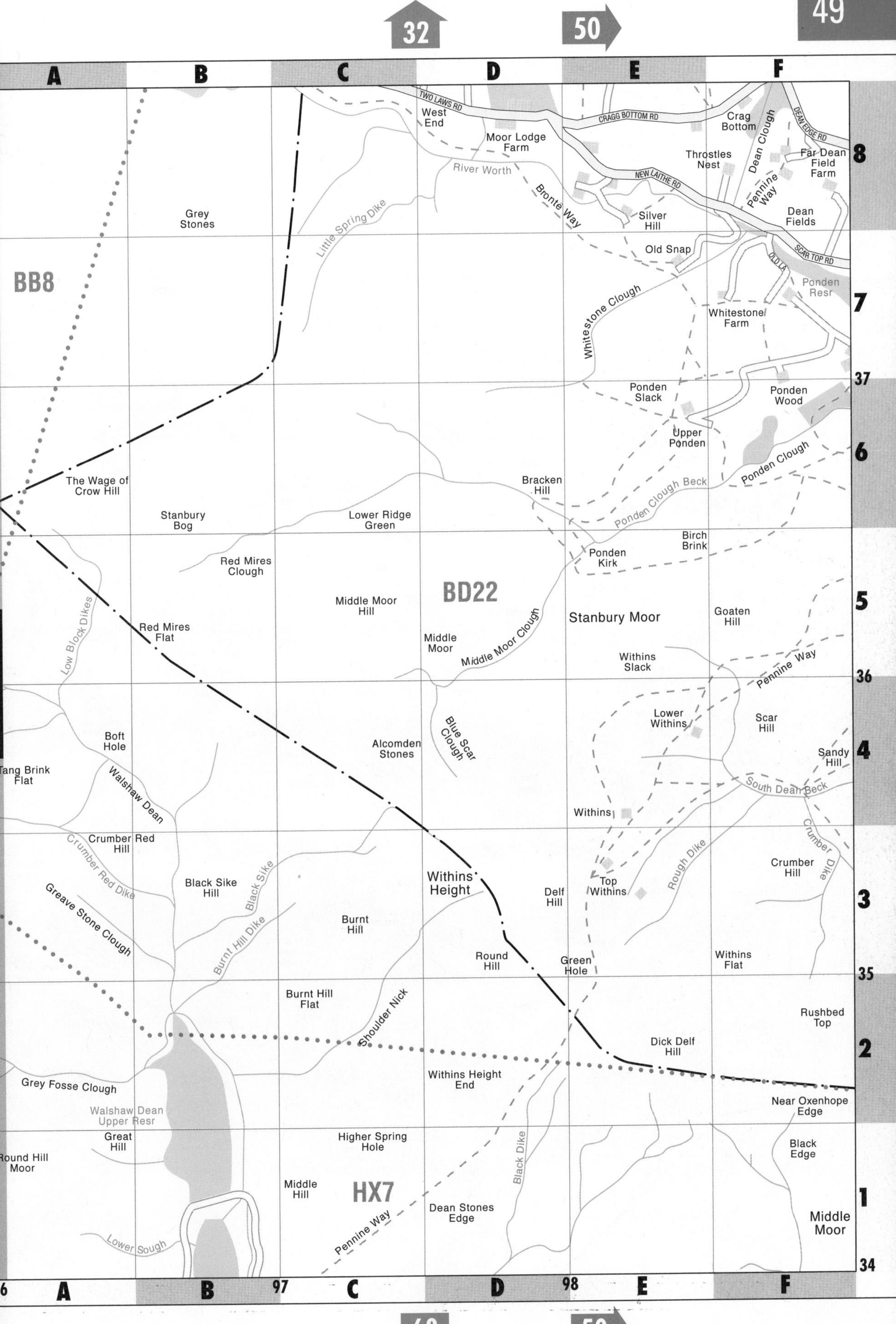

A B C D E F

8

Two Laws Rd
West End
CRAGG BOTTOM RD
Crag Bottom
DEAN EDGE RD
Moor Lodge Farm
Throstles Nest
Far Dean Field Farm
River Worth
NEW LAITHE RD
Dean Clough
Pennine Way
Dean Fields

BB8

Little Spring Dike
Bronte Way
Silver Hill
Dean Fields
Old Snap
Scar Top Rd

7

Grey Stones
Whitestone Clough
Whitestone Farm
OLD LA
Ponden Resr

37

Ponden Slack
Ponden Wood

The Wage of Crow Hill
Upper Ponden
Ponden Clough

6

Bracken Hill
Ponden Clough Beck

Stanbury Bog
Lower Ridge Green
Birch Brink

Red Mires Clough
Ponden Kirk

BD22

Low Block Dikes
Middle Moor Hill
Stanbury Moor
Goaten Hill

5

Red Mires Flat
Middle Moor
Middle Moor Clough
Withins Slack
Pennine Way

36

Boft Hole
Alcomden Stones
Blue Scar Clough
Lower Withins
Scar Hill
Sandy Hill

4

Tang Brink Flat
Walshaw Dean
Withins
South Dean Beck
Crumber Dike

Crumber Red Hill
Crumber Red Dike
Black Sike Hill
Black Sike
Black Sike Dike
Withins Height
Delf Hill
Top Withins
Rough Dike
Crumber Hill

3

Greave Stone Clough
Burnt Hill
Burnt Hill Dike
Round Hill
Green Hole
Withins Flat

35

Burnt Hill Flat
Shoulder Nick
Dick Delf Hill
Rushbed Top

2

Grey Fosse Clough
Withins Height End
Near Oxenhope Edge

Walshaw Dean Upper Resr
Great Hill
Higher Spring Hole
Black Edge

Round Hill Moor
Middle Hill
HX7
Black Dike
Middle Moor

1

Lower Sough
Pennine Way
Dean Stones Edge

34

96 A B 97 C D 98 E F

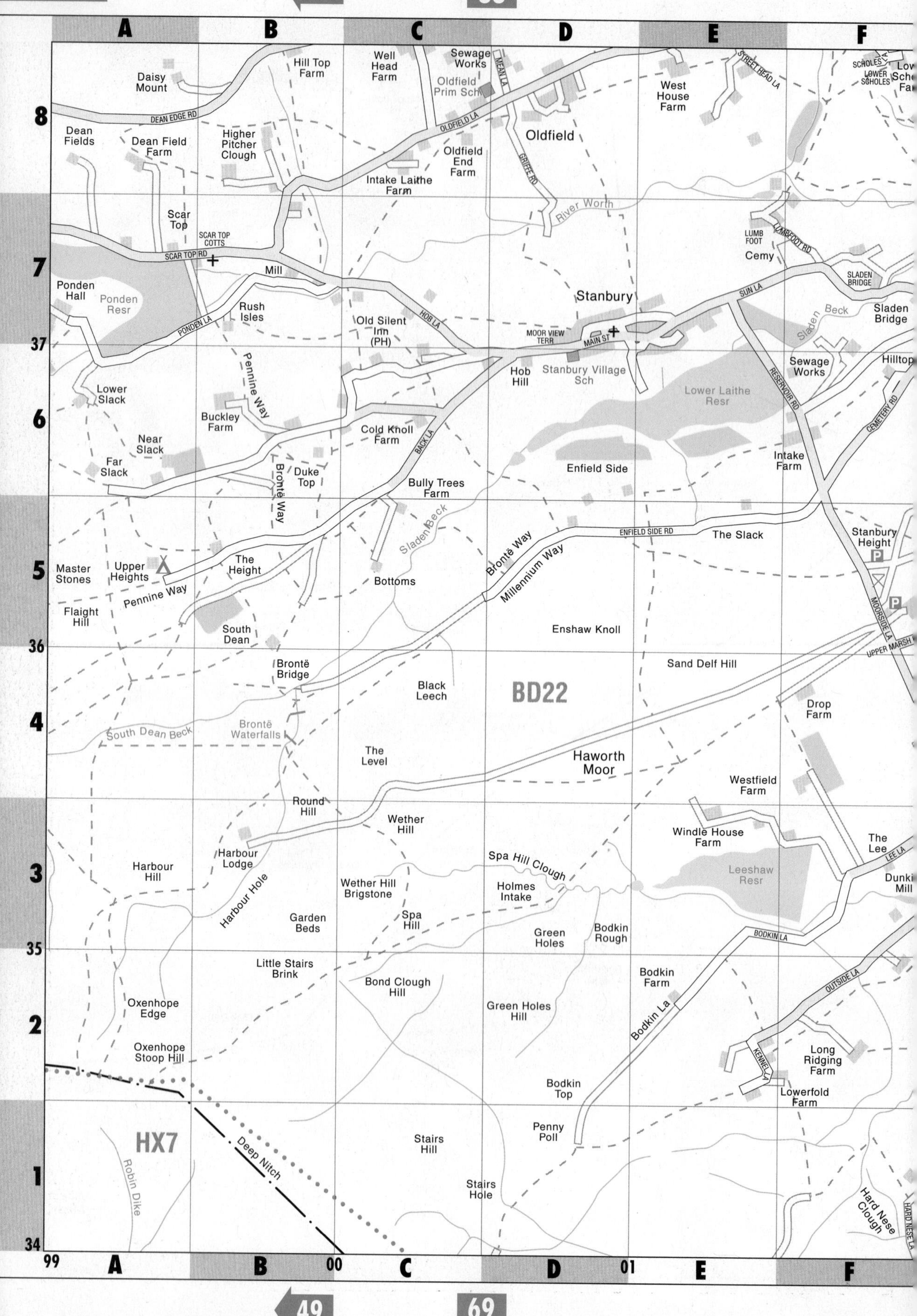

A   B   C   D   E   F

8

Daisy Mount
Dean Edge Rd
Dean Fields
Dean Field Farm
Higher Pitcher Clough
Hill Top Farm
Well Head Farm
Sewage Works
Oldfield Prim Sch
MELA LA
West House Farm
SCHOLES LOWER SCHOLES
Lower Scho Far
Oldfield
Oldfield La
Oldfield End Farm
GREEN RD
STREET HEAD LA
Intake Laithe Farm
River Worth
LUMB FOOT RD
LAMBFOOT RD

7

Scar Top
Scar Top Cotts
Scar Top Rd
Mill
Ponden La
Rush Isles
Cemy
SLADEN BRIDGE
Ponden Hall
Ponden Resr
Old Silent Inn (PH)
HOB LA
Stanbury
SUN LA
Sladen Beck
Sladen Bridge

37

Moor View Terr
Main St
Sewage Works
Hilltop
RESERVOIR RD
Pennine Way
Hob Hill
Stanbury Village Sch
CEMETERY RD

6

Lower Slack
Buckley Farm
Cold Knoll Farm
BACK LA
Lower Laithe Resr
Intake Farm
Near Slack
Far Slack
Duke Top
Bronté Way
Bully Trees Farm
Enfield Side

5

Master Stones
Upper Heights
The Height
Sladen Beck
Bottoms
Bronté Way
Millennium Way
Enfield Side Rd
The Slack
Stanbury Height
P
Pennine Way
Flaight Hill

36

South Dean
Bronté Bridge
Black Leech
Enshaw Knoll
Sand Delf Hill
P
UPPER MARSH
MOORSIDE LA

4

South Dean Beck
Bronté Waterfalls
The Level
BD22
Haworth Moor
Drop Farm

3

Harbour Hill
Harbour Lodge
Harbour Hole
Round Hill
Wether Hill
Spa Hill Clough
Holmes Intake
Windle House Farm
Westfield Farm
The Lee
LEE LA
Leeshaw Resr
Dunki Mill
Wether Hill Brigstone
Garden Beds
Spa Hill
Green Holes
Bodkin Rough
Bodkin Farm
BODKIN LA

35

Little Stairs Brink
Bond Clough Hill
Green Holes Hill
Bodkin La
OUTSIDE LA

2

Oxenhope Edge
Oxenhope Stoop Hill
Bodkin Top
Long Ridging Farm
KENNEL LA
Lowerfold Farm

1

HX7
Deep Nitch
Stairs Hill
Penny Poll
Robin Dike
Stairs Hole
Hard Nese Clough
HARD NESE LA

34

99   A   B   00   C   D   01   E   F

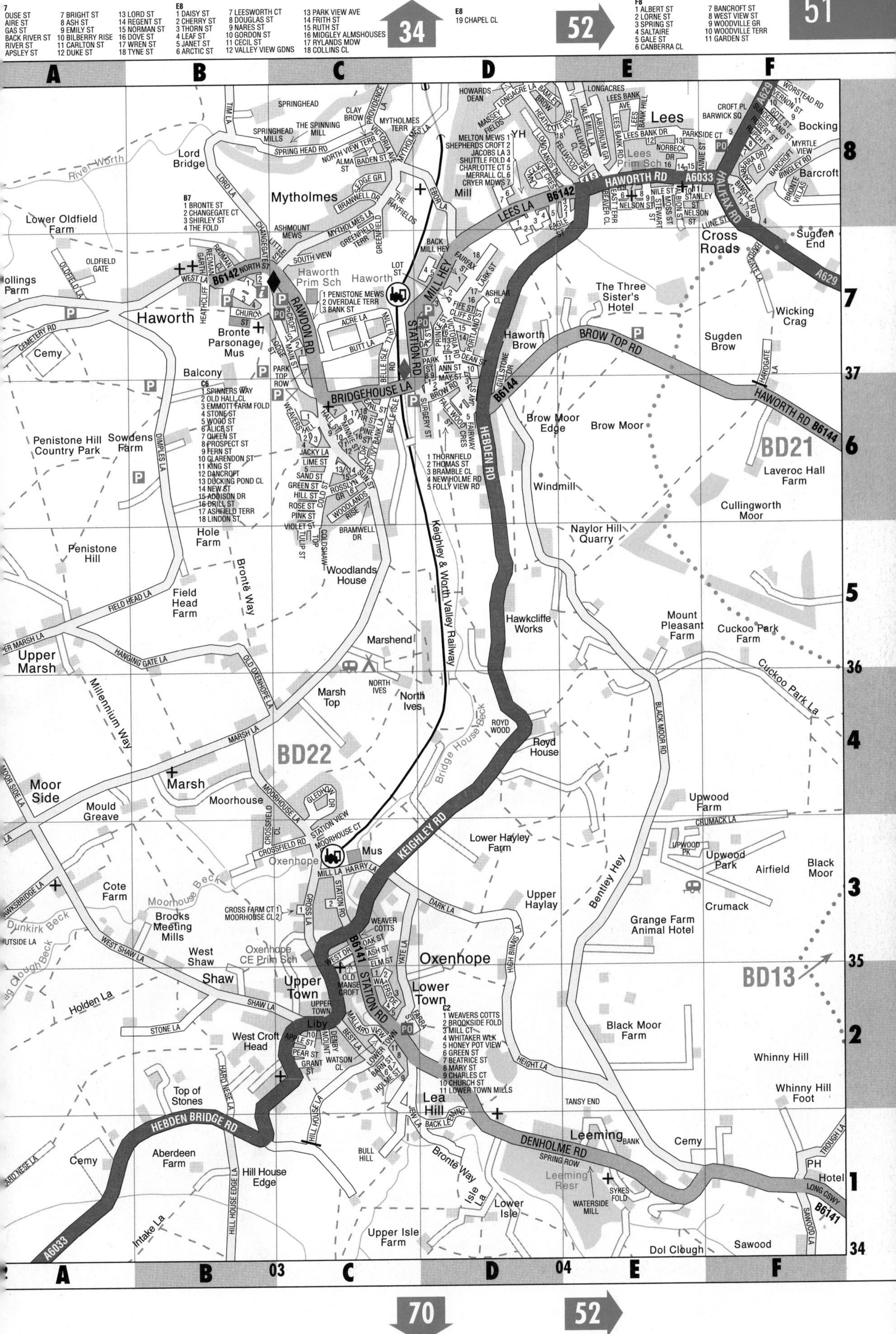
51
7 OUSE ST
AIRE ST
GAS ST
BACK RIVER ST
RIVER ST
APSLEY ST
7 BRIGHT ST
8 ASH ST
9 EMILY ST
10 BILBERRY RISE
11 CARLTON ST
12 DUKE ST
13 LORD ST
14 REGENT ST
15 NORMAN ST
16 DOVE ST
17 WREN ST
18 TYNE ST
E8
1 DAISY ST
2 CHERRY ST
3 THORN ST
4 LEAF ST
5 JANET ST
6 ARCTIC ST
7 LEESWORTH CT
8 DOUGLAS ST
9 NARES ST
10 GORDON ST
11 CECIL ST
12 VALLEY VIEW GDNS
13 PARK VIEW AVE
14 FRITH ST
15 RUTH ST
16 MIDGLEY ALMSHOUSES
17 RYLANDS MDW
18 COLLINS CL
34
E8
19 CHAPEL CL
52
F8
1 ALBERT ST
2 LORNE ST
3 SPRING ST
4 SALTAIRE
5 GALE ST
6 CANBERRA CL
7 BANCROFT ST
8 WEST VIEW ST
9 WOODVILLE GR
10 WOODVILLE TERR
11 GARDEN ST
A
B
C
D
E
F
8
7
37
6
5
36
4
3
35
2
1
34
03
04
Lees
Lord Bridge
Mytholmes
Mill
Lower Oldfield Farm
Haworth
Bronte Parsonage Mus
Haworth Prim Sch
Cross Roads
Sugden End
Bocking
Barcroft
The Three Sister's Hotel
Wicking Crag
Sugden Brow
Haworth Brow
BROW TOP RD
Brow Moor Edge
Brow Moor
BD21
Laveroc Hall Farm
Cullingworth Moor
Windmill
Naylor Hill Quarry
B7
1 BRONTE ST
2 CHANGEGATE CT
3 SHIRLEY ST
4 THE FOLD
C6
1 SPINNERS WAY
2 OLD HALL CL
3 EMMOTT FARM FOLD
4 STONE ST
5 WOOD ST
6 ALICE ST
7 QUEEN ST
8 PROSPECT ST
9 FERN ST
10 CLARENDON ST
11 KING ST
12 DANCROFT
13 DUCKING POND CL
14 NEW ST
15 ADDISON DR
16 DRILL ST
17 ASHFIELD TERR
18 LINDON ST
1 PENISTONE MEWS
2 OVERDALE TERR
3 BANK ST
1 THORNFIELD
2 THOMAS ST
3 BRAMBLE CL
4 NEW HOLME RD
5 FOLLY VIEW RD
Penistone Hill Country Park
Sowdens Farm
Balcony
Cemy
Penistone Hill
Hole Farm
Field Head Farm
Brontë Way
Woodlands House
Keighley & Worth Valley Railway
HEBDEN RD
Hawkcliffe Works
Mount Pleasant Farm
Cuckoo Park Farm
Cuckoo Park La
Marshend
Upper Marsh
Millennium Way
Marsh Top
North Ives
Royd House
BD22
BLACK MOOR RD
Moor Side
Marsh
Mould Greave
Moorhouse
Upwood Farm
CRUMACK LA
Upwood Park
Airfield
Black Moor
Lower Hayley Farm
KEIGHLEY RD
Mus
Oxenhope
Cote Farm
Moorhouse Beck
Dunkirk Beck
Brooks Meeting Mills
Upper Haylay
Bentley Hey
Crumack
Grange Farm Animal Hotel
CROSS FARM CT 1
MOORHOUSE CL 2
West Shaw
Shaw
Oxenhope CE Prim Sch
Upper Town
Lower Town
BD13
Holden La
C2
1 WEAVERS COTTS
2 BROOKSIDE FOLD
3 MILL CT
4 WHITAKER WLK
5 HONEY POT VIEW
6 GREEN ST
7 BEATRICE ST
8 MARY ST
9 CHARLES CT
10 CHURCH ST
11 LOWER TOWN MILLS
Black Moor Farm
Whinny Hill
Whinny Hill Foot
West Croft Head
Liby
Top of Stones
Lea Hill
TANSY END
Leeming
Cemy
HEBDEN BRIDGE RD
DENHOLME RD
Aberdeen Farm
Hill House Edge
Bull Hill
Brontë Way
Leeming Resr
WATERSIDE MILL
SYKES FOLD
PH
Hotel
Lower Isle
Isle La
Intake La
Upper Isle Farm
Dol Clough
Sawood
A6033
B6141
70
52

51
35

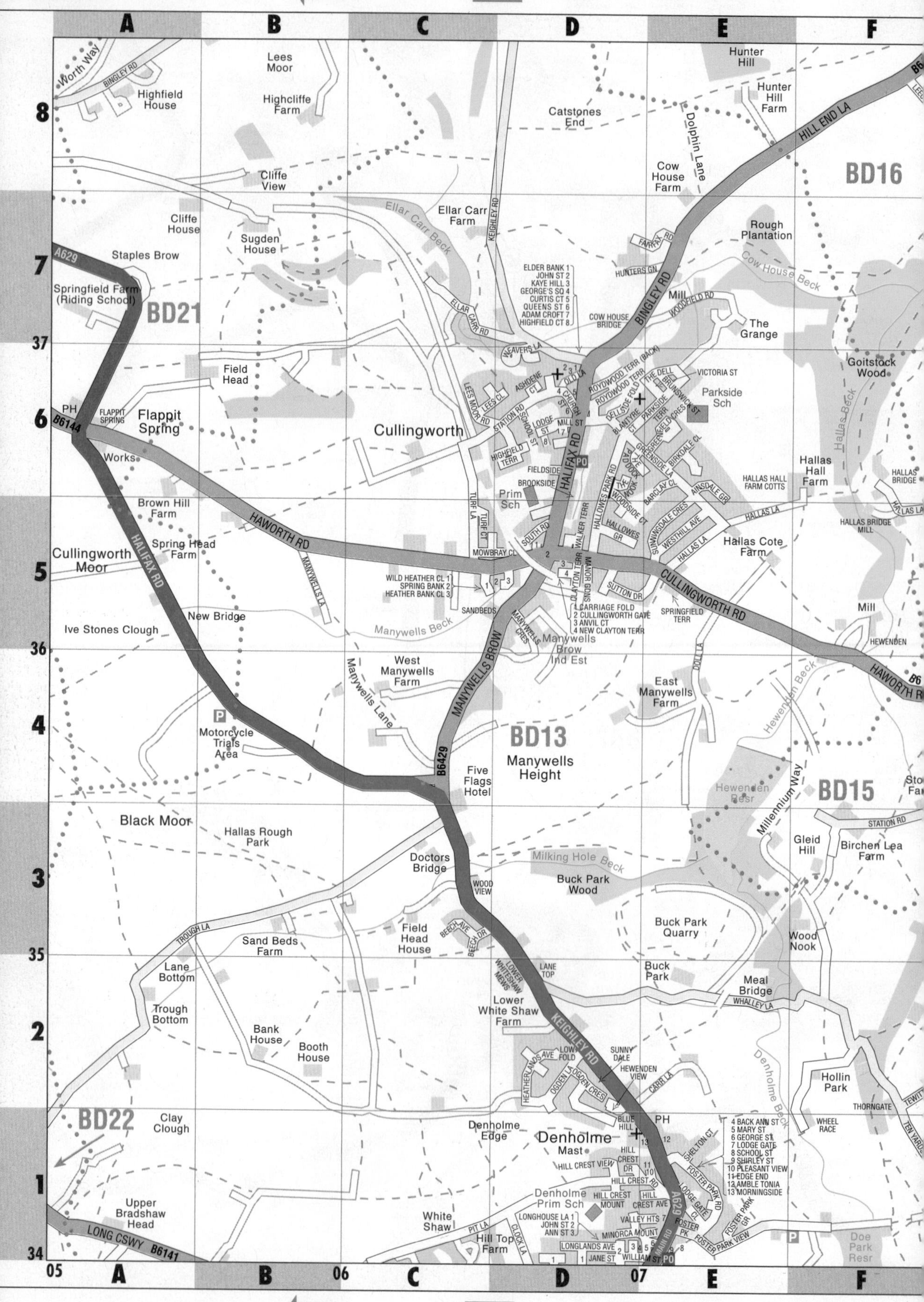
A
B
C
D
E
F
8
7
37
6
5
36
4
3
35
2
1
34
05
06
07
Lees Moor
Worth Way
Bingley Rd
Highfield House
Highcliffe Farm
Catstones End
Dolphin Lane
Hunter Hill
Hunter Hill Farm
Hill End La
BD16
Cow House Farm
Cliffe View
Cliffe House
Sugden House
Ellar Carr Beck
Ellar Carr Farm
Keighley Rd
Rough Plantation
Fairfax Rd
Hunters Gn
Cow House Beck
A629
Staples Brow
Springfield Farm (Riding School)
BD21
Elder Bank 1
John St 2
Kaye Hill 3
George's Sq 4
Curtis Ct 5
Queens St 6
Adam Croft 7
Highfield Ct 8
Ellar Carr Rd
Cow House Bridge
Mill
Woodfield Rd
The Grange
Weavers La
Field Head
Roydwood Terr (Back)
Roydwood Terr
Victoria St
Goitstock Wood
Parkside Sch
Old La
Church St
Ashdene Ct
Lees Cl
Lees Moor Rd
Station Rd
School St
Lodge St
Mill St
The Dell
Brunswick St
Dellside Fold
Blantyre Ct
Parkside Terr
Greenfield Cres
PH
Flappit Spring
B6144
Cullingworth
Halifax Rd
Highfield Terr
Fieldside
Brookside
Greenside La
Birkdale Cl
Hallas Beck
Works
PO
The Paddock
The Nook
Hallowes Park Rd
Woodside Ct
Barclay Cl
Ainsdale Gr
Hallas Hall Farm Cotts
Hallas Hall Farm
Hallas Bridge
Brown Hill Farm
Prim Sch
Turf La
Turf Ct
South Rd
Walker Terr
Hallowes Gr
Sunningdale Cres
Westhill Ave
Hallas La
Hallas Bridge Mill
Haworth Rd
Cullingworth Moor
Spring Head Farm
Manywells La
Mowbray Cl
Hallas Cote Farm
Wild Heather Cl 1
Spring Bank 2
Heather Bank Cl 3
Clayton Terr
Manor Gdns
Sutton Dr
Cullingworth Rd
1 Carriage Fold
2 Cullingworth Gate
3 Anvil Ct
4 New Clayton Terr
Springfield Terr
Sandbeds
Manywells Beck
New Bridge
Mill
Ive Stones Clough
Manywells Cres
Manywells Brow Ind Est
Hewenden
West Manywells Farm
Manywells Brow
Doll La
East Manywells Farm
Hewenden Beck
Manywells Lane
BD13
Manywells Height
P
Motorcycle Trials Area
B6429
Five Flags Hotel
Hewenden Resr
Millennium Way
BD15
Black Moor
Hallas Rough Park
Station Rd
Gleid Hill
Birchen Lea Farm
Doctors Bridge
Milking Hole Beck
Wood View
Buck Park Wood
Trough La
Beech Ave
Beech Dr
Field Head House
Sand Beds Farm
Buck Park Quarry
Wood Nook
Lane Bottom
Lower Whitshaw Mews
Lane Top
Buck Park
Meal Bridge
Whalley La
Lower White Shaw Farm
Trough Bottom
Bank House
Booth House
Keighley Rd
Sunny Dale
Low Fold
Heatherlands Ave
Ogden La
Ogden Cres
Hewenden View
Carr La
Denholme Beck
Hollin Park
BD22
Clay Clough
Denholme Edge
Blue Hill
PH
Denholme
Mast
Thorngate
Wheel Race
4 Back Ann St
5 Mary St
6 George St
7 Lodge Gate
8 School St
9 Shirley St
10 Pleasant View
11 Edge End
12 Amble Tonia
13 Morningside
Shelton Ct
Hill Crest View
Hill Crest Dr
Hill Crest Rd
Foster Park Rd
Lodge Gate Cl
Denholme Prim Sch
Hill Crest Mount
Crest Ave
Upper Bradshaw Head
White Shaw
Longhouse La 1
John St 2
Ann St 3
Valley Hts
Foster Park Gr
Foster Pk
Foster Park View
P
Doe Park Resr
Long Cswy
B6141
Pit La
Hill Top Farm
Clock La
Minorca Mount
Longlands Ave
Jane St
William St
Main Rd
PO

51
71

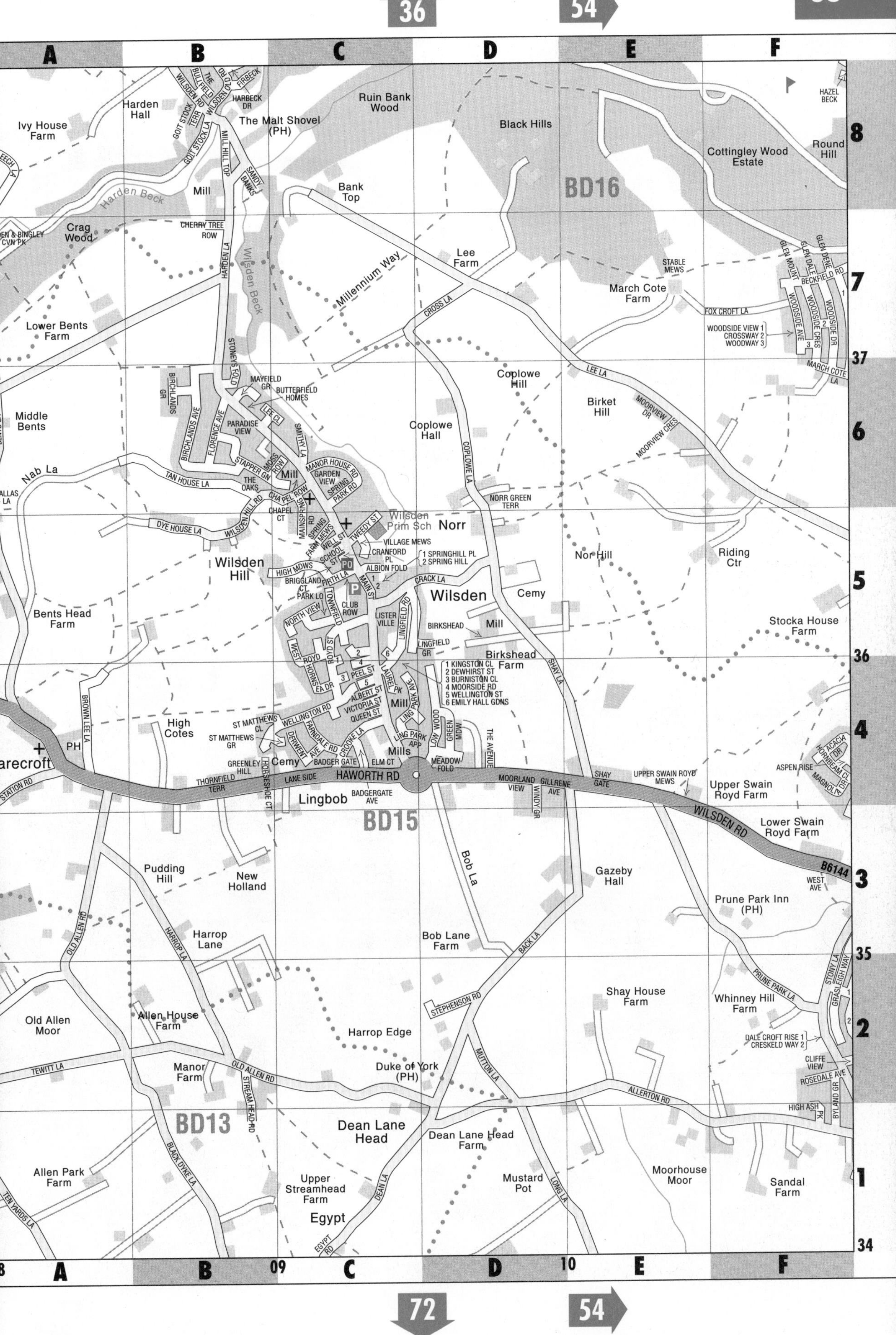
36
54
A
B
C
D
E
F
8
7
37
6
5
36
4
3
35
2
1
34
09
10
Harden Hall
Ivy House Farm
The Malt Shovel (PH)
Ruin Bank Wood
Black Hills
Cottingley Wood Estate
Round Hill
HAZEL BECK
BD16
Mill
Harden Beck
Bank Top
Crag Wood
Wilsden Beck
Millennium Way
Lee Farm
March Cote Farm
Lower Bents Farm
Coplowe Hill
Birket Hill
Middle Bents
Coplowe Hall
Nab La
Wilsden Prim Sch
Norr
Nor Hill
Riding Ctr
Wilsden Hill
Wilsden
Cemy
Bents Head Farm
Birkshead Farm
Stocka House Farm
High Cotes
Mills
Upper Swain Royd Farm
Lower Swain Royd Farm
Lingbob
BD15
HAWORTH RD
WILSDEN RD
B6144
Pudding Hill
New Holland
Bob La
Gazeby Hall
Prune Park Inn (PH)
Harrop Lane
Bob Lane Farm
Old Allen Moor
Allen House Farm
Harrop Edge
Shay House Farm
Whinney Hill Farm
Manor Farm
Duke of York (PH)
BD13
Dean Lane Head
Dean Lane Head Farm
Allen Park Farm
Upper Streamhead Farm
Egypt
Mustard Pot
Moorhouse Moor
Sandal Farm
1 KINGSTON CL
2 DEWHIRST ST
3 BURNISTON CL
4 MOORSIDE RD
5 WELLINGTON ST
6 EMILY HALL GDNS
1 SPRINGHILL PL
2 SPRING HILL
WOODSIDE VIEW 1
CROSSWAY 2
WOODWAY 3
DALE CROFT RISE 1
CRESKELD WAY 2
72
54

53
37
E8
1 HIRST WOOD CRES
2 WOODSIDE AVE
3 DALLAM GR
4 ALBERT WLK
5 PETERSGARTH
F8
1 AMELIA ST
2 WILLIAM HENRY ST
3 LOWER SCHOOL ST
4 HIGHER SCHOOL ST
5 LOCKWOOD ST
6 MAWSON ST
7 EXHIBITION RD
8 UPPER ADA ST
9 UPPER MARY ST
10 KATHERINE ST
11 MYRTLE PL
12 DAISY PL
13 HAROLD PL
14 ALEXANDRA S
15 FERNCLIFFE R
16 RICHMOND PL
17 RICHMOND R
18 VICTORIA CT
A
B
C
D
E
F
8
7
6
5
4
3
2
1
37
36
35
34
11
12
13
Rye Loaf Hill
Cemy
Crem
Saltaire
River Aire
Bankfield Hotel
Nab Wood
Cottingley Park
Round Hill
Cottingley
Recn Gd
Nab Wood Sch
Moorhea
A7
1 MIDWAY AVE
2 THE PARADE
3 MANOR CT
4 GRANGE CT
B6
1 POLLARD ST
2 MITTON ST
3 HERBERT ST
4 OLD VICARAGE CL
5 BUTTERFIELD HOMES
6 OBERON WAY
7 TITANIA CL
8 GOODFELLOW CL
1 CRAIG VIEW
2 NAB WOOD CL
3 NAB WOOD GDNS
New Close Farm
BD18
Cottingley Village Prim Sch
Cottingley Moor
New Brighton
Cliff Farm
Shipley High Moor
BD16
Stoney Ridge
Bunkers Hill
Heaton Shay
Norman Rae Playing Fie
Shay Grange Farm
Heaton Royds
Noon Nick
Belle Vue Girls Sch
Works
Cliff Wood
Belle Vue Boys Sch
Thorn Park Sch for Deaf Children
West House Farm
Royds Cli Wood
Sandy Lane
Sandy Lane Prim Sch
Heaton Prim Sch
Liby
Works
Chellow Heights
BD9
Heaton
Chellow Dean
Chellow Dean Resrs
Lynfield Mount
BD15
1 PLANETREES ST
2 UPPER FERNDOWN GN
3 GARFIELD PL
4 CHAPEL ROW
Daisy Hill
Bradford Royal
1 WELLINGTON ST
2 GRAPE ST
3 PROSPECT TERR
The Preparatory Sch
Bradford Coll Girls' Gram Sch
BD8
BROCKLESBY DR 1
TERRACOTTA DR 2
BRADFORD RD
BINGLEY RD
COTTINGLEY NEW RD
COTTINGLEY CLIFFE RD
COTTINGLEY MOOR RD
HAWORTH RD
TOLLER LA
BINGLEY RD
53
73
F1
1 COMO DR
2 COMO GDNS
3 COMO AVE
4 ST LEONARD'S CT
5 GIRLINGTON RD

55
A7
1 WELLINGTON CT
2 AVONDALE GR
3 SCARBOROUGH GR
4 BACK ST PAUL'S RD
5 ASHDOWN CT
6 ROSSENDALE PL
A8
1 WESTEND TERR
2 MILL VIEW
3 AIRE VIEW AVE
4 PARK AVE
5 PARK TERR
6 MELBOURNE ST
B7
1 The Arndale Sh Ctr
2 WINDSOR CT
3 WESTCLIFFE MEWS
4 BIRKLANDS TERR
5 SUNNY BANK
6 WOOLCOMBERS HALL
B8
1 UPPER ASHLEY LA
2 WAINMAN ST
3 ATKINSON ST
4 NEW KIRKGATE
5 CROSSE ROSSE ST
6 BANK ST
D5
1 MAFEKING TERR
2 ORCHID CL
3 CAMELLIA CT
4 BLUEBELL CL
5 LAVENDER CT
6 LABURNUM RD
38
D8
1 WOODVILLE TERR
2 WOODVILLE ST
3 WOOD TOP
56
E8
1 IDLE MOOR
F8
1 LONGROYD
2 LOWER HOUSE CL
3 COTE FARM LA
4 BALE DR
A B C D E F
8 7 6 5 4 3 2 1
37 36 35 34 15 16
SHIPLEY
Shipley
Saltaire Rd A657
Leeds Rd
Wood End
West Royd
Windhill
Wrose Hill
Low Ash
Idle Hill
Idle Moor
BD10
BD17
BD18
BD2
BD9
BD8
BD1
BD3
Frizinghall
Owlet
Wrose
Gaisby Hill
Swain House
Bolton Woods
Bolton
Heaton Grove
Manningham
Clifton Villas
Girlington
Norman Rae Playing Fields
Lister Park
Cartwright Hall Art Gall & Mus
Bradford Gram Sch
St Joseph's RC Coll
Bradford Bsns Pk
Football Gd
Peel Park
Old Hill
Hanson Sch
Westminster CE Prim Sch
Margaret McMillan Prim Sch
Heaton St Barnabas CE Prim Sch
St Bede's RC Gram Sch
Poplars Farm Prim Sch
Low Ash Prim Sch
Windhill CE Prim Sch
St Anthony's RC Prim Sch
Shipley CE Prim Sch
High Crags Prim Sch
Leeds & Liverpool Canal
River Aire
Bradford Beck
Bradford Rd A6038
Otley Rd
Valley Rd
Keighley Rd
Canal Rd
Manningham La A650
Queen's Rd
Toller La
Whetley La A6177
Lister La A6176
A6037
A6177
B6149
B6144
74
56
A1
1 NORTHROP CL
2 WOODLANDS RD
3 LOWER WESTFIELD RD
B1
1 ANVIL CT
2 ANVIL ST
3 SILVER ST
4 BARDEN ST
5 MIDDLETON ST
6 WHITE'S TERR
7 ABERFORD RD
8 ASHWELL ST
C1
1 LIBBY ST
2 CHURCH GN
3 ST PAUL'S CL
4 COWGILL ST
5 TREES ST
6 QURESHI VIEW
7 HIGHFIELD PL
8 ASHDOWN PL
9 GREENFIELD PL
10 ASPLEY VILLAS
11 LINCOLN CL
12 ARNOLD ST
13 Carlisle Mills Bsns Ctr
C2
1 LISTER GDNS
2 BACK LINDUM ST
3 BACK BLENHEIM MOUNT
4 QUBA CT
5 ROSE BANK
6 FERN TERR
D1
1 GROSVENOR TERR
2 GROSVENOR ST
D1
3 COTTINGLEY TERR
4 SOUTH PAR
5 SPRINGLODGE PL
6 BACK SPRINGFIELD PL
7 CORNWALL TERR
8 MILLHAVEN MEWS
9 CAMDEN TERR
10 Thorncliffe Park Ind Est
F1
1 WESTMINSTER PL
2 WESTMINSTER TERR
3 STANACRE PL
4 SOUTHAMPTON ST
5 PORTSMOUTH AVE
6 DOVER ST
F3
1 KINGSDALE GR
2 ASHBOURNE DR

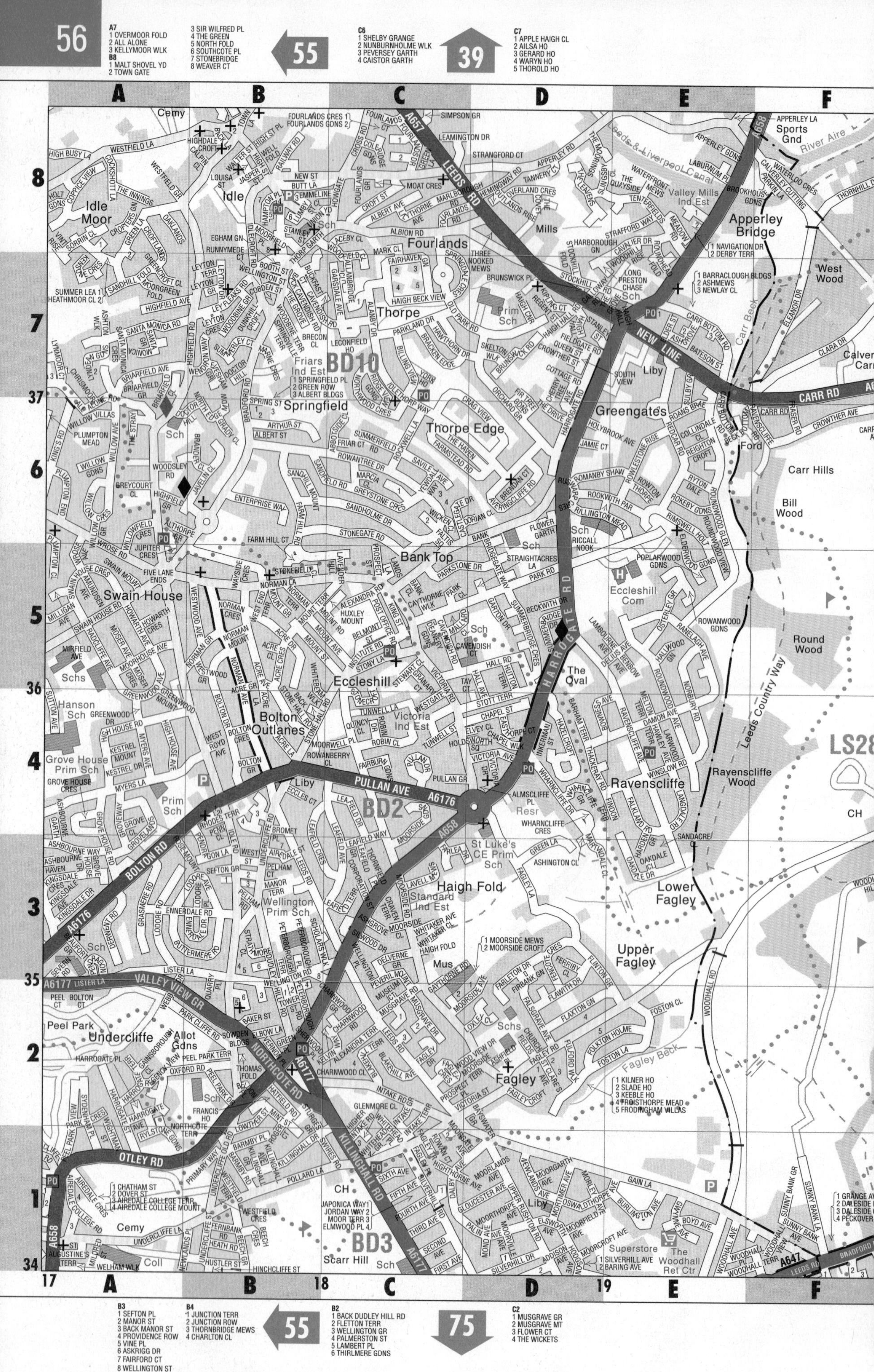

40
58
BD10
LS19
LS18
LS13
LS28
Calverley Wood
Lodge Wood
Lodge Farm
Works
Woodbottom Farm
Woodbottom
Woodbottom Mills
Low Hall
Paris Restaurant (PH)
Park Lane Coll Horsforth Ctr
Swaine Wood
Calverley
Calverley CE Prim Sch
Calverley House Farm
Victoria Park
Owl Bridge (swing)
Leeds & Liverpool Canal
River Aire
The Grange
Rodley Fold Farm
Holly Park Mills
Red Beck
Wood Hill
Hazelbrae
Crossfield Farm
The Rein
Kirklees Knowl
Bagley
Rodley
Mills
Priesthorpe
PUDSEY
The Green
Farsley Spring Bank Jun Sch
Farsley Beck Bottom
Cape Mills Ind Est
Summerfield Prim Sch
Woodhall Hills
Farsley
Half Mile
Stanningley Park
Stanningley Prim Sch
Farsley Farfield Prim Sch
Priesthorpe Sch
Marsden Meml Homes
Recn Ctr
Civic Hall
West Royd Park
Thornbury Barracks
New Pudsey
Owlcotes Ctr
Stanningley
Foundry Ind Est
Grangefield Ind Est
Pudsey Primrose Hill Prim Sch
First Avenue Ind Est
CARR RD
TOWN GATE
RODLEY LA
CALVERLEY LA
HORSFORTH NEW RD
BROADWAY
RAWDON RD
RING RD FARSLEY
TOWN ST
BRADFORD RD
STANNINGLEY RD
STANNINGLEY BY-PASS
A65
A6120
A657
A647
B6156
B6157
B6155
B6154
D1
1 HARKER TERR
2 HUDSON ST
3 STANHALL AVE
4 SPRINGFIELD TERR
5 CONWAY ST
6 WILSONS YD
7 DAWSON ST
8 WILLIAM ST
9 WEST TERRACE ST
10 WEST GROVE ST
D2
1 BEVERLEY CT
2 YORK HO
3 LINCOLN CT
4 BECKBURY CL
5 BECKBURY ST
6 PROSPECT TERR
7 NEW PARK WLK
8 DONALD ST
9 PROVIDENCE ST
10 MELBOURNE ST
11 TENNYSON ST
12 ARMSTRONG ST
13 ANDREW ST
14 SOUTHCOTE ST
15 ARNCLIFFE GARTH
16 PROSPECT SQ
17 POPLAR SQ
18 ASHVILLE TERR
19 WEST VIEW
D3
1 GLADSTONE ST
2 OAKWELL TERR
3 MARSDEN CT
4 ANDREW SQ
5 TURNER ST
6 EBENEZER ST
7 HAINSWORTH SQ
8 GAMBLES HILL
9 OLD FOLD
10 RIPON HO
76
11 DURHAM CT
12 ST JOHN'S AVE
13 WILLIAMS CT
E1
1 TEMPERANCE ST
2 BOOCOCK ST
3 CAVENDISH SQ
4 PROVIDENCE PL
5 PRIMROSE HILL
6 ASHFIELD GR
58
E2
1 BRANSBY CT
2 TURBARY AVE
3 FERN TERR
4 GROVE ST
5 NORTH VIEW TERR
6 KEIGHLEY PL
7 BACK BANK TERR
8 BANK TERR
F2
1 VICTORIA TERR
2 VICTORIA CT
3 GRANVILLE ST
4 ROSEBERY TERR
5 GLADSTONE CT
6 BACK BRIGHT ST
7 STANNINGLEY CT
8 HARRISONS AVE
9 BROAD LA
10 BRITANNIA ST
11 BRITANNIA CL

B7
1 FEATHERBANK WLK
2 BACK FEATHERBANK TERR
3 FEATHERBANK TERR
4 FEATHERBANK CT
5 SUNNYBANK AVE
6 BACK SUNNYBANK AVE
7 SUNNYBANK RD
8 HOPEWELL TERR
9 BACK CLARENCE RD
10 NEWLAY WOOD FOLD
11 FAIRBURN HO

B8
1 FEAST FIELD

57

2 STONEYTHORPE
3 STONEYCROFT
4 BROADWAY DR
5 FEATHERBANK GR
6 FEATHERBANK MOUNT
7 BACK TOWN ST

41

C7
1 WARWICK CT
2 NEWLAY BRIDLE PATH
3 NEWLAY WOOD GDNS
4 THROSTLE NEST VIEW
5 BACK OUTWOOD LA
6 BACK CRAGGWOOD RD
7 CRAGGWELL TERR
8 CRAGGWOOD TERR
9 WOODBINE TERR
10 REGENT CT
11 GLENWOOD VILLAS

F8
1 RING RD WEST PK
2 CLAYTON GRANGE
3 LATCHMERE CROSS
4 LATCHMERE CREST
5 LATCHMERE GN
6 OLD FARM WLK
7 LINTON CROFT
8 MOOR GRANGE CT

A B C D E F

HORSFORTH

LS18 Cragg Hill · Horsforth Hall Park · Low Fold · Horsforth Woodside · Hawksworth · LS16 · Newlay · Newlay Locks · Bramley Fall · Fall Park · Whitecote · Moorside · Forge Locks · LS5 · Kirkstall Lock · Kirkstall Abbey · Rossett Bsns Pk · Sandford · Intake · LS13 · Bramley · Beecroft Mast Hill · Swinnow · LS28 · Raynville · Hill Top · Town End

23 A B 24 C D 25 E F

C1
1 ELDER MOUNT
2 ELDER PL
3 ELDER ST
4 CLEOPATRA PL
5 BRAMLEY ST
6 WEST CT
7 BRAMLEY GRANGE

C2
1 HENLEY AVE
2 HENLEY GR
3 HENLEY ST
4 WARREL'S ROW
5 BK ROSEMONT WLK
6 ROSEMONT WLK
7 ROSEMONT AVE
8 ROSEMONT GR
9 NANSEN AVE
10 NANSEN GR
11 NANSEN MOUNT
12 STATION GR
13 ASHDOWN ST
14 BATH GR
15 BACK BATH RD
16 HOUGH GR
17 HOUGH TERR
18 BACK MELBOURNE GR
19 WARREL'S TERR

57

C3
1 WESTOVER TERR
2 WESTOVER ST
3 WESTOVER GR
4 WARREL'S AVE
5 WESTOVER VIEW
6 WESTOVER AVE
7 HAYLEIGH TERR
8 HAYLEIGH ST
9 HAYLEIGH AVE
10 WESTOVER MOUNT

77

D1
1 HOUGH END CT
2 HOUGH END GDNS
3 DAISY ROW
4 WINDSOR CT

D2
1 NEW SCARBRO' RD
2 DAISYFIELD RD
3 ROSSEFIELD CL
4 ASHBY MOUNT
5 ROSSEFIELD WLK
6 McLAREN FIELDS
7 SNOWDEN WLK
8 ROSSEFIELD GDNS

D4
1 WESTMORELAND MOUNT
2 BACK WESTMORELAND MT
3 WELLINGTON GARTH
4 BELLMOUNT GN

E1
1 SOUTH END TERR
2 SOUTH END MOUNT
3 EASTLAND WLK

E2
1 BACK ASTON PL
2 BACK ASTON TERR
3 BACK ASTON VIEW
4 BACK HIGHFIELD RD

E3
1 RAYNVILLE APP
2 RAYNVILLE CT
3 RAYNVILLE GRANGE
4 RAYNVILLE PL

F1
1 WYTHER PARK CL
2 COCKSHOTT CL
3 ARMLEY GRANGE DR

F2
1 WENSLEYDALE MEWS
2 WENSLEYDALE CL
3 WENSLEYDALE RISE

A5
1 KEPSTORN RISE

A6
1 LATCHMERE AVE
2 OLD FARM GARTH
3 LINTON CROFT
4 LATCHMERE WLK

D5
1 CHAPEL SQ
2 ASH TERR
3 ASH VIEW
4 BACK ASH VIEW
5 CROSS CHAPEL ST
6 Arndale Ctr

7 GRUNBERG ST
8 GRANBY MOUNT
9 CROSS GRANBY TERR
10 CHAPEL TERR
11 CHAPEL PL
12 TRELAWN CRES
13 ALMA COTTS

D6
1 GROVEWOOD
2 HOLLY BANK
3 SEFTON CT
4 VICTORIA TERR
5 BACK HEATHFIELD TERR
6 BACK BURTON CRES

7 HEATHFIELD SQ
8 TEMPLE VUE
9 ODDY PL
10 SOWDEN'S YD
11 ST CHADS PAR
12 ELLIS TERR

E6
1 MONK BRIDGE PL
2 MONK BRIDGE GR
3 BACK MONK BRIDGE PL
4 SPRINGHILL GR
5 BACK WILTON GR
6 CLAIRE CT

E6
7 CLAREMOUNT
8 HEDDON ST
9 BROOKFIELD TERR

E7
1 CROSS GREENWOOD MOUNT
2 GREEN CHASE
3 GREEN ROW
4 BACK GREENWOOD MOUNT
5 SUNSET AVE
6 SUNSET DR

42

60

59

K NORMAN MOUNT
PER GR
PER TERR
PER PL
ING BANK
ORIA HO
ORIA TERR

For full street detail of the highlighted area see page 205.

78

60

C5
1 BACK ROKEBY GDNS
2 WINSTON GDNS
3 BACK WINSTON GDNS
4 GRIMTHORPE AVE
5 BACK GRIMTHORPE ST

E5
1 ASHFIELD PK
2 CONISTON AVE
3 BACK WOODLAND PARK RD
F6
1 BENTLEY CT
2 MEANWOOD VALLEY GR
3 BACK BENTLEY AVE
4 KING'S SQ
5 GORDON PL

6 MONK BRIDGE DR
7 BK MONK BRIDGE DR
8 CLIPSTON AVE
9 CLIPSTON TERR
10 MONK BRIDGE MOUNT
11 MONK BRIDGE AVE

For full street detail of the highlighted area see pages 204, 206 and 207.

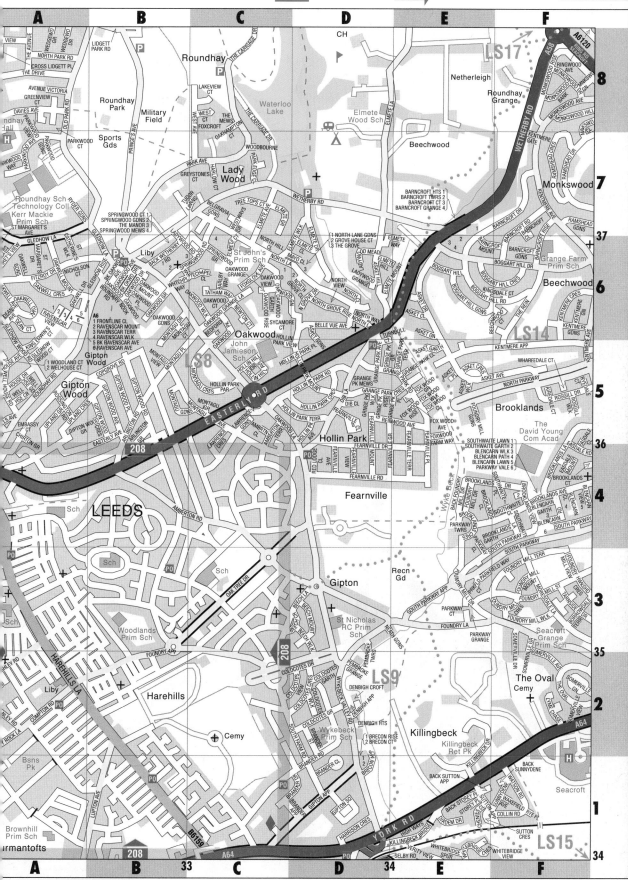

For full street detail of the highlighted area see page 208.

A5
1 RAMSHEAD HTS
2 ELIZABETH PL
3 BAILEYS CL

A8
1 RINGWOOD MOUNT
2 WHINMOOR CRES
3 MONKSWOOD AVE
4 MONKSWOOD HILL
5 MONKSWOOD CL
6 MONKSWOOD GATE

61

B8
1 HATHAWAY WLK
2 WHITE LAITHE GARTH
3 WHITE LAITH CT

45

D5
1 LANGBAR GDNS
2 ASH TREE CT
3 PENNWELL CROFT
4 ASH TREE VIEW
5 ASH TREE WALK
6 BRAYTON GARTH
7 BRAYTON SQ
8 BRAYTON PL
9 LANGBAR GRANGE

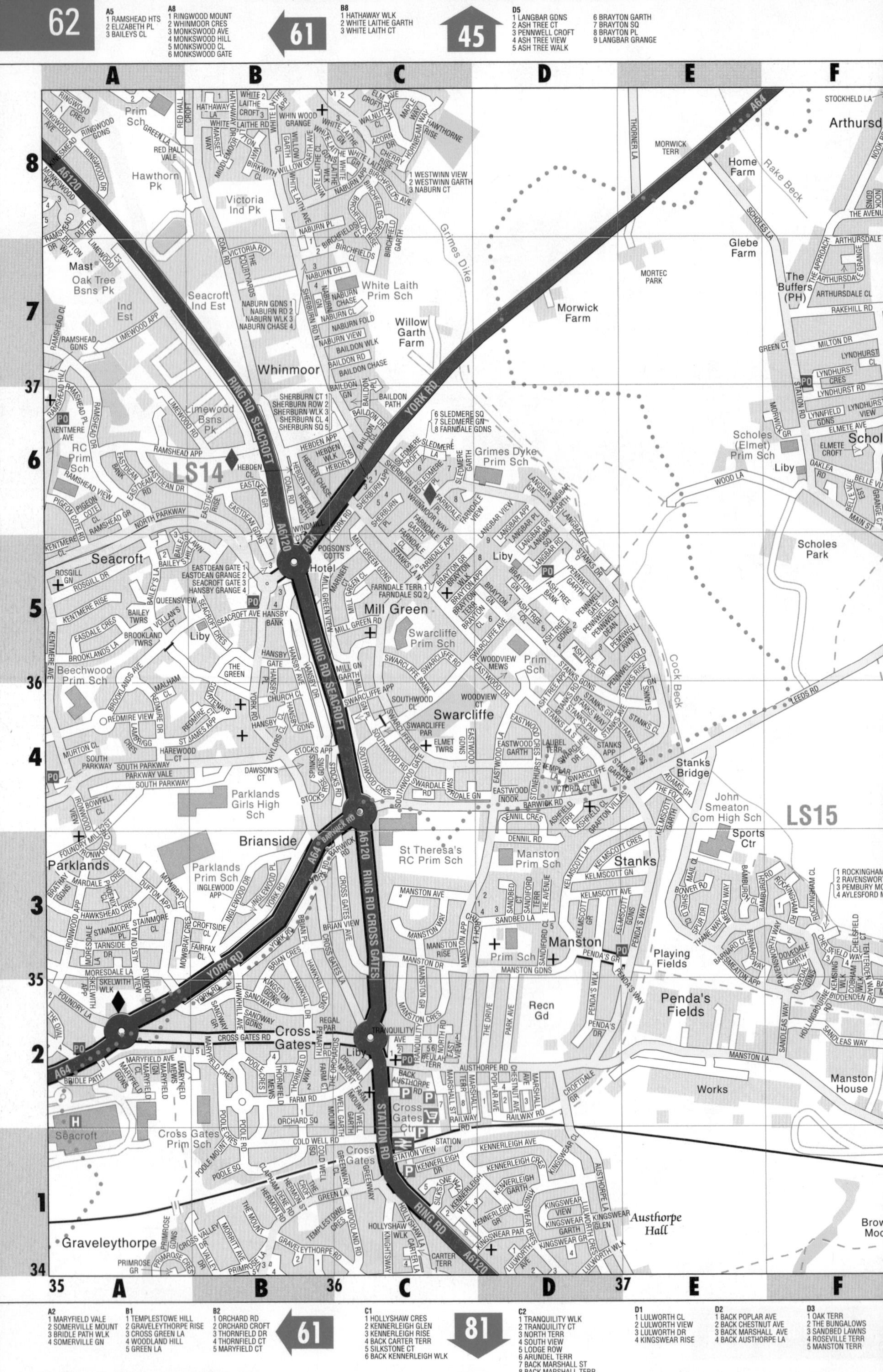

A2
1 MARYFIELD VALE
2 SOMERVILLE MOUNT
3 BRIDLE PATH WLK
4 SOMERVILLE GN

B1
1 TEMPLESTOWE HILL
2 GRAVELEYTHORPE RISE
3 CROSS GREEN LA
4 WOODLAND HILL
5 GREEN LA

B2
1 ORCHARD RD
2 ORCHARD CROFT
3 THORNFIELD DR
4 THORNFIELD CT
5 MARYFIELD CT

61

C1
1 HOLLYSHAW CRES
2 KENNERLEIGH GLEN
3 KENNERLEIGH RISE
4 BACK CARTER TERR
5 SILKSTONE CT
6 BACK KENNERLEIGH WLK

81

C2
1 TRANQUILITY WLK
2 TRANQUILITY CT
3 NORTH TERR
4 SOUTH VIEW
5 LODGE ROW
6 ARUNDEL TERR
7 BACK MARSHALL ST
8 BACK MARSHALL TERR

D1
1 LULWORTH CL
2 LULWORTH VIEW
3 LULWORTH DR
4 KINGSWEAR RISE

D2
1 BACK POPLAR AVE
2 BACK CHESTNUT AVE
3 BACK MARSHALL AVE
4 BACK AUSTHORPE LA

D3
1 OAK TERR
2 THE BUNGALOWS
3 SANDBED LAWNS
4 ROSEVILLE TERR
5 MANSTON TERR

46
64

A
B
C
D
E
F
STOCKHELD LA
Stockheld Grange Farm
Rake Hill
Rakehill Farm
RAKEHILL RD
Rake Beck
Ford
DARK LA
Mill
MEADOW VIEW
POTTERTON LA
POTTERTON CL
MAYPOLE MEWS
THE BOYLE
CHURCH FARM VIEW
POTTERTON CT
ELMWOOD CT
PH
PO
THE CROSS
SCHOOLGATE
ABERFORD RD
FIELDHEAD DR
Ass Bridge
Potterton Beck
Sewage Works
LS 25
ELMWOOD AVE
ELMWOOD CHASE
WENDEL AVE
ELMWOOD LA
MAIN ST
TITHE BARN FOLD
WELFARE AVE
CHAPEL LA
PARLINGTON CT
Barwick in Elmet CE Prim Sch
Barwick in Elmet
CROFT WAY
CARRFIELD RD
CARRFIELD DR
CARRFIELD
CARRFIELD LA
Leeds Country Way
RICHMONDFIELD GARTH
PEAR TREE GDNS
RICHMONDFIELD WAY
RICHMONDFIELD MOUNT
ELMET DR
ELMET RD
1 RICHMONDFIELD CL
2 RICHMONDFIELD GR
3 RICHMONDFIELD CROSS
4 RICHMONDFIELD WLK
RICHMONDFIELD LA
GASCOIGNE VIEW
THE COPPICE
THE MOUNT
THE CLOSE
FLATS LA
GASCOIGNE RD
GASCOIGNE CT
RICHMONDFIELD CRES
RICHMONDFIELD DR
RICHMONDFIELD AVE
PARLINGTON MDW
BECK MDW
GASCOIGNE AVE
SHAWS LA
Limekiln Hill
LEEDS RD
Longlane Beck
MAIN ST
TAYLOR LA
LS15
Barwick Bank
Highfield Farm
HIGHFIELD LA
HIGHFIELD LA
LONG LA
Honesty Farm
Barnbow Carr
BARNBOW LA
BOG LA
Carr Beck
Upper Barnbow Farm
Cock Beck
Throstlenest Bridge
Throstle Nest Farm
PARLINGTON LA
Leeds Country Way
BARNBOW LA
Barnbow Wood
CH
Laverack
Parlington Hollins
The Lake
ELLIS LA
LS25
Cock Beck
Lake Cottage
BARWICK RD
Manor Farm Cottage
Lazencroft Farm
Shippen House Farm
Sports Ground
Barnbow Common
The Manor House
M1
MANSTON LA
LC
M1
8
7
37
6
5
36
4
3
35
2
1
34
39
40

82
64

63
47

LS15
The Ridge
Bankside Plantation
Potterton Beck
Cock Beck
Leyfield Farm
Becca Banks
Folly Corner
Green Hill
Sewage Works
The R
ST JOHN'S GARTH
THE DALE
PINFOLD RISE
REIN CT
HAYTON WOOD VIEW
HIGHFIELD RD
RAPER VIEW
FIELD LA
ABBOTS CL
MARKHAM COTTS
BECCA LA
MAIN ST
Cock Beck
Aberford Bridge
ABERFORD BY-PASS
A1(M)
KINGFISHER LA
FIELD LA
Barwick Lodge Plantation
Chantryhill Plantation
PARLINGTON HO
WATERSIDE MDWS
CATTLE LA
BEECH VIEW
PARLINGTON DR
PARLINGTON VILLAS
BRIDGE COTTS
PH
Aberford
PO
Barwick Bank
Hungerhills Plantation
The Belt
SCHOOL LA
Aberford CE Prim Sch
MANOR CT
BECKSIDE
WINDMILL RISE
STOCKING LA
Willowgarth Plantation
Cherry Strip
LOTHERTON LA
BUNKERS HILL
YOUNG'S CT
WIDOW'S ROW
Whitehouse Farm
Cooper Wood
Triumphal Arch
The Terraces
Aberford Park
Old Wood
LS15
Priory Park
Home Farm
Wilderness
Hangings Plantation
Hicklam House
Parlington Gardens
Hicklam Mill
PARLINGTON LA
LS25
Hicklam Mill Farm
COLLIER LA
Gamekeepers Cottage
Dawson's Wood
The Staith Cottage
Bathingwell Plantation
Parlington Park
Parlington Hollins
Wakefield Lodge
Hook Moor
44
Fox Covert
Park House Farm
48
B1217 ABERFORD RD
Hook Moor Cottage
M1
Lilly Pit Cottage
Beech Plantation
M1
47
A462
A656
Hawk's Nest Wood
Sutton Dyke
Ridge Road Farm
The Weigh House
1 SILKSTONE CL
2 MOULE RISE
CEDAR RIDGE
A462
A656
A1(M)
A B C D E F
8 7 6 5 4 3 2 1
37 36 35 34
41 42 43

63
83

A   B   C   D   E   F

8

Hayton Wood

South Dyke

LS24

Low Lead Farm

Lead Mill Farm

7

Woodhouse Grange

B1217

The Rein

Crow Hill

37

STOCKING LA

Reform Place

Lead Hall Farm

+

DAM LA

6

LOTHERTON LA

The Crooked Billet (PH)

Galton Cottages

Lotherton Lodge

Lotherton Park Farm

West Field

5

COLLIER LA

P

P

Captain Wood

COPLEY LA

36

Lotherton Hall

+

4

Deer Park

Lotherton Hall Estate

Rose Cottage

North Yorkshire STREET ATLAS

LS25

COLDHILL LA

Vevers Bushes

Coldhill Pond

Lower Cold Hill Farm

3

Bragdale

Ringhay Wood

The Avenue

Coldhill Farm

Cold Hill

35

Coburnhill Wood

Far Fox Covert

2

Scott's Wood

Near Fox Covert

Middle Fox Covert

Weet Wood

The Marsh

1

Daniel Hartly's Wood

LAITH STAID LA

34

A   B   45   C   D   46   E   F

Cock Beck

A B C D E F

8

Grey Stone Hill

Western Hills

Fold Ho Top

Great Edge Flat

7

Small Edge

Rakes Clough

Coal Pit Pasture

Extwistle Moor

Birkin Clough

Old Hay Dike

Flaught Hill

Great Edge Bottom

Round Hill

33

Swinden Water

Clattering Stones

Burnley Way

Scar Hollow

6

Standing Stone Height

Birkin Clough Head

The Brinks

Hameldon

Wether Edge

5

GORPLE RD

Smallshaw Clough

Gorple Rd

Burnley Way

Gorple Stones

Little Hill

Gorple Gate

Dicken Dike

HX7

BB10

Shuttleworth Moor

32

Hare Stones Hill

Gorple

Black Moor

4

Hazel Edge

Rams Clough

Thistleden Dean

Gorple Upper Resr

3

Gorple Bottom

Whinberry

31

Cant Clough Resr

Hameldon Holes

Whinberry Flat

2

Black Clough

Wicken Clough

Red Carr Clough

1

Worsthorne Moor

OL14

Whinberry Clough

Three Nook Bit

Long Rut

Tongue

30

90 A B 91 C D 92 E F

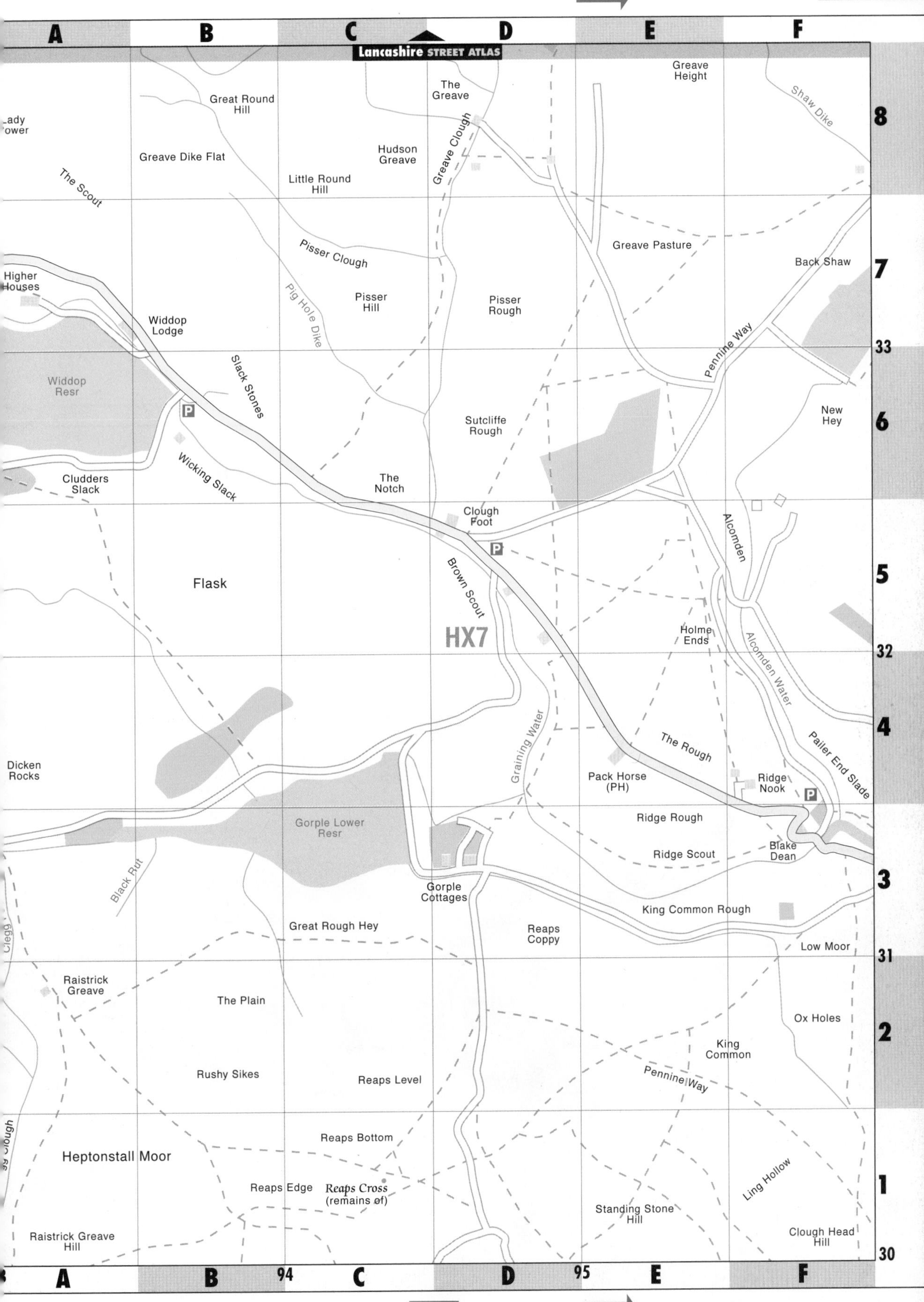

A   B   C   D   E   F

8

Greave
Height

Shaw Dike

The Greave

Great Round
Hill

Greave Clough

Greave Dike Flat

Hudson
Greave

Little Round
Hill

Back Shaw   7

The Scout

Pisser Clough

Greave Pasture

33

Pig Hole Dike

Higher
Houses

Pisser
Hill

Pisser
Rough

Pennine Way

Widdop
Lodge

Slack Stones

New
Hey   6

Widdop
Resr

P

Sutcliffe
Rough

Alcomden

Wicking Slack

Cludders
Slack

The
Notch

Clough
Foot

Alcomden Water

Flask

P

5

Brown Scout

HX7

Holme
Ends

32

Dicken
Rocks

Graining Water

The Rough

Pailer End Slade

4

Pack Horse
(PH)

Ridge
Nook   P

Gorple Lower
Resr

Ridge Rough

Blake
Dean

Black Rut

Gorple
Cottages

Ridge Scout

King Common Rough   3

Great Rough Hey

Reaps
Coppy

Low Moor

31

Clegg

Raistrick
Greave

The Plain

Ox Holes   2

King
Common

Rushy Sikes

Reaps Level

Pennine Way

Clough

Reaps Bottom

Heptonstall Moor

Ling Hollow   1

Reaps Edge   Reaps Cross
(remains of)

Standing Stone
Hill

Raistrick Greave
Hill

Clough Head
Hill

30

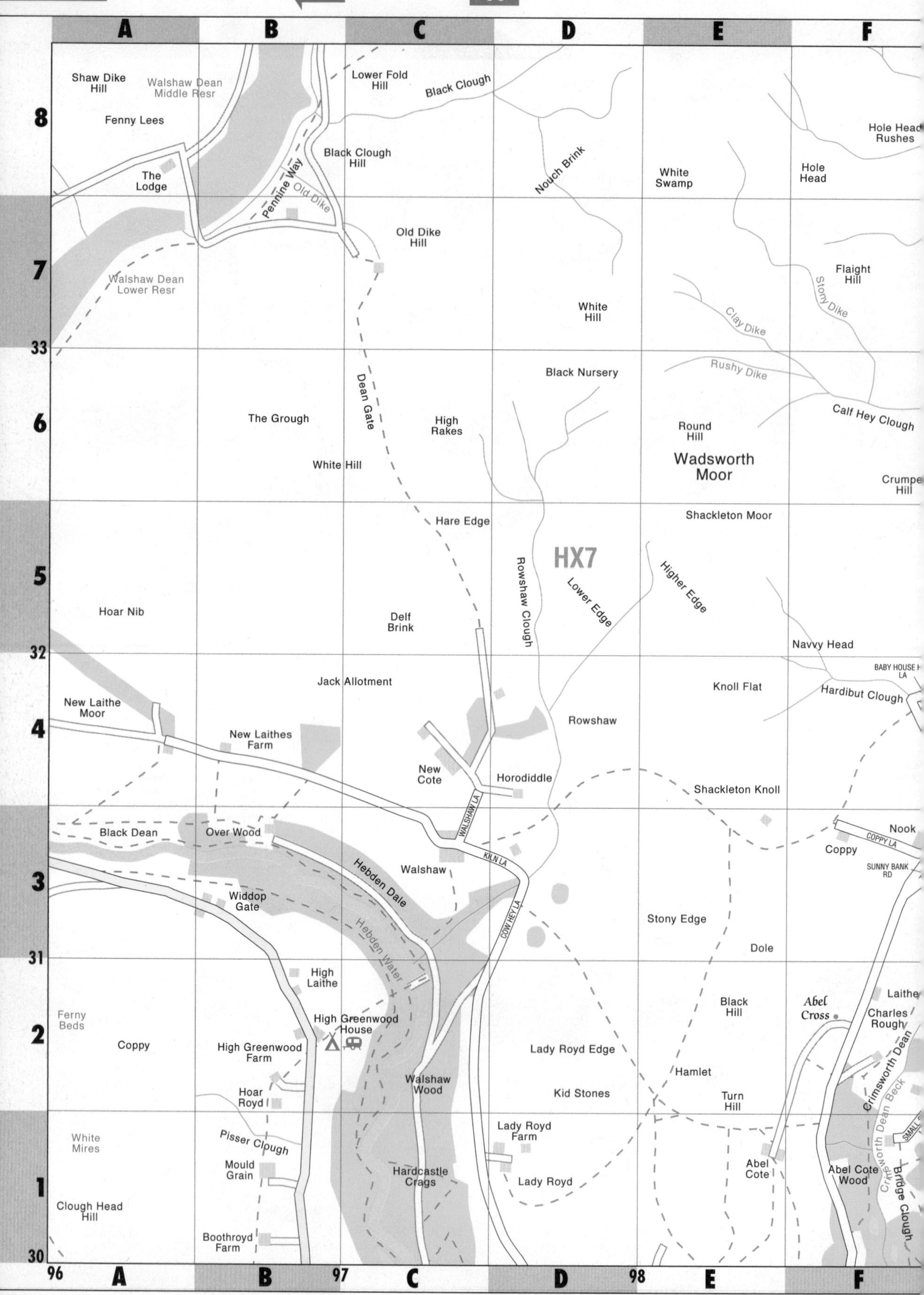

	A	B	C	D	E	F

8

Shaw Dike Hill

Walshaw Dean Middle Resr

Lower Fold Hill

Black Clough

Hole Head Rushes

Fenny Lees

Black Clough Hill

Nouch Brink

White Swamp

Hole Head

The Lodge

Pennine Way

Pennine Old Dike

7

Walshaw Dean Lower Resr

Old Dike Hill

White Hill

Flaight Hill

Stony Dike

Clay Dike

33

Dean Gate

Rushy Dike

Calf Hey Clough

6

The Grough

High Rakes

Black Nursery

Round Hill

Crumpet Hill

White Hill

Wadsworth Moor

Hare Edge

Shackleton Moor

5

Hoar Nib

Delf Brink

Rowshaw Clough

HX7

Lower Edge

Higher Edge

Navvy Head

32

Jack Allotment

BABY HOUSE LA

Hardibut Clough

New Laithe Moor

Knoll Flat

4

New Laithes Farm

New Cote

Horodiddle

Rowshaw

Shackleton Knoll

WALSHAW LA

Black Dean

Over Wood

Walshaw

Nook

COPPY LA

Coppy

3

Widdop Gate

Hebden Dale

KILN LA

COW HEY LA

Stony Edge

SUNNY BANK RD

31

Hebden Water

High Laithe

Dole

Ferny Beds

Coppy

High Greenwood House

Black Hill

Abel Cross

Laithe

Charles Rough

2

High Greenwood Farm

Lady Royd Edge

Hamlet

Crimsworth Dean

Hoar Royd

Walshaw Wood

Kid Stones

Turn Hill

Abel Cote

Abel Cote Wood

White Mires

Pisser Clough

Lady Royd Farm

Crimsworth Dean Beck

SMALL

Bridge Clough

1

Mould Grain

Hardcastle Crags

Lady Royd

Clough Head Hill

Boothroyd Farm

30

96	A	B	97	C	D	98	E	F

50
70

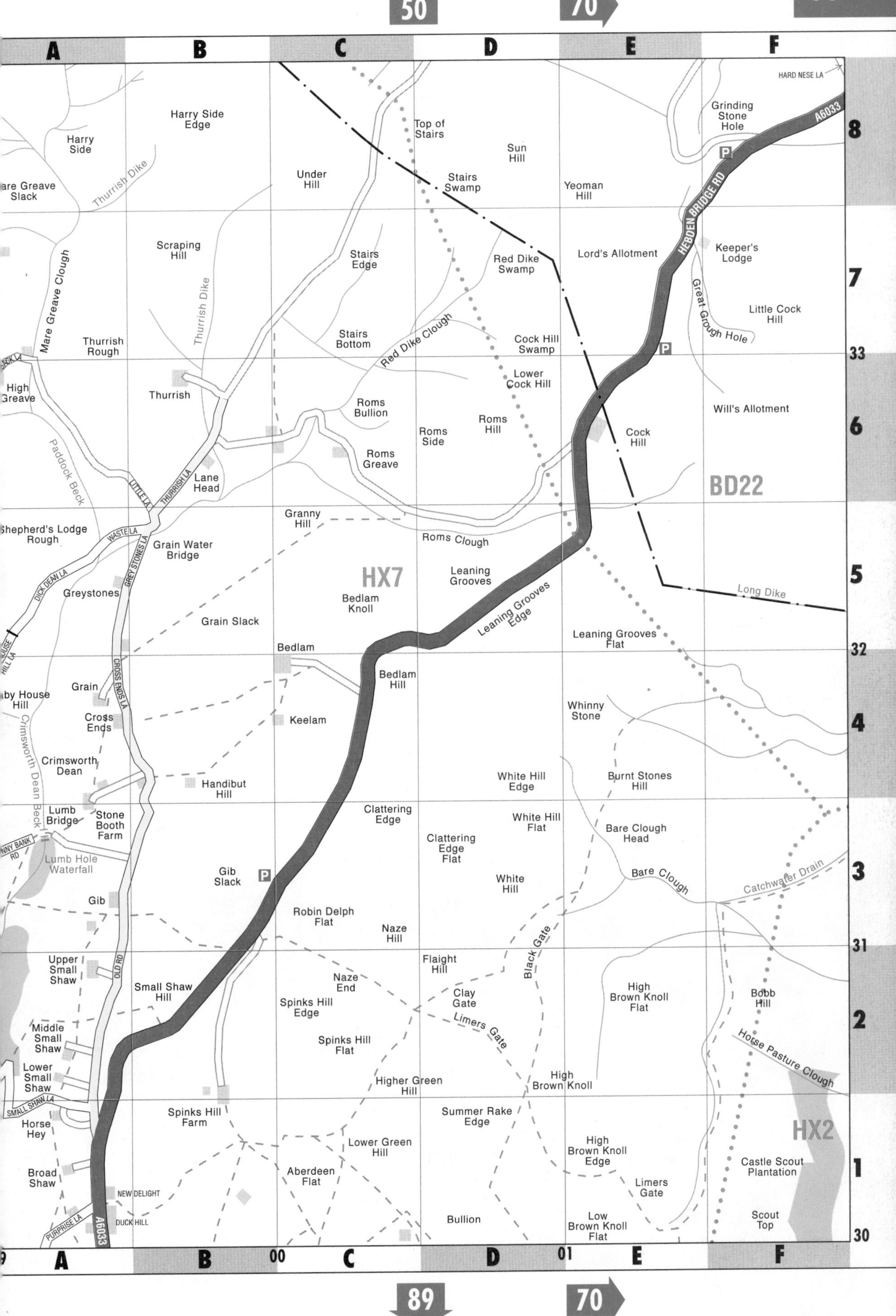
A
B
C
D
E
F
HARD NESE LA
A6033
Harry Side Edge
Harry Side
Mare Greave Slack
Thurrish Dike
Top of Stairs
Sun Hill
Grinding Stone Hole
Under Hill
Stairs Swamp
Yeoman Hill
HEBDEN BRIDGE RD
Scraping Hill
Stairs Edge
Red Dike Swamp
Lord's Allotment
Keeper's Lodge
Mare Greave Clough
Thurrish Dike
Great Clough Hole
Little Cock Hill
Thurrish Rough
Stairs Bottom
Red Dike Clough
Cock Hill Swamp
High Greave
Thurrish
Lower Cock Hill
Roms Bullion
Roms Hill
Roms Side
Will's Allotment
Cock Hill
Paddock Beck
Roms Greave
Lane Head
LITTLE LA
THURRISH LA
BD22
Granny Hill
Shepherd's Lodge Rough
WASTE LA
Grain Water Bridge
Roms Clough
GREY STONES LA
DICK DEAN LA
HX7
Leaning Grooves
Greystones
Bedlam Knoll
Leaning Grooves Edge
Long Dike
Grain Slack
Leaning Grooves Flat
Bedlam
Bedlam Hill
Grain
CROSS ENDS LA
Cross Ends
Keelam
Whinny Stone
Crimsworth Dean
Crimsworth Dean Beck
Handibut Hill
White Hill Edge
Burnt Stones Hill
Lumb Bridge
Stone Booth Farm
Clattering Edge
White Hill Flat
Bare Clough Head
Lumb Hole Waterfall
Clattering Edge Flat
Gib Slack
White Hill
Bare Clough
Catchwater Drain
Gib
Robin Delph Flat
Naze Hill
Black Gate
Upper Small Shaw
OLD RD
Flaight Hill
Small Shaw Hill
Naze End
Clay Gate
High Brown Knoll Flat
Bobb Hill
Spinks Hill Edge
Limers Gate
Middle Small Shaw
Spinks Hill Flat
Horse Pasture Clough
Lower Small Shaw
Higher Green Hill
High Brown Knoll
SMALL SHAW LA
Spinks Hill Farm
Summer Rake Edge
HX2
Horse Hey
Lower Green Hill
High Brown Knoll Edge
Castle Scout Plantation
Broad Shaw
Aberdeen Flat
Limers Gate
NEW DELIGHT
PURPRISE LA
DUCK HILL
Bullion
Low Brown Knoll Flat
Scout Top
A6033
8
7
33
6
5
32
4
3
31
2
1
30
00
01

89
70

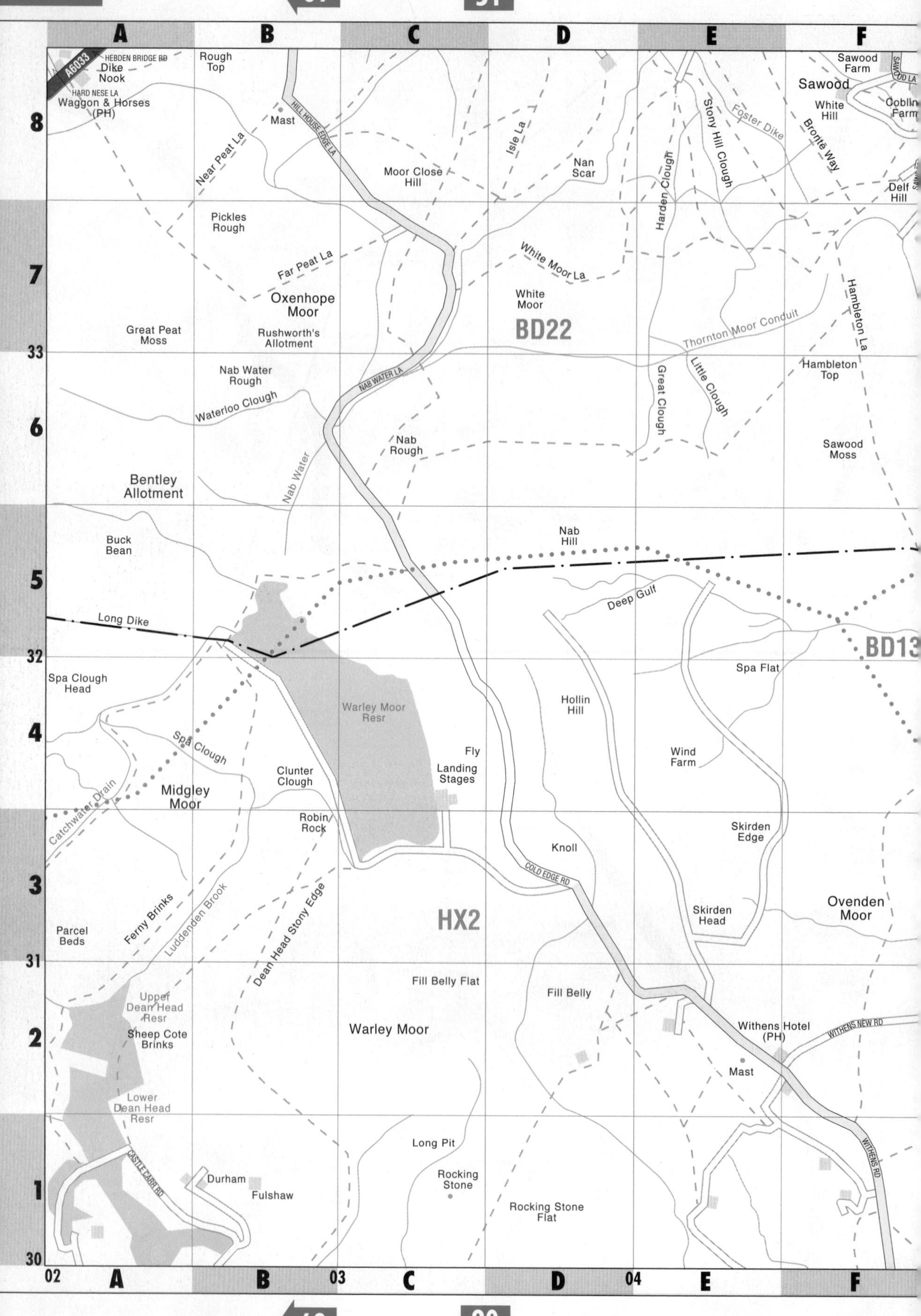

| A | B | C | D | E | F |

8 Dike Nook — A6033 HEBDEN BRIDGE RD — HARD NESE LA — Waggon & Horses (PH) — Rough Top — Mast — HILL HOUSE EDGE LA — Moor Close Hill — Isle La — Nan Scar — Harden Clough — Stony Hill Clough — Foster Dike — Bronte Way — Sawood Farm — Sawood — White Hill — Goblin Farm — SAWOOD LA — Delf Hill

7 Pickles Rough — Far Peat La — Near Peat La — Oxenhope Moor — White Moor La — White Moor — Great Clough — Little Clough — Hambleton La — Hambleton Top

33 Great Peat Moss — Rushworth's Allotment — BD22 — Thornton Moor Conduit

6 Nab Water Rough — Waterloo Clough — NAB WATER LA — Nab Water — Nab Rough — Sawood Moss

Bentley Allotment

5 Buck Bean — Long Dike — Nab Hill — Deep Gulf — BD13

32 Spa Clough Head — Spa Flat

4 Spa Clough — Catchwater Drain — Midgley Moor — Clunter Clough — Warley Moor Resr — Fly Landing Stages — Hollin Hill — Wind Farm

Robin Rock — Knoll — Skirden Edge

3 Ferny Brinks — Luddenden Brook — Dean Head Stony Edge — COLD EDGE RD — HX2 — Skirden Head — Ovenden Moor

Parcel Beds

31 Upper Dean Head Resr — Fill Belly Flat — Fill Belly — Withens Hotel (PH) — WITHENS NEW RD

2 Sheep Cote Brinks — Warley Moor — Mast

Lower Dean Head Resr — WITHENS RD

1 CASTLE CARR RD — Durham — Fulshaw — Long Pit — Rocking Stone — Rocking Stone Flat

30

52 72

A B C D E F

ntry Hill
WOOD LA
B6141
LONG CSWY
Pit La
Spring Row
NETHERWOOD 1
EASTFIELD 2
CHAPEL ST 3
SOUTH ST 4
MOULSON TERR 5
NEW ST 6
COMMERCIAL ST 7
FORESTER CT 8
THE DRIVE
KIRKCROFT
CLOCK LA
LONGHOUSE LA
LONGHOUSE DR
WOODTHORPE
BURNHOLME
MAIN RD
A629
Liby
PARKINSON RD
9 KNOWLES ST
10 CLAPHAM ST
11 SCHOOL ST
12 MILTON ST
13 BUCK ST
14 STRADMORE RD
Sewage Works
Doe Park Resr
STATION RD
ALBION ST
FAIRFIELD CRES
CARPERLEY
CLIFFE TERR
Millennium Way
Lower Shay Farm
Mills
Carperley Beck
Bark Hill
8
Bracken Hall
FOSTER SQ 15
DENTON ROW 16
TUNNEL ST 17
WELL ST 18
MOUNT PLEASANT 19
GLADSTONE PL 20
NEW RD
B6141
OLD RD
HALIFAX RD
Stubden Beck
7
Thornton Moor Resr
Stubden Resr
THORNTON MOOR RD
Stubden
Works
Denholme Gate Inn (PH)
Denholme Beck
33
Morton Farm
CROFT ROW
DENHOLME GATE
WHITEMOOR WAY
Brontë Way
SMITHY HILL
A644
Denholme Clough
CLOUGH CT 1
MONARCH GATE 2
JOHN HANSON CT 3
HIGHGATE
BD22
6
BLACK EDGE LA
BRIGHOUSE RD
WELL HEADS
Thornton Moor
BD13
Black Edge
Keelham Prim Sch
Keelham
CRAGG LA
KEELHAM PL
PH
B6145
Foreside La
CRAGG TOP
CRAGG LA
The Copper Kettle (PH)
THORNTON RD
Denholme Gate
BRIGHOUSE AND DENHOLME RD
5
Bottomley Holes
Foreside
FORESIDE BOTTOM LA
COUNTY BRIDGE
HALIFAX RD
A644
The Shay
32
Foreside Top
Sun Side
4
Cockhill Hill
Far Shay Farm
New Moss Farm
Works
The Borders
COAL LA
Soil Hill
The Pastures
White Wall End
Great Scar
Soil Hill Farm
Back La
The Goose Inn (PH)
3
Mast
Cloth Hall Farm
Ogden Plantation
Mount Pleasant
Skirden Clough
CAUSEWAY FOOT
Causeway Foot Inn (PH)
NED HILL RD
TAYLOR LA
31
Round Hill
Spice Cake Hills
Ogden Resr
OGDEN LA
P
GREYSHAW SYKE
Delves Farm
Laverock Hall Farm
Ogden Water Country Park
HX2
SYKE LA
2
Ogden
WITHENS NEW RD
JANE GN
KEIGHLEY RD
Ash Farm
Rosemary Hall
BRADSHAW ROW
Mixenden Ings
Ogden Water Visitor Centre
Black Hill
Middle Grain Beck
Rodger Leys
Hebble Brook
Cock Hill Gate
COW HILL GATE LA
Ingham Lane Farm
SOUTHLANDS
1
Wamesley Scar
Carrs Beck
Hall Banks
UNION LA
TRIPPING GN
ROCKS LA
INGHAM LA
PH
Bradshaw Prim Sch
BRADSHAW LA
LYNTON GR
WEST VIEW TERR
The Carrs
P
CH
Odd Moor
A629
INGHAM CL
30

05 A B 06 C D 07 E F

91 72

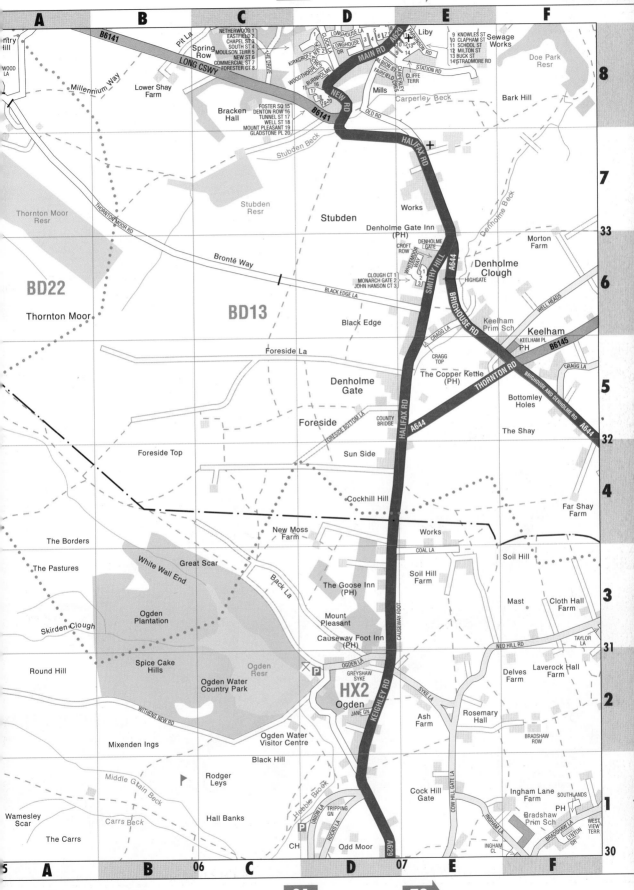

← 71

↑ 53

Map grid references A–F (columns), 1–8, 30–33 (rows)

Law Farm
The Roughs
Rock and Heifer (PH)
Bell Dean
Upper Pikeley
BD15
Aldersley Farm
Lower Bailey Fold Farm
Spring Hall Farm
Back Heights
School Ridge
Packington St
HOBB END
Spring View
Salt Pie
Pitty Beck
Spring Hall Farm
World End View
Ring O' Bells (PH)
Hill Top
Long Row
White Horse Inn (PH)
Well Heads
Close Head Row
Cemy
Brontë Way
Thornton Prim Sch
Thornton
Thornton Hall Farm
Brooklands Ave
Fireclay Bsns Pk
B6145
THORNTON RD
B61
Aldersholes La
Green Clough
BD13
Upper Headley
Carr House Farm
Squirrel Hill
Black Carr
Pinch Beck
CH
Headley La
Deep La
Upper Sandal
New Royd Gate
BD14
Mavis Farm
Hole Bottom Beck
A644
Raggalds Farm
Law Hill
West Scholes
The Junction (PH)
Yews Gn
Hollingwell Hill
Clayton Edge Farm
Sun Farm
The Raggalds Inn (PH)
Perseverance Rd
BRIGHOUSE AND DENHOLME RD
Lanes Farm
Foxhill Prim Sch
Low Fold Farm
QUEENSBURY
Scarlet Height
HX2
Mountain
Pineberry Inn (PH)
Masts
ALBERT RD
BRIGHOUSE RD
Scarlet Hts
A64
Bradshaw
Four Seasons Elder Lea
Bradshaw Tavern (PH)
Woodland Farm
Roper Farm
Warmleigh Cvn Pk
A647 WEST END
Mills
Hunger Hill
Vale Gr

← 71

↓ 92

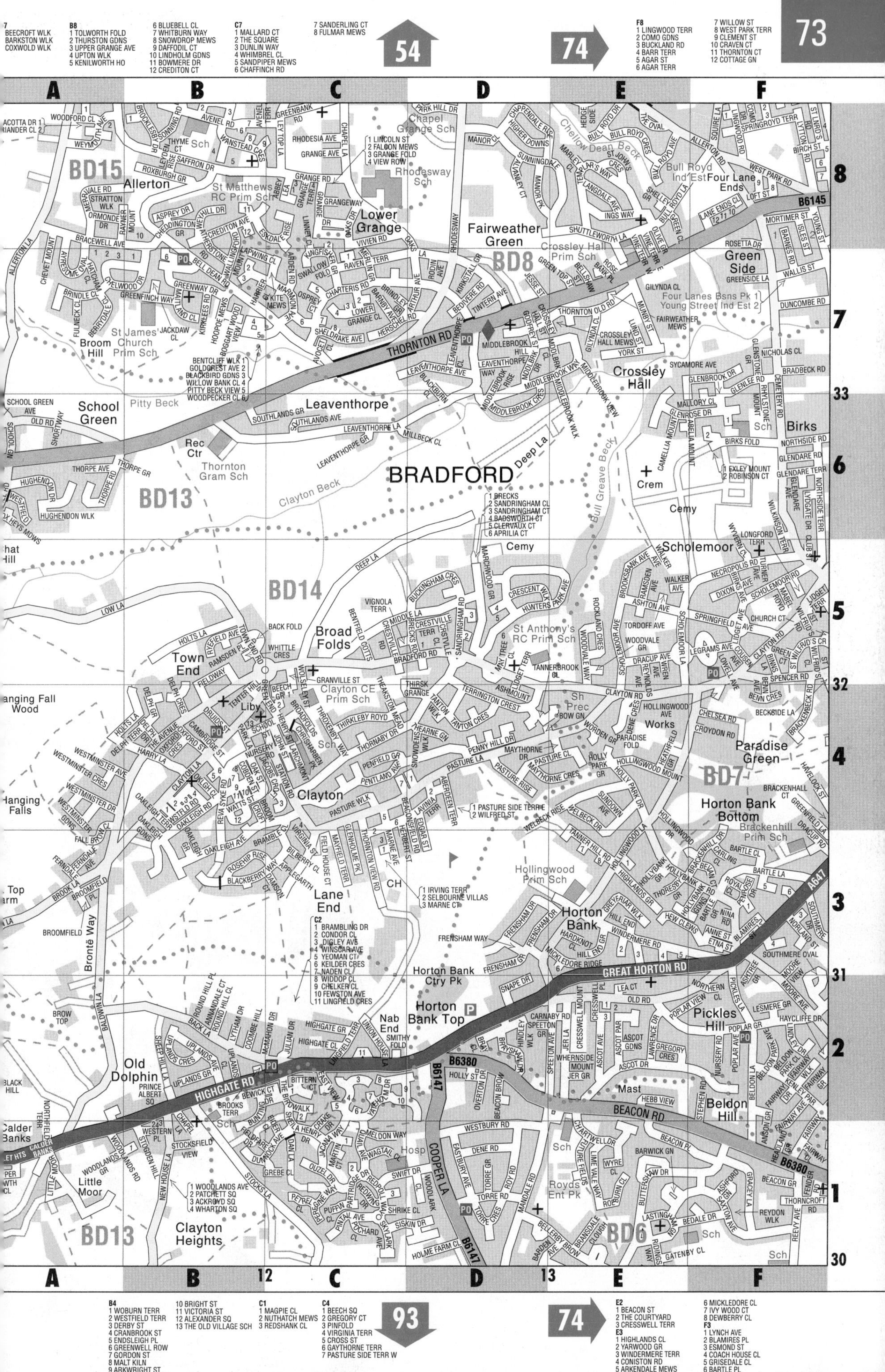
A7
BEECROFT WLK
BARKSTON WLK
COXWOLD WLK
B8
1 TOLWORTH FOLD
2 THURSTON GDNS
3 UPPER GRANGE AVE
4 UPTON WLK
5 KENILWORTH HO
6 BLUEBELL CL
7 WHITBURN WAY
8 SNOWDROP MEWS
9 DAFFODIL CT
10 LINDHOLM GDNS
11 BOWMERE DR
12 CREDITON CT
C7
1 MALLARD CT
2 THE SQUARE
3 DUNLIN WAY
4 WHIMBREL CL
5 SANDPIPER MEWS
6 CHAFFINCH RD
7 SANDERLING CT
8 FULMAR MEWS
54
74
F8
1 LINGWOOD TERR
2 COMO GDNS
3 BUCKLAND RD
4 BARR TERR
5 AGAR ST
6 AGAR TERR
7 WILLOW ST
8 WEST PARK TERR
9 CLEMENT ST
10 CRAVEN CT
11 THORNTON CT
12 COTTAGE GN
A
B
C
D
E
F
8
7
33
6
5
32
4
3
31
2
1
30
BD15
Allerton
Thyme Sch
St Matthews RC Prim Sch
Chapel Grange Sch
Rhodesway Sch
Lower Grange
Fairweather Green
BD8
Crossley Hall Prim Sch
Chellow Dean Beck
Bull Royd Ind Est
Four Lane Ends
B6145
Green Side
Four Lanes Bsns Pk
Young Street Ind Est
Broom Hill
St James Church Prim Sch
THORNTON RD
Crossley Hall
School Green
Pitty Beck
Leaventhorpe
Rec Ctr
Thornton Gram Sch
BD13
Clayton Beck
BRADFORD
Deep La
Bull Greave Beck
Crem
Cemy
Birks
Scholemoor
BD14
Broad Folds
Town End
St Anthony's RC Prim Sch
Clayton CE Prim Sch
Liby
Sh Prec
Works
Paradise Green
BD7
Horton Bank Bottom
Brackenhill Prim Sch
Clayton
Hanging Falls
Hanging Fall Wood
Lane End
Hollingwood Prim Sch
Horton Bank
CH
Bronte Way
Horton Bank Ctry Pk
GREAT HORTON RD
A647
Nab End
Horton Bank Top
Pickles Hill
Old Dolphin
HIGHGATE RD
B6380
B6147
COOPER LA
BEACON RD
Mast
Beldon Hill
Calder Banks
Little Moor
Hosp
Sch
Royds Ent Pk
BD6
BD13
Clayton Heights
C2
1 BRAMBLING DR
2 CONDOR CL
3 DIGLEY AVE
4 WINSCAR AVE
5 YEOMAN CT
6 KEILDER CRES
7 NADEN CL
8 WIDDOP CL
9 CHELKER CL
10 FEWSTON AVE
11 LINGFIELD CRES
1 BRECKS
2 SANDRINGHAM CL
3 SANDRINGHAM CT
4 BADSWORTH CT
5 CLERVAUX CT
6 APRILIA CT
1 IRVING TERR
2 SELBOURNE VILLAS
3 MARNE CT
1 PASTURE SIDE TERR E
2 WILFRED ST
1 WOODLANDS AVE
2 PATCHETT SQ
3 ACKROYD SQ
4 WHARTON SQ
1 EXLEY MOUNT
2 ROBINSON CT
1 LINCOLN ST
2 FALCON MEWS
3 GRANGE FOLD
4 VIEW ROW
BENTCLIFF WLK 1
GOLDCREST AVE 2
BLACKBIRD GDNS 3
WILLOW BANK CL 4
PITTY BECK VIEW 5
WOODPECKER CL 6
A
B
12
C
D
13
E
F
B4
1 WOBURN TERR
2 WESTFIELD TERR
3 DERBY ST
4 CRANBROOK ST
5 ENDSLEIGH PL
6 GREENWELL ROW
7 GORDON ST
8 MALT KILN
9 ARKWRIGHT ST
10 BRIGHT ST
11 VICTORIA ST
12 ALEXANDER SQ
13 THE OLD VILLAGE SCH
C1
1 MAGPIE CL
2 NUTHATCH MEWS
3 REDSHANK CL
C4
1 BEECH SQ
2 GREGORY CT
3 PINFOLD
4 VIRGINIA TERR
5 CROSS ST
6 GAYTHORNE TERR
7 PASTURE SIDE TERR W
93
74
E2
1 BEACON ST
2 THE COURTYARD
3 CRESSWELL TERR
E3
1 HIGHLANDS CL
2 YARWOOD GR
3 WINDERMERE TERR
4 CONISTON RD
5 ARKENDALE MEWS
6 MICKLEDORE CL
7 IVY WOOD CT
8 DEWBERRY CL
F3
1 LYNCH AVE
2 BLAMIRES PL
3 ESMOND ST
4 COACH HOUSE CL
5 GRISEDALE CL
6 BARTLE PL

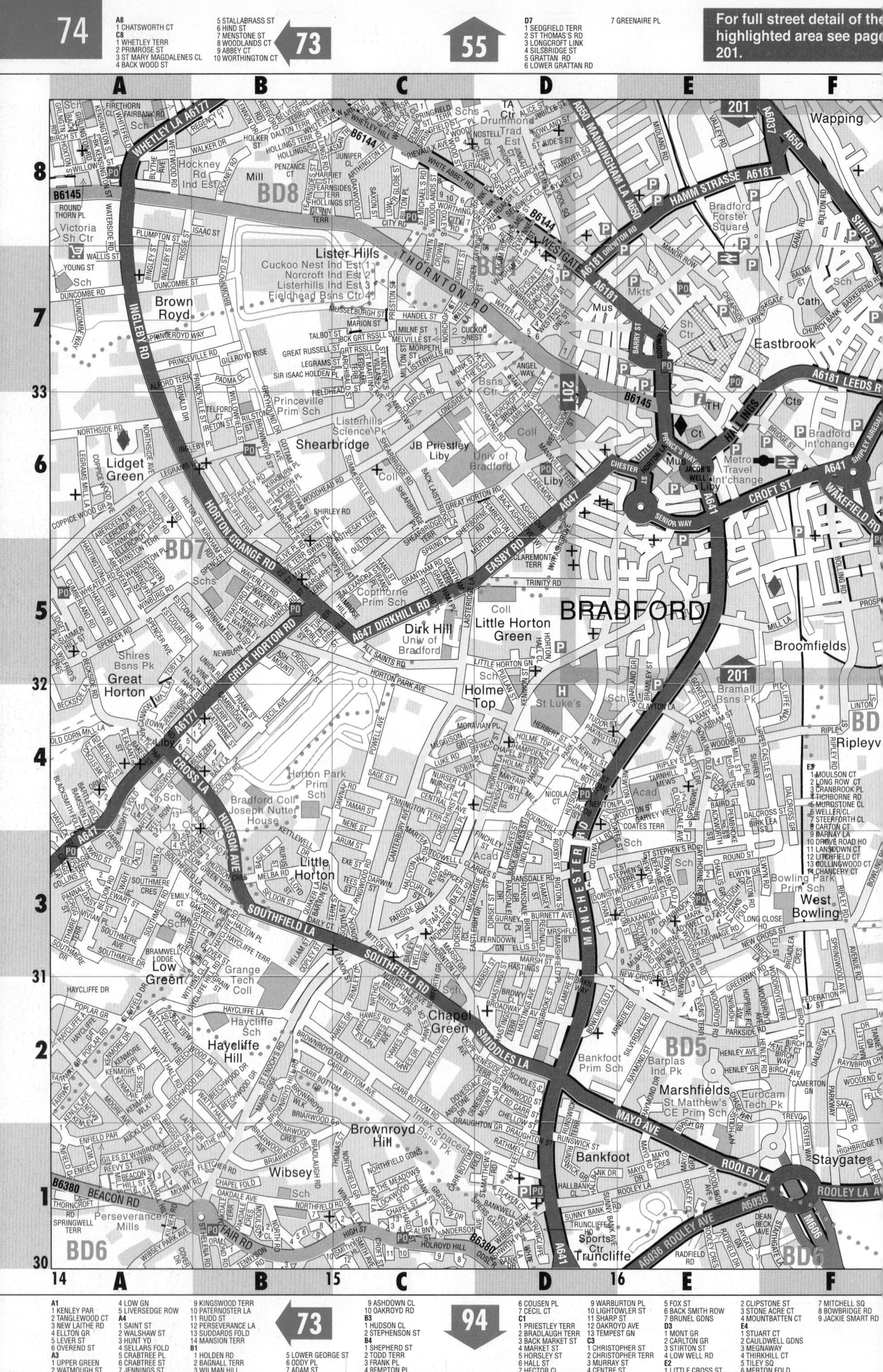
A8
1 CHATSWORTH CT
C8
1 WHETLEY TERR
2 PRIMROSE ST
3 ST MARY MAGDALENES CL
4 BACK WOOD ST
5 STALLABRASS ST
6 HIND ST
7 MENSTONE ST
8 WOODLANDS CT
9 ABBEY CT
10 WORTHINGTON CT
73
55
D7
1 SEDGFIELD TERR
2 ST THOMAS'S RD
3 LONGCROFT LINK
4 SILSBRIDGE ST
5 GRATTAN RD
6 LOWER GRATTAN RD
7 GREENAIRE PL
For full street detail of the highlighted area see page 201.
A
B
C
D
E
F
8
7
33
6
5
32
4
3
31
2
1
30
14
15
16
BD8
BD7
BD5
BD6
BRADFORD
Wapping
Lister Hills
Brown Royd
Victoria Sh Ctr
Shearbridge
Lidget Green
Great Horton
Dirk Hill
Little Horton Green
Holme Top
Broomfields
Eastbrook
Bradford Forster Square
Little Horton
Low Green
West Bowling
Chapel Green
Haycliffe Hill
Marshfields
Brownroyd Hill
Wibsey
Bankfoot
Staygate
Truncliffe
Perseverance Mills
Ripleyville
Univ of Bradford
JB Priestley Liby
Bradford Int'change
Metro Travel Int'change
St Luke's
Bramall Bsns Pk
Bowling Park Prim Sch
Eurocam Tech Pk
Barplas Ind Pk
St Matthew's CE Prim Sch
Bankfoot Prim Sch
Imex Spaces Bsns Pk
Grange Tech Coll
Haycliffe Sch
Horton Park Prim Sch
Bradford Coll Joseph Nutter House
Shires Bsns Pk
Copthorne Prim Sch
Princeville Prim Sch
Listerhills Science Pk
Cuckoo Nest Ind Est
Norcroft Ind Est
Listerhills Ind Est
Fieldhead Bsns Ctr
Hockney Rd Ind Est
Drummond Trad Est
Sports Ctr
THORNTON RD
INGLEBY RD
HORTON GRANGE RD
GREAT HORTON RD
MANCHESTER RD
SOUTHFIELD LA
SMIDDLES LA
MAYO AVE
ROOLEY LA
HAMM STRASSE A6181
MANNINGHAM LA A650
WAKEFIELD RD
LEEDS RD
CROFT ST
A647 DIRKHILL RD
EASBY RD
BEACON RD
HOLROYD HILL
WHETLEY LA A6177
ROOLEY AVE
201

or full street detail of the
ighlighted area see page
01.

56

D5
1 NUNROYD HO
2 LENDAL HO
3 SHERWOOD HO
4 KENTMERE HO
5 KELSTERN HO
6 NORWOOD HO
7 PONSFORD HO
8 NUNBURY HO
9 MARKFIELD HO

76

D6
1 WELLESLEY HO
2 FORTESCUE HO
3 NORTON HO
4 PORTLAND HO
5 WAINCLIFFE HO

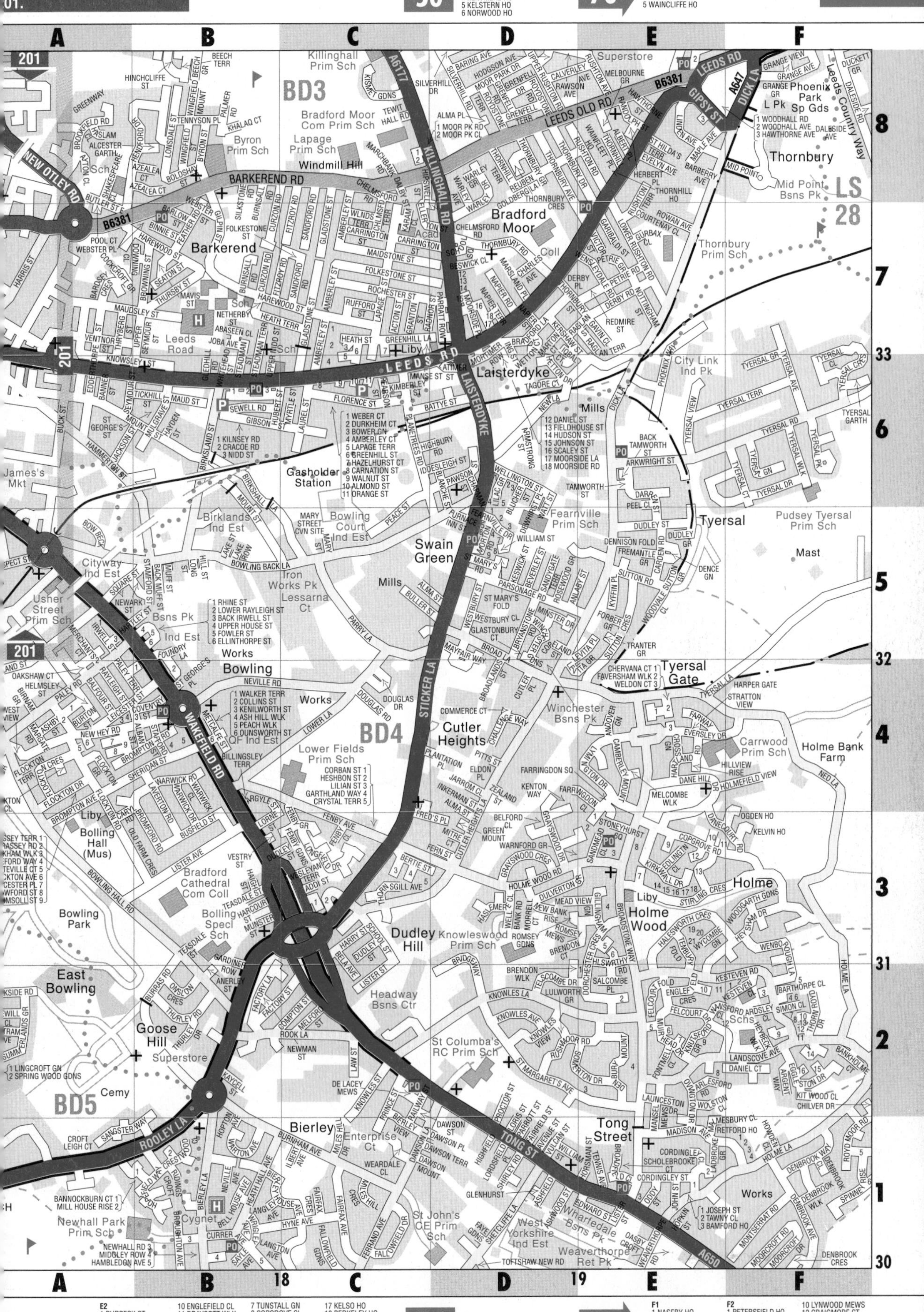
A
B
C
D
E
F
201
BD3
BD4
BD5
LS 28
Barkerend
Bradford Moor
Laisterdyke
Thornbury
Tyersal
Tyersal Gate
Swain Green
Bowling
Cutler Heights
Holme
Holme Wood
Dudley Hill
East Bowling
Goose Hill
Bierley
Tong Street
Windmill Hill
Leeds Road
Phoenix Park Sp Gds
Leeds Country Way
LEEDS RD
LEEDS OLD RD
BARKEREND RD
KILLINGHALL RD
STICKER LA
WAKEFIELD RD
TONG ST
ROOLEY LA
NEW OTLEY RD
A6177
A647
A650
B6381
8
7
33
6
5
32
4
3
31
2
1
30
18
19

E2
1 PURBECK CT
2 WAREHAM CNR
3 COPPLESTONE WLK
4 TIVERTON WLK
5 HORSHAM RD
6 MUIRHEAD CT
7 MUIRHEAD FOLD
8 LEAMSIDE WLK
9 KNUTSFORD MEWS
10 ENGLEFIELD CL
11 DRAYCOTT WLK
12 SANDGATE WLK

E3
1 FARRINGDON DR
2 STONEYHURST WAY
3 THE PARADE
4 BIDEFORD MOUNT
5 DORCHESTER CT
6 PEVERELL CL
7 TUNSTALL GN
8 COPGROVE CL
9 EASTFIELD GDNS
10 INGLEBOROUGH CL
11 MIDDLEHAM CT
12 COPGROVE CT
13 KILNSEA MOUNT
14 WORMALD LEA
15 LEITH HO
16 FORBES HO
17 KELSO HO
18 BERKELEY HO
19 SEFTON HO
20 DENHAM HO
21 MANSFIELD HO

95

76

F1
1 NASEBY HO
2 BROUGHTON HO
3 DENBY HO
4 AYTON HO
5 KIRKDALE WAY
6 SKELLOW DR

F2
1 PETERSFIELD HO
2 LENTON HO
3 BOWATER CT
4 BARTHORPE HO
5 KENNERLEIGH WLK
6 PURSTON HO
7 LINGMELL CRES
8 TYNWALD HO
9 KESTEVEN CT
10 LYNWOOD MEWS
12 CRAIGMORE CT
11 CRAIGMORE HO
13 LYNWOOD HO
14 LANSDALE CT
15 LANDSHOLME CT
16 GREENHOLME CT

A8
1 CHATSWORTH AVE
2 CHATSWORTH DR
3 GALLOWAY CT
4 MOORLAND CRES
E5
1 HILLTHORPE SQ

2 HILLTHORPE ST
3 HILLTHORPE TERR
4 REGENCY PARK GR
E6
1 RADCLIFFE TERR
2 RADCLIFFE GR
3 CHAPEL FOLD

E6
4 SANDRINGHAM AVE
E7
1 CRAWSHAW CL
2 CRAWSHAW HILL
3 PARKFIELD TERR
4 PARK AVE

E7
5 MANOR HOUSE ST
6 THE IVIES
7 WESLEY SQ
8 BOOTHS YD
E8
1 CLARENCE TR

2 CARLTON TR
3 RUTLAND CT
4 SURREY RD
5 PEMBROKE DR
6 CROFT HOUSE CT
7 BROUGHTON TR
8 NORTH ST

9 OAKROYD TR
10 QUEENS CT
11 MNT PLEASANT CT
12 CLIFTON MEWS
13 WESLEY VIEW
14 WESLEY ROW
15 CLIFTON CT

F5
1 WEAVERS CT
2 LEAFIELD DR
3 MARLOWE CL
F7
1 LONGFIELD MNT
2 LONGFIELD GR

3 LONGFIELD AVE
4 HAMMERTON GR
5 HUGGAN ROW
6 HILLSIDE GR
7 BROADLANDS PL
8 BROADLANDS CT

F8
1 WHITELANDS
2 FAIRFIELD AVE
3 MNT PLEASANT
4 ROSEMONT ST
5 ROSEMONT CT
6 EAST VIEW CTS

75

57

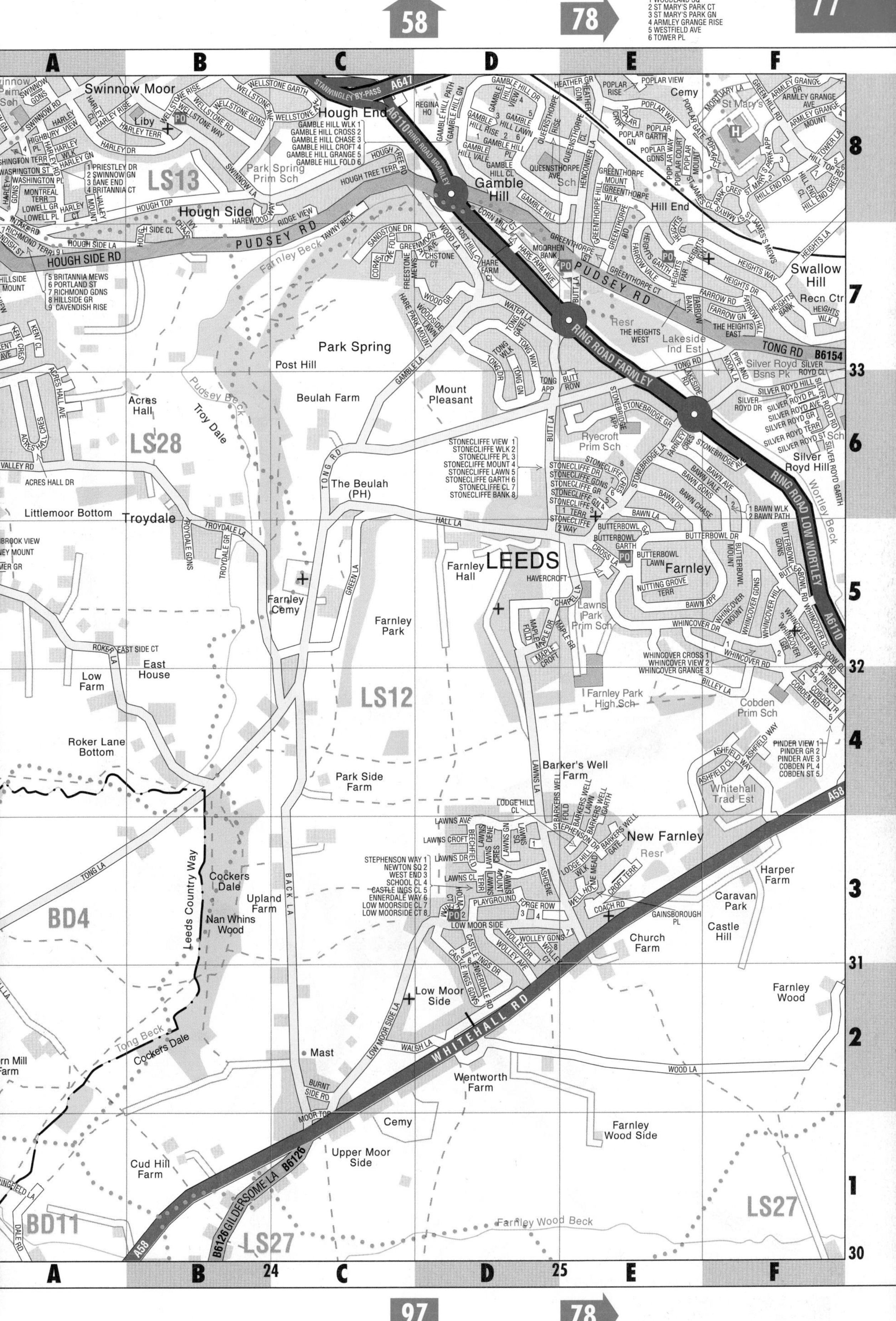

For full street detail of the highlighted area see pages 209, 210 and 213.

77   98

For full street detail of the
highlighted area see pages
211, 212, 214 and 215.

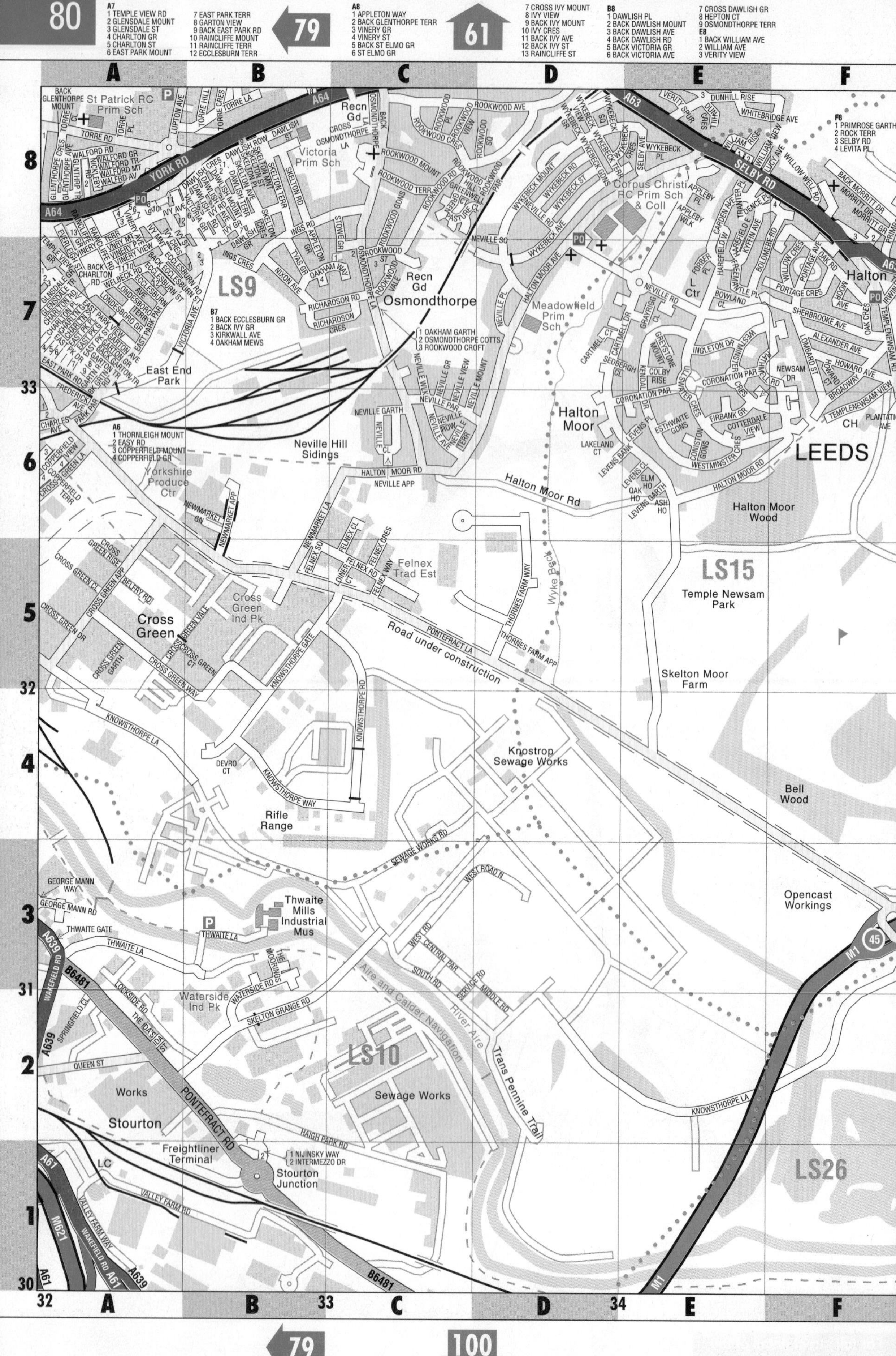

80
A7
1 TEMPLE VIEW RD
2 GLENSDALE MOUNT
3 GLENSDALE ST
4 CHARLTON GR
5 CHARLTON ST
6 EAST PARK MOUNT
7 EAST PARK TERR
8 GARTON VIEW
9 BACK EAST PARK RD
10 RAINCLIFFE MOUNT
11 RAINCLIFFE TERR
12 ECCLESBURN TERR
79
A8
1 APPLETON WAY
2 BACK GLENTHORPE TERR
3 VINERY GR
4 VINERY ST
5 BACK ST ELMO GR
6 ST ELMO GR
61
7 CROSS IVY MOUNT
8 IVY VIEW
9 BACK IVY MOUNT
10 IVY CRES
11 BACK IVY AVE
12 BACK IVY ST
13 RAINCLIFFE ST
B8
1 DAWLISH PL
2 BACK DAWLISH MOUNT
3 BACK DAWLISH AVE
4 BACK DAWLISH RD
5 BACK VICTORIA GR
6 BACK VICTORIA AVE
7 CROSS DAWLISH GR
8 HEPTON CT
9 OSMONDTHORPE TERR
E8
1 BACK WILLIAM AVE
2 WILLIAM AVE
3 VERITY VIEW
A B C D E F
8 7 6 5 4 3 2 1
33 32 31 30
F8
1 PRIMROSE GARTH
2 ROCK TERR
3 SELBY RD
4 LEVITA PL
B7
1 BACK ECCLESBURN GR
2 BACK IVY GR
3 KIRKWALL AVE
4 OAKHAM MEWS
C7
1 OAKHAM GARTH
2 OSMONDTHORPE COTTS
3 ROOKWOOD CROFT
A6
1 THORNLEIGH MOUNT
2 EASY RD
3 COPPERFIELD MOUNT
4 COPPERFIELD GR
St Patrick RC Prim Sch
Victoria Prim Sch
Recn Gd
YORK RD
A64
A63
SELBY RD
Corpus Christi RC Prim Sch & Coll
LS9
Osmondthorpe
Meadowfield Prim Sch
Halton
East End Park
Halton Moor
LEEDS
Neville Hill Sidings
Yorkshire Produce Ctr
Halton Moor Rd
Halton Moor Wood
LS15
Temple Newsam Park
Felnex Trad Est
Cross Green Ind Pk
Cross Green
Road under construction
PONTEFRACT LA
Skelton Moor Farm
Knostrop Sewage Works
Bell Wood
Rifle Range
Wyke Beck
Opencast Workings
Thwaite Mills Industrial Mus
Waterside Ind Pk
Aire and Calder Navigation
River Aire
Trans Pennine Trail
LS10
Sewage Works
Works
Stourton
Freightliner Terminal
1 NIJINSKY WAY
2 INTERMEZZO DR
Stourton Junction
PONTEFRACT RD
KNOWSTHORPE LA
LS26
M1
M621
A61
A639
B6481
45
32 33 34

62
82
101
82

A8
1 PRIMROSE CRES
2 PRIMROSE AVE
3 BARLEY FIELD CT
4 OVERDALE TERR
5 BACK OVERDALE TERR
6 BACK GRAVELEY ST

7 CROSS PARK ST
8 PARK VIEW TERR
9 WHEATON CT
10 CHAPEL CT
11 CHAPEL FOLD
12 THE ORCHARD

B8
1 GREEN LA
2 WILFRED ST
3 CHARLOTTE GR
4 PROSPECT GDNS
5 TEMPLESTOWE GDNS
6 TEMPLESTOWE HILL

C8
1 GRAVELEYTHORPE RD
2 CARTER AVE
3 TEMPLESTOWE DR
4 HOLLYSHAW TERR
5 BACK HOLLYSHAW TERR
6 CARTER LA

81
63

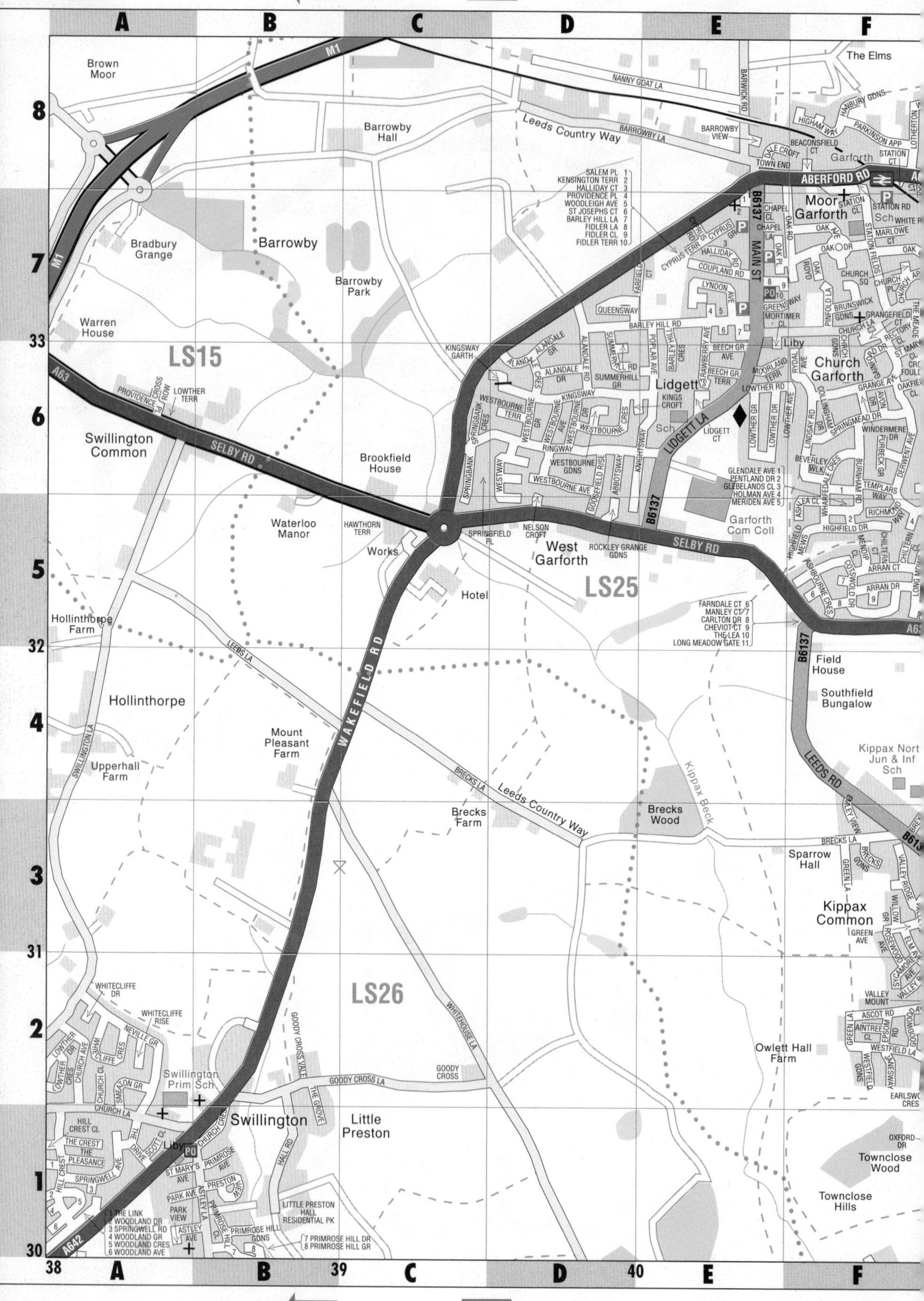
A
B
C
D
E
F
Brown Moor
M1
NANNY GOAT LA
BARWICK RD
The Elms
Barrowby Hall
Leeds Country Way
BARROWBY LA
BARROWBY VIEW
BEACONSFIELD CT
DALE CROFT
TOWN END
Garforth
STATION CT
ABERFORD RD
SALEM PL 1
KENSINGTON TERR 2
HALLIDAY CT 3
PROVIDENCE PL 4
WOODLEIGH AVE 5
ST JOSEPHS CT 6
BARLEY HILL LA 7
FIDLER LA 8
FIDLER CL 9
FIDLER TERR 10
B6137
MAIN ST
Moor Garforth
STATION RD
CHAPEL CL
OAK RD
OAK AVE
OAK DR
MARLOWE CT
Bradbury Grange
Barrowby
Barrowby Park
CYPRUS TERR
HALLIDAY RD
COUPLAND RD
LYNDON AVE
GREENSWAY
MORTIMER CL
CHURCH SQ
BRUNSWICK GDNS
GRANGEFIELD CT
QUEENSWAY
BARLEY HILL RD
Warren House
LS15
A63
PROVIDENCE PL
LOWTHER TERR
KINGSWAY GARTH
ALANDALE GR
ALANDALE DR
ALANDALE RD
SUMMERHILL GR
POPLAR AVE
BEECH GR AVE
BEECH GR TERR
MOORLAND TERR
Liby
Church Garforth
Lidgett
KINGS CROFT
LOWTHER RD
LOWTHER GR
LOWTHER DR
LOWTHER AVE
Swillington Common
SELBY RD
WESTBOURNE TERR
WESTBOURNE CRES
RINGWAY
KINGSWAY
LIDGETT LA
LIDGETT CT
Sch
SPRINGMEAD DR
WINDERMERE DR
Brookfield House
WESTBOURNE GDNS
WESTBOURNE AVE
WESTWAY
SPRINGBANK CRES
GOOSEFIELD RISE
ABBOTSWAY
KNIGHTSWAY
GLENDALE AVE 1
PENTLAND DR 2
GLEBELANDS CL 3
HOLMAN AVE 4
MERIDEN AVE 5
BEVERLEY WLK
TEMPLARS WAY
RICHMOND WAY
HIGHFIELD DR
Waterloo Manor
HAWTHORN TERR
Works
SPRINGFIELD PL
NELSON CROFT
West Garforth
ROCKLEY GRANGE GDNS
Garforth Com Coll
LS25
Hotel
ARRAN CT
ARRAN DR
Hollinthorpe Farm
FARNDALE CT 6
MANLEY CT 7
CARLTON DR 8
CHEVIOT CT 9
THE LEA 10
LONG MEADOW GATE 11
LEEDS LA
WAKEFIELD RD
Field House
Southfield Bungalow
Hollinthorpe
Mount Pleasant Farm
Kippax North Jun & Inf Sch
LEEDS RD
Upperhall Farm
SWILLINGTON LA
BRECKS LA
Leeds Country Way
Brecks Farm
Kippax Beck
Brecks Wood
Sparrow Hall
GREEN LA
Kippax Common
GREEN AVE
VALLEY MOUNT
ASCOT RD
AINTREE CL
WESTFIELD LA
LS26
WHITECLIFFE DR
WHITECLIFFE RISE
NEVILLE GR
GOODY CROSS VALE
WHITEHOUSE LA
Owlett Hall Farm
GOODY CROSS
GOODY CROSS LA
Swillington Prim Sch
CHURCH LA
Swillington
THE GROVE
Little Preston
HILL CREST CL
THE CREST
THE PLEASANCE
SPRINGWELL AVE
SCOTT CL
CHURCH CRES
ST MARY'S AVE
PRIMROSE AVE
PRESTON VIEW
HALL RD
LITTLE PRESTON HALL RESIDENTIAL PK
PARK AVE
PARK VIEW
ASTLEY AVE
PRIMROSE HILL GDNS
1 THE LINK
2 WOODLAND DR
3 SPRINGWELL RD
4 WOODLAND GR
5 WOODLAND CRES
6 WOODLAND AVE
7 PRIMROSE HILL DR
8 PRIMROSE HILL GR
A642
EARLSWOOD CRES
OXFORD DR
Townclose Wood
Townclose Hills
8
7
33
6
5
32
4
3
31
2
1
30
38
39
40

81
102

A   B   C   D   E   F

1 ANNING FOLD
2 CEDAR RIDGE
3 WOODBRIDGE AVE
4 ASHLEY PARK MEWS
5 EAST RIDGE VIEW

East Garforth Prim Sch

East Garforth

Ash Plantation

Well House Farm

Old Micklefield

8

Three Acre Plantation

7

Sturton Grange Farm

33

East Garforth Sports Ctr

Roman Ridge Bridge

6

1 NINELANDS VIEW
2 GREENACRE CT
3 CRICKETERS CL
4 GREEN LANE VILLAS

Stub Wood

Garforth Green Lane Prim Sch

Peckfield Bsns Pk

Phoenix Ave

Ninelands Prim Sch

Warren Farm

5

GARFORTH

LS25

Clifftop Park

32

Peckfield House Farm

4

SELBY RD

Roach Grange Farm

Limekiln House

Warren House

Quarryfield Plantation

Peckfield Common

Roach Hill

Warrenhouse Plantation

3

The Fruit Gardens

31

The Hills

Ledston Luck Enterprise Park

Kippax

Ledston Luck

Sheepcote Wood

2

Kippax Greenfield Prim Sch

Kippax Ash Tree Prim Sch

Sheepcotes Farm

Liby

HIGH ST

1

1 PARK LA
2 LONGDIKE LA
3 CORONATION BGLWS

Ledston Engine

B6137

30

A   B   C   D   E   F

42
43

A1
1 THE GREEN
2 CROSS HILLS GDNS
3 CROSS HILLS CT

A2
1 MOORGATE CL
2 MOORGATE RISE
3 GREENFIELD CL
4 GREENFIELD GARTH

B1
1 ROGER FOLD
2 BRAMHAM'S YD
3 THE INTAKE
4 MANOR TERR
5 PARK VIEW
6 MALTKILN LA
7 LONGDIKE CT
8 MOUNT PLEASANT
9 MOUNT PLEASANT GDNS

10 APPLE TREE MEWS
11 HALL PARK CROFT
12 APPLE TREE WLK
13 PEASEFOLD

A   B   C   D   E   F

8

Old Micklefield

HALL FARM CL
CHURCH CL
CHURCHVILLE DR
ST HELEN'S DR
Grange Farm
NEW ROW
OLDFIELD CL

PO

1 CHURCHVILLE AVE
2 CHURCHVILLE TERR
3 ST MARY'S WLK

PH
Micklefield CE Prim Sch

Manor Farm

Micklefield

7

Daniel Hartly's Wood

Hartly Wood

Sewage Works

Sheep Dike

Huddleston Hall

LAITH STAID LA

Huddleston Old Wood

33

PIT LA

RAILWAY COTTS

P

GREAT NORTH RD
GARDEN VILLAGE

Micklefield

Newthorpe Farm

6

Enterprise Ct
PROSPECT TERR 1
CLIFFE TERR 2
WEST VIEW 3

PIT LA

SUNNYBANK

THE CRESCENT
EAST VIEW
Newton Farm

Highroyds Wood

Brookfield House

Newthorpe Barrack

Newthorpe Beck

Newthorpe Grange

New Micklefield

HONEYSUCKLE CL

Woodlands

Castle Hills

Highfield

Newthorpe Quarry

HALL LA

LC

5

LS25

HIGHFIELD LA

The New Inn (PH)

Newthorpe

B1222

32

Peckfield Plantation

Micklefield Plantation

WHITECOTE LA

4

A63

SELBY RD

The Boot and Shoe (PH)

Whitecote Plantation

Quarryfield Plantation

Beacon Plantation

B1222

Pointer Farm

3

31

Wellington Plantation

Ledston Lodge

NEW RD

Peckfield Lodge

WESTFIELD LA

A1(M)

2

Ledston Park

Hundred Acre Plantation

Scat House Farm

1

Sheepcote Farm

Long Plantation

Old Vicarage

PARK LA

Dale Plantation

Selby Fork Hotel

A63

30

WF10

44   A   B   45   C   D   46   E   F

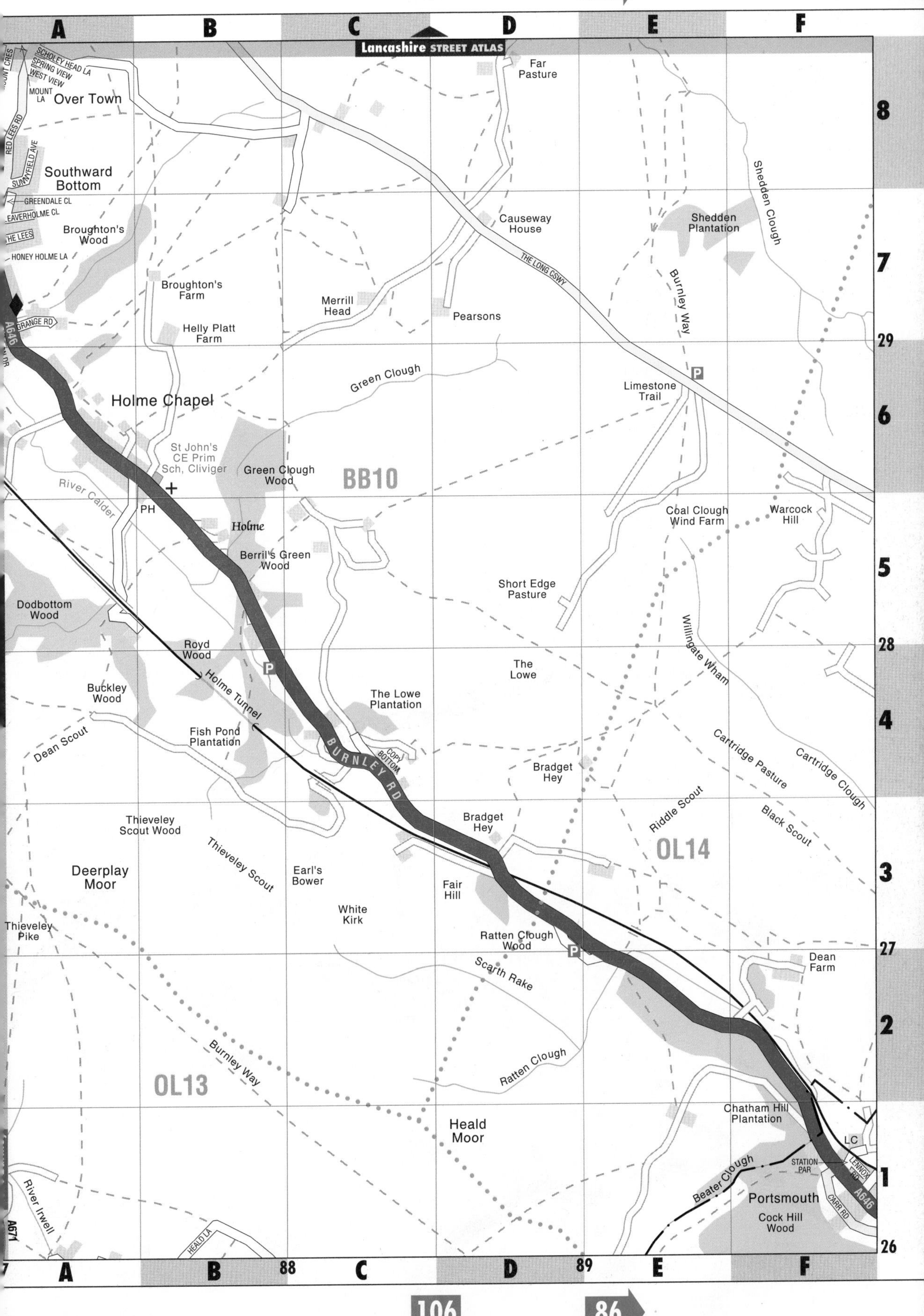

Lancashire STREET ATLAS

A   B   C   D   E   F

SCHOLEY HEAD LA
SPRING VIEW
WEST VIEW
MOUNT CRES
RED LEES RD
SUNNYFIELD AVE
MOUNT LA
Over Town

8

Far Pasture

Shedden Clough

Southward Bottom

GREENDALE CL
BEAVERHOLME CL
THE LEES
HONEY HOLME LA

Broughton's Wood

Causeway House

THE LONG CSWY

Shedden Plantation

7

A646
GRANGE RD

Broughton's Farm

Merrill Head

Pearsons

Burnley Way

29

Helly Platt Farm

Green Clough

Limestone Trail

P

6

Holme Chapel

River Calder

St John's CE Prim Sch, Cliviger

Green Clough Wood

BB10

Coal Clough Wind Farm

Warcock Hill

PH

Holme

Short Edge Pasture

5

Berril's Green Wood

Willingate Wham

Dodbottom Wood

The Lowe

28

Royd Wood

P

Holme Tunnel

The Lowe Plantation

COPY BOTTOM

Buckley Wood

BURNLEY RD

Cartridge Pasture

Cartridge Clough

4

Fish Pond Plantation

Bradget Hey

Riddle Scout

Black Scout

Dean Scout

Thieveley Scout Wood

Bradget Hey

OL14

Thieveley Scout

Earl's Bower

Fair Hill

Deerplay Moor

White Kirk

3

Thieveley Pike

Ratten Clough Wood

P

Dean Farm

27

Scarth Rake

2

Burnley Way

Ratten Clough

OL13

Chatham Hill Plantation

LC

Heald Moor

LENNOX RD
CARR RD
A646

River Irwell

A671

Beater Clough

STATION PAR

1

HEALD LA

Portsmouth

Cock Hill Wood

26

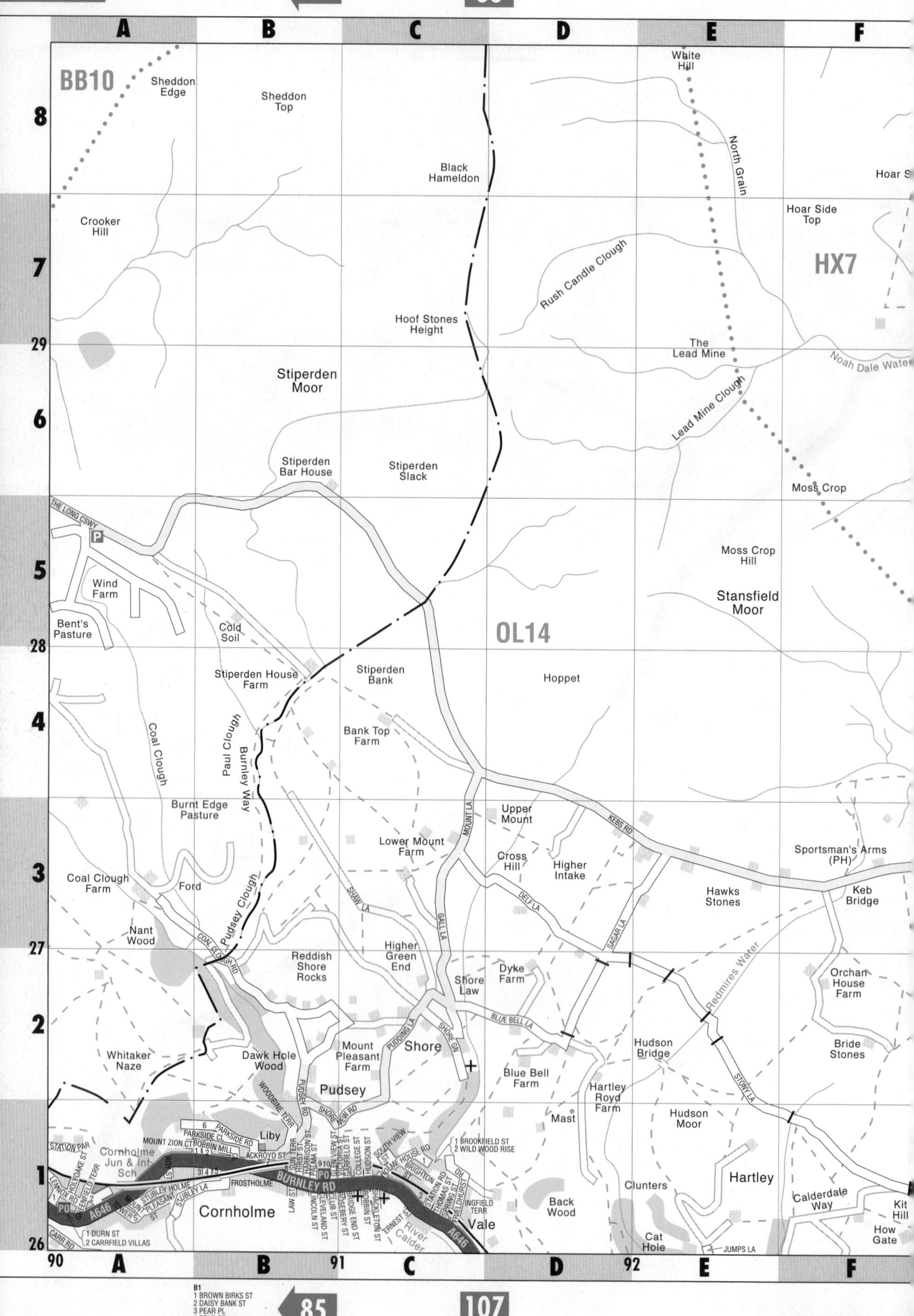

A   **B**   **C**   **D**   **E**   **F**

BB10

8 — Sheddon Edge · Sheddon Top · White Hill · Hoar S

Crooker Hill · Black Hameldon · Hoar Side Top

HX7

7

Rush Candle Clough · North Grain

29 — Hoof Stones Height · The Lead Mine · Noah Dale Wate

Stiperden Moor · Lead Mine Clough

6 — Stiperden Bar House · Stiperden Slack · Moss Crop

The Long Cswy · P

5 — Wind Farm · Cold Soil · Moss Crop Hill · Stansfield Moor

Bent's Pasture

28 — Stiperden House Farm · Stiperden Bank · Hoppet

OL14

4 — Coal Clough · Paul Clough · Bank Top Farm · Burnley Way · Burnt Edge Pasture

Upper Mount · Kebs Rd · Sportsman's Arms (PH)

3 — Coal Clough Farm · Ford · Pudsey Clough · Lower Mount Farm · Cross Hill · Higher Intake · Hawks Stones · Keb Bridge

Nant Wood · Coal Clough Rd · Reddish Shore Rocks · Higher Green End · Shore Law · Dyke Farm · Segar La · Redmires Water · Orchard House Farm

27 — Sharp La · Gall La · Delf La

Whitaker Naze · Dawk Hole Wood · Mount Pleasant Farm · Shore · Blue Bell La · Hudson Bridge · Bride Stones

2 — Pudding La · Shore Gm · Woodbine Terr · Pudsey · Blue Bell Farm · Hartley Royd Farm · Hudson Moor

Liby · Mast · Back Wood · Clunters · Hartley · Calderdale Way

Parkside Cl · Parkside Rd · Bobbin Mill · Mount Zion Ct · Ackroyd St · South View · 1 Brookfield St · 2 Wild Wood Rise · Kit Hill

1 — Station Par · Cornholme Jun & Inf Sch · Frostholme · BURNLEY RD · Ingfield Terr · How Gate

Stubley Holme · Shackleton St · Brighton St · River Calder · Vale · Cat Hole · Jumps La

26 — Lenny Rd · PO · A646 · 1 Durn St · 2 Carrfield Villas · Cornholme

A   **B**   **C**   **D**   **E**   **F**

B1
1 BROWN BIRKS ST
2 DAISY BANK ST
3 PEAR PL
4 PEAR ST
5 SPRING VILLAS
6 STANSFIELD TERR
7 CORNHOLME TERR
8 OAKLEIGH TERR
9 SUNNY BANK TERR
10 GLADSTONE ST

67
88

A B C D E F

Cabin Hill
Rushy Field
Flaight Clough
Egypt
Popples Close
Black Mires
Park
Lane Side
Rough Hey La
Rough Hey
Moth Hole La
Everhill Shaw
8
Colden Water
Middle Fold
Pennine Bridleway
Hoar Side
Lower Fold
Park La
New Edge
Higher Heath
Colden Water
Crabtree Field
Lower Ear Lees
Moor La
Stony Turgate Hill
7
Noah Dale
Low Ling La
Edge La
Long Tail La
Hot La
Old Edge
Noah Dale
Pad Laithe
Slade
Top o' th' Hill
Greenland
Rodmer Clough Farm
Dark La
Longtail
29
Greenland Rd
School Land La
Noon Hill
Three Gates End
Scotland
School Land
Higher Colden
Colden La
Clunters
Lord Piece
6
The Rush Beds
Cross Clough
Four Gates End
New Rd
Moorcock Hill
Field Head Farm
Moorcock La
Higher Strines
Moorhall Farm
Lower Strines Farm
HX7
5
Brown Hill Bottom
Moorcock Rd
New Shaw La
Redmires
Brown Hill La
28
Dukes Cut
Halifax La
Brown Hill
Burnt Edge La
Moss Hall Slades
Blackshaw Head
Earnshaw Water
Trimmer La
Warcock La
Moss Hall La
Higher Back La
4
West Bar
Old Shaw La
Earnshaw Hole Moor
Lower Back La
Badger La
Well Hill
Long Cswy
Pennine View
Moor House View
Pole Hill
Higher Moss Hall
Lane Side
Lane Bottom
Causeway Fold
Mast
Lower La
Harleywood Gate
Daisy Bank
Kebs Rd
Davey La
Keb Hill
Daisy Bank Clough
3
Raw Pole
Barley Croft
Hippins
Ingham Pastures
Clunters
Hippins Clough
Hippins Bridge
Long Row
27
Staups La
Posset
Back of Behind
Bride Stones Moor
Calderdale Way
Staups Moor
2
Great Bride Stones
Eastwood Rd
Chisley Stones
Windy Harbour La
Keelham La
Keelham Farm
OL14
Great Rock
Mast
Keelham Heights
Broad La
1
Harley Wood Slack
Black Stone Hill
Stony La
Higher Winsley Farm
Windy Harbour
Higher Birks
Crossley New Rd
Whirlaw Common
Hey Head La
Upper La
Butts La
Lower Winsley Farm
Grey Stone La
26

93 A B 94 C D 95 E F

108
88

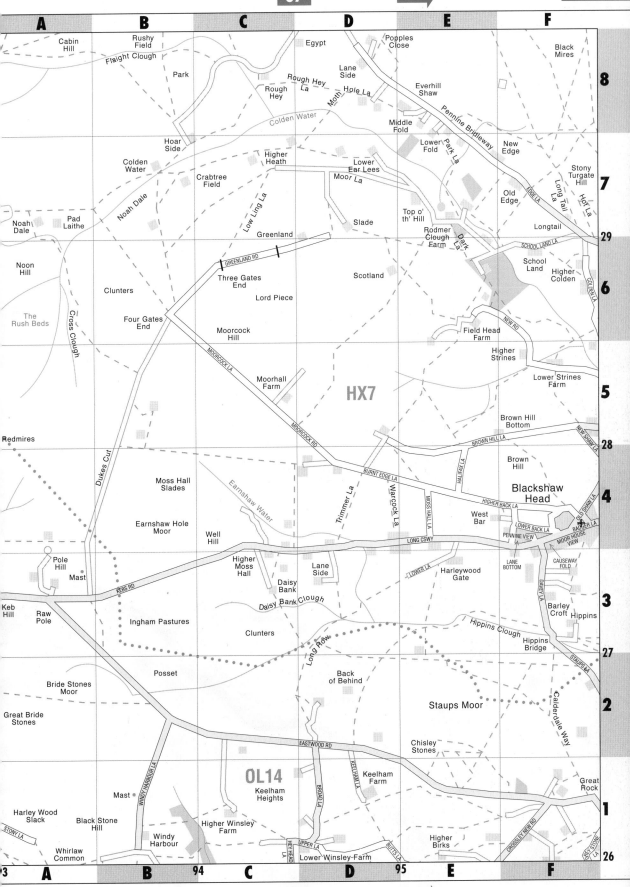

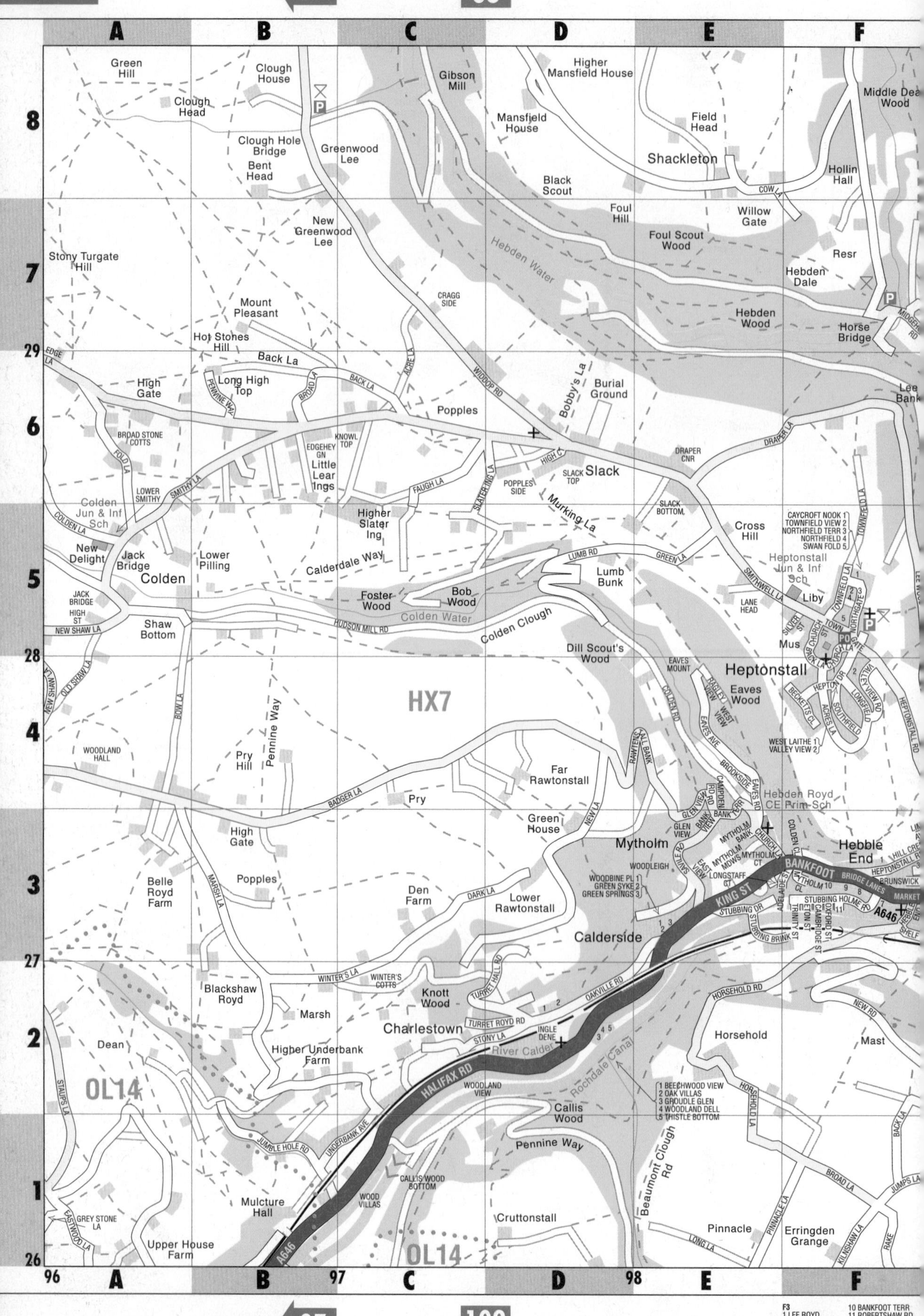

87
68
87
109

F3
1 LEE ROYD
2 ALBION TERR
3 QUEENS TERR
4 MELBOURNE ST
5 HANGINGROYD RD
6 SALEM ST
7 CALDER TERR
8 RIVER ST
9 CALDER PL

10 BANKFOOT TERR
11 ROBERTSHAW RD

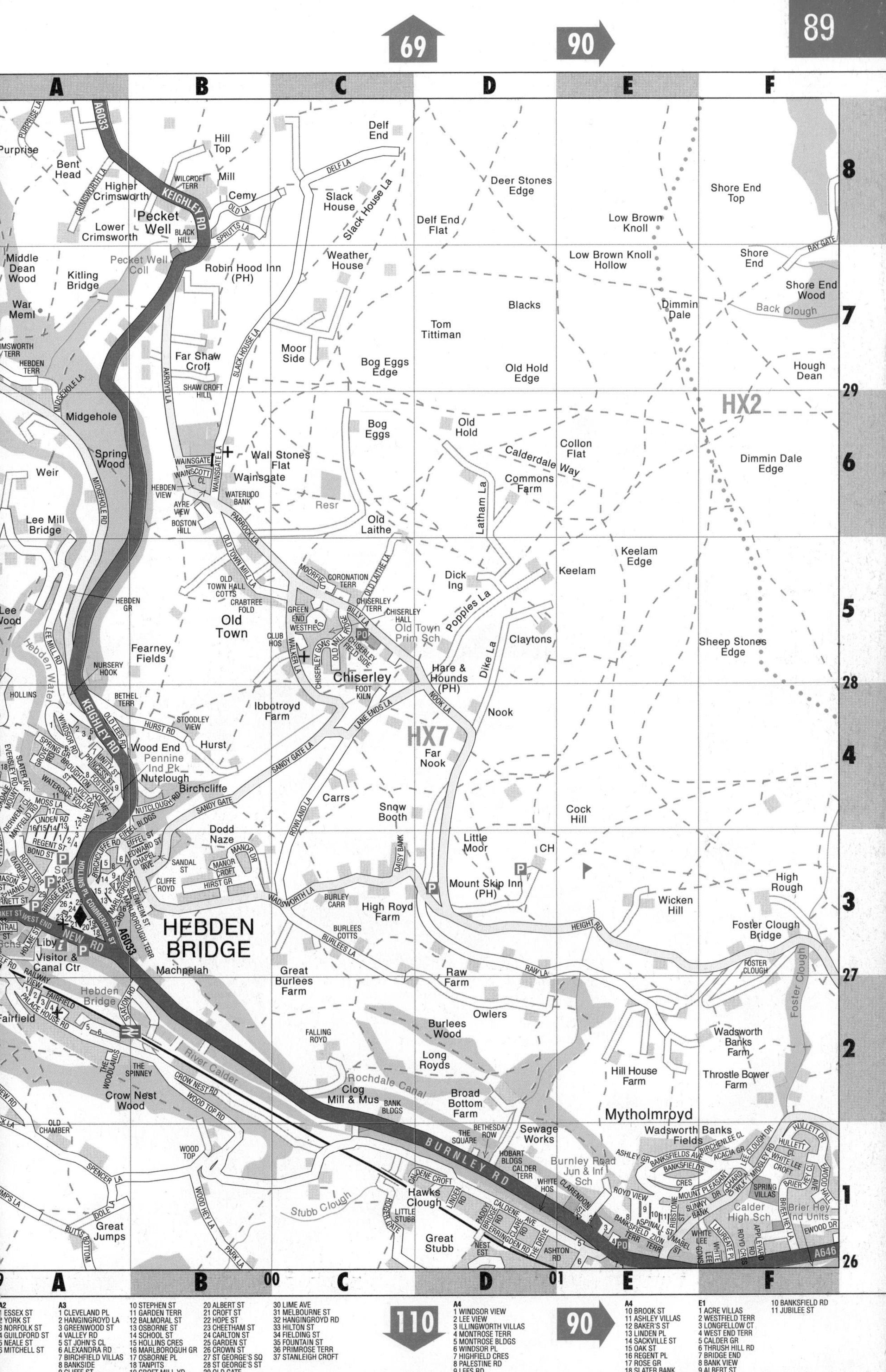

A B C D E F

8
7
29
6
5
28
4
27
2
1
26

Map labels

Purprise La
Bent Head
Higher Crimsworth
Lower Crimsworth
Pecket Well
Middle Dean Wood
Kitling Bridge
War Meml
Midgehole
Spring Wood
Weir
Lee Mill Bridge
Lee Wood
Fearney Fields
Nursery Hook
Bethel Terr
Hollins
HEBDEN BRIDGE
Machpelah
Hebden Bridge
Fairfield
Crow Nest Wood
Great Jumps
Great Stubb

Hill Top
Mill
Cemy
Pecket Well Coll
Robin Hood Inn (PH)
Far Shaw Croft
Shaw Croft Hill
Wainsgate
Waterloo Bank
Ayre View
Boston Hill
Old Town
Hebden Gr
Ibbotroyd Farm
Hurst
Wood End
Pennine Ind Pk
Nutclough
Birchcliffe
Dodd Naze
Manor Croft
Cliffe Royd
Hirst Gr

Delf End
Slack House
Weather House
Moor Side
Bog Eggs Edge
Bog Eggs
Old Laithe
Coronation Terr
Crabtree Fold
Green End
Westfield
Club Hos
Chiserley
Foot Kiln
Carrs
Snow Booth
High Royd Farm
Burley Carr
Burlees Cotts
Burlees La
Great Burlees Farm
Falling Royd
Long Royds
Rochdale Canal
Clog Mill & Mus
Hawks Clough
Great Stubb

Deer Stones Edge
Delf End Flat
Tom Tittiman
Old Hold Edge
Old Hold
Latham La
Dick Ing
Hare & Hounds (PH)
Nook
Far Nook
Little Moor
Mount Skip Inn (PH)
Raw Farm
Owlers
Burlees Wood
Broad Bottom Farm
Sewage Works
Burnley Road Jun & Inf Sch

Low Brown Knoll
Low Brown Knoll Hollow
Blacks
Dimmin Dale
Collon Farm
Calderdale Way
Commons Farm
Keelam
Keelam Edge
Claytons
Sheep Stones Edge
Cock Hill
Wicken Hill
Hill House Farm
Mytholmroyd
Wadsworth Banks Fields
Banksfields

Shore End Top
Shore End
Shore End Wood
Back Clough
Hough Dean
HX2
Dimmin Dale Edge
High Rough
Foster Clough Bridge
Foster Clough
Wadsworth Banks Farm
Throstle Bower Farm
Calder High Sch

HX7

Street index

89
70

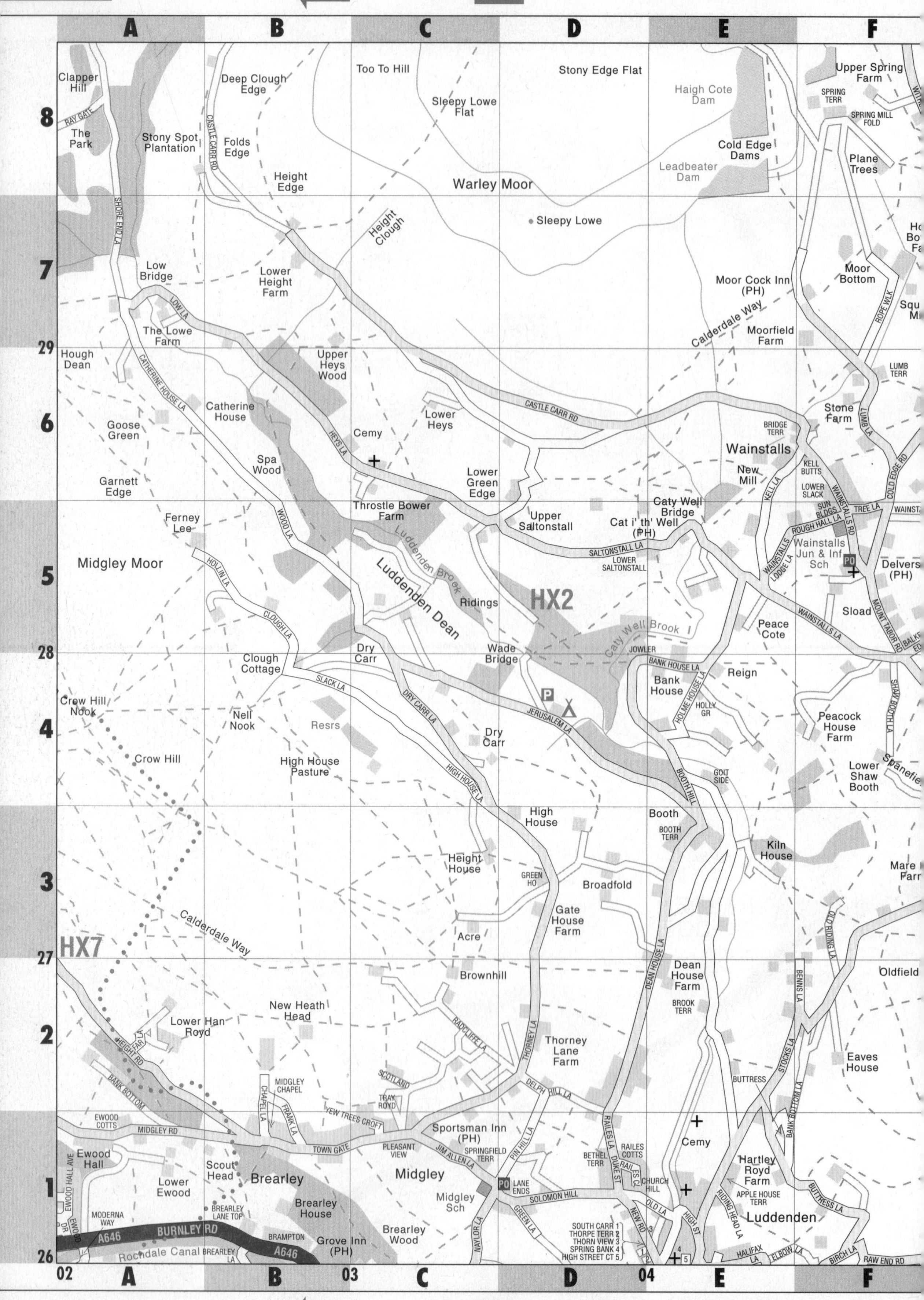
A
B
C
D
E
F
Clapper Hill
Deep Clough Edge
Too To Hill
Stony Edge Flat
Haigh Cote Dam
Upper Spring Farm
The Park
Stony Spot Plantation
Folds Edge
Sleepy Lowe Flat
Cold Edge Dams
Plane Trees
Height Edge
Warley Moor
Leadbeater Dam
Sleepy Lowe
Height Clough
Low Bridge
Lower Height Farm
Moor Cock Inn (PH)
Moor Bottom
The Lowe Farm
Calderdale Way
Moorfield Farm
Hough Dean
Upper Heys Wood
Catherine House
Lower Heys
Stone Farm
Goose Green
Cemy
Wainstalls
Spa Wood
Lower Green Edge
New Mill
Garnett Edge
Throstle Bower Farm
Upper Saltonstall
Caty Well Bridge
Cat i' th' Well (PH)
Ferney Lee
Luddenden Brook
Wainstalls Jun & Inf Sch
Midgley Moor
Luddenden Dean
Delvers (PH)
Ridings
HX2
Sload
Caty Well Brook
Peace Cote
Dry Carr
Wade Bridge
Clough Cottage
Bank House
Reign
Crow Hill Nook
Nell Nook
Resrs
Dry Carr
Peacock House Farm
Crow Hill
High House Pasture
Lower Shaw Booth
High House
Booth
Kiln House
Height House
Broadfold
Mare Farm
Gate House Farm
HX7
Acre
Dean House Farm
Oldfield
Brownhill
New Heath Head
Lower Han Royd
Thorney Lane Farm
Eaves House
Sportsman Inn (PH)
Cemy
Ewood Hall
Scout Head
Brearley
Midgley
Hartley Royd Farm
Lower Ewood
Midgley Sch
Brearley House
Luddenden
Grove Inn (PH)
Brearley Wood
Rochdale Canal
A646 BURNLEY RD
8
7
29
6
5
28
4
3
27
2
1
26
02
03
04

89
111

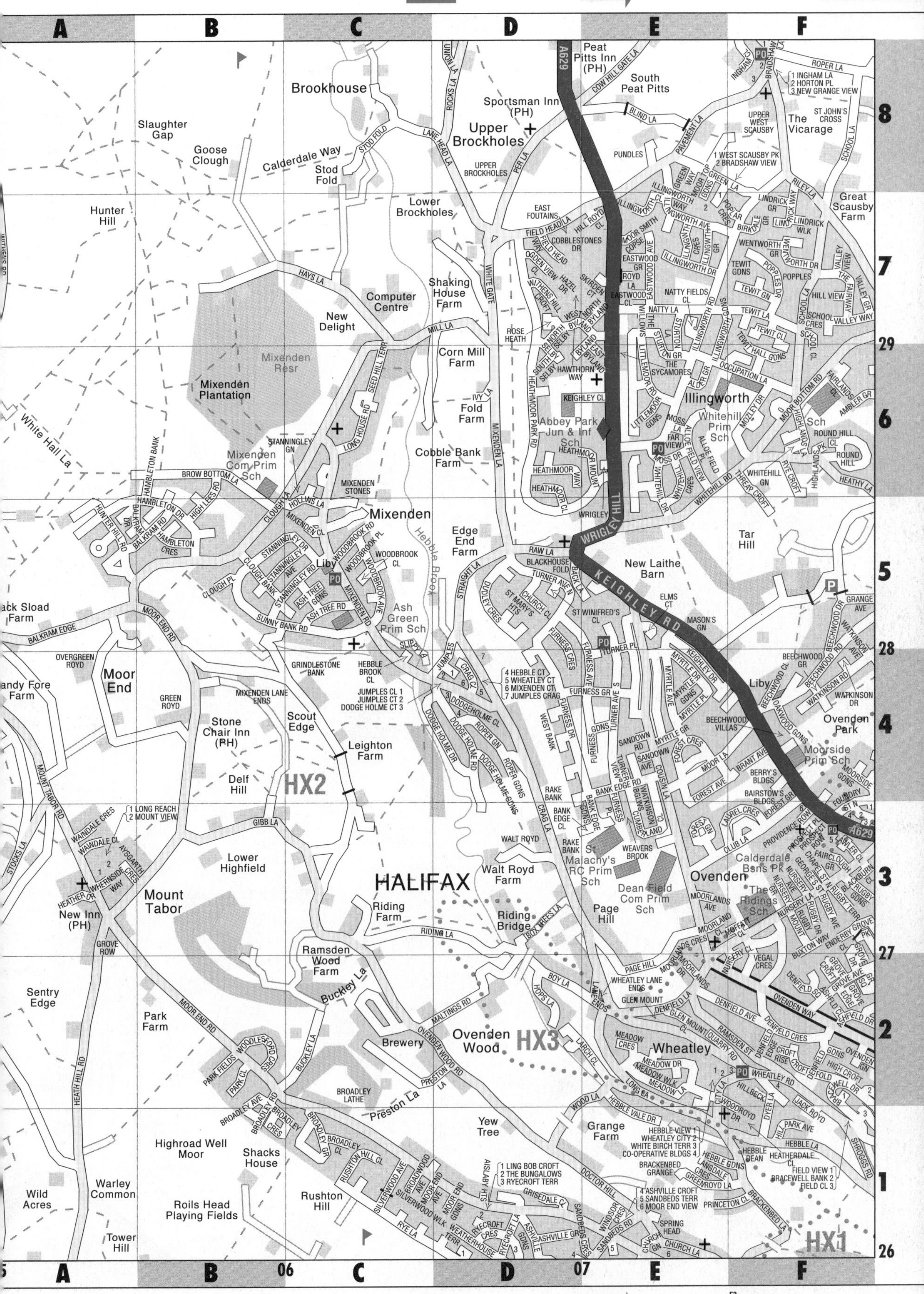

A B C D E F

8
7
29
6
5
28
4
3
27
2
26

A B 06 C D 07 E F

HX2

HALIFAX

HX3

HX1

Brookhouse
Slaughter Gap
Goose Clough
Calderdale Way
Stod Fold
Hunter Hill
Lower Brockholes
Upper Brockholes
Sportsman Inn (PH)
Upper Brockholes
Peat Pitts Inn (PH)
South Peat Pitts
Blind La
St John's Cross
The Vicarage
Upper West Scausby
Great Scausby Farm
White Hall La
New Delight
Computer Centre
Shaking House Farm
Mill La
Rose Heath
Corn Mill Farm
East Fountains
Field Head La
Cobblestones Dr
Hill Royd
Illingworth
Mixenden Resr
Mixenden Plantation
Seed Hill Terr
Fold Farm
Keighley Cl
Abbey Park Jun & Inf Sch
The Sycamores
Illingworth
Whitehill Prim Sch
Round Hill
Stanningley Gn
Mixenden Com Prim Sch
Mixenden Stones
Liby
Mixenden
Cobble Bank Farm
Heathmoor
Wrigley Hill
New Laithe Barn
Tar Hill
White Hall La
Moor End
Green Royd
Overgreen Royd
Mixenden Lane Ends
Ash Green Prim Sch
Grindlestone Bank
Hebble Brook Cl
Edge End Farm
Blackhouse Fold
Raw La
St Mary's
St Winifred's Cl
Mason's Gn
Liby
Ovenden Park
Beechwood
Mount Tabor
New Inn (PH)
Grove Row
Delf Hill
Scout Edge
Leighton Farm
Gibb La
Lower Highfield
Jumples Cl
Dodgeholme Cl
Beechwood Villas
Moorside Prim Sch
St Malachy's RC Prim Sch
Walt Royd Farm
Page Hill
Dean Field Com Prim Sch
Ovenden
Calderdale Bsns Pk
The Ridings Sch
Sentry Edge
Park Farm
Ramsden Wood Farm
Buckley La
Brewery
Ovenden Wood
Riding Farm
Riding Bridge
Wheatley Lane Ends
Glen Mount
Wheatley
Highroad Well Moor
Shacks House
Broadley Lathe
Preston La
Yew Tree
Grange Farm
Wild Acres
Warley Common
Tower Hill
Roils Head Playing Fields
Rushton Hill
Spring Head

A629

Keighley Rd

F3
1 BURNS ST
2 HOPKINSON ST
3 JUBILEE ST N
4 HOPKINSONS BLDGS
5 MASON SQ
6 CLUB HOUSES

C8
1 MOOR CLOSE FARM MEWS
2 CAPE OF GOOD HOPE
3 ELDER BANK
4 WESTERCROFT GARTH
5 PLEASANT ROW
6 FLOWERPOT LA

C8
7 OXFORD RD
8 DOLPHIN TERR
9 BALMORAL PL
10 CLARENDON PL
11 SUNNY VIEW TERR
12 MYRTLE GR

D8
1 CONISTON AVE
2 CONISTON CL
3 LEE ST
4 HAINSWORTH MOOR GARTH
5 HAINSWORTH MOOR CRES
6 HAINSWORTH MOOR DR

A1
1 BRACEWELL DR
2 BRACEWELL GR
3 WHEATLEY CL
4 WHEATLEY RD
5 LEE MOUNT GDNS
6 PEABODY ST
7 ELLISON ST
8 BUXTON ST
9 MATLOCK ST
10 GRANGE ST
11 LIVINGSTONE ST
12 TENNYSON ST
13 CLIFTON ST
14 LAWRENCE ST
15 OVENDEN CL
16 RUSHWORTH ST
17 GARFIELD ST
18 COLUMBUS ST
19 ASHVILLE ST
20 WASHINGTON ST
21 BRIGHTON ST
22 MELBOURNE ST
23 INGHAMS CT
24 RUSKIN TERR
25 WOODVILLE ST
26 MELROSE ST
27 CONCRETE ST
28 BATLEY ST
A2
1 FRIENDLY ST
2 BETHEL ST
3 AMY ST

A2
4 CLEVEDON PL
5 EARL TERR
6 LENTILFIELD TERR
7 FRIENDLY FOLD HO
8 EASTWOOD ST
9 ROBERT ST
10 OVENDEN ROAD TERR
B1
1 SALISBURY TERR
2 CHESTER CT
3 CHESTER GR

B1
4 OLIVIA CT
5 BANKFIELD YD
6 CHESTER CL
7 LINCOLN WAY
8 CHESTER PL
9 GILMOUR ST
B2
1 TURNER'S CT
2 McBURNEY CL
3 WESTERN HO
4 BRUNEL CT

5 BUTLERS VIEW
6 SIMPSON ST
7 UTTLEY S
8 FERNFIELD TERR
9 IONA PL
10 CATHCART ST
C1
1 SUNNY SIDE ST
2 ALL SOULS' ST
3 ALL SOULS' ST
4 SUNNY BANK TERR
5 LAURA ST

6 ADA ST
7 LYTTON ST
8 WOODLANDS VIEW
9 LOWER RANGE
10 AMBLERS ST
11 BROUGHAM RD
12 BROUGHAM ST
13 BROUGHAM TERR
14 OLD SCHOOLS GDNS
15 CHURCH SIDE CL
16 CHURCH SIDE DR
17 SCHOOL YARD VIEW

C2
1 RINGBY TERR
2 BREWERY ST
3 ROBERT ST N
4 CLAREMOUNT TERR
5 ROYD MOUNT
6 THORN VIEW

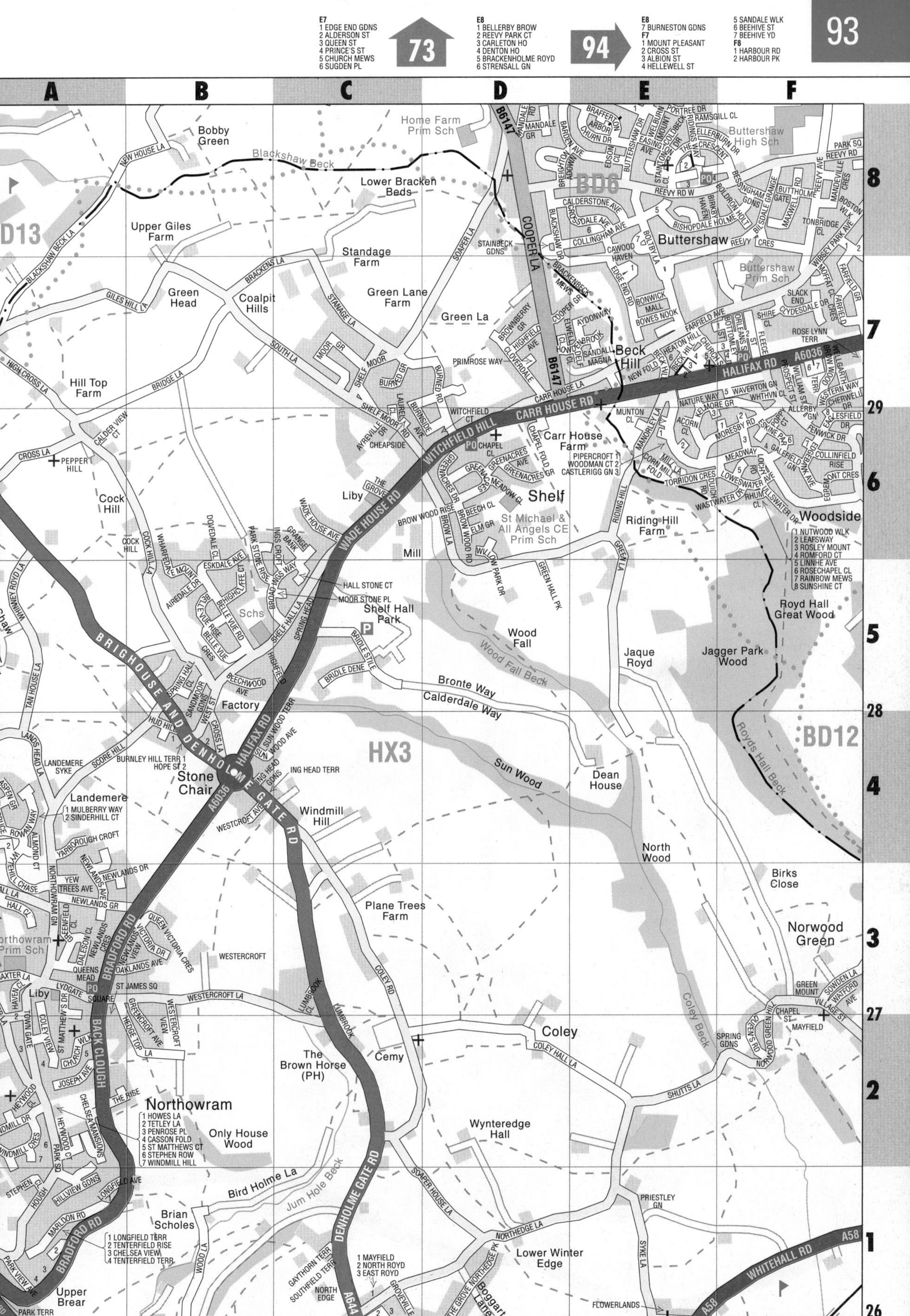
A
B
C
D
E
F
8
7
29
6
5
28
4
3
27
2
1
26
12
13
BD13
BD6
BD12
HX3
Bobby Green
Blackshaw Beck
Lower Bracken Beds
Home Farm Prim Sch
Buttershaw High Sch
Upper Giles Farm
Standage Farm
Buttershaw
Buttershaw Prim Sch
Green Head
Coalpit Hills
Green Lane Farm
Green La
Beck Hill
Hill Top Farm
HALIFAX RD
A6036
B6147
COOPER LA
CARR HOUSE RD
WITCHFIELD HILL
Carr House Farm
Pepper Hill
Cock Hill
Liby
Shelf
St Michael & All Angels CE Prim Sch
Riding Hill Farm
Woodside
1 NUTWOOD WLK
2 LEAFSWAY
3 ROSLEY MOUNT
4 ROMFORD CT
5 LINNHE AVE
6 ROSECHAPEL CL
7 RAINBOW MEWS
8 SUNSHINE CT
Mill
WADE HOUSE RD
Schs
Shelf Hall Park
Royd Hall Great Wood
Wood Fall
Wood Fall Beck
Jaque Royd
Jagger Park Wood
Bronte Way
Calderdale Way
BRIGHOUSE AND DENHOLME GATE RD
Factory
Royds Hall Beck
Landemere
1 MULBERRY WAY
2 SINDERHILL CT
Stone Chair
Sun Wood
Dean House
Windmill Hill
North Wood
Birks Close
Plane Trees Farm
Norwood Green
Northowram Prim Sch
BRADFORD RD
WESTERCROFT
Coley
Coley Beck
The Brown Horse (PH)
Cemy
Northowram
1 HOWES LA
2 TETLEY LA
3 PENROSE PL
4 CASSON FOLD
5 ST MATTHEWS CT
6 STEPHEN ROW
7 WINDMILL HILL
Only House Wood
Wynteredge Hall
Bird Holme La
Jum Hole Beck
DENHOLME GATE RD
Brian Scholes
1 LONGFIELD TERR
2 TENTERFIELD RISE
3 CHELSEA VIEW
4 TENTERFIELD TERR
1 MAYFIELD
2 NORTH ROYD
3 EAST ROYD
Lower Winter Edge
Boggart Lane
WHITEHALL RD
A58
A644
Upper Brear
PARK TERR
FLOWERLANDS

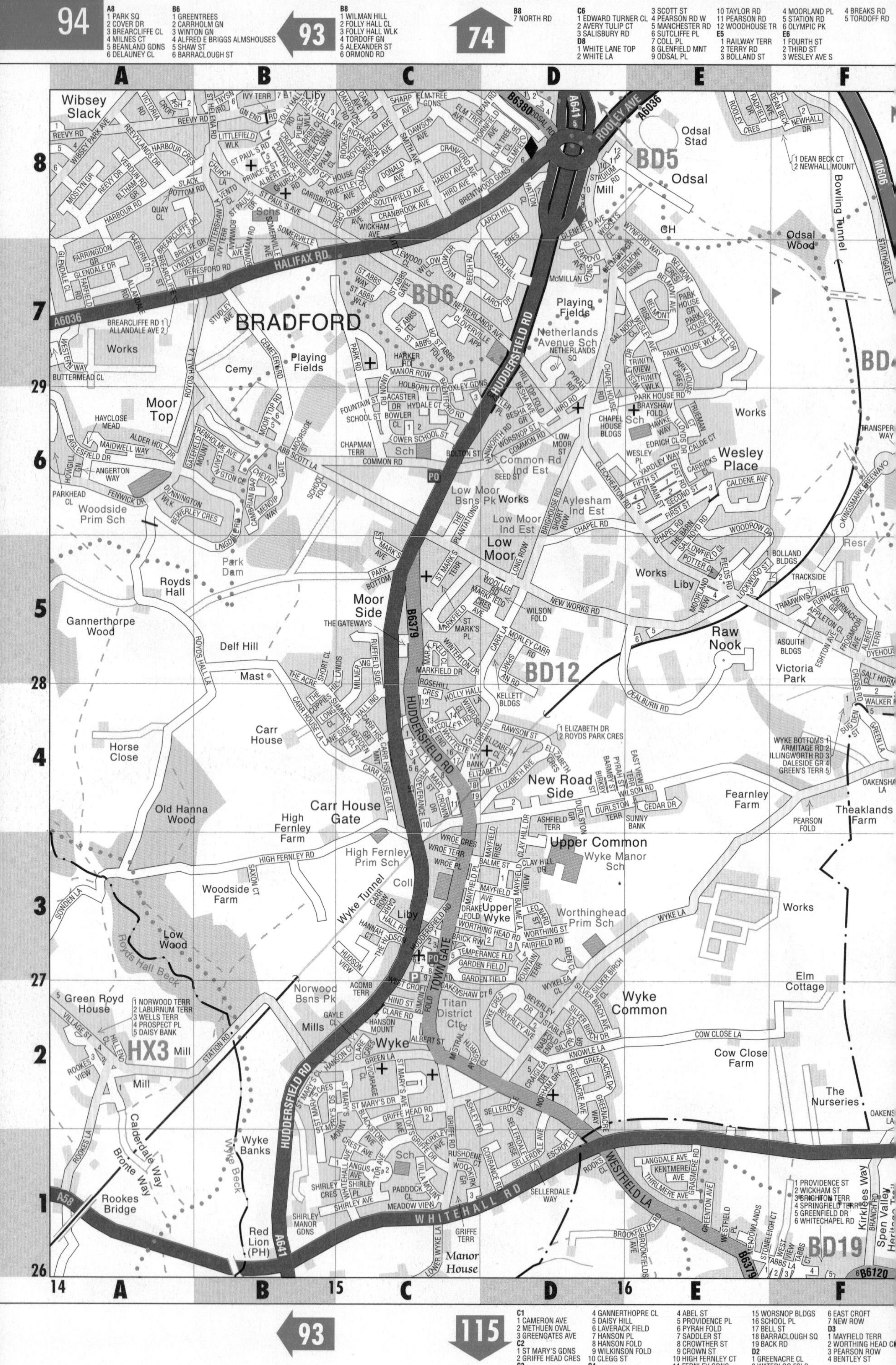

75
96
A
B
C
D
E
F
BD5
Bierley
Waggon House Farm
West Yorkshire Ind Est
Toftshaw Moor Side
Model Farm
Lockwood Farm
East Bierley
East Bierley CE Fst Sch
Toftshaw Bottom
Mill Carr Hill
Euroway Trad Est
Hunsworth Hill
Cheesecake House Farm
Upper Chatts Farm
BD4
Hagg Hall Farm
Upper House Park Farm
Copley House Farm
Copley Springs Farm
Clifford House Farm
Chatts Hill
Kirklees Way
BD11
Lower Woodlands
Chatts Wood
Bluehills Farm
Oakenshaw
BD12
Works
Hanging Wood
Hunsworth Lodge Farm
Lodge Garage
Hunsworth
BD19
Drub
Mast
Hillside Works Ind Est
Merchant Fields
Mills
Spen Trad Est
Lands Farm
Cleckheaton
Moorend
Moorlands Ind Ctr
Egypt
Round Hill
Cemy
M62
M606
A58
A638
A650
A651
B6121
B6120
WHITEHALL RD
WHITEHALL RD W
BRADFORD RD
HUNSWORTH LA
18
19
26
27
28
29
8
7
6
5
4
3
2
1
116
96

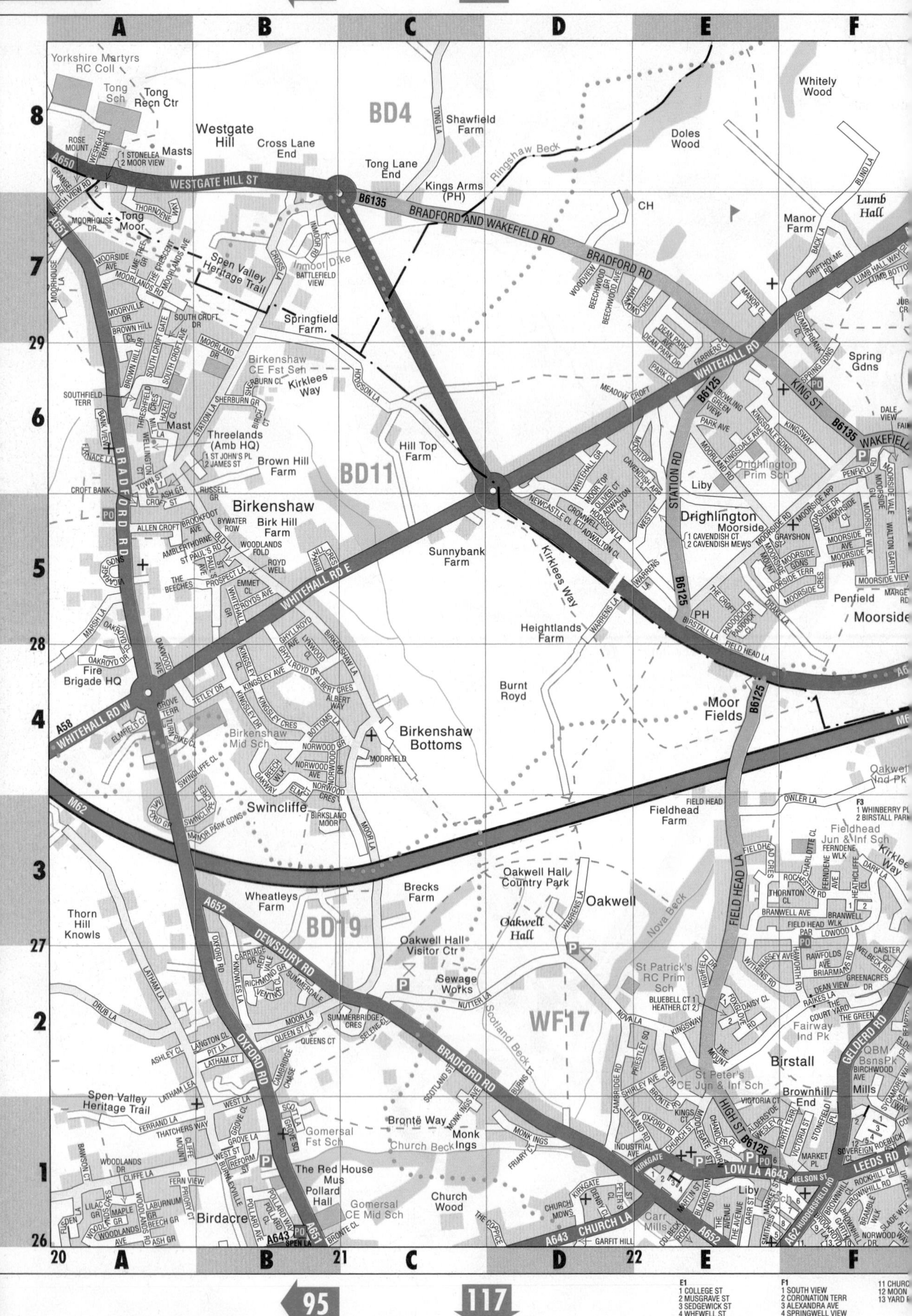

77
98

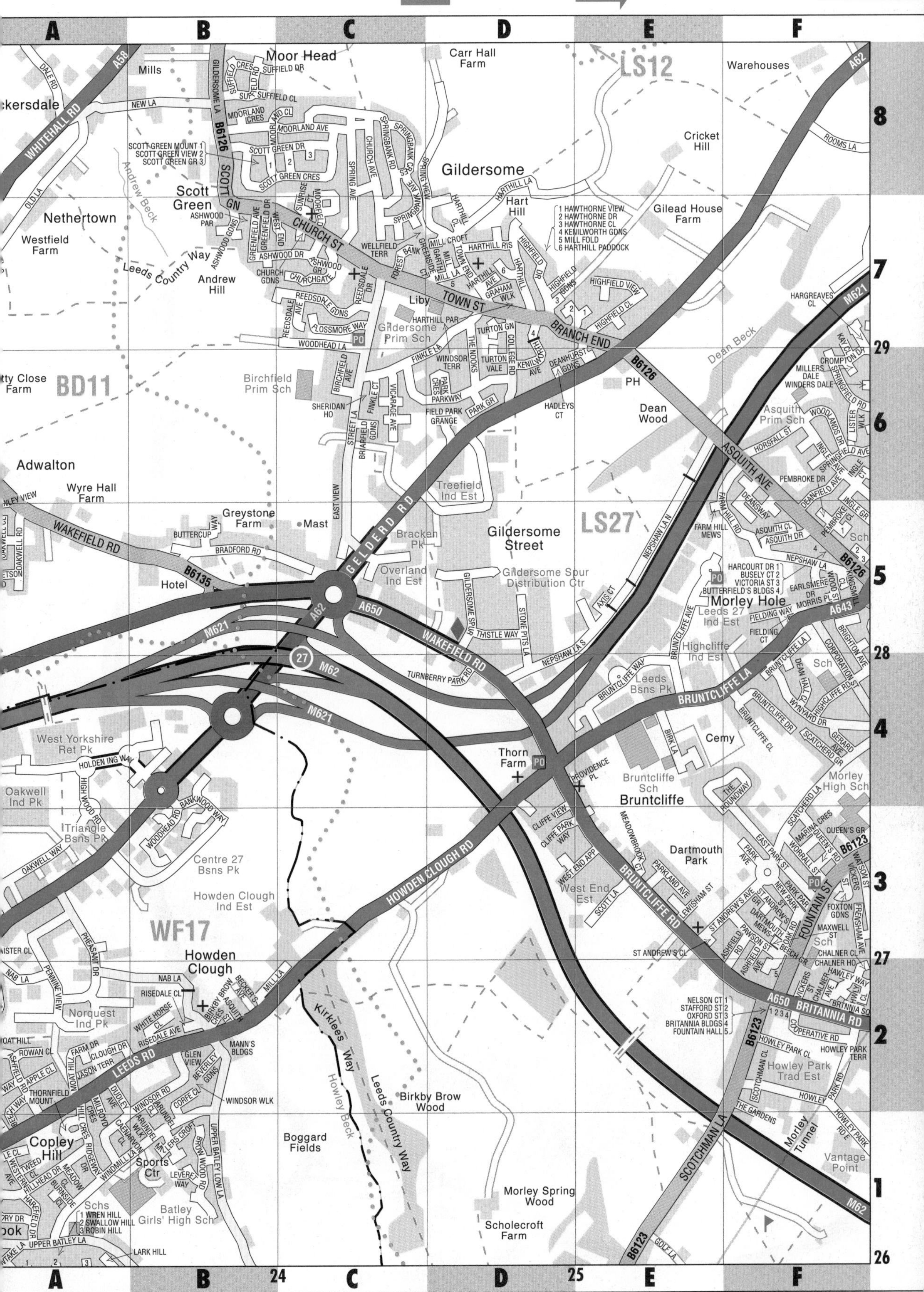
A
B
C
D
E
F
Moor Head
Carr Hall Farm
LS12
Warehouses
Mills
Gildersome
Cricket Hill
Scott Green
Nethertown
Westfield Farm
Hart Hill
Gilead House Farm
Andrew Hill
Leeds Country Way
Liby
Gildersome Prim Sch
Birchfield Prim Sch
BD11
Adwalton
Wyre Hall Farm
Greystone Farm
Mast
Treefield Ind Est
Bracken Pk
Gildersome Street
LS27
Overland Ind Est
Gildersome Spur Distribution Ctr
Dean Wood
Asquith Prim Sch
Morley Hole
Leeds 27 Ind Est
Highcliffe Ind Est
Leeds Bsns Pk
Hotel
West Yorkshire Ret Pk
Oakwell Ind Pk
Triangle Bsns Pk
Centre 27 Bsns Pk
Howden Clough Ind Est
WF17
Howden Clough
Norquest Ind Pk
Thorn Farm
Cemy
Bruntcliffe Sch
Bruntcliffe
Morley High Sch
Dartmouth Park
West End Est
Howley Park Trad Est
Kirklees Way
Howley Beck
Birkby Brow Wood
Boggard Fields
Morley Spring Wood
Scholecroft Farm
Morley Tunnel
Vantage Point
Copley Hill
Sports Ctr
Batley Girls' High Sch
Schs
WAKEFIELD RD
GELDERD RD
HOWDEN CLOUGH RD
BRUNTCLIFFE LA
BRUNTCLIFFE RD
ASQUITH AVE
BRITANNIA RD
LEEDS RD
SCOTCHMAN LA
TOWN ST
CHURCH ST
BRANCH END
WHITEHALL RD
M621
M62
A62
A650
A643
A58
B6126
B6135
B6123
8
7
29
6
5
28
4
3
27
2
1
26
24
25

118
98

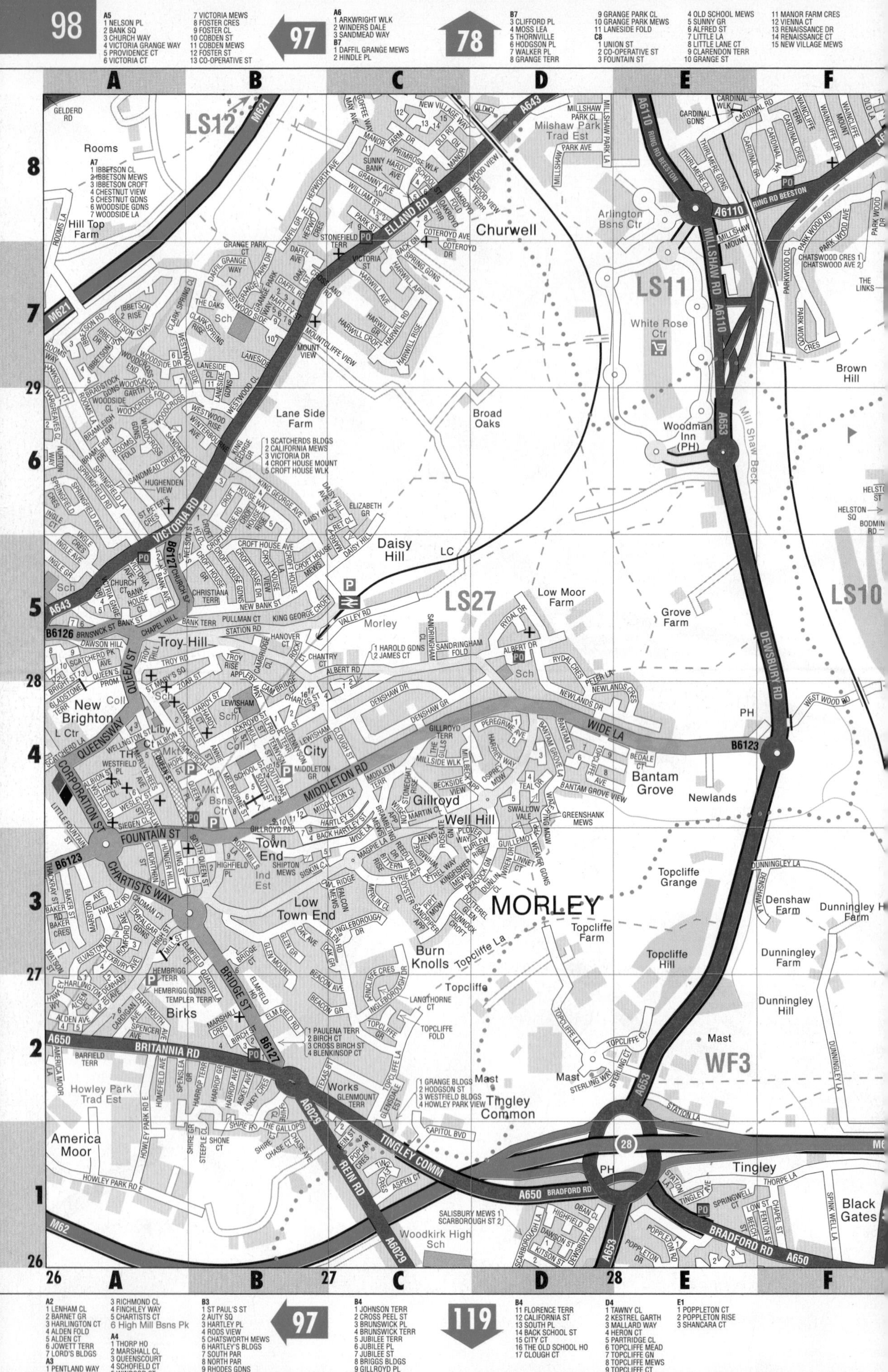
A5
1 NELSON PL
2 BANK SQ
3 CHURCH WAY
4 VICTORIA GRANGE WAY
5 PROVIDENCE CT
6 VICTORIA CT
7 VICTORIA MEWS
8 FOSTER CRES
9 FOSTER CL
10 COBDEN ST
11 COBDEN MEWS
12 FOSTER ST
13 CO-OPERATIVE ST
97
A6
1 ARKWRIGHT WLK
2 WINDERS DALE
3 SANDMEAD WAY
B7
1 DAFFIL GRANGE MEWS
2 HINDLE PL
78
B7
3 CLIFFORD PL
4 MOSS LEA
5 THORNVILLE
6 HODGSON PL
7 WALKER PL
8 GRANGE TERR
9 GRANGE PARK CL
10 GRANGE PARK MEWS
11 LANESIDE FOLD
C8
1 UNION ST
2 CO-OPERATIVE ST
3 FOUNTAIN ST
4 OLD SCHOOL MEWS
5 SUNNY GR
6 ALFRED ST
7 LITTLE LA
8 LITTLE LANE CT
9 CLARENDON TERR
10 GRANGE ST
11 MANOR FARM CRES
12 VIENNA CT
13 RENAISSANCE DR
14 RENAISSANCE CT
15 NEW VILLAGE MEWS
A
B
C
D
E
F
8
7
29
6
5
28
4
3
27
2
1
26
LS12
LS11
LS27
LS10
WF3
Rooms
Hill Top Farm
A7
1 IBBETSON CL
2 IBBETSON MEWS
3 IBBETSON CROFT
4 CHESTNUT VIEW
5 CHESTNUT GDNS
6 WOODSIDE GDNS
7 WOODSIDE LA
Churwell
Milshaw Park Trad Est
Arlington Bsns Ctr
White Rose Ctr
Brown Hill
Lane Side Farm
Broad Oaks
Woodman Inn (PH)
Mill Shaw Beck
1 SCATCHERDS BLDGS
2 CALIFORNIA MEWS
3 VICTORIA DR
4 CROFT HOUSE MOUNT
5 CROFT HOUSE WLK
Daisy Hill
Low Moor Farm
Grove Farm
Morley
Troy Hill
New Brighton
1 HAROLD GDNS
2 JAMES CT
City
Gillroyd
Well Hill
Bantam Grove
Newlands
Town End
Low Town End
MORLEY
Topcliffe Grange
Denshaw Farm
Dunningley Hill Farm
Topcliffe Farm
Burn Knolls
Topcliffe
Topcliffe Hill
Dunningley Farm
Dunningley Hill
Birks
1 PAULENA TERR
2 BIRCH CT
3 CROSS BIRCH ST
4 BLENKINSOP CT
Howley Park Trad Est
Works
1 GRANGE BLDGS
2 HODGSON ST
3 WESTFIELD BLDGS
4 HOWLEY PARK VIEW
Tingley Common
Mast
America Moor
Tingley
Black Gates
SALISBURY MEWS 1
SCARBOROUGH ST 2
Woodkirk High Sch
M621
M62
A643
A6110
A653
B6123
B6127
B6126
A650
A6029
DEWSBURY RD
ELLAND RD
VICTORIA RD
QUEENSWAY
CORPORATION ST
FOUNTAIN ST
MIDDLETON RD
WIDE LA
CHARTISTS WAY
BRIDGE ST
BRITANNIA RD
TINGLEY COMM
BRADFORD RD
RING RD BEESTON
MILLSHAW RD
26
27
28
A2
1 LENHAM CL
2 BARNET GR
3 HARLINGTON CT
4 ALDEN FOLD
5 ALDEN CT
6 JOWETT TERR
7 LORD'S BLDGS
A3
1 PENTLAND WAY
2 SUTTON GR
3 RICHMOND CL
4 FINCHLEY WAY
5 CHARTISTS CT
6 High Mill Bsns Pk
A4
1 THORP HO
2 MARSHALL CL
3 QUEENSCOURT
4 SCHOFIELD CT
5 WINDSOR CT
6 HAYDN CT
B3
1 ST PAUL'S ST
2 AUTY SQ
3 HARTLEY PL
4 RODS VIEW
5 CHATSWORTH MEWS
6 HARTLEY'S BLDGS
7 SOUTH PAR
8 NORTH PAR
9 RHODES GDNS
97
B4
1 JOHNSON TERR
2 CROSS PEEL ST
3 BRUNSWICK PL
4 BRUNSWICK TERR
5 JUBILEE TERR
6 JUBILEE PL
7 JUBILEE ST
8 BRIGGS BLDGS
9 GILLROYD PL
10 AIREDALE TERR
119
B4
11 FLORENCE TERR
12 CALIFORNIA ST
13 SOUTH PL
14 BACK SCHOOL ST
15 CITY CT
16 THE OLD SCHOOL HO
17 CLOUGH CT
D4
1 TAWNY CL
2 KESTREL GARTH
3 MALLARD WAY
4 HERON CT
5 PARTRIDGE CL
6 TOPCLIFFE MEAD
7 TOPCLIFFE GN
8 TOPCLIFFE MEWS
9 TOPCLIFFE CT
E1
1 POPPLETON CT
2 POPPLETON RISE
3 SHANCARA CT

99
79
100
120
GROVEHALL DR
OAKHURST ST
OAKHURST AVE
CHAPEL HILL
STRAITHE GDNS
3 TURNSTONE CT
4 AVOCET GARTH
5 SANDERLING GARTH
6 DUNLIN CT
7 DUNLIN FOLD
8 DUNLIN CROFT
D8
1 WINROSE HILL
2 CORNUS GDNS
3 THE SPINDLES
4 BLACKTHORN CT
5 GORSE LEA
6 WHITEBEAM LA
F7
1 KENSINGTON WAY
2 KENSINGTON GDNS
3 SOUTH HILL CROFT
4 LEA PARK GDNS
5 LEA PARK GARTH
6 HOPES FARM MOUNT
7 HOPES FARM RD
8 HOPES FARM VIEW
9 GRANGE FIELDS MOUNT
F4
1 LEDBURY GN
2 LEDBURY GR
3 LEDBURY CROFT
4 LEDBURY CL
C4
1 LINGWELL MEWS
2 LINGWELL VIEW
3 LINGWELL GDNS
4 LINGWELL APP
5 LINGWELL WLK
6 LINGWELL GN
1 GOODWOOD
2 BURGHLEY MEWS
3 THIRSK GR
CRANMORE GN 1
CRANMORE GARTH 2
South Leeds Stadium
Leeds Coll of Tech
Park Farm Ind Est
LS11
Park Wood
Beeston Park Side
Cockburn Coll of Arts
Middleton Wood
The Clearings
Middleton Park
Park Halt
Middleton Rly
Windmill PrimSch
Merlyn Rees Com High Sch
Belle Isle
LEEDS
Broomfield Sch
Clapgate Prim Sch
St Philip's RC Prim Sch
St Mary's CE Prim Sch
Wtr Twr
Sharp Lane Prim Sch
Middleton District Ctr
L Ctr
LS10
Sharp House Farm
Middleton
Throstle Carr Beck
Middleton Prim Sch
Sissons Farm
MIDDLETON LA
Thorpe Hall
THORPE LA
THORPE LOWER LA A654
Chy Foundry
Low Street Farm
Thorpe on the Hill
Thorpe Prim Sch
LINGWELL GATE LA
B6135
LONG THORPE LA
M62
M1
A61
A653
WF3
Recn Gd
Ardsley Common
Owlett Hall Farm
Thorpe Lane
DUNNINGLEY LA
STATION LA
CH
PH
Liby
PO
A B C D E F
8 7 29 6 5 28 4 3 27 2 1 26
30 31

A B C D E F
8 7 29 6 5 28 4 3 27 2 1 26
LS10
LS26
WF3
Rothwell Haigh
Leeds Valley Pk
Bell Hill
Rose Cottage Farm
Haigh Cottage Farm
Rothwell Haigh
Haigh House
Glebe Farm
Haigh Side Farm
Haigh Beck
Rothwell Victoria Jun Sch
Rothwell Haigh Road Inf Sch
Cemy
ROTHWELL
Churchfields
Hope's Farm
Hopefield Farm
Middle Shutts
Carlton Fields
Matty La
Rothwell Prim Sch
Rothwell St Mary's RC Prim Sch
West Bridge
Bridge End Farm
West Beck
Carlton Prim Sch
Sherwood Ind Est
Robin Hood
Carlton
Carlton Beck
Carlton Carr
Swithen's Farm
Green End Farm
Robin Hood Prim Sch
The Grange
Town End
Ouzlewell Green
Bushy Cliffe Wood
Dungeon Lane Farm
Lee Moor Beck
Rodillian Sch
Lofthouse
WAKEFIELD RD
LEEDS RD
LEADWELL LA
CARLTON LA
MARSH ST
OULTON LA
LOWER LA
LONG THORPE LA
GREEN LA
A639
A654
A61
M1
M621
M62
B6481
B6135
A654THORPE

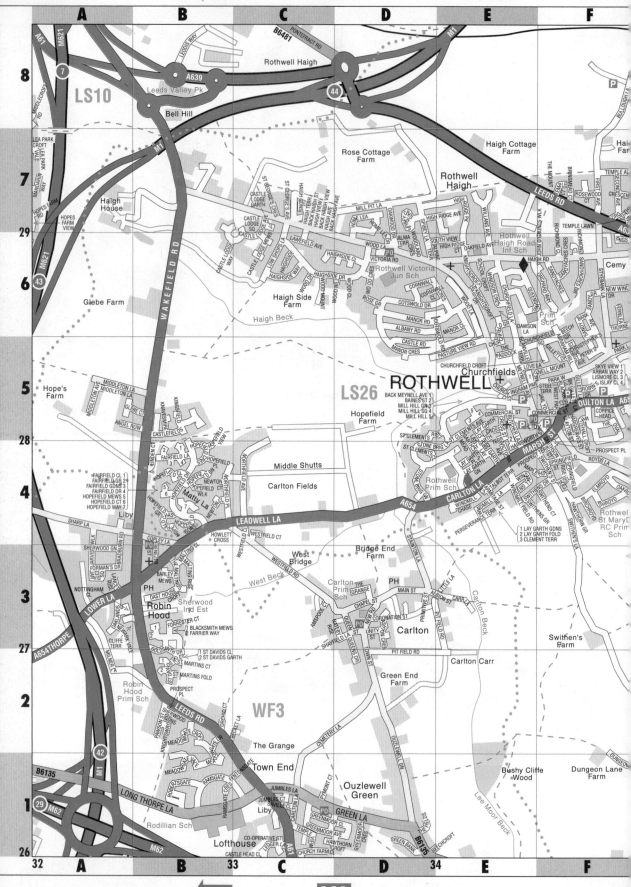

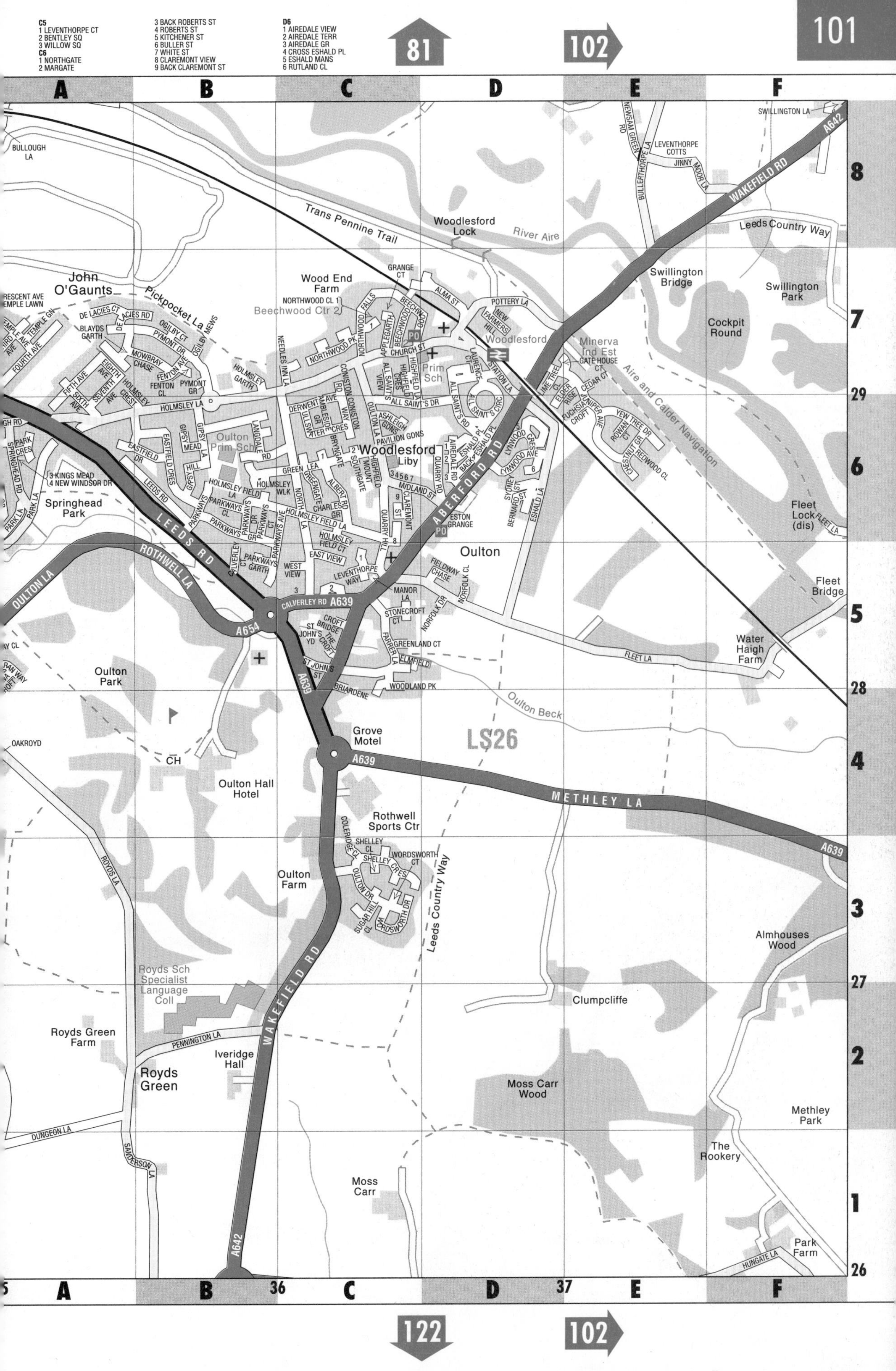
C5
1 LEVENTHORPE CT
2 BENTLEY SQ
3 WILLOW SQ
C6
1 NORTHGATE
2 MARGATE
3 BACK ROBERTS ST
4 ROBERTS ST
5 KITCHENER ST
6 BULLER ST
7 WHITE ST
8 CLAREMONT VIEW
9 BACK CLAREMONT ST
D6
1 AIREDALE VIEW
2 AIREDALE TERR
3 AIREDALE GR
4 CROSS ESHALD PL
5 ESHALD MANS
6 RUTLAND CL
81
102
A
B
C
D
E
F
BULLOUGH LA
Trans Pennine Trail
Woodlesford Lock
River Aire
Leeds Country Way
WAKEFIELD RD
A642
NEWSAM GREEN RD
LEVENTHORPE COTTS
BULLERTHORPE LA
JINNY MOOR LA
SWILLINGTON LA
Swillington Bridge
Swillington Park
Cockpit Round
John O'Gaunts
Pickpocket La
Wood End Farm
Beechwood Ctr
Woodlesford
Minerva Ind Est
Aire and Calder Navigation
Prim Sch
Oulton Prim Sch
Woodlesford Liby
HOLMSLEY LA
LEEDS RD
ROTHWELL LA
OULTON LA
A654
ABERFORD RD
A639
CALVERLEY RD
Springhead Park
Oulton
Fleet Lock (dis)
Fleet Bridge
FLEET LA
Water Haigh Farm
Oulton Park
Oulton Beck
LS26
Grove Motel
OAKROYD
CH
Oulton Hall Hotel
METHLEY LA
Rothwell Sports Ctr
Oulton Farm
Leeds Country Way
ROYDS LA
Almhouses Wood
Royds Sch Specialist Language Coll
Clumpcliffe
Royds Green Farm
PENNINGTON LA
Iveridge Hall
Royds Green
Moss Carr Wood
Methley Park
DUNGEON LA
SANDERSON LA
The Rookery
Moss Carr
HUNGATE LA
Park Farm
8
7
29
6
5
28
4
3
27
2
1
26
36
37
122
102

101
82

A B C D E F
8 7 29 6 5 28 4 3 27 2 1 26
38 39 40
Home Farm
Astley Lane Ind Est
Leeds Country Way
Swillington Park
Fleakingley Bridge
ASTLEY LA
Old Hall Farm
Great Preston
LS25
Station Road Ind Est
Great Preston CE Prim Sch
Brigshaw High Sch
Hollinhurst Wood
QUEEN ST
Woodend
Opencast Workings
Iron Bridge
LS26
WF10
Lemonroyd Lock
Trans Pennine Trail
River Aire
A639 METHLEY LA
Mickletown
Lower Mickletown
Methley Park
Melwood House Farm
Wood Row
Mulberry Bridge
LEEDS RD
STATION RD
CHURCH LA
Methley Prim Sch
PINFOLD LA
White Cross Field
Coney Moor
Church Side
Methley
CHURCH SIDE
Moorhouse Farm
Coney Moor Common
Crooked Park
Pinder Green
Pinder Green Bridge
Watergate
WATERGATE
B6135
BARNSDALE RD
Windmill Moor
Low Common
Dunford House
A639
1 BURNLEYS VIEW
2 GREEN ROW
3 GREEN ROW FOLD

101
123

83
104
124
104
A
B
C
D
E
F
8
7
29
6
5
28
4
3
27
2
1
26
42
43
LS25
WF10
LS26
B6137
LONGDIKE LA
RIDGE RD A656
BARNSDALE RD
LOCK LA A656
Kippax Mill
Kippax Park
Owl Wood
Sewage Works
Sheffield Beck
Pit Plantation
Whin Covert
Little Plantation
Home Farm
Sheldon Hill
North Park
Ledston Hall
Elm Tree Farm
Lady Elizabeth Hastings CE Prim Sch
Ledston
Ledston Intake
Chestnut Farm
Allerton Bywater Prim Sch
Allerton Bywater
Liby
Allerton Bywater Network Ctr
Lin Dyke
Fairburn Ings Nature Reserve
The Boat (PH)
Arrow La
Spoil Heap
River Aire
Willow Grove Farm
Ledston Ings
Allerton Ings
Aire and Calder Navigation Castleford Cut
The Oxbow Lakes
Castleford Ings
The Aire & Calder Ind Pk
Works
River Calder
JUNCTION HOUSES
Parlour Pit Wood
BACK NEWTON LA
SPARTAL LA
LEDSTON MILL LA
GREEN LA
MANOR PK
MAIN ST
WHITE HORSE FOLD
DOVECOTE DR
HALL LA
PARK LA
PARK AVE
HAIGH MOOR WAY
SILKSTONE SQ
STATION RD
NEWTON LA
INGS LA
LEEDS RD
BLANDS AVE
BLANDS GR
BLANDS TERR
BLANDS CRES
DOCTORS LA
WESTFIELD AVE
WESTFIELD GR
WESTFIELD TERR
GRANGE PARK CL
MANOR PARK AVE
VICARS TERR
BICKERDIKE PL
ST MARY'S CT
MAIN ST
VICTORIA ST
VICTORIA CL
WHITLEY PL
BEESTON WAY
ROBINSON ST
BACK LA
PROVIDENCE PL
BOAT LA
LOWER MICKLETOWN
STATION RD
ROOKWOOD AVE
LYNDALE
HOLLINS BECK CL
BRIGSHAW LA
CROMWELL RISE
HALL PARK MDWS
1 TATEFIELD GR
2 HALL PARK ORCHS
MOUNT PLEASANT
WOODLANDS CROFT
WOODLANDS VIEW
PARK LA
WOODLANDS GR
1 HALL PARK CROFT
2 APPLE TREE LA
3 APPLE TREE MEWS
4 MOUNT PLEASANT GDNS
5 WOODLANDS CT
NAVIGATION RD
GREEN ST
JAMES ST
WILLIAM ST
HUNT ST
MILL LA
AIRE TERR 1
WATER VIEW 2
WEIR VIEW 3
RIVER VIEW
POTTERY ST
QUEEN ST
RYEBREAD
ELLAND ST
WILLIAM ST
THOMAS ST
SWISS ST
NEW ST
SCHOOL ST
PRINCESS ST
WHELDON RD
HEPWORTH ST
CORONATION ST
INGS LA
GREEN LA
SMITH ST
PH
PO
P

A B C D E F

Park Lane Farm
Hastings Plantation
Hill Top Farm
ST JOHN'S HOSPITAL (ALMSHOUSES)
HOLY ROOD LA
PH
Plaster Pits
Park House Farm
Ledsham
MANOR GARTH
NEWFIELD LA
Wormstall Wood
A63
A1246
CLAYPIT LA
LS25
Capon Hill
Horselock Dale
Madbanks
Lambkin Plantation
Lambkin Hill
Newfield Farm
BACK NEWTON LA
Newfield Plantation
Newfield La
Caudle Hill Plantation
Haugh Hill Plantation
Beckfield House
WF11
Newton Farm
Newton
BECKFIELD LA
CLIFF HILL TERR
CAUDLE HILL
Newton Abbey (rems of)
NEWTON LA
RSPB Visitor Ctr
Fairburn Ings Nature Reserve
Newton Ings
Fairburn Ings
River Aire
New Fryston
BROOK ST
WF10
NORTH ST
Aire Bridge
SMITH COTTS
WILLIAM ST
HOPE ST
SMITH ST
Spoil Heap
SOUTH VIEW
Sewage Works
Spoil Heap
WHELDALE LA
Wheldale Ings
Well Wood
Sewage Works
AIREDALE DR
KESWICK DR
LANGDALE CL
CUMBERLAND RD
PENRITH CRES
Hall Farm
Water Fryston
WHELDON RD
PARK DALE
ST ANDREW'S RD
ASKHAM RD
FAIRFIELD CL
PO
GRANGE RD
TARN CL
FAIR VIEW
FRYSTON RD
DELACY CRES
Wheldale
BORROWDALE DR
Fryston Hall Farm
Whin Covert
HADRIAN CL
SUNDERLAND CRES
LANCASTER ST
ELMETE RD
AMBLESIDE RD
WATLING RD
STANSFIELD RD
WHELDALE CT
PARK DALE
HULME SQ
DERWENT DR
HILLTOP CL
HEALDFIELD RD
ELIZABETH DR
SCHOLES RD
KENDAL DR
BOWNESS AVE
PEMBERTON RD
STANSFIELD CL
FOSS WLK
NIDD DR
WOOD SIDE
Sch
GRASMERE CL
8
7
29
6
5
28
4
3
27
2
1
26
44
45
46

A B C D E F

A1(M) Wetherby (A1)

A162 Tadcaster

A63 Selby

MAIN ST   A63

Pollums House Farm

Monk Fryston Lodge

LC

Betteras Hill Rd

Hillam

Betteras Hill

29

Running La

LS25

West Park Farm

1 PIPER HILL DR
2 CRAG TOP
3 SCHOOL TERR
4 OLD GARTH CROFT
5 CHAPEL YD

Fairburn Com Prim Sch

Ox Moor

28

LUMNFIELDS LA

Fairburn

WF11

VICTORIA COTTS

RAILWAY COTTS

Burton Salmon Com Prim Sch

Hall Farm

Burton Common La

Cow La

WATERSIDE

Top Stone Drain

Fairburn Ings Nature Reserve

Plough Inn (PH)

Burton Salmon

NEW LA

LC

POOLE ROW

POOLE

27

Poole Belt

Spoil Heap

WF10

Byram Park

Coppering Kilns

The Dales

Foxcliff

P

Byram Hall

River Aire

A1(M)

A1246

A162

A7
1 WESLEY TERR
2 FIELD TOP
3 ROCHESTER CL
4 CAPTAIN ST
5 HALLEY ST
6 DEER ST
7 RICHARD ST
8 COMET ST
9 WRIGHT ST
10 HILLSIDE CRES
11 MELROSE TERR

85

| A | B | C | D | E | F |

8
7
25
6
5
24
4
3
23
2
1
22

THE MOORLANDS
FELL VIEW
HEALD LA
HEALD CL
Wambs Farm
Weir
WEIR BOTTOM
Scar End Hey
Scar End Brook
Mean Hey
Far Old Meadows Farm
Old Meadows
Stake Moss
Sharneyford
Sharneyford Prim Sch
HIGHER CHANGE VILLAS
Higher Change
Parrock Farm
BACUP
The Flowers (PH)
Greave
Beech Ind Est
Pasture Bottom Farm
Lower Reaps Farm
Hoyle Hey Clough
St Mary's RC Prim Sch
Mast
Hogshead Law Hill
Higher Hogshead
Heald Top Farm
Greens Clough
Carr and Craggs Moor
FLOWER SCAR RD
Slate Pit Hill
Clough Head
Little Tooter Hill
BACUP RD
Works
Holden Gate
OL14
Plan Eart The Ctr Astronomy Ctr
Rossendale Way
Tooter Hill
UMBERS GATE
Midgelden Pasture
Maden Pasture
Reaps Moss
Counting Hill
OL12
OL13
TODMORDEN RD
TODMORDEN OLD RD
River Irwell
Irwell Valley Way
A671 Bacup Burnley Rd
A671 Burnley
A681 Rawtenstall
A671 Rochdale
ROCHDALE RD
A671
Lancashire STREET ATLAS

| A | B | C | D | E | F |
87   88   89

A1
1 FOXDALE CL
2 LANE END LA
3 THE FERNS
4 MERSEY ST
5 BRIAR ST
6 MOORLANDS TERR
7 PINE ST
8 GREEN HILL RD
9 GREEN HILL
10 FIR MOUNT
11 BARKER CT

A2
1 BATH ST
2 CO-OPERATION ST
3 GLADSTONE CRES
4 REGENT ST
5 CRIMEA ST
6 INKERMAN ST
7 THORN CRES
8 MYRTLE COTTS

A3
1 GREENSNOOK TERR
2 GREENSNOOK MEWS
3 CARLTON ST
4 CHRIST CHURCH ST
5 OAK ST
6 ELM ST
7 THE COURTYARD
8 GREAVE CRES
9 ARBOUR ST
10 GREEN END CL
11 CROSS ST
12 SPRING GDNS
13 WARKWORTH TERR
14 COWGILL ST
15 ASHWORTH ST
16 HANNAH ST
17 BEAVER TERR
18 EDWARD ST

B3
1 GREAVE CLOUGH CL
2 GREAVE TERR
3 NUTTALL ST
4 GREAVE CL
5 ROSENDALE CL

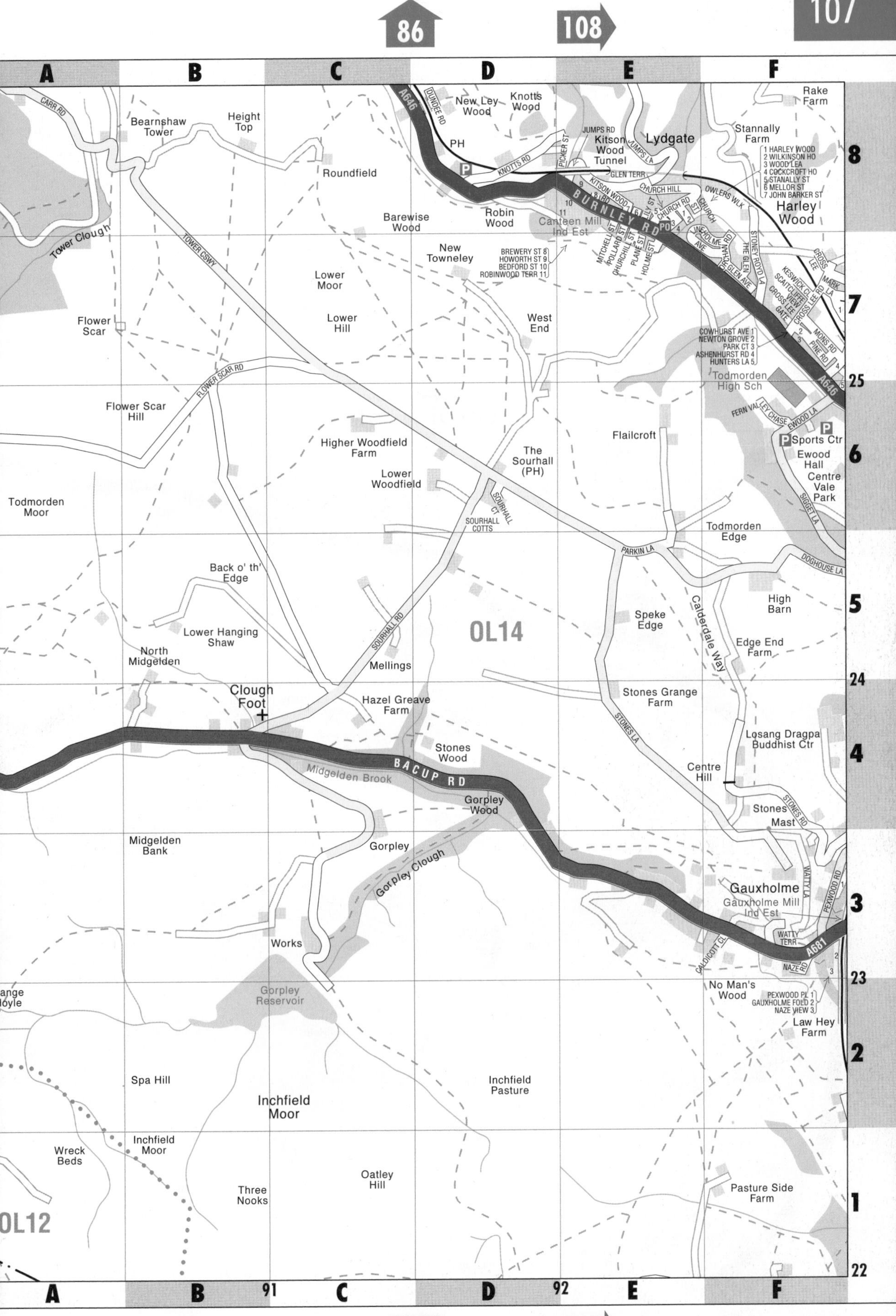
86
108
A
B
C
D
E
F
Bearnshaw Tower
Height Top
Roundfield
New Ley Wood
Knotts Wood
Rake Farm
Stannally Farm
Lydgate
Kitson Wood Tunnel
PH
Robin Wood
Barewise Wood
Canteen Mill Ind Est
Harley Wood
1 HARLEY WOOD
2 WILKINSON HO
3 WOOD LEA
4 COCKCROFT HO
5 STANALLY ST
6 MELLOR ST
7 JOHN BARKER ST
BURNLEY RD
A646
Tower Clough
TOWER CSWY
Lower Moor
New Towneley
BREWERY ST 8
HOWORTH ST 9
BEDFORD ST 10
ROBINWOOD TERR 11
Flower Scar
Lower Hill
West End
COWHURST AVE 1
NEWTON GROVE 2
PARK CT 3
ASHENHURST RD 4
HUNTERS LA 5
Todmorden High Sch
FLOWER SCAR RD
Flower Scar Hill
Higher Woodfield Farm
Lower Woodfield
The Sourhall (PH)
Flailcroft
Sports Ctr
Ewood Hall
Centre Vale Park
Todmorden Moor
SOURHALL COTTS
Todmorden Edge
PARKIN LA
DOGHOUSE LA
Back o' th' Edge
OL14
High Barn
Speke Edge
Lower Hanging Shaw
Calderdale Way
Edge End Farm
North Midgelden
Mellings
SOURHALL RD
Clough Foot
Hazel Greave Farm
Stones Grange Farm
STONES LA
Losang Dragpa Buddhist Ctr
Stones Wood
BACUP RD
Midgelden Brook
Centre Hill
Gorpley Wood
Stones Mast
Midgelden Bank
Gorpley
Gorpley Clough
Gauxholme
Gauxholme Mill Ind Est
Works
A681
Gorpley Reservoir
No Man's Wood
PEXWOOD PL 1
GAUXHOLME FOLD 2
NAZE VIEW 3
Law Hey Farm
Spa Hill
Inchfield Pasture
Inchfield Moor
Wreck Beds
Inchfield Moor
Three Nooks
Oatley Hill
Pasture Side Farm
OL12
8
7
25
6
5
24
4
3
23
2
1
22
91
92
128
108

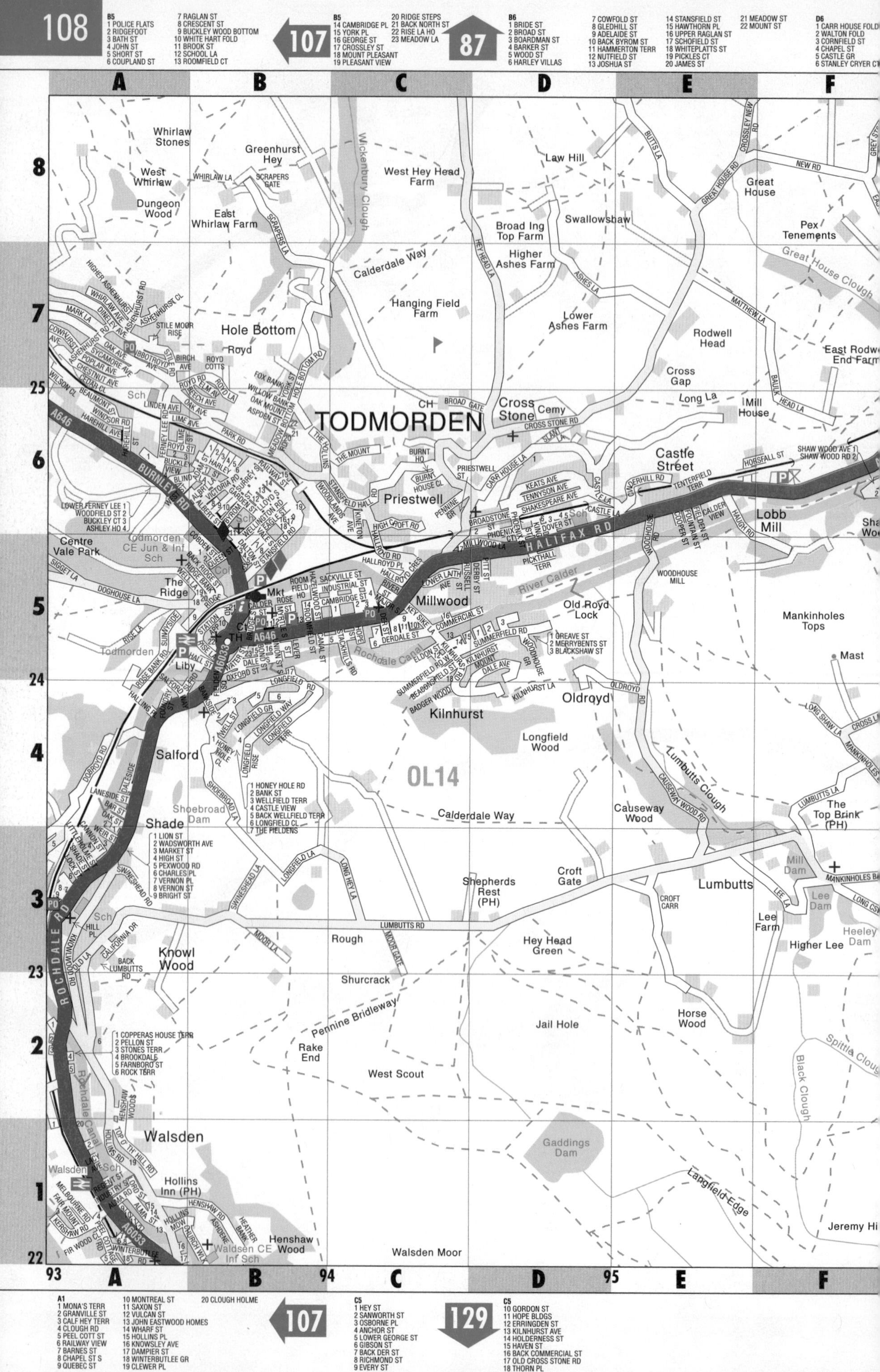

108

B5
1 POLICE FLATS
2 RIDGEFOOT
3 BATH ST
4 JOHN ST
5 SHORT ST
6 COUPLAND ST

7 RAGLAN ST
8 CRESCENT ST
9 BUCKLEY WOOD BOTTOM
10 WHITE HART FOLD
11 BROOK ST
12 SCHOOL LA
13 ROOMFIELD CT

107

B5
14 CAMBRIDGE PL
15 YORK PL
16 GEORGE ST
17 CROSSLEY ST
18 MOUNT PLEASANT
19 PLEASANT VIEW

20 RIDGE STEPS
21 BACK NORTH ST
22 RISE LA HO
23 MEADOW LA

87

B6
1 BRIDE ST
2 BROAD ST
3 BOARDMAN ST
4 BARKER ST
5 WOOD ST
6 HARLEY VILLAS

7 COWFOLD ST
8 GLEDHILL ST
9 ADELAIDE ST
10 BACK BYROM ST
11 HAMMERTON TERR
12 NUTFIELD ST
13 JOSHUA ST

14 STANSFIELD ST
15 HAWTHORN PL
16 UPPER RAGLAN ST
17 SCHOFIELD ST
18 WHITEPLATTS ST
19 PICKLES CT
20 JAMES ST

21 MEADOW ST
22 MOUNT ST

D6
1 CARR HOUSE FOLD
2 WALTON FOLD
3 CORNFIELD ST
4 CHAPEL ST
5 CASTLE GR
6 STANLEY CRYER C

A1
1 MONA'S TERR
2 GRANVILLE ST
3 CALF HEY TERR
4 CLOUGH RD
5 PEEL COTT ST
6 RAILWAY VIEW
7 BARNES ST
8 CHAPEL ST S
9 QUEBEC ST

10 MONTREAL ST
11 SAXON ST
12 VULCAN ST
13 JOHN EASTWOOD HOMES
14 WHARF ST
15 HOLLINS PL
16 KNOWSLEY AVE
17 DAMPIER ST
18 WINTERBUTLEE GR
19 CLEWER PL

20 CLOUGH HOLME

107

C5
1 HEY ST
2 SANWORTH ST
3 OSBORNE PL
4 ANCHOR ST
5 LOWER GEORGE ST
6 GIBSON ST
7 BACK DEAN ST
8 RICHMOND ST
9 EVERY ST

129

C5
10 GORDON ST
11 HOPE BLDGS
12 ERRINGDEN ST
13 KILNHURST AVE
14 HOLDERNESS ST
15 HAVEN ST
16 BACK COMMERCIAL ST
17 OLD CROSS STONE RD
18 THORN PL

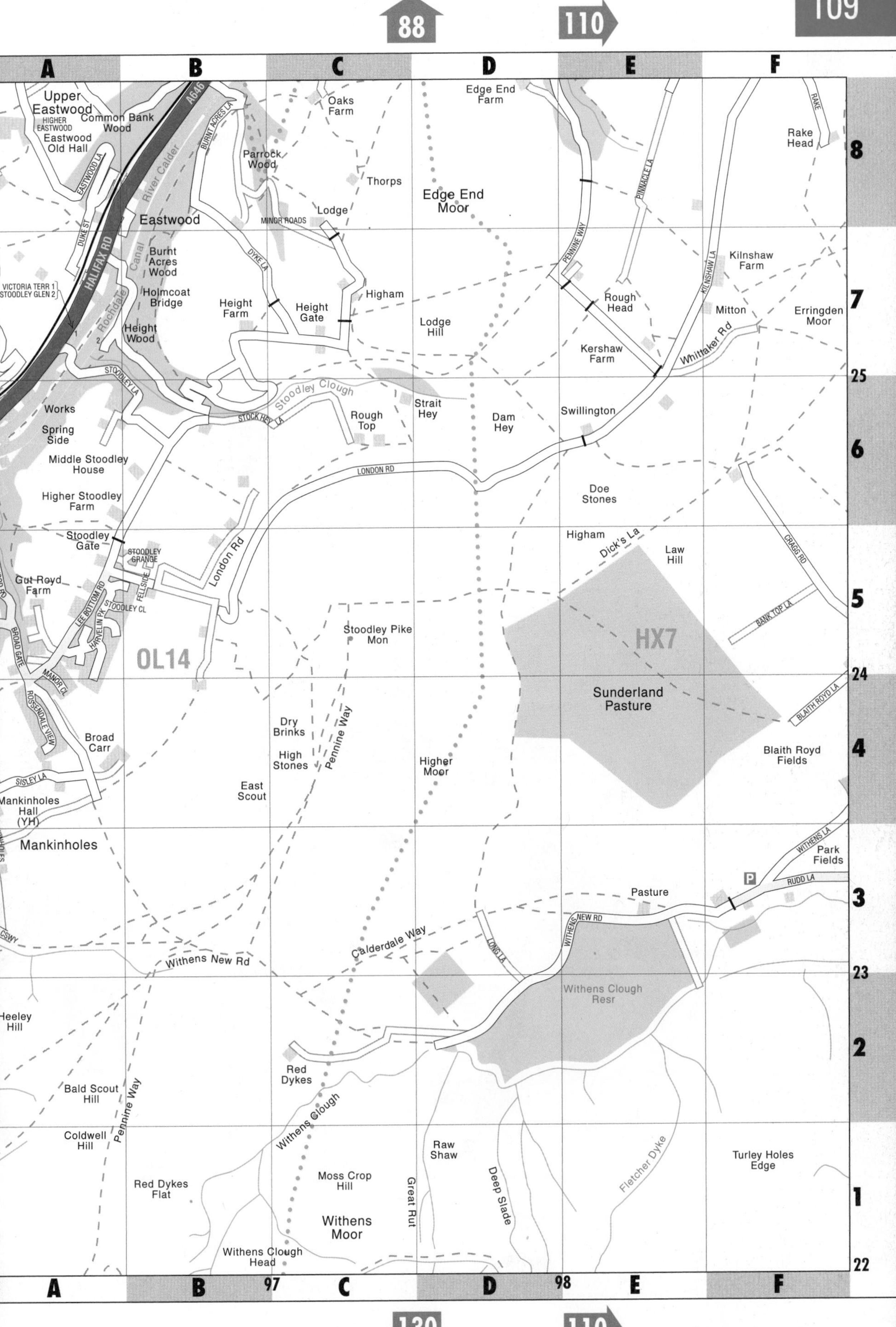
88
110
A
B
C
D
E
F
Upper Eastwood
HIGHER EASTWOOD
Common Bank Wood
Eastwood Old Hall
Eastwood
Burnt Acres Wood
Holmcoat Bridge
Height Wood
Parrock Wood
Oaks Farm
Thorps
Lodge
MINOR ROADS
Higham
Height Farm
Height Gate
Edge End Farm
Edge End Moor
Lodge Hill
Rake Head
Kilnshaw Farm
Mitton
Erringden Moor
Rough Head
Kershaw Farm
Whittaker Rd
Swillington
Strait Hey
Dam Hey
Rough Top
Stoodley Clough
STOCK HEY LA
LONDON RD
London Rd
Works
Spring Side
Middle Stoodley House
Higher Stoodley Farm
Stoodley Gate
STOODLEY GRANGE
Gut Royd Farm
Doe Stones
Higham
Dick's La
Law Hill
HX7
Sunderland Pasture
OL14
Stoodley Pike Mon
Dry Brinks
High Stones
Pennine Way
East Scout
Higher Moor
Broad Carr
Mankinholes Hall (YH)
Mankinholes
Blaith Royd Fields
Park Fields
Pasture
Withens New Rd
Calderdale Way
Withens Clough Resr
Heeley Hill
Red Dykes
Bald Scout Hill
Coldwell Hill
Withens Clough
Red Dykes Flat
Moss Crop Hill
Withens Moor
Withens Clough Head
Great Rut
Raw Shaw
Deep Slade
Fletcher Dyke
Turley Holes Edge
A646
HALIFAX RD
VICTORIA TERR 1
STOODLEY GLEN 2
River Calder
Rochdale Canal
DUKE ST
EASTWOOD LA
BURNT ACRES LA
DYKE LA
PENNINE WAY
PINNACLE LA
KILNSHAW LA
RAKE
CRAGG RD
BANK TOP LA
BLAITH ROYD LA
WITHENS LA
RUDD LA
WITHENS NEW RD
LONG LA
STOODLEY LA
LEE BOTTOM RD
HARVELIN PK
STOODLEY CL
FELLSIDE
BROAD GATE
MANOR CL
ROSSENDALE VIEW
SISLEY LA
8
7
25
6
5
24
4
3
23
2
1
22
97
98
130
110

109
89

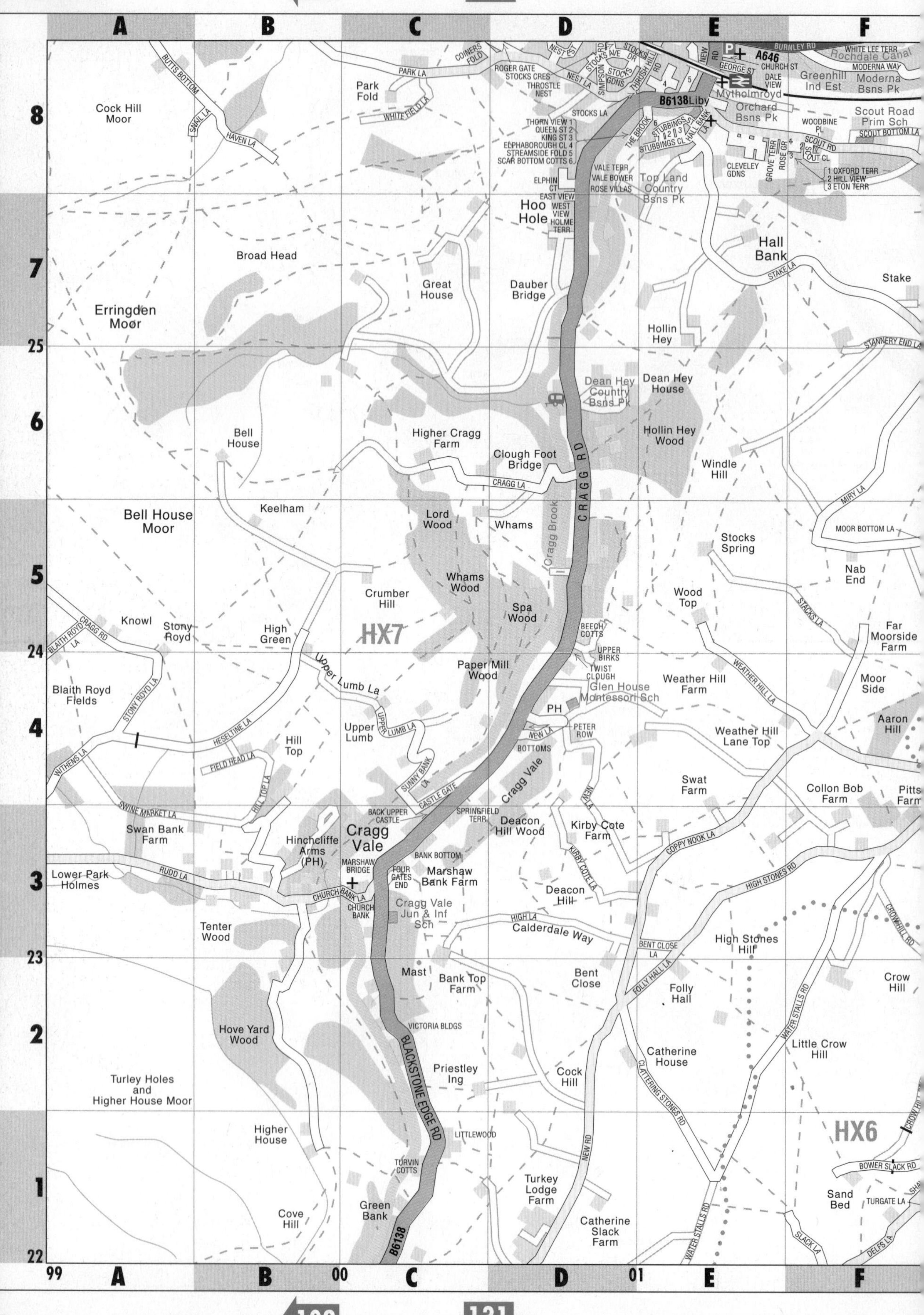
A
B
C
D
E
F
8
7
6
5
4
3
2
1
25
24
23
22
99
00
01
Cock Hill Moor
Park Fold
Mytholmroyd
Orchard Bsns Pk
Greenhill Ind Est
Moderna Bsns Pk
Scout Road Prim Sch
Rochdale Canal
A646
B6138
Hoo Hole
Top Land Country Bsns Pk
Hall Bank
Broad Head
Great House
Dauber Bridge
Stake
Erringden Moor
Hollin Hey
Dean Hey Country Bsns Pk
Dean Hey House
Hollin Hey Wood
Bell House
Higher Cragg Farm
Clough Foot Bridge
Windle Hill
CRAGG RD
Bell House Moor
Keelham
Lord Wood
Whams
Cragg Brook
Stocks Spring
Nab End
Whams Wood
Crumber Hill
Wood Top
Knowl
Stony Royd
High Green
HX7
Spa Wood
Far Moorside Farm
Blaith Royd Fields
Upper Lumb La
Paper Mill Wood
Weather Hill Farm
Moor Side
Glen House Montessori Sch
Upper Lumb
Hill Top
PH
Weather Hill Lane Top
Aaron Hill
Cragg Vale
Swat Farm
Collon Bob Farm
Swan Bank Farm
Cragg Vale
Hinchcliffe Arms (PH)
Deacon Hill Wood
Kirby Cote Farm
Lower Park Holmes
Marshaw Bank Farm
Deacon Hill
Cragg Vale Jun & Inf Sch
Tenter Wood
Calderdale Way
High Stones Hill
Mast
Bank Top Farm
Bent Close
Folly Hall
Crow Hill
Hove Yard Wood
BLACKSTONE EDGE RD
Catherine House
Little Crow Hill
Priestley Ing
Cock Hill
Turley Holes and Higher House Moor
Higher House
HX6
Turkey Lodge Farm
Sand Bed
Cove Hill
Green Bank
Catherine Slack Farm
NEW RD
WATER STALLS RD
CLATTERING STONES RD
HIGH STONES RD
COPPY NOOK LA
RUDD LA
HESELTINE LA
WITHENS LA
SWINE MARKET LA
STAKE LA
MIRY LA
MOOR BOTTOM LA
STACKS LA
WEATHER HILL LA
HAVEN LA
PARK LA
CRAGG LA

109
131

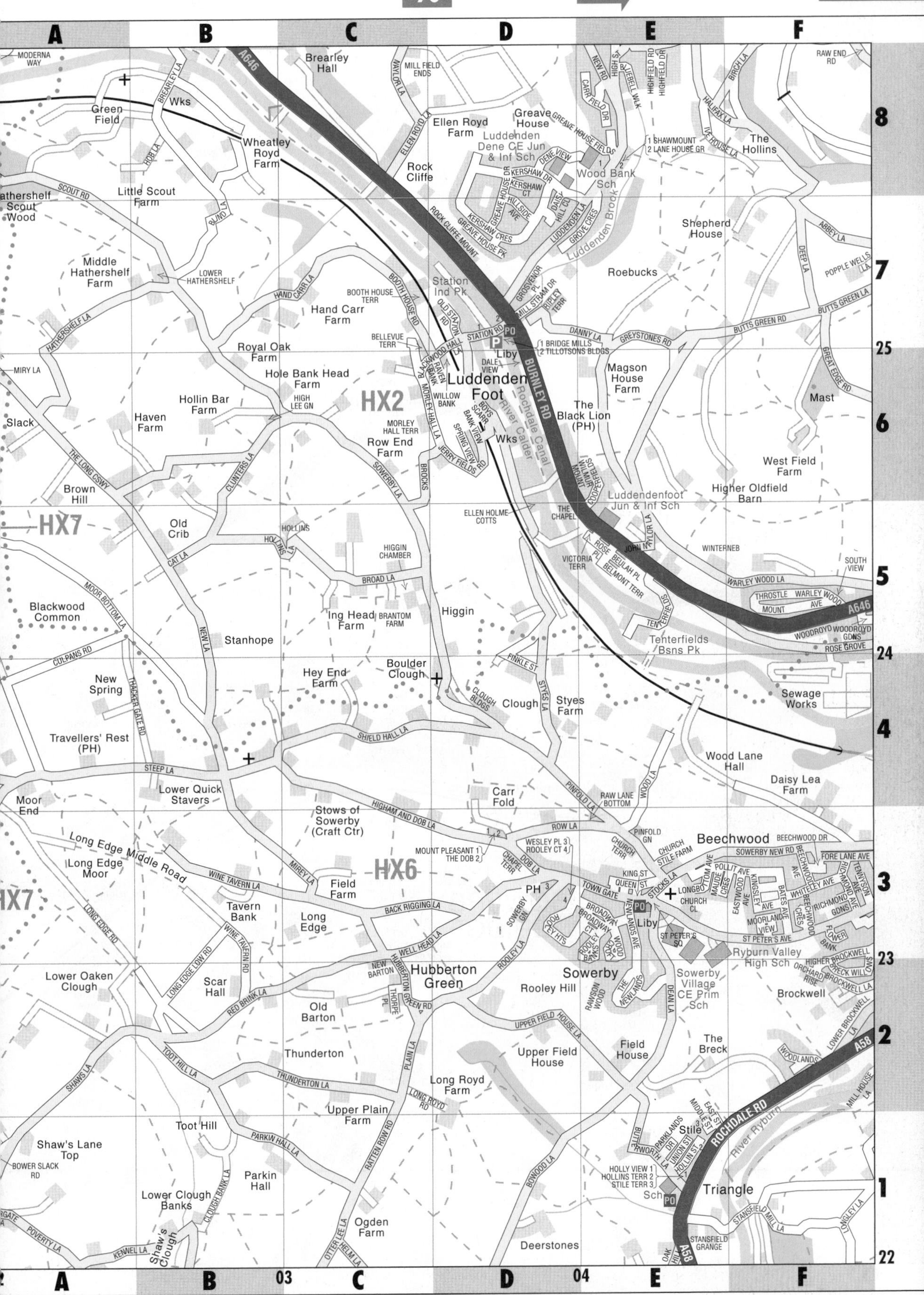
90
112
Brearley Hall
Green Field
Wks
Wheatley Royd Farm
Ellen Royd Farm
Greave House
Luddenden Dene CE Jun & Inf Sch
Wood Bank Sch
The Hollins
Rock Cliffe
Little Scout Farm
Hathershelf Scout Wood
Middle Hathershelf Farm
Shepherd House
Roebucks
Station Ind Pk
Hand Carr Farm
Royal Oak Farm
Hole Bank Head Farm
Luddenden Foot
Magson House Farm
HX2
Hollin Bar Farm
Haven Farm
The Black Lion (PH)
Mast
Slack
Row End Farm
West Field Farm
Higher Oldfield Barn
Brown Hill
Luddendenfoot Jun & Inf Sch
HX7
Old Crib
Blackwood Common
Stanhope
Ing Head Farm
Higgin
Tenterfields Bsns Pk
New Spring
Hey End Farm
Boulder Clough
Clough
Styes Farm
Sewage Works
Travellers' Rest (PH)
Wood Lane Hall
Daisy Lea Farm
Moor End
Lower Quick Stavers
Carr Fold
Stows of Sowerby (Craft Ctr)
Beechwood
Long Edge Moor
Long Edge Middle Road
HX6
Field Farm
Tavern Bank
Long Edge
Hubberton Green
Sowerby
Ryburn Valley High Sch
Sowerby Village CE Prim Sch
Lower Oaken Clough
Scar Hall
Old Barton
Rooley Hill
Brockwell
Thunderton
Upper Field House
Field House
The Breck
Long Royd Farm
Upper Plain Farm
Toot Hill
Stile
Shaw's Lane Top
Parkin Hall
Triangle
Lower Clough Banks
Ogden Farm
Shaw's Clough
Deerstones
BURNLEY RD
ROCHDALE RD
A646
A58
River Calder
Rochdale Canal
River Ryburn
03
04
132
112

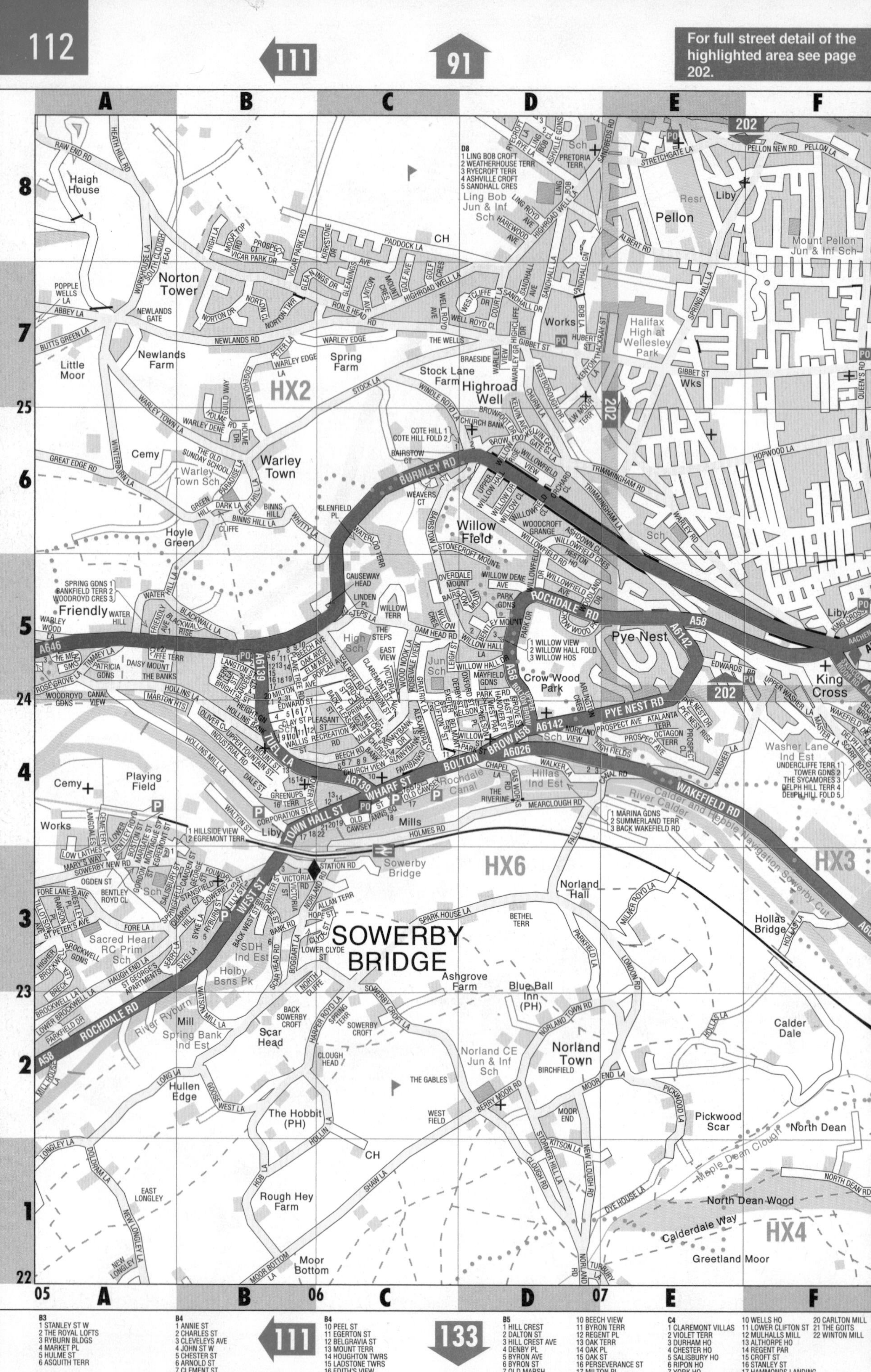

For full street detail of the highlighted area see pages 202 and 203.
92
114
113
A
B
C
D
E
F
202
203
HALIFAX
Birks Hall La
Ind Est
Shroggs Rd
Carriage Dr
Pellon La
Sch
Bsns Ctr
PO
Gibbet St
Cemy
Hopwood La
Princess Mary Ctr
Coll
King Cross St
King Cross Rd
Aachen Way
Haugh Shaw Rd
Savile Park Rd
Arden Rd
Ovenden Rd
Burdock Way
A629
A647 Haley Hill
Lee Bridge
Dean Clough
New Bank
Godley Rd
Godley La A58
Old Godley La
Claremount Rd
Beacon Hill Rd
Charlestown Rd
L Ctr
Liby
TH
Mus
Mkts
Art Ctr
Broad St
Cow Gn
Orange St
Northgate
Winding Rd
King St
Charles St
Horton St
Church St
Square
Fountain St
Ward's End
Portland Pl
Prescott St
Skircoat Rd
Halifax
Eureka! Mus
Bailey Hall Rd
South Par
Water La
Shay Syke
TA Ctr
The Shay Stad
Shaw Hill
Heath Rd
Siddal New Rd
Cemy
Shibden Park
Shibden Hall
Mus
Park Farm
The Russetts
Shibden Hall Rd
Shibden Hall Croft
Beacon Hill Tunnel
Miss Lister's Rd
Barrowclough La
Field House
Beacon Hill
Southowram Bank
Long La
Stub Thorn La
Marsh Delves La
Marsh Delves
Green La
Blaithroyd La
Blaithroyd Ct
Beaconsfield St
Bennett St
Trooper La
High Grove La
Marsh La
Bank Top
1 South Cliffe
2 East Cliffe
3 Merrion St
4 Epsom Gr
Law Hill
Twinge La
Belle Vue Terr
Higgin La
Hill Cres
Broadway
Sun Way
High Field Farm
Southowram
Pit Farm
Pinnar La
Law La
Mast
Free School La
HX1
Savile Park
The Mackintosh Memorial Homes
Regent Ct
Skircoat Moor Rd
Manor Heath
Delph Hill
HX2
Long Wood
The Gleddings Prep Sch
Woodhall Cres
Birdcage Hill
Birdcage La
Longwood Cl
Heath Villas
Heath Gdns
Linden Rd
Clifton Rd
Bath Rd
Knightsbridge Ct
Heathfield Terr
Cheltenham Ct
Mansion La
Heath Royd
Whinney Field
Stafford Ave
Huddersfield Rd
Abbott's Ladies Home
Dryclough La
A646
Liby
The Calderdale Royal
Westbourne Terr
Westbourne Gr
Phoebe La Ind Est
Shaw La
Whitegate
Whitegate Terr
Woodford Ave
Siddal Gr
Rosebery Ave
Longbottom Terr
Cleveland Ave
Browning Ave
Oxford Ct
Siddal View
Keswick Cl
Stoney Royd Terr
HX3
Snydal Farm
Whitegate Top
Coalpit La
Siddal Top La
Siddal Top
Siddal
Siddal La
Mortons Cl
Roselee Cl
Rosemary La
West La
Westfield Gate
Salterhebble
Salterhebble Hill
Backhold Hall
Backhold Dr
Backhold La
The Bungalows
Park La
Change
Change La
Park Nook
Park Gate
Calderdale Way
Exley
Exley Bank
Exley Gdns
Lower Exley
Exley La
Upper Exley
Elland Park Wood
Elland Wood Bottom
HX5
Plains La
Crem
Skircoat Green
Skircoat Green Rd
Green Park Rd
Godfrey Rd
Dudwell La
Dudwell Ave
Dudwell Terr
Works
Bankhouse La
Huddersfield Rd
A6026
B6112
Stainland Rd
Ravenscliffe High Sch
Spring Wood Dr
Spring Wood Ave
Riverwood Dr
Copley
Wakefield Rd
Copley Mill Ho
Railway Terr
Lydbrook Pk
Calder Terr
Springwood Gdns
North Dean Rd
Calder and Hebble Navigation
River Calder
Sewage Works
North Dean Wood (Nature Trail)
North Dean Bsns Pk
Calderdale Way
HX4
Moor Bottom La
Scholes La
Dean Wood View
8
7
25
6
5
24
4
3
23
2
1
22
09
10
134
114
A4
1 STONE CLIFFE
2 ROSE TERR
3 ROCKS VIEW
4 VICTORIA TERR
5 DELPH HILL
6 NORLAND VIEW
7 EASTWOOD CT
B4
1 WARWICK CL
2 RUFFORD PL
3 HEATHERSTONES
4 RUFFORD VILLAS
5 GRANDSMERE PL
6 SECOND AVE
7 MARLBOROUGH AVE
8 AVONDALE PL
9 LEICESTER TERR
10 PARKSIDE
C4
1 HEATHFIELD GR
2 HEATHFIELD PL
3 ELM VIEW
D3
1 SALTERHEBBLE TERR
2 DONCASTER ST
3 BRISTOL ST
4 HILLAS CT
E3
1 ASHGROVE AVE
2 DYSON PL
3 ASHGROVE PL
4 BARKER HO

113
93

A
B
C
D
E
F
8
7
25
6
5
24
4
3
23
2
1
22
11
12
13
A58 LEEDS RD
Lower Brear Farm
Denmark Farm
WOOD LA
BREAK NECK
Fenny Royd Est
HORTON TERR
LANE ENDS TERR
SHIBDEN HALL RD
SHIBDEN GARTH
HALIFAX RD
HALIFAX OLD RD
SHIBDEN HALL CROFT
LANE ENDS GN
WATERGATE
TANHOUSE HILL
STATION RD
A644
DENHOLME GATE RD
Wks
WEST ROYD
LANGLEA TERR
TENNYSON PL
GARDEN FOLD
GARDENER'S SQ
TOWNGATE
WELLCROFT GDNS
COBDEN TERR
SPRINGFIELD ST
SPRINGFIELD TERR
BROOKE GREEN
KIRK LA
BRADLEY CL
THE GROVE
Dominion Ind Pk
ASH
Sch
BRAMLEY LA
CRAIGLANDS
THE AVENUE
HOLLY BANK DR
BRAMLEY FOLD
LEYBURN AVE
UPPER SUTHERLAND RD
FLOWERLANDS
MOUNTFIELDS
BRAMLEY VIEW
SYKE LA
A58
CH
LEEDS RD
SUTHERLAND RD
KNOWLE TOP RD
CECIL AVE
KNOWLE TOP DR
Lightcliffe
1 HAWTHORN ST
2 ROYDLANDS TERR
3 HIGHLAND VILLE
4 ROCK TERR
PO
P
A649
Hipperholme
WAKEFIELD RD
PARK CL
Lydgate
Cliffe Hill Nurseries
Cliffe Hill
A64
WHITEHALL AVE
AMISFIELD RD
THE CRESCENT
ASTRAL AVE
THE DRIVE
ASTRAL CL
GEORGE ST
SANDHOLME CRES
WELBURN AVE
VICTORIA RD
WESTFIELD AVE
WESTFIELD DR
SUNNYSIDE
CRIMBLE CL
PARK VIEW
BROOKELEA
IVY TERR
IVY CRES
HILL TOP
ST GILES RD
Dark La
Lower Place Farm
BADGER LA
UNDERCLIFFE PL
Upper Place Farm
LEES BLDGS 1
GLEN TERR 2
WAVERLEY TERR 3
WAVERLEY CRES 4
SOUTH EDGE TERR 5
BROOKEVILLE AVE 6
SUNNY MOUNT
THE BROWNINGS
BRIGHOUSE RD
1 BROOKLANDS
2 GLAISDALE GR
3 ROYDLANDS ST
4 VICTORIA TERR
5 SANDHOLME FOLD
6 OSBORNE GR
7 WESTFIELD
8 PARK TERR
Factory
NORCLIFFE LA
SUNNY BANK LA
Brow Mills Ind Est
Hipperholme & Lightcliffe High Sch & Sports Coll
COACH RD
Cliffe Hill Com Prim Sch
Sunny Bank Farm
MARSH LA
Upper Lake
SUNNYVALE GDNS
SUTCLIFFE WOOD LA
BROAD OAK LA
BROAD OAK PL
BROAD OAK ST
SOUTH VIEW CT
Lightcliffe Wks
WESTMINSTER RD
Crowhurst
Hipperholme Wks
HX3
LOWER FINKIL ST
CH
NEWTON PK
CATHERINE ST
WALTER CLOUGH LA
BROW COTTS
Red Beck
WARREN PK
WARREN PARK CL
SPOUT HOUSE LA
ADAMS CT
ST GILES CL
GREEN LA
WELL GR
SEFTON DR
SEFTON CRES
Ivy House
Walter Clough Hall
Stony La
CHAPEL ST
HARDY PL
ST CHAD'S AVE
UPPER GREEN LA
WELL GREEN LA
St Joseph's RC Prim Sch
Brighouse High Sch
Hove Edge
LAVEROCK LA
WHITLEY LA
HALF HOUSE LA
SOUTH GR
STUDLEIGH TERR
WOOD TOP
RIDGEWAY GDNS
MARYVILLE AVE
FINKIL ST
Withinfields Prim Sch
Sutcliffe Wood Farm
Lower Clay Royd Farm
BROOKLYN TERR
HALIFAX RD
SMITH HOUSE CRES 1
LAVEROCK CRES 2
HUNTOCK PL 3
LAVEROCK PL 4
PINNAR CROFT
LAW LA
FAIRFAX CRES
FREEMAN RD
CREST VIEW 1
CREST PL 2
YEW PS 3
WITHINFIELDS
WITHINFIELD CT
RUSTIC AVE
Southowram
CROMWELL CT
Barker Royd
Upper Clay Royd Farm
WOOD BOTTOM LA
GRANNY HALL GR 1
GRANNY HALL PK 2
BLACKBURN RD 3
THE COPSE 4
SLEAD AVE
SLEAD CRES
YEW TREES
ADGIL CRES
CROMWELL RD
Pasture House
FAIRBURN
Near Wood Bottom Farm
Slead Syke
SLEAD GR
GRANNY HALL LA
TOWNLEY AVE
Liby
MOUNT PLEASANT
CAIN LA
1 KINGS VIEW
2 QUEENS DR
3 THE PARK TOWNGATE
Malt Shovel Inn (PH)
Cross Platts Farm
COW LA
South Holme La
Wet Shod La
CLOG SOLE RD
SLEAD CT
AUSTIN
MAURICE AVE
COALPIT LA
UPPER BELL CROFT
YEADON DR
CHARLES AVE
ANNE'S CT
NEW ST
CROSS PLATTS
CHURCH LA
MILL HILL LA
WOOD GR
GARDE
CHAPEL LA
SCHOOL LA
CROMWELL VIEW
Dark La
BARRINGTON CL
SOUTH VIEW
GRANGE HTS
GRANGE CT
JERUSALEM SQ
A644
SYCAMORE VIEW
Brookfoot Ind Est
WINTER HILL
HALL INGS
WEST LA
PROVIDENCE BLDGS
Milking Hill
BROOKFOOT LA
Brookfoot Bsns Pk
Wks
WOODLAND DR
RYDINGS WLK
HELEN TERR
MILTON ST
COOKSON ST
ELMWOOD DR
BRIGHOUSE WOOD LA
Wks
ASHDAY LA
Ashday
Cromwell Wood
Calderdale Way
Wood La
Brookfoot
Vine Ind Est
BRIGHOUSE WOOD ROW
HD6
Binns Top
BRIER LA
NORTH CUT
Mills
WOOD LA
ELLAND RD
GROVE COTTS
GROVE TERR
The Lillands
Binns Wood
BINNS TOP LA
Wks
Wks
CROMWELL BOTTOM DR
Cromwell Bottom
LILLANDS LA
LILLANDS TERR
LILLANDS AVE
JUBILEE MOUNT
OAKLANDS
Elland Park Wood
Rawson's Arms (PH)
Calder & Hebble Navigation
River Calder
Reins Wood
CALDER VIEW 1
CLOSES RD 2
LONGROYDE RD 3
CLOSE LEA 4
CLOSE LEA DR 5
CASTLE AVE 6
LONGROYDE CL 7
WOOD CROFT 8
Schs
PARK RD
River Calder
HX5
Low Fields
RIVER BANK WAY
LOCK VIEW
Power Sta
A6025
Sch
FOXCROFT DR
RIDGE LEA
FIELD TOP RD
CLOSE LEA

113
135

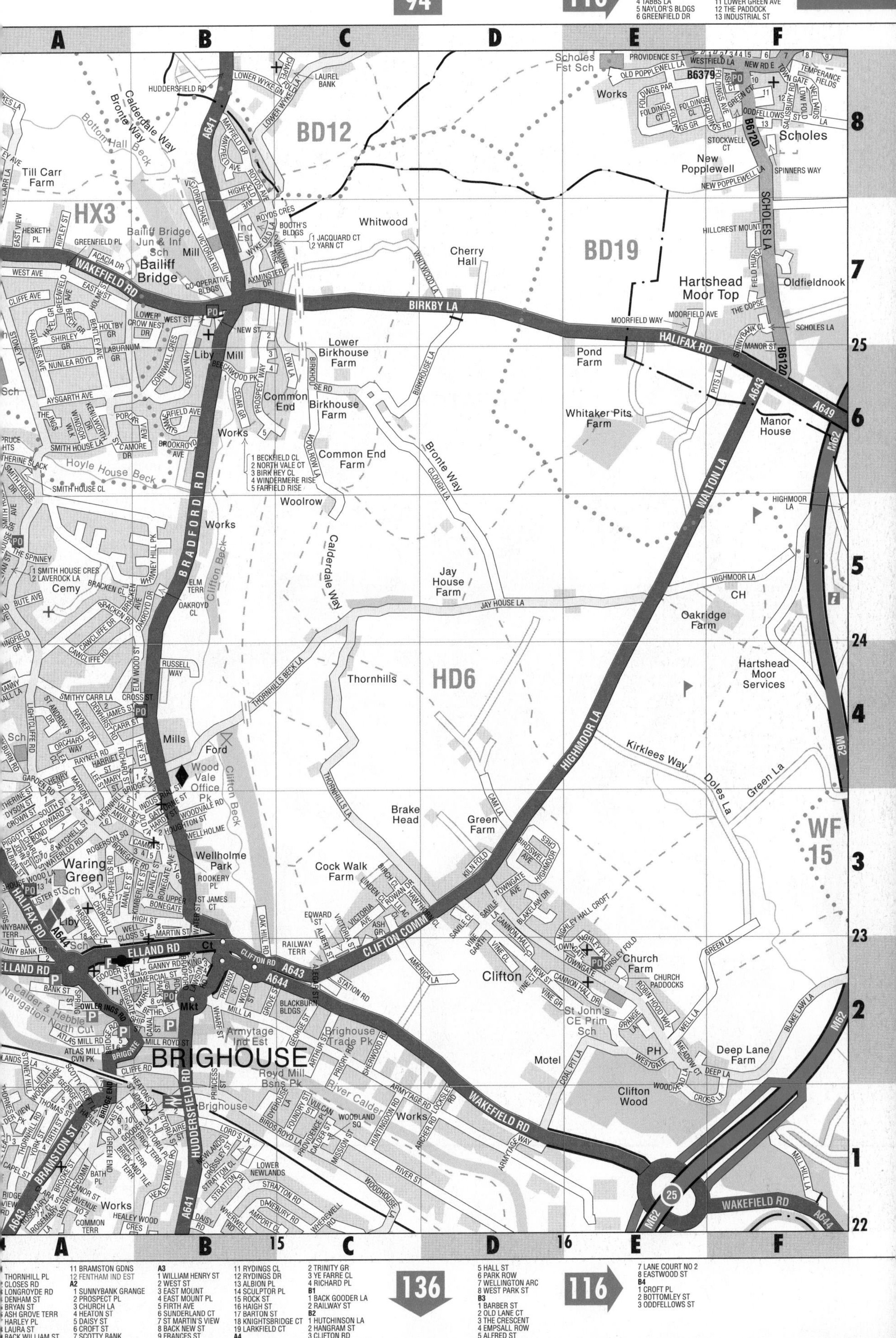

D7
1 CARLTON CL
2 CARLTON WAY
3 GLADSTONE ST
4 BADEN TERR
5 CROSS CROWN ST
6 HOLDSWORTH CT

7 PLATT SQ
8 BUTTS YD
9 OLD ROBIN
D8
1 BEATRICE ST
2 ALICE ST
3 JOHN WILLIAM ST

4 CANARY ST
5 TENNYSON PL
6 LYNTON TERR
7 CROWTHER ST
8 CLAREMONT ST
9 YORK PL
10 WHITFIELD ST

11 CAROLINE ST
12 PROSPECT ST
E7
1 MARKET PL
2 HORNCASTLE ST
3 SPRINGFIELD HOUSE
4 CHURCH GRANGE

5 CENTRAL ARC
6 CENTRAL PAR
7 ST JOHN'S PL
8 CROSS CHURCH ST
9 FAIRFIELD TERR
10 ASHFIELD TERR
11 SUNFIELD TERR

12 MAYFIELD TERR
13 BEECHFIELD TERR
14 WOODHEAD ST
15 PAVEMENT ST
E8
1 COACH LA
2 PROVIDENCE ST

CLECKHEATON

BD19

HD6

WF15

WF14

Whitechapel Middle Sch
Whitcliffe Mount Coll
West End
St Luke's Mid Sch
Hartshead Moor Side
Moorside
Hightown Heights
Upper Blacup
Lower Blacup
Hightown
Lawnbank
Springfield Farm
Rawfolds
Marsh
Mount Pleasant
Fusden Wood
Works
Hartsoil Farm
Hartshead Moor Services
Windy Bank Farm
High Bank Fst Sch
RM Grylls Mid Sch
Hightown Fst Sch
Clough Beck
Lands Beck
Upper House Farm
Soap House
Church Farm
Church Field Farm
Beggerington
Grey Ox Inn (PH)
Kirklees Way
Hartshead Jun & Inf Sch
Hollin Wood
Lawn Wood
Kirklees Hall
Triangle Farm
Bullace Trees Farm
Cemy
Moorside
Pogg Myres
Church Farm
Roberttown
Roberttown CE Jnr & Inf Sch
Little Thorpe
New Inn (PH)
Hartshead
Dockentail Wood
Spen Valley Heritage Trail
Grove Cottage
Taylor Hall

WHITECHAPEL RD
WHITCLIFFE RD
WESTGATE
MOORSIDE
MOOR BOTTOM
HALIFAX RD
BRADFORD RD
DEWSBURY RD
ST PEG LA
SPEN BANK
SPEN LA
WINDY BANK LA
PEEP GREEN RD
BRONTE WAY
FALL LA
B6120
B6119
A649
A643
M62
A62
A638

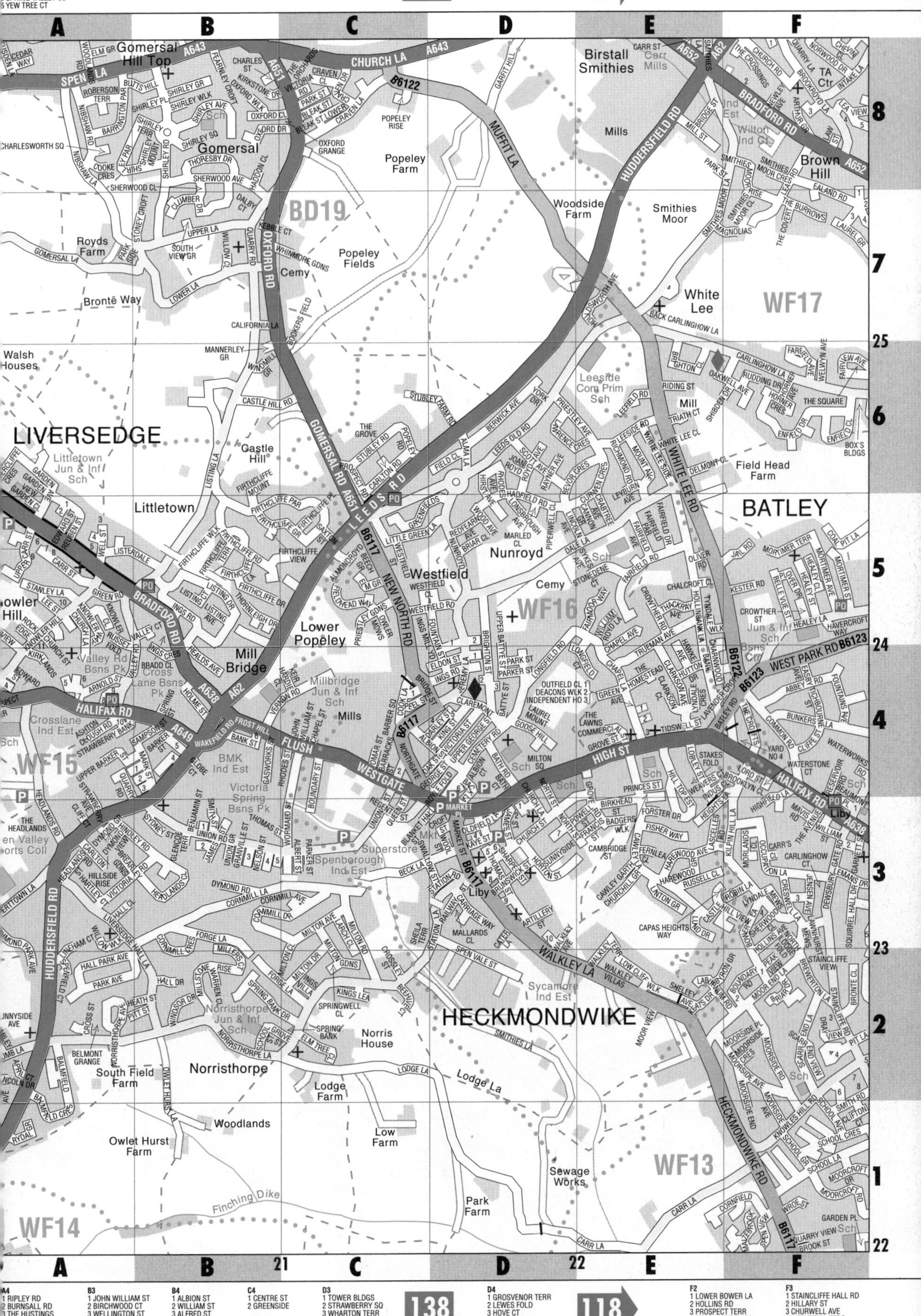

96
118

138
118

117
97

C5
1 CHURCHFIELD ST
2 HENRIETTA ST
3 BK HENRIETTA ST
4 BK PROVIDENCE ST
5 MARKET SQ
6 MARKET PL
7 BRUNSWICK ST
8 HUME CREST
9 COBDEN CL
10 BAYLDONS PL
11 WARDS HILL CT

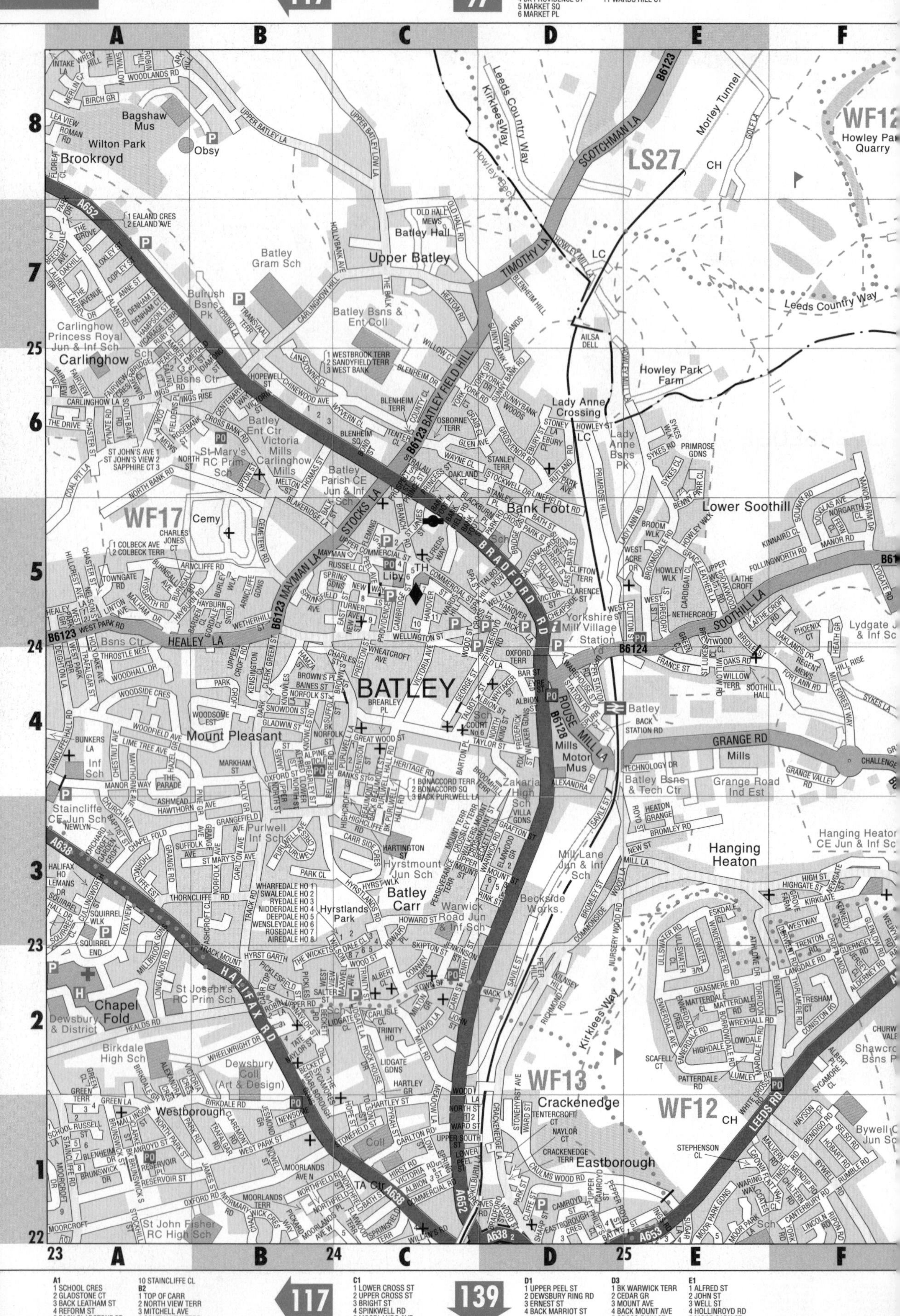

117
139

A1
1 SCHOOL CRES
2 GLADSTONE CT
3 BACK LEATHAM ST
4 REFORM ST
5 BACK GLADSTONE ST
6 HANOVER CT
7 FAIRFIELD MEWS
8 FAIRFIELD CRES
9 FIR BANK
10 STAINCLIFFE CL

B2
1 TOP OF CARR
2 NORTH VIEW TERR
3 MITCHELL AVE
4 SOUTH VIEW TERR
5 MARLBRO' TERR

C1
1 LOWER CROSS ST
2 UPPER CROSS ST
3 BRIGHT ST
4 SPINKWELL RD
5 MOORLANDS AVE

D1
1 UPPER PEEL ST
2 DEWSBURY RING RD
3 ERNEST ST
4 BACK MARRIOT ST

D3
1 BK WARWICK TERR
2 CEDAR GR
3 MOUNT AVE
4 BACK MOUNT AVE
5 CROSS RINK ST
6 RINK TERR
7 RINK PAR

E1
1 ALFRED ST
2 JOHN ST
3 WELL ST
4 HOLLINROYD RD
5 MOOR PARK CT

98
120

A
B
C
D
E
F
M62
Woodkirk High Specialist Science Sch
Howley Park Brick Works
LS27
Howley Park Quarry Farm
Leeds Country Way
QUARRY LA
Woodkirk Int Freight Terminal
WF17
Manor Farm
SOOTHILL LA
B6124
Croft House Farm
Soothill Manor
LEEDS RD
WF12
Grange Farm
Lees House Farm
SYKES LA
GRANGE RD
CHALLENGE WAY
Shaw Cross Inf Sch
Chidswell
1 CHIDSWELL GDNS
2 FIELDHEAD GDNS
3 WINDSOR GDNS
4 SMALLWOOD GDNS
5 HILLESLEY RD
6 MANOR GDNS
7 JOHN ORMSBY V C WAY
CHIDSWELL LA
MANOR PK
OWL LA
WINDSOR RD
The Huntsman (PH)
FLAGSHIP SQ
WINDSOR CT
Shawcross Bsns Pk
Shaw Cross
Tower
HALL CL
Savile Pit La
DEWSBURY RD
REIN RD
A6029
A653
SCARBOROUGH ST 1
SCARBOROUGH LA 2
TURNBERRY DR 3
TURNBERRY CL 4
SYKE TERR
Woodkirk
Baghill
ARMITAGE BLDGS
Scargill Wood
HEYBECK LA
Dum Wood
Hey Beck
SCHOOL ST
WOODLAND VIEW
PH
Upper Green
West Ardsley
Beggarington Hill
Westerton Prim Sch
FAIRFIELD AVE
WESTERTON RD
1 LONGWOOD FOLD
2 LONGWOOD GARTH
3 HEATHERDALE CT
4 POPPLETON RD
5 POPPLETON WAY
6 POPPLETON RISE
7 FOLLY HALL MOUNT
Westerton
WF3
8 BLACKGATES CT
9 BLACKGATES RISE
10 BLACKGATES FOLD
11 LEIGH VIEW
12 FAIRLEIGH CRES
13 CRABTREE WAY
14 HEATHFIELD CL
Blackgates Prim Sch
A650
BRADFORD RD
Nook Farm
Ardsley Resr
Boyle Hall Farm
Haigh Moor
Hill Top Prim Sch
Common Side
BATLEY RD
Haigh Hall Spring Wood
Haigh Hall Farm
WF2
Dogloitch Wood
Red Lodge
WF5
Lower Park Farm
New Park Grange
Gawthorpe La
GAWTHORPE LA
Highfield Sch
Gawthorpe
Sch
A638
B6128
Tufty Farm
8
7
25
6
5
24
4
3
23
2
1
22
27
28

140
120

119
99

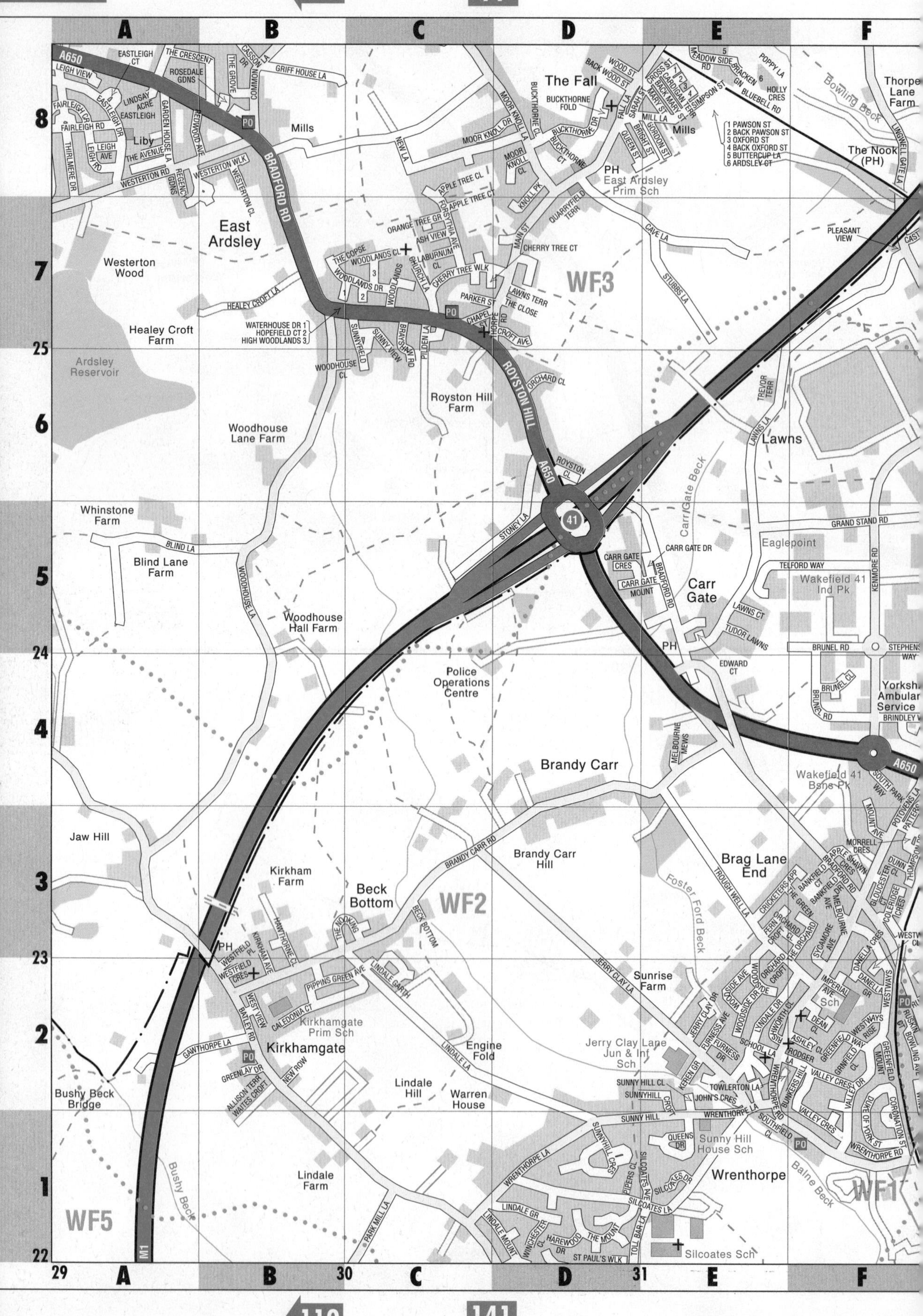
East Ardsley
Westerton Wood
Healey Croft Farm
Ardsley Reservoir
Liby
Mills
The Fall
Thorpe Lane Farm
The Nook (PH)
East Ardsley Prim Sch
WF3
Royston Hill Farm
Woodhouse Lane Farm
Whinstone Farm
Blind Lane Farm
Woodhouse Hall Farm
Lawns
Eaglepoint
Wakefield 41 Ind Pk
Carr Gate
Police Operations Centre
Brandy Carr
Wakefield 41 Bsns Pk
Jaw Hill
Kirkham Farm
Beck Bottom
WF2
Brandy Carr Hill
Brag Lane End
Sunrise Farm
Kirkhamgate
Kirkhamgate Prim Sch
Engine Fold
Jerry Clay Lane Jun & Inf Sch
Bushy Beck Bridge
Lindale Hill
Warren House
Sunny Hill House Sch
Lindale Farm
Wrenthorpe
WF1
WF5
Silcoates Sch
A650
M1
BRADFORD RD
ROYSTON HILL
1 PAWSON ST
2 BACK PAWSON ST
3 OXFORD ST
4 BACK OXFORD ST
5 BUTTERCUP LA
6 ARDSLEY CT
WATERHOUSE DR 1
HOPEFIELD CT 2
HIGH WOODLANDS 3

119
141

100
122

A B C D E F

M1
M62
CASTLE HEAD CL
WESTGATE CT
A61
CHURCH CROFT
CHURCH FARM CL
B6135 OUZLEWELL GN
M62
B6135
Castle Head Farm
Westgate
BROADLAND WAY
WESTGATE GR
WESTGATE CL
WESTGATE LA
VALENTINE MEWS
CASTLE HEAD LA
CASTLE GATE
PREMIER WAY
PATRICK GN
CONEY WARREN LA
8
THE POPLARS
SHOP LA
Langley
WESTGATE LA
ACRES RD
PH
LS26
WOODSIDE VIEW
LEE BECK GR
LEE MOOR LA
MOORLAND PL
LINGWELL NOOK LA
Lingwell Gate
Lingwell Gate Beck
Lofthouse Hill
Lee Moor
COMMON RD
FENTON RD
7
Springfield Farm
WF3
PARK DR
Stanley Arms (PH)
HIGH BROOK FALL
PARK AVE
25
JOHNS AVE
LEEDS RD
PARK SQ
Lofthouse Gate
MOOR RD
MOOR GR
MOOR AVE
LEE MOOR RD
VIRGINIA CL
VIRGINIA GDNS
VIRGINIA DR
MOORE RD
LINGWELL GATE LA
Lee Moor
ROGERS CT
PHILIP'S GR
PARK VIEW
Canal Hill
6
RIDINGS MEWS
CONISTON CT
LINGWELL NOOK LA
MILLCROFT CL
MILLCROFT RISE
1 CONSTABLE GR
2 TENNYSON AVE
3 SHELLEY WLK
PRIORY MEWS
Lee Mount
RIDINGS GDNS
RIDINGS LA
RHODES GDNS
LINGWELL CHASE
POTOVENS CT
Lofthouse Gate Prim Sch
BLACK CARR LODGE
RIDINGS WAY
OAKDALE CL
RIDINGS CT
PARTONS PL
CANAL LA
STANMOOR DR
HAYDN AVE
BYRON GR
CHAUCER AVE
LONGFELLOW GR
CANAL WLK
MOUNT RD
GDNS WALLACE
POTTERS CROFT
MILTON CT
LAKE LOCK DR
Wakefield 41 Ind Pk
COLLIERY APP
WINDEN CL
POLLARD ST
POPLAR ST
WOOLFORD WAY
ELGAR WLK
KENTS GR
CROXALL DR
FIRTH CT
GAINSBOROUGH WAY
Stanley Lane Ends
GRAND STAND RD
Outwood
GATEWAYS
QUEENSBURY AVE
SHERIDAN ST
CANAL CT
LANGDALE AVE
SAMUEL DR
WORDSWORTH GR
Sch
BINGHAM PL
CHANDLERS CL
WINDEN GR
THE HAWTHORNS
MICHAEL AVE
RAE CT
NEWLANDS DR
HARGREAVES AV
NOOK RD
LONG CSWY
Liby
WF2
RAILWAY TERR
LINGWELL GATE CRES
CLAYTON RISE
CHARLES AVE
EDWARD DR
HOLLY CT
BELFRY CT
ANAHEIM DR
HAZELWOOD RD
MEADOWCROFT
BAKER LA
NEWLANDS WLK
CHAPEL ST
LAKE LOCK RD
CHURCH RD
LINGWELL GATE DR
RYECROFT CL
BROADMEADOWS
MEADOW CROFT
NEWLANDS
STONECROFT
LANE ENDS VIEW
INTAKE LA
MARSHALL ST
BEAUMONT RD
BEAUMONT CL
5
BRAMBLE CT
POTOVENS LA
KINGSLEY AVE
NEW CRES
GEORGE ST
PHILIP GARTH
MEADOW GARTH
MEADOW CL
WHISPERWOOD RD
RUSHWORTH GR
BARDWELL CT
AYNDALE DR
ORCHARD SHIRES GR
ASHBURY CHASE
SPRINGHILL CL
KINGSLEY GARTH
KINGSLEY CL
CHURCH LA
VICARAGE CL
ROYDS GR
BEVIN CL
BEVIN CRES
MOUNTBATTEN CRES
MEADOW VALE
BRACKENWOOD CT
HEATHER CT
THISTLEWOOD RD
AUTY MEWS
AUTY CRES
INTAKE CL
A642
STEPHENSON WAY
SPRINGHILLS
MOUNTBATTEN AVE
RINGWOOD CT
HAZELWOOD CT
NEWSTEAD AVE
PO
MONKWOOD RD
CHURCH LANE AVE
LEEDS RD
MOXON WAY
BINKS ST
COACH RD
BRIARWOOD CL
ATTLEE GR
GRANGEWOOD CT
ROOK'S NEST RD
1 MEADOWCROFT CT
2 BRACKENWOOD CT
3 WHISPERWOOD CL
CLIFTON AVE
ASH CRES
ELM AVE
24
Outwood
MOXON ST
MOUNTBATTEN GR
LEDGER LA
Ledger Lane Sch
Cemy
COBHAM PAR
KINGSWELL AVE
Stanley
BEECH AVE
OAK AVE
LIME PIT LA
Robin Hood Bridge
LEDGER PL
JUBILEE CRES
JUBILEE AVE
OAK ST
STANLEY LA
WATER LA
Outwood Grange Coll of Tech
THE AVENUE
ANNIE ST
PRINCESS ST
QUEEN ST
4
BOLUS LA
BOLUS CL
Rook's Nest Jun & Inf Sch
SPA FOLD
ELSTONE VIEW
OUTWOOD PARK CT
BRAMLEY CRES
NEWTON CT
WILSON DR
WILSON CT
MARGARET ST
VICTORIA ST
Liby
OUCHTHORPE FOLD
Stanley Marsh Nature Reserve
PARK AVE
KING GEORGE ST
NEWTON LA
QUEEN ELIZABETH ST
VICTORIA WAY
VICTORIA APP
NEWTON DR
Hatfeild Hall
Stanley Grove Prim Sch
GREY CL
GREY ST
3
BARNES AVE
GREY CT
FARN CT
Ouchthorpe Farm
Leeds Country Way
RUSKIN AVE
HEDLEY CRES
WILLOW GN
LYNTON GR
SILVER ST
MONTCALM CRES
WESLEY HALL CT
ABERFORD RD
ASH LEA
23
Newton Hill
WILLOW PK
SECOND AVE
FINKIN LA
FWKIN AVE
FINKIN CROFT
ASH GR
ASH ST
RIVERDALE GR
KINGSWAY
FERRY LA
WF1
THIRD AVE
CLARKE HALL RD
RIVERDALE RD
OUCHTHORPE LA
Snow Hill
Paragon Bsns Village
RED HALL AVE
FIRST AVE
FOURTH AVE
Field Head
BALK CRES
2
PARAGON AVE
RIVERDALE AVE
BROOM HALL AVE
Newton Hill Jun & Inf Sch
HATFIELD VIEW
PARKSIDE LA
BROOM HALL CRES
RED HALL CT
HERRIOT WAY
NEWTON AVE
EAST ST
RIVERDALE CRES 1
RIVERDALE DR 2
ST SWITHINS GR 3
ST SWITHINS CT 4
ST SWITHINS DR 5
Red Hall
Fieldhead
RED HALL LA
1 WINDSOR CRES
2 WRENTHORPE RD
H
RED HALL LA
BOUNDARY DR
WICKET DR
Stanley Hall
SNOW HILL CL
THE OVAL
BRADFORD RD
SNOW HILL RISE
NEWTON GN
SPINNERS AVE
BAR LA
HALDANE CRES 1
BIRCHTREE CL 2
FOUNTAINS WAY
1
WHITEHALL AVE
Pinders Fields
NEWTON CL
NEWTON GDNS
1 TRENT BRIDGE WAY
2 PAVILION WAY
3 BOWLERS CT
LONG CSWY
H
CLARKE HALL FARM
GLASTONBURY AVE
CLARKE GR
BARNSTONE VALE
FOREST CL
HALDANE CRES
WHITEGATES CL
A650
FOX LA
WHITEHALL CRES
A61
HEADINGLEY MEWS
WESTFIELD VIEW
Pinderfields General
A642
Clark Hall
BARLEYCORN
22

A B 33 C D 34 E F

142
122

A
B
C
D
E
F
SANDERSON LA
M62
30
Hungate
HUNGATE LA
Scholey Hill
B6135
8
Patrick Green
CASTLE GATE
SANDERSON LA
Royds Hall Riding Sch
A642
LS26
Savile Park Farm
NEWMARKET LA
CASTLE GATE
Methley Lanes
7
West Farm
West Hall Farm
MOORHOUSE VIEW
MOORHOUSE TERR
SCARTH TERR
CHARLESWORTH PL
MOORHOUSE GR
MOORHOUSE CL
MOORHOUSE AVE
Trans Pennine Trail
Leeds Country Way
25
Roman Station Farm
Kingsland Prim Sch
MEADOWFIELD RISE
ST PETER'S CRES
BOTTOM BOAT RD
6
HOLMFIELD CHASE
NETTLETON ST
BARKER ST
PO
Lake Lock
THE CHASE
ABERFORD RD
Bottom Boat
Old Canal
WF3
KINGS RD
Altofts Ings
LOCK DR
LAKE
LAKE LOCK RD
LAKE YD
River Calder
King's Road Lock
FOXHOLES LA
A642
LAKE LOCK GR
5
Aire and Calder Navigation
Birkwood Lock
FERNLEY HILL DR
ROSE FARM CL
HIGHGROVE CT 1
HEY'S BLDGS 2
SILKSTONE CT 3
24
ROSE FARM APP
ROSE FARM MWS
ROSE FARM RISE
TEMPLE GDNS
KING ST
Sewage Works
Cemy
HILLCREST
4
Birkwood Farm
WF6
HASTINGS GR
BOSWORTH AVE
Liby
CHURCH RD
PRIORY CL
BANNOCKBURN WAY
MARSTON WLK
AGINCOURT DR
FREESTONE WAY
CHURCH FARM CL
OAKWOOD DR
OAKWOOD CL
THE CRESCENT
CHURCHFIELD CROFT
ST MARY'S AVE
LAWNS VIEW
LAWNS CL
PARKER AVE
Martin Frobisher Inf Sch
Top Farm
ILLINGWORTH AVE
CORONATION AVE
MARTIN FROBISHER DR
WOOD CL
YORK ST
Altofts
ST MARY'S RD
BIRKWOOD RD
GARFORTH DR
FAIRFIELD AVE
HIGH GREEN RD
EAST VIEW
BROOK ST
LEE BRIG
3
Hilltop Farm
GARFORTH CL
ALTOFTS LODGE DR
PO
GEORGE ST
STATION RD
Lee Brigg Inf Sch
PATIENCE LA
DRURY LA
LODGE FARM GDNS
HIGH ST
CALVERLEY GREEN RD
CROFT AVE
HANBY AVE
Altofts Jun Sch
Birkwood Plantation
The Ship Inn (PH)
ST SWITHINS DR
23
FERRY LA
GARDEN ST
GREENBANK RD
NEWLAND VIEW
GREENBANK GR
Stanley Ferry
WARD LA
VICTORIA
BALK LA
BALK CRES
BALK AVE
EAST ST
Ramsdens Bridge
AIRE AND CALDER COTTS
2
Newland Park
NEWLAND LA
St John's Field
Altofts Brickworks
Trans Pennine Trail
NEWLAND LA
Newland Hall
1
WF1
PARK
LODGE LA
22
35
36
37

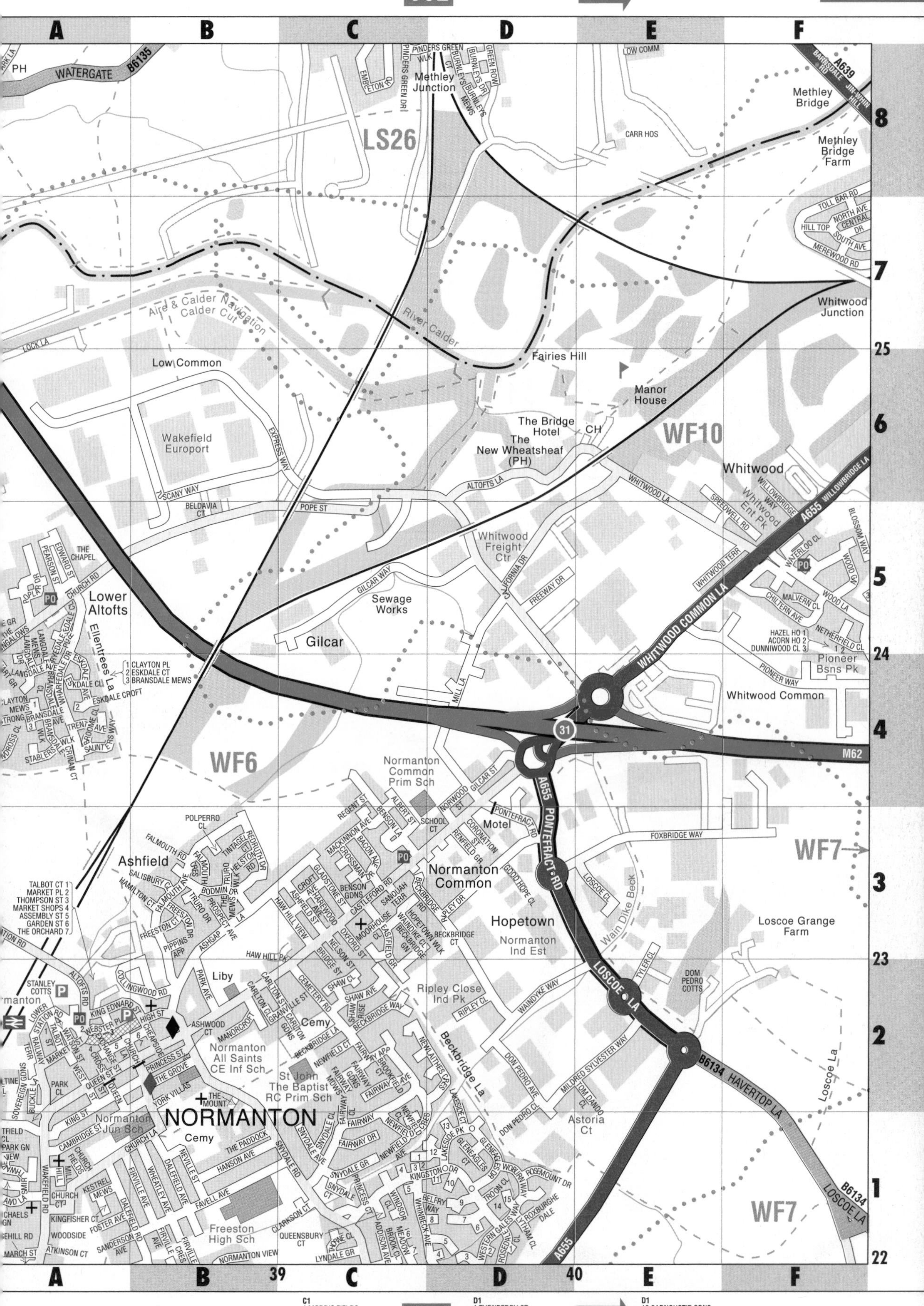

CASTLEFORD (LAGENTIVM)

WF10

WF6

WF7

WF8

North Featherstone

Glass Houghton

Half Acres

Cutsyke

Hightown

Whitwood Mere

The Island

River Calder

River Calder (old course)

Raglan Ind Est

Savile Prec

Liby & Mus

Wheldon Inf Sch

The Maltins

Castleford High Sch (Tech Coll)

Queen's Park

Civic Ctr

Glasshoughton Inf Sch

Three Lane Ends Com Prim Sch

Methley Road Ind Pk

Bsns Ctr

Bretton Hall Coll (Annexe)

Castleford Normanton & District (General)

Wakefield Coll (Whitwood Ctr)

Round Hill

Ackton Bridge

Ackton Pasture

Netherfield Farm

Ackton Pasture Wood

Wood House Farm

Low Laithe Farm

Mickle Hill

Spoil Heap

Glass Houghton

Xscape

Freeport

Sterling Ind Pk

Carr Wood Ind Est

Race Course

Mast

Park Farm

Park Grange Farm

Cemy

Parkfield Farm

St Wilfrid's RC High Sch

Quarry Plantation

Ackton Hall Farm

All Saints CE Jun & Inf Sch

Wr Twr

M62

Four Lane Ends

Leeds Barnsdale Rd

Methley Rd

Lumley St

High St

Aketon Rd

Cutsyke Rd

Castleford La

Willow La

Ackton La

Park La

Colorado Way

Pontefract Rd

Leeds Rd

Front St

A6032 A655 A6539 A656 B6134 B6421

D1
1 CROSSTHWAITE CT
2 SPINK HO
3 CASTLE GR
4 MICKLEGATE SQ
5 ROBINSON ST
6 HARROP WELL LA
7 HORSE FAIR FLATS
8 RICHMOND TERR
9 RICHMOND AVE

D1
10 RICHMOND CT
11 JUBILEE GDNS
12 NORTHLAND VIEW
13 BAILEYGATE CT
14 PIPER HO

F1
1 WHITEBEAM GN
2 HORNBEAM GN
3 ACACIA GN
4 CHESTNUT GN
F3
1 QUEENSWAY PL

125
105

A
B
C
D
E
F
WF10
Brotherton
Hotel
1 QUEEN MARGARETS CL
2 QUEEN MARGARETS AVE
3 CROMWELL CL
4 SUMMERFIELD CL
Husseydales
BYRAM PARK RD
Ferrybridge Power Station
Byram
Sutton
Hall Farm
Village Farm
DISH HILL FLY-OVER
Cooling Towers
Marsh Drain
Ferrybridge
Brotherton Marsh
WF11
River Aire
Aire and Calder Navigation
THE SQUARE
1 STATION RD
2 BROUGHTONS YD
3 DONCASTER SQ
4 CLAYFIELD BGLWS
5 CORONATION BGLWS
STRANGLANDS LA
FERRYBRIDGE BY-PASS
Ferrybridge Workspace
Ferrybridge Bsns Pk
Roundhill Jun Sch
Ferrybridge Inf Sch
Cemy
North Court Ind Est
FISHERGATE
FERRYBRIDGE RD
HILL TOP
Clifton Forge Bsns Pk
Superstore
Liby
Myson Chair
The Vale Jun & Inf Sch
Ferrybridge Hill
Knottingley
PONTEFRACT RD
Works
WF8
A1 Bsns Pk
Pear Tree Farm
Simpson's Lane Jun & Inf Sch
KNOTTINGLEY RD
Longbull Hill
Shilling Hill
Long Dales
Ferrybridge Services
Motel
Doveroyd House
Throstle Farm Jun & Inf Sch
Crow Crowns
Mast
Cattlelaith
Holy Family & St Michaels RC Prim Sch
Cobbler's Lane Prim Sch
Greavefield Closes
M62
A1(M)
A1
A1246
A162
A645
B6136
8
7
25
6
5
24
4
3
23
2
1
22
47
48
49

125
147

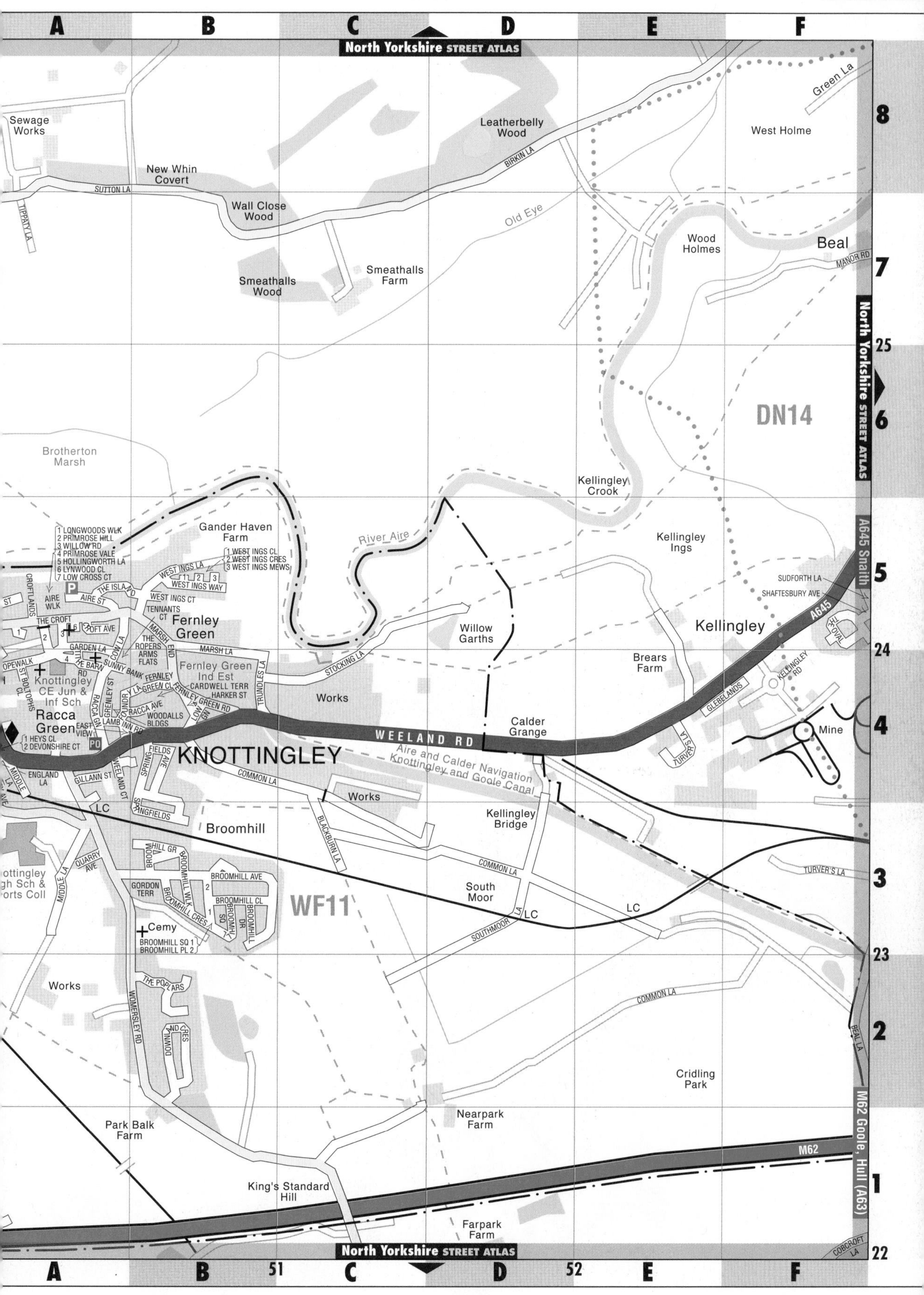

8

Sewage
Works

New Whin
Covert

Leatherbelly
Wood

West Holme

Green La

TIPPETY LA

SUTTON LA

Wall Close
Wood

Smeathalls
Wood

Smeathalls
Farm

Old Eye

BIRKIN LA

Wood
Holmes

Beal

MANOR RD

7

North Yorkshire STREET ATLAS

25

DN14

6

Brotherton
Marsh

Gander Haven
Farm

River Aire

Kellingley
Crook

Kellingley
Ings

A645 Snaith

1 LONGWOODS WLK
2 PRIMROSE HILL
3 WILLOW RD
4 PRIMROSE VALE
5 HOLLINGWORTH LA
6 LYNWOOD CL
7 LOW CROSS CT

CROFTLANDS

P

WEST INGS LA
THE ISLA RD
WEST INGS WAY

1 WEST INGS CL
2 WEST INGS CRES
3 WEST INGS MEWS

1 2 3

SUDFORTH LA
SHAFTESBURY AVE

A645

5

Aire
WLK

AIRE ST

WEST INGS CT

Kellingley
Ings

Kellingley

CHY CHY

KELLINGLEY RD

THE CROFT

CROFT AVE

Fernley
Green

MARSH LA

STOCKING LA

Willow
Garths

Brears
Farm

GLEBELANDS

24

OPEWALK

GARDEN LA

THE BARN

SUNNY BANK

Knottingley
CE Jun &
Inf Sch

Racca
Green

GREENLEY ST

THE
ROPERS
ARMS
FLATS

FERNLEY
FERNLEY LA

RACCA AVE

LAMB INN RD

Fernley Green
Ind Est

CARDWELL TERR
HARKER ST
FERNLEY GREEN RD

WOODALLS
BLDGS

TRUNDLES LA

Works

Calder
Grange

Mine

TURVERS LA

4

1 HEYS CL
2 DEVONSHIRE CT

PO

KNOTTINGLEY

WEELAND RD

Aire and Calder Navigation
Knottingley and Goole Canal

Kellingley
Bridge

VISTA

ENGLAND LA

GILLANN ST

SPRING
FIELDS

SPRINGFIELDS

COMMON LA

Works

Kellingley
Bridge

COMMON LA

LC

LC

3

ottingley
gh Sch &
orts Coll

MIDDLE LA

QUARRY AVE

LC

Broomhill

BLACKBURN LA

South
Moor

SOUTHMOOR

LC

WF11

HILL GR

BROOMHILL WAY
BROOMHILL CRES

GORDON
TERR

BROOMHILL AVE

BROOMHILL SQ

BROOMHILL CL

BROOMHILL
DR

23

Cemy

BROOMHILL SQ 1
BROOMHILL PL 2

Works

WOMERSLEY RD

THE POPLARS

COMMON LA

2

WOMD
CRES

Cridling
Park

BEAL LA

M62 Goole, Hull (A63)

Park Balk
Farm

Nearpark
Farm

M62

1

King's Standard
Hill

Farpark
Farm

COBCROFT
LA

22

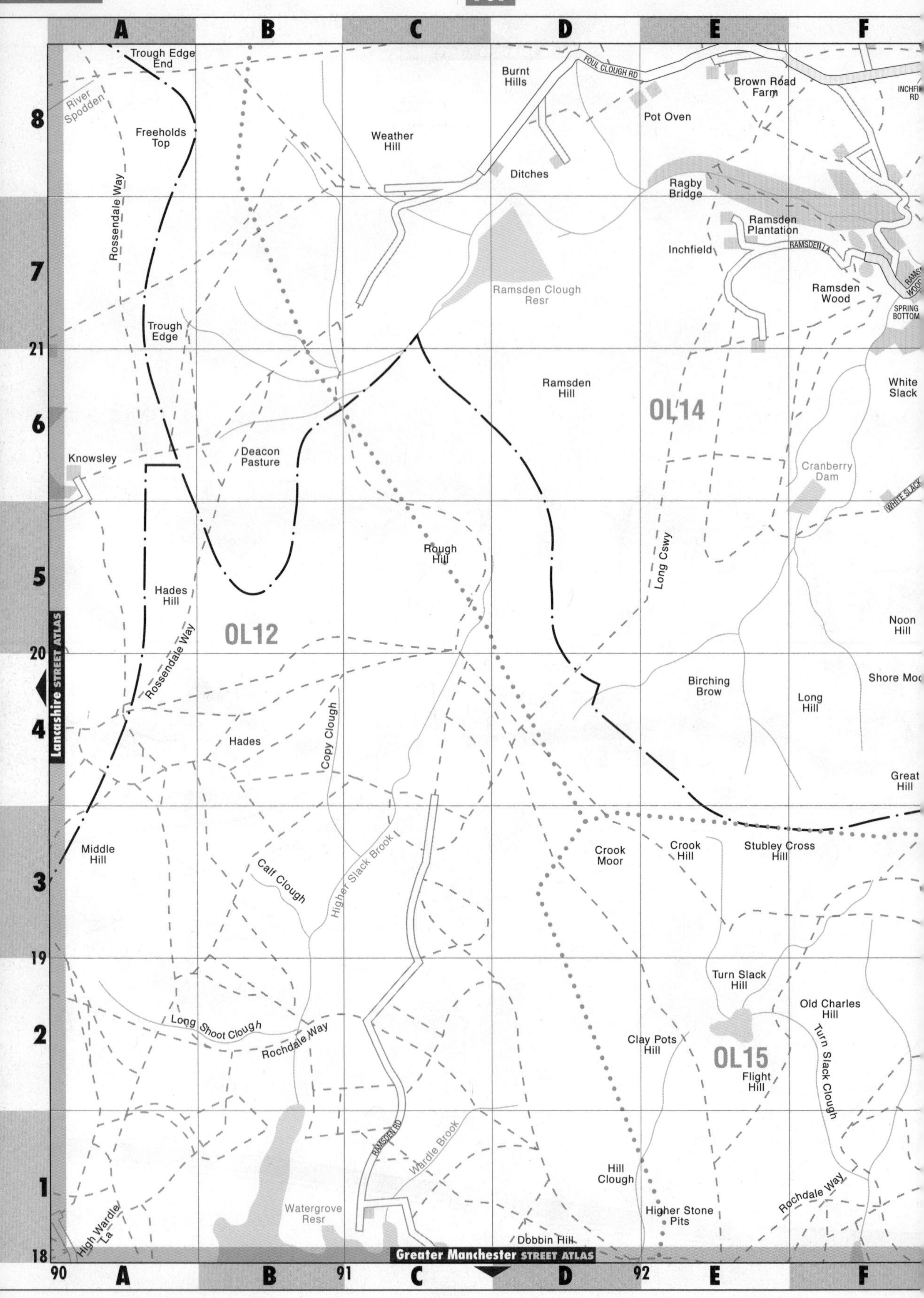

A **B** **C** **D** **E** **F**

Trough Edge
End

River
Spodden

Freeholds
Top

8

Rossendale Way

Burnt
Hills

FOUL CLOUGH RD

Brown Road
Farm

INCHFI
RD

Weather
Hill

Pot Oven

Ditches

Ragby
Bridge

Ramsden
Plantation

RAMSDEN LA

7

Inchfield

Ramsden Clough
Resr

Ramsden
Wood

SPRING
BOTTOM

21

Trough
Edge

Ramsden
Hill

OL14

White
Slack

6

Knowsley

Deacon
Pasture

Cranberry
Dam

WHITE SLACK

Rough
Hill

Long Cswy

Hades
Hill

OL12

Rossendale Way

5

Noon
Hill

Shore Moo

20

Copy Clough

Birching
Brow

Long
Hill

4

Hades

Great
Hill

Middle
Hill

Calf Clough

Higher Slack Brook

Crook
Moor

Crook
Hill

Stubley Cross
Hill

3

19

Turn Slack
Hill

Old Charles
Hill

Long Shoot Clough

Rochdale Way

2

Clay Pots
Hill

OL15

Flight
Hill

Turn Slack Clough

RAMSDEN RD

Wardle Brook

Hill
Clough

Rochdale Way

1

High Wardle
La

Watergrove
Resr

Higher Stone
Pits

18

Dobbin Hill

90 **A** **B** **91** **C** **D** **92** **E** **F**

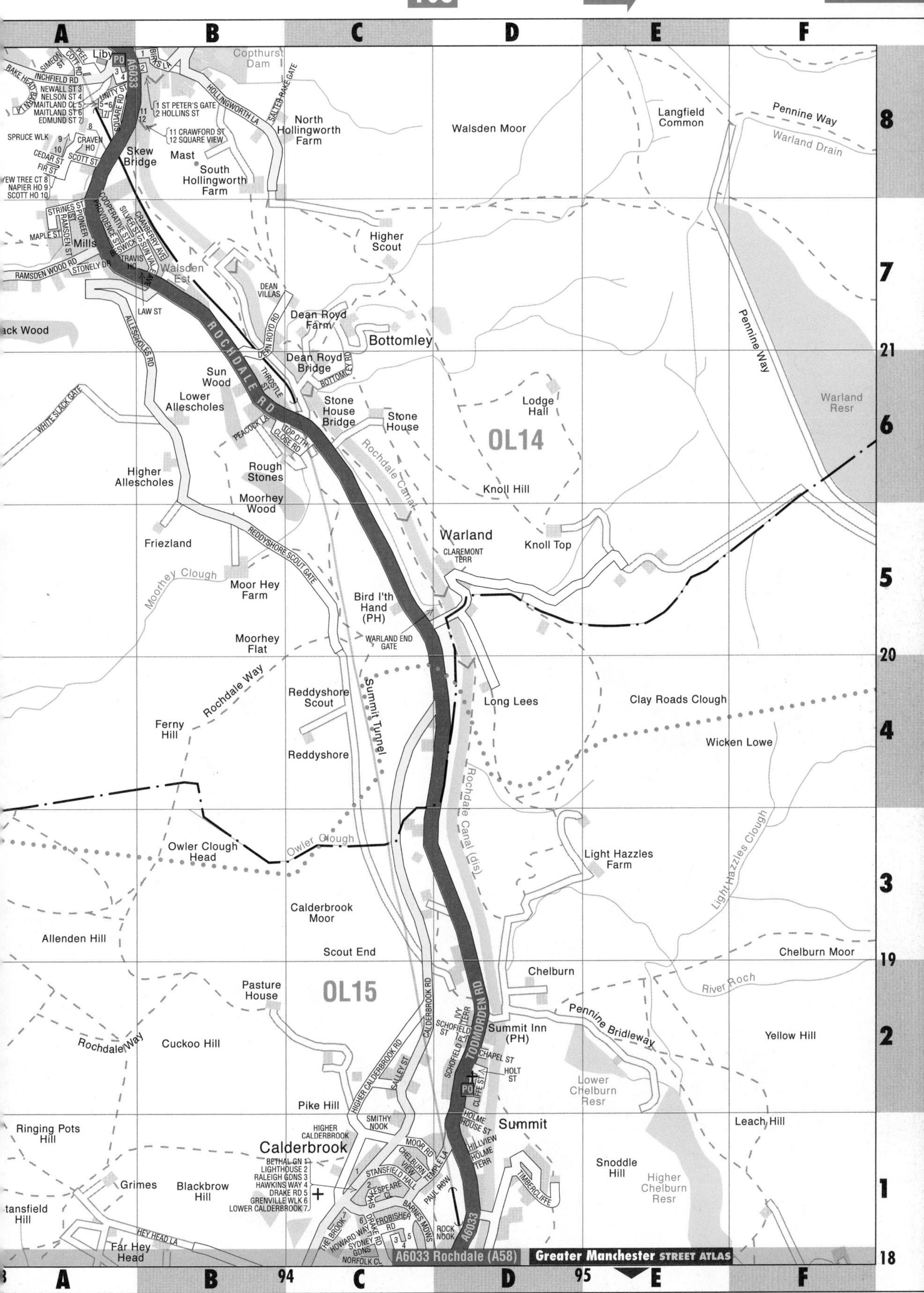

A6033 Rochdale (A58) **Greater Manchester** STREET ATLAS

129
109

A
B
C
D
E
F
8
7
21
6
5
20
4
3
19
2
1
18
96
97
98
Pennine Way
Warland Drain
Warland Drain
Bird Nest Hill
Turley Holes and Higher House Moor
HX7
Blake Moor
White Holme Drain
Little Dove Lowe
OL14
White Holme Moss
Turvin Clough
Round Hills
Light Hazzles Resr
Little Moor Clough
Saw Gill Hollow
BLACKSTONE EDGE RD
White Holme Resr
Little Moor
Round Hill
Captains Mark Hill
Farther Hill
Light Hazzles Edge
Chelburn Moor
Pennine Way
Toad La
OL15
HX6
Soyland Moor
Cold Laughton Drain
Middle Hill
Knave Holes Hollow
Knave Holes Hill
Utley Edge
Byron Edge
Nigher Hill
TURVIN RD
Head Drain
Black Castle Drain
Rush Bed Hill
Cow Head
Black Castle Hill
Blackstone Edge Resr
ROCHDALE RD
Fairy Hill
B6138
A58
HALIFAX RD
Slate Pit Hill

129
148

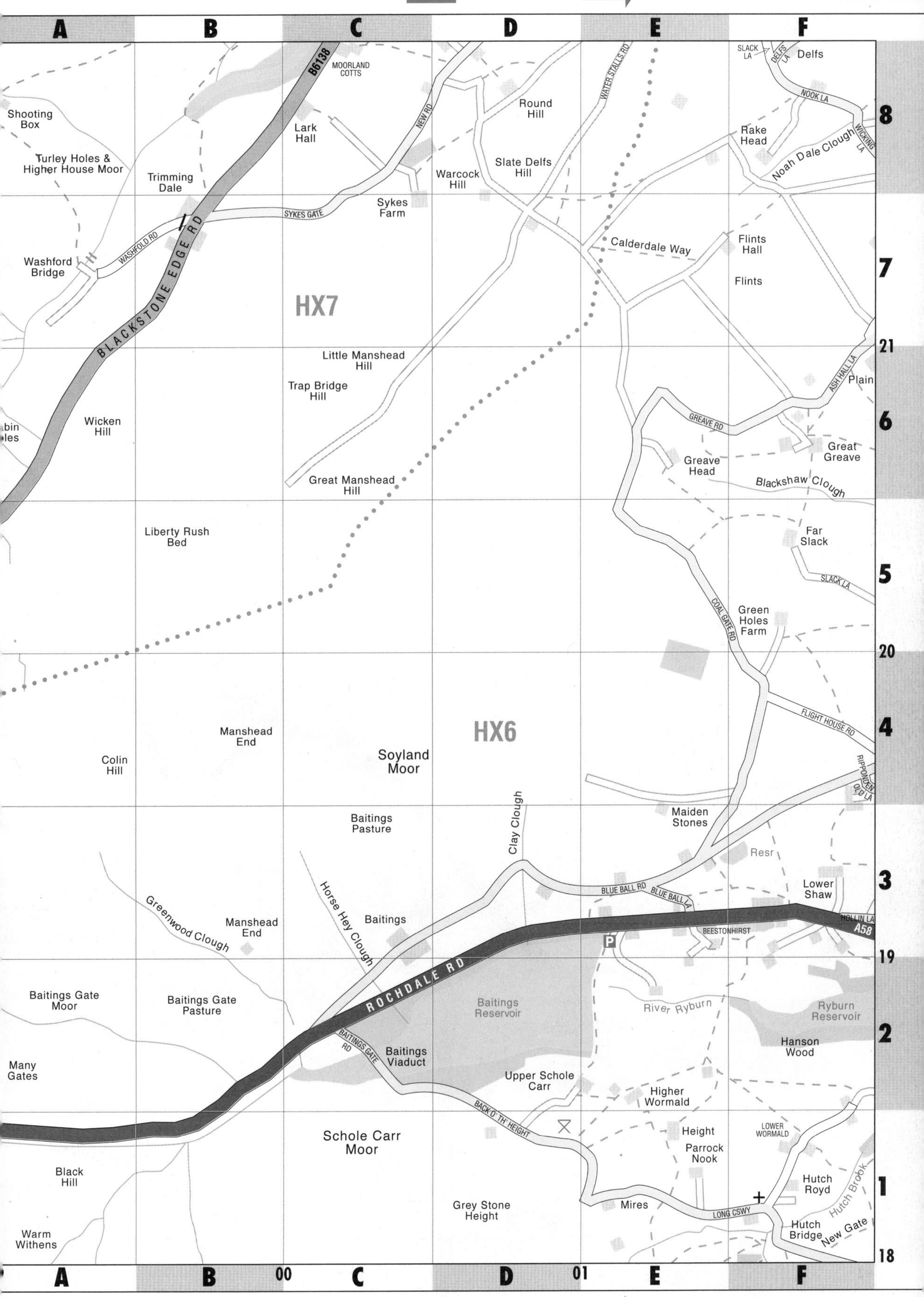

A B C D E F

8

Shooting Box

MOORLAND COTTS

B6138

NEW RD

Round Hill

Delfs

SLACK LA

DELFS LA

NOOK LA

Rake Head

Noah Dale Clough

VICKERS LA

Turley Holes & Higher House Moor

Lark Hall

Warcock Hill

Slate Delfs Hill

Trimming Dale

Sykes Gate

Sykes Farm

Calderdale Way

Flints Hall

Flints

7

Washfold Rd

Washford Bridge

BLACKSTONE EDGE RD

HX7

21

Plain

ASH HALL LA

6

bin les

Wicken Hill

Little Manshead Hill

Trap Bridge Hill

GREAVE RD

Greave Head

Great Greave

Blackshaw Clough

Great Manshead Hill

Far Slack

5

Liberty Rush Bed

COAL GATE RD

SLACK LA

Green Holes Farm

20

Colin Hill

Manshead End

Soyland Moor

HX6

Maiden Stones

FLIGHT HOUSE RD

RIPPONDEN OLD LA

4

Baitings Pasture

Clay Clough

Resr

Lower Shaw

3

Baitings

Greenwood Clough

Horse Hey Clough

Manshead End

BLUE BALL RD

BLUE BALL LA

Beestonhirst

HOLLIN LA

A58

19

Baitings Gate Moor

Baitings Gate Pasture

ROCHDALE RD

BAITINGS GATE RD

Baitings Reservoir

P

River Ryburn

Ryburn Reservoir

Hanson Wood

2

Many Gates

Baitings Viaduct

Upper Schole Carr

BACK O'TH' HEIGHT

Higher Wormald

Height

Parrock Nook

LOWER WORMALD

Hutch Royd

Hutch Brook

1

Black Hill

Schole Carr Moor

Grey Stone Height

Mires

LONG CSWY

Hutch Bridge

New Gate

Warm Withens

18

A B 00 C D 01 E F

131
111

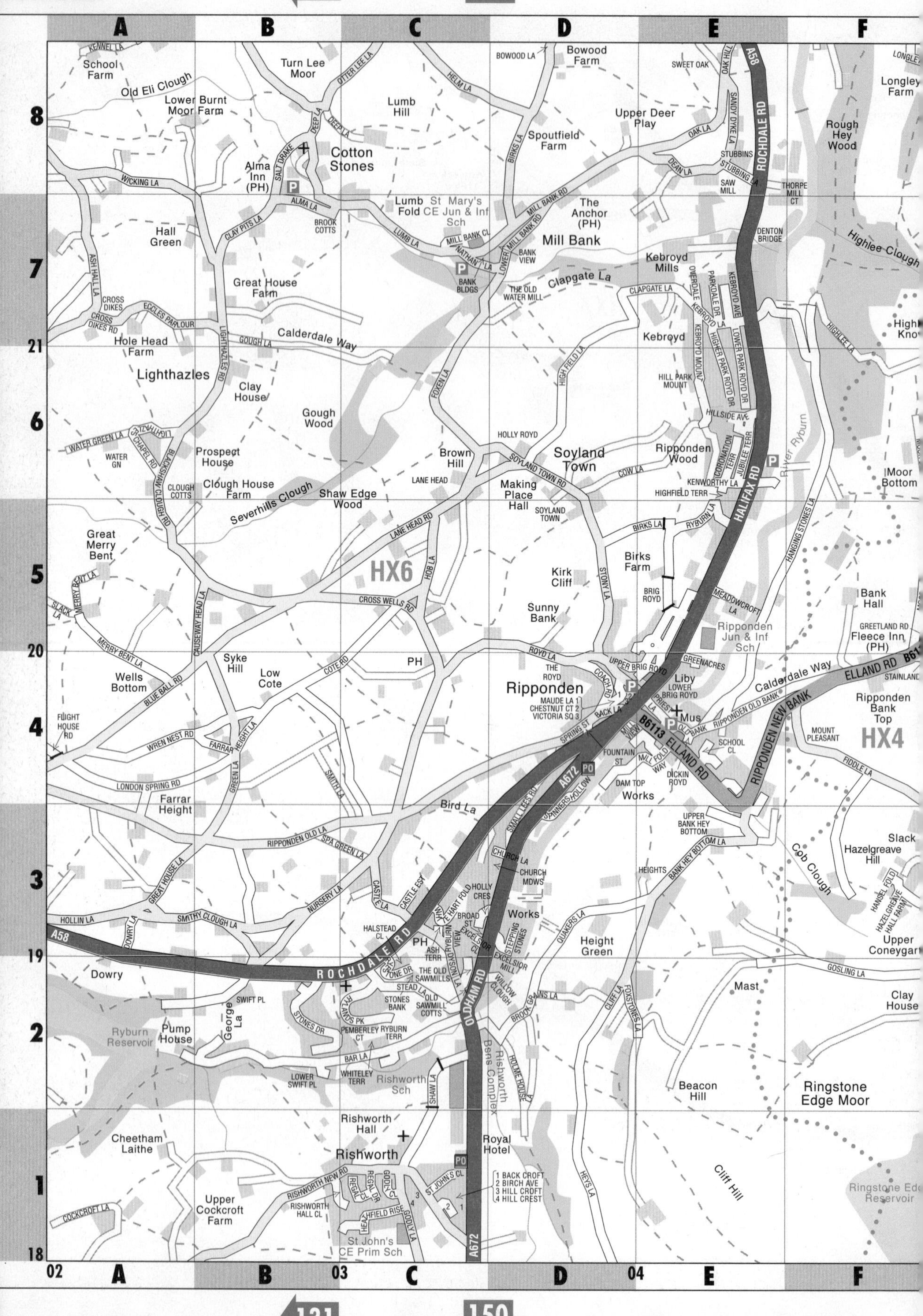
School Farm
Old Eli Clough
Turn Lee Moor
Lower Burnt Moor Farm
Lumb Hill
Bowood Farm
Upper Deer Play
Longley Farm
Rough Hey Wood
Cotton Stones
Alma Inn (PH)
Spoutfield Farm
Lumb Fold
St Mary's CE Jun & Inf Sch
The Anchor (PH)
Mill Bank
Hall Green
Kebroyd Mills
Highlee Clough
Great House Farm
Clapgate La
Calderdale Way
Hole Head Farm
Kebroyd
Lighthazles
Clay House
Gough Wood
Soyland Town
Ripponden Wood
Brown Hill
Prospect House
Clough House Farm
Making Place Hall
Moor Bottom
Severhills Clough
Shaw Edge Wood
Great Merry Bent
HX6
Kirk Cliff
Birks Farm
Sunny Bank
Bank Hall
Ripponden Jun & Inf Sch
Fleece Inn (PH)
Syke Hill
Low Cote
Wells Bottom
Ripponden
Ripponden Bank Top
HX4
Farrar Height
Bird La
Works
Slack
Hazelgreave Hill
Cob Clough
Height Green
Upper Coneygarth
Dowry
Mast
Clay House
Ryburn Reservoir
Pump House
George La
Rishworth Sch
Rishworth Bsns Complex
Beacon Hill
Ringstone Edge Moor
Cheetham Laithe
Rishworth Hall
Rishworth
Royal Hotel
Cliff Hill
Upper Cockcroft Farm
St John's CE Prim Sch
Ringstone Edge Reservoir
ROCHDALE RD
HALIFAX RD
OLDHAM RD
ELLAND RD
RIPPONDEN NEW BANK
A58
A672
B6113
1 BACK CROFT
2 BIRCH AVE
3 HILL CROFT
4 HILL CREST
MAUDE LA 1
CHESTNUT CT 2
VICTORIA SQ 3
A B C D E F
8 7 21 6 5 20 4 3 19 2 1 18
02 03 04

131
150

112
134
A
B
C
D
E
F
8
7
21
6
5
20
4
3
19
2
1
18
06
07
151
134
Bilberry Hall
Moor Side
Moorcock Inn (PH)
Turgate Delph
Lamb Hill
Stockley House
Higher Turbury
Far Turbury
Lower Otterworth End
Calderdale Way
Norland Moor
Vicar's Lot
Sportsman's Inn (PH)
Upper Greetland
Spring Head
HX6
Spring Rock Inn (PH)
ROCHDALE RD
B6113
Cat La
Ladstone House
Spring Hill
Crawstone Hall
Gallows Pole Hill
Greetland Wall Nook
Lower High Trees
B6114
Branch Road Inn (PH)
Gate Head Farm
The New Rock Inn (PH)
Abbots Royd
Bowers
Barsey Green
GREETLAND RD
Near Barsey Farm
Pannier Top
Stone Stile
SADDLEWORTH RD
Far Barsey
Stubbing Wood
Bold Hall
Stubbing
Wood Royd
Sandyfoot Clough
Barsey Clough
Black Brook
Bowers Mill Ind Est
Eaves Top Wood
Barkisland Hall
Barkisland
Barkisland CE Prim Sch
Cross Villa
Recreation Ground
Barkisland Clough
Beestones Wood
HX4
B6112
Elland Scholes
Liby
Howroyde
Park Nook
Slack Lane End Farm
Bottomley Clough
Pierce Hey
Stainland
Howroyd Hill
Hill House
Bottomley
Mill
Hard Platts
Calf Hey
STAINLAND RD
New Laithe Farm
Mill
Krumlin Hall
Ringstone Royd
Waterloo Farm
Dean Farm
Prospect Place
Peat Pits
Krumlin
Bank Royd
Refuse Tip
Firth House Mills
Sowood Green
Wholestone Hill
Penny Hill
Dean Lodge
Mount Pleasant Farm
Forest
Broom House
Dog and Partridge (PH)
CLAY PIT LA

134
C7
1 LINDWELL PL
2 LINDWELL GR
3 LOWER WELLGATE
4 ROAD END
5 LINDWELL AVE
6 HOLLYNS TERR
D6
1 MIDDLE DEAN ST
2 BACK QUEEN ST
3 EXCHANGE ST
4 FEATHERBED CL
5 FEATHER BED LA
6 WOODSIDE TERR
133
D7
1 ELIZABETH ST
2 LAMBERT ST
3 PRINCESS ST
4 NORTH ST
5 GEORGE ST
6 UNION ST
7 CROSS ST
8 HIGH ST
9 GARWICK TERR
113
F6
1 NORTHFIELD CL
2 TALBOT HO
3 TIMBER ST
4 TOWN HALL ST
5 ROCHESTER PL
6 GRANVILLE ST
7 BEDFORD ST
8 Burley Bsns Ctr
9 DEAN ST
10 AINLEY ST
11 BURLEY ST
12 FRANCES ST
13 ALBION ST
14 JOHN WILLIAM ST
15 PARKFIELD AVE
16 CATHERINE CRES
F7
1 TOWNGATE HO
2 WEST HO
3 MEXBOROUGH HO
4 YORK HO
5 RIPON HO
6 REGENT HO
7 SAVILE HO
8 ELAND HO
9 MARLBOROUGH HO
10 CALDER HO
11 CROFT HO
12 ST MARYS GATE
13 CHURCH HO
14 PORTLAND HO
15 CONISTON HO
16 CORNWALL HO
17 CASTLEGAT
18 PROVIDENC
A B C D E F
8 7 21 6 5 20 4 3 19 2 1 18
Upper Scholes Farm
B8
1 GOLDFIELDS CL
2 GOLDFIELDS VIEW
3 MOORLANDS CT
B7
1 THORNFIELD ST
2 THORNFIELD RISE
Moor Bottom Farm
Greetland
Greetland Prim Sch
Lindwell
Calderdale Way
HX3
Cemy
Elland Tunnel
Mill
Elland Hall Farm
ELLAND HALL FARM CVN PK
CALDERDALE WAY
HALIFAX RD
ROCHDALE RD
Cross Hill
Brow Bridge
Works
SADDLEWORTH RD
Sunnybank
West Vale
Calder and Hebble Navigation
River Calder
Mill
Black Brook
The Park
Liby
Works
Bradley Mill Farm
ELLAND
The Brooksbank Sch
STAINLAND RD
CH
Ravenstone Wood
CH
Cross Lane Prim Sch
HX5
HX4
Brookwoods Ind Est
Old Dan La
Broad Carr
Bsns Pk Mill
Blackley
Greaves Farm
Holywell Green
Works
Hollins Hey Clough
Golden Fleece Inn (PH)
Kew Hill
Refuse Tip
Jagger Dean
Carr Hall La
Shavey Clough
Copriding Farm
Haigh House
Harrow Clough
Old Lindley
Helen Hill Farm
Holywell Brook
Clough Head
Martin Nest
Works
Peat Ponds Farm
Lee Green
Turley Cote Farm
Kirklees Way
Wappy Spring Inn (PH)
HD3
Gosport Clough
Old Lindley Moor
LINDLEY MOOR RD
New Lea
Laund Hill
Brewery Farm
Leys
NEW HEY RD
A643
Sowood Hill
Mount
Moorlands Prim Sch
M62
A640
08 09 10
A4
1 THORNE ST
2 OAK TERR
3 GLADSTONE ST
B4
1 NORTH VIEW
2 CROSS ST
3 WELL ST
4 GREEN ST
133
152
F1
1 MAPLIN DR
2 DEER CROFT RD
3 DEER CROFT CRES
4 RYNDLESIDE
5 LOW HILLS LA

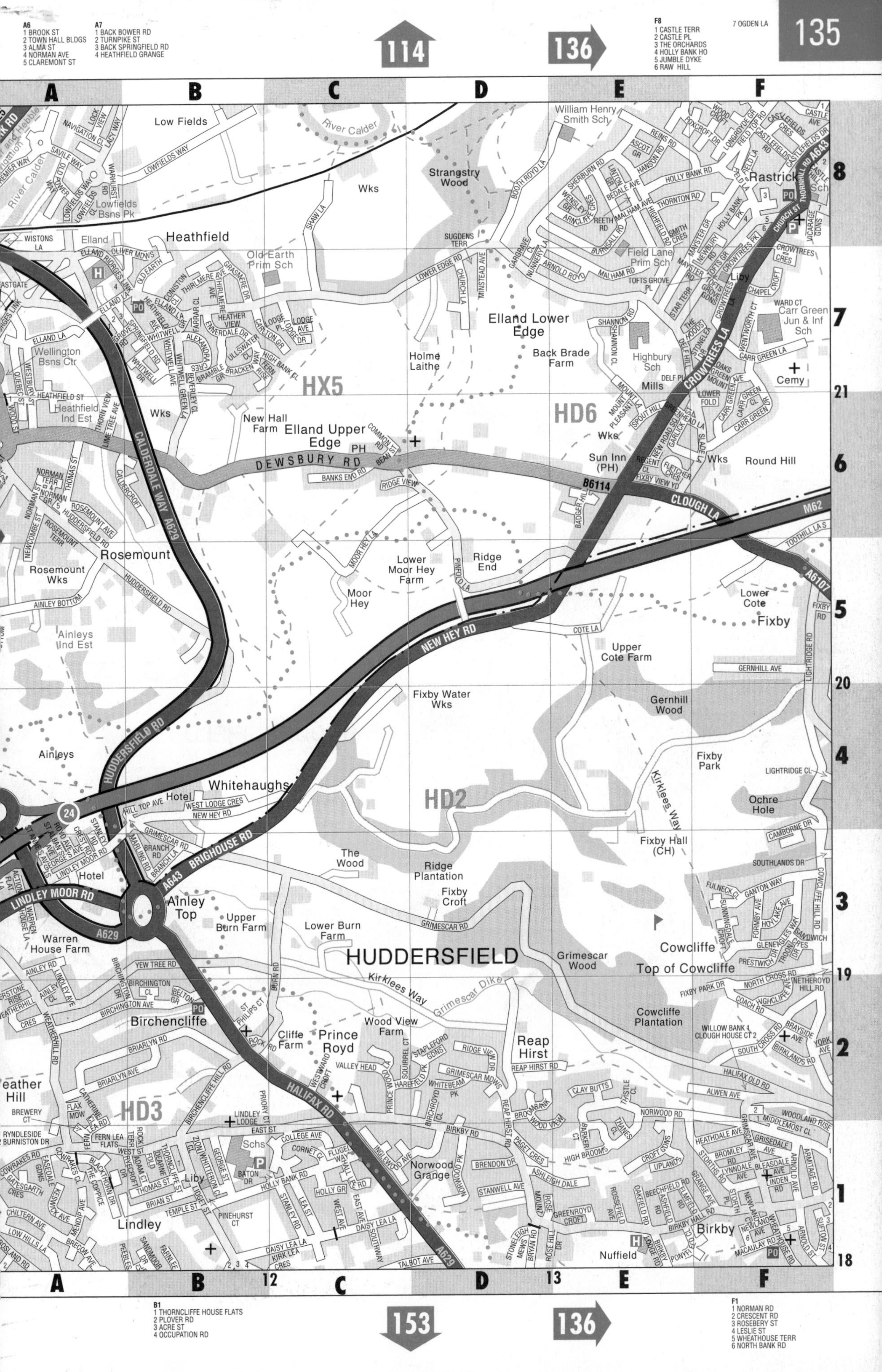
A6
1 BROOK ST
2 TOWN HALL BLDGS
3 ALMA ST
4 NORMAN AVE
5 CLAREMONT ST
A7
1 BACK BOWER RD
2 TURNPIKE ST
3 BACK SPRINGFIELD RD
4 HEATHFIELD GRANGE
114
136
F8
1 CASTLE TERR
2 CASTLE PL
3 THE ORCHARDS
4 HOLLY BANK HO
5 JUMBLE DYKE
6 RAW HILL
7 OGDEN LA
A
B
C
D
E
F
Low Fields
River Calder
William Henry Smith Sch
Strangstry Wood
Wks
Rastrick
Lowfields Bsns Pk
Elland
Heathfield
Old Earth Prim Sch
Field Lane Prim Sch
Elland Lower Edge
Carr Green Jun & Inf Sch
Holme Laithe
Back Brade Farm
Highbury Sch
Wellington Bsns Ctr
HX5
Mills
Cemy
Heathfield Ind Est
New Hall Farm
Elland Upper Edge
HD6
DEWSBURY RD
Sun Inn (PH)
Round Hill
B6114
CLOUGH LA
M62
CALDERDALE WAY A629
Rosemount
Rosemount Wks
Lower Moor Hey Farm
Ridge End
Moor Hey
Lower Cote
Fixby
NEW HEY RD
Upper Cote Farm
Ainleys Ind Est
Fixby Water Wks
Gernhill Wood
HUDDERSFIELD RD
Ainleys
Fixby Park
Kirklees Way
Ochre Hole
Whitehaughs
Hotel
HD2
BRIGHOUSE RD
A643
Fixby Hall (CH)
The Wood
Ridge Plantation
LINDLEY MOOR RD
Ainley Top
Fixby Croft
Warren House Farm
Upper Burn Farm
Lower Burn Farm
A629
HUDDERSFIELD
Grimescar Wood
Cowcliffe
Top of Cowcliffe
Cowcliffe Plantation
Birchencliffe
Cliffe Farm
Prince Royd
Wood View Farm
Reap Hirst
Heather Hill
HD3
HALIFAX RD
Norwood Grange
Lindley
Birkby
Nuffield
21
20
19
18
12
13
8
7
6
5
4
3
2
1
153
136
B1
1 THORNCLIFFE HOUSE FLATS
2 PLOVER RD
3 ACRE ST
4 OCCUPATION RD
F1
1 NORMAN RD
2 CRESCENT RD
3 ROSEBERY ST
4 LESLIE ST
5 WHEATHOUSE TERR
6 NORTH BANK RD

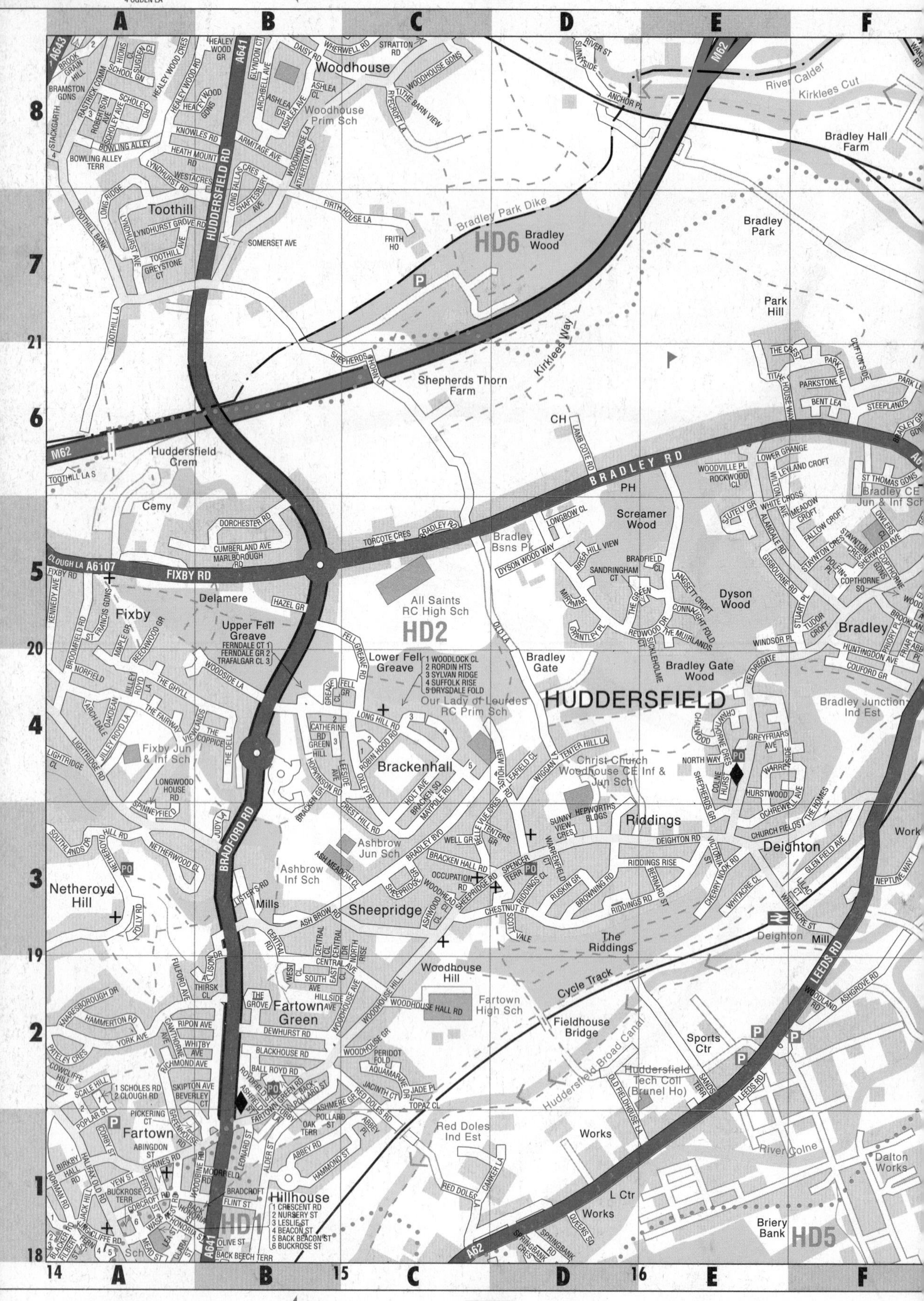

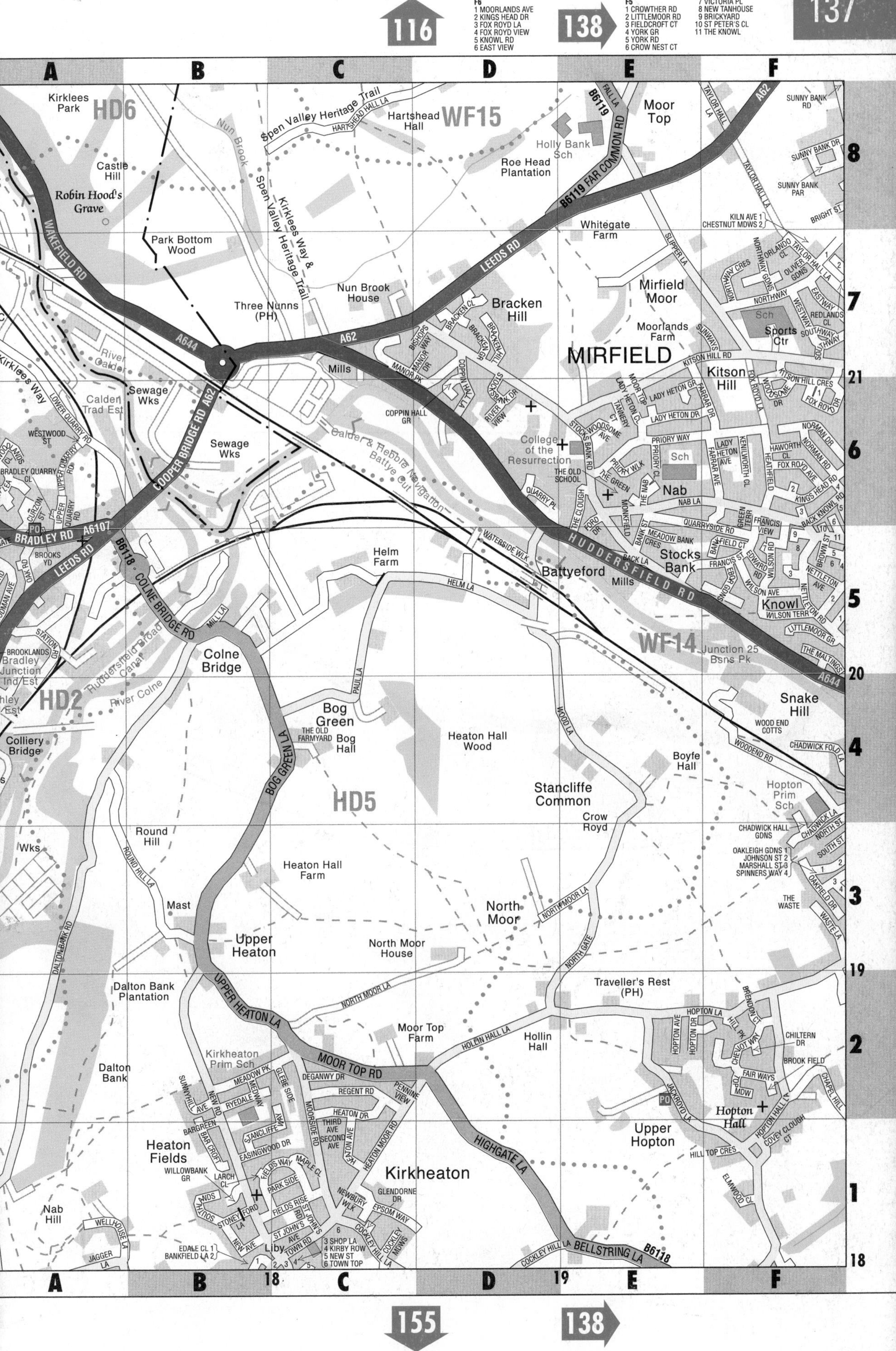

A6
1 TALBOT VIEW
2 STONEHURST RD
3 WATER ROYD DR
4 FERNHURST CL
5 FERNHURST WAY

137   117

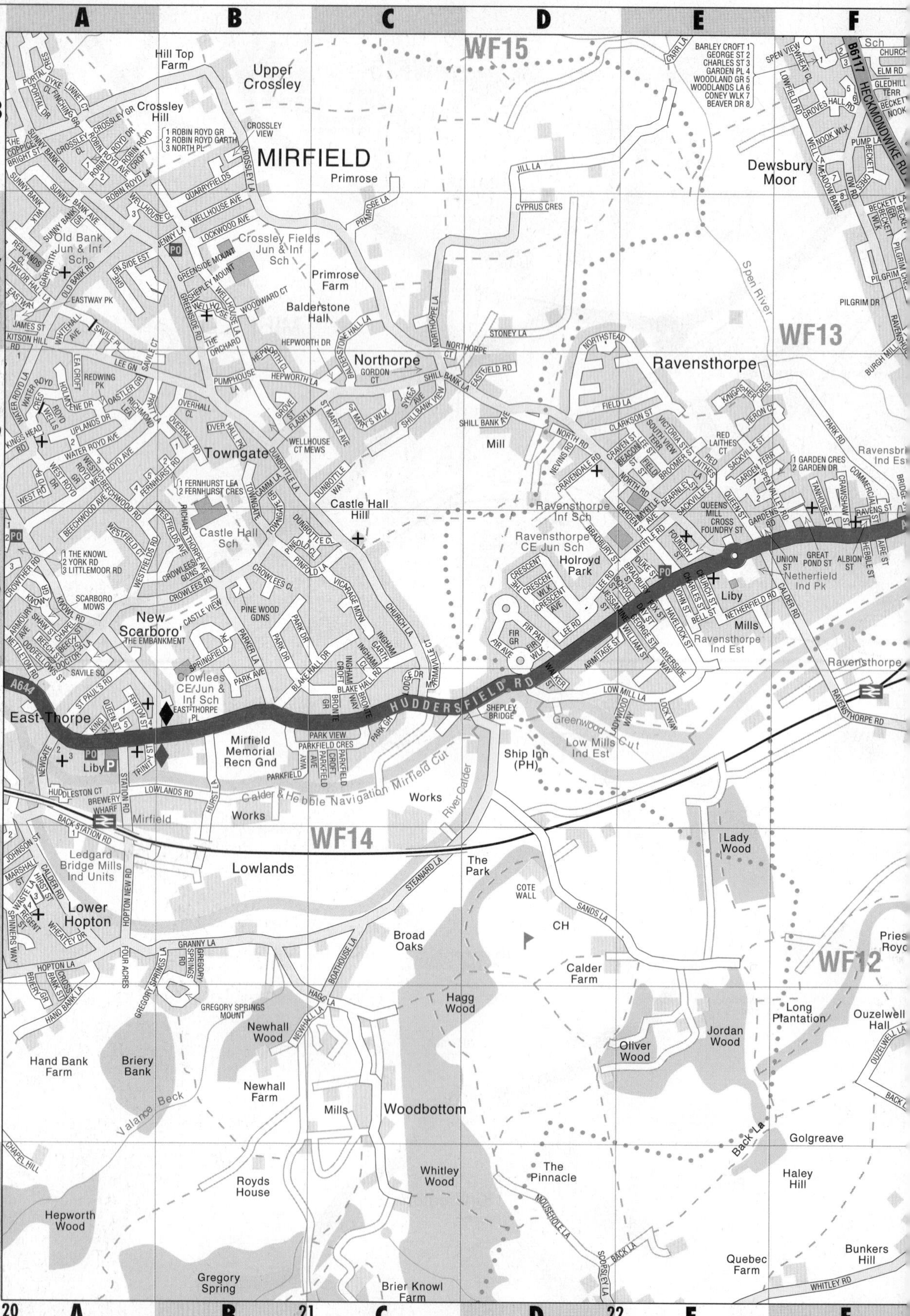

A | B | C | D | E | F

WF15

BARLEY CROFT 1
GEORGE ST 2
CHARLES ST 3
GARDEN PL 4
WOODLAND GR 5
WOODLANDS LA 6
CONEY WLK 7
BEAVER DR 8

Hill Top Farm
Upper Crossley

Crossley Hill

8

Crossley View

MIRFIELD
Primrose

1 ROBIN ROYD GR
2 ROBIN ROYD GARTH
3 NORTH PL

Dewsbury Moor

HECKMONDWIKE

Old Bank Jun & Inf Sch
Crossley Fields Jun & Inf Sch
Primrose Farm
Balderstone Hall

JILL LA
CYPRUS CRES

7

WF13

Eastway Pk

21

Northorpe

STONEY LA

Ravensthorpe

6

Towngate
Mill
Ravensbri Ind Est

1 FERNHURST LEA
2 FERNHURST CRES

Castle Hall Hill

Ravensthorpe Inf Sch

1 GARDEN CRES
2 GARDEN DR

Castle Hall Sch

Ravensthorpe CE Jun Sch
Holroyd Park

QUEENS MILL CROSS FOUNDRY ST

5

1 THE KNOWL
2 YORK RD
3 LITTLEMOOR RD

Scarboro Mdws

Pine Wood Gdns

Liby
Ravensthorpe Ind Est

Netherfield Ind Pk

New Scarboro'
THE EMBANKMENT

Ravensthorpe Mills

20

A644

Crowlees CE/Jun & Inf Sch
EAST-THORPE PL

HUDDERSFIELD RD

Ravensthorpe

East-Thorpe
Liby

Mirfield Memorial Recn Gnd
PARK VIEW

SHEPLEY BRIDGE
Greenwood Cut
Low Mills Ind Est

4

Ship Inn (PH)

Works

BREWERY WHARF
Mirfield

LOWLANDS RD

Calder & Hebble Navigation Mirfield Cut

River Calder

Works

BACK STATION RD

WF14

Lady Wood

Ledgard Bridge Mills Ind Units

Lowlands

The Park

COTE WALL

3

Lower Hopton

CH

SANDS LA

Calder Farm

WF12

19

Broad Oaks

Hagg Wood

Long Plantation
Ouzelwell Hall

Gregory Springs Mount
Newhall Wood

Oliver Wood
Jordan Wood

2

Hand Bank Farm
Briery Bank

Newhall Farm
Mills
Woodbottom

Back La
Golgreave

Valance Beck

Haley Hill

1

Hepworth Wood

Royds House
Whitley Wood

The Pinnacle

Quebec Farm
Bunkers Hill

18

Chapel Hill

Gregory Spring
Brier Knowl Farm

WHITLEY RD

20 | A | 21 | B | C | 22 | D | E | F

137   156

A3
1 LEDGARD WHARF
2 SOUTH ST
3 CO-OPERATIVE ST
4 SPENCER ST

A4
1 REGENCY RD
2 CALDER HO
3 ST PAUL'S TERR
4 TOWN HALL ST
5 PRINCESS ST

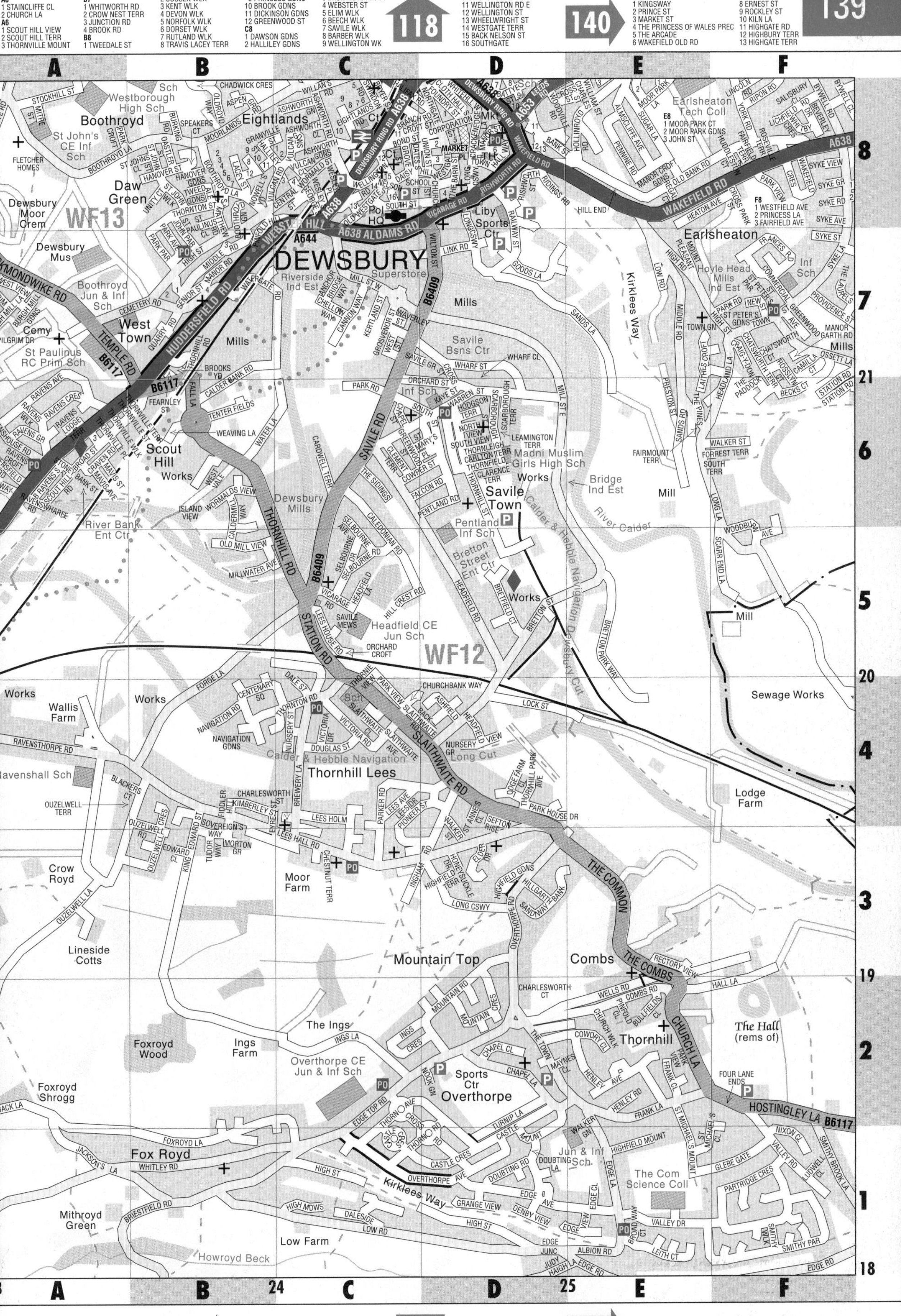

118

140

157

140

139

119

D5
1 DUNDALK CT
2 OLD CHURCH ST
3 WELLGATE
4 OAKWOOD COTTS
5 SANFORD CT
6 QUEEN'S TERR

D6
1 MOORCROFT CT
2 WOODHEAD CL
3 KINGSWAY HO
4 TURNER CL

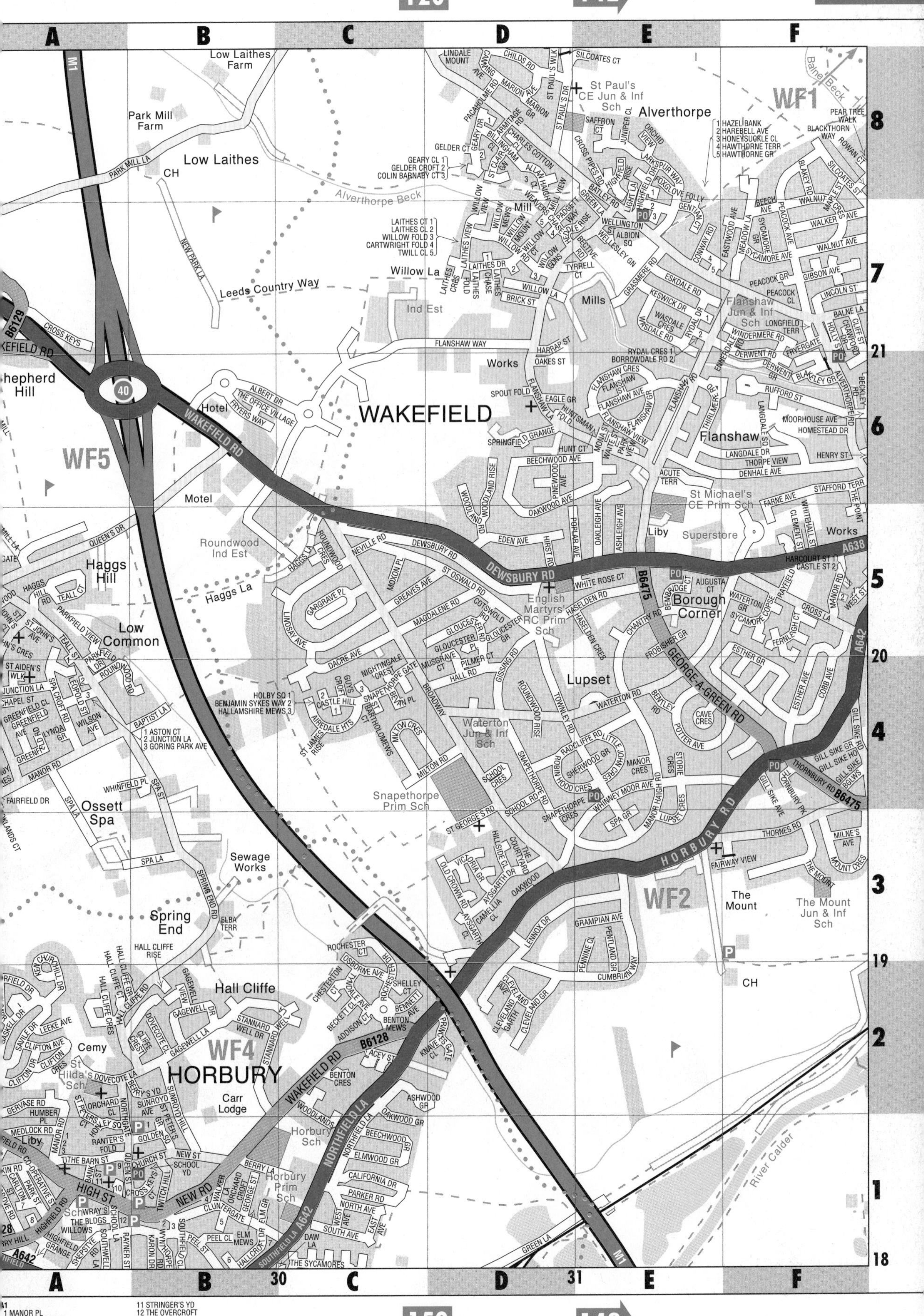

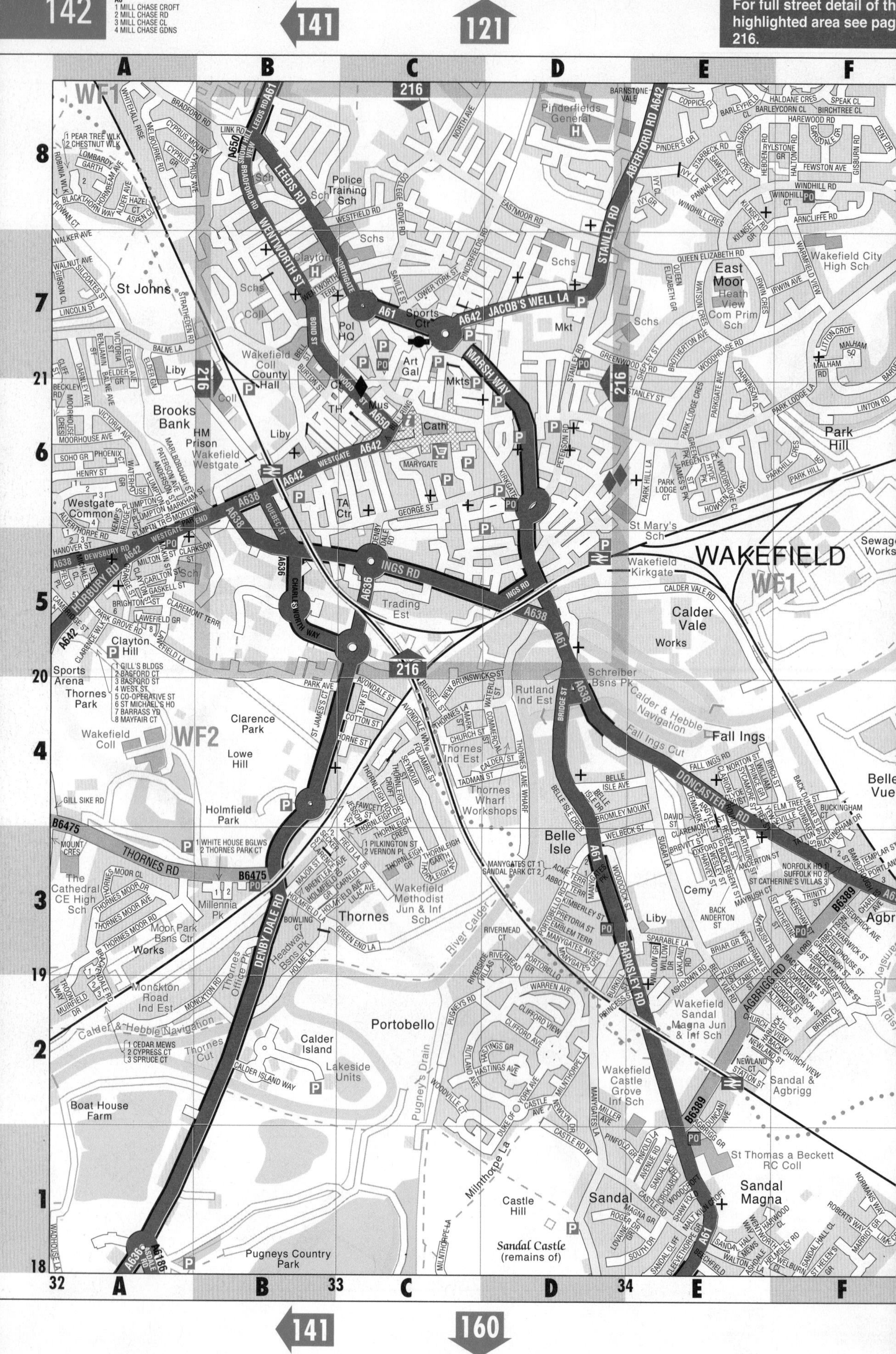

122
144
A
B
C
D
E
F
8
7
21
6
5
20
4
3
19
2
1
18
36
37
Old Park Farm
WELBECK LA
PARK LODGE LA
Aire & Calder Navigation
Calder Cut
Southern Washlands Nature Reserve
River Calder
Broadreach Lock
LC
Kirkthorpe
WILLOW LA
WOODLAND AVE
CHURCH AVE
PARK AVE
PO
FRESTON DR
FRESTON AVE
Church Field
Peas Hill
HALF MOON LA
KIRKTHORPE LA
Goosehill
GOOSEHILL LA
WF6
SYLVESTER AVE
WAKEFIELD RD
Woodhouse Common
Cross Hills Farm
The Plough (PH)
BOUNDARY LA
WARMFIELD LA
A655
CROFT HEAD LA
Plump Hill
PINEAPPLE COTTS
ELSICKER LA
Warmfield
Pineapple Inn (PH)
CROSSLEY ST
Low Wood
WF1
Gled Hill
Heath Hall Farm
Mount Tarry by it
RED LA
OLD HALL COURT YD
Heath Hall
Penhill Field
Heath
HEATH MANOR
P
HELL LA
Caravan Park
Trans Pennine Trail
Heath Common
WOODLAND VIEW
Heath Farm
WEST VIEW
Horse & Groom (PH)
HORSE RACE END
Dean Field
BLACK RD
Black Hill
Burcroft Farm
A655
LC
Bracken Hill
LC
Mount Pleasant
Sewage Works
CAMBRIDGE CRES
RUTLAND DR
RISE
KENDAL DR
KENDAL
KINGSLEY AVE
KINGSLEY CL
A645
WEELAND RD
A645
Oakenshaw Grange
DONCASTER RD
Oakenshaw Farm
Barnsley Canal (dis)
Motel
WF4
B6378 LODGE LA
Brand Hill
PONTEFRACT RD
B6378
PH
COCK LA
HALL PARK AVE
PARKWAY
A638
OAKENSHAW LA
BRAND HILL DR
BRAND HILL APP
THE AVENUE
WOODLANDS
CHESTNUT GR
ASHDENE AVE
Crofton
ASHDENE APP
ASHDENE GARTH
ASHDENE DR
SHAY LA
SHAY CT
HOLLY CRES
HOLLY CL
HAWTHORN AVE
HAWTHORN CT
HARRISON RD
ASHDENE CRES
CHURCHFIELDS
WF1
CHEVET TERR
WF2
WF2
B6378
THORNTREE CT
THORNTREE AVE
Sch
CHURCH HILL
FARM
FARNHAM WAY 1
CRAYFORD DR 2
GARDEN ROW 3
HOPE TERR 4
HIGH ST
ROSE GARTH
SANDOWN AVE
Sch
161
144

143
123

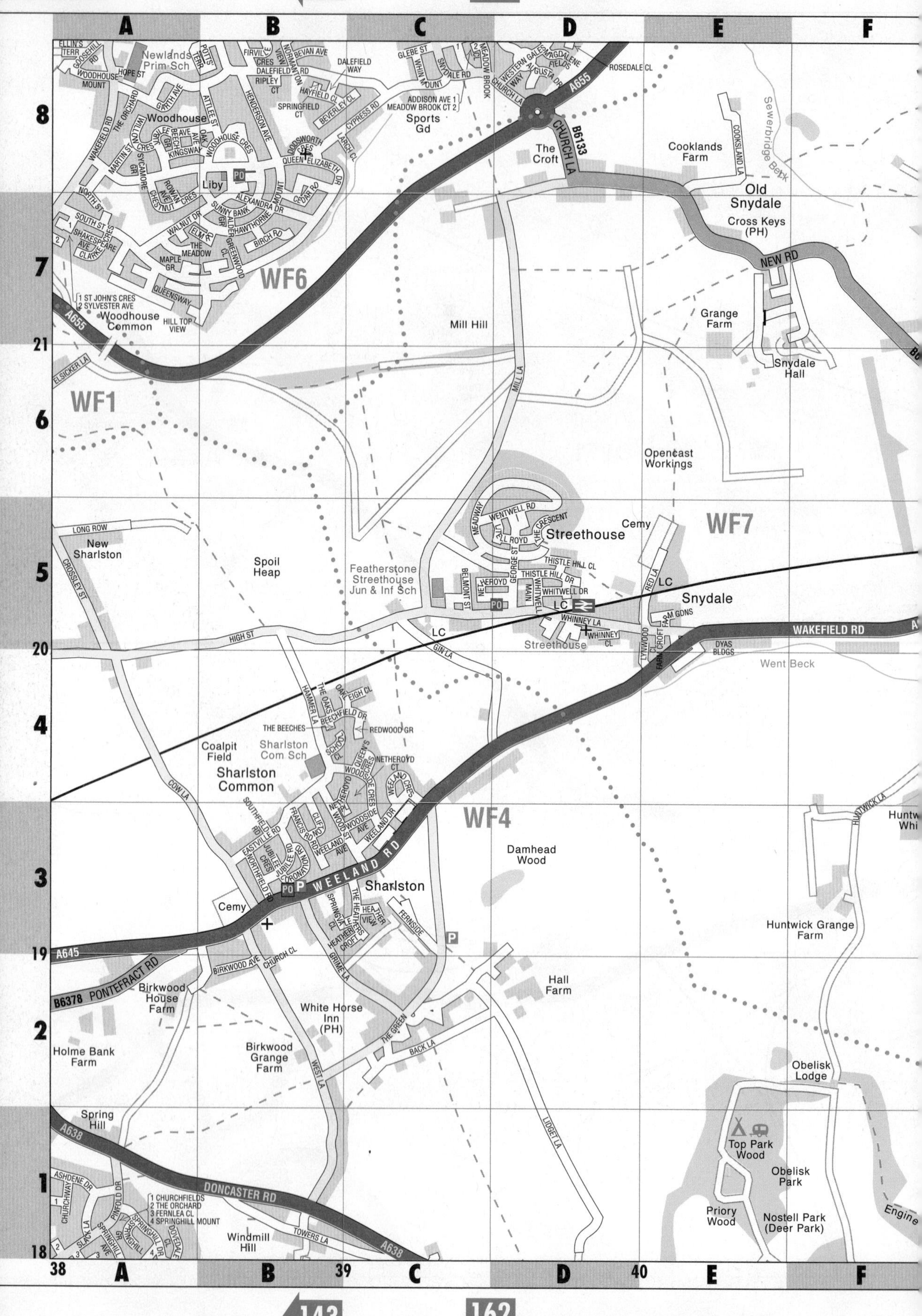
A
B
C
D
E
F
8
7
21
6
5
20
4
3
19
2
1
18
38
39
40
Newlands Prim Sch
Woodhouse
Liby
PO
WF6
WF1
WF7
WF4
A655
B6133
CHURCH LA
Sports Gd
The Croft
Cooklands Farm
COOKSLAND LA
Sewerbridge Beck
Old Snydale
Cross Keys (PH)
NEW RD
Grange Farm
Snydale Hall
Woodhouse Common
HILL TOP VIEW
1 ST JOHN'S CRES
2 SYLVESTER AVE
ELSICKER LA
Mill Hill
MILL LA
Opencast Workings
Streethouse
Cemy
LC
Snydale
RED LA
FARM GDNS
WAKEFIELD RD
DYAS BLDGS
Went Beck
Whinney La
Featherstone Streethouse Jun & Inf Sch
LONG ROW
New Sharlston
CROSSLEY ST
Spoil Heap
HIGH ST
GIN LA
Coalpit Field
Sharlston Common
Sharlston Com Sch
COW LA
WEELAND RD
Sharlston
Damhead Wood
Huntwick Grange Farm
HUNTWICK LA
A645
B6378 PONTEFRACT RD
BIRKWOOD AVE
CHURCH CL
Birkwood House Farm
White Horse Inn (PH)
Hall Farm
Holme Bank Farm
Birkwood Grange Farm
WEST LA
BACK LA
THE GREEN
LIDGET LA
Obelisk Lodge
Spring Hill
A638
DONCASTER RD
Top Park Wood
Obelisk Park
Priory Wood
Nostell Park (Deer Park)
Windmill Hill
TOWERS LA
1 CHURCHFIELDS
2 THE ORCHARD
3 FERNLEA CL
4 SPRINGHILL MOUNT
ASHDENE DR
Engine

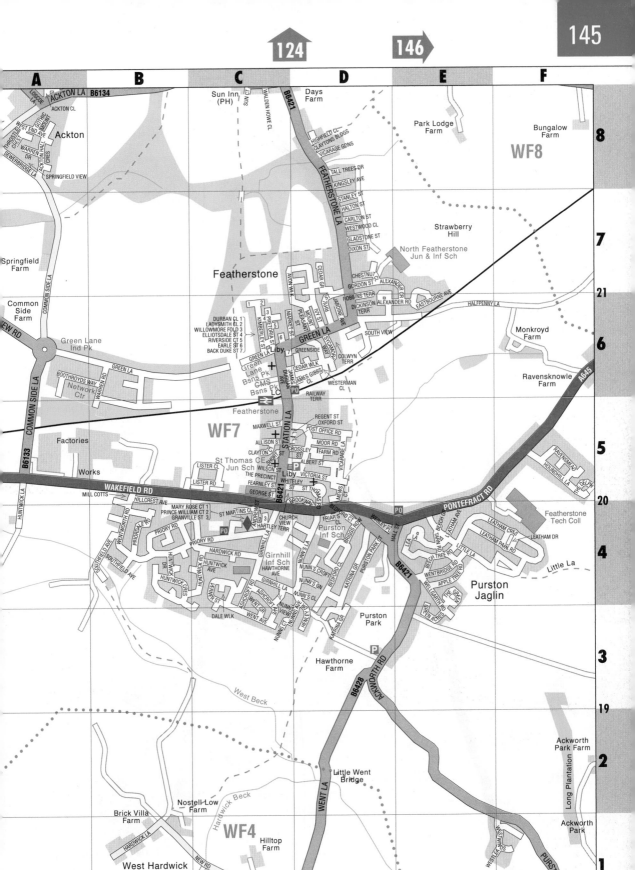

A   B   C   D   E   F

ACKTON LA B6134

Sun Inn (PH)   Days Farm

B6421

Park Lodge Farm   Bungalow Farm

Ackton
ACKTON CL
WEST END AVE
GOTHIC MOUNT
WARREN DR
JACKTON CRES
SPRINGFIELD VIEW

8

WF8

HIGHFIELD CL
CLAYTONS BLDGS
VICARAGE GDNS

Strawberry Hill

7

FEATHERSTONE LA

TALL TREES DR
KINGSLEY AVE
STANLEY ST
CARLTON ST
WESTWOOD CL
GLADSTONE ST
DIXON ST

North Featherstone Jun & Inf Sch

21

Springfield Farm

Featherstone

CHESTNUT
GORDON ST
JARDINE AVE
ALEXANDER DR
ROBBINS TERR
DICKINSON TERR
Alexander Rd
Eastbourne Ave
Halfpenny La

6

Common Side Farm

COMMON SIDE LA

GREEN LA

AVON WK
CEDAR GR
IVY ST
RYAN
MOUNT PLEASANT ST
MARKET ST
PRETORIA ST
KIMBERLEY ST
SOUTH VIEW
SYCAMORE WAY
COLWYN TERR

Monkroyd Farm

NEW RD

DURBAN CL 1
LADYSMITH CL 2
WILLOWMORE FOLD 3
ELLIOTSDALE ST 4
RIVERSIDE CT 5
EARLE ST 6
BACK DUKE ST 7

Liby

Green Lane Bsns Pk
GMS
Bsns Pk

GREENSIDE
CEDAR WLK
JAMES GIBBS
DUKE
WESTERMAN CL

Ravensknowle Farm

A645

Green Lane Ind Pk
BOOTHROYDS WAY
Network Ctr
WARREN RD
GREEN LA

LC

Featherstone

Railway Terr

5

B6133

WF7

STATION LA

MAXWELL ST
ALLISON ST
CLAYTON ST
LISTER CL
LISTER RD
MILL COTTS
HILLCREST AVE

St Thomas CE Jun Sch
THE PRECINCT
FEARNLEY ST
GEORGE ST

Liby

REGENT ST
OXFORD ST
POST OFFICE RD
MOOR RD
FARM ST
VICARAGE RD
CROSSLEY ST
ALBERT ST
Victoria St
WHITELEY
ST
ST THOMAS ST
BROOKWAY
MEWS

P

RAVENSMEAD
HOUNDHILL LA
THE SELBY TREE

Factories

Works

WAKEFIELD RD

B6421

PONTEFRACT RD

Featherstone Tech Coll

20

HUNTWICK LA

MARY ROSE CT 1
PRINCE WILLIAM CT 2
GRANVILLE ST 3

ST MARTINS CL
ANDREW
HARTLEY TERR
CHURCH VIEW

BEDFORD CT
FRIARS CL
BRIGGS ROW
WESLEY PL
HALL ST
BECH GR
LITTLE LA
BEECH TREE RD
LEATHAM CRES
LEATHAM PARK RD
LEATHAM DR

Little La

SOUTHGATE AVE
WENTWORTH RD
PRIORDALE RD
PRIORY RD
HARDWICK RD
HUNTWICK RD
HUNTWICK AVE
HUNTWICK CRES
DALE WLK
WENT AVE
ASHCROFT AVE
GIRNHILL LA

Girnhill Inf Sch
HAWTHORNE AVE
Purston Inf Sch

NUNN'S CROFT
NUNN'S GN
NUNN'S CL
KATRINA GR
PURSTON PARK CT
KATRINA GR

Purston Jaglin

WENTBRIDGE AV
APPLE TREE RD
WELLGARTH
THE GROVE
GREEN ACRES

4

PO

B6421

SOUTHFIELD AVE
JAMES ST
ASHCROFT VIEW
NUNNS CT
HENLEY

Purston Park

WENT LA

Hawthorne Farm

P

ACKWORTH RD

B6428

3

West Beck

19

Ackworth Park Farm

2

Long Plantation

Little Went Bridge

Brick Villa Farm
HARDWICK LA

Nostell Low Farm

Hardwick Beck

WF4

Hilltop Farm

NEW RD

WENT LA

B6428

Ackworth Park

WEST LA

PURSTON LA

B6421

West Hardwick

HILL TOP LA

HESSLE LA

Owlett Hall

Ackworth Old Hall

1

18

A   B   C   D   E   F

42   43

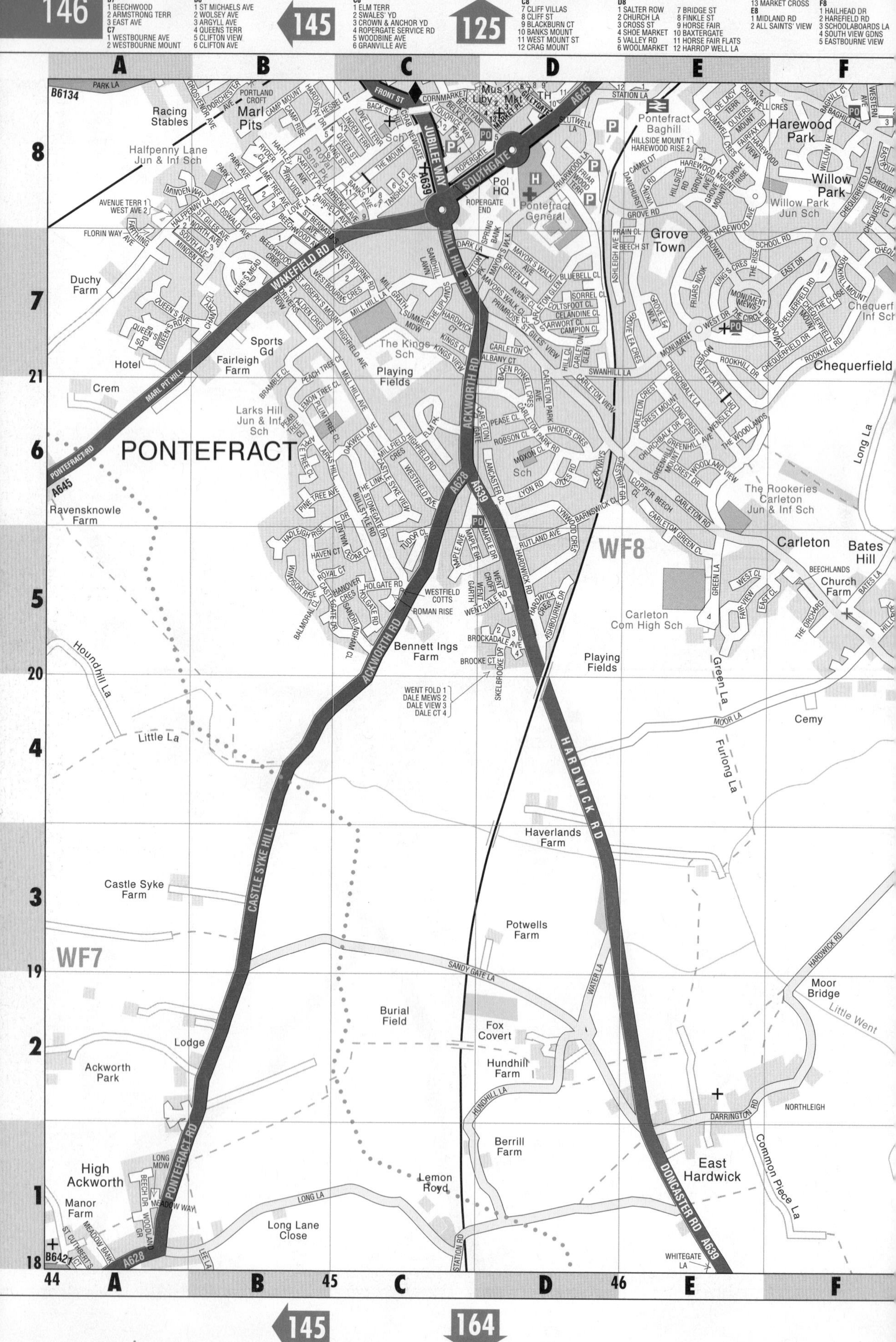

126

A
B
C
D
E
F
Cobbler's Lane Prim Sch
Greavefield Closes
GROVEHALL LA
GREAVEFIELD LA
GROVE HALL PARK HOMES
Grove Hall Farm
Grove Hall
Trinity Farm
1 SHARNALEY CT
2 POMFRET CT
3 LAYTHORPE CT
EASTBOURNE VIEW
EASTBOURNE CL
WF11
8
7
21
6
5
20
4
3
19
2
1
18
Spital Gap
LONG LA
Hodgewood Farm
Hodge Wood
A1(M)
40
A1
SPITALGAP LA
STREET FURLONG LA
HODGEWOOD LA
Hunters Wood
Bickering Wood
Millhill Fields
Darrington
Church Farm
Darrington CE Jun & Inf Sch
LEYS RD
LEYS LA
HAVERCROFT LA
CH
Valley Plantation
MARLPIT LA
ASH GR
ELM CL
SOTHERON CROFT
DENBY RD
PARK AVE
PARK CL
PHILIP'S LA
DENBY CREST
MILL HILL CL
WENTWORTH PARK RISE
HILLCROFT CL
BEECH CRES
NORWOOD
TUMBLING HILL
CARLETON RD
West End Farm
PO
ESTCOURT RD
CHURCH LA
MANOR PK
MANOR PARK RISE
ORCHARD LA
NEW ROW
ORCHARD VIEW
GREENROYD CT
THORNTREE CL
MILNER'S LA
ESTCOURT DR
VALLEY GDNS
FAIRWAYS CT
VALLEY RD
BANK WOOD RD
NORTH LODGE LA
Machir
Manasseh
Darrington Windmill (disused)
WF8
Darrington Hall
ASH TREE FOLD
West Valley
Chestnut House Hotel
North Yorkshire STREET ATLAS
Long Plantation
Stapleton Park
West Field
WICK RD
WESTFIELD LA
WEST PARK TERR
PH
WEST PARK DR
Caravan Park
Fletcher's Spring Covert
MOOR LA
Thorntree Closes
Round Ash Closes
Went Hill
B6474
Kirkdike Plantation
Long Plantation
Dale Field
Horse Race Closes
Wenthill Plantation
48
49

165

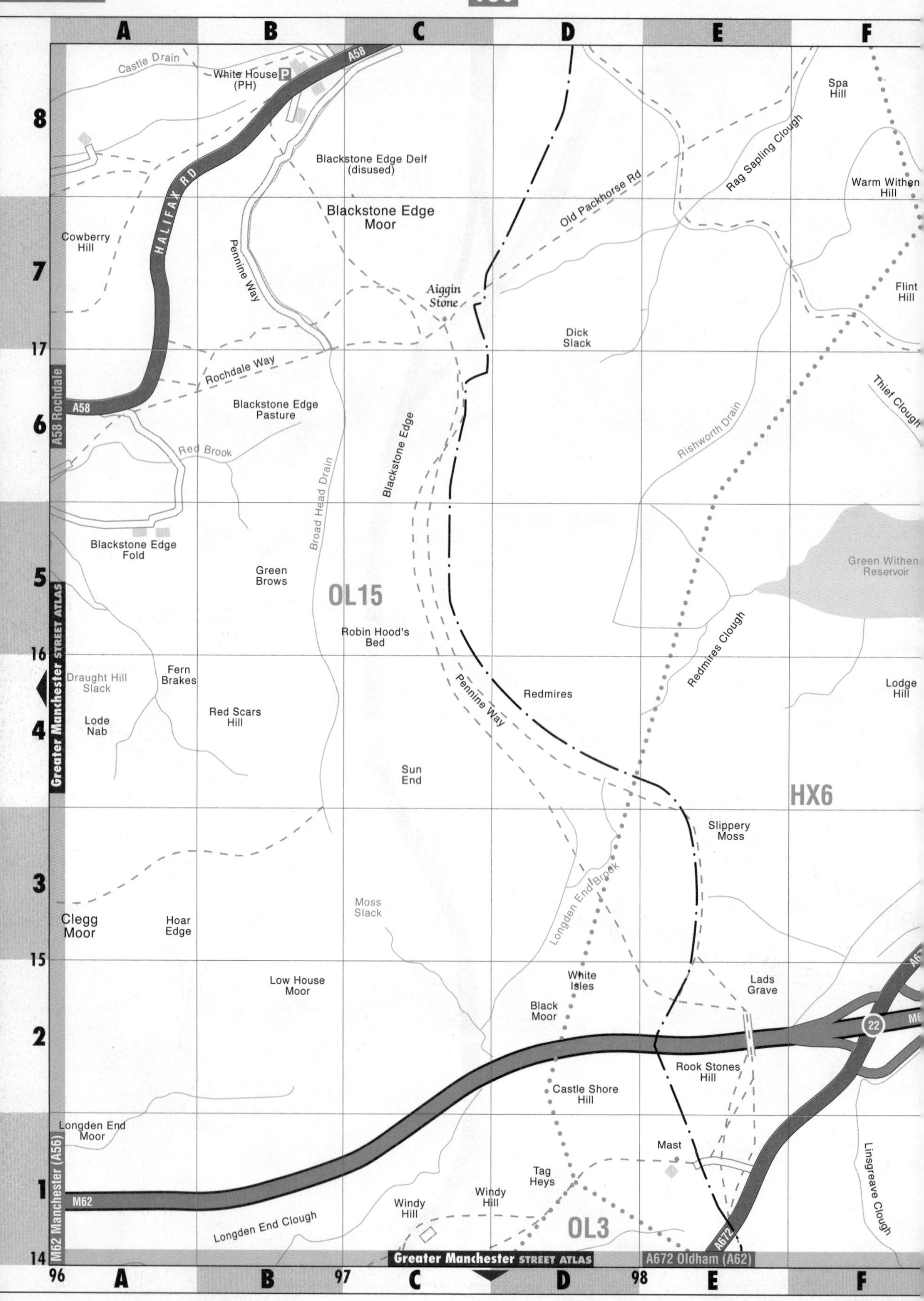

130

Castle Drain

White House (PH)

A58

Cowberry Hill

HALIFAX RD

Blackstone Edge Delf (disused)

Blackstone Edge Moor

Spa Hill

Rag Sapling Clough

Warm Withen Hill

Pennine Way

Aiggin Stone

Old Packhorse Rd

Flint Hill

Dick Slack

A58 Rochdale

A58

Rochdale Way

Blackstone Edge Pasture

Blackstone Edge

Thief Clough

Red Brook

Broad Head Drain

Rishworth Drain

Blackstone Edge Fold

Green Withen Reservoir

Green Brows

OL15

Robin Hood's Bed

Redmires Clough

Greater Manchester STREET ATLAS

Draught Hill Slack

Fern Brakes

Pennine Way

Redmires

Lodge Hill

Lode Nab

Red Scars Hill

Sun End

HX6

Slippery Moss

Clegg Moor

Hoar Edge

Moss Slack

Longden End Brook

Low House Moor

White Isles

Lads Grave

Black Moor

22

Rook Stones Hill

Castle Shore Hill

Longden End Moor

Mast

Linsgreave Clough

M62 Manchester (A56)

M62

Tag Heys

Windy Hill

OL3

A672

Windy Hill

Longden End Clough

A672 Oldham (A62)

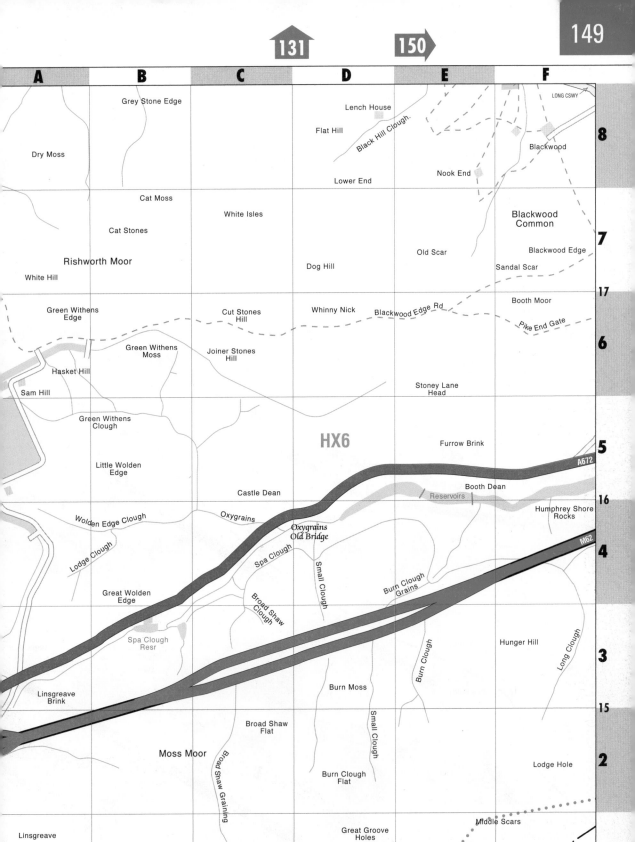

A   B   C   D   E   F

Grey Stone Edge

LONG CSWY

Lench House

Flat Hill

Black Hill Clough

8

Dry Moss

Blackwood

Lower End

Nook End

Cat Moss

White Isles

Blackwood Common

Cat Stones

7

Rishworth Moor

Old Scar

Blackwood Edge

Dog Hill

Sandal Scar

White Hill

17

Green Withens Edge

Cut Stones Hill

Whinny Nick

Blackwood Edge Rd

Booth Moor

Pike End Gate

6

Green Withens Moss

Joiner Stones Hill

Hasket Hill

Sam Hill

Stoney Lane Head

Green Withens Clough

HX6

Furrow Brink

5

A672

Little Wolden Edge

Castle Dean

Booth Dean

16

Reservoirs

Wolden Edge Clough

Oxygrains

Humphrey Shore Rocks

Oxygrains Old Bridge

M62

Lodge Clough

Spa Clough

Small Clough

Burn Clough Grains

4

Great Wolden Edge

Broad Shaw Clough

Hunger Hill

Long Clough

3

Spa Clough Resr

Burn Clough

Linsgreave Brink

Burn Moss

15

Broad Shaw Flat

Moss Moor

Broad Shaw Graining

Small Clough

Lodge Hole

2

Burn Clough Flat

Linsgreave

Great Groove Holes

Middle Scars

1

Way Stone Edge

Way Pit Holes

Moss Moor Edge

HD7

Way Stone

14

A   B   00   C   D   01   E   F

149
132

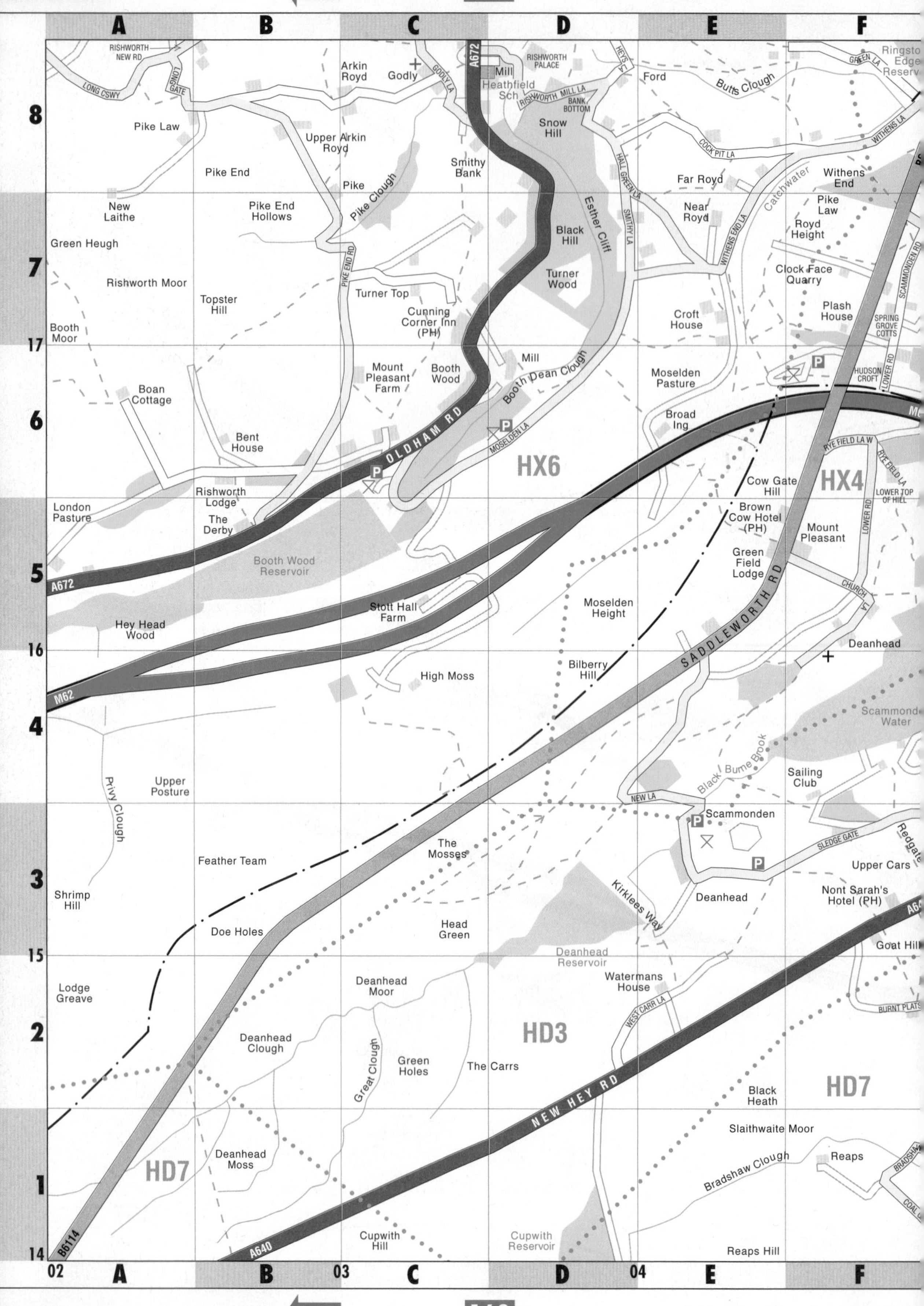
A
B
C
D
E
F
8
7
17
6
5
16
4
3
15
2
1
14
02
03
04
RISHWORTH NEW RD
LONG CSWY
LONG GATE
Arkin Royd
Godly
GODLY LA
A672
Mill
Heathfield Sch
RISHWORTH PALACE
RISHWORTH MILL LA
BANK BOTTOM
HEYS LA
Ford
Butts Clough
GREEN LA
Pike Law
Upper Arkin Royd
Smithy Bank
Snow Hill
COCK PIT LA
WITHENS LA
Withens End
Pike End
Pike
Pike Clough
Esther Cliff
HALL GREEN LA
SMITHY LA
Far Royd
Catchwater
New Laithe
Pike End Hollows
Black Hill
Near Royd
WITHENS END LA
Pike Law
Royd Height
Green Heugh
PIKE END RD
Turner Wood
Clock Face Quarry
SCAMMONDEN RD
Rishworth Moor
Turner Top
Topster Hill
Cunning Corner Inn (PH)
Croft House
Plash House
SPRING GROVE COTTS
Booth Moor
Mill
Mount Pleasant Farm
Booth Wood
Booth Dean Clough
Moselden Pasture
HUDSON CROFT
LOWER RD
Boan Cottage
Broad Ing
MOSELDEN LA
OLDHAM RD
Bent House
HX6
RYE FIELD LA W
RYE FIELD LA
Cow Gate Hill
HX4
LOWER TOP OF HILL
Rishworth Lodge
London Pasture
The Derby
Brown Cow Hotel (PH)
Mount Pleasant
LOWER RD
Booth Wood Reservoir
Green Field Lodge
A672
SADDLEWORTH RD
CHURCH LA
Moselden Height
Stott Hall Farm
Hey Head Wood
Deanhead
Bilberry Hill
High Moss
M62
Scammonden Water
Black Burne Brook
Sailing Club
Upper Posture
Privy Clough
NEW LA
Scammonden
The Mosses
SLEDGE GATE
Redgate
Feather Team
Upper Cars
Kirklees Way
Deanhead
Nont Sarah's Hotel (PH)
Shrimp Hill
Doe Holes
Head Green
Goat Hill
Deanhead Reservoir
Lodge Greave
Deanhead Moor
Watermans House
WEST CARR LA
BURNT PLATS
HD3
Deanhead Clough
Great Clough
Green Holes
The Carrs
NEW HEY RD
Black Heath
HD7
Slaithwaite Moor
Deanhead Moss
HD7
Bradshaw Clough
Reaps
BRADSHAW
COAL
Cupwith Hill
Cupwith Reservoir
Reaps Hill
A640
B6114

149
168

133
152

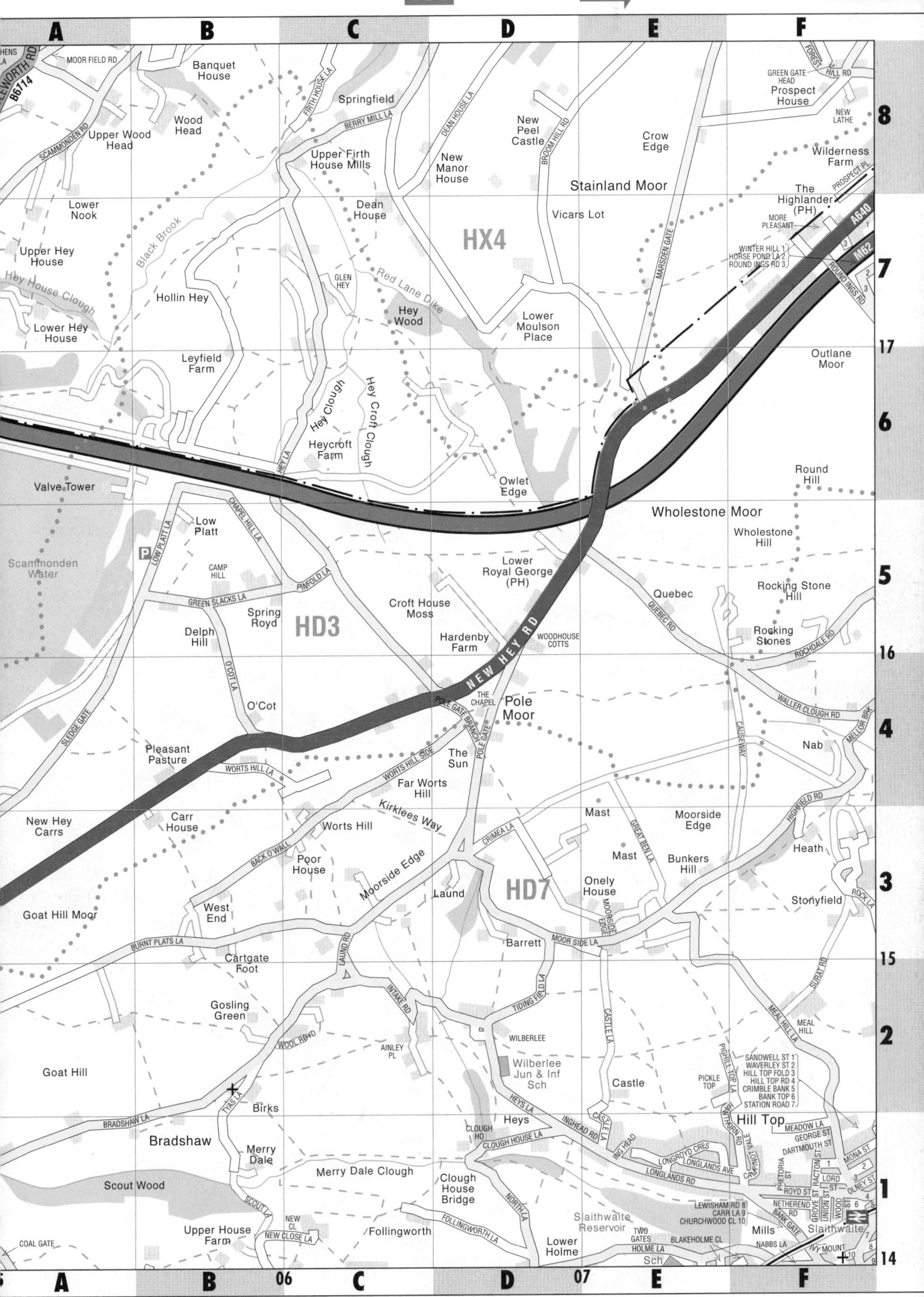
A
B
C
D
E
F
Banquet House
Springfield
Wood Head
Upper Wood Head
Upper Firth House Mills
New Manor House
New Peel Castle
Crow Edge
Prospect House
Wilderness Farm
Stainland Moor
Lower Nook
Dean House
Vicars Lot
The Highlander (PH)
HX4
Upper Hey House
Hollin Hey
Hey Wood
Lower Moulson Place
Lower Hey House
Leyfield Farm
Outlane Moor
Hey Clough
Hey Croft Clough
Heycroft Farm
Owlet Edge
Valve Tower
Round Hill
Low Platt
Wholestone Moor
Wholestone Hill
Scammonden Water
Lower Royal George (PH)
Quebec
Rocking Stone Hill
Spring Royd
Croft House Moss
Delph Hill
HD3
Hardenby Farm
Rocking Stones
O'Cot
Pole Moor
Nab
Pleasant Pasture
The Sun
Far Worts Hill
Mast
Moorside Edge
New Hey Carrs
Carr House
Worts Hill
Kirklees Way
Heath
Poor House
Bunkers Hill
Moorside Edge
Laund
HD7
Onely House
Stonyfield
Goat Hill Moor
West End
Barrett
Cartgate Foot
Gosling Green
Goat Hill
Wilberlee Jun & Inf Sch
Castle
Birks
Heys
Hill Top
Bradshaw
Merry Dale
Merry Dale Clough
Scout Wood
Clough House Bridge
Upper House Farm
Follingworth
Lower Holme
Slaithwaite Reservoir
Mills
Slaithwaite
NEW HEY RD
M62
A640
B6114
17
16
15
14
8
7
6
5
4
3
2
1
06
07

169
152

151
134

A
B
C
D
E
F
8
7
6
5
4
3
2
1
17
16
15
14
08
09
10
HD3
HD7
HD4
Lower Hurst
Upper Hirst
Snow Lea
Salendine Nook
Slack
Shaw Farm
Whin Gate
Pendle Hill
Pighill Wood
Longwood Edge
Leys Farm
Compensation Resr
Longwood Resr
Dodlee
Hotel
Nettleton Hill
Kirklees Way
Scapegoat Hill Jun & Inf Sch
Greenroyd Farm
Scapegoat Hill
Parkwood Mills
Firm Mills
Longwood
Golcar
Whitwam Bank
Hillside
Hall Ings
Golcar Flat
Leymoor
Mast
Masts
Haughs Green
Town End
Ridings
Colne Valley Mus
Liby
Schs
Scar Wood
Golcar Lilly (PH)
Clough Head Jun & Inf Sch
Bolster Moor
Heath House Mill
Harden Road Farm
Upper Wellhouse
Wellhouse
Lower Wellhouse
Sunny Bank
Wellhouse Jun & Inf Sch
Wood End Farm
Crimble
Crimble Clough
Westwood House
Westwood Mills
Linthwaite
Spa Fields Ind Est
Linthwaite Bsns Ctr
Linthwaite Ardron CE Jun & Inf Sch
Colne Valley Bsns Pk
Colne Valley High Sch
Linthwaite Clough Jun & Inf Sch
Rye Croft Edge
Holme Mills Ind Est
Huddersfield New Coll
Salendine Nook High Sch
Slaithwaite
Works
Mill
Huddersfield Narrow Canal
River Colne
Longwood Brook
Clay Wood Brook
NEW HEY RD
MANCHESTER RD (LINTHWAITE)
SCAR LA
A640
M62
A62
B6111
B6112
HUBERT ST 1
MOOR HILL CT 2
MAPLIN AVE 3
DEER CROFT DR 4
HEATHER CT 5
BEAUMONT ST 1
ROYD ST 2
RUTLAND RD 3
BOTHAM FIELDS 4
1 STEEPLE VIEW
2 BOBBIN CT
3 BOBBIN CL
4 DEAL LA
5 PARK LANE W
6 PARK LANE E
7 THE ORCHARD
1 EDGE VIEW
2 WOODVILLE AVE
3 HEATHFIELD MEWS
FIRST AVE 1
SECOND AVE 2
THIRD AVE 3
AINLEY ST 4
1 INGFIELD TERR
2 KNOWLE RD
1 CROFTON CL
2 THE RIDGEWAYS
3 WAINGATE PK
4 HUMBER CL

151
170

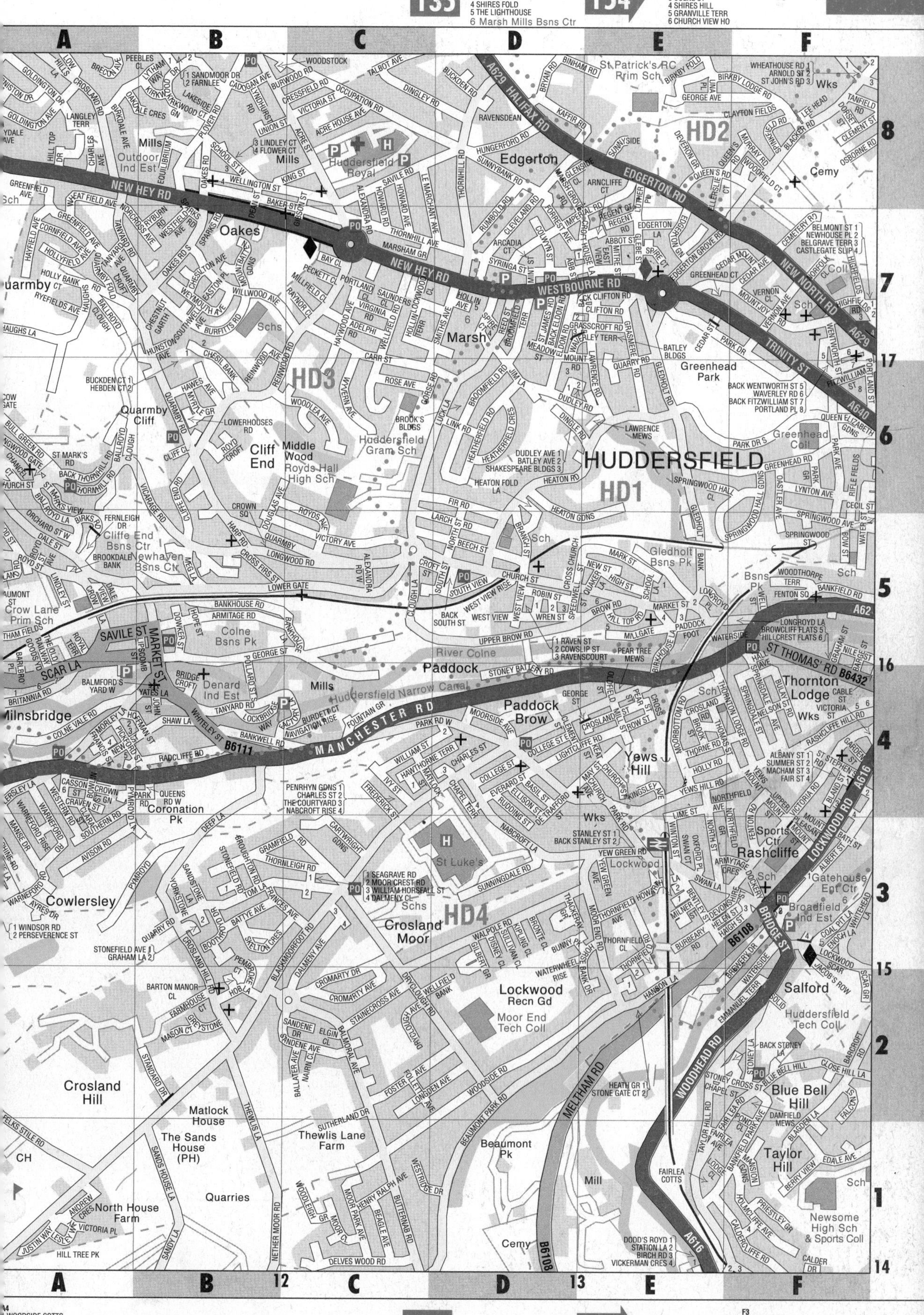

135
D7
1 JAMES MASON CT
2 CROSS COTTS
3 HOLME PL
4 SHIRES FOLD
5 THE LIGHTHOUSE
6 Marsh Mills Bsns Ctr

154
E5
1 GRANBY FLATS
2 THE TRIANGLE
3 COLNE ST
4 SHIRES HILL
5 GRANVILLE TERR
6 CHURCH VIEW HO

A4
1 WOODSIDE COTTS
2 FARADAY SQ
3 PICKFORD SQ
4 FRANCIS AVE
5 WILSON GDNS
6 MOUNT ST
7 SCARWOOD TERR

F3
1 CROWTHER ST
2 WATER ST
3 NEALE RD
4 WOOD END
5 Sovereign Bsns Ctr
6 Perserverance Mills

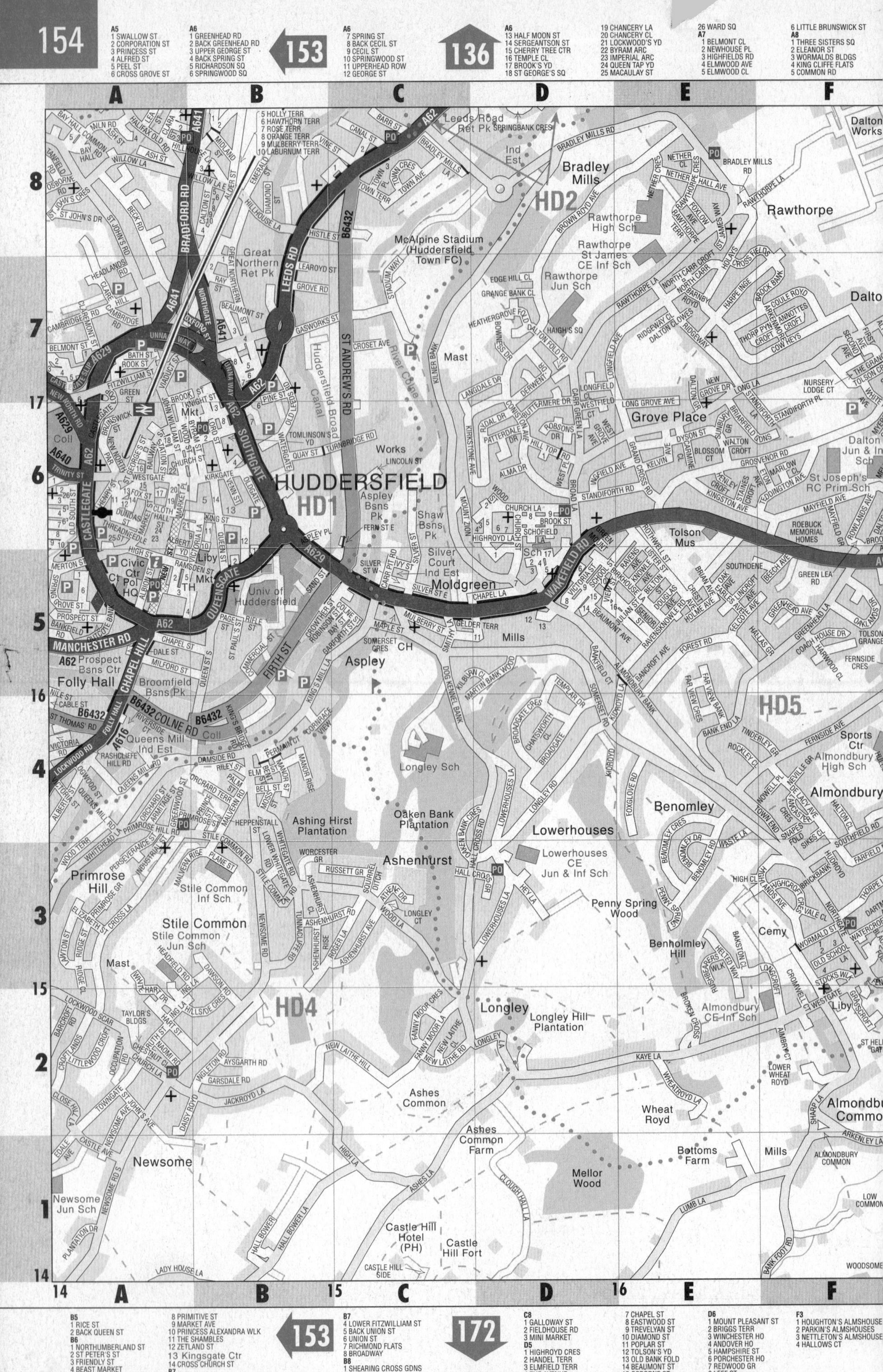
154
A5
1 SWALLOW ST
2 CORPORATION ST
3 PRINCESS ST
4 ALFRED ST
5 PEEL ST
6 CROSS GROVE ST
A6
1 GREENHEAD RD
2 BACK GREENHEAD RD
3 UPPER GEORGE ST
4 BACK SPRING ST
5 RICHARDSON SQ
6 SPRINGWOOD SQ
153
A6
7 SPRING ST
8 BACK CECIL ST
9 CECIL ST
10 SPRINGWOOD ST
11 UPPERHEAD ROW
12 GEORGE ST
136
A6
13 HALF MOON ST
14 SERGEANTSON ST
15 CHERRY TREE CTR
16 TEMPLE CL
17 BROOK'S YD
18 ST GEORGE'S SQ
19 CHANCERY LA
20 CHANCERY CL
21 LOCKWOOD'S YD
22 BYRAM ARC
23 IMPERIAL ARC
24 QUEEN TAP YD
25 MACAULAY ST
26 WARD SQ
A7
1 BELMONT CL
2 NEWHOUSE PL
3 HIGHFIELDS RD
4 ELMWOOD AVE
5 ELMWOOD CL
6 LITTLE BRUNSWICK ST
A8
1 THREE SISTERS SQ
2 ELEANOR ST
3 WORMALDS BLDGS
4 KING CLIFFE FLATS
5 COMMON RD
A B C D E F
HUDDERSFIELD
HD1
HD2
HD4
HD5
Bradley Mills
Rawthorpe
Rawthorpe High Sch
Rawthorpe St James CE Inf Sch
Rawthorpe Jun Sch
McAlpine Stadium (Huddersfield Town FC)
Great Northern Ret Pk
Leeds Road Ret Pk
Dalton Works
Dalton
Grove Place
Huddersfield Broad Canal
River Colne
Moldgreen
Tolson Mus
Aspley
Folly Hall
Prospect Bsns Ctr
Broomfield Bsns Pk
Queens Mill Ind Est
Univ of Huddersfield
Longley Sch
Ashing Hirst Plantation
Oaken Bank Plantation
Ashenhurst
Lowerhouses
Lowerhouses CE Jun & Inf Sch
Benomley
Almondbury
Almondbury High Sch
Penny Spring Wood
Benholmley Hill
Primrose Hill
Stile Common
Stile Common Inf Sch
Stile Common Jun Sch
Longley
Longley Hill Plantation
Almondbury CE Inf Sch
Ashes Common
Ashes Common Farm
Wheat Royd
Bottoms Farm
Mellor Wood
Newsome
Newsome Jun Sch
Castle Hill Hotel (PH)
Castle Hill Fort
WOODSOME
14 A B 15 C D 16 E F
B5
1 RICE ST
2 BACK QUEEN ST
B6
1 NORTHUMBERLAND ST
2 ST PETER'S ST
3 FRIENDLY ST
4 BEAST MARKET
5 Pack Horse Ctr
6 IBBOTSON FLATS
7 LONSBROUGH FLATS
8 PRIMITIVE ST
9 MARKET AVE
10 PRINCESS ALEXANDRA WLK
11 THE SHAMBLES
12 ZETLAND ST
13 Kingsgate Ctr
14 CROSS CHURCH ST
B7
1 MYRTLE ST
2 LOWER VIADUCT ST
3 WILLIAM ST
153
B7
4 LOWER FITZWILLIAM ST
5 BACK UNION ST
6 UNION ST
7 RICHMOND FLATS
8 BROADWAY
B8
1 SHEARING CROSS GDNS
2 WHITESTONE LA
3 CROFT COTTAGE LA
4 HEBBLE ST
172
C8
1 GALLOWAY ST
2 FIELDHOUSE RD
3 MINI MARKET
D5
1 HIGHROYD CRES
2 HANDEL TERR
3 ELMFIELD TERR
4 THE AVENUE
5 OLD WAKEFIELD RD
6 VICTORIA PL
7 CHAPEL ST
8 EASTWOOD ST
9 TREVELYAN ST
10 DIAMOND ST
11 POPLAR ST
12 TOLSON'S YD
13 OLD BANK FOLD
14 BEAUMONT ST
15 OSBORNE ST
16 ROSEDALE AVE
17 POPLAR TERR
D6
1 MOUNT PLEASANT ST
2 BRIGGS TERR
3 WINCHESTER HO
4 ANDOVER HO
5 HAMPSHIRE ST
6 PORCHESTER HO
7 REDWOOD GR
8 LEEF ST
9 BATLEY ST
F3
1 HOUGHTON'S ALMSHOUSE
2 PARKIN'S ALMSHOUSES
3 NETTLETON'S ALMSHOUSE
4 HALLOWS CT

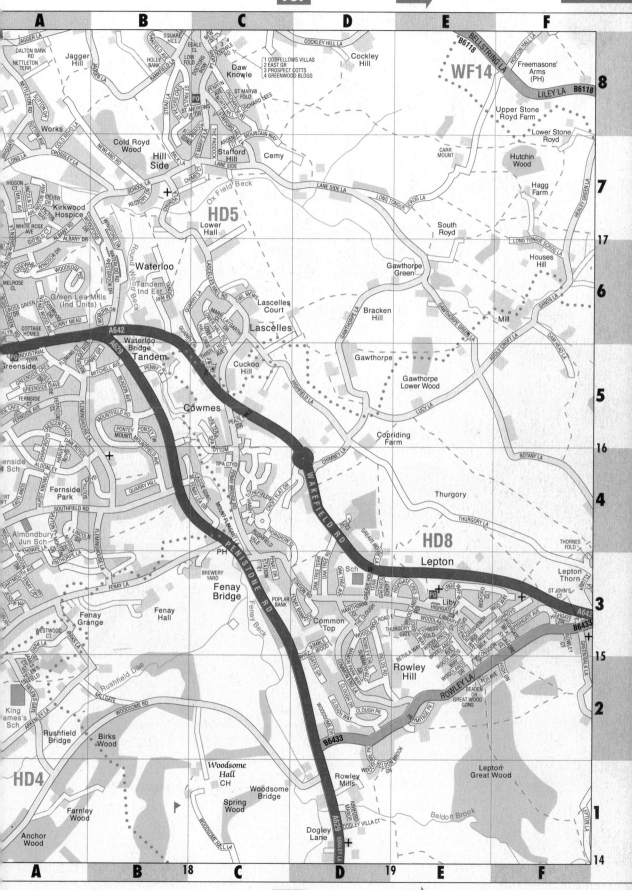

155
138

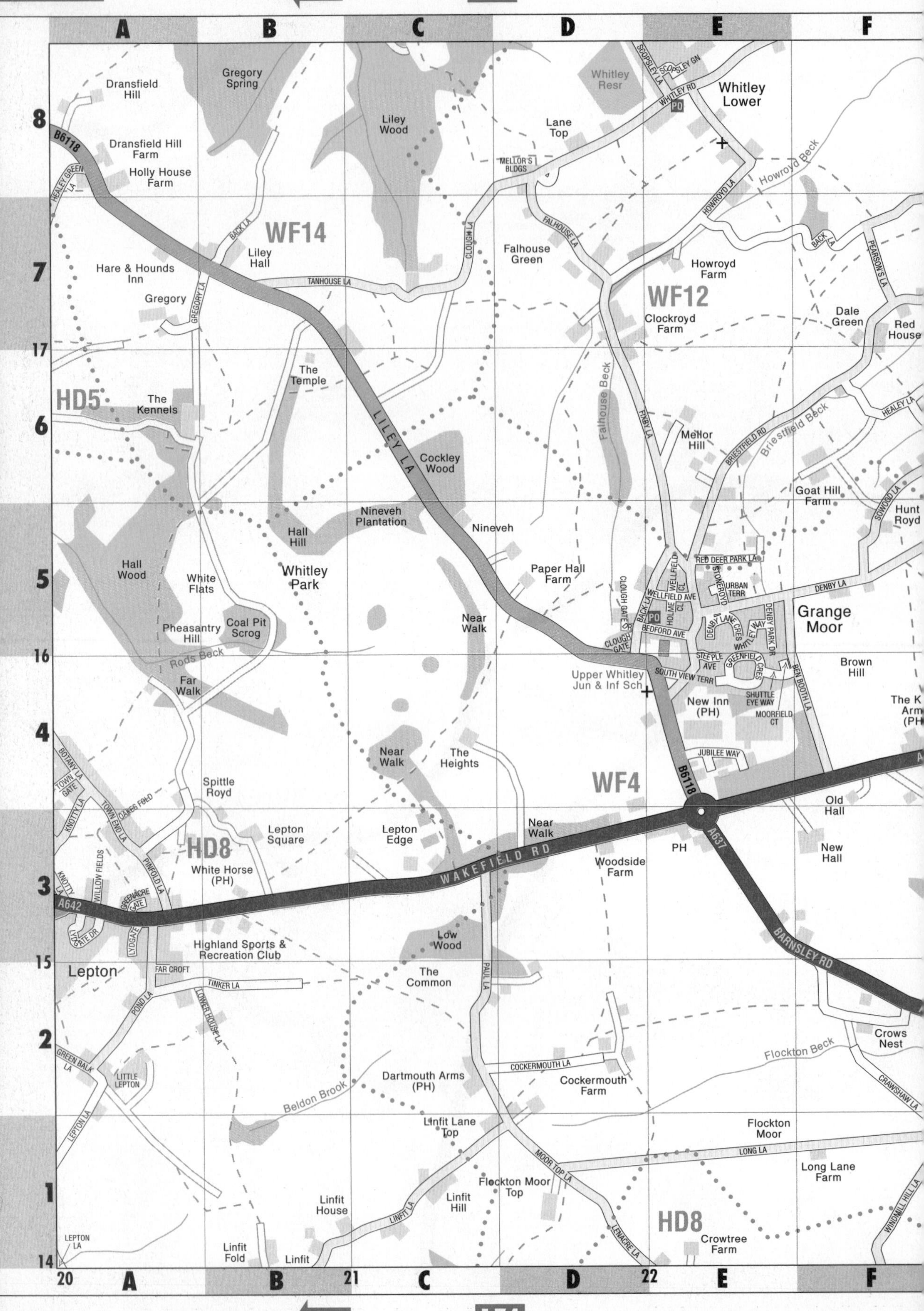
Dransfield Hill
Gregory Spring
Liley Wood
Lane Top
Whitley Resr
Whitley Lower
Dransfield Hill Farm
Holly House Farm
MELLOR'S BLDGS
Howroyd Beck
WF14
Liley Hall
Falhouse Green
Howroyd Farm
Hare & Hounds Inn
Gregory
TANHOUSE LA
WF12
Clockroyd Farm
Dale Green
Red House
The Temple
HD5
The Kennels
LILEY LA
Fathouse Beck
Mellor Hill
Briestfield Beck
Cockley Wood
Goat Hill Farm
Hunt Royd
Nineveh Plantation
Hall Hill
Nineveh
Hall Wood
White Flats
Whitley Park
Paper Hall Farm
DENBY LA
Grange Moor
Near Walk
Pheasantry Hill
Coal Pit Scrog
Rods Beck
Brown Hill
Upper Whitley Jun & Inf Sch
New Inn (PH)
Far Walk
Near Walk
The Heights
WF4
Spittle Royd
Old Hall
Near Walk
Lepton Square
Lepton Edge
HD8
PH
New Hall
WAKEFIELD RD
White Horse (PH)
Woodside Farm
A642
Highland Sports & Recreation Club
Low Wood
BARNSLEY RD
Lepton
The Common
Crows Nest
Flockton Beck
Dartmouth Arms (PH)
Cockermouth Farm
Beldon Brook
Linfit Lane Top
Flockton Moor
Long Lane Farm
Flockton Moor Top
Linfit House
Linfit Hill
HD8
Crowtree Farm
Linfit Fold
Linfit
B6118
A637
A B C D E F
20 21 22
14 15 16 17
1 2 3 4 5 6 7 8

155
174

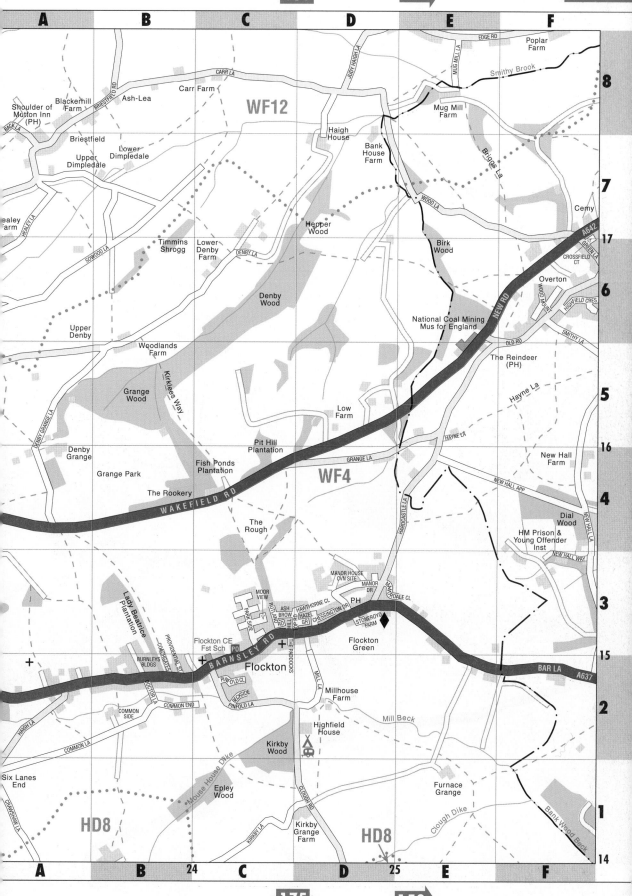

A B C D E F

8
7
17
6
5
16
4
15
3
2
1
14

WF12

Shoulder of Mutton Inn (PH)
Blackerhill Farm
Ash-Lea
Carr Farm
Briestfield
Upper Dimpledale
Lower Dimpledale
Healey Farm
BACK LA
BRIESTFIELD RD
HEALEY LA
SOWOOD LA
CARR LA
JUDY HAIGH LA

Haigh House
Bank House Farm
Mug Mill Farm
Poplar Farm
EDGE RD
MUG MILL LA
Smithy Brook

Timmins Shrogg
Lower Denby Farm
Hepper Wood
Birk Wood
DENBY LA
Briggs La
Cemy
A642
GREEN LA
CROSSFIELD CT
17

Upper Denby
Denby Wood
National Coal Mining Mus for England
NEW RD
Overton
WOOD LA
WOOD MOUNT
HIGHFIELD CRES
6

Woodlands Farm
KIRKLEES WAY
OLD RD
SMITHY LA
The Reindeer (PH)

Grange Wood
DENBY GRANGE LA
Low Farm
Hayne La
HAYNE LA
New Hall Farm
16

Denby Grange
Pit Hill Plantation
GRANGE LA
NEW HALL APP
NEW HALL LA

Grange Park
Fish Ponds Plantation
WF4
Dial Wood
4

The Rookery
WAKEFIELD RD
HARDCASTLE LA
HM Prison & Young Offender Inst
NEW HALL WAY

The Rough
MANOR HOUSE OVN SITE
MANOR DR
MANORDALE CL

Lady Beatrice Plantation
MOOR VIEW
PARK SIDE
RUTLAND ST
ASH BROW
HAWTHORNE CL
HAZEL GR
CHESSINGTON DR
PH
Stoneroyd Farm
3

Flockton CE Fst Sch
PROVIDENTIAL ST
COACHGATES
BARNSLEY RD
THE PADDOCKS
Flockton Green
BAR LA
A637
15

BURNLEYS BLDGS
PO
Flockton
MILL LA
2

COMMON SIDE
DOCTOR LA
COMMON END
PINFOLD CL
BECKSIDE
PINFOLD LA
Millhouse Farm
Mill Beck

HAGH LA
COMMON LA
MOUSE HOUSE DIKE
Highfield House
Kirkby Wood
CLOUGH RD

Six Lanes End
CRAWSHAW LA
Epley Wood
KIRKBY LA
Kirkby Grange Farm
Furnace Grange
Clough Dike
Bank Wood Beck
1

HD8
HD8
14

A B 24 C D 25 E F

157
140

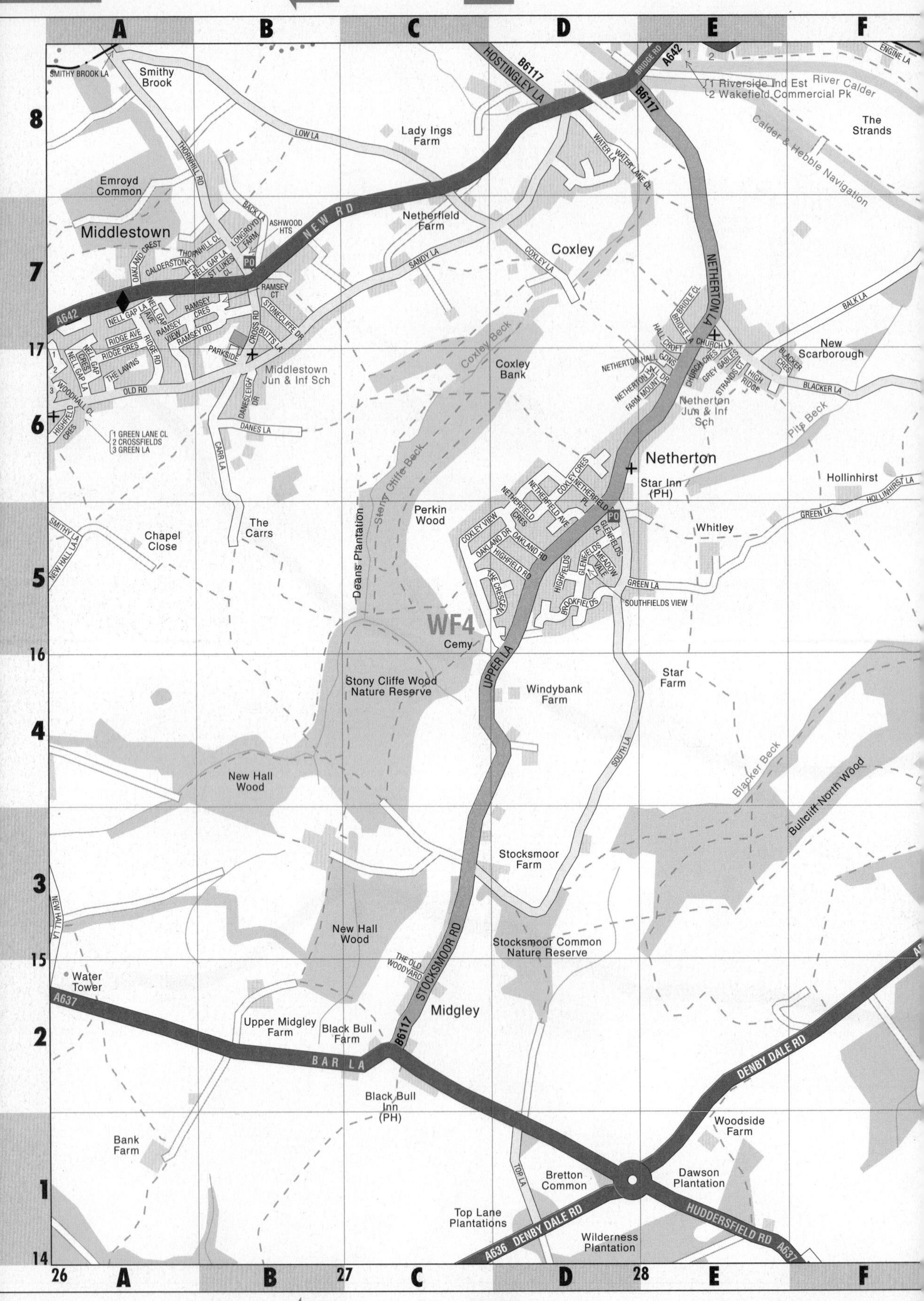
A
B
C
D
E
F
8
7
17
6
5
16
4
3
15
2
1
14
26
27
28
SMITHY BROOK LA
Smithy Brook
HOSTINGLEY LA
B6117
BRIDGE RD
A642
1 Riverside Ind Est
2 Wakefield Commercial Pk
River Calder
ENGINE LA
The Strands
Calder & Hebble Navigation
Lady Ings Farm
LOW LA
THORNHILL RD
Emroyd Common
WATER LA
WATER LANE CL
Middlestown
BACK LA
ASHWOOD HTS
LONGROYD FARM
NEW RD
Netherfield Farm
OAKLAND CREST
CALDERSTON CL
THORNHILL CL
NELL GAP LA
ST LUKES CL
PO
SANDY LA
Coxley
COXLEY LA
NETHERTON LA
A642
NELL GAP LA
RAMSEY CT
RAMSEY CRES
STONECLIFFE DR
BALK LA
BRIDLE CL
BRIDLE LA
HALL CROFT
CHURCH LA
New Scarborough
BLACKER CRES
RIDGE AVE
RIDGE CRES
RIDGE RD
RAMSEY VIEW
RAMSEY RD
CROSS RD
BUTTS LA
PARKSIDE
THE LAWNS
OLD RD
Middlestown Jun & Inf Sch
Coxley Beck
Coxley Bank
NETHERTON HALL GDNS
NETHERTON HALL RD
FARM MOUNT DR
CHURCH CRES
GREY GABLES
STRANDS CT
HIGH RIDGE
BLACKER LA
WOODHALL CL
HIGHFIELD CRES
1 GREEN LANE CL
2 CROSSFIELDS
3 GREEN LA
DANESLEIGH DR
DANES LA
CARR LA
Netherton Jun & Inf Sch
Pits Beck
Netherton
Star Inn (PH)
Hollinhirst
HOLLINHIRST LA
GREEN LA
Whitley
Stony Cliffe Beck
Perkin Wood
Deans Plantation
COXLEY CRES
NETHERFIELD PL
NETHERFIELD AVE
NETHERFIELD CRES
COXLEY VIEW
OAKLAND DR
OAKLAND RD
HIGHFIELD RD
THE CRESCENT
HIGHFIELDS
GLENFIELDS
MEADOW VALE
BROOKFIELDS
GREEN LA
SOUTHFIELDS VIEW
SMITHY LA
NEW HALL LA
Chapel Close
The Carrs
WF4
Cemy
UPPER LA
Stony Cliffe Wood Nature Reserve
Windybank Farm
Star Farm
SOUTH LA
New Hall Wood
Blacker Beck
Bullcliff North Wood
Stocksmoor Farm
NEW HALL LA
New Hall Wood
Stocksmoor Common Nature Reserve
THE OLD WOODYARD
STOCKSMOOR RD
Water Tower
A637
Midgley
Upper Midgley Farm
Black Bull Farm
B6117
BAR LA
DENBY DALE RD
Black Bull Inn (PH)
Woodside Farm
Bank Farm
Bretton Common
TOP LA
Dawson Plantation
Top Lane Plantations
A636
DENBY DALE RD
HUDDERSFIELD RD
A637
Wilderness Plantation

157
176

141
160

HORBURY
Addingford
Mill
The Wyke
Sewage Works
Horbury Junction
Navigation Inn (PH)
Ind Est
Wks
Horbury Cut
Calder and Hebble Navigation
River Calder
Broad Cut
Hartley Bank Wood
Broad Cut Farm
Greenfield Farm
Cedar Court Hotel
Cedar Court Office Pk
Durkar
Durkar Hall Farm
WF2
WF4
Calder Grove
Brice Hill
British Oak (PH)
Brice Hill Plantation
St James CE Jun & Inf Sch
Cemy
Crigglestone
Great Cliff
Mackie Hill Jun & Inf Sch
Blacker Hall Farm
The Station (PH)
Painthorpe
Blacker Beck
Dennington Beck
Bullcliff Beck
Bullcliff Wood
Blacker Hall Spring
Birch Lathe Farm
Wakefield City Farm
Dennington
Reddie Carr Ing
Broad Carr
Hollingthorpe
Stag Royd Wood
Low Moor
Dane Royd Jun & Inf Sch
Hall Green
Burn Bank
Jenkin Wood
Woolley Moor Farm
Woolley Moor House
Woolley Moor
Totty Spring
Woolley Edge
Gate Royd Wood
Woolley Edge Services
A642
SOUTHFIELD LA
A636
DENBY DALE RD
M1
39
BLACKER LA
DENBY DALE RD
CLIFF RD
HAVEROID LA
DENNINGTON LA
WOOLLEY LOW MOOR LA
LOW MOOR LA
BOLTON WIFE HILL
GALLOWS LA
INTAKE LA
COMMON LA
BRETTON LA
BRANCH RD
DAW LA
HOLLINGTHORPE LA
HOLLINGTHORPE RD
PAINTHORPE LA
HIGH ST
CALDER MOUNT
STANDBRIDGE LA
BULL LA
A B C D E F
30 31
8 7 6 5 4 3 2 1
17 16 15 14

177
160

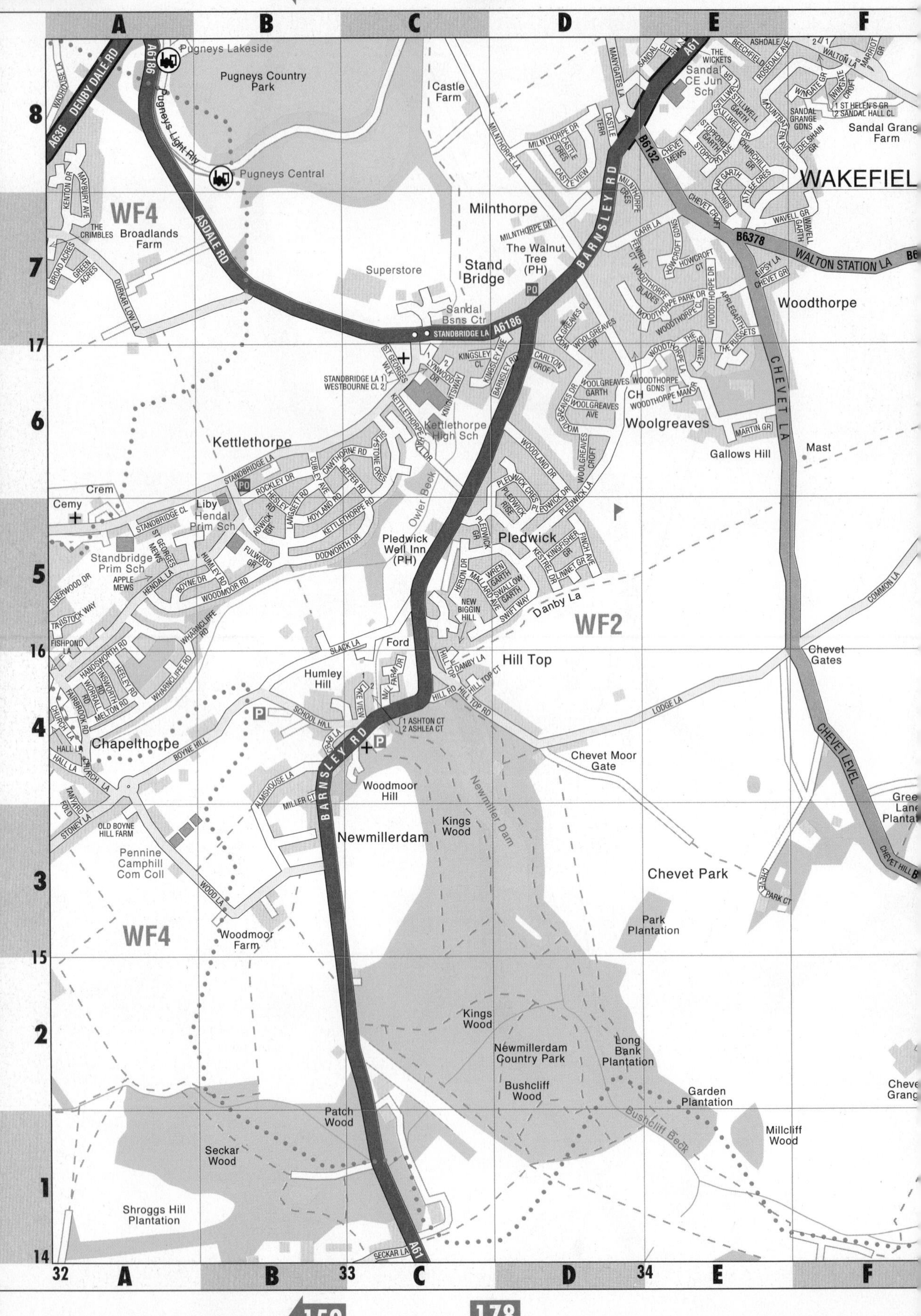

159
142

A   B   C   D   E   F

8

Pugneys Lakeside

Pugneys Country Park

Castle Farm

Sandal CE Jun Sch

Ashdale

THE WICKETS

Sandal Grang Farm

WAKEFIEL

Pugneys Light Rly

Pugneys Central

WF4

THE CRIMBLES

Broadlands Farm

Milnthorpe

7

Superstore

Stand Bridge

The Walnut Tree (PH)

Woodthorpe

BARNSLEY RD

B6378

WALTON STATION LA

17

Sandal Bsns Ctr

STANDBRIDGE LA

A6186

Woolgreaves

Woodthorpe CH

STANDBRIDGE LA 1
WESTBOURNE CL 2

Kingsley High Sch

Kettlethorpe

Woolgreaves

Gallows Hill

Mast

6

Kettlethorpe

Crem

Cemy

Liby
Hendal Prim Sch

Pledwick

Pledwick Well Inn (PH)

Pledwick

Owler Beck

Standbridge Prim Sch

Apple Mews

5

NEW BIGGIN HILL

Danby La

WF2

16

Fishpond La

Ford

Hill Top

Humley Hill

4

Chapelthorpe

Chevet Moor Gate

CHEVET LEVEL

1 ASHTON CT
2 ASHLEA CT

BARNSLEY RD

Woodmoor Hill

Kings Wood

Newmiller Dam

Gree Lane Planta

Old Boyne Hill Farm

Pennine Camphill Com Coll

Newmillerdam

Chevet Park

3

WF4

Woodmoor Farm

Park Plantation

15

Kings Wood

Long Bank Plantation

Chevet Grang

2

Newmillerdam Country Park

Bushcliff Wood

Garden Plantation

Patch Wood

Millcliff Wood

Bushcliff Beck

Seckar Wood

1

Shroggs Hill Plantation

14

32   A   B   33   C   D   34   E   F

SECKAR LA

A61

159
178

143
162

WF1
WF2
WF4
Walton
Overtown
The Balk
Rose Farm
Walton Jun Sch
Walton Grove Inf Sch
Liby
Brook Farm
Thorntree Farm
Highwood Farm
Hare Park Junction
Harepark Farm
Thorntree Hill
Hare Park Wood
Crofton High Sch
Walton Park
Water Gate
Walton Hall
Anglers Country Park
Stubbs Wood
The Heronry
Haw Park
Clay Royd Bridge
Briery Hall Farm
Visitor Ctr
Wintersett Resr
Cold Hiendley Resr
Rough Bottom Plantation
Haw Park Bridge
Bleakley Bridge
Haw Park Beck
Cold Hiendley Bridge
Works
Rose Farm
Cold Hiendley
Ryhill Pits
Trans Pennine Trail
Barnsley Canal (dis)
Drain Beck
SHAY LA
B6378
B6132
CHEVET LA
HAW PARK LA
COLD HIENDLEY COMMON LA
RYHILL PITS LA
STATION RD
SIKE LA
THE BALK
BROCKSWOOD CT
FERRY TOP LA
RECTORY CRES
PARK LA
HARE PARK LA
HIGH ST
SLACK LA
SMITHY
WALTON VIEW
CLAREMONT CRES 1
HARE PARK VIEW 2
Sch
WOOD YARD COTTS
MANOR GARTH
MANOR CRES
MANOR RISE
MANOR RD
OAKENSHAW LA
ELMWOOD GARTH
ELMWOOD AVE
ELMWOOD CL
ELMWOOD DR
SCHOOL LA
THE STABLES
WALTON LOCKS
BEECH CROFT
ORCHARD CROFT
CHERRY TREE DR
CHERRY TREE CRES
CHERRY TREE RD
BROOKLANDS VIEW
BROOKLANDS RD
BROOKLANDS AVE
GROVE CRES
THE GROVE
THORNHILL CROFT
HILL DR
PRIORY SQ
WATERTON CL
AMBLESIDE DR
OAKLANDS CROFT
HIGH MDWS
SPURR GR
COPPER BEECH CT
WOODFIELD PK
LAKELAND WAY
LANGDALE
OAK TREE MOUNT
KENDAL RISE
1 CHESTNUT AVE
2 BUTTERMERE CROFT
COMMON LA
CH
36
37
A B C D E F
1 2 3 4 5 6 7 8
14 15 16 17

179
162

161
144

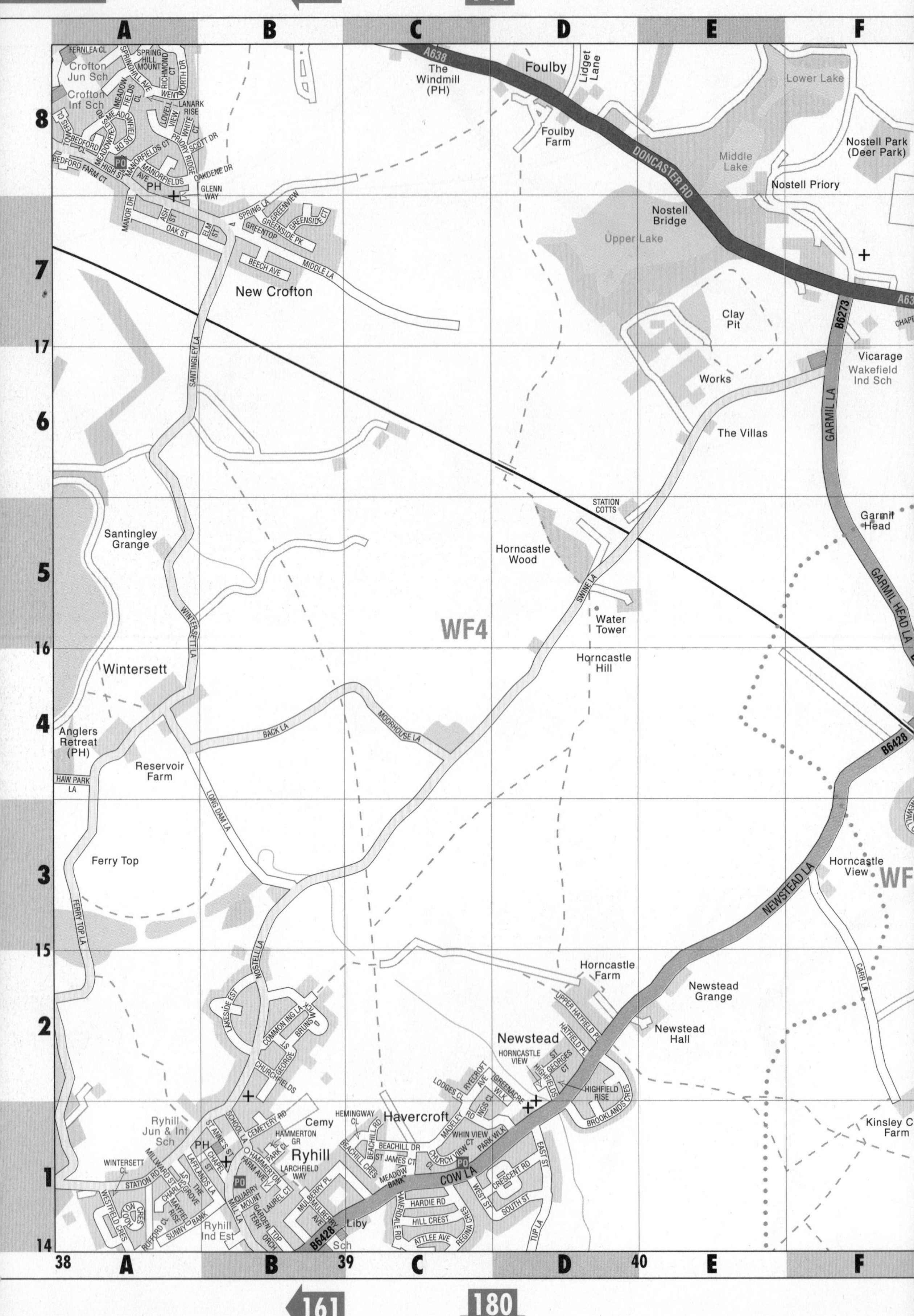
A
B
C
D
E
F
Crofton Jun Sch
Crofton Inf Sch
The Windmill (PH)
Foulby
Lidget Lane
Foulby Farm
Lower Lake
Middle Lake
Nostell Park (Deer Park)
Nostell Priory
Nostell Bridge
Upper Lake
A638
DONCASTER RD
New Crofton
Clay Pit
B6273
Vicarage
Wakefield Ind Sch
Works
The Villas
GARMIL LA
SANTINGLEY LA
Santingley Grange
STATION COTTS
Garmil Head
Horncastle Wood
GARMIL HEAD LA
SWINE LA
Water Tower
WF4
Horncastle Hill
WINTERSETT LA
Wintersett
Anglers Retreat (PH)
BACK LA
MOORHOUSE LA
B6428
Reservoir Farm
HAW PARK LA
LONG DAM LA
Ferry Top
FERRY TOP LA
Horncastle View
NEWSTEAD LA
NOSTELL LA
Horncastle Farm
Newstead Grange
CARR LA
Newstead Hall
LAKESIDE EST
COMMON ING LA
Newstead
HIGHFIELD RISE
BROOKLANDS CRES
Kinsley C Farm
Ryhill Jun & Inf Sch
Cemy
Havercroft
Ryhill
COW LA
HARDIE RD
HILL CREST
ATTLEE AVE
Ryhill Ind Est
Liby
Sch
EAST ST
WEST ST
SOUTH ST
TUP LA
STATION RD
WINTERSETT CL
8
7
17
6
5
16
4
3
15
2
1
14
38
39
40

161
180

145
164

Wragby
Engine Wood
Roebuck Wood
Ash Wood
The Bushes
Hessle Cottage
Hessle
Hessle Hall
WF4
Spread Eagle (PH)
Constitution Hill
Ackworth Sch
Ackworth Moor Top
Constitution Hill Farm
Wragby Grange
DONCASTER RD
WF7
Offley Bridge
Taylor Wood
Onward Bsns Pk
Brackenhill Bridge
Sewage Works
Fishpond Plantation
Poplar Farm
Liby
Kinsley Green Farm
Brackenhill
WAKEFIELD RD
Ray Winfield Ind Est
Fitzwilliam Prim Sch
Rhyddings Farm
Oakfield Park Sch
Priory Bsns Pk
Fitzwilliam
Outgang
WF9
Bingley Spring Wood
Kinsley Prim Sch
Ings Farm
Kinsley Common
Hoyle Mill Dam
Hagg Wood
Kinsley
Ashmount Ind Est
Hemsworth Turkey Farms
Depot
Hemsworth Water Park
Hemsworth Marsh
Marsh Farm
Common Side Farm
Vale Head Park
B6428
B6273
A628
A638

181
164

163
146

High Ackworth
Court Farm
Townend Farm
Ackworth Grange
Green Lane Farm
Ackworth House
Ackworth Sch
Low Ackworth
Howard CE Jun & Inf Sch
South Lodge
The Chestnuts
Kennels Farm
Low Grange Farm
WF8
Tan House Dike
Low Farm
Sewage Works
Burnhill Bridge
WF7
Mill Dam Jun & Inf Sch
Moorhouse Farm
Rockingham Gorse
Cemy
Cherry Tree Farm
Firth Field
Oakfield Park Sch
Shepherd's Hill
WF9
Badsworth Common
Ninevah Farm
The Grove
Rogerthorpe Manor (Hotel)
Lanes Farm
Hall Farm
Badsworth CE Jun & Inf Sch
Brookside Farm
Badsworth Grange
Badsworth
Marsh Whin Covert
Royd Moor Farm
DONCASTER RD
BARNSLEY RD
PONTEFRACT RD
RIGG LA
WHITEGATE LA
ACKWORTH BRIDLE RD
BURNHILL LA
ROCKINGHAM LA
FIRTHFIELD LA
OWLERS LA
THORPE LA
BEACONFIELD RD
NEW RD
ROYD MOOR LA
OAKTREE LA
TAN HOUSE LA
LOW FARM LA
1 HOWARD DR
2 STRATUS CL
1 GRANGE CT
2 BADSWORTH MEWS
3 MANOR FARM
4 NEW ROW

163
182

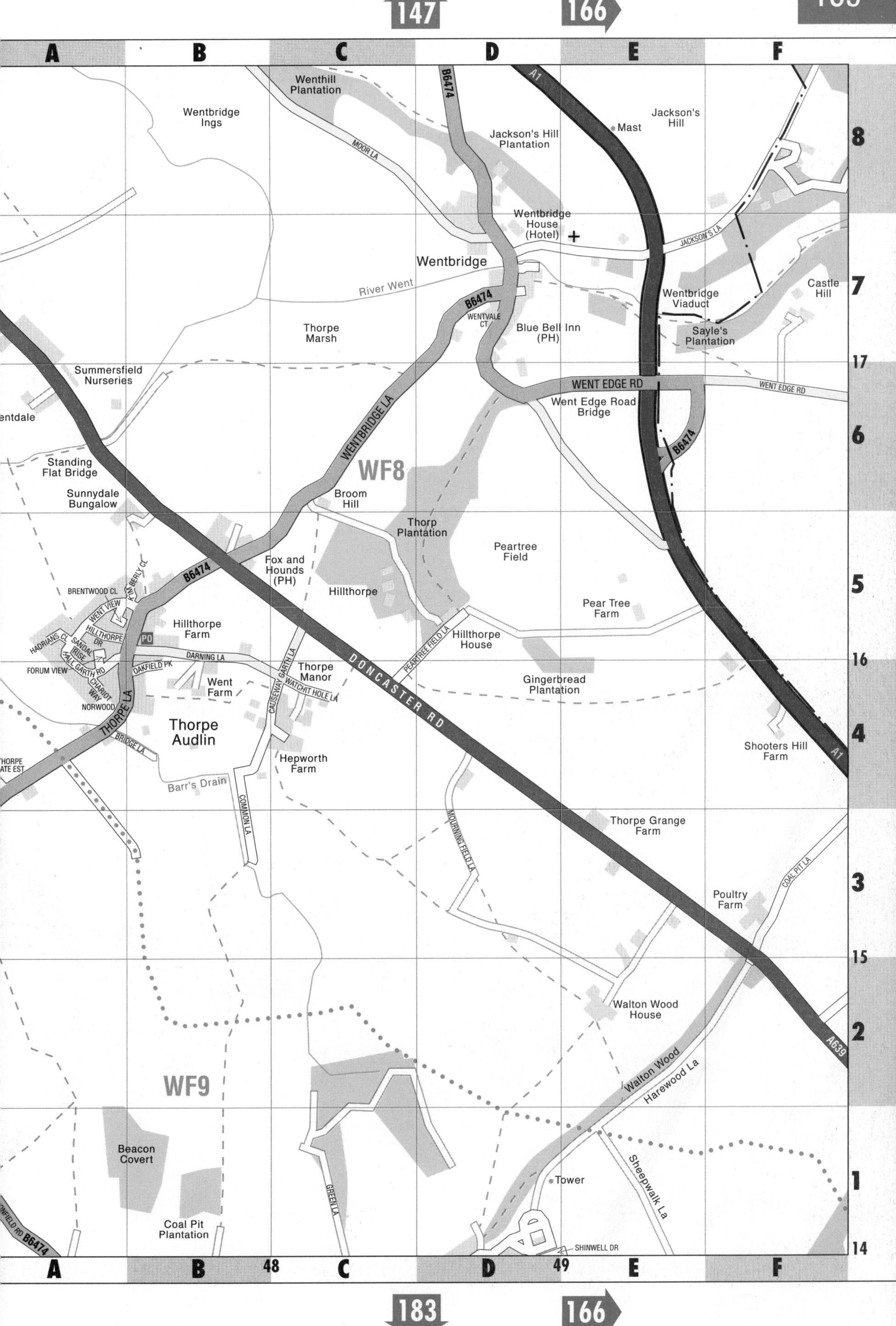

A B C D E F

8

Wenthill
Plantation

Wentbridge Ings

Jackson's Hill
Plantation

Mast

Jackson's
Hill

B6474

A1

MOOR LA

Wentbridge House
(Hotel)

JACKSON'S LA

Wentbridge

7

River Went

Thorpe
Marsh

B6474

WENTVALE
CT

Blue Bell Inn
(PH)

Wentbridge
Viaduct

Castle
Hill

Sayle's
Plantation

17

Summersfield
Nurseries

WENT EDGE RD

WENT EDGE RD

Went Edge Road
Bridge

B6474

6

entdale

Standing
Flat Bridge

WF8

Broom
Hill

Thorp
Plantation

Peartree
Field

Sunnydale
Bungalow

WENTBRIDGE LA

Pear Tree
Farm

5

BRENTWOOD CL

KINGSBERRY CL

B6474

Fox and
Hounds
(PH)

Hillthorpe

Hillthorpe
House

PEARTREE FIELD LA

Went
View

HILLTHORPE
DR

SANDAL
RISE

PO

Hillthorpe
Farm

Gingerbread
Plantation

16

HADRIANS CL

TALL GARTH RD

CHARIOT
WAY

OAKFIELD PK

DARNING LA

DONCASTER RD

FORUM VIEW

NORWOOD

THORPE LA

CAUSEWAY GARTH LA

WATCHIT HOLE LA

Went
Farm

Thorpe
Manor

Shooters Hill
Farm

A1

4

Thorpe
Audlin

HORPE
ATE EST

BRIDGE LA

Hepworth
Farm

Thorpe Grange
Farm

Barr's Drain

COMMON LA

MOURNING FIELD LA

Poultry
Farm

COAL PIT LA

3

15

WF9

Walton Wood
House

A639

2

Walton Wood

Harewood La

Beacon
Covert

GREEN LA

Sheepwalk La

Tower

1

INFIELD RD B6474

Coal Pit
Plantation

SHINWELL DR

14

A B 48 C D 49 E F

165

North Yorkshire STREET ATLAS

DN6

Smeaton Leys

Brockadale Plantation

Brockadale

Smeaton Pasture

LEYS LA

SMEATLEY'S LA

CHURCHFIELD LA

WENT EDGE RD

River Went

CHAPEL LA

HODGE LA

The Fox (PH)

MOU PLEAS...

Went Edge Field

Kirk Smeaton CE Prim Sch PH

WENTDALE

STAN VALLEY

Riverside Farm

Little Smeaton

TOP HOUSE CT

MAIN ST

PO

RECTORY CT

WATER LA

SPRINGFIELD CRES

Willow Bridge

Kirk Smeaton

MANOR CL

Manor House

PINFOLD LA

PINFOLD CROSS

WF8

Little Bottom Plantation

NORTON AND KIRK SMEATON RD

SPITTLERUSH LA

MIDDLEFIELD LA

Middle Field

Westfield

Upper Wells

COAL PIT LA

A1

Broomfield Plantation

Westfield Farm

Highfield Farm

Long Close Plantation

WESTFIELD LA

GREENGATE RD

CRAB TREE LA

LONG LA

Mutton Hall Farm

Sewage Wks

Barnsdale Bar Quarry

Old Whin Fox Covert

Motel

Quarry

FOX COVERT ROAD OR WHIN COVERT LA

White Ley Plantation

A639

DONCASTER RD

Barnsdale Bar Service Area

Windhill Plantation

Cusworth Hill

DN6

Quarry

Barnsdale

WHITE LEY RD

Glebe Farm

A1

Barnsdale Wood

WF9

50

A

B

51

C

D

52

E

F

165
184

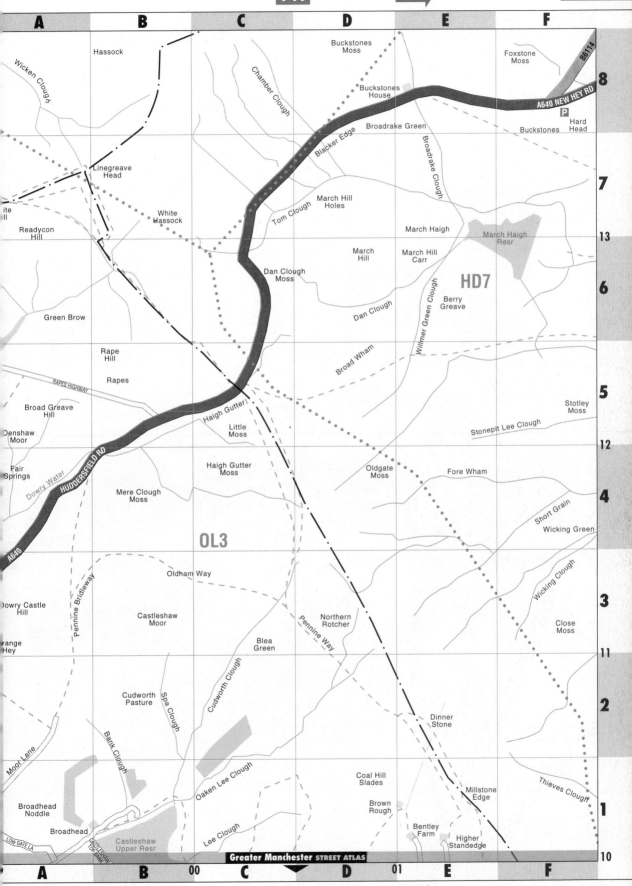

149
168

A
B
C
D
E
F
8
7
13
6
5
12
4
3
11
2
1
10
Hassock
Wicken Clough
Buckstones Moss
Chamber Clough
Foxstone Moss
B6114
Buckstones House
A640 NEW HEY RD
P
Hard Head
Buckstones
Broadrake Green
Blacker Edge
Broadrake Clough
Linegreave Head
March Hill Holes
Tom Clough
White Hassock
Readycon Hill
March Haigh
March Haigh Resr
March Hill
March Hill Carr
Dan Clough Moss
HD7
Willmer Green Clough
Berry Greave
Dan Clough
Green Brow
Rape Hill
Broad Wham
Rapes
RAPES HIGHWAY
Broad Greave Hill
Haigh Gutter
Little Moss
Stotley Moss
Stonepit Lee Clough
Denshaw Moor
Fair Springs
HUDDERSFIELD RD
Dowry Water
Haigh Gutter Moss
Oldgate Moss
Fore Wham
Mere Clough Moss
Short Grain
Wicking Green
OL3
A640
Oldham Way
Pennine Bridleway
Wicking Clough
Dowry Castle Hill
Castleshaw Moor
Northern Rotcher
Pennine Way
Close Moss
Grange Hey
Blea Green
Cudworth Clough
Cudworth Pasture
Spa Clough
Dinner Stone
Bank Clough
Moor Lane
Coal Hill Slades
Oaken Lee Clough
Thieves Clough
Millstone Edge
Broadhead Noddle
Brown Rough
Broadhead
Bentley Farm
Lee Clough
Higher Standedge
LOW GATE LA
CASTLESHAW TOP BANK
Castleshaw Upper Resr
00
01

168

167
150

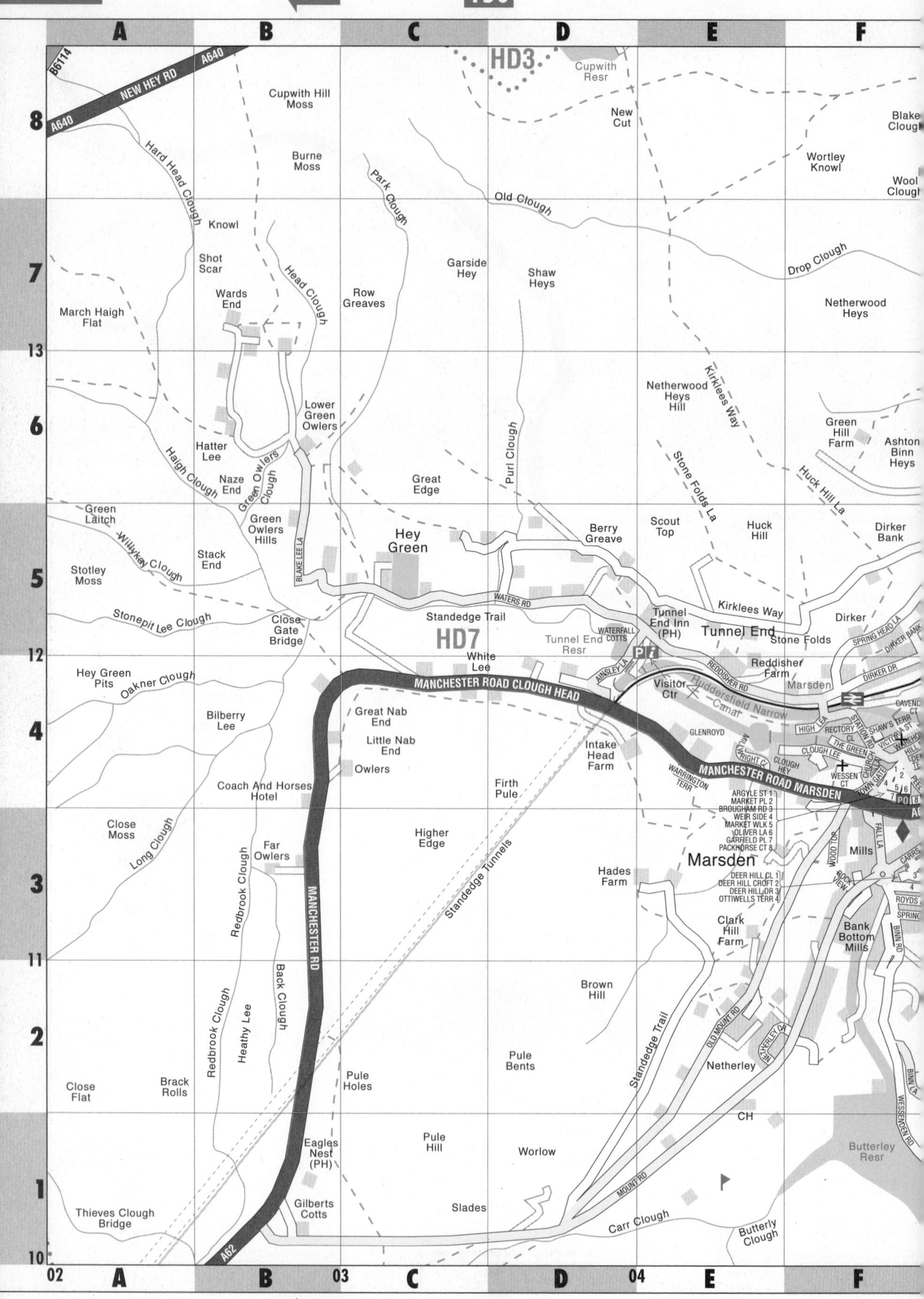
HD3
Cupwith Resr
New Cut
Cupwith Hill Moss
Burne Moss
NEW HEY RD
A640
B6114
Hard Head Clough
Park Clough
Old Clough
Wortley Knowl
Blake Clough
Wool Clough
Knowl
Shot Scar
Wards End
Head Clough
Row Greaves
Garside Hey
Shaw Heys
Drop Clough
Netherwood Heys
March Haigh Flat
Kirklees Way
Netherwood Heys Hill
Lower Green Owlers
Hatter Lee
Naze End
Haigh Clough
Green Owlers Clough
Purl Clough
Great Edge
Stone Folds La
Green Hill Farm
Ashton Binn Heys
Huck Hill La
Green Laitch
Green Owlers Hills
Hey Green
Berry Greave
Scout Top
Huck Hill
Dirker Bank
Willykay Clough
Stack End
Stotley Moss
BLAKE LEE LA
WATERS RD
Stonepit Lee Clough
Close Gate Bridge
Standedge Trail
HD7
Tunnel End Inn (PH)
Tunnel End
Kirklees Way
Dirker
Stone Folds
Tunnel End Resr
WATERFALL COTTS
White Lee
Hey Green Pits
Oakner Clough
MANCHESTER ROAD CLOUGH HEAD
AINSLEY LA
Visitor Ctr
Huddersfield Narrow Canal
REDDISHER RD
Reddisher Farm
Marsden
SPRING HEAD LA
DIRKER BANK
DIRKER DR
Great Nab End
Little Nab End
Bilberry Lee
Intake Head Farm
GLENROYD
HIGH LEA
RECTORY CL
STATION RD
SHAW'S TERR
VICTORIA ST
THE GREEN
CLOUGH LEE
MILLWRIGHT CL
CLOUGH HEY
CHURCH LA
WESSEN CT
TOWN GATE
Owlers
Coach And Horses Hotel
Firth Pule
WARRINGTON TERR
MANCHESTER ROAD MARSDEN
ARGYLE ST 1
MARKET PL 2
BROUGHAM RD 3
WEIR SIDE 4
MARKET WLK 5
OLIVER LA 6
GARFIELD PL 7
PACKHORSE CT 8
PO
Close Moss
Long Clough
Higher Edge
Far Owlers
Redbrook Clough
Standedge Tunnels
Marsden
Hades Farm
WOOD TOP
FALL LA
Mills
DEER HILL CL 1
DEER HILL CROFT 2
DEER HILL DR 3
OTTIWELLS TERR 4
ROCK VIEW
CARRS
ROYDS
SPRING
MANCHESTER RD
Clark Hill Farm
Bank Bottom Mills
BINN RD
Back Clough
Brown Hill
Redbrook Clough
Heathy Lee
Standedge Trail
OLD MOUNT RD
HATHERLEY DR
Netherley
Close Flat
Brack Rolls
Pule Holes
Pule Bents
CH
BINN LA
WESSENDEN RD
Eagles Nest (PH)
Pule Hill
Worlow
Butterley Resr
MOUNT RD
Thieves Clough Bridge
Gilberts Cotts
Slades
Carr Clough
Butterly Clough
A62
A B C D E F
8 7 6 5 4 3 2 1
13 12 11 10
02 03 04

167
185

151
170

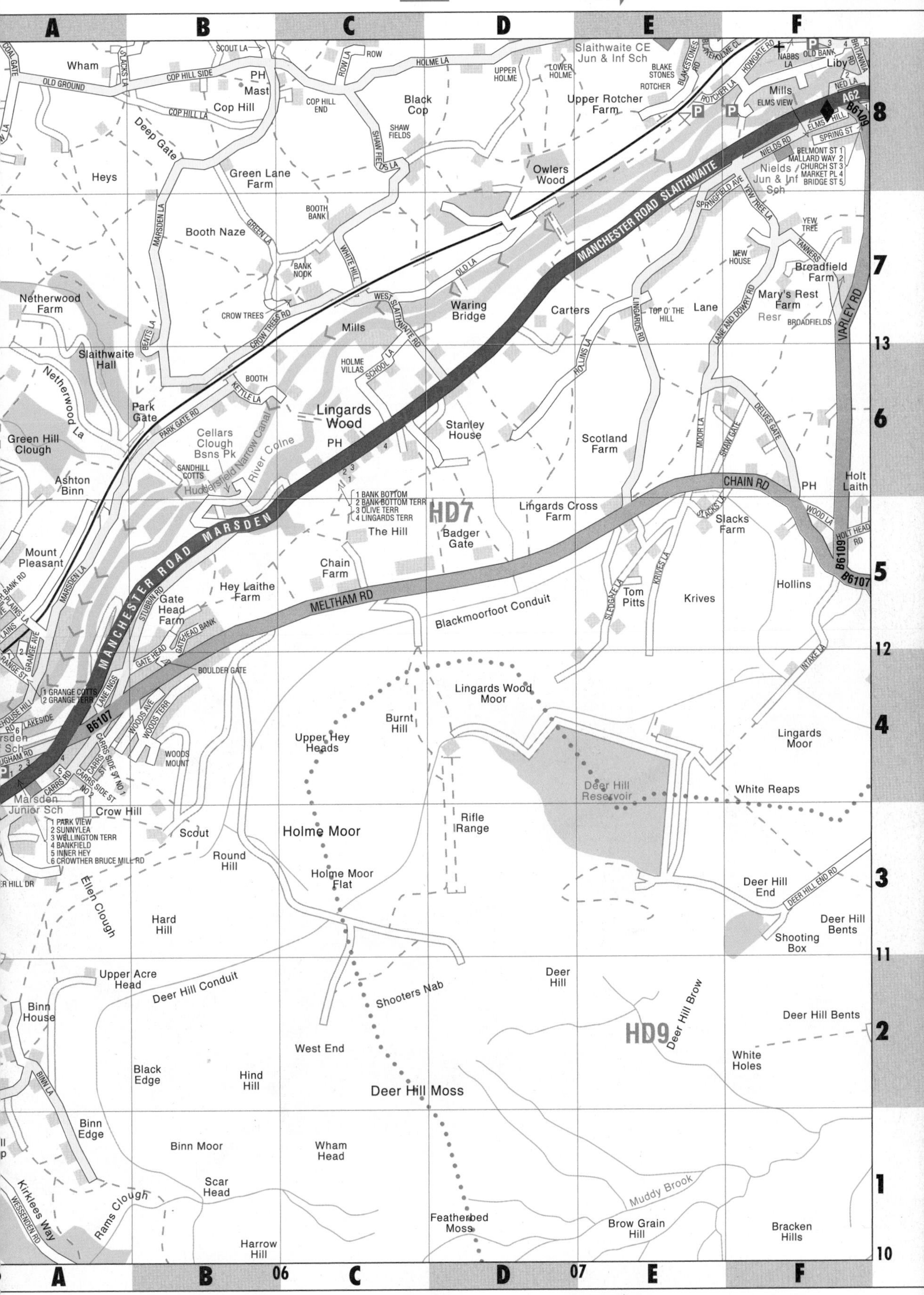
Wham
Heys
Cop Hill
Mast
Black Cop
Green Lane Farm
Booth Naze
Netherwood Farm
Slaithwaite Hall
Green Hill Clough
Ashton Binn
Mount Pleasant
Park Gate
Cellars Clough Bsns Pk
Lingards Wood
Mills
Waring Bridge
Carters
Owlers Wood
Upper Rotcher Farm
Slaithwaite CE Jun & Inf Sch
Liby
Nields Jun & Inf Sch
Broadfield Farm
Mary's Rest Farm
Resr
Lane
Stanley House
Scotland Farm
Holt Laith
Lingards Cross Farm
Slacks Farm
Badger Gate
The Hill
Chain Farm
Hey Laithe Farm
Gate Head Farm
Tom Pitts
Krives
Hollins
MANCHESTER ROAD SLAITHWAITE
MANCHESTER ROAD MARSDEN
MELTHAM RD
CHAIN RD
Blackmoorfoot Conduit
HD7
Lingards Wood Moor
Burnt Hill
Upper Hey Heads
Lingards Moor
White Reaps
Deer Hill Reservoir
Rifle Range
Holme Moor
Holme Moor Flat
Scout
Round Hill
Crow Hill
Marsden Junior Sch
Ellen Clough
Hard Hill
Deer Hill End
Deer Hill Bents
Shooting Box
Upper Acre Head
Deer Hill Conduit
Deer Hill
Shooters Nab
Binn House
Deer Hill Brow
HD9
Deer Hill Bents
White Holes
West End
Black Edge
Hind Hill
Deer Hill Moss
Binn Edge
Binn Moor
Wham Head
Scar Head
Muddy Brook
Rams Clough
Kirklees Way
Featherbed Moss
Brow Grain Hill
Bracken Hills
Harrow Hill
A62
B6109
B6107

186
170

169
152

Liby Mills
River Colne
MANCHESTER RD (LINTHWAITE) A62
Kitchen Clough
Heywoods Farm
High House
HD7
Lower Clough
Black Rock Mills
Upper Clough
Height
Observatory
Jerusalem Farm
Bethany Farm
Blackmoorfoot
Bulls Head (PH)
HD4
Hey
Jubilee Quarries (dis)
Blackmoorfoot Reservoir
Green Gate
Black Moor
Holt Head
Cottage Home Farm
Edge Moor
Orange Wood
Cop End Farm
Moor Top Farm
Meltham Edge
Will's O'Nat's (PH)
Helme
Laund Farm
Meltham Cop
Queen Mary's Farm
Laund
Blackmoorfoot Conduit
Helme CE Jun & Inf Sch
Far Fields
Hall Heys Wood
Upper Hey
Helme Hall
Lower Hey Farm
Meltham Grange Farm
SLAITHWAITE RD
Travellers' Rest (PH)
HD9
Hassocks Rd
Meltham
Wks
Meltham Moor Prim Sch
Catchwater Drain
Deer Hill Bents
Britain
Town Gate
New Bridge
Albion Mills
Golcar Brow
Mill
Brow Grains Dike
Liby
Hotel
Halfroods Farm
Legards Slack
Oldfield Hill
Thick Hollins CH
Calmlands
HUDDERSFIELD RD
HOLMFIRTH RD
B6107
B6108
B6109
A B C D E F
8 7 6 5 4 3 2 1
13 12 11 10
08 09 10

169
187

153
172

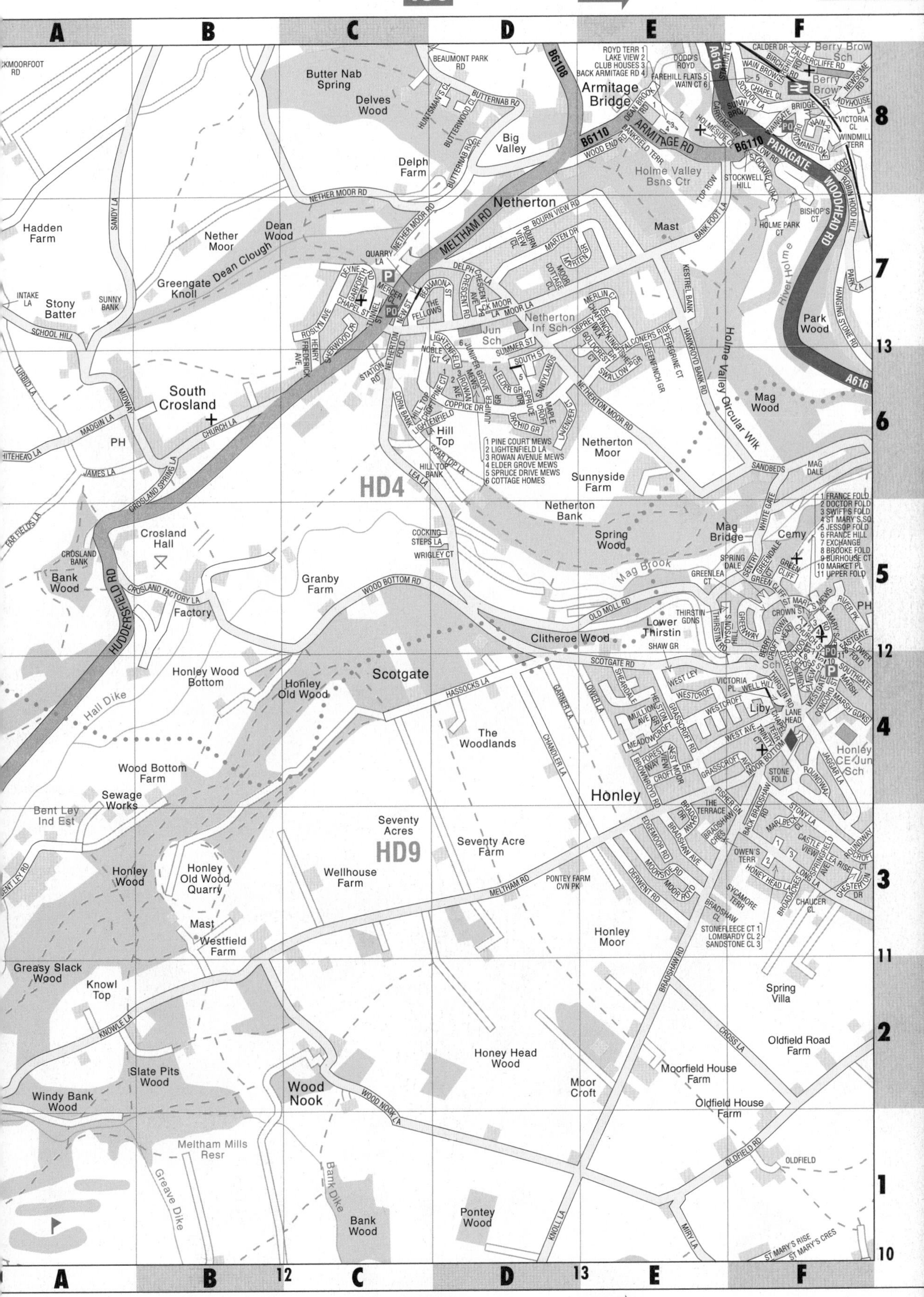
A
B
C
D
E
F
8
7
13
6
5
12
4
3
11
2
1
10
Butter Nab Spring
Delves Wood
Big Valley
Delph Farm
Armitage Bridge
B6108
B6110
ARMITAGE RD
A616
PARKGATE
WOODHEAD RD
Berry Brow Sch
Holme Valley Bsns Ctr
Netherton
NETHER MOOR RD
MELTHAM RD
Hadden Farm
Nether Moor
Dean Wood
Greengate Knoll
Dean Clough
Stony Batter
SCHOOL HILL
Mast
Park Wood
Netherton Inf Sch
Jun Sch
South Crosland
CHURCH LA
PH
Hill Top
Holme Valley Circular Wlk
River Holme
Mag Wood
Netherton Moor
Sunnyside Farm
HD4
Netherton Bank
Spring Wood
Mag Bridge
Cemy
Crosland Hall
Bank Wood
HUDDERSFIELD RD
Granby Farm
WOOD BOTTOM RD
Factory
Mag Brook
Lower Thirstin
Clitheroe Wood
Scotgate
Honley Wood Bottom
Honley Old Wood
Hall Dike
The Woodlands
Liby
Honley CE Jun Sch
Wood Bottom Farm
Sewage Works
Bent Ley Ind Est
Honley
Seventy Acres
HD9
Seventy Acre Farm
Honley Wood
Honley Old Wood Quarry
Wellhouse Farm
PONTEY FARM CVN PK
Mast
Westfield Farm
Honley Moor
Greasy Slack Wood
Knowl Top
Spring Villa
Oldfield Road Farm
Honey Head Wood
Moorfield House Farm
Slate Pits Wood
Windy Bank Wood
Wood Nook
Moor Croft
Oldfield House Farm
Meltham Mills Resr
Greave Dike
Bank Dike
Bank Wood
Pontey Wood
OLDFIELD
1 PINE COURT MEWS
2 LIGHTENFIELD LA
3 ROWAN AVENUE MEWS
4 ELDER GROVE MEWS
5 SPRUCE DRIVE MEWS
6 COTTAGE HOMES
1 FRANCE FOLD
2 DOCTOR FOLD
3 SWIFT'S FOLD
4 ST MARY'S SQ
5 JESSOP FOLD
6 FRANCE HILL
7 EXCHANGE
8 BROOKE FOLD
9 BURHOUSE CT
10 MARKET PL
11 UPPER FOLD
ROYD TERR 1
LAKE VIEW 2
CLUB HOUSES 3
BACK ARMITAGE RD 4
FAREHILL FLATS 5
WAIN CT 6
STONEFLEECE CT 1
LOMBARDY CL 2
SANDSTONE CL 3
12
13

171
154

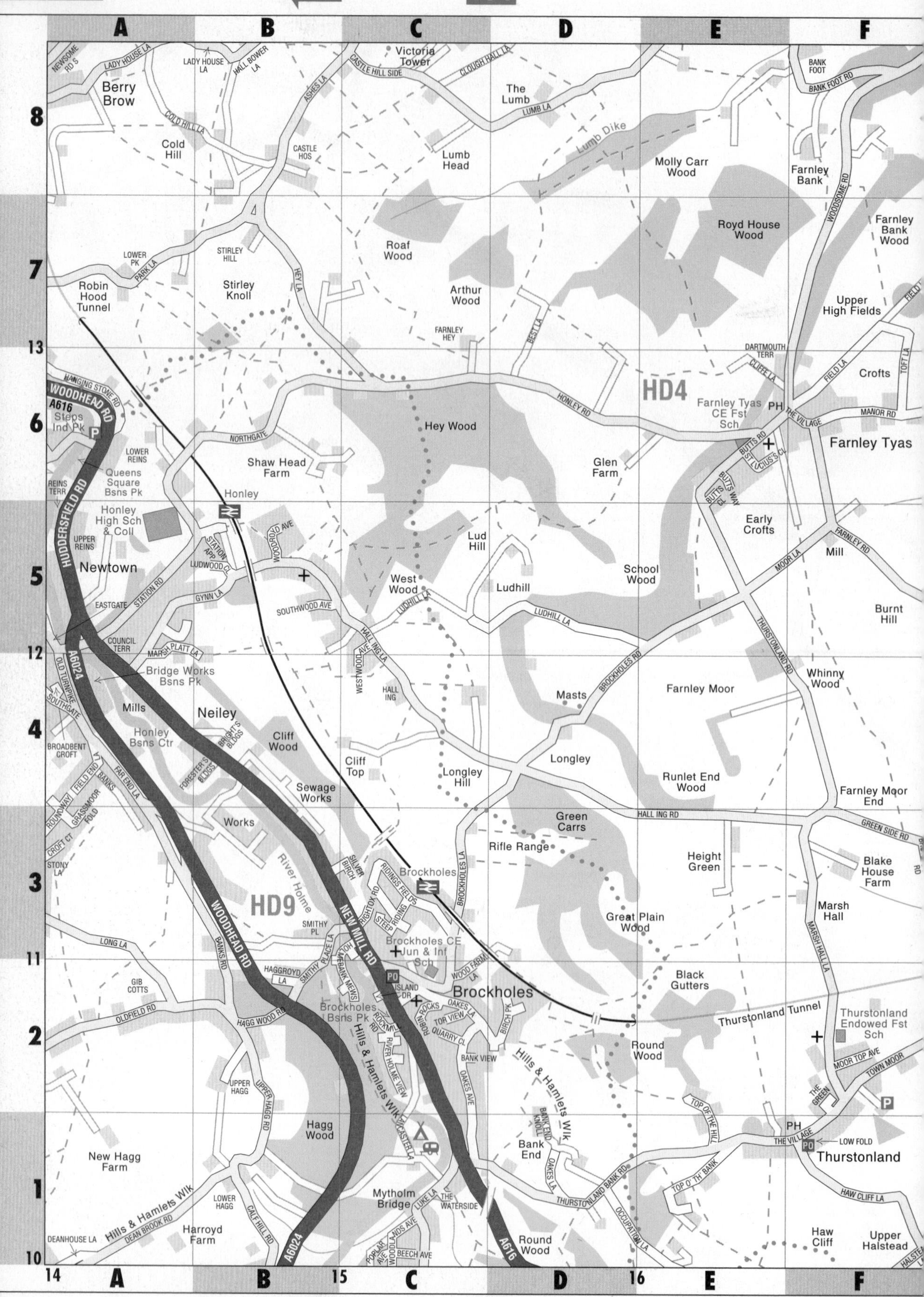
Berry Brow
Cold Hill
Victoria Tower
The Lumb
Lumb Head
Molly Carr Wood
Farnley Bank
Roaf Wood
Royd House Wood
Farnley Bank Wood
Robin Hood Tunnel
Stirley Knoll
Arthur Wood
Upper High Fields
HD4
Crofts
Farnley Tyas CE Fst Sch
Farnley Tyas
Hey Wood
Shaw Head Farm
Glen Farm
Honley
Queens Square Bsns Pk
Honley High Sch & Coll
Early Crofts
Newtown
Lud Hill
Ludhill
School Wood
West Wood
Mill
Burnt Hill
Bridge Works Bsns Pk
Neiley
Farnley Moor
Whinny Wood
Mills
Masts
Honley Bsns Ctr
Cliff Wood
Cliff Top
Longley Hill
Longley
Runlet End Wood
Farnley Moor End
Sewage Works
Works
Green Carrs
Rifle Range
Height Green
Blake House Farm
HD9
River Holme
Brockholes
Great Plain Wood
Marsh Hall
Brockholes CE Jun & Inf Sch
Black Gutters
Brockholes Bsns Pk
Thurstonland Tunnel
Thurstonland Endowed Fst Sch
Round Wood
Hills & Hamlets Wlk
Hagg Wood
Bank End
New Hagg Farm
Thurstonland
Mytholm Bridge
Harroyd Farm
Round Wood
Haw Cliff
Upper Halstead
WOODHEAD RD
HUDDERSFIELD RD
NEW MILL RD
HONLEY RD
HALL ING RD
BROCKHOLES RD
THURSTONLAND BANK RD
MARSH HALL LA
WOODSOME RD
A616
A6024

171
189

155
174

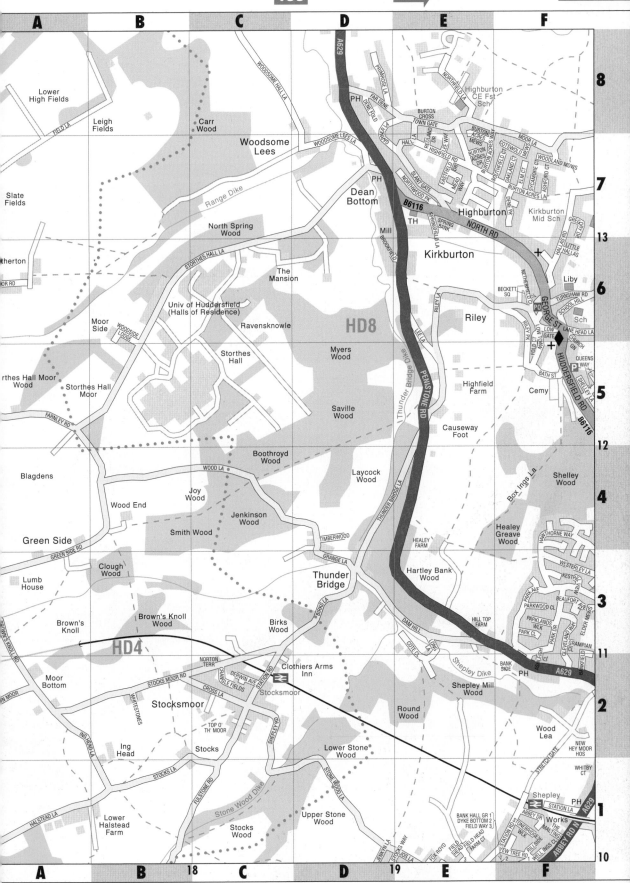
Lower
High Fields
Leigh
Fields
Carr
Wood
Woodsome
Lees
Slate
Fields
Range Dike
North Spring
Wood
Dean
Bottom
Highburton
CE Fst
Sch
Highburton
Kirkburton
Mid Sch
Kirkburton
TH
Mill
The
Mansion
Univ of Huddersfield
(Halls of Residence)
Ravensknowle
HD8
Riley
Liby
Sch
Moor
Side
Storthes
Hall
Myers
Wood
Storthes Hall
Moor
Highfield
Farm
Cemy
Saville
Wood
Causeway
Foot
Thunder Bridge Dike
Boothroyd
Wood
Blagdens
Laycock
Wood
Shelley
Wood
Joy
Wood
Wood End
Jenkinson
Wood
Box Ings La
Healey
Greave
Wood
Green Side
Smith Wood
Clough
Wood
Lumb
House
Thunder
Bridge
Hartley Bank
Wood
Brown's
Knoll
Brown's Knoll
Wood
Birks
Wood
HD4
Clothiers Arms
Inn
Stocksmoor
Moor
Bottom
Shepley Dike
Shepley Mill
Wood
Round
Wood
Wood
Lea
Ing
Head
Stocks
Lower Stone
Wood
Stone Wood Dike
Shepley
Works
Lower
Halstead
Farm
Stocks
Wood
Upper Stone
Wood
A629
B6116
PENISTONE RD
NORTH RD
GEORGE ST
HUDDERSFIELD RD
WOODSOME HALL LA
WOODSOME LEES LA
STORTHES HALL LA
FIELD LA
FARNLEY RD
WOOD LA
GREEN SIDE RD
GRANGE LA
TIMBERWOOD
THUNDER BRIDGE LA
LEE LA
RILEY LA
DAM HILL
COTE CL
LONG LA
BIRKS LA
STOCKS MOOR RD
STATION RD
SHEPLEY RD
STOCKS LA
ING HEAD LA
HALSTEAD LA
FULSTONE RD
STONE WOOD LA
STRETCH GATE
STATION LA
ABBEY RD N
HAWTHORNE WAY
WESTERLEY LA
PARK AVE
PARKWOOD CL
PARKLANDS WLK
PARK CL
PARK DR
CLEVELAND WAY
BEAUFORT AVE
GRAMPIAN CL
ELDER MEWS
BANKFIELD
ASHLEIGH CL
HILL TOP FARM
HEALEY FARM
BANK SIDE
PRIMROSE LA
FAR DENE
DENE FOLD
NORTHFIELD LA
BURTON CROSS
TOWN GATE
MOOR LA
WOODLAND MDWS
NORTHWOOD PK
SLANT GATE
SPRINGFIELD LA
SPRING BANK
BROOKFIELD
HALLAS RD
LITTLE HALLAS
TURNSHAW RD
SCHOOL HILL
LANE HEAD LA
CHURCH GN
QUEENS WAY
BATH ST
SHELLEY LA
BECKETT SQ
NETHERFIELD CL
RILEY PK
LOW TOWN
LOW GATE
WOODSIDE LODGE
NORTON TERR
CRANGLE FIELDS
DERWIN AVE
CROSS LA
WHITESTONES
TOP O' TH' MOOR
NEW HEY MOOR HOS
WHITBY CT
BANK HALL GR 1
DYKE BOTTOM 2
FIELD WAY 3
FOX ROYD
FIELD HEAD
FIELD HEAD FARM CT
JENKYN LA
STOCKS WAY
STONEBRIDGE WLK
RILLSIDE
WELL INGS CL
YEW TREE RD
THE MALTINGS
ABBEY DR
PH
PO
A B C D E F
8 7 13 6 5 12 4 3 11 2 1 10
18 19

190
174

WF4

Manor Mill Farm

Yew Tree Farm

Butts Top

Rock Wood Farm

Emley Moor

LEPTON LA

LINDET LA

MOOR LA

BURTON ROYD LA

Burton Royd La

THORNCLIFF

THORNCLIFF LA

PLAIN LA

CINDER HILL

Sheep Cote

LENACRE LA

Cross Roads

FACTORY LA

COMMON LA

WINDMILL HILL LA

WESTFIELD LA

The Heater

BURTON ACRES LA

Sch

TURNSHAWS AVE

PADDOCK RD

THE CRESCENT

TURNSHAW

PH

ROYDS MOUNT

LANESIDE

HALLAS LA

BURTON ROYD LA

THORNCLIFF GREEN RD

Thorncliff Spring Farm

Highfield House

Mast

JAGGER LA

P

Mast

Mast

Moor Head Plantation

TURNSHAW RD

OAKROYD

Common Side

Carr House

TITUS LA

Moor Head

High Wood

HIGH WOOD LA

Lane Head

LANE HEAD LA

Highwood

GRYCE HALL

The Three Acres (PH)

DRINKER LA

ROYDHOUSE

Roydhouse

High Chamber

Lane Head Farm

Folly Hall House

QUEENSWAY

FAIRFIELD RISE

CROSS LA

Standinghurst Farm

Lane End

Wool Row Farm

Radcliffe Wood

B6116

SHELLEY LA

WOOL ROW LA

HD8

Rough Piece Wood

Lightcliff Wood

Silver Ings

Wood Nook Farm

HUDDERSFIELD RD

PILLING TOP LA

GREEN HOUSE HILL

Green House

GREEN HOUSE LA

Baildon Dike

Baildon Place

VANTHORNE WAY

WESTERLEY CL

WESTERLEY WAY

PUSSY LA

PH

Town End

Shelley

EAST VIEW TERR

BARK HOUSE LA

KIRKLEA

Windmill Hill

Peace Wood

Springs Wood

WESTERLEY LA

BACK LA

BACK LA

FAR BANK

FLOCKTON RD

Shelley Woodhouse

Hopstrines Farm

STRIKE LA

BOGG

STATION TERR

DAMHEAD

ELDER MEWS

Shelley First Sch

SCHOOL TERR

FAR BANK CL

1 WATER LA
2 DOCTOR LA

HORSE CROFT LA

HUDDERSFIELD RD

JUBILEE AVE

STONELEIGH CT

NEAR BANK

Woodhouse Farm

STEAD GATE

ROUND HILL CL

Round Hill

RESERVOIR VIEW

Skelmanthorpe Common

Common End

STATION RD

WOOD S

PH

B61

GLEN VIEW RD

A629

Brook Bridge

BROOK HOUSE LA

Shelley Coll

GARRETT CL

HEATHER FOLD

PADDC

ABBEY RD

A629

WHITBY CT

THE KNOWLE

COPLEY LA

Long Moor

LONG MOOR LA

Shelley

Kirklees Light Railway

BARNCLIFFE HILL

SHELLEY WOODHOUSE LA

Mount Pleasant Farm

Cliffe Hill Farm

Cumberworth Common

COAL PIT LA

PONKER LA

Ponker

BEDALE DR

CUMBERWORTH LA

LIDGETT RISE

DENE RD

WESTFIELD AVE

LIDGETT LA

PONKER NOOK LA

WILLC

A B C D E F

WF4
Clough Bridge
CLOUGH RD
WF4
CRAWSHAW LA
KIRKBY LA
Out Lane Dike
LEISURE LA
8
Upper Crawshaw
RECTORY LA
GRANGE DR
CROSS LA
RECTORY GARDEN
THORNCLIFFE LA
BROOM FIELD LA
STRINGER HOUSE LA
MOORLAND VIEW
Emley
ST MICHAEL'S GDNS
ASPEN CT 1
NORTH LANE CT 2
CHURCH ST
Emley Fst Sch
RODLEY LA
Little Dike
7
SPRINGFIELD TERR
BROOMFIELD CL
SCHOOL LA
JAGGER LA
OUT LA
ST MICHAEL'S CL
Hutt Farm
BEAUMONT ST
PO
THE CROFTS
SAVILE ST
SAVILE AVE
MOUNT PLEASANT
GLEBE CL
TIPPING LA
CHAPEL LA
MANDERLAY GDNS
UPPER LA
ASH LA
WOODHOUSE LA
13
WENTWORTH DR
WENTWORTH AVE
ELLMONT AVE
FOX CL
SUMMER LA
PHOENIX AVE
RISHWORTH AVE
VIKING AVE
WARBURTON
Emley Moor Bsns Pk
LEYS LA
TYBURN LA
GREEN ACRES CL
BROOMHEY AVE
White Cross
Tyburn Hill
SAXON CL
6
Leys Farm
HAG HILL
Churchill Farm
HAG HILL LA
Owlers Wood
FRANK LA
BACK LA
OLD HALL LA
Low House Farm
5
KILN LA
Taylor Hill
Emley Old Hall
PARK LA
12
HD8
PARK FARM
Lady Oak
Park Lane House
Nineclogs Dike
Uppler Owlers Wood
COLLIERS WAY
4
Emley Park
A636
LANGLEY LA
WOODBINE TERR
Park Gate
Emley Lodge
CROWN BLDGS 1
HIGSON ROW 2
CROWN TERR 3
RAILWAY CT 4
STATION CT 5
SCOTT'S COTTS 6
PARK AVE
LONG LA
PARK RD
Blacker Farm
3
BACK LA
HAIGH ROW
Park Gate Dike
Clayton West
PARK MILL WAY
Blacker Wood
INGS MILL AVE
Skelmanthorpe
Dearne Way
SCOTT HILL
Kirklees Light Railway
ALL SAINTS CL
STATION RD
INGS MILL DR
11
SPENCER ST
LAUREL BANK
MARSDEN ST
Cuckoo's Nest Halt
VINERY CL
PILLING LA
CHURCH LA
1 DALE ST
2 THE FOLDINGS
3 MANOR CROFT
4 ARMITAGE CL
5 STATION TERR
SAVILLE RD
THE CLOSE
LANGLEY CT
DEARNE PK
GROVE HOUSE DR
VICTORIA ST
ALBERT RD
THE INGS
PENNINE RISE
SUNNYMEAD
RIVERSIDE
NEWLANDS AVE
HOLMFIELD RD
Sch
SCORE LEA
CROFT HEAD
TENTER CL
Bsns Pk
PENNINE DR
PENNINE WAY
CHAPEL HILL
CLIFFE ST
CLIFFE VIEW
2
DALE CROFT
GIB LA TERR
Skelmanthorpe
THE BUNGALOWS
WAKEFIELD RD
CLIFFEWOOD RISE
HOLMFIELD CL
ELM ST
Scissett Mid Sch
QUEEN ST
LODGE ST
KING ST
Skelmanthorpe Fst Sch
Scissett CE Fst Sch
SPRING GR
DUKE ST
WOOD RD
HIGH ST
6 POPLAR RISE
7 LABURNUM GR
8 WILLOW CL
9 RADCLIFFE ST
10 PROSPECT SQ
POST OFFICE ROW
Clayton West
OLDFIELD LA
COMMERCIAL RD
KINGS CT
SPRINGFIELD AVE
PO
P
NEW ST
CHAPEL CL
BEECHFIELD AVE
MANOR DR
MEWS
TALLOW
CHURCH TERR
PO
BARNSLEY RD
HOLMFIELD AVE 8
HOLMFIELD TERR 9
SCHOOL TERR 10
VICTORIA TERR 11
HOLMFIELD 12
BILHAM RD 13
CHERRY LA 14
CLIFTON VIEW 15
HILL TOP TERR 16
HILL TOP 17
Hill Top Farm
OAKFIELD GR
SMITHY LA
PARK LODGE VIEW
BARRONSTEAD
Kirklees Way
BUSKER LA
B6116
BLENHEIM CHASE
Lower Common
Sch
BIRCHFIELD GR
MANOR RISE
MANORSTEAD
WOODLANDS DR
WHARFEDALE CRES
EAST FOLD
WATER ST
FLETCHER ST
STANHOPE ST
DEARNE TERR
1
SMITHY CL
WINDSOR DR
PICKLES LA
WINDMILL CRES
Nortonthorpe Hall Sch
LOWER COMMON LA
Mast
1 DEARNE ST
2 SAVILLE ST
3 MARSHALL MILL CT
4 DEARNE ROYD
5 BRIDGE CL
6 SPRINGFIELD CL
7 RIDINGWOOD RISE
Riding Wood
MATHERVILLE
MEADOW VIEW
NEW LA
WOOL PL
NEW ST
CROWN ST
CROWN VILLAS
UPPER COMMON LA
RIDGE CL
ASHFIELD AVE
CROSS LA
THORPES CRES
HIGHBRIDGE LA
WOOD ST
ROCK VILLAS
Skelmanthorpe Cemy
Nortonthorpe Ind Est
Scissett
A636
CUTTLEHURST
10

A B 24 C D 25 E F

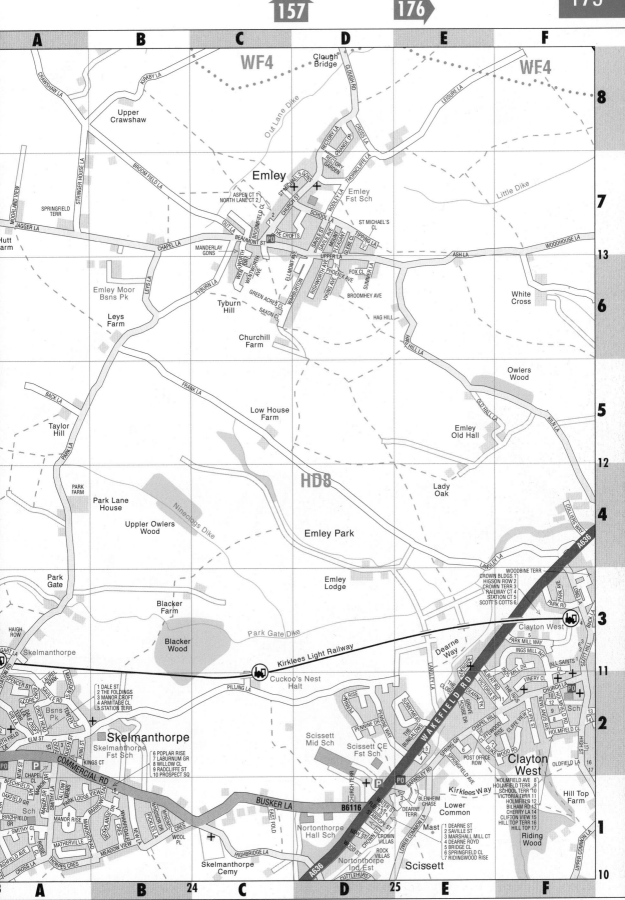

175
158

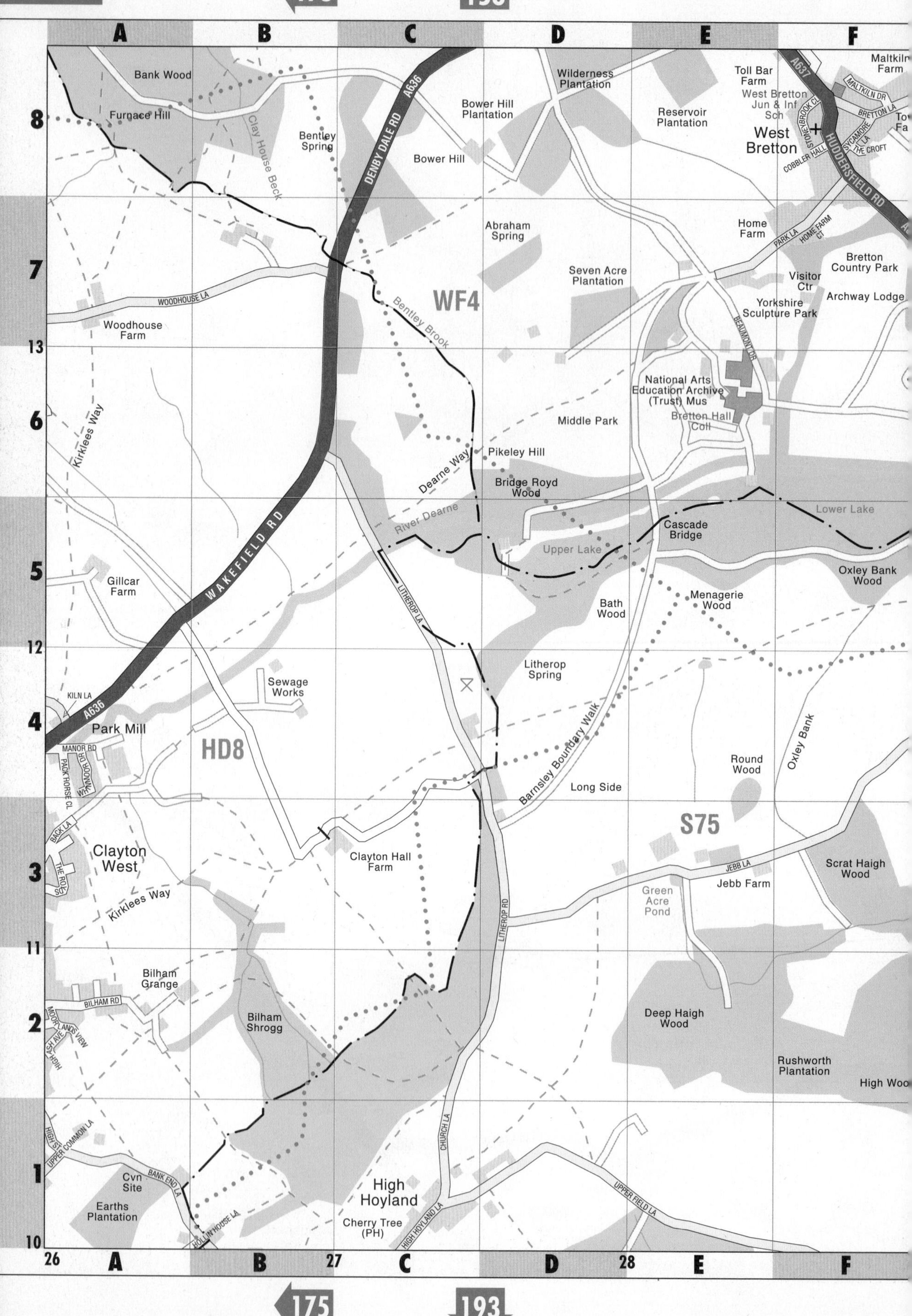
A
B
C
D
E
F
Bank Wood
Furnace Hill
Clay House Beck
Bentley Spring
DENBY DALE RD
A636
Bower Hill Plantation
Bower Hill
Wilderness Plantation
Reservoir Plantation
Toll Bar Farm
West Bretton Jun & Inf Sch
West Bretton
Maltkiln Farm
MALTKILN DR
BRETTON LA
SYCAMORE LA
THE CROFT
STONEBROOK CL
COBBLER HALL
A637
HUDDERSFIELD RD
Abraham Spring
Home Farm
PARK LA
HOME FARM CT
Bretton Country Park
Seven Acre Plantation
Visitor Ctr
Archway Lodge
Yorkshire Sculpture Park
WOODHOUSE LA
Woodhouse Farm
WF4
Bentley Brook
BEAUMONT DR
National Arts Education Archive (Trust) Mus
Bretton Hall Coll
Middle Park
Kirklees Way
Pikeley Hill
Dearne Way
Bridge Royd Wood
River Dearne
Lower Lake
Cascade Bridge
Upper Lake
WAKEFIELD RD
Gillcar Farm
LITHEROP LA
Oxley Bank Wood
Bath Wood
Menagerie Wood
Litherop Spring
Sewage Works
KILN LA
A636
Park Mill
HD8
Barnsley Boundary Walk
Round Wood
Oxley Bank
MANOR RD
PACK HORSE CL
MANOR DR
Long Side
S75
BACK LA
Clayton West
THE ROYD
Clayton Hall Farm
JEBB LA
Jebb Farm
Scrat Haigh Wood
Kirklees Way
Green Acre Pond
LITHEROP RD
Bilham Grange
BILHAM RD
MOORLANDS VIEW
HIGH ASH AVE
Bilham Shrogg
Deep Haigh Wood
Rushworth Plantation
High Woo
HIGH ST
UPPER COMMON LA
CHURCH LA
BANK END LA
Cvn Site
High Hoyland
UPPER FIELD LA
Earths Plantation
HOLLIN HOUSE LA
Cherry Tree (PH)
HIGH HOYLAND LA
8
7
13
6
5
12
4
3
11
2
1
10
26
27
28

175
193

159
178

A
B
C
D
E
F
Woolley Edge Service Area
BRETTON LA
BRAMLEY LA
M1
Mast
Bimshaw Wood
WOOLLEY LOW MOOR LA
COMMON LA
COMMON LA
GALLOWS LA
WATER LA
Mast
8
INTAKE LA
High Moor
Common Doles
Sewage Works
Savin Royd Wood
Beacon Hill
WF4
Eccle Hill
7
BACKHOUSE LA
FINKLE ST
FINKLE CL
Rose Farm
Ash Farm
Woolley
WENTWORTH CL
HIGH ST
MOLLY HURST LA
High House Farm
CHURCH ST
13
Church Farm
BACK LA
Dearne Way & Barnsley Boundary Walk
HUDDERSFIELD RD
HAIGH LA
MIDDLE FIELD LA
6
Bretton Country Park
Smithy Ridge
Moor House Spring
WOOLLEY EDGE LA
Jobson Wood
HAIGH HILL
GIPSY LA
Visitor Ctr
P
HAWTOP LA
Sewage Works
HAIGH MEWS
Near Moor Farm
MOORHOUSE LA
CLAPHOUSE FOLD
5
HAIGH LA
Haigh
Haw Top
12
Spoil Heap
Barnsley Boundary Walk
JEBB LA
38
S75
4
Haigh Hall
Low Swithen
HUDDERSFIELD RD
PH
WINDHILL LA
Sheep Lane Head
Windhill Gate
Riverside Farm
Windhill Wood
Swithen House
Colliery
3
Husband Wood
River Dearne
TOP ROW
Upper Swithen
SWITHEN HILL
WOOLLEY COLLIERY RD
BLUEBELL RD
ish Pond Halt
LOW ROW
11
Mast
PARK HILL
Sewage Works
2
Dearne Way
Spoil Heap
High Wood
Walk Royd Hill
WOOLLEY COLLIERY RD
Birthwaite Hall
BLOOMHOUSE LA
KINGSWAY
Bloomhouse
Cowcroft Wood
Spring Ram Bsns Pk
FOUNTAIN SQ
BLOOMHOUSE LA
BLOOMFIELD RISE 1
OAKS FARM CL 2
MONTROSE AVE 3
DARTON HALL CL 4
APPLEBY CL
CRANBORNE DR
BLOOMFIELD RD
HUDDERSFIELD RD
FALCON KNOWL ING 1
HIGH CL 2
ALLENDALE RD 3
Darton
FOUNTAIN CL
HOWDEN CL
SACKUP LA
1
Brook Hill
BALLFIELD LA
M1
SCHOOL ST
BRIDGE ST
DEARNE ST
DARTON HALL DR
Darton Prim Sch
OAKS FARM DR
LAWNDALE FOLD
Squirrel Hall
SIKE CL
A637
LAMBE FLATT
MIDDLE CL
FALCONER CL
M1 Sheffield (A6109)
A637 Barnsley (A635)
P
PO
CHURCH ST
MILL LA
STATION RD
ROCKWOOD CL
BIRTHWAITE RD
South Yorkshire STREET ATLAS
B6131
P
CHURCH CL
B6131
10
9
A
B
30
C
D
31
E
F

178

A1
1 BLOOMFIELD RISE
2 BLOOMFIELD RD
3 OAKS FARM DR
4 PRIEST ROYD
5 CROFT CL

B1
1 TOWNGATE MEWS

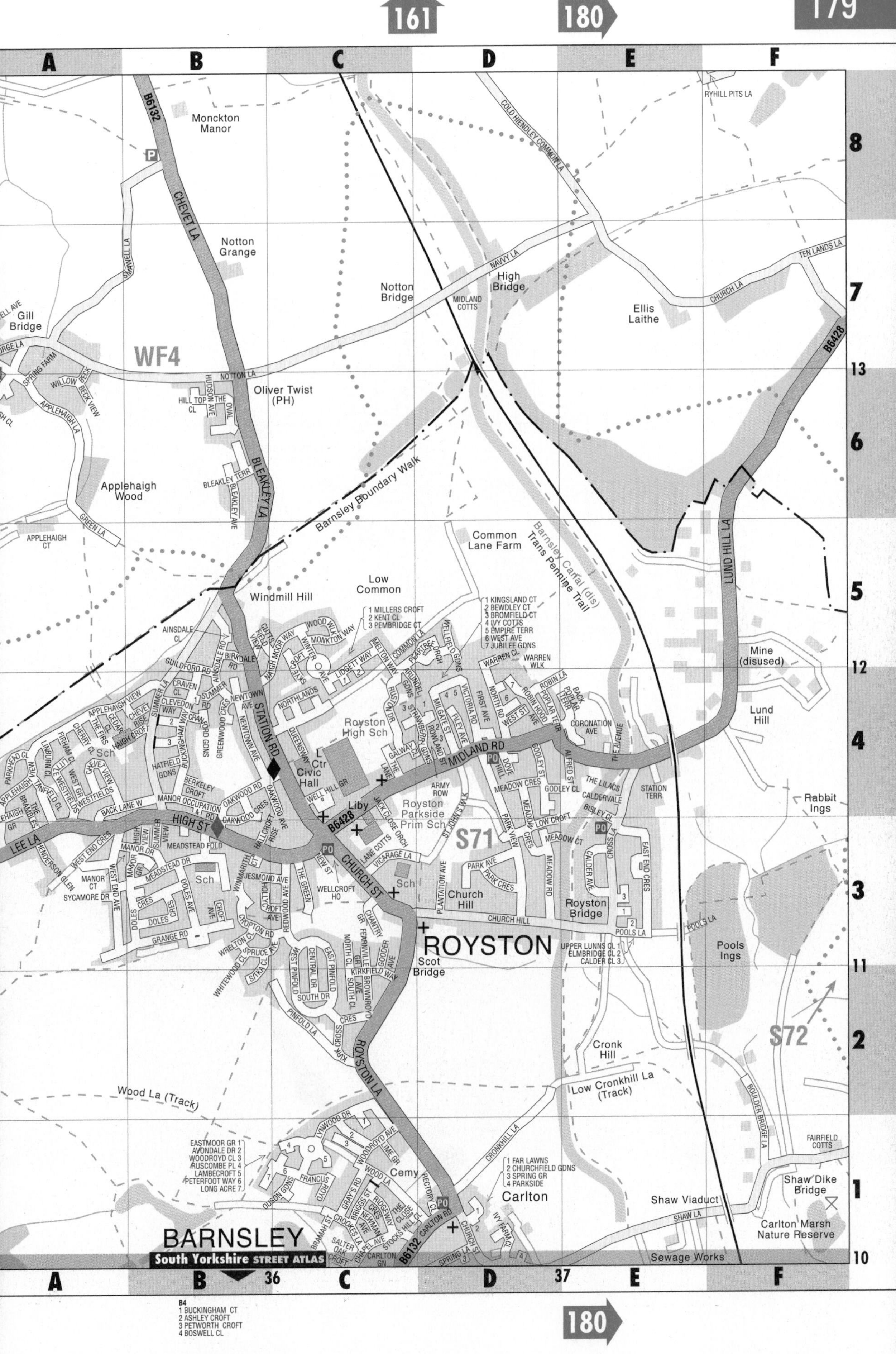

179
162

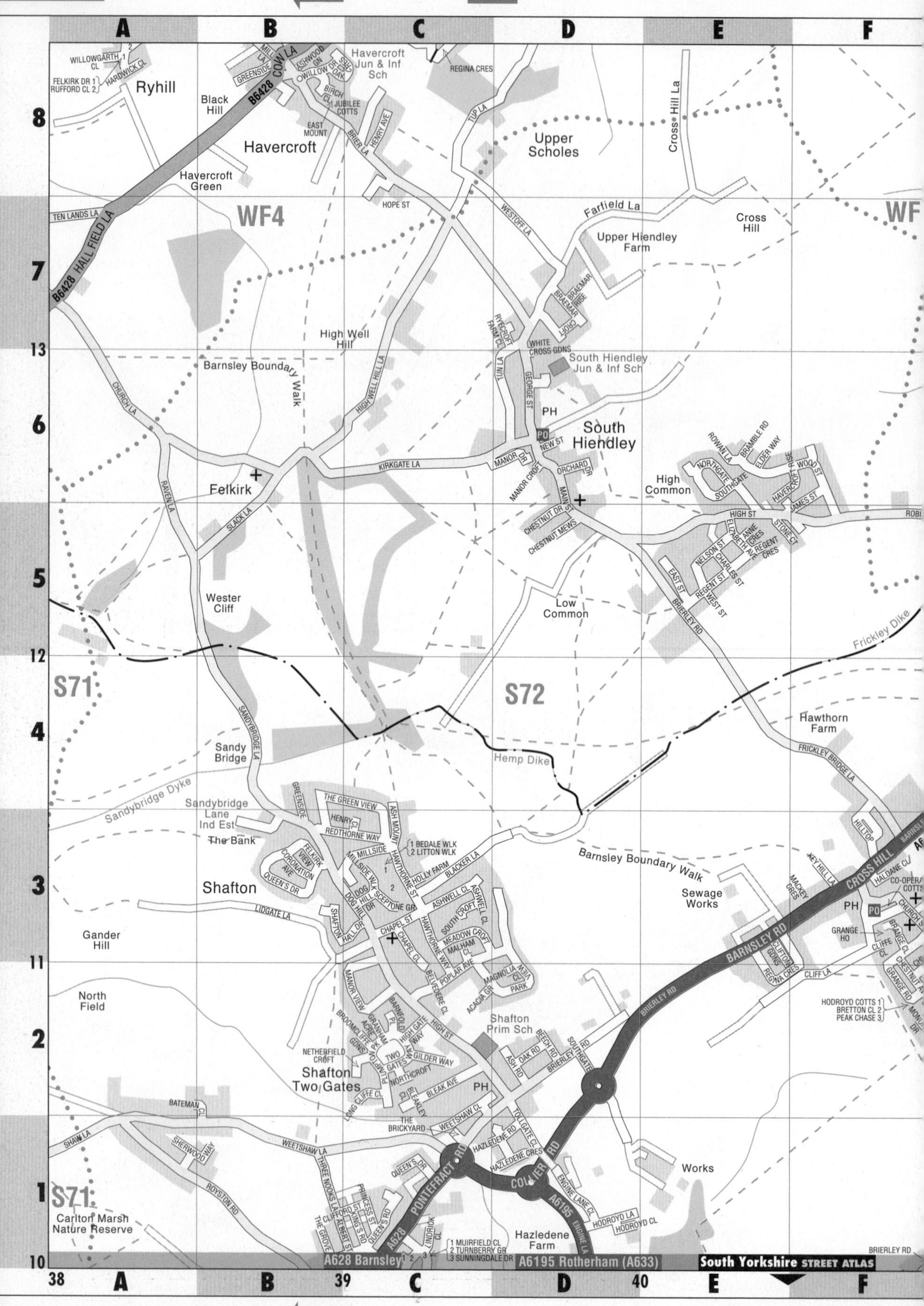
A
B
C
D
E
F
8
7
13
6
5
12
4
3
11
2
1
10
38
39
40
WILLOWGARTH CL
HARDWICK CL
FELKIRK DR 1
RUFFORD CL 2
Ryhill
MILL LA
GREENSIDE
COW LA
B6428
ASHWOOD GR
WILLOW DR
OAK RD
BIRCH CL
JUBILEE COTTS
EAST MOUNT
Havercroft Jun & Inf Sch
REGINA CRES
Black Hill
Havercroft
Havercroft Green
HENRY AVE
BRIER LA
TUP LA
Upper Scholes
Cross Hill La
HOPE ST
TEN LANDS LA
HALL FIELD LA
B6428
WF4
WESTOFF LA
Farfield La
Cross Hill
WF
Upper Hiendley Farm
BRAEMAR RISE
BRAEMAR
CORO
RYECROFT FARM CL
WHITE CROSS GDNS
High Well Hill
South Hiendley Jun & Inf Sch
Barnsley Boundary Walk
HIGH WELL HILL LA
TUN LA
GEORGE ST
PH
CHURCH LA
PO
NEW ST
South Hiendley
ROWAN LA
BRAMBLE RD
ELDER WAY
NORTHGATE
SOUTHGATE
HAVERCROFT RISE
WOOD ST
JAMES ST
KIRKGATE LA
MANOR DR
MANOR CROFT
ORCHARD DR
High Common
Felkirk
RAVEN LA
SLACK LA
MAIN ST
CHESTNUT DR
CHESTNUT MEWS
HIGH ST
ELIZABETH AVE
ANNE CRES
REGENT CRES
STONE CT
ROBI
NELSON ST
CHARLES ST
REGENT ST
WEST ST
EAST ST
BRIERLEY RD
Wester Cliff
Low Common
Frickley Dike
S71
S72
SANDYBRIDGE LA
Hawthorn Farm
Sandy Bridge
Hemp Dike
FRICKLEY BRIDGE LA
Sandybridge Dyke
Sandybridge Lane Ind Est
GREENSIDE
THE GREEN VIEW
HENRY CL
ASH MOUNT
REDTHORNE WAY
The Bank
1 BEDALE WLK
2 LITTON WLK
MILLSIDE
HAWTHORNE ST
HOLLY FARM
BLACKER LA
HILLTOP
Barnsley Boundary Walk
FELKIRK VIEW
CORONATION AVE
QUEEN'S DR
MILLSIDE WLK
DOG HILL DR
SCEPTONE GR
ASHWELL CL
KEY HILL LA
HALDANE CL
CROSS HILL
Shafton
Sewage Works
MACKEY CRES
CO-OPERA COTTS
PH
PO
CHURCH
LIDGATE LA
SHAFTON HALL DR
CHAPEL ST
CHAPEL CL
HAWTHORNE WAY
SOUTH CROFT
MEADOW CROFT
MALHAM CL
GRANGE HO
GRANGE CL
Gander Hill
BARNSLEY RD
CLIFTON GDNS
REGINA CRES
CLIFF LA
CLIFFE CL
CHESTNUT
GRANGE RD
POPLAR AVE
MAGNOLIA CL
VIEW
PARK
BELVEDERE CL
ACACIA GR
MANOR VIEW
North Field
BRIERLEY RD
HODROYD COTTS 1
BRETTON CL 2
PEAK CHASE 3
BARNFOLD PL
GRANHAM ACRE
BROOMCLIFFE GDNS
HIGH GATE WAY
HIGH ST
Shafton Prim Sch
BEECH RD
OAK RD
ASH RD
BRIERLEY RD
SOUTHGATE
NETHERFIELD CROFT
TWO GATES
GILDER WAY
NORTHCROFT
Shafton Two Gates
PH
LONG CLIFFE CL
BLEAKLEY CL
BLEAK AVE
BATEMAN CL
THE BRICKYARD
WEETSHAW CL
TOLLGATE CL
HAZLEDENE RD
HAZLEDENE CRES
SHAW LA
SHERWOOD WAY
WEETSHAW LA
PONTEFRACT RD
COLLIER RD
Works
THREE NOOKS LA
QUEEN'S DR
ROYSTON RD
ENGINE LANE CL
S71
PRINCESS ST
A6195
ENGINE LA
HODROYD LA
HODROYD CL
Carlton Marsh Nature Reserve
CLIFFORD ST
KING'S RD
QUEEN'S RD
ALBERT ST
THE GROVE
A628
LINDRICK CL
1 MUIRFIELD CL
2 TURNBERRY GR
3 SUNNINGDALE DR
Hazledene Farm
BRIERLEY RD
A628 Barnsley
A6195 Rotherham (A633)

179

163 D6
1 NETTLETON HO
2 JACKSON HO
3 COOPER HO
4 STARLING HO

182 E6
1 HAZELWOOD GDNS
2 ST OSWALD CT
3 BAYLEE ST
4 PONTEFRACT TERR

181

A B C D E F

8

HEMSWORTH

Shaw Hill
Hollins Bank
B6273
WAKEFIELD RD
Marsh Plantation

Church Field
Cemy
West End Prim Sch
St Helen's Ave
The Old Orchard

Sports Centre
Hemsworth Arts & Com Coll
Low Field
Little Hemsworth
Common End

Green Hill
Cross Hill
Highfield
B6422

Vissitt Manor
ARCHBISHOP HOLGATE HOSPL
ROBIN LA
Hotel Kennels Farm
St Helens CE Jun & Inf Sch

Moor Top Farm
B6273

WF9

Road under construction
Hague Hall Cotts

HEMSWORTH RD
WATER LA
B6422

Hague Hall Beck

South Moor
SOUTHMOOR RD

Ball Park Wood

Brierley
Brierley CE Prim Sch
Recn Gd
Pudding Hill Elms Farm House

S72

Hemsworth Gate
Cob Carr Plantation

Dunsley

Burntwood Sports & L Ctr
Brierley Common

Holmsley La

Barnsley Boundary Walk
Willowgarth High Sch
Tom Bank Wood
Windmill Hill

Brierley Gap
Mast
PH
B6273
Ringstone Hill

South Kirkby Common
Common Rd

1 A 42 B C 43 D E F 10

A B C D E F

8

7

13

6

5

WF9

12

4

3

11

2

1

10

44 A B 45 C D 46 E F

Royd Moor La
Royd Moor House
Royd Moor
Royd Moor Dairy Farm
Grey Cocks
Elmsall Lodge Farm
The Lawn
Long Plantation
Great Breaks
The Manor
DONCASTER RD
A628
A638
A638
Wheat Royds
LOWFIELD RD
Road under construction
Spoil Heap
North Elmsall Common
Mosley Mires
Bullenshaw Villas
Sewage Works
Hague Plantation
Hague Hall Farm
WATER LA
Minsthorpe Com Coll
Minsthorpe
Sports Ctr
Kirkby Bridge
Lower North Field
Upper North Field
HEMSWORTH RD
B6422
Limphill Green Farm
Moorthorpe Prim Sch
BARNSLEY RD
B6422
Moorthorpe
Moorthorpe
WHITE APRON ST
Northfield Prim Sch
Liby
CROWN YD
Park View
Langthwaite Grange Ind Est
South Kirkby
Burntwood Jun & Inf Sch
Onward Way
Common Road Inf Sch
Stockingate Mill Jun Sch
Langthwaite Beck
Broadway Terr
Broadway

BLUEBELL WAY 1
DAISY FOLD 2
PENARTH TERR 3

F2
1 GRIMETHORPE ST
2 FIELD CRES
3 WESTFIELD BGLWS
4 ALBANY ST
5 ALBANY PL
6 WOODLEA

165
184

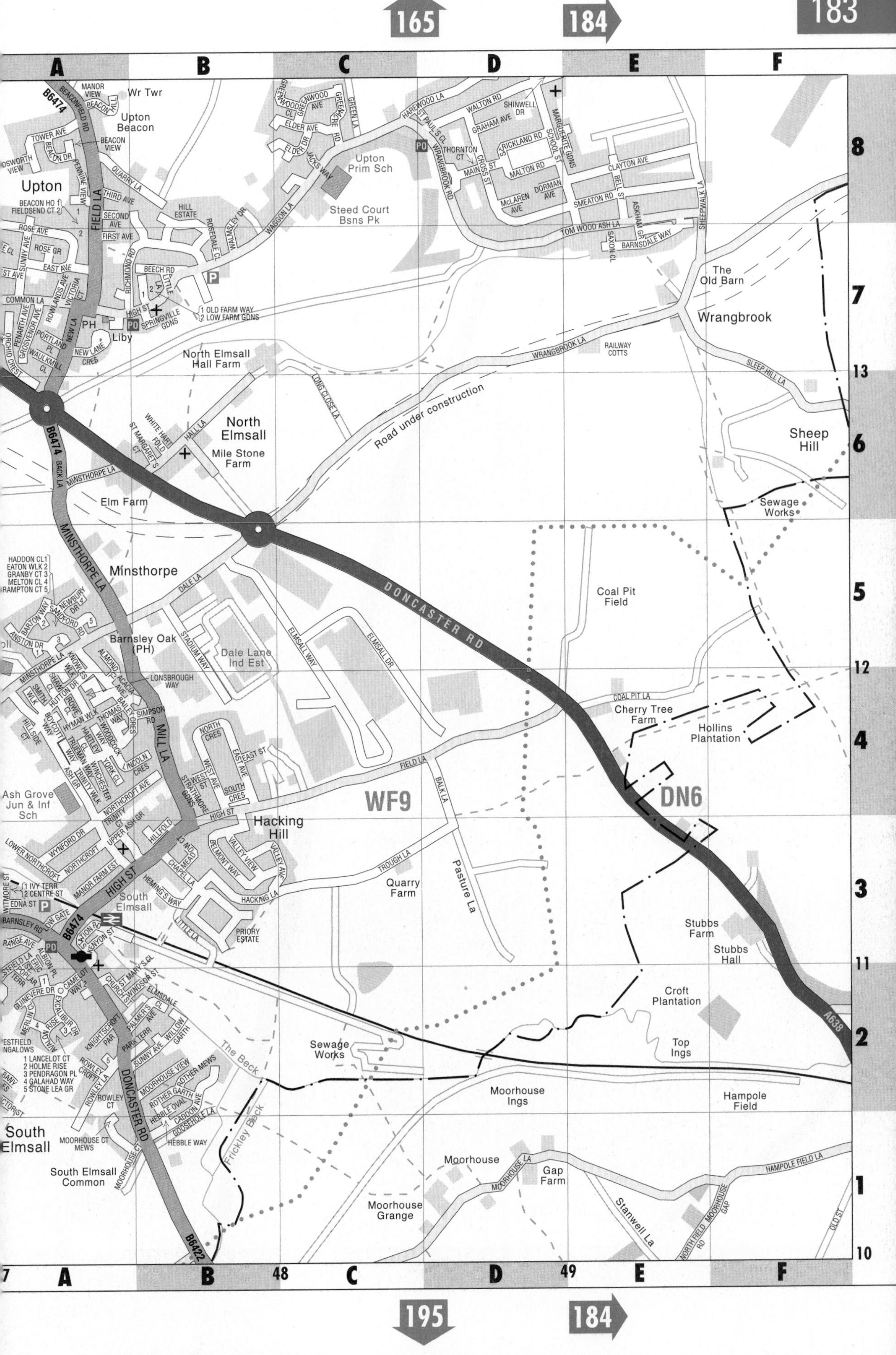
A
B
C
D
E
F
8
7
6
5
4
3
2
1
13
12
11
10
48
49
7
B6474
BEACONFIELD RD
MANOR VIEW
BEACON HILL
Wr Twr
Upton Beacon
TOWER AVE
BEACON DR
BEACON VIEW
PENNINE VIEW
FIELD LA
Upton
BEACON HO 1
FIELDSEND CT 2
QUARRY LA
THIRD AVE
SECOND AVE
FIRST AVE
HILL ESTATE
ROSE AVE
ROSE GR
SUNNY AVE
EAST AVE
COMMON LA
ROWLANDS AVE
VICTORIA CT
RICHMOND RD
BEECH RD
LITTLE LA
HIGH ST
SPRINGVILLE GDNS
1 OLD FARM WAY
2 LOW FARM GDNS
PENARTH AVE
GROSVENOR AVE
PORTLAND PL
NEW LA
PH
Liby
NEW LANE CRES
WALKMILL CL
ORCHID CREST
ROSEDALE CL
WALMSLEY DR
WAGGON LA
JACKS WAY
GREENWOOD CL
GREENWOOD AVE
ELDER AVE
ELDER DR
GREEN LA
Upton Prim Sch
Steed Court Bsns Pk
HAREWOOD LA
ST PAUL'S CL
WRANGBROOK RD
THORNTON CT
MAIN ST
CROSS ST
WALTON RD
SHINWELL DR
GRAHAM AVE
STRICKLAND RD
MALTON RD
McLAREN AVE
DORMAN AVE
SCHOOL ST
MARGUERITE GDNS
CLAYTON AVE
BELL ST
SMEATON RD
ASKHAM GR
TOM WOOD ASH LA
SAXON CL
BARNSDALE WAY
SHEEPWALK LA
The Old Barn
Wrangbrook
WRANGBROOK LA
RAILWAY COTTS
SLEEP HILL LA
North Elmsall Hall Farm
LONG CLOSE LA
Road under construction
North Elmsall
WHITE HART FOLD
ST MARGARET'S CT
HALL LA
Mile Stone Farm
BACK LA
MINSTHORPE LA
Elm Farm
Sheep Hill
Sewage Works
Minsthorpe
HADDON CL 1
EATON WLK 2
GRANBY CT 3
MELTON CL 4
RAMPTON CT 5
DALE LA
DONCASTER RD
Coal Pit Field
BARTON WAY
SANDFORD RD
NEWBURY DR
ANSTON DR
Barnsley Oak (PH)
STADIUM WAY
Dale Lane Ind Est
ELMSALL WAY
ELMSALL DR
ALMOND AVE
LONSBROUGH WAY
KNOWLES WLK
SMITH WLK
HUTTON DR
ROWE CT
HYMAN WLK
THOMAS WAY
BAILEY CRES
SIMPSON RD
HILLSIDE CT
BOYCOTT WAY
HARDLEY CL
WOODCOCK WAY
TRUEMAN WAY
ASH GR
YORK CL
LINCOLN CRES
WINCHESTER WAY
TRINITY WLK
NORTHCROFT AVE
MILL LA
NORTH CRES
WEST AVE
WEST ST
EAST AVE
EAST ST
SOUTH CRES
STRATHMORE GDNS
COAL PIT LA
Cherry Tree Farm
Hollins Plantation
FIELD LA
BALK LA
WF9
DN6
Ash Grove Jun & Inf Sch
HIGH ST
Hacking Hill
TRINITY CT
UPPER ASH GR
HILLFOLD
MEAD CL
CHAPEL LA
BELMONT WAY
VALLEY VIEW
VALLEY AVE
WYNFORD DR
LOWER NORTHCROFT
NORTHCROFT
MANOR FARM EST
TROUGH LA
Quarry Farm
Pasture La
HEMING'S WAY
HACKING LA
1 IVY TERR
2 CENTRE ST
EDNA ST
WITMORE ST
South Elmsall
BARNSLEY RD
LONG GATE
STATION RD
CANYON ST
LITTLE LA
PRIORY ESTATE
Stubbs Farm
Stubbs Hall
RANGE AVE
PO
ALBION PL
CHURCH ST
ST MARY'S CL
WINDSOR ST
ELMSDALE CL
CAMELOT WAY
POPLAR TERR
GUINEVERE DR
MERLIN CT
EXCALIBUR DR
AVALON RISE
KNIGHTSCROFT PAR
PALMER'S AVE
Croft Plantation
A638
Sewage Works
The Beck
PARK TERR
SUNNY AVE
WILLOW GARTH
Top Ings
ESTFIELD
NGALOWS
1 LANCELOT CT
2 HOLME RISE
3 PENDRAGON PL
4 GALAHAD WAY
5 STONE LEA GR
ROWLEY CROFT
ROWLEY LA
ROWLEY CT
DONCASTER RD
MOORHOUSE VIEW
ROTHER MEWS
ROTHER GARTH
HEBBLE OVAL
CADDON AVE
GOOSEHOLE LA
HEBBLE WAY
Frickley Beck
Moorhouse Ings
Hampole Field
South Elmsall
MOORHOUSE CT
MEWS
MOORHOUSE CT
South Elmsall Common
Moorhouse
MOORHOUSE LA
Gap Farm
HAMPOLE FIELD LA
Stanwell La
Moorhouse Grange
NORTH FIELD RD
MOORHOUSE GAP
OLD ST
B6422

195
184

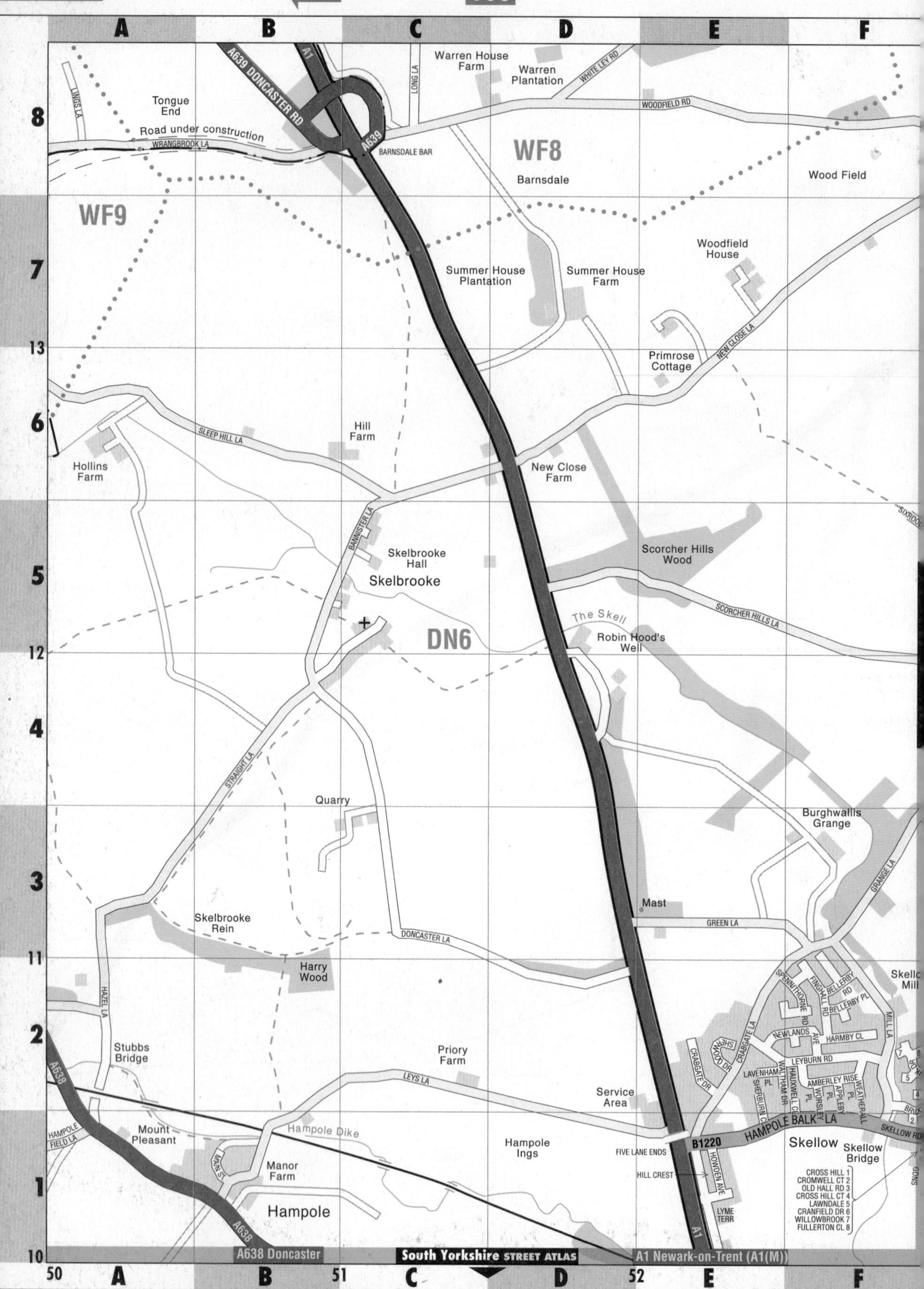

A B C D E F

8

Tongue End

Road under construction

WRANGBROOK LA

BARNSDALE BAR

WF8

Barnsdale

Warren House Farm

Warren Plantation

WHITE LEY RD

WOODFIELD RD

Wood Field

WF9

Woodfield House

7

Summer House Plantation

Summer House Farm

NEW CLOSE LA

13

Primrose Cottage

SIXROO...

6

SLEEP HILL LA

Hill Farm

New Close Farm

Hollins Farm

BANNISTER LA

Skelbrooke Hall

Scorcher Hills Wood

SCORCHER HILLS LA

5

Skelbrooke

The Skell

12

DN6

Robin Hood's Well

4

STRAIGHT LA

Quarry

Burghwallis Grange

GRANGE LA

3

Skelbrooke Rein

DONCASTER LA

Mast

GREEN LA

11

HAZEL LA

Harry Wood

Skello... Mill

MILL LA

SPENNTHORPE RD

TINGHALL RD

BELLERBY RD

BELLERBY PL

2

Stubbs Bridge

A638

Priory Farm

LEYS LA

Service Area

NEWLANDS AVE

HARMBY CL

LEYBURN RD

CRABGATE DR

MOORW...

OXSPRING LA

LAVENHAM PL

SHERBURN CL

WATTHAM DR

HAUXWELL CL

AMBERLEY RISE

WINSLEY PL

APPLEBY PL

WEATHERALL

SKELLOW RD

HAMPOLE FIELD LA

Mount Pleasant

Manor Farm

Hampole Dike

Hampole Ings

HILL CREST

FIVE LANE ENDS

B1220

HAMPOLE BALK LA

Skellow

Skellow Bridge

HOWDEN LA

LYME TERR

1

TRAIN S

A638

Hampole

CROSS HILL 1
CROMWELL CT 2
OLD HALL RD 3
CROSS HILL CT 4
LAWNDALE 5
CRANFIELD DR 6
WILLOWBROOK 7
FULLERTON CL 8

10

50

51

52

A B C D E F

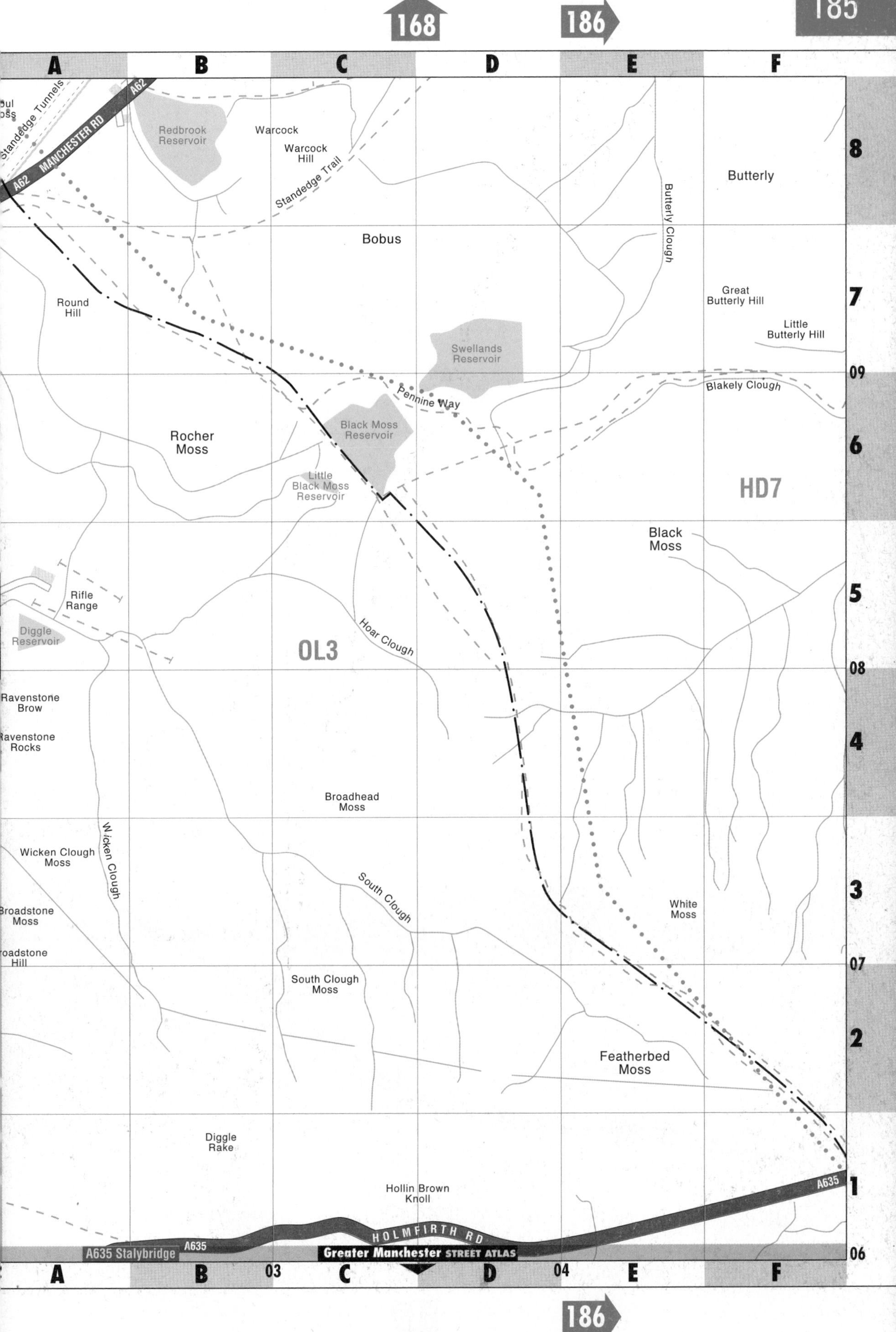

A   B   C   D   E   F

Standedge Tunnels

A62 MANCHESTER RD

Redbrook Reservoir

Warcock

Warcock Hill

Standedge Trail

Bobus

Butterly

Butterly Clough

8

Round Hill

Great Butterly Hill

Little Butterly Hill

7

09

Swellands Reservoir

Pennine Way

Blakely Clough

Rocher Moss

Black Moss Reservoir

HD7

6

Little Black Moss Reservoir

Black Moss

Rifle Range

5

Diggle Reservoir

OL3

Hoar Clough

08

Ravenstone Brow

Ravenstone Rocks

4

Broadhead Moss

Wicken Clough Moss

Wicken Clough

South Clough

White Moss

3

Broadstone Moss

Broadstone Hill

07

South Clough Moss

Featherbed Moss

2

Diggle Rake

Hollin Brown Knoll

A635

1

HOLMFIRTH RD

A635 Stalybridge   A635

Greater Manchester STREET ATLAS

06

A   B   03   C   D   04   E   F

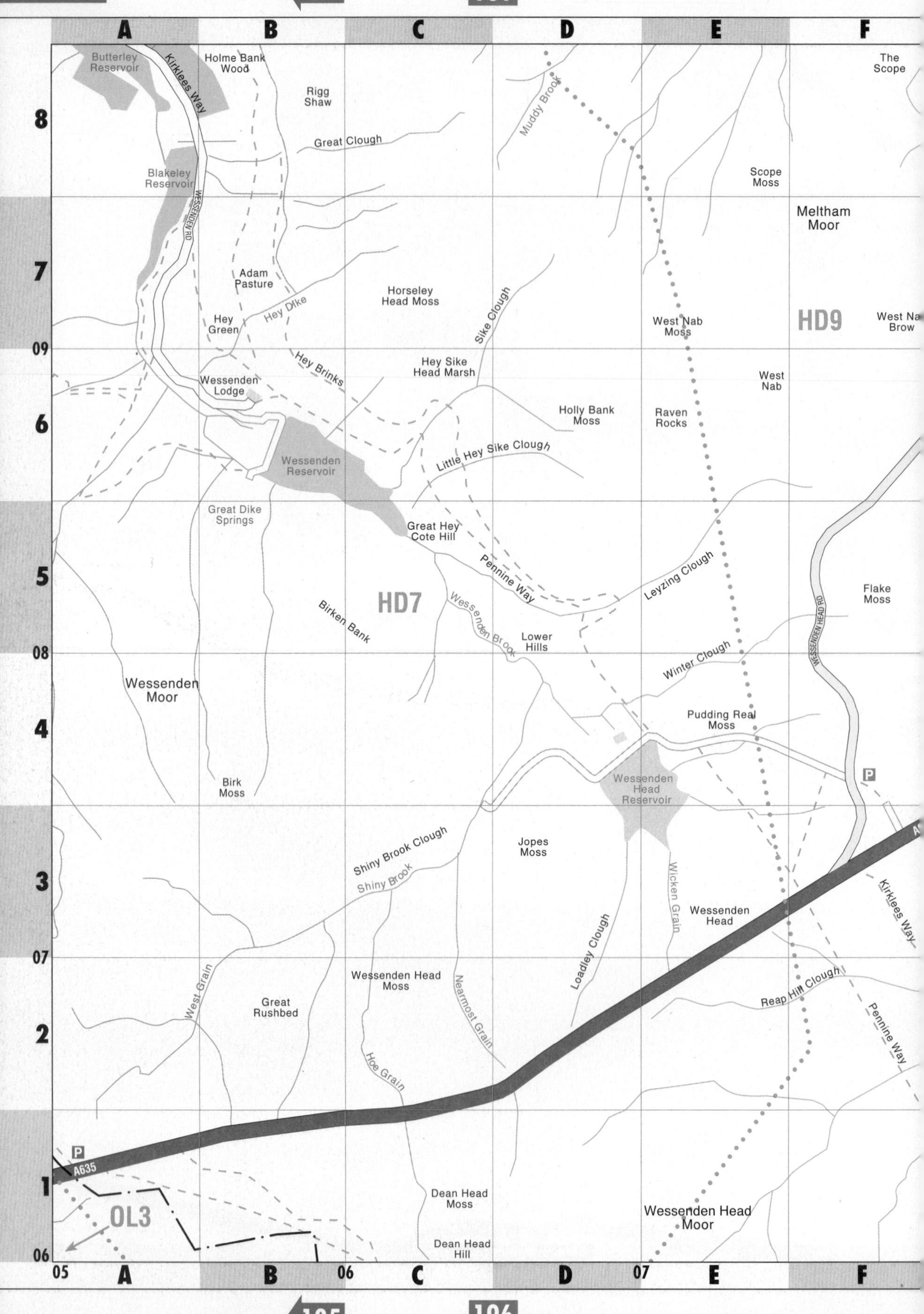

A B C D E F

8

Butterley
Reservoir

Holme Bank
Wood

Rigg
Shaw

Great Clough

Muddy Brook

The
Scope

Scope
Moss

Meltham
Moor

Blakeley Reservoir

7

Adam
Pasture

Hey Dike

Horseley
Head Moss

Sike Clough

West Nab
Moss

HD9

West Nab
Brow

Hey
Green

09

Hey Brinks

Hey Sike
Head Marsh

West
Nab

6

Wessenden
Lodge

Holly Bank
Moss

Raven
Rocks

Wessenden
Reservoir

Little Hey Sike Clough

Great Dike
Springs

Great Hey
Cote Hill

Leyzing Clough

Flake
Moss

5

Birken Bank

HD7

Pennine Way

Wessenden Brook

Winter Clough

Wessenden Head Rd

08

Wessenden
Moor

Lower
Hills

Pudding Real
Moss

4

Birk
Moss

Wessenden
Head
Reservoir

P

Shiny Brook Clough

Jopes
Moss

Wicken Grain

Wessenden
Head

3

Shiny Brook

Loadley Clough

West Grain

Reap Hill Clough

Kirklees Way

07

Great
Rushbed

Wessenden Head
Moss

Nearmost Grain

Pennine Way

2

Hoe Grain

P
A635

1

Dean Head
Moss

Wessenden Head
Moor

OL3

Dean Head
Hill

06

05 A B 06 C D 07 E F

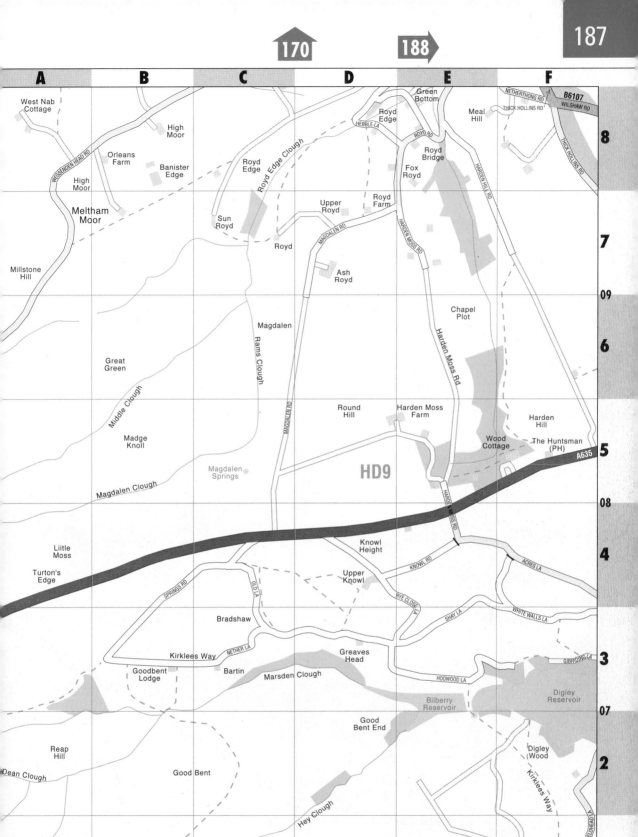

170
188
197
188

A B C D E F

8 7 09 6 5 08 4 3 07 2 1 06

West Nab Cottage
High Moor
Orleans Farm
Banister Edge
Royd Edge
Green Bottom
Royd Edge
Meal Hill
NETHERTHONG RD
THICK HOLLINS RD
WILSHAW RD
B6107
THICK HOLLINS RD
HEBBLE LA
ROYD RD
Royd Bridge
Fox Royd
Royd Farm
HARDEN HILL RD
High Moor
WESSENDEN HEAD RD
Meltham Moor
Sun Royd
Royd
Upper Royd
MAGDALEN RD
Royd Edge Clough
HARDEN MOSS RD
Millstone Hill
Ash Royd
Chapel Plot
Magdalen
Rams Clough
Great Green
Harden Moss Rd
Middle Clough
Round Hill
Harden Moss Farm
Harden Hill
The Huntsman (PH)
Wood Cottage
A635
Madge Knoll
MAGDALEN RD
Magdalen Springs
HD9
Magdalen Clough
Liitle Moss
Turton's Edge
Knowl Height
HARDEN MOSS RD
ACRES LA
Upper Knowl
KNOWL RD
WHITE WALLS LA
SPRINGS RD
OLD LA
RYE CLOSE LA
SHAY LA
Bradshaw
NETHER LA
Kirklees Way
Bartin
Greaves Head
HOOWOOD LA
GIBRIDING LA
Digley Reservoir
Goodbent Lodge
Marsden Clough
Bilberry Reservoir
Digley Wood
Reap Hill
Good Bent End
Kirklees Way
Dean Clough
Good Bent
Hey Clough
FIELDHEAD LA
Black Dike
Pennine Way
Stopes Moor
Issues Rd
Cliff Rd
Statham
Meal Hill
NEAL HILL RD
WOODHEAD RD
A6024
Holme Jun & Inf Sch

187
171

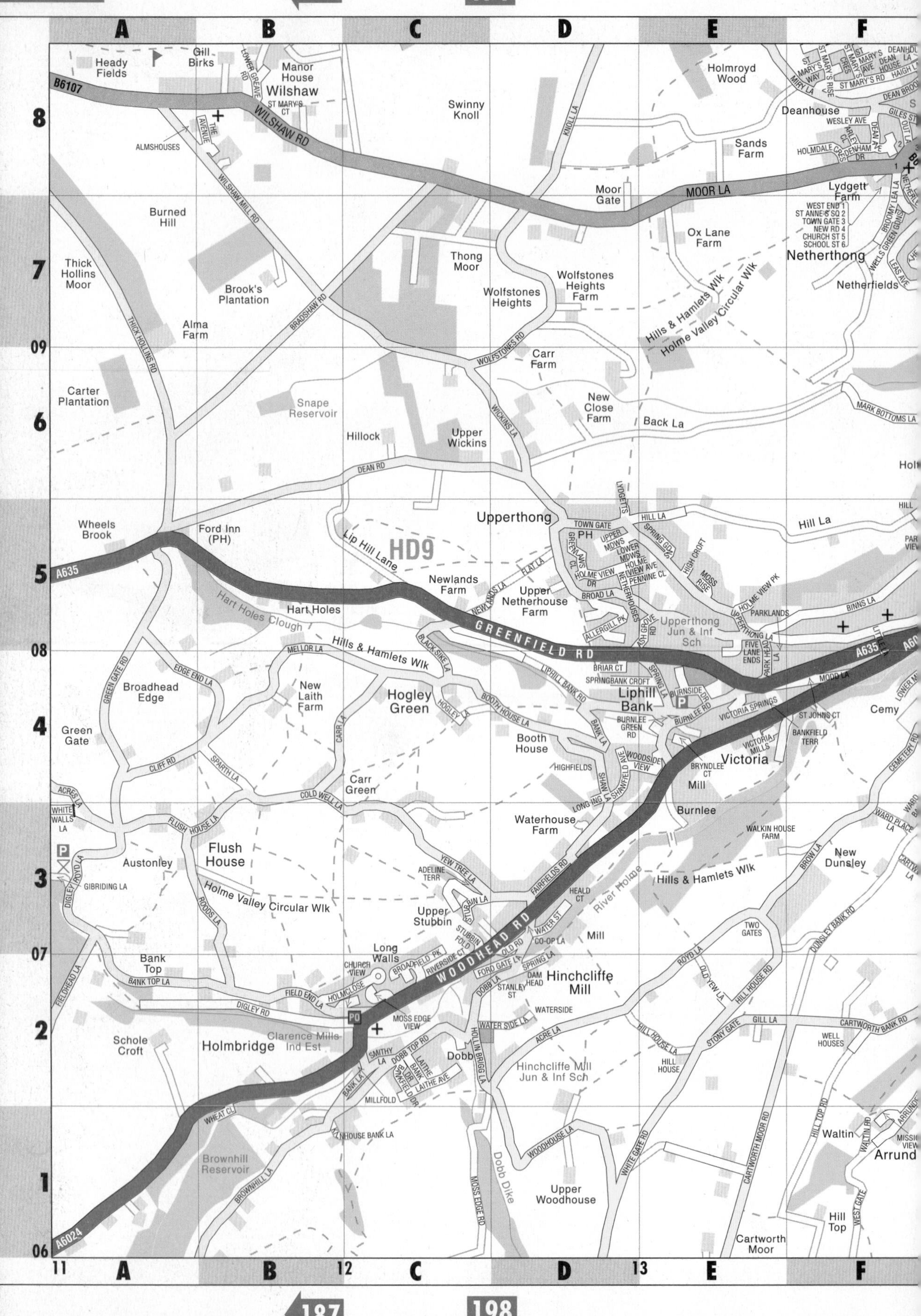
A
B
C
D
E
F
Heady Fields
Gill Birks
Manor House
Wilshaw
Holmroyd Wood
B6107
WILSHAW RD
Swinny Knoll
Deanhouse
Sands Farm
MOOR LA
Moor Gate
Lydgett Farm
Burned Hill
Ox Lane Farm
Netherthong
Thick Hollins Moor
Brook's Plantation
Thong Moor
Wolfstones Heights Farm
Wolfstones Heights
Netherfields
Alma Farm
Hills & Hamlets Wlk
Holme Valley Circular Wlk
Carr Farm
Carter Plantation
Snape Reservoir
New Close Farm
Back La
Hillock
Upper Wickins
Wheels Brook
Ford Inn (PH)
Upperthong
Hill La
HD9
A635
Newlands Farm
Upper Netherhouse Farm
Hart Holes
Hart Holes Clough
GREENFIELD RD
Upperthong Jun & Inf Sch
Broadhead Edge
New Laith Farm
Hogley Green
Liphill Bank
Green Gate
Booth House
Cemy
Victoria
Mill
Carr Green
Burnlee
Waterhouse Farm
Flush House
Austonley
New Dunsley
Holme Valley Circular Wlk
Hills & Hamlets Wlk
River Holme
Upper Stubbin
WOODHEAD RD
Mill
Bank Top
Long Walls
Hinchcliffe Mill
Schole Croft
Holmbridge
Clarence Mills Ind Est
Dobb
Hinchcliffe Mill Jun & Inf Sch
Hill House
Waltin
Arrund
Brownhill Reservoir
Dobb Dike
Upper Woodhouse
Hill Top
A6024
Cartworth Moor
8
7
09
6
5
08
4
3
07
2
1
06
11
12
13

187
198

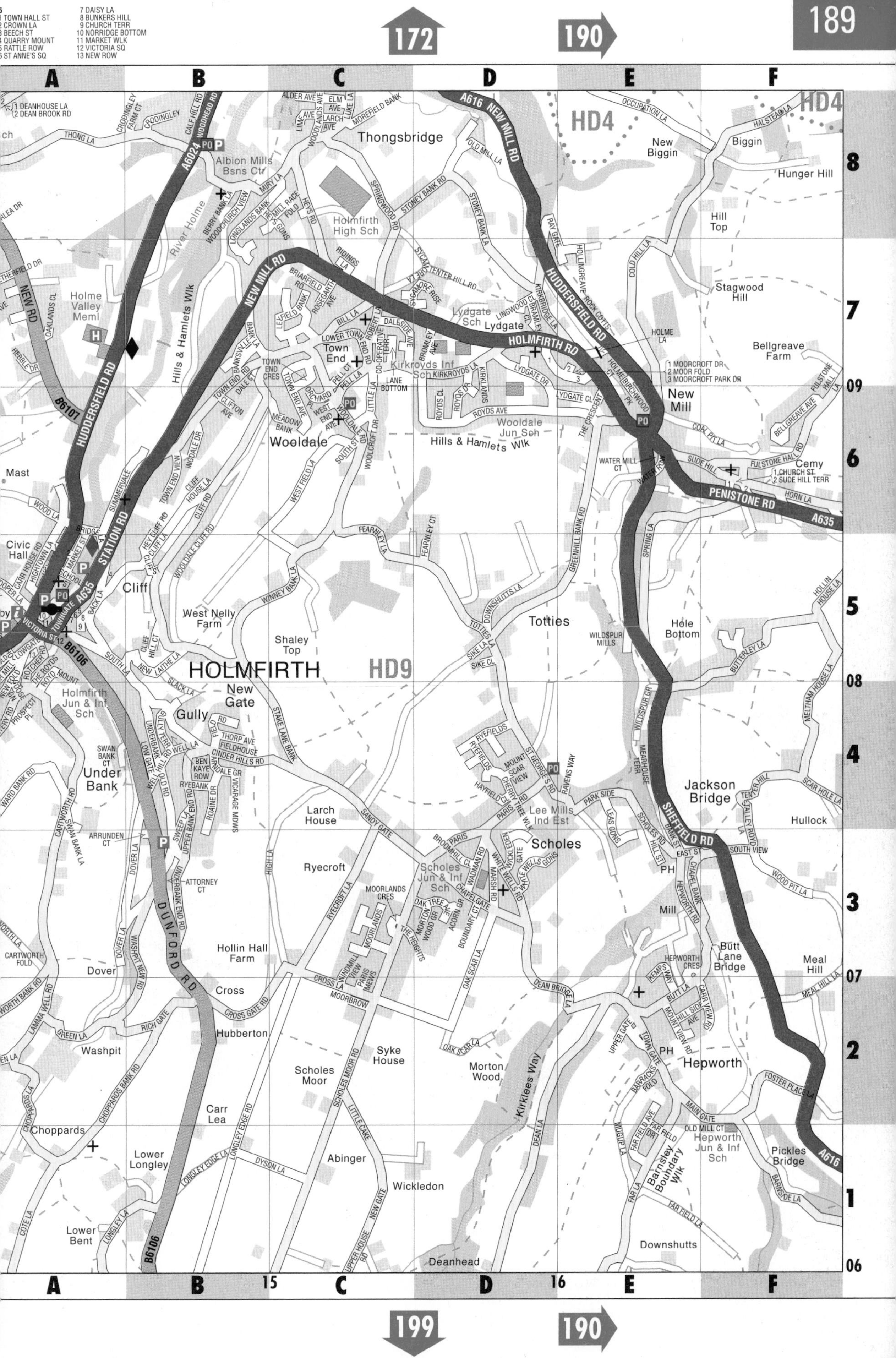

172
190
199
1 TOWN HALL ST
2 CROWN LA
3 BEECH ST
4 QUARRY MOUNT
5 RATTLE ROW
6 ST ANNE'S SQ
7 DAISY LA
8 BUNKERS HILL
9 CHURCH TERR
10 NORRIDGE BOTTOM
11 MARKET WLK
12 VICTORIA SQ
13 NEW ROW
1 DEANHOUSE LA
2 DEAN BROOK RD
1 MOORCROFT DR
2 MOOR FOLD
3 MOORCROFT PARK DR
1 CHURCH ST
2 SUDE HILL TERR
A
B
C
D
E
F
8
7
09
6
5
08
4
3
07
2
1
06
15
16
HD4
HD9
HOLMFIRTH
Thongsbridge
Albion Mills Bsns Ctr
River Holme
Holmfirth High Sch
Holme Valley Meml
Hills & Hamlets Wlk
Lydgate Sch
Lydgate
Town End
Kirkroyds Inf Sch
Wooldale Jun Sch
Wooldale
New Biggin
Biggin
Hunger Hill
Hill Top
Stagwood Hill
Bellgreave Farm
New Mill
Cemy
Mast
Civic Hall
Cliff
West Nelly Farm
Shaley Top
Totties
Wildspur Mills
Hole Bottom
New Gate
Gully
Holmfirth Jun & Inf Sch
Under Bank
Larch House
Lee Mills Ind Est
Scholes
Jackson Bridge
Hullock
Ryecroft
Scholes Jun & Inf Sch
Mill
Butt Lane Bridge
Meal Hill
Hollin Hall Farm
Dover
Cross
Hubberton
Washpit
Syke House
Scholes Moor
Morton Wood
Kirklees Way
Hepworth
Carr Lea
Choppards
Lower Longley
Abinger
Wickledon
Hepworth Jun & Inf Sch
Barnsley Boundary Wlk
Pickles Bridge
Lower Bent
Deanhead
Downshutts
A6024 WOODHEAD RD
A616 NEW MILL RD
HUDDERSFIELD RD
NEW MILL RD
HOLMFIRTH RD
PENISTONE RD
A635
SHEFFIELD RD
A616
STATION RD
B6107
NEW RD
B6106
DUNFORD RD

A **B** **C** **D** **E** **F**

8

Halstead Wood

HD4

Matthewman's Wood

Hall Syke

Fox Royd

Stocks Way

The Square

Abbey Rd S A629

The Knowle

1 LONG LA
2 DYKE BOT
3 BANK HALL

Croft Bottom Farm

WOOD END

Shepley

North Row

Cliffe

Shepley Fst Sch

War Meml

7

Fulstone Hall La

Acre La

White Ley Bank

FULSTONE

Long Close

Wood End La

Shepley Marsh

Marsh La

Dob Royd

Dobroyd Farm

Cliffe House Ctr

Lane Head Rd

Shepley Carr

Fulston Hall Farm

Horn Cote La

Ebson House La

Long Close La

Row Gate

09

Highfield Ct

Cross La

Carr La

Sovereign Ind Est

6

Horn Cote La

Horn Hill

Acre La

Horn La

Snowgate Head

PENISTONE RD

Nabscliffe

Holmfirth Rd

St Marks Ct

Lane Head

Piper Well La

Appleton Quarries

Barnsley Rd

Sovereign Inn

Cumberworth La

5

A635

Hollin House La

Holme House La

Gate Foot La

Crossroads Inn (PH)

Gate Foot

The Gully

Hirst Brow

Scaly Gate

Kirklees Way

Deershaw La

Wall Nook

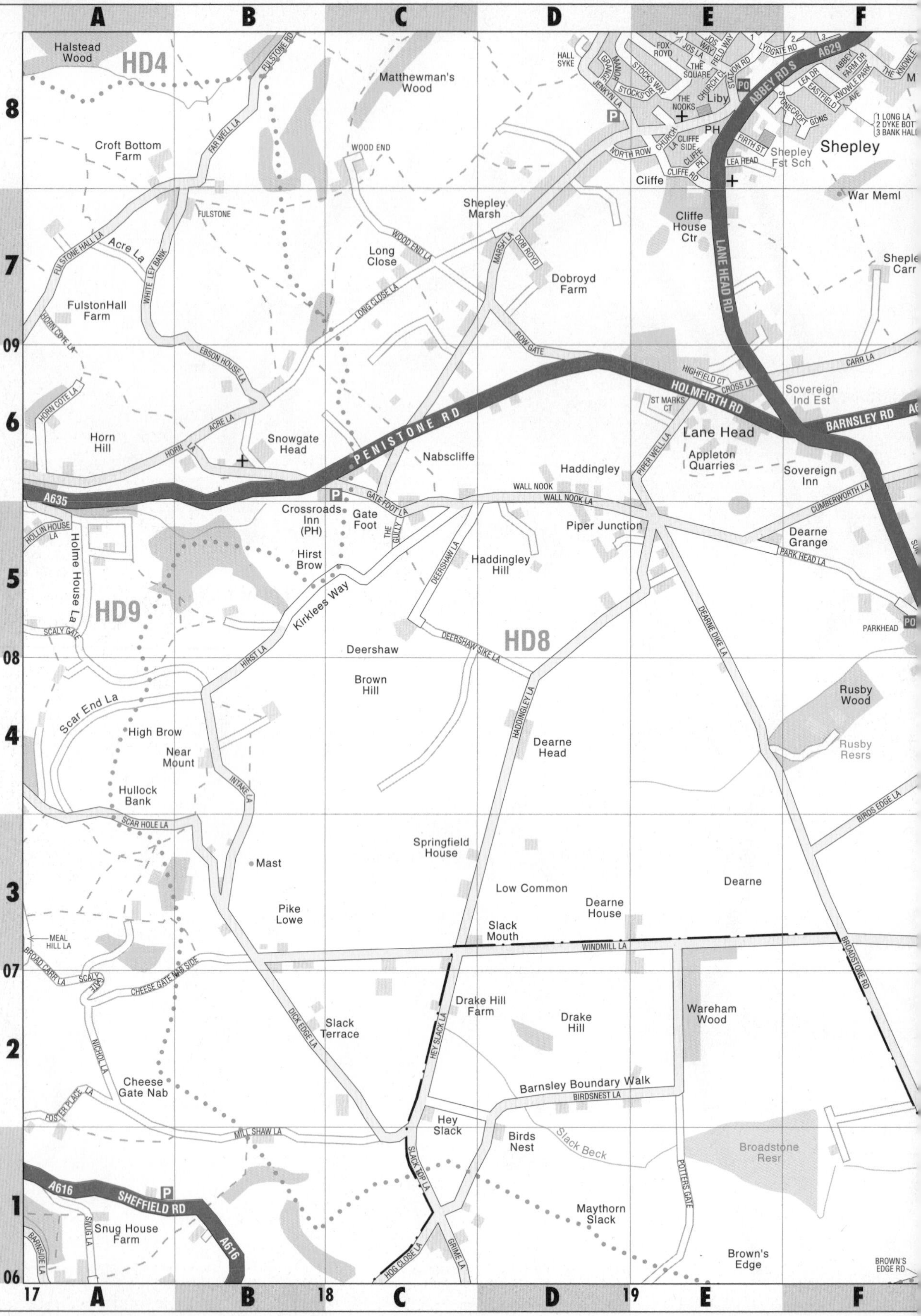

Wall Nook La

Haddingley

Haddingley Hill

Piper Junction

Park Head La

Dearne Grange

PARKHEAD

08

Hirst La

Deershaw

Deershaw Sike La

Brown Hill

HD8

Dearne Dike La

Rusby Wood

4

HD9

Scar End La

High Brow

Near Mount

Intake La

Dearne Head

Rusby Resrs

Hullock Bank

Scar Hole La

3

Meal Hill La

Broad Carr La

Scaly La

Mast

Pike Lowe

Springfield House

Low Common

Slack Mouth

Dearne House

Dearne

Windmill La

Broadstone Rd

07

Cheese Gate Nab Side

Dick Edge La

Hey Slack La

Slack Terrace

Drake Hill Farm

Drake Hill

Wareham Wood

2

Nichol La

Cheese Gate Nab

Mill Shaw La

Slack Top La

Hey Slack

Barnsley Boundary Walk

Birdsnest La

Birds Nest

Slack Beck

Potters Gate

Broadstone Resr

1

A616

Foster Place

Sheffield Rd

P

A616

Snug House Farm

Snug La

Horn Close La

Grime La

Maythorn Slack

Brown's Edge

Brown's Edge Rd

06

Barnside La

17 **A** **18** **B** **C** **18** **D** **19** **E** **F**

174
192

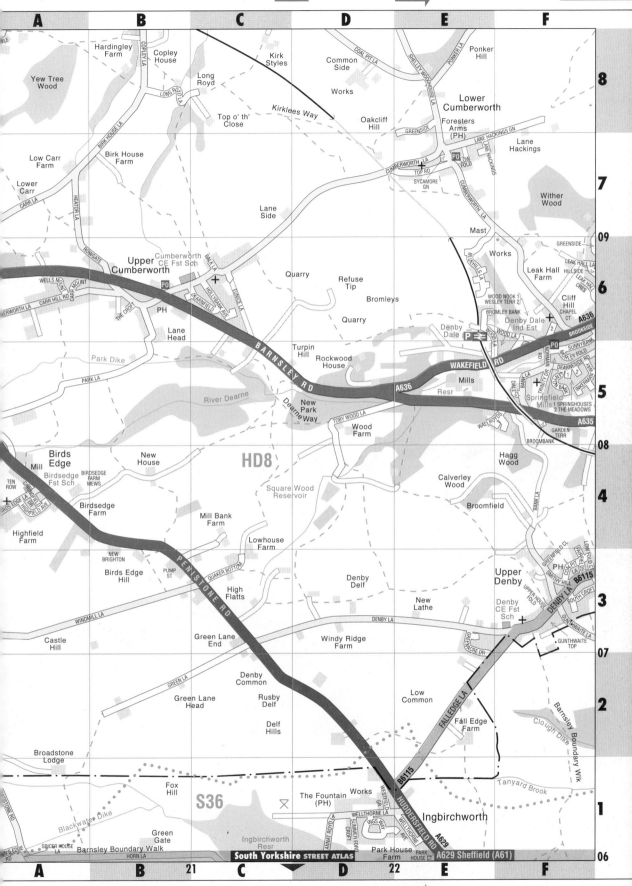
A
B
C
D
E
F
Hardingley Farm
Copley House
Yew Tree Wood
Long Royd
Kirk Styles
Common Side
Ponker Hill
Works
Lower Cumberworth
Kirklees Way
Top o' th' Close
Oakcliff Hill
Foresters Arms (PH)
Lane Hackings
Low Carr Farm
Birk House Farm
Lower Carr
Sycamore Gn
Wither Wood
Lane Side
Mast
Upper Cumberworth
Cumberworth CE Fst Sch
Quarry
Refuse Tip
Bromleys
Leak Hall Farm
Cliff Hill
PH
Lane Head
Denby Dale
Denby Dale Ind Est
Turpin Hill
Rockwood House
Park Dike
Mills
River Dearne
Resr
New Park Way
Dearne
Wood Farm
Springfield Mills
Birds Edge
Mill
Birdsedge Fst Sch
New House
HD8
Hagg Wood
Calverley Wood
Square Wood Reservoir
Broomfield
Birdsedge Farm
Highfield Farm
Mill Bank Farm
Lowhouse Farm
New Brighton
Birds Edge Hill
Pump St
High Flatts
Denby Delf
Upper Denby
New Lathe
Denby CE Fst Sch
Castle Hill
Green Lane End
Windy Ridge Farm
Denby Common
Rusby Delf
Green Lane Head
Low Common
Delf Hills
Fall Edge Farm
Barnsley Boundary Wlk
Clough Dike
Broadstone Lodge
Fox Hill
S36
The Fountain (PH)
Works
Tanyard Brook
Ingbirchworth
Blackwater Dike
Green Gate
Ingbirchworth Resr
Barnsley Boundary Walk
Park House Farm
BARNSLEY RD
WAKEFIELD RD
PENISTONE RD
HUDDERSFIELD RD
FALLEDGE LA
DENBY LA
WINDMILL LA
GREEN LA
A636
A635
A629
B6115
A629 Sheffield (A61)
8
7
09
6
5
08
4
3
07
2
1
06
21
22

192

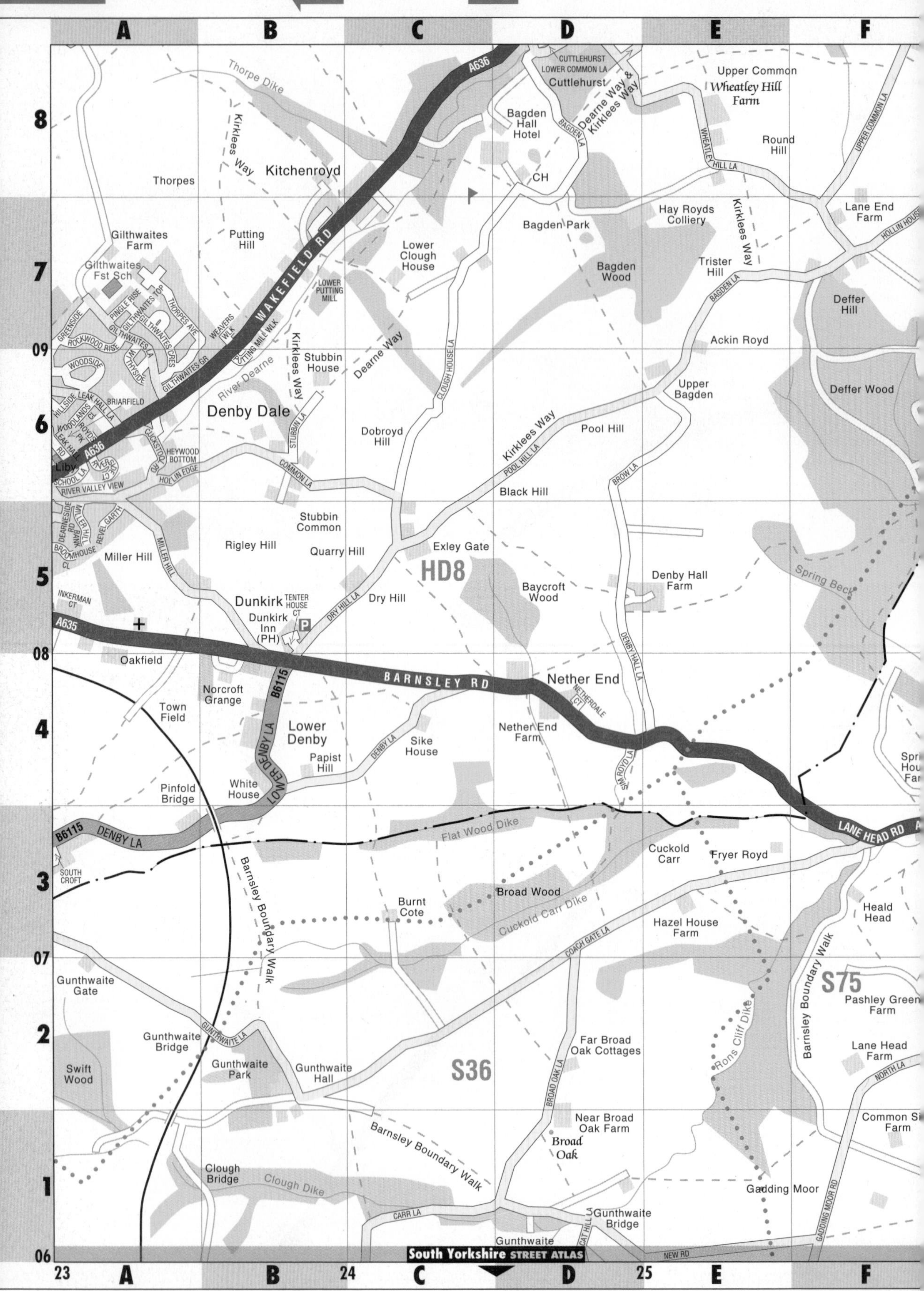
Thorpe Dike
Kirklees Way
Kitchenroyd
Thorpes
Gilthwaites Farm
Putting Hill
Gilthwaites Fst Sch
WAKEFIELD RD
A636
CUTTLEHURST
LOWER COMMON LA
Cuttlehurst
Dearne Way & Kirklees Way
Bagden Hall Hotel
BAGDEN LA
CH
Upper Common
Wheatley Hill Farm
Round Hill
WHEATLEY HILL LA
UPPER COMMON LA
Lane End Farm
HOLLIN HOUSE
Hay Royds Colliery
Bagden Park
Lower Clough House
LOWER PUTTING MILL
Bagden Wood
Trister Hill
Deffer Hill
Ackin Royd
Deffer Wood
Upper Bagden
Stubbin House
Dearne Way
CLOUGH HOUSE LA
River Dearne
Denby Dale
Dobroyd Hill
Pool Hill
POOL HILL LA
Black Hill
BROW LA
Stubbin Common
Rigley Hill
Quarry Hill
Exley Gate
Miller Hill
HD8
Dunkirk
TENTER HOUSE CT
Dunkirk Inn (PH)
Dry Hill
DRY HILL LA
Baycroft Wood
Denby Hall Farm
Spring Beck
A635
Oakfield
INKERMAN CT
BARNSLEY RD
Nether End
NETHERDALE CT
DENBY HALL LA
B6115
Norcroft Grange
Town Field
Lower Denby
Papist Hill
DENBY LA
Sike House
Nether End Farm
SIM ROYD LA
Pinfold Bridge
White House
LOWER DENBY LA
DENBY LA
Flat Wood Dike
LANE HEAD RD
Cuckold Carr
Fryer Royd
SOUTH CROFT
Barnsley Boundary Walk
Broad Wood
Burnt Cote
Cuckold Carr Dike
Hazel House Farm
Heald Head
COACH GATE LA
S75
Pashley Green Farm
Gunthwaite Gate
Rons Cliff Dike
Gunthwaite Bridge
GUNTHWAITE LA
Far Broad Oak Cottages
Lane Head Farm
Swift Wood
Gunthwaite Park
Gunthwaite Hall
S36
NORTH LA
BROAD OAK LA
Near Broad Oak Farm
Common Side Farm
Broad Oak
Clough Bridge
Clough Dike
Barnsley Boundary Walk
Gadding Moor
GADDING MOOR RD
CARR LA
Gunthwaite Bridge
CAT HILL LA
Gunthwaite
NEW RD
GREENSIDE
PINGLE RISE
ROCKWOOD RISE
GILTHWAITES LA
GILTHWAITES TOP
GILTHWAITES CRES
GILTHWAITES GR
THORPES AVE
WEAVERS WLK
PUTTING MILL WLK
WOODSIDE
WHYSIDE
LEAK HALL LA
BRIARFIELD
HILLSIDE
WOODLANDS
STUBBIN LA
COMMON LA
HEYWOOD BOTTOM
HOLLIN EDGE
Liby
SCHOOL LA
RIVER VALLEY VIEW
MILLER HILL
BROOMHOUSE CL

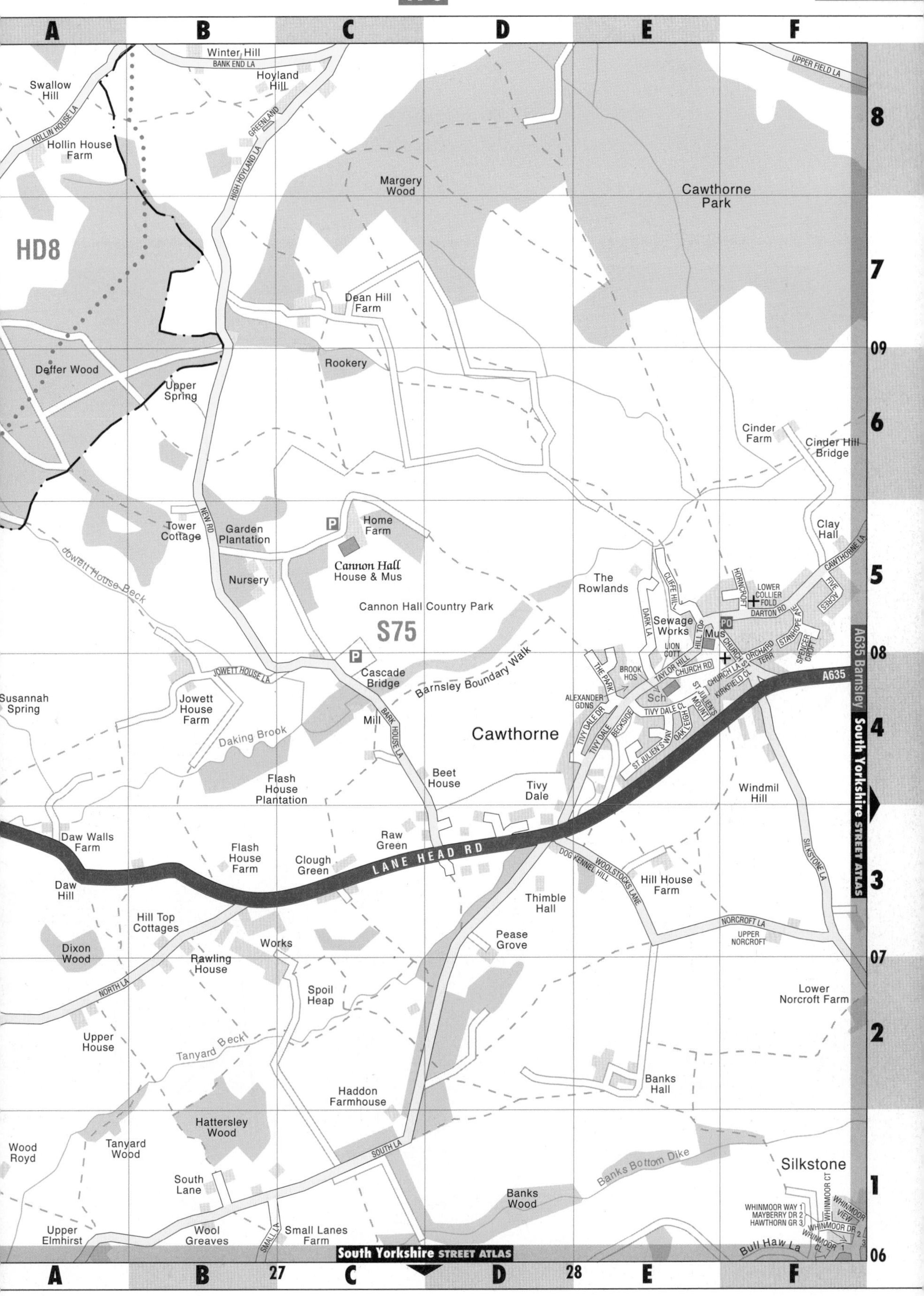

A | B | C | D | E | F

8
7
09
6
5
08
4
3
07
2
1
06

HD8

Swallow Hill

Hollin House Farm

Winter Hill
BANK END LA

Hoyland Hill

Margery Wood

Cawthorne Park

Dean Hill Farm

Deffer Wood

Upper Spring

Rookery

Cinder Farm

Cinder Hill Bridge

Clay Hall

Tower Cottage

Garden Plantation

Home Farm

Nursery

Cannon Hall House & Mus

The Rowlands

Cannon Hall Country Park

S75

Sewage Works

LOWER COLLIER FOLD

Barnsley Boundary Walk

Cascade Bridge

Susannah Spring

Jowett House Farm

Mill

Cawthorne

Windmil Hill

Daking Brook

Flash House Plantation

Beet House

Tivy Dale

Daw Walls Farm

Flash House Farm

Clough Green

Raw Green

LANE HEAD RD

DOG KENNEL HILL

Hill House Farm

Daw Hill

Hill Top Cottages

Works

Thimble Hall

NORCROFT LA

UPPER NORCROFT

Dixon Wood

Rawling House

Pease Grove

Lower Norcroft Farm

Spoil Heap

Upper House

Tanyard Beck

Haddon Farmhouse

Banks Hall

Wood Royd

Tanyard Wood

Hattersley Wood

Banks Bottom Dike

Silkstone

South Lane

Banks Wood

WHINMOOR WAY 1
MAYBERRY DR 2
HAWTHORN GR 3

Upper Elmhirst

Wool Greaves

Small Lanes Farm

SOUTH LA

Bull Haw La

Jowett House Beck

A635 Barnsley
South Yorkshire STREET ATLAS

A635

182

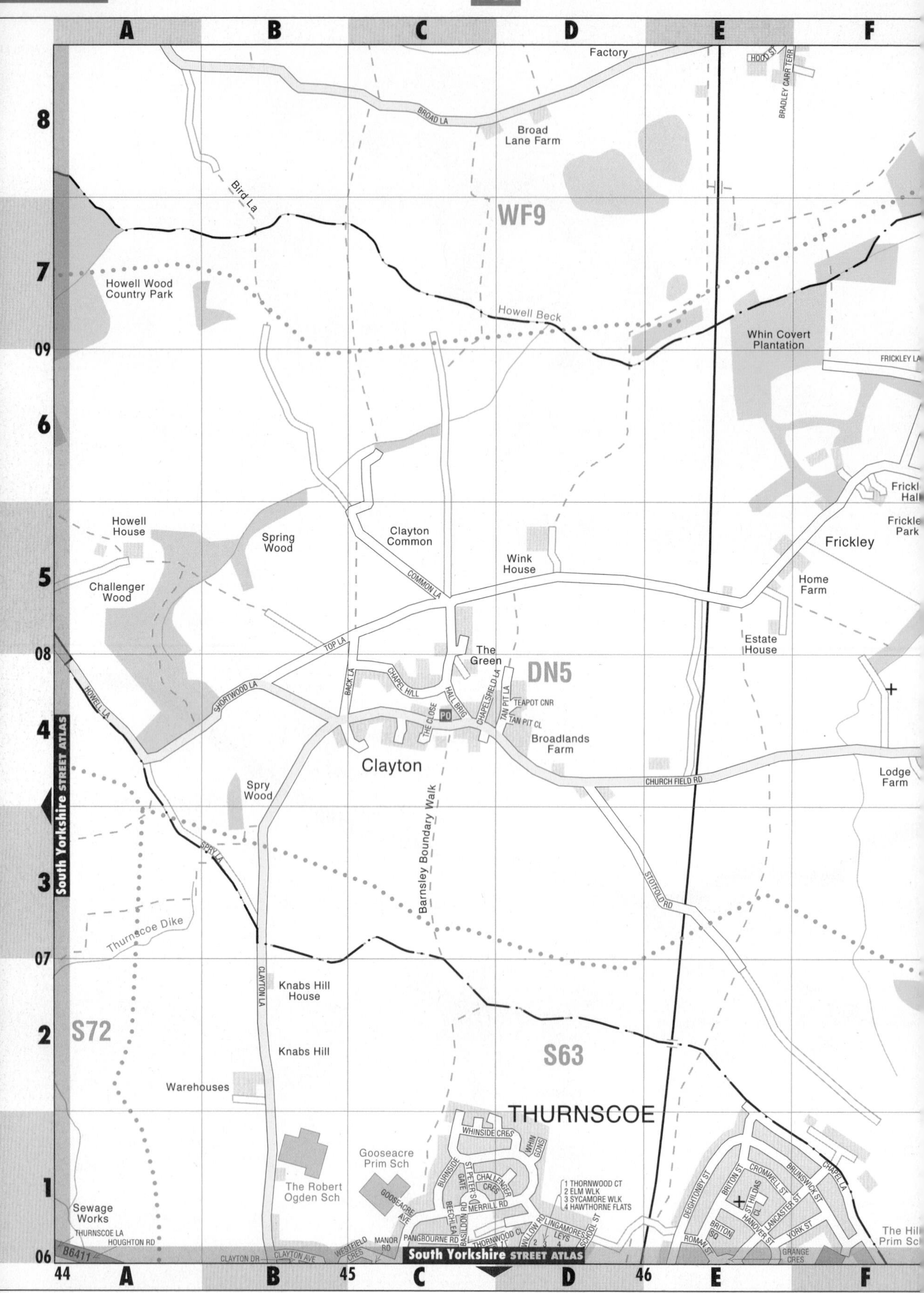
Factory
HOOD ST
BRADLEY CARR TERR
BROAD LA
Broad Lane Farm
Bird La
WF9
Howell Wood Country Park
Howell Beck
Whin Covert Plantation
FRICKLEY LA
Howell House
Spring Wood
Clayton Common
Wink House
Frickley Hall
Frickley Park
Frickley
Challenger Wood
COMMON LA
Home Farm
TOP LA
The Green
Estate House
DN5
HOWELL LA
SHORTWOOD LA
BACK LA
CHAPEL HILL
HALL BRIG
CHAPELSFIELD LA
TAN PIT LA
TEAPOT CNR
TAN PIT CL
THE CLOSE
PO
Broadlands Farm
Clayton
Lodge Farm
Spry Wood
CHURCH FIELD RD
Barnsley Boundary Walk
SPRY LA
STOTFOLD RD
Thurnscoe Dike
CLAYTON LA
Knabs Hill House
S72
Knabs Hill
S63
Warehouses
THURNSCOE
WHINSIDE CRES
WHIN GDNS
Gooseacre Prim Sch
The Robert Ogden Sch
BURNSIDE
ST PETER'S GATE
CHALLENGER CRES
GOOSEACRE AVE
BEECHLEA
BASILDON RD
MERRILL RD
1 THORNWOOD CT
2 ELM WLK
3 SYCAMORE WLK
4 HAWTHORNE FLATS
DEIGHTONBY ST
BRITON ST
CROMWELL ST
BRUNSWICK ST
CHAPEL LA
ST HILDAS CL
LANCASTER ST
HANOVER ST
BRITON SQ
YORK ST
ROMAN ST
GRANGE CRES
Sewage Works
THURNSCOE LA
HOUGHTON RD
B6411
CLAYTON DR
CLAYTON AVE
WESTFIELD CRES
MANOR RD
PANGBOURNE RD
THORNWOOD CL
WILLOW RD
LINGAMORE LEYS
SCHOOL ST
The Hill Prim Sch
South Yorkshire STREET ATLAS
A
B
C
D
E
F
8
09
7
6
5
08
4
3
07
2
1
06
44
45
46

A   B   C   D   E   F

WF9

B6422

Moorhouse Common

MOORHOUSE LA

FRICKLEY LA

DN6

8

Hooton Thorn Covert

ELMSALL LA

NORTH FIELD RD

LENNY BALK

7

The Ashes

North Field

OLD ST

OLD ST

09

South Yorkshire STREET ATLAS

6

Hooton Pagnell Wood

BROAD BALK

Back Field

Hooton Pagnell

Hooton Pagnell Common

Church Plantation

Hooton Pagnell All Saints CE Prim Sch

HOME FARM CT

BACK LA

NARROW BALK

Lound Hill

5

CHURCH FIELD RD

CLAYTON LA

PO

Redroof

Bluegate Flatt Plantation

LOUND LA

08

Mapple Yard

Mapple Yard Plantation

Black Plantation

Hooton Pagnell Hall

Bread Walls Plantation

Broadrick Holt

4

Cemy

DN5

WHITE LA

Cricket Ground

BUTT LA

B6422

HOOTON RD

Norman Hill

Second Plantation

BILHAM ROW

Third Plantation

WATCHLEY LA

STREET LA

3

07

Little Watchley

Bilham Grange

Watchley Crag

BILHAM LA

Fish Pond Plantation

Bilham Lodge

2

The Wilderness

Bilham Park

Bilham Wood

Stotfold Farm

Bilham House Farm

Summer House Plantation

Wr Twr

1

Hickleton Spring

A   B   48   C   D   49   E   F

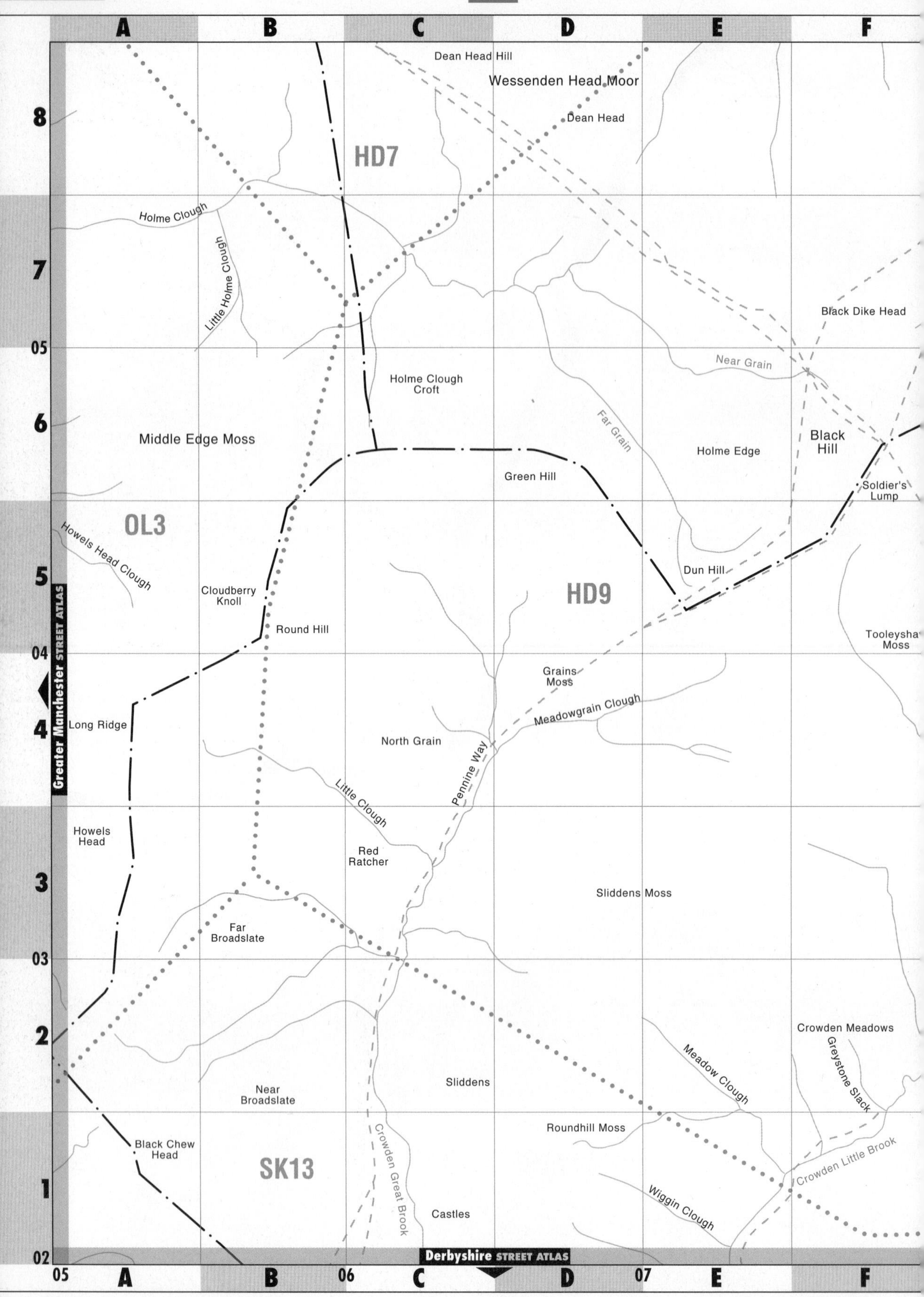

Derbyshire STREET ATLAS

Greater Manchester STREET ATLAS

Dean Head Hill

Wessenden Head Moor

Dean Head

HD7

Holme Clough

Little Holme Clough

Black Dike Head

Near Grain

05

Holme Clough Croft

Far Grain

Black Hill

6

Middle Edge Moss

Holme Edge

Soldier's Lump

Green Hill

OL3

HD9

Howels Head Clough

Dun Hill

5

Cloudberry Knoll

Round Hill

Tooleysha Moss

04

Grains Moss

Long Ridge

Meadowgrain Clough

4

North Grain

Pennine Way

Howels Head

Little Clough

Red Ratcher

Sliddens Moss

3

Far Broadslate

Crowden Meadows

03

Greystone Slack

2

Near Broadslate

Sliddens

Meadow Clough

Roundhill Moss

Crowden Great Brook

Black Chew Head

SK13

Castles

Wiggin Clough

Crowden Little Brook

1

02

05   A   B   06   C   D   07   E   F

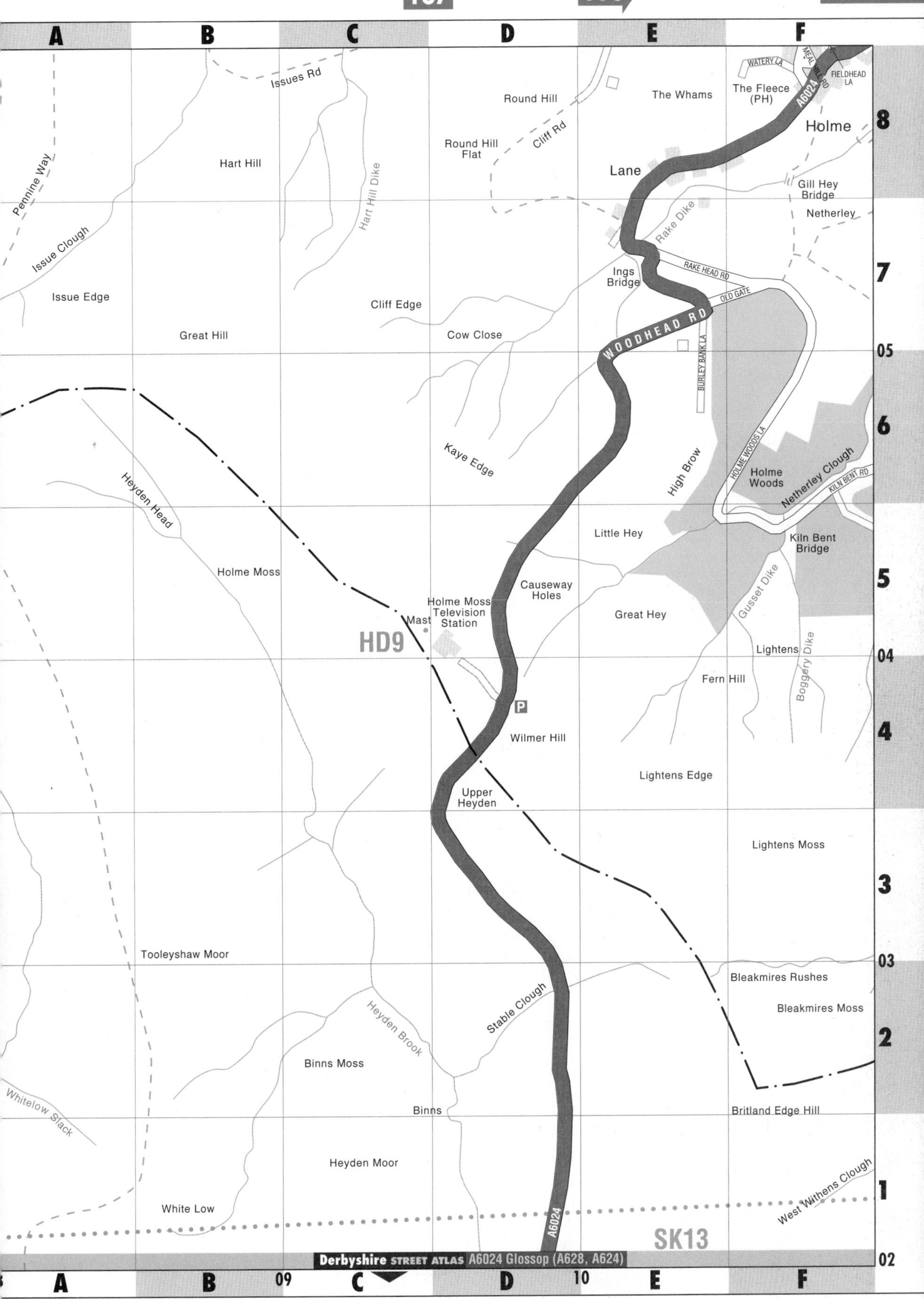

A B C D E F

Watery La
The Fleece (PH)
FIELDHEAD LA
Holme
8

Issues Rd
Round Hill
The Whams
Pennine Way
Hart Hill
Round Hill Flat
Cliff Rd
Lane
Gill Hey Bridge
Netherley
7

Issue Clough
Hart Hill Dike
Cliff Edge
Ings Bridge
Rake Dike
RAKE HEAD RD
OLD GATE
WOODHEAD RD
05

Issue Edge
Great Hill
Cow Close
BURLEY BANK LA
6

Kaye Edge
High Brow
HOLME WOODS LA
Holme Woods
Netherley Clough
KILN BENT RD

Heyden Head
Little Hey
Kiln Bent Bridge
5

Holme Moss
Causeway Holes
Great Hey
Gusset Dike
Lightens
Boggery Dike
04

Mast
Holme Moss Television Station
Fern Hill

HD9
P
Wilmer Hill
Lightens Edge
4

Upper Heyden
Lightens Moss
3

Tooleyshaw Moor
03

Heyden Brook
Bleakmires Rushes
Bleakmires Moss
2

Binns Moss
Stable Clough
Binns
Britland Edge Hill

Whitelow Stack
Heyden Moor
West Withens Clough
1

White Low
A6024
SK13
02

A B 09 C D 10 E F

197
188

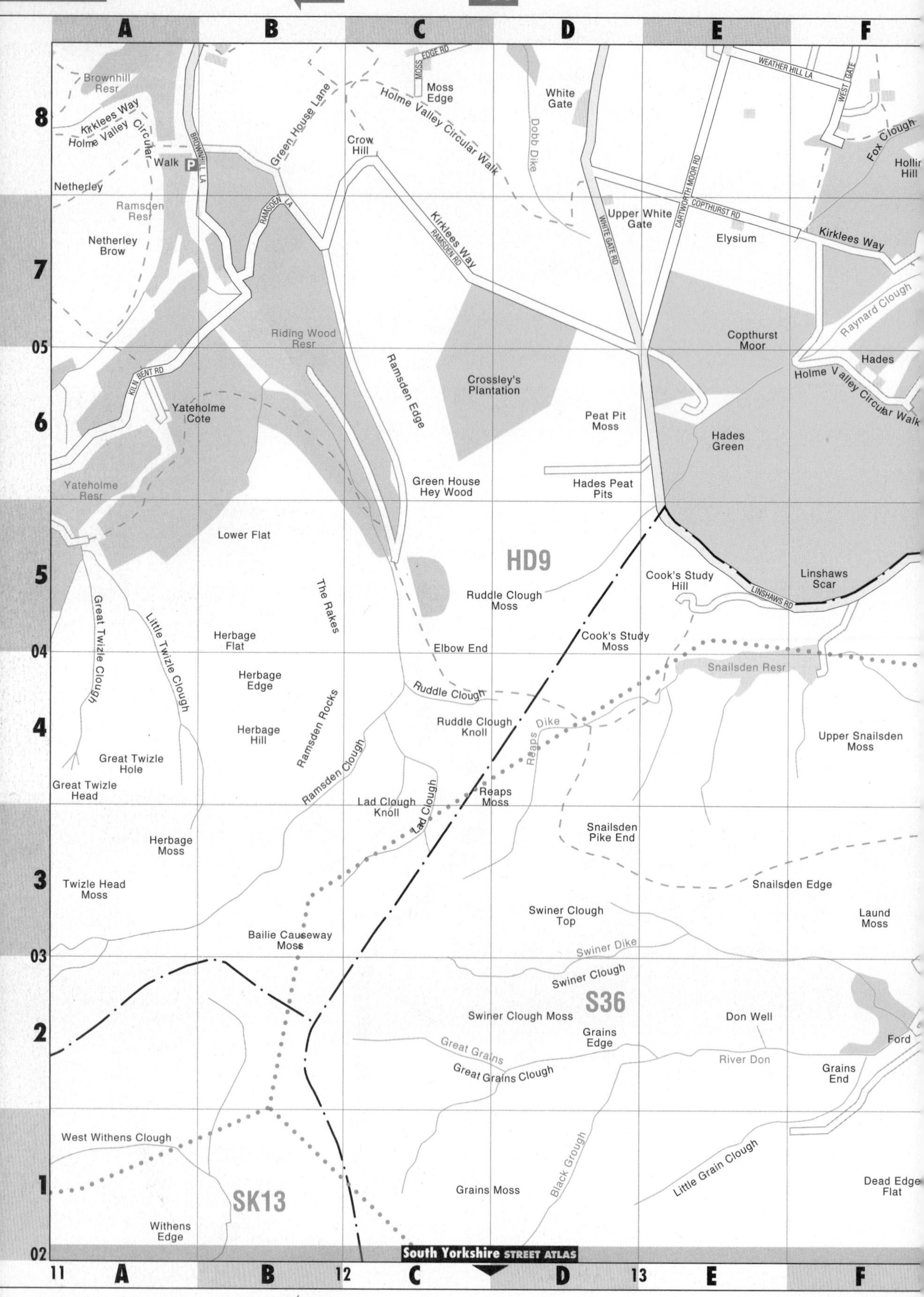
A
B
C
D
E
F
8
7
05
6
5
04
4
3
03
2
1
02
11
12
13
Brownhill Resr
Kirklees Way
Holme Valley Circular Walk
Netherley
Ramsden Resr
Netherley Brow
BROWNHILL LA
Green House Lane
RAMSDEN LA
MOSS EDGE RD
Moss Edge
Holme Valley Circular Walk
Crow Hill
White Gate
Dobb Dike
WEATHER HILL LA
WEST GATE
Fox Clough
Hollin Hill
Kirklees Way
RAMSDEN RD
Upper White Gate
WHITE GATE RD
CARTWORTH MOOR RD
COPTHURST RD
Elysium
Kirklees Way
Raynard Clough
Riding Wood Resr
Ramsden Edge
Copthurst Moor
Hades
KILN BENT RD
Yateholme Cote
Crossley's Plantation
Peat Pit Moss
Holme Valley Circular Walk
Hades Green
Yateholme Resr
Green House Hey Wood
Hades Peat Pits
Lower Flat
HD9
Cook's Study Hill
Linshaws Scar
LINSHAWS RD
The Rakes
Ruddle Clough Moss
Great Twizle Clough
Little Twizle Clough
Herbage Flat
Elbow End
Cook's Study Moss
Snailsden Resr
Herbage Edge
Ruddle Clough
Ruddle Clough Knoll
Reaps Dike
Upper Snailsden Moss
Herbage Hill
Ramsden Rocks
Great Twizle Hole
Ramsden Clough
Great Twizle Head
Lad Clough Knoll
Lad Clough
Reaps Moss
Snailsden Pike End
Herbage Moss
Twizle Head Moss
Snailsden Edge
Swiner Clough Top
Laund Moss
Bailie Causeway Moss
Swiner Dike
Swiner Clough
S36
Swiner Clough Moss
Grains Edge
Don Well
Ford
Great Grains
Great Grains Clough
River Don
Grains End
West Withens Clough
Black Grough
Little Grain Clough
Grains Moss
Dead Edge Flat
SK13
Withens Edge
South Yorkshire STREET ATLAS

197

A B C D E F

8 7 6 5 4 3 2 1

Mount
Hade Edge Jun & Inf Sch
Kirklee Way
Hade Edge
Bay Horse Hotel (PH)
Strines Moor
Fields Head
Crimes House
Berristal Top
Ing Royd
Ox Lee
Crow Hill
New House Farm
Berristal Head
Moorside
Cote
Law Farm
Long Ing
Daisy Lee Moor
Little Law
Bradshaw Edge
Wild Boar Clough
Lane House
HD9
Green Gate
Lower Snittlegate
Law Head
Ellentree Brow
Snittlegate
Barnsley Boundary Walk
Fox House Moss
Harden Clough
Harden
Harden Edge
Tinker Hill
Harden Reservoir
Cocker Edge
Snailsden
Lower Snailsden Moss
Wetshaw Edge
Sand Ridge Moss
Sand Ridge
Little Shepherd's Castle
Booth Hill Flat
S36
Lower Town Head
Railway Cotts
Townhead
Upper Town Head
Broad Hill Bank
Dearden Foot Plantation
Banks
Winscar Reservoir
Dunford Bridge
Lower Dead Edge
River Don
Trans Pennine Trail
Black Bank
Stanhope Arms Hotel
Shepley Ings
Woodhead Tunnel (dis)
Dunford Bridge
Dick Royd
Bance Edge Plantation

COTE LA, LONGLEY LA, DUNFORD RD, BENT LA, LONGLEY EDGE RD, BOSHAW, B6106, HILL TOP VIEW, BAYFIELD CL, SCHOLES MOOR RD, UPPER HOUSE RD, COWCLIFF HILL RD, DEAN LA, FAR LA, GREAVE RD, CLOUGH FOOT LA, HOPEFIELD CT, ABBEY CL, ABBEY CT, LONG ING RD, GREEN ABBEY, STRINES MOOR RD, OX LEE LA, BENT RD, PENISTONE RD, DAISY LEE LA, SNITTLE RD, LAW SLACK RD, BEDDING EDGE RD, FLINT LA, ROUND CLOSE RD, LAW COMMON RD, LINSHAWS RD, BARE BONES RD, FLIGHT HILL, DUNFORD RD, BROOK HILL LA, DON VIEW, WINDLE EDGE

05 04 03 02

15 16

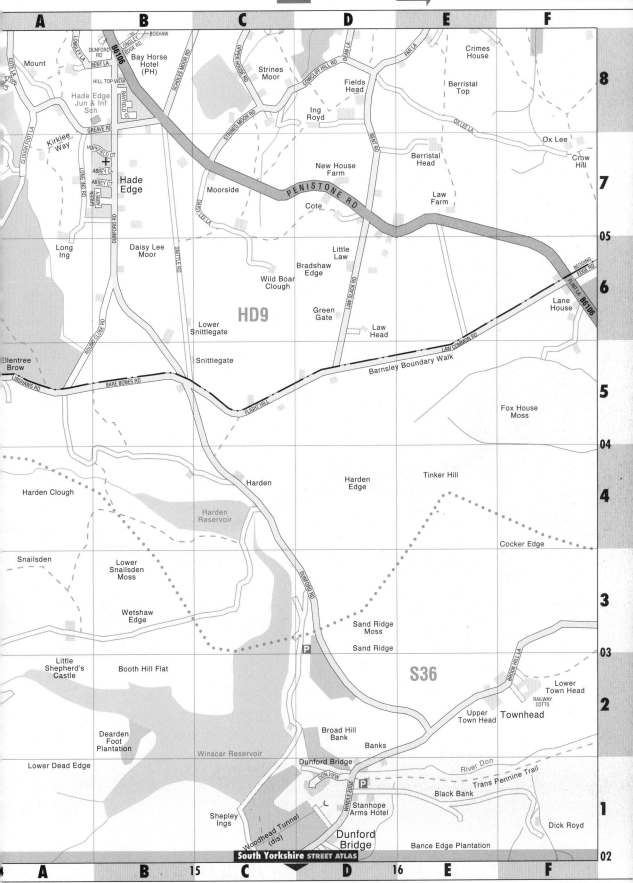

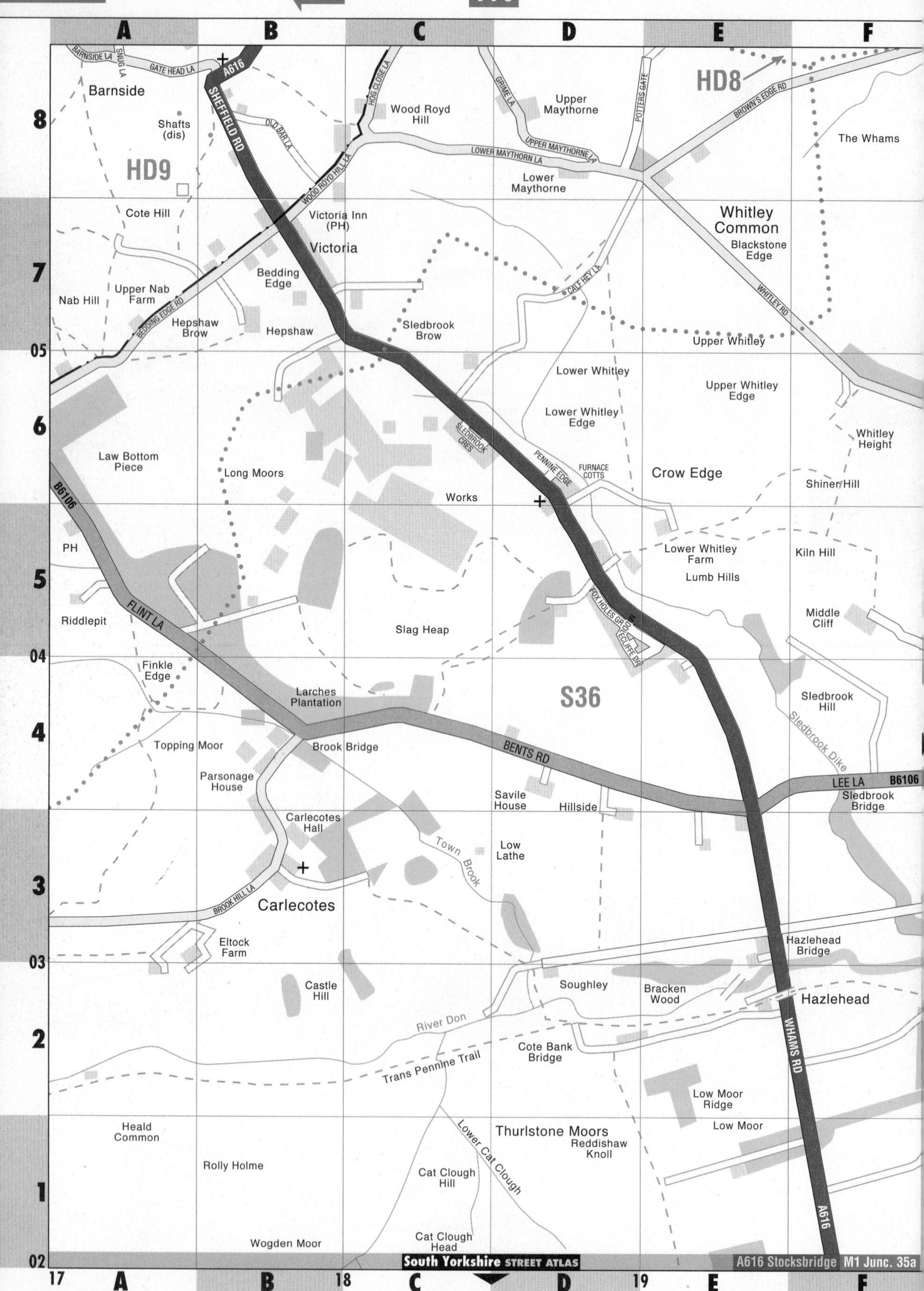
A
B
C
D
E
F
8
7
05
6
5
04
4
3
03
2
1
02
17
18
19
BARNSIDE LA
SNUG LA
GATE HEAD LA
A616
SHEFFIELD RD
Barnside
Shafts (dis)
HD9
OLD BAR LA
HOG CLOSE LA
Wood Royd Hill
GRIME LA
Upper Maythorne
POTTERS GATE
HD8
BROWN'S EDGE RD
The Whams
UPPER MAYTHORNE LA
LOWER MAYTHORN LA
Lower Maythorne
WOOD ROYD HILL LA
Cote Hill
Victoria Inn (PH)
Victoria
Whitley Common
Blackstone Edge
Bedding Edge
CALF HEY LA
WHITLEY RD
Nab Hill
Upper Nab Farm
BEDDING EDGE RD
Hepshaw Brow
Hepshaw
Sledbrook Brow
Upper Whitley
Lower Whitley
Upper Whitley Edge
Lower Whitley Edge
SLEDBROOK CRES
Whitley Height
Law Bottom Piece
PENNINE EDGE
FURNACE COTTS
Crow Edge
Long Moors
Shiner Hill
B6106
Works
PH
Lower Whitley Farm
Kiln Hill
Lumb Hills
FOX HOLES GR
ECLIFFE DR
Middle Cliff
Riddlepit
FLINT LA
Slag Heap
Finkle Edge
Larches Plantation
S36
Sledbrook Hill
Sledbrook Dike
Topping Moor
Brook Bridge
BENTS RD
LEE LA
B6106
Sledbrook Bridge
Parsonage House
Savile House
Hillside
Carlecotes Hall
Town Brook
Low Lathe
BROOK HILL LA
Carlecotes
Eltock Farm
Hazlehead Bridge
Castle Hill
Soughley
Bracken Wood
Hazlehead
River Don
Cote Bank Bridge
WHAMS RD
Trans Pennine Trail
Low Moor Ridge
Low Moor
Heald Common
Thurlstone Moors
Reddishaw Knoll
Lower Cat Clough
Rolly Holme
Cat Clough Hill
A616
Wogden Moor
Cat Clough Head

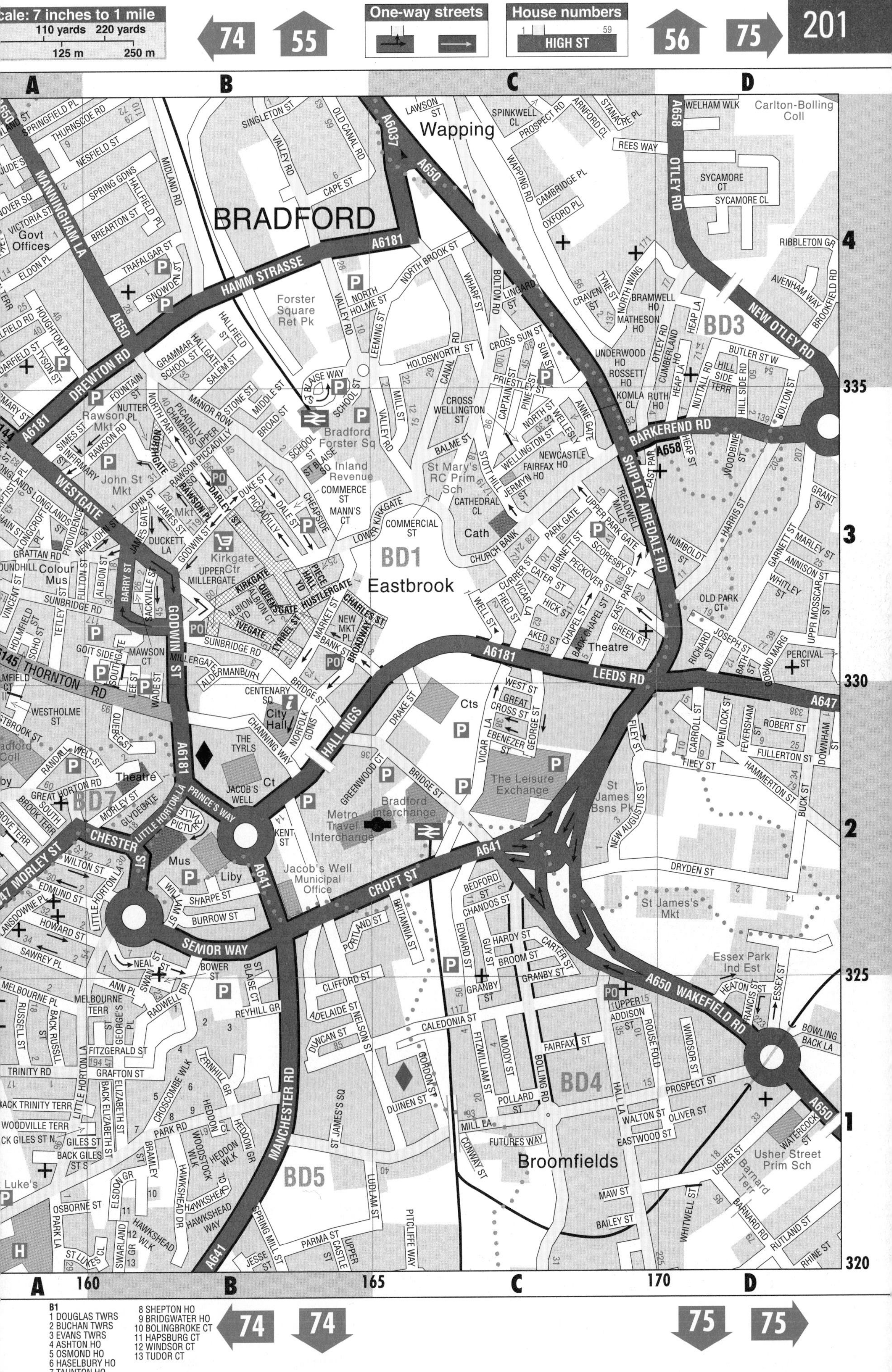

C3
1 WOLSELEY TERR
2 OAK TERR
3 ROSE TERR
4 OAK LA
5 BOWMAN PL
6 BOWMAN ST
7 BAKER FOLD
8 RAGLAN CT
9 CRYSTAL CT
10 LIGHTOWLER CL
11 GROSVENOR TERR
12 BACK CAVENDISH TERR
13 CAVENDISH TERR
14 CAVENDISH ST
15 GLADSTONE RD
16 HEYWOOD ST

Scale: 7 inches to 1 mile
0   110 yards   220 yards
0   125 m   250 m

B1
1 VAUGHN ST
2 THORNTON TERR
3 AUTUMN ST
4 POHLMAN ST
5 RALEIGH ST
6 BURLEIGH ST
7 MAPLE ST

B1
8 CANNON ST
9 MOORGATE ST
10 LEADENHALL ST

C1
1 WEST ROYD VILLAS
2 TRAFALGAR SQ
3 TRAFALGAR ST
4 HAWTHORN ST
5 HAWTHORN TERR
6 WOODBINE ST
7 WOODBINE TERR
8 MAYFIELD ST
9 MAYFIELD TERR S
10 UPPER HAUGH SHAW
11 LAUREL BANK
12 FIELDHOUSE COTTS
13 HAUGH SHAW CROFT
14 LAUREL MOUNT
15 ROCKVILLE TERR
16 ELDROTH MOUNT
17 SAVILE PARK TERR
18 INGRAM SQ
19 WALSH'S SQ
20 BELL HALL MOUNT

One-way streets
House numbers
HIGH ST
59
A3
1 CROMWELL TERR
2 BACK CROMWELL TERR
3 MILTON TERR
4 BRUNSWICK GDNS
5 SUNDERLAND ST
92
B3
1 CULVER ST
2 TOWN HALL ST E
3 WESLEY CT
4 HIND'S CHAMBERS
5 LANDOWN HO
113
B3
6 BANK CHAMBERS
7 GILL'S CT
8 THE OLD ARCADE
9 UPPER GEORGE YD
10 BLACK SWAN PAS
11 BLACK SWAN GINNELL
12 GEORGE SQ
13 BARUM TOP
14 POWELL ST
15 BACK COMMERCIAL ST
16 CARRIER ST
203
A
B
C
4
255
3
250
2
245
1
240
HALIFAX
HX1
HX3
Lee Bridge Ind Est
Dean Clough Office Pk
Birks Hall La
Snake Hill
Beech Hill Jun & Inf Sch
St Joseph's RC Prim Sch
North Bridge L Ctr
Margram Bsns Ctr
Green Mount Ret Pk
Halifax Ret Pk
Royal Ind Pk
Liby
Calderdale Industrial Mus
Borough Mkt
Westgate
Piece Hall
Square Chapel
The Victoria Theatre
Halifax Playhouse
Halifax
Eureka! The Museum for Children
Bailey Hall Bsns Pk
St Mary's RC Prim Sch
Brunswick Ind Est
Holy Trinity CE Prim Sch
Swimming Pool
TA Ctr
The Shay (Halifax Town FC & Halifax Blue Sox RLFC)
Queen's Sports Club
Clover Hill Wlk
Cemy
OVENDEN RD
BURDOCK WAY
NEW BANK
GODLEY RD
A58
A629
A647
HALEY HILL
ORANGE ST
BROAD ST
COW GN
FOUNTAIN ST
PORTLAND PL
SKIRCOAT RD
KING CROSS ST
CHARLESTOWN RD
1 EDGECUMBE HOUSE APARTMENTS
2 RAWSON APARTMENTS
3 BALDWIN APARTMENTS
4 KITCHENMAN APARTMENTS
5 McCREA APARTMENTS
085
090
095
A
B
C
A1
1 LANGWITH CT
2 BISHOPDALE CT
3 PORTER APARTMENTS
4 CROSSLEY APARTMENTS
5 APPLEYARD APARTMENTS
6 SIMPSON APARTMENTS
7 PRINCESS APARTMENTS
8 RICHMOND HOUSE APARTMENTS
9 WHITAKER HOUSE APARTMENTS
A2
1 HENRY ST
2 WEST PARADE FLATS
3 DERALD HO
113
B2
1 CARLTON PL
2 BACK FERGUSON ST
3 CADNEY CROFT
4 CARLTON TERR
5 SEDAN ST
6 POWELL ST
7 HOPE HALL TERR
8 BACK HOPE HALL TERR
113
C2
1 CROSS ST
2 WELLINGTON PL
3 BATH ST
4 JUBILEE TERR

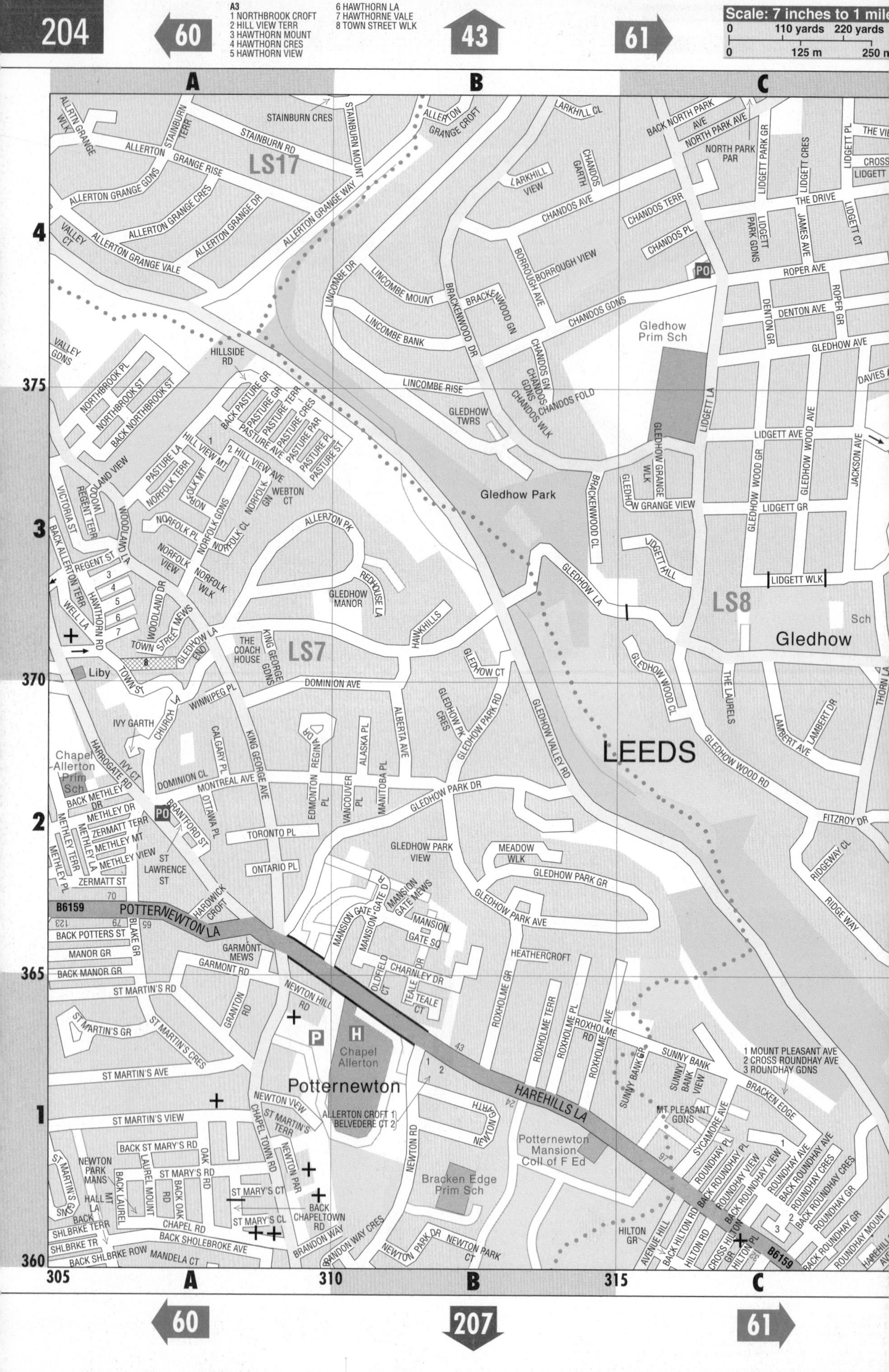
60
43
61
A3
1 NORTHBROOK CROFT
2 HILL VIEW TERR
3 HAWTHORN MOUNT
4 HAWTHORN CRES
5 HAWTHORN VIEW
6 HAWTHORN LA
7 HAWTHORNE VALE
8 TOWN STREET WLK
Scale: 7 inches to 1 mile
0
110 yards
220 yards
125 m
250 m
A
B
C
4
375
3
370
2
365
1
360
305
310
315
LS17
LS7
LS8
LEEDS
Gledhow Park
Gledhow
Potternewton
Chapel Allerton
Gledhow Prim Sch
Chapel Allerton Prim Sch
Bracken Edge Prim Sch
Potternewton Mansion Coll of F Ed
Sch
Liby
PO
B6159
POTTERNEWTON LA
HAREHILLS LA
STAINBURN CRES
STAINBURN RD
STAINBURN MOUNT
STAINBURN TERR
ALLERTON GRANGE CROFT
ALLERTON GRANGE WAY
ALLERTON GRANGE GDNS
ALLERTON GRANGE CRES
ALLERTON GRANGE DR
ALLERTON GRANGE VALE
ALLERTON GRANGE RISE
ALLRTN GRANGE WLK
VALLEY CT
VALLEY GDNS
LARKHILL CL
LARKHILL VIEW
CHANDOS GARTH
CHANDOS AVE
CHANDOS TERR
CHANDOS PL
CHANDOS GDNS
CHANDOS GN
CHANDOS FOLD
CHANDOS WLK
BACK NORTH PARK AVE
NORTH PARK AVE
NORTH PARK PAR
LIDGETT PARK GR
LIDGETT CRES
LIDGETT PL
LIDGETT PARK GDNS
LIDGETT CT
LIDGETT AVE
LIDGETT GR
LIDGETT WLK
LIDGETT HILL
LIDGETT LA
THE DRIVE
JAMES AVE
ROPER AVE
ROPER GR
DENTON AVE
DENTON GR
GLEDHOW AVE
DAVIES AVE
GLEDHOW WOOD GR
GLEDHOW WOOD AVE
JACKSON AVE
LINCOMBE DR
LINCOMBE MOUNT
LINCOMBE BANK
LINCOMBE RISE
BRACKENWOOD DR
BRACKENWOOD GN
BRACKENWOOD CL
BORROUGH AVE
BORROUGH VIEW
GLEDHOW TWRS
GLEDHOW GRANGE WLK
GLEDHOW GRANGE VIEW
GLEDHOW LA
GLEDHOW WOOD CL
GLEDHOW WOOD RD
THE LAURELS
LAMBERT AVE
LAMBERT DR
THORN
FITZROY DR
RIDGEWAY CL
RIDGE WAY
HILLSIDE RD
NORTHBROOK PL
NORTHBROOK ST
BACK NORTHBROOK ST
BACK PASTURE GR
PASTURE GR
PASTURE TERR
PASTURE CRES
PASTURE AVE
PASTURE PAR
PASTURE PL
PASTURE ST
PASTURE LA
HILL VIEW MT
HILL VIEW AVE
WEBTON CT
LAND VIEW
NORFOLK TERR
NORFOLK MT
NORFOLK GDNS
NORFOLK GN
NORFOLK PL
NORFOLK CL
NORFOLK VIEW
NORFOLK WLK
VICTORIA ST
REGENT TERR
REGENT ST
WOODLAND LA
WOODLAND DR
BACK ALLERTON TERR
WELL LA
HAWTHORN RD
TOWN STREET MEWS
TOWN ST
GLEDHOW LA END
ALLERTON PK
GLEDHOW MANOR
REDHOUSE LA
HAWKHILLS
THE COACH HOUSE
KING GEORGE GDNS
GLEDHOW CT
DOMINION AVE
GLEDHOW PK CRES
GLEDHOW PARK RD
GLEDHOW VALLEY RD
GLEDHOW PARK DR
GLEDHOW PARK VIEW
MEADOW WLK
GLEDHOW PARK GR
GLEDHOW PARK AVE
IVY GARTH
IVY CT
CHURCH LA
WINNIPEG PL
CALGARY PL
KING GEORGE AVE
REGINA DR
ALASKA PL
ALBERTA AVE
EDMONTON PL
VANCOUVER PL
MANITOBA PL
HARROGATE RD
DOMINION CL
MONTREAL AVE
OTTAWA PL
BRANTFORD ST
TORONTO PL
ONTARIO PL
BACK METHLEY DR
METHLEY DR
ZERMATT TERR
METHLEY MT
METHLEY LA
METHLEY TERR
METHLEY VIEW
METHLEY PL
ZERMATT ST
ST LAWRENCE ST
HARDWICK CROFT
BACK POTTERS ST
BLAKE GR
MANOR GR
BACK MANOR GR
GARMONT MEWS
GARMONT RD
MANSION GATE DR
MANSION GATE MEWS
MANSION GATE
MANSION GATE SQ
OLDFIELD CT
CHARNLEY DR
TEALE DR
TEALE CT
HEATHERCROFT
ROXHOLME GR
ROXHOLME TERR
ROXHOLME PL
ROXHOLME RD
ROXHOLME AVE
SUNNY BANK GR
SUNNY BANK VIEW
SUNNY BANK AVE
ST MARTIN'S RD
ST MARTIN'S GR
ST MARTIN'S CRES
ST MARTIN'S AVE
ST MARTIN'S VIEW
ST MARTIN'S TERR
GRANTON RD
NEWTON HILL RD
NEWTON VIEW
NEWTON GARTH
NEWTON RD
NEWTON PAR
NEWTON PARK MANS
NEWTON PARK DR
NEWTON PARK CT
ALLERTON CROFT 1
BELVEDERE CT 2
CHAPELTOWN RD
BACK CHAPELTOWN RD
BACK ST MARY'S RD
ST MARY'S RD
ST MARY'S CT
ST MARY'S CL
LAUREL MOUNT
BACK LAUREL MT
BACK OAK RD
OAK RD
HALL LA
CHAPEL RD
BACK SHOLEBROKE AVE
BACK SHLBRKE TERR
SHLBRKE TR
BACK SHLBRKE ROW
MANDELA CT
BRANDON WAY
BRANDON WAY CRES
1 MOUNT PLEASANT AVE
2 CROSS ROUNDHAY AVE
3 ROUNDHAY GDNS
BRACKEN EDGE
MT PLEASANT GDNS
SYCAMORE AVE
ROUNDHAY PL
BACK ROUNDHAY PL
ROUNDHAY VIEW
BACK ROUNDHAY VIEW
ROUNDHAY AVE
BACK ROUNDHAY AVE
ROUNDHAY CRES
BACK ROUNDHAY CRES
ROUNDHAY GR
BACK ROUNDHAY GR
ROUNDHAY MOUNT
HILTON GR
AVENUE HILL
BACK HILTON RD
HILTON RD
CROSS HILTON GR
HILTON PL
60
207
61

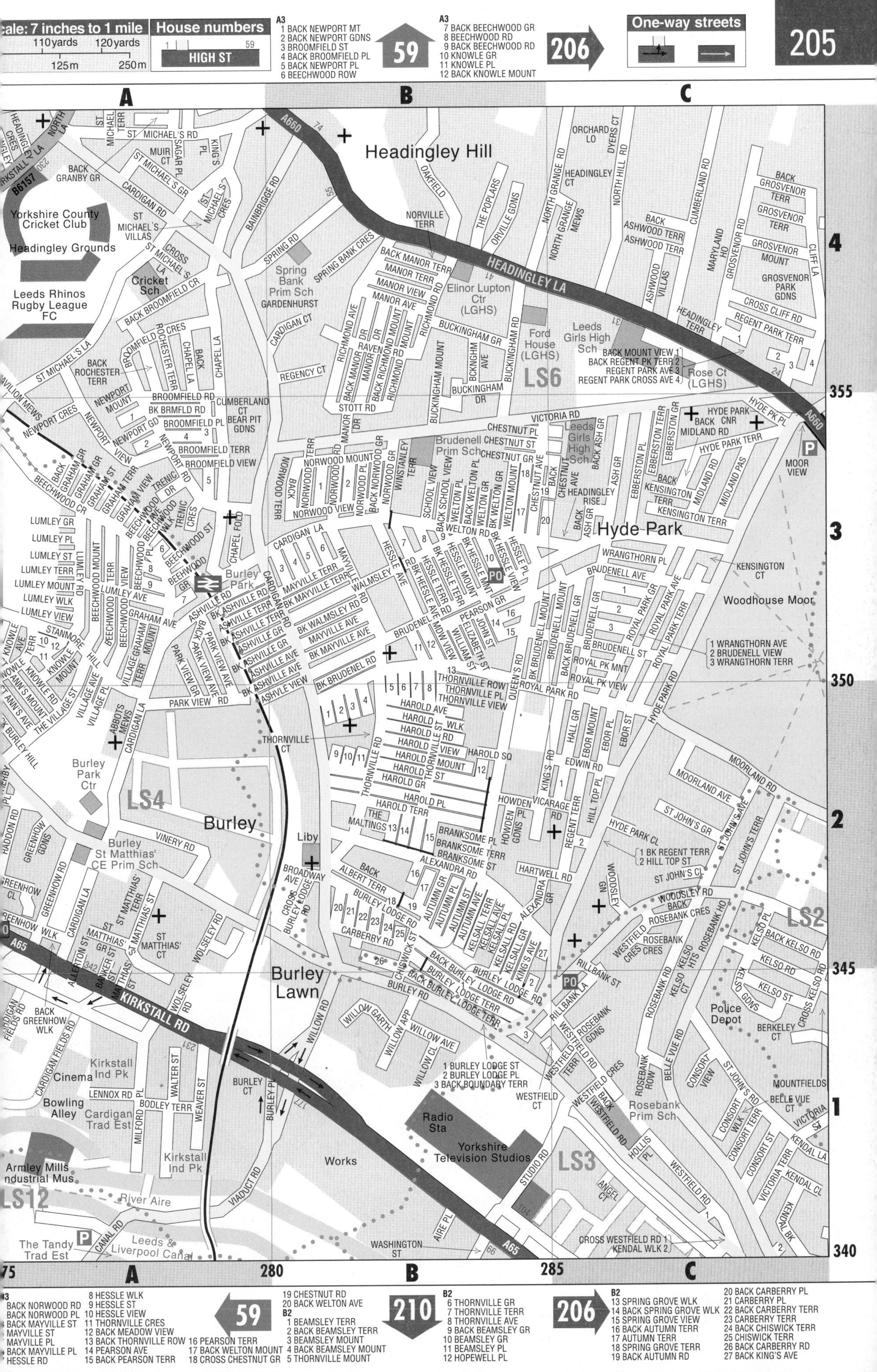

Scale: 7 inches to 1 mile
110yards 120yards
125m   250m

House numbers
1   59
HIGH ST

A3
1 BACK NEWPORT MT
2 BACK NEWPORT GDNS
3 BROOMFIELD ST
4 BACK BROOMFIELD PL
5 BACK NEWPORT PL
6 BEECHWOOD ROW

59

A3
7 BACK BEECHWOOD GR
8 BEECHWOOD RD
9 BACK BEECHWOOD RD
10 KNOWLE GR
11 KNOWLE PL
12 BACK KNOWLE MOUNT

206

One-way streets

205

A3
BACK NORWOOD RD
BACK NORWOOD RD
BACK MAYVILLE ST
MAYVILLE ST
MAYVILLE PL
BACK MAYVILLE ST
HESSLE RD

8 HESSLE WLK
9 HESSLE ST
10 HESSLE VIEW
11 THORNVILLE CRES
12 BACK MEADOW VIEW
13 BACK THORNVILLE ROW
14 PEARSON AVE
15 BACK PEARSON TERR

16 PEARSON TERR
17 BACK WELTON MOUNT
18 CROSS CHESTNUT GR

59

19 CHESTNUT RD
20 BACK WELTON AVE
B2
1 BEAMSLEY TERR
2 BACK BEAMSLEY TERR
3 BEAMSLEY MOUNT
4 BACK BEAMSLEY MOUNT
5 THORNVILLE MOUNT

210

B2
6 THORNVILLE GR
7 THORNVILLE TERR
8 THORNVILLE AVE
9 BACK BEAMSLEY GR
10 BEAMSLEY GR
11 BEAMSLEY PL
12 HOPEWELL PL

206

B2
13 SPRING GROVE WLK
14 BACK SPRING GROVE WLK
15 SPRING GROVE VIEW
16 BACK AUTUMN TERR
17 AUTUMN TERR
18 SPRING GROVE TERR
19 BACK AUTUMN RD

20 BACK CARBERRY PL
21 CARBERRY PL
22 BACK CARBERRY TERR
23 CARBERRY TERR
24 BACK CHISWICK TERR
25 CHISWICK TERR
26 BACK CARBERRY RD
27 BACK KING'S AVE

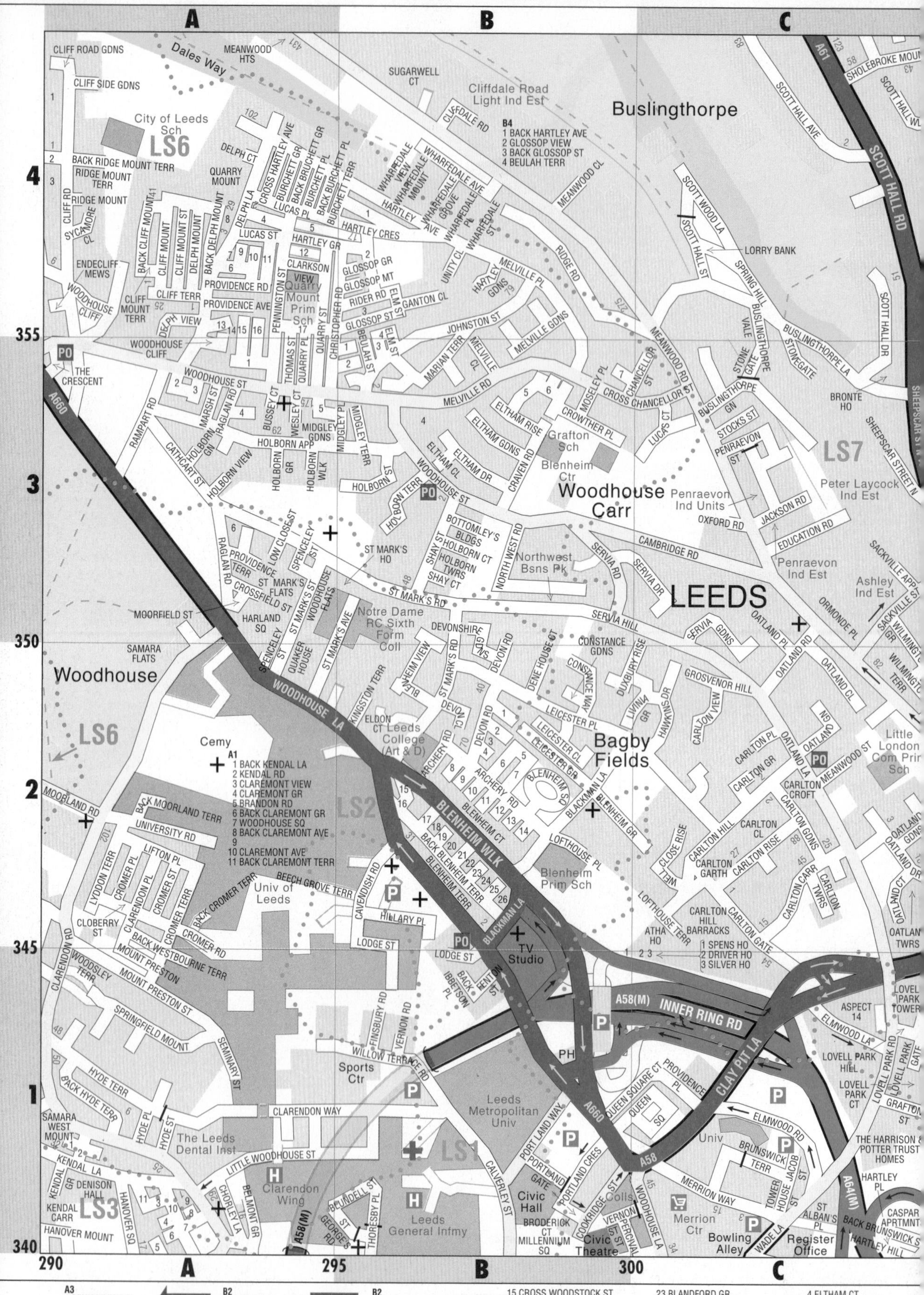

A4
1 CLIFF CT
2 BACK MONTPELIER TR
3 MONTPELIER TERR
4 BACK LUCAS ST
5 BACK HARTLEY GR

6 QUARRY MOUNT ST
7 RIDGEWAY TERR
8 INGLEWOOD TERR
9 QUARRY MOUNT PL
10 QUARRY MOUNT TERR
11 BACK QUARRY MOUNT TERR

12 BACK CLARKSON VIEW
13 BACK PROVIDENCE AVE
14 PENNINGTON CT
15 PENNINGTON TERR
16 PENNINGTON GR
17 CROSS QUARRY ST

B4
1 BACK HARTLEY AVE
2 GLOSSOP VIEW
3 BACK GLOSSOP ST
4 BEULAH TERR

A1
1 BACK KENDAL LA
2 KENDAL RD
3 CLAREMONT VIEW
4 CLAREMONT GR
5 BRANDON RD
6 BACK CLAREMONT GR
7 WOODHOUSE SQ
8 BACK CLAREMONT AVE
9 CLAREMONT AVE
10 CLAREMONT AVE
11 BACK CLAREMONT TERR

A3
1 PENNINGTON PL
2 PLEASANT CT
3 MARSH VALE
4 HOLBURN GDNS
5 LESLIE TERR
6 THE HARRISON &
  POTTER TRUST HOMES

B2
1 WINFIELD PL
2 WINFIELD TERR
3 BACK WINFIELD GR
4 WINFIELD GR
5 BLENHEIM CRES
6 BLENHEIM AVE
7 BACK BLENHEIM AVE

B2
8 BACK ARCHERY PL
9 ARCHERY PL
10 BACK ARCHERY TERR
11 ARCHERY TERR
12 BACK ARCHERY ST
13 ARCHERY ST
14 BACK ARCHERY RD

15 CROSS WOODSTOCK ST
16 BACK WOODSTOCK ST
17 MARLBOROUGH GDNS
18 BACK MARLBOROUGH GDNS
19 MARLBOROUGH GR
20 BACK MARLBOROUGH GR
21 BLANDFORD GDNS
22 BACK BLANDFORD GDNS

23 BLANDFORD GR
24 BACK BLANDFORD GR
25 CHURCHILL GDNS
26 BACK CHURCHILL GDNS
B3
1 BEULAH VIEW
2 BEULAH MOUNT
3 BEULAH GR

4 ELTHAM CT
5 CROSS SPEEDWELL ST
6 SPEEDWELL MOUNT
7 SPEEDWELL ST

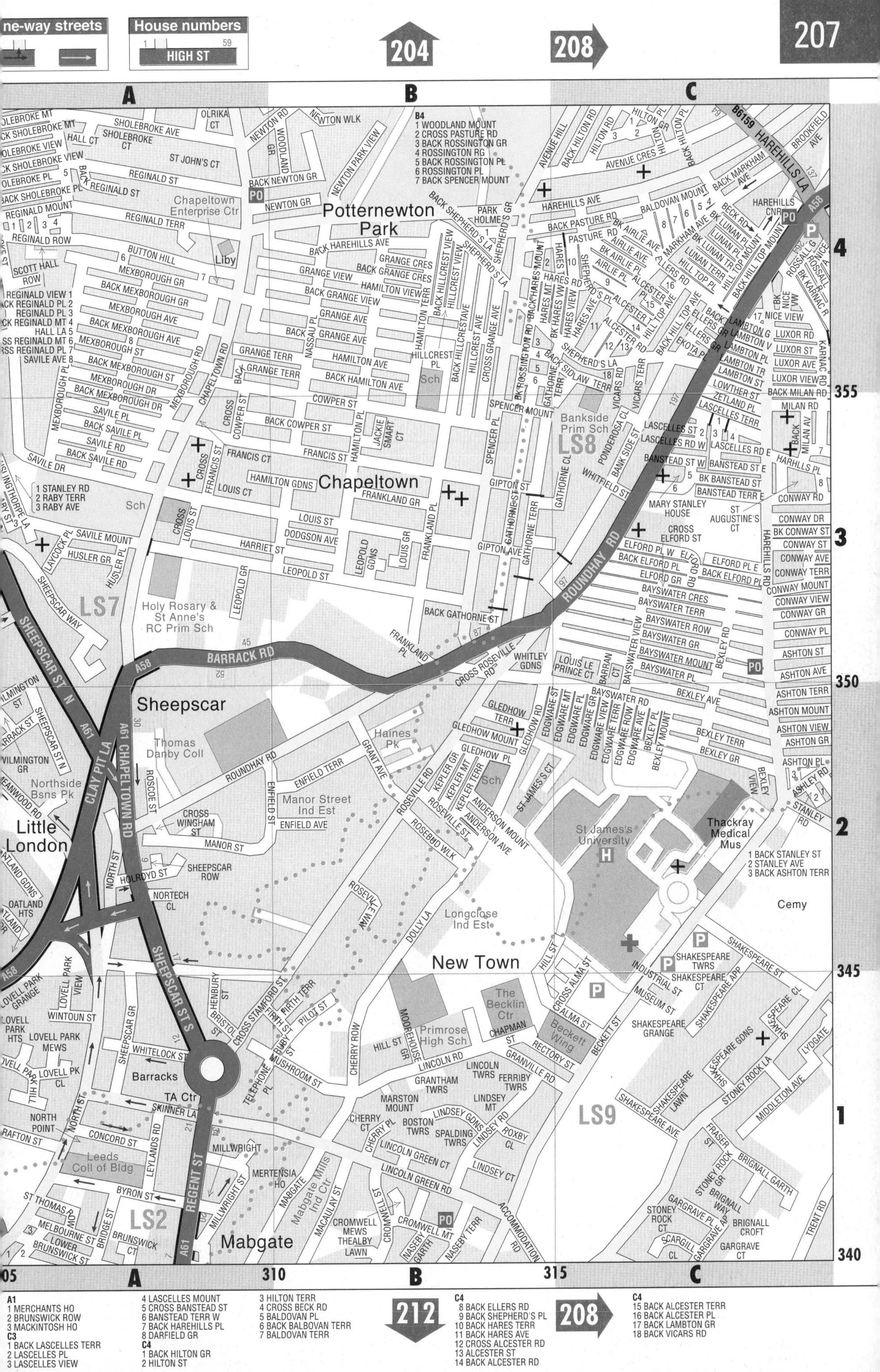

One-way streets
House numbers
1
59
HIGH ST
204
208
207
A
B
C
B4
1 WOODLAND MOUNT
2 CROSS PASTURE RD
3 BACK ROSSINGTON GR
4 ROSSINGTON RG
5 BACK ROSSINGTON PL
6 ROSSINGTON PL
7 BACK SPENCER MOUNT
Potternewton Park
Chapeltown Enterprise Ctr
Liby
Chapeltown
LS7
LS8
LS9
LS2
Holy Rosary & St Anne's RC Prim Sch
Bankside Prim Sch
MARY STANLEY HOUSE
ST AUGUSTINE'S CT
Sheepscar
Thomas Danby Coll
Haines Pk
Manor Street Ind Est
Northside Bsns Pk
Little London
St James's University
Thackray Medical Mus
Cemy
Longclose Ind Est
New Town
The Becklin Ctr
Beckett Wing
Primrose High Sch
Barracks
TA Ctr
Leeds Coll of Bldg
Mabgate Mills Ind Ctr
Mabgate
SHAKESPEARE GRANGE
BARRACK RD
ROUNDHAY RD
HAREHILLS LA
B6159
A58
A61
A64
CHAPELTOWN RD
SHEEPSCAR ST N
SHEEPSCAR ST S
SHEEPSCAR WAY
CLAY PIT LA
REGENT ST
1 STANLEY RD
2 RABY TERR
3 RABY AVE
1 BACK STANLEY ST
2 STANLEY AVE
3 BACK ASHTON TERR
REGINALD VIEW 1
BACK REGINALD PL 2
REGINALD PL 3
BACK REGINALD MT 4
HALL LA 5
BACK REGINALD MT 6
BACK REGINALD PL 7
SAVILE AVE 8
355
350
345
340
4
3
2
1
305
310
315
212
208
A1
1 MERCHANTS HO
2 BRUNSWICK ROW
3 MACKINTOSH HO
C3
1 BACK LASCELLES TERR
2 LASCELLES PL
3 LASCELLES VIEW
4 LASCELLES MOUNT
5 CROSS BANSTEAD ST
6 BANSTEAD TERR W
7 BACK HAREHILLS PL
8 DARFIELD GR
C4
1 BACK HILTON GR
2 HILTON ST
3 HILTON TERR
4 CROSS BECK RD
5 BALDOVAN PL
6 BACK BALBOVAN TERR
7 BALDOVAN TERR
C4
8 BACK ELLERS RD
9 BACK SHEPHERD'S PL
10 BACK HARES TERR
11 BACK HARES AVE
12 CROSS ALCESTER RD
13 ALCESTER ST
14 BACK ALCESTER RD
C4
15 BACK ALCESTER TERR
16 BACK ALCESTER PL
17 BACK LAMBTON GR
18 BACK VICARS RD

207
61
61

One-way Streets

House numbers
1 59 HIGH ST

Scale: 7 inches to 1 mile
0 110 yards 220 yards
0 125 m 250 m

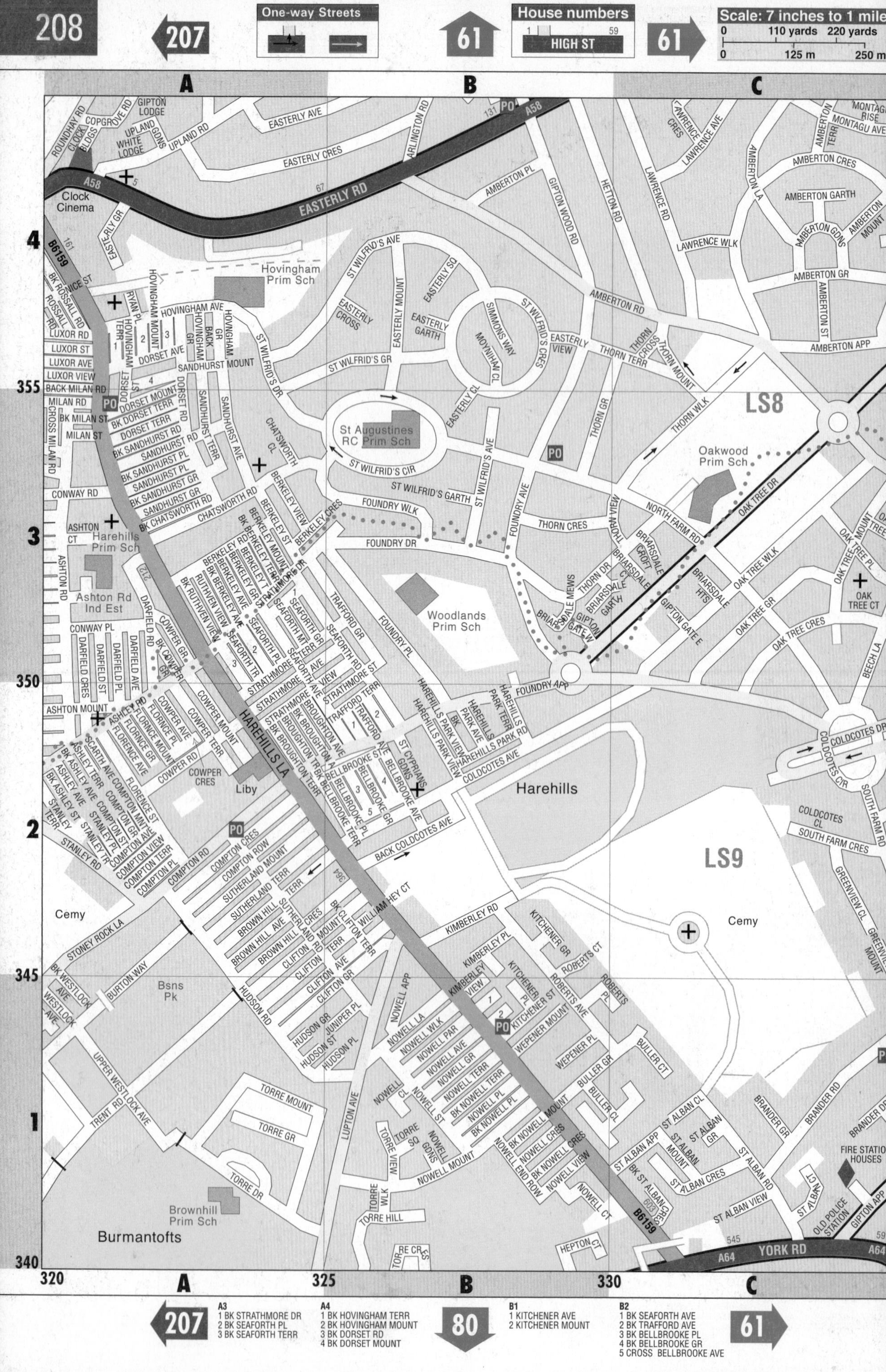

A B C
EASTERLY RD
A58
B6159
HAREHILLS LA
Clock Cinema
Hovingham Prim Sch
St Augustines RC Prim Sch
Oakwood Prim Sch
Harehills Prim Sch
Ashton Rd Ind Est
Woodlands Prim Sch
LS8
LS9
Harehills
Liby
Cemy
Bsns Pk
Brownhill Prim Sch
Burmantofts
YORK RD
A64
FIRE STATION HOUSES
OLD POLICE STATION
4
355
3
350
2
345
1
340
320
325
330

A3
1 BK STRATHMORE DR
2 BK SEAFORTH PL
3 BK SEAFORTH TERR

A4
1 BK HOVINGHAM TERR
2 BK HOVINGHAM MOUNT
3 BK DORSET RD
4 BK DORSET MOUNT

B1
1 KITCHENER AVE
2 KITCHENER MOUNT

B2
1 BK SEAFORTH AVE
2 BK TRAFFORD AVE
3 BK BELLBROOKE PL
4 BK BELLBROOKE GR
5 CROSS BELLBROOKE AVE

207
80
61

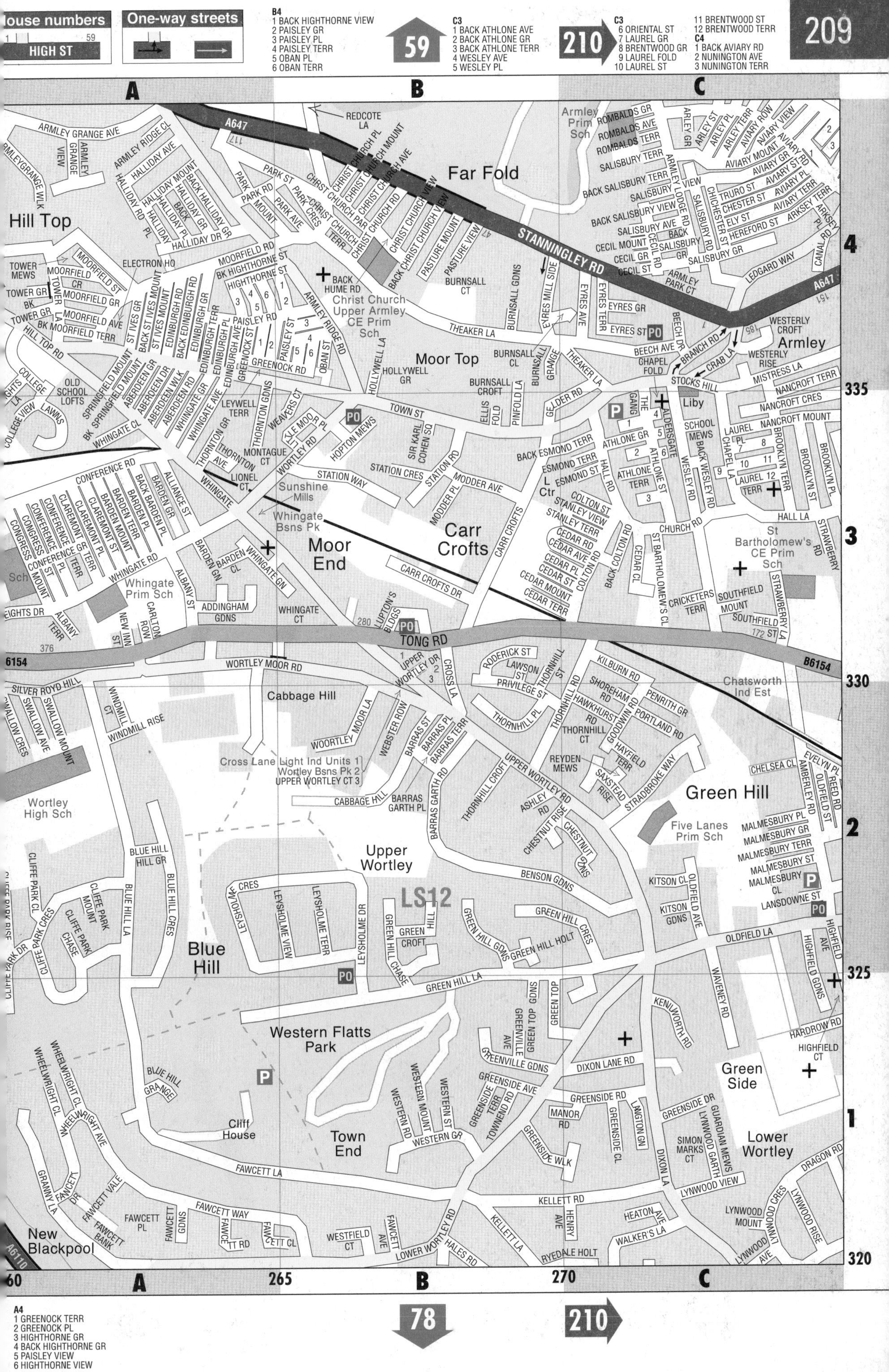

House numbers
1
59
HIGH ST
One-way streets
B4
1 BACK HIGHTHORNE VIEW
2 PAISLEY GR
3 PAISLEY PL
4 PAISLEY TERR
5 OBAN PL
6 OBAN TERR
59
C3
1 BACK ATHLONE AVE
2 BACK ATHLONE GR
3 BACK ATHLONE TERR
4 WESLEY AVE
5 WESLEY PL
210
C3
6 ORIENTAL ST
7 LAUREL GR
8 BRENTWOOD GR
9 LAUREL FOLD
10 LAUREL ST
11 BRENTWOOD ST
12 BRENTWOOD TERR
C4
1 BACK AVIARY RD
2 NUNINGTON AVE
3 NUNINGTON TERR
209
A
B
C
4
3
2
1
335
330
325
320
A647
STANNINGLEY RD
Far Fold
Hill Top
Armley Prim Sch
Moor Top
Armley
Christ Church Upper Armley CE Prim Sch
Moor End
Carr Crofts
Sunshine Mills
Whingate Bsns Pk
Whingate Prim Sch
St Bartholomew's CE Prim Sch
TONG RD
B6154
Cabbage Hill
Chatsworth Ind Est
Cross Lane Light Ind Units 1
Wortley Bsns Pk 2
UPPER WORTLEY CT 3
Green Hill
Five Lanes Prim Sch
Wortley High Sch
Upper Wortley
LS12
Blue Hill
Western Flatts Park
Cliff House
Town End
Green Side
Lower Wortley
New Blackpool
ARMLEY GRANGE AVE
ARMLEY RIDGE CL
HALLIDAY AVE
HALLIDAY DR
ELECTRON HO
MOORFIELD RD
HIGHTHORNE ST
PAISLEY RD
GREENOCK RD
TOWN ST
THEAKER LA
HOLLYWELL LA
STATION WAY
STATION CRES
MODDER AVE
CARR CROFTS DR
WHINGATE RD
CONFERENCE RD
WORTLEY MOOR RD
UPPER WORTLEY RD
SILVER ROYD HILL
WINDMILL RISE
CABBAGE HILL
BENSON GDNS
GREEN HILL LA
OLDFIELD LA
GREEN HILL HOLT
DIXON LANE RD
GREENSIDE RD
FAWCETT LA
FAWCETT WAY
KELLETT RD
LOWER WORTLEY RD
RYEDALE HOLT
LYNWOOD VIEW
STOCKS HILL
CHURCH RD
HALL LA
KILBURN RD
STRADBROKE WAY
60
265
270
A
B
C
78
210
A4
1 GREENOCK TERR
2 GREENOCK PL
3 HIGHTHORNE GR
4 BACK HIGHTHORNE GR
5 PAISLEY VIEW
6 HIGHTHORNE VIEW

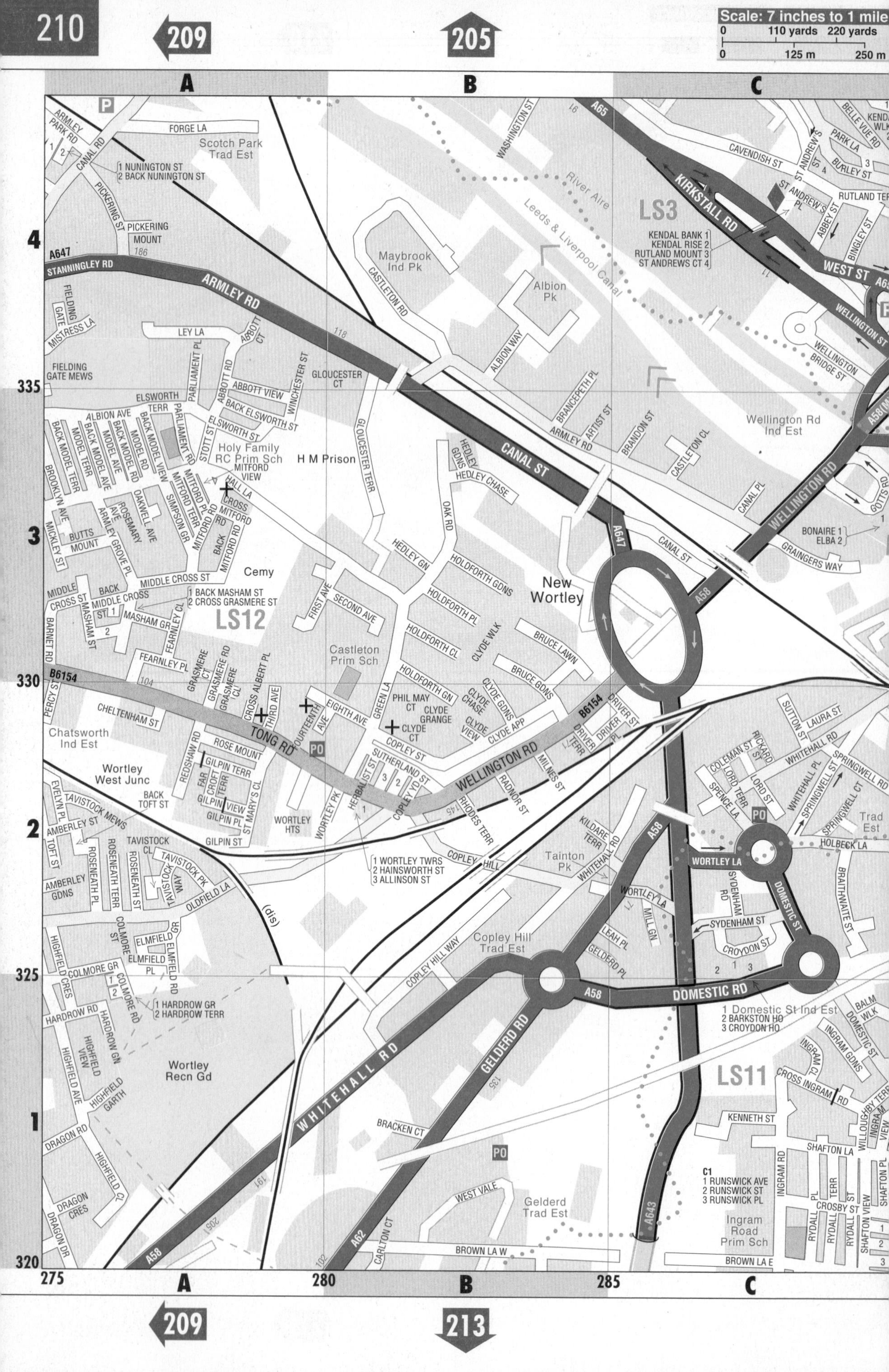

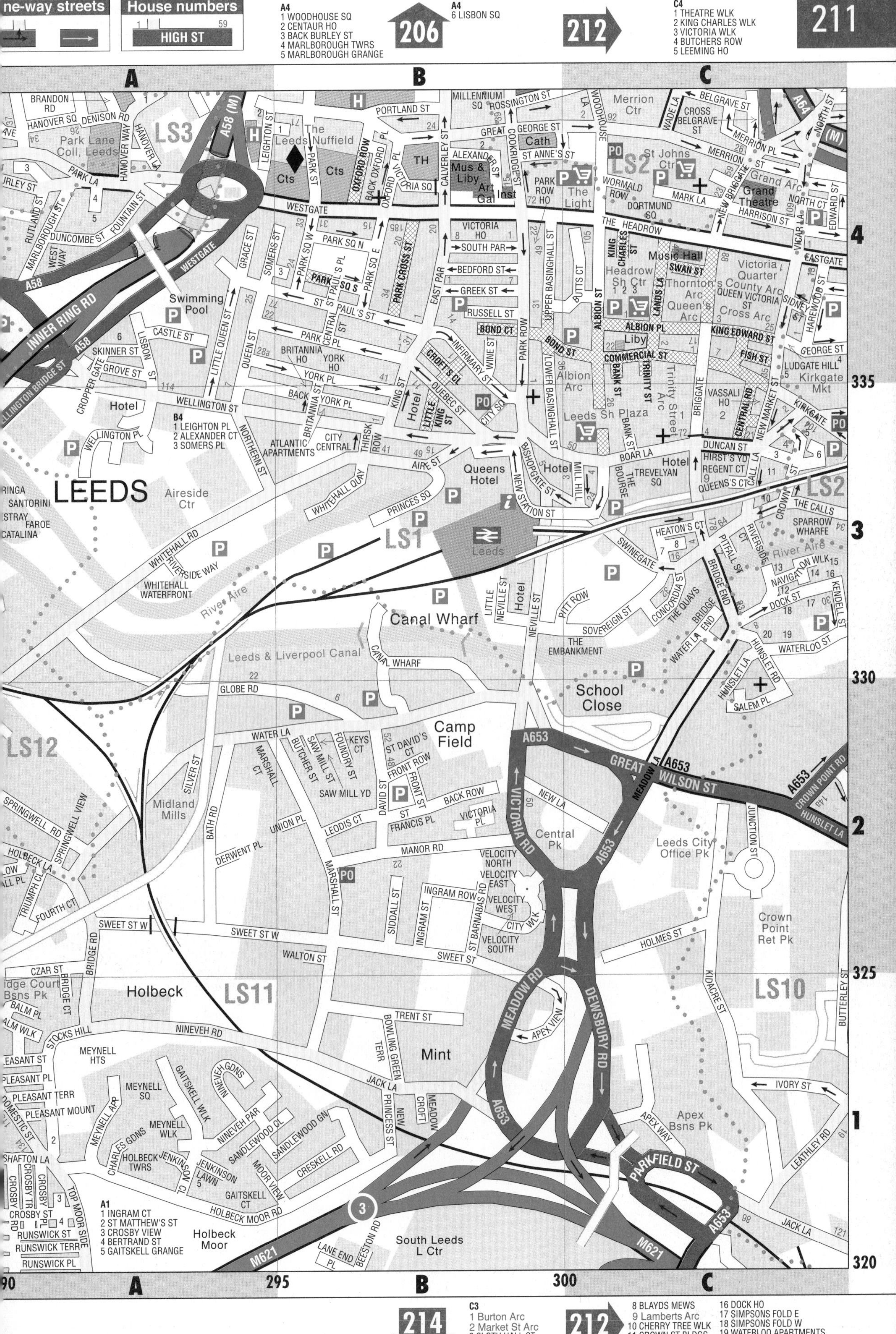
One-way streets
House numbers
HIGH ST
A4
1 WOODHOUSE SQ
2 CENTAUR HO
3 BACK BURLEY ST
4 MARLBOROUGH TWRS
5 MARLBOROUGH GRANGE
206
A4
6 LISBON SQ
212
C4
1 THEATRE WLK
2 KING CHARLES WLK
3 VICTORIA WLK
4 BUTCHERS ROW
5 LEEMING HO
A
B
C
LS3
LS2
LS1
LS12
LS11
LS10
LEEDS
Park Lane Coll, Leeds
The Leeds Nuffield
Merrion Ctr
St Johns Ctr
Grand Theatre
Mus & Liby
Art Gal
Cath
The Light
Music Hall
Victoria Quarter
Thornton's Arc
Queen's Arc
County Arc
Cross Arc
Kirkgate Mkt
Liby
Albion Arc
Leeds Sh Plaza
Trinity Street Arc
Swimming Pool
Queens Hotel
Leeds
Aireside Ctr
Whitehall Waterfront
River Aire
Canal Wharf
Leeds & Liverpool Canal
School Close
Camp Field
Midland Mills
Central Pk
Leeds City Office Pk
Crown Point Ret Pk
Holbeck
Mint
Apex Bsns Pk
Holbeck Moor
South Leeds L Ctr
INNER RING RD
WESTGATE
THE HEADROW
WELLINGTON ST
BOAR LA
GREAT WILSON ST
VICTORIA RD
DEWSBURY RD
MEADOW RD
PARKFIELD ST
NINEVEH RD
SWEET ST
WATER LA
GLOBE RD
JACK LA
HUNSLET RD
A58(M)
A58
A64
A653
M621
B4
1 LEIGHTON PL
2 ALEXANDER CT
3 SOMERS PL
A1
1 INGRAM CT
2 ST MATTHEW'S ST
3 CROSBY VIEW
4 BERTRAND ST
5 GAITSKELL GRANGE
4
335
3
330
2
325
1
320
90
295
300
214
C3
1 Burton Arc
2 Market St Arc
3 CLOTH HALL ST
4 Corn Exchange
5 CROWN CT
6 ASSEMBLY ST
7 BLAYD'S YD
212
8 BLAYDS MEWS
9 Lamberts Arc
10 CHERRY TREE WLK
11 CROWN ST BLDGS
12 CHIPPENDALE HO
13 FLAX HO
14 FLYBOAT HO
15 AIRE HO
16 DOCK HO
17 SIMPSONS FOLD E
18 SIMPSONS FOLD W
19 WATERLOO APARTMENTS
20 THE BRIDGE

211

A3
1 NEW YORK ST
2 PINE CT
3 BACK YORK ST

A4
1 BELL ST
2 CROSS BELL ST

B4
1 THEALBY PL
2 CROMWELL HTS
3 NASEBY GRANGE
4 NASEBY GDNS

207

One-way streets

80

Scale: 7 inches to 1 mile

0   110 yards   220 yards
0   125 m   250 m

A   **B**   **C**

TRAFALGAR ST · NILE ST · HOPE RD · ARGYLE RD · MACAULAY ST · CROMWELL ST · NASEBY PL · NASEBY TERR · NIPPET LA · ST STEPHEN'S CT · SCARGILL GRANGE
GOWER ST · NEW YORK RD · REGENT ST · MABGATE GN · THEALBY CL · NASEBY VIEW · NASEBY WLK · BECKETT ST · ST STEPHEN'S RD · TORRE RD · TRENT RD · APPLETON SQ
A64 (M) · TEMPLAR PL · MABGATE · BRIDGE · ST PETER'S CE PRIM SCH · ST MARY'S ST · ST MARY'S LA · RIDER ST · BURMANTOFTS ST · RIGTON LAWN · RIGTON DR · TORRE GN · OXTON WAY · TORRE GDNS
TEMPLAR LA · LADYBECK CL · ST MARY'S HALL · RIGTON APP · Ebor Gardens Prim Sch · HASLEWOOD GDNS · OXTON MOUNT · HASLEWOOD MEWS · SAVILLE GN
LYDIA ST · LADY LA · A61 · The W Yorks Playhouse · Quarry Hill · A64 (M) · YORK RD · A64 · HASLEWOOD DR · HASLEWOOD PL · HASLEWOOD GN

EASTGATE · UNION ST · GEORGE ST · Kirkgate Mkt · LS2 · DUKE ST · ST PETER'S · JOSEPH STONES HO · Leeds Coll of Music · MARSH LA · SHANNON ST · PLAID ROW · Liby · CROSS AYSGARTH MOUNT · ALL SAINTS RICHMOND HILL CE PRIM SCH · AYSGARTH DR · AYSGARTH CL · GLENSDALE RD · TEMPLE VIEW RD

335

HARPER ST · CROSS YORK ST · CHURCH WLK · YORK ST · BRUSSELS ST · RAILWAY ST · GREENFIELD RD · EAST FIELD ST · DOLPHIN · WESLEY ST · Richmond Hill · PONTEFRACT LANE CL · ASCOT TERR · TEMPLE VIEW TERR · GLENSDALE MOUNT
KIRKGATE · HIGH CT · CHANTRELL CT · CROSS MAUDE ST · FOUNDRY ST · SAXTON LA · PROVIDENCE · CATHERINE ST · Richmond Hill · HALL PL · LAVENDER WLK · GLENSDALE TERR

3 · WHARF ST · The CALLS · CHURCH · MAUDE ST · MILL ST · FLAX · The GARTH · The CLOSE · DOLPHIN CT · CROSS · Bank · UPPER ACCOMMODATION RD · RICHMOND ST · BUTTERFIELD ST · BACK PROSPECT TERR · EAST PARK RD

Brewery Wharf · CALDER HO · LANGTONS WHARF · The CHANDLERS · MERCHANTS QUAY · STEANDER · SAXTON GDNS · The LANE · The DRIVE · The PARADE · CHURCH RD · Richmond Hill CL · The SPINNEY · SUSSEX ST · WALTER CRES · HAMPTON TERR · DENT ST · KITSON ST · OXLEY ST · CLARK MOUNT · CLARK AVE

BREWERY PL · REGENTS QUAY · TURLOW CT · TRINITY ONE · NEPTUNE ST · EAST KING ST · RICHMOND ST · Mount St Mary's RC High Sch · HAMPTON CL · LONG CLOSE LA · BACK KITSON ST · BACK MOUNT · CLARK TERR · CLARK ROW
BOWMAN LA · CROMWELL ST · St JAMES QUAY · The DYKE WORKS · The ENGINE HO · EAST ST · ELLERBY · WILLIS ST · RICHMOND GREEN ST · SPINNEYFIELD CT 2 · MEADOWCROFT MEWS 3 · MULLINS CT · KIPPAX PL · CLARK CRES · CLARK GR
BALMORAL PL · ARMOURIES WAY · The Royal Armouries Mus · Fearn's Island · MORRETH PL · Cavalier Hill · SPRING CLOSE GDNS · MILNER GDNS · SIMMONS · Richmond Hill Prim Sch

330 · MAGELLAN HO · MACKENZIE HO · LS9 · SPRING CLOSE AVE · DIAL ST · EASY RD · CHARLES ST

CROWN POINT RD · BLACK BULL ST · CHADWICK ST · McCLURE HO · ARMOURIES DR · River Aire · SPRING CL ST · SPRING CLOSE WLK · MAY TERR · CAVALIER CT · FEWSTON CT · BACK CAUTLEY RD

A653 · SHEAF ST · CUDBEAR ST · HUNSLET RD · CARLISLE RD · Trans Pennine Trail · LOW FOLD · CAVALIER APP · CAVALIER VIEW · CAVALIER GN · ST HILDA'S RD · CAUTLEY · COPPERFIELD

2 · A653 · SOVEREIGN BSNS PK · SAYNER RD · VICTORIA ST · INGHAM ST · BROOKFIELD TERR · CHADWICK ST S · CLARENCE RD · CAVALIER MEWS · CAVALIER GATE · CROSS GREEN CRES · GLENCOE VIEW

NEAL PL · SCALA CT · WARD ST · PO · LS10 · Works · SAYNER LA · CROSS GREEN LA · BACK CROSS GN CRES · FEWSTON AVE · KNOWSTHORPE CRES

325 · LEATHLEY RD · LEATHLEY ST · MULBERRY ST · A653 HUNSLET RD · BROOKFIELD ST · SOUTH ACCOMMODATION RD · BRIDGEWATER RD · Road under construction · LONG CSWY · Cross Green Ind Pk · KNOWSTHORPE

A61 · Pottery Field · KITSON ST · Hunslet Bsns Pk · ATKINSON ST · FOX WAY · Knowsthorpe

1 · PEARSON ST · LOW WHITEHOUSE ROW · DEWSTHORPE ST · EMSLEY PL · GOODMAN ST · NATIONAL RD · YARN ST · LARCHFIELD RD

JACK LA · GRAPE ST · ST HELENS · WHITEHOUSE ST · GLASSHOUSE ST · A61 · A639 · FORSTER ST

320

305   A   310   B   315   C

C2
1 THORNLEIGH GR
2 THORNLEIGH VIEW
3 THORNLEIGH MOUNT
4 THORNLEIGH ST
5 COPPERFIELD TERR
6 COPPERFIELD WLK
7 COPPERFIELD ROW
8 COPPERFIELD DR
9 COPPERFIELD PL
10 COPPERFIELD CRES
11 COPPERFIELD VIEW
12 COPPERFIELD GR
13 ST HILDA'S MOUNT
14 ST HILDA'S AVE

215

C2
15 ST HILDA'S GR
16 CROSS GREEN GR
17 CROSS GREEN AVE
18 BACK CROSS GREEN LA

C3
1 EAST PARK DR
2 CAIN CL
3 O'GRADY SQ

80

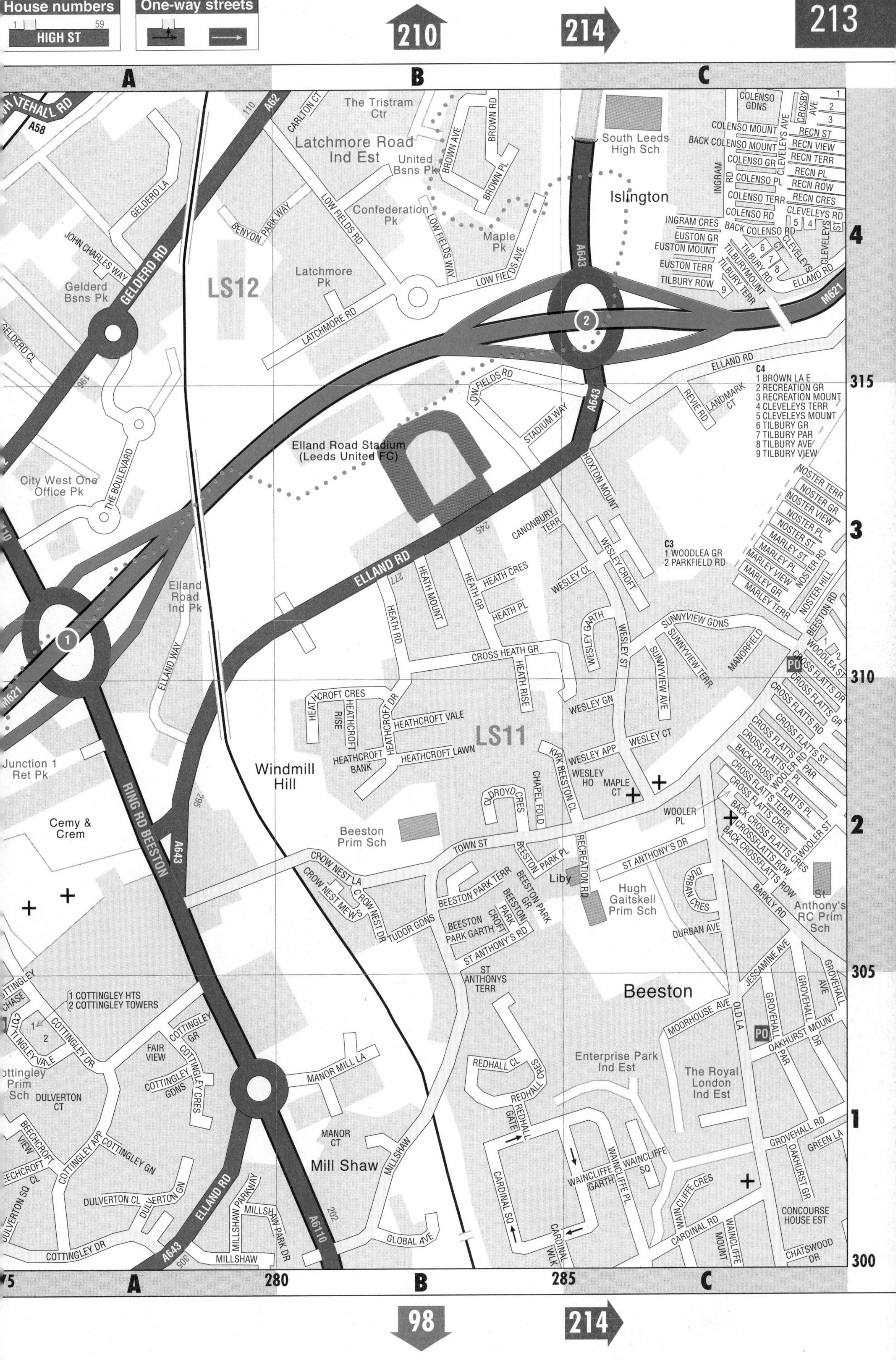
A
B
C
WHITEHALL RD
A58
A62
110
CARLTON CT
The Tristram Ctr
Latchmore Road Ind Est
United Bsns Pk
BROWN AVE
BROWN RD
BROWN PL
South Leeds High Sch
Islington
COLENSO GDNS
CROSBY AVE
COLENSO MOUNT
BACK COLENSO MOUNT
CLEVELEYS AVE
RECN ST
RECN VIEW
RECN TERR
RECN PL
RECN ROW
RECN CRES
INGRAM RD
COLENSO GR
COLENSO PL
COLENSO TERR
COLENSO RD
CLEVELEYS RD
CLEVELEYS ST
INGRAM CRES
EUSTON GR
EUSTON MOUNT
EUSTON TERR
TILBURY ROW
BACK COLENSO RD
TILBURY RD
TILBURY MOUNT
TILBURY TERR
CLEVELEYS CT
CLEVELEYS TERR
ELLAND RD
M621
GELDERD LA
BENYON PARK WAY
LOW FIELDS RD
Confederation Pk
LOW FIELDS WAY
Maple Pk
LOW FIELDS AVE
JOHN CHARLES WAY
GELDERD RD
Gelderd Bsns Pk
LS12
Latchmore Pk
LATCHMORE RD
A643
4
GELDERD CL
196
LOW FIELDS RD
STADIUM WAY
REVIE RD
LANDMARK CT
C4
1 BROWN LA E
2 RECREATION GR
3 RECREATION MOUNT
4 CLEVELEYS TERR
5 CLEVELEYS MOUNT
6 TILBURY GR
7 TILBURY PAR
8 TILBURY AVE
9 TILBURY VIEW
315
Elland Road Stadium (Leeds United FC)
THE BOULEVARD
City West One Office Pk
HOXTON MOUNT
CANONBURY TERR
245
NOSTER TERR
NOSTER GR
NOSTER VIEW
NOSTER PL
NOSTER ST
MARLEY ST
MARLEY PL
MARLEY VIEW
MARLEY GR
MARLEY TERR
NOSTER RD
NOSTER HILL
3
C3
1 WOODLEA GR
2 PARKFIELD RD
WESLEY CROFT
WESLEY CL
HEATH CRES
HEATH PL
HEATH MOUNT
HEATH GR
HEATH RD
277
ELLAND RD
Elland Road Ind Pk
ELLAND WAY
WESLEY GARTH
WESLEY ST
SUNNYVIEW GDNS
SUNNYVIEW TERR
SUNNYVIEW AVE
MANORFIELD
BEESTON RD
WOODLEA ST
CROSS FLATTS DR
CROSS HEATH GR
HEATH RISE
310
HEATHCROFT CRES
HEATHCROFT RISE
HEATHCROFT DR
HEATHCROFT VALE
HEATHCROFT BANK
HEATHCROFT LAWN
LS11
WESLEY GN
WESLEY CT
WESLEY APP
WESLEY HO
KIRK BEESTON CL
CHAPEL FOLD
MAPLE CT
CROSS FLATTS GR
CROSS FLATTS RD
CROSS FLATTS ST
CROSS FLATTS PAR
CROSS FLATTS PL
BACK CROSS FLATTS PL
CROSS FLATTS TERR
CROSS FLATTS CRES
CROSS FLATTS ROW
BACK CROSS FLATTS CRES
BACK CROSSFLATTS ROW
WOOLER PL
WOOLER ST
Junction 1 Ret Pk
Windmill Hill
OLDROYD CRES
295
Cemy & Crem
RING RD BEESTON
A643
Beeston Prim Sch
TOWN ST
BEESTON PARK PL
RECREATION RD
ST ANTHONY'S DR
2
Liby
Hugh Gaitskell Prim Sch
DURBAN CRES
BARKLY RD
St Anthony's RC Prim Sch
CROW NEST LA
CROW NEST MEWS
CROW NEST DR
TUDOR GDNS
BEESTON PARK TERR
BEESTON PARK GARTH
BEESTON PARK GR
BEESTON PARK CROFT
BEESTON PARK
ST ANTHONY'S RD
ST ANTHONYS TERR
DURBAN AVE
JESSAMINE AVE
GROVEHALL AVE
305
COTTINGLEY CHASE
1 COTTINGLEY HTS
2 COTTINGLEY TOWERS
COTTINGLEY VALE
COTTINGLEY DR
Beeston
MOORHOUSE AVE
OLD LA
GROVEHALL PAR
OAKHURST MOUNT
GROVEHALL DR
FAIR VIEW
COTTINGLEY GR
COTTINGLEY GDNS
COTTINGLEY CRES
Cottingley Prim Sch
DULVERTON CT
MANOR MILL LA
REDHALL CL
REDHALL CRES
Enterprise Park Ind Est
The Royal London Ind Est
REDHALL GATE
BEECHCROFT VIEW
BEECHCROFT
COTTINGLEY APP
COTTINGLEY GN
MANOR CT
Mill Shaw
MILLSHAW
1
GROVEHALL RD
GREEN LA
OAKHURST GR
WAINCLIFFE GARTH
WAINCLIFFE PL
WAINCLIFFE SQ
WAINCLIFFE CRES
CARDINAL SQ
DULVERTON SQ
DULVERTON CL
DULVERTON GN
ELLAND RD
MILLSHAW PARKWAY
MILLSHAW PARK DR
202
A6110
GLOBAL AVE
CARDINAL WLK
CARDINAL RD
WAINCLIFFE MOUNT
WAINCLIFFE DR
CONCOURSE HOUSE EST
CHATSWOOD DR
COTTINGLEY DR
A643
305
MILLSHAW
300
75
280
285

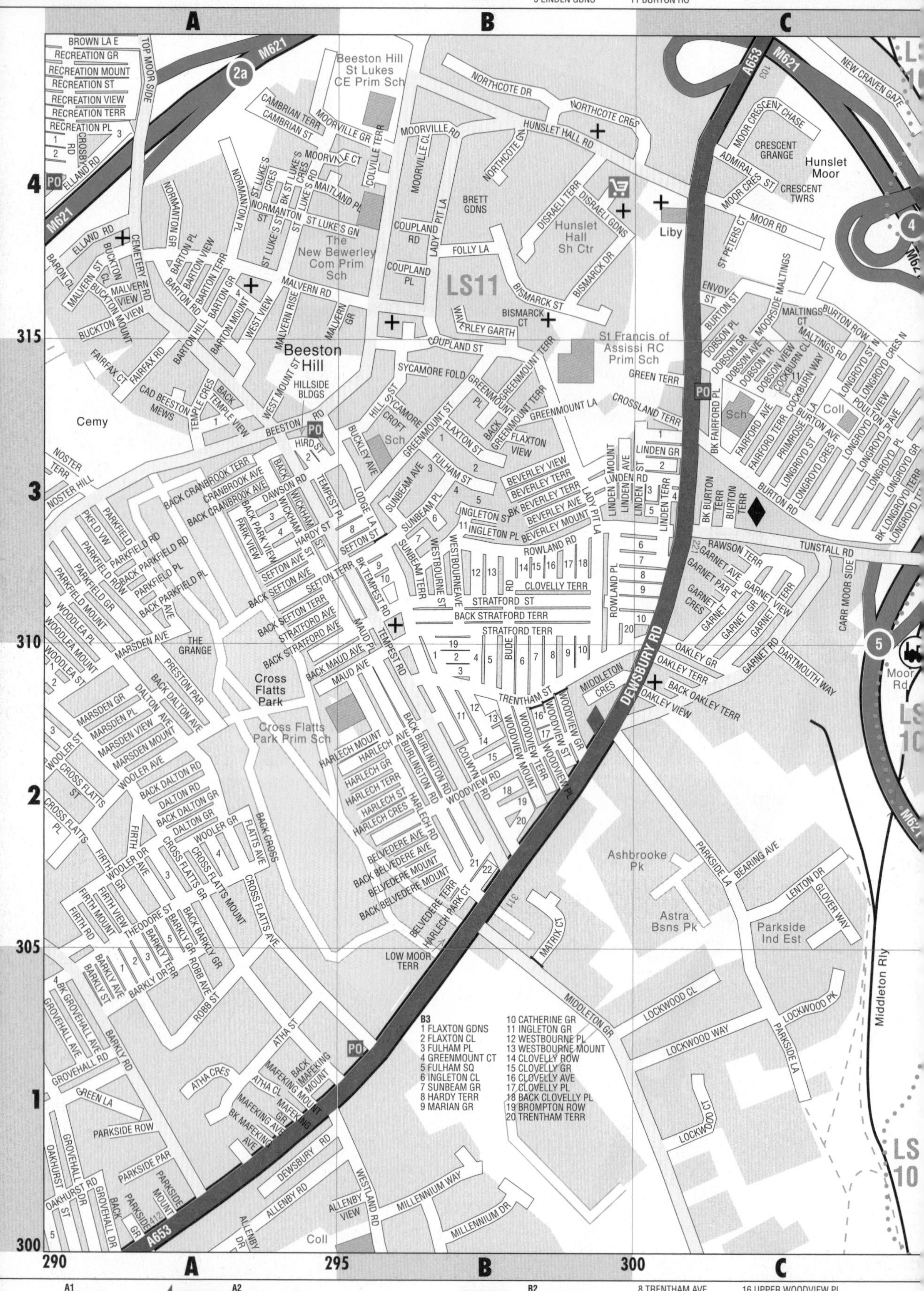

A3
1 BACK MIDDLETON VIEW
2 BACK TEMPEST RD
3 HARDY VIEW
4 HARDY GR

A4
1 RECREATION ROW
2 RECREATION CRES
3 RECREATION AVE
4 ST LUKE'S VIEW

C3
1 BK CROSSLAND TERR
2 BACK LINDEN GR
3 LINDEN PL
4 CROSS LINDEN TERR
5 LINDEN GDNS

6 ROWLAND TERR
7 BACK ROWLAND TERR
8 CAMBERLEY ST
9 BACK CAMBERLEY ST
10 BACK STRATFORD ST
11 BURTON HO

Scale: 7 inches to 1 mile
0   110 yards   220 yards
0   125 m   250 m

B3
1 FLAXTON GDNS
2 FLAXTON CL
3 FULHAM PL
4 GREENMOUNT CT
5 FULHAM SQ
6 INGLETON CL
7 SUNBEAM GR
8 HARDY TERR
9 MARIAN GR

10 CATHERINE GR
11 INGLETON GR
12 WESTBOURNE PL
13 WESTBOURNE MOUNT
14 CLOVELLY ROW
15 CLOVELLY GR
16 CLOVELLY AVE
17 CLOVELLY PL
18 BACK CLOVELLY PL
19 BROMPTON ROW
20 TRENTHAM TERR

A1
1 BARKLY PL
2 BARKLY PAR
3 BACK BARKLY PAR
4 OAKHURST MOUNT
5 OAKHURST AVE

A2
1 WOOLER RD
2 CROSS FLATTS DR
3 BACK CROSS FLATTS GR
4 BACK CROSS FLATTS MOUNT
5 BACK BARKLY TERR

B2
1 BACK LODGE LA
2 BROMPTON GR
3 BROMPTON VIEW
4 BROMPTON MOUNT
5 BROMPTON MOUNT
6 TRENTHAM ROW
7 TRENTHAM GR

8 TRENTHAM AVE
9 TRENTHAM PL
10 BACK TRENTHAM PL
11 BACK COLWYN VIEW
12 COLWYN VIEW
13 LODGE TERR
14 COLWYN AVE
15 COLWYN MOUNT

16 UPPER WOODVIEW PL
17 CROSS WOODVIEW ST
18 COLWYN TERR
19 COLWYN PL
20 BACK COLWYN PL
21 BURLINGTON PL
22 BACK BURLINGTON PL

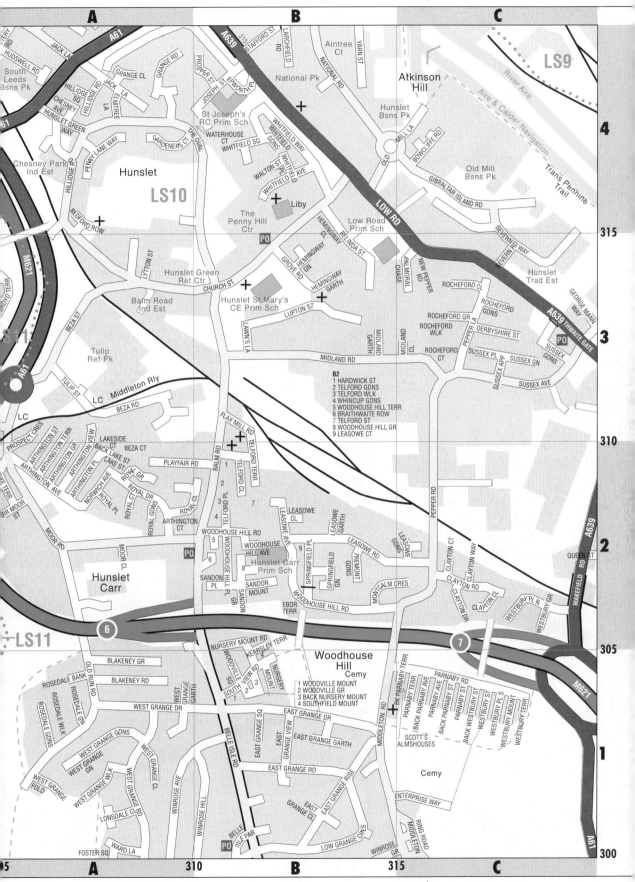

House numbers
1 | 59
HIGH ST

212
80

A   B   C

LS9

River Aire

Aire & Calder Navigation

Trans Pennine Trail

A61

HUDSWELL RD

South Leeds Bsns Pk

JACK LANE

GRANGE RD

GRANGE CL

HILLIDGE SQ

HILLIDGE RD

JACK LA

EL MTREE

PROSPER ST

EPWORTH PL

STAFFORD ST

LARCHFIELD

Aintree Ct

YARN ST

NATIONAL RD

Atkinson Hill

A639

HILLIDGE AVE

HUNSLET GREEN WAY

PENNY LANE WAY

GARDENERS CT

THE OVAL

JOSEPH ST

St Joseph's RC Prim Sch

WATERHOUSE CT

WHITFIELD SQ

National Pk

Hunslet Bsns Pk

Old Mill La

BOWCLIFFE RD

GIBRALTAR ISLAND RD

Old Mill Bsns Pk

HILLIDGE RD

Chesney Park Ind Est

Hunslet

LS10

BEDFORD ROW

WHITFIELD WAY

WHITFIELD GDNS

WALTON PL

WHITFIELD PL

WHITFIELD AVE

WHITFIELD

Liby

LOW RD

Low Road Prim Sch

SEVERN RD WAY

Hunslet Trad Est

4

M621

LLOYD TERR

LYTTON ST

Hunslet Green Ret Ctr

CHURCH ST

PO

The Penny Hill Ctr

HEMINGWAY CL

HEMINGWAY GN

GROVE RD

HEMINGWAY GARTH

BELINDA ST

PALMORAL CHASE

NEW PEPPER RD

ROCHEFORD CL

ROCHEFORD GDNS

SEVERN RD WAY

Hunslet Trad Est

315

S11

BEZA ST

Balm Road Ind Est

Hunslet St Mary's CE Prim Sch

LAWN'S LA

LUPTON ST

GARTH

MIDLAND GARTH

MIDLAND CL

ROCHEFORD GR

ROCHEFORD WLK

ROCHEFORD CT

PEPPER LA

DERBYSHIRE ST

SUSSEX GDNS

PO

A639 THWAITE GATE

GEORGE MANN WAY

3

A61

Tulip Ret Pk

TULIP ST

LC

Middleton Rly

BEZA RD

LC

MIDLAND RD

SUSSEX PL APP

SUSSEX GN

SUSSEX AVE

PROSPECT CRES

ARTHINGTON ST

ARTHINGTON TERR

ARTHINGTON GR

ARTHINGTON VIEW

Lakeside Ct

BACK LAKE ST

LAKE ST

BEZA CT

FLAX MILL RD

TELFORD TERR

B2
1 HARDWICK ST
2 TELFORD GDNS
3 TELFORD WLK
4 WHINCUP GDNS
5 WOODHOUSE HILL TERR
6 BRAITHWAITE ROW
7 TELFORD ST
8 WOODHOUSE HILL GR
9 LEASOWE CT

310

AVE TERR

ARTHINGTON AVE

ARTHINGTON PL

NORWICH AVE

ROYAL GDNS

ROYAL GR

ROYAL DR

ROYAL PL

ROYAL CT

ARTHINGTON CT

PLAYFAIR RD

BALM RD

TELFORD PL

TELFORD CL

1

2

3

4

7

LEASOWE CL

LEASOWE AVE

LEASOWE GARTH

LEASOWE RD

LEASOWE GDNS

FREMONT GDNS

LEASOWE

PEPPER RD

CLAYTON CT

CLAYTON WAY

A639

QUEEN ST

WAKEFIELD RD

2

MOOR RD

MOOR CL

WOODHOUSE HILL RD

5

WOODHOUSE HILL AVE

6

8

Hunslet Carr Prim Sch

SANDON PL

SANDON MOUNT

SPRINGFIELD PL

SPRINGFIELD GN

MONTCALM CRES

CLAYTON DR

CLAYTON RD

CLAYTON CL

CLAYTON PL

WESTBURY PL N

WESTBURY GR

Hunslet Carr

SANDON PL

WOODHOUSE HILL RD

EBOR TERR

WOODHOUSE HILL RD

M621

6

7

305

LS11

ROSEDALE BANK

OLD RUN RD

BLAKENEY GR

BLAKENEY RD

WEST GRANGE GARTH

NURSERY MOUNT RD

KEARSLEY TERR

WOODVILLE SQ

SOUTH VIEW RD

NURSERY MOUNT

Woodhouse Hill Cemy

1 WOODVILLE MOUNT
2 WOODVILLE GR
3 BACK NURSERY MOUNT
4 SOUTHFIELD MOUNT

MIDDLETON RD

BK PARNABY TERR

PARNABY TERR

PARNABY RD

BACK PARNABY AVE

PARNABY AVE

BACK PARNABY ST

PARNABY ST

WESTBURY ST

WESTBURY PL S

WESTBURY MOUNT

WESTBURY TERR

ROSEDALE WLK

ROSEDALE GDNS

WEST GRANGE DR

WEST GRANGE GDNS

EAST GRANGE SQ

EAST GRANGE DR

EAST GRANGE VIEW

EAST GRANGE GARTH

SCOTT'S ALMSHOUSES

Cemy

WEST GRANGE GN

WEST GRANGE WLK

WEST GRANGE RD

BELLE ISLE RD

WINROSE AVE

WINROSE HILL

EAST GRANGE RD

EAST GRANGE CL

EAST GRANGE RISE

LOW GRANGE CRS

WINROSE GR

MIDDLETON

RING ROAD

ENTERPRISE WAY

1

WEST GRANGE FOLD

LONSDALE CL

FOSTER SQ

WARD LA

BELLE ISLE PAR

PO

A61

300

A   310   B   315   C

99
80

One-way streets

House numbers
1 ▮▮▮ 59
HIGH ST

WAKEFIELD

WF1

WF2

H Pinderfields General
1 ELM APARTMENTS
2 MAPLE APARTMENTS
3 BIRCH APARTMENTS
4 CEDAR APARTMENTS
5 CHALONER GN
6 ASH APARTMENTS

1 BACK HAMBLETON ST
2 HAMBLETON ST
3 MARIZON GR
4 CLARENDON ST
5 LOWER YORK CT

Council Offices

St John's CE Jun & Inf Sch

Police Training Sch

Queen Elizabeth Gram & Jun Gram Sch

Wakefield Girls High Sch

City Art Gall

Wakefield Coll

West Yorkshire Pol HQ Offs

Council Offs

Wakefield Coll

County Hall

HM Prison

Wakefield Westgate

Coll

Liby

Theatre

Theatre

TA Ctr

Cath

Ridings Sh Ctr

Cinema

Cinema

Albion Mills Ret Pk

Westgate Ret & L Pk

Cathedral Ret Pk

Trad Est

Trinity Bsns Pk

Thornhill Street Bglws

Chantry Bridge Ind Est

Thornes Ind Est

Thornes Trad Est

Rutland Ind Est

Kirkgate Bsns Ctr

Calder & Hebble Navigation

River Calder

Trinity Bsns Ctr

Wakefield Kirkgate

Govt Offs

Council Office

Pinderfields General

Wakefield Pinders Prim Sch

Queen Elizabeth Rd

St Austin's RC Prim Sch

St Mary's Sch

Eagles Yard Bsns Pk

Roads
LEEDS RD · A61 · A650 · BRADFORD RD · LINK RD · CYPRUS MOUNT · WENTWORTH ST · NORTHGATE · BOND ST · WOOD ST · A642 · MARSH WAY · JACOB'S WELL LA · STANLEY RD · GREENWOOD RD · WESTGATE · A638 · WESTGATE END · QUEBEC ST · PICCADILLY · CHARLESWORTH WAY · A636 · DENBY DALE RD · INGS RD · KIRKGATE · CALDER VALE RD · DONCASTER RD · LAWEFIELD LA

Scale: 7 inches to 1 mile
0 — 110 yards — 220 yards
0 — 125 m — 250 m
← 142
↔ 142
142 →

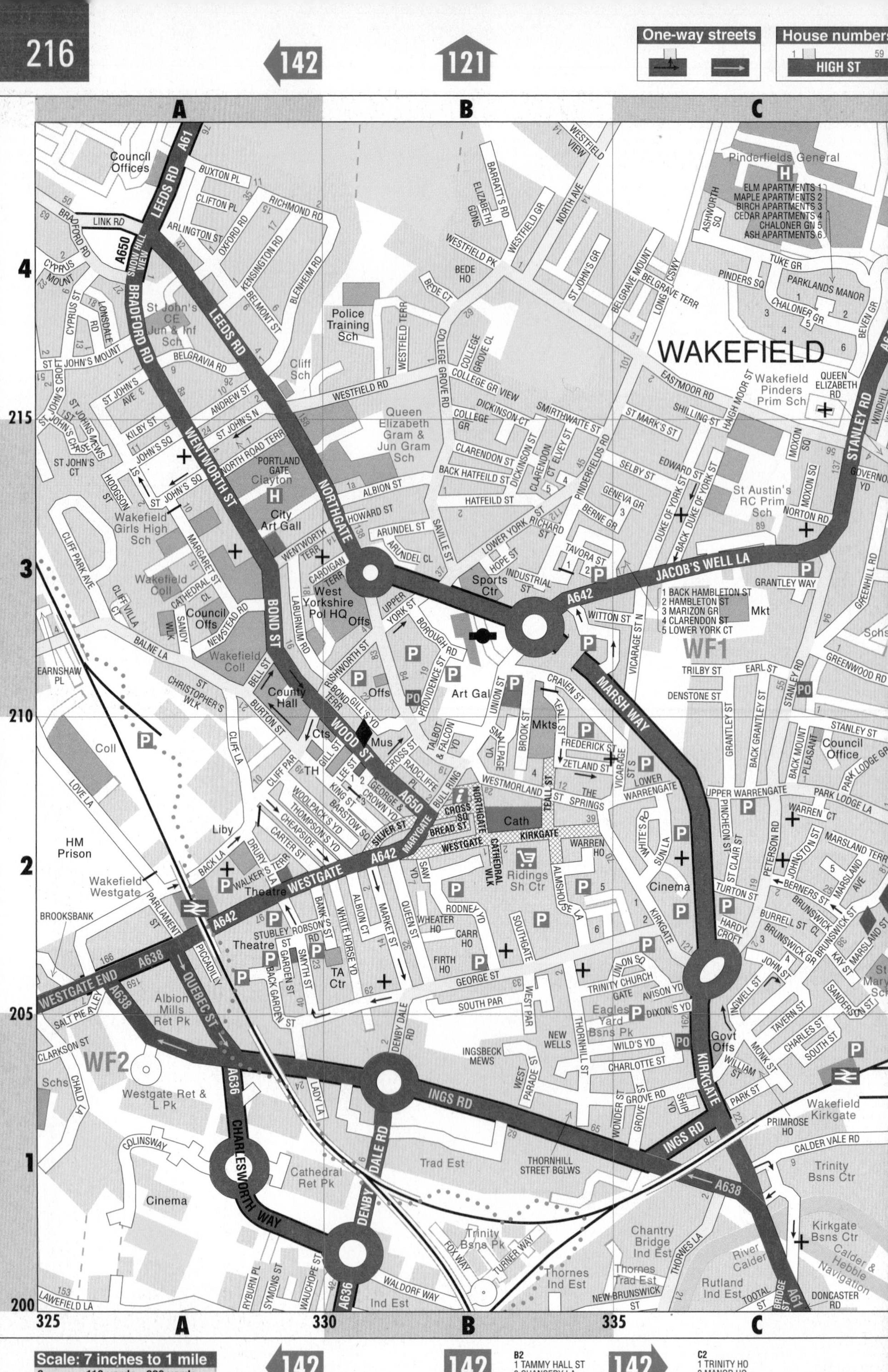

B2
1 TAMMY HALL ST
2 CHANCERY LA
3 CROWN CT
4 WESTMORLAND HO
5 TUDOR HO
6 GREENWOOD HO

C2
1 TRINITY HO
2 MANOR HO
3 INGWELL CT
4 CRYSTAL PL
5 MARSLAND PL

Index

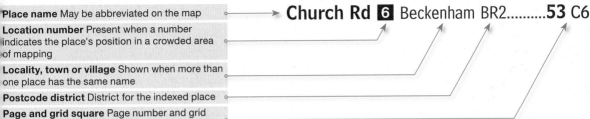

Place name May be abbreviated on the map

Location number Present when a number indicates the place's position in a crowded area of mapping

Locality, town or village Shown when more than one place has the same name

Postcode district District for the indexed place

Page and grid square Page number and grid reference for the standard mapping

Public and commercial buildings are highlighted in **magenta** **Places of interest** are highlighted in **blue** with a star★

Abbreviations used in the index

Abbreviation	Meaning
Acad	Academy
App	Approach
Arc	Arcade
Ave	Avenue
Bglw	Bungalow
Bldg	Building
Bsns, Bus	Business
Bvd	Boulevard
Cath	Cathedral
Cir	Circus
Cl	Close
Cnr	Corner
Coll	College
Com	Community
Comm	Common
Cott	Cottage
Cres	Crescent
Cswy	Causeway
Ct	Court
Ctr	Centre
Ctry	Country
Cty	County
Dr	Drive
Dro	Drove
Ed	Education
Emb	Embankment
Est	Estate
Ex	Exhibition
Gd	Ground
Gdn	Garden
Gn	Green
Gr	Grove
H	Hall
Ho	House
Hospl	Hospital
HQ	Headquarters
Hts	Heights
Ind	Industrial
Inst	Institute
Int	International
Intc	Interchange
Junc	Junction
L	Leisure
La	Lane
Liby	Library
Mdw	Meadow
Meml	Memorial
Mkt	Market
Mus	Museum
Orch	Orchard
Pal	Palace
Par	Parade
Pas	Passage
Pk	Park
Pl	Place
Prec	Precinct
Prom	Promenade
Rd	Road
Recn	Recreation
Ret	Retail
Sh	Shopping
Sq	Square
St	Street
Sta	Station
Terr	Terrace
TH	Town Hall
Univ	University
Wk, Wlk	Walk
Wr	Water
Yd	Yard

Index of localities, towns and villages

A

Aberford ... 64 E7
Ackton ... 145 A8
Ackworth Moor Top ... 163 E6
Addingford ... 159 A8
Addingham ... 6 E8
Addingham Moorside ... 6 F4
Adel ... 42 D4
Adel East Moor ... 42 E4
Adwalton ... 97 A6
Agbrigg ... 142 F3
Ainley Top ... 135 B3
Airedale ... 125 B7
Aireworth ... 35 E8
Akroydon ... 92 B1
Allerton ... 73 B8
Allerton Bywater ... 103 B4
Almondbury ... 154 F4
Almondbury Common ... 154 F2
Altofts ... 122 F3
Alverthorpe ... 141 E8
Alwoodley ... 43 B5
Alwoodley Gates ... 43 E6
Alwoodley Park ... 43 A6
Ambler Thorn ... 92 C7
America Moor ... 98 A1
Apperley Bridge ... 56 F8
Armitage Bridge ... 171 E8
Armley ... 209 C4
Arrunden ... 188 F1
Arthington ... 25 D6
Arthursdale ... 62 F8
Ashenhurst ... 154 C3
Ashfield ... 123 B3
Askwith ... 9 F5
Aspley ... 154 C5
Atkinson Hill ... 215 C4
Austhorpe ... 81 E8

B

Bacup ... 106 B4
Badsworth ... 164 E2
Bagby Fields ... 206 B2
Bagley ... 57 E4
Baildon ... 38 B3
Baildon Green ... 38 B2
Baildon Holmes ... 38 C1
Baildon Wood Bottom ... 38 C1
Bailey Hills ... 36 E4
Bailiff Bridge ... 115 B7
Bank ... 212 B3
Bankfoot ... 74 D1
Bank Foot ... 118 D5
Bankhouse ... 76 D5
Bank Top
 Halifax ... 113 F6
 Shipley ... 56 C5
Bantam Grove ... 98 E4
Bardsey ... 28 D4
Barkerend ... 75 B7
Barkisland ... 133 B4
Barnbow Carr ... 63 C5
Barnside ... 200 A8
Barnsley ... 179 B1
Barrowby ... 82 B7
Barwick in Elmet ... 63 E7
Batley ... 118 C4
Batley Carr ... 118 C3
Battyeford ... 137 E5
Beal ... 127 F7
Beamsley ... 2 F5
Beck Bottom ... 120 C3
Beck Hill ... 93 E7
Beechcliffe ... 18 B1
Beechwood
 Horsforth ... 41 A3
 Leeds ... 61 F6
 Sowerby Bridge ... 111 F3
Beeston ... 213 C1
Beeston Hill ... 214 A3
Beeston Park Side ... 99 A7
Beldon Hall ... 73 F2
Belle Isle
 Leeds ... 99 E7
 Wakefield ... 142 D3
Belle Vue ... 142 F4
Benomley ... 154 E4
Ben Rhydding ... 8 E3
Berry Brow ... 172 A8
Bickerton ... 15 C8
Bierley ... 95 C8
Bingley ... 37 C3
Birchencliffe ... 135 B2
Birdacre ... 96 B1
Birkby ... 135 F1
Birkenshaw ... 96 B5
Birkenshaw Bottoms ... 96 C4
Birks
 Bradford ... 73 F6
 Morley ... 98 A2
Birstall ... 96 F2
Birstall Smithies ... 117 E8
Black Gates ... 98 F1
Black Hill ... 34 F8
Blackley ... 134 E4
Black Moor ... 43 A4
Blackmoorfoot ... 170 D7
Blackshaw Head ... 87 F4
Blackwood ... 44 B4
Blue Bell Hill ... 153 F2
Blue Hill ... 209 A2
Bog Green ... 137 C4
Bogthorn ... 34 E3
Bolster Moor ... 152 B4
Bolton ... 55 F3
Bolton Abbey ... 2 E8
Bolton Outlanes ... 56 B4
Bolton Woods ... 55 E4
Booth Naze ... 169 B7
Boothroyd ... 139 A8
Boothtown ... 92 B2
Borough Corner ... 141 E5
Boston Spa ... 30 D7
Botany ... 19 E2
Bottom Boat ... 122 C6
Bottomley ... 129 C7
Bowling ... 75 B4
Bracken Bank ... 34 F3
Brackenhall ... 136 C4
Brackenhill ... 163 D5
Bracken Hill ... 137 D7
Bradford ... 201 B4
Bradford Moor ... 75 D7
Bradley ... 136 F5
Bradley Mills ... 154 D8
Bradshaw
 Huddersfield ... 151 B1
 Queensferry ... 72 A1
Brag Lane End ... 120 E3
Braithwaite ... 34 E8
Bramham ... 30 D3
Bramhope ... 24 D4
Bramley ... 58 B2
Brandon ... 44 E6
Brandy Carr ... 120 D4
Brearley ... 90 B1
Brianside ... 62 B3
Brierley ... 181 A3
Brighouse ... 115 B2
Broad Carr ... 134 C4
Broad Folds ... 73 C5
Brockholes ... 172 C2
Brodsworth ... 195 F4
Brookfoot ... 114 E3
Brookhouse ... 91 C8
Brooklands ... 61 F5
Brookroyd ... 118 A8
Brooks Bank ... 142 A6
Broomfields ... 201 C1
Broomhill ... 127 B3
Brotherton ... 126 D8
Brown Hill ... 117 F8
Brown Moor ... 81 F8
Brown Royd ... 74 A7
Brownroyd Hill ... 74 C1
Brownroyd Oak ... 74 C1
Bruntcliffe ... 97 E4
Brunthwaite ... 6 A1
Burghwallis ... 184 E5
Burley ... 205 A2
Burley in Wharfedale ... 9 D1
Burley Lawn ... 205 B1
Burley Woodhead ... 21 C6
Burmantoffs ... 208 A1
Burn Knolls ... 98 C3
Burton Salmon ... 105 E3
Buslingthorpe ... 206 C4
Buttershaw ... 93 E8
Byram ... 126 E7

C

Calderbrook ... 129 C1
Calder Grove ... 159 D6
Calderside ... 88 D3
Calder Vale ... 142 E5
Calmlands ... 170 E1
Calverley ... 57 B7
Cambridge ... 23 B6
Camp Field ... 211 B2
Camp Town ... 43 B3
Canal Wharf ... 211 B3
Carlecotes ... 200 B3
Carleton ... 146 F5
Carlinghow ... 118 A6
Carlton
 Barnsley ... 179 D1
 Rothwell ... 100 D3
Carr Crofts ... 209 B3
Carr Gate ... 120 E5
Carr House Gate ... 94 C4
Carr Manor ... 43 C1
Castleford ... 124 F8
Castleford Ings ... 103 E1
Castle Street ... 108 E6
Castley ... 25 B8
Cavalier Hill ... 212 B2
Cawthorne ... 193 D4
Chapel Allerton ... 60 C7
Chapel Fold ... 118 A2
Chapel Green ... 74 C2
Chapelthorpe ... 160 A4
Chapeltown ... 207 B3
Charlestown
 Baildon ... 38 E2
 Hebden Bridge ... 88 C2
Chequerfield ... 146 F7
Chickenley ... 140 B8
Chidswell ... 119 B3
Chiserley ... 89 C5
Churchfields ... 100 E5
Church Garforth ... 82 F6
Church Hill ... 38 D4
Churwell ... 98 D8
City ... 98 B4
Clayton
 Bradford ... 73 C4
 Thurnscoe ... 194 C4
Clayton Heights ... 73 B1
Clayton West ... 175 F2
Cleckheaton ... 116 C6
Cliff ... 189 B5
Cliff End ... 153 B6
Clifford ... 30 D5
Clifton
 Brighouse ... 115 D2
 Otley ... 10 E5
Clifton Villas ... 55 D2
Clough Foot ... 107 B4
Cockersdale ... 97 A8
Colden ... 88 A5
Cold Hiendley ... 161 E1
Coley ... 93 D2
Collingham ... 29 B8
Colne Bridge ... 137 B5
Colton ... 81 D6
Combs ... 139 E3
Compton ... 29 D6
Cononley ... 4 A3
Cookridge ... 41 D6
Copley ... 113 A2
Copley Hill ... 97 A1
Cornholme ... 86 B1
Cottingley ... 54 A7
Cotton Stones ... 132 C8
Cowcliffe ... 135 E3
Cowlersley ... 153 A3
Cowling ... 32 C7
Cowmes ... 155 C5
Coxley ... 158 D7
Crackenedge ... 118 D1
Cragg Hill ... 58 C8
Cragg Vale ... 110 C3
Crigglestone ... 159 E5
Crimble ... 152 A2
Crimbles ... 76 F7
Cringles ... 5 F6
Crofton ... 143 F1
Crosland Hill ... 153 A2
Crosland Moor ... 153 C3
Crossflatts ... 36 E6
Cross Gates ... 62 B2
Cross Green ... 80 A5
Cross Hills ... 16 E7
Crossley Hall ... 73 E7
Cross Roads
 Huddersfield ... 174 E8
 Keighley ... 51 F7
Cross Stone ... 108 D6
Crow Nest ... 37 B3

Index of streets, hospitals, industrial estates, railway stations, schools, shopping centres, universities and places of interest

A

A1 Bsns Pk WF11 126 C3
Aachen Way HX1 202 C1
Aaron Wilkinson Ct WF9 182 A2
Abaseen Cl BD3 75 B7
Abbey Ave LS5 58 F3
Abbey Cl
  Addingham LS29 7 A8
  Holmfirth HD9 199 B7
Abbey Ct
  [9] Bradford BD8 74 C8
  Holmfirth HD9 199 B7
  Horsforth LS18 58 B6
Abbeydale Garth LS5 58 E6
Abbeydale Gdns LS5 58 E6
Abbeydale Gr LS5 58 E6
Abbeydale Mount LS5 58 E6
Abbeydale Oval LS5 58 E6
Abbeydale Vale LS5 58 E6
Abbeydale Way LS5 58 E6
Abbey Dr HD8 173 F1
Abbey Farm Dr HD8 190 F8
Abbeyfield Ct [16] LS29 8 B4
Abbey Garth LS19 40 B6
Abbey Gdns WF8 125 D3
Abbey Gorse LS5 59 A5
Abbey Grange CE High Sch LS16 58 F8
Abbey House Mus★ LS5 58 F5
Abbey La HX2 111 F7
Abbey Lea BD15 73 C8
Abbey Mews WF8 125 D3
Abbey Mount LS5 58 F3
Abbey Park Jun & Inf Sch HX2 91 D6
Abbey Pl HD2 136 C1
Abbey Rd
  Batley WF17 117 F4
  Huddersfield HD2 136 B1
  Leeds LS5 58 E6
  Shepley HD8 174 A2
Abbey Rd N HD8 173 F1
Abbey Rd S HD8 190 E8
Abbey Ret Pk LS5 59 A4
Abbey St LS3 210 C4
Abbey Terr LS5 58 F3
Abbey View LS5 59 A5
Abbey Wlk
  Halifax HX3 113 C4
  Leeds LS5 58 F5
  Pontefract WF8 125 D3
Abbey Wlk S HX3 113 D4
Abbot La WF4 178 B6
Abbotside Cl BD10 56 C6
Abbots Mews LS4 205 A2
Abbots Pl HD2 136 F5
Abbot St HD1 153 E7
Abbotsway LS25 82 D6
Abbots Wood BD9 55 A3
Abbott's Ladies Home HX3 113 C3
Abbott Ct LS12 210 A4
Abbott Rd LS12 210 A4
Abbotts Cl LS25 64 E8
Abbotts Terr HX1 202 C3
Abbott Terr WF1 142 D3
Abbott View LS12 210 A4
Abb Scott La BD12, BD6 94 B6
Abb St HD1 153 D7
Abelia Mount BD7 73 F6
Abel St [4] BD12 94 C4
Aberdeen Dr LS12 209 A4
Aberdeen Gr LS12 209 A4
Aberdeen Pl BD7 74 A5
Aberdeen Rd LS12 209 A3
Aberdeen Terr
  Bradford BD14 73 D4
  Bradford, Lidget Green BD7 74 A6
Aberdeen Wlk LS12 209 A3
Aberfield Bank LS10 99 E6
Aberfield Cl LS10 99 E7
Aberfield Crest LS10 99 E6
Aberfield Dr
  Crigglestone WF4 159 E4
  Leeds LS10 99 E6
Aberfield Gate LS10 99 E7
Aberfield Gdns LS10 99 E6
Aberfield Mount LS10 99 E6
Aberfield Rd LS10 99 E7
Aberfield Rise LS10 99 E7
Aberfield Wlk LS10 99 E6
Aberford By-Pass LS25 64 F7
Aberford CE Prim Sch LS25 64 E7
Aberford Rd
  Aberford LS25 64 C2
  Barwick in E LS15 63 E7
  Bradford BD8 74 B8
  Bramham LS23 30 D2
  Garforth LS25 83 A8
  Lofthouse Gate WF3 121 F3
  Rothwell LS26 101 D6
  Wakefield WF1 142 E8
Abingdon St
  Bradford BD8 55 B1
  Huddersfield HD2 136 A1
Abraham Hill LS26 100 F5
Abraham Ormerod Day Hospl OL14 108 B5
Abram St BD5 74 E4
Abu Hurairah Acad BD3 75 C7
Acacia Ave WF9 183 A4
Acacia Cl WF10 125 D6
Acacia Dr
  Bradford BD15 54 A4
  Brighouse HX3 115 A7
  Castleford WF10 125 D6
Acacia Gn [8] WF8 125 F1
Acacia Gr
  Mytholmroyd HX7 89 F1
  Shafton S72 180 C2
Acacia Ho [8] WF10 124 E7
Acacia Park Cres BD10 39 F2
Acacia Park Dr BD10 39 F2
Acacia Park Terr LS19 40 A2
Acacia Wlk WF11 126 D3
Acaster Dr
  Bradford BD12 94 C6
  Garforth LS25 83 B5
Accommodation Rd LS9 207 B1
Acer Cl BD20 16 F5
Acer Way [8] BD19 115 F8
Ackroyd Ct [13] BD13 72 D6
Ackroyd Sq BD13 73 B1
Ackroyd St
  Morley LS27 98 B4
  Todmorden OL14 86 B1
Ackton Cl WF7 145 A8
Ackton Hall Cres WF7 145 A8
Ackton La WF7 124 C1
Ackton Pasture La WF7 124 B4
Ackton Pastures Prim Sch WF10 124 A6
Ackworth Ave LS19 40 C6
Ackworth Bridle Rd WF8 164 E6
Ackworth Cres LS19 40 C6
Ackworth Dr LS19 40 D6
Ackworth House Cl WF7 164 A8
Ackworth Rd
  Pontefract WF7, WF8 146 C5
  Purston Jaglin WF7 145 D3
Ackworth Sch WF7 164 A7
Ackworth St BD5 74 E4
Acland Hall BD16 37 A5
Acme Terr WF1 142 D3
Acomb Terr BD12 94 C2
Acorn Bsns Pk BD23 4 A7
Acorn Cl BD6 93 E6
Acorn Dr LS14 62 C8
Acorn Gr HD9 189 D3
Acorn Ho WF10 123 F5
Acorn Pk BD17 38 E2
Acorn Pk Ind Est BD17 38 E2
Acorn St
  Halifax HX1 202 C3
  Keighley BD21 35 B5
Acorn Way LS21 24 D6
Acre Ave BD2 56 B5
Acre Cir LS10 99 C4
Acre Cl
  Bradford BD2 56 B5
  Middleton LS10 99 B3
Acre Cres
  Bradford BD2 56 B5
  Middleton LS10 99 C4
Acre Ct LS10 99 C4
Acre Dr BD2 56 B5
Acre Fold LS29 6 E8
Acre Gr
  Bradford BD2 56 B5
  Middleton LS10 99 C4
Acre House Ave HD3 153 C8
Acrehowe Rise BD17 38 E4
Acre La
  Bradford BD2 56 B4
  Bradford, Brownroyd Hill BD6 74 C1
  Haworth BD22 51 C7
  Heptonstall HX7 88 C6
  Holmfirth, Hinchcliffe Mill HD9 188 D2
  Meltham HD9 170 F1
  Shepley HD9 190 B6
Acre Mount LS10 99 C4
Acre Pl LS10 99 C4
Acre Rd LS10 99 C4
Acre Rise BD17 38 C4
Acres Hall Ave LS28 77 A6
Acres Hall Cres LS28 77 A6
Acres Hall Dr LS28 77 A6
Acres La
  Heptonstall HX7 88 F4
  Holmfirth HD9 187 F4
Acre Sq LS10 99 C4
Acres Rd WF3 121 C8
Acres St BD21 35 B6
Acre St
  Huddersfield HD3 153 C8
  Middleton LS10 99 D4
Acres The
  Addingham LS29 7 A8
  Beamsley LS29 3 A1
  Sutton-in-C BD20 16 C4
Acre Terr LS10 99 D4
Acre The BD12 94 B5
Acre Villas [1] HX7 89 E1
Acton Flat La HD3 135 A3
Acton St BD3 75 C7
Acute Terr WF2 141 E6
Ada's Pl LS28 57 E2
Adam Croft BD13 52 D6
Adam Ct HD3 135 B1
Adams Croft LS21 22 F7
Adams Ct HD6 114 E5
Adams Gr LS15 62 E4
Adam St
  [7] Bradford BD6 74 B1
  Todmorden OL14 108 B6
Ada St
  Baildon BD17 38 E2
  [6] Halifax HX3 92 C1
  [11] Keighley BD21 35 A7
  [8] Queensbury BD13 72 D1
  Shipley BD18 54 F8
Addersgate La HX13 92 E4
Addingford Cl WF4 159 A8
Addingford Dr WF4 159 A8
Addingford La WF4 159 A8
Addingham Gdns LS12 209 A3
Addingham Prim Sch LS29 2 F1
Addison Ave
  Bradford BD3 56 D1
  Normanton WF6 123 C1
Addison Ct
  Horbury WF4 141 C2
  Leeds LS15 81 D6
Addison Dr [15] BD22 51 C6
Addi St BD4 75 C3
Addle Croft La HD8 155 F5
Addlethorpe La LS22 12 A5
Addy Cres WF9 182 F3
Adelaide Ho BD16 37 B2
Adelaide Rise [1] BD17 38 C1
Adelaide St
  Bradford BD5 201 B1
  Halifax HX1 202 B3
  Hebden Bridge HX7 88 F3
  [9] Todmorden OL14 108 B6
Adelaide Terr HX4 133 F3
Adel Garth LS16 42 D5
Adel Gn LS16 42 D4
Adel Grange Cl LS16 42 C2
Adel Grange Croft LS16 42 C2
Adel Grange Mews LS16 42 C2
Adeline Terr HD9 188 C3
Adel La LS16 42 C3
Adel Mead LS16 42 D4
Adel Mill LS16 42 D6
Adel Park Cl LS16 42 C3
Adel Park Croft LS16 42 C3
Adel Park Ct LS16 42 C3
Adel Park Dr LS16 42 C3
Adel Park Gdns LS16 42 C3
Adel Pasture LS16 42 C3
Adelphi Rd HD3 153 C7
Adel Prim Sch LS16 42 D3
Adel St John the Baptist CE Prim Sch LS16 42 D4
Adel Towers Cl LS16 42 D3
Adel Towers Ct LS16 42 D3
Adel Vale LS16 42 D4
Adel Wood Cl LS16 42 D3
Adel Wood Dr LS16 42 D3
Adel Wood Gdns LS16 42 D3
Adel Wood Gr LS16 42 D3
Adel Wood Pl LS16 42 D3
Adel Wood Rd LS16 42 D3
Adgil Cres HX3 114 A4
Admiral Ct LS10 212 A3
Admiral St LS11 214 C4
Admiral Way [8] BD21 35 C8
Adowsley Cl WF7 163 E6
Adwalton Cl BD11 96 D5
Adwalton Gn BD11 96 D5
Adwalton Gr BD13 72 F1
Adwick Gr WF2 160 B5
Adwick Pl LS4 59 C2
Adwick Terr WF8 125 E2
Agar St [5] BD8 73 F8
Agar Terr [6] BD8 73 F8
Agbrigg Gr WF2 142 E2
Agbrigg Rd WF1, WF2 142 E2
Agincourt Dr
  Bingley BD16 37 B3
  Normanton WF6 122 E4
Agnes St BD20 18 C1
Ailsa Dell WF17 118 E7
Ailsa Ho [2] BD10 56 C7
Aimbry Ct HD5 154 F2
Ainley Bottom HX5 135 A5
Ainley Cl HD3 135 A2
Ainley Pk HD7 152 E4
Ainley Pl HD7 151 C2
Ainley Rd HD3 135 A3
Ainleys Ind Est HX5 135 A5
Ainley St
  [10] Elland HX5 134 F6
  Huddersfield HD7 152 D4
Ainsbury Ave
  Baildon BD10 39 B3
  Bradford BD10 39 C3
Ainsdale Cl S71 179 B5
Ainsdale Gr BD13 52 E6
Ainsdale Rd S71 179 B5
Ainsley La HD7 168 D4
Ainsty Cres LS22 13 E7
Ainsty Dr LS22 13 E7
Ainsty Garth LS22 13 E7
Ainsty Rd LS22 13 D7
Ainsty View LS22 13 E7
Aintree Cl LS25 82 F2
Aintree Ct LS10 215 B4
Airebank BD16 36 F3
Aireburn Ave BD20 17 D5
Aire & Calder Cotts WF3 122 B2
Aire & Calder Ind Pk The WF10 103 D1
Aire Cl BD17 38 B1
Aire Cres BD20 16 E6
Aire Ct [5] BD20 17 E8
Airedale Ave BD16 54 A7
Airedale Bsns Ctr BD23 4 A8
Airedale Cliff LS13 58 C5
Airedale College Mount BD3 56 A1
Airedale College Rd BD3 56 A1
Airedale College Terr BD3 56 A1
Airedale Com Bsns Ctr WF10 125 C7
Airedale Cres BD3 56 A1
Airedale Croft LS13 57 F5
Airedale Ct LS14 61 F5
Airedale Dr
  Castleford WF10 104 C2
  Garforth LS25 83 B6
  Horsforth LS18 57 F8
  Shelf HX3 93 B5
Airedale Gdns LS13 57 F5
Airedale General Hospl BD20 17 B6
Airedale Gr
  Horsforth LS18 57 F8
  [3] Rothwell LS26 101 D6
Airedale High Sch WF10 125 D7
Airedale Ho WF13 118 C2
Airedale Hts WF2 141 C4
Airedale Mews BD20 5 E1
Airedale Mount
  Keighley BD20 36 C8
  Pudsey LS13 57 E5
Airedale Pl BD17 38 E2
Airedale Quay LS13 58 A4
Airedale Rd
  Bradford BD3 55 F1
  Castleford WF10 125 B7
  [5] Keighley BD21 35 E8
  Keighley BD21 35 F8
  Rothwell LS26 101 D6
Airedale Sh Ctr BD21 35 C7
Airedale St
  Bingley BD16 36 F3
  Bradford BD2 56 B3
Airedale Terr
  [4] Baildon BD17 38 D2
  [10] Morley LS27 98 B4
  [2] Rothwell LS26 101 D6
Airedale Trad Pk BD20 16 E7
Airedale View
  Glusburn BD20 16 D7
  Pudsey LS13 57 F5
  [1] Rothwell LS26 101 D6
  Yeadon LS19 40 D3
Airedale Wharf LS13 57 F4
Aire Gr LS19 40 C6
Aire Ho [15] LS10 211 C3
Aire Mount LS22 13 D7
Aire Pl LS3 205 B1
Aire Rd LS22 13 D7
Aireside BD20 4 B2
Aireside Ave BD20 4 B2
Aireside Ctr LS1 211 A3
Aireside Rd BD17 38 D1
Aireside Terr BD20 4 A3
Aire St
  Bingley BD16 36 E6
  Bradford BD10 39 A1
  Brighouse HD6 115 B1
  Castleford WF10 124 D8
  Dewsbury WF13 138 F5
  Glusburn BD20 16 E6
  [2] Haworth BD22 51 D7
  Keighley BD21 35 D8
  Knottingley WF11 127 A5
  Leeds LS1 211 B3
Aire Terr WF10 103 D1
Aire Valley Cl BD20 4 B6
Aire Valley Ct BD16 36 F2
Aire Valley Dr BD20 4 B6
Aire Valley Mount WF10 125 A7
Airevalley Rd BD21 36 B7
Aire View
  Brotherton WF11 126 C8
  Cononley BD20 4 A2
  Keighley BD20 18 F2
  Keighley BD20 36 B8
  Knottingley WF11 126 D5
  Silsden BD20 5 E1
  Yeadon LS19 40 C6
Aire View Ave
  [3] Shipley BD18 55 A8
  Shipley, Cottingley BD16 54 B8
Aireview Cres BD17 38 A1
Aire View Dr BD20 36 C7
Aire View Inf Sch BD20 5 E1
Aireview Terr BD21 35 E6
Aireville Ave BD9 55 B5
Aireville Cl
  Keighley BD20 18 A2
  Shipley BD18 55 B5
Aireville Cres
  Shipley BD9 55 B4
Aireville Cres *continued*
  Silsden BD20 5 E
Aireville Dr
  Shipley BD18 55 E
  Silsden BD20 5 F
Aireville Gr BD18 55 E
Aireville Grange BD18 55 E
Aireville Mount
  Keighley BD20 36 C
  Silsden BD20 5 F
Aireville Rd BD9 55 C
Aireville Rise BD9 55 E
Aireville St BD20 18 A
Aireville Terr LS29 9 E
Aire Way BD17 38 A
Aire Wlk WF11 127 A
Aireworth Cl [11] BD21 18 E
Aireworth Gr BD21 35 E
Aireworth Mills BD21 35 E
Aireworth Rd BD21 35 E
Aireworth St BD21 35 B
Airey St BD21 35 A
Airlie Ave LS8 207 C
Airlie Pl LS8 207 C
Aislaby Hts HX2 91 D
Akam Rd BD1 74 D
Aked's Rd HX1 203 A
Aked St BD1 201 C
Aketon Dr WF10 124 C
Aketon Rd WF10 124 C
Akroyd Ct HX3 203 E
Akroyd La HX7 89 E
Akroyd Pl HX1 203 B
Akroyd Terr HX2 202 E
Alabama St [4] HX1 202 E
Alanby Dr BD10 56 C
Alan Cres LS15 81 A
Alan Ct BD13 72 D
Alandale Cres LS25 82 D
Alandale Dr LS25 82 D
Alandale Gr LS25 82 D
Alandale Rd
  Garforth LS25 82 D
  Huddersfield HD2 136 E
Alaska Pl LS7 204 B
Albans Cl LS17 28 E
Alban St BD4 75 B
Albany Cres WF9 182 F
Albany Ct
  Keighley BD20 35 A
  Pontefract WF8 146 D
Albany Dr HD5 155 A
Albany Pl [5] WF9 182 F
Albany Rd
  Huddersfield HD5 155 A
  Rothwell LS26 100 D
Albany St
  Bradford BD5 74 E
  Bradford, Brownroyd Hill BD6 74 C
  Halifax HX3 203 C
  Huddersfield HD1 153 F
  Leeds LS12 209 A
  [4] South Elmsall WF9 182 F
Albany Terr
  Halifax HX3 203 C
  Leeds LS12 209 A
Albany Wlk LS29 8 B
Alberta Ave LS7 204 B
Albert Ave
  Bradford BD10 56 C
  Halifax HX2 202 A
  Shipley BD18 37 F
Albert Bldgs BD10 56 B
Albert Cl WF17 118 C
Albert Cres
  Birkenshaw BD11 96 B
  Queensbury BD13 72 E
Albert Ct HX2 202 A
Albert Dr
  Halifax HX2 202 A
  Morley LS27 98 D
  Wakefield WF5 141 B
Albert Edward St [4] BD13 72 E
Albert Gdns HX2 202 A
Albert Gr LS6 59 D
Albert La OL14 108 B
Albert Mount LS18 58 D
Albert Pl
  Batley WF12 118 F
  Bradford BD3 75 E
  Horsforth LS18 41 C
  Mickletown LS26 102 B
Albert Prom HX3 113 A
Albert Rd
  Clayton West HD8 175 E
  Glusburn BD20 16 D
  Halifax, Pellon HX2 202 A
  Morley LS27 98 C
  Queensbury BD13 72 E
  Rothwell LS26 101 C
  Shipley BD18 54 F
  Sowerby Bridge HX6 112 C
Albert Simmons Way LS29 9 E
Albert Sq
  [8] Silsden BD20 5 E
  [12] Yeadon LS19 40 C
Albert St
  [2] Baildon BD17 38 C
  Bradford BD6 94 B
  Bradford, Springfield BD10 56 B
  Bradford, Wyke BD12 94 C

Albert St *continued*
Brighouse HD6 **115** C2
Castleford WF10 **124** D8
Cleckheaton BD19 **116** D8
Cudworth S72 **180** C1
Elland HX5 **134** F6
Featherstone WF7 **145** D5
Halifax HX1 **203** A3
1 Haworth BD22 **51** F8
20 Hebden Bridge HX7 **89** A3
Huddersfield HD1 **153** F3
Keighley BD21 **35** B7
Liversedge WF15 **117** C3
9 Mytholmroyd HX7 **89** E1
Normanton WF6 **123** C3
Pudsey LS28 **76** D6
Queensbury BD13 **72** F1
Sutton-in-C BD20 **16** E5
Thornton BD13 **72** D6
Todmorden OL14 **108** B6
Wilsden BD15 **53** C4
Albert Terr
Bradford, Raw Nook BD12 **94** F5
5 Bradford, Wyke Common BD12 **94** D2
Shipley BD18 **37** F1
11 Yeadon LS19 **40** C7
Albert View HX2 **202** A4
Albert Way BD11 **96** B4
Albert Wlk 4 BD18 **54** E8
Albert Yd
Huddersfield HD1 **154** A5
6 Keighley BD21 **35** C6
Albion Arc LS1 **211** C4
Albion Ave LS12 **210** A3
Albion Cl LS23 **30** D5
Albion Croft WF5 **140** E6
Albion Ct
Batley WF16 **117** D4
Bradford BD1 **201** B3
Halifax HX1 **203** B3
Meltham HD9 **170** C2
Wakefield WF1 **216** B2
Albion Fold BD15 **53** C5
Albion Mills Bsns Ctr HD9 **189** B8
Albion Mills Ret Pk WF2 **216** A1
Albion Pk LS12 **210** B4
Albion Pl
13 Brighouse HD6 **115** A3
Guiseley LS20 **22** E1
Leeds LS1 **211** C4
South Elmsall WF9 **183** A3
Thornton BD13 **72** C6
Albion Rd
Bradford BD10 **56** C8
Dewsbury WF12 **139** E1
Pudsey LS28 **57** E2
Albion Sq WF2 **141** E7
Albion St
Bacup OL13 **106** A3
Batley, Heckmondwike WF16 **117** D4
Batley WF17 **118** D4
Bradford BD1 **201** B3
3 Bradford, Buttershaw BD6 **93** F7
Brighouse HD6 **115** A3
Castleford WF10 **124** C8
Cleckheaton BD19 **116** E7
Clifford LS23 **30** D5
Denholme BD13 **71** D8
Dewsbury, Ravensthorpe WF13 **138** F5
Dewsbury WF13 **118** C1
Elland HX5 **135** A6
Fitzwilliam WF9 **163** A3
Halifax HX1 **203** B3
Haworth BD22 **51** E8
Huddersfield HD1 **154** A5
Leeds LS1, LS2 **211** C4
1 Liversedge WF15 **117** B4
Morley LS27 **98** A4
Otley LS21 **23** B7
Queensbury BD13 **72** D1
Rothwell WF3 **100** D3
Wakefield WF1 **216** B3
Albion Terr
Clifford LS23 **30** D5
2 Hebden Bridge HX7 **88** F3
Albion Way LS12 **210** B4
Albion Yd BD1 **201** B3
Alcester Garth BD3 **75** B8
Alcester Pl LS8 **207** C4
Alcester Rd LS8 **207** C4
Alcester St 13 LS8 **207** C4
Alcester Terr LS8 **207** C4
Aldams Rd WF12 **139** C7
Alden Ave LS27 **98** A2
Alden Cl LS27 **98** A2
Alden Cres WF8 **146** B7
Alden Ct 5 LS27 **98** A2
Alden Fold 4 LS27 **98** A2
Alder Ave
Holmfirth HD9 **189** C8
Keighley BD21 **35** E5
Wakefield WF2 **142** A8
Alder Carr BD17 **38** B3
Alder Cl S75 **178** A1
Alder Dr LS28 **76** A8
Alder Garth LS28 **76** B8
Alder Gr
Halifax HX2 **91** E6
Normanton WF6 **144** B7
Alder Hill Ave LS7 **60** A7
Alder Hill Gr LS7 **60** A7
Alder Holt Dr BD6 **94** A6
Aldermanbury BD1 **201** B3
Alderney Rd WF12 **118** F2
Alderscholes Cl 9 BD13 **72** D6
Alderscholes La BD13 **72** C5
Aldersgate LS12 **209** C3
Alderson St 2 BD6 **93** E7
Alder St HD1, HD2 **136** B1
Alderstone Rise HD3 **135** A2
Aldersyde WF17 **96** E1
Aldersyde Rd LS20 **39** D8
Aldersyde Way LS20 **39** D8
Alderton Bank LS17 **42** F2
Alderton Cres LS17 **43** A2
Alderton Hts LS17 **42** F2
Alderton Mount LS17 **42** F2
Alderton Pl LS17 **42** F2
Alderton Rise LS17 **43** A2
Aldonley HD5 **155** A4
Alegar St HD6 **115** C2
Alexander Ave LS15 **80** F7
Alexander Cres WF7 **145** E7
Alexander Ct
Keighley BD20 **36** D7
2 Leeds LS1 **211** B4
Alexander Gdns S75 **193** E4
Alexander Rd WF7 **145** D6
Alexander Sq 12 BD14 **73** B4
Alexander St
5 Bradford BD6 **94** B8
Leeds LS1 **211** B4
Alexander Terr HX1 **202** B3
Alexandra Ave 3 WF17 **96** F1
Alexandra Cl HX6 **112** C4
Alexandra Cres
Dewsbury WF13 **118** A2
Elland HX5 **135** B7
Ilkley LS29 **8** A4
Alexandra Dr WF6 **144** B7
Alexandra Gr
Leeds LS6 **205** B2
Pudsey LS28 **76** D6
Alexandra Pl 3 LS29 **8** A4
Alexandra Rd
Batley WF17 **118** D4
Bradford BD2 **56** C5
6 Hebden Bridge HX7 **89** A3
Horsforth LS18 **58** C8
Huddersfield HD3 **153** C7
Leeds LS6 **205** B2
Pudsey LS28 **76** C6
Shipley BD18 **55** A7
Alexandra Rd W HD3 **153** C5
Alexandra Sq 14 BD18 **54** F8
Alexandra St
Bradford BD7 **74** C5
Halifax HX1 **203** B3
4 Liversedge WF15 **117** A4
Queensbury BD13 **72** E1
Alexandra Terr
Bradford BD2 **56** C2
7 Yeadon LS19 **40** C7
Alford Terr BD7 **74** A7
Alfred E Briggs Almshouses
4 BD12 **94** B6
Alfred St E HX1 **203** C3
Alfred St
4 Batley, Heckmondwike WF16 **117** D3
Batley, Mount Pleasant WF17 **118** B4
5 Brighouse HD6 **115** B3
1 Dewsbury WF13 **118** E1
Elland HX4 **134** D7
Halifax HX1 **202** B3
4 Huddersfield HD1 **154** A5
3 Liversedge WF15 **117** B4
6 Morley LS27 **98** C8
Royston S71 **179** E4
Alfreds Way WF17 **118** C5
Alice St
Bradford BD8 **74** D8
2 Cleckheaton BD19 **116** D8
6 Haworth BD22 **51** C6
Keighley BD21 **35** C7
Alkincote St BD21 **35** C6
All Alone 2 BD10 **56** A7
All Alone Rd BD2, BD10 **56** A6
Allanbridge Cl BD10 **56** C7
Allandale Ave BD6 **94** A7
Allandale Rd BD6 **94** A7
Allanfield Gr LS22 **13** E7
Allanfield Terr LS22 **13** E8
Allan Haigh Cl WF2 **141** D8
Allan Terr HX6 **112** C3
Allenby Cres LS11 **99** A8
Allenby Dr LS11 **99** A8
Allenby Gdns LS11 **99** A8
Allenby Gr LS11 **99** A8
Allenby Pl LS11 **99** A8
Allenby Rd LS11 **99** A8
Allenby View LS11 **214** B1
Allen Croft BD11 **96** A5
Allendale Rd S75 **177** D1
Allerby Gn BD6 **93** F6
Allergill Pk HD9 **188** D5
Allerton Ave LS17 **43** D2
Allerton Bywater Network Ctr WF10 **103** D4
Allerton Bywater Prim Sch WF10 **103** B5
Allerton Cl BD15 **54** B1
Allerton Dr LS17 **28** C6
Allerton Gr LS17 **43** D2
Allerton Grange Ave LS17 **43** E1
Allerton Grange Cl LS17 **60** C8
Allerton Grange Cres LS17 **204** A4
Allerton Grange Croft LS8 **204** B4
Allerton Grange Dr
Bradford BD15 **54** B1
Leeds LS17 **204** A4
Allerton Grange Gdns LS17 **204** A4
Allerton Grange Rise LS17 **204** A4
Allerton Grange Sch LS17 **43** E1
Allerton Grange Vale LS17 **204** A4
Allerton Grange Way LS17, LS8 **204** A4
Allerton Grange Wlk LS17 **204** A4
Allerton High Sch LS17 **43** B3
Allerton Hill LS7 **60** C7
Allerton La BD13, BD15 **73** A7
Allerton Lo 10 LS17 **43** C1
Allerton Mews 8 LS17 **43** C2
Allerton Pk LS7 **204** B3
Allerton Pl
Halifax HX1 **202** C3
Leeds LS17 **43** D2
Allerton Prim Sch BD15 **54** B1
Allerton Rd BD15 **54** B1
Allerton St LS4 **205** A2
Allerton Upper Gn BD15 **72** E8
Allescholes Rd OL14 **129** B7
Alliance St LS12 **209** A3
Allinson St LS12 **210** B2
Allison Dr HD2 **136** B2
Allison La BD2 **55** D4
Allison St WF7 **145** C5
Allison Terr WF2 **120** B2
Alloe Field Pl HX2 **91** E6
Alloe Field View HX2 **91** E6
Allott Cl WF9 **182** F3
All Saint's Circ LS26 **101** D6
All Saint's Dr LS26 **101** C6
All Saint's Rd LS26 **101** D6
All Saint's View LS26 **101** C7
All Saints' CE Jun & Inf Sch HX3 **113** C2
All Saints' CE Prim Sch BD5 **74** D5
All Saints' View 2 WF8 **146** E8
All Saints CE Prim Sch LS29 **8** A4
All Saints Cl HD8 **175** F3
All Saints Ct
13 Keighley BD21 **35** B7
Otley LS21 **23** A8
All Saints Featherstone CE Jun & Inf Sch WF7 **124** D1
All Saints Ind Est WF8 **125** E1
All Saints Prim Sch LS21 **23** B7
All Saints RC High Sch HD2 **136** C5
All Saints Rd BD7 **74** C5
All Saints Richmond Hill CE Prim Sch LS9 **212** C4
All Saints Terr 14 BD21 **35** B7
All Souls' Rd HX3 **92** C1
All Souls' St 3 HX3 **92** C1
All Souls' Terr 2 HX3 **92** C1
Allums La LS21 **25** F5
Alma Cl LS28 **57** C3
Alma Cotts 13 LS6 **59** D5
Alma Dr HD5 **154** D6
Alma Gr BD18 **55** D8
Alma La
Batley WF16 **117** D6
Ripponden HX6 **132** B7
Alma Pl
Bradford BD3 **75** D8
Keighley BD21 **35** C5
Alma Rd
Leeds LS6 **59** E5
Walsden OL14 **108** A1
Alma St
Bacup OL13 **106** A2
Bradford, Cutler Heights BD4 **75** D3
Bradford, Swain Green BD4 **75** D5
3 Elland HX5 **135** A6
Haworth BD22 **51** C8
Keighley BD21 **35** C5
Leeds LS9 **207** C1
Queensbury BD13 **72** D1
Rothwell LS26 **101** D7
Shipley BD18 **55** D8
Walsden OL14 **108** A1
Yeadon LS19 **40** C7
Alma Terr
Keighley BD21 **35** C5
Keighley, Green End BD20 **19** E1
Rothwell LS26 **100** D6
Almondbury Bank HD5 **154** E5
Almondbury CE Inf Sch HD5 **154** F2
Almondbury Cl HD5 **155** A3
Almondbury Comm HD4 **154** F1
Almondbury High Sch HD5 **154** F4
Almondbury Jun Sch HD5 **155** A4
Almond Cl WF9 **183** A5
Almond Ct HX3 **93** A4
Almondroyd WF16 **117** C5
Almond St BD3 **75** C6
Almond Way WF17 **96** F1
Almscliffe Ave WF12 **139** E8
Almscliffe Pl BD2 **56** D4
Almscliffe Terr 3 LS21 **23** B7
Almshouse Hill LS23 **30** D2
Almshouse La
Crigglestone WF2 **160** B4
Wakefield WF1 **216** B2
Almshouses HD9 **188** A8
Alnwick View LS16 **59** C7
Alpha St BD21 **35** D6
Alpine Cl WF17 **118** B4
Alpine Ct
Castleford WF10 **124** E5
Hemsworth WF9 **181** D8
Alpine Rise BD13 **72** D6
Alpine Terr LS26 **100** D6
Alpine View WF9 **181** D8
Alston Cl BD9 **54** D1
Alston La LS14 **62** A3
Alston Rd BD21 **18** D1
Alston Ret Pk BD21 **18** D1
Altar Dr
Bradford BD9 **55** A3
Keighley BD20 **19** A1
Altar La BD16 **36** C4
Althorpe Gr BD10 **56** A6
Althorpe Ho 13 HX6 **112** C4
Altinkool St WF1 **142** F2
Altofts Hall Rd WF6 **122** F4
Altofts Jun Sch WF6 **122** F3
Altofts La WF10 **123** D6
Altofts Lodge Dr WF6 **122** E3
Altofts Rd WF6 **123** A2
Alton Ave HD5 **154** F7
Alton Gr
Bradford BD9 **54** F3
Shipley BD18 **55** B5
Alton Way S75 **178** A1
Alum Ct BD9 **55** A3
Alum Dr BD9 **55** A3
Alvanley Ct BD8 **73** D8
Alva Terr BD18 **55** B6
Alverthorpe Rd WF2 **141** F6
Alwen Ave HD2 **135** F2
Alwoodley Chase LS17 **43** E5
Alwoodley Court Gdns LS17 **43** A6
Alwoodley Ct LS17 **42** F5
Alwoodley Gates LS17 **43** E6
Alwoodley Gdns LS17 **43** A5
Alwoodley La LS17 **43** C6
Alwoodley Prim Sch LS17 **43** A3
Amberley Ct BD3 **75** C6
Amberley Gdns LS12 **209** C2
Amberley Rd LS12 **209** C2
Amberley Rise DN6 **184** F2
Amberley St
Bradford BD3 **75** C7
Leeds LS12 **210** A2
Amber St WF17 **118** A6
Amberton App LS8 **208** C4
Amberton Cl LS8 **61** C5
Amberton Cres LS8 **208** C4
Amberton Garth LS8 **208** C4
Amberton Gdns LS8 **208** C4
Amberton Gr LS8 **208** C4
Amberton La LS8 **208** C4
Amberton Mount LS8 **208** C4
Amberton Pl LS8 **208** B4
Amberton Rd LS8, LS9 **208** C4
Amberton St LS8 **208** C4
Amberton Terr LS8 **61** C5
Ambler Gr HX2 **91** F6
Amblers Croft BD10 **39** B2
Amblers Ct LS28 **76** E6
Amblers Mews
4 Baildon BD17 **38** C4
East Morton BD20 **36** D8
Amblers Row BD17 **38** C4
Ambler St
Bradford BD8 **55** C1
Castleford WF10 **124** E7
Keighley BD21 **35** D7
Amblers Terr 10 HX3 **92** C1
Amblerthorne BD11 **96** B5
Ambler Way BD13 **92** C7
Ambleside Ave BD9 **54** F2
Ambleside Dr WF2 **161** A6
Ambleside Gdns LS28 **76** C7
Ambleside Gr LS26 **101** C6
Ambleside Rd WF10 **104** E1
Ambleside Wlk LS22 **13** B6
Amble Tonia BD13 **52** E1
Ambleton Way BD13 **92** C8
Amelia St 1 BD18 **54** F8
America La
Brighouse HD6 **115** C2
Sutton-in-C BD20 **16** E1
America Moor La LS27 **98** A2
Amisfield Rd HX3 **114** D8
Amos St HX1 **202** B3
Amport Cl HD6 **115** B1
Amspool Ct WF3 **100** C3
Amundsen Ave BD2 **56** A5
Amy Busfield Gn LS29 **9** E1
Amyroyce Dr BD18 **55** E7
Amy St
9 Bingley BD16 **37** A3
3 Halifax HX3 **92** A2
Anaheim Dr WF1 **121** D5
Ancaster Cres LS16 **59** B7
Ancaster Rd LS16 **59** B7
Ancaster View LS16 **59** B7
Anchorage The BD16 **36** F4
Anchor Bridge Way WF12 **139** C7
Anchor Pl HD6 **136** D8
Anchor St
Huddersfield HD1 **154** B7
4 Todmorden OL14 **108** C5
Andersen Ct WF10 **125** C5
Anderson Ave LS8 **207** B2
Anderson Ho BD17 **38** B1
Anderson Mount LS8 **207** B2
Anderson St
Bradford BD8 **55** C1
Pontefract WF8 **125** C1
Wakefield WF2 **142** A6
Anderton St
Glusburn BD20 **16** D7
Wakefield WF1 **142** E3
Andover Gn BD4 **75** E4
Andover Ho 4 HD5 **154** D6
Andrew Cl HX3 **114** A4
Andrew Cres
Huddersfield HD4 **153** A1
Lofthouse Gate WF1 **121** B5
Andrews Gr WF7 **163** F6
Andrew Sq 4 LS28 **57** D3
Andrew St
13 Pudsey LS28 **57** D2
Purston Jaglin WF7 **145** C4
Wakefield WF1 **216** A4
Anerley St BD4 **75** B2
Angel Ct LS3 **205** C1
Angel Rd HX1 **202** C4
Angel Row LS26 **100** B5
Angel St BD17 **38** D4
Angel Way BD7 **74** D7
Angerton Way BD6 **94** A6
Anglers Ctry Pk* WF4 **161** F5
Angus Ave BD12 **94** C1
Anlaby St BD4 **75** D5
Annandale Ct
Bradford BD13 **73** B2
Ilkley LS29 **8** B3
Annat Royd La S36 **191** D1
Anne's Ct HX3 **114** A4
Anne Cres S72 **180** E5
Anne Gate BD1 **201** C3
Anne St
Batley WF17 **118** A7
Bradford BD7 **73** F3
Annie St
Fitzwilliam WF9 **163** A4
Haworth BD22 **51** F8
Keighley BD21 **18** C1
Lofthouse Gate WF1 **121** B4
Morley LS27 **98** B4
Shipley BD18 **55** C6
1 Sowerby Bridge HX6 **112** B4
Anning Fold LS25 **83** B8
Annison St BD3 **201** D3
Annottes Croft HD5 **154** F7
Ann Pl BD5 **201** B1
Ann St
Denholme BD13 **52** D1
Haworth BD22 **51** D7
Keighley BD21 **35** B6
Anroyd St WF13 **118** A1
Anson Gr BD7 **73** F2
Anston Dr WF9 **183** A5
Anstone Dr BD5 **74** C2
Anthony La BD16 **36** B2
Antony Cl HD3 **134** D1
Anvil Ct
1 Bradford BD8 **55** B1
Cullingworth BD13 **52** D5
Anvil St
2 Bradford BD8 **55** B1
Brighouse HD6 **115** A3
Apex Bsns Ctr LS11 **211** C1
Apex View LS11 **211** B1
Apex Way LS11 **211** C1
Apperley Gdns BD10 **56** E8
Apperley La BD10, LS19 **39** F2
Apperley Rd BD10 **56** D8
Appleby Cl
Darton S75 **177** F1
Queensbury BD13 **72** D1
Appleby La LS25 **83** B7
Appleby Pl
Leeds LS15 **80** E8
Skellow DN6 **184** F2
Appleby Way
Morley LS27 **98** B4
Wetherby LS22 **13** E7
Appleby Wlk LS15 **80** E8
Apple Cl WF17 **97** A2
Applegarth
Bradford BD14 **73** C3
Rothwell LS26 **101** C7
Wakefield WF2 **160** E7
Apple Haigh Cl 1 BD10 **56** C7
Applehaigh Ct WF4 **179** A5
Applehaigh Gr S71 **179** A4
Applehaigh La WF4 **179** A6
Applehaigh View S71 **179** A4
Apple House Terr HX2 **90** E1
Apple Mews WF2 **160** A5
Apple Shawn Cres WF2 **120** F3
Apple St
Keighley BD21 **35** A3
Oxenhope BD22 **51** C2
Appleton Cl
Bingley BD16 **37** B5
Bradford BD12 **94** F5
3 Leeds LS9 **212** C4
Appleton Ct
Crigglestone WF2 **159** F8
2 Leeds LS9 **212** C4
Thornton BD13 **72** D6
Appleton Gr LS9 **80** B7
Appleton Sq LS9 **212** C4
Appleton Way LS9 **212** C4
Appletree Cl LS23 **30** D7
Apple Tree Cl
East Ardsley WF3 **120** C8
Pontefract WF8 **146** B6

Apple Tree Ct WF3 120 C7
Apple Tree Gdns LS29 7 F4
Apple Tree La LS25 83 B1
Apple Tree Mews 10 LS25 83 B1
Apple Tree Rd WF7 145 E4
Apple Tree Wlk 12 LS25 83 B1
Appleyard Apartments 5 HX1 203 A1
Appleyard Rd HX7 89 F1
Approach The LS15 62 F7
April Ct WF15 117 A2
April Gdns BD13 72 E1
Aprilia Ct BD14 73 D5
Apsley Cres BD8 55 C1
Apsley St
6 Haworth BD22 51 D7
8 Keighley BD21 35 B5
Oakworth BD22 34 D3
Apsley Terr BD22 34 D3
Aquamarine Dr HD2 136 C2
Aquila Way WF15 116 D5
Arborary La HD4, HD7 170 F6
Arbour St 9 OL13 106 A3
Arbour The
Farnhill BD20 4 D1
Ilkley LS29 8 A6
Arcade Royale HX1 203 B3
Arcade The
5 Dewsbury WF12 139 D8
Knottingley WF11 126 E4
Arcadia Ct HD1 153 D7
Arcadia St 12 BD21 35 B5
Archbell Ave HD6 136 B8
Archbishop Cranmer CE Prim Sch LS17 43 B3
Archbishop Holgate Hospl WF9 181 A6
Archer Rd HD6 115 D1
Archer St WF10 124 C6
Archery Pl 9 LS2 206 B2
Archery Rd LS2 206 B2
Archery St 13 LS2 206 B2
Archery Terr 11 LS2 206 B2
Arches St HX1 203 A2
Arches The HX3 92 D1
Archibald St BD7 74 C7
Arctic Par BD7 74 A4
Arctic St
6 Haworth BD22 51 E8
Keighley BD20 18 B1
Arden Ct
Horbury WF4 159 A8
Kirkheaton HD5 155 C7
Ardennes Cl BD2 55 F4
Arden Rd
Bradford BD8 73 C7
Halifax HX1 203 A2
Ardsley Cl BD4 75 F2
Ardsley Ct WF3 120 E8
Argent Way BD4 75 F2
Argie Ave LS4 59 B3
Argie Gdns 3 LS4 59 C2
Argie Rd LS4 59 C2
Argie Terr LS4 59 C2
Argyle Rd
Knottingley WF11 126 C5
Leeds LS9 212 A4
Argyle St
Bradford BD4 75 B4
Keighley BD21 35 B7
Marsden HD7 168 F4
Shipley BD18 55 B6
Wakefield WF1 142 E4
Argyll Ave 3 WF8 146 B8
Argyll Cl
Baildon BD17 38 E2
Horsforth LS18 41 B4
Argyl Mews LS17 28 C5
Arkendale Mews 5 BD7 73 E3
Arkenley La HD4, HD8 155 A2
Arkenmore HD5 154 F7
Arksey Pl LS12 209 C4
Arksey Terr LS12 209 C4
Arkwright Ct 9 WF15 117 A5
Arkwright St
9 Bradford, Clayton BD14 73 B4
Bradford, Tyersal BD4 75 E6
Arkwright Wlk 1 LS27 98 A6
Arlesford Rd BD4 75 E2
Arley Cl HD9 188 F8
Arley Gr LS12 209 C4
Arley Pl LS12 209 C4
Arley St 5 LS12 59 C1
Arley Terr LS12 209 C4
Arlington Bsns Ctr LS11 98 E8
Arlington Cres HX2 112 D4
Arlington Gr
Castleford WF10 124 F7
Leeds LS8 61 B5
Arlington Rd LS8 61 B5
Arlington St WF1 216 A4
Arlington Way HD5 155 A7
Armadale Ave BD4 95 B8
Armgill La BD2 55 D4
Armidale Way BD2 55 F3
Armitage Ave HD6 136 B8
Armitage Bldgs WF12 119 B6
Armitage Cl HD8 175 A2
Armitage Rd
Bradford BD12 94 F4
Halifax HX1 202 B1
Huddersfield, Armitage Bridge HD4 171 E8
Huddersfield, Birkby HD2 135 F1
Armitage Rd *continued*
Huddersfield HD3 153 B5
Wakefield WF2 141 D8
Armitage Sq 2 LS28 76 D6
Armitage St
Castleford WF10 124 C8
Dewsbury WF13 138 D5
Huddersfield HD4 154 A4
Rothwell LS26 100 E4
Armitage The BD20 36 B8
Armley Grange Ave LS12 209 A4
Armley Grange Cres LS12 58 F1
Armley Grange Dr LS12 77 F8
Armley Grange Mount LS12 77 F8
Armley Grange Oval LS12 58 F1
Armley Grange Rise 4 LS12 77 F8
Armley Grange View LS12 209 A4
Armley Grange Wlk LS12 209 A4
Armley Grove Pl LS12 210 A3
Armley Lodge Rd LS12 209 C4
Armley Mills Ind Mus* LS12 205 A1
Armley Park Ct LS12 209 C4
Armley Park Rd LS12 59 C1
Armley Prim Sch LS12 209 C4
Armley Rd LS12 210 B3
Armley Ridge Cl LS12 209 A4
Armley Ridge Rd
Leeds, Moor Top LS12 209 B4
Leeds, Upper Armley LS12 59 A1
Armley Ridge Terr LS12 59 A1
Armouries Dr LS10 212 A2
Armouries Way LS10 212 A3
Armoury Ave WF14 138 A5
Armstrong Cl WF6 123 A4
Armstrong St
Bradford BD4 75 D6
12 Pudsey LS28 57 D2
Armstrong Terr 2 WF8 146 B7
Army Row S71 179 D4
Armytage Cres HD1 153 F3
Armytage Ind Est HD6 115 B2
Armytage Rd HD6 115 D1
Armytage Way HD6 115 D1
Armytage Wlk WF9 182 C3
Arncliffe Ave 1 BD22 35 A5
Arncliffe Cres
Brighouse HD6 135 E8
Morley LS27 98 C2
Arncliffe Ct HD1 153 E7
Arncliffe Dr WF11 126 C4
Arncliffe Garth 15 LS28 57 D2
Arncliffe Gdns WF17 118 B5
Arncliffe Gr 16 BD22 35 A6
Arncliffe Grange LS17 43 D2
Arncliffe Rd
Batley WF17 118 B5
Keighley BD22 35 A6
Leeds LS16 59 A8
Wakefield WF1 142 F8
Arncliffe St LS28 57 D2
Arncliffe Terr BD7 74 B6
Arncliff Pl 17 BD21 35 A6
Arndale Ctr 6 LS6 59 D5
Arndale Gr HD9 189 B4
Arndale Sh Ctr The 1 BD18 55 B7
Arnford Cl BD3 201 C4
Arnhem Cl BD16 37 B3
Arnold Ave HD2 135 F1
Arnold Pl BD8 74 C8
Arnold Royd HD6 135 E7
Arnold St
12 Bradford BD8 55 C1
Halifax HX1 202 C3
Huddersfield HD2 135 F1
Liversedge WF15 117 A4
6 Sowerby Bridge HX6 112 B4
Arnside Ave BD20 18 E1
Arnside Cl WF10 125 D8
Arnside Cres WF10 125 D8
Arnside Rd BD5 74 E2
Arran Cl HD7 152 D5
Arran Ct LS25 82 F5
Arran Dr
Garforth LS25 82 F5
Horsforth LS18 41 B4
Arran Way LS26 100 F5
Arrunden Ct HD9 189 B3
Arrunden La HD9 188 F2
Arthington Ave LS10 215 A2
Arthington Cl WF3 119 D7
Arthington Ct LS10 215 A2
Arthington Garth LS21 24 F6
Arthington Gr LS10 215 A2
Arthington La
Arthington LS21 25 D6
Pool LS21 24 E6
Arthington Lawns LS21 24 E6
Arthington Pl LS10 215 A2
Arthington Rd LS16 25 C2
Arthington St
Bradford BD8 74 C8
Leeds LS10 215 A2
Arthington Terr LS10 215 A2
Arthington View LS10 215 A2
Arthur Ave BD8 73 D7
Arthur Gr WF17 117 F8
Arthursdale Cl LS15 62 F7
Arthursdale Dr LS15 62 F7
Arthursdale Grange LS15 62 F7
Arthur St
Bacup OL13 106 B3
Bingley BD16 36 F3
Arthur St *continued*
Bradford BD10 56 B6
Brighouse HD6 115 C2
Huddersfield HD7 152 E4
Oakworth BD22 34 C2
Pudsey, Farsley LS28 57 D2
Pudsey LS28 57 E2
Wakefield WF1 142 E3
Artillery St WF16 117 D3
Artist St LS12 210 B3
Arum St BD5 74 C3
Arundel Cl
Batley WF17 97 B2
Wakefield WF1 216 B3
Arundel Gdns S71 179 C4
Arundel St
Garforth LS25 83 B8
Halifax HX1 202 B3
Pudsey LS28 76 E8
Wakefield WF1 216 B3
Arundel Terr 6 LS15 62 C2
Arundel Wlk WF17 97 B1
Ascham Hall BD16 37 A5
Ascot Ave BD7 73 E2
Ascot Dr BD7 73 E2
Ascot Gdns
Bradford BD7 73 E2
Middleton LS10 99 D3
Ascot Gr HD6 135 E8
Ascot Par BD7 73 E2
Ascot Rd LS25 82 F2
Ascot Terr LS9 212 C3
Asdale Rd WF2 160 B7
Ash Apartments WF1 216 C4
Ash Ave LS6 59 D5
Ashbourne Ave
Bradford BD2 55 F3
Cleckheaton BD19 116 D6
Ashbourne Bank BD2 55 F3
Ashbourne Cl BD2 55 F4
Ashbourne Cres
Bradford BD2 55 F3
Garforth LS25 82 F5
Queensbury BD13 72 D1
Ashbourne Croft BD19 116 D6
Ashbourne Dr
2 Bradford BD2 55 F3
Cleckheaton BD19 116 D6
Pontefract WF8 146 D5
Ashbourne Garth BD2 56 A4
Ashbourne Gdns
Bradford BD2 55 F3
Cleckheaton BD19 116 D6
Ashbourne Gr
Bradford BD2 55 F3
Halifax HX1 202 B3
Ashbourne Haven BD2 55 F3
Ashbourne Mount BD2 55 F3
Ashbourne Oval BD2 55 F3
Ashbourne Rd
Bradford BD2 55 F3
Keighley BD21 35 A5
Ashbourne Rise BD2 55 F3
Ashbourne View BD19 116 D6
Ashbourne Way
Bradford BD2 55 F3
Cleckheaton BD19 116 D6
Ashbrook Cl WF5 140 D7
Ashbrooke Pk LS11 214 C2
Ash Brow WF4 157 C3
Ashbrow Inf Sch HD2 136 B3
Ashbrow Jun Sch HD2 136 C3
Ash Brow Rd HD2 136 B3
Ashburn Cl LS22 13 D7
Ashburn Croft LS22 13 D7
Ashburn Dr LS22 13 D7
Ashburn Gr
Baildon BD17 38 C4
Wetherby LS22 13 D7
Ashburnham Gr BD9 55 B3
Ashburn Pl LS29 8 A3
Ashburn Way LS22 13 D7
Ashbury Chase WF1 121 A5
Ashby Ave LS13 58 D1
Ashby Cl WF15 116 F1
Ashby Cres LS13 58 D1
Ashby Mount 4 LS13 58 D2
Ashby Sq LS13 58 D2
Ashby St BD4 75 A4
Ashby Terr LS13 58 D2
Ashby View LS13 58 D2
Ash Cl
Brighouse HX3 114 D8
Ilkley LS29 7 E4
Ossett WF5 140 D5
Ashcombe Dr WF11 126 F3
Ash Cres
Leeds LS6 59 D5
Lofthouse Gate WF3 121 F5
Ash Croft BD6 94 A8
Ashcroft Ave WF7 145 C4
Ashcroft Cl WF17 118 B3
Ashcroft Rd WF7 145 C4
Ash Ct BD19 115 F8
Ashdale WF2 142 E1
Ashdale La LS22 13 D8
Ashday La HX3, HD6 114 B3
Ashdene
Gildersome LS12 77 D3
Walsden OL14 108 B1
Ashdene App WF4 143 F1
Ashdene Ave WF4 143 F1
Ashdene Cl LS28 76 E5
Ashdene Cres
Crofton WF4 143 F1
Pudsey LS28 76 E5
Ashdene Ct BD13 52 D6
Ashdene Dr WF4 143 F1
Ashdene Garth WF4 143 F1
Ashdene Gr WF8 125 F4
Ashdown Cl
9 Bradford BD6 74 B1
Halifax HX2 112 D6
Ashdown Ct 5 BD18 55 A7
Ashdown Pl 8 BD8 55 C1
Ashdown Rd WF1 142 E3
Ashdown St 13 LS13 58 C2
Ashenhurst Ave HD4 154 C3
Ashenhurst Cl
Huddersfield HD4 154 B3
Todmorden OL14 108 A7
Ashenhurst Rd
Huddersfield HD4 154 B3
Todmorden OL14 108 A7
Ashenhurst Rise HD4 154 B3
Asherton Gr LS23 30 E7
Ashes La
Huddersfield HD4 154 C1
Todmorden OL14 108 D7
Ashfield
Bradford BD4 75 D1
Dewsbury WF12 139 D4
Leeds LS12 78 A4
Wetherby LS22 13 F6
Ashfield Ave
Morley LS27 97 F3
Shipley BD18 55 B5
Skelmanthorpe HD8 175 A1
Ashfield Cl
Halifax HX3 91 F2
Leeds, New Farnley LS12 77 F4
Leeds, Stanks LS15 62 D4
Ashfield Cres
Bingley BD16 37 A2
Pudsey LS28 57 E1
Ashfield Ct 14 BD16 37 A2
Ashfield Dr
Baildon BD17 38 D3
Halifax HX3 92 A2
Shipley BD9 55 B5
Ashfield Gr
6 Pudsey LS28 57 E1
Shipley BD9 55 B5
Ashfield Ho WF9 181 D6
Ashfield Paddock LS23 30 F7
Ashfield Pk 1 LS6 59 E5
Ashfield Pl
Bradford BD2 56 D2
Otley LS21 22 F7
Ashfield Prim Sch LS21 10 E1
Ashfield Rd
Batley WF17 97 A2
Bradford BD10 39 C1
Elland HX4 134 B7
Hemsworth WF9 181 D5
Huddersfield HD2 135 E1
Morley LS27 97 F3
Pudsey LS28 57 E1
Shipley BD18 54 E7
Thornton BD13 72 D6
Ashfield St
Huddersfield HD2 136 B2
9 Keighley BD21 35 B6
Normanton WF6 123 C3
Ashfield Terr
Bradford BD12 94 D4
10 Cleckheaton BD19 116 E7
Elland HX4 134 B8
17 Haworth BD22 51 C6
Leeds LS15 62 D4
Middleton WF3 99 F2
Ashfield Way LS12 77 F4
Ashford Ct HD8 173 F7
Ashford Dr LS28 76 F6
Ashford Gn BD6 73 F1
Ashford Manor HD8 155 D1
Ashford Pk HD7 152 D5
Ashgap La WF6 123 B3
Ash Gdns LS6 59 D5
Ash Ghyll Gdns BD16 36 F4
Ash Gn WF8 125 F1
Ash Gr
Bingley BD16 37 A1
Birkenshaw BD11 96 A6
Brighouse HD6 115 C2
Cleckheaton BD19 116 B6
Cleckheaton, Birdacre BD19 96 A1
Darrington WF8 147 C5
Horsforth LS18 41 C2
Ilkley LS29 8 C5
Keighley BD21 35 B4
Leeds LS6 205 C3
Lofthouse Gate WF3 121 F2
Otley LS21 22 F7
Pudsey LS28 76 E6
South Elmsall WF9 183 A4
Sutton-in-C BD20 16 D5
Ash Green Prim Sch HX2 91 C5
Ashgrove
Bradford, Apperley Bridge BD10 56 E7
Bradford BD7 74 D6
Bradford, Haigh Fold BD2 56 C3
Steeton BD20 17 D5
Ashgrove Ave 1 HX3 113 E3
Ashgrove Cres LS25 83 B3
Ashgrove Croft LS25 83 B2
Ash Grove Jun & Inf Sch WF9 183 A4
Ashgrove Mews LS13 57 F4
Ashgrove Mount LS25 83 A3
Ashgrove Pl 3 HX3 113 E3
Ashgrove Rd
Huddersfield HD2 136 F2
Keighley BD20 18 A2
Ash Grove Rd HD9 188 E5
Ash Grove Terr 6 HD6 115 A
Ash Hall La HX6 132 A
Ash Hill Dr LS17 44 F
Ash Hill Garth LS17 44 F
Ash Hill Gdns LS17 44 F
Ash Hill La LS17 44 F
Ash Hill Wlk BD4 75 B
Ash Ho LS15 80 E
Ashington Cl BD2 56 D
Ash La
Emley HD8 175 E
Garforth LS25 83 A
Ashlands Prim Sch LS29 8 C
Ashlands Rd LS29 8 C
Ashlar Cl BD22 51 D
Ashlar Gr
Castleford WF10 124 F
Queensbury BD13 92 D
Ash Lea
Fairburn WF11 105 B
Lofthouse Gate WF3 121 F
Ashlea Ave HD6 136 B
Ashlea Cl
Brighouse HD6 136 B
Garforth LS25 82 F
Ashlea Ct
Crigglestone WF2 160 C
Leeds LS13 58 C
Ashlea Dr HD6 136 B
Ashlea Gate LS13 58 C
Ashlea Gn LS13 58 C
Ashleigh S72 181 A
Ashleigh Ave
Pontefract WF8 146 D
Wakefield WF2 141 E
Ashleigh Cl HD8 173 F
Ashleigh Dale HD2 135 E
Ashleigh Gdns
Ossett WF5 140 C
Rothwell LS26 101 C
Ashleigh Rd LS16 59 A
Ashleigh St BD21 35 C
Ashley Ave LS9 208 A2
Ashley Cl
Cleckheaton BD19 96 A2
Wakefield WF2 120 F2
Ashley Croft 2 S71 179 B4
Ashley Ct WF9 181 F1
Ashley Gr HX7 89 E1
Ashley Ho OL14 108 A6
Ashley Ind Est
Huddersfield HD2 137 A4
Leeds LS7 206 C3
Ossett WF5 140 E7
Ashley La BD17 55 B8
Ashley Park Mews LS25 83 B8
Ashley Rd
Bingley BD16 37 A2
Bradford BD12 94 C2
Leeds LS9 208 A2
Leeds, Upper Wortley LS12 209 B2
Ashley St
Halifax HX1 202 B3
Shipley BD17 55 B8
Ashley Terr LS9 208 A2
Ashley Villas 11 HX7 89 A4
Ashmead
Batley WF17 118 A3
Clifford LS23 30 D5
Ash Meadow Cl HD2 136 C3
Ashmere Gr HD2 136 C2
Ashmews BD10 56 E7
Ashmore Dr WF5 119 C1
Ashmore Gdns BD4 95 B8
Ashmount BD14 73 D4
Ash Mount
Bradford BD7 74 B5
Keighley BD21 35 A5
Shafton S72 180 C3
Ashmount Ind Est WF9 163 B2
Ashmount Mews BD22 51 C7
Ash Rd
Leeds LS6 59 C5
Shafton S72 180 D2
Ashroyd LS26 100 F4
Ash St
Cleckheaton BD19 116 C7
Crofton WF4 162 A7
Glusburn BD20 16 D6
8 Haworth BD22 51 D7
Huddersfield HD1 154 A8
Ilkley LS29 8 C5
Lofthouse Gate WF3 121 F2
Oxenhope BD22 51 C3
Ash Terr
Bingley BD16 36 F2
Garforth LS25 83 A8
2 Leeds LS6 59 D5
Ripponden HX6 132 C3
Ashtofts Mount LS20 22 E1
Ashton Ave
Bradford BD7 73 E5
Leeds LS8 207 C3
Ashton Clough Rd WF15 117 A4
Ashton Cres WF3 100 D3
Ashton Ct
Crigglestone WF2 160 C4
Leeds LS8 208 A3
Ashton Gr LS8 207 C2
Ashton Ho 4 BD5 201 B1
Ashton Mount LS8 208 A2
Ashton Pl LS8 207 C2
Ashton Rd
Castleford WF10 124 D6
Leeds LS8 208 A3
Mytholmroyd HX7 89 E1
Ashton Road Ind Est LS8 208 A3

shton St
Bradford BD1 74 D7
Castleford WF10 124 D7
Leeds LS8 207 C3
shton Terr LS8 207 C2
shton View LS8 207 C2
shton Wlk BD10 56 A7
sh Tree App LS14 62 D4
sh Tree Ave BD13 72 B6
sh Tree Bank LS14 62 D5
sh Tree Cl LS14 62 D5
sh Tree Ct 2 LS14 62 D5
sh Tree Fold WF8 147 D4
sh Tree Gdns
Halifax HX2 91 C5
Leeds LS14 62 D5
Normanton WF6 122 F3
shtree Gr BD7 73 F3
sh Tree Gr
Kippax LS25 83 B1
Leeds LS14 62 D5
sh Tree Pk LS25 83 B1
sh Tree Rd HX2 91 C5
sh Tree View 4 LS14 62 D5
shtree Way WF10 125 F7
sh Tree Wlk
Burley in W LS29 9 E1
5 Leeds LS14 62 D5
sh View
East Ardsley WF3 120 C7
3 Leeds LS6 59 D5
shville Ave LS6 205 B3
shville Croft 4 HX2 112 D8
shville Gdns HX2 112 D8
shville Gr
Halifax HX2 91 D1
Leeds LS6 205 A3
shville Rd LS4, LS6 205 A3
shville St 19 HX3 92 A1
shville Terr
Glusburn BD20 16 D6
Leeds LS6 205 A3
Oakworth BD22 34 D3
18 Pudsey LS28 57 D2
shville View LS6 205 B2
shway LS23 15 C1
shwell Cl S72 180 C3
shwell La BD9 55 A4
shwell Rd
Bradford BD8 55 B1
Shipley BD9 55 A4
shwell St 8 BD8 55 B1
sh Wlk HD7 152 E5
shwood LS14 45 B1
shwood Cl HD2 136 C3
shwood Ct
Normanton WF6 123 B2
Ossett WF5 119 C1
shwood Dr
Gildersome LS27 97 C7
Keighley BD20 19 A1
shwood Gdns LS27 97 B7
shwood Gr
Gildersome LS27 97 C7
Horbury WF4 141 C2
shwood Grange WF4 159 E6
shwood Hts WF4 158 B7
shwood Par LS27 97 B7
shwood St BD4 75 D1
shwood Terr LS6 205 C4
shwood Villas LS6 205 C4
shworth Cl WF13 139 C8
shworth Gdns WF13 139 C8
shworth Gn WF13 139 C8
shworth Pl BD6 74 D1
shworth Rd
Dewsbury WF13 139 C8
Pontefract WF8 125 E3
shworth Sq WF1 216 C4
shworth St 15 OL13 106 A3
skam Ave WF8 125 F4
sket Ave LS14 61 F5
sket Cl LS14 61 E6
sket Cres LS14 61 E5
sket Dr LS14 61 E6
sket Garth LS14 61 E5
sket Gdns LS8 61 D6
sket Gn LS14 61 E6
sket Hill LS8 61 D6
sket Pl LS14 61 E5
sket Wlk LS14 61 E5
skey Ave LS27 98 B2
skey Cres LS27 98 B2
skham Gr WF9 183 E7
skham Rd WF10 104 D1
skrigg Dr 6 BD2 56 B3
skwith La LS21 10 A6
skwith Prim Sch LS21 9 F5
spden St OL14 108 B6
spect 14 LS2 206 C1
spect Gdns LS28 76 D8
spect Terr LS28 76 C8
spen Cl
Keighley BD21 35 E5
Wakefield WF2 142 A8
spen Ct
Emley HD8 175 C7
Morley WF3 98 C1
spen Gr
Dewsbury WF13 139 B8
Northowram HX3 93 A4
spen Mount LS16 41 E2
spen Rise BD15 53 F4
spen Way WF10 124 F4
spinall St
Halifax HX1 202 B2
Mytholmroyd HX7 89 E1
spley Bsns Pk HD1 154 C6
Aspley Pl HD1 154 B6
Aspley Villas 10 BD8 55 C1
Asprey Dr BD15 73 B8
Asquith Ave LS27 97 F6
Asquith Bldgs BD12 94 F5
Asquith Cl LS27 97 F5
Asquith Dr LS27 97 F5
Asquith Prim Sch LS27 97 F6
Asquith St WF17 97 B2
Asquith Terr 6 HX6 112 B3
Assembly St
6 Leeds LS2 211 C3
Normanton WF6 123 A2
Asthall Cl 16 BD21 35 B7
Astley Ave LS26 82 A1
Astley La LS26 102 C8
Astley Lane Ind Est LS26 102 B8
Astley Way LS26 102 B8
Aston Ave LS13 58 E2
Aston Chase WF9 181 D6
Aston Cl WF15 116 F2
Aston Court Bsns Pk LS13 58 E2
Aston Cres LS13 58 E2
Aston Ct WF5 141 A4
Aston Dr LS13 58 E2
Aston Gr LS13 58 E2
Aston Mount LS13 58 E2
Aston Pl LS13 58 E2
Aston Rd
Bradford BD5 74 E3
Leeds LS13 58 D2
Aston St LS13 58 D2
Aston Terr LS13 58 E2
Aston View LS13 58 E2
Astor Gr LS13 58 A2
Astoria Ct WF6 123 E1
Astor St LS13 58 A2
Astra Bsns Pk LS11 214 C2
Astral Ave HX3 114 D8
Astral Cl HX3 114 D8
Astral View BD6 74 A2
Astronomy Ctr The★
OL14 106 F4
Astura Ct LS7 60 B5
Astwick Cl BD20 19 A1
Atalanta Terr HX2 112 E4
Atha Cl LS11 214 A1
Atha Cres LS11 214 A1
Atha Ho LS2 206 C2
Atha St LS11 214 A1
Athelstan La LS21 11 A1
Athene Dr HD4 154 C3
Atherstone Rd BD15 73 B7
Atherton La HD6 136 B8
Athlone Dr WF12 118 E2
Athlone Gr LS12 209 C3
Athlone Rise LS25 83 B7
Athlone St LS12 209 C3
Athlone Terr LS12 209 C3
Athol Cl HX3 92 A3
Athol Cres HX3 92 A3
Athold Dr WF5 140 F5
Athold St WF5 140 F5
Athol Gdns HX3 92 A3
Athol Gn HX3 92 A3
Athol Rd
Bradford BD9 55 B2
Halifax HX3 92 A3
Athol St
Halifax HX3 92 A3
15 Keighley BD21 18 E1
Atkinson Ct WF6 123 A1
Atkinson La WF8 125 F2
Atkinson St
Leeds LS10 212 B1
3 Shipley BD18 55 B8
Atlanta St LS13 58 A2
Atlantic Apartments LS1 211 B3
Atlas Com Prim Sch BD8 74 C8
Atlas Mill Cvn Pk HD6 115 A2
Atlas Mill Rd HD6 115 A2
Atlas St BD8 55 B1
Attlee Ave WF4 162 C1
Attlee Cres WF2 160 E8
Attlee Gr WF1 121 C4
Attlee St WF6 144 B8
Attorney Ct HD9 189 B3
Auckland Rd BD6 74 A1
Audby Cl LS22 13 F6
Audby Ct LS22 13 F6
Audby La LS22 13 F6
Audrey St WF5 140 E4
Audsley's Yd WF4 140 E1
Augusta Ct WF2 141 F5
Augusta Dr WF6 144 D8
Aurelia Ho BD8 55 C2
Austhorpe Ave LS15 81 E7
Austhorpe Ct LS15 81 E7
Austhorpe Dr LS15 81 E7
Austhorpe Gdns LS15 81 F8
Austhorpe Gr LS15 81 E8
Austhorpe La LS15 62 D1
Austhorpe Prim Sch LS15 81 E8
Austhorpe Rd LS15 62 D2
Austhorpe View LS15 81 D8
Austin Ave HD6 114 F4
Austin Rd WF10 125 D8
Austin St 18 BD21 35 D8
Austwick Cl S75 178 A2
Authorpe Rd LS6 59 F6
Autumn Ave
Leeds LS6 205 B2
Wetherby LS22 13 E8
Autumn Cres LS18 58 D7
Autumn Gr LS6 205 B2
Autumn Pl LS6 205 B2
Autumn St
3 Halifax HX1 202 B1
Autumn St *continued*
Leeds LS6 205 B2
Autumn Terr 17 LS6 205 B2
Auty Cres WF3 121 F5
Auty Mews WF3 121 F5
Auty Sq 2 LS27 98 B3
Avalon Rise WF9 183 A2
Avenel Rd BD15 73 B8
Avenel Terr BD15 73 B8
Avenham Way BD3 201 D4
Avens Cl WF8 146 D7
Avenue A LS23 15 B3
Avenue B LS23 15 B1
Avenue C E LS23 15 C2
Avenue Cres LS8 207 C4
Avenue C W LS23 15 C2
Avenue D LS23 15 B1
Avenue Des Hirondelles
LS21 24 D6
Avenue E E LS23 15 C1
Avenue E W LS23 31 B8
Avenue F LS23 15 D1
Avenue Gdns LS17 43 A5
Avenue Hill LS8 207 C4
Avenue Lawns LS17 42 F5
Avenue No 2 HD6 115 A1
Avenue Rd
Bradford BD5 74 F3
Wakefield WF2 142 E1
Avenue St BD4 75 D1
Avenue Terr
Otley LS21 22 F7
Pontefract WF8 146 A8
Yeadon LS19 40 D7
Avenue The
Barwick in E LS15 62 F8
Batley, Birstall WF17 96 E1
Batley, Carlinghow WF17 118 A7
Batley WF17 117 F3
Bradford BD14 73 B4
Brighouse HX3 114 D8
Collingham LS22 13 A1
Crofton WF4 143 E1
East Ardsley WF3 120 A8
Guiseley BD10, BD17 39 E2
Harewood LS17 27 A6
Horsforth LS18 40 F1
4 Huddersfield HD5 154 D5
Leeds, Alwoodley LS17 43 A5
Leeds, Bank LS9 212 B3
Leeds, Colton LS15, LS26 81 E4
Leeds, Gledhow LS8 61 A8
Leeds, Manston LS15 62 D3
Leeds, Park Villas LS8 44 A1
Lofthouse Gate WF1 121 B4
Meltham HD9 188 B8
Royston S71 179 E4
Shipley BD16 54 B8
Wilsden BD15 53 D4
Avenue Victoria LS8 61 A8
Averingcliffe Rd BD10 56 D6
Avery Tulip Ct 2 BD12 94 C6
Aviary Gr LS12 209 C4
Aviary Mount LS12 209 C4
Aviary Pl LS12 209 C4
Aviary Rd LS12 209 C4
Aviary Row LS12 209 C4
Aviary St LS12 209 C4
Aviary Terr LS12 209 C4
Aviary View LS12 209 C4
Avison Rd HD4 153 A3
Avison Yd WF1 216 C2
Avocet Cl BD8 73 C7
Avocet Garth 4 LS10 99 D5
Avon Cl LS17 44 F4
Avon Croft WF5 140 C5
Avon Ct LS17 44 E5
Avondale BD20 35 A8
Avondale Cres BD18 55 A7
Avondale Ct LS17 43 D3
Avondale Dr
Barnsley S71 179 C1
Lofthouse Gate WF3 121 E5
Avondale Gr 2 BD18 55 A7
Avondale Mount BD18 55 A7
Avondale Pl 8 HX3 113 B4
Avondale Rd BD18 54 F7
Avondale St
Leeds LS13 58 C1
Wakefield WF2 142 C4
Avondale Villas LS14 45 E3
Avondale Way WF2 142 C4
Avon Dr LS25 82 F6
Avon Garth LS22 13 C5
Avon Wlk WF7 145 C7
Axis Ct LS27 97 E5
Axminster Dr BD19 115 B7
Aydon Way HX3 93 E7
Aygill Ave BD9 54 D3
Aylesbury St 8 BD21 35 A4
Aylesford Mount LS15 62 F3
Aylesham Ind Est BD12 94 D6
Aynholme Cl LS29 6 F8
Aynholme Dr LS29 7 A8
Aynsley Gr BD15 54 B1
Ayres Dr HD4 153 A3
Ayresome Ave LS8 44 A2
Ayresome Oval BD15 73 A7
Ayresome Terr LS8 43 F2
Ayre View HX7 89 B6
Ayreville Dr HX3 93 C6
Ayrton Cres 21 BD16 37 A3
Aysgarth Ave HX3 115 A6
Aysgarth Cl
Bradford BD12 94 C2
Leeds LS9 212 C3
Wakefield WF2 141 D3
Aysgarth Cres HX2 91 A3
Aysgarth Dr
Leeds LS9 212 C3
Wakefield WF2 141 D3
Aysgarth Fold LS10 99 C4
Aysgarth Pl LS9 212 C3
Aysgarth Rd
Batley WF17 118 A5
Huddersfield HD4 154 B2
Aysgarth Wlk LS9 212 C3
Ayton Cl BD3 75 A8
Ayton Ho 4 BD4 75 F1
Ayton Rd HD3 152 E6
Azealea Ct BD3 75 B8

B

Baby House Hill La HX7 69 A4
Bachelor La LS18 41 C2
Back Acres St 8 BD21 35 B6
Back Ada St 10 BD21 35 A7
Back Aireview Terr BD21 35 E6
Back Aireville St BD20 18 A2
Back Airlie Pl LS8 207 C4
Back Albert Gr LS6 59 D6
Back Albert Terr LS6 205 B2
Back Alcester Pl 16 LS8 207 C4
Back Alcester Rd 14 LS8 207 C4
Back Alcester Terr 15
LS8 207 C4
Back Allerton Terr LS7 204 A3
Back Alma St 6 LS19 40 C7
Back Anderton St WF1 142 E3
Back Ann St BD13 52 E1
Back Archery Pl 8 LS2 206 B2
Back Archery Rd 14 LS2 206 B2
Back Archery St 12 LS2 206 B2
Back Archery Terr 10
LS2 206 B2
Back Armitage Rd HD4 171 E8
Back Ash Gr LS6 205 C3
Back Ashgrove (W) BD7 74 D6
Back Ashley Ave LS9 208 A2
Back Ashley St LS9 208 A2
Back Ash View 4 LS6 59 D5
Back Ashville Ave LS6 205 B3
Back Ashville Gr LS6 205 B3
Back Ashville Rd LS6 205 A3
Back Ashville Terr LS6 205 A3
Back Ashwood Terr LS6 205 C4
Back Aston Pl 1 LS13 58 E2
Back Aston Rd LS13 58 D2
Back Aston St LS13 58 D2
Back Aston Terr 2 LS13 58 E2
Back Aston View 3 LS13 58 E2
Back Athlone Ave 1
LS12 209 C3
Back Athlone Gr 2 LS12 209 C3
Back Athlone Terr 3
LS12 209 C3
Back Atlanta St LS13 58 A2
Back Austhorpe La 4
LS15 62 D2
Back Austhorpe Rd LS15 62 C2
Back Autumn Rd 19 LS6 205 B2
Back Autumn Terr 16
LS6 205 B2
Back Aviary Rd 1 LS12 209 C4
Back Aylesbury St 4
BD21 35 A4
Back Baker St BD18 55 A8
Back Baldovan Terr 6
LS8 207 C4
Back Balfour St
Bingley BD16 36 F2
5 Keighley BD21 35 B6
Back Bank St WF10 124 D8
Back Bank Terr 7 LS28 57 E2
Back Banstead St LS8 207 C3
Back Barden Pl LS12 209 A3
Back Barkly Gr LS11 214 A2
Back Barkly Par 3 LS11 214 A1
Back Barkly Terr 5
LS11 214 A2
Back Barrowby View LS15 81 F7
Back Bath Rd 15 LS13 58 C2
Back Beacon St HD2 136 A1
Back Beamsley Gr 9
LS6 205 B2
Back Beamsley Mount 4
LS6 205 B2
Back Beamsley Terr 2
LS6 205 B2
Back Beaumont St WF17 118 C3
Back Beck La LS29 6 F8
Back Beech St BD16 36 F2
Back Beech Terr HD1 136 B1
Back Beechwood Gr 7
LS4 205 A3
Back Beechwood Rd 9
LS4 205 A3
Back Bellbrooke Gr LS9 208 B2
Back Bellbrooke Pl LS9 208 B2
Back Bellbrooke Terr
LS9 208 B2
Back Belvedere Ave
LS11 214 B2
Back Belvedere Mount
LS11 214 B2
Back Bentley Ave 3 LS6 59 F6
Back Bentley Gr LS6 59 F6
Back Berkeley Ave LS8 208 A3
Back Berkeley Terr LS8 208 A3
Back Beverley Terr LS11 214 B3
Back Blackwood Gr HX1 202 B4
Back Blandford Gdns 22
LS2 206 B2
Back Blandford Gr 24
LS2 206 B2
Back Blenheim Ave 7
LS2 206 B2
Back Blenheim Mount 3
BD8 55 C2
Back Blenheim Terr LS2 206 B2
Back Boundary Terr LS3 205 B1
Back Bower Rd 1 HX5 135 A7
Back Bowling Green Rd
HX4 133 F3
Back Bowman St WF1 142 F3
Back Bradshaw Rd HD9 171 F3
Back Branch Pl 12 LS12 78 A4
Back Breary Ave LS18 41 D1
Back Breary Terr LS18 41 D1
Back Briggate 7 BD20 5 E2
Back Bright St 6 LS28 57 F2
Back Broad La LS13 58 D4
Back Broomfield Cres
LS6 205 A4
Back Broomfield Pl 4
LS6 205 A3
Back Broomfield Rd
5 Keighley BD21 35 B7
Leeds LS4 205 A3
Back Broomfield St 6
BD21 35 B7
Back Broughton Ave
LS9 208 A2
Back Broughton Terr
LS9 208 A2
Back Brudenell Gr LS6 205 C3
Back Brudenell Mount
LS6 205 B3
Back Brudenell Rd LS6 205 B3
Back Brunswick St
Dewsbury WF13 118 A1
Leeds LS2 206 C1
Back Burchett Gr LS6 206 A4
Back Burchett Pl LS6 206 A4
Back Burley Hill LS4 205 A2
Back Burley Lodge Rd
LS6 205 B1
Back Burley Lodge Terr
LS6 205 B1
Back Burley St 3 LS3 211 A4
Back Burlington Pl 22
LS11 214 B2
Back Burlington Rd
LS11 214 B2
Back Burton Cres 6 LS6 59 D6
Back Burton Terr LS11 214 C3
Back Buxton St 4 BD21 35 D7
Back Byrl St BD21 18 C1
Back Byrom St 10 OL14 108 B6
Back Caister St 4 BD21 35 B4
Back Caledonia Rd 2
BD21 35 D8
Back Camberley St 9
LS11 214 C3
Back Carberry Pl 20 LS6 205 B2
Back Carberry Rd 26
LS6 205 B2
Back Carberry Terr 22
LS6 205 B2
Back Carlinghow La
WF17 117 E7
Back Carter Mount LS15 81 C8
Back Carter Terr 4 LS15 62 C1
Back Cartmel Rd 12 BD21 35 A7
Back Castle Rd BD21 35 B8
Back Cautley Rd LS9 212 C2
Back Cavendish Rd BD10 56 B7
Back Cavendish St BD21 35 C7
Back Cavendish Terr 12
HX1 202 C3
Back Cecil St 8 HD1 154 A6
Back Chapel La LS6 205 A4
Back Chapel St BD1 201 C3
Back Chapeltown Rd
LS7 204 A1
Back Charles St 10 HD6 115 A3
Back Charlton Rd LS9 80 A7
Back Chatsworth Rd LS8 208 A3
Back Chestnut Ave
2 Leeds, Cross Gates
LS15 62 D2
Leeds, Hyde Park LS6 205 C3
Back Chiswick Terr 24
LS6 205 B2
Back Christ Church View
LS12 209 B4
Back Churchill Gdns 26
LS2 206 B2
Back Church La
Leeds, Adel LS16 42 D5
Leeds, Kirkstall LS5 59 A4
Back Church View WF1 142 F2
Back Claremont Ave 8
LS2 206 A1
Back Claremont Gr 6
LS3 206 A1
Back Claremont St 9
LS26 101 C6
Back Claremont Terr 11
LS3 206 A1
Back Clarence Rd 9 LS18 58 B7
Back Clarence St HX1 203 A3
Back Clarendon Pl HX1 202 C2
Back Clarkson View 12
LS6 206 A4
Back Cliff Mount LS6 206 A4
Back Clifton Rd HD1 153 E7
Back Clifton Terr LS9 208 B2

Back Clipston Ave LS6 . . . . 59 F6
Back Clock View St BD20 . 18 B2
Back Clough HX3 . . . . 93 A2
Back Clovelly Pl 18 LS11. 214 B3
Back Coldcotes Ave LS9 . 208 B2
Back Colenso Mount
  LS11 . . . . 213 C4
Back Colenso Rd
  9 Keighley BD21 . . . . . 18 E1
  Leeds LS11 . . . . 213 C4
Back Colne Rd BD20 . . . . . 16 D6
Back Colton Rd LS12 . . . . 209 C3
Back Colwyn Pl 20 LS11. 214 B3
Back Colwyn View 11
  LS11 . . . . 214 B2
Back Commercial St 15
  HX1 . . . . 203 B3
Back Commerical St 16
  OL14 . . . . 108 C5
Back Compton St 11
  BD21 . . . . 35 D8
Back Conway St LS8 . . . . 207 C4
Back Cowper Gr LS8 . . . . 208 A3
Back Cowper St LS7 . . . . 207 B3
Back Craggwood Rd 6
  LS18 . . . . 58 C7
Back Crag Rd BD18 . . . . . 55 C7
Back Cranbrook Ave
  . . . . 214 A3
Back Cranbrook Terr
  LS11 . . . . 214 A3
Back Croft HX6 . . . . 132 C1
Back Croft House La
  BD20 . . . . 18 A2
Back Cromer Ave 16 BD21 35 B5
Back Cromer Gr 1 BD21 . 35 B4
Back Cromer Terr LS2. . 206 A2
Back Cromwell Terr 2
  HX1 . . . . 203 A3
Back Cross Flatts Ave
  LS11 . . . . 214 A2
Back Cross Flatts Cres
  LS11 . . . . 213 C2
Back Cross Flatts Gr 3
  LS11 . . . . 214 A2
Back Cross Flatts Mount 4
  LS11 . . . . 214 A2
Back Cross Flatts Pl
  LS11 . . . . 213 C2
Back Crossflatts Row
  LS11 . . . . 213 C2
Back Cross Green Cres
  LS9. . . . . 212 C2
Back Cross Green La 18
  LS9. . . . . 212 C2
Back Cross La HX5 . . . . . 134 E6
Back Crossland Terr 1
  LS11 . . . . 214 C3
Back Cunliffe Rd 5 LS29 . .8 B4
Back Dalton Ave LS11 . . . 214 A1
Back Dalton Gr LS11 . . . . 214 A2
Back Dalton Rd LS11 . . . . 214 A1
Back Dawlish Ave 3 LS9. 80 B8
Back Dawlish Mount 2
  LS9. . . . . 80 B8
Back Dawlish Rd 4 LS9. . 80 B8
Back De Lacy Mount LS5 . 59 A5
Back Delph Mount LS6. . 206 A4
Back Dent St LS9 . . . . . . 212 C3
Back Der St 7 OL14. . . . 108 C5
Back Devonshire La LS8. . 44 A2
Back Dorset Mount 4
  LS8. . . . . 208 A4
Back Dorset Rd 3 LS8 . . 208 A4
Back Dorset Terr LS8 . . . 208 A3
Back Dudley Hill Rd 1
  BD2 . . . . 56 B2
Back Dudwell Terr HX3 . 113 C2
Back Duke of York St
  WF1. . . . . 216 C3
Back Duke St WF7 . . . . . 145 C6
Back Dunbar St 1 . . . . . 142 F4
Back East Park Rd 9 LS9. 80 A7
Back Eaton St 2 BD21 . . 35 A4
Back Ecclesburn Gr 1
  LS9. . . . . 80 B7
Back Ecclesburn St LS9. . 80 A7
Back Edensor Rd 9 BD21 35 A7
Back Edinburgh Rd LS12 209 A4
Back Eldon Rd HD1 . . . . 153 D7
Back Elford Pl LS8 . . . . . 207 C3
Back Elizabeth St BD5. . 201 B1
Back Ellers Gr LS8 . . . . . 207 C4
Back Ellers Rd 8 LS8 . . . 207 C4
Back Elmfield Terr HX1 . 203 A1
Back Elsworth St LS12 . 210 A3
Back Emily St
  10 Keighley BD21 . . . . 35 C8
  18 Keighley BD21 . . . . 35 D8
Back Eric St
  Keighley BD21 . . . . 35 C8
  Leeds LS13 . . . . 58 C5
Back Eshald Pl LS26. . . . 101 D6
Back Esmond Terr LS12 209 C4
Back Estcourt Ave LS6 . . 59 C4
Back Estcourt Terr LS6. . 59 C4
Back Eversley Mount
  HX2 . . . . 202 A4
Back Fairford Pl LS11 . 214 C3
Back Featherbank Terr 2
  LS18. . . . . 58 C7
Back Ferguson St
  HX1 . . . . 203 B2
Back Field BD13 . . . . 72 D6
Back Fitzwilliam St HD1. 153 F6

Back Florist St 8 BD21. . . 18 E1
Back Fold BD14 . . . . 73 B5
Back Foster Rd 2 BD21. . 35 B4
Back Foundry Mill Dr LS8 61 E4
Back Garden St
  Castleford WF10 . . . . 124 D6
  Wakefield WF1 . . . . 216 A2
Back Garton Rd LS9. . . . . . 80 A7
Back Garton Terr LS9 . . . . 80 A7
Back Gathorne St LS8 . . 207 B3
Back Gerrard St HX1 . . . 203 A3
Back Giles St N BD5. . . . 201 B1
Back Giles St S BD5. . . . 201 B1
Back Gillett La LS26. . . . 100 F5
Back Girlington Rd BD8 . 54 F1
Back Gladstone St
  Bingley BD16 . . . . 36 F2
  5 Dewsbury WF13 . . . 118 A1
Back Glebe Terr LS16 . . . 59 D7
Back Glen Terr HX1 . . . . 203 A1
Back Glenthorpe Mount
  LS9. . . . . 80 A8
Back Glenthorpe Terr 2
  LS9. . . . . 80 A8
Back Glossop St LS6 . . . 206 B4
Back Gn
  Elland HD3. . . . . 152 A6
  Morley LS27. . . . . 98 C7
Back Gooder La 1 HD6 . 115 B1
Back Gordon St WF1 . . . 142 F2
Back Gordon Terr LS6. . . 59 F6
Back Graham Gr LS4 . . . 205 A3
Back Granby Gr LS6. . . . 205 A4
Back Grange Ave LS7 . . 207 B4
Back Grange Cres LS7. . 207 B4
Back Grange Terr LS7. . 207 B4
Back Grange View LS7. . 207 B4
Back Grantley St WF1 . 216 C2
Back Grant St BD21 . . . . 35 A7
Back Granville Terr LS20. 22 F2
Back Graveley St 6 LS6. 81 A8
Back Great Russell St
  BD7 . . . . 74 C7
Back Greaves St BD5. . . . 74 D3
Back Greenhead Rd 2
  HD1 . . . . 154 A6
Back Greenhow Wlk LS4 205 A2
Back Greenmount Terr
  LS11 . . . . 214 B3
Back Greenwood Mount 4
  LS6. . . . . 59 E7
Back Grimthorpe St 5
  LS6. . . . . 59 C5
Back Grosvenor Terr
  Halifax HX1 . . . . 202 C3
  Leeds LS6 . . . . 205 C4
Back Grouse St BD21. . . . 35 D8
Back Grove Gdns LS6 . . . 59 E6
Back Grovehall Ave
  LS11 . . . . 214 A1
Back Grovehall Dr LS11 214 A1
Back Grove Rd 6 LS29 . . .8 B4
Back Haigh Ave LS26. . . 100 C7
Back Haigh St LS26 . . . . 100 C7
Back Haigh View LS26. . 100 C7
Back Halliday Gr LS12. . 209 A4
Back Halliday Pl LS12 . . 209 A4
Back Hambleton St WF1. 216 B3
Back Hamilton Ave LS7. 207 B4
Back Hamilton View LS7 207 B4
Back Harehills Ave LS7. 207 B4
Back Harehills Park View
  LS9. . . . . 208 B2
Back Harehills Pl 7 LS8. 207 C4
Back Hares Ave 11 LS8 . 207 C4
Back Hares Mount LS8 . 207 C4
Back Hares Terr 10 LS8. 207 C4
Back Hares View LS8. . . 207 C4
Back Harold Gr LS6 . . . . 205 B2
Back Hartley Ave LS6 . . 206 B4
Back Hartley Gr 5 LS6. . 206 A4
Back Hartley St LS27. . . . 98 C3
Back Hatfeild St WF1 . . 216 B3
Back Hawksworth Gr LS5. 58 D6
Back Headingley Ave LS6. 59 C5
Back Headingley Mount
  LS6. . . . . 59 C5
Back Heathfield Terr 5
  LS6. . . . . 59 D6
Back Heddon Pl LS6 . . . . 59 E6
Back Heddon St LS6 . . . . 59 E6
Back Heights Rd BD13. . . 72 B8
Back Henrietta St 3
  WF17 . . . . 118 C5
Back Hessle Ave LS6. . . 205 B3
Back Hessle Mount LS6 . 205 B3
Back Hessle Terr LS6 . . 205 B3
Back Hessle View LS6. . 205 B3
Back Heston Rd 9 LS29. . .8 B4
Back Highbury Terr LS6. 59 E6
Back Highfield Rd 4
  LS13. . . . . 58 E2
Back High St
  12 Thornton BD13. . . . 72 D6
  Yeadon LS19 . . . . 40 B7
Back Highthgorne View 1
  LS12. . . . . 209 B4
Back Highthorne Gr 4
  LS12. . . . . 209 A4
Back Highthorne St
  LS12. . . . . 209 A4
Back Hillcrest Ave LS7 . 207 B4
Back Hillcrest View LS7. 207 B4
Back Hill Top Ave LS8. . 207 C4
Back Hill Top Mount
  LS8. . . . . 207 C4
Back Hilton Gr 1 LS8 . . 207 C4
Back Hilton Pl LS8 . . . . 207 C4

Back Hilton Rd LS8 . . . . . 207 C4
Back Hird St 7 BD21. . . . 35 B6
Backhold Ave HX3 . . . . . 113 E2
Backhold Dr HX3 . . . . . . 113 E2
Backhold Hall HX3 . . . . . 113 E3
Backhold La HX3. . . . . . . 113 D2
Backhold Rd HX3 . . . . . . 113 C2
Back Hollyshaw Terr 5
  LS15. . . . . 81 C8
Back Holywell La LS17 . . 44 D5
Back Honoria St HD1. . . . 136 A1
Back Hope Hall Terr 8
  HX1 . . . . 203 B2
Backhouse La WF4. . . . . 177 F7
Back Hovingham Mount 2
  LS8. . . . . 208 A4
Back Hovingham Terr 1
  LS8. . . . . 208 A4
Back Hume Rd LS12. . . . 209 B4
Back Hyde Gr 3 BD21. . . 35 D8
Back Hyde Terr LS2 . . . . 206 A1
Back Ibbetson Pl LS2 . . 206 B1
Back Ingledew Cres LS8. . 44 B2
Back Irwell St BD4 . . . . . . 75 A5
Back Ivy Ave 11 LS9 . . . . 80 A8
Back Ivy Gr 2 LS9 . . . . . . 80 B7
Back Ivy Mount 9 LS9 . . 80 A8
Back Ivy St 12 LS9. . . . . . 80 A8
Back John St BD13. . . . . . 72 D6
Back Karnac Rd LS8. . . . 207 C4
Back Kelso Rd LS2 . . . . . 205 C2
Back Kendal La 1 LS2 . . 206 A1
Back Kennerleigh Wlk 6
  LS15. . . . . 62 C1
Back Kensington St
  Bradford BD8. . . . . 55 A1
  Bradford, Brown Royd BD8 . 74 A8
Back Kensington Terr
  LS6. . . . . 205 C3
Back King's Ave 27 LS6. 205 B2
Back Kirby St BD21. . . . . 35 D8
Back Kirkgate BD18. . . . . 55 A7
Back Kitson St LS9 . . . . 212 C1
Back Knowle Mount 12
  LS4. . . . . 205 A3
Back Knowl Rd WF14. . . 137 F6
Back La
  Badsworth WF9 . . . . 164 E2
  Batley WF16 . . . . 117 D4
  Birkenshaw BD11 . . . . . . 96 F7
  Bradford BD10. . . . . 56 B8
  Bradford, Clayton Heights BD13,
    BD14. . . . . 73 B2
  Bramham LS23 . . . . 30 D3
  Burley in W LS29. . . . . . . .9 F1
  Clayton DN5. . . . . 194 C4
  Clayton West HD8 . . . . 176 A3
  Crofton WF4 . . . . 144 C2
  Dewsbury WF12 . . . . . . 138 F2
  Dewsbury, Whitley Lower
    WF12. . . . . 156 F7
  Emley HD8 . . . . 175 A5
  Gildersome LS12 . . . . . . 77 C3
  Grange Moor WF4 . . . . 156 E5
  Guiseley LS20 . . . . 39 D8
  Halifax HX2 . . . . 91 D5
  Haworth BD22 . . . . 50 C6
  Hebden Bridge HX7. . . . . 88 F1
  Heptonstall HX7 . . . . . . 88 F4
  Holmfirth HD9 . . . . 189 A5
  Hooton Pagnell DN5 . . . 195 D5
  Horsforth LS18 . . . . 58 B8
  Keighley, East Morton BD20 19 D1
  Kippax WF10 . . . . 103 B4
  Laycock BD20, BD22. . . . 34 B7
  Leeds LS13 . . . . 58 B7
  Lepton WF14 . . . . 156 B7
  Middlestown WF4 . . . . . 158 B7
  Mirfield WF14 . . . . 137 E5
  Ossett WF5 . . . . 140 D5
  Pudsey LS28 . . . . 57 D3
  Ripponden HX6 . . . . . . 132 D4
  Ryhill WF4 . . . . 162 B4
  Shelley HD8 . . . . 174 B3
  Shipley BD9 . . . . 55 A4
  Sicklinghall LS22 . . . . . . 12 C5
  Silsden BD20 . . . . .5 E2
  Skipton BD23 . . . . .4 C8
  South Elmsall WF9. . . . . 183 A6
  Thornton BD13 . . . . 72 E7
  Wadsworth Moor HX7. . . 69 A6
  Wakefield WF1 . . . . 216 A2
  Wilsden BD15 . . . . 53 D3
  Woolley WF4 . . . . 178 A6
  Yeadon LS19 . . . . 40 A6
Back Laisteridge La BD7 . 74 C6
Back Lake St LS10 . . . . . 215 A2
Back Lambton Gr 17 LS8 207 C4
Back Landseer Ave LS13. . 58 E3
Back Landseer Gr LS13. . 58 E3
Back Landseer Terr LS13. 58 E3
Back Lane W S71 . . . . . . 179 A4
Back Langdale Gdns LS6 . 59 C4
Back Langdale Terr LS6. . 59 C4
Back Lascelles Terr 1
  LS8. . . . . 207 C3
Back Laurel Mount LS7. 204 A1
Back Leatham St 3
  WF13. . . . . 118 A1
Back Leeming BD22. . . . . 51 D1
Back Lime St BD21. . . . . . 35 B8
Back Linden Gr 2 LS11 . 214 C3
Back Lindum St 2 BD8. . 55 C2
Back Lodge La 1 LS11 . 214 B2
Back Lombard St LS19 . . 40 A4
Back Longroyd Terr
  LS11 . . . . 214 C3

Back Lord St HX1 . . . . 203 A3
Back Low La LS18. . . . . . . 41 D1
Back Lucas St 4 LS6. . . . 206 A4
Back Lumbutts Rd OL14 . 108 A3
Back Lunan Pl LS8 . . . . . 207 C4
Back Lunan Terr LS8 . . . 207 C4
Back Lyon St BD13 . . . . . . 72 F1
Back Lytton St HX3 . . . . . 92 C1
Back Mafeking Ave LS11 214 A1
Back Mafeking Mount
  LS11 . . . . 214 A1
Back Malt St 7 BD22 . . . 35 A4
Back Mannville Rd 11
  BD21 . . . . 35 A6
Back Manor Dr LS6 . . . . 205 B4
Back Manor Gr LS7 . . . . 204 A2
Back Manor St 3 BD2. . . 56 B3
Back Manor Terr LS6. . . 205 B4
Back Market St 3 BD6. . . 74 C1
Back Markham Ave LS8 . 207 C4
Back Marlborough Gdns 18
  LS2. . . . . 206 B2
Back Marlborough Gr 20
  LS2. . . . . 206 B2
Back Marriot St 4
  WF13. . . . . 118 D1
Back Marshall Ave 3
  LS15. . . . . 62 D2
Back Marshall St 7 LS15. 62 C2
Back Marshall Terr 8
  LS15. . . . . 62 C2
Back Mary St
  East Ardsley WF3 . . . . . 120 E8
  Glusburn BD20 . . . . 16 D8
Back Masham St LS12. . 210 A3
Back Maud Ave LS11 . . . 214 B2
Back Mayville Ave LS6 . 205 B3
Back Mayville Pl 6 LS6. 205 B3
Back Mayville St LS6. . . 205 B3
Back Mayville Terr LS6. 205 B3
Back Meadow View 12
  LS6. . . . . 205 B3
Back Melbourne Gr 18
  LS13. . . . . 58 C2
Back Methley Dr LS7 . . 204 A2
Back Mexborough Ave
  LS7. . . . . 207 A4
Back Mexborough Dr
  LS7. . . . . 207 A4
Back Mexborough Gr
  LS7. . . . . 207 A4
Back Mexborough St
  LS7. . . . . 207 A4
Back Meynell Ave LS26. 100 E5
Back Middle Cross St
  LS12. . . . . 210 A3
Back Middleton Rd 2
  LS29. . . . . .8 A4
Back Middleton View 1
  LS11 . . . . 214 A1
Back Midland Rd LS6 . . 205 C3
Back Milan Ave LS8 . . . 207 C3
Back Milan Rd LS8 . . . . 207 C3
Back Milan St LS8 . . . . . 208 A3
Back Mill Hey BD22 . . . . 51 D7
Back Minnie St 10 BD21. 35 B6
Back Mitchell Terr BD16 . 36 F2
Back Mitford Rd LS12 . . 210 A3
Back Model Ave LS12 . . 210 A3
Back Model Rd LS12 . . . 210 A3
Back Model Terr LS12. . 210 A3
Back Model View LS12. 210 A3
Back Monk Bridge Dr 7
  LS6. . . . . 59 F6
Back Monk Bridge Pl 8
  LS6. . . . . 59 F6
Back Monk Bridge St LS6. 59 F6
Back Montague St WF1 . 142 F3
Back Montpelier Terr 2
  LS6. . . . . 206 A4
Back Moorfield St HX1 . 202 C1
Back Moorfield Terr
  LS12. . . . . 209 A4
Back Moor La HD4. . . . . 171 D7
Back Moorland Terr LS2 206 A2
Back Morning St 12 BD21. 35 B4
Back Morritt Dr LS15. . . 80 F8
Back Mount Ave 4
  WF17. . . . . 118 D3
Back Mount Pleasant
  Middleton LS10 . . . . 99 C5
  Wakefield WF1 . . . . 216 C2
Back Mount View LS6. . 205 C4
Back Muff St BD4 . . . . . . 75 B5
Back Myrtle Ave BD16. . . 36 F2
Back Myrtle Terr BD22. . 34 F1
Back Nansen St LS13. . . . 58 A2
Back Nelson Rd 13 LS29. . .8 A4
Back Nelson St WF13. . . 139 C8
Back Newport Gdns 2
  LS6. . . . . 205 A3
Back Newport Mount 1
  LS6. . . . . 205 A3
Back Newport Pl 5 LS6. 205 A3
Back New St
  Bradford BD12. . . . . 95 B5
  8 Brighouse HD6. . . . . 115 A3
Back Newton Gr LS7 . . . 207 B4
Back Newton La
  Ledsham WF10. . . . . 104 B5
  Ledston WF10 . . . . 103 E7
Back Nice View LS8. . . . 207 C4
Back Norfolk St WF17. . . 118 B4
Back Norman Mount 1
  LS5. . . . . 59 A4
Back Norman Pl LS8 . . . . 44 A2
Back Norman Terr LS8. . 44 A2
Back Northbrook St LS7. 204 A3

Back Northgate WF8 . . . . 125 C
Back North Park Ave
  LS8. . . . . 204 C
Back North St
  Bradford BD12. . . . . 95 A
  21 Todmorden OL14 . . . 108 B
Back Norwood Gr LS6. . . 205 E
Back Norwood Pl 2 LS6 205 E
Back Norwood Rd 1
  LS6. . . . . 205 E
Back Norwood Terr LS6 . 205 E
Back Nowell Cres LS8 . . 208 E
Back Nowell Mount LS9. 208 E
Back Nowell Pl LS9 . . . . 208 E
Back Nowell Terr LS9 . . 208 E
Back Nunington St LS12. 210 A
Back Nunington View 3
  LS12. . . . . 59 C
Back Nunroyd Rd 2 LS17 43 C
Back Nursery Mount
  LS10. . . . . 215 B
Back O' Dam HD7. . . . . . 170 A
Back o' Th' Height HX6. . 131 C
Back O'Wall HD7. . . . . . . 151 B
Back Oak Ave BD16 . . . . . 36 F
Back Oakfield Terr LS6. . 59 F
Back Oakley St WF3. . . . . 99 F
Back Oakley Terr LS11 . 214 C
Back Oak Rd LS7. . . . . . 204 A
Back Oakwood Ave LS8 . 61 E
Back Oakwood Dr LS8. . . 61 E
Back Osmondthorpe La
  LS9. . . . . 80 C
Back Otterburn St 2
  BD21 . . . . 35 B
Back Outwood La 5 LS18 58 C
Back Overdale Terr 5
  LS15. . . . . 81 A
Back Oxford Pl LS1 . . . . 211 E
Back Oxford St
  East Ardsley WF3 . . . . . 120 E
  7 Keighley BD21 . . . . . 35 A
Back Paget St 7 BD21 . . 35 A
Back Parish Ghyll Rd LS29. .8 D
Back Park Cres LS8 . . . . . 44 B
Back Parkfield Pl LS11 . 214 A
Back Parkfield Rd LS11 . 214 A
Back Park Terr HX1 . . . . 202 C
Back Park View LS11 . . 214 A
Back Park View Ave LS4. 205 A
Back Parnaby Ave LS10. 215 C
Back Parnaby St LS10. . 215 C
Back Parnaby Terr LS10. 215 C
Back Pasture Gr LS7 . . . 204 A
Back Pasture Rd LS8. . . 207 C
Back Pawson St WF3. . . 120 E
Back Pearson Terr 15
  LS6. . . . . 205 B
Back Pleasant St HX6 . . 112 C
Back Pollard La LS13. . . . 58 C
Back Pollard St HD2 . . . . 136 B
Back Poplar Ave 1 LS15. 62 D
Back Poplar Terr S71 . . . 179 B
Back Potternewton La
  LS7. . . . . 60 C
Back Potters St LS7. . . . 204 A
Back Prospect Pl BD18 . 35 B
Back Prospect Terr LS9. 212 C
Back Providence Ave 13
  LS6. . . . . 206 A
Back Providence St 4
  WF17. . . . . 118 C
Back Purlwell Hall Rd
  WF17. . . . . 118 C
Back Purlwell La WF17 . 118 C
Back Quarry Mount Terr 11
  LS6. . . . . 206 A
Back Queen St
  2 Elland HX4 . . . . 134 C
  1 Huddersfield HD1. . . 154 B
Back Ravenscar Ave 5
  LS8. . . . . 61 A
Back Ravens St WF13 . . 139 C
Back Raynville Mount
  LS13. . . . . 58 E
Back Rd 19 BD12. . . . . . . 94 C
Back Regent Park Terr
  LS6. . . . . 205 C
Back Regent St 1 . . . . . 142 E
Back Regent Terr LS6. . 205 C
Back Reginald Mount
  LS7. . . . . 207 A
Back Reginald Pl LS7 . . 207 A
Back Reginald St LS7 . . 207 A
Back Rhodes St HX1 . . . 203 A
Back Ribble St BD21 . . . . 35 B
Back Richardson St BD12. 95 A
Back Richmond Mount
  LS6. . . . . 205 B
Back Ridge Mount Terr
  LS6. . . . . 206 A
Back Ridge St OL14 . . . . 108 B
Back Ridge View LS7. . . . 60 A
Back Rigging La HX6. . . . 111 C
Back Ripley St 2 BD20. . 18 F
Back Ripon St HX1. . . . . 202 A
Back Ripon Terr HX3. . . . 92 B
Back River St 4 BD22. . . 51 D
Back Roberts St 3 LS26. 101 C
Back Rochester Terr
  LS6. . . . . 205 A
Back Rokeby Gdns 1 LS6 59 C
Back Roman Gr LS8. . . . . 44 A
Back Roman Pl LS8 . . . . . 44 A
Back Roman St LS8 . . . . . 44 B
Back Rose Ave LS18. . . . . 58 B

ack Rosebank Cres LS3 205 C2
ack Rosemont Wlk 5 LS13 58 C2
ack Rossall Rd LS8 208 A4
ack Rossington Gr 3 LS8 207 B4
ack Rossington Pl 5 LS8 207 B4
ack Rossington Rd LS8 207 B4
ack Roundhay Ave LS8 204 C1
ack Roundhay Cres LS8 204 C1
ack Roundhay Gr LS8 204 C1
ack Roundhay Pl LS8 204 C1
ack Roundhay View LS8 204 C1
ack Row LS11 211 B2
ack Rowland Terr 7 LS11 214 C3
ack Rowsley St 2 BD21 35 D7
ack Rupert St BD21 35 C8
ack Russell St BD5 201 A1
ack Ruthven View LS8 208 A3
ack Rydal St 5 BD22 35 A6
ack Rylstone St 2 BD21 35 E8
ack St Alban Cres LS9 208 C1
ack St Elmo Gr 5 LS9 80 A8
ack Saint Ives Mount LS12 209 A4
ack St Luke's Cres LS11 214 A4
ack St Mary's Rd LS7 204 A1
ack St Paul's Rd 4 BD18 55 A7
ack Salisbury Gr LS12 209 C4
ack Salisbury Terr LS12 209 C4
ack Salisbury View LS12 209 C4
ack Saltaire Rd N BD17 55 B8
ack Sandhurst Gr LS8 208 A3
ack Sandhurst Pl LS8 208 A3
ack Sandhurst Rd LS8 208 A3
ack Savile Par HX1 203 A1
ack Savile Pl LS7 207 A3
ack Savile Rd LS7 207 A3
ack School St 14 LS27 98 B4
ack School View LS6 205 B3
ack Seaforth Ave 1 LS9 208 B2
ack Seaforth Pl 2 LS9 208 A3
ack Seaforth Terr 3 LS9 208 A3
ack Sefton Ave LS11 214 A3
ack Sefton Terr LS11 214 A3
ack Shaftesbury Ave LS8 44 A2
ack Shaw La BD21 35 D3
ack Shepherd's La LS7 207 B4
ack Shepherd's Pl 9 LS8 207 C4
ack Sholebroke Ave LS7 204 A1
ack Sholebroke Mount LS7 207 A4
ack Sholebroke Pl LS7 207 A4
ack Sholebroke Row LS7 204 A1
ack Sholebroke Terr LS7 204 A1
ack Sholebroke View LS7 207 A4
ack Sidlaw Terr LS8 207 C4
ack Simpson St 1 BD21 35 A7
ack Sladen St 5 BD21 35 A7
ack Slaithwaite Rd WF12 139 C4
ack Smith Row 6 BD5 74 C3
ack South End Gr LS13 58 E1
ack Southfield Sq BD8 55 C1
ack South St HD1 153 D5
ack Sowerby Croft HX6 112 B2
ack Spencer Mount 7 LS8 207 B4
ack Springfield Mount LS12 209 A4
ack Springfield Pl 6 BD8 55 D1
ack Springfield Rd 3 HX5 135 A7
ack Spring Grove Wlk 14 LS6 205 B2
ack Spring St 4 HD1 154 A6
ack St
Bramham LS23 30 C2
Pontefract WF8 146 C8
ack Stanley St
Huddersfield HD1 153 E3
Leeds LS9 207 C2
ack Stanmore Pl LS4 59 C3
ack Stanmore St LS4 59 C3
ack Station Rd
Batley WF17 118 D4
Glusburn BD20 16 D7
Mirfield WF14 138 A3
ackstone Gill La LS17 27 E1
ack Stone Hall Rd BD2 56 B4
ackstone La LS29 8 C3
ackstone Way LS29 8 D4
ack Stoney La HD4 153 F2
ack Storey Pl LS14 61 E1
ack Stratford Ave LS11 214 A3
ack Stratford St 10 LS11 214 C3
ack Stratford Terr LS11 214 B3
Back Strathmore Dr 1 LS9 208 A3
Back Sunnybank Ave 6 LS18 58 B7
Back Sunnydene LS14 61 F1
Back Sutton App LS14 61 E1
Back Swinton St HX1 202 B2
Back Sycamore Ave BD16 36 F2
Back Tamworth St BD4 75 E6
Back Tempest Rd
2 Leeds LS11 214 A3
Leeds LS11 214 B3
Back Temple View LS11 214 A3
Back Thornhill Rd HD3 153 A6
Back Thornhill St LS28 57 B6
Back Thornville Row 13 LS6 205 B3
Back Toft St LS12 210 A2
Back Tower Gr LS12 209 A4
Back Town St 7 LS18 58 B8
Back Trafford Ave 2 LS9 208 B2
Back Trentham Pl 10 LS11 214 B2
Back Trinity Terr BD5 201 A1
Back Union St 5 HD1 154 B7
Back Unity St N BD16 36 F2
Back Unity St S 15 BD16 37 A2
Back Upper Castle HX7 110 C3
Back Vicars Rd 18 LS8 207 C4
Back Victoria Ave 6 LS9 80 B8
Back Victoria Gr 5 LS9 80 B8
Back Victoria St HX1 203 B3
Back Victor Terr HX1 202 C4
Back Wakefield Rd HX6 112 D4
Back Walmsley Rd LS6 205 B3
Back Walnut St 14 BD21 35 B4
Back Warwick Terr 1 WF17 118 D3
Back Webster St 3 WF13 139 C8
Back Welburn Ave LS16 59 B7
Back Wellfield Terr OL14 108 B4
Back Welton Ave 20 LS6 205 B3
Back Welton Gr LS6 205 B3
Back Welton Mount 17 LS6 205 B3
Back Welton Pl LS6 205 B3
Back Wentworth St HD1 153 F7
Back Wesley Rd LS12 209 C3
Back Wesley St WF10 124 D8
Back Westbourne Terr LS2 206 A2
Back Westbury St LS10 215 C1
Back Westfield Rd LS3 205 C1
Back Westlock Ave LS9 208 A1
Back Westmoreland Mount 2 LS13 58 D4
Back Westover Rd LS13 58 C3
Back West St HX6 112 B3
Back Wetherby Gr 4 LS4 59 C2
Back Wetherby Rd LS8 61 B6
Back Wheat St 5 BD22 35 A4
Back Wickham St LS11 214 A3
Back William Ave 1 LS15 80 E8
Back William St 9 HD6 115 A1
Back Wilton Gr 5 LS6 59 E6
Back Winfield Gr 3 LS2 206 B2
Back Winston Gdns 3 LS6 59 C5
Back Winterburn St BD21 35 C8
Back Wolsley Terr 2 HX1 202 B3
Back Woodbine Terr LS6 59 E6
Back Woodland Park Rd 3 LS6 59 E5
Back Woodlands Ave LS28 57 C1
Back Woodlands Gr LS28 57 C1
Back Woodlands Terr LS28 57 C1
Back Wood St
4 Bradford BD8 74 C8
East Ardsley WF3 120 D8
Back Woodstock St 16 LS2 206 B2
Back Wright Ave BD22 34 D3
Back York Pl LS1 211 B3
Back York St 3 LS2 212 A3
Bacon Ave WF6 123 C3
Bacon St LS20 39 F8
Bacup Rd OL14 107 D4
Baddeley Gdns BD10 39 A1
Baden Powell Cres WF8 146 D7
Baden St BD22 51 C8
Baden Terr 4 BD19 116 D7
Badger Brow HD9 170 D2
Badger Cl
Crigglestone WF4 159 F7
Ilkley LS29 7 E4
Badger Gate
Meltham HD9 170 D2
Wilsden BD15 53 C4
Badgergate Ave BD15 53 C4
Badger Hill HD6 135 E6
Badger La
Blackshaw Head HX7 88 B4
Brighouse HX3 114 B7
Badgers Drift BD20 18 B2
Badgers Gate LS29 3 E4
Badgers Mount LS15 62 F2
Badgerstone Cl BD20 19 D1
Badgers Way BD2 55 E4
Badgers Wlk WF16 117 E3
Badger Wood OL14 108 C4
Badger Wood Glade LS22 13 E7
Badminton Dr LS10 99 D3
Badminton View LS10 99 D3
Badsworth CE Jun & Inf Sch WF9 164 E2
Badsworth Ct
Badsworth WF9 164 E3
Bradford BD14 73 D5
Badsworth Mews WF9 164 E2
Badsworth View WF9 183 A8
Bagden La
Denby Dale HD8 192 D8
Denby Dale, Trister Hill HD8 192 E7
Baghill Ct WF8 146 F8
Baghill Gn WF3 119 D6
Baghill La WF8 146 F8
Baghill Rd WF3 119 D6
Bagley La LS28 57 E4
Bagnall Terr 2 BD6 74 B1
Bagshaw Mus* WF17 118 A8
Baildon Ave LS25 83 B3
Baildon CE Prim Sch BD17 38 E4
Baildon Chase LS14 62 C7
Baildon Cl LS14 62 C6
Baildon Dr LS14 62 C6
Baildon Gn LS14 62 C6
Baildon Holmes BD17 38 C1
Baildon Path LS14 62 C6
Baildon Pl LS14 62 C6
Baildon Rd
Baildon BD17 38 D2
Leeds LS14 62 C7
Baildon Sta BD17 38 E3
Baildon Wlk LS14 62 C7
Baildon Wood Ct BD17 38 C2
Bailes Rd LS7 60 A5
Bailey's Hill LS14 62 B5
Bailey's La LS14 62 A5
Bailey's Lawn LS14 62 A5
Bailey Cres WF9 183 A4
Baileygate Ct 13 WF8 125 D1
Bailey Hall Bank HX3 203 C3
Bailey Hall Bsns Pk HX3 203 C3
Bailey Hall Rd HX3 203 C2
Bailey Hall View HX3 203 C3
Bailey Hills Rd BD16 36 E4
Baileys Cl 3 LS14 62 A5
Bailey St BD4 201 C1
Bailey Twrs LS14 62 A5
Bailey Wells Ave BD5 74 C3
Bailey Wlk WF4 159 F3
Bailiff Bridge Jun & Inf Sch HD6 115 B7
Bainbridge Wharf BD20 4 D1
Bainbrigge Rd LS6 205 A4
Baines St
Batley WF17 118 B4
Halifax HX1 202 C4
Rothwell LS26 100 E5
Baird St BD5 74 E4
Bairstow's Bldgs HX2 91 F4
Bairstow Ct HX6 112 C6
Bairstow La HX6 112 C6
Bairstow Mount HX6 112 D5
Bairstow St BD15 54 A3
Baitings Gate Rd HX6 131 C2
Baker's St 12 HX7 89 A4
Baker Cres LS27 98 A3
Baker Fold 7 HX1 202 C3
Baker La WF3 121 D5
Baker Rd LS27 98 A3
Baker St N HX2 92 A5
Baker St
Bradford BD2 56 B2
Huddersfield HD3 153 B8
Morley LS27 98 A3
Shipley BD18 55 A8
Bakes St BD7 74 A4
Bakston Cl HD5 154 E3
Balbec Ave LS6 59 E5
Balbec St LS6 59 E5
Balderstone Hall La WF14 138 C7
Baldovan Mount LS8 207 C4
Baldovan Pl 5 LS8 207 C4
Baldovan Terr 7 LS8 207 C4
Baldwin Apartments HX1 203 B1
Baldwin La BD13, BD14 73 A2
Baldwin Terr HX3 203 C3
Bale Dr 4 BD10 55 F8
Balfour St
Bingley BD16 36 F2
Bradford BD4 75 A4
6 Keighley BD21 35 B6
Balk Ave WF3 122 A2
Balkcliffe La LS10, LS11 99 A6
Balk Cres WF3 122 A2
Balk La
Bradford BD7 74 B4
Denby Dale HD8 191 C6
Kirkheaton HD5 155 B7
Lofthouse Gate WF3 122 B1
Netherton WF4 158 F7
Shelley HD8 174 C3
South Elmsall WF9 183 D4
Balkram Dr HX2 91 A5
Balkram Edge HX2 91 A5
Balkram Rd HX2 91 B5
Balks WF15 116 F4
Balk St WF17 118 B5
Balk The
Batley WF17 118 C7
Darton S75 178 C2
Walton WF2 161 B6
Ballantyne Rd BD10 39 A2
Ballater Ave HD4 153 C2
Ballfield La S75 177 C1
Ballroyd Clough
Huddersfield HD3 153 A6
Huddersfield, Quarmby HD3 153 A7
Ballroyd La HD3 153 A5
Ball Royd Rd HD2 136 B2
Ball St BD13 72 E6
Balme La BD12 94 D3
Balme Rd BD19 116 D8
Balme St
Bradford BD1 201 C3
Bradford, Upper Common BD12 94 D3
Balmfield WF15 117 A2
Balmfield Cres WF15 117 A1
Balmford's Yard W HD3 153 B4
Balmoral Ave HD4 153 C2
Balmoral Chase LS10 215 C3
Balmoral Cl WF8 146 B5
Balmoral Dr
Knottingley WF11 126 C4
Mickletown LS26 102 C3
Balmoral Pl
Halifax HX1 203 B2
Leeds LS10 212 A3
9 Queensbury BD13 92 C8
Balmoral St 12 HX7 89 A3
Balmoral Way LS19 40 D6
Balm Pl LS11 211 A1
Balm Rd LS10 215 B2
Balm Road Ind Est LS10 215 A3
Balm Wlk LS11 211 A1
Balne Ave WF2 142 A7
Balne La WF2 142 A7
Bamborough St WF1 142 F3
Bamburgh Cl LS15 62 E3
Bamburgh Rd LS15 62 E3
Bamford Ho BD4 75 E1
Bamlett Brow BD22 51 D8
Banbury Rd WF8 125 E3
Bancroft Ave HD5 154 E5
Bancroft St 7 BD22 51 F8
Bangor Gr 14 LS12 78 A4
Bangor Pl LS12 78 A4
Bangor St LS12 78 A4
Bangor Terr LS12 78 A4
Bangor View 13 LS12 78 A4
Bank
Bradford BD10 56 D6
Oxenhope BD22 51 E1
Bank Ave
Horsforth LS18 58 B8
Morley LS27 98 A5
Bank Bldgs
Hebden Bridge HX7 89 C2
Meltham HD9 170 E1
Sowerby Bridge HX6 132 C7
Bank Bottom
Cragg Vale HX7 110 C3
Halifax HX1, HX3 203 C3
Marsden HD7 169 C6
Mytholmroyd HX7 90 A2
Ripponden HX6 150 D8
Bank Bottom La HX2 90 E1
Bank Bottom Terr HD7 169 C6
Bank Chambers 6 HX1 203 B3
Bank Cl BD10 56 C5
Bank Crest BD17 38 C3
Bank Crest Rise BD18 54 C7
Bank Dr BD6 74 D1
Bank Edge Cl HX2 91 E3
Bank Edge Gdns HX2 91 E3
Bank Edge Rd HX2 91 E4
Bank End
Elland HX4 133 D7
Slaithwaite HD7 152 C4
Bank End La
Clayton West HD8 176 A1
Huddersfield HD5 154 E4
Bank End Rd HD7 152 C3
Banker St LS4 205 A2
Bankfield
Bardsey LS17 28 D4
Marsden HD7 169 A4
Shelley HD8 173 F2
Bankfield Ave
Kirkheaton HD5 155 B8
Shipley BD18 54 D7
Bankfield Cl WF5 140 F4
Bankfield Ct
Huddersfield HD5 154 D5
Mirfield WF14 137 F5
Wakefield WF2 120 F3
Bankfield Dr
Holmfirth HD9 188 C2
Keighley BD22 34 E7
Shipley BD18 54 D7
Wakefield WF2 120 F3
Bankfield Gdns
Halifax HX3 113 F6
1 Leeds LS4 59 C2
Bankfield Gr
Leeds LS4 59 C3
Shipley BD18 54 D6
Bank Field Grange HX4 134 C7
Bankfield La HD5 155 B8
Bankfield Mount BD22 34 E7
Bankfield Mus* HX3 92 C1
Bankfield Park Ave HD4 153 F1
Bankfield Rd
Huddersfield HD1 153 F5
Keighley BD22 34 E8
Leeds LS4 59 C2
Shipley BD18 54 D7
Bank Field Rd WF17 118 C5
Bankfield St BD22 34 E8
Bankfield Terr
Baildon BD17 38 D2
Bankfield Terr *continued*
Holmfirth HD9 188 F4
Huddersfield HD4 171 E8
Leeds LS4 59 C2
Sowerby Bridge HX6 112 A5
Bankfield View HX3 92 B1
Bankfield Wlk BD22 34 E7
Bankfield Yd 5 HX3 92 B1
Bankfoot HX7 88 F3
Bank Foot HD4 172 F8
Bank Foot La HD4 171 E7
Bank Foot Pl WF17 118 C5
Bankfoot Prim Sch BD5 74 D2
Bank Foot Rd HD4 172 F8
Bank Foot St WF17 118 C5
Bankfoot Terr 10 HX7 88 F3
Bank Gate HD7 151 F1
Bank Gdns LS18 58 B8
Bank Gr WF12 140 A7
Bank Hall Gr HD8 190 F8
Bank Hey Bottom La HX6 132 E3
Bank Ho HX4 133 D4
Bankholme Ct BD4 75 F2
Bankhouse LS28 76 D5
Bank House Cl LS27 98 A5
Bankhouse Ct LS28 76 D5
Bankhouse La
Halifax HX3 113 D2
Huddersfield HX3 153 C5
Pudsey LS28 76 D5
Bank House La HX2 90 E4
Bankhouse Rd HD3 153 B5
Bank La
Denby Dale HD8 191 F4
Holmfirth HD9 188 C2
Holmfirth, Liphill Bank HD9 188 D4
Holmfirth, Town End HD9 189 B7
Silsden BD20 5 E8
Banklands BD20 5 E2
Banklands Ave BD20 5 F2
Banklands La BD20 5 F2
Bank Nook HD7 169 C7
Bank Par LS21 22 F7
Bank Rd
Glusburn BD20 16 D7
Sowerby Bridge HX6 112 B3
Bank Royd La HX4 133 B1
Banks HD9 172 A4
Banks App HD7 152 D5
Banks Ave
Ackworth M T WF7 163 E5
Huddersfield HD7 152 D5
Pontefract WF8 146 C8
Banks Cres HD7 152 D5
Banks Dr HD7 152 D5
Banks End La HD9 172 D1
Banks End Rd HX5 135 C6
Banksfield Ave LS19 40 B8
Banksfield Cl LS19 40 B8
Banksfield Cres LS19 40 B8
Banksfield Gr LS19 40 B8
Banksfield Mount LS19 40 B8
Banksfield Rd 10 HX7 89 E1
Banksfield Rise LS19 40 B8
Banksfields Ave HX7 89 E1
Banksfields Cres HX7 89 E1
Banksfield Terr
Mytholmroyd HX7 89 E1
14 Yeadon LS19 40 B7
Banks Garth WF11 126 F4
Banks Gr HD7 152 D5
Bankside
8 Hebden Bridge HX7 89 A3
Todmorden OL14 108 B4
Bank Side HD8 173 F2
Bankside Prim Sch LS8 207 C3
Bank Side St LS8 207 C3
Bankside Terr 3 BD17 38 B2
Banks La
Keighley BD20 18 E3
Knottingley WF11 126 F4
Banks Mount 10 WF8 146 C8
Bank Sq 2 LS27 98 A5
Banks Rd
Honley HD9 172 B3
Huddersfield HD7 152 D5
Slaithwaite HD7 170 B8
Banks Side HD7 152 D5
Banks St WF17 118 C4
Bank St
Bradford BD1 201 B3
Bradford, Brownroyd Hill BD6 74 C1
Brighouse HD6 115 A2
Castleford WF10 124 D8
Cleckheaton BD19 116 C7
Dewsbury WF12 139 D8
Haworth BD22 51 C7
Hemsworth WF9 181 D7
Holmfirth HD9 189 E4
Horbury WF4 141 A1
5 Keighley BD21 35 C7
Leeds LS1 211 C3
Liversedge WF15 117 B4
Mirfield WF14 137 E5
Morley LS27 98 A5
Ossett WF5 140 D5
Shipley BD18 55 B7
6 Shipley BD18 55 B8
Todmorden OL14 108 B4
Wakefield WF1 216 B2
Wetherby LS22 13 E5
Banks The HX6 112 A5

Banksville HD9 . . . . 189 B7
Bank Terr
  Hebden Bridge HX7 . . . . . . 88 E4
  Morley LS27 . . . . 98 B5
  8 Pudsey LS28 . . . . 57 E2
Bank Top
  Elland HX4 . . . . 134 C8
  Halifax HX3 . . . . 113 F5
  Slaithwaite HD7 . . . . 151 F1
Bank Top Dr BD20 . . . . . . 18 F2
Bank Top La
  Hebden Bridge HX7 . . . . . . 109 F5
  Holmfirth HD9 . . . . 188 A2
Bank Top Way BD21 . . . . . . 35 F6
Bank View
  Baildon BD17 . . . . 38 B2
  Birkenshaw BD11 . . . . 96 A6
  Dewsbury WF12 . . . . 140 A8
  Hebden Bridge HX7 . . . . . . 88 E3
  Honley HD9 . . . . 172 C2
  Leeds LS7 . . . . 60 B7
  Luddenden Foot HX2 . . . . . 111 D6
  8 Mytholmroyd HX7 . . . . . . 89 E1
  Sowerby Bridge, Mill Bank
    HX6 . . . . 132 D7
Bank View Ho BD17 . . . . . . 38 C2
Bankwell Fold BD6 . . . . . . 74 D1
Bankwell Rd HD3 . . . . 153 B4
Bank Wlk BD17 . . . . 38 C4
Bankwood WF17 . . . . 97 B4
Bank Wood Rd WF8 . . . . 147 F4
Bankwood Way WF17 . . . . . . 97 B3
Bannerman BD12 . . . . 95 A5
Banner St BD3 . . . . 75 A6
Bannister La DN6 . . . . 184 C5
Bannockburn Ct BD5 . . . . . 75 B1
Bannockburn Way WF6 . . . . 122 E4
Banstead St E LS8 . . . . . . 207 C3
Banstead St W LS8 . . . . . . 207 C3
Banstead Terr E LS8 . . . . 207 C3
Banstead Terr W 6 LS8 . . 207 C3
Bantam Cl LS27 . . . . 98 D4
Bantam Grove La LS27 . . . 98 D4
Bantam Grove View LS27 . 98 D4
Bantree Ct BD10 . . . . 39 A2
Baptist Fold BD13 . . . . . . 72 E1
Baptist La WF5 . . . . 141 B4
Baptist Pl BD1 . . . . 201 A3
Baptist St WF17 . . . . 118 A3
Baptist Way LS13 . . . . 58 A2
Barber Row HD7 . . . . 152 D1
Barberry Ave BD3 . . . . 75 E8
Barber Sq WF16 . . . . 117 C4
Barber St 1 HD6 . . . . 115 B3
Barber Wlk 8 WF13 . . . . . . 139 C8
Barclay Cl BD13 . . . . 52 E6
Barclay St LS7 . . . . 207 A1
Barcroft BD22 . . . . 51 F8
Bar Croft HD5 . . . . 137 B1
Barcroft Gr LS19 . . . . 40 A6
Barcroft Rd HD4 . . . . 154 A2
Barden Ave BD6 . . . . 93 D8
Barden Cl
  Batley WF17 . . . . 118 B5
  Leeds LS12 . . . . 209 A3
Barden Dr BD16 . . . . 37 C4
Barden Gn LS12 . . . . 209 A3
Barden Gr LS12 . . . . 209 A3
Barden Mount LS12 . . . . . . 209 A3
Barden Pl LS12 . . . . 209 A3
Barden Rd WF1 . . . . 142 F7
Barden St 4 BD8 . . . . 55 B1
Barden Terr LS12 . . . . 209 A3
Bardon Hall Gdns LS16 . . 59 C8
Bardon Hall Mews LS16 . . 59 C8
Bardsey Cres BD3 . . . . 75 A7
Bardsey Prim Sch LS17 . . 28 C3
Bardwell Ct WF3 . . . . 121 E1
Bare Bones Rd HD9 . . . . . . 199 B5
Bare Head La HX3 . . . . 92 D5
Barewell Hill S72, WF9 . . 181 B5
Barfield Ave LS19 . . . . . . 40 A6
Barfield Cres LS17 . . . . . 43 F5
Barfield Dr LS19 . . . . 40 A6
Barfield Gr LS17 . . . . 44 A5
Barfield Mount LS17 . . . . 44 A5
Barfield Rd HX3 . . . . 114 C7
Barfield Terr LS27 . . . . . 98 A2
Bargate HD7 . . . . 152 D1
Bargess Terr LS25 . . . . . . 83 B1
Barge St HD1 . . . . 153 F4
Bargrange Ave BD18 . . . . . 55 B6
Bargreen HD5 . . . . 137 B1
Barham Terr BD10 . . . . 56 D4
Bar House La BD20 . . . . . . 17 F3
Bar House Row LS21 . . . . . 24 B5
Baring Ave BD3 . . . . 75 D8
Baring-Gould Way WF4 . . . 140 E1
Baring Sq BD20 . . . . 16 D4
Bark Cl HD8 . . . . 174 A3
Barker's Rd WF4 . . . . 159 E6
Barker Cl HX3 . . . . 113 E3
Barker Ct
  11 Bacup OL13 . . . . 106 A1
  Huddersfield HD2 . . . . 135 C1
Barkerend Prim Sch BD3 . 75 A8
Barkerend Rd BD1, BD3 . . 75 B8
Barker Ho 4 HX3 . . . . 113 E3
Barker Rd WF4 . . . . 140 F2
Barker St
  Liversedge WF15 . . . . 117 B4
  Lofthouse Gate WF3 . . . . 122 B6
  24 Todmorden OL14 . . . . . 108 B6
Barkers Well Fold LS12 . 77 D4

Barkers Well Garth LS12 . 77 E3
Barkers Well Gate LS12 . 77 E3
Barkers Well Lawn LS12 . 77 E3
Bark House La
  Cawthorne S75 . . . . 193 C4
  Shelley HD8 . . . . 174 C3
Barkisland CE Prim Sch
  HX4 . . . . 133 A5
Bark La LS29 . . . . 7 A8
Barkly Ave LS11 . . . . 214 A1
Barkly Dr LS11 . . . . 214 A1
Barkly Gr LS11 . . . . 214 A2
Barkly Par 2 LS11 . . . . . . 214 A1
Barkly Pl 1 LS11 . . . . 214 A1
Barkly Rd LS11 . . . . 214 A1
Barkly Terr LS11 . . . . 214 A2
Barkston Ho LS11 . . . . 210 C2
Barkston Wlk 2 BD15 . . . 73 A7
Bar La
  Bramham LS23 . . . . 31 A6
  Garforth LS25 . . . . 83 A7
  Horsforth LS18 . . . . 57 F8
  Keighley BD20 . . . . 18 F1
  Lofthouse Gate WF1 . . . . 121 D1
  Netherton WF4 . . . . 158 B2
  Ripponden HX6 . . . . 132 C2
  West Bretton WF4 . . . . . . 158 B2
Barlbro' Pl HD4 . . . . 153 A4
Barleycorn Cl WF3 . . . . . . 121 E1
Barley Cote Ave BD20 . . . 19 A2
Barley Cote Cotts BD20 . . 19 A2
Barley Cote Gr BD20 . . . . 19 A2
Barley Cote Rd BD20 . . . . 19 A2
Barley Croft WF13 . . . . . . 138 F8
Barleyfield Ct WF1 . . . . . 142 E8
Barley Field Ct 3 LS15 . 81 A8
Barleyfields Cl LS22 . . . 13 E7
Barleyfields Ct LS22 . . . 13 E6
Barleyfields La LS22 . . . 13 E6
Barleyfields Mews LS22 . 13 E6
Barleyfields Rd LS22 . . . 13 E7
Barleyfields Terr 5 LS22 . 13 E6
Barleyfields Wlk LS22 . . 13 E6
Barley Hill Cres LS25 . . 82 E6
Barley Hill La LS25 . . . . 82 E7
Barley Hill Rd LS25 . . . . 82 E7
Barley Mews WF3 . . . . 100 B3
Barley St BD22 . . . . 35 A4
Barlow Rd BD21 . . . . 35 B8
Barlow St BD3 . . . . 75 B7
Barmby Cl WF5 . . . . 140 F4
Barmby Cres WF5 . . . . 141 A4
Barmby Fold WF5 . . . . 140 F4
Barmby Pl BD2 . . . . 56 B1
Barmby Rd BD2 . . . . 56 B1
Barmby St BD12 . . . . 94 D4
Bar Mount LS25 . . . . 83 A7
Barmouth Terr BD3 . . . . . . 55 F2
Barnaby Rd BD16 . . . . 37 C4
Barnard Cl LS15 . . . . 62 E3
Barnard Rd BD4 . . . . 201 D1
Barnard Rd BD4 . . . . 201 D1
Barnard Way LS15 . . . . 62 E3
Barnbow La
  Barwick in E, Barnbow Carr
    LS15 . . . . 63 B5
  Barwick in E LS15 . . . . . 63 B3
Barnbrough St LS4 . . . . . . 59 C2
Barnby Ave BD8 . . . . 73 C7
Barnby Royd HD5 . . . . 154 E7
Barn Cl LS29 . . . . 21 F4
Barncliffe Hill HD8 . . . . 174 C1
Barncroft Cl LS14 . . . . . . 61 F7
Barncroft Ct LS14 . . . . . . 61 F6
Barncroft Dr LS14 . . . . . . 61 F7
Barncroft Gdns LS14 . . . . 61 F6
Barncroft Grange LS14 . . 61 E6
Barncroft Hts LS14 . . . . . 61 E7
Barncroft Mount LS14 . . . 61 F6
Barncroft Rd LS14 . . . . . . 61 F7
Barncroft Rise LS14 . . . . 61 F6
Barncroft Twrs LS14 . . . . 61 E6
Barnes Mdws OL15 . . . . 129 C1
Barnes Rd
  Bradford BD8 . . . . 73 F7
  Castleford WF10 . . . . 124 D6
Barnes St 2 OL14 . . . . 108 A1
Barnet Gr 2 LS27 . . . . 98 A2
Barnet Rd LS12 . . . . 210 A3
Barnfold Pl S72 . . . . 180 C2
Barnsdale Bar DN6 . . . . . . 184 C8
Barnsdale Est WF10 . . . . . 124 B6
Barnsdale Rd
  Kippax WF10 . . . . 103 D4
  Mickletown LS26 . . . . 102 E1
Barnside Way WF9 . . . . 183 E7
Barnside La HD9 . . . . 189 F1
Barnsley Beck Gr BD17 . . 38 D3
Barnsley Rd
  Ackworth M T WF7 . . . . . . 164 A6
  Brierley S72 . . . . 181 A4
  Clayton West HD8 . . . . . . 175 E1
  Crigglestone WF2, WF4 . . 160 B4
  Denby Dale HD8 . . . . 191 C5
  Flockton WF4 . . . . 157 C3
  Hemsworth WF9 . . . . 181 C6
  South Elmsall WF9 . . . . . 182 A3
  Wakefield WF1, WF2 . . . . 142 E2
  Wakefield WF1, WF2 . . . . 160 D7
  Woolley WF4 . . . . 178 C6
Barn St BD22 . . . . 51 C2
Barnstone Vale WF1 . . . . . 121 E1
Barnswick Cl WF8 . . . . 146 D8
Barnswick View LS16 . . . . 41 E4
Barn The BD12 . . . . 94 E6

Baron Cl LS11 . . . . 214 A4
Baronscourt LS15 . . . . 81 D8
Baronsmead LS15 . . . . 81 D8
Baronsway LS15 . . . . 81 C8
Barplas Ind Pk BD5 . . . . 74 E2
Barrack Rd LS7 . . . . 207 A3
Barracks Fold HD9 . . . . . . 189 E2
Barracks St WF16 . . . . 117 C4
Barrack St LS7 . . . . 207 A2
Barraclough Bldgs BD10 . 56 E7
Barraclough Sq 18 BD12 . 94 B6
Barraclough St 6 BD12 . . 94 B6
Barran Ct LS8 . . . . 207 C3
Barran St 8 BD16 . . . . 37 A3
Barras Garth Pl LS12 . . . 209 B2
Barras Garth Rd LS12 . . . 209 B2
Barras Pl LS12 . . . . 209 B2
Barras St LS12 . . . . 209 B2
Barrass Yd WF2 . . . . 142 A5
Barras Terr LS12 . . . . 209 B2
Barratt's Rd WF1 . . . . 216 B4
Barrett Pl BD20 . . . . 16 D5
Barrett St BD20 . . . . 5 D1
Barrington Cl HX3 . . . . . . 114 A4
Barrington Par BD19 . . . . 117 A8
Barrowby Ave LS15 . . . . . . 81 E7
Barrowby Cl LS29 . . . . 22 B4
Barrowby Cres LS15 . . . . . 81 E8
Barrowby Dr LS15 . . . . 81 F7
Barrowby La
  Garforth LS25 . . . . 82 A6
  Leeds LS15 . . . . 81 E8
Barrowby Rd LS15 . . . . 81 F7
Barrowby View LS15 . . . . . 82 E8
Barrowclough La HX3 . . . . 113 F7
Barrows La BD20 . . . . 17 C4
Barrowstead HD8 . . . . 175 B1
Barr St HD1 . . . . 154 C8
Barr Terr 4 BD8 . . . . 73 F8
Barry St BD1 . . . . 201 B3
Barsey Green La HX4 . . . . 133 C6
Bar St
  Batley WF17 . . . . 118 D4
  Todmorden OL14 . . . . 108 A4
Barstow Fall WF8 . . . . 125 E3
Barstow Sq WF1 . . . . 216 B2
Barthorpe Ave LS17 . . . . . 60 B8
Barthorpe Cl BD4 . . . . 75 F2
Barthorpe Cres LS17 . . . . 60 C8
Barthorpe Ho 4 BD4 . . . . 75 F2
Bartle Cl BD7 . . . . 73 F3
Bartle Fold BD7 . . . . 74 A4
Bartle Gill Dr BD17 . . . . 38 E4
Bartle Gill Rise BD17 . . 38 E4
Bartle Gill View BD17 . . 38 E4
Bartle Gr BD7 . . . . 73 F3
Bartle La BD7 . . . . 73 F3
Bartle Pl 6 BD7 . . . . 73 F3
Bartle Sq BD7 . . . . 74 A4
Barton Ct LS15 . . . . 81 D7
Barton Gr LS11 . . . . 214 A4
Barton Hill LS11 . . . . 214 A4
Barton Manor Cl HD4 . . . . 153 B2
Barton Mount LS11 . . . . . . 214 A4
Barton Pl
  Batley WF17 . . . . 118 C4
  Leeds LS11 . . . . 214 A4
Barton Rd LS11 . . . . 214 A4
Barton St
  Bradford BD5 . . . . 74 B3
  17 Brighouse HD6 . . . . . . 115 A3
Barton Terr LS11 . . . . 214 A4
Barton View LS11 . . . . 214 A4
Barton Way WF9 . . . . 183 A5
Barum Top 13 HX1 . . . . 203 B3
Barwick Gn BD6 . . . . 73 E1
Barwick in Elmet CE Prim
  Sch LS15 . . . . 63 E7
Barwick Rd
  Barwick in E LS15, LS25 . 63 E2
  Leeds LS14, LS15 . . . . . . 62 D4
Barwick Sq BD22 . . . . 51 F8
Basford Ct WF2 . . . . 142 A5
Basford St WF2 . . . . 142 A5
Basildon Rd S63 . . . . 194 C1
Basil St
  Bradford BD5 . . . . 74 B3
  Huddersfield HD4 . . . . . . 153 D4
Baslow Gr BD9 . . . . 54 F2
Bassenthwaite Wlk
  WF11 . . . . 126 E2
Batcliffe Dr LS6 . . . . 59 C6
Batcliffe Mount LS6 . . . . 59 C5
Bateman Cl S72 . . . . 180 B2
Bateman St BD8 . . . . 55 D1
Bates Ave HX6 . . . . 111 F3
Bates La WF8 . . . . 146 F5
Bateson St BD10 . . . . 56 E7
Bath Cl LS13 . . . . 58 C2
Bath Ct WF16 . . . . 117 D4
Bath Gr 14 LS13 . . . . 58 C2
Bath La LS13 . . . . 58 C2
Bath Pl
  Brighouse HD6 . . . . 115 A1
  Cleckheaton BD19 . . . . . . 116 D7
  Halifax HX3 . . . . 92 B1
Bath Rd
  Batley WF16 . . . . 117 D4
  Cleckheaton BD19 . . . . . . 116 D7
  Halifax HX3 . . . . 113 C4
  Leeds, Holbeck LS11 . . . . 211 A2
  Leeds LS13 . . . . 58 C2
Bath St
  1 Bacup OL13 . . . . 106 A2
  Batley WF17 . . . . 118 D5
  Bradford BD3 . . . . 201 D3
  Dewsbury WF13 . . . . 118 C1
  Elland HX5 . . . . 134 F6

Bath St continued
  3 Halifax HX1 . . . . 203 C2
  Huddersfield HD1 . . . . . . 154 A7
  Huddersfield, Rashcliffe
    HD1 . . . . 153 F3
  Ilkley LS29 . . . . 8 C5
  Keighley BD21 . . . . 35 D7
  Kirkburton HD8 . . . . 173 F5
  3 Todmorden OL14 . . . . . . 108 B5
Batley Ave HD1 . . . . 153 D6
Batley Bldgs HD1 . . . . 153 E7
Batley Bsns Ctr WF17 . . . 118 B6
Batley Bsns & Ent Coll
  WF17 . . . . 118 C7
Batley Bsns & Tech Ctr
  WF17 . . . . 118 E4
Batley Ct BD17 . . . . 38 D4
Batley Ent Ctr WF17 . . . . 118 B6
Batley Field Hill WF17 . . 118 C4
Batley Girls' High Sch
  WF17 . . . . 97 B1
Batley Gram Sch WF17 . . . 118 B7
Batley Parish CE Jun & Inf
  Sch WF17 . . . . 118 C6
Batley Rd
  Batley WF16 . . . . 117 F4
  East Ardsley WF2, WF3 . . 119 E5
  Wakefield WF2 . . . . 120 B2
Batley St
  28 Halifax HX3 . . . . 92 A1
  9 Huddersfield HD5 . . . . 154 D6
Batley Sta WF17 . . . . 118 D4
Baton La S19 . . . . 40 C4
Batter La LS19 . . . . 40 C4
Battinson Rd HX1 . . . . 202 B1
Battinson St HX3 . . . . 113 E5
Battlefield View BD4,
  BD11 . . . . 96 B7
Battyeford CE Prim Sch
  WF14 . . . . 137 E6
Battye St
  Batley WF16 . . . . 117 D4
  Bradford BD4 . . . . 75 D6
  Dewsbury WF13 . . . . 139 D8
Baulk Head La OL14 . . . . . 108 F6
Bavaria Pl BD8 . . . . 55 B1
Bawn App LS12 . . . . 77 F5
Bawn Ave LS12 . . . . 77 F6
Bawn Chase LS12 . . . . 77 E6
Bawn Dr LS12 . . . . 77 E6
Bawn Gdns LS12 . . . . 77 E6
Bawn La LS12 . . . . 77 E6
Bawn Path LS12 . . . . 77 F6
Bawn Vale LS12 . . . . 77 F6
Bawn Wlk LS12 . . . . 77 F6
Bawson Dr BD19 . . . . 96 A1
Baxandall St BD5 . . . . 74 E3
Baxtergate 10 WF8 . . . . . . 146 D8
Baxter La HX3 . . . . 93 A3
Baxter Wood BD20 . . . . 16 C7
Bay Cl HD3 . . . . 153 C7
Bayfield Cl HD9 . . . . 199 B8
Bay Hall HD1 . . . . 154 A8
Bay Hall Common Rd
  HD1 . . . . 154 A8
Bay Ho LS23 . . . . 30 D2
Bay Horse Ct 8 LS21 . . . . 23 A8
Bay Horse La LS14, LS17 . 45 A6
Bayldons Pl 10 WF17 . . . . 118 C5
Baylee St 3 WF9 . . . . 181 E6
Bayne Dr BD4 . . . . 95 B8
Bay of Biscay BD9 . . . . . . 54 B4
Bayswater Cres LS8 . . . . . 207 C3
Bayswater Gr
  Bradford BD2 . . . . 56 D2
  Leeds LS8 . . . . 207 C3
Bayswater Mount LS8 . . . . 207 C3
Bayswater Pl LS8 . . . . 207 C3
Bayswater Rd LS8 . . . . 207 C3
Bayswater Row LS8 . . . . . . 207 C3
Bayswater Terr
  Halifax HX3 . . . . 113 C3
  Leeds LS8 . . . . 207 C3
Bayswater View LS8 . . . . . 207 C3
Bayton La LS18, LS19 . . . . 40 E5
Beachill Cres WF4 . . . . . . 162 C1
Beachill Dr WF4 . . . . 162 C1
Beachill Rd WF4 . . . . 162 C1
Beacon Ave LS27 . . . . 98 C2
Beacon Brow BD6 . . . . 73 D2
Beacon Cl BD16 . . . . 37 B3
Beacon Dr WF9 . . . . 183 A8
Beaconfield Rd WF9 . . . . . 164 F1
Beacon Gr
  Bradford BD6 . . . . 73 F1
  Morley LS27 . . . . 98 C2
Beacon Hill WF9 . . . . 183 A8
Beacon Hill Rd HX3 . . . . . 113 E7
Beacon Ho WF9 . . . . 183 A8
Beacon Pl BD6 . . . . 73 E1
Beacon Rd BD6 . . . . 73 E2
Beacon Rise LS29 . . . . 7 E4
Beaconsfield Ct LS25 . . . 82 F8
Beaconsfield Rd BD14 . . . 73 D4
Beaconsfield St
  Halifax HX3 . . . . 113 E6
  Todmorden OL14 . . . . 108 C5
Beacon St
  Addingham LS29 . . . . 7 A8
  Bradford BD6 . . . . 74 A1
  1 Bradford, Horton Bank
    BD7 . . . . 73 E2
  Dewsbury WF13 . . . . 138 E6
  Huddersfield HD2 . . . . . . 136 A1
Beacon View
  South Kirkby WF9 . . . . . . 182 C3
  Upton WF9 . . . . 183 A8

Beaden Dr HD8 155
Beadon Ave HD5 155
Beagle Ave HD4 153
Beal La DN14 127
Beamshaw WF9 182
Beamsley Gr
  Bingley BD16 37
  10 Leeds LS6 205
Beamsley Ho BD18 55
Beamsley La BD23 2
Beamsley Mount 3 LS6 . . 205
Beamsley Pl 11 LS6 205
Beamsley Rd
  Bradford BD9 55
  Shipley BD18 55
Beamsley Terr 1 LS6 . . . 205
Beamsley View LS29 7
Beamsley Wlk BD9 55
Beancroft Rd WF10 124
Beancroft St WF10 124
Beanland Gdns 5 BD6 . . . 94
Beanlands Dr BD20 16
Beanlands Par LS29 8
Beanlands Pl BD20 16
Bean St HX5 135
Bearing Ave LS11 214
Bear Pit Gdns LS6 205
Beastfair WF8 146
Beast Market 4 HD1 154
Beatrice St
  1 Cleckheaton BD19 . . . 116
  Keighley BD21 18
  7 Oxenhope BD22 51
Beaufort Ave HD8 173
Beaufort Gr BD2 56
Beaufort Mews WF7 164
Beaufort Rd OL13 106
Beaumont Ave
  Huddersfield HD5 154
  Leeds LS8 44
  South Elmsall WF9 182
Beaumont Dr WF4 176
Beaumont Park Rd HD4 . . 153
Beaumont Pl WF17 117
Beaumont Rd BD8 55
Beaumont Sq 5 LS28 76
Beaumont St
  Batley WF17 118
  Emley HD8 175
  Huddersfield HD1 154
  Huddersfield, Longwood
    HD3 152
  14 Huddersfield, Moldgreen
    HD5 154
  Huddersfield, Netherton
    HD4 171
  Lofthouse Gate WF3 121
  Todmorden OL14 108
Beauvais Dr BD20 36
Beaver Cl BD22 51
Beaver Dr WF13 138
Beaver Terr 17 OL13 106
Becca La LS25 64
Beck Bottom
  Pudsey LS28 56
  Wakefield WF2 120
Beckbridge Ct WF6 123
Beckbridge Gn WF6 123
Beckbridge La WF6 123
Beckbridge Rd WF6 123
Beckbridge Way WF6 123
Beckbury Cl 4 LS28 57
Beckbury St 5 LS28 57
Beckenham Pl HX1 202
Becker's Ave WF17 97
Becket La WF3 100
Beckett's Park Cres LS6 . 59
Beckett's Park Dr LS6 . . 59
Beckett's Park Rd LS6 . . 59
Beckett Cl WF4 141
Beckett Cres WF13 138
Beckett Ct LS15 81
Beckett Gr WF13 138
Beckett Ho LS6 59
Beckett La WF13 138
Beckett Nook WF13 138
Beckett Rd WF13 118
Becketts Cl HX7 88
Beckett Sq HD8 173
Beckett St
  Batley WF17 118
  Leeds LS9 207
Beckett Terr LS9 207
Beckett Wlk WF13 138
Beckfield Cl
  Brighouse BD19 115
  Glusburn BD20 16
Beckfield La WF11 104
Beckfield Rd BD16 54
Beckfoot La BD16 36
Beckfoot Mill BD16 36
Beckfoot Sch BD16 37
Beck Hill BD6 93
Beckhill App LS7 60
Beckhill Ave LS7 60
Beckhill Chase LS7 60
Beckhill Cl LS7 60
Beckhill Dr LS7 60
Beckhill Fold LS7 60
Beckhill Garth LS7 60
Beckhill Gate LS7 60
Beckhill Gdns LS7 60
Beckhill Gn LS7 60
Beckhill Gr LS7 60
Beckhill Lawn LS7 60
Beckhill Row LS7 60

Beckhill Vale LS7 60 A7
Beckhill View LS7 60 A6
Beckhill Wlk LS7 60 A7
Beck Ho BD16 37 A4
Beck La
Bingley BD16 37 A4
Collingham LS22 13 B1
Liversedge WF16 117 C3
Beckley Rd WF2 142 A6
Beck Mdw LS15 63 E6
Beck Rd
Huddersfield HD1 154 A8
Leeds LS8 207 C4
Micklethwaite BD16 36 E8
Beck Rise WF9 181 D7
Becks Ct WF12 139 F6
Beckside
Aberford LS25 64 E6
Cawthorne S75 193 E4
Beck Side 3 BD21 35 C6
Beckside Cl
Addingham LS29 6 F8
Burley in W LS29 9 E1
Beckside Ct BD20 5 E2
Beckside Gdns
Huddersfield HD5 155 C4
Leeds LS16 59 D7
Beckside La BD7 74 A4
Beckside Rd BD7 74 A5
Beckside View LS27 98 C4
Beckside Works WF17 118 D3
Becks Rd BD21 35 A6
Beck St BD21 35 C6
Beck View WF4 179 A6
Beckwith Dr BD10 56 D5
Bective Rd WF2 141 E7
Bedale WF3 119 D8
Bedale Ave
Brighouse HD6 135 E8
Skelmanthorpe HD8 174 F1
Bedale Cl HD8 174 F1
Bedale Ct LS27 98 E4
Bedale Dr
Bradford BD6 73 F1
Knottingley WF11 126 E2
Skelmanthorpe HD8 174 F1
Bedale Wlk S72 180 C3
Bedding Edge Rd HD9 200 A7
Bede's Cl BD13 72 D6
Bede Ct WF1 216 B4
Bede Ho WF1 216 B4
Bedford Ave WF4 156 E5
Bedford Cl
Crofton WF4 162 A8
Leeds LS16 41 E3
Lepton HD8 155 E3
Purston Jaglin WF7 145 D4
Bedford Ct
Horsforth LS18 41 C1
Leeds LS8 61 C6
Purston Jaglin WF7 145 D4
Bedford Dr LS16 41 E3
Bedford Farm Ct WF4 162 A8
Bedford Garth LS16 41 E3
Bedford Gdns LS16 41 E3
Bedford Gn LS16 41 E3
Bedford Gr LS16 41 E2
Bedford Mount LS16 41 E2
Bedford Pl
3 Guiseley LS20 39 E8
Otley LS21 23 C8
Bedford Row LS10 215 A4
Bedford St N HX1 203 A3
Bedford St
Bradford BD4 201 C2
Cleckheaton BD19 116 C7
7 Elland HX5 134 F6
Halifax HX1 203 A3
Keighley BD21 35 B7
Leeds LS1 211 B4
Todmorden OL14 107 E8
Bedford View LS16 41 E3
Bedivere Rd BD8 73 D7
Bedlam La LS21 25 F4
Beech Ave
Crofton WF4 162 B7
Denholme BD13 52 C3
Holmfirth HD9 172 C1
Horsforth LS18 58 C7
Huddersfield HD5 154 F5
Huddersfield, Leymoor
HD7 152 E5
Leeds LS12 209 C4
Lofthouse Gate WF3 121 F4
Sowerby Bridge HX6 112 B5
Todmorden OL14 108 B6
Wakefield WF2 141 F7
Beech Cl
Bacup OL13 106 A3
Bradford BD10 39 B2
Brierley S72 181 A3
Menston LS29 22 A6
Shelf HX3 93 D6
South Kirkby WF9 182 B2
Beech Cotts HX7 110 D5
Beech Cres
Baildon BD17 37 F1
Bradford BD3 56 B1
Castleford WF10 125 D5
Darrington WF8 147 C5
Leeds LS9 61 D3
Beechcroft WF3 100 D1
Beech Croft
Pontefract WF8 125 E3
Walton WF2 161 A7
Beechcroft Cl LS11 213 A1
Beechcroft Mead LS17 44 A4
Beechcroft View LS11 213 A1
Beech Ct
Baildon BD17 38 B1
Castleford WF10 124 E6
Ossett WF5 140 C6
Beechdale Ave WF17 118 A7
Beech Dr
Ackworth M T WF7 146 A1
Denholme BD13 52 C3
Horsforth LS18 58 B7
Leeds LS12 209 C4
Beecher St
Halifax HX3 92 B2
Keighley BD21 18 E1
Beeches End LS23 30 E7
Beeches Rd BD21 35 E8
Beeches The
Baildon BD17 38 D4
Birkenshaw BD11 96 A5
Crofton WF4 144 B4
Guiseley LS20 22 E2
Pool LS21 24 D7
Pudsey LS28 76 B8
Wetherby LS22 14 A6
Beechfield
Gildersome LS12 77 D3
Wakefield WF2 160 E8
Beechfield Ave HD8 175 A1
Beechfield Dr WF4 144 B4
Beechfield Rd HD2 135 E1
Beechfield Terr 13 BD19 116 E7
Beech Gdns WF10 125 D6
Beech Gr
Bingley BD16 37 C5
Bradford BD3 56 B1
Bradford, Clayton BD14 73 C4
Brighouse HX3 115 A7
Burton Salmon LS25 105 E3
Cleckheaton BD19 96 A1
Fitzwilliam WF9 163 A2
Liversedge WF16 117 C5
Menston LS29 22 A3
Mirfield WF14 138 A5
Morley LS27 97 F3
Normanton WF6 144 A8
Purston Jaglin WF7 145 E4
Rothwell LS26 100 F6
Silsden BD20 5 D1
Beech Grove Ave LS25 82 E6
Beech Grove Terr
Garforth LS25 82 E6
Leeds LS2 206 B2
Beech Hill
Otley LS21 23 A8
Pontefract WF8 125 E1
Beech Hill Jun & Inf Sch
HX1 203 A4
Beech Ho LS16 59 C8
Beech Ind Est OL13 106 A3
Beech Inf & Jun Sch
HD7 152 E5
Beech La LS9 61 D3
Beechlands WF8 146 F5
Beechlea S63 194 C1
Beech Lees LS28 57 C4
Beech Mount LS9 61 D3
Beechmount Cl BD17 38 D4
Beechnut La WF8 125 C1
Beech Rd
Boston Spa LS23 30 C8
Bradford BD6 94 C7
Shafton S72 180 D2
Sowerby Bridge HX6 112 C4
Upton WF9 183 B7
Beechroyd LS28 76 E6
Beechroyd Terr BD16 36 F2
Beech Spinney LS22 13 E8
Beech Sq 1 BD14 73 C4
Beech St
Bacup OL13 106 A3
Bingley BD16 36 F2
East Ardsley WF3 98 E1
Elland, Holywell Green
HX4 134 A4
Elland HX5 134 F6
Glusburn BD20 16 D6
Halifax HX1 203 A4
3 Holmfirth HD9 189 A5
Huddersfield HD1 153 D5
Keighley BD21 35 E8
Mirfield WF14 138 A5
Pontefract WF8 146 E7
South Elmsall WF9 182 E1
Steeton BD20 17 C5
Beech Terr BD3 75 B8
Beechtree Ct BD17 38 A2
Beech Tree Rd WF7 145 E4
Beech View
Aberford LS25 64 D7
Castleford WF10 125 F7
Crigglestone WF4 159 F3
10 Sowerby Bridge HX6 112 B5
Beech Way WF17 97 A2
Beech Wlk
Birkenshaw BD11 96 B4
6 Dewsbury WF13 139 C8
Leeds, Gipton LS9 61 D3
Leeds LS16 42 D2
Beechwood
1 Pontefract WF8 146 B7
Rothwell LS26 101 D7
Beechwood Ave
Birkenshaw BD11 96 D7
Bradford BD6 74 B2
Halifax HX2, HX3 92 A5
Keighley BD20 18 F1
Leeds LS4 205 A3
Mirfield WF14 138 A5
Pontefract WF8 146 B7
Beechwood Ave *continued*
Shelf HX3 93 B5
Shipley BD18 54 E7
Sowerby Bridge HX6 111 F3
Wakefield WF2 141 D6
Beechwood Cl
Halifax HX2 91 F4
Horsforth LS18 41 A3
Beechwood Cres
Hemsworth WF9 181 C6
Leeds LS4 205 A3
Pontefract WF8 146 B7
Sowerby Bridge HX6 111 F3
Beechwood Ct
Leeds, Beechwood LS14 61 F6
Leeds LS16 42 B5
Beechwood Ctr LS26 101 C7
Beechwood Dale WF7 164 B7
Beechwood Dr
Bradford BD6 74 B2
Halifax HX2 91 F5
Sowerby Bridge HX6 111 F3
Beechwood Gr
Birkenshaw BD11 96 D7
Bradford BD6 74 B2
Halifax HX2 91 F4
Horbury WF4 141 C1
Huddersfield HD2 136 A4
Ilkley LS29 7 F4
Leeds LS4 205 A3
Shipley BD18 54 E7
Beechwood Mount
Hemsworth WF9 181 D6
Leeds LS4 205 A3
Beechwood Pk BD19 115 B6
Beechwood Pl LS4 205 A3
Beechwood Prim Sch
LS14 62 A4
Beechwood Rd
Bradford BD6 74 A2
Halifax HX2 91 F4
8 Leeds LS4 205 A3
Mirfield WF14 138 A6
Beechwood Rise LS22 13 E7
Beechwood Row 6 LS4 205 A3
Beechwood St
Leeds LS4 205 A3
Pudsey LS28 57 C1
Beechwood Terr LS4 205 A3
Beechwood View
Hebden Bridge HX7 88 D2
Leeds LS4 205 A3
Beechwood Villas HX2 91 F4
Beechwood Wlk LS4 205 A3
Beecroft Cl LS13 58 B3
Beecroft Cres LS13 58 B3
Beecroft Gdns LS13 58 B3
Beecroft Mount 3 LS13 58 B3
Beecroft Prim Sch LS4 59 B3
Beecroft St
Keighley BD21 35 D7
Leeds LS5 59 A3
Beecroft Wlk 1 BD15 73 A7
Beehive Ct WF15 117 C2
Beehive St 6 BD6 93 F7
Beehive Yd 7 BD6 93 F7
Beeston Hill St Luke's CE
Prim Sch LS11 214 B4
Beestonhirst HX6 131 E3
Beestonley HX4 133 E4
Beestonley La HX4 133 E4
Beeston Park Croft LS11 213 B2
Beeston Park Garth
LS11 213 B2
Beeston Park Gr LS11 213 B2
Beeston Park Pl LS11 213 B2
Beeston Park Terr LS11 213 B2
Beeston Prim Sch LS11 213 B2
Beeston Rd LS11 214 A3
Beeston Way WF10 103 C4
Beevers Ct LS16 41 F2
Bela Ave BD4 75 C3
Belcross Dr HX3 203 C4
Beldavia Ct WF6 123 B5
Beldon Brook Gn HD8 155 D1
Beldon La BD7 73 F2
Beldon Park Ave BD7 73 F2
Beldon Park Cl BD7 73 F2
Beldon Pl BD2 56 B2
Beldon Rd BD7 74 A3
Belfast St HX1 202 B2
Belford Cl BD4 75 D3
Belford Ct LS6 42 E1
Belfry Ct WF1 121 C5
Belfry Rd LS9 80 A5
Belfry The LS19 40 C6
Belfry Way WF6 123 D1
Belgrave Ave
Halifax HX3 203 C4
Ossett WF5 140 E4
Belgrave Cl HX3 203 C4
Belgrave Cres HX3 113 E8
Belgrave Dr HX3 113 E8
Belgrave Gdns HX3 203 C4
Belgrave Gr HX3 203 C4
Belgrave Mews LS19 40 A4
Belgrave Mount
Halifax HX3 92 D1
Wakefield WF1 216 C4
Belgrave Pk HX3 203 C4
Belgrave Rd
Bingley BD16 37 A3
Keighley BD21 35 B8
Belgrave St
Leeds LS2 211 C4
Ossett WF5 140 E4
12 Sowerby Bridge HX6 112 B4
Belgrave Terr
Huddersfield HD1 153 F7
Wakefield WF1 216 C4
Belgravia Gdns LS8 61 C7
Belgravia Rd WF1 216 A4
Belinda St LS10 215 B3
Bell Bank View BD16 36 E4
Bellbrooke Ave LS9 208 B2
Bellbrooke Gr 4 LS9 208 B2
Bellbrooke Pl 3 LS9 208 B2
Bellbrooke St LS9 208 B2
Bell Dean Rd BD15, BD8 73 B7
Belle Isle BD22 51 C6
Belle Isle Ave WF1 142 D4
Belle Isle Cir LS10 99 E8
Belle Isle Cl LS10 99 E8
Belle Isle Cres WF1 142 D4
Belle Isle Dr WF1 142 D4
Belle Isle Par LS10 215 B1
Belle Isle Rd
Haworth BD22 51 C7
Leeds LS10 99 E7
Bellerby Brow BD6 73 E1
Bellerby Pl DN6 184 F2
Bellerby Rd DN6 184 F2
Belle Vue
Bradford BD8 55 D1
Ilkley LS29 8 C3
Queensbury BD13 92 E7
Belle Vue Ave
Barwick in E LS15 62 F6
Leeds LS8 61 D6
Belle Vue Boys Sch BD9 54 C4
Belle Vue Cl BD10 39 B1
Belle Vue Cres
Huddersfield HD2 136 C3
Shelf HX3 93 B5
Belle Vue Ct LS3 205 C1
Belle Vue Dr LS28 57 C3
Belle Vue Est LS15 62 F6
Belle Vue Girls Sch BD9 54 C5
Belle Vue Rd
Barwick in E LS15 62 F6
Leeds LS3 205 C1
Shelf HX3 93 B5
Wakefield WF1 142 E2
Belle Vue Rise HX3 93 B5
Belle Vue St WF17 117 F5
Bellevue Terr HX2 111 C7
Belle Vue Terr
Guiseley LS20 39 E8
Halifax HX3 113 E5
Keighley BD21 35 D6
Bell Gr LS13 58 D3
Bellgreave Ave HD9 189 F6
Bell Hall Mount 20 HX1 202 C1
Bell Hall Terr HX1 202 C1
Bell Hall View HX1 203 A1
Bell House Ave BD4 75 B1
Bellhouse Cres BD4 95 B8
Bell La
Ackworth M T WF7 163 F5
Leeds LS13 58 D3
Bell Lane Prim Sch WF7 163 F5
Bellmont Cres WF9 181 E6
Bellmount Cl LS13 58 D3
Bellmount Gdns LS13 58 C4
Bellmount Gn 4 LS13 58 D4
Bellmount Pl LS13 58 D4
Bellmount View LS13 58 D3
Bell Rd LS13 58 C3
Bellshaw St BD8 73 E7
Bell Sq 6 BD20 5 E2
Bell St
17 Bradford BD12 94 C4
Dewsbury WF13 138 E5
Halifax HX3 203 C4
Huddersfield HD4 154 B4
1 Leeds LS9 212 A4
Upton WF9 183 E8
Wakefield WF1 216 A3
Bellstring La WF14 137 E1
Bellwood Ave LS23 30 D6
Belmont WF11 105 C1
Belmont Ave
Baildon BD17 38 B3
Bradford BD12 94 E7
Otley LS21 10 F1
Belmont Cl
Baildon BD17 38 B3
1 Huddersfield HD1 154 A7
Belmont Cres
Bradford BD12 94 E7
Shipley BD18 55 A8
Belmont Gdns BD12 94 D7
Belmont Gr
Bradford BD6 94 D7
Leeds LS2 206 A1
Yeadon LS19 40 C5
Belmont Grange WF15 117 A2
Belmont Mews 14 BD16 37 A3
Belmont Pl HX1 202 C2
Belmont Rd LS29 8 E4
Belmont Rise
Baildon BD17 38 B3
Bradford BD12 94 E7
Belmont St
Bradford BD2 56 C5
Featherstone WF7 144 C5
Halifax HX3 113 E8
Huddersfield HD1 154 A7
Slaithwaite HD7 169 F8
Sowerby Bridge HX6 112 C4
Wakefield WF1 216 A4
Belmont Terr
Luddenden Foot HX2 111 E5
Middleton WF3 99 F2
Shipley BD18 55 A8
Belmont Way WF9 183 B3
Belton Cl BD7 74 A3
Belton Gr HD3 135 B2
Belton Rd BD20 17 E8
Belton St HD5 154 E5
Belvedere Ave
Leeds, Alwoodley Gates
LS17 43 D4
Leeds LS11 214 B2
Belvedere Cl S72 180 C2
Belvedere Ct
Leeds LS17 43 E4
Leeds, Potternewton LS7 204 B1
Belvedere Gdns LS17 43 E4
Belvedere Gr LS17 43 D4
Belvedere Mount LS11 214 B2
Belvedere Rd
Batley WF17 118 B4
Leeds LS17 43 D4
Belvedere Terr
Bradford BD8 74 B8
Leeds LS11 214 B2
Belvedere View LS17 43 E4
Belvoir Dr WF11 126 E4
Belvoir Gdns HX3 113 C3
Bembridge Ct WF2 141 E5
Bempton Ct 5 BD7 74 B4
Bempton Gr WF17 96 F2
Bempton Pl 4 BD7 74 B4
Ben Booth La WF4 156 F4
Benbow Ave BD10 56 E5
Bendigo Rd WF12 118 F1
Benjamin St
Liversedge WF15 117 B3
Wakefield WF2 142 A7
Benjamin Sykes Way
WF2 141 C4
Ben Kaye Row HD9 189 B4
Benn Ave BD7 73 F4
Benn Cres BD7 73 F4
Bennet Ct LS15 81 D8
Bennett Ave WF4 141 C2
Bennett Ct LS21 10 F1
Bennett La WF12 118 F2
Bennett Rd LS6 59 D5
Bennett St
Halifax HX3 203 C2
5 Liversedge WF15 117 B4
Benn La HD3 152 F6
Benns La HX2 90 F2
Benny La HD7 152 B3
Benny Parr Cl WF17 118 E5
Benomley Cres HD5 154 E4
Benomley Dr HD5 154 E3
Benomley Rd HD5 154 E3
Ben Rhydding Dr LS29 8 F3
Ben Rhydding Prim Sch
LS29 8 E4
Ben Rhydding Rd LS29 8 D3
Ben Rhydding Sta LS29 8 E4
Benroyd Terr HX4 134 C4
Benson Ct BD2 55 D5
Benson Gdns
Leeds LS12 209 B2
Normanton WF6 123 C3
Benson La WF6 123 C3
Benson St LS7 207 A2
Bentcliffe Ave LS17 43 E2
Bentcliffe Cl LS17 43 E1
Bentcliffe Ct LS17 43 E1
Bentcliffe Dr LS17 43 E2
Bentcliffe Gdns LS17 43 E1
Bentcliffe Gr LS17 43 E1
Bentcliffe La LS17 43 D2
Bentcliffe Mount LS17 43 E1
Bentcliff Wlk BD15 73 B7
Bent Close La HX7 110 E3
Bent Est OL13 106 A7
Bent Farm Cotts BD20 16 B5
Bentfield Cotts BD14 73 C5
Bentham Way S75 178 A2
Bentinck Ho 3 BD16 37 A2
Bent La
Holmfirth HD9 199 B8
Sutton-in-C BD20 16 C5
Bent Lea HD2 136 F6
Bentley Ave HX3 115 A7
Bentley Cl BD17 38 B4
Bentley Ct 1 LS6 59 F6
Bentley Gdns LS6 59 F6
Bentley Gr LS6 59 F6
Bent Ley Ind Est HD9 171 A3
Bentley La LS6, LS7 59 F6
Bentley Mount
Leeds LS6 59 F6
Sowerby Bridge HX6 112 D5
Bentley Par LS6 59 F6
Bentley Rd WF2 141 E4
Bent Ley Rd HD9 171 A3
Bentley Royd Cl HX6 112 A3
Bentley Sq 2 LS26 101 C5
Bentley St
4 Bradford BD12 94 D3
Huddersfield HD1 153 E3
Benton Cres WF4 141 C2
Benton Mews WF4 141 C2
Benton Park Ave LS19 40 C5
Benton Park Cres LS19 40 C5
Benton Park Dr LS19 40 C5
Benton Park Rd LS19 40 C5
Benton Park Sch LS19 40 B5
Bent Rd HD9 199 D7
Bents La
Marsden HD7 169 B6
Wilsden BD15 53 A6

Bents Rd S36 200 D4
Bent St HD4 154 B4
Benyon Park Way LS12 213 A4
Beresford Rd BD6 94 B7
Beresford St BD12 95 A5
Beringa LS12 211 A3
Berkeley Ave LS8 208 A3
Berkeley Cres LS8 208 A3
Berkeley Croft S71 179 B4
Berkeley Ct LS3 205 C1
Berkeley Gr LS8 208 A3
Berkeley Ho 18 BD4 75 E3
Berkeley Mount LS8 208 A3
Berkeley Rd LS8 208 A3
Berkeley St LS8 208 A3
Berkeley Terr LS8 208 A3
Berkeley View LS8 208 A3
Berking Ave LS9 212 C4
Bermondsey Mews 9 LS21 23 B8
Bermondsey St 10 LS21 23 B8
Bernard St
Huddersfield HD2 136 E3
Rothwell LS26 101 D6
Berne Gr WF1 216 B3
Berners St WF1 216 C2
Berrington Way BD22 34 B3
Berry's Bldgs HX2 91 F4
Berry's Yd WF4 141 B2
Berry Bank La HD9 189 B8
Berry Brow Inf Sch HD4 171 F8
Berry Brow Sta HD4 171 F8
Berry Croft HD9 171 F5
Berrydale Cl BD15 73 A7
Berryfield Garth WF5 140 D8
Berry La
Halifax HX1 203 C3
Horbury WF4 141 B1
Keighley BD21 35 B6
Kippax LS26 102 E8
Berry Mill La HD3, HX4 151 C8
Berry Moor Rd HX6 112 D2
Berry Rd HD9 170 C3
Berry St 6 BD21 35 D7
Berry View HD4 153 F1
Bertha St LS28 57 D2
Bertie St BD4 75 C3
Bertram Dr BD17 38 B2
Bertram Rd BD8 55 C2
Bertrand St 4 LS11 211 A1
Berwick Ave WF16 117 D6
Berwick Ct BD6 73 B2
Berwick St HX1 203 C3
Bescaby Gr BD17 38 E3
Bescot Way BD18 55 E5
Besha Ave BD12 94 D6
Besha Gr BD12 94 D6
Bessingham Gdns BD6 93 F8
Best La
Kirkburton HD4 172 D7
Oxenhope BD22 51 C2
Beswick Cl BD3 75 D7
Beswick St OL14 129 A7
Bethal Gn OL15 129 C1
Bethel Rd BD18 55 D8
Bethel St
Brighouse HD6 115 B2
East Morton BD20 36 D8
2 Halifax HX3 92 A2
Bethel Terr
Halifax HX2 90 D1
Hebden Bridge HX7 89 A4
Sowerby Bridge HX6 112 D3
Bethesda Row HX7 89 D1
Betteras Hill Rd LS25 105 F7
Betula Way HD8 155 E3
Beulah Gr 3 LS6 206 B3
Beulah Mount 2 LS6 206 B3
Beulah Pl HX2 111 E5
Beulah St LS6 206 B3
Beulah Terr
Leeds, Cross Gates LS15 62 C2
Leeds LS6 206 B4
Beulah View 1 LS6 206 B3
Bevan Ave WF6 144 B8
Bevan Ct BD7 73 F3
Bevan Pl WF2 141 C4
Beven Gr WF1 216 C4
Beverley Ave
Bradford BD12 94 D2
Leeds LS11 214 B3
Beverley Cl
Elland HX5 135 B7
Normanton WF6 144 B8
Beverley Ct
Huddersfield HD2 136 B2
1 Pudsey LS28 57 D2
Beverley Dr
Bradford BD12 94 D2
Dewsbury WF12 139 F8
Beverley Garth WF7 164 A5
Beverley Gdns WF17 97 B2
Beverley Mount LS11 214 B3
Beverley Pl HX3 92 B1
Beverley Rise LS29 7 E4
Beverley St BD4 75 D5
Beverley Terr
Halifax HX3 92 B1
Leeds LS11 214 B3
Beverley View LS11 214 B3
Beverley Wlk LS25 82 F6
Bevin Cl WF1 121 C5
Bevin Cres WF1 121 C5
Bevitt St WF1 142 E3
Bevor Cres WF16 117 D6
Bewdley Ct S71 179 D4
Bewerley Cres BD6 94 A6
Bewick Gr LS10 99 F7
Bexhill Cl WF8 125 F2
Bexley Ave LS8 207 C2
Bexley Gr LS8 207 C2
Bexley Mount LS8 207 C2
Bexley Pl LS8 207 C2
Bexley Rd LS8 207 C3
Bexley Terr LS8 207 C2
Bexley View LS8 207 C2
Beza Ct LS10 215 A2
Beza Rd LS10 215 A3
Beza St LS10 215 A3
Bickerdike Pl WF10 103 B4
Bickerdike Terr LS25 83 A1
Bickerton Way LS21 10 E1
Biddenden Rd LS15 62 F2
Bidder Dr WF3 99 C1
Bideford Ave LS8 43 F2
Bideford Mount 4 BD4 75 E3
Bierley Hall Gr BD4 95 B7
Bierley House Ave BD4 75 C1
Bierley La BD4 95 B8
Bierley Marsh BD4 95 F7
Bierley View BD4 75 C1
Big Meadow Dr LS29 6 D8
Bilberry Cl BD14 73 C3
Bilberry Rise 10 BD22 51 D7
Bilham La DN5 195 D2
Bilham Rd HD8 176 A2
Bilham Row DN5 195 F3
Billam's Hill LS21 10 F1
Billey La LS12 77 E4
Billingbauk Dr LS13 58 D1
Billingbaulk Ct LS12, LS13 58 D1
Billing Ct LS19 40 D3
Billing Dr LS19 40 E3
Billingham Cl WF2 141 D8
Billingsley Terr BD4 75 B4
Billing View
Bradford BD10 56 C7
Yeadon LS19 40 D3
Billingwood Dr LS19 40 D3
Bill La HD9 189 C7
Billy La HX7 89 C5
Bilsdale Grange BD6 93 F8
Bilsdale Way BD17 38 A2
Bilton Pl BD8 74 C8
Bingham Pl WF1 121 A5
Bingley Bank LS17 28 C2
Bingley Five Rise Locks* BD16 36 F4
Bingley Gram Sch BD16 36 E4
Bingley Hospl BD16 37 A3
Bingley Lands 18 LS20 22 E1
Bingley Rd
Baildon BD17 38 B6
Bradford BD9 54 D4
Cullingworth BD13 35 B1
Guiseley BD16, LS20, LS29 21 C2
Haworth BD22 51 F8
Menston LS29 21 F3
Shipley BD18 54 E8
Bingley St
Bradford BD8 74 A7
Leeds LS3 210 C4
Bingley Sta BD16 36 F3
Binham Rd HD2 153 D8
Binks Fold 3 BD12 94 D2
Binks St WF1 121 C4
Binn HD7 170 A7
Binnie St BD3 75 B7
Binn La HD7 169 A2
Binn Rd HD7 168 F3
Binns Hill HX2 112 B6
Binns Hill La HX2 112 B6
Binns La
Bradford BD7 73 F5
Glusburn BD20 16 A6
Holmfirth HD9 188 F5
Binns St BD16 37 A3
Binns Top La HX3 114 B2
Binswell Fold 9 BD17 38 C4
Bircham Cl BD16 37 C5
Birch Apartments WF1 216 C4
Birch Ave
Bradford BD5 74 F2
Leeds LS15 81 A8
Lepton HD8 155 E2
Ripponden HX6 132 C1
Todmorden OL14 108 A7
Birch Cl
Bradford BD5 74 F2
Brighouse HD6 115 C3
Havercroft WF4 180 B8
Birch Cliff BD17 38 B2
Birchcliffe Rd HX7 89 A3
Birch Close La BD16 37 F8
Birch Cres LS15 81 A8
Birch Ct
Birkenshaw BD11 96 B6
Morley LS27 98 B2
Birchdale BD16 36 F5
Birch Dr LS25 83 A3
Birchen Ave WF5 140 C6
Birchen Cl WF10 124 A5
Birchencliffe Hill Rd HD3 135 B2
Birchen Hills WF5 140 C5
Birchenlee Cl HX7 89 F1
Birches The
Bramhope LS16 24 F2
Guiseley LS20 22 E2
Birchfield HX6 112 D2
Birchfield Ave LS27 97 C6
Birchfield Garth LS14 62 C8
Birchfield Gr HD8 175 A1
Birchfield Prim Sch LS27 97 C6
Birchfields Ave LS14 62 C8
Birchfields Cl LS14 62 C7
Birchfields Cres LS14 62 C8
Birchfields Ct LS14 62 C8
Birchfields Rise LS14 62 C8
Birchfield Villas 7 HX7 89 A3
Birch Gn WF8 125 F1
Birch Gr
Batley WF17 118 A8
Bradford BD5 74 E1
Castleford WF10 125 D6
Huddersfield HD7 152 E5
Keighley BD21 35 B4
Kippax LS25 83 A3
Birch Hill Rise LS18 58 E8
Birch Ho 7 WF10 124 E7
Birchington Ave HD3 135 B2
Birchington Cl HD3 135 B2
Birchington Dr HD3 135 A2
Birch La
Bradford BD5 74 E3
Bradford, Staygate BD5 74 F2
Luddenden HX2 111 F8
Birchlands Ave BD15 53 B6
Birchlands Gr BD15 53 B6
Birch Mews LS16 42 D2
Birch Pk HD9 172 D2
Birch Rd
Huddersfield HD4 171 F8
Kippax LS25 83 A3
Normanton WF6 144 B7
Birchroyd LS26 100 F4
Birchroyd Cl HD2 135 D2
Birch St
Bradford BD8 74 A8
Morley LS27 98 B2
Wakefield WF1 142 F4
Birchtree Cl WF1 142 F8
Birch Tree Gdns BD21 35 E6
Birchtree Way LS16 41 E2
Birchtree Wlk WF11 126 D3
Birch Way BD5 74 F2
Birchwood Ave
Batley WF17 96 F2
Keighley BD20 18 B2
Leeds LS17 44 A3
Birchwood Ct
Ilkley LS29 8 A4
2 Liversedge WF15 117 B3
Birchwood Dr BD20 18 B2
Birchwood Hill LS17 44 A4
Birchwood Mount LS17 44 A4
Birchwood Pk HD9 189 E6
Birchwood Rd BD20 18 A2
Birdale Field La LS22 29 D8
Birdcage Ct LS21 23 B6
Birdcage Hill HX3 113 A3
Birdcage La HX3 113 B3
Birdcage Wlk LS21 23 A6
Birdsedge Farm Mews HD8 191 A4
Birdsedge First Sch HD8 191 A4
Birds Edge La HD8 190 F4
Birdsnest La HD8 190 D2
Birds Royd La HD6 115 C1
Birdswell Ave HD6 115 D3
Birdwalk The BD6 73 C2
Birfed Cres LS4 59 B3
Birkby Brow Cres WF17 97 B2
Birkby Fold HD2 153 E8
Birkby Hall Rd HD2 135 E1
Birkby Haven BD6 93 E8
Birkby Jun Sch HD1 136 A1
Birkby La HD6 115 D7
Birkby Lodge Rd HD2 153 F8
Birkby Rd HD2 135 D1
Birkby St BD12 94 D4
Birkdale Ave HD3 153 A8
Birkdale Cl
Cullingworth BD13 52 E6
Leeds LS17 43 B4
Birkdale Ct BD20 18 A3
Birkdale Dr LS17 43 B4
Birkdale Gn LS17 43 B4
Birkdale Gr
Dewsbury WF13 118 A1
Halifax HX2 91 F7
Leeds LS17 43 A4
Birkdale High Sch WF13 118 A2
Birkdale Mount LS17 43 B4
Birkdale Pl LS17 43 A4
Birkdale Rd
Dewsbury WF13 118 B1
Royston S71 179 B5
Birkdale Rise LS17 43 A4
Birkdale Way LS17 43 B4
Birkdale Wlk LS17 43 A4
Birkenshaw CE Fst Sch BD11 96 B6
Birkenshaw La BD11 96 C4
Birkenshaw Mid Sch BD11 96 B4
Birkett St BD19 116 D8
Birkhead St WF16 117 E3
Birk Hey Cl BD19 115 B6
Birkhill WF10 125 C8
Birkhill Cres BD11 96 B5
Birkhouse La
Brighouse HD6 115 D6
Huddersfield HD5 154 E5
Huddersfield, Yews Hill HD1, HD4 153 E5
Birk House La HD8 191 B8
Birkhouse Rd HD6 115 C6
Birkin La WF11 127 D8
Birk La LS27 97 E4
Birklands Rd
Huddersfield HD2 135 F2
Shipley BD18 55 B7
Birklands Terr 4 BD18 55 B7
Birk Lea St BD5 74 F4
Birkmyre Ho 2 LS22 13 F6
Birks Ave BD7 73 F5
Birks Fold BD7 73 F6
Birkshall La BD4, BD3 75 B6
Birks Hall St HX1 202 C4
Birks Hall Terr HX1 202 C4
Birkshead BD15 53 D5
Birks La
Huddersfield HD4, HD5, HD8 155 A3
Kirkburton HD8 173 D3
Ripponden HX6 132 E5
Sowerby Bridge HX6 132 D8
Todmorden OL14 129 B8
Birksland Ind Est BD4 75 B5
Birksland Moor BD11 96 B3
Birksland St BD3 75 B6
Birks Rd HD3 153 A5
Birkwith Cl LS14 62 B8
Birkwood Ave WF4 144 B2
Birkwood Rd WF6 122 C3
Birmingham La HD9 170 C3
Birnam Gr BD4 75 A4
Birr Rd BD9 55 B3
Birstall La BD11 96 E5
Birstall Park Ct 2 WF17 96 F3
Birstall Prim Sch WF17 96 F1
Birthwaite Rd S75 177 B1
Bishop's Ct HD4 171 F7
Bishopdale Ct 2 HX1 203 A1
Bishopdale Dr LS22 13 A1
Bishopdale Holme BD6 93 E8
Bishopgate St LS1 211 B3
Bishop St BD9 55 B2
Bishops Way
Meltham HD9 170 E2
Mirfield WF14 137 D7
Bishop Way WF3 119 F8
Bisley Cl S71 179 E4
Bismarck Ct LS11 214 B4
Bismarck Dr LS11 214 B4
Bismarck St LS11 214 B4
Bittern Ct BD6 73 C2
Bittern Rise LS27 98 C3
Bk Airlie Ave LS8 207 C4
Black Abbey La BD20 16 C6
Blackberry Way
Bradford BD14 73 B3
Halifax HX3 113 E4
Blackbird Gdns BD8 73 B7
Black Brook Way HX4 134 C6
Black Bull St LS10 212 A2
Blackburn Bldgs HD6 115 C2
Blackburn Cl
Bradford BD8 73 D7
Halifax HX3 91 F3
Blackburn Ct
9 Pontefract WF8 146 C8
Rothwell LS26 100 F5
Blackburn Ho HX3 92 A3
Blackburn La WF11 127 C3
Blackburn Pl WF17 118 D5
Blackburn Rd
Batley WF17 96 E1
Brighouse HD6 115 A4
Black Carr Lo WF3 121 A6
Black Dyke La BD13 53 B1
Black Edge La BD13 71 D6
Blacker Cres WF4 158 E6
Blacker La
Netherton WF4 159 B5
Shafton S72 180 C3
Blacker Rd
Darton S75 178 C1
Huddersfield HD1, HD2 153 F8
Blackers Ct WF12 139 B4
Blackett St LS28 57 B7
Blackgates Cres WF3 119 F8
Black Gates Ct WF3 119 F8
Blackgates Dr WF3 119 F8
Blackgates Fold WF3 119 F8
Blackgates Prim Sch WF3 119 F8
Black Gates Rise WF3 119 F8
Black Hill
Bradford BD13 73 A2
Wadsworth Moor HX7 89 B8
Black Hill La
Bramhope LS16 25 D1
Keighley BD20 17 E1
Black Hill Rd LS21 25 C5
Blackhouse Fold HX2 91 D5
Blackhouse Rd HD2 136 B2
Black La HD7 170 E7
Blackledge HX1 203 C3
Blackley Rd HX5 134 E4
Blackman La LS2 206 B2
Blackmires HX2 92 A5
Blackmoor Ct LS17 42 F5
Blackmoorfoot Rd
Huddersfield HD4 153 E4
Linthwaite HD7 170 D7
Blackmoor La LS17 28 A1
Black Moor Rd
Leeds LS17 43 A2
Oxenhope BD22 51 E4
Blackpool Gr 7 LS12 78 A4
Blackpool Pl LS12 78 A4
Blackpool St 9 LS12 78 A4
Blackpool Terr 8 LS12 78 A4
Blackpool View 10 LS12 78 A4
Black Rd WF1, WF4 143 B3
Black Rock Mills HD7 170 D8
Blackshaw Beck La BD13 93 A
Blackshaw Clough Rd HX6 132 A
Blackshaw Dr BD6 93 D
Blackshaw St OL14 108 D
Black Sike La HD9 188 C
Blacksmith Fold BD7 74 A
Blacksmith La LS16 25 F
Blacksmith Mews WF3 100 B
Blacksmiths Fold HD5 154 F
Blackstone Ave BD12 94 C
Blackstone Edge Rd
Hebden Bridge HX7 131 B
Littleborough HX6, HX7 130 F
Black Swan Ginnell 11 HX1 203 E
Black Swan Pas 10 HX1 203 E
Blackthorn Ct 4 LS10 99 D
Blackthorn Dr HD3 135 A
Blackthorn Rd LS29 8 D
Blackthorn Way WF2 142 A
Blackwall HX1 203 B
Blackwall La HX6 112 E
Blackwall Rise HX6 112 E
Black Wlk WF8 125 E
Blackwood Ave LS16 41 D
Blackwood Gdns LS16 41 D
Blackwood Gr HX1 202 B
Black Wood Gr LS16 41 D
Blackwood Hall La HX2 111 D
Black Wood Mount LS16 41 D
Black Wood Rise LS16 41 D
Blacup Moor View BD19 116 D
Blagden La HD4 153 F
Blairsville Gdns LS13 58 B
Blairsville Gr LS13 58 C
Blaithroyd Ct HX3 113 E
Blaithroyd La HX3 113 E
Blaith Royd La HX7 109 F
Blake Cres LS20 39 F
Blake Gr LS7 204 A
Blake Hall Dr WF14 138 C
Blake Hall Rd WF14 138 C
Blake Hill HX3 92 E
Blakehill Ave BD2 56 C
Blake Hill End HX3 92 F
Blakehill Prim Sch BD10 56 A
Blakehill Terr BD2 56 C
Blakeholme Cl HD7 169 E
Blakelaw Dr HD6 115 D
Blake Law La
Brighouse WF15 115 F
Liversedge HD6 116 A
Blake Lee La HD7 168 E
Blakeley Gr WF2 141 F
Blakeney Gr LS10 215 A
Blakeney Rd LS10 215 A
Blakeridge La WF17 118 E
Blake Stones HD7 169 E
Blakestones Rd HD7 169 E
Blakey Rd WF2 141 F
Blamires Pl 2 BD7 73 F
Blamires St BD7 73 F
Blanche St BD4 75 D
Bland's Cl WF10 124 E
Blandford Gdns 21 LS2 206 E
Blandford Gr 23 LS2 206 E
Blands Ave WF10 103 A
Blands Cres WF10 103 A
Blands Gr WF10 103 A
Bland St
Halifax HX1 203 A
Huddersfield HD1 153 F
Blands Terr WF10 103 A
Blanket Hall St WF16 117 D
Blantyre Ct BD13 52 D
Blayd's Yd 7 LS1 211 C
Blayds Garth LS26 101 A
Blayds Mews 8 LS1 211 C
Blayds St LS9 212 C
Bleach Mill La LS29 21 E
Bleak Ave S72 180 C
Bleakley Ave WF4 179 B
Bleakley Cl S72 180 C
Bleakley La WF4 179 B
Bleakley Terr WF4 179 B
Bleak St Lower BD19 117 C
Bleak St BD19 117 C
Bleasdale Ave
Huddersfield HD2 135 F
Knottingley WF11 126 F
Blencarn Cl LS14 61 F
Blencarn Garth LS14 61 F
Blencarn Lawn LS14 61 F
Blencarn Path LS14 61 F
Blencarn Rd LS14 61 F
Blencarn View LS14 61 F
Blencarn Wlk LS14 61 F
Blenheim Ave 6 LS2 206 E
Blenheim Chase HD8 175 E
Blenheim Cl WF11 126 C
Blenheim Cres 5 LS2 206 E
Blenheim Ct
Halifax HX1 203 A
Leeds LS2 206 B
Blenheim Ctr LS6 206 E
Blenheim Dr
Batley WF17 118 C
Dewsbury WF13 118 A
Blenheim Gr LS2 206 E
Blenheim Hill WF17 118 D
Blenheim Mount BD8 55 C
Blenheim Pl BD10 39 B
Blenheim Prim Sch LS2 206 E
Blenheim Rd
Bradford BD8 55 C
Wakefield WF1 216 A

enheim Sq
Batley WF17 118 C6
Leeds LS2 206 B2
enheim St
Hebden Bridge HX7 89 B3
10 Keighley BD21 35 B5
enheim Terr
Batley WF17 118 C6
Leeds LS2 206 B2
enheim View LS2 206 B2
enheim Wlk LS2 206 B2
enkinsop Ct LS27 98 B2
ind La
Bickerton LS24 15 F8
Birkenshaw BD11 96 F8
East Ardsley WF3 120 A5
Halifax HX2 91 E8
Harden BD16 36 D3
Luddenden Foot HX2 111 B7
Shadwell LS17 44 E4
Todmorden OL14 108 B6
loomfield Rd S75 177 F1
loomfield Rise S75 177 F1
loomfield Sq 9 LS21 23 A7
loomhouse La S75 177 F1
lossom Ct HD5 154 E6
lossom Way WF10 125 F3
lucher St BD4 75 D6
lue Ball La HX6 131 E3
lue Ball Rd HX6 131 E3
luebell Cl
6 Bradford BD15 73 B8
Pontefract WF8 146 D7
4 Shipley BD18 55 D5
luebell Ct WF17 96 E2
lue Bell Hill HD4 153 F2
lue Bell La OL14 86 D2
luebell Rd
Darton S75 177 E3
East Ardsley WF3 120 E8
luebell Way WF9 182 F7
luebell Wlk HX2 111 E8
luebird Wlk BD16 37 C4
lue Butts WF5 140 D5
luecoat Ct LS22 28 F8
lue Hill BD13 52 D1
lue Hill Cres LS12 209 A2
lue Hill Gr LS12 209 A2
lue Hill Grange LS12 209 A1
lue Hill La LS12 209 A2
luehills La HD8 191 E6
lundell St
Leeds LS1 206 B1
South Elmsall WF9 182 E3
lythe Ave BD8 74 A8
lythe St BD7 74 D7
MK Ind Est WF15 117 B4
oardman St 3 OL14 108 B6
oar La LS1 211 C3
oathouse La WF14 138 C3
oat La
Kippax WF10 103 B3
Mickletown WF10 103 A3
oatman's Wharfe BD17 55 C8
obbin Cl HD7 152 D4
obbin Ct HD7 152 D4
obbin Mill Cl
Steeton BD20 17 C5
Todmorden OL14 86 B1
obbin Mill Ct BD20 17 C5
obbin St OL14 86 C1
ob La HX2 112 D7
odiham Hill LS25 83 B8
odkin La BD22 50 E3
odley Terr LS4 205 A1
odmin App LS10 99 A5
odmin Ave BD18 55 F7
odmin Cres LS10 99 B5
odmin Croft LS10 99 B4
odmin Dr WF6 123 B3
odmin Garth LS10 99 A4
odmin Gdns LS10 99 A4
odmin Pl LS10 99 B4
odmin Rd LS10 99 A5
odmin Sq LS10 99 A4
odmin St LS10 99 A4
odmin Terr LS10 99 A4
oggart Hill LS14 61 E6
oggart Hill Cres LS14 61 F6
oggart Hill Dr LS14 61 F6
oggart Hill Gdns LS14 61 E6
oggart Hill Rd LS14 61 E6
oggart La
Skelmanthorpe HD8 175 A3
Sowerby Bridge HX6 112 B3
oggart Wood View BD15 73 B7
og Green La HD5 137 C4
og La LS15 63 A5
oland Ct BD22 34 E3
oldgrove St WF12 140 A6
oldmere Rd LS15 80 E7
oldron Holt BD6 93 F8
oldshay St BD3 75 B8
olehill Pk HD6 114 E6
olingbroke Ct 10 BD5 201 B1
olingbroke St BD5 74 D2
olland Bldgs BD12 94 F5
olland St 3 BD12 94 E5
olling Hall (Mus)★ BD4 75 A3
olling Rd
Bradford BD4 201 C1
Ilkley LS29 8 D4
olling Specl Sch BD4 75 B3
olsover Cl LS25 83 B7
olster Gr HD7 152 B3
olstermoor Rd HD7 152 A4
oltby La BD6 93 E8
olton Abbey Sta★ BD23 2 C7
Bolton Bridge Ct 5 LS29 8 A4
Bolton Bridge Rd LS29 8 A4
Bolton Brow HX6 112 D4
Bolton Brow Jun & Inf Sch
HX6 112 D4
Bolton Cres BD2 56 B4
Bolton Ct BD2 56 A2
Bolton Dr BD2 56 B4
Bolton Gr BD2 56 B4
Bolton Grange LS19 40 C6
Bolton Hall Rd BD2 55 E5
Bolton La BD2 55 E3
Bolton Rd
Addingham LS29 2 F4
Bradford BD2, BD3 55 F2
Bradford, Bolton Outlanes
BD2 56 A3
Silsden BD20, LS29 5 F4
Yeadon LS19 40 C6
Bolton Royd Primary Sch
LS28 76 A8
Bolton St
Bradford BD3 201 D3
Bradford, Low Moor BD12 94 C6
Bolton Terr BD20 5 E2
Bolton Way LS23 30 C7
Bolton Wife Hill WF4 159 F1
Bolus Cl WF1 121 C4
Bolus La WF1 121 C4
Bonaccord Sq WF17 118 C4
Bonaccord Terr WF17 118 C4
Bonaire LS12 210 C3
Bond Ct LS1 211 B4
Bondgate
Harewood LS17 27 A7
Otley LS21 23 A7
Pontefract WF8 125 F2
Bond St
6 Batley, Birstall WF17 96 E1
Batley WF17 118 C6
Brighouse HD6 115 A3
Dewsbury WF13 139 C8
Halifax HX1 203 A2
Hebden Bridge HX7 89 A3
Leeds LS1 211 B4
Pontefract WF8 125 E2
Todmorden OL14 108 B5
Wakefield WF1 216 A3
Bond Terr WF1 216 B3
Bonegate Ave HD6 115 B3
Bonegate Rd HD6 115 B3
Bonn Rd BD9 55 A2
Bonwick Mall BD6 93 E7
Boocock St 2 LS28 57 E1
Bookers Field BD19 117 C7
Booth's Bldgs HD6 115 B7
Booth HD7 169 B6
Bootham Pk BD9 54 D2
Booth Bank HD7 169 C7
Booth Hill HX2 90 E4
Booth House La HD9 188 D4
Booth House Rd HX2 111 C7
Booth House Terr HX2 111 C7
Boothman Wlk 4 BD21 35 A5
Booth Royd BD10 39 B1
Boothroyd Dr
Huddersfield HD4 153 B3
Leeds LS6 59 F5
Booth Royd Dr BD10 39 B1
Boothroyd Gn WF13 139 B8
Boothroyd Jun & Inf Sch
WF13 139 A7
Boothroyd La WF13 139 A8
Booth Royd La HD6 135 D8
Boothroyds Way WF7 145 A6
Booth St
Bradford BD10 56 B7
Burley in W LS29 9 E2
Castleford WF10 124 D8
Cleckheaton BD19 116 D8
5 Queensbury BD13 72 D1
Shipley BD18 55 D7
Booths Yd 8 LS28 76 E7
Booth Terr HX2 90 E3
Boothtown Rd HX3 92 B2
Border Cl HD3 134 F1
Boroughgate LS21 23 A8
Borough Mkt HX1 203 B3
Borough Rd WF1 216 B3
Borrins Way BD17 38 D3
Borrough Ave LS8 204 B4
Borrough View LS8 204 B4
Borrowdale Cres LS12 58 F2
Borrowdale Croft LS19 40 B7
Borrowdale Dr WF10 104 D1
Borrowdale Rd
Batley WF12 118 E2
Wakefield WF2 141 E7
Borrowdale Terr LS14 61 F3
Boshaw HD9 199 B8
Boston Ave LS5 58 F3
Boston Hill HX7 89 B6
Boston Mews LS23 30 E7
Boston Rd
Clifford LS23 30 D6
Wetherby LS22 13 E3
Boston Spa Sch LS23 30 B7
Boston St
Castleford WF10 124 E8
Halifax HX1 202 B3
Sowerby Bridge HX6 112 A3
Boston Twrs LS9 207 B1
Boston Wlk BD6 93 F8
Boswell Cl 4 S71 179 B4
Bosworth Ave WF6 122 E4
Bosworth Cl BD15 54 B1
Botany Ave BD2 55 F4
Botany Dr BD20 19 E2
Botany La HD8 155 F4
Botham Fields HD3 153 A5
Botham Hall Rd HD3 152 F5
Bottom Boat Rd WF3 122 D6
Bottomley's Bldgs LS6 206 B3
Bottomley La HX4 133 C2
Bottomley Rd OL14 129 C6
Bottomley St
Bradford BD5 74 D4
Bradford, Buttershaw BD6 93 F7
2 Brighouse HD6 115 B4
Bottoms
Cragg Vale HX7 110 D4
Halifax HX3 113 D3
Bottoms La BD11 96 B4
Boulder Bridge La S71 179 F1
Boulder Gate HD7 169 B4
Boulevard The
Leeds LS12 213 A3
Pudsey LS28 57 D2
Boundary Ave BD20 16 D6
Boundary Cl
Baildon BD17 38 D5
Leeds LS15 81 E7
Boundary Ct HD9 189 D3
Boundary Dr S72 181 A3
Boundary Farm Rd LS17 43 A3
Boundary La WF1, WF6 143 F7
Boundary Rd WF13 117 F2
Boundary St WF16 117 C4
Boundary The BD8 54 E1
Bounday Dr WF1 121 C1
Bourbon Cl BD6 94 B8
Bourne Ct S75 178 C2
Bourne St BD10 39 B2
Bourne Wlk S75 178 C2
Bourn View Cl HD4 171 D7
Bourn View Rd HD4 171 D7
Bourse The LS2 211 C3
Bowater Ct 3 BD4 75 F2
Bow Beck BD4 75 A5
Bowbridge Rd 8 BD5 74 E4
Bowcliffe Rd
Bramham LS23 30 D2
Leeds LS10 215 C4
Bower Gn BD3 75 C7
Bower La WF13 117 F3
Bower Rd LS15 62 E3
Bowers La HX4 133 D6
Bower Slack Rd HX6 110 F1
Bowers Mill Ind Est HX4 133 D5
Bower St BD5 201 B1
Bower The 1 WF17 117 F7
Bowes Nook BD6 93 E7
Bowfell Cl LS14 62 A4
Bow Gn BD7 73 D4
Bow La HX7 88 A4
Bowland Ave BD17 37 E1
Bowland Cl LS15 80 E7
Bowland St BD1 74 D8
Bowler Cl BD12 94 C6
Bowlers Ct WF1 121 C1
Bowling Alley HD6 136 A8
Bowling Alley Terr HD6 136 A8
Bowling Ave WF2 120 F2
Bowling Back La BD4 75 B5
Bowling Court Ind Est
BD4 75 C5
Bowling Ct
Brighouse HD6 114 F3
Wakefield WF2 142 B3
Bowling Dyke HX3 203 B4
Bowling Green Ct
Elland HX4 133 F3
Huddersfield HD3 152 E7
Bowling Green Prim Sch
HX4 133 F3
Bowling Green Rd HX4 133 F3
Bowling Green Terr
LS11 211 B1
Bowling Green View
BD11 96 E6
Bowling Hall Rd BD4 75 A3
Bowling Old La
Bradford, Bankfoot BD5 74 D2
Bradford BD5 74 E4
Bowling Park Cl BD4 74 F4
Bowling Park Dr BD4 74 F3
Bowling Park Prim Sch
BD5 74 F3
Bowling St HD4 153 A4
Bowman Ave BD6 94 B7
Bowman Gr HX1 202 C3
Bowman La LS10 212 A3
Bowman Pl 5 HX1 202 C3
Bowman Rd BD6 94 B7
Bowman St
6 Halifax HX1 202 C3
Wakefield WF1 142 F3
Bowman Terr HX1 202 C3
Bowmere Dr 11 BD15 73 B8
Bownas Rd LS23 30 C8
Bowness Ave
Bradford BD10 56 D4
Castleford WF10 104 E1
Bowness Dr HD5 154 D7
Bowood Ave LS7 60 A7
Bowood Cres LS7 60 A7
Bowood Gr LS7 60 A7
Bowood La HX6 111 D1
Bowood Rd HX5 134 F5
Bow St
Huddersfield HD1 153 F5
Keighley BD21 35 C7
Leeds LS9 212 B3
Bowwood Dr BD20 36 C8
Box's Bldgs WF17 117 F6
Boxhall Rd HX5 134 F7
Box La WF8 125 E2
Box Tree Cl BD8 54 E1
Box Tree Gr BD21 35 E6
Box Trees La HX2 91 D3
Boycott Dr WF7 164 A5
Boycott Way WF9 183 A4
Boyd Ave BD3 56 E1
Boy La
Bradford BD4 95 B7
Halifax HX3 91 D2
Boyle & Petyt Prim Sch The
BD23 2 F6
Boyle The LS15 63 D8
Boyne Dr WF2 160 A5
Boyne Hill WF4 160 A4
Boyne St HX1 203 A3
Boynton St BD5 74 E3
Boynton Terr BD5 74 E3
Boys La HX3 203 C1
Boys Scarr HX2 111 D6
Bracewell Ave BD15 73 A8
Bracewell Bank HX3 92 A2
Bracewell Dr HX3 91 F2
Bracewell Gr 2 HX3 92 A1
Bracewell Rd HD9 170 D1
Bracewell St BD21 35 F7
Bracken Ave HD6 115 A5
Bracken Bank Ave BD22 34 F3
Bracken Bank Cres BD22 35 A3
Bracken Bank Gr BD22 34 F3
Bracken Bank Way BD22 34 F3
Bracken Bank Wlk BD22 34 F2
Brackenbeck Mews HX3 93 D7
Brackenbeck Rd BD7 73 F4
Brackenbed Grange HX2 91 E1
Brackenbed La HX2 91 F1
Bracken Cl
Brighouse HD6 115 A5
Mirfield WF14 137 D7
Bracken Ct
Leeds, Carr Manor LS17 43 C1
Leeds LS12 210 B1
Brackendale BD10 39 A2
Brackendale Ave BD10 39 A2
Brackendale Dr BD10 38 F2
Brackendale Gr BD10 38 F2
Brackendale Par BD10 38 F2
Brackendale Rd WF2 142 A2
Bracken Edge
Bradford BD10 56 C7
Leeds LS8 204 C1
Bracken Edge Prim Sch
LS7 204 B1
Bracken Ghyll Dr BD20 5 D2
Bracken Gn WF3 120 E8
Bracken Gr
Huddersfield HD2 136 B4
Mirfield WF14 137 D7
Bracken Hall Countryside
Ctr★ BD17 37 E3
Brackenhall Ct BD7 73 F4
Bracken Hall Rd HD2 136 C3
Bracken Hill
Ackworth M T WF7 163 D6
Leeds LS17 43 C1
Mirfield WF14 137 D7
South Kirkby WF9 182 D4
Brackenhill Dr BD7 73 F3
Brackenhill Prim Sch BD7 73 F3
Brackenholme Royd 5
BD6 93 E8
Brackenhurst Dr 5 LS17 43 C2
Brackenhurst Pl 6 LS17 43 C2
Bracken Mount BD20 5 D2
Bracken Pk
Bingley BD16 37 C3
Gildersome LS27 97 C5
Scarcroft LS14 45 A7
Bracken Rd
Brighouse HD6 115 A5
Keighley BD22 35 A4
Steeton BD20 17 A5
Brackens La HX3 93 B7
Bracken Sq HD2 136 C4
Bracken St BD21 35 B4
Bracken Way HX5 135 B7
Brackenwood Cl
Ilkley LS29 8 E4
Leeds LS8 204 B3
Brackenwood Ct WF1 121 D5
Brackenwood Dr LS8 204 B4
Brackenwood Gn LS8 204 B4
Brackenwood Rd WF1 121 D5
Bradbeck Rd BD7 73 F7
Bradburn Rd WF3 100 A3
Bradbury St WF13 138 E5
Bradcroft HD1 136 B1
Bradd Cl WF15 117 B5
Bradfield Cl HD2 136 E5
Bradford Bsns Pk BD1 55 E1
Bradford Cathedral Com Coll
BD4 75 B3
Bradford Christian Sch
BD2 55 D4
Bradford Coll BD7 74 D6
Bradford Coll Joseph Nutter
Ho BD5 74 B4
Bradford Coll McMillan Bldg
BD5 74 D5
Bradford Forster Sq Sta
BD1 201 B3
Bradford Girls' Gram Sch
BD9 54 F1
Bradford Gram Sch BD9 55 C3
Bradford & Heckmondwike
Rd BD4 95 F8
Bradford Ind Mus★ BD2 56 C3
Bradford Interchange Sta
BD1 201 C2
Bradford La BD3 75 D7
Bradford Moor Com Prim
Sch BD3 75 C8
Bradford Old Rd
Halifax HX3 92 C2
Shipley BD16 54 B7
Bradford Playhouse
(Theatre)★ BD1 201 C3
Bradford Rd
Batley WF17 118 D5
Bingley BD16 37 A1
Birkenshaw BD11 96 A5
Birkenshaw, Drighlington
BD11 96 D7
Bradford BD10 56 B6
Bradford, Clayton BD14 73 D5
Bradford, Oakenshaw BD12,
BD19 95 B3
Brighouse HD6 115 B2
Brighouse HD6 115 B5
Burley in W LS29 21 F8
Cleckheaton BD19 116 E8
Cleckheaton, Birstall BD19,
WF17 96 C2
East Ardsley WF3 120 B8
Gildersome BD11, LS27 97 B5
Guiseley LS29 22 B3
Huddersfield HD1, HD2 136 B3
Keighley BD20, BD21 18 E1
Keighley, Eastwood BD21 35 D8
Liversedge WF15 117 B4
Lofthouse Gate WF2 120 E5
Menston LS29 22 B3
Northowram HX3 93 A1
Northowram HX3 93 A3
Otley LS21 22 D6
Pudsey LS28 57 C1
Shipley BD18 55 B6
Shipley, Nab Wood BD18 54 C7
Wakefield WF2 120 F3
Bradford Royal Infmy BD9 54 F1
Bradfords Cl LS23 30 C3
Bradford St
Dewsbury WF13 118 D1
Keighley BD21 35 D8
Bradford & Wakefield Rd BD4,
BD11 96 C7
Bradlaugh Rd BD6 74 B1
Bradlaugh Terr 2 BD6 74 C1
Bradley Ave
Castleford WF10 124 C8
Silsden BD20 5 D2
Bradley Bsns Pk HD2 136 D5
Bradley Bvd HD2 136 C3
Bradley Carr Terr WF9 194 E8
Bradley CE Jun & Inf Sch
HD2 136 F5
Bradley Dr BD20 5 D2
Bradley Gr BD20 5 D2
Bradley Grange Gdns
HD2 136 F6
Bradley Hill LS13 58 A2
Bradley Junction Ind Est
HD2 136 F4
Bradley La
Elland HX4 134 B6
Pudsey LS28 76 B7
Bradley Mills La HD1 154 C8
Bradley Mills Rd HD5 154 D8
Bradley Quarry Cl HD2 137 A6
Bradley Rd
Huddersfield HD2 136 D6
Silsden BD20 5 D2
Bradley Rise BD20 5 D2
Bradleys Both Com Prim Sch
BD20 4 C6
Bradley St
Bingley BD16 36 F3
Castleford WF10 124 D8
Shipley BD9 55 C4
Bradley Terr LS17 44 A4
Bradley View HX4 134 B4
Bradshaw Ave HD9 171 E3
Bradshaw Cl HD9 171 E3
Bradshaw Cres HD9 171 E3
Bradshaw Dr HD9 171 E3
Bradshaw La
Halifax HX2 72 A2
Marsden HD7 151 A1
Bradshaw Primary Sch
HX2 71 F1
Bradshaw Rd
Honley HD9 171 E2
Meltham HD9 188 B7
Bradshaw Row HX2 71 F2
Bradshaw View
Halifax HX2 91 E7
Queensbury BD13 72 C1
Bradstock Gdns LS27 98 A6
Bradwell La WF5 140 E5
Brae Ave BD2 55 F3
Braemar Croft S72 180 D7
Braemar Dr LS25 83 B8
Braemar Rise S72 180 D7
Braeside HX2 112 D7
Brafferton Arbor BD6 93 E8
Braine Rd LS22 13 F6
Braithwaite Ave BD22 34 F7
Braithwaite Cres BD22 34 F7
Braithwaite Ct WF9 181 E8
Braithwaite Dr BD22 34 F7
Braithwaite Edge Rd
BD22 34 D8

Braithwaite Gr BD22 34 F7
Braithwaite Rd BD22 34 E8
Braithwaite Row 6 LS10 215 B2
Braithwaite Sch BD22 34 E8
Braithwaite St
Darton S75 178 C1
Leeds LS11 210 C2
Braithwaite Way BD22 34 F7
Braithwaite Wlk BD22 34 F7
Bramah St S71 179 C1
Bramall Bsns Pk BD5 74 E4
Bramble Ave LS23 30 B7
Bramble Cl
Bradford BD14 73 C3
Halifax HX3 113 E4
Haworth BD22 51 D6
Pontefract WF8 146 B7
Bramble Ct
Lofthouse Gate WF3 121 A5
Pool LS21 24 D6
Bramble Gr
Elland HX5 135 B7
Pool LS21 24 D6
Bramble Mews LS17 44 C5
Bramble Rd S72 180 E6
Brambles The
Ilkley LS29 7 F4
Royston S71 179 A4
Bramble Wlk WF17 96 F1
Brambling Dr 1 BD6 73 C2
Brambling Mews LS27 98 C3
Bramblings The WF10 124 A5
Bramham's Yd 2 LS25 83 B1
Bramham Dr BD17 38 D4
Bramham La LS17, LS23 29 B3
Bramham Park Ct LS10 99 D3
Bramham Park House & Gardens★ LS23 46 F8
Bramham Prim Sch LS23 30 D4
Bramham Rd
Bingley BD16 37 A4
Castleford WF10 124 A6
Clifford LS23 30 D4
Thorner LS14 46 C7
Bramhope Prim Sch LS16 24 E2
Bramhope Rd BD19 116 C8
Bramleigh Dr LS27 98 A6
Bramleigh Gr LS27 98 A6
Bramley Cl
Holmfirth HD9 189 D7
Oakworth BD22 34 B3
Bramley Cres WF1 121 B4
Bramley Ctr LS13 58 D3
Bramley Fold HX3 114 D8
Bramley Gdns LS14 45 C1
Bramley Grange 7 LS13 58 C1
Bramley La
Brighouse HX3 114 D8
West Bretton WF4 177 B8
Bramley Prim Sch LS13 58 B2
Bramley St Peter's CE Prim Sch LS13 58 C2
Bramley St
Bradford BD5 74 E4
Bradford BD5 201 B1
5 Leeds LS13 58 C1
Bramley Sta LS13 58 B1
Bramley View HX3 114 E8
Brampton HX2 90 B1
Brampton Ct WF9 183 A5
Bramstan Ave LS13 58 A3
Bramstan Cl LS13 58 A3
Bramstan Gdns LS13 58 A3
Bramston Gdns 11 HD6 115 A1
Bramston St HD6 115 A1
Bramwell Dr BD22 51 C6
Bramwell Ho BD3 201 C4
Bramwell Lo BD7 74 A3
Bramwell Way HX1 203 A1
Branby Ave BD20 19 A1
Brancepeth Pl LS12 210 B3
Branch Cl LS12 78 A4
Branch End LS27 97 E7
Branch La HD2 135 B3
Branch Pl LS12 78 A4
Branch Rd
Batley WF17 118 C5
Brighouse BD19 94 F1
Crigglestone WF4 159 C4
Dewsbury WF13 139 C8
Elland HX4 133 D5
Huddersfield HD2 135 B4
Leeds, Armley LS12 209 C4
Leeds LS12 78 A4
Branch St
Huddersfield HD1 153 D5
Leeds LS12 78 A4
Brander App LS9 61 D1
Brander Cl
Bradford BD10 56 B6
Leeds LS9 61 D1
Brander Dr LS9 61 D1
Brander Gr LS9 208 C1
Brander Rd LS9 61 D1
Brander St LS9 61 D2
Brandfort St BD7 74 A5
Brand Hill App WF4 143 E1
Brand Hill Dr WF4 143 E1
Brandling Ct LS10 99 C5
Brandon Cres LS17 44 F6
Brandon Ct LS17 44 C5
Brandon La LS17 44 F6
Brandon Rd 5 LS3 206 A1
Brandon St LS12 210 C3
Brandon Terr LS17 44 C5
Brandon View LS17 44 D5
Brandon Way LS7 204 A1
Brandon Way Cres LS7 204 B1
Brandy Carr Rd WF2 120 C3
Branksome Cres BD9 54 F2
Branksome Ct BD9 54 F2
Branksome Dr BD18 54 D8
Branksome Gr BD18 54 C8
Branksome Pl LS6 205 B2
Branksome St LS6 205 B2
Branksome Terr LS6 205 B2
Bransby Cl LS28 57 E2
Bransby Ct 1 LS28 57 E2
Bransby Rise LS28 57 E2
Bransdale Ave
Guiseley LS20 39 E8
Normanton WF6 123 A4
Bransdale Cl
Baildon BD17 38 A2
4 Guiseley LS20 39 E8
Normanton WF6 123 A4
Bransdale Clough BD6 73 E1
Bransdale Garth 5 LS20 39 E8
Bransdale Gdns LS20 39 E8
Bransdale Mews WF6 123 A4
Bransdale Wlk WF6 123 A4
Branshaw Dr BD22 34 E5
Branshaw Gr BD22 34 E5
Branshaw Mount BD22 34 E5
Branshaw Sch BD22 35 A6
Bran St BD21 35 B4
Branstone Gr WF5 119 D1
Brant Ave HX2 91 F4
Brant Bank La LS29 7 D6
Brantcliffe Dr BD17 38 C4
Brantcliffe Way BD17 38 C5
Brantdale Cl BD9 54 C4
Brantdale Rd BD9 54 C4
Brantford St LS7 204 A2
Brantom Farm HX2 111 C5
Brantwood Ave BD9 54 C4
Brantwood Cl BD9 54 C4
Brantwood Cres BD9 54 C4
Brantwood Dr BD9 54 C4
Brantwood Gr BD9 54 B4
Brantwood Oval BD9 54 C4
Brantwood Rd BD9 54 B4
Brantwood Villas BD9 54 C4
Branwell Ave WF17 96 F3
Branwell Ct BD9 54 E2
Branwell Dr BD22 51 C8
Branwell Lo BD10 39 F1
Branwell Wlk WF17 96 F3
Branxholme Ind Est HD6 115 B7
Brassey Rd BD4 75 A4
Brassey St HX1 203 A2
Brassey Terr BD4 75 A4
Brathay Gdns LS14 62 A3
Braybrook Ct BD8 55 C3
Bray Cl BD7 73 D2
Brayshaw Dr BD7 73 D2
Brayshaw Fold BD12 94 E6
Brayshaw Rd WF3 120 C7
Brayside Ave HD2 135 F2
Brayton App LS14 62 C5
Brayton Cl LS14 62 C5
Brayton Garth 6 LS14 62 D5
Brayton Gn LS14 62 D5
Brayton Gr LS14 62 C5
Brayton Pl 8 LS14 62 D5
Brayton Sq 7 LS14 62 D5
Brayton Terr LS14 62 C5
Brayton Wlk LS14 62 C5
Brazil St WF10 124 E8
Bread St WF1 216 B2
Breakmoor Ave BD20 5 E3
Break Neck HX3 114 A8
Breaks Rd 4 BD12 94 E6
Bream Ave BD19 116 C7
Brearcliffe Cl 3 BD6 94 A8
Brearcliffe Dr BD6 94 A8
Brearcliffe Gr BD6 94 A7
Brearcliffe Rd BD6 94 B7
Brearcliffe St BD6 94 A7
Brearley Gdns WF15 117 A3
Brearley La HX2 111 B8
Brearley Lane Top HX2 90 B1
Brearley Pl WF17 118 C4
Brearley St WF17 118 B4
Brearton St BD1 201 B4
Breary Ave LS18 41 D1
Breary Ct LS16 24 E3
Breary La LS16 24 E3
Breary La E LS16 25 A3
Breary Rise LS16 24 E3
Breary Terr LS18 41 D1
Breary Wlk LS18 41 D1
Breck Lea HX6 112 A3
Brecks BD14 73 D5
Brecks Gdns LS25 82 F3
Brecks La
Kippax LS25 82 F3
Swillington LS26 82 C4
Brecks Rd BD14 73 D5
Breck Willows HX6 111 F2
Brecon App LS9 61 D1
Brecon Ave HD3 135 A1
Brecon Cl BD10 56 B7
Brecon Ct LS9 61 D1
Brecon Rise LS9 61 D1
Bredon Ave BD18 55 F7
Bredon Cl WF9 181 F7
Breighton Adown BD6 93 D8
Bremner St LS21 23 B8
Brendan Ct BD10 56 D6
Brendon Ct
Bradford BD4 75 D3
Brendon Ct *continued*
Mirfield WF14 137 F2
Brendon Dr HD2 135 D1
Brendon Wlk BD4 75 D2
Brentford Rd BD12 94 C6
Brentlea Ave WF2 142 B3
Brentwood Cl
Batley WF17 118 E5
Thorpe Audlin WF8 165 A5
Brentwood Gdns BD6 94 D8
Brentwood Gr 8 LS12 209 C3
Brentwood St 11 LS12 209 C3
Brentwood Terr 12 LS12 209 C3
Bretfield Ct WF12 139 D5
Brettegate WF9 181 C7
Brett Gdns LS11 214 B4
Bretton Cl S72 180 F2
Bretton Ctry Pk★ WF4 176 F7
Bretton Ctry Pk Visitor Ctr★ S75 177 A6
Bretton Hall Coll WF4 176 E6
Bretton Hall Coll (Annexe) WF10 124 C7
Bretton La WF4 159 B2
Bretton Park Way WF12 139 E5
Bretton St WF12 139 D5
Bretton Street Ent Ctr WF12 139 D5
Brewerton La WF13 117 F2
Brewery Ct HD3 135 A1
Brewery Dr HD4 153 F1
Brewery La
Dewsbury WF12 139 C4
Knottingley WF11 126 F4
Queensbury BD13 72 D3
Queensbury, Shibden Head BD13 92 C7
Brewery Pl LS10 212 A3
Brewery Rd
Ilkley LS29 8 C4
Keighley BD21 35 A3
Brewery St
5 Batley WF16 117 D3
2 Halifax HX3 92 C2
Keighley BD21 35 D7
Todmorden OL14 107 E8
Brewery Wharf WF14 138 A4
Brewery Yd HD8 155 C3
Brexdale Ave LS25 82 F3
Brian Ave HD5 154 E5
Brian Cres LS15 62 B3
Brian Pl LS15 62 B3
Brian Royd La HX4 133 F7
Brian St HD3 135 B1
Brian View LS15 62 C3
Briar Ave HD9 170 C3
Briar Bank WF9 163 A2
Briar Cl
Batley WF16 117 D5
Elland HX5 134 E5
Pudsey LS28 57 D3
Briar Ct HD9 188 D4
Briardale Rd BD9 54 B4
Briardene LS26 101 C5
Briar Dr WF13 117 F2
Briarfield HD8 192 A6
Briarfield Ave BD10 56 A7
Briarfield Cl
Bradford BD10 56 A7
Ilkley LS29 8 D3
Briarfield Gdns
Gildersome LS27 97 C6
Huddersfield HD5 154 E6
Shipley BD18 55 C6
Briarfield Gr BD10 56 A7
Briarfield Rd
Holmfirth HD9 189 C7
Shipley BD18 55 C5
Briar Gate LS22 13 E7
Briar Gr
Brierley S72 181 A3
Wakefield WF1 142 E3
Briarlea Cl LS19 39 F5
Briarlyn Ave HD3 135 A2
Briarlyn Rd HD3 135 B2
Briarmains Rd WF17 96 F2
Briar Rhydding BD17 38 E2
Briarsdale Croft LS8 208 C3
Briarsdale Ct LS8 208 C3
Briarsdale Garth LS8 208 B3
Briarsdale Hts LS9 208 C3
Briarsdale Mews LS8 208 B3
Briar St 5 OL13 106 A1
Briar Wood BD18 55 E7
Briarwood Ave
Bradford BD6 74 B1
Keighley BD20 18 F1
Briarwood Cl WF1 121 D5
Briarwood Cres BD6 74 B1
Briarwood Dr BD6 74 B1
Briarwood Gr BD6 74 B2
Briary Cl WF1 142 F2
Brickbank HD5 154 F3
Brickfield Gr HX2 92 A5
Brickfield La HX2 92 A5
Brickfield Terr HX2 92 A5
Brick Mill Rd LS28 76 F6
Brick Row
Bradford BD12 94 C3
Halifax HX3 113 D4
Brick St
Cleckheaton BD19 116 C7
Keighley BD21 35 C6
Leeds LS9 212 A3
Wakefield WF2 141 D7
Brick Terr HD6 115 B1
Brick & Tile Terr HD6 115 A1
Brickyard 9 WF14 137 F5
Brickyard The S72 180 C1
Bride St 1 OL14 108 B6
Bridge Ave LS21 23 A8
Bridge Cl
Boston Spa LS23 30 E8
Clayton West HD8 175 E2
Horbury WF4 140 E1
Bridge Cotts LS25 64 E7
Bridge Court Bsns Pk LS11 211 A1
Bridge Croft HD3 153 B4
Bridge Ct
Fitzwilliam WF9 163 A2
Leeds LS11 211 A1
Morley LS27 98 B3
Bridge End
Brighouse HD6 115 A1
Glusburn BD20 16 B6
Leeds LS1 211 C3
7 Mytholmroyd HX7 89 E1
Bridge End St OL14 86 C1
Bridge Fold LS5 59 A4
Bridge Foot LS23 30 E8
Bridge Garth LS23 30 D6
Bridge Gate HX7 89 A3
Bridgegate Way BD10 56 D5
Bridgehouse La BD22 51 C6
Bridge Ind Est WF12 139 E6
Bridge La
Holmfirth HD9 189 A6
Ilkley LS29 8 A4
Knottingley WF11 126 F5
Shelf HX3 93 B7
Thorpe Audlin WF8 165 B4
Bridge Lanes HX7 88 F3
Bridge Mills HX2 111 D7
Bridge Paddock LS22 13 B1
Bridge Pl LS18 41 C3
Bridge Rd
Boston Spa LS23 30 E8
Brighouse HD6 115 A2
Horbury WF4 140 E1
Leeds, Holbeck LS11 211 A2
Leeds, Kirkstall LS5 59 A4
Pudsey LS13 57 E5
9 Silsden BD20 5 E2
Sutton-in-C BD20 16 D5
Bridge St
Batley, Bank Foot WF17 118 D5
Batley, Birstall Smithies WF17 117 E8
Bradford BD1 201 C2
Castleford WF10 124 E8
Darton S75 177 E1
Dewsbury WF13 138 F6
Huddersfield HD4 171 F8
Huddersfield, Rashcliffe HD4 153 F3
Keighley BD21 35 B6
Leeds LS2 212 A4
Liversedge WF16 117 C4
Morley LS27 98 B2
Normanton WF6 123 C3
Oakworth BD22 34 B2
Otley LS21 23 A8
7 Pontefract WF8 146 D8
Silsden BD20 5 E2
Slaithwaite HD7 152 A1
Sowerby Bridge HX6 112 B3
1 Thornton BD13 72 E6
Todmorden OL14 108 B5
Wakefield WF1 142 D4
Bridge Terr
Glusburn BD20 16 D5
Halifax HX2 90 E6
Bridge The 20 LS10 211 C3
Bridge View LS13 57 E6
Bridgewater Ct LS6 59 F6
Bridgewater Park Dr DN6 184 F2
Bridgewater Rd LS9 212 C1
Bridgeway BD4 75 D3
Bridge Wood Cl LS18 41 D2
Bridge Wood View LS18 41 D2
Bridge Works Bsns Pk HD9 172 A4
Bridgland Ave LS29 22 A5
Bridgwater Ho 9 BD5 201 B1
Bridgwater Rd BD9 55 A2
Bridle Ave WF5 140 C8
Bridle Cl WF4 158 E7
Bridle Dene HX3 93 C5
Bridle La
Netherton WF4 158 E7
Ossett WF5 140 C8
Bridle Path LS15 62 A2
Bridle Path Rd LS17 44 E5
Bridle Path Wlk 3 LS15 62 A2
Bridle Pl WF5 140 D8
Bridle St WF17 118 E5
Bridle Stile HX3 93 C5
Bridle Stile La BD13 72 E2
Bridley Brook HD7 170 A5
Bridley Dr HD7 170 A8
Bridon Way BD19 116 E6
Brierdene 5 BD20 5 E2
Brier Hey Cl HX7 89 F1
Brier Hey Ind Units HX7 89 F1
Brier Hey La HX7 89 F1
Brier Hill Cl BD19 116 A6
Brier Hill View HD2 136 D5
Brier La
Brighouse HD6 114 E2
Havercroft WF4 180 C8
Brierlands Cl LS25 83 B8
Brierlands Fold LS25 83 B8
Brierlands La LS25 83 B8
Brierley CE Prim Sch S72 181
Brierley Cl BD18 55
Brierley Cres WF9 182
Brierley Rd
Brierley S72 181
Shafton S72 180
Shafton S72 180
South Hiendley S72 180
Brier St
Halifax HX3 92
Keighley BD21 35
Briery Cl LS29 7
Briery Field BD18 55
Briery Gr WF14 138
Briestfield Rd WF12 156
Brigg's Ave WF10 124
Briggate
Brighouse HD6 115
Elland HX5 134
Huddersfield HD5 155
Leeds LS1 211
Shipley BD17 55
Shipley, Windhill BD18 55
Silsden BD20 5
Brigg Gdns BD22 34
Briggland Ct BD15 53
Briggs Ave BD6 74
Briggs Bldgs 8 LS27 98
Briggs Gr BD6 74
Briggs Pl BD6 74
Briggs Row WF7 145
Briggs St
Barnsley S71 179
Queensbury BD13 72
Briggs Terr 2 HD5 154
Brighouse & Denholme Gate Rd HX3 93
Brighouse & Denholme Rd BD13 72
Brighouse High Sch
Brighouse HD6 115
Brighouse, Hove Edge HD6 114
Brighouse Rd
Bradford BD12 94
Brighouse HX3 114
Denholme BD13 71
Huddersfield HD3 135
Shelf BD13, HX3 92
Brighouse Sta HD6 115
Brighouse Trade Pk HD6 115
Brighouse Wood La HD6 114
Brighouse Wood Row HD6 114
Bright's Bldgs HD9 172
Brighton Ave LS27 97
Brighton Cl WF17 117
Brighton Cliff LS13 58
Brighton Gr
Halifax HX1 202
Leeds LS13 58
Brighton Rd LS29 8
Brighton St
Batley WF16 117
Bradford BD10 39
21 Halifax HX3 92
Shipley BD17 55
Todmorden OL14 86
Wakefield WF2 142
Brighton Terr BD19 94
Bright St
Bradford BD15 54
10 Bradford, Clayton BD14 73
3 Dewsbury WF13 118
East Ardsley WF3 120
Farnhill BD20 4
7 Haworth BD22 51
Mirfield WF14 138
Morley LS27 98
Pudsey LS28 57
Queensbury BD13 72
Sowerby Bridge HX6 112
Todmorden OL14 108
Brignall Croft LS9 207
Brignall Garth LS9 207
Brignall Way LS9 207
Brig Royd HX6 132
Brigshaw Dr WF10 102
Brigshaw High Sch WF10 102
Brigshaw La LS25, WF10 103
Brindle Cl BD15 73
Brindle Park Dr WF10 125
Brindley Gr BD8 73
Brindley Rd BD20 17
Brindley Way WF2 120
Brinsmead Ct LS26 100
Brisbane Ave BD2 55
Briscoe La HX4 134
Bristol Ave BD20 36
Bristol St
3 Halifax HX3 113
Leeds LS7 207
Britannia Ave OL13 106
Britannia Bldgs LS27 97
Britannia Bsns Ent Ctr WF5 140
Britannia Cl 11 LS28 57
Britannia Ct LS13 77
Britannia Ho LS1 211
Britannia Mews LS28 77
Britannia Mills Trad Est HD3 152
Britannia Rd
Huddersfield HD3, HD7 152
Morley LS27 98
Slaithwaite HD7 169

itannia Sq LS27 97 F2
itannia St
Bingley BD16 37 A3
Bradford BD5 201 C2
Leeds LS1 211 B3
Pudsey LS28 58 A2
itannia Terr BD19 116 D8
iton Sq S63 194 E1
iton St S63 194 E1
itton St BD19 116 F6
oadacre Rd WF5 140 F5
oadacres HD9 171 F3
oad Acres WF4 160 A7
oadacres Dr LS22 13 C5
oadacre Way BD17 38 F4
oad Balk DN5 195 E6
oadbent Croft HD9 172 A4
oad Carr La
Elland HX4 134 C4
Shepley HD9 190 A2
oad Carr Terr HX4 134 D5
oadcroft Chase WF3 119 E7
oadcroft Dr WF3 119 E8
oadcroft Gr WF3 119 E8
oadcroft Way WF3 119 E8
oad Cut Rd WF4 159 D7
oad Dale Cl BD20 19 B1
oadfield Cl BD4 75 E1
oadfield Ind Est HD1 153 F3
oadfield Pk HD9 188 C2
oadfields
5 Horsforth LS18 41 C1
Slaithwaite HD7 169 F7
oadfield Way LS29 6 D8
oadfolds BD14 73 C4
oadgate
Elland HX4 134 A2
Huddersfield HD5 154 D4
Ossett WF5 140 E5
oad Gate
Todmorden, Cross Stone
OL14 108 D6
Todmorden OL14 109 A5
oadgate Ave LS18 41 D1
oadgate Cres
Horsforth LS18 58 C8
Huddersfield HD5 154 D4
oadgate Ct LS18 58 D8
oadgate Dr LS18 41 D1
oadgate La LS18 41 C1
oadgate Prim Sch LS18 41 C1
oadgate Rise LS18 58 D8
oadgate Wlk LS18 58 C8
oad Head La BD22 33 D3
oad Ings Way HX3 93 C5
oad La
Bradford BD4 75 D5
Hebden Bridge HX7 88 F1
Heptonstall HX7 88 B6
Holmfirth HD9 188 D5
Huddersfield HD5 154 D6
Leeds LS5, LS13, LS28 58 C3
Luddenden Foot HX2 111 C5
Pontefract WF8 125 D1
South Elmsall WF9 182 E1
South Kirkby WF9 194 C8
Todmorden OL14 87 D1
oadlands BD20 35 A8
oadlands Ave LS28 76 F7
oadlands Ct 8 LS28 76 F7
oadlands Pl 7 LS28 76 F7
oadlands Rd HD9 170 D3
oadlands St BD4 75 D4
oadland Way WF3 121 C8
oad Lane Bsns Ctr
WF9 182 F1
oad Lane Cl LS13 58 E4
oadlea Ave LS13 58 E4
oadlea Cl LS13 58 E4
oadlea Cres
Bradford BD5 74 F3
Leeds LS13 58 E4
oadlea Gdns LS13 58 E4
oadlea Gr LS13 58 E4
oadlea Hill LS13 58 E4
oadlea Mount LS13 58 F3
oadlea Oval LS13 58 E4
oadlea Pl LS13 58 E3
oadlea Rd LS13 58 E4
oadlea St LS13 58 E4
oadlea Terr LS13 58 F4
oadlea View LS13 58 D4
oadley Ave HX2 91 B2
oadley Cl HX2 91 C1
oadley Cres HX2 91 C1
oadley Gr HX2 91 C1
oadley Lathe HX2 91 C2
oadley Rd HX2 91 B1
oadmead WF10 124 F8
oadmeadows WF1 121 D5
oad Oak HD7 152 E2
oad Oak La
Brighouse HX3 114 D6
Ingbirchworth S36 192 D2
oad Oak Pl HX3 114 D6
oadoaks Cl WF12 140 A7
oad Oak St HX3 114 D6
oadowler La WF5 140 F5
oad Royd HX4 133 E3
oad St
Bradford BD1 201 B3
Dewsbury WF13 139 A6
Halifax HX1 203 B3
Pudsey LS28 57 C3
Ripponden HX6 132 C3
2 Todmorden OL14 108 B6
oad Stone Cotts HX7 88 A6
oadstone Rd HD8 190 F3

Broadstone St OL14 108 D6
Broadstone Way BD4 75 E3
Broad Tree Rd HX3 92 A2
Broad View WF5 140 F5
Broadwalk The LS21 10 E1
Broadway
Bingley BD16 37 A2
Bradford BD1 201 B3
Darton S75 178 B1
Guiseley LS20 39 C8
Halifax HX3 113 F5
Horsforth LS18 58 C8
8 Huddersfield HD1 154 B7
Leeds, Halton LS15 80 F7
Leeds, Hawksworth LS5 58 E7
Pontefract WF8 146 E7
South Elmsall WF9 182 E1
Sowerby Bridge HX6 111 E3
Wakefield WF2 141 D4
Broadway Ave
Bradford BD5 74 D2
Leeds LS6 205 B2
Broadway Cl BD5 74 D2
Broadway Ct HX6 111 E3
Broad Way Ct WF12 139 E1
Broadway Dr 4 LS18 58 B8
Broadway Terr WF9 182 E1
Broadwell Dr BD18 55 E6
Broadwell Rd WF5 140 F5
Broadwood Ave HX2 91 C1
Brockadale Ave WF8 146 D5
Brock Bank HD5 154 F7
Brockholes Bsns Pk
HD9 172 C2
Brockholes CE Jun & Inf Sch
HD9 172 C2
Brockholes La HD9 172 C3
Brockholes Rd HD4 172 D4
Brockholes Sta HD9 172 C3
Brocklebank Cl BD20 19 B1
Brocklesby Dr BD15 73 B8
Brocklyn Yd HX1 203 C2
Brocks HX2 111 C6
Brockstones HX4 133 F7
Brockswood Ct WF2 161 C5
Brockwell Gdns HX6 112 A3
Brockwell La HX6 112 A2
Broderick Ct LS1 206 B1
Brodetsky Prim Sch LS17 43 C4
Brodley Cl HX3 114 C8
Brodrick Ct LS6 59 D5
Brodrick Dr LS29 8 B3
Brodwell Grange LS18 58 E8
Brogans Yd LS21 23 B7
Broken Cross HD5 154 E2
Broken Way BD5 74 D2
Bromet Pl BD2 56 B4
Bromfield Ct S71 179 D4
Bromford Rd BD4 75 B3
Bromley Ave HD9 189 D7
Bromley Bank HD8 191 E6
Bromley Gr BD22 34 E5
Bromley Mount WF1 142 D4
Bromley Rd
Batley WF17 118 E3
Bingley BD16 36 F4
Huddersfield HD2 135 F1
Shipley BD18 54 E8
Bromley St WF17 118 D3
Brompton Ave BD4 75 A4
Brompton Gr 2 LS11 214 B2
Brompton Mount 5
LS11 214 B2
Brompton Rd BD4 75 B4
Brompton Row 19 LS11 214 B3
Brompton Terr 4 LS11 214 B2
Brompton View 3 LS11 214 B2
Bronshill Gr BD15 54 C1
Bronte Ave WF11 126 B4
Bronte Cl
Batley WF13 117 F2
Bradford BD9 54 E2
Cleckheaton BD19 96 B1
Huddersfield HD4 153 D3
Bronte Ct WF8 125 D2
Bronte Dr BD22 34 F3
Bronte Gr
Hemsworth WF9 181 C6
Mirfield WF14 138 C4
Bronte Ho LS7 206 C3
Bronte House Sch BD10 39 F2
Bronte Old Rd BD13 72 E6
Bronte Parsonage Mus*
BD22 51 B7
Bronte Pl BD13 72 E6
Bronte Rd WF17 96 E1
Bronte Rise WF10 125 D5
Bronte St
1 Haworth BD22 51 B7
Keighley BD21 35 D8
Bronte Villas BD22 51 F8
Bronte Way WF14 138 C4
Brook's Bldgs HD1 153 D6
Brook's Yd 17 HD1 154 A6
Brook Cl WF5 140 F3
Brook Cotts HX6 132 B7
Brookdale OL14 108 A2
Brookdale Ave WF5 119 D1
Brookdale Bank HD3 153 A5
Brook Dr HX4 134 C4
Brooke Ct WF8 146 D5
Brooke Fold HD9 171 F4
Brooke Gn HX3 114 C8
Brookelea HX3 114 E7
Brooke St
8 Batley WF16 117 D3
Brighouse HD6 115 A1
Cleckheaton BD19 116 E7

Brookeville Ave HX3 114 C7
Brookfield HD8 173 E6
Brook Field WF14 137 F2
Brookfield Ave
Castleford WF10 124 F7
Cleckheaton BD19 95 E1
Leeds LS8 207 C4
Pudsey LS13 57 D6
Shipley BD18 55 D8
Brookfield Ct
Normanton WF6 123 C2
Pudsey LS13 57 D6
Brookfield Dr WF7 164 C8
Brookfield Gdns LS13 57 D6
Brookfield Pl LS6 59 E6
Brookfield Rd
Bradford BD3 75 A8
Leeds LS6 59 E6
Shipley BD18 55 D8
Brookfields WF4 158 D5
Brookfields Ave BD12 94 E1
Brookfields Rd BD12 94 E1
Brookfield St
Leeds LS10 212 A1
Todmorden OL14 86 C1
Brookfield Terr
Cleckheaton BD19 95 E1
9 Leeds, Far Headingley
LS6 59 E6
Leeds, Pottery Field LS10 212 A1
Brookfield View BD19 95 E1
Brookfoot Ave BD11 96 A5
Brookfoot Bsns Pk HD6 114 F3
Brookfoot Ind Est HD6 114 E3
Brookfoot La HD6 114 E3
Brook Gdns
10 Dewsbury WF13 139 B8
Meltham HD9 170 D3
Brook Grain Hill HD6 136 A8
Brook Grains La HX6 132 D2
Brook Hill BD17 38 D3
Brookhill Ave LS17 43 E4
Brookhill Cl LS17 43 E4
Brookhill Cres LS17 43 E4
Brookhill Dr LS17 43 E4
Brookhill Gr LS17 43 E4
Brook Hill La
Carlecotes S36 200 B3
Dunford Bridge S36 199 F2
Brook Hos S75 193 E4
Brookhouse Gdns BD10 56 F8
Brook House La HD8 174 B2
Brook La
Bradford BD14 73 A3
Cleckheaton WF15 116 C4
Huddersfield HD7 152 D4
Brooklands
Brighouse HX3 114 D7
East Keswick LS17 28 C5
Huddersfield HD2 136 F5
Leeds LS8 44 A2
Brooklands Ave
Elland HX4 134 B4
Leeds LS14 62 A4
Thornton BD13 72 F6
Walton WF2 161 B7
Brooklands Cl
Elland HX4 134 B4
Leeds LS14 61 E4
Menston LS29 22 B5
Brooklands Cres
Leeds LS14 61 E4
Ryhill WF4 162 D1
Yeadon LS19 40 B6
Brooklands Ct WF5 141 A4
Brooklands Dr
Leeds LS14 61 E4
Yeadon LS19 40 B6
Brooklands Garth LS14 61 F4
Brooklands Gr LS29 22 B5
Brooklands La
Leeds LS14 61 F4
Menston LS29 22 B5
Brooklands Rd WF2 161 C7
Brooklands View
Leeds LS14 61 F4
Walton WF2 161 C7
Brooklands Way LS29 22 A5
Brooklands Wlk LS29 22 B5
Brookland Twrs LS14 62 A5
Brookleigh LS28 57 B6
Brooklyn Ave
Huddersfield HD5 155 A6
Leeds LS12 210 A3
Brooklyn Cl WF13 117 F4
Brooklyn Ct BD19 116 D8
Brooklyn Dr BD19 116 D8
Brooklyn Grange BD19 116 D8
Brooklyn Pl LS12 209 C3
Brooklyn Rd BD19 116 D8
Brooklyn St
Keighley BD20 18 A2
Leeds LS12 209 C3
Brooklyn Terr
Brighouse HD6 114 E5
Leeds LS12 209 C3
Brook Rd 4 WF12 139 B7
Brook Row BD22 34 D1
Brookroyd Ave HD6 115 B6
Brookroyd Gdns 3
WF17 117 F8
Brookroyd La WF17 117 F8
Brooksbank WF2 216 A2
Brooksbank Ave BD7 73 E5
Brooksbank Dr LS15 81 A8
Brooksbank Gdns HX5 134 F6
Brooksbank Sch The
HX5 134 E6

Brooksfield WF9 182 D4
Brookside
Collingham LS22 29 B8
Cullingworth BD13 52 D6
Denby Dale HD8 191 F6
Hebden Bridge HX7 88 E4
Hemsworth WF9 181 E7
Leeds LS17 43 E5
Brook Side HD7 152 A2
Brookside Fold 2 BD22 51 C2
Brookside St WF9 182 F3
Brookside Terr WF9 182 F3
Brook St
Bradford BD12 95 B5
Castleford WF10 104 C3
Dewsbury WF13 117 F1
1 Elland HX5 135 A6
10 Hebden Bridge HX7 89 A4
Huddersfield HD1 154 A7
Huddersfield, Moldgreen
HD5 154 D6
Huddersfield, Yews Hill
HD1 153 E4
Ilkley LS29 8 B4
11 Keighley BD21 35 B5
Normanton WF6 122 F3
Ossett WF5 140 D5
11 Todmorden OL14 108 B5
Wakefield WF1 216 B2
Brooks Terr BD13 73 B2
Brooks Yd
Dewsbury WF13 139 B7
Huddersfield HD2 137 A5
Brook Terr
Halifax HX2 90 E2
Slaithwaite HD7 152 A2
Brook The
Calderbrook OL15 129 C1
Mytholmroyd HX7 110 E8
Brookwater Cl HX3 113 D3
Brookwater Dr BD18 55 E5
Brookway WF7 145 D5
Brookwoods Ind Est HX4 134 B5
Broombank
Denby Dale HD8 191 F5
Huddersfield HD2 135 D2
Broom Cl
Darton S75 178 A1
Leeds LS10 99 F7
Broomcliffe Gdns S72 180 C2
Broom Cres LS10 99 E7
Broomcroft BD14 73 B4
Broomcroft Rd WF5 140 D4
Broom Cross LS10 99 E7
Broome Ave BD2 55 E3
Broome Cl WF6 123 A4
Broomer St WF13 138 E6
Broomfield
Bradford BD14 73 A3
Elland HX5 134 D6
Leeds LS16 42 B4
Broomfield Ave HX3 113 B3
Broomfield Bsns Pk HD1 154 A4
Broomfield Cl HD8 175 C7
Broomfield Cres LS6 205 A4
Broom Field La HD8 175 B7
Broomfield Pl
Bradford BD14 73 A3
3 Keighley BD21 35 B7
Leeds LS6 205 A3
Broomfield Rd
Huddersfield HD2 136 A5
Huddersfield, Marsh HD1 153 D6
4 Keighley BD21 35 B7
Leeds LS6 205 A4
Broomfield Sch LS10 99 F7
Broomfield St
Keighley BD21 35 B7
3 Leeds LS6 205 A3
Queensbury BD13 72 E1
Broomfield Terr
Cleckheaton BD19 116 B7
Huddersfield HD1 153 D7
Leeds LS6 205 A3
Broomfield View LS6 205 A3
Broom Garth LS10 99 F7
Broom Gdns LS10 99 E7
Broom Gr LS10 99 F6
Broom Hall Ave WF1 121 A2
Broom Hall Cres WF1 121 A2
Broomhey Ave HD8 175 D6
Broomhill WF10 125 A6
Broomhill Ave
Keighley BD21 35 A5
Knottingley WF11 127 B3
Leeds LS17 43 D1
Broomhill Cl
Holmfirth HD9 189 D3
Knottingley WF11 127 B3
Broomhill Cres
Knottingley WF11 127 B3
Leeds LS17 43 D2
Broomhill Dr
2 Keighley BD21 35 A5
Knottingley WF11 127 B3
Leeds LS17 43 C1
Broomhill Gr
Keighley BD21 35 A5
Knottingley WF11 127 B3
Broomhill Mount BD21 35 A5
Broomhill Pl WF11 127 B3
Broom Hill Rd HX4 151 D8
Broomhill Sq WF11 127 B3
Broomhill St BD21 35 A4
Broomhill Terr WF17 118 D4
Broomhill Way BD21 35 B5
Broomhill Wlk
Keighley BD21 35 A5

Broomhill Wlk *continued*
Knottingley WF11 127 B3
Broomhouse Cl HD8 192 A5
Broom Lawn LS10 99 E7
Broom Mills Rd LS28 57 E3
Broom Mount LS10 99 F6
Broom Nook LS10 99 F7
Broom Pl LS10 99 F6
Broom Rd LS10 99 E7
Broomroyd HD3 152 F6
Broomsdale Rd WF17 118 E5
Broom St
Bradford BD4 201 C2
Cleckheaton BD19 116 B6
7 Keighley BD21 35 C6
Broom Terr
Leeds LS10 99 F7
Oakworth BD22 34 D3
Broom View LS10 99 F7
Broom Wlk
Batley WF17 118 E5
Leeds LS10 99 F6
Broomy Lea La HD9 188 F7
Broster Ave BD22 34 F7
Brotherton Ave WF1 142 E7
Brotherton & Byram Com
Prim Sch WF11 126 C7
Brougham Rd
11 Halifax HX3 92 C1
Marsden HD7 169 A4
Brougham St 12 HX3 92 C1
Brougham Terr 13 HX3 92 C1
Broughton Ave
Bradford BD4 75 B1
Leeds LS9 208 A2
Broughton Ho 2 BD4 75 F1
Broughton Rd HD4 153 B3
Broughton St HX7 89 A4
Broughtons Yd WF11 126 C5
Broughton Terr
Leeds LS9 208 A2
7 Pudsey LS28 76 E8
Brow Bottom La HX2 91 B6
Browcliff BD20 5 E2
Browcliff Flats HD1 153 F4
Brow Cotts HD6 114 D5
Browfield Terr 2 BD20 5 E2
Browfield View BD22 34 E5
Browfoot BD18 55 D8
Browfoot Dr HX2 112 D6
Brow Foot Gate La HX2 112 D6
Browgate BD17 38 C4
Brow Grains Rd HD9 170 B2
Brow La
Denby Dale HD8 192 D6
Halifax HX3 92 B6
Holmfirth HD9 188 F3
Northowram HX3 92 E4
Shelf HX3 93 D6
Thornton BD14 72 F3
Brow Mills Ind Est HX3 114 D6
Brown's Edge Rd HD9,
S36 200 E8
Brown's Knoll Rd HD4 173 A3
Brown's Pl WF17 118 B4
Brown's St WF17 118 C4
Brown Ave LS11 213 B4
Brown Bank La BD20 6 B4
Brown Bank Terr BD20 16 E7
Brownberrie Ave LS18 41 C3
Brownberrie Cres LS18 41 B3
Brownberrie Dr LS18 41 C3
Brownberrie Gdns LS18 41 B3
Brownberrie La LS18 41 B3
Brownberrie Wlk LS18 41 C3
Brownberry Gr HX3 93 D7
Brown Birks St 1 OL14 86 B1
Brown Hill Ave LS9 208 A2
Brownhill Cl WF17 96 F1
Brown Hill Cl BD11 96 A7
Brownhill Cres WF9 163 A1
Brown Hill Cres LS9 208 A2
Brown Hill Dr BD11 96 A6
Brownhill Garth WF17 96 F1
Brownhill Inf Sch WF17 97 A1
Brownhill La HD9 198 B8
Brown Hill La HX7 87 E5
Brownhill Prim Sch LS9 208 A1
Brownhill Rd WF17 96 F1
Brown Hill Terr LS9 208 A2
Browning Ave HX3 113 D4
Browning Rd HD2 136 D3
Browning St BD3 75 B7
Brownings The HX3 114 C7
Brown La E LS11 210 C1
Brown La W LS11, LS12 210 B1
Brownlea Cl LS19 39 F5
Brown Lee La BD15 53 A4
Brown Pl LS11 213 B4
Brown Rd LS11 213 B4
Brownroyd Ave S71 179 C2
Brown Royd Ave HD5 154 D8
Brownroyd Fold BD5 74 B2
Brownroyd Hill Rd BD6 74 B2
Brownroyd Rd HD9 171 E4
Brownroyd St
Bradford BD8 74 B7
Bradford, Shearbridge BD7 74 B6
Brownroyd Wlk BD6 74 B2
Browns Ct BD20 4 C6
Brown Springs La BD22 34 E4
Brown St
17 Keighley BD21 35 D8
Mirfield WF14 137 F5

Brow Rd
Haworth BD22 51 D6
Huddersfield HD1 153 E5
Browsfield Rd LS29 6 D8
Browsholme St 2 BD21 35 C6
Brow St BD21 35 D6
Brow Top BD14 73 A2
Brow Top Rd BD22 51 E7
Brow Wood Cres BD2 55 E3
Brow Wood Rd
Batley WF17 97 B1
Shelf HX3 93 D6
Brow Wood Rise HX3 93 D6
Brow Wood Terr BD6 93 F7
Bruce Gdns LS12 210 B3
Bruce Lawn LS12 210 B3
Bruce St HX1 202 B2
Brudenell Ave LS6 205 C3
Brudenell Gr LS6 205 C3
Brudenell Mount LS6 205 C3
Brudenell Prim Sch LS6 205 B3
Brudenell Rd LS6 205 B3
Brudenell St LS6 205 C3
Brudenell View LS6 205 C3
Brunel Cl
Bradford BD9 55 A2
Lofthouse Gate WF2 120 F4
Brunel Ct 4 HX3 92 B2
Brunel Gdns 7 BD5 74 C3
Brunel Rd WF2 120 F4
Brunswick WF4 162 B2
Brunswick Arc BD21 35 C7
Brunswick Cl WF1 216 C2
Brunswick Ct LS2 207 A1
Brunswick Dr WF13 118 A1
Brunswick Gdns
Garforth LS25 82 F7
4 Halifax HX1 203 A3
Brunswick Gr WF1 216 C2
Brunswick Ho BD16 37 B2
Brunswick Ind Est HX1 203 A2
Brunswick Pl
Bradford BD10 56 D7
3 Morley LS27 98 B4
Brunswick Rd
Bradford BD10 56 D7
Pudsey LS28 76 E8
Brunswick Row 2 LS2 207 A1
Brunswick St
Batley, Heckmondwike WF16 117 D3
7 Batley WF17 118 C5
Bingley BD16 37 B3
Cullingworth BD13 52 E6
Dewsbury WF13 118 A1
Hebden Bridge HX7 88 F3
Huddersfield HD1 154 A6
Morley LS27 98 A5
1 Queensbury BD13 72 F1
Thurnscoe S63 194 F1
Wakefield WF1 216 C2
Brunswick Terr
Leeds LS2 206 C1
4 Morley LS27 98 B4
Bruntcliffe Ave LS27 97 E5
Bruntcliffe Cl LS27 97 F4
Bruntcliffe Dr LS27 97 F4
Bruntcliffe La LS27 97 E4
Bruntcliffe Rd LS27 97 E3
Bruntcliffe Sch LS27 97 E4
Bruntcliffe Way LS27 97 E4
Brunthwaite Bridge La BD20 18 A8
Brunthwaite La BD20 6 B1
Brussels St LS9 212 A3
Bryan Cl WF10 124 A8
Bryan Rd
Elland HX5 134 D6
Huddersfield HD2 135 D1
Bryan St
5 Brighouse HD6 115 A1
Pudsey LS28 57 D3
Bryanstone Rd BD4 75 D5
Bryan Terr HD3 152 E6
Bryer St WF13 139 C8
Bryndlee Ct HD9 188 E4
Bryngate LS26 101 C6
Bryony Ct LS10 99 F5
Bubwith Gr HX2 202 A2
Buchan Twrs 2 BD5 201 B1
Buckden Ct
Huddersfield HD3 153 B7
Silsden BD20 5 E2
Buckden Rd HD3 153 D8
Buckfast Ct BD10 56 B7
Buckingham Ave LS6 205 B4
Buckingham Cres BD14 73 D5
Buckingham Ct
1 Royston S71 179 B4
Wakefield WF1 142 F4
Buckingham Dr
Leeds LS6 205 B4
Wakefield WF1 142 F3
Buckingham Gr LS6 205 B4
Buckingham Mount LS6 205 B3
Buckingham Rd LS6 205 B4
Buckingham Way
Byram WF11 126 E7
Castleford WF10 124 C7
Royston S71 179 B4
Buck La BD17 38 F3
Buckland Pl HX1 202 A2
Buckland Rd 3 BD8 73 F8
Bucklar Hill BD20 16 E8
Buckle La
Menston LS29 22 C4
Normanton WF6 123 A2
Buckley Ave LS11 214 B3
Buckley Ct OL14 108 A6
Buckley La HX2 91 C2
Buckley View OL14 108 A6
Buckley Wood Bottom 9 OL14 108 B5
Buck Mill La BD10 39 A2
Buckrose St HD1 136 A1
Buckrose Terr HD1 136 A1
Buck St
Bradford BD3 201 D2
Denholme BD13 71 E8
Buck Stone Ave LS17 42 F4
Buck Stone Cl LS17 43 A4
Buck Stone Cres LS17 43 A4
Buckstone Dr LS19 40 B3
Buck Stone Dr LS17 42 F4
Buckstone Garth BD20 19 D1
Buck Stone Gdns LS17 43 A4
Buck Stone Gn LS17 42 F4
Buck Stone Gr LS17 42 F4
Buck Stone La BD20 16 A1
Buck Stone Mount LS17 42 F4
Buck Stone Oval LS17 42 F4
Buck Stone Rd LS17 42 F5
Buck Stone Rise LS17 42 F4
Buckstones Cl HX4 134 B4
Buck Stone View LS17 42 F4
Buck Stone Way LS17 42 F4
Buckthorne Cl WF3 120 D8
Buckthorne Ct WF3 120 D8
Buckthorne Dr WF3 120 D8
Buckthorne Fold WF3 120 D8
Buckton Cl LS11 214 A4
Buckton Mount LS11 214 A4
Buckton View LS11 214 A4
Bude Rd
Bradford BD5 74 F1
Leeds LS11 214 B3
Bugler Terr WF4 140 E1
Bula Cl LS25 83 B2
Bulay Rd HD1 153 F4
Bullace Trees La WF15 116 E3
Bull Close La HX1 203 B2
Bullenshaw Rd WF9 181 D6
Buller Cl LS9 208 B1
Buller Ct LS9 208 C1
Buller Gr LS9 208 B1
Buller St
Bradford BD4 75 C5
6 Rothwell LS26 101 C6
Bullerthorpe La LS15, LS26 81 E4
Bullfields Cl WF12 139 E2
Bullfield The BD16 53 B8
Bull Gn HX1 203 B3
Bull Green Rd HD3 152 F6
Bull Hill BD22 51 C1
Bull La
Crigglestone WF4 159 F5
South Kirkby WF9 182 C2
Bullough La
Leeds LS26 81 A1
Rothwell LS26 100 F8
Bull Ring WF1 216 B2
Bull Royd Ave BD8 73 E8
Bull Royd Cres BD8 73 E8
Bull Royd Dr BD8 73 E8
Bull Royd Ind Est BD8 73 E8
Bull Royd La BD8 73 E8
Bullstyle Rd WF8 146 C6
Bulrush Bsns Pk WF17 118 B7
Bungalow Rd BD20 16 C6
Bungalows The
Clayton West HD8 175 E2
Glusburn BD20 16 B7
Halifax HX2 91 D1
Halifax, Salterhebble HX3 113 E2
2 Leeds LS15 62 D3
Normanton WF6 123 A5
Ossett WF5 140 C6
Bunker's Hill La BD22 34 D5
Bunkers Hill
Aberford LS25 64 E6
Guiseley BD17 39 B5
8 Holmfirth HD9 189 A5
Wakefield WF2 120 F2
Bunkers La WF17 117 F4
Bunney Gn HX3 92 F4
Bunny Pk HD4 153 D3
Bunting Dr BD6 73 B2
Burbeary Rd HD1 153 E3
Burberry Cl BD4 95 C8
Burchett Gr LS6 206 A4
Burchett Pl LS6 206 A4
Burchett Terr LS6 206 B4
Burcote Dr HD3 134 B1
Burdale Pl BD7 74 B6
Burdett Ct HD3 153 C4
Burdett Terr 5 LS4 59 C2
Burdock Way HX1 203 A3
Burfitts Rd HD3 153 B7
Burghley Mews LS10 99 D3
Burghley Wlk BD18 55 E6
Burgh Mill Gdns WF13 139 A7
Burgh Mill La WF13 139 A7
Burhouse Ct HD9 171 F4
Burkill St WF1 142 D2
Burking Rd WF13 139 B8
Burlees Cotts HX7 89 C3
Burlees La HX7 89 C3
Burleigh St 6 HX1 202 B1
Burley Bank La HD9 197 E6
Burley Bsns Ctr 8 HX5 134 F6
Burley Carr HX7 89 C3
Burley Ct
Leeds LS4 205 A1
Steeton BD20 17 C5
Burley Grange Rd 2 LS4 59 C2
Burley Hill Cres LS4 59 B3
Burley Hill Dr LS4 59 C3
Burley in Wharfedale Sta LS29 21 E8
Burley La
Horsforth LS18 58 B7
Menston LS29 21 F5
Burley Lodge Pl LS6 205 B1
Burley Lodge Rd LS6 205 B2
Burley Lodge St LS6 205 B1
Burley Lodge Terr LS6 205 B1
Burley Mews BD20 17 C5
Burley Oaks Prim Sch LS29 9 F1
Burley Park Ctr LS4 205 A2
Burley Park Sta LS4 205 A3
Burley Pl LS4 205 B1
Burley Rd
Leeds LS3, LS4 205 A2
Menston LS29 22 A6
Burley St Matthias' CE Prim Sch LS4 205 A2
Burley St
11 Elland HX5 134 F6
Leeds LS3 210 C4
Shipley BD2 55 D4
Burley Wlk WF17 118 B5
Burley Wood Cres LS4 59 C2
Burley & Woodhead CE Prim Sch LS29 21 F8
Burley Wood La LS4 59 C3
Burley Wood Mount LS4 59 C3
Burley Wood View LS4 59 C3
Burlington Ave BD3 56 E1
Burlington Pl 21 LS11 214 B2
Burlington Rd LS11 214 B2
Burlington St
Bradford BD8 55 D1
3 Halifax HX1 202 B3
Burmantofts St LS9 212 B4
Burned Gr HX3 93 C7
Burned Rd HX3 93 D7
Burneston Gdns 7 BD6 93 E8
Burnett Ave BD5 74 D3
Burnett Pl BD5 74 D3
Burnett Rise BD13 92 C8
Burnett St BD1 201 C3
Burnham Ave
Bradford BD4 75 C1
Darton S75 178 B1
Burnham Ct LS22 13 C6
Burnham Rd LS25 82 F6
Burnhill La WF9 164 F5
Burnholme BD13 71 D8
Burniston Cl BD15 53 C4
Burniston Dr HD3 153 A8
Burnlee Green Rd HD9 188 E4
Burnlee Rd HD9 188 E4
Burnley Hill Terr HX3 93 B4
Burnley Rd
Bacup OL13 85 A1
Halifax, Willow Field HX2, HX6 112 C6
Holme Chapel BB10 85 C4
Luddenden Foot HX2 111 D6
Todmorden OL14 85 C4
Burnley Road Jun & Inf Sch HX7 89 E1
Burnleys Bldgs WF4 157 B2
Burnleys Ct LS26 123 D8
Burnleys Dr LS26 123 D8
Burnleys Mews LS26 123 D8
Burnleys View LS26 102 D1
Burnleyville BD19 96 B1
Burn Rd HD2, HD3 135 C3
Burnroyd Ave BD20 16 D6
Burnsall Ave WF17 118 A5
Burnsall Cl LS12 209 C4
Burnsall Croft LS12 209 B3
Burnsall Ct LS12 209 B4
Burnsall Gdns LS12 209 B4
Burnsall Grange LS12 209 B4
Burnsall Mews BD20 5 E2
Burnsall Rd
Batley WF17 118 A5
Bradford BD3 75 B7
Brighouse HD6 135 E8
Liversedge WF15 116 F4
Burns Ave WF9 181 F1
Burns Ct WF17 96 D2
Burnsdale BD15 54 A3
Burnshaw Mews LS10 99 C3
Burns Hill LS29 6 E8
Burnside
3 Addingham LS29 6 F8
Thurnscoe S63 194 C1
Burnside Ave HX3 93 C6
Burnside Cl WF17 97 A1
Burnside Dr HD9 188 E4
Burns St 1 HX3 91 F3
Burns Way LS23 30 D5
Burnt Acres La OL14 109 B8
Burnt Edge La HX7 87 D4
Burnt Ho OL14 108 C6
Burnt House Cl OL14 108 C6
Burnt Plats La HD7 151 B3
Burnt Side Rd LS12 77 C2
Burntwood Ave WF9 182 C2
Burntwood Bank WF9 181 D5
Burnt Wood Cres WF9 182 C2
Burntwood Dr WF9 182 C1
Burntwood Gr WF9 182 C1
Burntwood Jun & Inf Sch WF9 182 C2
Burnt Wood La S72 181 E1
Burntwood Sports & L Ctr S72 181 C2
Burnup Gr BD19 116 C7
Burnwells BD10 39 A2
Burnwells Ave BD10 39 A2
Burrage St BD16 36 F3
Burras Ave LS21 22 F7
Burras Dr LS21 22 F7
Burras La LS21 22 F7
Burras Rd BD4 75 B2
Burrel Cl LS22 14 A5
Burrell St WF1 216 C2
Burrow St BD5 201 B2
Burrows The WF17 117 F7
Burr Tree Dr LS15 81 D7
Burr Tree Garth LS15 81 D7
Burr Tree Vale LS15 81 D7
Burrwood Terr HX4 134 B5
Burrwood Way HX4 134 B5
Burton Acres Dr HD8 173 E7
Burton Acres La HD8 173 F7
Burton Acres Mews HD8 173 E7
Burton Acres Way HD8 173 E7
Burton Arc 1 LS1 211 C3
Burton Ave LS11 214 C3
Burton Common La LS25 105 F4
Burton Cres LS6 59 D6
Burton Cross HD8 173 E8
Burton Ho
1 Leeds, Alwoodley Gates LS17 43 F4
11 Leeds LS11 214 C3
Burton Mews LS17 43 D5
Burton Rd LS11 214 C3
Burton Row LS11 214 C4
Burton Royd La HD8 174 B7
Burton Salmon Com Prim Sch LS25 105 E3
Burton St
Bradford BD4 75 A4
Halifax HX2 92 A5
Keighley BD20 18 B1
Leeds LS11 214 C4
Pudsey LS28 57 D3
South Elmsall WF9 182 F2
Wakefield WF1 216 A3
Burton Terr LS11 214 C3
Burton Way LS9 208 A1
Burwood Rd HD3 153 C8
Bury La BD20 19 C2
Busely Ct LS27 97 F5
Busfield St
Bingley BD16 36 F3
Bradford BD4 75 B3
Bushill Fold BD13 72 C2
Bush St WF9 181 E6
Busker La HD8 175 C1
Buslingthorpe Gn LS7 206 C3
Buslingthorpe La LS7 206 C4
Buslingthorpe Vale LS7 206 C4
Bussey Ct LS6 206 A3
Busy La BD18 38 E1
Butcher Hill
Hemsworth WF9 181 E8
Leeds LS16, LS18 58 F8
Butcher La LS26 100 E5
Butchers Row 4 LS2 211 C4
Butcher St LS11 211 B2
Bute Ave HD6 115 A5
Bute St BD2 55 D4
Butler's Fold BD16 36 F7
Butler La BD17 38 D4
Butler St E BD3 75 A7
Butler St W BD3 201 D4
Butlers View 5 HX3 92 B2
Butler Way LS28 57 E2
Butterbowl Dr LS12 77 F5
Butterbowl Garth LS12 77 E5
Butterbowl Gdns LS12 77 F5
Butterbowl Gr LS12 77 E5
Butterbowl Lawn LS12 77 E5
Butterbowl Mount LS12 77 F5
Butterbowl Rd LS12 77 F5
Buttercup Cl WF9 182 F7
Buttercup La WF3 120 E8
Buttercup Way
Castleford WF10 124 A5
Gildersome BD11 97 B5
Butterfield's Bldgs LS27 97 F5
Butterfield Homes
6 Baildon BD17 38 C4
Glusburn BD20 16 C6
5 Shipley BD16 54 B6
Wilsden BD15 53 B6
Butterfield Ind Est BD17 38 C1
Butterfield St LS9 212 C3
Butterley La HD9 189 F5
Butterley St LS10 211 C1
Buttermead Cl BD6 94 A7
Buttermere Ave LS22 13 C6
Buttermere Croft WF2 161 A6
Buttermere Dr HD5 154 D6
Buttermere Rd BD2 56 B3
Buttermere Wlk WF11 126 E2
Butternab Rd HD4 171 D8
Butternab Ridge HD4 171 D8
Buttershaw Dr BD6 73 E1
Buttershaw High Sch BD6 93 F8
Buttershaw La
Bradford BD6 94 B8
Cleckheaton WF15 116 B5
Buttershaw Prim Sch BD6 93 F7
Butterton Cl S75 178 C1
Butterwick Gdns LS22 13 C5
Butterwood Cl HD4 171 D8
Butterworth End La HX4, HX6 133 A7
Butterworth Hill HD3 152 A7
Butterworth La HX6 111
Butt Hill LS25 83
Buttholme Gate BD6 93
Butt La
Bradford BD10 56
Haworth BD22 51
Holmfirth HD9 189
Hooton Pagnell DN5 195
Leeds LS12, LS13 77
Button Hill LS7 207
Button Pk WF8 146
Buttress HX2 90
Buttress La HX2 90
Butt Row LS12 77
Butts Cl HD4 172
Butts Ct LS1 211
Butts Garth LS14 45
Butts Garth Ct LS14 45
Butts Garth View LS14 45
Butts Green La HX2 112
Butts Green Rd HX2 111
Butts Hill BD19 117
Butts La
6 Guiseley LS20 22
Middlestown WF4 158
South Milford LS25 105
Todmorden OL14 108
Butts Mount LS12 210
Butts Rd HD4 172
Butts Terr 8 LS20 22
Butts The
East Morton BD20 36
Pontefract WF8 125
Butts Way HD4 172
Butts Yd 8 BD19 116
Buxton Ave BD9 55
Buxton La BD9 55
Buxton Pl WF1 216
Buxton St
Bradford BD9 55
8 Halifax HX3 92
3 Keighley BD21 35
Buxton Way HX3 91
Byeway LS20 22
Byland HX2 91
Byland Cl LS23 30
Byland Gr BD15 53
Bylands Ave BD20 18
Byram Arc 22 HD1 154
Byram Park Ave WF11 126
Byram Park Rd WF11 126
Byram St HD1 154
Byre Way BD22 34
Byrl St 1 BD21 35
Byrom St OL14 108
Byron Ave 5 HX6 112
Byron Cl WF11 126
Byron Gr
Batley WF13 117
Lofthouse Gate WF3 121
Byron Ho LS29 8
Byron Mews BD16 37
Byron Prim Sch BD3 75
Byron St
Bradford BD3 75
Halifax HX1 202
Leeds LS2 207
6 Sowerby Bridge HX6 112
Byron Terr 11 HX6 112
Bywater Row BD11 96
Byways The WF8 146
Bywell CE Jun Sch WF12 118
Bywell Cl WF12 140
Bywell Rd WF12 118

C

Cabbage Hill LS12 209
Cabin Rd LS21 24
Cable St HD1 154
Cad Beeston Mews LS11 214
Caddon Ave WF9 183
Cadman Ct LS27 98
Cadney Croft 3 HX1 203
Cadogan Ave HD3 153
Caenarvon Cl WF17 97
Caernarvon Ave LS25 83
Cain Cl 2 LS9 212
Cain La HX3 114
Cairn Ave LS20 22
Cairn Cl BD20 18
Cairn Garth LS20 22
Cairns Cl BD2 55
Cairn View LS29 8
Caister Cl WF17 97
Caister Gr 5 BD21 35
Caister St 3 BD21 35
Caister Way BD21 35
Caistor Garth 4 BD10 56
Calde Ct BD12 94
Caldene Ave
Bradford BD12 94
Mytholmroyd HX7 89
Caldene Croft HX7 89
Calder HX4 133
Calder Ave
Halifax HX2 202
Royston S71 179
Calder Bank Rd WF13 139
Calder Banks BD13 73
Calderbrook Rd OL15 129
Calder Cl
Castleford WF10 125
Crigglestone WF2 159
Elland HX4 134
Ossett WF5 140
Royston S71 179

alder Cl *continued*
Wetherby LS22 . . . . **13** D8
Aldercliffe Rd HD4 . . . . . **153** F1
aldercroft HX5 . . . . **135** B6
Alderdale Bsns Pk HX2 . . **91** F3
Alderdale Coll HX1 . . . . . **202** C2
Alderdale Industrial Mus★
HX1 . . . . **203** C3
Alderdale Royal Hospl The
HX3 . . . . **113** D3
alderdale Way HX5 . . . . . **135** B6
alder Dr HD4 . . . . **171** F8
alder Gr 5 HX7 . . . . **89** E1
alder High Sch HX7 . . . . . **89** F1
alder Ho
10 Elland HX5 . . . . **134** F7
Leeds LS10 . . . . **212** A3
2 Mirfield WF14 . . . . . . **138** A4
aldermill Way WF2 . . . . . **142** B2
alder Island Way WF2 . . . **142** B2
aldermill Way WF13 . . . . **139** B6
alder Mount WF4 . . . . . . **159** E5
alder Pl 9 HX7 . . . . **88** F3
alder Rd
Dewsbury WF13 . . . . . . **138** F5
Mirfield WF14 . . . . **138** A3
alder St
Brighouse HD6 . . . . **115** C1
Castleford WF10 . . . . . . **124** C8
Elland HX4 . . . . **134** D7
Halifax HX3 . . . . **203** C2
Todmorden OL14 . . . . . **108** B5
Wakefield WF1 . . . . **142** D4
alderstone Ave BD6 . . . . . **93** E8
alderstone Cl WF4 . . . . . **158** A7
alder Terr
Elland HX3 . . . . **113** A1
1 Hebden Bridge HX7 . . **88** F3
Horbury WF4 . . . . **159** C8
Mytholmroyd HX7 . . . . . **89** D1
alder Trad Est HD5 . . . . . **137** A6
aldervale S71 . . . . **179** E4
Calder Vale Rd
Horbury WF4 . . . . **159** C8
Wakefield WF1 . . . . **142** E5
Calder View
Brighouse HD6 . . . . **115** A1
Crigglestone WF4 . . . . . **159** E5
Ossett WF5 . . . . **140** B5
Todmorden OL14 . . . . . **108** E6
Calder Way HX3 . . . . **93** A6
Calder Way BD20 . . . . . . **17** E8
Calderwood Cl BD18 . . . . **55** F3
Caldicott Cl OL14 . . . . . . **107** F3
Caledonia Ct WF2 . . . . . . **120** B2
Caledonian Rd WF12 . . . . **139** C5
Caledonia Rd
Batley WF17 . . . . **118** C5
Keighley BD21 . . . . **35** D8
Caledonia St BD4, BD5 . . . **201** C1
Calf Hey La S36 . . . . **200** D7
Calf Hey Terr 3 OL14 . . . **108** A1
Calf Hill Rd HD9 . . . . **172** B1
Calgary Pl LS7 . . . . **204** A2
California Dr
Castleford WF10 . . . . . . **123** D5
Horbury WF4 . . . . **141** C1
Todmorden OL14 . . . . . **108** A3
California La DB19 . . . . . **117** B7
California Mews LS27 . . . . **98** B4
California St 12 LS27 . . . . **98** B4
Callis Wood Bottom HX7 . **88** C1
Call La LS1 . . . . **211** D3
Calls The LS14 . . . . **212** A3
Calmlands Rd HD9 . . . . . **170** D1
Calpin Cl BD10 . . . . **56** B8
Calton Gr 3 BD21 . . . . . **35** F6
Calton Rd BD21 . . . . **35** F6
Calton St
Huddersfield HD1 . . . . . **154** B8
2 Keighley BD21 . . . . . **35** B5
1 Keighley BD21 . . . . . **35** B6
Calver Ave BD21 . . . . . . **35** A8
Calver Gr BD21 . . . . **35** A7
Calverley Ave
Bradford BD3 . . . . **75** D8
Leeds LS13 . . . . **58** B3
Calverley Bridge LS13 . . . **57** E6
Calverley CE Prim Sch
LS28 . . . . **57** B7
Calverley Ct
Leeds LS13 . . . . **58** B3
Rothwell LS26 . . . . **101** B5
Calverley Cutting BD10 . . **56** F8
Calverley Dr LS13 . . . . . . **58** B3
Calverley Garth LS13 . . . . **58** B3
Calverley Gdns LS13 . . . . **58** A4
Calverley Gr 1 LS13 . . . . **58** B3
Calverley Green Rd WF6 . . **122** F3
Calverley La
Horsforth LS18 . . . . **58** A8
Leeds LS13 . . . . **58** A3
Pudsey LS28 . . . . **57** C5
Yeadon LS18 . . . . **57** E7
Calverley Moor Ave LS28 . **57** A1
Calverley Parkside Prim Sch
LS28 . . . . **57** B6
Calverley Rd LS26 . . . . . . **101** C5
Calverley St WlK **206** B1
Calverley Terr 2 LS13 . . . **58** B3
Calver Rd BD21 . . . . **35** A7
Calversyke St BD21 . . . . . **35** A7
Calvert Cl LS25 . . . . **83** A3
Calvert Ho 3 BD16 . . . . . **37** A2
Calverts Wlk WF5 . . . . . . **140** E4
Camargue Rd BD2 . . . . . . **55** F4
Camberley Cl LS28 . . . . . **76** E6
Camberley Mount BD4 . . . **75** E4
Camberley St 8 LS11 . . . . **214** C3

Camberley Way LS28 . . . . **76** E6
Camborne Dr HD2 . . . . . . **135** F3
Camborne Way BD22 . . . . **34** E5
Cambrian Bar BD12 . . . . . **94** B6
Cambrian St LS11 . . . . . . **214** A4
Cambrian Terr LS11 . . . . . **214** A4
Cambridge Chase BD19 . . . **96** B2
Cambridge Cl LS27 . . . . . **98** B5
Cambridge Cres WF4 . . . . **143** C3
Cambridge Ct LS27 . . . . . **98** B4
Cambridge Dr
Leeds LS13 . . . . **58** B3
Otley LS21 . . . . **23** C7
Cambridge Gdns LS13 . . . **58** B3
Cambridge Gr
Kippax LS25 . . . . **83** A5
Otley LS21 . . . . **23** B7
Cambridge Pl
Bradford BD3 . . . . **201** C4
13 Queensbury BD13 . . . **72** E1
14 Todmorden OL14 . . . **108** B5
Cambridge Rd
Batley WF17 . . . . **96** D2
Huddersfield HD1 . . . . . **154** A7
Leeds LS6 . . . . **206** C3
Cambridge St
Batley, Heckmondwike
WF16 . . . . **117** E4
Batley WF17 . . . . **118** C5
Bradford BD7 . . . . **74** B4
Bradford, Town End BD14 . **73** B4
Castleford WF10 . . . . . . **124** D7
5 Guiseley LS20 . . . . . . **22** E1
Hebden Bridge HX7 . . . . **88** F3
Normanton WF6 . . . . . . **123** A1
Otley LS21 . . . . **23** B7
Queensbury BD13 . . . . . **72** F1
South Elmsall WF9 . . . . **182** A3
Todmorden OL14 . . . . . **108** C5
Wakefield WF2 . . . . **142** A5
Cambridge Terr 4 LS21 . . . **23** B7
Cambridge Way LS21 . . . . **23** B7
Camden St WF10 . . . . **125** D8
Camden St HX6 . . . . **112** B3
Camden Terr 7 BD8 . . . . . **55** D1
Camellia Cl WF2 . . . . **141** D3
Camellia Ct 3 BD18 . . . . . **55** D5
Camellia Mount BD7 . . . . **73** E6
Camelot Ct WF8 . . . . **146** E8
Camelot Way WF9 . . . . . . **183** A2
Cameron Ave 1 BD12 . . . . **94** C1
Cameronian St 8 BD21 . . . **35** C7
Camerton Gn BD5 . . . . . . **74** F2
Camilla Ct WF12 . . . . **139** F7
Cam La HD6 . . . . **115** D3
Camm La WF14 . . . . **138** B6
Camm St HD6 . . . . **115** B3
Camomile Ct BD13 . . . . . . **72** B6
Campbell St
Glusburn BD20 . . . . **16** D7
Keighley BD21 . . . . **35** C7
Pudsey LS28 . . . . **57** E2
Queensbury BD13 . . . . . **72** F1
Campden St HX7 . . . . **88** E4
Camp Hill HD3 . . . . **151** B5
Campinot Vale HD7 . . . . . **151** F1
Campion Cl WF8 . . . . **146** D7
Camp Mount WF8 . . . . . . **146** B8
Camp Rd
Bramhope LS16 . . . . **24** E1
South Kirkby WF9 . . . . . **181** F1
Camp Rise WF8 . . . . **146** B8
Camp Sq LS15 . . . . **45** F5
Campus Rd BD7 . . . . **74** C6
Camroyd St WF13 . . . . . . **118** D1
Camwood Ct BD20 . . . . . . **19** B1
Canada Cres LS19 . . . . . . **40** C4
Canada Dr LS19 . . . . **40** C5
Canada Rd LS19 . . . . **40** C5
Canada Terr LS19 . . . . . . **40** C4
Canalbank View LS13 . . . . **57** F5
Canal Ct WF3 . . . . **121** D6
Canal La
Lofthouse Gate WF3 . . . . **121** E6
Silsden BD20 . . . . **18** A7
Canal Pl LS12 . . . . **210** C3
Canal Rd
Bingley BD16 . . . . **36** F5
Bradford BD1 . . . . **201** C4
Halifax HX6 . . . . **112** C4
Keighley BD20 . . . . **18** E1
Leeds LS12 . . . . **210** A4
Pudsey LS13 . . . . **57** E5
Shipley BD1, BD2 . . . . . **55** D3
Canal St
Brighouse HD6 . . . . **115** B2
Halifax HX3 . . . . **203** C4
Huddersfield HD1 . . . . . **154** C8
Leeds LS10 . . . . **210** B3
Todmorden OL14 . . . . . **108** B5
Canal View HX6 . . . . **112** A5
Canal Wharf LS11 . . . . . . **211** B3
Canal Wlk WF3 . . . . **121** F6
Canary Dr BD15 . . . . **37** C4
Canary St BD19 . . . . **116** D8
Canberra Cl 6 BD22 . . . . . **51** F8
Canberra Dr BD22 . . . . . . **51** F8
Canby Gr HD5 . . . . **155** B5
Canford Dr BD15 . . . . . . **54** C1
Canford Rd BD15 . . . . . . **54** C1
Canker La
Halifax HX3 . . . . **92** A3
Huddersfield HD2 . . . . . **136** D1
Canning Ave WF2 . . . . . . **141** D8
Cannon Gr WF16 . . . . **117** E5
Cannon Hall Cl HD6 . . . . . **115** F3

Cannon Hall Ctry Pk★
S75 . . . . **193** D5
Cannon Hall Dr HD6 . . . . **115** F3
Cannon Hall House & Mus★
S75 . . . . **193** C5
Cannon St
6 Bingley BD16 . . . . . . **37** A2
Castleford WF10 . . . . . . **124** C5
8 Halifax HX1 . . . . **202** B1
Todmorden OL14 . . . . . **108** A3
Cannon Way WF13 . . . . . . **139** C7
Canonbury Terr LS11 . . . . **213** B3
Canteen Mill Ind Est
OL14 . . . . **107** E8
Canterbury Ave BD5 . . . . **74** C4
Canterbury Cres HX3 . . . . **92** B1
Canterbury Ct WF8 . . . . . **125** E3
Canterbury Dr LS6 . . . . . **59** C4
Canterbury Ho 9 HX6 . . . . **112** C4
Canterbury Rd
Dewsbury WF12 . . . . . . **118** F1
Leeds LS6 . . . . **59** C4
Canter The LS10 . . . . **99** D3
Canwick Cl BD20 . . . . . . **19** B1
Capas Heights Way
WF16 . . . . **117** E3
Capel Ct LS28 . . . . **57** B6
Capel St
Brighouse HD6 . . . . **115** A1
Pudsey LS28 . . . . **57** B6
Cape Mills Ind Est LS28 . . **57** E3
Cape Of Good Hope 2
BD13 . . . . **92** C8
Cape St BD1 . . . . **201** B4
Capitol Bvd LS27 . . . . . . **98** C1
Capitol Par LS6 . . . . **59** F7
Caprington Ct 2 WF6 . . . . **123** D1
Captain St
4 Bacup OL13 . . . . **106** A7
Bradford BD1 . . . . **201** C3
Caraway Ct 2 LS6 . . . . . . **42** F1
Caraway Dr LS6 . . . . **42** F1
Caraway Drive Apartments
3 LS6 . . . . **42** F1
Caraway Mews LS6 . . . . . **42** F1
Carberry Pl 21 LS6 . . . . . **205** B2
Carberry Rd LS6 . . . . **205** B2
Carberry Terr 23 LS6 . . . . **205** B2
Cardan Dr LS19 . . . . **8** C4
Carden Ave LS15 . . . . . . **80** E8
Carden Rd BD4 . . . . **75** E5
Cardigan Ave LS27 . . . . . **98** A2
Cardigan Cl WF17 . . . . . . **118** E5
Cardigan Fields Rd LS4 . . . **205** A2
Cardigan La
Leeds, Burley LS4, LS6 . . . **205** A2
Leeds LS6 . . . . **205** B3
Ossett WF5 . . . . **141** A3
Cardigan Rd LS6 . . . . **205** B3
Cardigan St BD13 . . . . . . **72** F1
Cardigan Terr
East Ardsley WF3 . . . . . **120** E8
Wakefield WF1 . . . . **216** B3
Cardigan Trad Est LS4 . . . **205** A1
Cardinal Ave LS11 . . . . . **98** E8
Cardinal Cl HD9 . . . . **170** E2
Cardinal Cres LS11 . . . . . **98** E8
Cardinal Gdns LS11 . . . . . **98** E8
Cardinal Gr LS11 . . . . . . **98** E8
**Cardinal Heenan RC High
Sch** LS6 . . . . **43** A1
Cardinal Rd LS11 . . . . . . **213** C1
Cardinal Sq LS11 . . . . . . **213** B1
Cardinal Wlk LS11 . . . . . . **98** F8
Cardwell Terr
Dewsbury WF12 . . . . . . **139** C6
Knottingley WF11 . . . . . **127** B4
Carisbrooke BD6 . . . . **94** C8
Carisbrooke La LS25 . . . . **83** B8
Carisbrooke Rd LS16 . . . . **59** B7
Cark Rd BD21 . . . . **35** C8
Carlby Gr 3 BD22 . . . . . . **35** A6
Carlby St BD22 . . . . **35** A6
Carleton Cl
Boston Spa LS23 . . . . . . **30** B8
Pontefract WF8 . . . . . . **146** D7
Carleton Com High Sch
WF8 . . . . **146** E5
Carleton Crest WF8 . . . . . **146** E6
Carleton Dr LS23 . . . . . . **30** B7
Carleton Gate WF8 . . . . . **146** D6
Carleton Glen WF8 . . . . . **146** D7
Carleton Green Cl WF8 . . . **146** E6
Carleton Ho 8 BD6 . . . . . **93** E8
Carleton Park Ave WF8 . . . **146** D6
Carleton Park Jun & Inf Sch
WF8 . . . . **146** D6
Carleton Park Rd WF8 . . . **146** D6
Carleton Rd WF8 . . . . . . **146** E6
Carleton St BD20 . . . . . . **18** C1
Carleton View WF8 . . . . . **146** D6
Carlile St HD9 . . . . **170** E2
Carling Cl BD7 . . . . **73** F3
Carlinghow Cl WF13 . . . . **117** F3
Carlinghow Hill WF17 . . . . **118** B2
Carlinghow La WF17 . . . . **117** F6
Carlinghow Mills WF17 . . . **118** B2
**Carlinghow Princess Royal
Jun & Inf Sch** WF17 . . . **118** A2
Carlisle Ave LS19 . . . . . . **40** C6
Carlisle Cl WF13 . . . . **118** C2
Carlisle Dr LS28 . . . . **76** E6
Carlisle Gr LS28 . . . . **76** D6
Carlisle Mills Bsns Ctr 13
BD8 . . . . **55** C1
Carlisle Pl BD8 . . . . **55** C1

Carlisle Rd
Bradford BD8 . . . . **55** C1
Leeds LS10 . . . . **212** A3
Pudsey LS28 . . . . **76** D6
Carlisle St
Bradford BD8 . . . . **55** C1
Halifax HX2 . . . . **202** A4
Keighley BD21 . . . . **35** D7
Pudsey LS28 . . . . **57** C1
Carlisle Terr BD8 . . . . . . **55** C1
Carlrayne La LS29 . . . . . . **22** A5
Carlton App LS22 . . . . . . **13** C6
Carlton Ave
Batley WF17 . . . . **118** B3
Castleford WF10 . . . . . . **124** F7
Pudsey LS28 . . . . **76** E7
Shipley BD18 . . . . **54** F8
Carlton Bolling Coll BD3 . **56** A1
Carlton Carr LS7 . . . . **206** C2
Carlton Cl
1 Cleckheaton BD19 . . . **116** D7
Hemsworth WF9 . . . . . . **181** C5
Leeds LS7 . . . . **206** C2
Normanton WF6 . . . . . . **123** C2
Carlton Croft
Cleckheaton BD19 . . . . . **116** D8
Leeds LS12 . . . . **213** B4
Ossett WF5 . . . . **140** D6
Carlton Ct
Leeds LS12 . . . . **213** B4
Leeds LS7 . . . . **206** C2
Carlton Dr
Baildon BD17 . . . . **38** C4
Garforth LS25 . . . . **82** F5
Guiseley LS20 . . . . **22** F2
Shipley, Frizinghall BD18 . . **55** A5
Shipley, Heaton BD9 . . . . **55** B4
Carlton Garth
Leeds, Blackwood LS17 . . **44** A5
Leeds LS7 . . . . **206** C2
Carlton Gate LS7 . . . . . . **206** C2
Carlton Gdns
Leeds LS7 . . . . **206** C2
Normanton WF6 . . . . . . **123** C2
South Elmsall WF9 . . . . **182** F3
Carlton Gn S71 . . . . **179** C1
Carlton Gr
2 Bradford BD5 . . . . . . **74** D3
Elland HX5 . . . . **135** C7
Leeds LS7 . . . . **206** C2
Shipley BD18 . . . . **55** B5
Carlton Grange LS19 . . . . **40** C7
Carlton Hill LS2, LS7 . . . . **206** C2
Carlton Hill Barracks
LS7 . . . . **206** C2
Carlton House Terr HX1 . . . **202** C1
Carlton Jun & Inf Sch
Dewsbury WF13 . . . . . . **118** C1
South Elmsall WF9 . . . . **182** F3
Carlton La
East Carlton LS19 . . . . . **23** C3
Rothwell, Lofthouse LS26 . . **100** C1
Rothwell LS26 . . . . **100** E4
Carlton Moor Mews LS10 . **99** F5
Carlton Mount LS19 . . . . . **40** C8
Carlton Pl
1 Halifax HX1 . . . . **203** B2
Leeds LS7 . . . . **206** C2
Carlton Prim Sch WF3 . . . **100** D3
Carlton Rd
Barnsley S71 . . . . **179** C1
Batley WF16 . . . . **117** C6
Dewsbury WF13 . . . . . . **118** C1
Liversedge WF15 . . . . . **117** A3
Shipley BD18 . . . . **54** E8
South Elmsall WF9 . . . . **182** F3
Carlton Rise
Leeds LS7 . . . . **206** C2
Pudsey LS28 . . . . **76** E7
Carlton Row LS12 . . . . . . **209** A3
Carlton St
3 Bacup OL13 . . . . **106** A3
Bradford BD7 . . . . **74** D6
Castleford WF10 . . . . . . **124** D8
Featherstone WF7 . . . . . **145** D7
Halifax HX1 . . . . **203** B2
11 Haworth BD22 . . . . . **51** D7
24 Hebden Bridge HX7 . . **89** A3
Horbury WF4 . . . . **141** A1
Normanton WF6 . . . . . . **123** C2
Otley LS21 . . . . **23** B7
Wakefield WF2 . . . . **142** A3
Carlton Terr
Dewsbury WF12 . . . . . . **139** D6
4 Halifax HX1 . . . . **203** B2
2 Pudsey LS28 . . . . . . **76** E8
5 Yeadon LS19 . . . . . . **40** C7
Carlton Twrs LS7 . . . . . . **206** C2
Carlton View
Kippax WF10 . . . . **102** F6
Leeds LS7 . . . . **206** C2
Carlton Way BD19,
OL2 . . . . **116** D7
Carlton Wlk BD18 . . . . . . **54** F8
Carlyle Cres WF10 . . . . . . **125** B7
Carlyle Rd WF10 . . . . **125** B7
Carmel Rd HX3 . . . . **92** C2
Carmine Cl HD5 . . . . **154** E6
Carmona Gdns BD18 . . . . **55** B5
Carnaby Rd BD7 . . . . **73** C6
Carnation St BD3 . . . . . . **75** C6
Carnegie Coll LS6 . . . . . . **59** B6
Carnegie Ct LS29 . . . . . . **8** C4

Carnegie Dr BD18 . . . . . **55** C7
Carnlea Gr WF2 . . . . **142** C3
Carnoustie Gdns 10
WF6 . . . . **123** D1
Carnoustie Gr BD16 . . . . . **54** B7
Carolan Ct HD7 . . . . **152** D5
Caroline St
10 Cleckheaton BD19 . . . **116** D8
Shipley BD18 . . . . **54** F8
Carperley Cres BD13 . . . . **71** E8
Carr's Cl WF13 . . . . **117** F3
Carr Bank
Keighley BD20 . . . . **19** C1
Otley LS21 . . . . **11** A2
Carr Bank Bottom LS21 . . **10** F2
Carr Beck Dr WF10 . . . . . **124** A5
Carr Beck Rd WF10 . . . . . **124** A5
Carr Beck View WF10 . . . **124** A5
Carr Bottom Ave BD5 . . . **74** C2
Carr Bottom Fold BD5 . . . **74** C1
Carr Bottom Gr BD5 . . . . **74** B2
Carr Bottom Rd
Bradford BD10 . . . . **56** E7
Bradford, Brownroyd Hill
BD5 . . . . **74** C2
Carr Bridge Ave LS16 . . . **41** D3
Carr Bridge Cl LS16 . . . . **41** D3
Carr Bridge Dr LS16 . . . . **41** D3
Carr Bridge View LS16 . . . **41** D3
Carr Cl LS19 . . . . **40** D3
Carr Croft Ct 8 LS29 . . . . **8** A4
Carr Crofts LS12 . . . . . . **209** B3
Carr Crofts Dr LS12 . . . . **209** B3
Carrfield Dr LS15 . . . . . . **63** D7
Carr Field Dr HX2 . . . . . . **111** E8
Carrfield La LS15 . . . . . . **63** C7
Carrfield Rd LS15 . . . . . . **63** D7
Carrfield Villas OL14 . . . . **86** A1
Carr Furlong S71 . . . . . . **178** F1
Carrgate WF9 . . . . **163** B2
Carr Gate Cres WF2 . . . . **120** D5
Carr Gate Dr WF2 . . . . . . **120** E5
Carr Gate Mount WF2 . . . **120** D5
Carr Gr BD20 . . . . **19** A1
Carr Green Ave HD6 . . . . **135** F6
Carr Green Cl HD6 . . . . . **135** F6
Carr Green Dr HD6 . . . . . **135** F6
Carr Green Jun & Inf Sch
HD6 . . . . **135** F7
Carr Green La
Brighouse HD6 . . . . **135** F7
Huddersfield HD5 . . . . . **154** D6
Carr Hall Ave HX4 . . . . . . **134** A4
Carr Hall Rd BD12 . . . . . **94** C3
Carr Head La BD20 . . . . . **16** A5
Carr Hill Ave LS28 . . . . . **57** A6
Carr Hill Dr LS28 . . . . . . **57** A6
Carr Hill Gr LS28 . . . . . . **57** A6
Carr Hill Nook LS28 . . . . **57** A6
Carr Hill Rd
Denby Dale HD8 . . . . . . **191** A6
Pudsey LS28 . . . . **57** A6
Carr Hill Rise LS28 . . . . . **57** A6
Carr Ho WF1 . . . . **216** B2
Carrholm Cres LS7 . . . . . **60** B7
Carrholm Dr LS7 . . . . . . **60** B7
Carrholm Gn 2 LS7 . . . . . **94** B6
Carrholm Gr LS7 . . . . . . **60** B7
Carrholm Mount LS7 . . . . **60** B7
Carrholm Rd LS7 . . . . . . **60** B7
Carrholm View LS7 . . . . . **60** B7
Carr Hos LS26 . . . . **123** E8
Carr House Fold 1
OL14 . . . . **108** D6
Carr House Gate BD12 . . . **94** C4
Carr House Gr BD12 . . . . **94** C4
Carr House La
Bradford BD12 . . . . **94** B4
Shelf HX3 . . . . **93** D7
Todmorden OL14 . . . . . **108** D6
Carr House Mount BD12 . . **94** C4
Carr House Rd
Holmfirth HD9 . . . . **189** A5
Shelf HX3 . . . . **93** D7
Carriage Dr
Cleckheaton BD19 . . . . . **96** B2
Halifax HX1 . . . . **202** C4
Huddersfield HD4 . . . . . **171** F8
Carriage Dr The
Elland, Holywell Green
HX4 . . . . **134** A4
Elland HX4 . . . . **134** C8
Leeds LS8 . . . . **61** C8
Carriage Fold BD13 . . . . . **52** D5
Carriage Way WF16 . . . . . **117** D3
Carricks Cl BD12 . . . . . . **94** E6
Carrier St 16 HX1 . . . . . . **203** B3
Carrington St BD3 . . . . . . **75** C7
Carrington Terr LS20 . . . . **39** D8
Carr La
Bradford BD12 . . . . **94** D5
Castleford WF10 . . . . . . **124** F6
Denholme BD13 . . . . . . **52** E2
Dewsbury, Heckmondwike
WF16 . . . . **117** B1
Dewsbury WF12 . . . . . . **157** C8
East Morton BD20 . . . . . **36** D8
Hemsworth WF4, WF9 . . . **162** F2
Holmfirth HD9 . . . . **188** B4
Ingbirchworth S36 . . . . . **192** D4
Keighley, Riddlesden BD20 . **19** A1
Micklethwaite BD16 . . . . **36** E8
Middlestown WF4 . . . . . **158** B6
Rothwell WF3 . . . . **100** E3

Carr La continued
Shepley HD8 . . . . **190** F6
Shipley BD18 . . . . **55** D7
Slaithwaite HD7. . . . . **152** A1
South Kirkby WF9 . . . . **182** D4
Thorner LS14, LS17 . . . . . . **45** D5
Wakefield WF2 . . . . **160** E7
Wetherby LS22 . . . . **14** A7
Yeadon LS19 . . . . **40** D3
Carr Lane Ave WF10. . . . **124** E5
Carr Manor Ave LS17 . . . **43** B1
Carr Manor Cres LS17 . . . **60** B8
Carr Manor Croft LS17 . . **60** B7
Carr Manor Dr LS17 . . . . . **60** B8
Carr Manor Garth 2 LS17 **43** B1
Carr Manor Gdns LS17 . . **60** B8
Carr Manor Gr LS17 . . . . . **60** B8
Carr Manor High Sch
LS17 . . . . **60** A7
Carr Manor Mount LS17. . **60** B8
Carr Manor Par LS17 . . . . **60** B8
Carr Manor Pl LS17 . . . . . **60** B8
Carr Manor Prim Sch
LS17. . . . . **60** B8
Carr Manor Rd LS17. . . . . **60** B8
Carr Manor View LS17 . . . **60** C8
Carr Manor Wlk LS17 . . . . **60** B7
Carr Mills WF17. . . . . **117** E6
Carr Moor Side LS11 . . . **214** C3
Carr Moor St LS10 . . . . . **215** A2
Carr Mount
Denby Dale HD8 . . . . **191** A6
Kirkheaton HD5 . . . . **155** E7
Carroll Ct WF9. . . . . **182** E3
Carroll St BD3 . . . . **201** D2
Carr Pit Rd HD5. . . . . **154** C5
Carr Rd
3 Bradford BD12. . . . . . . **94** C3
Pudsey LS28 . . . . **57** A7
Todmorden OL14 . . . . **107** A8
Carr Row BD12 . . . . **94** C3
Carr Side Cres WF17 . . . **118** C3
Carrs Rd HD7. . . . . **169** A4
Carrs Side St No 1 HD7. **169** A4
Carrs Side St No 2 HD7. **169** A4
Carrs St HD7 . . . . **169** A4
Carr St
Batley, Batley Carr
WF17. . . . . **118** C2
Batley, Birstall WF17 . . . . . **96** E1
Bradford BD5. . . . . **74** D2
Brighouse HD6 . . . . **115** A4
Cleckheaton BD19 . . . . . . **116** D7
Huddersfield HD3 . . . . **153** C7
Keighley BD21 . . . . **35** C7
Liversedge WF15 . . . . **117** A5
Carr Top Cl WF17 . . . . . . **118** B2
Carr Top La HD7 . . . . **152** D4
Carr View WF9 . . . . **182** C3
Carr View Rd HD9. . . . . . **189** F2
Carr Wood Cl LS28 . . . . . **57** A6
Carr Wood Gdns LS28 . . . **57** A7
Carr Wood Ind Est WF10 **124** F5
Carr Wood Rd WF10 . . . . **124** F5
Carr Wood Way LS28. . . . **57** A7
Carter's La LS29 . . . . **8** E7
Carter Ave 2 LS15 . . . . . **81** C8
Carter La
6 Leeds LS15. . . . . **81** C8
Queensbury BD13 . . . . **72** D3
Carter Mount LS15 . . . . . **81** C8
Carter Terr LS15 . . . . **62** C1
Cartlon Lanes Sh Ctr 8
. . . . **124** D8
Cartmell La BD20 . . . . **17** C5
Cartmell Ct LS15. . . . . **80** D7
Cartmell Dr LS15. . . . . **80** D7
Cartmel Rd BD21. . . . . **35** A7
Carton Ct 8 BD5 . . . . **74** E3
Cartworth Bank Rd HD9 **188** F2
Cartworth Fold HD9. . . . . **189** A3
Cartworth La HD9. . . . . . . **189** A3
Cartworth Moor Rd
Holme HD9 . . . . **198** E8
Holmfirth HD9 . . . . **188** E1
Cartworth Rd HD9 . . . . . . **189** A4
Cartwright Fold WF2. . . . **141** D7
Cartwright Gdns HD4 . . . **153** C3
Cartwright Hall Art Gall &
Mus* BD9 . . . . **55** C3
Cartwright Ho 7 WF15. . **117** A5
Cartwright St BD19 . . . . . **116** F6
Carver St BD19 . . . . **116** D8
Caryl Rd BD4 . . . . **75** A3
Cashmere St BD21 . . . . . . **35** A7
Caspar Apartments LS2 . **206** C1
Casson Ave WF3 . . . . **99** B1
Casson Dr WF3 . . . . **120** B8
Casson Fold HX3. . . . . **93** A2
Casson Gr WF3 . . . . **99** B1
Casson St HD4 . . . . **153** E3
Castle Ave
Brighouse HD6 . . . . **135** F8
Huddersfield HD4 . . . . **154** A1
Wakefield WF2 . . . . **142** D2
Castle Carr Rd
Halifax HX2 . . . . **90** D6
Wadsworth Moor HX2. . . . . **70** A1
Castle Chain WF2 . . . . . . **125** E1
Castle Cl
Bardsey LS17. . . . . **28** D3

Castle Cl continued
Batley WF17 . . . . **97** A1
Castle Cres
Dewsbury WF12 . . . . **139** D1
Wakefield WF2 . . . . **160** D8
Castle Croft BD16 . . . . . . **36** A1
Castle Ct 1 BD21 . . . . **35** C8
Castle Est HX4 . . . . **132** C3
Castlefield Ct WF10 . . . . **124** D8
Castlefields LS26 . . . . . . **100** B5
Castlefields Cres HD6 . . . **135** F8
Castlefields Dr HD6 . . . . . **135** F8
Castlefields Ind Est BD16 . **36** D5
Castlefields Inf Sch HD6 **114** F1
Castlefields La BD16 . . . . **36** E5
Castlefields Rd
Bingley BD16 . . . . **36** D6
Brighouse HD6 . . . . **135** F8
Castleford Airedale Inf Sch
WF10 . . . . **125** C7
Castleford Airedale Jun Sch
WF10 . . . . **125** C7
Castleford High Sch (Tech
Coll) WF10 . . . . **124** F8
Castleford La
Featherstone WF7. . . . . . . **124** B2
Knottingley WF11 . . . . **126** B5
Castleford Mus* WF10 . . **124** D8
Castleford Normanton &
District Hospl (General)
WF10 . . . . **124** B6
Castleford Rd WF6 . . . . . . **123** C3
Castleford Sta WF10 . . . . **124** D7
Castleford Townville Inf Sch
WF10 . . . . **125** C7
Castle Garth WF8 . . . . . . **125** E1
Castle Gate
Cragg Vale HX7 . . . . **110** C4
Ilkley LS29 . . . . **8** B4
Lofthouse Gate LS26 . . . . **122** A8
Wetherby LS22 . . . . **13** E5
Castlegate Dr
Bradford BD10. . . . . **56** C6
Pontefract WF8 . . . . **146** C5
Castlegate Ho 17 HX5. . . **134** F7
Castlegate Loop HD1 . . . **154** A6
Castlegate Slip HD1. . . . . **154** A7
Castle Gr
Bardsey LS17. . . . . **28** C3
Harden BD16 . . . . **36** A1
Horbury WF4 . . . . **159** C8
3 Pontefract WF8 . . . . . . **125** D1
5 Todmorden OL14 . . . . **108** D6
Castle Grange LS19 . . . . . **40** D6
Castle Grove Ave LS6 . . . . **59** D7
Castle Grove Dr LS6. . . . . **59** D6
Castle Hall Sch WF14 . . . **138** B5
Castle Head Cl WF13 . . . **100** C1
Castle Head La WF3. . . . . **121** A8
Castle Hill
Brighouse HD6 . . . . **135** F8
Ilkley LS29 . . . . **8** B4
Wakefield WF4 . . . . **141** C4
Castle Hill Fort* HD4 . . . . **154** C1
Castle Hill Prim Sch
OL14. . . . . **108** D6
Castle Hill Rd BD19 . . . . **117** B6
Castle Hill Side HD4. . . . **172** C6
Castle Hill View
Bardsey LS17. . . . . **28** C3
Batley WF16 . . . . **117** F3
Castle Hos HD4 . . . . **172** B8
Castle Ings Cl LS12. . . . . . **77** D3
Castle Ings Dr LS12 . . . . . **77** D3
Castle Ings Gdns LS12. . . **77** D2
Castle Keep LS22 . . . . **13** E5
Castle La
Ripponden HX6 . . . . **132** C3
Slaithwaite HD7. . . . . **151** E2
Todmorden OL14 . . . . **108** D6
Castle Lodge Ave LS26 . . **100** C6
Castle Lodge Garth LS26 **100** C7
Castle Lodge Mews
LS26. . . . . **100** C6
Castle Lodge Sq LS26 . . . **100** C7
Castle Lodge Way LS26. . **100** B6
Castle Mdws WF4. . . . . . . **159** F3
Castlemore Rd BD17 . . . . . **38** D2
Castle Mount WF2 . . . . . . **139** D1
Castle Par WF10 . . . . **124** F6
Castle Pl 2 HD6 . . . . **135** F8
Castle Rd
Ilkley LS29 . . . . **8** B4
Keighley BD21 . . . . **35** B8
Rothwell LS26 . . . . **100** D5
Shipley BD18 . . . . **55** B7
Wakefield WF2 . . . . **142** E1
Castle Rd W WF2 . . . . . . **142** D1
Castlerigg Gn BD6 . . . . **93** E6
Castleshaw Top Bank
OL3 . . . . **167** B1
Castle St
Leeds LS1 . . . . **211** A4
Wakefield WF2 . . . . **141** F5
Castle Syke View WF8. . . **146** C6
Castle Terr
1 Brighouse HD6. . . . . . . **135** F8
Wakefield WF2 . . . . **160** D8
Castleton Cl LS12 . . . . . . **210** C3
Castleton Prim Sch LS12 **210** B3
Castleton Rd LS12 . . . . . . **210** B4
Castletown Dr OL13. . . . . **106** B1
Castle Vale WF8 . . . . **125** F2
Castle View
Honley HD9 . . . . **171** F3
Horbury WF4 . . . . **159** C8

Castle View continued
Leeds LS17 . . . . **43** B1
Mirfield WF14 . . . . **138** B5
Pontefract WF8 . . . . **125** D1
Todmorden OL14 . . . . **108** B4
Wakefield WF2 . . . . **160** D8
Castle Wood Cl
Harewood LS17 . . . . **27** A7
Horsforth LS18 . . . . **58** D8
Castle Yd 1 LS29 . . . . **8** B4
Castley La
Castley LS21 . . . . **25** B8
Pool LS21. . . . . **24** E8
Catalina LS12. . . . . **211** A3
Cater La WF16 . . . . **117** D3
Cater St BD1. . . . . **201** C3
Cathcart St
10 Halifax HX3 . . . . **92** B2
Leeds LS6 . . . . **206** A3
Cath Church of St Peter
The* BD1. . . . . **201** C3
Cathedral CE High Sch The
WF2 . . . . **142** A3
Cathedral Church of All
Saints The HX1 . . . . . . **216** B2
Cathedral Cl
Bradford BD1. . . . . **201** C3
Wakefield WF1 . . . . **216** A3
Cathedral Ret WF2. . . . . . **216** A1
Cathedral Wlk WF1 . . . . . **216** B2
Catherine Cl HD3 . . . . **135** A2
Catherine Cres 16 HX5 . . **134** F4
Catherine Gr 10 LS11. . . . **214** B3
Catherine House La HX2 . . **90** A6
Catherine Rd HD2. . . . . . . **136** B4
Catherine Slack
Brighouse HD6 . . . . **114** F6
Queensbury BD13 . . . . **92** C6
Catherine St
Brighouse HD6 . . . . **115** A3
Elland HX5 . . . . **134** F6
Fitzwilliam WF9 . . . . **163** A4
5 Keighley BD21 . . . . **35** B5
Cat Hill La S36. . . . . **192** D1
Cat La HX2 . . . . **111** B5
Catlow St WF10 . . . . **124** C7
Cattle La LS25 . . . . **64** E7
Cattlelaith La WF11 . . . . **126** D2
Cattle Market St LS21 . . . . **23** A8
Caudle Hill WF11 . . . . **104** F4
Cauldwell Gdns 2 BD5. . . **74** E4
Caulms Wood Rd WF13. . **118** D1
Causeway
Halifax HX1 . . . . **203** C3
Ripponden HX4 . . . . **133** A2
Slaithwaite HD3, HD7 . . . . **151** F4
Causeway Cres HD7. . . . . **152** D1
Causeway Fold HX7 . . . . . . **87** F4
Causeway Foot HX2 . . . . . **71** D3
Causeway Garth La WF8 **165** C4
Causeway Head HX6 . . . . **112** C5
Causeway Head La HX6 . **132** B5
Causeway Side HD7. . . . . **152** D1
Causeway Wood Rd
OL14 . . . . **108** E4
Cautley Rd LS9 . . . . **212** C2
Cavalier App LS9 . . . . **212** C2
Cavalier Cl LS9 . . . . **212** C2
Cavalier Ct LS9 . . . . **212** C2
Cavalier Dr BD10. . . . . **56** E8
Cavalier Gate LS9 . . . . . . **212** C2
Cavalier Gdns LS9 . . . . . . **212** C2
Cavalier Gn LS9. . . . . **212** C2
Cavalier Mews LS9 . . . . . **212** C2
Cavalier View LS9. . . . . . **212** C2
Cave Cres WF2 . . . . **141** E4
Cave Hill HX3. . . . . **92** F4
Cave La WF3 . . . . **120** E7
Cavendish App BD11. . . . . **96** E6
Cavendish Ave WF8 . . . . . **125** E3
Cavendish Ct
Birkenshaw, Drighlington
BD11. . . . . **96** E5
Bradford BD10. . . . . **56** C5
2 Keighley BD21 . . . . **35** C7
Marsden HD7. . . . . **168** F4
Cavendish Dr
Bingley BD16 . . . . **37** B4
Guiseley LS20 . . . . **39** D8
Cavendish Gr LS20 . . . . . . **39** D8
Cavendish Mews
Birkenshaw, Drighlington
BD11. . . . . **96** E6
Leeds LS17 . . . . **43** D4
Cavendish Pl LS28 . . . . . . **57** E1
Cavendish Prim Sch
BD10. . . . . **56** D5
Cavendish Rd
Bradford, Bank Top BD2 . . . **56** C5
Bradford, Thorpe BD10 . . . . **56** B7
Guiseley LS20 . . . . **39** D8
Leeds LS2 . . . . **206** D2
Cavendish Rise LS28 . . . . **77** A7
Cavendish Sq 3 LS28 . . . . **57** E1
Cavendish St
14 Halifax HX1 . . . . **202** C3
Keighley BD21 . . . . **35** C7
Leeds LS3 . . . . **210** C4
Pudsey LS28 . . . . **77** A7
3 Yeadon LS19 . . . . **40** C7
Cavendish Terr 13 HX1 . . **202** C3
Cavewell Cl WF5 . . . . **140** F3
Cavewell Gdns WF5 . . . . . **140** F3
Cawcliffe Dr HD6 . . . . **115** A5
Cawcliffe Rd HD6. . . . . . . **115** A4
Cawley Garth WF16 . . . . . **117** E3
Cawley La WF16 . . . . **117** E3

Cawley Lane Jun & Inf Sch
WF16 . . . . **117** E4
Cawood Haven BD6. . . . . . **93** E8
Cawthorne Ave HD2. . . . . **136** A2
Cawthorne CE Prim Sch
S75 . . . . **193** E4
Cawthorne La S75 . . . . . . **193** F5
Cawthorne Mus* S75. . . . **193** E5
Cawthorne Rd WF2 . . . . . **160** B6
Caxton Gdns WF8 . . . . . . **125** D3
Caxton Rd LS21 . . . . **22** E7
Caxton St LS22. . . . . **13** E5
Caycroft Nook HX7. . . . . . **88** F5
Caygill Terr HX1 . . . . **203** B2
Caythorne Wlk BD10 . . . . **56** C5
Caythorpe Rd LS16. . . . . . **59** B7
Cecil Ave
Baildon BD17 . . . . **38** C4
Bradford BD7. . . . . **74** B4
Brighouse HX3. . . . . **114** E8
Cecil Ct 7 BD7. . . . . **74** B4
Cecil Gr LS12 . . . . **209** C4
Cecil Mount LS12 . . . . . . **209** C4
Cecil Rd LS12 . . . . **209** C4
Cecil St
11 Haworth BD22. . . . . . . **51** E8
9 Huddersfield HD1. . . . . **154** A6
Leeds LS12 . . . . **209** C4
Cedar Apartments WF1 . **216** C4
Cedar Ave
Huddersfield HD1 . . . . **153** F7
Leeds LS12 . . . . **209** C4
Ossett WF5 . . . . **140** E4
Cedar Cl
Huddersfield HD7 . . . . **152** F5
Leeds LS12 . . . . **209** C3
Pontefract WF8 . . . . **146** C5
Royston S71. . . . . **179** A4
Todmorden OL14 . . . . **108** A7
Cedar Court Office Pk
WF4 . . . . **159** D6
Cedar Covert LS22 . . . . . . **13** E8
Cedar Ct
Castleford WF10 . . . . **124** E7
Rothwell LS26 . . . . **101** C2
Cedar Dr
Bradford BD12. . . . . **94** E4
Dewsbury WF12 . . . . **140** B7
Cedar Gr
2 Batley WF17. . . . . **118** C3
Brighouse BD19 . . . . **115** B6
Elland HX4. . . . . **134** B7
Featherstone WF7. . . . . . . **145** D7
Sutton-in-C BD20. . . . . **16** C5
Cedar Mews WF2 . . . . . . **142** A3
Cedar Mount
Huddersfield HD1 . . . . **153** F7
Leeds LS12 . . . . **209** C4
Cedar Pl LS12 . . . . **209** C4
Cedar Rd
Dewsbury WF12 . . . . **140** A7
Leeds LS12 . . . . **209** C3
Normanton WF6 . . . . **144** B7
Cedar Ridge LS25 . . . . **64** B1
Cedar St
Bingley BD16 . . . . **36** E5
Halifax HX1 . . . . **202** B5
Huddersfield HD1 . . . . **153** E7
Keighley BD21 . . . . **35** B4
Leeds LS12 . . . . **209** C4
Todmorden OL14 . . . . **129** A8
Cedars The LS16 . . . . **24** F2
Cedar Terr LS12 . . . . **209** C3
Cedar Way BD19 . . . . **117** A8
Cedar Wlk
Featherstone WF7 . . . . **145** D6
Knottingley WF11 . . . . **126** E2
Celandine Ave HD3 . . . . . **152** E8
Celandine Cl WF8. . . . . . . **146** D7
Celandine Dr HD3. . . . . . . **152** E8
Celete Ind Pk BD19 . . . . . **116** C7
Cellars Clough Bsns Pk
HD7. . . . . **169** B6
Cemetery La
Keighley BD20 . . . . **18** B2
Rothwell WF3 . . . . **100** C2
Sowerby Bridge HX6 . . . . . **112** C4
Cemetery Rd
Batley, Heckmondwike
WF16 . . . . **117** D4
Batley WF17 . . . . **118** B5
Bingley BD16 . . . . **36** D8
Bradford, Birks BD7, BD8 . . **73** F6
Bradford, Moor Top BD12,
BD6. . . . . **94** B7
Dewsbury WF13 . . . . **139** B7
Guiseley LS19 . . . . **23** D1
Haworth BD22. . . . . **50** F6
Hemsworth WF9 . . . . **181** C8
Holmfirth HD9 . . . . **188** F4
Huddersfield HD1 . . . . **153** F7
Leeds LS11 . . . . **214** A4
Normanton WF6 . . . . **123** C2
Pudsey LS28 . . . . **76** D8
Ryhill WF4 . . . . **162** B1
Centaur Ho 2 LS1 . . . . . . **211** A4
Centenary Rd BD17 . . . . . . **38** F4
Centenary Sq
Bradford BD1. . . . . **201** B2
Dewsbury WF12 . . . . **139** B4
Leeds LS2, LS9 . . . . **212** A4
Centenary Way WF17 . . . **118** B6
Central Arc 5 BD19. . . . . **116** E7
Central Ave
Baildon BD17 . . . . **38** B2
Bradford BD5. . . . . **74** C4
Cleckheaton WF15. . . . . . **116** B5
Fitzwilliam WF9 . . . . **163** A4

Central Ave continued
Huddersfield HD2 . . . . **136** B3
Keighley BD22 . . . . **34** F1
Shipley BD18 . . . . **55** B2
South Elmsall WF9 . . . . . . **182** F1
Central Cl HD2. . . . . **136** B3
Central Dr
Castleford WF10 . . . . **124** A3
Huddersfield HD2 . . . . **136** B3
Keighley BD22 . . . . **34** F1
Royston S71. . . . . **179** C2
Central Par
6 Cleckheaton BD19 . . . **116** E7
Leeds LS9 . . . . **80** C7
Central Pk
Halifax HX1 . . . . **203** A1
Leeds LS11 . . . . **211** B3
Central Rd
Huddersfield HD2 . . . . **136** B3
Leeds LS1 . . . . **211** C3
Central St
Dewsbury WF13 . . . . **139** C2
Halifax HX1 . . . . **203** B3
Hebden Bridge HX7 . . . . . . **89** A3
Leeds LS1 . . . . **211** B4
Central Street Inf Sch
HX7. . . . . **89** A4
Central View OL13. . . . . . **106** A3
Centre 27 Bsns Pk WF17 . **97** B3
Centre St
4 Bradford BD5. . . . . **74** C3
Hemsworth WF9 . . . . **181** D8
1 Liversedge WF16 . . . . . **117** C4
South Elmsall WF9 . . . . . . **183** A3
Centuria Wlk HD3. . . . . . . **152** E8
Centurion Way BD19 . . . . **95** C2
Century Pl BD8 . . . . **55** C1
Century Rd HX5. . . . . **134** F2
Century Way LS15. . . . . . . **81** F2
Ceres Rd LS22 . . . . **14** A5
Chaddlewood Cl 3 LS18 . **41** C1
Chadwell Springs BD16 . . **54** A7
Chadwick Cres WF13. . . . **118** B3
Chadwick Fold La WF14 . **137** F4
Chadwick Hall Gdns
WF14. . . . . **137** F3
Chadwick La WF14. . . . . . **137** F4
Chadwick St S LS10 . . . . . **212** A2
Chadwick St LS10. . . . . . . **212** A2
Chaffinch Rd 6 BD8 . . . . . **73** C7
Chaffinch Wlk HD4. . . . . . **171** E7
Chain Bar Rd BD19. . . . . . **95** D1
Chain St
Meltham HD7. . . . . **170** A5
Slaithwaite HD7. . . . . **169** F6
Chaln St
Bradford BD1. . . . . **201** A3
Castleford WF10 . . . . **124** C8
Chak Gdns BD9 . . . . **54** D5
Chalcroft Cl WF16 . . . . . . **117** E5
Chald La WF2. . . . . **216** A1
Chalfont Rd LS16 . . . . **59** B8
Chalice Cl LS10 . . . . **99** F7
Challenge Coll BD8 . . . . . . **55** D3
Challenger Cres S63 . . . . **194** D1
Challenge Way
Batley WF12, WF17 . . . . . **119** A3
Bradford BD4. . . . . **75** D4
Challis Gr BD5 . . . . **74** E3
Chalner Ave LS27 . . . . **97** F2
Chalner Cl LS27. . . . . **97** F2
Chalner Ho LS27 . . . . **97** F2
Chaloner Gn WF1 . . . . **216** C4
Chaloner Gr WF1 . . . . **216** C4
Chalwood HD2. . . . . **136** E4
Chaly Fields LS23 . . . . **30** D7
Champion Ave WF10 . . . . **124** E5
Chancel Ct HD3. . . . . **153** A6
Chancellor St LS6. . . . . . . **206** C3
Chancery Cl 20 HD3. . . . . **154** A6
Chancery Ct 14 BD5. . . . . **74** E3
Chancery La
19 Huddersfield HD1. . . . **154** A6
Ossett WF5 . . . . **140** C6
2 Wakefield WF1. . . . . . . **216** B2
Chancery Rd WF5. . . . . . . **140** B8
Chandler Cl WF17 . . . . **96** E1
Chandler La HD9. . . . . **171** D4
Chandlers Cl WF1. . . . . . . **121** B5
Chandlers The LS2. . . . . . **212** A3
Chandlers Wharf LS13. . . . **57** E6
Chandos Ave LS8 . . . . **204** B4
Chandos Fold LS8. . . . . . . **204** B3
Chandos Garth LS8 . . . . . **204** B4
Chandos Gdns LS8 . . . . . **204** B4
Chandos Gn LS8 . . . . **204** B4
Chandos Pl LS8. . . . . **204** C4
Chandos St
Bradford BD4. . . . . **201** C2
4 Keighley BD21 . . . . **35** B5
Chandos Terr LS8. . . . . . . **204** C4
Chandos Wlk LS8 . . . . **204** B3
Change Cl OL13. . . . . **106** B4
Changegate BD22. . . . . **51** B7
Changegate Ct 2 BD22. . . **51** B7
Changegate Ho 9 BD21. . **35** C7
Change La HX3. . . . . **113** E2
Channing Way BD1 . . . . . **201** B2
Chantrell Ct LS2 . . . . **212** A3
Chantry Bridge Ind Est
WF1 . . . . **216** C1
Chantry Cl
Ilkley LS29 . . . . **8** D3
Pontefract WF8 . . . . **146** E6
Chantry Croft
Fitzwilliam WF9 . . . . **163** A2
Leeds LS15 . . . . **81** D7
Chantry Ct LS27 . . . . **98** B5

hantry Dr LS29 8 B4
hantry Garth LS15 81 D7
hantry Gr S71 179 C3
hantry La LS24 48 E5
hantry Rd WF2 141 E5
hapel Allerton Hospl LS7 204 B1
hapel Allerton Prim Sch LS7 204 A2
hapel Ave
Barnsley S71 179 C1
Batley WF16 117 E5
Hebden Bridge HX7 89 B3
hapel Bank HD9 189 E3
hapel Cl
Cononley BD20 4 A3
Dewsbury WF12 139 D2
Elland HX4 134 B4
Garforth LS25 82 E7
Huddersfield HD4 171 F8
Shafton S72 180 C3
Shelf HX3 93 D6
Skelmanthorpe HD8 175 A2
West Hardwick WF4 163 A7
hapel Croft
Brighouse HD6 135 F7
Laycock BD22 34 C7
hapel Ct
1 Addingham LS29 6 F8
Denby Dale HD8 191 F6
10 Leeds LS15 81 A8
Meltham HD9 170 D2
Sicklinghall LS22 12 C5
Wilsden BD15 53 C6
hapelfields WF9 182 B1
hapel Fold
Batley WF17 118 A3
Bradford BD6 74 B1
Brighouse BD12 115 C8
Leeds, Beeston LS11 213 B2
Leeds, Burley LS6 205 A3
Leeds LS12 209 C3
11 Leeds LS15 81 A8
Oakworth BD22 34 B3
3 Pudsey LS28 76 E6
Shelf HX3 93 D6
hapel Garth WF7 164 A6
hapelgate HD9 189 D3
hapel Gn 1 LS28 76 D6
hapel Gr BD16 36 E5
hapel Grange Sch BD15 73 D8
hapel Hill
Clayton DN5 194 C4
Clayton West HD8 175 E2
Huddersfield HD1 154 A5
1 Middleton LS10 99 D5
Mirfield WF14 137 F2
Morley LS27 98 A5
Slaithwaite HD7 152 D1
2 Yeadon LS19 40 B7
Chapel Hill La
Castley LS21 25 B8
Marsden HD3 151 B5
Chapel Hill Rd LS21 24 C7
Chapel House Bldgs BD12 94 D6
Chapel House Rd BD12 94 D7
Chapel La
Badsworth WF9 164 E2
Barwick in E LS15 63 E7
6 Batley, Birstall WF17 96 F1
Batley WF16 117 E4
Bingley BD16 36 F3
Bradford, Clayton Heights BD13 73 B2
Bradford, Lower Grange BD15 73 C8
Clifford LS23 30 D5
Dewsbury WF12 139 D2
Emley HD8 175 B7
Garforth LS25 82 E7
Guiseley BD17 39 C5
Halifax HX3 113 D3
Halifax, Midgley HX2 90 B2
Halifax, Southowram HX3 114 B4
Halton East BD23 1 E8
Huddersfield, Moldgreen HD5 154 D5
Huddersfield, Wellhouse HD7 152 D4
Ilkley LS29 8 A4
Keighley BD21 35 B7
Kippax LS25 83 B1
Kirk Smeaton WF8 166 E6
Laycock BD22 34 C7
Leeds, Armley LS12 209 C3
Leeds, Farnley LS12 77 E5
Leeds, Headingley Hill LS6 205 A4
Queensbury BD13 72 E1
South Elmsall WF9 183 B3
Sowerby Bridge HX6 112 D4
Thurnscoe S63 194 F1
Yeadon LS19 40 B7
Chapel Mews
Clifford LS23 30 D6
Darton S75 178 C1
Chapel Pl 11 LS6 59 D5
Chapel Rd
Bingley BD16 36 E5
Bradford BD12 94 E6
Bradford, Low Moor BD12 94 D6
Leeds LS7 204 A1
Steeton BD20 17 C5
Chapel Row
Bradford BD15 54 B1
Pool LS21 24 C7
Wilsden BD15 53 C6
Chapel St N HX3 91 F3
Chapel St S 8 OL14 108 A1
Chapelsfield La DN5 194 C4
Chapel Sq 1 LS6 59 D5
Chapel St
Addingham LS29 6 F8
Bingley BD16 36 E5
Bradford BD1 201 C3
Bradford, Brownroyd Hill BD6 74 C1
Bradford, Eccleshill BD2 56 D4
Bradford, Holme Top BD5 74 D4
Brighouse, Hove Edge HD6 114 E5
Brighouse, Norwood Green HX3 93 F2
Calderbrook OL15 129 D2
Cleckheaton BD19 116 E8
Cleckheaton, Hightown WF15 116 C5
Denholme BD13 71 D8
Dewsbury WF12 139 C6
East Ardsley, Black Gates WF3 98 F1
East Ardsley WF3 120 C7
Elland HX4 134 B4
Halifax HX2 202 A4
19 Haworth BD22 51 E8
Huddersfield, Blue Bell Hill HD4 153 E2
Huddersfield HD1 154 A5
7 Huddersfield, Moldgreen HD5 154 D5
Huddersfield, Netherton HD4 171 C7
Knottingley WF11 127 A5
Leeds, Halton LS15 81 A8
Leeds, Headingley LS6 59 D5
Liversedge WF15 117 C4
Lofthouse Gate WF3 121 E5
Mirfield WF14 138 A5
Ossett WF5 141 A4
Pudsey, Calverley LS28 57 B6
Pudsey, Rodley LS13 57 E5
Pudsey, Stanningley LS28 57 E1
Queensbury BD13 72 E1
Rothwell WF3 100 D3
Ryhill WF4 162 B1
Shafton S72 180 C3
Silsden BD20 5 E2
Slaithwaite HD7 152 B5
Thornton BD13 72 D6
4 Todmorden OL14 108 D6
Yeadon LS19 40 B4
Chapel Terr
Bradford BD15 54 B1
Honley HD9 171 F4
Huddersfield HD4 153 D4
10 Leeds LS6 59 D5
Ripponden HX6 133 C7
Sowerby Bridge HX6 111 D3
14 Thornton BD13 72 D6
Chapel The
Luddenden Foot HX2 111 D5
Normanton WF6 123 A5
Slaithwaite HD3 151 D4
Chapeltown
Halifax HX1 203 B3
Pudsey LS28 76 D6
Chapeltown Bsns Ctr LS7 207 A4
Chapeltown Enterprise Ctr LS7 207 A4
Chapeltown Rd LS7 207 A4
Chapel Wlk BD2 56 D4
Chapel Yd
Fairburn WF11 105 A4
Leeds LS15 81 D6
Chapman St
Bradford BD4 75 D6
Leeds LS9 207 B1
Chapman Terr BD12 94 C6
Chariot Way WF8 165 A4
Charles Ave
Bradford BD3 75 D7
Halifax HX3 114 A4
Huddersfield HD3 153 A8
Leeds LS9 212 C2
Lofthouse Gate WF1 121 B5
Wakefield WF1 142 F3
Charles Cotton Cl WF2 141 D8
Charles Ct 9 BD22 51 C2
Charles Gdns LS11 211 A1
Charles Gr LS26 101 C6
Charles Jones Ct WF17 118 A5
Charles Pl OL14 108 A3
Charles St
Batley WF17 118 C4
Bingley BD16 36 F3
Bradford BD1 201 B3
Brighouse HD6 115 A3
Castleford WF10 124 E7
Cleckheaton BD19 117 B8
Dewsbury, Dewsbury Moor WF13 138 F8
Dewsbury, Ravensthorpe WF13 138 E5
Dewsbury WF12 139 E8
Elland HX5 134 F6
Halifax HX1 203 C3
Horbury WF4 159 D7
Horsforth LS18 58 B7
Huddersfield HD4 153 D4
Morley LS27 98 B4
Ossett WF5 140 F3
Otley LS21 23 A7
Pudsey LS28 57 D3
Queensbury BD13 72 D1
Ryhill WF4 162 A1
Shipley BD17 55 B8
Charles St *continued*
South Hiendley S72 180 E5
2 Sowerby Bridge HX6 112 B4
Wakefield WF1 216 C1
Charlestown Est WF7 164 A4
Charlestown Rd HX1, HX3 203 C4
Charles View WF4 159 F3
Charlesworth's Bldgs 3 WF4 141 A1
Charlesworth Ct WF12 139 D2
Charlesworth Gr HX2 202 A4
Charlesworth Pl WF3 122 C6
Charlesworth Sq BD19 117 A8
Charlesworth St WF12 139 C4
Charlesworth Terr HX2 202 A4
Charlesworth Way WF2 216 A1
Charleville WF9 182 E4
Charlotte Cl
Batley WF17 96 F3
Halifax HX1 203 B1
Charlotte Ct
Bradford BD7 74 B3
Haworth BD22 51 D8
Charlotte Gr
3 Leeds LS15 81 B8
Ossett WF5 140 F4
Charlotte St WF1 216 C1
Charlton Cl 4 BD2 56 B4
Charlton Ct HX2 202 A4
Charlton Gr
4 Leeds LS9 80 A7
Silsden BD20 17 F8
Charlton Pl LS9 80 A7
Charlton Rd LS9 80 A7
Charlton St 5 LS9 80 A7
Charnley Dr LS7 204 B2
Charnock Cl HX1 203 B1
Charnwood Bank WF16 117 E4
Charnwood Cl BD2 56 C2
Charnwood Gr BD2 56 C2
Charnwood Rd BD2 56 C2
Charterhouse Rd BD10 39 C2
Charteris Rd BD8 73 C7
Chartists Ct 5 LS27 98 A3
Chartists Way LS27 98 A3
Chartwell Ct LS17 44 B5
Chartwell Dr BD6 73 E1
Charville Gdns LS17 44 F3
Chase Ave LS27 98 B1
Chase Ct LS27 98 B1
Chase The
Burley in W LS29 22 A7
Garforth LS25 83 B7
Keighley BD21 34 F8
Lofthouse Gate WF3 122 A6
Wetherby LS22 13 F6
Yeadon LS19 40 A4
Chase Way BD5 74 E2
Chassum Gr BD9 55 B2
Chaster St WF17 118 A6
Chatham St
Bradford BD3 56 A1
Halifax HX1 203 A3
9 Sowerby Bridge HX6 112 B5
Chat Hill Rd BD13, BD14 72 F5
Chatswood Ave LS11 98 F8
Chatswood Cres LS11 98 F8
Chatswood Dr LS11 213 C1
Chatsworth Ave
Pontefract WF8 125 E3
1 Pudsey LS28 76 A8
Chatsworth Cl
Huddersfield HD5 154 D4
Leeds LS8 208 A3
Chatsworth Cres LS28 76 A8
Chatsworth Ct
1 Bradford BD8 74 A8
Dewsbury WF12 139 F7
Chatsworth Dr
2 Pudsey LS28 76 A8
Wetherby LS22 13 C6
Chatsworth Fall LS28 76 A8
Chatsworth Ind Est LS12 210 A2
Chatsworth Mews 5 LS27 98 B3
Chatsworth Pl BD8 55 B2
Chatsworth Rd
Leeds LS8 208 A3
Pudsey LS28 76 A8
Chatsworth Rise LS28 76 A8
Chatsworth St BD21 35 D7
Chatsworth Terr WF12 139 F7
Chatts Wood Fold BD12 95 B5
Chaucer Ave
Lofthouse Gate WF3 121 E6
Pudsey LS28 76 F6
Chaucer Cl HD9 171 F3
Chaucer Gdns LS28 76 F6
Chaucer Gr LS28 76 F6
Chaucer St HX1 202 B2
Cheapside
Batley WF17 118 D5
Bradford BD1 201 B3
Cleckheaton BD19 116 E7
Halifax HX1 203 B3
Normanton WF6 123 B2
Shelf HX3 93 C6
Wakefield WF1 216 A2
Checkstone Ave WF10 124 A5
Cheddington Gr BD15 73 B8
Cheese Gate Nab Side HD8, HD9 190 A2
Cheetham St 23 HX7 89 A3
Chelburn View OL15 129 C1
Chelker Cl 9 BD13 73 C2
Chellowfield Ct BD9 54 C3
Chellow Grange Rd BD9 54 C3
Chellow La BD9 54 D1
Chellow St BD5 74 D2
Chellow Terr BD9 54 D1
Chellow Way WF12 139 C7
Chelmsford Rd BD3 75 C8
Chelmsford Terr BD3 75 C7
Chelsea Cl LS12 209 C2
Chelsea Mans HX3 93 A2
Chelsea Rd BD7 73 F4
Chelsea St 3 BD21 35 B5
Chelsfield Ct LS15 62 F3
Chelsfield Way LS15 62 F3
Chelston Pk BD16 36 B1
Cheltenham Ave LS29 8 F4
Cheltenham Ct HX3 113 D4
Cheltenham Gdns HX3 113 D4
Cheltenham Pl HX3 113 D4
Cheltenham Rd BD2 55 F5
Cheltenham St LS12 210 A2
Chelwood Ave LS8 43 E3
Chelwood Cres LS8 43 F2
Chelwood Dr
Bradford BD15 73 A7
Leeds LS8 43 F2
Chelwood Gr LS8 43 F3
Chelwood Mount LS8 43 F3
Chelwood Pl LS8 43 E3
Chenies Cl LS14 61 E1
Chepstow Cl LS25 83 B7
Chepstow Dr LS10 99 D3
Chequerfield Ave WF8 146 F8
Chequerfield Cl WF10 124 A6
Chequerfield Dr WF8 146 F7
Chequerfield Inf Sch WF8 146 F7
Chequerfield La WF8 146 F8
Chequerfield Mount WF8 146 F7
Chequerfield Rd WF8 146 F7
Chequers Cl WF8 146 F7
Chequers Ct WF8 146 F8
Chequers The HD9 170 E2
Cherington Ct LS29 21 F8
Cheriton Dr BD13 72 F1
Cherry Cl S71 179 A4
Cherry Ct
Halifax HX1 202 C4
Leeds, Miles Hill LS6 59 F5
Leeds, New Town LS9 207 B1
Cherry Fields BD2 55 E4
Cherry Garth WF9 181 C6
Cherry Gr
Ilkley LS29 7 F4
Leeds LS6 59 F5
Cherry Hills S75 178 A1
Cherry La HD8 175 F2
Cherry Lea Ct LS19 40 B5
Cherry Nook Rd HD2 136 E3
Cherry Pl LS9 207 B1
Cherry Rise LS14 62 C8
Cherry Row LS9 207 B1
Cherry St
2 Haworth BD22 51 E8
Keighley BD21 35 E8
Cherry Tree Ave
Bradford BD10 56 D7
Knottingley WF11 126 E3
Cherrytree Cl WF9 163 B2
Cherry Tree Cl
Castleford WF10 124 A5
Darton S75 178 C1
Huddersfield HD7 152 F5
Cherry Tree Cres
Pudsey LS28 57 D3
Walton WF2 161 B7
Cherry Tree Ct WF3 120 C7
Cherry Tree Ctr 15 HD1 154 A6
Cherry Tree Dr
Elland HX4 134 C7
Pudsey LS28 57 D3
Walton WF2 161 B7
Cherry Tree Gdns BD10 38 F1
Cherry Tree Rd WF2 161 B7
Cherry Tree Rise BD21 35 E6
Cherry Tree Row BD16 53 B7
Cherry Tree Wlk
East Ardsley WF3 120 C7
Holmfirth HD9 189 D4
10 Leeds LS2 211 C3
Cherrywood Cl LS14 45 B1
Cherrywood Gdns LS14 45 B1
Chervana Ct BD4 75 E4
Cherwell Croft LS25 83 B5
Cherwell Dr BD6 93 F7
Chesham St BD21 35 D8
Chesil Bank HD3 153 B6
Chesilton Ave HD3 153 B7
Chesney Ave LS10 215 A4
Chesney Park Ind Est LS10 215 A4
Chessington Dr WF4 157 D3
Chester Cl 6 HX3 92 B1
Chester Ct 2 HX3 92 B1
Chester Gr 3 HX3 92 B1
Chester Ho 4 HX6 112 C4
Chester Pl 8 HX3 92 B1
Chester Rd HX3 92 B1
Chester St
Bradford BD5 201 B2
Halifax, Woodside HX3 92 B1
Leeds LS12 209 C4
5 Sowerby Bridge HX6 112 B4
Chester Terr HX3 92 B1
Chesterton Ct
Horbury WF4 141 C2
Leeds LS15 81 D6
Chesterton Dr HD9 171 F3
Chestnut Ave
Batley WF17 118 A4
Boston Spa LS23 30 C8
Brierley S72 180 F2
Leeds, Cross Gates LS15 62 D2
Leeds, Hyde Park LS6 205 B3
Todmorden OL14 108 A7
Walton WF2 161 A6
Wetherby LS22 13 D6
Chestnut Cl
Elland HX4 134 B7
Featherstone WF7 145 D7
Huddersfield HD4 154 A2
Ilkley LS29 8 E3
Keighley BD22 34 F6
Chestnut Cres WF6 144 A7
Chestnut Ct
Ripponden HX6 132 D4
Shipley BD18 54 F7
Chestnut Dr
Leeds LS16 42 B5
South Hiendley S72 180 D5
Chestnut End LS23 30 E7
Chestnut Garth HD3 153 B7
Chestnut Gdns
Leeds LS12 209 B2
5 Morley LS27 98 A7
Chestnut Gn 4 WF8 125 F1
Chestnut Gr
Boston Spa LS23 30 C8
Crofton WF4 143 F1
Hemsworth WF9 181 F6
Leeds LS6 205 B3
Pontefract WF8 146 D6
Pudsey LS28 57 B6
Rothwell LS26 101 E6
Shipley BD2 55 E4
Chestnut Mdws WF14 137 F8
Chestnut Mews S72 180 D5
Chestnut Pl LS6 205 B3
Chestnut Rd 19 LS6 205 B3
Chestnut Rise LS12 209 B2
Chestnut St
Glusburn BD20 16 D6
Halifax HX1 202 B2
Huddersfield HD2 136 D3
Leeds LS6 205 B3
South Elmsall WF9 182 F1
Chestnuts The WF8 126 A4
Chestnut Terr WF12 139 C3
Chestnut View 4 LS27 98 A7
Chestnut Way LS16 42 B5
Chestnut Wlk
Knottingley WF11 126 D3
Wakefield WF2 142 A8
Chevet Croft WF2 160 E7
Chevet Gr WF2 160 E7
Chevet Hill WF2 160 F3
Chevet La
Notton WF4 179 B8
Wakefield WF2, WF4 160 F6
Walton WF2 161 B2
Chevet Level WF2 160 F4
Chevet Mews WF2 160 E8
Chevet Mount BD15 73 A8
Chevet Park Ct WF2 160 E3
Chevet Rise S71 179 B4
Chevet Terr WF1 143 A1
Chevet View S71 179 A4
Chevin Ave
Menston LS29 22 A5
Otley LS21 23 B6
Chevin Ct 6 LS21 23 A8
Chevinedge Cres HX3 113 D1
Chevin End Rd LS20 22 D3
Chevin Forest Pk* LS21 23 D5
Chevington Ct LS19 40 A3
Chevins Cl WF17 117 F8
Chevin Side LS21 23 A6
Chevin Terr LS21 23 A6
Chevin View LS21 24 C7
Cheviot Ave HD9 170 F1
Cheviot Cl WF9 181 F7
Cheviot Ct LS25 82 F5
Cheviot Gate BD12 94 B6
Cheviot Pl WF11 126 F4
Cheviot Way WF14 137 F2
Cheyne Wlk 12 BD22 35 A6
Chichester St LS12 209 C4
Chickenley La WF12 140 B7
Chickenly Com Jun & Inf Sch WF12 140 A7
Chidswell Gdns WF12 119 B3
Chidswell La
Batley WF12 119 A3
Ossett WF5, WF12 119 B2
Child La WF15 116 F1
Childs La BD18 55 E6
Childs Rd WF2 141 D8
Chiltern Ave
Castleford WF10 123 F5
Huddersfield HD3 135 A1
Knottingley WF11 126 E4
Chiltern Cl LS25 82 F5
Chiltern Ct
Ackworth M T WF7 163 F5
Garforth LS25 82 F5
Hemsworth WF9 181 F7
Pudsey LS13 57 E5
Chiltern Dr
Ackworth M T WF7 163 F5
Mirfield WF14 137 F2
Chiltern Rd WF12 118 F1
Chiltern Way WF15 116 D5
Chilver Dr BD4 76 A2

Chilwell Cl S71 178 F1
Chilwell Gdns S71 178 F1
Chilwell Mews S71 178 F1
Chimes Ct HD5 155 C7
Chimney La HD8 155 D4
Chinewood Ave WF17 118 B6
Chippendale Ct LS29 22 B4
Chippendale Ho 12 LS10 211 C3
Chippendale Rise
  Bradford BD8 73 D8
  Otley LS21 11 A1
Chirton Gr LS8 61 A5
Chiserley Field Side HX7 89 C5
Chiserley Gdns HX7 89 C5
Chiserley Hall HX7 89 C5
Chiserley Terr HX7 89 C5
Chislehurst Pl BD5 74 C4
Chiswick St LS6 205 B2
Chiswick Terr 25 LS6 205 B2
Choppards Bank Rd HD9 189 A2
Choppards La HD9 189 A2
Chrisharben Pk BD14 73 C4
Chrismoor BD10 56 A7
Christ Church Ave LS12 209 B4
Christ Church CE Jun Sch HX6 112 C5
Christ Church Mount LS12 209 B4
Christ Church Par LS12 209 B4
Christ Church Pellon CE Prim Sch HX2 112 D8
Christ Church Pl LS12 209 B4
Christ Church Rd LS12 209 B4
Christ Church St 4 OL13 106 A3
Christ Church Terr LS12 209 B4
Christ Church Upper Armley CE Prim Sch LS12 209 B4
Christ Church View LS12 209 B4
Christ Church Woodhouse CE Inf & Jun Sch HD2 136 D4
Christiana Terr LS27 98 B5
Christopher Rd LS6 206 A4
Christopher St 1 BD5 74 C3
Christopher Terr 2 BD5 74 C3
Christ the King RC Prim Sch LS13 58 E1
CHs
  6 Halifax HX2 91 F3
  Huddersfield HD4 171 E8
Church App LS25 82 F7
Church Ave
  Crofton WF1 143 C7
  Gildersome LS27 97 C8
  Horsforth LS18 41 B1
  Huddersfield, Linthwaite HD7 152 E2
  Huddersfield, Yews Hill HD4 153 E4
  Leeds LS6 59 F7
  South Kirkby WF9 182 C2
  Swillington LS26 82 A2
Churchbalk Dr WF8 146 E6
Churchbalk La WF8 146 E6
Church Bank
  Bradford BD1 201 C3
  Cragg Vale HX7 110 C3
  Halifax, Highroad Well HX2 112 D6
  Sowerby Bridge HX6 112 C4
Church Bank La HX7 110 C3
Churchbank Way WF12 139 C4
Church Cl
  Crofton WF4 144 B2
  Darton S75 177 E1
  Halifax HX1 203 A3
  Halifax, Ovenden HX2 91 D5
  Hemsworth WF9 181 D7
  Leeds LS14 62 B4
  Micklefield LS25 84 A8
  Oakworth BD22 34 B2
  Pool LS21 24 C7
  Shepley HD8 190 E8
  Sowerby Bridge HX6 111 E3
  Steeton BD20 17 C5
  Swillington LS26 82 A2
Church Cres
  Horsforth LS18 41 B1
  Leeds LS17 43 C3
  Netherton WF4 158 E6
  Swillington LS26 82 B1
  Yeadon LS19 40 A6
Church Croft WF3 121 C8
Church Cswy LS23 14 F1
Church Ct
  Bradford BD7 73 F5
  Keighley BD20 18 F2
  Morley LS27 98 A5
  Normanton WF6 123 A1
  Ossett WF5 140 D7
  Yeadon LS19 40 B6
Church Dr
  Brierley S72 180 F3
  East Keswick LS17 28 B5
  South Kirkby WF9 182 C2
Church Farm LS14 45 F6
Church Farm Cl
  Normanton WF6 122 F4
  Rothwell WF3 100 C1
Church Farm Garth LS17 44 F4
Church Farm View LS15 63 E7
Churchfield Cl 5 WF15 117 A4
Churchfield Croft
  Normanton WF6 122 F4
  Rothwell LS26 100 F5
Churchfield Gdns S71 179 D1
Churchfield Gr LS26 100 E6
Churchfield La
  Castleford WF10 124 F7
  Kirk Smeaton WF8 166 F7
  Rothwell LS26 100 E6
Churchfield Rd LS26 100 F5
Church Field Rd DN5 194 E4
Churchfields
  Huddersfield HD2 136 F3
  Ryhill WF4 162 B2
Church Fields
  Bradford BD2 56 D2
  Huddersfield HD2 136 F3
  Normanton WF6 123 A1
Church Fields Mews WF10 124 F6
Churchfields Rd HD6 115 A3
Churchfield St 1 WF17 118 C5
Churchfield Terr 6 WF15 117 A4
Church Garth
  Castleford WF10 124 F6
  Pool LS21 24 C7
Churchgate
  Bramhope LS16 24 D3
  Gildersome LS27 97 C7
Church Gate LS18 41 B1
Church Gdns
  Garforth LS25 82 F6
  Gildersome LS27 97 C7
  Leeds LS17 43 D3
Church Gn
  2 Bradford BD8 55 C1
  Halifax HX2 91 E1
  Kirkburton HD8 173 F6
Church Gr
  Horsforth LS18 41 B1
  Leeds LS6 59 F7
  South Kirkby WF9 182 C2
Church Grange 4 BD19 116 E7
Church Hill
  Baildon BD17 38 D4
  Bramham LS23 30 D2
  Bramhope LS16 24 D3
  Halifax HX2 90 D1
  Royston S71 179 D3
  Thorner LS14 46 A6
  Todmorden OL14 107 E8
Church Hill Farm WF4 143 F1
Church Hill Gdns LS28 57 F2
Church Hill Gn LS28 57 F2
Church Hill Mount LS28 57 F2
Church Ho 13 HX5 134 F7
Churchill Flats LS21 24 C7
Churchill Gdns 25 LS2 206 B2
Churchill Gr
  Batley WF16 117 E3
  Wakefield WF2 160 E8
Churchill Rd BD13 72 F6
Churchill St OL14 107 E8
Churchill Way BD20 16 E7
Church La
  Bardsey LS17 28 C2
  Batley WF16 117 D3
  Bradford BD6 94 B8
  Brighouse, Elland Lower Edge HD6 135 D7
  3 Brighouse HD6 115 A2
  Brighouse, Southowram HX3 114 C4
  Brighouse, Waring Green HD6 115 A3
  Cawthorne S75 193 F4
  Clayton West HD8 175 F2
  Cleckheaton BD19 117 C8
  Clifton LS21 10 B2
  Collingham LS22 13 B1
  Crigglestone WF4 160 A4
  Darrington WF8 147 D5
  Dewsbury, Dewsbury Moor WF13 138 F8
  Dewsbury, Thornhill WF12 139 E2
  East Ardsley, Upper Green WF3 119 D7
  East Ardsley WF3 120 C7
  Elland HX4 134 A4
  Featherstone WF7 124 C1
  Garforth LS25 82 F7
  Guiseley BD17 39 C5
  Halifax HX2 91 E1
  Harewood LS17 26 F7
  Hebden Bridge HX7 88 E3
  Heptonstall HX7 88 F5
  High Hoyland S75 176 C1
  Horsforth LS18 41 B1
  Huddersfield HD4 171 B6
  Huddersfield, Moldgreen HD5 154 D6
  Huddersfield, Newsome HD4 154 A2
  Kippax LS25 83 B1
  Kirkheaton HD5 155 B7
  Leeds, Adel LS16 42 C5
  Leeds, Bank LS2 212 A3
  Leeds, Chapel Allerton LS7 204 A2
  Leeds, Hill Top LS6 59 F7
  Leeds, Manston LS15 62 D3
  Liversedge, Knowler Hill WF15 117 A5
  Liversedge WF15 116 B3
  Lofthouse Gate WF1 121 B5
  Marsden HD7 168 F4
  Marsden, Scammonden HX4 150 F5
  Micklefield LS25 83 F7
  Mickletown LS26 102 C2
  Mirfield WF14 138 C5
Church La *continued*
  Netherton WF4 158 E7
  Normanton, Old Snydale WF6, WF7 144 D8
  Normanton WF6 123 B1
  2 Pontefract WF8 146 D8
  Pool LS21 24 C7
  Pudsey LS28 76 E7
  Ripponden HX6 132 D3
  Ryhill, Felkirk WF4 180 A6
  Ryhill S71 179 F7
  Shepley HD8 190 E8
  Slaithwaite HD7 152 E1
  Swillington LS26 82 A1
Church Lane Ave WF1 121 B5
Church Mdws
  Batley WF17 96 D1
  Bramham LS23 30 D3
  Ripponden HX6 132 D3
Church Mews
  Boston Spa LS23 30 D8
  5 Bradford BD6 93 E7
  Leeds LS5 58 E6
Church Mount
  Horsforth LS18 41 B1
  South Kirkby WF9 182 C2
Church Paddocks HD6 115 E2
Church Pk WF15 116 E2
Church Pl
  Garforth LS25 82 F7
  Halifax HX1 203 A3
Church Rd
  Batley WF17 117 F8
  Bradford BD6 94 B8
  Cawthorne S75 193 E4
  Horsforth LS18 41 B1
  Kippax LS26 102 E8
  Leeds, Bank LS9 212 B3
  Leeds LS12 209 C3
  Liversedge FW15 116 E2
  Lofthouse Gate WF3 121 F5
  Normanton WF6 122 E4
  Sutton-in-C BD20 16 D5
  Todmorden OL14 107 E8
Church Row
  Denton LS29 9 A6
  Leeds LS2 212 A3
Church Side LS26 102 C2
Church Side Cl 15 HX3 92 C1
Church Side Dr 16 HX3 92 C1
Churchside Villas LS26 102 C2
Church Sq LS25 82 F7
Church St
  Addingham LS29 7 A8
  Barnsley, Carlton S71 179 D1
  Batley, Birstall WF17 96 E1
  Batley, Heckmondwike WF16 117 D3
  Bingley BD16 37 A2
  Boston Spa LS23 30 D8
  Bradford BD8 55 C1
  Bradford, Beck Hill BD6 93 E7
  Brierley S72 181 A2
  Brighouse HD6 135 F8
  Brotherton WF11 126 C8
  Castleford WF10 124 D8
  Cawthorne S75 193 F4
  Cleckheaton BD19 116 E7
  Cleckheaton, Hightown WF15 116 C5
  Cullingworth BD13 52 D6
  Darton S75 177 E1
  Dewsbury, Ravensthorpe WF13 138 E5
  Dewsbury WF13 139 D8
  Elland HX5 134 F7
  Elland, West Vale HX4 134 D7
  Emley HD8 175 C7
  Gildersome LS27 97 C7
  Glusburn BD20 16 D7
  Guiseley LS20 22 F1
  Halifax HX1 203 C2
  Haworth BD22 51 B7
  Heptonstall HX7 88 F5
  Holmfirth, Netherthong HD9 188 F8
  Holmfirth, New Mill HD9 189 F6
  Honley HD9 171 F5
  Horbury WF4 141 B1
  Huddersfield HD1 154 B6
  Huddersfield, Longwood HD3 153 A6
  Huddersfield, Moldgreen HD5 154 D6
  Huddersfield, Paddock HD1 153 D5
  Huddersfield, Town End HD7 152 D4
  Huddersfield, Yews Hill HD4 153 E4
  Ilkley LS29 8 B4
  Keighley BD21 35 C6
  Keighley, Eastwood BD21 35 D7
  Leeds, Kirkstall LS5 59 A4
  Leeds LS10 215 B3
  Liversedge WF15 117 A5
  Mapplewell S75 178 C1
  Morley LS27 98 A5
  Mytholmroyd HX7 110 E8
  Ossett WF5 140 D7
  10 Oxenhope BD22 51 C2
  Rothwell, Churchfields LS26 100 E5
  Rothwell, Woodlesford LS26 101 C7
  Royston S71 179 C3
  Shipley BD18 55 D8
  Slaithwaite HD7 169 F8
Church St *continued*
  South Elmsall WF9 183 A2
  Todmorden OL14 107 E8
  Wakefield WF1 142 C4
  Wetherby LS22 13 E5
  Woolley WF4 177 F7
  Yeadon LS19 40 A6
Church Stile Farm HX6 111 E3
Church Terr
  Clayton West HD8 175 D1
  9 Holmfirth HD9 189 A5
  Sowerby Bridge HX6 111 E3
Church Top WF9 182 C2
Churchtown Cres OL13 106 B1
Church View
  Cleckheaton BD19 116 B8
  Crigglestone WF4 159 F5
  Featherstone WF7 145 C5
  Holmfirth HD9 188 C2
  Kippax LS25 83 D2
  Leeds LS5 59 B4
  Pool LS21 24 C7
  South Kirkby WF9 182 C2
  Sowerby Bridge HX6 112 C4
  Thorner LS14 45 F6
  Wakefield WF1 142 E2
Church View Cl WF4 162 C1
Church View Mews LS23 30 D5
Church Villas WF9 182 C2
Churchville LS25 84 A8
Churchville Ave LS25 83 F7
Churchville Dr LS25 84 A7
Churchville Terr LS25 84 A7
Church Way
  Keighley BD21 35 C6
  3 Morley LS27 98 A5
Church Wlk
  Batley WF17 118 A3
  Dewsbury WF12 139 E2
  Leeds LS2 212 A3
  Northowram HX3 93 A2
  Walsden OL14 108 B1
Church Wood Ave LS16 59 C7
Churchwood Cl HD7 151 F1
Church Wood Mount LS16 59 C7
Church Wood Rd LS16 59 C6
Churn Dr BD6 93 E8
Churn La HX2 112 D7
Churn Milk La HX3 92 A4
Churwell Ave 3 WF13 117 F3
Churwell Cl WF10 124 D6
Churwell Prim Sch LS27 98 B7
Churwell Vale WF12 119 A2
Cinder Hill HD8 174 B7
Cinderhill Rd OL14 108 E6
Cinderhills La HX3 113 E3
Cinder Hills Rd HD9 189 B4
Cinder La
  Castleford WF10 124 C8
  Clifford LS23 30 E6
  Lindley LS21 11 F5
Circle The WF8 146 E7
Cirrus View WF7 163 F4
City Art Gall★ WF1 216 A3
City Central LS1 211 B3
City Ct 15 LS27 98 B4
City La HX3 91 E2
City Link Ind Pk BD4 75 E6
City of Leeds Coll of Music LS2 206 B1
City of Leeds Sch LS6 206 A4
City Park Ind Est LS12 78 C3
City Rd BD8 74 C8
City Sq LS1 211 B3
City Varieties Music Hall★ LS1 211 C4
Cityway Ind Est BD4 75 A5
City West One Office Pk LS12 213 A3
City Wlk LS11 211 B2
Claire Ct 6 LS6 59 E6
Clapgate LS21 23 A8
Clapgate La HX6 132 E7
Clapgate Prim Sch LS10 99 F5
Clapham Dene Rd LS15 62 B1
Clapham St BD13 71 E8
Claphouse Fold S75 177 A5
Clapton Ave HX1 202 C2
Clara Dr LS28 57 A8
Clara Rd BD2 55 F5
Clara St
  Brighouse HD6 115 A1
  Huddersfield, Cowlersley HD4 153 A3
  Huddersfield, Fartown HD1 136 A1
  Huddersfield HD1 154 A8
  Pudsey LS28 57 D2
Clare Cres BD12 94 C2
Clare Ct HX1 203 B2
Clare Hall La HX1 203 B2
Clare Hill HD1 154 A7
Claremont
  Batley WF16 117 D4
  Bradford BD7 74 D6
  Pudsey LS28 76 F8
Claremont Ave
  10 Leeds LS3 206 A1
  Shipley BD18 55 E6
Claremont Cres
  Crofton WF4 161 F8
  Leeds LS6 59 F5
  Shipley BD18 55 E6
Claremont Ct LS6 59 E6
Claremont Dr LS6 59 E6
Claremont Gdns
  Bingley BD16 37 A4
Claremont Gdns *continued*
  Pudsey LS28 57 D
Claremont Gr
  4 Leeds LS3 206 A
  Pudsey LS28 76 E
  Shipley BD18 55 F
Claremont Pl LS12 209 A
Claremont Rd
  Dewsbury WF13 118 B
  Leeds LS6 59 E
  Shipley BD18 55 E
Claremont St
  7 Cleckheaton BD19 116 D
  5 Elland HX5 135 A
  Huddersfield HD1 154 A
  Leeds LS12 209 A
  Rothwell LS26 101 C
  Sowerby Bridge HX6 112 C
  Wakefield WF1 142 E
Claremont Terr
  Bradford BD5 74 D
  Leeds LS12 209 A
  Todmorden OL14 129 D
  Wakefield WF2 142 A
Claremont View
  3 Leeds LS3 206 A
  8 Rothwell LS26 101 C
Claremont Villas
  9 Leeds LS2 206 A
  1 Sowerby Bridge HX6 112 C
Claremount 7 LS6 59 E
Claremount Rd HX3 92 C
Claremount Terr 4 HX3 92 C
Clarence Dr
  Horsforth LS18 58 B
  Menston LS29 21 F
Clarence Gdns LS18 58 B
Clarence Gr LS18 58 B
Clarence Mews LS18 58 B
Clarence Mills Ind Est HD9 188 B
Clarence Rd
  Horsforth LS18 58 B
  Leeds LS10 212 B
  Shipley BD18 54 F
  Wakefield WF2 142 B
Clarence St
  Batley WF17 118 D
  Cleckheaton BD19 116 D
  Halifax HX1 203 A
  Leeds LS13 58 C
Clarence Terr
  Dewsbury WF12 139 D
  1 Pudsey LS28 76 E
Clarence Wlk WF2 142 A
Clarendon Cotts WF5 140 E
Clarendon Ct WF1 216 B
Clarendon Pl
  Halifax HX1 202 C
  Leeds LS2 206 A
  10 Queensbury BD13 92 C
Clarendon Rd
  Bingley BD16 37 B
  Boston Spa LS23 30 C
  Leeds LS2 206 A
Clarendon St
  10 Haworth BD22 51 C
  Keighley BD21 35 B
  Mytholmroyd HX7 89 E
  Wakefield WF1 216 B
Clarendon Terr
  9 Morley LS27 98 C
  Pudsey LS28 76 E
Clarendon Way LS2 206 A
Clare Rd
  Bradford BD12 94 C
  Cleckheaton BD19 116 D
  Halifax HX1 203 B
  Mytholmroyd HX7 89 D
Clare St HX1 203 B
Clarges St BD5 74 D
Clarion Field LS29 22 D
Clarion St WF1 142 E
Clark Ave LS9 212 C
Clark Cres LS9 212 C
Clark Ct WF7 124 C
Clarke Cres WF6 144 A
Clarke Gr WF1 121 E
Clarke Hall Farm WF1 121 E
Clarke Hall Rd WF3 121 E
Clarke La HD9 170 E
Clarke Rd WF3 119 E
Clarke St
  Dewsbury WF13 118 A
  Pudsey LS28 57 B
Clark Gr LS9 212 C
Clark La LS9 212 C
Clark Mount LS9 212 C
Clark Rd LS9 212 C
Clark Row LS9 212 C
Clarkson Ave WF16 117 E
Clarkson Cl WF16 117 E
Clarkson Ct WF6 123 C
Clarkson Dr LS25 105 E
Clarkson St
  Dewsbury WF13 138 E
  Wakefield WF2 142 A
Clarkson View LS6 206 A
Clark Spring Cl LS27 98 A
Clark Spring Rise LS27 98 B
Clark Terr LS9 212 C
Clark View LS9 212 C
Clarydon Pl 4 WF16 117 D
Clattering Stones Rd HX7 110 E
Clayborn View BD19 116 E
Clay Brow BD22 51 C
Clay Butts HD2 135 E

layfield Bglws WF11 ...126 C4
layfield Dr BD7 ....74 A2
lay Hill Dr BD12 ......94 D4
lay House La HX4 .....134 D7
lay La HD7 ....152 A1
laypit La
  Ledsham LS25 ....104 C7
  Thorner LS14 ....45 F5
lay Pit La
  Elland, Sowood Green
  HX4 ....133 F1
  Leeds LS2, LS7 ....206 C1
lay Pits La
  Halifax HX1 ....202 B4
  Ripponden HX6 ....132 B7
lay St
  Halifax HX1 ....202 B3
  Sowerby Bridge HX6 ...112 B4
layton Ave
  Kippax LS25 ....83 C2
  Thurnscoe S63 ....194 B1
  Upton WF9 ....183 E8
layton CE Prim Sch
  BD14 ....73 C4
layton Cl LS10 ....215 C2
layton Ct
  Featherstone WF7 .....145 C5
  Leeds, West Park LS16 ..58 F8
  Leeds, Woodhouse Hill
  LS10 ....215 C2
layton Dr
  Leeds LS10 ....215 C2
  Thurnscoe S63 ....194 B1
layton Fields HD2 .....153 F8
layton Fold BD20 ......16 E6
layton Gr LS19 ....40 B7
layton Grange 2 LS16 ..58 F8
layton Holt WF9 ....182 B1
layton Hospl WF1 .....216 A3
layton La
  Bradford BD5 ....74 E4
  Bradford, Clayton BD14 ..73 B4
  Hooton Pagnell DN5 ...195 C5
  Thurnscoe S63 ....194 B2
layton Mews WF6 .....123 A4
layton Pk LS16 ....41 F1
layton Pl WF6 ....123 A4
layton Rd
  Bradford BD7 ....73 F5
  Leeds LS10 ....215 C2
layton Rise
  Keighley BD20 ....35 A8
  Lofthouse Gate WF1 ...121 B5
laytons Bldgs WF5 ....145 D8
laytons Cl LS26 ....102 B3
laytons Cotts 2 WF4 ..141 A1
layton St
  Rothwell LS26 ....100 F5
  Wakefield WF2 ....142 A5
layton Terr BD13 ....52 D5
layton View WF9 ......182 B1
Clayton Village Prim Sch
  BD14 ....73 C4
Clayton West Sta ☀ HD8 .175 F3
Clayton Wood Bank LS16 ..41 F1
Clayton Wood Cl LS16 ...41 F1
Clayton Wood Ct LS16 ...41 F1
Clayton Wood Rd LS16 ...41 F1
Clayton Wood Rise LS16 ..41 F1
Clay Well HD7 ....152 D4
Clearings The LS10 ......99 D8
Cleasby Rd LS29 ....22 A4
Cleavesty La LS17 ....28 B6
Cleckheaton Rd BD12 ...94 D6
Cleeve Hill LS19 ....40 B4
Cleevethorpe Gr WF2 ...142 E1
Clegg La HX4 ....133 F7
Clegg St 10 BD12 ....94 C3
Clement Cl 3 WF6 .....123 D1
Clement Ct HX1 ....202 C4
Clement St
  9 Bradford BD8 ....73 F8
  Huddersfield HD1 .....153 F8
  Huddersfield, Paddock Brow
  HD4 ....153 D4
  7 Sowerby Bridge HX6 .112 B4
  Wakefield WF2 ....141 F5
Clement Terr
  Dewsbury WF12 ......139 C6
  Rothwell LS26 ....100 F5
Cleopatra Pl 4 LS13 ...58 C1
Clerk Green St WF17 ...118 B4
Clervaux Ct BD14 ......73 D5
Clevedon House Prep Sch
  LS29 ....9 A2
Clevedon Pl 4 HX3 .....92 A2
Clevedon Way S71 .....179 B4
Cleveland Ave
  Halifax HX3 ....113 D4
  Horbury WF2 ....141 D2
  Knottingley WF11 ....126 E4
  Meltham HD9 ....170 F1
Cleveland Garth WF2 ...141 D2
Cleveland Garth 4 WF2 .141 D2
Cleveland Pl 1 HX7 ....89 A3
Cleveland Rd
  Bradford BD9 ....55 B3
  Huddersfield HD1 .....153 D7
Cleveland St OL14 ......86 B1
Cleveland Way HD8 ....173 F3
Cleveley Gdns HX7 .....110 C8
Cleveleys Ave
  Leeds LS11 ....213 C4
  3 Sowerby Bridge HX6 .112 B4
Cleveleys Ct LS11 .....213 C4
Cleveleys Gdns 18 HX6 .112 B5

Cleveleys Mount 5
  LS11 ....213 C4
Cleveleys Rd LS11 .....213 C4
Cleveleys St LS11 .....213 C4
Cleveleys Terr 4 LS11 .213 C4
Clewer Pl 19 OL14 .....108 A1
Cliff Cl HD3 ....153 B6
Cliff Cres
  Halifax HX2 ....202 A1
  Kippax LS25 ....83 C1
Cliff Ct
  1 Leeds LS6 ....206 A4
  Liversedge WF15 .....117 A3
Cliffdale Rd LS7 ....206 B4
Cliffdale Road Light Ind Est
  LS7 ....206 B4
Cliff Dr WF4 ....159 D5
Cliffe HX2 ....112 B6
Cliffe Ash HD7 ....152 D4
Cliffe Ave
  Baildon BD17 ....38 C3
  Brighouse HX3 ....115 A4
  Harden BD16 ....36 A1
Cliffe Castle Mus ☀ BD20 ..18 B1
Cliffe Cl S72 ....180 F3
Cliffe Com Bsns Pk HD1 .153 F5
Cliffe Cres BD20 ....36 B8
Cliffe Crest WF4 ......141 B2
Cliffe Ct BD21 ....35 B8
Cliffe Dr LS19 ....40 B3
Cliffe End Bsns Ctr HD3 .153 A5
Cliffe End Rd HD3 .....153 B6
Cliffe Hill S75 ....193 E5
Cliffe Hill Com Prim Sch
  HX3 ....115 A6
Cliffe House Ave LS25 ..83 A5
Cliffe La
  Baildon BD17 ....38 C1
  Cleckheaton BD19 ....95 F1
  Kirkburton HD4 ......172 E6
  Thornton BD13 ....72 E7
  Yeadon LS19 ....40 C3
Cliffe La S BD17 ......38 C1
Cliffe La W BD17 ......38 C2
Cliffe Mill Fold BD20 ..36 E8
Cliffe Mount BD19 .....96 A1
Cliffe Park Chase LS12 .209 A2
Cliffe Park Cl LS12 ...209 A2
Cliffe Park Cres LS12 .209 A2
Cliffe Park Dr LS12 ...209 A2
Cliffe Park Mount LS12 .209 A2
Cliffe Park Rise LS12 .209 A2
Cliffe Park Way LS27 ..97 D3
Cliffe Pk HD8 ....190 E8
Cliffe Rd
  Bradford BD3 ....55 F1
  Brighouse HD6 ......115 B2
  Keighley BD21 ....35 B4
  Shepley HD8 ....190 E8
Cliffe Royd HX7 ....89 B3
Cliffe Side HD8 ....190 E8
Cliffe Terr
  Batley WF17 ....117 F4
  Calderbrook OL15 ...129 D2
  Clayton West HD8 ...175 F2
  Dewsbury WF13 .....118 D1
  9 Hebden Bridge HX7 .89 A3
  Keighley BD21 ....35 B8
  Thornton BD13 ......72 D7
Cliffestone Dr BD20 ...36 D8
Cliffe Terr
  Baildon BD17 ....38 C1
  Bradford BD8 ....55 D1
  Denholme BD13 ......71 D8
  Halifax, Skircoat Green
  HX3 ....113 C2
  Keighley BD21 ....35 C4
  Micklefield LS25 .....84 B6
  Rothwell WF3 ....100 A3
  Sowerby Bridge HX6 .112 A5
  Wetherby LS22 ....13 E5
Cliffe View
  Bradford BD15 ....53 F2
  Clayton West HD8 ...175 F2
  Morley LS27 ....97 D3
Cliffe Villas BD16 .....54 C5
Cliffe Wood Cl BD9 ....54 E3
Cliffewood Rise HD8 ...175 E2
Cliff Gdns
  Halifax HX2 ....202 A1
  Shipley BD18 ....55 B6
Cliff Gr WF4 ....159 C4
Cliff Hill Ct HD9 ......189 B6
Cliff Hill La HX2 ......112 B6
Cliff Hill Terr WF11 ..104 F4
Cliff Hollins La BD12, BD4 ..95 C6
Cliff House La HD9 ....189 B6
Cliff La
  Brierley WF17 ....180 F2
  Holmfirth HD9 ....189 B6
  Leeds LS6 ....205 C4
  Ripponden HX6 ......132 D2
  Wakefield WF1 ....216 A2
Cliff Mount LS6 ....206 A4
Cliff Mount St LS6 ....206 A4
Cliff Mount Terr LS6 ..206 A4
Clifford Ave
  Ilkley LS29 ....8 A5
  Wakefield WF2 ....142 A2
Clifford Ct
  Clifford LS23 ....30 E5
  Ossett WF5 ....140 C6
Clifford Mill LS23 .....30 E5
Clifford Moor Rd LS23 ..30 C7
Clifford Pl 3 LS27 .....98 B7
Clifford Rd
  Baildon BD17 ....38 C2
  Boston Spa LS23 .....30 E7

Clifford Rd continued
  Bramham LS23 ....30 D3
  Ilkley LS29 ....8 A5
  South Kirkby WF9 ...182 B2
Clifford St
  Bradford BD5 ....201 B1
  Cudworth S72 ....180 C1
  Silsden BD20 ....5 D2
  South Elmsall WF9 ..182 F2
Clifford View WF2 .....142 D2
Cliff Par WF1 ....216 A4
Cliff Park Ave WF1 ...216 A3
Cliff Rd
  Crigglestone WF4 ...159 D4
  Holmfirth, Cliff HD9 ..189 B6
  Holmfirth, Flush House
  HD9 ....188 A4
  Leeds LS6 ....206 A4
Cliff Road Gdns LS6 ..206 A4
Cliff Side Gdns LS6 ..206 A4
Cliff St
  Haworth BD22 ....51 D7
  Holmfirth HD9 ....189 B5
  8 Pontefract WF8 ...146 C8
  Wakefield WF2 ......141 F7
Cliff Terr LS6 ....206 A4
Cliff Vale Rd BD18 .....55 B5
Cliff Villa Ct WF1 .....216 A3
Cliff Villas 7 WF8 ....146 C8
Cliff Wood Ave BD18 ..55 B6
Clifton Ave
  Halifax HX1 ....202 B2
  Holmfirth HD9 ....189 B6
  Horbury WF4 ....141 A2
  Leeds LS9 ....208 B2
  Lofthouse Gate WF1 .121 C5
  6 Pontefract WF8 ...146 B8
Clifton Cl WF4 ....141 A2
Clifton Comm HD6 ...115 C3
Clifton Cres
  Barnsley S71 ....178 E1
  Horbury WF4 ....141 A2
Clifton Ct
  Batley WF16 ....117 E2
  14 Pudsey LS28 ......76 E8
Clifton Dr
  Horbury WF4 ....141 A2
  Pudsey LS28 ....76 E8
Clifton Forge Bsns Pk
  WF11 ....126 E4
Clifton Gdns S72 .....180 E3
Clifton Gr LS9 ....208 B1
Clifton Hill LS28 ....76 E8
Clifton Inf Sch WF4 ...140 F2
Clifton La
  Clifton LS21 ....10 E5
  Meltham HD9 ....170 E2
Clifton Mews 12 LS28 ..76 E8
Clifton Mount LS9 ....208 A2
Clifton Pl
  Pudsey LS28 ....76 F8
  Shipley BD18 ....55 B6
  Wakefield WF1 ......216 A4
Clifton Rd
  3 Brighouse HD6 ...115 B2
  Crofton WF4 ....144 B3
  Halifax HX3 ....113 C4
  Horbury WF4 ....141 A2
  Huddersfield HD1 ...153 E7
  Ilkley LS29 ....8 D3
  Pudsey LS28 ....76 E8
Clifton Side HD2 .....136 F6
Clifton St
  Bradford BD8 ....55 D1
  13 Halifax HX3 ....92 A1
  Hemsworth WF9 ....181 C6
  Keighley BD21 ....35 A6
  10 Queensbury BD13 ..72 E1
  4 Sowerby Bridge HX6 .112 C4
Clifton Terr
  Batley WF17 ....118 D5
  Leeds LS9 ....208 A2
  Ossett WF5 ....140 C8
Clifton View
  Clayton West HD8 ...175 F2
  5 Pontefract WF8 ...146 B8
Clifton Villas
  Bradford BD8 ....55 D1
  Otley LS21 ....22 F6
Clipston Ave LS6 ....59 F6
Clipstone St 2 BD5 ....74 E2
Clipstone Mount 8 LS6 .59 F6
Clipston St LS6 ....59 F6
Clipston Terr 9 LS6 ...59 F6
Cliveden Ave BD13 .....72 E6
Clive Pl BD7 ....74 B5
Clive Terr BD7 ....74 B5
Cloberry St LS2 ......206 A2
Clock Bldgs LS8 ......208 A4
Clock La BD13 ....71 D8
Clock Row Ave WF9 ..182 D3
Clock Row Gr WF9 ...182 D3
Clock Row Mount WF9 .182 D3
Clock View St BD20 ...18 B8
Clog Bridge 4 BD20 ...5 E1
Clog Mill & Mus ☀ HX7 .89 C2
Clog Sole Rd HD6 ....114 F4
Cloisters The HX1 ....202 C1
Close Head BD13 ....72 B6
Close Head Dr BD13 ...72 B6
Close Head La BD13 ...72 B6
Close Hill La HD4 .....153 F2
Close Lea HD6 ....115 A8
Close Lea Ave HD6 ...114 F1
Close Lea Dr HD6 ....114 F1
Close Lea Way HD6 ...114 F1
Close Rd WF10 ....124 F7

Closes Rd 2 HD6 .....115 A1
Close St WF9 ....181 C7
Close The
  Barnsley S71 ....179 C1
  Barwick in E LS15 ...63 D6
  Boston Spa LS23 .....30 E8
  Bradford BD2 ....55 F6
  Clayton DN5 ....194 C4
  Collingham LS22 .....29 B8
  Crigglestone WF4 ...159 E7
  East Ardsley WF3 ...120 D7
  East Keswick LS17 ...28 C5
  Guiseley LS20 ....39 C8
  Kippax LS25 ....83 A1
  Leeds, Alwoodley LS17 .43 A5
  Leeds, Bank LS9 .....212 B3
  Pontefract WF8 .....146 F7
  Thorner LS14 ....46 A6
Cloth Hall St
  Dewsbury WF13 ....139 D8
  Huddersfield HD1 ...154 A6
  3 Leeds LS2 ....211 C3
Cloudsdale Ave BD5 ...74 E4
Clough Ave BD20 ......17 C6
Clough Bank HX2 .....91 B5
Clough Bank La
  Goose Eye BD22 ......34 B6
  Sowerby Bridge HX6 .111 B1
Clough Bldgs HX6 ....111 D4
Clough Cotts HX6 ....132 A6
Clough Ct
  Denholme BD13 ......71 E6
  17 Morley LS27 ......98 B4
Clough Dr
  Batley WF17 ....97 A2
  Lepton HD8 ....155 D2
  Linthwaite HD7 .....170 D8
Clough Foot La HD9 ...199 A7
Clough Gate
  Grange Moor WF4 ...156 D5
  Oakworth BD22 ......34 D2
Clough Gate Dr WF4 ..156 D5
Clough Hall La HD4 ...154 D1
Clough Head
  Slaithwaite HD7 .....152 A4
  Sowerby Bridge HX6 .112 C2
Clough Head Jun & Inf Sch
  HD7 ....152 A4
Clough Hey HD7 ......168 E4
Clough Ho HD7 ....151 D1
Clough Holme 20 OL14 .108 B7
Clough House Dr HD2 .135 F2
Clough House La
  Denby Dale HD8 ....192 C6
  Ripponden HX4 .....133 B2
  Slaithwaite HD7 ....151 D1
Clough La
  Brighouse, Bailiff Bridge
  HD6 ....115 D6
  Brighouse, Elland Lower Edge
  HD6 ....135 F6
  Halifax HX2 ....91 B5
  Huddersfield, Paddock HD1,
  HD2 ....153 C5
  Lepton HD8 ....156 C7
  Liversedge WF15 ...116 D3
  Oakworth BD22 ......34 D3
  Wadsworth Moor HX2 .90 B5
Clough Lee HD7 ......168 F4
Clough Pk HD8 ....155 D2
Clough Pl HX2 ....91 B5
Clough Rd
  Bacup OL13 ....106 A3
  Emley WF4 ....157 D1
  Huddersfield HD2 ...136 A3
  Slaithwaite, Crimble HD7 .152 A2
  Slaithwaite HD7 ....152 A4
  4 Walsden OL14 ....108 A1
Clough St
  Bradford BD5 ....74 E3
  Morley LS27 ....98 C4
Clough The
  Lepton HD8 ....155 D3
  Mirfield WF14 ......137 E6
Clough Way HD8 .....155 D2
Clovelly Ave 16 LS11 .214 B3
Clovelly Gr 11 LS11 ..214 B3
Clovelly Pl 17 LS11 ..214 B3
Clovelly Row 14 LS11 .214 B3
Clovelly Terr LS11 ...214 B3
Clover Cres LS28 .....57 A7
Clover Ct LS28 ....57 A7
Cloverdale HX3 ....93 D7
Clover Hill WF15 .....116 D5
Clover Hill Cl HX1 ....203 A1
Clover Hill Rd HX1 ...203 A1
Clover Hill Terr HX1 .203 A1
Clover Hill View HX1 .203 A1
Clover Rise BD21 ......35 E7
Clover St
  Bacup OL13 ....106 A3
  Bradford BD5 ....74 B3
Cloverville App BD6 ...94 C7
Clover Wlk WF9 ......183 A4
Club Hos HX7 ....89 C5
Clubhouses Croft 8
  WF4 ....141 A1
Club La
  Halifax HX2 ....91 F3
  Pudsey LS13 ....57 E5
Club Row
  Leeds LS7 ....204 A3
  Wilsden BD15 ....53 C5
  Yeadon LS19 ....40 C7
Club St
  Bradford BD7 ....73 F5

Cla–Coc 237

Club St continued
  Todmorden OL14 .....86 B1
Club Terr WF9 ....163 B3
Clumber Dr BD19 .....117 B7
Cluntergate WF4 .....141 B1
Clunters La HX2 ......111 B6
Clutton St WF17 ......118 C5
Clyde App LS12 ......210 B2
Clyde Chase LS12 ....210 B2
Clyde Ct LS12 ....210 B2
Clyde Gdns LS12 .....210 B2
Clyde Grange LS12 ..210 B2
Clydesdale Dr BD6 ....93 F7
Clyde St
  Bingley BD16 ....36 F3
  Sowerby Bridge HX6 .112 C3
  Wakefield WF1 ......142 E4
Clyde View LS12 .....210 B2
Clyde Wlk LS12 ......210 B3
CMS Bsns Pk WF7 ....145 C6
Coach Fold HX3 ......203 B4
Coach Gate La S36 ...192 D3
Coachgates WF4 .....157 B2
Coach House Cl 4 BD7 .73 F3
Coach House Dr HD5 ..154 F5
Coach House The LS7 .204 A3
Coach La
  1 Cleckheaton BD19 .116 B8
  Lindley LS21 ....11 F6
  Thornton BD13 ....72 F6
Coach Rd
  Baildon BD17 ....38 A1
  Brighouse HD6 ......114 F6
  Gildersome LS12 ....77 E3
  Guiseley LS20 ....39 D7
  Huddersfield HD2 ...135 F2
  Lofthouse Gate WF1 .121 C4
  Meltham HD9 ....170 F1
  Ripponden HX6 .....132 D4
Coal Clough Rd OL14 ..86 B2
Coal Gate HD7 ....151 A1
Coal Gate Rd HX6 ...131 E5
Coal Hill Dr LS13 .....57 F4
Coal Hill Fold LS13 ...57 F4
Coal Hill Gate LS13 ...57 F4
Coal Hill Gdns LS13 ..57 F4
Coal Hill Gn LS13 ....57 F4
Coal Hill La LS28, LS13 .57 F4
Coal La HX2 ....71 E3
Coalpit La
  Denby Dale HD8 ....191 F3
  Halifax HX3 ....113 F4
Coal Pit La
  Bacup OL13 ....106 B3
  Batley WF17 ....118 A6
  Brighouse HD6 .....115 E2
  Denby Dale HD8 ....191 D8
  Holmfirth HD9 ......189 F6
  Huddersfield HD4 ..153 F3
  Skelmanthorpe HD8 .174 D1
  South Elmsall WF9 .183 E4
  Upton WF8 ....165 E4
Coal Pit Mews WF17 .118 A6
Coal Rd
  Leeds LS14, LS17 ....45 A2
  Leeds, Whinmoor LS14 .62 B6
  Scarcroft LS17 ....44 E8
Coate's La BD20 ....4 F4
Coates Cl WF12 ......118 F1
Coates St BD5 ....74 D4
Coates Terr BD5 .....74 D4
Cobb Ave WF4 ....141 F4
Cobbler's La WF8 ...147 A8
Cobbler's Lane Prim Sch
  WF8 ....147 A8
Cobbler Hall WF4 ...176 F8
Cobbles The HD9 ...170 E2
Cobblestones Dr HX2 .91 D7
Cobbydale Ct BD20 .....5 D1
Cobcroft La WF11 ...127 F1
Cobcroft Rd HD1, HD2 .136 A1
Cobden Ave 3 LS12 ...78 A4
Cobden Cl 9 WF17 ...118 C5
Cobden Ct HX1 ......203 A4
Cobden Gr 4 LS12 ....78 A4
Cobden Mews 11 LS27 .98 A5
Cobden Pl LS12 ....77 F4
Cobden Prim Sch LS12 .77 F4
Cobden Rd
  6 Leeds, New Blackpool
  LS12 ....77 F4
  Leeds LS12 ....78 A4
Cobden St
  Bradford, Allerton BD15 .54 B1
  Bradford, Clayton BD14 .73 B4
  Bradford, Springfield BD10 .56 B7
  Leeds LS12 ....77 F4
  10 Morley LS27 ......98 A5
  Queensbury BD13 ...72 F1
  Todmorden OL14 ...108 B5
Cobden Terr
  Brighouse HX3 ......114 C8
  Elland HX5 ....134 F4
  Leeds LS12 ....77 F4
Cobham Par WF1 ....121 B4
Cobham Wlk LS15 ....62 F2
Cockburn Cl LS11 ...214 C3
Cockburn Coll of Arts
  LS11 ....99 A7
Cockburn Way LS11 .214 C3
Cockcroft Fold BD16 ..36 B2
Cockcroft Gr BD3 .....75 A7
Cockcroft Ho OL14 ...107 E8
Cockcroft La HX6 ....132 A1
Cockermouth La WF4 .156 D2

Cock Hill HX3 .... 93 B6
Cock Hill La HX3 .... 93 B6
Cocking La LS29 .... 6 E6
Cocking Steps La HD4 .. 171 D5
Cockin La BD14 .... 72 E4
Cockley Hill La HD5 .... 155 D8
Cockley Mdws HD5 ...... 137 C1
Cock Pit La HX4 .... 150 E8
Cockshott Cl 2 LS12 .... 58 F1
Cockshott Dr LS12 .... 58 F1
Cockshott Hill LS28 ...... 57 D3
Cockshott La
 Bradford BD10 .... 56 A8
 Leeds LS12 .... 58 F1
Cockshott Pl LS29 .... 6 E6
Coiners Fold HX7 .... 110 C8
Colbeck Ave WF17 .... 118 A5
Colbeck Row WF17 .... 96 E1
Colbeck Terr WF17 ...... 118 A5
Colbert Ave LS29 .... 8 E5
Colby Rise LS15 .... 80 E7
Coldbeck Dr BD6 .... 93 E8
Cold Edge Rd
 Halifax HX2 .... 70 D3
 Halifax, Wainstalls HX2 ... 90 F6
Colden Cl HX7 .... 88 F3
Colden Jun & Inf Sch
 HX7 .... 88 A5
Colden La HX7 .... 88 A5
Colden Rd HX7 .... 88 E4
Colders Dr HD9 .... 170 D1
Colders Gn HD9 .... 170 D2
Colders La HD9 .... 170 D1
Cold Hiendley Common La
 WF2 .... 161 D1
Coldhill La LS25 .... 65 E4
Cold Hill La
 Holmfirth HD9 .... 189 E7
 Huddersfield HD4 ...... 172 A8
Cold Royd La HD5 .... 155 A7
Coldshaw Top BD22 ...... 51 C6
Cold St BD22 .... 51 C6
Cold Well La HD9 .... 188 B4
Cold Well Rd LS15 .... 62 B1
Coldwells Hill HX4 ...... 133 F3
Cold Well Sq LS15 .... 62 B1
Coldwell St HD7 .... 152 D1
Coleman St
 Bradford BD1 .... 55 F1
 Leeds LS12 .... 210 C2
Colenso Gr
 10 Keighley BD21 .... 18 E1
 Leeds LS11 .... 213 C4
Colenso Mount LS11 .... 213 C4
Colenso Pl LS11 .... 213 C4
Colenso Rd LS11 .... 213 C4
Colenso Terr LS11 ...... 213 C4
Colenso Way 13 BD21 ... 18 E1
Colenso Wlk 14 BD21 ... 18 E1
Coleridge Cl LS26 ...... 101 C3
Coleridge Cres WF 120 F3
Coleridge Gdns BD10 .... 56 C8
Coleridge La LS28 .... 76 F5
Coleridge St HX1 .... 203 B2
Coleridge Way WF8 .... 125 D2
Coleshill Way BD4 .... 95 C8
Coles Way BD20 .... 18 D2
Coley Hall La HX3 .... 93 D2
Coley Rd HX3 .... 93 C3
Coley View HX3 .... 93 A2
Colin Barnaby Ct WF2 .. 141 D8
Colinsway WF2 .... 216 A1
Collbrook Ave BD6 ...... 94 C8
Colleen Rd WF4 .... 159 E5
College Ave HD3 .... 135 C1
College Cres BD20 .... 4 D6
College Ct BD20 .... 4 C5
College Dr LS29 .... 8 B3
College Farm La LS22 ... 13 B3
College Gr
 Castleford WF10 ...... 124 A6
 Wakefield WF1 .... 216 B4
College Grove Cl WF1 .. 216 B4
College Grove Rd WF1 .. 216 B4
College Grove View
 WF1 .... 216 B4
College La BD20 .... 4 D6
College Lawns LS12 .... 209 A4
College Rd
 Bingley BD16 .... 37 A6
 Castleford WF10 ...... 125 B7
 Gildersome LS27 .... 97 D6
 Low Bradley BD20 ...... 4 D5
College St E HD4 .... 153 D4
College St
 1 Halifax HX1 .... 96 E1
 Huddersfield HD4 ..... 153 D4
 Todmorden OL14 .... 86 C1
College Terr
 Ackworth M T WF7 .... 163 E6
 Halifax HX1 .... 203 B2
College View
 Ackworth M T WF7 .... 163 E6
 Leeds LS12 .... 209 A3

College Wlk 6 BD21 .... 35 C7
Collier La
 Aberford LS25 .... 65 A5
 Baildon BD17 .... 38 C4
Collier Rd S72 .... 180 D1
Colliers Cl BD18 .... 54 E7
Colliers La LS17 .... 44 E4
Colliers Way HD8 ...... 175 F4
Colliery App WF3 ...... 121 B6
Collindale Cl BD10 ...... 56 E6
Collinfield Rise BD6 ..... 93 F6
Collingham Ave BD6 ..... 93 E8
Collingham Dr LS25 ..... 82 F6
Collingham Lady Elizabeth
 Hastings CE Prim Sch
 LS22 .... 13 A1
Collingwood Ct 13 BD5 .. 74 E3
Collingwood Rd WF6 ... 123 B2
Collin Moor La HX4 .... 134 C8
Collin Rd LS14 .... 61 F1
Collins Cl 18 BD22 ...... 51 E8
Collinson St BD19 ...... 116 D8
Collins St
 Bradford, Bowling BD4 .. 75 B4
 Bradford, Low Green BD7 .. 74 A3
Coll of the Resurrection
 WF14 .... 137 E6
Coll Pl 7 BD6 .... 94 D8
Collyer View LS29 .... 8 E5
Colmore Gr LS12 ...... 210 A1
Colmore Rd LS12 ...... 210 A1
Colmore St LS12 .... 210 A2
Colne HX4 .... 133 D4
Colne Bridge Rd HD2 .. 137 B5
Colne Bsns Pk HD3 .... 153 B5
Colne Hurst HD2 .... 136 E4
Colne Rd
 Glusburn BD20 .... 16 B6
 Huddersfield HD1 ..... 154 A4
Colne Rd (Chapel La)
 BD22 .... 34 C2
Colne Rd (Church St)
 BD22 .... 34 B2
Colne Rd (Goodley) BD22 . 34 C2
Colne St
 Huddersfield, Aspley
  HD1 .... 154 C5
 3 Huddersfield HD1 ... 153 D5
Colne Vale Rd HD3 .... 153 A4
Colne Valley Bsns Pk
 HD7 .... 152 D1
Colne Valley High Sch
 HD7 .... 152 E1
Colne Valley Mus* HD7 . 152 D4
Colne View HD7 .... 152 A1
Colonel's Wlk WF8 .... 125 C1
Colorado Way WF10 .. 124 E4
Colour Mus* BD1 ...... 201 A3
Colston Cl BD8 .... 54 E1
Colston Dr LS29 .... 21 D8
Colton Croft LS15 ...... 81 D7
Colton Ct LS15 .... 81 D7
Colton Garth LS15 ...... 81 D7
Colton La LS15 .... 81 D7
Colton Prim Sch LS15 .. 81 E6
Colton Rd
 Leeds, Armley LS12 ... 209 C3
 Leeds LS15 .... 81 C7
Colton Rd E LS15 .... 81 E6
Colton Ret Pk LS15 ..... 81 E7
Colton St LS12 .... 209 C3
Coltsfoot Cl WF8 ...... 146 D7
Columbus St 18 HX3 .... 92 A1
Colville Terr
 East Ardsley WF3 ...... 99 E1
 Leeds LS11 .... 214 B4
Colwyn Ave 14 LS11 ... 214 B2
Colwyn Mount 15 LS11 . 214 B2
Colwyn Pl 19 LS11 ..... 214 B2
Colwyn Rd LS11 .... 214 B2
Colwyn St HD1 .... 153 D7
Colwyn Terr
 Featherstone WF7 .... 145 D6
 18 Leeds LS11 .... 214 B2
Colwyn View 12 LS11 .. 214 B2
Colyton Mount BD15 .... 54 A1
Combs Rd WF12 .... 139 E2
Combs The WF12 ...... 139 E3
Comet St 8 OL13 ...... 106 A7
Commerce Ct BD4 ...... 75 D4
Commerce St BD1 ..... 201 B3
Commercial Bldgs BD12 . 95 B4
Commercial Rd
 Dewsbury WF13 .... 118 C1
 Leeds LS5 .... 59 A3
 Skelmanthorpe HD8 .. 175 B2
Commercial St
 Batley, Heckmondwike
  WF16 .... 117 E4
 Batley WF17 .... 118 C5
 Bradford BD1 .... 201 C3
 Brighouse HD6 .... 115 B2
 6 Castleford WF10 ... 124 D8
 Cleckheaton BD19 .... 116 E4
 Denholme BD13 ...... 71 D8
 Dewsbury, Earlsheaton
  WF12 .... 139 F7
 Dewsbury, Ravensthorpe
  WF13 .... 138 F5
 Halifax HX1 .... 203 B3
 Hebden Bridge HX7 ... 89 A3
 Huddersfield HD1 .... 154 B5
 Leeds LS1 .... 211 C4
 Morley LS27 .... 98 B4
 Oakworth BD22 ...... 34 B2
 4 Queensbury BD13 ... 72 D1
 Rothwell LS26 .... 100 F5
 Shipley BD18 .... 55 B8

Commercial St continued
 Slaithwaite HD7 ...... 170 A8
 3 Thornton BD13 ..... 72 E6
 Todmorden OL14 ..... 108 C5
 Wakefield WF1 .... 142 D4
Commercial Villas LS28 . 76 D6
Commondale Way BD4 . 95 A6
Common End WF4 ..... 157 B2
Common End La HD8 .. 155 D2
Common Holme La LS29 . 7 E6
Common Ing La WF4 .. 162 B2
Common La
 Clayton DN5 .... 194 C5
 Denby Dale HD8 ...... 192 B6
 East Ardsley WF3 ..... 99 C1
 Emley HD8 .... 174 E7
 Flockton WF4 .... 157 A2
 Halifax HX3 .... 113 F5
 Knottingley, Broomhill
  WF11 .... 127 B4
 Knottingley, South Moor
  WF11 .... 127 D3
 Royston S71 .... 179 C5
 Thorpe Audlin WF8 .. 165 B3
 Wakefield WF2 .... 160 F5
 Woolley WF4 .... 177 F8
Common Rd
 Batley WF17 .... 117 F4
 Bradford BD12 .... 94 C6
 Brierley S72 .... 181 B2
 Elland HX5 .... 135 C6
 Fitzwilliam WF9 ..... 163 A4
 5 Huddersfield HD1 .. 154 A8
 Lofthouse Gate WF3 . 121 F7
 South Kirkby S72, WF9 . 181 E1
Common Road Ave WF2 . 182 A1
Common Road Ind Est
 BD12 .... 94 D6
Common Road Inf Sch
 WF9 .... 182 A1
Commonside
 Batley WF17 .... 118 D3
 Liversedge FW15 ..... 116 E2
Common Side WF4 .... 157 B2
Common Side La WF7 . 145 A6
Common Terr HD6 ..... 115 A1
Como The WF12 .... 139 E3
Como Ave 3 BD8 .... 54 F1
Como Dr BD8 .... 73 F8
Como Gdns 2 BD8 ..... 54 F1
Como Gr BD8 .... 54 F1
Compeigne Ave BD21 .. 18 F1
Compton Ave LS9 ..... 208 A2
Compton Cres LS9 .... 208 A2
Compton Ct 4 LS22 ... 29 B8
Compton Gr LS9 ...... 208 A2
Compton La LS17, LS22 . 29 B6
Compton Mount LS9 .. 208 A2
Compton Pl LS9 ...... 208 A2
Compton Rd LS9 ..... 208 A2
Compton Row LS9 .... 208 A2
Compton St
 Bradford BD4 .... 75 C2
 12 Keighley BD21 .... 35 D8
 Leeds LS9 .... 208 A2
Compton Terr LS9 .... 208 A2
Compton View LS9 ... 208 A2
Com Science Coll The
 WF12 .... 139 E1
Concordia St LS1 ..... 211 C3
Concord St
 Honley HD9 .... 171 F4
 Leeds LS2 .... 207 A1
Concourse House Est
 LS11 .... 213 C1
Concrete St 27 HX3 .... 92 A1
Condor Cl 2 BD6 ...... 73 C2
Conduit St BD8 .... 55 C1
Coney La BD21 .... 35 C7
Coney Moor Gr S26 .. 102 F3
Coney Park Ind Pk LS19 . 23 E1
Coney Warren La WF3 . 121 E8
Coney Wlk WF13 ..... 138 F8
Confederation Pk LS12 . 213 B4
Conference Gr LS12 .. 209 A3
Conference Pl LS12 .. 209 A3
Conference Rd LS12 .. 209 A3
Conference Terr LS12 . 209 A3
Congress Mount LS12 . 209 A3
Congress St LS12 .... 209 A3
Congreve App LS17 ... 28 E6
Congreve Way LS17 .. 28 E6
Conisborough Cl LS29 . 21 D8
Conisborough La LS25 . 83 B7
Conisborough Way WF9 . 181 B2
Coniston Ave
 Darton S75 .... 178 A2
 Huddersfield HD5 .... 154 D6
 1 Leeds LS6 .... 59 E5
 1 Queensbury BD13 .. 72 D1
Coniston Cl
 Elland HX5 .... 135 B7
 2 Queensbury BD13 .. 92 D8
Coniston Ct WF3 ..... 121 B6
Coniston Dr WF10 ... 125 E7
Conistone Cres WF1 . 142 E8
Coniston Gdns
 Castleford WF10 .... 124 A7
 Leeds LS15 .... 80 E6
Coniston Gr
 Baildon BD17 .... 37 F1
 Bradford BD9 .... 54 F2
Coniston Ho 15 HX5 . 134 F7
Coniston Pl WF11 ... 126 E1
Coniston Rd
 Batley WF12 .... 118 F2
 4 Bradford BD7 ..... 73 E3
 Meltham HD9 .... 170 E1

Coniston Rd continued
 Rothwell LS26 .... 101 C7
Coniston Way
 Bacup OL13 .... 106 A4
 Wetherby LS22 ...... 13 B5
Connaught Fold HD2 . 136 E5
Connaught Rd LS29 ... 8 D3
Cononley Bsns Pk BD20 . 4 B2
Cononley Com Prim Sch
 BD20 .... 4 A3
Cononley La BD20 .... 4 B2
Cononley Rd BD20 ... 16 B8
Cononley Sta BD20 ... 4 A2
Consort St LS3 ...... 205 C1
Consort Terr LS3 .... 205 C1
Consort View LS3 ... 205 C1
Consort Wlk LS3 .... 205 C1
Constable Dr WF5 ... 140 D6
Constable Gr WF3 ... 121 E6
Constable Rd
 East Ardsley WF3 .... 119 F8
 Ilkley LS29 .... 8 E3
Constance Gdns LS7 . 206 B2
Constance St BD18 ... 54 F8
Constance Way LS7 .. 206 B2
Constitutional St HX1 . 202 C1
Convent Ave WF2 .... 182 C2
Conway Ave LS8 ..... 207 C3
Conway Cres
 Batley WF17 .... 118 C2
 Meltham HD9 .... 170 D1
Conway Dr LS8 ...... 207 C3
Conway Gr LS8 ...... 207 C3
Conway Mount LS8 .. 207 C3
Conway Pl LS8 ...... 208 A3
Conway Rd
 Leeds LS8 .... 208 A3
 Wakefield WF2 ..... 141 E7
Conway St
 Bradford BD5 .... 201 C1
 Halifax HX1 .... 202 C2
 Leeds LS8 .... 207 C3
 1 Pudsey LS28 ..... 57 D1
Conway Terr LS8 .... 207 C3
Conway View LS8 ... 207 C3
Cooke Cres BD19 .... 117 A8
Cooke La
 10 Keighley BD21 ... 35 C7
 5 Silsden BD21 ..... 35 C7
Cook La WF16 .... 117 C4
Cookridge Ave LS16 . 41 E6
Cookridge Dr LS16 .. 41 E6
Cookridge Gr LS16 .. 41 E6
Cookridge Hospl LS16 . 41 E2
Cookridge La LS16 .. 41 E7
Cookridge Prim Sch LS16 . 41 E4
Cookridge St
 Leeds LS1 .... 206 B1
 Leeds LS1, LS2 ..... 211 B4
Cooksland La WF7 .. 144 E8
Cookson Cl WF10 ... 125 D5
Cookson St HD6 .... 114 F3
Coombe Hill BD13 ... 73 B2
Coombe Rd HD3 .... 152 F5
Co-op Bldgs HX3 .... 91 F7
Co-operation St
 2 Bacup OL13 ...... 106 A2
 11 Leeds LS12 ..... 78 A4
Co-operative Bldgs HD6 . 115 B7
Co-operative Cotts S72 . 180 F3
Cooperative Rd LS27 . 97 F2
Cooperative St OL14 . 129 A7
Co-operative St
 Dewsbury WF12 ..... 140 B8
 Horbury WF4 .... 141 A1
 Keighley BD21 ...... 35 A3
 3 Mirfield WF14 .... 138 A3
 13 Morley, Churwell LS27 . 98 A5
 2 Morley LS27 ..... 98 C8
 Rothwell WF3 ...... 100 C1
 Wakefield WF2 ..... 142 A4
Co-operative Terr
 Elland HX4 .... 133 F4
 Holmfirth HD9 ...... 189 C7
Cooper Bridge Rd HD5,
 WF14 .... 137 B6
Cooper Cl BD16 ..... 37 A5
Cooperfields HX2 .... 111 E6
Cooper Gr HX3 ...... 93 D7
Cooper Hill LS28 .... 76 F5
Cooper Ho 3 WF9 ... 181 D6
Cooper La
 Bradford BD6 .... 93 D8
 Holmfirth HD9 ...... 189 A4
Cooper Lane Prim Sch
 BD6 .... 73 D1
Cooper Rd LS22 ..... 13 E5
Coopers Cl WF7 ..... 163 E6
Cooper St OL14 ..... 108 E6
Co-op La HD9 .... 188 D3
Copeland St BD4 .... 75 D5
Copeworth Dr WF4 . 159 F3
Copgrove Cl 8 BD4 .. 75 E3
Copgrove Ct 12 BD4 . 75 E3
Copgrove Rd
 Bradford BD4 .... 75 E3
 Leeds LS8 .... 61 B5
Cop Hill End HD7 ... 169 C8
Cop Hill La HD7 .... 169 B8
Cop Hill Side HD7 .. 169 B8
Copley Ave
 Halifax HX2 .... 202 B1
 Meltham HD9 .... 170 D2
Copley Bank Rd HD7 . 152 C3
Copley Cl HX3 ...... 113 B1
Copley Glen HX3 .... 113 B2
Copley Gr HX3 ..... 113 B2
Copley Hall St HX3 .. 113 B2
Copley Hall Terr HX3 . 113 B2

Copley Hill
 Batley WF17 .... 96 F1
 Leeds LS12 .... 210 B2
Copley Hill Trad Est
 LS12 .... 210 B2
Copley Hill Way LS12 . 210 B2
Copley La
 Aberford LS25 ...... 65 D1
 Halifax HX3 .... 113 B1
 Rothwell WF3 ...... 100 B2
 Shepley HD8 .... 174 B3
Copley Mill Ho HX3 . 113 A1
Copley Mount HX3 .. 113 B1
Copley Prim Sch HX3 . 113 B1
Copley St
 Batley WF17 .... 118 A5
 Bradford BD5 .... 74 B4
 Halifax HX3 .... 203 B1
 Leeds LS12 .... 210 B2
Copley Terr HX3 .... 113 B1
Copley View HX3 ... 113 B1
Copley Yd LS12 ..... 210 B2
Coplowe La BD15 .... 53 D5
Copmanroyd LS21 ... 11 A2
Copperas House Terr
 OL14 .... 108 A4
Copperas Row HX4 .. 133 E5
Copper Beech Cl WF8 . 146 E6
Copper Beech Ct WF2 . 161 A7
Copperfield Ave LS9 . 212 C1
Copperfield Cres 10 LS9 . 212 C1
Copperfield Dr 8 LS9 . 212 C1
Copperfield Gr 4 LS9 . 80 A7
Copperfield Mount 3
 LS9 .... 80 A7
Copperfield Pl 9 LS9 . 212 C1
Copperfield Row 7 LS9 . 212 C1
Copperfield Terr LS9 . 80 A7
Copperfield View 11 LS9 . 212 C1
Copperfield Wlk 6 LS9 . 212 C1
Coppertop Mews WF8 . 125 E1
Coppice Cl WF1 ..... 142 E4
Coppice Dr HD4 .... 171 D6
Coppice Grange LS19 . 40 B7
Coppice Head LS26 . 100 F5
Coppice The
 Barwick in E LS15 ... 63 D7
 Batley WF17 .... 96 D1
 Glusburn BD20 ..... 16 C6
 Halifax HX1 .... 203 A1
 Huddersfield, Fixby HD2 . 136 B1
 Huddersfield, Lindley HD3 . 135 A1
 Ilkley LS29 .... 8 A4
 Mirfield WF14 ..... 138 A8
 Yeadon, Westfield LS19 . 39 F7
Coppice View BD10 . 56 A8
Coppice Way LS8 .... 61 A6
Coppice Wood Ave
 Bradford BD7 .... 74 A5
 Yeadon LS19, LS20 .. 40 A8
Coppice Wood Cl LS19 . 23 A1
Coppice Wood Cres LS19 . 23 A1
Coppice Wood Gr
 Bradford BD7 .... 74 A6
 Yeadon LS20 .... 40 A8
Coppice Wood Rise LS19 . 40 B8
Coppies The BD12 .. 94 B4
Coppin Hall Gr WF14 . 137 D6
Coppin Hall La WF14 . 137 D6
Copplestone Wlk 3 BD4 . 75 C2
Coppy Cl BD16 ..... 54 A6
Coppy La
 Haworth BD22 ...... 33 C7
 Leeds LS13 .... 58 C4
 Wadsworth Moor HX7 . 68 F1
Coppy Nook La HX7 . 110 E3
Coppy Rd
 Addingham LS29 .... 6 E8
 Steeton BD20 ...... 17 B5
Coppy Row BD22 .... 34 B2
Coppy Wood Dr LS29 . 8 B7
Copse The
 Bingley BD16 .... 37 D3
 Boston Spa LS23 ... 14 C1
 Brighouse, Hartshead Moor Top
  BD19 .... 115 F7
 Brighouse, Hove Edge HD6 . 114 F4
 Burley in W LS29 ... 21 E8
 East Ardsley WF3 .. 120 B7
 Featherstone WF7 .. 124 C1
Copthorne Gdns HD2 . 136 F5
Copthorne Prim Sch BD7 . 74 C5
Copthorne Sq HD2 .. 136 F5
Copthurst Rd HD9 .. 198 E7
Copt Royd Gr LS19 . 40 A7
Copy Bottom BB10 . 85 C4
Corban St BD4 ..... 75 C3
Corby St HD2 ...... 136 A1
Cordingley Cl BD4 .. 75 E1
Cordingley St BD4 .. 75 E1
Corfe Cl WF17 ..... 97 B2
Coriander Cl BD15 .. 73 A8
Corn Bank HD4 .... 171 C6
Cornerstones Cl LS29 . 7 A8
Cornet Cl HD3 ..... 135 C1
Corn Exchange 4 LS1 . 211 C3
Cornfield WF13 .... 117 F1
Cornfield Ave HD3 .. 153 A7
Cornfield St 3 OL14 . 108 C6
Cornholme Jun & Inf Sch
 OL14 .... 86 A1
Cornholme Terr 7 OL14 . 86 B1
Cornmarket WF8 ... 146 C8
Corn Market HX1 .. 203 B3
Corn Mill LS29 ..... 22 B4
Cornmill Ave WF15 . 117 C3
Cornmill Cl LS17 ... 28 D3
Cornmill Cres WF15 . 117 B3

Corn Mill Ct LS13 ... 77 D7
Cornmill Dr WF15 ... 117 B3
Corn Mill Fold BD6 ... 93 E6
Cornmill La
Bardsey LS17 ... 28 D3
Liversedge WF15 ... 117 B3
Corn Mill La
Otley LS29 ... 10 A1
Thornton BD13 ... 72 F5
Corn Mill Wlk BD20 ... 16 E5
Cornrace View HD4 ... 154 B4
Corn St BD21 ... 35 A4
Cornstone Fold LS12 ... 77 C7
Cornus Gdns 2 LS10 ... 99 D8
Cornwall Ave BD20 ... 5 C1
Cornwall Cl LS26 ... 100 D6
Cornwall Cres
Baildon BD17 ... 38 B4
Brighouse HD6 ... 115 B6
Rothwell LS26 ... 100 D6
Cornwall Ho 16 HX5 ... 134 F7
Cornwall Pl BD8 ... 55 D1
Cornwall Rd
Bingley BD16 ... 37 B2
Bradford BD8 ... 55 D1
12 Keighley BD21 ... 18 E1
Cornwall Terr 7 BD8 ... 55 D1
Coronation Ave
Guiseley BD10 ... 39 D4
Kippax LS25 ... 83 C1
Normanton WF6 ... 122 F3
Royston S71 ... 179 E4
Shafton S72 ... 180 B3
Coronation Bglws
Kippax LS25 ... 83 C1
Knottingley WF11 ... 126 D4
Meltham HD9 ... 170 E1
Coronation Bsns Ctr
BD21 ... 18 D1
Coronation Hospl LS29 ... 8 C3
Coronation Mount BD22 ... 34 F7
Coronation Par LS15 ... 80 E7
Coronation Rd
Crofton WF4 ... 144 B3
Halifax HX3 ... 113 D4
Coronation St
Bradford BD12 ... 95 A4
Castleford WF10 ... 103 F1
Elland HX5 ... 134 F6
Elland, Lindwell HX4 ... 134 C7
Normanton WF6 ... 123 D3
Rothwell WF3 ... 100 D3
Wakefield WF2 ... 120 F1
Coronation Terr
2 Batley WF17 ... 96 F1
Castleford WF10 ... 125 A6
Ripponden HX6 ... 132 E6
Wadsworth Moor HX7 ... 89 C5
Coronation Way BD22 ... 34 F8
Coronation Wlk BD22 ... 34 F8
Corporal La HX3 ... 92 F6
Corporation St
Bradford BD2 ... 56 C3
Dewsbury WF13 ... 139 D8
Halifax HX3 ... 203 B4
2 Huddersfield HD1 ... 154 A5
Morley LS27 ... 98 A4
Sowerby Bridge HX6 ... 112 B4
Corpus Christi RC Coll
LS9 ... 80 E8
Corpus Christi RC Prim Sch
LS9 ... 80 D8
Corrance Rd BD12 ... 94 D1
Corrie St BD13 ... 72 E6
Cote Cl HD8 ... 173 E3
Cote Farm La
Bradford BD17 ... 38 F1
3 Shipley BD10 ... 55 F8
Cotefields Ave LS28 ... 57 C2
Cote Gap BD13 ... 72 D7
Cote Hill HX2 ... 112 C6
Cote Hill Fold HX2 ... 112 D6
Cote La
Bradford BD15 ... 54 A1
Brighouse HD2 ... 135 E5
Holmfirth HD9 ... 199 A8
Pudsey LS28 ... 57 C2
Cote Rd HX6 ... 132 B4
Coteroyd Ave LS27 ... 98 C8
Coteroyd Dr LS27 ... 98 C7
Cote The LS28 ... 57 C2
Cote Wall WF14 ... 138 D3
Cotewall Rd BD5 ... 74 D3
Cotswold Ave BD18 ... 55 E7
Cotswold Cl WF9 ... 181 F7
Cotswold Dr
Cleckheaton WF15 ... 116 D5
Garforth LS25 ... 82 F5
Knottingley WF11 ... 126 E4
Rothwell LS26 ... 100 D6
Cotswold Mews HD8 ... 173 F7
Cotswold Rd
Rothwell LS26 ... 100 E6
Wakefield WF2 ... 141 D5
Cottage Gn 12 BD8 ... 73 F8
Cottage Homes
Huddersfield, Dalton
HD5 ... 155 A6
Huddersfield, Netherton
HD4 ... 171 D7
Cottage Rd
Bradford BD10 ... 56 D7
Leeds LS6 ... 59 D6
Cottages The BD16 ... 36 C2
Cottam Ave BD7 ... 74 B6
Cottam Croft WF9 ... 181 E7
Cottam Terr BD7 ... 74 B6
Cotterdale BD15 ... 54 A3
Cotterdale Holt LS22 ... 13 A1
Cotterdale View LS15 ... 80 E6
Cotterill Rd WF11 ... 126 D3
Cottingley App LS11 ... 213 A1
Cottingley Chase LS11 ... 213 A1
Cottingley Cliffe Rd BD16 ... 54 C6
Cottingley Cres LS11 ... 213 A1
Cottingley Dr
Morley LS11 ... 78 C2
Shipley BD16 ... 54 A8
Cottingley Fold LS11 ... 78 C2
Cottingley Gdns LS11 ... 213 A1
Cottingley Gn LS11 ... 213 A1
Cottingley Gr LS11 ... 213 A1
Cottingley Hts LS11 ... 213 A1
Cottingley Manor Pk
BD16 ... 54 B7
Cottingley Moor Rd BD16 ... 54 A5
Cottingley New Rd BD16 ... 54 B7
Cottingley Prim Sch LS11 ... 78 C1
Cottingley Rd
Bradford BD15 ... 54 A4
Morley LS11 ... 78 C2
Cottingley Sta LS11 ... 78 C1
Cottingley Terr 3 BD8 ... 55 D1
Cottingley Twrs LS11 ... 213 A1
Cottingley Vale LS11 ... 213 A1
Cottingley Village Prim Sch
BD16 ... 54 B6
Cotton St
Leeds LS9 ... 212 A3
Wakefield WF2 ... 142 C4
Couford Gr HD2 ... 136 F4
Coule Royd HD5 ... 154 F7
Coultas Cl LS29 ... 22 B4
Council Terr HD9 ... 172 A5
County Arc LS1 ... 211 C4
County Bridge BD13 ... 71 D5
County Cl WF17 ... 118 C6
Coupe Gr WF6 ... 122 F5
Coupland Pl LS11 ... 214 B4
Coupland Rd
Garforth LS25 ... 82 E7
Leeds LS11 ... 214 B4
Coupland St
Leeds LS11 ... 214 B3
6 Todmorden OL14 ... 108 B5
Courtenay Cl BD3 ... 75 E7
Courtenays LS14 ... 62 B4
Courthouse St LS21 ... 23 A8
Court La HX2 ... 112 D7
Court No 6 WF17 ... 118 C4
Courts Leet 1 BD12 ... 94 C4
Court The
Leeds LS17 ... 42 F5
Liversedge WF15 ... 116 E4
Shipley BD18 ... 54 E7
Courtway The WF7 ... 164 B8
Courtyard Mews BD20 ... 17 F6
Courtyards The LS14 ... 62 B7
Courtyard The
7 Bacup OL13 ... 106 A3
Batley WF17 ... 96 F2
2 Bradford BD7 ... 73 E2
Huddersfield HD4 ... 153 D4
Keighley BD21 ... 18 D1
Pontefract WF8 ... 125 E3
Shipley BD18 ... 54 E7
Wakefield WF2 ... 141 D3
Court Yard The WF4 ... 178 A7
Cousen Ave BD7 ... 73 F5
Cousen Pl 6 BD7 ... 74 B4
Cousen Rd BD7 ... 74 B4
Cousin La HX2 ... 91 E4
Coutances Way LS29 ... 9 B3
Coventry St
Bradford BD4 ... 75 B4
Halifax HX2 ... 202 A3
Coverdale Garth 2 LS22 ... 29 A8
Coverdale Way BD17 ... 38 E4
Cover Dr 2 BD6 ... 94 A8
Coverley Garth LS19 ... 39 F7
Coverley Rise LS19 ... 39 F7
Covert The WF17 ... 117 F7
Covet The BD10 ... 56 D8
Covey Clough Ct WF14 ... 137 F1
Cow & Calf* LS29 ... 8 E2
Cowcliffe Hill Rd HD2 ... 135 F3
Cowcliff Hill Rd HD9 ... 199 D8
Cow Close Gr LS12 ... 78 A4
Cow Close La BD12 ... 94 E2
Cow Close Rd LS12 ... 78 A4
Cowdray Dr 9 BD19 ... 115 F8
Cowdry Cl WF12 ... 139 E2
Cowfold St 7 OL14 ... 108 B6
Cow Gate HD3 ... 152 F6
Cowgill St
14 Bacup OL13 ... 106 A3
4 Bradford BD8 ... 55 C1
Cow Gn HX1 ... 203 B3
Cow Hey La HX7 ... 68 D3
Cow Heys HD5 ... 154 F7
Cow Hill Gate La HX2 ... 71 E1
Cow House Bridge BD13 ... 52 D7
Cowhurst Ave OL14 ... 108 A7
Cow La
Brighouse HX3 ... 114 D4
Crofton WF4 ... 144 A4
Halifax HX3 ... 113 C2
Knottingley WF11 ... 127 A4
Ripponden HX6 ... 132 D6
Ryhill WF4 ... 162 C1
Wadsworth Moor HX7 ... 88 E8
Cowlersley La HD4, HD7 ... 152 F3
Cowlersley Prim Sch
HD4 ... 152 F3
Cowley Cres BD9 ... 54 D4
Cowley Rd LS13 ... 57 F5
Cowpasture Rd LS29 ... 8 C3
Cowper Ave LS9 ... 208 A2
Cowper Cres LS9 ... 208 A2
Cowper Gr LS8 ... 208 A3
Cowper Mount LS9 ... 208 A2
Cowper Rd LS9 ... 208 A2
Cowper St
Dewsbury WF12 ... 139 C6
Leeds LS7 ... 207 B3
Cowper Terr LS9 ... 208 A2
Cowrakes Cl HD3 ... 135 A1
Cowrakes Rd HD3 ... 135 A1
Cowroyd Pl HX3 ... 203 C4
Cowslip St HD1 ... 153 D5
Cowtoot La OL13 ... 106 A4
Coxley Cres WF4 ... 158 D6
Coxley La WF4 ... 158 D7
Coxley View WF4 ... 158 C5
Coxwold Hill LS22 ... 13 E7
Coxwold View LS22 ... 13 E6
Coxwold Wlk 3 BD15 ... 73 A7
Crabgate Dr DN6 ... 184 E2
Crabgate La DN6 ... 184 E2
Crab Hill WF8 ... 146 C8
Crab La
Crigglestone WF2 ... 160 B4
Leeds LS12 ... 209 C4
Crabtree Ave
Bacup OL13 ... 106 A1
Batley WF16 ... 117 E5
Crabtree Fold HX7 ... 89 B5
Crabtree Gn LS22 ... 29 B7
Crabtree Hill LS22 ... 29 B8
Crabtree La LS17 ... 28 C7
Crab Tree La WF8 ... 166 B3
Crabtree Pl 5 BD7 ... 74 A4
Crabtree St
6 Bradford BD7 ... 74 A4
Halifax HX1 ... 202 B3
Crabtree Way WF3 ... 119 F7
Crackenedge La WF13 ... 118 D1
Crackenedge Terr WF13 ... 118 D1
Crack La BD15 ... 53 D5
Cracoe Rd BD3 ... 75 B6
Crag Cl
Halifax HX2 ... 91 D4
Sutton-in-C BD20 ... 16 C5
Crag Ct HX2 ... 91 D4
Cragg Ave LS18 ... 58 C8
Cragg Bottom Rd BD22 ... 49 E8
Crag Gdns LS23 ... 30 D2
Cragg Dr LS29 ... 8 F3
Cragg Hill LS18 ... 58 C8
Cragg La
Bradford BD7 ... 74 A3
Denholme BD13 ... 71 E6
Mytholmroyd HX7 ... 110 D6
Thornton BD13 ... 72 A5
Cragg Rd
Hebden Bridge, Cragg Vale
HX7 ... 109 F5
Horsforth LS18 ... 58 C8
Mytholmroyd HX7 ... 110 D6
Cragg Side HX7 ... 88 C7
Cragg St BD7 ... 74 A3
Cragg Terr
Bradford BD7 ... 74 A3
Horsforth LS18 ... 58 B8
Yeadon LS19 ... 40 B2
Cragg Top BD13 ... 71 E5
Cragg Vale Jun & Inf Sch
HX7 ... 110 C3
Cragg View
15 Addingham LS29 ... 6 F8
Pool LS21 ... 24 B5
Silsden BD20 ... 5 E2
Craggwell Terr 7 LS18 ... 58 C7
Craggwood Cl LS18 ... 58 C7
Cragg Wood Dr LS19 ... 40 A2
Craggwood Rd LS18 ... 58 C7
Craggwood Terr 8 LS18 ... 58 C7
Crag Hill Ave LS16 ... 41 E6
Crag Hill Rd BD10 ... 39 A2
Crag Hill View LS16 ... 41 E6
Crag La
Halifax HX2 ... 91 D3
Leeds LS17 ... 42 F5
Low Bradley BD20 ... 4 C4
Sutton-in-C BD20 ... 16 C4
Crag Mount 12 WF8 ... 146 C8
Crag Pl BD21 ... 35 C4
Crag Rd BD18 ... 55 C7
Cragside BD10 ... 38 F1
Cragside Cl LS5 ... 58 E7
Cragside Cres LS5 ... 58 E7
Cragside Gdns LS5 ... 58 E7
Cragside Gr LS5 ... 58 D6
Cragside Mount LS5 ... 58 E7
Cragside Pl LS5 ... 58 E6
Cragside Wlk LS5 ... 58 E7
Crag The LS23 ... 30 D2
Crag Top WF11 ... 105 A4
Crag Vale Terr BD20 ... 16 B6
Crag View
Bradford BD10 ... 56 D6
Cononley BD20 ... 4 A1
Sutton-in-C BD20 ... 16 C5
Craig Cl WF17 ... 118 C6
Craiglands HX3 ... 114 D8
Craiglands Pk LS29 ... 8 C3
Craiglands Rd LS29 ... 8 C3
Craiglea Dr BD12 ... 94 D2
Craigmore Ct 12 BD4 ... 75 F2
Craigmore Dr LS29 ... 8 E4
Craigmore Ho 11 BD4 ... 75 F2
Craig View BD18 ... 54 E7
Craig-y-don WF12 ... 139 F7
Crake Dr BD6 ... 73 C1
Cranberry Ave OL14 ... 129 B7
Cranborne Dr S75 ... 177 F1
Cranbourne Rd BD9 ... 54 D1
Cranbrook Ave
Bradford BD6 ... 94 C8
Leeds LS11 ... 214 A3
Cranbrook Ho 1 BD16 ... 37 A2
Cranbrook Pl 3 BD5 ... 74 E3
Cranbrook St
Bradford BD5 ... 74 E3
4 Bradford, Clayton BD14 ... 73 B4
Cranbrook View LS28 ... 77 A5
Cranbrook Way WF8 ... 125 E3
Cranewells Dr LS15 ... 81 D6
Cranewells Gn LS15 ... 81 C6
Cranewells Rise LS15 ... 81 C6
Cranewells Vale LS15 ... 81 C6
Cranewells View LS15 ... 81 C7
Cranfield Dr DN6 ... 184 F2
Cranford Gdns
Ilkley LS29 ... 7 F3
Royston S71 ... 179 B4
Cranford Pl BD15 ... 53 C5
Crangle Fields HD4 ... 173 C2
Cranleigh Mount BD21 ... 35 A5
Cranmer Bank LS17 ... 43 A3
Cranmer Cl LS17 ... 43 A3
Cranmer Gdns
Leeds LS17 ... 43 A3
Meltham HD9 ... 170 F2
Cranmer Rd
Bradford BD3 ... 55 F1
Leeds LS17 ... 43 A3
Cranmer Rise LS17 ... 43 A3
Cranmore Cres LS10 ... 99 E5
Cranmore Dr LS10 ... 99 F6
Cranmore Garth LS10 ... 99 E5
Cranmore Gdns LS10 ... 99 E5
Cranmore Gn LS10 ... 99 E5
Cranmore Gr LS10 ... 99 E5
Cranmore La LS10 ... 99 F5
Cranmore Rd LS10 ... 99 E5
Cranmore Rise LS10 ... 99 F5
Cranwood Dr HD5 ... 155 A6
Craven Ave
Silsden BD20 ... 5 E1
Thornton BD13 ... 72 E6
Craven Cl
Cleckheaton BD19 ... 117 C8
Royston S71 ... 179 B4
Craven Cres LS29 ... 6 E8
Craven Ct
10 Bradford BD8 ... 73 F8
Halifax HX1 ... 202 C3
Silsden BD20 ... 5 F1
Cravendale Rd WF13 ... 138 D6
Craven Dr
Cleckheaton BD19 ... 117 C8
Silsden BD20 ... 5 E1
Craven Edge HX1 ... 202 C2
Craven Gr BD20 ... 5 F1
Craven Ho OL14 ... 129 A8
Craven La BD19 ... 117 C8
Craven Mount HX1 ... 202 C2
Craven Pk LS29 ... 21 F5
Craven Rd
Dewsbury WF13 ... 139 A6
Hemsworth WF9 ... 181 D6
Keighley BD21 ... 35 E8
Leeds LS6 ... 206 B3
Craven St
Bradford BD3 ... 201 C4
Dewsbury WF13 ... 138 E6
Huddersfield HD4 ... 153 A4
Otley LS21 ... 23 B7
Wakefield WF1 ... 216 B3
Craven Terr
Bradford BD2 ... 56 C3
Halifax HX1 ... 202 C2
6 Otley LS21 ... 23 B7
Crawford Ave BD6 ... 94 C8
Crawford Dr WF2 ... 141 F7
Crawford St
Bradford BD4 ... 75 A4
Todmorden OL14 ... 129 B8
Crawley Ave WF9 ... 182 D3
Crawshaw Ave LS28 ... 76 F7
Crawshaw Cl 1 LS28 ... 76 E7
Crawshaw Gdns LS28 ... 76 F7
Crawshaw Hill 2 LS28 ... 76 E7
Crawshaw La
Emley HD8 ... 175 A8
Flockton, Six Lanes End HD8,
WF4 ... 157 A1
Flockton WF4 ... 156 F2
Crawshaw Pk LS28 ... 76 E7
Crawshaw Rd LS28 ... 76 E7
Crawshaw Rise LS28 ... 76 E6
Crawshaw Sch LS28 ... 76 F7
Crawshaw St WF13 ... 138 F6
Crawthorne Cres HD2 ... 136 E4
Crayford Dr WF4 ... 143 F1
Cray La HX4 ... 133 E2
Crediton Ave BD15 ... 73 B8
Crediton Ct 12 BD15 ... 73 B8
Crescent Ave
Dewsbury WF13 ... 138 D5
Huddersfield HD4 ... 171 D7
Rothwell LS26 ... 100 F7
Crescent Bglws WF3 ... 99 D2
Crescent Ct
11 Ilkley LS29 ... 8 B4
Leeds LS17 ... 42 F6
Crescent Gdns LS17 ... 43 D4
Crescent Grange LS11 ... 214 C4
Crescent Rd
Huddersfield, Fartown
HD2 ... 136 A1
Crescent Rd *continued*
Huddersfield, Netherton
HD4 ... 171 D7
Ryhill WF4 ... 162 D1
Crescent Royd HD5 ... 155 A5
Crescent St 8 OL14 ... 108 B5
Crescent Terr 12 LS29 ... 8 B4
Crescent The
Baildon BD17 ... 38 C2
Bingley BD16 ... 36 E6
Birkenshaw BD11 ... 96 A7
Bradford BD6 ... 93 E8
Brighouse, Hipperholme
HX3 ... 114 D8
3 Brighouse, Waring Green
HD6 ... 115 B3
Burley in W LS29 ... 21 E8
Castleford WF10 ... 124 F6
Cleckheaton WF15 ... 116 D5
Dewsbury WF13 ... 138 D5
East Ardsley WF3 ... 120 A8
Elland, Holywell Green
HX4 ... 134 A4
Elland HX5 ... 134 F5
Featherstone WF7 ... 144 D5
Garforth LS25 ... 83 A7
Guiseley LS20 ... 39 C8
Halifax HX3 ... 113 F6
Holmfirth HD9 ... 189 E6
Ilkley LS29 ... 8 E5
Kippax LS25 ... 83 A1
Kirkburton HD8 ... 174 A7
Leeds, Alwoodley LS17 ... 42 F6
Leeds LS16 ... 42 B4
Leeds, Whitkirk LS15 ... 81 B8
Leeds, Woodhouse LS6 ... 206 A3
Menston LS29 ... 22 B4
Micklefield LS25 ... 84 A6
Netherton WF4 ... 158 D5
Normanton WF6 ... 122 F4
Otley LS21 ... 11 A2
Pudsey LS28 ... 76 F8
Sicklinghall LS22 ... 12 C5
Crescent Twrs LS11 ... 214 C4
Crescent View
Keighley BD22 ... 35 A3
Leeds LS17 ... 42 F6
Crescent Wlk
Bradford BD14 ... 73 D5
Dewsbury WF13 ... 138 D5
Creskeld Cres LS16 ... 24 F3
Creskeld Dr LS16 ... 24 F3
Creskeld Garth LS16 ... 24 F3
Creskeld Gdns LS16 ... 24 F3
Creskeld La
Arthington LS21 ... 25 A5
Bramhope LS16 ... 24 F3
Creskeld Pk LS16 ... 24 F3
Creskeld View LS16 ... 24 E3
Creskeld Way BD15 ... 53 F2
Creskell Rd LS11 ... 211 B1
Cressfield Rd HD3 ... 153 C8
Cresswell Mount BD7 ... 73 E2
Cresswell Pl BD7 ... 73 E2
Cresswell Terr 3 BD7 ... 73 E2
Crest Ave
Bradford BD12 ... 94 C1
Huddersfield HD5 ... 154 E5
Crest Dr WF8 ... 146 E6
Crestfield Ave HX5 ... 134 E6
Crestfield Cres HX5 ... 134 E5
Crestfield Dr
Elland HX5 ... 134 E5
Halifax HX2 ... 202 A1
Crestfield Rd HX5 ... 134 E5
Crest Hill Rd HD2 ... 136 C3
Crest Mount WF8 ... 146 E6
Crest Pl HD6 ... 114 E5
Crest Rd HD3 ... 135 A3
Crest The
Huddersfield HD2 ... 136 E6
Kippax LS25 ... 83 A1
Swillington LS26 ... 82 A1
Crest View HD6 ... 114 E5
Crestville Cl BD14 ... 73 D5
Crestville Rd BD14 ... 73 C5
Crestville Terr BD14 ... 73 D5
Crestwood Cl BD5 ... 75 B1
Creswell La WF13 ... 117 F3
Crewe Ave WF11 ... 126 B4
Crewe Rd WF10 ... 125 D7
Crib La HX3 ... 203 B4
Cricketers App WF2 ... 120 E3
Cricketers Cl
Ackworth M T WF7 ... 164 A5
Garforth LS25 ... 83 A7
Cricketers Fold
Halifax HX3 ... 113 D2
Shadwell LS17 ... 44 E4
Cricketers Gn LS19 ... 40 C5
Cricketers Terr LS12 ... 209 C3
Cricketers The LS5 ... 59 B4
Cricketers View LS17 ... 44 E4
Cricketers Wlk
Leeds LS15 ... 81 E7
Steeton BD20 ... 17 D5
Cricklegate LS15 ... 81 B8
Crimble Bank HD7 ... 152 A1
Crimble Cl HX3 ... 114 E7
Crimble Clough Rd HD7 ... 152 A3
Crimbles Ct LS28 ... 76 F7
Crimbles Pl LS28 ... 76 F7
Crimbles Rd LS28 ... 76 F7
Crimbles Terr LS28 ... 76 F7
Crimbles The WF4 ... 160 A7

Crimea La HD7 151 E4
Crimea St 5 OL13 106 A2
Crimple Gn LS25 83 B6
Crimshaw La BD18 55 D5
Crimsworth Dean* HX7 68 F2
Crimsworth La HX7 89 A8
Crimsworth Terr HX7 89 A7
Crinan Ct WF6 123 A4
Cringles La BD20 5 F7
Cripplegate HX1 203 C3
Cripple Syke LS18 41 C2
Crodingley HD9 189 B8
Crodingley Farm Ct HD9 189 B8
Croft's Ct LS1 211 B4
Croft Ave
Bingley BD16 36 D6
East Ardsley WF3 120 D7
Knottingley WF11 127 A5
Normanton, Altofts WF6 122 F3
Normanton, Normanton Common WF6 123 C3
Otley LS21 10 F1
Pudsey LS28 57 D3
Royston S71 179 B3
Croft Bank BD11 96 A5
Croft Bridge LS26 101 C5
Croft Carr OL14 108 E3
Croft Cl
5 Darton S75 178 A1
Menston LS29 21 F4
Croft Cottage La 3 HD1 154 B8
Croft Ct
Honley HD9 171 F3
Horsforth LS18 41 C1
Menston LS29 21 F4
Croftdale Gr LS15 62 D2
Croft Dr
Bramham LS23 30 D3
Darton S75 178 B1
Honley HD9 171 E4
Menston LS29 22 A4
Croft End LS22 13 C5
Crofters Gn BD10 56 A8
Crofters Lea LS19 39 F7
Crofters Mill BD20 16 D5
Croft Field BD20 17 E8
Croft Flat Dr HD8 155 C4
Croft Fold HX3 91 F2
Croft Foulds Ct LS25 82 F7
Croft Gdns HD2 135 E1
Croft Head
Guiseley LS20 22 E1
Skelmanthorpe HD8 175 A2
Croft Head La WF1 143 E6
Croft Head Terr BD20 16 C6
Croft Hill BD20 16 C5
Croft Ho 11 HX2 134 F7
Croft House Ave LS27 98 B5
Croft House Cl
Bradford BD6 94 B8
Morley LS27 98 B5
Croft House Ct 6 LS28 76 E8
Croft House Dr
Morley LS27 98 B5
Otley LS21 10 F1
Croft House Fold LS29 7 A8
Croft House Gdns LS27 98 B5
Croft House Gr LS27 98 B5
Croft House La
Huddersfield HD1 153 E7
Keighley BD20 18 A2
Morley LS27 98 B5
Croft House Mews LS27 98 B5
Croft House Mount LS27 98 B6
Croft House Rd
Bradford BD6 94 B8
Morley LS27 98 B5
Croft House Rise LS27 98 B6
Croft House View LS27 98 B5
Croft House Way LS27 98 B6
Croft House Wlk LS27 98 B6
Croft La
Newton Kyme LS24 31 E6
Walton LS23 15 A4
Croftlands
Batley WF12 118 F2
Bradford BD10 56 A8
Huddersfield HD4 154 A2
Knottingley WF11 127 A5
Ossett WF5 140 E5
Croft Leigh Ct BD5 75 A1
Croft Mill Yd 19 HX7 89 A3
Crofton Cl HD7 170 D8
Crofton Ct BD9 54 F4
Crofton High Sch WF4 161 F8
Crofton Inf Sch WF4 162 A8
Crofton Jun Sch WF4 162 A8
Crofton Rd
Bradford BD9 54 F3
Shipley BD9 55 A4
Crofton Rise LS17 45 A4
Crofton Terr LS17 45 A4
Croft Pk LS29 21 F4
Croft Pl
1 Brighouse HD6 115 B4
Haworth BD22 51 F8
Croft Rd
Bingley BD16 36 D6
Bramham LS23 30 D3
Keighley BD20 19 D1
Croft Rise
Halifax HX3 91 F2
Menston LS29 22 A4
Croft Row BD13 71 E6
Croftside Cl LS14 62 B3
Croft St
Birkenshaw BD11 96 A5
Bradford BD10 56 C8
Bradford, Brownroyd Hill BD6 74 C1
Bradford, Eastbrook BD1, BD4, BD5 201 C2
6 Brighouse HD6 115 A2
Dewsbury WF13 139 C8
Glusburn BD20 16 C6
Haworth BD22 51 C7
21 Hebden Bridge HX7 89 A3
Huddersfield HD1 153 C5
Keighley BD21 35 B6
Liversedge WF16 117 D3
Otley LS21 23 B7
Pudsey LS28 57 D3
Shipley BD18 55 B8
15 Sowerby Bridge HX6 112 C4
Steeton BD20 17 C5
Crofts The
Batley WF17 117 F4
Emley HD8 175 D7
Farnhill BD20 4 E1
Sutton-in-C BD20 16 C4
Croft Terr
Gildersome LS12 77 E3
Oakworth BD22 34 D2
Croft The
Badsworth WF9 164 D3
Birkenshaw BD11 96 E5
Castleford WF10 124 F6
Collingham LS22 29 A8
Denby Dale HD8 191 B6
Draughton BD23 1 D5
East Ardsley WF12 119 D5
Knottingley WF11 127 A5
Leeds LS15 62 B1
Rothwell LS26 101 C5
Scarcroft LS14 45 D8
West Bretton WF4 176 F8
Croftway LS15 63 E7
Croft Way LS29 22 A4
Croisdale Cl WF15 116 E4
Cromack View LS28 76 C7
Cromarty Ave HD4 153 C2
Cromarty Dr HD4 153 C2
Cromer Ave 15 BD21 35 B5
Cromer Gr 17 BD21 35 B5
Cromer Pl LS2 206 A2
Cromer Rd
Keighley BD21 35 B5
Leeds LS2 206 A2
Cromer St
Halifax HX1 202 B1
14 Keighley BD21 35 B5
Leeds LS2 206 A2
Cromer Terr LS2 206 A2
Crompton Dr LS27 97 F6
Cromwell Bottom Dr HD6 114 D2
Cromwell Cl
Byram WF11 126 D8
Halifax HX3 114 A4
Cromwell Cres WF8 146 E8
Cromwell Ct
Birkenshaw BD11 96 D5
Huddersfield HD5 154 F2
Leeds LS10 212 A3
Shipley BD9 54 C5
Skellow DN6 184 F1
Cromwell Hts 2 LS9 212 B4
Cromwell Mews LS9 207 B1
Cromwell Mount
Leeds, Mabgate LS9 207 B1
Leeds, Woodhouse Hill LS10 99 D8
Pontefract WF8 125 D2
Cromwell Pl WF5 140 E7
Cromwell Rd
Castleford WF10 125 D7
Halifax HX3 114 A4
Cromwell Rise LS25 103 B8
Cromwell St
Leeds LS9 207 B1
Thurnscoe S63 194 E1
Cromwell Terr 1 HX1 203 A3
Cromwell View HX3 114 B4
Cronkhill La S71 179 D1
Crooked La
Bradford BD10 38 F1
Halifax HX3 92 B6
Crooke La BD15 53 C4
Crookes La S71 179 C1
Crook Farm Cvn Pk BD17 37 F3
Cropper Gate LS1 211 A4
Cropredy Cl BD13 72 F1
Cropstones LS23 30 D2
Cropton Rd S71 179 B3
Crosby Ave LS11 213 C4
Crosby Pl LS11 211 A1
Crosby Rd LS11 211 A1
Crosby St
Keighley BD21 35 B8
Leeds LS11 210 C1
Crosby Terr LS11 211 A1
Crosby View 3 LS11 211 A1
Croscombe Wlk BD5 201 B1
Croset Ave HD1 154 C7
Crosland Bank HD4 171 A5
Crosland Ct HD3 134 F1
Crosland Edge HD9 170 F4
Crosland Factory La HD4 171 B5
Crosland Hill Rd HD4 153 B3
Crosland Moor Jun Sch HD4 153 C3
Crosland Rd
Huddersfield, Lidley HD3 135 A1
Huddersfield, Yews Hill HD1 153 E4
Crosland Spring La HD4 171 B6
Crosland St HD4 153 E4
Crosley View BD16 37 C2
Crosley Wood Rd BD16 37 B2
Cross Albert Pl LS12 210 A2
Cross Alcester Rd 12 LS8 207 C4
Cross Alma St LS9 207 C1
Cross Arc LS1 211 C4
Cross Aston Gr LS13 58 E2
Cross Ave LS26 100 F7
Cross Aysgarth Mount LS9 212 C4
Cross Bank Rd WF17 118 B6
Cross Banks BD18 55 B7
Cross Bank St WF14 138 A2
Cross Banstead St 5 LS8 207 C3
Cross Bath Rd LS13 58 C2
Crossbeck Cl LS29 8 B3
Crossbeck Rd LS29 8 C3
Cross Beck Rd 4 LS8 207 C4
Cross Belgrave St LS2 211 C4
Cross Bellbrooke Ave 5 LS9 208 B2
Cross Bell St 2 LS9 212 A4
Cross Bentley La LS6 59 F6
Cross Birch St LS27 98 B2
Cross Burley Lodge Rd LS6 205 B2
Cross Cardigan Terr LS4 59 C1
Cross Catherine St LS9 212 B3
Cross Chancellor St LS6 206 B3
Cross Chapel St 5 LS6 59 D5
Cross Chestnut Gr 18 LS6 205 B3
Cross Church St
8 Cleckheaton BD19 116 E7
14 Huddersfield HD1 154 B6
Huddersfield, Paddock HD1 153 D5
Cross Cliff Rd LS6 205 C4
Cross Cotts 2 HD1 153 D7
Cross Cowper St LS7 207 A3
Cross Crown St 5 BD19 116 D7
Crossdale Ave BD6 93 E8
Cross Dawlish Gr 7 LS9 80 B8
Cross Dikes HX6 132 A7
Cross Dikes Rd HX6 132 A7
Cross Easy Rd LS9 212 C2
Cross Elford St LS8 207 C3
Cross Emily St 11 BD21 35 C8
Cross End Fold LS29 7 A8
Cross Ends La HX7 69 A4
Cross Eric St LS13 58 C5
Cross Eshald Pl 4 LS26 101 D6
Cross Evanston Ave LS4 59 C2
Cross Farm Ct BD22 51 C3
Cross Field HX4 134 A4
Crossfield Cl BD22 51 B3
Crossfield Ct WF4 157 F6
Crossfield Rd BD22 51 C3
Crossfields WF4 158 A6
Cross Fields HD5 154 E7
Crossfield St LS2 206 A3
Cross Firs St HD3 153 B5
Cross Flatts Ave LS11 214 A2
Cross Flatts Cres LS11 213 C2
Cross Flatts Dr LS11 213 C2
Cross Flatts Gr LS11 214 A2
Cross Flatts Mount LS11 214 A2
Cross Flatts Par LS11 213 C2
Cross Flatts Park Prim Sch LS11 214 B2
Cross Flatts Pl LS11 213 C2
Crossflatts Prim Sch BD16 36 E7
Cross Flatts Rd LS11 213 C2
Crossflatts Row LS11 213 C2
Cross Flatts St LS11 213 C2
Crossflatts Sta BD16 36 E5
Cross Flatts Terr LS11 213 C2
Cross Foundry St WF13 138 E5
Cross Francis St LS7 207 A3
Crossgate
Darton S75 178 B1
Otley LS21 23 A7
Cross Gate Rd HD9 189 B2
Cross Gates Ave LS15 62 C3
Cross Gates Ctr LS15 62 C2
Cross Gates La
Harden BD16 36 C3
Leeds LS15 62 B3
Cross Gates Prim Sch LS15 62 B2
Cross Gates Rd LS15 62 B2
Cross Gates Sta LS15 62 C1
Cross Glen Rd LS16 59 C7
Cross Gn
Bradford BD4 75 E4
Otley LS21 23 B8
Cross Granby Terr 9 LS6 59 D5
Cross Grange Ave LS7 207 B4
Cross Grasmere St LS12 210 A3
Cross Green App LS9 80 A5
Cross Green Ave 17 LS9 212 C2
Cross Green Cl LS9 80 A5
Cross Green Cres LS9 212 C2
Cross Green Ct LS9 80 B5
Cross Green Dr
Huddersfield HD5 155 A6
Leeds LS9 80 A5
Cross Green Garth LS9 80 A5
Cross Green Gr 16 LS9 212 C2
Cross Green Ind Pk
Leeds, Cross Green LS9 80 B5
Leeds, Knowsthorpe LS9 212 C1
Cross Green La
Leeds, Knowsthorpe LS9 212 C2
Leeds LS15 81 B8
Cross Green Rd
Huddersfield HD5 155 A6
Leeds LS9 212 C2
Cross Green Rise LS9 80 A5
Cross Green Row LS6 59 E7
Cross Green Vale LS9 80 B5
Cross Green Way LS9 80 A5
Cross Greenwood Mount 1 LS6 59 E7
Cross Grove St 6 HD1 154 A5
Cross Hands La WF4 163 B6
Cross Hartley Ave LS6 206 A4
Cross Heath Gr LS11 213 B3
Cross Henley Rd LS13 58 C2
Cross Hill
Brierley S72 180 F3
Elland HX4 134 C7
Fairburn WF11 105 A4
Hemsworth WF9 181 D7
Skellow DN6 184 F1
Cross Hill Ct DN6 184 F2
Cross Hill La WF15 116 C1
Cross Hills
Halifax HX1 203 B4
Kippax LS25 83 B1
Cross Hills Ct 3 LS25 83 A1
Cross Hills Dr LS25 83 A1
Cross Hills Ent Ctr BD20 16 E7
Cross Hills Gdns 2 LS25 83 A1
Crosshills Mount HX4 134 C7
Crosshills Rd BD20 4 A2
Cross Hilton Gr LS8 204 C1
Cross House Ct BD12 95 A4
Cross Ingledew Cres LS8 44 B2
Cross Ingram Rd LS11 210 C1
Crossings The WF17 117 F8
Cross Ivy Mount 7 LS9 80 A8
Cross Kelso Rd LS2 205 C1
Cross Keys WF5 141 A7
Cross Keys Ct WF4 141 B1
Cross La
Bingley BD16 36 F3
Birkenshaw BD4, BD11 96 B7
Bradford BD7 74 A4
Brighouse HD6 115 F1
Elland HX5 134 E6
Emley HD8 175 D8
Guiseley LS20 23 A4
Holmfirth HD9 189 C2
Honley HD9 171 F2
Huddersfield HD4 154 A3
Kirkburton HD8 174 B5
Kirkburton, Stocksmoor HD4 173 C2
Leeds, Farnley LS12 77 E5
Leeds LS12 209 B3
Oxenhope BD22 51 C3
Queensbury BD13 92 C8
Royston S71 179 E3
Shelf HX3 93 A6
Shelf, Stone Chair HX3 93 B4
Shepley HD8 190 E6
Skelmanthorpe HD8 175 A1
Todmorden OL14 108 F4
Wakefield WF2 141 F5
Wilsden BD16 53 D7
Crossland Rd LS27 98 B7
Crossland Terr LS11 214 C3
Cross Lane Bsns Pk WF15 117 B4
Cross Lane Ct BD20 4 C5
Crosslane Ind Est WF15 117 A4
Cross Lane Light Ind Units LS12 209 B3
Cross Lane Mill BD20 4 C5
Cross Lane Prim Sch HX5 134 E5
Cross Lea Farm Rd LS5 58 F7
Cross Lee OL14 107 F7
Cross Leeds St BD21 35 B7
Cross Lee Gate OL14 107 F7
Cross Lee Rd OL14 107 F7
Crossley Apartments 4 HX1 203 A1
Crossley Cl WF14 138 A8
Crossley Fields Jun & Inf Sch WF14 138 B7
Crossley Gdns HX1 202 C3
Crossley Gr WF14 138 A8
Crossley Hall Mews BD8 73 E7
Crossley Hall Prim Sch BD8 73 E8
Crossley Hall St BD8 73 D7
Crossley Heath Sch The HX3 113 A4
Crossley Hill HX3 113 D3
Crossley La
Huddersfield HD5 155 A7
Mirfield WF14 138 B8
Crossley New Rd OL14 87 F1
Crossley Ret Pk HX1 203 A4
Crossley St
Batley WF15 117 C2
Bradford BD7 74 B5
Brighouse HD6 115 B1
Crofton WF1, WF4 143 F6
Featherstone WF7 145 D5
Halifax HX1 203 B3
Queensbury BD13 72 F1
17 Todmorden OL14 108 B5
Wetherby LS22 13 E5
Crossley Street Prim Sch LS22 13 E
Crossley Terr WF17 118 C
Crossley Terr N HX3 92 A
Crossley Terr S HX3 92 A
Crossley View WF14 138 B
Cross Lidgett Pl LS8 204 C
Cross Linden Terr 4 LS11 214 C
Cross Lister St 10 BD21 35 A
Cross Louis St LS7 207 A
Crossman Dr WF6 123 C
Cross Maude St LS2 212 A
Cross Milan Rd LS8 208 A
Cross Mitford Rd LS12 210 A
Cross Moor Cl BD20 5 C
Crossmount St WF17 118 C
Cross Normanton St WF4 159 C
Cross Osmondthorpe La LS9 80 C
Cross Park Ave WF10 124 F
Cross Park St
Batley WF17 118 D5
Dewsbury WF12 139 F8
7 Horbury WF4 141 A1
7 Leeds LS15 81 A8
Cross Pasture Rd 2 LS7 207 B4
Cross Peel St 2 LS27 98 B4
Cross Pipes Rd WF2 141 E8
Cross Platts HX3 114 C4
Cross Quarry St 17 LS6 206 A4
Cross Queen St WF6 123 A2
Cross Rd
Bradford, Fourlands BD10 56 C8
Bradford, Girlington BD8 55 B1
Bradford, Oakenshaw BD12 94 F4
Crigglestone WF4 159 F3
Dewsbury WF12 139 D1
Horsforth LS18 58 A8
Middlestown WF4 158 B7
Cross Reginald Mount LS7 207 A4
Cross Reginald Pl LS7 207 A4
Cross Rink St 5 WF17 118 D3
Cross River St 6 BD21 18 E1
Crossroads Cotts LS24 47 E5
Cross Roseville Rd LS8 207 B3
Cross Rosse St 5 BD18 55 B8
Cross Roundhay Ave LS8 204 C1
Cross Row LS15 82 A6
Cross Rydal St 6 BD22 35 A6
Cross Ryecroft St WF5 140 C7
Cross St Michael's La LS6 205 A4
Cross St W HX2 202 A4
Cross Speedwell St 5 LS6 206 B3
Cross Sq WF1 216 B2
Cross St
11 Bacup OL13 106 A3
Batley WF17 118 C5
2 Bradford, Buttershaw BD6 93 F7
5 Bradford, Clayton BD14 73 C4
Bradford, Oakenshaw BD12 95 A4
Brighouse HD6 115 B4
Castleford WF10 124 C8
Dewsbury, Savile Town WF12 139 D7
Dewsbury WF12 139 E8
East Ardsley WF3 120 E8
2 Elland, Holywell Green HX4 134 B4
7 Elland, West Vale HX4 134 D7
Halifax HX1 203 B3
1 Halifax HX1 203 C2
Hemsworth WF9 181 C7
Honley HD9 171 F4
3 Horbury WF4 141 B1
Huddersfield HD4 153 E4
Leeds LS15 81 A8
Liversedge WF15 117 A2
Ossett WF5 119 C1
3 Pontefract WF8 146 D8
Rothwell LS26 100 E5
Slaithwaite HD7 152 A1
Upton WF9 183 D8
Wakefield WF1 216 B2
Wetherby LS22 13 E5
Cross Stamford St LS7 207 A1
Cross Stone Rd OL14 108 D6
Cross Sun St BD1 201 C4
Cross Terr LS26 100 E5
Cross The
Barwick in E LS15 63 E7
Bramhope LS16 24 D3
Crossthwaite Ct 1 WF8 125 D1
Cross Valley Dr LS15 62 B1
Cross View BD22 34 D3
Crossway BD16 53 F7
Crossways The LS21 11 A2
Cross Wellington St BD1 201 C3
Cross Wells Rd HX6 132 C5
Cross Westfield Rd LS3 205 C1
Cross Wingham St LS7 207 A2
Cross Woodstock St 15 LS2 206 B2
Cross Woodview St 17 LS11 214 B2
Cross York St LS2 212 A3
Crowgill Rd BD18 55 B8
Crow Hill Rd HX6, HX7 110 F2
Crow La
Huddersfield HD3 153 A5
Otley LS21 23 A7

Crow Lane Prim & Foundation Scheme Sch HD3 153 A5
Crowlees CE Jun & Inf Sch WF14 138 B4
Crowlees Cl WF14 138 B5
Crowlees Gdns WF14 138 B5
Crowlees Rd WF14 138 B5
Crown & Anchor Yd 3 WF8 146 C8
Crown Bldgs HD8 175 F3
Crown Cl WF12 140 A7
Crown Ct
  5 Leeds LS2 211 C3
  3 Wakefield WF1 216 B2
Crown Dr BD12 94 C4
Crow nest Ct 6 WF14 137 F5
Crow Nest Dr LS11 213 B2
Crownest La BD16 37 A3
Crow Nest La LS11 213 B2
Crow Nest Mews LS11 213 B2
Crownest Rd BD16 37 A3
Crow Nest Rd HX7 89 B2
Crow Nest Terr 2 WF13 139 B7
Crow Nest View WF13 139 A7
Crown Flatt Way WF12 118 E1
Crown Gn HD4 153 A4
Crown La 2 HD9 189 A5
Crownlands La WF5 140 D6
Crown Point Cl WF5 140 C6
Crown Point Dr WF5 140 C7
Crown Point Rd
  Leeds LS10 212 A3
  Ossett WF5 140 C6
Crown Point Ret Pk LS10 211 C2
Crown Rd HX3 92 B2
Crown St Bldgs 11 LS2 211 C3
Crown Sq HD3 153 B5
Crown St
  9 Bradford, Carr House Gate BD12 94 C4
  Bradford, Lister Hills BD1 74 C7
  Brighouse HD6 115 A3
  Burley in W LS29 9 F1
  Clayton West HD8 175 D1
  Cleckheaton BD19 116 D7
  Elland HX5 134 F7
  Halifax HX1 203 B3
  26 Hebden Bridge HX7 89 A3
  Honley HD9 171 F5
  Leeds LS2 211 C3
  Ossett WF5 140 E3
Crown Terr HD8 175 F3
Crown Villas HD8 175 D1
Crown Yd WF9 182 D3
Crowther Ave LS28 56 F6
Crowther Bruce Mill Rd HD7 169 A4
Crowther Cl HD7 152 A2
Crowther Fold BD16 36 B1
Crowther Pl
  Castleford WF10 124 D7
  Leeds LS6 206 B3
Crowther Rd
  Batley WF16 117 E5
  Mirfield WF14 138 A5
Crowther St
  Batley WF17 117 F5
  Bradford BD10 56 D7
  8 Bradford, Carr House Gate BD12 94 C4
  Castleford WF10 124 D7
  6 Cleckheaton BD19 116 D8
  Huddersfield, Aspley HD1 154 B5
  1 Huddersfield, Rashcliffe HD1 153 F3
Crow Tree Cl BD17 38 D3
Crow Tree La BD8 54 E1
Crow Trees HD7 169 C7
Crowtrees Cres HD6 135 F7
Crowtrees Ct LS19 40 B3
Crowtrees La HD6 135 F7
Crowtrees Pk HD6 135 F8
Crow Trees Pk LS19 40 B4
Crow Trees Rd HD7 169 B7
Crow Wood La HX4 133 D2
Crow Wood Pk HX2 112 D5
Croxall Dr WF3 121 E5
Croydon Ho LS11 210 C2
Croydon Rd BD7 73 F4
Croydon St
  Leeds LS11 210 C2
  12 Queensbury BD13 72 E1
Crumack La BD22 51 F3
Crummock Pl WF11 126 E2
Crunwelle Ct BD15 54 A4
Cryer Mdws BD22 51 D8
Cryer Row BD20 16 D4
Crystal Ct 9 HX1 202 C3
Crystal Pl 4 WF1 216 C2
Crystal Terr BD4 75 C3
Crystal Way WF10 124 E5
Cubley Ave WF2 160 B6
Cuckoo's Nest Halt* HD8 175 C2
Cuckoo La HD9 171 F4
Cuckoo Nest BD7 74 C7
Cuckoo Nest Ct BD16 36 C2
Cuckoo Nest Ind Est BD7 74 C7
Cuckstool Rd HD8 192 A6
Cudbear St LS10 212 A2
Cullingworth Gate BD13 52 D5
Cullingworth Prim Sch BD13 52 D6
Cullingworth Rd BD13 52 E5
Cullingworth St WF13 118 A3
Culpans Rd HX6 111 A5
Culver St 1 HX1 203 B3
Cumberland Ave HD2 136 B5
Cumberland Cl HX2 91 E3
Cumberland Ct LS6 205 A3
Cumberland Ho BD3 201 D4
Cumberland Rd
  Bradford BD7 74 A5
  Castleford WF10 104 E2
  Leeds LS6 205 C4
Cumberworth CE Fst Sch HD8 191 B6
Cumberworth La
  Denby Dale, Lower Cumberworth HD8 191 E7
  Shepley HD8 190 F6
Cumberworth Rd HD8 174 F1
Cumbrian Way WF2 141 E2
Cuniver Ct WF15 116 C5
Cunliffe La BD17 39 B5
Cunliffe Rd
  Bradford BD8 55 D3
  Ilkley LS29 8 B4
Cunliffe Terr BD8 55 D2
Cunliffe Villas BD8 55 D3
Cupstone Cl BD20 19 D1
Cure Hill BD22 34 B3
Curlew Cl
  Castleford WF10 124 D6
  Ilkley LS29 7 E4
Curlew Ct BD20 17 B6
Curlew Rise LS27 98 D3
Curlew St BD5 74 C3
Curly Hill LS29 8 B6
Currer Ave BD4 75 B1
Currerbell Mews BD13 72 F6
Currer La LS29 3 C4
Currer St
  Bradford BD1 201 C3
  Bradford, Oakenshaw BD12 95 A4
Currer Wlk BD20 17 B6
Curtis Ct BD13 52 D6
Curwen Cres WF16 117 E6
Curzon Rd BD3 75 B7
Curzon St HD2 137 A6
Cusworth Cl HX1 202 B4
Cuthberts Cl BD13 92 D8
Cutler Heights La BD4 75 D3
Cutler La LS26 102 E4
Cutler Pl BD4 75 D4
Cut Rd
  Brotherton WF11 105 C1
  Fairburn WF11 105 A4
Cutsyke Ave WF10 124 B5
Cutsyke Crest WF10 124 B5
Cutsyke Rd
  Castleford WF7 124 B3
  Featherstone WF7 124 B3
Cutsyke Wlk WF10 124 C5
Cuttlehurst HD8 175 D1
Cutts Field View S71 179 B5
Cygnet Hospl BD4 75 B1
Cyndor Ct WF10 125 E6
Cypress Ct WF2 142 A2
Cypress Fold HD8 155 E3
Cypress Ho 10 WF10 124 E7
Cypress Rd WF6 144 C8
Cyprus Ave
  Bradford BD10 38 F1
  Wakefield WF1 142 A8
Cyprus Cres WF14 138 D7
Cyprus Dr BD10 39 A1
Cyprus Gr
  Garforth LS25 82 E7
  Wakefield WF1 142 A8
Cyprus Mount WF1 142 A8
Cyprus Rd LS25 82 E7
Cyprus St
  Ossett WF5 140 C8
  Wakefield WF1 216 A4
Cyprus Terr LS25 82 E7
Czar St LS11 211 A2

D

Dacre Ave WF2 141 C4
Dacre Cl WF15 116 F5
Daffels Wood Cl BD4 95 B8
Daffil Ave LS27 98 B7
Daffil Gr LS27 98 B8
Daffil Grange Mews 1 LS27 98 B7
Daffil Grange Way LS27 98 B7
Daffil Rd LS27 98 B7
Daffodil Ct 9 BD15 73 B8
Dahl Dr WF10 125 C5
Daily Ct BD5 74 B3
Daisy Bank
  Brighouse HX3 94 A2
  Halifax HX1 203 A1
  Hebden Bridge HX7 89 C3
Daisy Bank St 2 OL14 86 B1
Daisy Cl WF17 96 E2
Daisy Croft BD20 5 F1
Daisyfield Rd 2 LS13 58 D2
Daisy Fold WF9 182 F7
Daisy Gn HD7 170 C7
Daisy Hill
  5 Bradford BD12 94 C3
  Dewsbury WF13 139 C8
  Morley LS27 98 C5
  Silsden BD20 5 F1
Daisy Hill Ave LS27 98 C6
Daisy Hill Back La BD9 54 E2
Daisy Hill Cl
  Luddenden HX2 111 D7
  Morley LS27 98 C6
Daisy Hill Gr BD9 54 E2
Daisy Hill La BD9 54 E2
Daisy La 7 HD9 189 A5
Daisy Lea HD3 152 A8
Daisy Lea La HD3 135 C1
Daisy Lee La HD9 199 C7
Daisy Mount HX6 112 A5
Daisy Pl 12 BD18 54 F8
Daisy Rd HD6 136 B8
Daisy Row 3 LS13 58 D1
Daisy Royd HD4 154 A2
Daisy St
  Bradford BD7 74 A3
  5 Brighouse HD6 115 A2
  Halifax HX1 203 A2
  1 Haworth BD22 51 E8
Daisy Vale Mews WF3 99 E1
Daisy Vale Terr WF3 99 E1
Dalby Ave BD3 56 C1
Dalby Ct BD19 117 B7
Dalby St BD3 75 C8
Dalcross Gr BD5 74 F4
Dalcross St BD5 74 F4
Dale Ave OL14 108 D5
Dale Cl
  Batley WF17 118 C3
  Denby Dale HD8 191 F5
  Guiseley LS20 39 B8
  Ossett WF5 140 E6
Dale Cres BD20 17 C5
Dale Croft
  Garforth LS25 82 E8
  Ilkley LS29 7 E4
  Skelmanthorpe HD8 175 A2
Dale Croft Rise BD15 54 A2
Dale Ct
  Holmfirth HD9 189 B7
  Ossett WF5 140 D6
  Pontefract WF8 146 D5
Dalefield Ave WF6 123 B1
Dalefield Rd WF6 144 B8
Dalefield Way WF6 144 B8
Dale Garth BD17 38 B3
Dale Gr BD10 38 E1
Dale House Ind Sch WF17 118 A6
Dale La
  Batley WF16 117 E5
  South Elmsall WF9 183 B5
Dale Lane Ind Est WF9 183 B5
Dale Mews WF8 146 D5
Dale Park Ave LS16 41 D4
Dale Park Cl LS16 41 D4
Dale Park Gdns LS16 41 D4
Dale Park Rise LS16 41 D4
Dale Park View LS16 41 D4
Dale Park Wlk LS16 41 D4
Dale Rd BD11 97 A8
Dales Dr LS20 39 B8
Daleside
  Dewsbury WF12 139 C1
  Elland HX4 134 A7
  Todmorden OL14 108 A4
Daleside Ave
  Holmfirth HD9 189 C7
  Pudsey LS28 76 A8
Daleside Cl LS28 56 F1
Daleside Gr
  Bradford BD12 94 F4
  Pudsey LS28 76 A7
Daleside Rd
  Keighley BD20 19 A1
  Pudsey LS28 75 F8
  Shipley BD18 55 E8
Daleside Wlk BD5 74 F2
Daleson Cl HX3 93 A3
Dale St
  Bradford BD1 201 B3
  Dewsbury WF12 139 C4
  Huddersfield, Folly Hall HD1 154 A5
  Huddersfield HD3 153 A5
  7 Keighley BD21 18 E1
  Ossett WF5 140 D6
  Shipley BD18 55 B7
  Skelmanthorpe HD8 175 A2
  Sowerby Bridge HX6 112 B4
  Todmorden OL14 108 B5
Dale Stone Cl WF11 105 C1
Dalesview Cotts BD23 1 D5
Dalesway BD16 37 B5
Dales Way LS20 39 B8
Dale The LS25 47 E1
Dale View
  Birkenshaw, Drighlington BD11 96 F6
  Hemsworth WF9 181 F6
  Huddersfield HD3 153 A5
  Ilkley LS29 7 E4
  Luddenden Foot HX2 111 D6
  Mytholmroyd HX7 110 E8
  Pontefract WF8 146 D5
  Silsden BD20 5 E2
  Steeton BD20 17 C5
Dale View Cl BD21 35 E6
Daleview Ct BD17 38 A2
Dale View Gr BD21 35 E6
Dale View Rd BD21 35 E6
Dale Villas
  Castleford WF10 125 C7
  Horsforth LS18 58 D7
Dale Wlk WF7 145 C4
Dallam Ave BD18 54 E8
Dallam Gr 3 BD18 54 E8
Dallam Rd BD18 54 E8
Dallam Wlk BD18 54 F8
Dalmeny Ave HD4 153 C3
Dalmeny Cl HD4 153 C3
Dalton Ave LS11 214 A2
Dalton Bank Rd HD2, HD5 137 A3
Dalton Clowes HD5 154 E7
Dalton Fold Rd HD5 154 D7
Dalton Gr
  Huddersfield HD5 154 E7
  Leeds LS11 214 A2
Dalton Green La HD5 155 A6
Dalton Jun & Inf Sch HD5 154 F6
Dalton La
  Collingham LS23 29 E3
  Keighley BD21 35 E7
Dalton Mills Bsns Complex BD21 35 D7
Dalton Rd
  Keighley BD21 35 E7
  Leeds LS11 214 A2
Dalton St
  2 Sowerby Bridge HX6 112 B5
  Todmorden OL14 108 B5
Dalton Terr
  Bradford BD8 74 B8
  Castleford WF10 124 D7
  Keighley BD21 35 E8
Dalton Works HD5 136 F1
Damask St HX1 203 A4
Damems La BD22 35 A2
Damems Rd BD21 35 A3
Damems Sta* BD22 35 A2
Damfield Mews HD4 153 F2
Dam Head
  Holmfirth HD9 188 D2
  Northowram HX3 92 E3
Dam Head La HD8 155 F6
Dam Head Rd HX6 112 C5
Dam Hill HD8 173 E3
Dam La
  Aberford LS24 65 F6
  Yeadon LS19 40 C7
Damon Ave BD10 56 E4
Dampier St 17 OL14 108 A1
Damside BD21 35 B6
Damside Rd HD4 154 B4
Damson Ct BD14 73 C3
Dam Top HX6 132 D4
Danby Ave BD4 95 B8
Danby La WF2 160 C4
Danby Wlk LS9 212 C3
Dancroft 12 BD22 51 C6
Dandy Mill Ave WF8 125 F2
Dandy Mill Croft WF8 125 F2
Dandy Mill View WF8 125 F3
Danebury Rd HD6 115 B1
Danecourt Rd BD4 75 F3
Danefield Terr LS21 23 B8
Dane Hill Dr BD4 75 E4
Danehurst WF8 146 E8
Danella Cres WF2 120 F3
Danella Gr WF2 120 F2
Dane Royd Jun & Inf Sch WF4 159 F2
Danes La WF4 158 B6
Danesleigh Dr WF4 158 B6
Daniel Cl BD21 35 A3
Daniel Ct BD4 75 F2
Daniel St BD3 75 D7
Dan La BD6 73 C1
Danny La HX2 111 D7
Dansk Way LS29 8 D5
Danum Dr BD17 38 C2
Darbyfields HD7 152 E6
Darcey Hey La HX2 202 A1
Darcy Ct LS15 81 C8
Darfield Ave LS8 208 A3
Darfield Cres LS8 208 A3
Darfield Gr 8 LS8 207 C3
Darfield Pl LS8 208 A3
Darfield Rd LS8 208 A3
Darfield St
  Bradford BD1 201 A4
  Leeds LS8 208 A3
Darkfield La WF8 125 F4
Dark La
  Barwick in E LS15 63 D8
  Batley, Birstall WF17 96 F3
  Batley, Mount Pleasant WF17 118 B4
  Blackshaw Head HX7 88 C3
  Cawthorne S75 193 E5
  Halifax HX2 112 B6
  Haworth BD22 33 F1
  Huddersfield HD4 155 A3
  Oxenhope BD22 51 D3
  Pontefract WF8 146 C7
Darkwood Cl LS17 44 A4
Darkwood Way LS17 44 A4
Darley Ave LS10 99 D7
Darley Rd WF15 116 F5
Darley St
  Batley WF16 117 D4
  Bradford BD1 201 B3
  Keighley BD20 18 B1
Darnay La 9 BD5 74 E3
Darnes Ave HX2 202 A1
Darning La WF8 165 B5
Darnley Ave WF2 142 A6
Darnley Cl HD9 170 E1
Darnley La LS15 81 C7
Darnley Rd LS16 59 B7
Darren St BD4 75 E6
Darrington CE Jun & Inf Sch WF8 147 D5
Darrington Rd WF8 146 E2
Dartmouth Ave
  Huddersfield HD5 155 A3
  Morley LS27 98 A2
Dartmouth Mews LS27 97 F3
Dartmouth St HD7 151 F1
Dartmouth Terr
  Bradford BD8 55 C2
  Kirkburton HD4 172 E6
Dartmouth Way LS11 214 C2
Darton Hall Cl S75 177 F1
Darton Hall Dr S75 177 F1
Darton La S75 178 B1
Darton Prim Sch S75 177 F1
Darton Rd S75 193 F5
Darton Sta S75 177 E1
Darwin St BD5 74 C3
Davey La HX7 87 F3
David La WF13 118 C2
David St
  Leeds LS11 211 B2
  Wakefield WF1 142 E4
David Young Com Acad The LS14 61 F4
Davies Ave LS8 61 A8
Davis Ave WF10 125 D6
Dawes Ave WF10 124 F6
Daw Green Ave WF4 159 E4
Daw La
  Crigglestone WF4 159 D4
  Horbury WF4 159 C8
Dawlish Ave LS9 80 B8
Dawlish Cres LS9 80 B8
Dawlish Gr LS9 80 B7
Dawlish Mount LS9 80 B8
Dawlish Pl 1 LS9 80 B8
Dawlish Rd LS9 80 B8
Dawlish Row LS9 80 B8
Dawlish St LS9 80 B8
Dawlish Terr LS9 80 B8
Dawnay Rd BD5 74 C4
Daw Royds HD5 155 A4
Dawson's Cnr LS28 57 C2
Dawson's Ct LS14 62 B4
Dawson's Terr LS28 57 C2
Dawson Ave BD6 94 C8
Dawson Gdns 1 WF13 139 C8
Dawson Hill LS27 98 A5
Dawson Hill Yd 4 WF4 141 B1
Dawson Ho LS13 58 F3
Dawson La
  Birkenshaw BD4 76 E2
  Bradford BD4 75 C1
  Rothwell LS26 100 E6
Dawson Mount BD4 75 C1
Dawson Pl
  Bradford BD4 75 D1
  Keighley BD21 35 C5
Dawson Rd
  Huddersfield HD4 154 B3
  Keighley BD21 35 C5
  Leeds LS11 214 A3
Dawsons Mdw LS28 57 C2
Dawson St
  Bradford, Bierley BD4 75 C2
  Bradford, Thackley BD10 39 B2
  East Ardsley WF3 98 D1
  7 Pudsey LS28 57 D1
Dawson Terr BD4 75 C1
Dawson Way BD21 35 C5
Dawtrie Cl WF10 125 D7
Dawtrie St WF10 125 D7
Day St
  Dewsbury WF13 138 E5
  Huddersfield HD1 154 C5
Deacon Cl HD9 170 E2
Deaconess Ct LS29 8 B3
Deacons Wlk WF16 117 E4
Deacon View HX3 203 C4
Deadmanstone HD4 171 F8
Dealburn Rd BD12 94 E4
Deal La HD7 152 D4
Deal St
  Halifax HX1 203 C2
  Keighley BD21 35 E8
Dean Ave
  Holmfirth HD9 188 F8
  Leeds LS8 61 A6
Dean Beck Ave BD6 74 E1
Dean Beck Ct BD6 94 F8
Dean Bridge La HD9 189 E2
Dean Brook Rd
  Holmfirth HD9 172 A1
  Huddersfield HD4 171 E8
Dean Cl
  Bradford BD8 54 D1
  Wakefield WF2 120 F2
Dean Clough HX3 203 B4
Dean Clough Office Pk HX3 203 A4
Dean Ct
  Elland HX3 113 A2
  Leeds LS8 61 A6
Dean Edge Rd BD22 50 A8
Dean End HX4 134 C8
Deanery Gdns BD10 56 C5
Deanfield Ave LS27 97 F6
Dean Field Com Prim Sch HX2 91 E3
Dean Hall Cl LS27 97 F4
Dean Head LS18 41 A8
Deanhouse HD9 188 F8
Deanhouse La HD9 189 A8
Dean House La
  Elland HX4 133 D1
  Halifax HX2 90 E2
Deanhurst Gdns LS27 97 E6
Dean La
  East Carlton LS16 24 A1
  Goose Eye BD22 34 A6

Dean La *continued*
Guiseley LS20 38 F8
Holmfirth HD9 189 D1
Horsforth LS18 41 A8
Sowerby Bridge HX6 132 E8
Sowerby Bridge, Sowerby HX6 111 E2
Wilsden BD13 53 C1
Dean Park Ave BD11 96 E7
Dean Park Dr BD11 96 E6
Dean Rd
Bradford BD6 94 D8
Holmfirth HD9 188 C6
Deanroyd Rd OL14 129 B7
Deans Ct WF8 125 D1
Deans Laithe BD21 35 D7
Dean St
9 Elland HX5 134 F6
Elland, West Vale HX4 134 D7
Haworth BD22 51 D7
Huddersfield HD3 153 B8
Ilkley LS29 8 C5
Deans Terr HX3 92 C3
Deanstones Cres BD13 92 E8
Deanstones La BD13 92 E8
Deansway LS27 97 F6
Deanswood Cl LS17 43 A3
Deanswood Dr LS17 42 F3
Deanswood Garth 2 LS17 43 A3
Deanswood Gdns LS17 42 F3
Deanswood Gn LS17 42 F3
Deanswood Hill LS17 43 A3
Deanswood Pl LS17 43 A3
Deanswood Rise 1 LS17 43 A3
Deanswood View LS17 43 A3
Dean View WF17 96 F2
Dean Villas OL14 129 B7
Deanwood Ave BD15 54 A3
Deanwood Cres BD15 54 A2
Dean Wood View HX3 113 C2
Deanwood Wlk BD15 54 A2
Dearden St
Ossett WF5 140 D5
Sowerby Bridge HX6 112 B5
Dearne Croft LS22 13 E8
Dearne Dike La HD8 190 E5
Dearne Fold HD3 135 B1
Dearne Pk HD8 175 E2
Dearne Royd HD8 175 E2
Dearneside Rd HD8 191 F5
Dearne St
Clayton West HD8 175 D1
Darton S75 177 F1
South Elmsall WF9 182 F3
Dearne Terr HD8 175 E1
Dearnfield HD8 191 C6
Dearnley St WF13 138 E6
Dee Ct BD22 34 C2
Deep Dale LS23 14 C1
Deepdale Cl BD17 38 A2
Deepdale Ho WF13 118 C2
Deepdale La LS23 14 C1
Deep La
Bradford BD13 73 C5
Brighouse HD6 115 F2
Halifax HX2 111 F7
Huddersfield HD4 153 B3
Sowerby Bridge HX6 132 B8
Thornton BD13 72 A5
Deer Croft Ave HD3 152 F8
Deer Croft Cres HD3 152 F8
Deer Croft Dr HD3 152 F8
Deer Croft Rd 2 HD3 134 F1
Deer Hill Cl HD7 168 F3
Deer Hill Croft HD7 168 F3
Deer Hill Ct HD9 170 C2
Deer Hill Dr HD7 168 F3
Deer Hill End Rd HD9 170 A4
Deerplay Ct OL13 106 A8
Deerplay Dr OL13 106 A8
Deershaw La HD8 190 C5
Deershaw Sike La HD8 190 C5
Deer St 6 OL13 106 A7
Deerstone Ridge LS22 13 E8
Defarge Ct BD5 74 E3
Deffer Rd WF2 160 C6
Deganwy Dr HD5 137 C2
Deightonby St S63 194 E1
Deighton Cl LS22 13 F6
Deighton Gates Prim Sch LS22 13 E8
Deighton La WF17 118 A4
Deighton Rd
Huddersfield HD2 136 E3
Wetherby LS22 13 E7
Deighton Sta HD2 136 E3
Deighton View LS6 42 E1
De Lacey Mews BD4 75 C2
De Lacies Ct LS26 101 A7
De Lacies Rd LS26 101 B8
De Lacy Ave
Bradford BD4 95 B8
Featherstone WF7 124 C1
Huddersfield HD5 154 F4
Delacy Cres WF10 104 D1
De Lacy Mount LS5 59 A4
De Lacy Terr WF8 146 E8
Delamere St BD5 74 D2
Delauney Cl 6 BD6 94 A8
Delaware Ct BD4 95 B8
Delf Cl HX3 93 E7
Delf Hill HD6 135 E7
Delf La
Todmorden OL14 86 D3
Delf La *continued*
Wadsworth Moor HX7 89 C8
Delf Pl HD6 135 E7
Delfs La HX6 110 F1
Delius Ave BD10 56 E5
Dell Croft BD20 5 C2
Dellside Fold BD13 52 D6
Dell The
Bardsey LS17 28 D3
Castleford WF10 124 A6
Cullingworth BD13 52 E6
Huddersfield HD2 136 B4
Delmont Cl WF17 117 E6
Delph Brow HX3 112 F4
Delph Cres BD14 73 B4
Delph Croft View BD21 35 D6
Delph Ct LS6 206 A4
Delph Dr BD14 73 B4
Delph Gr BD14 73 B4
Delph Hill
10 Baildon BD17 38 C4
5 Halifax HX2 113 A4
Pudsey LS28 76 E8
Delph Hill Fold HX2 112 F4
Delph Hill La HX2 90 D2
Delph Hill Rd HX2 112 F4
Delph Hill Terr HX2 112 F4
Delph La
Huddersfield HD4 171 D7
Leeds LS6 206 A4
Delph Mount LS6 206 A4
Delph St HX1 203 A2
Delph Terr BD14 73 B4
Delph The WF7 145 F5
Delph View LS6 206 A4
Delph Wood Cl BD16 37 C3
Delverne Gr BD2 56 C3
Delves Gate HD7 169 F6
Delves Wood Rd HD4 153 C1
Denard Ind Est HD4 153 B4
Denbigh App LS9 61 D2
Denbigh Croft LS9 61 D2
Denbigh Hts LS9 61 D2
Denbrook Ave BD4 75 F1
Denbrook Cl BD4 75 F1
Denbrook Cres BD4 95 F8
Denbrook Way BD4 75 F1
Denbrook Wlk BD4 75 F1
Denbury Mount BD4 75 E2
Denby CE Fst Sch HD8 191 F3
Denby Cl
Batley WF17 96 D1
Liversedge WF15 116 F5
Denby Crest WF8 147 D5
Denby Ct BD22 34 B2
Denby Dale Ind Est HD8 191 F6
Denby Dale Rd
Crigglestone WF4 159 C5
Wakefield WF2 142 B3
West Bretton WF4 158 E2
Denby Dale Rd E WF4 159 F7
Denby Dale Rd W WF4 159 D6
Denby Dale Sta HD8 191 E6
Denby Dr BD17 38 B1
Denby Grange La WF4 157 A5
Denby Hall La HD8 192 D4
Denby Hill Rd BD22 34 B2
Denby Ho 3 BD4 75 F1
Denby La
Bradford BD15 54 B1
Denby Dale, Lower Denby HD8 192 C4
Denby Dale, Upper Denby HD8 191 F3
Flockton WF4, WF12 157 C6
Denby Lane Cres WF4 156 E5
Denby Mount BD22 51 C2
Denby Park Dr WF4 156 E5
Denby Pl 4 HX6 112 B5
Denby Rd
Darrington WF8 147 C5
Keighley BD21 35 C5
Denby St BD8 74 C8
Denby View WF12 139 D1
Dence Gn BD4 75 E5
Dence Pl LS15 80 E8
Dendrum Cl BD22 34 C3
Dene Bank BD16 37 A6
Dene Cl HX5 134 E5
Dene Cres BD7 73 E4
Dene Fold HD8 173 D8
Dene Gr BD20 5 E2
Denehill BD9 54 D2
Dene Hill BD17 37 F3
Dene House Ct LS2 206 B2
Dene Mount BD15 54 C1
Dene Pk HD8 173 F7
Dene Pl HX1 203 A4
Dene Rd
Bradford BD6 73 D1
Skelmanthorpe HD8 174 F1
Dene Royd Cl HX4 133 F3
Dene Royd Ct HX4 133 F3
Deneside WF5 140 C7
Deneside Mount BD5 74 D2
Deneside Terr BD5 74 D2
Denesway LS25 83 A5
Dene View HX2 111 D8
Deneway LS28 57 C2
Denfield Ave HX3 91 F2
Denfield Cres HX3 91 F2
Denfield Edge HX3 91 F2
Denfield Gdns HX3 91 F2
Denfield La HX3 91 E2
Denfield Sq HX3 91 F2
Denhale Ave WF2 141 F6
Denham Ave LS27 98 A2
Denham Ct WF17 118 A7
Denham Dr HD9 188 F8
Denham Ho 20 BD4 75 E3
Denham St
Batley WF17 118 A7
4 Brighouse HD6 115 A1
Denholme Dr WF5 140 D7
Denholme Gate BD13 71 E6
Denholme Gate Rd HX3 93 C1
Denholme Mdw WF9 182 F4
Denholme Prim Sch BD13 52 D1
Denholme Rd BD22 51 D1
Denison Hall LS3 206 A1
Denison Rd LS3 211 A4
Denison St
Batley WF17 118 C4
Yeadon LS19 40 B7
Denmark St WF1 142 E4
Dennil Cres LS15 62 D4
Dennil Rd LS15 62 D3
Dennington La WF4 159 C3
Dennis La BD20 5 A4
Dennison Fold BD4 75 E5
Dennison Hill 4 LS21 23 B8
Dennistead Cres LS6 59 D5
Denshaw Dr LS27 98 C4
Denshaw Gr LS27 98 C4
Denshaw La WF3 98 F4
Denstone St WF1 216 C3
Dent Dr WF1 142 F8
Denton Ave LS8 204 C4
Denton Bridge HX6 132 E7
Denton Dr BD16 37 C4
Denton Gdns WF7 164 A5
Denton Gr LS8 204 C4
Denton Ho 4 BD6 93 E8
Denton Rd
Denton LS29 9 A6
Ilkley, Ben Rhydding LS29 8 E4
Ilkley LS29 8 A5
Ilkley LS29 8 D5
Denton Row
Denholme BD13 71 D8
Elland HX4 134 C4
Denton Terr WF10 124 E8
Dent St LS9 212 C3
Denwell Terr WF8 125 D1
Derald Ho 3 HX1 203 A2
Derby Pl BD3 75 D7
Derby Rd
Bradford BD3 75 E7
Yeadon LS19 40 B4
Derbyshire St LS10 215 C3
Derby St
Bingley BD16 36 F3
3 Bradford, Clayton BD14 73 B4
Bradford, Great Horton BD7 74 B4
Queensbury BD13 72 D1
Sowerby Bridge HX6 112 D4
Todmorden OL14 108 D5
Derby Terr
Bradford BD10 56 E8
Marsden HD7 168 F4
Derdale St OL14 108 C5
Derry Hill LS29 21 F4
Derry Hill Gdns LS29 21 F4
Derry La LS29 21 F4
Der St OL14 108 C5
Derwent Ave
Baildon BD17 37 E1
Garforth LS25 82 F6
Rothwell LS26 101 C6
Wilsden BD15 53 C4
Derwent Cl HX7 89 A4
Derwent Ct BD20 17 E8
Derwent Dr
Castleford WF10 104 E1
Huddersfield HD5 154 D7
Leeds LS16 42 D4
Derwent Gr WF2 141 F6
Derwent Pl
Knottingley WF11 126 E1
Leeds LS11 211 A2
6 Queensbury BD13 72 C2
Derwent Rd
Batley WF12 118 F2
Bradford BD2 56 A3
Honley HD9 171 E3
Meltham HD9 170 E1
Wakefield WF2 141 F6
Derwent Rise LS22 13 D8
Derwent St BD21 35 F8
Derwentwater Gr LS6 59 D5
Derwentwater Terr LS6 59 D5
Derwin Ave HD4 173 C2
De Trafford St HD4 153 D4
Detroit Ave LS15 81 E8
Detroit Dr LS15 81 E8
Deveron Gr HD2 153 E8
Devon Cl LS2 206 B2
Devon Gr WF5 140 C4
Devon Rd LS2 206 B2
Devonshire Ave LS8 44 A2
Devonshire Cl LS8 44 A2
Devonshire Cres LS8 44 A1
Devonshire Ct WF11 127 A4
Devonshire Gdns LS2 206 B3
Devonshire La LS8 44 A2
Devonshire Pl 3 LS19 40 B7
Devonshire St W BD21 35 A7
Devonshire St
Huddersfield HD1 153 E3
Keighley BD21 35 B7
Devonshire Terr BD9 55 C2
Devon St HX1 202 B2
Devon Way HD6 115 B6
Devon Wlk 4 WF13 139 B8
Devro Ct LS9 80 B4
Dewar Cl LS22 13 B1
Dewberry Cl 8 BD7 73 E3
Dewfield Cres BD4 95 C8
Dewhirst Cl BD17 38 D2
Dewhirst Pl BD4 75 D6
Dewhirst Rd
Baildon BD17 38 D2
Brighouse HD6 115 A4
Dewhirst St BD15 53 C5
Dewhurst Rd HD2 136 B2
Dewsbury Coll WF13 118 C1
Dewsbury Coll (Art & Design) WF13 118 B2
Dewsbury District Golf Course WF14 138 D3
Dewsbury & District Hospl WF13 118 A2
Dewsbury Gate Rd WF13 117 F3
Dewsbury Mills WF12 139 C6
Dewsbury Mus* WF13 139 A7
Dewsbury Rd
Cleckheaton BD19 96 B2
Cleckheaton, Marsh BD19 116 E7
East Ardsley WF3, WF12 119 C7
Elland HD6, HX5 135 C6
Leeds LS11 211 C1
Leeds LS11 214 C2
Middleton LS27, WF3 98 F5
Ossett WF5 140 D7
Wakefield WF2 141 D5
Dewsbury Sta WF13 139 C8
Deyne Rd HD4 171 C7
Diadem Dr LS14 61 E1
Dial St LS9 212 C2
Diamond Ave WF9 182 E3
Diamond St
Batley WF17 118 B6
Halifax HX1 202 C4
Huddersfield HD1 154 B8
10 Huddersfield, Moldgreen HD5 154 D5
Keighley BD22 35 A4
Diamond Terr HX1 202 C4
Dibb La LS19 39 F7
Dib Cl LS8 61 D5
Dib La LS8 61 D5
Dick's Garth Rd LS29 21 F4
Dick Dean La HX7 69 A5
Dick Edge La HD8 190 B2
Dicken's St HX2 202 A3
Dickens Dr WF10 125 D5
Dickens St BD5 74 E3
Dickin Royd HX6 132 E4
Dickinson Ct WF1 216 B4
Dickinson Gdns 11 WF13 139 B8
Dickinson St
Horsforth LS18 41 C2
Wakefield WF1 216 B3
Dickinson Terr WF7 145 D6
Dick La BD3, BD4 75 E6
Dickson Fold WF15 116 F4
Dicky Sykes La WF7 163 D5
Digby Rd LS29 22 A4
Digley Ave 3 BD13 73 C2
Digley Rd HD9 188 B2
Digley Royd La HD9 188 A3
Digpal Rd LS27 78 C1
Dimple Gdns WF5 140 D4
Dimples La
East Morton BD20 36 D8
Haworth BD22 51 B6
Dimple Well Inf Sch WF5 140 D4
Dimple Wells Cl WF5 140 D4
Dimple Wells La WF5 140 D4
Dimple Wells Rd WF5 140 D4
Dineley Ave OL14 108 A7
Dingle Rd HD1 153 D6
Dingley Rd HD3 153 C8
Dinsdale's Bldgs LS19 40 A6
Dirker Ave HD7 169 A5
Dirker Bank Rd HD7 168 F5
Dirker Dr HD7 168 F4
Dirkhill Rd BD7 74 C5
Dirkhill St BD7 74 B5
Discovery Rd HX1 203 C2
Dish Hill WF11 126 D7
Dish Hill Fly-over WF11 126 D8
Disney Cl HD4 153 D3
Dispensary Wlk HX1 203 C3
Disraeli Gdns LS11 214 B4
Disraeli Terr LS11 214 B4
Dixon's Yd WF1 216 C2
Dixon Ave BD7 73 F5
Dixon Cl
Elland HX4 134 B8
Steeton BD20 17 C5
Dixon La LS12 209 C1
Dixon Lane Rd LS12 209 C1
Dixons City Acad BD5 74 E4
Dixon St
Featherstone WF7 145 D7
Sutton-in-C BD20 16 E5
Doals Gate OL13 106 A8
Dobb Kiln La BD16 37 B1
Dobb La HD9 188 C2
Dobb Top Rd HD9 188 C2
Dob La HX6 111 D3
Dob Park Rd LS21 10 E8
Dob Royd HD8 190 D7
Dobroyd Rd OL14 108 A4
Dobson Ave LS11 214 C3
Dobson Gr LS11 214 C3
Dobson Locks BD10 39 D1
Dobson Pl LS11 214 C3
Dobsons Wharf 3 BD20 17 E8
Dobson Terr LS11 214 C3
Dobson View LS11 214 C3
Dob The HX6 111 D3
Dockery HD1 153 F3
Dockfield Pl BD17 55 C8
Dockfield Rd BD17 55 C8
Dockfield Terr BD17 55 C8
Dock Ho 16 LS10 211 C3
Dock La BD17, BD18 55 C8
Dockroyd BD22 34 D1
Dockroyd La BD22 34 D2
Dock St LS10 211 C3
Doctor Fold HD9 171 F5
Doctor Hill
Bradford BD10 56 A6
Bradford BD10 56 B7
Halifax HX2 91 E1
Doctor La
Bradford BD10 39 B1
Flockton WF4 157 B2
Mirfield WF14 138 A5
Shelley HD8 174 A3
Doctors La WF10 103 A5
Doctors Row
Huddersfield HD7 152 D1
Kirkheaton HD5 155 C8
Dodd's Royd HD4 171 E8
Dodgeholme Cl HX2 91 D4
Dodge Holme Ct HX2 91 D4
Dodge Holme Dr HX2 91 D4
Dodge Holme Gdns HX2 91 D4
Dodge Holme Rd HX2 91 D4
Dodgson Ave LS7 207 B3
Dodgson St HX5 134 F5
Dodlee La HD3 152 E7
Dodsworth Cres WF6 144 B8
Dodworth Dr WF2 160 B5
Dog Hill S72 180 C3
Dog Hill Dr S72 180 C3
Doghouse La OL14 108 A5
Dog Kennel Bank HD5 154 C4
Dog Kennel Hill S75 193 E3
Dog Kennel La HX3 113 E5
Dog La
Elland, Stainland HX4 133 E2
Elland, Upper Greetland HX4 133 E7
Dogley La HD8 155 D1
Dogley Villa Ct HD8 155 D1
Dog Pits La OL13 106 A6
Doldram La HX6 112 A1
Dole La HX7 89 A1
Doles Ave S71 179 B3
Doles Cres S71 179 B3
Dole St BD13 72 E6
Dolfin Pl HD2 136 F5
Doll La BD13 52 E4
Dolly La LS9 207 B2
Dolphin Ct
Leeds, Cavalier Hill LS9 212 B3
Leeds LS13 58 B2
Dolphin La WF3 99 F2
Dolphin Rd LS10 99 E5
Dolphin St LS9 212 B3
Dolphin Terr 8 BD13 92 C8
Dombey St HX1 202 C3
Domestic Rd LS12 210 C1
Domestic St Ind Est LS11 210 C2
Domestic St LS11 210 C1
Dominion Ave LS7 204 B3
Dominion Cl LS7 204 A2
Dominion Ind Pk HX3 114 C8
Dom Pedro Cotts WF6 123 E2
Donald Aldred Dr LS29 21 E8
Donald Ave BD6 94 C8
Donald St 8 LS28 57 D2
Don Ave LS22 13 D8
Doncaster La DN6 184 C3
Doncaster Rd
Ackworth M T WF4 163 B6
Badsworth WF7 164 B3
Crofton WF4 143 C2
Hampole DN6, WF9 183 D5
Kirk Smeaton WF8 166 A1
Knottingley WF11 126 C4
South Elmsall DN6, WF9 183 A2
Thorpe Audlin WF8 165 C4
Upton WF9 182 E7
Wakefield WF1 142 E4
West Hardwick WF4 163 B6
Doncaster Road Est WF7 164 A5
Doncaster Sq WF11 126 D5
Doncaster St 2 HX3 113 D3
Don Ct BD20 5 E1
Donisthorpe St
Bradford BD5 74 E3
Leeds LS10 212 B1
Don Pedro Ave WF6 123 D2
Don Pedro Cl WF6 123 D2
Don St BD21 35 B8
Don View S36 199 D1
Dorchester Ave WF8 146 B8
Dorchester Cres
Baildon BD17 38 F4
Bradford BD4 75 E2
Dorchester Ct 5 BD4 75 E3
Dorchester Dr
Halifax HX2 202 A1
Yeadon LS19 40 D6
Dorchester Rd HD2 136 B5
Dorian Cl BD10 56 C6
Dorman Ave WF9 183 D8
Dorothy St BD21 35 A3
Dorset Ave LS8 208 A4
Dorset Cl
Bradford BD5 74 C3
Hemsworth WF9 181 D8
Dorset Gr LS28 76 E8
Dorset Mount LS8 208 A3

Dor–Eas 243

Dorset Rd LS8 208 A3
Dorset St
Bradford BD5 74 D3
Huddersfield HD1 153 F8
Leeds LS8 208 A4
Dorset Terr LS8 208 A3
Dorset Wlk 6 WF13 139 B8
Dortmund Sq LS2 211 C4
Dotterel Glen LS27 98 C3
Doubting La WF12 139 D1
Doubting Rd WF12 139 D1
Douglas Ave
Batley WF17 118 F5
Huddersfield, Cliff End HD3 153 B6
Huddersfield HD5 154 E5
Douglas Cres BD18 55 D6
Douglas Dr BD4 75 C4
Douglas Rd
Bacup OL13 106 A1
Bradford BD4 75 C4
Douglas St
Dewsbury WF12 139 C4
Halifax HX3 92 B2
8 Haworth BD22 51 E8
Douglas Twrs 1 BD5 201 B1
Dove Cl LS22 13 E8
Dovecote Cl WF4 141 B2
Dovecote Dr WF10 103 E6
Dovecote La WF4 141 A2
Dovedale WF8 125 D3
Dovedale Cl
Crofton WF4 144 A1
Shelf HX3 93 B6
Dovedale Garth LS15 62 F3
Dovedale Gdns LS15 62 F3
Dove Dr WF10 125 B8
Dove Hill S71 179 D4
Dovelands BD20 16 D4
Dover La HD9 189 B3
Dover St
Bradford BD3 56 A1
Garforth LS25 83 B7
Todmorden OL14 108 D5
Dovesdale Gr BD5 74 D2
Dovesdale Rd BD5 74 D2
Dove St
16 Haworth BD22 51 D7
Shipley BD18 54 F8
Dowkell La LS23 14 F1
Dowker St
Halifax HX1 202 B1
Huddersfield HD3 153 B5
Dowley Gap La BD16 37 B1
Downham St BD3 201 D2
Downing Cl BD3 75 B7
Downing St HD7 170 C8
Downland Cres WF11 127 B2
Downside Cres BD15 54 A1
Dowry La HX6 132 A3
Dracup Ave BD7 73 E5
Dracup Rd BD7 73 F3
Dradishaw Rd BD20 5 D1
Dragon Cres LS12 210 A1
Dragon Dr LS12 210 A1
Dragon Rd LS12 210 A1
Drake Fold BD12 94 C3
Drake La BD11 96 E5
Drake Rd OL15 129 C1
Drakes Ind Est HX3 92 A4
Drake St
Bradford BD1 201 C2
Keighley BD21 35 C8
Draper Cnr HX7 88 E6
Draper La HX7 88 F6
Draughton Gr BD5 74 D1
Draughton Hall Farm BD23 1 D6
Draughton St BD5 74 D1
Draycott Wlk 11 BD4 75 E2
Dray View WF13 117 F2
Drewry Rd BD21 35 B7
Drewton Rd BD1 201 B4
Driftholme Rd BD11 96 F7
Drighlington Prim Sch BD11 96 E6
Drill Hall Bsns Ctr LS29 8 C4
Drill Hall The HX1 203 B2
Drill Par BD8 55 D1
Drill St
16 Haworth BD22 51 C6
Keighley BD21 35 C7
Drinker La HD8 174 D6
Driver Ho LS2 206 C1
Driver Pl LS12 210 B2
Drivers Row WF8 146 B7
Driver St LS12 210 B2
Driver Terr
Leeds LS12 210 B2
Silsden BD20 5 E2
Drive The
Bardsey LS17 28 D5
Batley WF17 118 A6
Bingley BD16 36 E6
Bradford BD10 56 D6
Brighouse HX3 114 D8
Burley in W LS29 21 E8
Denholme BD13 71 C8
Kippax LS25 83 A1
Leeds, Alwoodley LS17 43 A6
Leeds, Bank LS9 212 B3
Leeds, Ireland Wood LS16 42 A4
Leeds LS8 61 A8
Leeds, Manston LS15 62 D2
Mytholmroyd HX7 89 D1
Swillington LS26 82 A1
Drove Road Ho 10 BD5 74 E3
Drovers Way BD2 55 E4
Drub La BD19 95 F2
Druggist La LS29 6 F8
Druids St BD14 73 B4
Druids View BD16 36 D6
Drummer La HD7 152 B4
Drummond Ave LS16 59 C7
Drummond Ct LS16 59 C6
Drummond Rd
Bradford BD8 55 C1
Leeds LS16 59 C7
Drummond Trad Est BD8 74 D8
Drury Ave LS18 58 B8
Drury Cl LS18 58 B8
Drury La
Elland HX4 133 F4
Horsforth LS18 58 B8
Normanton WF6 122 F3
Wakefield WF1 216 A2
Dry Carr La HX2 90 C4
Dryclough Ave HD4 153 C2
Dryclough CE Inf Sch HD4 153 C3
Dryclough Cl HX3 113 C3
Dryclough La HX3 113 C3
Dryclough Rd HD4 153 C2
Dryden St
Bingley BD16 36 F3
Bradford BD1 201 D2
Dry Hill La HD8 192 B5
Drysdale Fold HD2 136 C4
Dubb La 24 BD16 37 A3
Duchy Ave BD9 54 E3
Duchy Cres BD9 54 E3
Duchy Dr BD9 54 E3
Duchy Gr BD9 54 E3
Duchy Villas BD9 54 E3
Duchywood BD9 54 E3
Ducie St BD10 39 B1
Duckett Gr LS28 75 F8
Duckett La BD1 201 B3
Duck Hill HX7 69 A1
Ducking Pond Cl 13 BD22 51 C6
Duckworth Gr BD9 54 F1
Duckworth La BD9 54 F1
Duckworth Terr BD9 54 F1
Dudfleet La WF4 159 B8
Dudley Ave
Batley WF17 97 A2
Huddersfield HD1 153 D6
Dudley Cres HX2 91 D5
Dudley Gr BD4 75 E5
Dudley Hill Rd BD2 56 B3
Dudley Rd HD1 153 D6
Dudley St
Bradford BD4 75 B3
Bradford, Dudley Hill BD4 75 C3
Bradford, Tyersal BD4 75 E5
Dudwell Ave HX3 113 C2
Dudwell Gr HX3 113 C2
Dudwell La HX3 113 C2
Dufton App LS14 62 A3
Duich Rd BD6 93 E6
Duinen St BD5 201 C1
Duke of York Ave WF2 142 D1
Duke of York St
Wakefield WF1 216 C3
Wakefield, Wrenthorpe WF2 120 F1
Dukes Hill LS29 8 A6
Duke St
Bradford BD1 201 B3
Castleford WF10 124 B8
Dewsbury, Chickenley WF12 140 B7
Dewsbury, Ravensthorpe WF13 138 E5
Elland HX5 134 F6
Fitzwilliam WF9 163 A3
Halifax HX2 90 D1
12 Haworth BD22 51 D7
Keighley BD20 18 C1
Leeds LS9 212 A3
Todmorden OL14 109 A8
Duke Wood Rd HD8 175 F2
Dulverton Cl
Morley LS11 213 A1
Pontefract WF8 125 F3
Dulverton Ct LS11 213 A1
Dulverton Garth LS11 78 C1
Dulverton Gdns LS11 78 C2
Dulverton Gn LS11 213 A1
Dulverton Gr
Bradford BD4 75 D3
Morley LS11 78 C1
Dulverton Pl LS11 78 C1
Dulverton Rise WF8 125 F3
Dulverton Sq LS11 213 A1
Dulverton Way WF8 125 F3
Dunbar Croft BD13 72 F1
Dunbar Ct LS26 102 C3
Dunbar St WF1 142 F4
Dunbottle Cl WF14 138 C5
Dunbottle La WF14 138 B6
Dunbottle Way WF14 138 C6
Duncan Ave
Otley LS21 22 D6
Wakefield WF2 142 E2
Duncan St
Bradford BD5 201 B1
Leeds LS1 211 C3
Dunce Park Cl HX5 134 F5
Duncombe Rd BD8 74 A7
Duncombe St
Bradford BD8 74 A7
Leeds LS1 211 A4
Duncombe Way BD8 74 A7
Dundalk Ct 1 WF5 140 D5
Dundas St
Halifax HX1 202 B1
Dundas St *continued*
Huddersfield HD1 154 A6
Keighley BD21 35 D6
Dundee Rd OL14 107 D8
Dunderdale Cres WF10 104 D1
Dunford Rd
Dunford Bridge HD9 199 D3
Holmfirth, Hade Edge HD9 199 B7
Holmfirth HD9 189 B3
Dungeon La LS26 101 A1
Dunhill Cres LS9 80 E8
Dunhill Rise LS9 80 E8
Dunkhill Croft BD10 56 B7
Dunkirk Cres HX1 202 A2
Dunkirk Gdns HX1 202 A1
Dunkirk La HX1 202 B2
Dunkirk Rise BD20 18 E2
Dunkirk St HX1 202 A2
Dunkirk Terr HX1 202 B2
Dunlin Cl LS27 98 C3
Dunlin Croft 8 LS10 99 D5
Dunlin Ct 6 LS10 99 D5
Dunlin Dr LS10 99 D5
Dunlin Fold 7 LS10 99 D5
Dunlin Way 3 BD8 73 C7
Dunmore Ave BD13 72 C1
Dunn Cl WF2 120 F3
Dunningley La
Middleton, Black Gates WF3 98 F2
Middleton WF3 98 F3
Dunnington Wlk BD6 94 A6
Dunniwood Cl WF10 123 F5
Dunniwood Dr WF10 124 A5
Dunnock Ave BD6 73 C1
Dunnock Croft LS27 98 C3
Dunnock Rd HD9 170 C4
Dunrobin Ave LS25 83 B8
Dunsford Ave BD4 95 B8
Dunsil Villas WF9 182 F1
Dunsley Bank Rd HD9 188 F3
Dunsley Terr WF9 182 A2
Dunsmore Dr HD3 152 F8
Dunstan Cl WF5 140 E4
Dunstan Gr BD19 116 E8
Dunstarn Dr LS16 42 D3
Dunstarn Gdns LS16 42 E3
Dunstarn La LS16 42 D2
Durban Ave LS11 213 C2
Durban Cl WF7 145 C6
Durban Cres LS11 213 C2
Durham Ct 11 LS28 57 D3
Durham Ho 3 HX6 112 C4
Durham Rd BD8 55 A1
Durham St
Castleford WF10 124 E6
Halifax HX2 202 A3
Durham Terr BD8 55 A1
Durkar Fields WF4 159 F6
Durkar Hall Farm WF4 159 F7
Durkar La WF4 159 F6
Durkar Low La WF4 160 A7
Durkar Rise WF4 159 F6
Durkheim Ct BD3 75 C7
Durley Ave BD9 55 A3
Durling Dr BD18 55 E7
Durlston Gr BD12 94 D4
Durlston Terr BD12 94 D4
Durn St OL14 86 A1
Durrance St BD22 34 F6
Durrant Cl LS22 13 F4
Dutton Gn LS14 62 A8
Dutton Way LS14 62 A7
Duxbury Rise LS7 206 B2
Dyas Bldgs WF7 144 E5
Dyehouse Dr BD19 95 C2
Dyehouse Fold BD12 95 A5
Dyehouse La
Brighouse HD6 115 B1
Pudsey LS28 76 E4
Dye House La
Sowerby Bridge HX6 112 E1
Wilsden BD15 53 B5
Dyehouse Rd BD12 95 A5
Dyer La HX3 91 F2
Dyers Ct LS6 205 C4
Dyer St LS2 212 A4
Dye Works The LS9 212 B3
Dyke Bottom HD8 190 F8
Dyke Cl WF14 138 A8
Dyke End HD7 152 B3
Dyke La OL14 109 B7
Dymond Gr WF15 117 A3
Dymond Rd WF15 117 B3
Dymond View WF15 117 A3
Dyson's Hill HD9 171 F5
Dyson La
Holmfirth HD9 189 C1
Ripponden HX6 132 C2
Dyson Pl 2 HX3 113 E3
Dyson Rd HX1 202 B4
Dyson St
Bradford BD1 74 D7
Brighouse HD6 115 A3
Huddersfield HD5 154 E6
Shipley BD9 55 A4
Dyson Wood Way HD2 136 D5

E

Eagle Gr WF2 141 D6
Eaglepoint WF2 120 E5
Eaglesfield Dr BD6 94 A6
Eagle St
Haworth BD22 51 E8
Keighley BD21 35 B7
Todmorden OL14 108 B6
Eagles Yard Bsns Pk WF1 216 B1
Ealand Ave WF17 118 A7
Ealand Cres WF17 118 A7
Ealand Rd
Batley, Brown Hill WF17 117 F7
Batley, Carlinghow WF17 118 A7
Ealing Ct WF17 118 A6
Earles Ave HD5 154 E5
Earle St WF7 145 C6
Earlsheaton Inf Sch WF12 139 F7
Earlsheaton Tech Coll WF12 139 E8
Earlsmere Dr LS27 97 F5
Earl St
Dewsbury WF12 140 B8
Fitzwilliam WF9 163 A3
Haworth BD22 51 C6
Keighley BD21 35 B8
Wakefield WF1 216 C3
Earls View BD20 16 C4
Earlswood Ave LS8 43 F2
Earlswood Chase LS28 76 E6
Earlswood Cl LS28 76 E5
Earlswood Cres LS25 83 A2
Earlswood Mead LS28 76 E6
Earl Terr 5 HX3 92 A2
Earnshaw Pl WF2 216 A3
Easby Ave WF17 117 F4
Easby Cl LS29 7 F4
Easby Dr LS29 7 F4
Easby Rd BD7 74 D5
Easdale Cl LS14 61 F5
Easdale Cres LS14 62 A5
Easdale Mount LS14 61 F4
Easdale Rd LS14 61 F4
Easedale Gdns HD3 135 A1
Easington Ave BD6 93 E8
Easingwood Dr HD5 137 B1
East Acres WF11 126 E7
East Ardsley Prim Sch WF3 120 D8
East Ave
Glusburn BD20 16 D6
Horbury WF4 141 C1
Huddersfield HD3 135 C1
Keighley BD21 35 C8
Pontefract WF8 146 B7
South Elmsall WF9 183 B4
Upton WF9 183 A7
East Bath St WF17 118 D5
East Beck Ct LS21 9 F5
East Bierley CE Fst Sch BD4 95 F7
Eastborough Cres WF13 118 D1
Eastborough Jun & Inf Sch WF13 139 D8
Eastbourne Ave WF7 145 E6
Eastbourne Cl WF8 147 A7
Eastbourne Cres WF8 147 A8
Eastbourne Dr WF8 147 A8
Eastbourne Rd BD9 55 B5
Eastbourne Terr WF8 147 A8
Eastbourne View WF8 147 A8
Eastburn Jun & Inf Sch BD20 16 F6
Eastbury Ave BD6 73 D1
East Busk La LS21 23 C8
East Byland HX2 91 E6
East Causeway Cl LS16 42 D5
East Causeway Cres LS16 42 D4
East Causeway Vale LS16 42 E4
East Chevin Rd LS21 23 C5
East Cl
Huddersfield HD2 136 B2
Pontefract WF8 146 F5
East Cliffe HX3 113 E6
East Croft 6 BD12 94 D2
East Cswy LS16 42 D5
East Dale Cl WF9 181 F7
Eastdean Bank LS14 62 A6
Eastdean Dr LS14 62 A6
Eastdean Gate LS14 62 B5
Eastdean Gdns LS14 62 B6
Eastdean Gr LS14 62 B6
Eastdean Grange LS14 62 B5
Eastdean Rd LS14 62 A6
Eastdean Rise LS14 62 B6
East Dene BD20 5 E2
East Down WF10 125 A8
East Dr WF8 146 F7
East End Cres S71 179 E3
Easterly Ave LS8 61 B5
Easterly Cl LS8 208 B3
Easterly Cres LS8 208 A4
Easterly Cross LS8 208 B4
Easterly Garth LS8 208 B4
Easterly Gr LS8 208 A4
Easterly Mount LS8 208 B4
Easterly Rd LS8 61 C5
Easterly Sq LS8 208 B4
Easterly View LS8 208 B4
Eastfield
Denholme BD13 71 D8
Shepley HD8 190 F8
Eastfield Ave WF11 126 F3
Eastfield Cres LS26 101 B6
Eastfield Dr
Kirkburton HD8 173 E7
Pontefract WF8 125 F1
Rothwell LS26 101 B6
Eastfield Gdns 9 BD4 75 E3
Eastfield Gr WF6 123 C3
Eastfield La
Burley in W LS29 22 A8
Castleford WF10 124 E8
Eastfield Pl BD20 16 D5
Eastfield Rd
Knottingley WF11 126 F3
Mirfield WF14 138 D6
East Field St LS9 212 B3
East Fold HD8 175 C1
East Foutains HX2 91 D7
East Garforth Prim Sch LS25 83 B8
East Garforth Sta LS25 83 A7
Eastgate
Bramhope LS16 24 D3
Elland HX5 134 F7
Hemsworth WF9 181 E6
Honley HD9 171 F5
Leeds LS2 212 A4
Eastgate Cl LS16 24 D3
East Gr HD5 155 C8
East Grange Cl LS10 215 B1
East Grange Dr LS10 215 B1
East Grange Garth LS10 215 B1
East Grange Rd LS10 215 B1
East Grange Rise LS10 215 B1
East Grange Sq LS10 215 B1
East Grange View LS10 215 B1
Easthorpe Ct BD2 56 D4
East King St LS9 212 B3
Eastlands HD5 155 A4
Eastland Wlk 3 LS13 58 E1
East Lee La OL14 109 A7
Eastleigh Ct WF3 120 A8
Eastleigh Dr WF3 120 A8
Eastleigh Gr BD5 74 C3
East Longley HX6 112 A1
East Moor Ave LS8 43 F1
East Moor Cres LS8 43 F2
East Moor Dr LS8 44 A1
Eastmoor Gr S71 179 C1
East Moor La LS16 42 D4
Eastmoor Rd WF1 216 C4
East Moor Rd LS8 43 F2
East Morton CE Prim Sch BD20 36 D8
East Mount
3 Brighouse HD6 115 A3
Havercroft WF4 180 B8
East Mount Pl 4 HD6 115 A3
Easton Pl HD3 153 B7
East Par
Baildon BD17 38 D4
Bradford BD1 201 C3
Ilkley LS29 8 C4
Keighley BD21 35 C7
Leeds LS1 211 B4
Menston LS29 22 A4
Sowerby Bridge HX6 112 D4
Steeton BD20 17 D5
East Park Dr LS9 80 A7
East Park Gr LS9 80 A7
East Park Mount 6 LS9 80 A7
East Park Par LS9 80 A7
East Park Pl LS9 80 A7
East Park Rd
Halifax HX3 92 A1
1 Leeds LS9 212 C3
East Park St
Leeds LS9 80 A7
Morley LS27 97 F3
East Park Terr 7 LS9 80 A7
East Park View LS9 80 A7
East Pinfold S71 179 C2
East Rd BD12 94 E6
East Riddlesden Hall* BD20 18 F1
East Ridge View LS25 83 C8
East Royd
Brighouse HX3 93 C1
Oakworth BD22 34 D2
East Side Ct LS28 77 A5
East Squire La BD8 55 C1
East St
Batley WF17 118 C5
Brighouse, Bailiff Bridge HX3 115 A7
Brighouse HD6 115 A1
Holmfirth HD9 189 E3
Huddersfield, Leymoor HD7 152 E4
Huddersfield, Lindley HD3 135 B1
Leeds LS2, LS9 212 B3
Lofthouse Gate, Newton Hill WF1 121 C2
Lofthouse Gate, Stanley Ferry WF3 122 A2
Ryhill WF4 162 D1
South Elmsall WF9 183 B4
South Hiendley S72 180 E5
Sowerby Bridge HX6 111 E1
East Terr BD22 51 E8
East-Thorpe Pl WF14 138 B4
East View
Bradford BD13 73 C2
Brighouse HX3 115 A7
Castleford WF10 124 A7
Cleckheaton BD19 116 A6
Gildersome LS27 97 C5
Glusburn BD20 16 D7
Hebden Bridge HX7 88 E3
Huddersfield HD1 153 E7
Kippax LS25 83 B2
Knottingley WF11 127 A4
Leeds LS15 62 C2
Micklefield LS25 84 B6
6 Mirfield WF14 137 F6
Mytholmroyd HX7 110 D7
Normanton WF6 122 E3

East View continued
Ossett WF5 . . . . **140** E3
Pudsey LS28 . . . . **76** E5
Rothwell LS26 . . . . **101** C5
Silsden BD20 . . . . **5** E1
Sowerby Bridge HX6 . . . . . . **112** C5
Thornton BD13 . . . . **72** E7
Yeadon LS19 . . . . **40** C6
Eastview Cotts HX4 . . . . . . **133** B5
East View Cotts 6 LS28 . . **76** F8
East View Rd LS19 . . . . . . **40** C6
East View Terr
Bradford BD12 . . . . **94** E4
7 Otley LS21 . . . . **23** B7
Shelley HD8 . . . . **174** B3
Eastville Rd WF4 . . . . **144** B3
Eastway WF14 . . . . **137** F7
Eastway Pk WF14 . . . . **138** A7
Eastwood Ave
Halifax HX2 . . . . **91** E7
Sowerby Bridge HX6 . . . . . . **111** F3
Wakefield WF2 . . . . **141** E7
Eastwood Cl
Crigglestone WF4 . . . . **159** F7
Halifax HX2 . . . . **91** E7
Eastwood Cres
Leeds LS14 . . . . **62** D4
Shipley BD16 . . . . **54** B8
Eastwood Ct
7 Halifax HX3 . . . . **113** A4
19 Keighley BD21 . . . . **35** D8
Eastwood Dr LS14 . . . . **62** D5
Eastwood Garth LS14 . . . . . **62** D4
Eastwood Gdns LS14 . . . . . **62** C4
Eastwood Gr
Garforth LS25 . . . . **83** A5
Halifax HX2 . . . . **91** E7
Eastwood La LS14 . . . . **62** D4
Eastwood Nook LS14 . . . . . **62** D4
Eastwood Prim Sch BD21 **35** D8
Eastwood Rd OL14 . . . . **87** D2
Eastwood St
Bradford BD4 . . . . **201** C1
8 Brighouse HD6 . . . . **115** B3
8 Halifax HX3 . . . . **92** A2
8 Huddersfield HD5 . . . . . **154** D5
Easy Rd LS9 . . . . **212** C2
Eaton Hill LS16 . . . . **41** F3
Eaton Mews LS10 . . . . **99** C5
Eaton Pl WF7 . . . . **181** E7
Eaton Rd LS29 . . . . **8** A3
Eaton Sq LS10 . . . . **99** C5
Eaton St 1 BD21 . . . . **35** A4
Eaton Wlk WF9 . . . . **183** A5
Eaves Ave HX7 . . . . **88** E4
Eaves Mount HX7 . . . . **88** E4
Eaves Rd HX7 . . . . **88** E4
Ebberston Gr LS6 . . . . **205** C3
Ebberston Pl LS6 . . . . **205** C3
Ebberston Terr LS6 . . . . . . **205** C3
Ebberton Cl WF9 . . . . **181** E8
Ebenezer Pl BD7 . . . . **74** A4
Ebenezer St
Bradford BD1 . . . . **201** C2
6 Pudsey LS28 . . . . **57** D3
Rothwell WF3 . . . . **100** B3
Ebony View BD22 . . . . **35** A4
Ebor Ct 14 BD21 . . . . **35** B6
Ebor Gardens Prim Sch
LS9 . . . . **212** C4
Ebor Gdns WF14 . . . . **137** F5
Ebor La BD22 . . . . **51** D8
Ebor Mount
Kippax LS25 . . . . **83** A2
Leeds LS6 . . . . **205** C2
Ebor Pl LS6 . . . . **205** C2
Ebor St LS6 . . . . **205** C2
Ebor Terr LS10 . . . . **215** B2
Ebridge Ct 20 BD16 . . . . **37** A3
Ebson House La HD9 . . . . . **190** B6
Ebury St WF17 . . . . **118** D6
Ebury St WF17 . . . . **118** D6
Ecclesburn Ave LS9 . . . . . . **80** A7
Ecclesburn Rd LS9 . . . . **80** A7
Ecclesburn St LS9 . . . . **80** A7
Ecclesburn Terr 12 LS9 . . **80** A7
Eccles Ct BD2 . . . . **56** B4
Eccleshill Com Hospl
BD10 . . . . **56** E5
Eccles Parlour HX6 . . . . . . **132** A7
Eccup La
Bramhope LS16 . . . . **25** F2
Harewood LS16 . . . . **26** A5
Eccup Moor Rd LS16 . . . . . . **42** E8
Echo St WF15 . . . . **116** F2
Edale Ave HD4 . . . . **153** F1
Edale Cl HD5 . . . . **137** B1
Edale Gr BD13 . . . . **92** C8
Edale Way LS16 . . . . **41** F3
Eddercliffe Cres WF15 . . . **117** A6
Edderthorpe St BD3 . . . . . . **75** A6
Eddison Cl LS16 . . . . **42** D5
Eddison St LS28 . . . . **57** D2
Eddison Wlk LS16 . . . . **42** D5
Eddystone Rise WF11 . . . . **126** D3
Edelshain Gr WF2 . . . . **160** F8
Eden Ave
Ossett WF5 . . . . **140** D6
Wakefield WF2 . . . . **141** D5
Eden Cl BD2 . . . . **94** D3
Eden Cres LS4 . . . . **59** B4
Edendale WF10 . . . . **124** F8
Eden Dr LS4 . . . . **59** C4
Eden Gdns LS4 . . . . **59** B3
Eden Gr LS4 . . . . **59** B3

Eden Mount LS4 . . . . **59** B3
Eden Rd LS4 . . . . **59** B4
Edensor Rd BD21 . . . . **35** A7
Eden Way LS4 . . . . **59** B3
Eden Wlk LS4 . . . . **59** B3
Ederoyd Ave LS28 . . . . **57** B1
Ederoyd Cres LS28 . . . . **57** B1
Ederoyd Dr LS28 . . . . **57** B1
Ederoyd Gr LS28 . . . . **57** B1
Ederoyd Mount LS28 . . . . . **57** B1
Ederoyd Rise LS28 . . . . **57** A1
Edgar St BD14 . . . . **73** D3
Edgbaston Cl LS17 . . . . **43** A6
Edgbaston Wlk LS17 . . . . . . **43** A6
Edge Ave WF12 . . . . **139** D1
Edgebank Ave BD6 . . . . **93** F6
Edge Cl
Dewsbury WF12 . . . . **139** E1
Huddersfield HD7 . . . . **152** E4
Edgecumbe House
Apartments HX1 . . . . **203** B1
Edge End BD13 . . . . **52** E1
Edge End Gdns 1 BD6 . . . . **93** E7
Edge End La BD13 . . . . **188** A4
Edge End Rd BD6 . . . . **93** E7
Edgefield Gr HX3 . . . . **113** A3
Edgehey Gn HX7 . . . . **88** B6
Edgehill Cl 7 BD13 . . . . **72** F1
Edge Hill Cl HD5 . . . . **154** D7
Edgeholme La HX2 . . . . **112** B7
Edge Junc WF12 . . . . **139** D1
Edge La
Dewsbury WF12 . . . . **139** E1
Heptonstall HX7 . . . . **87** F7
Edgemoor Cl
Bradford BD4 . . . . **95** E8
Halifax HX3 . . . . **113** B4
Edgemoor Rd
Crigglestone WF4 . . . . **159** F2
Honley HD9 . . . . **171** E3
Edge Rd WF12 . . . . **139** F1
Edgerton Gn HD1 . . . . **153** E7
Edgerton Grove Rd HD1 . . **153** E7
Edgerton La HD1 . . . . **153** E7
Edgerton Rd
Huddersfield HD1 . . . . **153** E8
Leeds LS16 . . . . **59** B8
Edge Terr HD3 . . . . **152** F7
Edge Top Rd WF12 . . . . **139** C2
Edge View
Dewsbury WF12 . . . . **139** E1
Huddersfield HD7 . . . . **152** E4
Edgeware Rd HD5 . . . . **155** A6
Edgware Ave LS8 . . . . **207** C2
Edgware Gr LS8 . . . . **207** C2
Edgware Mount LS8 . . . . . **207** C2
Edgware Pl LS8 . . . . **207** C2
Edgware Row LS8 . . . . **207** C2
Edgware St LS8 . . . . **207** B2
Edgware Terr LS8 . . . . **207** C2
Edgware View LS8 . . . . **207** C2
Edinburgh Ave LS12 . . . . . **209** A4
Edinburgh Gr LS12 . . . . . . **209** A4
Edinburgh Pl
Garforth LS25 . . . . **83** B7
Leeds LS12 . . . . **209** A4
Edinburgh Rd LS12 . . . . . . **209** A4
Edinburgh Terr LS12 . . . . . **209** A4
Edith's View 10 HX6 . . . . . . **112** B4
Edlington Cl BD4 . . . . **75** E3
Edmonton Pl LS7 . . . . **204** A2
Edmund St
Bradford BD5 . . . . **201** A2
Todmorden OL14 . . . . **129** A8
Edna St WF9 . . . . **183** A4
Edrich Cl BD12 . . . . **94** E6
Edroyd Pl LS28 . . . . **57** D3
Edroyd St LS28 . . . . **57** D3
Edson Cl BD6 . . . . **93** E8
Education Rd LS7 . . . . **206** C3
Edward Cl
Dewsbury WF12 . . . . **139** B3
Halifax HX3 . . . . **114** A4
Edward Ct WF2 . . . . **120** E5
Edward Dr WF1 . . . . **121** C5
Edward Rd WF14 . . . . **137** F5
Edwards Rd HX2 . . . . **202** A1
Edward St
18 Bacup OL13 . . . . **106** A3
Bradford BD4 . . . . **201** C2
Bradford, Tong Street BD4 . . **75** D4
Brighouse HD6 . . . . **115** C2
Brighouse, Waring Green
HD6 . . . . **115** A3
Hebden Bridge HX7 . . . . **89** A3
Leeds LS2 . . . . **211** C4
Liversedge, Knowler Hill
WF15 . . . . **117** A4
Liversedge, Littletown
WF15 . . . . **117** A5
Normanton WF6 . . . . **123** A5
4 Shipley BD18 . . . . **37** F1
Sowerby Bridge HX6 . . . . . . **112** B4
Wakefield WF1 . . . . **216** C3
Edward Turner Cl 1
BD12 . . . . **94** C6
Edwin Ave LS20 . . . . **22** D1
Edwin Rd LS6 . . . . **205** C2
Eelholme View St BD20 . . **18** B2
Eel Mires Garth LS22 . . . . . **13** F6
Effingham Rd BD16 . . . . **36** A1
Egerton Gr BD15 . . . . **54** A1
Egerton St 11 HX6 . . . . . . **112** B4
Egerton Terr LS19 . . . . **40** D3
Eggleston Dr BD4 . . . . **75** F2
Egglestone Sq LS23 . . . . . . **30** C7

Eggleston St LS13 . . . . **57** F5
Egham Gn BD10 . . . . **56** B7
Egmanton Rd S71 . . . . **178** F1
Egremont Cres BD6 . . . . **93** F6
Egremont St HX6 . . . . **112** A3
Egremont Terr HX6 . . . . . . **112** A3
Egypt Rd BD13 . . . . **72** C8
Eider Cl BD6 . . . . **73** C1
Eiffel Bldgs HX7 . . . . **89** A3
Eiffel St HX7 . . . . **89** A3
Eighth Ave
Cleckheaton WF15 . . . . **116** B5
Leeds LS12 . . . . **210** B2
Rothwell LS26 . . . . **101** A7
Eightlands Ave LS13 . . . . . . **58** D2
Eightlands La LS13 . . . . **58** D2
Eightlands Rd WF13 . . . . . **139** C8
Ekota Pl LS8 . . . . **207** C4
Elam Wood Rd BD20 . . . . . . **18** C3
Eland Ho 8 HX5 . . . . **134** F7
Elba LS12 . . . . **210** C3
Elba Terr WF4 . . . . **141** B3
Elbow La
Bradford BD2 . . . . **56** B2
Halifax HX2 . . . . **90** E1
Elder Ave
Upton WF9 . . . . **183** C8
Wakefield WF2 . . . . **142** A7
Elder Bank
Cullingworth BD13 . . . . **52** D6
8 Queensbury BD13 . . . . . . **92** C8
Elderberry Cl BD20 . . . . **19** B1
Elderberry Dr HX3 . . . . **113** E4
Elder Cl WF17 . . . . **96** F2
Elder Croft LS13 . . . . **58** C1
Elder Dr
Dewsbury WF12 . . . . **139** D3
Upton WF9 . . . . **183** C8
Elder Garth LS25 . . . . **83** B6
Elder Gn WF2 . . . . **142** A7
Elder Gr
Huddersfield HD4 . . . . **171** D6
Wakefield WF2 . . . . **142** A7
Elder Grove Mews HD4 . . **171** D6
Elder La HD2 . . . . **137** A5
Elder Lea HX2 . . . . **72** A1
Elder Mews HD8 . . . . **173** F3
Elder Mount 1 LS13 . . . . . . **58** C1
Elder Pl 2 LS13 . . . . **58** C1
Elder Rd LS13 . . . . **58** C1
Elder Rise LS26 . . . . **101** E7
Elder St
Bradford BD10 . . . . **56** E7
Keighley BD20 . . . . **18** A3
8 Leeds LS13 . . . . **58** C1
Elder Way S72 . . . . **180** E6
Elderwood Gdns BD10 . . . . **56** E5
Eldon Ct LS2 . . . . **206** B2
Eldon Ho 30 BD16 . . . . **37** A3
Eldon Mount 15 LS20 . . . . . **22** E1
Eldon Pl
Bradford BD1 . . . . **201** A4
Bradford, Cutler Heights
BD4 . . . . **75** D4
Cleckheaton BD19 . . . . **116** E7
Eldon Rd HD1 . . . . **153** D7
Eldon St
Batley WF16 . . . . **117** D4
Halifax HX3 . . . . **203** B4
Ossett WF5 . . . . **140** F4
Todmorden OL14 . . . . **108** C5
Eldon Terr BD1 . . . . **201** A4
Eldroth Mount 16 HX1 . . . **202** C1
Eldroth Rd HX1 . . . . **202** C1
Eldwick Beck BD16 . . . . **37** D6
Eldwick Croft BD16 . . . . **37** C5
Eldwick Prim Sch BD16 . . . **37** C4
Eleanor Dr BD10, LS28 . . . . **56** F7
Eleanor St
Brighouse HD6 . . . . **115** A1
2 Huddersfield HD1 . . . . . . **154** A8
Electron Ho LS12 . . . . **209** A4
Eleventh Ave WF15 . . . . . . **116** C5
Elford Gr LS8 . . . . **207** C3
Elford Pl E LS8 . . . . **207** C3
Elford Pl W LS8 . . . . **207** C3
Elford Rd LS8 . . . . **207** C3
Elgar Wlk WF3 . . . . **121** E6
Elgin Cl HD4 . . . . **153** C2
Elia St BD21 . . . . **35** D8
Elim Wlk 5 WF13 . . . . **139** C8
Elinor Lupton Ctr (Leeds
Girls High Sch) LS6 . . . . **205** B4
Eliot Gr LS20 . . . . **39** F8
Eliots Ct WF10 . . . . **125** C5
Eli St BD5 . . . . **74** F3
Elizabethan Ct WF8 . . . . . **125** E2
Elizabeth Ave
Bradford BD12 . . . . **94** D4
South Hiendley S72 . . . . **180** E5
Elizabeth Cl BD12 . . . . **94** D4
Elizabeth Cres BD12 . . . . . . **94** D4
Elizabeth Ct
Castleford WF10 . . . . **125** C8
7 Collingham LS22 . . . . **29** B8
Hemsworth WF9 . . . . **181** F6
Elizabeth Dr
Bradford BD12 . . . . **94** D4
Castleford WF10 . . . . **125** D8
Knottingley WF11 . . . . **126** C4
Elizabeth Gdns WF1 . . . . . **216** B4
Elizabeth Gr LS27 . . . . **98** C5
Elizabeth Pl 2 LS14 . . . . **62** A5
Elizabeth St
18 Bingley BD16 . . . . **37** A3
Bradford BD5 . . . . **201** B1
Bradford, New Road Side
BD12 . . . . **94** D4

Elizabeth St continued
Halifax HX5 . . . . **134** F6
1 Elland, West Vale HX4 . **134** D7
Huddersfield HD4 . . . . **154** A3
Keighley BD21 . . . . **35** F7
Leeds LS6 . . . . **205** B3
Liversedge FW15 . . . . **116** A4
Oakworth BD22 . . . . **34** D3
Wakefield WF1 . . . . **142** E2
Elland Bridge HX5 . . . . **134** F7
Elland CE Jun & Inf Sch
HX5 . . . . **134** F7
Elland Hall Farm Cvn Pk
HX5 . . . . **134** E7
Elland Hospl HX5 . . . . **135** A7
Elland La HX5 . . . . **135** A7
Elland Rd
Brighouse HD6, HX5 . . . . . . **114** C2
Leeds LS11 . . . . **213** B3
Morley LS11, LS27 . . . . **98** C8
Ripponden HX6 . . . . **132** C4
Elland Riorges Link HX5 . **135** A7
Elland Road Ind Pk LS11 **213** A3
Elland Road Stadium (Leeds
Utd FC) LS11 . . . . **213** B3
Elland St WF10 . . . . **103** E1
Elland Way LS11 . . . . **213** A3
Elland Wood Bottom HX5,
HX5 . . . . **113** D1
Ellar Carr Rd
Bradford BD10 . . . . **39** C1
Cullingworth BD13 . . . . **52** C7
Ellar Gdns LS29 . . . . **22** B6
Ella St WF9 . . . . **183** A4
Ellen Holme Cotts HX2 . . . **111** D5
Ellen Royd La HX2 . . . . **111** C8
Ellen Royd St HX3 . . . . **203** B4
Ellen St 18 BD16 . . . . **37** A3
Ellenthorpe Rd BD17 . . . . . . **37** E2
Ellerburn Dr BD6 . . . . **93** E8
Ellerby La LS9 . . . . **212** B2
Ellerby Rd LS9 . . . . **212** B3
Ellercroft Ave BD7 . . . . **74** A6
Ellercroft Rd BD7 . . . . **74** A6
Ellercroft Terr BD7 . . . . **74** A6
Ellerker La LS14 . . . . **46** B5
Ellerker Rd LS14 . . . . **46** A6
Ellers Gr LS8 . . . . **207** C4
Ellerslie Ct HD2 . . . . **153** E8
Ellers Rd
Leeds LS8 . . . . **207** C4
Sutton-in-C BD20 . . . . **16** D4
Ellerton St BD3 . . . . **75** C7
Ellicott Ct LS29 . . . . **22** A4
Ellin's Terr WF6 . . . . **144** A8
Ellingham Ct 9 BD13 . . . . . **72** E6
Ellinthorpe St BD4 . . . . **75** B5
Elliot Ct 11 BD13 . . . . **72** D1
Elliotsdale St WF7 . . . . **145** C6
Elliott St
Shipley BD18 . . . . **55** A8
Silsden BD20 . . . . **5** D1
Ellis Fold LS12 . . . . **209** B3
Ellis La LS25 . . . . **63** E3
Ellison St
7 Halifax HX3 . . . . **92** A1
Huddersfield HD4 . . . . **153** D4
Ellis St BD5 . . . . **74** D3
Ellis Terr 12 LS6 . . . . **59** D6
Elliston Ave S75 . . . . **178** C1
Ellistones Gdns HX4 . . . . . **134** A7
Ellistones La HX4 . . . . **134** A6
Ellistones Pl HX4 . . . . **134** A6
Ellmont Ave HD8 . . . . **175** D7
Ellton Gr 4 BD6 . . . . **74** A1
Ellwood Cl LS6 . . . . **59** F7
Elm Apartments WF1 . . . . **216** C4
Elm Ave
Holmfirth HD9 . . . . **189** C8
Kippax LS25 . . . . **82** F3
Lofthouse Gate WF3 . . . . . . **121** F4
Sowerby Bridge HX6 . . . . . . **112** B5
Todmorden OL14 . . . . **108** B6
Elmbridge Cl S71 . . . . **179** E3
Elm Cl
Darrington WF8 . . . . **147** C5
Ossett WF5 . . . . **140** E3
Pontefract WF8 . . . . **125** E2
Elm Cres
East Morton BD20 . . . . **36** D8
Fitzwilliam WF9 . . . . **163** B2
Elm Croft LS14 . . . . **62** C8
Elm Ct
Birkenshaw BD11 . . . . **96** B4
Kirkburton HD8 . . . . **173** F7
Wilsden BD15 . . . . **53** C4
Elmet Dr LS15 . . . . **63** E7
Elmete Ave
Barwick in E LS15 . . . . **62** F6
Leeds LS8 . . . . **61** D6
Elmete Cl LS8 . . . . **61** D6
Elmete Croft LS15 . . . . **62** F6
Elmete Ct LS8 . . . . **61** C6
Elmete Dr LS8 . . . . **61** D6
Elmete Gr LS8 . . . . **61** C7
Elmete Grange LS29 . . . . . . **22** A4
Elmete Hill LS8 . . . . **61** D6
Elmete La LS8 . . . . **61** D8
Elmete Mount LS8 . . . . **61** D6
Elmete Rd WF10 . . . . **104** D1
Elmete Way LS8 . . . . **61** D6
Elmete Wlk LS8 . . . . **61** D8
Elmete Wood Sch LS8 . . . . . **61** D8
Elmet Rd LS15 . . . . **63** E6
Elmet Twrs LS14 . . . . **62** C4
Elmfield
Baildon BD17 . . . . **38** D3
Rothwell LS26 . . . . **101** C5

Elmfield Ave HD3 . . . . **152** F
Elmfield Bsns Pk LS25 . . . . **83** A
Elmfield Ct
Birkenshaw BD11 . . . . **96** A
Morley LS27 . . . . **98** B
Elmfield Dr
Bradford BD6 . . . . **94** D
Skelmanthorpe HD8 . . . . . . **175** A
Elmfield Gr LS12 . . . . **210** A
Elmfield Ho LS27 . . . . **98** B
Elmfield Pl LS12 . . . . **210** A
Elmfield Rd
Glusburn BD20 . . . . **16** E
Huddersfield HD2 . . . . **135** E
Leeds LS12 . . . . **210** A
Morley LS27 . . . . **98** B
Elmfield Terr
Halifax HX1 . . . . **203** A
3 Huddersfield HD5 . . . . . . **154** D
Elmfield Way LS13 . . . . **58** D
Elm Gdns
Castleford WF10 . . . . **125** D
Halifax HX3 . . . . **203** B
Elm Gr
Burley in W LS29 . . . . **21** F
Cleckheaton BD19 . . . . **117** A
East Morton BD20 . . . . **36** D
Horbury WF4 . . . . **141** B
Keighley, Ingrow BD21 . . . . **35** B
Liversedge WF16 . . . . **117** C
Shelf HX3 . . . . **93** D
Shipley BD18 . . . . **55** E
Silsden BD20 . . . . **5** D
South Elmsall WF9 . . . . **182** F
Elm Ho LS15 . . . . **80** E
Elmhurst Cl LS17 . . . . **44** B
Elmhurst Gdns LS17 . . . . . . **44** A
Elmhurst Gr WF11 . . . . **126** F
Elm Mews WF4 . . . . **141** B
Elmore Terr BD20 . . . . **16** E
Elm Pk WF8 . . . . **146** C
Elm Pl
Knottingley WF11 . . . . **126** E
19 Sowerby Bridge HX6 . . **112** B
Elm Rd
Dewsbury WF13 . . . . **138** F
Hemsworth WF9 . . . . **181** E
Normanton WF6 . . . . **144** B
Shipley BD18 . . . . **55** D
Sutton-in-C BD20 . . . . **16** C
Elmroyd LS26 . . . . **100** F
Elmsall Dr WF9 . . . . **183** C
Elmsall La DN5, DN6 . . . . . **195** C
Elmsall Way WF9 . . . . **183** C
Elms Ct HX2 . . . . **91** E
Elmsdale Cl WF9 . . . . **183** B
Elmsham Fold WF9 . . . . . . **181** E
Elms Hill HD7 . . . . **169** F
Elmsley St BD20 . . . . **17** C
Elm St
6 Bacup OL13 . . . . **106** A
Crofton WF4 . . . . **162** B
Elland HX4 . . . . **134** A
Huddersfield HD4 . . . . **154** B
Leeds LS6 . . . . **206** B
Oxenhope BD22 . . . . **51** C
Skelmanthorpe HD8 . . . . . . **175** A
Elms The
Ackworth M T WF7 . . . . **163** F
Guiseley LS20 . . . . **22** E
Elms View HD7 . . . . **169** F
Elm Terr
Brighouse HD6 . . . . **115** B
Otley LS21 . . . . **23** C
1 Pontefract WF8 . . . . **146** C
Elmton Cl
Leeds LS10 . . . . **99** D
Leeds LS10 . . . . **99** E
Elm Tree Ave BD6 . . . . **94** C
Elm Tree Cl
Batley WF15 . . . . **117** C
Bradford BD6 . . . . **94** D
Keighley BD21 . . . . **35** D
Leeds LS15 . . . . **81** E
Elm Tree Gdns BD6 . . . . **94** C
Elmtree La LS10 . . . . **215** A
Elm Tree St WF1 . . . . **142** F
Elm View
3 Halifax HX3 . . . . **113** C
Steeton BD20 . . . . **17** B
Elm Way WF17 . . . . **97** A
Elm Wlk S63 . . . . **194** D
Elmwood Ave
Barwick in E LS15 . . . . **63** D
4 Huddersfield HD1 . . . . . **154** A
Walton WF2 . . . . **161** B
Elmwood Chase LS15 . . . . . **63** D
Elmwood Cl
5 Huddersfield HD1 . . . . . **154** A
Mirfield WF14 . . . . **137** F
Walton WF2 . . . . **161** B
Elmwood Ct LS15 . . . . **63** D
Elmwood Dr
Brighouse HD6 . . . . **114** F
Keighley BD22 . . . . **35** A
Walton WF2 . . . . **161** B
Elmwood Garth WF2 . . . . . **161** B
Elmwood Gr
Batley WF17 . . . . **118** D
Horbury WF4 . . . . **141** C
Elmwood La
Barwick in E LS15 . . . . **63** D
Leeds LS2 . . . . **206** C
Elmwood Pl BD2 . . . . **56** C
Elmwood Rd
Keighley BD22 . . . . **34** F
Leeds LS2 . . . . **206** C
Elmwood St HX1 . . . . **202** C

Elm Wood St HD6 . . . . 115 B4
Elmwood Terr
Dewsbury WF13 . . . . 118 C1
Keighley BD22 . . . . 34 F4
Elphaborough Cl HX7 . . . 110 E8
Elphin Ct HX7 . . . . 110 D8
Elsdon Gr BD5 . . . . 201 B1
Elsham Terr LS4 . . . . 59 C2
Elsicker La WF1 . . . . 143 F6
Elsie St BD20 . . . . 18 B2
Elsinore Ave HX5 . . . . 134 F5
Elsinore Ct HX5 . . . . 134 E6
Elston Dr BD20 . . . . 36 B8
Elstone View WF1 . . . . 121 A4
Elsworth Ave BD3 . . . . 56 D1
Elsworth Ho LS13 . . . . 58 F3
Elsworth St LS12 . . . . 210 A3
Elsworth Terr LS12 . . . . . . 210 A3
Eltham Cl LS6 . . . . 206 B3
Eltham Ct 4 LS6 . . . . 206 B3
Eltham Dr LS6 . . . . 206 B3
Eltham Gdns LS6 . . . . 206 B3
Eltham Gr BD6 . . . . 94 A8
Eltham Rise LS6 . . . . 206 B3
Elvaston Rd LS27 . . . . 98 A3
Elvey Cl BD2 . . . . 56 D4
Elvey St WF1 . . . . 216 B3
Elwell Cl HX3 . . . . 93 D7
Elwell St WF3 . . . . 99 E1
Elwyn Gr BD5 . . . . 74 E3
Elwyn Rd BD5 . . . . 74 F3
Ely St
Elland HX4 . . . . 134 D6
Leeds LS12 . . . . 209 C4
Embankment The
Leeds LS1 . . . . 211 C3
Mirfield WF14 . . . . 138 A5
Embassy Ct LS8 . . . . 61 A5
Emblem Ct BD13 . . . . 92 D8
Emblem Terr WF1 . . . . 142 D3
Embleton Rd LS26 . . . . 123 C8
Embsay & Bolton Abbey Steam Rly★ BD23 . . . . 1 C7
Emerald St
Batley WF17 . . . . 118 B6
Huddersfield HD1 . . . . 154 B8
Keighley BD22 . . . . 35 A4
Emerson Ave BD9 . . . . 54 D3
Emily Ct BD7 . . . . 74 B3
Emily Hall Gdns BD15 . . . . 53 C5
Emily St
9 Haworth BD22 . . . . 51 D7
Keighley BD21 . . . . 35 D8
South Kirkby WF9 . . . . 182 D3
Emily Way HX1 . . . . 203 B1
Emley Fst Sch HD8 . . . . . . 175 D7
Emley Moor Bsns Pk HD8 . . . . 175 B6
Emley View LS25 . . . . 82 F3
Emmanuel Terr HD4 . . . . 153 F2
Emmanuel Trad Est LS12 . . . . 210 C2
Emmeline Cl BD10 . . . . 56 B8
Emmet Cl BD11 . . . . 96 B5
Emmfield Dr BD9 . . . . 55 A4
Emm La BD9 . . . . 55 B3
Emmott Dr LS19 . . . . 40 E3
Emmott Farm Fold 3 BD22 . . . . 51 C6
Emmot View LS19 . . . . 40 E3
Empire Ho WF9 . . . . 182 F3
Empire Terr S71 . . . . 179 D4
Empsall Row 4 HD6 . . . . . 115 B3
Emscote Ave HX1 . . . . 202 C1
Emscote Gdns HX1 . . . . . . 202 C1
Emscote Gr HX1 . . . . 202 C1
Emscote Pl HX1 . . . . 202 C1
Emscote St S HX1 . . . . 202 C1
Emsley Cl BD4 . . . . 95 B8
Emsley Ho 2 BD16 . . . . 37 A2
Emsley Pl LS10 . . . . 212 B1
Emville Ave LS17 . . . . 44 C5
Endecliff Mews LS6 . . . . . . 206 A4
Enderby Cl HX3 . . . . 91 F3
Enderley Rd 8 BD13 . . . . . . 72 D6
Endor Cres LS29 . . . . 21 F7
Endor Gr LS29 . . . . 21 F7
Endsleigh Pl 5 BD14 . . . . . 73 B4
Enfield LS19 . . . . 40 B6
Enfield Ave LS7 . . . . 207 B2
Enfield Cl WF17 . . . . 117 F6
Enfield Dr
Batley WF17 . . . . 117 F6
Bradford BD6 . . . . 74 A1
Enfield Par BD6 . . . . 74 A1
Enfield Rd BD17 . . . . 38 C2
Enfield Side Rd BD22 . . . . . 50 E5
Enfield St
Keighley BD21 . . . . 35 B7
Leeds LS7 . . . . 207 A2
Enfield Terr LS7 . . . . 207 B2
Enfield Wlk BD6 . . . . 74 A1
Engine Ho The LS9 . . . . . . 212 A3
Engine La
Horbury WF4 . . . . 140 F1
Shafton S72 . . . . 180 D1
West Hardwick WF4 . . . . . 163 A7
Engine Lane Cl S72 . . . . . . 180 D1
England La WF11 . . . . 126 F3
England La Crossing WF11 . . . . 126 F3
England Lane Jun & Inf Sch WF11 . . . . 126 F3
Englefield Cl 10 BD4 . . . . . 75 E2
Englefield Cres BD4 . . . . . . 75 E2
English Martyrs' RC Prim Sch WF2 . . . . 141 D5
Ennerdale Ave WF12 . . . . 118 E2
Ennerdale Cl LS22 . . . . 13 C6
Ennerdale Cres WF12 . . . 118 E2
Ennerdale Dr
Bradford BD2 . . . . 56 B3
Elland HX5 . . . . 135 B7
Knottingley WF11 . . . . 126 E2
Ennerdale Rd
Batley WF12 . . . . 118 E2
Bradford BD2 . . . . 56 B3
Gildersome LS12 . . . . 77 D2
Wakefield WF2 . . . . 141 F7
Ennerdale Way LS12 . . . . . . 77 D3
Enoch La HD4 . . . . 153 F3
Enterprise Ct
Bradford BD4 . . . . 75 C1
Micklefield LS25 . . . . 84 A6
Enterprise Park Ind Est LS11 . . . . 213 C1
Enterprise Way
Bradford BD10 . . . . 56 B6
Castleford WF10 . . . . 124 C8
Middleton LS10 . . . . 215 C1
Skipton BD23 . . . . 4 A7
Envoy St LS11 . . . . 214 C4
Epsom Gr HX3 . . . . 113 E5
Epsom Rd LS25 . . . . 82 F2
Epsom Way HD5 . . . . 137 C1
Epworth Pl
Leeds LS10 . . . . 215 B4
Oakworth BD22 . . . . 34 B3
Equilibrium HD3 . . . . 153 B8
Eric St
Keighley BD21 . . . . 35 C8
Leeds LS13 . . . . 58 C5
South Elmsall WF9 . . . . . . 183 A3
Ernest St
8 Dewsbury WF13 . . . . . . 139 D8
Todmorden OL14 . . . . 86 C1
Erringden Rd HX7 . . . . 89 D1
Erringden St 12 OL14 . . . . 108 C5
Escroft Cl BD12 . . . . 94 D1
Eshald La LS26 . . . . 101 D6
Eshald Mans 5 LS26 . . . . 101 D6
Eshald Pl LS26 . . . . 101 D6
Esholt Ave LS20 . . . . 39 D7
Esholt La
Baildon BD17 . . . . 38 F4
Guiseley BD17 . . . . 39 A4
Esholt Lane Cvn Site BD17 . . . . 39 A4
Eshton Ave BD12 . . . . 94 F5
Eshton Ct S75 . . . . 178 A2
Esk Ave WF10 . . . . 125 B8
Eskdale Ave
Normanton WF6 . . . . 123 A4
Shelf HX3 . . . . 93 B5
Eskdale Cl
Batley WF12 . . . . 118 E3
Guiseley LS20 . . . . 39 E8
Normanton WF6 . . . . 123 A4
Eskdale Croft
Guiseley LS20 . . . . 39 E8
Normanton WF6 . . . . 123 A4
Eskdale Ct WF6 . . . . 123 A4
Eskdale Gr LS25 . . . . 83 A5
Eskdale Mount HX7 . . . . . . 89 A4
Eskdale Rd WF2 . . . . 141 E7
Eskdale Rise BD15 . . . . 73 C8
Esk Gdns LS22 . . . . 13 E8
Eskine Par BD6 . . . . 93 F6
Esmond St
3 Bradford BD7 . . . . 73 F3
Leeds LS12 . . . . 209 C3
Esmond Terr LS12 . . . . 209 C3
Essex Park Ind Est BD4 . . 201 D2
Essex St
Bradford BD4 . . . . 201 D1
Halifax HX1 . . . . 202 B2
1 Hebden Bridge HX7 . . . . 89 A2
Estcourt Ave LS6 . . . . 59 C4
Estcourt Dr WF8 . . . . 147 D4
Estcourt Gr BD7 . . . . 74 A5
Estcourt Rd
Bradford BD7 . . . . 74 A5
Darrington WF8 . . . . 147 C5
Estcourt Terr LS6 . . . . 59 C4
Esther Ave WF2 . . . . 141 F4
Esther Gr WF2 . . . . 141 F5
Esthwaite Gdns LS15 . . . . . 80 E6
Eston Grange LS26 . . . . . . 101 D6
Ethel St
Keighley BD20 . . . . 18 B1
Sutton-in-C BD20 . . . . 16 D4
Etna St BD7 . . . . 73 F3
Eton Ave HD5 . . . . 154 F6
Eton St
Halifax HX1 . . . . 202 B3
Hebden Bridge HX7 . . . . 88 F3
Eton Terr HX7 . . . . 110 F8
Euden Edge Rd HD7 . . . . . 152 A3
Eunice La HD8 . . . . 191 C6
Eureka! The Mus for Children★ HX1 . . . . 203 C2
Eurocam Tech Pk BD5 . . . . 74 E2
Euroway Trad Est BD4 . . . . 95 A7
Euston Gr LS11 . . . . 213 C4
Euston Mount LS11 . . . . . . 213 C4
Euston Terr LS11 . . . . 213 C4
Evanston Ave LS4 . . . . 59 C1
Evans Twrs 8 BD5 . . . . 201 B1
Evelyn Ave BD3 . . . . 75 E8
Evelyn Pl LS12 . . . . 209 C2
Evelyn Terr BD13 . . . . 72 C2
Evens Terr BD5 . . . . 74 E2
Everard St HD4 . . . . 153 D4
Everdale Mount
Hemsworth WF9 . . . . 181 C6
South Elmsall WF9 . . . . . . 182 E3
Everest Ave BD18 . . . . 55 E7
Evergreen Wlk BD16 . . . . . . 36 E5
Everleigh St LS9 . . . . 80 A7
Eversley Dr BD4 . . . . 75 E4
Eversley Mount HX2 . . . . . 202 A2
Eversley Pl HX2 . . . . 202 A2
Eversley Rd HX7 . . . . 89 A4
Eversley View LS14 . . . . 45 C7
Every St 9 OL14 . . . . 108 C5
Evesham Gr BD10 . . . . 56 B7
Ewart Pl BD7 . . . . 74 A3
Ewart St
Bradford BD7 . . . . 74 A3
Queensbury BD13 . . . . 72 E1
Ewood Cotts HX7 . . . . 90 A1
Ewood Dr HX7 . . . . 90 A1
Ewood Hall Ave HX7 . . . . . 89 F1
Ewood La OL14 . . . . 107 F6
Excalibur Dr WF9 . . . . 183 A2
Excelsior Cl HX6 . . . . 132 C3
Excelsior Mill HX6 . . . . . . 132 D3
Exchange HD9 . . . . 171 F5
Exchange Bldgs BD20 . . . . 16 D7
Exchange Ct BD19 . . . . 95 D1
Exchange St
Cleckheaton BD19 . . . . 95 D1
3 Elland HX4 . . . . 134 D6
Normanton WF6 . . . . 123 A2
South Elmsall WF9 . . . . . . 182 F3
Exe St BD5 . . . . 74 C3
Exeter Dr LS10 . . . . 99 E7
Exeter St
Halifax HX3 . . . . 113 D3
Sowerby Bridge HX6 . . . . . 112 C4
Exhibition Rd 7 BD18 . . . . 54 F8
Exley Ave BD21 . . . . 35 A4
Exley Bank HX3 . . . . 113 D2
Exley Bank Top HX3 . . . . . 113 D1
Exley Cres BD21 . . . . 35 A5
Exley Dr BD21 . . . . 35 A5
Exley Gdns HX3 . . . . 113 D2
Exley Gr BD21 . . . . 35 A5
Exley Head View BD22 . . . 34 E8
Exley La
Elland HX5 . . . . 134 E8
Halifax HX5 . . . . 113 E1
Exley Mount
Bradford BD7 . . . . 73 F6
Keighley BD21 . . . . 35 A5
Exley Rd BD21 . . . . 35 A5
Exley St BD22 . . . . 35 A6
Exley Way BD21 . . . . 35 A4
Exmoor St HX1 . . . . 202 B2
Exmouth Pl BD3 . . . . 55 F1
Express Way WF6 . . . . 123 B6
Eyres Ave LS12 . . . . 209 C4
Eyres Gr LS12 . . . . 209 C4
Eyres Mill Side LS12 . . . . . 209 B4
Eyres St LS12 . . . . 209 C4
Eyre St
Batley WF17 . . . . 118 D4
Dewsbury WF12 . . . . 139 B4
Eyres Terr LS12 . . . . 209 C4
Eyrie App LS27 . . . . 98 C3

F

Factory La
Bradford BD4 . . . . 75 B2
Huddersfield HD3 . . . . 153 B4
Factory St BD4 . . . . 75 B2
Fagley Cres BD2 . . . . 56 C2
Fagley Croft BD2 . . . . 56 D2
Fagley Dr BD2 . . . . 56 C2
Fagley La BD2 . . . . 56 D3
Fagley Pl BD2 . . . . 56 C1
Fagley Prim Sch BD2 . . . . . 56 D2
Fagley Rd BD2 . . . . 56 C1
Fagley Terr BD2 . . . . 56 C1
Fair Bank BD18 . . . . 55 C6
Fairbank Rd BD8 . . . . 55 A1
Fairbanks HX6 . . . . 112 C4
Fairbank Terr BD8 . . . . 55 A1
Fairbrook Rd WF2 . . . . 160 A4
Fairburn Com Prim Sch WF11 . . . . 105 A4
Fairburn Ct HX3 . . . . 114 A4
Fairburn Dr LS25 . . . . 83 B6
Fairburn Gdns BD2 . . . . 56 C4
Fairburn Ho 8 LS18 . . . . . . 58 B7
Fairburn Ings Nature Reserve★ WF10 . . . . 104 B4
Fairburn St WF10 . . . . 124 C8
Fairclough Gr HX3 . . . . 91 F3
Fairfax Ave
Birkenshaw BD11 . . . . 97 A5
Bradford BD4 . . . . 75 C1
Featherstone WF7 . . . . 124 C1
Knottingley WF11 . . . . 126 D3
Menston LS29 . . . . 22 A5
Fairfax Cl LS14 . . . . 62 B3
Fairfax Cres
Bradford BD4 . . . . 75 C1
Halifax HX3 . . . . 114 A5
Fairfax Ct LS11 . . . . 214 A3
Fairfax Dr WF8 . . . . 125 D1
Fairfax Flats 9 LS21 . . . . . 23 B7
Fairfax Gdns LS29 . . . . 22 A5
Fairfax Gr LS19 . . . . 39 F7
Fairfax Ho BD1 . . . . 201 C3
Fairfax Rd
Bingley BD16 . . . . 36 F5
Cullingworth BD13 . . . . 52 E7
Leeds LS11 . . . . 214 A3
Menston LS29 . . . . 22 A5
Pontefract WF8 . . . . 146 E8
Fairfax St
Bradford BD4 . . . . 201 C1
Haworth BD22 . . . . 51 D7
Otley LS21 . . . . 23 B7
Silsden BD20 . . . . 5 D1
Fairfax View
Birkenshaw BD4 . . . . 95 F7
Horsforth LS18 . . . . 41 B4
Fairfield
Denholme BD13 . . . . 71 D8
Fairburn WF11 . . . . 105 A5
Hebden Bridge HX7 . . . . 89 A2
Fairfield Ave
Batley WF16 . . . . 117 E5
3 Dewsbury WF12 . . . . . . 139 F8
East Ardsley WF3 . . . . 119 D7
Leeds LS13 . . . . 58 A2
Normanton WF6 . . . . 122 E3
Ossett WF5 . . . . 140 F4
Pontefract WF8 . . . . 146 B8
2 Pudsey LS28 . . . . 76 F8
Fairfield Cl
Castleford WF10 . . . . 104 E1
Leeds LS13 . . . . 58 B2
Ossett WF5 . . . . 140 F4
Rothwell LS26 . . . . 100 B4
Fairfield Cotts S71 . . . . . . 179 F1
Fairfield Cres
8 Dewsbury WF13 . . . . . . 118 A1
Leeds LS13 . . . . 58 B2
Fairfield Ct
Baildon BD17 . . . . 38 E4
Castleford WF10 . . . . 125 A7
Liversedge WF15 . . . . 116 F4
Fairfield Dr
Baildon BD17 . . . . 38 E4
Batley WF16 . . . . 117 E5
Ossett WF5 . . . . 140 F4
Rothwell LS26 . . . . 100 B4
Fairfield Gdns
Ossett WF5 . . . . 140 F5
Rothwell LS26 . . . . 100 B4
Fairfield Gr
Leeds LS13 . . . . 58 B2
Rothwell LS26 . . . . 100 B4
Fairfield Hill LS13 . . . . 58 B2
Fairfield La LS26 . . . . 100 B4
Fairfield Mews 7 WF13 . . 118 A1
Fairfield Mount
Leeds LS13 . . . . 58 B2
Ossett WF5 . . . . 140 F4
Fairfield Par WF16 . . . . . . 117 E5
Fairfield Rd
Batley WF16 . . . . 117 E5
Bradford BD8 . . . . 55 B1
Bradford, Upper Wyke BD12 . . . . 94 D3
Leeds LS13 . . . . 58 A2
Ossett WF5 . . . . 140 F4
Fairfield Rise HD8 . . . . . . 174 A5
Fairfields
Castleford WF10 . . . . 125 E7
Denby Dale HD8 . . . . 191 F3
Fairfield Sch WF16 . . . . . . 117 E5
Fairfield Sq LS13 . . . . 58 B2
Fairfields Rd HD9 . . . . 188 D3
Fairfield St
Bradford BD4 . . . . 75 D1
Leeds LS13 . . . . 58 B2
Fairfield Terr
9 Cleckheaton BD19 . . . . 116 E7
Dewsbury WF12 . . . . 139 F8
Leeds LS13 . . . . 58 B2
Ossett WF5 . . . . 140 E4
Fairfield Wlk WF5 . . . . 140 F4
Fairford Ave LS11 . . . . 214 C3
Fairford Ct 7 BD2 . . . . 56 B3
Fairford Mount LS6 . . . . . . 42 E1
Fairford Terr LS11 . . . . 214 C3
Fairhaven Gn BD10 . . . . 56 C7
Fair Isle Ct BD21 . . . . 35 C7
Fairlands Cl HX2 . . . . 91 F6
Fairlea Ave HD4 . . . . 153 E1
Fairlea Cotts HD4 . . . . 153 E1
Fair Lea Rd HD4 . . . . 153 E1
Fairleigh Cres WF3 . . . . . . 120 A8
Fairleigh Rd WF3 . . . . 120 A8
Fairless Ave HX3 . . . . 115 A7
Fairmoor Way WF16 . . . . . 117 E5
Fairmount BD9 . . . . 55 C2
Fair Mount OL14 . . . . 108 A1
Fairmount Pk BD18 . . . . 54 E7
Fairmount Terr
Dewsbury WF12 . . . . 139 E6
Keighley BD21 . . . . 35 F6
Fair Rd BD6 . . . . 74 B1
Fair St HD1 . . . . 153 F4
Fair View
Ackworth M T WF7 . . . . . . 164 A5
Castleford WF10 . . . . 104 B1
Liversedge WF15 . . . . 116 F5
Morley LS11 . . . . 213 A1
Pontefract WF8 . . . . 146 E5
Fairview Ave WF17 . . . . . . 117 F6
Fairview Cres WF17 . . . . . 118 A6
Fair View Cres OL13 . . . . . 106 B3
Fairview Ct BD17 . . . . 38 B1
Fairview Ho 1 LS22 . . . . . . 13 F6
Fairview Rd WF17 . . . . 118 A6
Fairview Terr HX3 . . . . 92 B1
Fairway
Bradford BD7 . . . . 73 F1
Guiseley LS20 . . . . 22 C1
Normanton WF6 . . . . 123 C1
Shipley BD18 . . . . 54 F7
Yeadon LS19 . . . . 40 A2
Fairway App WF6 . . . . 123 C2
Fairway Ave
Bradford BD7 . . . . 73 F2
Darton S75 . . . . 178 C2
Normanton WF6 . . . . 123 C2
Fairway Cl
Bradford BD7 . . . . 73 F1
Guiseley LS20 . . . . 39 C8
Normanton WF6 . . . . 123 C1
Fairway Cres BD22 . . . . 51 D6
Fairway Dr
Bradford BD7 . . . . 73 F2
Normanton WF6 . . . . 123 C1
Fairway Gdns WF6 . . . . . . 123 C2
Fairway Gr BD7 . . . . 74 A2
Fairway Ind Pk WF17 . . . . . 96 F2
Fairway Mdws WF6 . . . . . 123 C2
Fair Ways WF14 . . . . 137 F2
Fairways Ct WF8 . . . . 147 E4
Fairways The
Keighley BD20 . . . . 18 A3
Shipley BD9 . . . . 54 E5
Fairway The
Featherstone WF7 . . . . 124 D1
Halifax HX2 . . . . 91 F7
Huddersfield HD2 . . . . 136 A4
Leeds LS17 . . . . 43 B6
Pudsey LS28 . . . . 57 B1
Fairway View WF2 . . . . . . 141 F3
Fairway Wlk BD7 . . . . 73 F2
Fairweather Mews BD8 . . 73 E7
Fairy Dell BD16 . . . . 54 B7
Fairy Hill La WF8 . . . . 125 D5
Faith St WF9 . . . . 182 D4
Falcon Cl LS21 . . . . 23 A7
Falcon Cliffe BD20 . . . . 17 D5
Falcon Dr WF10 . . . . 124 C6
Falconer Cl S75 . . . . 177 D1
Falconers Ride HD4 . . . . . 171 E7
Falcon Knowl Ing S75 . . . 177 D1
Falcon Mews
Bradford BD8 . . . . 73 C8
Morley LS27 . . . . 98 C3
Falcon Rd
Bingley BD16 . . . . 36 F5
Dewsbury WF12 . . . . 139 D6
Falcon St
Bradford BD7 . . . . 74 B4
Halifax HX3 . . . . 113 D3
Huddersfield HD4 . . . . 153 F2
Falhouse La WF4 . . . . 156 D7
Falkland Cres LS17 . . . . 43 C1
Falkland Ct 22 BD16 . . . . . 37 A3
Falkland Gdns 1 LS17 . . . 43 D1
Falkland Gr LS17 . . . . 43 C1
Falkland Mount LS17 . . . . . 43 C1
Falkland Rd
Bradford BD10 . . . . 56 E4
Leeds LS17 . . . . 43 C1
Falkland Rise LS17 . . . . 43 C1
Falklands Ct 9 LS17 . . . . . 43 C1
Fall Brow Cl BD14 . . . . 73 A3
Falledge La HD8 . . . . 191 E2
Falling Royd HX7 . . . . 89 C2
Fall Ings Rd WF1 . . . . 142 E4
Fall La
Dewsbury WF13 . . . . 139 B6
East Ardsley WF3 . . . . 120 D8
Liversedge WF15 . . . . 116 D1
Marsden HD7 . . . . 168 F3
Northowram HX3 . . . . 92 D5
Sowerby Bridge HX6 . . . . . 112 D4
Fallow Croft HD2 . . . . 136 F5
Fallowfield Cl BD4 . . . . 95 C8
Fallowfield Dr BD4 . . . . 75 C1
Fallowfield Gdns BD4 . . . . 75 C1
Fallow La BD22 . . . . 34 A6
Fall Park Ct LS13 . . . . 58 D5
Fall Rd WF14 . . . . 137 E8
Fall Spring Gdns HX4 . . . 133 F3
Fall Spring Gn HX4 . . . . . 133 F3
Fallswood Gr LS13 . . . . 58 D4
Fall Wood St BD22 . . . . 51 D6
Falmouth Ave
Bradford BD3 . . . . 55 F1
Normanton WF6 . . . . 123 B3
Falmouth Cres WF6 . . . . . . 123 B3
Falmouth Rd WF6 . . . . 123 B3
Falsgrave Ave BD2 . . . . 56 D2
Faltis Sq BD10 . . . . 56 C6
Fanny Moor Cres HD4 . . . 154 C2
Fanny Moor La HD4 . . . . . 154 C2
Fanny St
Keighley BD21 . . . . 35 B6
3 Shipley BD18 . . . . 37 F1
Faraday Sq 2 HD3 . . . . . . 153 A4
Far Bank HD8 . . . . 174 B3
Farcliffe Pl BD8 . . . . 55 B1
Farcliffe Rd BD8 . . . . 55 B1
Farcliffe Terr BD8 . . . . 55 B1
Far Common Rd WF14 . . . 137 E8
Far Croft HD8 . . . . 156 A2
Far Croft Terr LS12 . . . . . 210 A2
Far Dene HD8 . . . . 173 D8
Fardene St BD20 . . . . 5 D2
Fardew Ct BD16 . . . . 36 F4
Farehill Flats HD4 . . . . 171 F8
Farehill Rd HD4 . . . . 171 F8
Far End La HD9 . . . . 172 A4
Farfield Ave
Batley WF17 . . . . 117 F6
Bradford BD6 . . . . 93 E7
Pudsey LS28 . . . . 57 C3
Far Field Ave HD9 . . . . . . 189 E1
Farfield Cres BD6 . . . . 93 F7

Farfield Ct
Garforth LS25 . . . . **82** D7
Leeds LS17 . . . . **43** E5
Farfield Dr LS28 . . . . **57** C2
Far Field Dr HD9 . . . . . . **189** E1
Farfield Gr
Bradford BD6 . . . . **93** F7
Pudsey LS28 . . . . **57** C3
Far Field La
Holmfirth HD9 . . . . **189** E1
Meltham HD4, HD9 . . . **170** F5
Farfield Rd
Baildon BD17 . . . . **38** D2
Bradford BD6 . . . . **94** A7
Huddersfield HD5 . . . . . **154** F3
Shipley BD18 . . . . **55** A7
Farfield Rise
Brighouse BD19 . . . . . . **115** B6
Pudsey LS28 . . . . **57** C3
Far Fields La HD4 . . . . **171** A5
Farfield St
Bradford BD9 . . . . **55** A2
Cleckheaton BD19 . . . . . **95** D1
Farfield Terr BD9 . . . . . **55** A2
Far La
Hebden Bridge HX2 . . . . **90** A2
Holmfirth HD9 . . . . **189** E1
Far Lawns S71 . . . . **179** D1
Farlea Dr BD2 . . . . **56** C3
Farleton Dr BD2 . . . . . . **56** D3
Farley Cres BD22 . . . . . . **34** B3
Far Low Bank BD22 . . . . **34** B3
Farm Croft WF7 . . . . . **144** E5
Farm Ct LS15 . . . . **62** B2
Far Mead Croft LS29 . . . . **9** E2
Farmfield Dr WF9 . . . . . **163** A3
Farm Gdns WF7 . . . . . **144** A5
Farm Hill Cres LS7 . . . . . **60** A5
Farm Hill Ct BD10 . . . . . **56** B5
Farm Hill Mews LS27 . . . **97** E5
Farm Hill N LS7 . . . . **60** A6
Farm Hill Rd
Bradford BD10 . . . . **56** B6
Morley LS27 . . . . **97** F5
Farm Hill Rise LS7 . . . . . **60** A5
Farm Hill S LS7 . . . . **60** A5
Farm Hill Way LS7 . . . . . **60** A5
Farmhouse Ct HD4 . . . . **153** B2
Farm La WF9 . . . . **163** A3
Farm Mount
Leeds LS15 . . . . **62** C2
Netherton WF4 . . . . . . **158** E6
Far Moss LS17 . . . . **43** A5
Farm Rd
Featherstone WF7 . . . . **145** D5
Leeds LS15 . . . . **62** B2
Farmstead Rd BD10 . . . . **56** C6
Farnboro St OL14 . . . . **108** A2
Farndale App LS14 . . . . . **62** C5
Farndale Cl
Leeds LS14 . . . . **62** C5
Wetherby LS22 . . . . **13** B6
Farndale Ct LS25 . . . . . . **82** F5
Farndale Garth LS14 . . . . **62** C6
Farndale Gdns LS14 . . . . **62** C6
Farndale Pl LS14 . . . . . . **62** C6
Farndale Rd
Baildon BD17 . . . . **38** A2
Wilsden BD15 . . . . **53** C4
Farndale Sq LS14 . . . . . **62** C5
Farndale Terr LS14 . . . . . **62** C6
Farndale View LS14 . . . . **62** C6
Farne Ave WF2 . . . . **141** F6
Farnham Cl
Baildon BD17 . . . . **38** C4
Leeds LS16 . . . . **59** C7
Leeds, Whinmoor LS14 . . . **45** B1
Farnham Croft LS14 . . . . **45** B1
Farnham Prim Sch BD7 . . **74** B5
Farnham Rd BD7 . . . . . . **74** B5
Farnham Way WF4 . . . . **143** F1
Farnlee HD3 . . . . **135** B1
Farnley CE Prim Sch
LS21 . . . . **11** D5
Farnley Cl LS29 . . . . **22** B4
Farnley Cres LS12 . . . . . . **77** E6
Farnley Hey HD4 . . . . . **172** C7
Farnley La LS21 . . . . **11** B3
Farnley Park High Sch
LS12 . . . . **77** E4
Farnley Pk LS21 . . . . **11** E2
Farnley Rd
Kirkburton HD4 . . . . . . **172** F5
Menston LS29 . . . . **22** B4
Farnley Tyas CE Fst Sch
HD4 . . . . **172** F6
Farnley View BD11 . . . . . **97** A6
Faroe LS12 . . . . **211** A3
Farrar Ave WF14 . . . . . **137** F6
Farrar Cl HX5 . . . . **135** B7
Farrar Croft LS16 . . . . . . **42** A4
Farrar Ct LS13 . . . . **58** C3
Farrar Dr WF14 . . . . . . **137** F6
Farrar Gr LS16 . . . . **42** A4
Farrar Height La HX6 . . **132** B4
Farrar La LS16 . . . . **42** A4
Farrar Mill La HX3 . . . . **113** D3
Farra St BD22 . . . . **51** C2
Far Reef Cl LS18 . . . . **41** C2
Farrer La LS26 . . . . **101** C5
Far Richard Cl WF5 . . . . **140** D7
Farriers Croft BD2 . . . . . **55** F4
Farriers Ct
Birkenshaw, Drighlington
BD11 . . . . **96** E6

Farriers Ct continued
Wetherby LS22 . . . . **13** F5
Farriers Pl WF10 . . . . . **125** B6
Farrier Way WF3 . . . . . **100** B3
Farringdon Cl BD4 . . . . . **75** E4
Farringdon Dr ◼ BD4 . . . **75** E3
Farringdon Gr BD4 . . . . . **94** A7
Farringdon Sq BD4 . . . . . **75** E4
Far Row LS21 . . . . **24** C5
Farrow Bank LS12 . . . . . **77** E7
Farrow Gn LS12 . . . . **77** E7
Farrow Hill LS12 . . . . **77** E7
Farrow Rd LS12 . . . . **77** E7
Farrow Vale LS12 . . . . . . **77** E7
Farr Royd LS29 . . . . **9** E2
Farr Royd Terr LS29 . . . . . **9** E2
Farside Gn BD5 . . . . **74** C3
Farsley Farfield Prim Sch
LS28 . . . . **57** C2
Farsley Spring Bank Jun Sch
LS28 . . . . **57** D3
Farsley Westroyd Inf Sch
LS28 . . . . **57** D2
Farthing Ave WF8 . . . . . **146** A7
Fartown LS28 . . . . **76** E5
Fartown Cl LS28 . . . . **76** E5
Fartown Green Rd HD2 . . **136** B2
Fartown High Sch HD2 . . **136** C2
Far View HX2 . . . . **91** E6
Far View Bank HD5 . . . . **154** E4
Far View Cres HD5 . . . . **154** E4
Farway BD4 . . . . **75** E4
Far Well Fold LS19 . . . . . **40** C3
Far Well La HD9 . . . . . . **190** B8
Far Well Rd LS19 . . . . **40** D3
Fascination Pl ◼ BD13 . . **72** C2
Faugh La HX7 . . . . **88** C6
Favell Ave WF6 . . . . . . **123** B1
Faversham Wlk BD4 . . . . **75** E4
Fawcett Ave LS12 . . . . . **209** A1
Fawcett Bank LS12 . . . . **209** A1
Fawcett Cl LS12 . . . . . . **209** A1
Fawcett Dr LS12 . . . . . . **209** A1
Fawcett Gdns LS12 . . . . **209** A1
Fawcett La LS12 . . . . . . **209** A1
Fawcett Pl
Bradford BD4 . . . . **95** C8
Leeds LS12 . . . . **209** A1
Fawcett Rd LS12 . . . . . . **209** A1
Fawcett St WF2 . . . . . . **142** C4
Fawcett Vale LS12 . . . . . **209** A1
Fawcett Way LS12 . . . . **209** A1
Fawkes Dr LS21 . . . . **22** D6
Faxfleet St BD5 . . . . **74** D2
Faye Gdns BD4 . . . . **75** D1
Fearnley Ave WF5 . . . . . **140** D7
Fearnley Cl LS12 . . . . . . **210** A3
Fearnley Croft BD19 . . . **117** B8
Fearnley Ct HD9 . . . . . . **189** D5
Fearnley Dr WF5 . . . . . **140** C7
Fearnley La HD9 . . . . . . **189** C6
Fearnley Pl LS12 . . . . . . **210** A3
Fearnley St
Dewsbury WF13 . . . . . . **139** B7
Featherstone WF7 . . . . **145** C5
Fearnside's Cl ◼◼ WF4 . . **141** A1
Fearnsides St BD8 . . . . . . **74** B8
Fearnsides Terr BD8 . . . . **74** B8
Fearnville Ave LS8 . . . . . **61** D4
Fearnville Cl LS8 . . . . **61** D5
Fearnville Dr
Bradford BD4 . . . . **75** D5
Leeds LS8 . . . . **61** D4
Fearnville Gr
Leeds LS8 . . . . **61** D4
Royston S71 . . . . **179** C3
Fearnville Mount LS8 . . . . **61** D4
Fearnville Pl LS8 . . . . **61** E4
Fearnville Prim Sch BD4 . . **75** D5
Fearnville Sch LS8 . . . . . . **61** D4
Fearnville Terr LS8 . . . . . **61** E4
Fearnville View LS8 . . . . . **61** D4
Feast Field LS18 . . . . **41** B1
Featherbank Ave LS18 . . . **58** B7
Featherbank Ct ◼◼ LS18 . . **58** B7
Featherbank Gr ◼ LS18 . . **58** B8
Featherbank La LS18 . . . . **58** B7
Featherbank Mount ◼
LS18 . . . . **58** B7
Featherbank Terr ◼ LS18 . . **58** B7
Featherbank Wlk ◼ LS18 . . **58** B7
Featherbed Cl ◼ HX4 . . **134** D6
Featherbed La LS24 . . . . . **15** E6
Feather Bed La ◼ HX4 . . **134** D6
Feather Rd BD3 . . . . **75** B7
Feather St BD21 . . . . **35** D6
Featherstone La WF7 . . **145** D7
Featherstone St WF7 . . **145** C6
Featherstone Streethouse
Jun & Inf Sch WF7 . . . . **144** C5
Featherstone Tech Coll
WF7 . . . . **145** F4
Federation St BD5 . . . . . **74** F2
Felbrigg Ave BD22 . . . . . **35** A6
Felcote Ave HD5 . . . . . . **154** E5
Felcourt Dr BD4 . . . . **75** E2
Felcourt Fold BD4 . . . . . . **75** E2
Felkirk Dr WF4 . . . . . . **180** A8
Felkirk View S72 . . . . . **180** B3
Felks Stile Rd HD4 . . . . **153** A1
Fell Cres BD22 . . . . **34** F6
Fell Gr
Huddersfield HD2 . . . . . **136** C4
Keighley BD22 . . . . **34** F6
Fell Greave Cres HD2 . . **136** C4
Fell Greave Rd HD2 . . . **136** C4
Fell La BD22 . . . . **34** F6

Fellowsides La WF5 . . . **140** E5
Fellowsides Mews WF5 . . **140** E5
Fellows The HD4 . . . . . . **171** C7
Fellside OL14 . . . . **109** B5
Fellside Cl BD5 . . . . **74** F2
Fell View OL13 . . . . **106** A8
Fellwood Ave BD22 . . . . . **51** E8
Fellwood Cl BD22 . . . . . . **51** E8
Felnex Cl LS9 . . . . **80** C6
Felnex Cres LS9 . . . . **80** C5
Felnex Rd LS9 . . . . **80** C5
Felnex Sq LS9 . . . . **80** B5
Felnex Trad Est LS9 . . . . . **80** C5
Felnex Way LS9 . . . . **80** C5
Fenay Bankside HD8 . . . **155** D3
Fenay Bridge Rd HD8 . . **155** C4
Fenay Cres HD5 . . . . . . **155** A3
Fenay Dr HD8 . . . . **155** C3
Fenay La HD5, HD8 . . . . **155** B3
Fenay Lea Dr HD5 . . . . . **155** C4
Fenby Ave BD4 . . . . **75** C3
Fenby Cl BD4 . . . . **75** C3
Fenby Gdns BD4 . . . . **75** C3
Fenby Gr BD4 . . . . **75** C3
Fencote Cres BD2 . . . . . . **56** D3
Fender Rd BD6 . . . . **73** F1
Fennec Rd BD17 . . . . **38** E4
Fennel Ct LS26 . . . . **102** C3
Fennell Ct WF2 . . . . **160** D7
Fenny Royd Est HX3 . . . **114** B8
Fentham Ind Est ◼◼ HD6 . **115** A1
Fenton Ave LS26 . . . . . . **101** B7
Fenton Cl
Rothwell LS26 . . . . **101** B7
South Kirkby WF9 . . . . . **182** B1
Fenton Rd
Halifax HX1 . . . . **202** B1
Huddersfield HD1 . . . . . **153** F3
Lofthouse Gate WF1 . . . **121** F7
Fentonsgate WF3 . . . . . **100** C1
Fenton Sq HD1 . . . . **153** F5
Fenton St
Burley in W LS29 . . . . **9** F1
East Ardsley WF3 . . . . . . **98** F1
Leeds LS2 . . . . **206** B1
Mirfield WF14 . . . . **138** A4
Fenwick Dr BD6 . . . . **94** A6
Ferguson St HX1 . . . . . . **203** B2
Fern Ave HD9 . . . . **170** C3
Fern Bank LS21 . . . . **23** B8
Fernbank Ave
◼◼ Bingley BD16 . . . . **37** A3
Keighley BD22 . . . . **34** F4
Pudsey LS13 . . . . **57** F3
Fernbank Cl LS13 . . . . . . **57** F3
Fernbank Dr
Baildon BD17 . . . . **38** A1
Bingley BD16 . . . . **37** A3
Pudsey LS13 . . . . **57** F3
Fernbank Gdns LS13 . . . . **57** F3
Fernbank Pl LS13 . . . . **57** F3
Fernbank Rd
Bradford BD3 . . . . **56** B1
Pudsey LS13 . . . . **57** F3
Fernbank St ◼◼ BD16 . . . . **37** A3
Fernbank Terr BD16 . . . . **37** A3
Fern Bank Terr LS19 . . . . **40** A7
Fernbank Wlk LS13 . . . . . **57** F3
Fern Chase LS14 . . . . **45** A7
Fern Cl WF17 . . . . **118** F5
Ferncliffe Dr
Baildon BD17 . . . . **38** B3
Keighley BD20 . . . . **18** A2
Ferncliffe Rd
Bingley BD16 . . . . **37** A3
Leeds LS13 . . . . **58** C2
◼◼ Shipley BD18 . . . . **54** F8
Ferncliffe Terr LS13 . . . . **58** C2
Ferncroft WF15 . . . . **116** C4
Fern Croft
Scarcroft LS14 . . . . **45** A7
Wakefield WF2 . . . . **120** E3
Ferndale BD14 . . . . **73** A3
Ferndale Ave BD14 . . . . . **73** A3
Ferndale Ct
Huddersfield HD2 . . . . . **136** B4
Ilkley LS29 . . . . **8** A3
Ferndale Gr
Huddersfield HD2 . . . . . **136** B4
Shipley BD9 . . . . **55** C4
Ferndale Pl WF9 . . . . . . **181** D6
Ferndene BD16 . . . . **37** B2
Ferndene Ave WF17 . . . . **96** F3
Ferndene Wlk WF17 . . . . **96** F3
Ferndown Gn BD5 . . . . . . **74** D3
Ferney Lee Prim Sch
OL14 . . . . **108** A6
Ferney Lee Rd OL14 . . . **108** A6
Fernfield Terr ◼ HX3 . . . . **92** B2
Fern Gdns LS29 . . . . **8** A3
Fernhill BD16 . . . . **37** A5
Fern Hill Ave BD18 . . . . . **54** F7
Fern Hill Gr BD18 . . . . . . **54** F7
Fern Hill Mount BD18 . . . **54** F7
Fern Hill Rd BD18 . . . . . . **54** F7
Fernhurst Cl ◼ WF14 . . . **138** A6
Fernhurst Cres WF14 . . **138** B6
Fernhurst Lea WF14 . . . **138** B6
Fernhurst Rd WF14 . . . **138** B6
Fernhurst Way ◼ WF14 . **138** A6
Fernlea LS26 . . . . **100** F6
Fern Lea BD13 . . . . **72** F1
Fernlea Cl
Batley WF16 . . . . **117** E3
Crofton WF4 . . . . **143** F2
Fern Lea Flats HD3 . . . . **135** A1
Fernlea Gr HD7 . . . . **152** E3

Fern Lea Rd HD3 . . . . . **135** A1
Fern Lea St HX6 . . . . . . **112** B5
Fern Lea View LS28 . . . . . **57** E2
Fernleigh Ct WF2 . . . . . **141** F5
Fernleigh Dr HD3 . . . . . **153** A5
Fernley Gdns ◼◼ BD12 . . . **94** C4
Fernley Green Cl WF11 . **127** B4
Fernley Green Ind Est
WF11 . . . . **127** B4
Fernley Green Rd WF11 . **127** B4
Fernley Hill Dr WF6 . . . **122** F5
Fern Pl BD18 . . . . **54** F8
Fern Rise HD5 . . . . **135** B7
Fern St E HD1 . . . . **154** C6
Fernside WF4 . . . . **144** C3
Fernside Ave HD5 . . . . . **154** F4
Fernside Cl HD5 . . . . . . **155** A5
Fernside Cres HD5 . . . . **155** A5
Fernside Rd HD5 . . . . . . **155** A5
Fern St
Bradford BD4 . . . . **75** D3
Halifax HX3 . . . . **92** B2
◼ Haworth BD22 . . . . **51** C6
Huddersfield HD1 . . . . . **136** A1
Keighley BD21 . . . . **35** C8
Ferns The ◼ OL13 . . . . . **106** A1
Fern Terr
◼ Bradford BD8 . . . . **55** C2
◼ Pudsey LS28 . . . . **57** E2
Fern Valley Chase OL14 . **107** F6
Fern View BD19 . . . . **96** A1
Fern Way LS14 . . . . **45** A7
Fernwood LS8 . . . . **44** A1
Fernwood Ct LS8 . . . . **44** A1
Ferrand Ave BD4 . . . . **95** C8
Ferrand La
Bingley BD16 . . . . **36** F3
Cleckheaton BD19 . . . . . **96** A1
Ferrands Cl BD16 . . . . . . **36** B1
Ferrands Park Way BD16 . **36** B1
Ferrand St ◼◼ BD16 . . . . . **37** A3
Ferriby Cl BD2 . . . . **56** D3
Ferriby Twrs LS9 . . . . . . **207** B1
Ferrybridge Bsns Pk
WF11 . . . . **126** D5
Ferrybridge By-Pass
WF11 . . . . **126** C5
Ferrybridge Inf Sch
WF11 . . . . **126** B5
Ferrybridge Power Sta
WF11 . . . . **126** B7
Ferrybridge Rd
Castleford WF10 . . . . . . **124** F7
Knottingley WF11 . . . . . **126** D4
Pontefract WF8 . . . . **125** F3
Ferrybridge Workspace
WF11 . . . . **126** C5
Ferry La WF3 . . . . **121** F2
Ferry Top La WF4 . . . . . **162** A3
Festival Ave BD18 . . . . . . **55** D5
Feversham Coll BD3 . . . . **55** F1
Feversham Grange HX3 . **113** B3
Feversham Prim Sch BD3 . **75** B7
Feversham St BD3 . . . . . **201** D2
Fewston Ave
◼◼ Bradford BD13 . . . . . . **73** C2
Leeds LS9 . . . . **212** C1
Wakefield WF1 . . . . **142** F8
Fewston Ct LS9 . . . . **212** C2
Fiddle La HX4 . . . . **132** F4
Fiddler Hill WF12 . . . . . **139** B4
Fidler Cl LS25 . . . . **82** E7
Fidler La LS25 . . . . **82** E7
Fidler Terr LS25 . . . . **82** E7
Field Cl
Batley WF16 . . . . **117** D6
Halifax HX3 . . . . **91** F1
Field Cres ◼ WF9 . . . . . **182** F2
Fieldcroft Ct ◼ WF14 . . **137** F5
Field Ct BD13 . . . . **72** E6
Fieldedge La BD20 . . . . . . **19** A2
Field End LS15 . . . . **81** A7
Field End Cl LS15 . . . . **81** A7
Field End Cres LS15 . . . . . **81** A7
Field End Ct LS15 . . . . **81** A7
Field End Garth LS15 . . . . **81** A7
Field End Gdns LS15 . . . . . **81** A7
Field End Gn LS15 . . . . . . **81** A7
Field End Gr LS15 . . . . **81** B8
Field End La
Holmfirth HD9 . . . . **188** B2
Honley HD9 . . . . **172** A4
Field End Mount LS15 . . . . **81** A7
Field End Rd LS15 . . . . **81** A6
Fieldens Pl WF17 . . . . . . **118** A6
Fielden Sq OL14 . . . . . . **108** B4
Fielden St OL14 . . . . . . **108** E6
Fieldens The OL14 . . . . **108** B4
Fieldfare Dr BD6 . . . . **73** B1
Fieldfares The BD20 . . . . . . **5** E1
Fieldgate Rd BD10 . . . . . . **56** D7
Field Head
Batley WF17 . . . . **96** E3
Huddersfield HD7 . . . . . **152** D5
Shepley HD8 . . . . **173** E1
Fieldhead Bsns Ctr BD7 . . **74** C7
Fieldhead Carr Prim Sch
LS14 . . . . **45** B1
Fieldhead Cl WF8 . . . . . **125** F1
Fieldhead Cres WF17 . . . . **96** E3
Fieldhead Cres LS23 . . . . **30** C7
Fieldhead Dr
Barwick in E LS15 . . . . . . **63** F8
Glusburn BD20 . . . . **16** D7
Guiseley LS20 . . . . **39** C8
Field Head Farm Ct HD8 . **173** E1
Fieldhead Gdns WF12 . . **119** B3
Fieldhead Gr LS20 . . . . . . **39** C8

Fieldhead Hospl WF1 . . . **121** C2
Fieldhead Jun & Inf Sch
WF17 . . . . **96** F3
Fieldhead La HD9 . . . . . **187** F1
Field Head La
Batley WF17 . . . . **96** E3
Cragg Vale HX7 . . . . **110** B3
Halifax HX2 . . . . **91** D7
Oxenhope BD22 . . . . **51** A5
Fieldhead Paddock LS23 . . **30** C8
Field Head Par WF17 . . . . **96** F3
Fieldhead Rd LS20 . . . . . . **39** C8
Fieldhead St BD7 . . . . **74** C7
Fieldhead Way WF16 . . . **117** C5
Field Head Way HX2 . . . . **91** D7
Fieldhouse HD9 . . . . **189** B4
Fieldhouse Cl LS17 . . . . . **43** C2
Field House LS22 . . . . **13** C5
Fieldhouse Cotts ◼◼ HX1 . **202** C1
Field House St BD14 . . . . **73** C3
Fieldhouse Dr
Leeds LS17 . . . . **43** C2
Slaithwaite HD7 . . . . . . **152** A1
Fieldhouse Gr LS28 . . . . . **57** C2
Fieldhouse Lawn LS17 . . . **43** C2
Fieldhouse Rd ◼ HD1 . . . **154** C8
Fieldhouse St
Bradford BD3 . . . . **75** D7
Wakefield WF1 . . . . **142** F3
Fieldhouse Wlk ◼ LS17 . . **43** C2
Field Hurst
Brighouse BD19 . . . . **115** F7
Ripponden HX4 . . . . **133** C5
Fieldhurst Ct BD4 . . . . . . **95** C8
Fielding Ct LS27 . . . . **97** F5
Fielding Gate LS12 . . . . **210** A4
Fielding Gate Mews
LS12 . . . . **210** A4
Fielding St ◼◼ HX7 . . . . . **89** A3
Fielding Way LS27 . . . . . . **97** F5
Field La
Aberford LS25 . . . . **64** E8
Batley WF17 . . . . **118** D4
Brighouse HD6 . . . . **135** F8
Dewsbury WF13 . . . . . . **138** D6
Kirkburton, Farnley Tyas
HD4 . . . . **172** F6
Kirkburton HD4 . . . . . . **173** A8
Ossett WF5 . . . . **140** D6
South Elmsall WF9 . . . . **183** C4
Upton WF9 . . . . **183** A8
Wakefield WF2 . . . . **142** C3
Field Lane Jun & Inf Sch
WF17 . . . . **118** D4
Field Lane Prim Sch
HD6 . . . . **135** E3
Fieldmoor Lo LS28 . . . . . **76** E6
Field Park Grange LS27 . . **97** D6
Field Pl WF2 . . . . **142** A5
Field Rd HD9 . . . . **189** B4
Fieldsend Ct WF9 . . . . . **183** A4
Fieldshead Bglws HD7 . . **170** D7
Fieldside BD13 . . . . **52** D6
Field Side HX1 . . . . **202** B4
Fieldside Rd WF9 . . . . . **163** B2
Fields Rd
Bradford BD12 . . . . **94** B4
Lepton HD8 . . . . **155** D2
Fields Rise HD5 . . . . **137** C1
Field St
Bradford BD1 . . . . **201** C3
Dewsbury WF13 . . . . . . **138** D6
Fields The WF3 . . . . **100** D1
Fields Way HD5 . . . . **137** C1
Field Terr LS15 . . . . **81** A8
Field Top ◼ OL13 . . . . . **106** A7
Field Top Rd HD6 . . . . . **114** F1
Field View
Castleford WF10 . . . . . . **124** A6
Halifax HX3 . . . . **91** F2
Fieldway
Bradford BD14 . . . . **73** B5
Ilkley LS29 . . . . **8** E4
Field Way HD8 . . . . **190** E6
Fieldway Ave LS13 . . . . . **58** A4
Fieldway Chase LS26 . . . **101** D5
Fieldway Cl LS13 . . . . **58** A4
Fieldway Rise LS13 . . . . . **58** A4
Fife St BD22 . . . . **51** D7
Fifth Ave
Bradford BD3 . . . . **56** C1
Rothwell LS26 . . . . **101** A7
Fifth Avenue E WF15 . . . **116** B5
Fifth Avenue W WF15 . . **116** B5
Fifth St BD12 . . . . **94** E6
Filbert St HD1 . . . . **136** A1
Filey St S71 . . . . **179** D4
Filey St BD1, BD3 . . . . . **201** C3
Filley Royd BD19 . . . . . . **116** E6
Fillingfir Dr LS16 . . . . **58** F8
Fillingfir Rd LS16 . . . . **58** F8
Fillingfir Wlk LS16 . . . . . . **58** F8
Finch Ave WF2 . . . . **160** D5
Finch Cl BD16 . . . . **37** C4
Finching Gr WF14 . . . . . **138** A8
Finchley St BD5 . . . . **74** D3
Finchley Way ◼ LS27 . . . . **98** A3
Finch St BD5 . . . . **74** D4
Findon Terr BD10 . . . . . . **56** E4
Fine Garth Cl LS23 . . . . . **30** D3
Finghall Rd DN6 . . . . . . **184** F2
Fink Hill LS18 . . . . **58** A8
Finkil St HD6 . . . . **114** F5
Finkin Ave WF3 . . . . **121** E2
Finkin Croft WF3 . . . . . **121** E2
Finkin La WF3 . . . . **121** E2
Finkle Cl WF4 . . . . **177** F7
Finkle Ct LS27 . . . . **97** C6

Fin-Fra 247

inkle La LS27 97 D6
inkle St
Pontefract WF8 125 D1
Sowerby Bridge HX6 111 D4
Woolley WF4 177 F7
insbury Dr BD2 55 F5
insbury Rd LS1 206 B1
inthorpe La HD5 155 A3
ir Ave WF13 138 D5
ir Bank 9 WF13 118 A1
irbank Gn BD2 56 D3
irbank Gr LS15 80 E6
irbeck BD16 53 B8
irbeck Rd LS23 30 D3
ireclay Bsns Pk BD13 72 A6
ire Station Houses LS9 208 C1
irethorn Cl BD8 74 A8
ir Gr WF13 138 D5
irham Cl S71 179 A4
ir Mount 10 OL13 106 A1
ir Par WF13 138 D5
ir Rd HD1 153 D6
ir St
Haworth BD22 51 C6
10 Keighley BD21 35 B4
Todmorden OL14 129 A8
irst Ave
Bardsey LS17 28 E5
Bradford BD3 56 C1
Cleckheaton WF15 116 C5
Fitzwilliam WF9 163 A4
Halifax HX3 113 B4
Horbury WF4 140 F1
Huddersfield, Dalton HD5 154 F7
Huddersfield, Town End HD7 152 D4
3 Keighley BD21 35 B6
Leeds LS12 210 A3
Lofthouse Gate WF1 121 C2
Pudsey LS28 57 E1
Rothwell LS26 100 F7
Royston S71 179 D4
South Kirkby WF9 181 F1
Upton WF9 183 A7
Wetherby LS22 13 F5
Yeadon LS19 40 C5
irst Avenue Ind Est LS28 57 E1
irs The
Royston S71 179 A4
Scarcroft LS14 45 C7
irst St BD12 94 E6
irth Ave
5 Brighouse HD6 115 A3
Leeds LS11 214 A2
irth Cl WF3 121 E5
irthcliffe Dr WF15 117 B5
irthcliffe Gr WF15 117 C5
irthcliffe La WF15 117 B5
irthcliffe Mount WF15 117 B5
irthcliffe Par WF15 117 B5
irthcliffe Pl WF15 117 C5
irthcliffe Rd WF15 117 B5
irthcliffe Terr WF15 117 B5
irthcliffe View WF15 117 B5
irthcliffe Wlk WF15 117 B5
irthfield La WF9 164 F4
irthfields LS25 83 A7
irth Gr LS11 214 A2
irth Ho WF1 216 B2
irth House La
Brighouse HD6 136 C7
Ripponden HX4 133 C1
irth La BD15 53 C5
irth Mount LS11 214 A2
irth Rd
Bradford BD9 55 A3
Leeds LS11 214 A2
irth Row BD4 95 B8
irth St
Brighouse HD6 115 A1
Huddersfield HD1 154 B5
Leeds LS9 207 B1
Shepley HD8 190 E8
4 Thornton BD13 72 D6
irth Terr LS9 207 B1
irth View LS11 214 A2
ir Tree App LS17 43 C3
irtree Ave LS25 83 B6
ir Tree Cl LS17 43 C4
ir Tree Gdns
Bradford BD10 56 D7
Leeds LS17 43 B4
ir Tree Gn LS17 43 C4
ir Tree Gr LS17 43 C4
ir Tree La LS17 43 D3
ir Tree Prim Sch LS17 43 C3
ir Tree Rise LS17 43 C3
ir Tree Vale LS17 43 C3
ir Tree View LS26 102 E3
irville Ave WF6 123 B1
irville Cres WF6 144 B8
ir Wlk WF13 138 D5
ir Wood Cl OL14 108 A1
ishbeck La BD20 6 A4
ishergate WF11 126 D5
isher Gn HD9 171 F4
isher Gr WF5 140 F4
isher St WF11 126 E4
isher Way WF15 117 E3
ishpond La WF2 159 F5
ishponds Dr WF4 159 F5
ish St LS1 211 C4
itts La LS17 27 A8
itzgerald Cl WF10 125 D5
itzgerald St BD5 201 B1
itzroy Dr LS8 61 A6
itzroy Rd BD3 75 C7

Fitzwilliam Prim Sch WF9 163 B4
Fitzwilliam St
Bradford BD4 201 C1
Fitzwilliam WF9 163 B1
Huddersfield HD1 154 A7
Fitzwilliam Sta WF9 163 A3
Five Acres S75 193 F5
Five Lane Ends
Bradford BD2 56 A5
Holmfirth HD9 188 E5
Leeds LS16 42 D8
Skellow DN6 184 E1
Five Lanes Prim Sch LS12 209 C2
Five Oaks BD17 38 A2
Five Rise BD16 36 F4
Fixby Ave HX2 202 A1
Fixby Jun & Inf Sch HD2 136 A4
Fixby La WF4 156 E6
Fixby Park Dr HD2 135 F2
Fixby Rd HD2 136 A5
Fixby View Yd HD6 135 E6
Flagship Sq WF12 119 A2
Flanshaw Ave WF2 141 E6
Flanshaw Cres WF2 141 E6
Flanshaw Gr WF2 141 E6
Flanshaw Jun & Inf Sch WF2 141 F7
Flanshaw La WF2 141 D6
Flanshaw Rd WF2 141 E6
Flanshaw St WF2 141 E6
Flanshaw View WF2 141 E6
Flanshaw Way WF2 141 D7
Flappit Spring BD21 52 A6
Flasby Ave BD20 36 B8
Flasby St BD21 35 C8
Flash La WF14 138 B6
Flass La WF10 124 C5
Flat Ho HD7 170 C8
Flat La HD9 188 D5
Flat Nook BD16 37 B3
Flats La LS15 63 D6
Flats The HX1 203 B2
Flavell Cl WF9 182 B1
Flawith Dr BD2 56 D2
Flaxen Ct BD6 74 D1
Flax Ho 13 LS10 211 C3
Flax Mdw HD3 135 A2
Flax Mill Rd LS10 215 B3
Flax Pl LS9 212 B3
Flaxton Cl 2 LS11 214 B3
Flaxton Gdns 1 LS11 214 B3
Flaxton Gn BD2 56 D2
Flaxton Pl BD7 74 B6
Flaxton St LS11 214 B3
Flaxton View LS11 214 B3
Fledborough Rd LS22 13 C5
Fleece St
Bradford BD6 93 F7
Keighley BD21 35 C7
Fleet La
Mickletown LS26 102 A3
Queensbury BD13 72 D1
Rothwell LS26 101 E5
Fleet St HD8 175 D1
Fleet Thro Rd LS18 58 B6
Fleming Ct HD5 155 A5
Fleminghouse La HD5 155 A5
Fleming St WF17 118 C5
Flemming Ct WF10 124 F4
Fletcher Ave BD20 5 E2
Fletcher Cres HD6 135 E6
Fletcher Homes WF13 139 A8
Fletcher La BD2 55 D4
Fletcher Rd BD6 74 B1
Fletton Terr 2 BD2 56 B2
Flexbury Ave LS27 98 A3
Flight Hill HD9 199 C5
Flight House Rd HX6 131 F4
Flint La HD9 200 A5
Flintmill La LS23 14 D3
Flinton Gr BD2 56 D3
Flint St HD1 136 B1
Flockton Ave BD4 75 A4
Flockton CE First Sch WF4 157 C2
Flockton Cl BD4 75 A4
Flockton Cres BD4 75 A4
Flockton Dr BD4 75 A4
Flockton Gr BD4 75 A4
Flockton Rd
Bradford BD4 75 A4
Shelley HD8 174 B3
Flockton Terr BD4 75 A4
Floral Ave LS7 60 C6
Floreat Cl WF17 118 A8
Florence Ave
Leeds LS9 208 A2
Wilsden BD15 53 B6
Florence Gr LS9 208 A2
Florence Mount LS9 208 A2
Florence Pl LS9 208 A2
Florence St
Bradford BD3 75 C6
Castleford WF10 124 D8
Halifax HX1 202 C3
Leeds LS9 208 A2
Florence Terr 11 LS27 98 B4
Florida Rd BD15 54 A4
Florin Way WF8 146 A7
Florist St BD21 18 E1
Flossmore Way LS27 97 C7
Flounders Hill WF7 163 F6
Flower Acre HX5 134 F6
Flower Bank
Bradford BD2 55 F4
Sowerby Bridge HX6 111 F3

Flower Cl LS19 40 A7
Flower Croft BD21 34 F5
Flower Ct 3 BD2 56 C2
Flower Garth BD10 56 D6
Flower Haven BD9 54 D4
Flower Hill BD9 54 F4
Flowerlands HX3 114 E8
Flower Mount
Baildon BD17 38 D4
9 Yeadon LS19 40 C7
Flowerpot La 6 BD13 92 C8
Flower Scar Rd OL14 107 B7
Floyd St BD5 74 B3
Flugel Way HD3 135 C1
Flush WF15 117 C4
Flushdyke Jun & Inf Sch WF5 140 F7
Flush House La HD9 188 A3
Flyboat Ho 14 LS10 211 C3
Focus Way LS19 40 B5
Fold Ct HD8 173 F5
Foldings Ave BD19 115 F8
Foldings Cl BD19 115 E8
Foldings Ct BD19 115 E8
Foldings Gr BD19 115 E8
Foldings Par BD19 115 E8
Foldings Rd BD19 115 F8
Foldings The HD8 175 A2
Fold La HX7 88 A6
Fold The
4 Haworth BD22 51 B7
Leeds LS15 62 E4
Foljambe St WF2 142 C4
Folkestone St BD3 75 C7
Folkton Holme BD2 56 E2
Follett Ave HD4 153 C2
Follingworth La HD7 151 D1
Follingworth Rd WF17 118 F5
Folly Hall HD1 154 A4
Folly Hall Ave BD6 94 B8
Folly Hall Cl 2 BD6 94 B8
Folly Hall Gdns The BD6 94 B8
Folly Hall La HX7 110 E2
Folly Hall Mount WF3 119 E8
Folly Hall Rd
Bradford BD6 94 B8
East Ardsley WF3 119 E8
Folly Hall Wlk 3 BD6 94 B8
Folly La
Bramham LS23 30 D2
Leeds LS11 214 B4
Folly Rd HD2 136 A3
Folly View LS23 30 D2
Folly View Rd BD22 51 D6
Fontmell Cl BD4 75 E2
Football LS19 40 C6
Footkiln HX7 89 C4
Forber Gr BD4 75 E5
Forber Pl LS15 80 E7
Forbes Ho 16 BD4 75 E3
Ford BD13 92 C8
Ford Dr WF14 137 E6
Ford Gate La HD9 188 D2
Ford Hill BD13 92 D8
Ford House (Leeds Girls High Sch) LS6 205 B4
Ford St
Fitzwilliam WF9 163 B1
3 Keighley BD21 18 E1
Fore La HX6 112 A3
Fore Lane Ave HX6 112 A3
Foreside Bottom La BD13 71 D5
Forest Ave HX2 91 E4
Forest Bank LS27 97 C7
Forest Cl WF1 121 F1
Forest Cres HX2 91 E4
Forester's Bldgs HD9 172 B4
Forester Cl WF9 163 A3
Forester Ct BD13 71 D8
Forest Gate LS21 23 A7
Forest Gn HX2 91 E3
Forest Gr HX2 91 F3
Forest Hill Gdns HD3 152 A8
Forest Hill Rd HX4 133 E1
Forest Rd HD5 154 E5
Forest Ridge WF3 99 C1
Forest Way HD9 171 E4
Forge Hill La WF11 126 E4
Forge La
Batley WF15 117 C2
Dewsbury WF12 139 B4
Harewood LS17 27 D1
Horbury WF4 159 C8
Leeds LS12 210 A4
Liversedge WF15 117 B3
Forge Row LS12 77 D3
Forge View BD20 17 C5
Forman's Dr WF3 100 A3
Formby Ave HD2 135 F3
Forrest Ave HD1 153 D7
Forrester Ct WF3 100 B3
Forresters HX4 133 F3
Forrest Terr WF12 139 E6
Forster Dr WF16 117 E3
Forster Pl LS12 78 B4
Forster Square Ret Pk BD1 201 B4
Forster St LS10 212 B1
Forsythia Ave WF3 120 C7
Fort Ann Rd WF17 118 F4
Fortescue Ho 2 BD4 75 D6
Fortis Way HD3 152 E8
Fortshot La LS17 27 B1
Forum View WF8 165 A5
Fossards Cl LS23 30 D2
Foss Ave LS22 13 D7
Fosse Way LS25 83 B6
Foss Wlk WF10 104 B1

Foster Ave
Huddersfield HD4 153 C2
Normanton WF6 123 A1
Silsden BD20 5 D2
Thornton BD13 72 F6
Foster Beaver Coll The BD9 54 F1
Foster Cl
Burley in W LS29 9 F1
9 Morley LS27 98 A5
Foster Clough HX7 89 F3
Foster Cres 8 LS27 98 A5
Foster Gdns BD22 34 F7
Foster La HX7 89 A4
Foster Park Gr BD13 52 E1
Foster Park Rd BD13 52 E1
Foster Park View BD13 52 E1
Foster Pk BD13 52 E1
Foster Place La HD9 189 F2
Foster Rd BD21 35 B4
Foster Sq
Denholme BD13 71 D8
Leeds LS10 99 D8
Foster St
12 Morley LS27 98 A5
1 Queensbury BD13 72 E1
Foster Terr LS13 58 D3
Foston Cl BD2 56 E2
Foston La BD2 56 E2
Fothergill Ave WF7 163 E6
Foulcauseway La LS21 23 D7
Foul Clough Rd OL14 128 D8
Foulds' Terr 7 BD16 37 A4
Foundation Ct 17 BD21 35 B4
Foundry App LS9 208 B2
Foundry Ave LS8, LS9 208 B3
Foundry Dr LS9 208 B3
Foundry Hill BD16 36 F3
Foundry Ho WF10 124 B7
Foundry La
Bradford BD4 75 B5
Knottingley WF11 127 A4
Leeds LS14, LS9 61 E3
Pudsey LS28 57 E2
Foundry Mill Cres LS14 61 F3
Foundry Mill Dr LS14 61 E3
Foundry Mill Gdns LS14 61 E5
Foundry Mill Mount LS14 61 F3
Foundry Mill St LS14 61 F3
Foundry Mill Terr LS14 61 F3
Foundry Mill View LS14 61 F3
Foundry Mill Wlk LS14 61 F3
Foundry Pl LS9 208 B3
Foundry St N HX3 91 F3
Foundry St
Brighouse HD6 115 C1
Dewsbury, Ravensthorpe WF13 138 E5
Dewsbury WF13 139 D8
Halifax HX1 203 B4
Leeds, Bank LS9 212 B3
Leeds, Camp Field LS11 211 B2
Sowerby Bridge HX6 112 B3
Todmorden OL14 108 A4
Foundry Terr BD19 116 E7
Foundry Wlk LS8 208 B3
Fountain Cl
Darton S75 177 E1
Liversedge WF15 116 F1
Fountain Ct S71 178 E1
Fountain Dr WF15 116 F1
Fountain Gr HD4 153 C4
Fountain Par S75 178 C1
Fountain Prim Sch LS27 97 F2
Fountains Ave
Batley WF17 117 F4
Boston Spa LS23 30 C7
Fountain Sq S75 177 E1
Fountain St
Batley WF16 117 D5
Bradford BD1 201 B4
Bradford, Low Moor BD12 94 C6
Halifax HX1 203 B2
35 Hebden Bridge HX7 89 A3
Leeds LS1 211 A4
Liversedge WF15 116 F1
3 Morley LS27 98 C8
14 Queensbury BD13 72 E1
Ripponden HX6 132 D4
7 Thornton BD13 72 D6
Todmorden OL14 108 E6
Fountains Way WF1 121 F1
Fountain Terr BD12 94 D3
Fountain Way BD18 55 C7
Four Acres WF14 138 A3
Four Gates End HX7 110 C3
Fourlands Cres BD10 56 C8
Fourlands Ct BD10 56 C8
Fourlands Dr BD10 56 C8
Fourlands Gdns BD10 56 C8
Fourlands Gr BD10 56 C8
Fourlands Rd BD10 56 C8
Four Lane Ends
Castleford WF10 124 A6
Dewsbury WF12 139 F2
Guiseley LS20 39 C7
Four Lanes Bsns Pk BD8 73 F8
Four Seasons HX2 72 A1
Fourteenth Ave LS12 210 A2
Fourth Ave
Bradford BD3 56 C1
Cleckheaton WF15 116 B5
9 Keighley BD21 35 A6
Lofthouse Gate WF1 121 B2
Rothwell LS26 101 A7
Wetherby LS22 13 F5
Fourth Ct LS11 211 A2
Fourth St 1 BD12 94 E6

Fowler's Pl LS28 57 E2
Fowler St BD4 75 B5
Fowler Street Ind Est BD4 75 B5
Fox Bank OL14 108 B7
Foxbridge Way WF6 123 E3
Fox Cl HD8 175 D6
Foxcliff WF11 105 D1
Fox Covert Rd or Whin Covert La WF8 166 E2
Foxcroft LS8 61 C8
Foxcroft Cl
Leeds LS6 59 B5
Queensbury BD13 92 C7
Foxcroft Dr HD6 114 F1
Foxcroft Gn LS6 59 B5
Fox Croft La BD16 53 F7
Foxcroft Mount LS6 59 C5
Foxcroft Rd LS6 59 B5
Foxcroft Way LS6 59 B5
Foxcroft Wlk LS6 59 B5
Fox Ct
Crigglestone WF4 159 F7
Elland HX4 134 D7
Foxdale Cl 1 OL13 106 A1
Foxen La HX6 132 C6
Foxford Gr WF9 164 D3
Foxglove Ave LS8 61 C6
Foxglove Folly WF2 141 E8
Foxglove Rd
Batley WF17 96 E2
Huddersfield HD5 154 E4
Fox Heads La LS22, HG3 12 A8
Foxhill
Baildon BD17 38 B3
Wetherby LS22 13 E6
Foxhill Ave
Leeds LS16 42 C1
Queensbury BD13 72 D1
Foxhill Cl BD13 72 D1
Foxhill Cres LS16 42 D1
Foxhill Ct LS16 42 C1
Foxhill Dr
Leeds LS16 42 D1
Queensbury BD13 72 D1
Foxhill Gn LS16 42 D1
Foxhill Gr
Leeds LS16 42 D1
Queensbury BD13 72 D1
Foxhill Prim Sch BD13 72 D2
Foxhills The LS16 41 D4
Foxhole La LS28 57 B6
Foxholes Cres LS28 57 B6
Fox Holes Gr S36 200 D5
Foxholes La WF6 122 F5
Foxhunters Way WF9 182 F1
Fox La
Crigglestone WF4 159 F7
Wakefield WF1 121 A1
Foxlow Ave HD5 154 E8
Fox Royd HD8 173 E1
Fox Royd Ave WF14 137 F6
Fox Royd Dr WF14 137 F6
Foxroyd La WF12 139 B1
Fox Royd La 3 WF14 137 F6
Fox Royd View 4 WF14 137 F6
Fox St
Batley WF17 118 D4
Bingley BD16 36 F3
5 Bradford BD5 74 C3
Cleckheaton BD19 116 B7
Dewsbury WF13 138 E5
Huddersfield HD1 154 A6
Foxstone Rise BD17 38 E3
Foxstones La HX6 132 D2
Fox Terr WF8 125 E1
Foxton Gdns LS27 97 F3
Fox View WF13 118 A3
Fox Way
Leeds LS10 212 B1
Wakefield WF2 216 B1
Fox Wood Ave LS8 61 E5
Fox Wood Cl LS8 61 E5
Foxwood Farm Way LS8 61 E5
Fox Wood Gr LS8 61 E5
Fox Wood Rise LS8 61 E5
Foxwood Wlk LS22 13 F7
Fox Wood Wlk LS8 61 E5
Frain Cl WF8 146 E7
France Fold HD9 171 F5
France Hill HD9 171 F5
Frances Ave HD4 153 C3
Frances Rd WF12 139 F7
Frances St
9 Brighouse HD6 115 A3
12 Elland HX5 134 F6
Keighley BD21 35 A8
Pudsey LS28 57 D2
France St WF17 118 E4
Francis Ave 4 HD3 153 A4
Francis Cl HX1 202 C3
Francis Ct LS7 207 A3
Francis Ho BD2 56 B2
Francis Rd WF4 144 B3
Francis St
Ackworth M T WF7 163 D5
Batley WF16 117 E3
Bradford BD4 201 D1
Castleford WF10 124 E8
Halifax HX1 202 C2
Huddersfield HD3 153 A4
Leeds LS7 207 B3
Mirfield WF14 137 F5
Francis Terr WF7 163 D5
Francis View WF14 137 F5
Francus Royd S71 179 C1

Frank Cl WF12 139 E2
Frank La
Dewsbury WF12 139 E2
Emley HD8 175 C5
Hebden Bridge HX2 90 B1
Frankland Gr LS7 207 B3
Frankland Pl LS7 207 B3
Franklin St HX1 202 B3
Frank Parkinson Ct 19 LS20 22 E1
Frank Parkinson Homes 2 LS20 22 E1
Frank Peel Cl 6 WF16 117 D4
Frank Pl 3 BD7 74 B4
Frank St
Bradford BD7 74 B4
Halifax HX1 202 C2
Fraser Ave LS18 58 A8
Fraser Rd LS28 56 F6
Fraser St
Bradford BD8 74 C8
Leeds LS9 207 C1
Freakfield La WF15 116 B2
Fred's Pl BD4 75 C3
Frederick Ave
Leeds LS9 80 A6
Wakefield WF1 142 F3
Frederick Cl BD10 38 F1
Frederick St
Huddersfield HD4 153 C4
Keighley BD21 35 D7
5 Liversedge WF15 117 B3
Pudsey LS28 57 C3
Wakefield WF1 216 B2
Frederick Walker Gdns WF17 118 D4
Fred St BD21 35 B6
Freely Fields LS23 30 D2
Freely La LS23 30 D2
Freeman Rd HX3 114 A5
Freemans Way LS22 14 A6
Freemantle Pl LS15 80 E7
Freemont St LS13 58 A2
Freeport WF10 124 F5
Free School La HX1, HX3 203 A1
Freeston Ct WF6 123 B3
Freeston Dr WF6 123 B3
Freestone Mews LS12 77 C7
Freestone Way WF6 122 E4
Freeston High Sch WF6 123 B1
Freeway Dr WF10 123 D5
Fremantle Gr BD4 75 E5
Frensham Ave LS27 97 F3
Frensham Dr
Bradford BD7 73 D3
Castleford WF10 125 D6
Frensham Gr BD7 73 D3
Frensham Way BD7 73 D3
Freshfield Gdns BD15 54 B1
Fresh Mdws 3 WF6 123 C1
Freston Ave WF1 143 D7
Freston Dr WF1 143 D7
Friar's Cl WF7 145 D4
Friar Ct BD10 56 C6
Friar Pl HD2 136 F5
Friars Ind Est BD10 56 B7
Friars Nook WF8 146 E7
Friarwood La WF8 146 D8
Friary Ct WF17 96 D1
Frickley Bridge La S72 180 F4
Frickley La DN5, DN6, WF9 195 A8
Frieldhurst Rd OL14 86 C1
Friendly Ave HX6 112 A5
Friendly Fold Ho 7 HX3 92 A2
Friendly Fold Rd HX3 92 A2
Friendly St
1 Halifax HX3 92 A2
3 Huddersfield HD1 154 B6
Thornton BD13 72 D6
Frimley Dr BD5 74 C2
Frith Ho HD6 136 C7
Frith St 14 BD22 51 E8
Frizinghall Prim Sch BD9 55 C5
Frizinghall Rd BD9 55 C4
Frizinghall Sta BD9 55 C4
Frizley Gdns BD9 55 C4
Frobisher Gr WF2 141 E5
Frobisher Rd OL15 129 C1
Frodingham Villas BD2 56 D2
Froebelian Sch The LS18 58 B7
Frogmoor Ave BD12 94 F5
Froisthorpe Mead BD2 56 D2
Frontline Cl 1 LS8 61 A6
Front Row LS11 211 B2
Front St
Bramham LS23 30 C2
Castleford WF10 124 F6
Leeds LS11 211 B2
Pontefract WF8 146 C8
Frost Hill WF15 117 B4
Frostholme OL14 86 B1
Fruit St BD21 35 E8
Fryergate WF2 141 F7
Fryers Way WF5 141 B6
Fryston La WF11 125 F7
Fryston Rd WF10 125 C7
Fuchsia Croft LS26 101 E6
Fulford Ave HD2 136 A2
Fulford Cl
Darton S75 178 A1
5 Normanton WF6 123 D1
Fulford St WF10 124 C7
Fulford Wlk BD2 56 D2
Fulham Pl 3 LS11 214 B3
Fulham Sq 5 LS11 214 B3
Fulham St LS11 214 B3
Fullerton Cl DN6 184 F2
Fullerton St BD3 201 D2
Fullerton Terr 8 LS22 29 B8
Fullwood Dr HD7 152 D4
Fulmar Ct LS10 99 D5
Fulmar Mews 8 BD8 73 C7
Fulmar Rd WF10 124 C6
Fulneck LS28 76 E5
Fulneck Cl
Bradford BD15 73 A7
Huddersfield HD2 135 F3
Leeds LS11 99 A7
Fulneck Ct LS28 76 F5
Fulneck Mews LS28 76 F5
Fulneck Sch LS28 76 E4
Fulstone HD9 190 B7
Fulstone Hall La HD9 190 A7
Fulstone Hall Rd HD9 189 F6
Fulstone Rd HD4 173 C1
Fulton Pl LS16 59 C7
Fulton St BD1 201 A3
Fulwood Gr WF2 160 B5
Furnace Cotts S36 200 D6
Furnace Gr BD12 94 F5
Furnace Inn St BD4 75 D5
Furnace La BD11 96 A6
Furnace Rd
Bradford BD4 95 A6
Bradford, Raw Nook BD12 94 F5
Furnbrook Gdns HD5 155 C8
Furness Ave
Halifax HX2 91 E4
Wakefield WF2 120 E2
Furness Cres HX2 91 D5
Furness Dr
Halifax HX2 91 D4
Wakefield WF2 120 E2
Furness Gdns HX2 91 E4
Furness Gr HX2 91 E4
Furness Pl HX2 91 E3
Fusden La BD19 96 A1
Future Fields BD6 73 E1
Futures Way BD4 201 C1
Fyfe Cres BD17 38 D2
Fyfe Gr BD17 38 E2
Fyfe La BD17 38 E2

G

Gable End Terr LS28 76 F7
Gables The
Baildon BD17 38 E3
Horsforth LS18 41 C2
13 Keighley BD21 35 A7
Pontefract WF8 125 F2
Sowerby Bridge HX6 112 C2
Gadding Moor Rd S75 192 F1
Gagewell Dr WF4 141 B2
Gagewell La WF4 141 B2
Gagewell View WF4 141 B2
Gainest HX2 202 B1
Gainford Dr LS25 82 F6
Gain La BD2, BD3 56 E1
Gainsborough Ave LS16 42 B5
Gainsborough Cl BD3 56 A2
Gainsborough Dr LS16 42 B5
Gainsborough Pl LS12 77 E3
Gainsborough Way WF3 121 E5
Gaisby La BD18 55 D5
Gaisby Mount BD18 55 D5
Gaisby Pl BD18 55 D6
Gaisby Rise BD18 55 D5
Gaitskell Ct LS11 211 A1
Gaitskell Grange 5 LS11 211 A1
Gaitskell Wlk LS11 211 A1
Galahad Way WF9 183 A2
Galefield Gn BD6 93 F6
Gale St
5 Haworth BD22 51 F8
Keighley BD21 35 C8
Gall La OL14 86 C3
Gallogate La LS17 25 F8
Gallon Croft WF9 182 E3
Gallops The LS27 98 B1
Galloway Ct 3 LS28 76 A8
Galloway La LS28 57 A1
Galloway Rd BD10 56 D7
Galloway St 1 HD1 154 C8
Gallows Hill WF10 125 D7
Gallows La WF4 159 F1
Galsworthy Ave BD9 54 D3
Galway Cl S71 179 C4
Gamble Hill LS13 77 D8
Gamble Hill Chase LS13 77 D8
Gamble Hill Cl LS13 77 D8
Gamble Hill Croft LS13 77 D8
Gamble Hill Cross LS13 77 D8
Gamble Hill Dr LS13 77 D8
Gamble Hill Fold LS13 77 D8
Gamble Hill Gn LS13 77 D8
Gamble Hill Grange LS13 77 D8
Gamble Hill Lawn LS13 77 D8
Gamble Hill Path LS13 77 D8
Gamble Hill Pl LS13 77 D8
Gamble Hill Rise LS13 77 D8
Gamble Hill Vale LS13 77 D8
Gamble Hill View LS13 77 D8
Gamble Hill Wlk LS13 77 D8
Gamble La LS12 77 C6
Gambles Hill 8 LS28 57 D3
Gamel View BD20 17 B6
Game Scar La or Goose Eye Brow BD22 34 B6
Gang The LS12 209 C3
Ganners Cl LS13 58 C4
Ganners Garth LS13 58 D4
Ganners Gn LS13 58 C4
Ganners Gr LS13 58 D4
Ganners Hill LS13 58 D4
Ganners La LS13 58 C4
Ganners Mount LS13 58 C4
Ganners Rd LS13 58 C4
Ganners Rise LS13 58 D4
Ganners Way LS13 58 C4
Ganners Wlk LS13 58 C4
Gannerthorpe Cl 4 BD12 94 C3
Gannet Cl WF10 124 C6
Ganny Rd HD6 115 B2
Ganton Cl LS6 206 B4
Ganton Ct 4 WF6 123 D1
Ganton Way HD2 135 F3
Gaol La HX1 203 B3
Garden Ave WF15 117 A6
Garden Cl
Bradford BD12 94 C4
Glusburn BD20 16 B6
Liversedge WF15 117 A5
Ossett WF5 140 E3
Garden Cres WF13 138 E6
Garden Croft WF17 118 A3
Garden Dr WF13 138 E6
Gardener's Sq HX3 114 C8
Gardeners Ct LS10 215 A4
Garden Field BD12 94 D3
Garden Fold HX3 114 C8
Garden House Cl LS26 102 D3
Garden House La WF3 120 A8
Gardenhurst LS6 205 B4
Garden La
Bradford BD9 54 F3
Knottingley WF11 127 A5
Ripponden HX6 133 C7
Garden Par 1 WF15 117 A5
Garden Pl
Dewsbury WF13 117 F1
Sutton-in-C BD20 16 E5
Garden Rd HD6 115 A4
Garden Row WF4 143 F1
Garden St N HX3 203 C4
Gardens Rd WF13 138 F5
Gardens St BD9 54 F4
Garden St
Ackworth M T WF7 163 D5
6 Batley WF16 117 D3
Castleford, Airedale WF10 125 A6
Castleford WF10 124 D6
Dewsbury WF13 138 E5
11 Haworth BD22 51 F8
25 Hebden Bridge HX7 89 A3
Huddersfield HD1 153 F4
Normanton, Altofts WF6 122 E3
Normanton WF6 123 B2
Todmorden OL14 108 B6
Wakefield WF1 216 A2
Gardens The
Bingley BD16 37 D3
Halifax HX1 203 B1
Middleton LS10 99 C4
Morley LS27 97 F2
Pudsey LS28 57 C3
Garden Street Mill HX3 203 C4
Garden Terr
Bradford BD9 55 A3
Crigglestone WF4 159 E4
Denby Dale HD8 191 F5
Dewsbury WF13 138 E6
11 Hebden Bridge HX7 89 A3
Ryhill WF4 162 B1
Garden View
Bingley BD16 37 C3
Liversedge WF15 117 A6
Wilsden BD15 53 C6
Garden View Ct LS8 44 B1
Garden Village LS25 84 A6
Garden Wlk 2 WF15 117 A5
Gardiner Row BD4 75 B3
Garfield Ave BD8 55 B2
Garfield Pl
Bradford BD15 54 A1
Marsden HD7 168 F4
Garfield St
Bradford BD15 54 A1
17 Halifax HX3 92 A1
Todmorden OL14 86 C1
Garfit Hill BD19 117 D8
Garforth Ave BD20 17 C6
Garforth Cl WF6 122 E3
Garforth Com Coll LS25 82 E5
Garforth Ct WF14 138 A7
Garforth Dr WF6 122 E3
Garforth Green Lane Prim Sch LS25 83 B6
Garforth Rd BD21 35 E8
Garforth St
Bradford BD15 54 B1
Huddersfield, Aspley HD1 154 C5
Huddersfield, Netherton HD4 171 C7
Garforth Sta LS25 82 F8
Gargrave App LS9 207 C1
Gargrave Cl HD6 135 D7
Gargrave Cres WF9 181 C6
Gargrave Ct LS9 207 C1
Gargrave Pl
Hemsworth WF9 181 C6
Leeds LS9 207 C1
Wakefield WF2 141 C5
Garibaldi St BD3 75 E7
Garland Dr LS15 81 D8
Garlick St HD6 135 E6
Garmil Head La WF9 162 F5
Garmil La WF4 162 F6
Garmont Mews LS7 204 A2
Garmont Rd LS7 204 A2
Garner La
Honley HD9 171 D4
Kirkburton HD8 173 D8
Garnet Ave LS11 214 C3
Garnet Cres LS11 214 C3
Garnet Gr LS11 214 C3
Garnet La LS24 48 F8
Garnet Par LS11 214 C3
Garnet Pl LS11 214 C3
Garnet Rd LS11 214 C2
Garnet Terr LS11 214 C3
Garnett St
Batley WF13 117 F3
Bradford BD3 201 D3
Hebden Bridge HX7 89 A3
Otley LS21 23 B8
Garnet View LS11 214 C3
Garrett Cl HD8 174 F2
Garsdale Ave BD10 56 C7
Garsdale Cres BD17 38 E4
Garsdale Fold LS22 13 A1
Garsdale Gr WF1 142 F8
Garsdale Rd HD4 154 B2
Garsdale Wlk WF11 126 E2
Garth Ave
Collingham LS22 29 B8
Leeds LS17 43 B1
Normanton WF6 144 A8
Garth Barn Cl BD9 55 A4
Garth Dr LS17 43 B1
Garth End LS22 29 B8
Garth Gr LS29 22 A4
Garthland Way BD4 75 C3
Garth Rd LS17 43 B1
Garth St
Castleford WF10 124 C6
Keighley BD21 35 A7
Garth The
Collingham LS22 29 B8
Garforth LS25 83 A7
Leeds LS9 212 B3
Garthwaite Mount BD15 54 B2
Garth Wlk LS17 43 C1
Garton Ave LS9 80 A7
Garton Dr BD10 56 D5
Garton Gr LS9 80 A7
Garton Rd LS9 80 A7
Garton Terr LS9 80 A7
Garton View 8 LS9 80 A7
Garvey View BD5 74 E4
Garwick Terr 9 HX4 134 D7
Gascoigne Ave LS15 63 D6
Gascoigne Ct LS15 63 E6
Gascoigne Ho WF8 125 D2
Gascoigne Rd
Barwick in E LS15 63 D6
East Ardsley WF3 99 E1
Gascoigne View LS15 63 D6
Gashouse La LS22 13 F5
Gaskell Dr WF4 141 A2
Gaskell St WF2 142 A5
Gas St 3 BD22 51 D7
Gas Works La
Boston Spa LS23 30 F7
Elland HX5 134 F7
Gas Works Rd
Keighley BD21 35 F7
Sowerby Bridge HX6 112 D4
Gasworks St
Huddersfield HD1 154 B7
Liversedge WF15 117 B4
Gatefield Mount BD6 94 B6
Gate Foot La HD8, HD9 190 C5
Gate Head
Elland HX4 133 F6
Marsden HD7 169 B4
Gatehead Bank HD7 169 B5
Gate Head La
Elland HX4 133 F6
Holmfirth HD9 200 A8
Gate House Ct LS26 101 E7
Gatehouse Ent Ctr HD1 153 F3
Gateland Dr LS17 44 E4
Gateland La LS17 44 E4
Gatenby Cl BD6 73 E1
Gateon House La LS17 28 B4
Gatesgarth Cres HD3 135 A1
Gatesway BD16 36 B1
Gate Way Dr LS19 40 A6
Gateways WF1 121 C5
Gateways Sch LS17 27 A6
Gateways The BD12 94 C5
Gathorne Cl LS8 207 C3
Gathorne St
Bradford BD7 74 B4
Brighouse HD6 115 B3
Leeds LS8 207 B3
Gathorne Terr LS8 207 B3
Gaukroger La HX1, HX3 203 C1
Gauk St
Brotherton WF11 126 C8
Fairburn WF11 105 A4
Gaunts Pl LS28 57 E3
Gauxholme Fold OL14 107 F3
Gauxholme Mill Ind Est OL14 107 F3
Gavin Cl BD3 75 E7
Gawcliffe Rd BD18 55 C7
Gawthorpe Ave BD16 37 A5
Gawthorpe Dr BD16 37 A5
Gawthorpe Green La HD5, HD8 155 E6
Gawthorpe La
Bingley BD16 37 A4
Kirkheaton HD8 155 D6
Ossett WF5 119 E2
Gawthorpe La *continued*
Wakefield WF2 120 A2
Gay La LS21 23 A7
Gayle Cl BD12 94 C2
Gaynor St BD8 74 D8
Gaythorne Rd
Bradford, Haigh Fold BD2 56 C2
Bradford, West Bowling BD5 74 E3
Gaythorne Terr 6 BD14 73 C4
Gaythorn Terr HX3 93 C1
Geary Cl WF2 141 D8
Geary Dr WF2 141 D8
Geecroft La LS22 12 B4
Geelong Cl BD2 55 F3
Gelder Croft WF2 141 D8
Gelder Ct WF2 141 D8
Gelderd Cl LS12 213 A4
Gelderd La LS12 213 A4
Gelderd Pl LS12 210 B2
Gelderd Rd WL27, LS27 97 C5
Gelderd Trad Est LS12 210 B1
Gelder Rd LS12 209 C3
Gelder Terr HD5 154 C5
Gemini Ct WF8 125 D2
Geneva Gr WF1 216 C3
Genista Dr LS10 99 D8
Gentian Ct WF2 141 E8
George's Sq
Cullingworth BD13 52 D6
16 Keighley BD21 35 B6
George's St HX3 91 F3
George-a-Green Rd WF2 141 E4
George Ave HD2 153 E8
George Buckley Ct WF9 182 A2
George & Crown Yd WF1 216 B2
George La
Notton WF4 178 E6
Ripponden HX6 132 B2
George Mann Rd LS10 80 A3
George Mann Way LS10 215 C3
George Sq 12 HX1 203 B3
George St
Addingham LS29 6 F8
6 Baildon BD17 38 C1
Batley, Heckmondwike WF16 117 D4
Batley WF17 118 C4
Bradford BD1 201 C2
Brighouse HD6 115 A1
Brighouse HD6 115 C
Brighouse, Hipperholme HX3 114 D
Cleckheaton BD19 116 D8
Darton S75 178 B
Denholme BD13 52 E
Dewsbury, Dewsbury Moor WF13 138 F8
Dewsbury, Ravensthorpe WF13 138 E5
Dewsbury WF13 139 C
Elland HX5 134 F
5 Elland, West Vale HX4 134 D
Featherstone, Streethouse WF7 144 D5
Featherstone WF7 145 C5
Halifax HX1 203 B3
Horbury WF4 141 B
12 Huddersfield HD1 154 A6
Huddersfield, Lindley HD3 135 B
Huddersfield, Milnsbridge HD3 153 B5
Huddersfield, Paddock Brow HD1 153 E
Kirkburton HD8 173 F
10 Liversedge WF15 117 A
Lofthouse Gate WF1 121 B
Mytholmroyd HX7 110 E
Normanton WF6 122 F
Ossett WF5 140 D
Ryhill WF4 162 B
Shipley BD18 54 F
Slaithwaite HD7 151 F
South Hiendley S72 180 D
Sowerby Bridge HX6 112 B
Thornton BD13 72 D
16 Todmorden OL14 108 B
Wakefield WF1 216 B
Yeadon LS19 40 B
Georgia Mews WF5 140 F
Geraldton Ave BD2 55 E
Gerard Ave LS27 97 F
Gerard Ho 3 BD10 56 C
Germaine Terr LS14 45 E
Gernhill Ave HD2 135 F
Gerrard St HX1 203 A
Gervase Rd WF4 141 A
Ghyllbank 1 BD20 5 E
Ghyll Beck Dr
Otley LS21 22 D
Yeadon LS19 40 E
Ghyll Cl BD20 17 C
Ghyll Dr BD22 51 C
Ghyll Mews LS29 8 A
Ghyll Mount LS19 39 F
Ghyll Rd LS6 59 A
Ghyllroyd LS19 40 A
Ghyll Royd
Guiseley LS20 39 E
Ilkley LS29 7 F
Ghyllroyd Ave BD11 96 B
Ghyllroyd Dr BD11 96 B
Ghyll Royd Sch LS29 9 D
Ghyll The
Huddersfield HD2 136 A
Shipley BD16 54 A

hyll Way BD23 4 A8
hyll Wood LS29 7 E3
hyll Wood Dr BD16 54 A8
ibbet St
Halifax, Highroad Well HX2 112 D7
Halifax HX1 202 B3
ibb La HX2 91 B3
ib Cotts HD9 172 A2
ib La HD8 175 A2
ibraltar Ave HX1 202 A2
ibraltar Island Rd LS10 215 C4
ibraltar Rd
Halifax HX1 202 A2
Pudsey LS28 76 B7
ibraltar Terr BD20 16 C5
ibriding La HD9 187 F3
ibson Ave WF2 141 F7
ibson Cl WF2 142 A7
ibson Dr LS15 81 C7
ibson La LS25 83 C2
ibson Mill★ HX7 88 C8
ibson St
Bradford BD3 75 B6
Huddersfield HD3 153 C7
6 Todmorden OL14 108 C5
ilbert Chase LS5 59 A3
ilbert Cl LS5 59 B3
ilbert Gr HD4 153 D3
ilbert Mount LS5 59 B3
ilbert St LS28 57 D2
ilcar St WF6 123 D4
ilcar Way WF6, WF10 123 D5
ildersome La LS27 77 B1
ildersome Prim Sch
_S27 97 C7
ildersome Spur LS27 97 D5
ildersome Spur Distribution
Ctr LS27 97 D5
ilder Way S72 180 C2
ilead Rd HD3 152 E7
iles Hill La HX3 93 A7
iles St
Bradford, Little Horton Green BD5 201 A1
Bradford, Wibsey BD6 74 A1
Holmfirth HD9 188 F8
ill's Bldgs WF2 142 A5
ill's Ct 7 HX1 203 B3
ill's Yd WF1 216 B3
illann St WF11 127 A4
ill Bank Rd LS29 8 A6
ill Beck Cl BD17 38 E4
ill Cl LS29 6 D8
illett Dr LS26 100 F5
illett La LS26 100 F5
illing Ave LS25 83 B8
illingham Gn BD4 75 E3
illion Cres WF4 159 E6
ill La
Guiseley BD17, LS19 39 F4
Holmfirth HD9 188 E2
Keighley BD22 34 A4
Nesfield LS29 7 C7
Yeadon, Henshaw LS19 40 A5
illrene Ave BD15 53 D4
illroyd La HD7 170 D8
illroyd Par LS27 98 B3
illroyd Pl 9 LS27 98 B4
illroyd Rise BD7 74 B7
illroyd Terr LS27 98 C4
ill Sike Ave WF2 141 F4
ill Sike Bglws WF2 141 F4
ill Sike Gr WF2 141 F4
ill Sike Ho WF2 141 F4
ill Sike Rd WF2 141 F4
ill St WF1 216 B2
ills The
Morley LS27 98 C4
Otley LS21 11 A2
illstone Dr BD22 51 D6
illygate WF8 146 D8
ilmour St 9 HX3 92 B1
ilpin Pl LS12 210 A2
ilpin St
Bradford BD3 75 B7
Leeds LS12 210 A2
ilpin Terr LS12 210 A2
ilpin View LS12 210 A2
ilstead Ct BD16 37 C3
ilstead Dr BD16 37 C3
ilstead La BD16 37 C3
ilstead Way LS29 8 B5
ilthwaites Cres HD8 192 A7
ilthwaites Fst Sch HD8 192 A7
ilthwaites Gr HD8 192 A6
ilthwaites La HD8 192 A7
ilthwaites Top HD8 192 A7
ilynda Cl BD8 73 E7
in La WF7 144 C4
innel The LS17 28 C2
ipsy Hill LS26 101 B6
ipsy La
Leeds LS11 99 A7
Rothwell LS26 101 B6
Wakefield WF2 160 E7
Woolley WF4 177 F6
ipsy Mead LS26 101 B6
ipsy St BD3 75 E8
ipton App LS9 61 D1
ipton Ave LS8 207 B3
ipton Gate E LS9 208 C3
ipton Gate W LS8 208 B3
ipton Lo LS8 208 A4
ipton Sq LS9 61 D1
ipton St LS8 207 B3
ipton Wood Ave LS8 61 B5
ipton Wood Cres LS8 61 B5
Gipton Wood Gr LS8 61 B5
Gipton Wood Pl LS8 61 B5
Gipton Wood Rd LS8 61 B5
Girlington Prim Sch BD8 74 A8
Girlington Rd BD8 55 A1
Girnhill Infants Sch WF7 145 C4
Girnhill La WF7 145 C4
Gisbourne Rd HD2 136 E5
Gisburn Rd WF1 142 F8
Gisburn St BD21 35 B8
Gissing Rd WF2 141 D4
Glade The
Pudsey LS28 57 A2
Scarcroft LS14 45 B7
Gladstonbury Ave WF1 121 F1
Gladstone Cres
3 Bacup OL13 106 A2
Yeadon LS19 40 B5
Gladstone Ct
2 Dewsbury WF13 118 A1
5 Pudsey LS28 57 F2
Gladstone Pl
Denholme BD13 71 D8
Oakworth BD22 34 D2
Gladstone Rd
15 Halifax HX1 202 C3
Yeadon LS19 40 B4
Gladstone St
Bacup OL13 106 A2
Bingley BD16 36 F2
Bradford, Barkerend BD3 75 C7
Bradford BD15 54 B1
3 Cleckheaton BD19 116 D7
3 Elland HX4 134 A4
Featherstone WF7 145 D7
Keighley BD21 35 B6
Normanton WF6 123 C3
1 Pudsey LS28 57 D3
Queensbury BD13 72 F1
10 Todmorden OL14 86 B1
Gladstone Terr
Castleford WF10 124 E8
Morley LS27 98 A4
Pudsey LS28 57 F2
Gladstone View HX3 113 E3
Gladwin St WF17 118 B4
Glaisdale Cl BD20 17 E8
Glaisdale Ct BD15 54 A3
Glaisdale Gr HX3 114 D7
Glamis Cl LS25 83 B8
Glanville Terr LS26 100 E5
Glass Houghton Cultural Ind
Ctr WF10 124 F6
Glasshoughton Inf Sch
WF10 124 F7
Glass Houghton Sta
WF10 124 F4
Glasshouse St LS10 212 A1
Glasshouse View LS10 99 B4
Glastonbury Ct BD4 75 D5
Glastonbury Dr HD3 152 F5
Glazier Rd BD13 72 C2
Gleanings Ave HX2 112 C7
Gleanings Dr HX2 112 C7
Glebe Ave LS5 59 B4
Glebe Cl HD8 175 D7
Glebe Ct LS26 100 D4
Glebe Field Chase LS22 13 D6
Glebe Field Cl LS22 13 D6
Glebe Field Croft LS22 13 D6
Glebe Field Dr LS22 13 D6
Glebe Field Garth LS22 13 D6
Glebe Field Holt LS22 13 D6
Glebe Gate WF12 139 F1
Glebe Gdns HX1 202 C1
Glebe La WF11 126 F4
Glebelands WF11 127 E4
Glebelands Cl LS25 82 F6
Glebelands Dr LS6 59 D6
Glebe Mount LS28 76 E6
Glebe Pl LS5 59 B4
Glebe Side HD5 137 C2
Glebe St
Castleford WF10 124 D7
Huddersfield HD1 153 E7
Normanton WF6 144 C8
Pudsey LS28 76 E6
Glebe Terr LS16 59 D7
Gledcliffe HX3 203 C4
Gleddings Cl HX3 113 A3
Gleddings Prep Sch The
HX3 113 A3
Gledhill Rd BD3 75 B6
Gledhill St 8 OL14 108 B6
Gledhill Terr WF13 138 F8
Gledholt Bank HD1 153 E5
Gledholt Bsns Pk HD1 153 E5
Gledholt Rd HD1 153 E6
Gledhow Ave LS8 204 C4
Gledhow Ct LS7 204 B3
Gledhow Dr BD22 51 C4
Gledhow Grange View
LS8 204 C3
Gledhow Grange Wlk
LS8 204 C3
Gledhow La LS7, LS8 204 B3
Gledhow Manor LS7 204 B3
Gledhow Mount LS8 207 B2
Gledhow Park Ave LS7 204 B2
Gledhow Park Cres LS7 204 B2
Gledhow Park Dr LS7 204 B2
Gledhow Park Gr LS7 204 B2
Gledhow Park Rd LS7 204 B2
Gledhow Park View LS7 204 B2
Gledhow Pl LS8 207 B2
Gledhow Prim Sch LS8 204 C4
Gledhow Rd LS8 207 B2
Gledhow Rise LS8 61 B6
Gledhow Terr LS8 207 B2
Gledhow Twrs LS8 204 B3
Gledhow Valley LS8 61 A5
Gledhow Valley Rd LS17, LS7,
LS8 204 B2
Gledhow Wood Ave LS8 204 C3
Gledhow Wood Cl LS8 204 C3
Gledhow Wood Ct LS8 61 A5
Gledhow Wood Gr LS8 204 C3
Gledhow Wood Rd LS8 204 C2
Gledmow Lane End LS7 204 A3
Glenaire BD18 38 E1
Glenaire Dr BD17 38 A1
Glenaire Prim Sch BD17 38 A2
Glen Ave
Batley WF17 118 C6
Todmorden OL14 107 F7
Glenbrook Dr BD7 73 F7
Glencoe Cl LS25 102 F8
Glencoe Croft LS25 102 F8
Glencoe Gdns LS25 102 F8
Glencoe Terr
Kippax LS25 102 F8
Liversedge WF15 117 B3
Glencoe View LS9 212 C2
Glen Ct WF10 124 A6
Glendale
Bingley BD16 37 C3
Horbury WF4 140 F1
Glen Dale BD16 53 F7
Glendale Ave LS25 82 F6
Glendale Cl BD6 94 A7
Glendale Ct HD3 152 A8
Glendale Dr BD6 94 A7
Glendare Ave BD7 73 F6
Glendare Rd BD7 73 F6
Glendare Terr BD7 73 F6
Glen Dene
Menston LS29 22 B4
Shipley BD16 53 F7
Glendorne Dr HD5 137 C1
Glendower Pk LS16 42 D2
Gleneagles Cl BD4 95 B8
Gleneagles Ct WF6 123 D1
Gleneagles Dr WF6 123 D1
Gleneagles Rd
Featherstone WF7 124 D1
Leeds LS17 43 B4
Gleneagles Way HD2 135 F3
Glenfield BD18 38 E1
Glenfield Ave
Bradford BD6 94 D8
Wetherby LS22 13 F4
Glen Field Ave HD2 136 F3
Glenfield Mount 8 BD6 94 D8
Glenfield Pl HX6 112 C6
Glenfields WF4 158 D5
Glenfields Cl WF4 158 D5
Glen Garth BD21 35 D5
Glen Gr LS27 98 B3
Glen Hey HD3 151 C7
Glenholme BD18 38 E1
Glenholme Heath HX1 202 A3
Glenholme Pk BD14 73 C3
Glenholme Rd
Bradford BD8 55 B1
Pudsey LS28 57 C2
Glenholme Terr WF5 119 C1
Glenholm Rd BD17 38 C3
Glen House Montessori Sch
HX7 110 D4
Glenhurst BD4 75 D1
Glenhurst Ave BD21 35 C5
Glenhurst Dr BD21 35 D5
Glenhurst Gr BD21 35 D5
Glenhurst Rd BD18 54 E8
Glenlea Cl LS28 58 A3
Glenlea Gdns LS28 58 A3
Glen Lee La BD21 35 D5
Glenlee Rd BD7 73 F7
Glenlow Rd WF12 118 F3
Glenlyon Ave BD20 18 A1
Glenlyon Dr BD20 18 A1
Glenmere Mount LS19 40 D7
Glenmore Cl BD2 56 C1
Glenmore Ct LS16 24 E3
Glen Mount
Halifax HX3 91 E2
Menston LS29 22 B3
Morley LS27 98 B3
Shipley BD16 53 F7
Glen Mount Cl HX3 91 E2
Glenmount Terr LS27 98 C2
Glenn Way WF4 162 A8
Glen Rd
Baildon BD17 37 D4
Leeds LS16 59 C7
Morley LS27 98 C3
Glen Rise BD17 38 A2
Glenrose Dr BD7 73 E6
Glenroyd
Marsden HD7 168 E4
Shipley BD18 38 E1
Glenroyd Ave BD6 94 D7
Glenroyd Cl LS28 76 C7
Glensdale Est LS27 98 C2
Glensdale Gr LS9 212 C3
Glensdale Mount LS9 212 C3
Glensdale Rd LS9 212 C3
Glensdale St LS9 212 C3
Glensdale Terr LS9 80 A7
Glenside Ave BD18 38 E1
Glenside Cl HD3 153 D8
Glenside Rd BD18 38 E1
Glen Side Rd HD7 170 A8
Glenstone Gr BD7 73 F7
Glen Terr
Brighouse HX3 114 C7
Glen Terr *continued*
Halifax HX1 203 A1
Todmorden OL14 107 E8
Glen The OL14 107 F7
Glenthorpe Ave LS9 80 A8
Glenthorpe Cres LS9 80 A8
Glenthorpe Terr LS9 80 A8
Glenton Sq BD9 55 A2
Glen View
Batley WF17 97 B2
Halifax HX1 203 A1
Harden BD16 36 B1
Hebden Bridge HX7 88 E3
Glenview Ave BD9 54 E3
Glenview Cl BD18 54 C7
Glenview Dr BD18 54 C6
Glenview Gr BD18 54 D7
Glenview Rd BD18 54 D7
Glen View Rd
Bingley BD16 37 C5
Hebden Bridge HX7 88 E4
Shelley HD8 174 A2
Glen View St OL14 86 B1
Glenview Terr BD18 54 F8
Glen Way BD16 37 C6
Glenwood Ave BD17 37 E1
Glenwood Villas 11 LS18 58 C7
Global Ave LS11 213 B1
Globe Ct WF15 117 B4
Globe Fold BD8 74 C8
Globe Rd LS11 211 A2
Glossop Gr LS6 206 B4
Glossop Mount LS6 206 B4
Glossop St LS6 206 B4
Glossop View LS6 206 B4
Gloucester Ave
Bradford BD3 56 D1
Silsden BD20 5 C1
Gloucester Ct
Leeds LS12 210 B4
Wakefield WF2 120 F3
Gloucester Gr WF2 141 D5
Gloucester Pl WF2 141 D5
Gloucester Rd
Bingley BD16 37 B2
Wakefield WF2 141 D5
Gloucester Terr LS12 210 B3
Glover Ct BD5 74 E4
Glovershaw La BD16 37 E6
Glover Way LS11 214 C2
Glusburn Com Prim Sch
BD20 16 C6
Glydegate BD1 201 B2
Glyndon Ct HD6 136 B8
Glynn Terr BD8 74 B8
Gobind Marg BD3 201 D3
Godfrey Rd HX3 113 C3
Godfrey St BD8 73 D7
Godley Branch Rd HX3 113 E8
Godley Cl S71 179 D4
Godley Gdns HX3 92 F1
Godley La
Halifax HX3 113 E8
Northowram HX3 92 F1
Godley Rd HX3 203 C4
Godley St S71 179 D4
Godly Cl HX6 132 C1
Godly La HX6 132 C1
Godwin Pl HD2 136 F5
Godwin St BD1 201 B3
Goffee Way LS27 98 C8
Goff Well La BD21 35 C2
Gog Hill HX5 134 F7
Goit Side
Bradford BD1 201 B3
Halifax HX2 90 E4
Goits The 21 HX6 112 C4
Goit Stock La BD16 53 B8
Goit Stock Terr BD16 53 B8
Golcar Brow Rd HD9 170 C2
Golcar Jun & Inf Sch
HD7 152 D4
Goldcrest Ave BD8 73 B7
Goldcrest Ct HD4 171 E6
Golden Acre Cnr LS16 25 A1
Golden Acre Pk & Gdns★
LS16 42 C8
Golden Bank LS18 41 C1
Golden Butts Rd LS29 8 C4
Golden Sq WF4 141 B1
Golden Terr LS12 78 A4
Golden View Dr BD21 35 F6
Goldfields Ave HX4 134 B8
Goldfields Cl 1 HX4 134 B8
Goldfields View 2 HX4 134 B8
Goldfields Way HX4 134 B8
Goldington Ave HD3 153 A8
Goldington Dr HD3 153 A8
Goldsmith Dr WF3 100 B2
Golf Ave HX2 112 C7
Golf Cres HX2 112 C7
Golf La LS27 118 E8
Gomersal CE Mid Sch
BD19 96 B1
Gomersal Fst Sch BD19 96 B1
Gomersal La BD19 117 A7
Gomersal Rd WF16 117 C6
Gomersal St Marys CE Fst
Sch BD19 117 B8
Gondal Ct BD5 74 C3
Goodcomb Pl LS25 83 C3
Gooder Ave S71 179 C3
Gooder La HD6 115 B1
Gooder St HD6 115 A2
Goodfellow Cl 8 BD16 54 B6
Good Hope Cl WF6 123 D3
Goodman St LS10 212 B1
Goodrick La LS17 43 B7
Goods La WF12 139 D7
Goodwin Ho 5 BD13 72 E1
Goodwin Rd LS12 209 C2
Goodwood
Ilkley LS29 7 F6
Middleton LS10 99 D3
Goodwood Ave LS25 83 A2
Goody Cross LS26 82 C2
Goody Cross La LS26 82 C2
Goody Cross Vale LS26 82 B2
Gooseacre Ave S63 194 C1
Gooseacre Prim Sch
S63 194 C1
Goose Cote La BD22 34 E2
Goose Cote Way BD22 34 E3
Goosedale Ct BD4 76 A1
Goose Eye BD22 34 B6
Goosefield Rise LS25 82 D6
Goose Gn HD9 189 A5
Goose Hill WF16 117 D4
Goosehill La WF6 143 E7
Goosehill Rd WF6 144 A8
Goosehole La WF9 183 B1
Goose La LS20 21 C1
Goose West La HX6 112 B2
Gordale Cl WF17 118 B5
Gordon Ave WF5 140 D6
Gordon Ct WF14 138 C6
Gordon Dr LS6 59 F6
Gordon Larking Ct LS21 22 E7
Gordon Pl
5 Leeds LS6 59 F6
South Elmsall WF9 182 F2
Gordonsfield WF7 163 F5
Gordon St
Bradford BD5 201 C1
7 Bradford, Clayton BD14 73 B4
East Ardsley WF3 120 E8
Elland HX5 134 F6
Featherstone WF7 145 D7
Halifax HX3 92 B2
10 Haworth BD22 51 E8
Ilkley LS29 8 C4
Keighley BD21 35 B7
Slaithwaite HD7 170 A8
Sowerby Bridge HX6 112 A3
Sutton-in-C BD20 16 D5
10 Todmorden OL14 108 C5
Wakefield WF1 142 F2
Gordon Terr
Bradford BD10 39 B1
Knottingley WF11 127 B3
Leeds LS6 59 F6
Slaithwaite HD7 152 D2
Gordon View LS6 59 F6
Goring Park Ave WF5 141 A4
Gorple Rd BB10 66 A5
Gorse Ave BD17 37 E1
Gorse Lea 5 LS10 99 D8
Gorse Rd HD3 153 C6
Gorton St WF9 163 B1
Gosling La HX4 132 F2
Gosport Cl HD3, HX4 152 A8
Gosport La HD3 152 A8
Gosside Gr 8 WF6 123 D1
Gothic Mount WF7 145 A8
Gothic St BD13 72 E1
Gott's Terr BD20 18 A2
Gotts Park Ave LS12 58 F1
Gotts Park View LS12 59 A2
Gotts Rd LS12 210 C3
Gott St BD22 51 F8
Gough La HX6 132 B7
Goulbourne St BD21 35 B6
Governor's Yd WF1 216 C3
Gower St
Bradford BD5 74 E4
Leeds LS2 212 A4
Gracechurch St BD8 74 D8
Grace Leather La WF17 118 E5
Grace St
Keighley BD21 35 D7
Leeds LS1 211 A4
Gracey La BD6 73 F1
Grady Cl BD10 56 B6
Grafton Cl
Baildon BD17 38 D4
Knottingley WF11 126 F5
Grafton Pl HX3 92 A3
Grafton Rd BD21 35 A5
Grafton Sch LS6 206 B3
Grafton St
Batley WF17 118 D3
Bradford BD5 201 B1
Castleford WF10 124 E5
Keighley BD21 35 B5
Leeds LS7 207 A1
Grafton Villas LS15 62 D4
Graham Ave
Leeds LS4 205 A3
Upton WF9 183 D8
Graham Dr WF10 125 B7
Graham Gr LS4 205 A3
Graham Ho LS13 58 F3
Graham La HD4 153 B3
Graham Mount LS4 205 A3
Graham St
Bradford BD9 55 A2
Huddersfield HD1 153 F5
Leeds LS4 205 A3
Graham Terr LS4 205 A3
Graham View LS4 205 A3
Graham Wlk LS27 97 D7
Graingers Way LS12 210 C3
Grain St BD5 74 B2

Gramfield Rd HD4 ....**153** C3
Grammar School St BD1.**201** B4
Grampian Ave WF2 ......**141** E3
Grampian Cl HD8 ....**173** F3
Granary Ct BD2 ....**56** C5
Granby Ave LS6 ....**59** D5
Granby Cl LS6 ....**59** D5
Granby Ct WF9 ....**183** A5
Granby Dr BD20 ....**18** F1
Granby Flats **1** HD1 ...**153** C5
Granby Gr LS6 ....**59** D5
Granby La BD20 ....**18** F1
Granby Mount **8** LS6 ..**59** D5
Granby Pl LS6 ....**59** D5
Granby Rd LS6 ....**59** D5
Granby St
  Bradford BD4 ....**201** C2
  Leeds LS6 ....**59** D5
  2 Queensbury BD13 ..**72** E1
Granby Terr LS6 ....**59** D5
Granby View LS6 ....**59** D5
Grandage Terr BD8 ......**74** B8
Grand Arc LS1 ....**211** C4
Grand Cross Rd HD5 ....**154** E6
Grandsmere Pl **5** HX3 ..**113** B4
Grand Stand HD7 ....**152** B5
Grand Stand Rd WF2 ....**120** F5
Grand Theatre★ LS1 ....**211** C4
Grand View **7** BD13 ...**72** C2
Grange Ave
  Batley WF17 ....**118** B3
  Birkenshaw BD4 ....**96** A8
  Bradford, Lower Grange
    BD15 ....**73** C4
  Bradford, Thornbury BD3. .**75** F8
  Garforth LS25 ....**82** F6
  Halifax HX2 ....**91** F5
  Huddersfield HD2 ......**135** F1
  Ilkley LS29 ....**8** D4
  Leeds LS7 ....**207** B4
  Marsden HD7 ....**169** A4
  Menston LS29 ....**21** F5
  Shipley BD18 ....**54** E8
  South Elmsall WF9 .....**183** A3
  Thorp Arch LS23 ....**15** A3
  Yeadon LS19 ....**40** C6
Grange Bank HX3 ....**93** C6
Grange Bank Cl HD5 ....**154** D7
Grange Bldgs LS27 ......**98** C2
Grange Cl
  Badsworth WF9 ....**164** E2
  Bardsey LS17 ....**28** D4
  Brierley S72 ....**180** F3
  Elland HD3 ....**152** A8
  Horsforth LS18 ....**57** F8
  Ilkley LS29 ....**8** D4
  Knottingley WF11 ......**126** E4
  Leeds LS10 ....**215** A4
Grange Cotts
  Cleckheaton BD19 ......**116** C8
  Marsden HD7 ....**169** A4
Grange Cres
  Keighley BD20 ....**18** E2
  Leeds LS7 ....**207** B4
  Thurnscoe S63 ....**194** E1
  Yeadon LS19 ....**40** C6
Grange Croft LS17 ......**43** C5
Grange Ct
  Badsworth WF9 ....**164** E2
  Barwick in E LS15 .....**62** F6
  Halifax HX3 ....**114** A4
  Leeds, Alwoodley LS17 ..**43** C5
  Leeds, Headingley Hill LS6 .**59** F5
  Rothwell LS26 ....**101** C7
  4 Shipley BD16 ....**54** A7
Grange Dr
  Bradford BD15 ....**73** C8
  Emley HD8 ....**175** D8
  Horsforth LS18 ....**57** F8
  Ossett WF5 ....**140** F3
Grange Est LS29 ....**8** D4
Grange Farm Cl LS29 ....**21** F5
Grange Farm Prim Sch
  LS14 ....**61** F6
Grangefield Ave
  Batley WF17 ....**118** B3
  Burley in W LS29 ....**9** F1
Grangefield Ct LS25 ....**82** F7
Grangefield Ind Est LS28. **57** F1
Grangefield Rd LS28 ....**57** F1
Grange Fields Mount **9**
  LS10 ....**99** F6
Grange Fields Rd LS10 ..**99** F6
Grange Fields Way LS10. .**99** F6
Grange Fold BD15 ....**73** C8
Grange Gr
  Bradford BD3 ....**75** C8
  Keighley BD20 ....**18** E1
Grange Ho S72 ....**180** F3
Grange Holt LS17 ....**43** C5
Grange Hts HX3 ....**114** A4
Grange La
  Brighouse HD6 ....**115** E2
  Flockton WF4 ....**157** D4
  Haworth BD22 ....**33** F3
  Kippax LS25 ....**83** B2
  Kirkburton HD8 ....**173** D3
  Skellow DN6 ....**184** F3
Grange Mount LS19 .....**40** C6
Grange Park Ave LS8 ....**61** D5
Grange Park Cl
  Kippax LS25 ....**103** A8
  Leeds LS8 ....**61** E5
  9 Morley LS27 ....**98** B7
Grange Park Cres LS8 ...**61** D5

Grange Park Ct LS27 ....**98** B7
Grange Park Dr
  Morley LS27 ....**98** B7
  Shipley BD16 ....**54** B8
Grange Park Gr LS8 .....**61** D5
Grange Park Mews
  Leeds LS8 ....**61** D5
  10 Morley LS27 ....**98** B7
Grange Park Pl LS8 .....**61** E5
Grange Park Rd
  Leeds LS8 ....**61** E5
  Shipley BD16 ....**54** A7
Grange Park Rise LS8 ...**61** E5
Grange Park Terr LS8 ...**61** E5
Grange Park Way LS27 ..**98** B7
Grange Park Wlk LS8 ...**61** D5
Grange Pk
  Baildon BD17 ....**38** E3
  Halifax HX3 ....**113** B3
Grange Rd
  Batley, Chidswell WF17 ..**119** A4
  Batley WF17 ....**118** A3
  Bingley BD16 ....**37** B4
  Bradford BD15 ....**73** C8
  Brierley S72 ....**180** F2
  Burley in W LS29 ....**9** F1
  Castleford WF10 ....**104** E1
  Cleckheaton BD19 ......**116** C8
  Farnhill BD20 ....**4** D1
  Holme Chapel BB10 ....**85** A7
  Huddersfield HD7 ......**152** E6
  Keighley BD20 ....**18** E1
  Leeds LS10 ....**215** A4
  Royston S71 ....**179** B3
  Steeton BD20 ....**17** A5
  Yeadon LS19 ....**40** C6
Grange Rd The LS16 .....**42** B1
Grange Rise WF9 ....**181** D7
Grange Road Ind Est
  WF17 ....**118** E4
Grange St
  10 Halifax HX3 ....**92** A1
  Keighley BD21 ....**35** C8
  Marsden HD7 ....**169** A4
  10 Morley LS27 ....**98** C8
  Wakefield WF2 ....**142** A5
Grange Tech Coll BD5 ...**74** B2
Grange Terr
  Bradford BD15 ....**73** C8
  Leeds LS7 ....**207** A4
  Marsden HD7 ....**169** A4
  8 Morley LS27 ....**98** B7
  Pudsey LS28 ....**76** E8
  Shipley BD18 ....**55** B6
  Steeton BD20 ....**17** A5
  5 Yeadon LS19 ....**40** C6
Grange The
  Garforth LS25 ....**83** B7
  Huddersfield HD5 ......**154** F7
  Leeds LS11 ....**214** A2
  Rothwell WF3 ....**100** D3
Grange Valley Rd WF17 .**118** F4
Grange View
  Bradford BD3 ....**75** F8
  Dewsbury WF12 ....**139** D1
  Hemsworth WF9 ....**181** D6
  Leeds, Colton LS15 .....**81** D6
  Leeds, Potternewton Park
    LS7 ....**207** B4
  Otley LS21 ....**10** F1
  Pudsey LS28 ....**76** E8
  Steeton BD20 ....**17** A5
  Wetherby LS22 ....**13** E4
Grange View Gdns LS17 .**44** F1
Grangeway
  Bradford BD15 ....**73** C8
  Hemsworth WF9 ....**181** D7
Grangewood Ct
  Leeds LS16 ....**42** B1
  Lofthouse Gate WF1 ...**121** D5
Grangewood Gdns LS16. .**42** B1
Granham Acre S72 ......**180** C2
Granhamthorpe LS13 ....**58** C2
Granholme Cl BD20 .....**16** D5
Granny Ave LS27 ....**98** C8
Granny Hall Gr HD6 .....**114** F4
Granny Hall La HD6 .....**114** F4
Granny Hall Pk HD6 .....**114** F4
Granny Hill Terr HX1 ....**202** B1
Granny La
  Leeds LS12 ....**209** A1
  Mirfield WF14 ....**138** B3
Grant Ave LS7 ....**207** B2
Grantham Pl
  Bradford BD7 ....**74** C5
  Halifax HX3 ....**92** B2
Grantham Rd
  Bradford BD7 ....**74** C5
  Halifax HX3 ....**92** B2
Grantham Terr BD7 .....**74** C5
Grantham Twrs LS7 .....**207** B1
Grantley Pl HD2 ....**136** D5
Grantley St WF1 ....**216** C2
Grantley Way WF1 ......**216** C3
Granton Rd LS7 ....**204** A1
Grant St
  Bradford BD3 ....**201** D3
  Keighley BD21 ....**35** A7
  Oxenhope BD22 ....**51** C2
Granville Ave **6** WF8 ..**146** C8
Granville Ct LS21 ......**22** F7
Granville Mount LS21 ...**22** F7
Granville Pl
  Bradford BD15 ....**73** C8
  Otley LS21 ....**22** F7
Granville Rd
  Leeds LS9 ....**207** B1

Granville Rd continued
  Shipley BD18 ....**55** C5
Granville St
  Bradford BD14 ....**73** C5
  Castleford WF10 ....**124** C5
  Dewsbury WF13 ....**139** B8
  6 Elland HX5 ....**134** F6
  Keighley BD21 ....**35** B7
  Liversedge WF15 ....**117** B3
  Normanton WF6 ....**123** B2
  Pudsey LS28 ....**76** C8
  3 Pudsey, Stanningley
    LS28 ....**57** F2
  Purston Jaglin WF7 ....**145** C4
  2 Walsden OL14 .....**108** A1
Granville Terr
  Bingley BD16 ....**37** A3
  Guiseley LS20 ....**22** F7
  5 Huddersfield HD1 ...**153** E5
  Otley LS21 ....**22** F7
  Shipley BD18 ....**55** B5
  2 Yeadon LS19 ....**40** C7
Grape St
  Bradford BD15 ....**54** C1
  Halifax HX1 ....**203** A2
  3 Keighley BD21 .....**35** E8
  Leeds LS10 ....**212** A1
Grasleigh Ave BD15 .....**54** A3
Grasleigh Way BD15 ....**53** F2
Grasmere Ave LS22 .....**13** C5
Grasmere Cl
  Castleford WF10 ....**104** E1
  Leeds LS12 ....**210** A2
Grasmere Cres S75 .....**178** A3
Grasmere Ct LS12 ......**210** A3
Grasmere Dr
  Elland HX5 ....**135** B7
  Wetherby LS22 ....**13** C5
Grasmere Rd
  Batley WF12 ....**118** E2
  Bradford BD2 ....**56** A3
  Brighouse BD12 ....**94** E1
  Knottingley WF11 ......**126** E2
  Leeds LS12 ....**210** A2
  Meltham HD9 ....**170** E1
  Wakefield WF2 ....**141** E7
Grasscroft HD5 ....**154** F2
Grasscroft Ave HD9 .....**171** F4
Grasscroft Rd
  Honley HD9 ....**171** E4
  Huddersfield HD1 ......**153** E7
Grassmere Rd HD1 ......**153** E7
Grassmoor Fold HD9 ....**172** A3
Gratrix La HX6 ....**112** C5
Grattan St **5** BD1 .....**74** D7
Graveleythorpe Rd LS15. .**62** B1
Graveleythorpe Rise **2**
  LS15 ....**62** B1
Gray's Rd S71 ....**179** C1
Gray Ave BD18 ....**55** D5
Gray Ct LS15 ....**81** D8
Gray Hall Cl HX4 ....**133** F3
Gray Ho **4** LS22 ......**13** E6
Grayrigg Cl LS15 ....**80** E7
Grayshon Dr BD6 ....**74** C1
Grayshon St BD11 ......**96** E5
Grayson Crest LS4 .....**59** B3
Grayson Hts LS4 ....**59** B3
Gray St FW15 ....**116** E4
Grayswood Cres BD4 ...**75** D3
Grayswood Dr BD4 .....**75** D3
Great Albion St HX1 ....**203** B3
Great Ben La HD7 ......**151** E3
Great Cross St BD1 .....**201** C2
Great Edge Rd HX2 .....**111** F6
Greatfield Cl WF5 ......**140** E6
Greatfield Dr WF5 ......**140** E6
Greatfield Gdns WF5 ...**140** E6
Greatfield Rd WF5 .....**140** E5
Great George St LS1, LS2 **211** B4
Great Horton Rd
  Bradford, Great Horton
    BD7 ....**74** B5
  Bradford, Horton Bank BD7. **73** E3
Great House La HX6 ....**132** A3
Great House Rd OL14 ...**108** E3
Great Northern Rd BD21. .**35** C6
Great Northern Ret Pk
  HD1 ....**154** B7
Great Northern St
  Huddersfield HD1 ......**154** B7
  Morley LS27 ....**98** A3
Great North Rd LS25 ...**84** A6
Great Pasture LS29 .....**9** F2
Great Pasture La LS29 ..**9** F2
Great Pond St WF13 ....**138** F5
Great Preston CE Prim Sch
  LS26 ....**102** E7
Great Russell Ct BD7 ...**74** C7
Great Russell St BD7 ...**74** C7
Great Wilson St LS11 ...**211** C2
Great Wood Gdns HD8 ..**155** C2
Great Wood St WF17 ...**118** C4
Greave Cl
  4 Bacup OL13 ....**106** B3
  Huddersfield HD2 ......**136** B4
Greave Clough Cl **1**
  OL13 ....**106** B3
Greave Clough Dr OL13 .**106** B3
Greave Cres **8** OL13 ..**106** A3
Greavefield La WF8,
  WF11 ....**126** B1
Greave House Dr HX2 ..**111** D7
Greave House Fields
  HX2 ....**111** E8
Greave House La HD8 ..**155** D3
Greave House Pk HX2 ..**111** D7
Greave House Terr HD8 .**155** D3

Greave Rd
  Bacup OL13 ....**106** B3
  Holmfirth HX9 ....**199** A8
  Rippondon HX6 ....**131** E6
Greaves Ave WF2 ....**141** C5
Greaves Croft HD8 .....**155** D3
Greaves Fold HX4 ......**134** C4
Greaves Pl HX4 ....**134** C4
Greaves Rd WF13 ......**118** D3
Greaves St
  Bradford BD5 ....**74** D3
  Castleford WF10 ....**124** D8
Greave St OL13 ....**108** D5
Greave Terr **2** OL13 ..**106** B3
Grebe Cl BD6 ....**73** C1
Greek St
  Castleford WF10 ....**124** E8
  Leeds LS1 ....**211** B4
Green's Sq HX2 ....**202** A4
Green's Terr BD12 .....**94** F4
Green Abbey HD9 ....**199** B8
Greenacre Ave BD12 ...**94** D2
Greenacre Cl **1** BD12 .**94** D2
Green Acre Cl BD17 ....**38** D3
Greenacre Ct LS25 .....**83** A7
Greenacre Dr
  Bradford BD12 ....**94** D2
  Denby Dale HD8 ....**191** E3
Greenacre Gate HD8 ...**156** A3
Greenacre Park Ave LS19. **40** B5
Greenacre Park Mews
  LS19 ....**40** C5
Greenacre Park Rise
  LS19 ....**40** C5
Greenacre Pk LS19 .....**40** B5
Greenacre Rd WF9 .....**183** C6
Greenacres
  Ossett WF5 ....**119** D1
  Rippondon HX6 ....**132** E4
  Shelf HX3 ....**93** D6
Green Acres
  Burley in W LS29 ......**21** D8
  Crigglestone WF4 ......**160** A7
  Featherstone WF7 .....**145** E3
Greenacres Ave HX3 ...**93** D6
Greenacres Cl WF5 .....**119** D1
Green Acres Cl HD8 ....**175** C6
Greenacres Ct WF10 ...**125** A8
Greenacres Dr
  Batley WF17 ....**97** A2
  Castleford WF10 ......**125** A8
  Keighley BD20 ....**18** A1
  Shelf HX3 ....**93** D6
Greenacres Gr HX3 ....**93** D6
Greenacre Way BD12 ..**94** D2
Greenacre Wlk WF4 ...**162** D2
Greenaire Pl **7** BD1 ..**74** D7
Green Ave
  Batley WF16 ....**117** E4
  Kippax LS25 ....**82** F3
  Silsden BD20 ....**5** D2
Green Balk La HD8 .....**155** F2
Green Bank
  Cleckheaton BD19 ....**116** F6
  Rothwell WF3 ....**100** D1
Greenbank Cl WF10 ....**124** A5
Green Bank Ct BD17 ....**38** B1
Greenbank Gr WF6 .....**122** F3
Greenbank Rd
  Bradford BD15 ....**73** C8
  Normanton WF6 ....**122** F4
Greenbanks Ave LS18 ..**41** C2
Greenbanks Cl LS18 ...**41** C2
Greenbanks Dr LS18 ...**41** B2
Green Chase **2** LS6 ..**59** E7
Green Cl
  Batley WF17 ....**118** C5
  Bradford BD8 ....**73** E8
  Dewsbury WF13 ....**118** A2
  Leeds LS6 ....**59** F7
  Low Bradley BD20 .....**4** C6
  Steeton BD20 ....**16** F6
Green Cliff HD9 ....**171** F5
Greencliffe Ave BD17 ..**38** C3
Green Cres
  Huddersfield HD7 ......**152** E5
  Leeds LS6 ....**59** E7
Green Croft WF9 ....**163** B2
Greencroft Ave HX3 ....**93** B3
Greencroft Cl BD10 ....**56** A7
Greencroft Mews LS20 .**22** E1
Green Ct
  Barwick in E LS15 .....**62** F7
  Bradford BD7 ....**73** F5
  Brighouse BD19 ....**115** F8
  Leeds LS17 ....**43** D2
Greendale Cl BB10 .....**85** A7
Greendale Ct HX3 ......**171** F5
Greendown Cl LS29 ....**8** D4
Green Edge HD7 ....**152** C6
Green End
  Bradford BD14 ....**73** B4
  Brighouse HD6 ....**115** A1
  Wadsworth Moor HX7...**89** C5
Green End **10** OL13 ...**106** A3
Green End La WF2 .....**142** C3
Green End Rd
  Bradford BD6 ....**94** B8
  Keighley BD20 ....**19** E2
Greenfell Cl BD22 .....**34** F6
Greenfield BD22 ....**51** C8
Greenfield Ave
  Brighouse HX3 ....**115** A7
  Gildersome LS27 ......**97** B2
  Guiseley LS20 ....**39** B7
  Huddersfield HD3 .....**153** A7
  Kippax LS25 ....**83** A2

Greenfield Ave continued
  Ossett WF5 ....**141** ▪
  Shipley BD18 ....**55** ◆
Greenfield Cl
  Burley in W LS29 ......**21** ▪
  Denby Dale HD8 ....**191** ▪
  Elland HX4 ....**133** ▪
  3 Kippax LS25 ......**83** ▪
  Northowram HX3 ......**93** ▪
  Ossett WF5 ....**141** ▪
  Wakefield WF2 ....**120** ▪
Greenfield Cres
  Cullingworth BD13 ....**52** ▪
  Grange Moor WF4 .....**156** ▪
Greenfield Ct
  Keighley BD16 ....**35** ▪
  Leeds LS16 ....**42** ▪
Greenfield Dr
  6 Brighouse BD19 ..**115** ▪
  Gildersome LS27 ......**97** ▪
Greenfield Garth **4** LS25. **83** ▪
Greenfield Gdns
  Barnsley S71 ....**178** ▪
  Steeton BD20 ....**16** ▪
Greenfield La
  Bradford, Bierley BD4 ..**95** ▪
  Bradford, Horton Bank Bottom
    BD7 ....**73** ▪
  Bradford, Thackley BD10. .**39** ▪
  Guiseley LS20 ....**39** ▪
Greenfield Mount WF2 ..**120** ▪
Greenfield Pl
  9 Bradford BD8 .....**55** ◆
  Brighouse HX3 ....**115** ▪
Greenfield Rd
  Hemsworth WF9 ......**181** ▪
  Holmfirth HD9 ....**188** ▪
  Leeds LS9 ....**212** ▪
  Normanton WF6 ......**122** ▪
  Ossett WF5 ....**141** ▪
Greenfield Rise LS25 ...**83** ▪
Greenfields WF16 ......**117** ◆
Greenfields Sch BD10 ..**39** ▪
Greenfields Way LS29 ..**21** ▪
Greenfield Terr
  Haworth BD22 ....**51** ◆
  Mickletown LS26 ......**102** ▪
  Todmorden OL14 ......**86** ▪
Greenfield Vale LS25 ...**83** ▪
Greenfield View LS25 ...**83** ▪
Greenfield Way WF2 ...**120** ▪
Greenfinch Dr HD4 .....**171** ▪
Greenfinch Way BD15 ..**73** ▪
Greenfold La LS22 .....**13** ▪
Greengate
  Rothwell LS26 ....**101** ◆
  Silsden BD20 ....**5** ▪
Green Gate Head HX4 ..**151** ▪
Green Gate La HD7 .....**170** ▪
Greengate Rd
  Keighley BD21 ....**35** ◆
  Norton WF8 ....**166** ▪
Green Gate Rd HD9 ....**188** ▪
Greengates Ave **3** BD12. .**94** ▪
Greengates Mill WF12....**140** ▪
Greengates Prim Sch
  BD10 ....**56** ◆
Green Gdns HD7 ....**152** ▪
Green Hall Pk HX3 .....**93** ▪
Green Head HD7 ....**170** ▪
Greenhead Ave HD5 ....**154** ▪
Green Head Ave BD20 ..**18** ▪
Greenhead Coll HD1 ...**153** ▪
Green Head Cl HD1 ....**153** ▪
Green Head Dr BD20 ...**18** ▪
Greenhead High Sch
  BD20 ....**18** ▪
Greenhead La
  Brighouse HD6 ....**135** ▪
  Huddersfield HD5 .....**154** ▪
Green Head La BD20 ...**18** ▪
Greenhead Rd
  Huddersfield HD1 ......**153** ▪
  Leeds LS16 ....**59** ▪
Green Head Rd BD20 ...**18** ▪
Green Hill
  9 Bacup OL13 ....**106** ▪
  Halifax HX2 ....**112** ▪
  Huddersfield HD2 .....**136** ▪
Greenhill Ave WF8 .....**146** ▪
Greenhill Bank Rd HD9. .**189** ▪
Green Hill Chase LS12 ..**209** ▪
Green Hill Cl LS12 .....**58** ▪
Green Hill Cres LS12 ...**209** ▪
Green Hill Croft LS12 ...**209** ▪
Greenhill Dr BD16 .....**36** ▪
Green Hill Dr LS13 .....**58** ▪
Green Hill Gdns LS12 ...**209** ▪
Green Hill Holt LS12 ...**209** ▪
Greenhill Ind Est HX7 ..**110** ▪
Greenhill La
  Bingley BD16 ....**36** ▪
  Bradford BD3 ....**75** ▪
Green Hill La LS12 .....**209** ▪
Greenhill Mount WF8 ..**146** ▪
Green Hill Mount LS13 ..**58** ▪
Green Hill Pl LS13 .....**58** ▪
Greenhill Prim Sch LS13. **77** ▪
Greenhill Rd
  Huddersfield HD3 .....**152** ▪
  Wakefield WF1 ....**216** ▪
Green Hill Rd
  8 Bacup OL13 ....**106** ▪
  Leeds LS12, LS13 ......**58** ▪
Greenhills LS19 ....**40** ▪
Greenhill St BD3 ....**75** ▪
Green Hill Way LS13 ...**58** ▪
Green Ho HX2 ....**90** ▪

reenholme Cl LS29 ....9 F2
reenholme Ct 16 BD4 .... 75 F2
reenholme Trad Est LS29..9 F2
reen House Hill HD8 .. 174 C4
reen House La HD8 ... 174 C4
reenhow Cl LS4 ...... 205 A2
reenhow Gdns LS4 ... 205 A2
reenhow Pk LS29 ..... 9 D1
reenhow Rd LS4 ...... 205 A2
reenhow Wlk LS4.. 205 A2
reen La
  Ackworth M T WF7....163 B6
  Addingham LS29 ...... 6 E8
  Baildon, Baildon Wood Bottom
    BD17.............38 B1
  Baildon BD17............38 A4
  Boston Spa LS23 .... 30 F6
  Bradford, Clifton Villas BD8 .. 55 C1
  Bradford, Fourlands BD10.. 56 C8
  Bradford, Haigh Fold BD2.. 56 D3
  Bradford, Idle Moor BD10.. 56 A8
  Bradford, Lidget Green BD7 74 A5
  Bradford, Oakenshaw BD12 94 F4
  Bradford, Wyke BD12 .... 94 C2
  Brighouse, Clifton HD6 .. 115 F2
  Brighouse, Hove Edge HD6 114 E4
  Burley in W LS29.... 9 E3
  Castleford, Castleford Ings
    WF10.............103 F1
  Castleford, Cutsyke WF10 124 C5
  Cleckheaton BD19.....95 E2
  Collingham LS22 .... 29 A8
  Denby Dale HD8 ...... 191 B2
  Dewsbury WF13 .... 118 A1
  Elland, Sowood Green HX4 133 F1
  Elland, West Vale HX4... 134 C6
  Featherstone WF7......145 B6
  Featherstone WF7......145 D6
  Garforth LS25 ....83 A7
  Glusburn BD20 ....16 B7
  Halifax, Bank Top HX3 .. 113 E6
  Halifax, Illingworth HX2 .. 91 E8
  Halifax, Midgley HX2.... 90 D1
  Halifax, Pye Nest HX2....202 A1
  Halifax, Shibden Dale HX2, HX3,
    HX4.............92 E6
  Halton East BD23 ...... 1 E8
  Haworth BD22.........33 F4
  Heptonstall HX7 ...... 88 E5
  Holmfirth HD9 .... 189 A2
  Horbury WF4 .... 159 C8
  Horsforth LS18 ...... 58 B7
  Kippax, Kippax Common
    LS25 ....82 F2
  Kippax LS25 ....82 F2
  Ledston WF10 .... 103 E6
  Leeds, Beeston LS11 ..... 214 A1
  Leeds, Cookridge LS16 .... 41 D5
  Leeds, Cross Gates LS15... 62 B1
  Leeds, Farnley LS12 ...... 77 C5
  Leeds, New Wortley LS12 . 210 B2
  Leeds, Whinmoor LS14 .... 62 A8
  Liversedge WF15........116 D3
  Low Bradley BD20 ...... 5 A6
  Marsden HD7.......... 169 B7
  Meltham HD9.......... 170 E1
  Menston LS29 .... 21 C5
  Mickletown LS26 ...... 102 F2
  Netherton, Overton WF4 .. 157 F6
  Netherton WF4 .... 158 E5
  Netherton WF4 .... 158 F5
  Notton WF4 .... 179 A5
  Oakworth BD22....... 34 D2
  Otley LS21 .... 10 F1
  Pontefract, Carleton WF8 . 146 F8
  Pontefract WF8....... 146 D7
  Pudsey LS28 .... 76 D6
  Queensbury BD13 ..... 72 B3
  Ripponden HX4, HX6 ..... 150 F8
  Ripponden, Syke Hill HX6 . 132 B4
  Rothwell WF3 .... 100 D1
  Shelf HX3........... 93 E6
  Skellow DN6 .... 184 E3
  South Kirkby WF9 ...... 182 B2
  Steeton BD20....... 17 A6
  Thornton BD13 ...... 72 E6
  Upton WF9........... 165 C1
  Wakefield WF2 .... 141 E7
  Yeadon LS19 .... 40 B5
reenland S75......... 193 B8
reenland Ave BD13 .... 92 E8
reenland Cotts BD13....72 E2
reenland Ct LS26 ..... 101 C5
reenland Rd HX7 ..... 87 C6
reenland Villas BD13 .. 92 E8
reen Lane Bsns Pk
  WF7..............145 C6
reen Lane Cl WF7 .... 145 C6
reen Lane Ind Pk WF7 145 A6
reen Lane Terr HD7... 152 C6
reen Lane Villas LS25.. 83 A7
reenlaws Cl HD9 ..... 188 D5
reenlay Dr WF2 ...... 120 B2
reen Lea LS26 .... 101 C5
reenlea Cl LS19 ..... 39 F6
reen Lea Cl LS23 .... 30 E7
reenlea Ct
  Honley HD9 ....171 F5
  Huddersfield HD5 .... 155 A6
reenlea Fold LS19 ... 39 F5
reen Lea Mills (Ind Units)
  HD5...............155 A6
reenlea Mount LS19 .. 39 F6
reenlea Rd LS19 ..... 39 F5
reen Lea Rd HD5 .... 154 F6
reenley Hill BD15.... 53 B4

Green Mdw BD15 .... 53 D4
Green Meadows Sch LS20 22 C1
Greenmoor Ave
  Leeds LS12 ....77 D7
  Rothwell WF3........100 C1
Greenmoor Cl WF3 .. 100 C1
Greenmoor Cres WF3 .. 100 C1
Green Mount
  4 Baildon BD17.......38 B2
  Bradford BD4.........75 D3
  Brighouse HX3........93 F3
  Huddersfield HD5 .... 154 D6
Greenmount Ct 4 LS11 214 B3
Greenmount La LS11... 214 B3
Greenmount Pl LS11 .. 214 B3
Green Mount Prim Sch
  LS11..............214 B3
Green Mount Ret Pk
  HX1...............203 A3
Greenmount St LS11 .. 214 B3
Greenmount Terr LS11 . 214 B3
Greenock Pl 2 LS12 .. 209 A4
Greenock Rd LS12 .... 209 A4
Greenock St LS12 .... 209 A4
Greenock Terr 1 LS12 .. 209 A4
Green Park Ave
  Halifax HX3 ....113 C2
  Horbury WF4 .... 140 F2
  Ossett WF5 .... 140 E3
Green Park Dr HX3 .. 113 C2
Green Park Gate HX3 . 113 C2
Green Park Rd HX3 .. 113 C2
Green Park St HX3 .. 113 C2
Green Pasture Cl LS9 .. 80 C8
Green Pk
  Leeds LS17 ....43 E2
  Wakefield WF1 ....142 E6
Green Pl BD2 .... 56 B2
Green Rd
  Baildon BD17........38 C2
  Leeds LS6 ....59 D4
  Liversedge WF15.......117 A5
Green Row
  Bradford BD10........56 B6
  3 Leeds LS6.........59 E7
  Mickletown LS26 ..... 102 D1
Green Row Fold LS26 .. 102 D1
Green Royd
  Elland HX4 ....134 C6
  Halifax HX2 ....91 B4
Greenroyd Ave
  Cleckheaton BD19 ...... 95 D2
  Halifax HX3 ....113 B3
Greenroyd Cl HX3.... 113 B2
Greenroyd Croft HD2.. 135 E1
Greenroyd Ct WF8 .... 147 C5
Greenroyd Dr BD20 ... 16 D4
Greenroyd Gr BD20 ... 16 D4
Greenroyd La HX2 .. 91 E1
Greens End Rd HD9 .. 170 D2
Greenset View S71.... 178 E1
Greenshank Mews LS27 .. 98 D3
Greenshaw Terr LS20 .. 22 D1
Greenside
  Bradford BD12........95 A4
  Cleckheaton BD19 ..... 116 E7
  Darton S75 .... 178 C1
  Denby Dale HD8 ..... 192 A4
  Featherstone WF7.......145 D6
  Havercroft WF4 ...... 180 B8
  2 Liversedge WF16 .... 117 C4
  Pudsey LS28 .... 76 D6
  Shafton S72 .... 180 B4
  Skelmanthorpe HD8 .. 191 E8
  Walton WF2 .... 161 A4
  Yeadon LS19 .... 40 A5
Greenside Ave
  Darton S75 ....178 C1
  Huddersfield HD5 .... 155 A5
  Leeds LS12 .... 209 B1
Greenside Cl LS12 ... 209 C1
Greenside Cres HD5 .. 155 A5
Greenside Ct
  Crofton WF4 ....162 B7
  Gildersome LS27 ...... 97 D7
Greenside Dr
  Huddersfield HD5 ... 155 A5
  Leeds LS12 .... 209 C1
Greenside Est WF14.. 138 A7
Greenside Gr 3 LS28 .. 76 D6
Greenside Inf Sch HD5 .. 155 A4
Greenside La
  Bradford BD8........73 F7
  Cullingworth BD13.... 52 E6
Greenside Mount WF14 138 B7
Greenside Pk WF4 .... 162 B7
Greenside Pl S75 ..... 178 C1
Greenside Prim Sch LS28 76 D6
Greenside Rd
  Leeds LS12 ....209 C1
  Mirfield WF14 ...... 138 B7
Green Side Rd HD4 ... 173 A3
Greenside Terr LS12 .. 209 B1
Greenside Wlk LS12.. 209 B1
Greens La OL13 ...... 106 A3
Green Slacks La HD3.. 151 B5
Greensnook La OL13 .. 106 A3
Greensnook Mews 2
  OL13..............106 A3
Greensnook Terr 1
  OL13..............106 A3
Green Springs HX7.... 88 E3
Green Sq LS25 .... 83 B1
Green St
  Bradford BD1.........201 C3
  Bradford, Lower Woodlands
    BD12..............95 B5

Green St continued
  Castleford WF10 ......103 D1
  4 Elland HX4 .... 134 B4
  Haworth BD22....... 51 C6
  Huddersfield HD1 .... 154 A7
  Meltham HD9........ 170 D2
  6 Oxenhope BD22.... 51 D2
Greensway LS25 ...... 82 E7
Green Syke HX7 ...... 88 B3
Green Sykes Rd BD22 .. 34 A7
Green Terr
  Dewsbury WF13 ......118 A2
  Guiseley LS20 .... 39 E8
  Mirfield WF14 ...... 137 F6
Green Terrace Sq HX1 .. 202 C1
Green The
  Addingham LS29 .... 2 E1
  Batley WF17 .... 96 F2
  Bingley BD16........ 37 A6
  Bingley, Eldwick Beck BD16. 37 C6
  Bingley, Gilstead BD16 ... 37 D3
  Birkenshaw BD4....... 95 F7
  Boston Spa LS23 ...... 30 E8
  4 Bradford BD10..... 56 B8
  Castleford WF10 ..... 125 D8
  Crofton WF4 .... 144 C2
  Garforth LS25 .... 83 A7
  Guiseley LS20 .... 39 E8
  Horsforth LS18 ...... 58 B8
  Huddersfield HD2 .... 136 D5
  1 Kippax LS25 ...... 83 A1
  Kirkburton HD4 ..... 172 F2
  Leeds, Hawksworth LS5 .. 58 E7
  Leeds LS14 .... 62 B5
  Leeds, Moortown LS17 ... 43 E2
  Marsden HD7........ 168 F4
  Micklethwaite BD16.... 36 E7
  Mirfield WF14 ...... 137 E6
  Ossett WF5 .... 140 E4
  Otley LS21 .... 10 F1
  Pudsey LS28 .... 57 D4
  Purston Jaglin WF7...... 145 E4
  Royston S71........ 179 C3
  South Kirkby WF9 ..... 182 C3
  Woolley WF4 .... 178 A7
  11 Yeadon LS19 ..... 40 B7
Greenthorpe Ct LS13.. 77 E7
Greenthorpe Hill LS13.. 77 E8
Greenthorpe Mount LS13 77 E8
Greenthorpe Rd LS13.. 77 E7
Greenthorpe St LS13 .. 77 E7
Greenthorpe Wlk LS13.. 77 E7
Greenthwaite Cl BD20.. 18 A1
Greenton Ave BD19 ... 94 E1
Greenton Cres BD13 .. 92 D8
Greentop
  Crofton WF4 ....162 B7
  Pudsey LS28 .... 76 D6
Green Top LS12 ...... 209 B1
Green Top Gdns LS12 .. 209 B1
Green Top St BD8..... 73 E7
Greentrees 1 BD6.... 94 B6
Greenups Mill 18 HX6 .. 112 B4
Greenups Terr HX6 .. 112 B4
Greenview 1 BD13.... 162 B7
Green View
  Leeds LS6 ....59 E7
  Scarcroft LS14 ...... 45 C3
Greenview Cl LS12 ... 208 C2
Greenview Ct LS8 ... 61 A8
Greenview Mount LS12 208 C2
Green View The S72 .. 180 C4
Greenville Ave LS12 .. 209 B1
Greenville Dr BD12.... 94 E7
Greenville Gdns LS12 .. 209 B1
Greenway
  Bradford BD3........75 A8
  Guiseley LS20 ...... 39 C7
  Honley HD9 .... 171 F5
  Huddersfield HD3 .... 152 F5
  Leeds LS15 .... 62 C1
Green Way
  Glusburn BD20 ....16 C7
  Halifax HX2 .... 91 E8
  Scarcroft LS14 ...... 45 C3
Greenway Cl LS15..... 62 C1
Greenway Dr BD15.... 73 B7
Greenway Rd BD5..... 74 E2
Greenwell Ct LS9 .... 80 C8
Greenwell Row 6 BD14.. 73 B4
Greenwood Ave
  Bradford BD2........56 A4
  Dewsbury WF12 ...... 139 F7
  Upton WF9......... 183 C8
Greenwood Bldgs HD5 .. 155 C8
Greenwood Cl
  Normanton WF6 ......144 B7
  Upton WF9......... 183 C8
Greenwood Cres S71.. 179 B4
Greenwood Ct
  Bradford BD1.........201 C2
  Leeds LS6 .... 59 E7
Greenwood Dr BD2 ... 56 A4
Greenwood Ho 6 WF1 216 B2
Greenwood Mount
  Bradford BD2........56 A4
  Leeds LS6 .... 59 E7
Green Wood Pk LS6.. 59 E7
Greenwood Rd
  Baildon BD17........38 B1
  East Ardsley WF3 ..... 119 F7
  Wakefield WF1 ...... 142 E6
Greenwood Row LS28.. 76 F7
Greenwood St
  Dewsbury, Savile Town
    WF12..............139 C6

Greenwood St continued
  Dewsbury WF12, WF13 .. 139 B8
  3 Hebden Bridge HX7.. 89 A3
  Huddersfield HD5 .... 154 A4
Greetland Prim Sch HX4 134 B7
Greetland Rd HX4..... 133 B6
Gregory Cres BD7.... 73 E2
Gregory Ct 2 BD14 ... 73 C4
Gregory Dr HD8....... 173 F7
Gregory La WF14 ..... 156 A7
Gregory Rd HD8...... 124 E5
Gregory Springs La
  WF14..............138 B3
Gregory Springs Mount
  WF14..............138 B2
Gregory Springs Rd
  WF14..............138 B3
Gregory St WF17...... 118 C5
Grenfell Dr BD3....... 75 D8
Grenfell Rd BD3...... 75 D8
Grenfell Terr BD3..... 75 D8
Grenley St WF11...... 127 A4
Grenville Wlk
  Calderbrook OL15 ....129 C1
  Crigglestone WF4 .... 159 F3
Gresham Ave BD2..... 55 F4
Gresley Ho LS18 ..... 41 C3
Gresley Rd BD21...... 35 C7
Gresley Road Ind Est
  BD21..............35 C7
Gretton Cl WF1 ..... 121 B3
Greycourt Cl
  Bradford BD10........56 A6
  Halifax HX1 .... 202 C1
Greycourt Ho HX1 ... 202 C2
Grey Ct WF1 .... 121 B3
Greyfriars Ave HD2 .. 136 E4
Greyfriar Wlk BD7 ... 73 E3
Grey Gables WF4 .... 158 E6
Grey Hall HX4 .... 133 F3
Greyhound Dr BD7 ... 74 B6
Grey Scar Ct BD22 ... 34 A2
Grey Scar Rd BD22 ... 34 A2
Greyshaw Syke HX2... 71 D2
Greyshiels Ave LS6.... 59 C4
Greyshiels Cl LS6.... 59 C4
Grey St WF1 .... 121 B3
Greystone HD4 ...... 153 B2
Greystone Ave HX5 ... 134 E5
Greystone Cl
  Boston Spa LS23 ......30 E7
  Burley in W LS29...... 9 E2
Greystone Cres BD10.. 56 C6
Greystone Ct HD6.... 136 A7
Greystone Mount LS15 .. 80 E7
Greystone Pk LS25 ... 47 E1
Greystones LS29 ..... 8 C3
Greystones Cl LS25 ... 47 E1
Greystones Ct LS8 ... 61 C7
Greystones Dr
  Keighley BD22 ....34 F3
  Ossett WF5 .... 140 E3
Greystones La BD22... 33 D7
Greystones Mount BD22.. 34 F3
Greystones Rd HX2 ... 111 E2
Greystones Rise BD22 .. 34 F3
Griffe BD12.......... 94 C1
Griffe Gdns BD22 .... 34 B2
Griffe Head Cres 2 BD12.. 94 C2
Griffe Head Rd BD12 .. 94 C2
Griffe Rd
  Bradford BD12........94 C1
  Haworth BD22....... 50 D8
Griffe Terr BD12 .... 94 C1
Griff House La WF3 .. 120 B8
Grime La
  Crofton WF4 ....144 B2
  Whitley Common HD9 .. 200 D8
Grimescar Mdws HD2.. 135 E2
Grimescar Rd HD2 .. 135 D3
Grimes Dyke Prim Sch
  LS14..............62 D6
Grimethorpe St 1 WF9 182 F2
Grimscar Ave HD2 ... 135 F1
Grimthorpe Ave 4 LS6.. 59 C5
Grimthorpe Pl LS6 ... 59 C5
Grimthorpe St LS6 ... 59 C5
Grimthorpe Terr LS6... 59 C5
Grindlestone Bank HX2.. 91 C4
Grisedale Ave HD2.... 135 F1
Grisedale Cl
  5 Bradford BD7.......73 F3
  Halifax HX2 .... 91 D1
Gritstone Cl LS29 ..... 9 E2
Grizedale Cl LS23 .... 13 B6
Grosmont Pl LS13 .... 58 C2
Grosmont Rd LS13 ... 58 C2
Grosmont Terr LS13.. 58 C3
Grosvenor Ave
  Lepton HD8 ....155 E3
  Pontefract WF8 ..... 146 B8
  Shipley BD18 .... 54 F8
  Upton WF9......... 183 A7
Grosvenor Ct LS16 ... 41 D4
Grosvenor Hill LS7... 206 C4
Grosvenor Mews LS19.. 40 A4
Grosvenor Mount LS6.. 205 C4
Grosvenor Park Gdns
  LS6...............205 C4
Grosvenor Pk LS7..... 60 C7
Grosvenor Pl HX2..... 111 C7
Grosvenor Rd
  Batley WF16........118 C6
  Bradford BD8........ 55 D1
  Huddersfield HD5 .... 154 F6
  Leeds LS6 .... 205 C4

Grosvenor Rd continued
  Shipley BD18 ....54 F7
Grosvenor St
  2 Batley WF16....... 117 D5
  2 Bradford BD8..... 55 D1
  Dewsbury WF12 ...... 139 C7
  Elland HX5.......... 134 F6
  Wakefield WF1 ...... 142 F3
Grosvenor Terr
  1 Batley WF16 ......117 D4
  1 Bradford BD8..... 55 D1
  11 Halifax HX1 ..... 202 C3
  Leeds LS6 .... 205 C4
  5 Otley LS21 ...... 23 B8
  Wetherby LS22 ..... 13 E6
Grosvenor Way HD8.. 155 E3
Groudle Glen HX7.... 88 C2
Grouse Moor La BD13.. 72 D2
Grouse St 10 BD21 ... 35 D8
Grove Ave
  Halifax HX3 ....92 A3
  Hemsworth WF9 ..... 181 E6
  Ilkley LS29......... 7 F3
  Leeds LS6 .... 59 E6
  Pontefract WF8 ..... 146 E8
  Pudsey LS28 .... 76 D7
  Shipley BD18 ...... 55 B5
  South Kirkby WF9 .... 182 C2
Grove Cl
  Bradford BD2........56 A4
  Cleckheaton BD19 .... 96 B1
Grove Cotts HD6 .... 114 E2
Grove Cres
  Boston Spa LS23 .....30 F7
  Luddenden Foot HX2 .. 111 F4
  Walton WF2 .... 161 B7
Grove Cres S LS23 ... 30 F7
Grove Croft HX3 ..... 91 F2
Grove Ct
  Halifax HX3 ....92 A2
  Leeds LS6 .... 59 E6
  Pudsey LS28 .... 76 D7
Grove Dr
  Halifax HX3 ....91 F3
  South Kirkby WF9 .... 182 B2
Grove Edge HX3 ..... 91 F2
Grove Farm WF17 .... 118 F3
Grove Farm Cl LS16 .. 41 F4
Grove Farm Cres LS16 .. 41 F4
Grove Farm Croft LS16 .. 41 F4
Grove Farm Dr LS16 .. 41 F4
Grove Gdns
  Boston Spa LS23 .....30 F7
  Dewsbury WF12 ..... 140 A6
  Halifax HX3 .... 92 A3
  Leeds LS6 .... 59 E6
Grovehall Ave LS11 .. 214 A1
Grovehall Dr LS11.... 214 A1
Grovehall La WF8, WF11 147 B8
Grovehall Par LS11.... 213 C1
Grove Hall Park Homes
  WF11..............147 D8
Grovehall Rd LS11 ... 213 C1
Grove Head WF9..... 182 B2
Grove Ho LS29......... 8 B3
Grove House Cres BD2.. 56 A4
Grove House Ct LS8... 61 D6
Grove House Dr
  Bradford BD2........56 A3
  Clayton West HD8 .... 175 E2
Grove House Prim Sch
  BD2...............56 A4
Grove House Rd BD2.. 56 A3
Grove La
  Badsworth WF9 ......164 E3
  Cleckheaton BD19 .... 96 B1
  Hemsworth WF9 ..... 181 E6
  Knottingley WF11 .... 126 E4
  Leeds LS6 .... 59 E6
  South Kirkby WF9 .... 182 B2
Grovelands BD2 ..... 56 A4
Grove Lea Cl WF9 .... 181 E6
Grove Lea Cres WF8 .. 146 E7
Grove Lea Prim Sch
  WF9...............181 E7
Grove Lea Wlk WF8 .. 146 E7
Grove Mill La HX3..... 92 A2
Grove Mount
  Pontefract WF8 ......146 E8
  South Kirkby WF9 .... 182 B2
Grove Nook HD3 ..... 152 F6
Grove Pk
  Crigglestone WF4 ....159 E6
  Halifax HX3 .... 92 A3
Grove Pl
  Boston Spa LS23 .....30 E7
  Hemsworth WF9 ..... 181 E6
Grove Prom The 7 LS29..8 B4
Grove Rd
  Batley WF16........117 E3
  Boston Spa LS23 ..... 30 E7
  Darton S75 .... 178 A1
  Elland HX5......... 135 B7
  Hebden Bridge HX7... 89 A4
  Horbury WF4 .... 141 A1
  Horsforth LS18 ..... 58 C8
  Huddersfield HD1 .... 154 B7
  Ilkley LS29......... 7 F3
  Leeds, Headingley Hill LS6 59 E5
  Leeds, Hunslet LS10 .. 215 B3
  Leeds LS15 .... 81 A7
  Menston LS29 ...... 22 A4
  Pontefract WF8 ..... 146 E8
  Pudsey LS28 .... 76 D7

Grove Rd continued
Shipley BD18 . . . . **55** B5
Wakefield WF1 . . . . **216** C1
Grove Rise
Leeds LS17 . . . . **42** F5
Pontefract WF8 . . . . **146** E8
Grove Row HX2 . . . . **91** A3
Grove Royd HX3 . . . . **92** A2
Grove St S 5 HX1 . . . . . . **202** B3
Groves Hall Rd WF13 . . **138** F8
Grove Sq
Cleckheaton BD19 . . . . . . **96** B1
Halifax HX3 . . . . **91** F2
Grove St
Bacup OL13 . . . . **106** A3
Batley, Heckmondwike
WF16 . . . . **117** E4
Batley, Norristhorpe
WF15 . . . . **117** C2
Brighouse HD6 . . . . **115** B2
Dewsbury WF13 . . . . **139** C8
Huddersfield HD3 . . . . . . **152** F6
Leeds LS1 . . . . **211** A4
Mirfield WF14 . . . . **138** B6
Ossett WF5 . . . . **140** D4
4 Pudsey LS28 . . . . **57** E2
Slaithwaite HD7 . . . . **151** F1
South Kirkby WF9 . . . . . **182** B2
Sowerby Bridge HX6 . . . . **112** D4
Wakefield WF1 . . . . **216** C1
Groves Terr LS21 . . . . . . **24** B5
Grove Terr
Birkenshaw BD11 . . . . **96** A4
Boston Spa LS23 . . . . **30** E7
Bradford BD7 . . . . **201** A2
Brighouse HD6 . . . . **114** E2
Hemsworth WF9 . . . . **181** E6
Mytholmroyd HX7 . . . . . . **110** E8
Pudsey LS28 . . . . **76** D7
Grove The
Baildon BD17 . . . . **38** C4
Batley, Brookroyd WF17 . **118** A7
Batley, Nunroyd WF16 . . **117** C6
Bingley BD16 . . . . **36** E6
Bradford, Greengates BD10 **56** D7
Bradford, Thorpe BD10 . . . **56** B7
Brighouse HX3 . . . . **114** D8
Cudworth S72 . . . . **180** B1
East Ardsley WF3 . . . . . . **120** B8
East Keswick LS17 . . . . . . **28** B6
Horsforth LS18 . . . . **41** B1
Huddersfield HD2 . . . . . . **136** B2
Ilkley LS29 . . . . **8** B4
Kippax LS25 . . . . **83** A1
Leeds, Alwoodley Park LS17 **42** F5
Leeds LS8 . . . . **61** D6
Meltham HD9 . . . . **170** F1
Normanton WF6 . . . . . . **123** B2
Pudsey LS28 . . . . **76** D7
7 Queensbury BD13 . . . . . **72** D1
Ryhill WF4 . . . . **162** A1
Shelf HX3 . . . . **93** C6
Shipley BD18 . . . . **54** E7
South Elmsall WF9 . . . . . **182** F4
Swillington LS26 . . . . **82** B2
Walton WF2 . . . . **161** B6
Yeadon, Nether Yeadon
LS19 . . . . **40** A4
Yeadon, Rufford Park LS19 **40** B6
Groveville HX3 . . . . **93** C1
Groveway BD2 . . . . **56** A4
Grove Way WF9 . . . . . . **182** B2
Grovewood 1 LS6 . . . . . **59** D6
Grunberg St 7 LS6 . . . . **59** D5
Grunberg St LS6 . . . . . . **59** D5
Gryce Hall HD8 . . . . . . **174** C6
Guard House Ave BD22 . . **35** A7
Guard House Dr BD22 . . . **35** A7
Guard House Gr BD22 . . . **34** F7
Guard House Prim Sch
BD22 . . . . **34** F7
Guard House Rd BD22 . . . **35** A7
Guardian Ct 17 LS29 . . . . . **8** B4
Guardian Mews LS12 . . **209** C1
Guernsey Rd WF12 . . . . **118** F2
Guildford Rd S71 . . . . . . **179** B5
Guildford St
4 Hebden Bridge HX7 . . . . **89** A2
Ossett WF5 . . . . **140** D4
Guild Way HX2 . . . . **112** B7
Guillemot App LS27 . . . . **98** D3
Guinevere Dr WF9 . . . . . **183** A2
Guiseley Dr LS29 . . . . . . **22** B2
Guiseley Inf Sch LS20 . . . . **22** E1
Guiseley Sch LS20 . . . . . . **39** D8
Guiseley Sta LS20 . . . . . . **22** D1
Gully Terr HD9 . . . . **189** B4
Gully The HD8 . . . . **190** C5
Gunson Cres WF5 . . . . . **140** D6
Gunter Rd LS22 . . . . **14** A5
Gunthwaite La S36 . . . . **192** B2
Gunthwaite Top HD8 . . . **191** F3
Gurbax Ct BD3 . . . . **75** E7
Gurney Cl BD5 . . . . **74** D3
Guycroft LS21 . . . . **22** F7
Guys Croft WF2 . . . . . . **141** C4
Guy St BD4 . . . . **201** C2
Gwynne Ave BD3 . . . . . . **56** E1
Gynn La HD9 . . . . **172** D5
Gypsy Ct WF10 . . . . **125** C6
Gypsy La WF10 . . . . **125** C5
Gypsy Wood Cl LS15 . . . . **81** D7
Gypsy Wood Crest LS15 . **81** D7

H

Hacking La WF9 . . . . **183** B3
Hadassah St HX3 . . . . . **113** D4
Haddingley La HD8 . . . . **190** D4
Haddon Ave
Halifax HX3 . . . . **113** C3
Leeds LS4 . . . . **59** C2
Haddon Cl
Cleckheaton BD19 . . . . . . **117** B8
South Elmsall WF9 . . . . . **183** A5
Haddon Pl LS4 . . . . **59** C2
Haddon Rd LS4 . . . . **205** A2
Hade Edge Jun & Inf Sch
HD9 . . . . **199** B8
Hadfield Rd WF16 . . . . . **117** D5
Hadleigh Ct LS17 . . . . . . **43** D2
Hadleigh Rise WF8 . . . . **146** B5
Hadleys Ct LS27 . . . . **97** D6
Hadrian's Cl HD3 . . . . . . **152** E8
Hadrian Cl WF10 . . . . . . **104** C1
Hadrians Cl WF10 . . . . . **165** A5
Hag Farm Rd
Burley in W LS29 . . . . **21** E7
Menston LS29 . . . . **21** E7
Hagg La WF14 . . . . **138** C2
Haggroyd La HD9 . . . . . **172** B2
Haggs Hill Rd WF5 . . . . **141** A5
Haggs La WF2 . . . . **141** C5
Hagg Wood Rd HD9 . . . . **172** B2
Hag Hill Hill HD8 . . . . . . **175** E6
Hag Hill La HD8 . . . . . . **175** E6
Hag La HX3 . . . . **92** D3
Hague Cres WF9 . . . . . . **181** E5
Hague Park Cl WF9 . . . . **182** B3
Hague Park Coppice
WF9 . . . . **182** B3
Hague Park Dr WF9 . . . . **182** B3
Hague Park Gdns WF9 . . **182** B3
Hague Park La WF9 . . . . **182** B3
Hague Park Wlk WF9 . . . **182** B3
Hague Terr WF9 . . . . . . **181** E6
Haigh's Sq HD5 . . . . . . **154** D7
Haigh Ave LS26 . . . . . . **100** C7
Haigh Beck View BD10 . . **56** D7
Haigh Cnr BD10 . . . . **56** D7
Haigh Croft S71 . . . . . . **179** B4
Haigh Ct HX3 . . . . **113** D4
Haighfield Cvn Pk LS17 . . **28** B2
Haigh Fold BD2 . . . . **56** C3
Haigh Gdns LS26 . . . . . **100** C7
Haigh Hall BD10 . . . . . . **56** D7
Haigh Hall Rd BD10 . . . . **56** D7
Haigh Hill S75 . . . . **177** C6
Haigh House Hill HD3 . . **134** E3
Haigh La
Flockton WF4 . . . . **157** A2
Halifax HX3 . . . . **113** D4
Holmfirth HD9 . . . . **188** F8
Woolley S75, WF4 . . . . . **177** C5
Haigh Mews S75 . . . . . . **177** C5
Haigh Moor Ave WF3 . . **119** E6
Haigh Moor Cres WF3 . . **119** E6
Haigh Moor Rd WF3 . . . **119** E6
Haigh Moor St WF1 . . . . **216** C4
Haigh Moor View WF3 . . **119** E6
Haigh Moor Way WF10 . **103** C4
Haigh Park Rd LS10 . . . . **80** B2
Haigh Rd LS26 . . . . **100** F6
Haigh Row HD8 . . . . . . **175** A3
Haighside LS26 . . . . **100** C6
Haighside Cl LS26 . . . . . **100** D6
Haighside Dr LS26 . . . . . **100** C6
Haighside Way LS26 . . . **100** C6
Haigh St
Bradford BD4 . . . . **75** B3
16 Brighouse HD6 . . . . . **115** A3
Elland HX4 . . . . **134** B7
Halifax HX1 . . . . **202** B4
Huddersfield HD1 . . . . . . **153** F3
Haigh Terr LS26 . . . . . . **100** C7
Haigh View LS26 . . . . . . **100** C7
Haigh Wood Cres LS16 . . **41** D3
Haigh Wood Gn LS16 . . . **41** D2
Haigh Wood Rd LS16 . . . **41** D2
Hailhead Dr WF8 . . . . . **125** F1
Haincliffe Pl 9 BD21 . . . **35** B4
Haincliffe Rd BD21 . . . . . **35** B4
Haines Pk LS7 . . . . **207** B2
Hainsworth Moor Cres 5
BD13 . . . . **92** D8
Hainsworth Moor Dr 6
BD13 . . . . **92** D8
Hainsworth Moor Garth 4
BD13 . . . . **92** D8
Hainsworth Moor Gr
BD13 . . . . **92** D8
Hainsworth Moor View
BD13 . . . . **92** D8
Hainsworth Rd BD20 . . . **17** F8
Hainsworth Sq 7 LS28 . . **57** D3
Hainsworth St
Leeds LS12 . . . . **210** B2
Rothwell BD20 . . . . **100** E4
5 Silsden BD20 . . . . **5** E1
Hainworth Croft Farm Cotts
BD21 . . . . **35** B3
Hainworth Crag Rd BD21 . **35** A2
Hainworth La BD21 . . . . . **35** B3
Hainworth Rd
Keighley, Hainworth BD21 . **35** B3
Keighley, The Pitts BD21 . . **35** A4
Hainworth Wood Rd BD21 **35** B4
Hainworth Wood Rd N
BD21 . . . . **35** C5
Haise Mount S75 . . . . . **178** A1
Halcyon Hill LS7 . . . . **60** C8

Halcyon Way BD5 . . . . . . **74** C3
Haldane Cl S72 . . . . **180** F3
Haldane Cres WF1 . . . . . **142** F8
Hales Rd LS12 . . . . **78** B4
Halesworth Cres BD4 . . . **75** C3
Haley's Yd LS13 . . . . **58** C3
Haley Ct HX3 . . . . **203** B4
Haley Hill HX3 . . . . **203** B4
Half Acre Rd BD13 . . . . . **72** B7
Half Acres Jun & Inf Sch
WF10 . . . . **124** C7
Half House La HD6 . . . . . **114** D5
Half Mile LS13 . . . . **57** F2
Half Mile Cl LS28 . . . . . . **57** F2
Half Mile Ct LS28 . . . . . . **57** F2
Half Mile Gdns LS13 . . . . **57** F2
Half Mile Gn LS28 . . . . . . **57** F2
Half Mile La LS13 . . . . . . **57** F2
Half Moon La WF1 . . . . . **143** C6
Half Moon St 13 HD1 . . . **154** A6
Halfpenny La WF8 . . . . . **146** A8
Halfpenny Lane Jun & Inf
Sch WF8 . . . . **146** B8
Half St BD21 . . . . **35** B8
Halifax High at Wellesley Pk
HX2 . . . . **202** A3
Halifax Ho WF17 . . . . . . **118** A3
Halifax Ind Ctr The HX1 . **202** C4
Halifax La
Blackshaw Head HX7 . . . . **87** E4
Luddenden HX2 . . . . . . **111** E8
Halifax Playhouse* HX1 **203** A2
Halifax Rd
Batley WF13, WF17 . . . . **118** B2
Bradford BD6 . . . . **94** B7
Brighouse, Hartshead Moor Top
HD6 . . . . **115** E7
Brighouse, Hipperholme
HX3 . . . . **114** B8
Brighouse, Hove Edge HD6 **114** E5
Brighouse, Waring Green
HD6 . . . . **115** A3
Cleckheaton WF15 . . . . . **116** C5
Cullingworth BD13 . . . . . . **52** D6
Cullingworth, Flappit Spring
BD13 . . . . **52** A5
Denholme, Denholme Gate
BD13 . . . . **71** C5
Denholme, Stubden BD13 . **71** E7
Elland HX5 . . . . **134** C7
Halifax HX3, HX5 . . . . . . **134** E8
Hebden Bridge HX7 . . . . . **88** C2
Keighley BD21, BD22 . . . . **35** A3
Littleborough OL15 . . . . . **148** A4
Northowram HX3 . . . . . . **93** B4
Queensbury BD13 . . . . . . **92** C7
Ripponden HX6 . . . . **132** C6
Slaithwaite HD7 . . . . **152** B5
Todmorden OL14 . . . . . . **108** D6
Halifax Ret Pk HX1 . . . . **203** A3
Halifax Sta HX1 . . . . . . **203** C2
Hallamfield LS20 . . . . . . **39** E8
Hallam La LS21 . . . . **10** B5
Hallamshire Mews WF2 . **141** C4
Hallam St LS20 . . . . **39** D8
Hallas Bridge BD13 . . . . . **52** F6
Hallas Bridge Mill BD13 . . **52** F5
Hallas Gr HD5 . . . . **154** F5
Hallas Hall Farm Cotts
BD13 . . . . **52** E6
Hallas La
Cullingworth BD13 . . . . . . **52** E5
Kirkburton HD8 . . . . **174** B7
Wilsden BD13 . . . . **52** F5
Hallas Rd HD8 . . . . **173** F6
Hall Ave
Bradford BD2 . . . . **56** D5
Huddersfield HD1 . . . . . . **153** F5
Sutton-in-C BD20 . . . . . . **16** D4
Hallbank Cl BD5 . . . . **74** D1
Hallbank Dr BD5 . . . . **74** D1
Hall Bank Dr BD16 . . . . . **36** F4
Hall Bank La HX7 . . . . . **110** E8
Hall Bower HD4 . . . . . . **154** B1
Hall Bower La HD4 . . . . **154** B1
Hall Brig DN5 . . . . **194** C4
Hall Cl
Boston Spa LS23 . . . . **30** E7
Bramhope LS16 . . . . **24** E4
Burley in W LS29 . . . . **9** D1
Hemsworth WF9 . . . . . . **181** D7
Liversedge WF15 . . . . . . **117** A3
Meltham HD9 . . . . **170** F2
Northowram HX3 . . . . **93** A3
Ossett WF5 . . . . **119** B1
Sutton-in-C BD20 . . . . . . **16** D4
Hallcliffe BD17 . . . . **38** D4
Hall Cliffe Cres WF4 . . . **141** A2
Hall Cliffe Ct WF4 . . . . . **141** A2
Hall Cliffe Gr WF4 . . . . . **141** A2
Hall Cliffe Rd WF4 . . . . . **141** A2
Hall Cliffe Rise WF4 . . . **141** B2
Hallcroft
Keighley BD16 . . . . **36** F5
Shipley BD18 . . . . **55** D8
Hall Croft WF4 . . . . **158** E6
Hallcroft Cl 6 WF4 . . . . **141** B1
Hallcroft Dr
Addingham LS29 . . . . **7** B7
Horbury WF4 . . . . **141** B1
Hallcroft Rise S71 . . . . . **179** B3
Hall Cross Gr HD5 . . . . . **154** D3
Hall Cross Rd HD5 . . . . . **154** D3
Hall Ct
Brotherton WF11 . . . . . . **126** C8
Leeds LS7 . . . . **207** A4
Sutton-in-C BD20 . . . . . . **16** D4

Hall Dr
Bramhope LS16 . . . . **24** E4
Burley in W LS29 . . . . **9** D1
Liversedge WF15 . . . . . . **117** B2
Sutton-in-C BD20 . . . . . . **16** D4
Hallfield Ave LS25 . . . . . . **83** F7
Hallfield Cres LS22 . . . . . **13** F5
Hallfield Ct 11 LS22 . . . . **13** F6
Hallfield Dr BD17 . . . . . . **38** C3
Hallfield La LS22 . . . . **13** F5
Hallfield Pl BD1 . . . . **201** B4
Hallfield Rd BD1 . . . . . . **201** A4
Hallfield St BD1 . . . . **201** B4
Hallfield Terr LS25 . . . . . **83** F7
Hall Garth Rd WF8 . . . . **165** A4
Hallgate BD1 . . . . **201** B4
Hallgate Ct LS17 . . . . **43** C4
Hall Gdns BD20 . . . . **4** E1
Hall Gr
Darton S75 . . . . **178** C1
Leeds LS6 . . . . **205** C2
Hall Green La HX6 . . . . . **150** D8
Halliday Ave LS12 . . . . . **209** A4
Halliday Ct LS25 . . . . **82** E7
Halliday Dr LS12 . . . . . . **209** A4
Halliday Gr LS12 . . . . . . **209** A4
Halliday Mount LS12 . . . **209** A4
Halliday Pl LS12 . . . . . . **209** A4
Halliday Rd
Garforth LS25 . . . . **82** E7
Leeds LS12 . . . . **209** A4
Halliday St LS28 . . . . **76** E8
Halliley Gdns 2 WF13 . . **139** C8
Halliley St WF13 . . . . . . **139** B8
Hall Ing HD9 . . . . **172** C4
Hall Ing La HD9 . . . . **172** C5
Halling Pl OL14 . . . . **108** A4
Hall Ing Rd HD4 . . . . . . **172** E3
Hall Ings
Bradford BD1 . . . . **201** B2
Halifax HX3 . . . . **114** A3
Hall La
Askwith LS21 . . . . **9** E6
Bradford BD4 . . . . **201** C1
Crigglestone WF4 . . . . . . **159** F4
Dewsbury WF12 . . . . . . **139** F2
Horsforth LS18 . . . . **41** A1
Kirkburton HD8 . . . . **173** E7
Ledston WF10 . . . . **103** F6
Leeds, Cookridge LS16 . . . **41** F6
Leeds, Farnley LS12 . . . . . **77** D5
Leeds LS12 . . . . **210** A3
Leeds, Potternewton LS7 . **207** A4
Newthorpe LS25 . . . . **84** F5
Northowram HX3 . . . . . . **92** A4
Shipley BD18 . . . . **55** D8
Slaithwaite HD3, HD7 . . . **152** B6
South Elmsall WF9 . . . . . **183** B6
Hall Lee Rd HD3 . . . . . . **135** C1
Hall Mews LS23 . . . . **30** E7
Hall Orchards Ave LS22 . . **14** A6
Hallowes Gr BD13 . . . . . . **52** D5
Hallowes Park Rd BD13 . . **52** D6
Hallows Ct 4 HD5 . . . . . **154** F3
Hallows Rd BD21 . . . . . . **18** E1
Hallows The BD20 . . . . . . **35** A8
Hall Park Ave
Crofton WF4 . . . . **143** F2
Horsforth LS18 . . . . **41** A1
Liversedge WF15 . . . . . . **117** A2
Hall Park Cl LS18 . . . . . . **41** A1
Hall Park Cres LS25 . . . . **83** B1
Hall Park Croft LS25 . . . . **83** B1
Hall Park Ct LS25 . . . . . . **83** B1
Hall Park Garth LS18 . . . . **41** A1
Hall Park Mdws LS25 . . **103** B8
Hall Park Mount LS18 . . . **41** A1
Hall Park Orch LS25 . . . . **83** B1
Hall Park Rd LS23 . . . . . . **15** B5
Hall Park Rise
Horsforth LS18 . . . . **41** B1
Kippax LS25 . . . . **83** B1
Hall Pl LS9 . . . . **212** C3
Hall Rd
Bradford BD2, BD10 . . . . . **56** D5
Leeds LS12 . . . . **209** C1
Swillington LS26 . . . . **82** B1
Wakefield WF2 . . . . **141** D4
Hall Rise
Bramhope LS16 . . . . **24** E3
Burley in W LS29 . . . . **9** D1
Hall Rise Cl LS16 . . . . **24** E3
Hall Rise Croft LS16 . . . . **24** E3
Hall Royd BD18 . . . . **55** B7
Hallroyd Cres OL14 . . . . **108** C5
Hallroyd Pl OL14 . . . . . . **108** C5
Hallroyd Rd OL14 . . . . . **108** C5
Hall St N HX3 . . . . **92** B2
Hallside Cl BD17 . . . . **38** F4
Hall Sq LS28 . . . . **57** B7
Hall St
5 Bradford BD6 . . . . **74** C1
5 Brighouse HD6 . . . . . . **115** B2
Glusburn BD20 . . . . **16** D7
Halifax HX1 . . . . **203** A3
Haworth BD22 . . . . **51** C6
Huddersfield HD3 . . . . . . **152** F7
Oakworth BD22 . . . . **34** D2
Purston Jaglin WF7 . . . . . **145** E4
Todmorden OL14 . . . . . . **108** B5
Hall Stone Ct HX3 . . . . . . **93** C5
Hall Syke HD8 . . . . **190** D8
Hall Way BD20 . . . . **16** D4
Hallwood Gn BD10 . . . . . **56** E5
Halstead Cl HX6 . . . . . . **132** C2
Halstead Dr LS29 . . . . . . **22** A5

Halstead Gr S75 . . . . . . **178** A
Halstead La HD4 . . . . . . **173** A
Halstead Pl BD7 . . . . **74** B
Halsteads Way BD20 . . . . **17** C
Halton Cl HD5 . . . . **154** F
Halton Dr LS15 . . . . **81** A
Halton Moor Ave LS9 . . . **80** D
Halton Moor Rd
Leeds, Halton Moor LS15 . . **80** E
Leeds, Osmondthorpe LS9 . **80** C
Halton Pl BD5 . . . . **74** B
Halton Rd WF1 . . . . **142** F
Halton St WF7 . . . . **145** D
Hambledon Ave
Bradford BD4 . . . . **95** B
Meltham HD9 . . . . **170** F
Hambleton Bank HX2 . . . **91** B
Hambleton Cotts BD23 . . . **2** B
Hambleton Cres HX2 . . . . **91** B
Hambleton Dr HX2 . . . . . **91** B
Hambleton St WF1 . . . . **216** B
Hamel Rise WF9 . . . . . . **181** C
Hame The HX4 . . . . **133** F
Hamilton Ave LS7 . . . . . **207** B
Hamilton Ct WF6 . . . . . . **123** B
Hamilton Gdns LS7 . . . . **207** B
Hamilton Pl LS7 . . . . . . **207** B
Hamilton Terr
Leeds LS7 . . . . **207** B
1 Otley LS21 . . . . **23** B
Hamilton View LS7 . . . . **207** B
Hammer La WF4 . . . . . . **144** B
Hammerstone Leach La
HX5 . . . . **134** D
Hammerstones Rd HX5 . **134** D
Hammerton Dr LS25 . . . . **83** A
Hammerton Farm Ave
WF4 . . . . **162** B
Hammerton Gr
4 Pudsey LS28 . . . . **76** F
Ryhill WF4 . . . . **162** B
Hammerton Rd HD2 . . . **136** A
Hammerton St
Bradford BD3 . . . . **75** A
Pudsey LS28 . . . . **76** E
Hammerton Terr 11
OL14 . . . . **108** B
Hammond Cres BD11 . . . . **96** E
Hammond Pl BD9 . . . . . . **55** A
Hammond Rd WF11 . . . . **126** D
Hammonds Landing 17
HX6 . . . . **112** C
Hammond Sq BD9 . . . . . **55** A
Hammond St
Halifax HX1 . . . . **202** B
Huddersfield HD2 . . . . . . **136** B
Hamm Strasse BD1 . . . . **201** B
Hampden Cl WF11 . . . . . **126** B
Hampden Pl
Bradford BD5 . . . . **74** C
Halifax HX1 . . . . **203** A
Hampden St BD5 . . . . **74** D
Hampole Balk La DN6 . . **184** B
Hampole Field La DN6 . . **183** F
Hampshire Cl
Ilkley LS29 . . . . **8** D
Pontefract WF8 . . . . **125** E
Hampshire St 5 HD5 . . . **154** D
Hampson St WF17 . . . . . **118** A
Hampton Ct 7 LS29 . . . . . **8** A
Hampton Pl
Bradford BD10 . . . . **56** B
Leeds LS9 . . . . **212** C
Hampton St HX1 . . . . . . **202** B
Hampton Terr LS9 . . . . . **212** C
Hamworth Dr BD22 . . . . . **34** D
Hamza St WF17 . . . . **118** B
Hanbury Gdns LS25 . . . . **82** F
Hanby Ave WF6 . . . . . . **122** F
Hanby Cl HD8 . . . . **155** C
Hand Bank La WF14 . . . . **138** A
Hand Carr La HX2 . . . . . **111** C
Handel St
Bradford BD7 . . . . **74** C
Huddersfield HD7 . . . . . . **152** D
Handel Terr 2 HD5 . . . . **154** D
Handsworth Rd WF2 . . . **160** A
Hanging Gate La BD22 . . **51** B
Hanging Heaton CE Jun & Inf
Sch WF17 . . . . **118** F
Hanging Royd HD7 . . . . **152** D
Hangingroyd Cl HX7 . . . . **89** A
Hangingroyd La 2 HX7 . . **89** A
Hangingroyd Rd 32 HX7 . **89** A
Hangingstone Rd LS29 . . . **8** B
Hanging Stone Rd HD4 . . **171** F
Hanging Stones La HX6 . **132** F
Hanging Wood Way BD19 **95** C
Hangram St 2 HD6 . . . . . **115** B
Hanley Rd LS27 . . . . **98** A
Hannah Ct BD12 . . . . **94** C
Hannah St 16 OL13 . . . . **106** A
Hanover Ave LS3 . . . . . . **211** A
Hanover Cl BD8 . . . . **55** B
Hanover Cres WF8 . . . . **146** C
Hanover Ct
6 Dewsbury WF13 . . . . . **118** A
Keighley BD20 . . . . **18** A
Morley LS27 . . . . **98** B
Hanover Gdns
Burley in W LS29 . . . . **21** E
Dewsbury WF13 . . . . . . **139** B
Hanover Ho WF2 . . . . . . **202** A
Hanover La LS3 . . . . **211** A
Hanover Mount LS3 . . . . **206** A
Hanover Pl
Batley WF17 . . . . **118** D
Brotherton WF11 . . . . . . **105** C

Han–Haw 253

Hanover Pl *continued*
Kippax LS25 83 B1
Hanover Sq
Bradford BD1 74 D8
Leeds LS3 211 A4
Hanover St
Batley WF17 118 C5
Dewsbury WF13 139 B8
Farnhill BD20 4 D1
Halifax HX1 203 A2
Keighley BD21 35 C7
Sowerby Bridge HX6 112 D4
Thurnscoe S63 194 E1
Wakefield WF2 142 A5
Hanover Way
Burley in W LS29 21 E8
Leeds LS3 211 A4
Hansby Ave LS14 62 B5
Hansby Bank LS14 62 B5
Hansby Cl LS14 62 B4
Hansby Dr LS14 62 B4
Hansby Gate LS14 62 B5
Hansby Gdns LS14 62 B4
Hansby Grange LS14 62 B5
Hansby Pl LS14 62 B5
Hansel Fold HX4 132 F3
Hanson Ave WF6 123 B1
Hanson Ct BD12 94 B2
Hanson Fold 8 BD12 94 C3
Hanson La
Halifax HX1 202 C3
Huddersfield HD4 153 E2
Hanson Mount BD12 94 C2
Hanson Pl 7 BD12 94 C3
Hanson Rd
Brighouse HD6 135 E8
Meltham HD9 170 C1
Hanson Sch BD2 56 A4
Hanson School 6th Form Ctr
BD2 56 A5
Hanworth Rd BD12 94 D6
Hapsburg Ct 11 BD5 201 B1
Harbeck Dr BD16 36 B1
Harborough Gn BD10 56 D8
Harbour Cres BD6 94 A8
Harbour Pk 2 BD6 93 F8
Harbour Rd BD6 94 A8
Harclo Rd BD21 35 E8
Harcourt Ave BD13 72 D7
Harcourt Dr
Addingham LS29 2 F1
Morley LS27 97 F5
Harcourt St
Bradford BD4 75 B3
Wakefield WF2 141 F5
Hardaker's La WF7 163 E6
Hardaker La BD17 38 A2
Hardakers App WF7 163 F5
Hardaker St BD8 74 D8
Hardcastle Ave WF8 125 C1
Hardcastle Crags* HX7 68 C1
Hardcastle La WF4 157 E4
Harden & Bingley Cvn Pk
BD16 53 A7
Harden Brow La BD16 36 A1
Harden Gr
Bradford BD10 56 E3
Keighley BD21 35 E5
Harden Hill Rd HD9 187 E8
Harden La BD15 53 B7
Harden Moss Rd
Holmfirth HD9 187 E4
Meltham HD9 187 E7
Harden Prim Sch BD16 36 B1
Harden Rd
Harden BD16 36 D2
Keighley BD21 35 F5
Hardgate La BD22 51 F7
Hardhill Hos BD16 36 B1
Hardie Rd WF4 162 C1
Harding Houses BD20 16 E7
Hardings La
Glusburn BD20 16 F7
Ilkley LS29 8 A7
Hard Ings Rd BD21 18 C1
Hardistry Dr WF8 146 B8
Hardknot Cl BD7 73 E3
Hard Nese La
Oxenhope BD22 51 B2
Oxenhope, Dike Nook BD22 50 F1
Hard Platts La HX4 133 F2
Hardrow Gn LS12 210 A1
Hardrow Gr LS12 210 A1
Hardrow Rd LS12 210 A1
Hardrow Terr LS12 210 A1
Hardwick Cl WF4 180 A8
Hardwick Cres WF8 146 D5
Hardwick Croft LS7 204 A2
Hardwick Ct WF8 146 C7
Hardwick La WF4 145 B1
Hardwick Rd
Darrington WF7, WF8 146 F3
Pontefract WF7, WF8 146 D5
Purston Jaglin WF7 145 C4
Hardwick St
8 Keighley BD21 35 A6
1 Leeds LS10 215 B2
Hardy Ave
Bradford BD6 94 C8
Morley LS27 98 C8
Hardy Croft WF1 216 C2
Hardy Ct LS27 98 B4
Hardy Gr 5 LS11 214 A3
Hardy Pl HD6 114 E5
Hardy St
Bradford BD4 201 C2
Bradford, Brownroyd Hill
BD6 74 C1
Hardy St *continued*
Brighouse HD6 115 B3
Leeds LS11 214 A3
Morley LS27 98 B4
Hardy Terr 8 LS11 214 B3
Hardy View 4 LS11 214 A3
Harebell Ave WF2 141 E7
Harecroft Rd LS21 11 A1
Haredon Cl S75 178 A2
Hare Farm Ave LS12 77 D7
Hare Farm Cl LS12 77 D7
Harefield Cl BD20 17 A5
Harefield Dr WF17 97 A1
Harefield E LS15 80 E7
Harefield Pk HD2 135 D2
Harefield Rd 2 WF8 146 F8
Harefield W LS15 80 E8
Harehill Ave OL14 108 A6
Harehill Cl BD10 39 B1
Harehill Rd BD10 39 B1
Harehills Ave LS7, LS8 207 C4
Harehills Cnr LS8 207 C4
Harehills La
Haworth BD22 33 D1
Leeds LS7, LS8, LS9 208 A2
Harehills Park Ave LS9 208 B2
Harehills Park Rd LS9 208 B2
Harehills Park Terr LS9 208 B2
Harehills Park View LS9 208 B2
Harehills Pl LS8 207 C3
Harehills Prim Sch LS8 208 A3
Harehills Rd LS8 207 C3
Harehill St OL14 108 A6
Hare La LS28 76 F4
Hare Park Ave WF15 116 C4
Hare Park Cl WF15 116 C4
Hare Park Dr WF15 116 C4
Hare Park La
Cleckheaton WF15 116 C4
Crofton WF4 161 F8
Hare Park Mount LS12 77 D7
Hare Park View WF4 161 F8
Hares Ave LS8 207 C4
Hares Mount LS8 207 B4
Hares Rd LS8 207 C4
Hare St HX1 202 C2
Hares Terr LS8 207 C4
Hares View LS8 207 C4
Harewood Ave
Batley WF16 117 E3
Halifax HX2 112 D8
Harewood LS17 27 D7
Normanton WF6 123 C3
Pontefract WF8 146 E8
Steeton BD20 17 A5
Harewood Cl WF11 126 C4
Harewood C of E Primary
Sch LS17 27 A7
Harewood Cres BD22 34 E2
Harewood Ct
Leeds LS17 43 D1
Leeds, The Green LS14 62 A4
Harewood Dr
Steeton BD20 17 A6
Wakefield WF2 120 D1
Harewood Gate LS17 27 A7
Harewood Gr WF16 117 E3
Harewood Hill BD22 34 E2
Harewood Ho* LS17 26 E6
Harewood La WF9 183 D8
Harewood Mews LS17 27 A7
Harewood Mount
Meltham HD9 170 F2
Pontefract WF8 146 E8
Harewood Pl HX2 202 A2
Harewood Rd
East Keswick LS17 28 C7
Keighley BD22 34 F3
Wakefield WF1 142 F8
Harewood Rise
Keighley BD22 34 F3
Pontefract WF8 146 E8
Harewood St
Bradford BD3 75 B7
Leeds LS2 211 C4
Harewood View WF8 146 E8
Harewood Way LS13 77 B8
Hargrave Cres LS29 21 F4
Hargreaves Ave WF3 121 E5
Hargreaves Cl LS27 98 A6
Hargreaves St
Glusburn BD20 16 E6
Rothwell LS26 100 F5
Harker Rd BD12 94 C7
Harker St
Knottingley WF11 127 B4
Sutton-in-C BD20 16 E5
Harker Terr 1 LS28 57 D1
Harland Cl BD2 55 E2
Harland Sq LS2 206 A3
Harlech Ave LS11 214 B2
Harlech Cres LS11 214 B2
Harlech Gr LS11 214 B2
Harlech Mount LS11 214 B2
Harlech Park Ct LS11 214 B2
Harlech Rd LS11 214 B2
Harlech St LS11 214 B2
Harlech Terr LS11 214 B2
Harlech Way LS25 83 B7
Harley Cl LS13 77 A8
Harley Ct LS13 77 A8
Harley Dr LS13 77 A8
Harley Gdns LS13 77 A8
Harley Gn LS13 77 A8
Harley Pl HD6 115 A1
Harley Rd LS13 77 A8
Harley Rise LS13 77 A8
Harley St
7 Brighouse HD6 115 A1
Todmorden OL14 108 B6
Harley Terr LS13 77 B8
Harley View LS13 77 A8
Harley Villas 6 OL14 108 B6
Harley Wlk LS13 77 A8
Harley Wood OL14 107 E8
Harlington Ct 3 LS27 98 A2
Harlington Rd LS27 98 A2
Harlock St WF1 142 E2
Harlow Ct LS8 61 C7
Harlow Rd BD7 74 A5
Harmby Cl DN6 184 F2
Harmon Cl BD4 95 C8
Harmony Pl BD13 72 C3
Harold Ave LS6 205 B2
Harold Gdns LS27 98 C4
Harold Gr LS6 205 B2
Harold Mount LS6 205 B2
Harold Pl
Leeds LS6 205 B2
13 Shipley BD18 54 F8
Harold Rd LS6 205 B2
Harold Sq LS6 205 B2
Harold St
Bingley BD16 36 E4
Leeds LS6 205 B2
Harold Terr LS6 205 B2
Harold View LS6 205 B2
Harold Wlk LS6 205 B2
Harpe Inge HD5 154 E7
Harper Ave BD10 39 B1
Harper Cres BD10 39 C1
Harper Gate BD4 75 F4
Harper Gr
Bradford BD10 39 B1
Sutton-in-C BD20 16 D4
Harper La LS19 40 B6
Harper Rock LS19 40 B6
Harper Royd La HX6 112 C2
Harpers Sq BD20 16 D4
Harper St LS2 212 A3
Harper Terr 8 LS19 40 B7
Harp Rd HD3 153 B5
Harrap St WF2 141 D7
Harrier Cl BD8 73 B7
Harriers Ct WF9 182 F1
Harrier Way LS27 98 D4
Harriet St
Bradford BD8 74 B8
Brighouse HD6 115 A4
Leeds LS7 207 A3
Harrington Ct HD9 170 F1
Harris Ct BD7 74 A4
Harrison Cres LS9 61 D1
Harrison La HD7, HD9 170 E5
Harrison Pl BD20 16 B6
Harrison & Potter Trust
Homes The
Leeds LS2 206 C1
6 Leeds, Woodhouse LS2 206 A3
Harrison Rd
Crofton WF4 143 F1
Halifax HX1 203 B2
Harrisons Ave 8 LS28 57 F2
Harrison St
17 Bingley BD16 37 A2
Leeds LS1 211 C4
Todmorden OL14 86 B1
Harris St
11 Bingley BD16 37 A2
Bradford BD1 201 D3
Harrogate Ave BD3 56 A2
Harrogate Par LS17 43 D2
Harrogate Pl BD3 56 A2
Harrogate Rd
Bradford BD10, BD2 56 D5
East Carlton LS16 23 F2
Harewood LS17 27 A4
Leeds, Alwoodley Gates
LS17 43 E5
Leeds, Chapel Allerton LS7 204 A2
Spofforth LS22 13 B7
Yeadon LS19 40 C5
Harrogate St BD3 56 A2
Harrogate Terr BD3 56 A2
Harrogate View LS17 44 C5
Harrop Ave LS27 98 B2
Harrop Gr LS27 98 B2
Harrop La BD15 53 B3
Harrop Terr LS27 98 B2
Harrop Well La 12 WF8 146 D8
Harrowby Cres LS16 59 B7
Harrowby Rd LS16 59 B7
Harrow St
Halifax HX1 202 B3
South Elmsall WF9 182 E3
Harrows The BD20 36 B8
Harry La
Bradford BD14 73 B4
Oxenhope BD22 51 C3
Harry St BD4 75 C3
Hart's Hole HD7 152 A5
Harthill LS27 97 D7
Harthill Ave LS27 97 D7
Harthill Cl LS27 97 D7
Harthill La LS27 97 D8
Harthill Paddock LS27 97 D7
Harthill Par LS27 97 D7
Harthill Rise LS27 97 D7
Hartington St
Batley WF17 118 C3
9 Keighley BD21 35 C8
Hartington Terr BD7 74 A5
Hartland Rd BD4 75 E4
Hartley's Bldgs 6 LS27 98 B3
Hartley's Sq BD20 19 D1
Hartley Ave LS6 206 B4
Hartley Cl WF9 183 A4
Hartley Cres LS6 206 B4
Hartley Ct WF15 117 A3
Hartley Gdns LS6 206 B4
Hartley Gr
Dewsbury WF13 118 C1
Leeds LS6 206 A4
Hartley Hill LS2 206 C1
Hartley Park Ave WF8 146 B8
Hartley Park View WF8 146 B8
Hartley Pl
Leeds LS2 206 C1
3 Morley LS27 98 B3
Hartley St
Bradford BD4 75 B5
Castleford WF10 124 C7
Dewsbury WF13 118 C1
Glusburn BD20 16 B6
Halifax HX1 202 C4
Morley, Churwell LS27 98 B7
Morley, Town End LS27 98 C4
Hartley Terr WF7 145 C4
Hartlington Ct BD17 38 E3
Hartman Pl BD9 54 F2
Hart Rhydding La LS29 6 F7
Hartshead Hall La WF15 116 D1
Hartshead Jun & Inf Sch
WF15 116 C2
Hartshead La WF15 116 C2
Hart St
Bradford BD7 74 B4
Huddersfield HD4 154 A2
Hartwell Rd LS6 205 B2
Harvelin Pk OL14 109 A5
Harvest Cl WF8 125 E3
Harvest Croft LS29 9 D1
Harvest Ct HX1 203 A3
Harvest Mews WF5 140 E3
Harvest Mount BD10 55 F8
Harvey Royd HD5 155 A4
Harvey St WF1 142 E3
Harwill App LS27 98 C7
Harwill Ave LS27 98 C7
Harwill Croft LS27 98 C7
Harwill Gr LS27 98 C7
Harwill Rd LS27 98 C7
Harwill Rise LS27 98 C7
Harwood Cl
Huddersfield HD5 154 F5
Wakefield WF2 142 E1
Haselbury Ho 6 BD5 201 B1
Haselden Cres WF2 141 E5
Haselden Rd WF2 141 E5
Haslam Cl BD3 75 A8
Haslam Gr BD18 55 E6
Haslemere Cl BD4 75 D3
Haslewood Cl LS9 212 B4
Haslewood Ct 1 LS9 212 C4
Haslewood Dene LS9 212 C4
Haslewood Dr LS9 212 C4
Haslewood Gdns LS9 212 C4
Haslewood Gn LS9 212 C4
Haslewood Mews LS9 212 C4
Haslewood Pl LS9 212 C4
Haslewood Sq LS9 212 C4
Haslewood View LS9 212 C4
Hasley Rd LS29 21 F8
Haslingden Dr BD9 54 F2
Hassocks La HD9 171 D4
Hassocks Rd HD9 170 C3
Haste St WF10 124 B8
Hastings Ave
Bradford BD5 74 D2
Wakefield WF2 142 D2
Hastings Cres WF10 125 B7
Hastings Ct
6 Collingham LS22 29 B8
Normanton WF6 122 E4
Shadwell LS17 44 E4
Hastings Gr WF2 142 D2
Hastings Pl BD5 74 D3
Hastings St BD5 74 D2
Hastings Terr BD5 74 D2
Hastings Way
Collingham LS22 28 F8
Halifax HX1 203 A1
Hastings Wlk WF10 125 B7
Hatcham Cl BD15 73 A7
Hatchet La BD12 95 A4
Hatfeild St WF1 216 B3
Hatfield Gdns S71 179 B4
Hatfield Pl WF4 162 D2
Hatfield Rd BD2 56 B2
Hatfield View WF1 121 C2
Hathaway Ave BD9 54 D3
Hathaway Dr LS14 45 B1
Hathaway La LS14 62 B8
Hathaway Mews LS14 45 B1
Hathaway Wlk 1 LS14 62 B8
Hathershelf La HX2 111 A7
Hatton Cl BD6 94 D8
Haugh End La HX6 112 A3
Haugh Rd OL14 108 E6
Haugh Shaw Croft 13
HX1 202 C1
Haugh Shaw Rd HX1 202 C1
Haugh Shaw Rd W HX1 202 B1
Haughs La HD3 153 A7
Haughs Rd HD3 153 A7
Hauxley Ct LS29 8 D5
Hauxwell Cl DN6 184 F2
Hauxwell Dr LS19 40 B6
Havelock Sq 2 BD13 72 E6
Havelock St
Bradford BD7 74 A4
Dewsbury WF13 138 E5
Thornton BD13 72 E6
Haven Chase LS16 41 E3
Haven Cl
Leeds LS16 41 F3
Northowram HX3 93 A3
Haven Croft LS16 41 F3
Haven Ct
Leeds LS16 41 F3
Pontefract WF8 146 B5
Haven Garth LS16 41 E3
Haven Gdns LS16 41 E3
Haven Gn LS16 41 E3
Haven La HX7 110 B8
Haven Mount LS16 41 E3
Haven Rise LS16 41 E3
Haven St 15 OL14 108 C5
Haven The
Bradford BD10 56 C6
Leeds LS15 81 D8
Haven View LS16 41 E3
Havercroft
Leeds LS12 77 E5
Ossett WF5 140 E5
Havercroft Jun & Inf Sch
WF4 180 B8
Havercroft La WF8 147 E5
Havercroft Rise S72 180 E6
Havercroft Way WF17 117 F5
Haverdale Rd WF4 162 C1
Haverlands The WF9 181 E6
Haveroid La WF4 159 F4
Haveroid Way WF4 159 F5
Haverthwaites Dr LS25 47 E1
Havertop La WF6 123 F2
Haw Ave LS19 40 C8
Hawber Cote Dr BD20 5 F2
Hawber Cote La BD20 5 F2
Hawber La BD20 5 F1
Haw Cliff La HD4 172 F1
Hawes Ave
Bradford BD5 74 C2
Huddersfield HD3 153 B6
Hawes Cl WF10 125 B8
Hawes Cres BD5 74 C2
Hawes Dr BD5 74 C2
Hawes Gr BD5 74 C2
Hawes Mount BD5 74 C2
Hawes Rd BD5 74 C2
Hawes Terr BD5 74 C2
Haweswater Cl LS22 13 B5
Haw Hill Pk WF6 123 C2
Haw Hill View WF6 123 C3
Hawk's Nest Gdns E LS17 43 D4
Hawk's Nest Gdns S LS17 43 D4
Hawk's Nest Gdns W LS17 43 D4
Hawk's Nest Rise LS17 43 D4
Hawkcliffe View BD20 5 C1
Hawke Ave WF16 117 E4
Hawke Way BD12 94 E6
Hawkhill Ave
Guiseley LS20 39 D8
Leeds LS15 62 B2
Hawkhill Dr LS15 62 B2
Hawkhill Gdns LS15 62 B2
Hawkhills LS7 204 B3
Hawkhurst Rd LS12 209 C2
Hawkingcroft Rd WF4 140 F1
Hawkins Dr LS7 206 C2
Hawkins Way OL15 129 C1
Hawkroyd Bank Rd HD4 171 E6
Hawksbridge La BD22 51 A3
Hawkshead Cl BD5 201 B1
Hawkshead Cres LS14 62 A3
Hawkshead Dr BD5 201 B1
Hawkshead Way BD5 201 B1
Hawkshead Wlk BD5 201 B1
Hawksley Ct LS27 98 A6
Hawk St 6 BD21 35 D8
Hawkstone Ave LS20 39 C7
Hawkstone Dr BD20 18 A1
Hawkstone View LS20 39 D7
Hawkswood Ave
Bradford BD9 54 F3
Leeds LS5 58 E7
Hawkswood Cres LS5 58 E7
Hawkswood Gr LS5 58 E7
Hawkswood Mount LS5 58 E7
Hawkswood Pl LS5 58 F6
Hawkswood St LS5 58 F6
Hawkswood Terr LS5 58 F6
Hawkswood View LS5 58 E7
Hawksworth Ave LS20 39 D8
Hawksworth CE Prim Sch
LS20 38 F8
Hawksworth Cl LS29 22 A3
Hawksworth Dr
Guiseley LS20 39 D7
Menston LS29 22 A4
Hawksworth Gr LS5 58 D6
Hawksworth La LS20 39 B7
Hawksworth Rd
Baildon BD17 38 C6
Horsforth LS18 58 D7
Hawksworth St 2 LS29 8 B4
Hawksworth Wood Prim Sch
LS16 58 E7
Haw La LS19 40 B8
Hawley Cl LS27 97 F2
Hawley Terr BD10 56 E4
Hawley Way LS27 97 F2
Haworth Cl
Halifax HX1 203 A1
Mirfield WF14 137 F6
Haworth Ct 1 LS19 40 B7
Haworth Gr BD9 54 E3
Haworth La LS19 40 B7

Haworth Prim Sch BD22 51 C7
Haworth Rd
Batley WF17 96 F2
Bradford BD9 54 C4
Haworth BD22 51 E8
Wilsden BD15 53 C4
Haworth Sta★ BD22 51 C7
Haw Park La
Ryhill WF4 161 F3
Walton WF2 161 B2
Hawthorn Ave
Batley WF17 118 A3
Crofton WF4 143 E1
Knottingley WF11 126 E3
Pool LS21 24 D6
Yeadon LS19 40 C7
Hawthorn Cl
Addingham LS29 6 D8
Brighouse HD6 115 C3
Hawthorn Cres
4 Leeds LS7 204 A3
Yeadon LS19 40 B7
Hawthorn Croft WF3 100 C1
Hawthorn Ct WF4 143 E1
Hawthorn Dr
Bradford BD10 56 C7
Pudsey LS13 57 D6
Yeadon LS19 40 C8
Hawthorne Ave
Bradford BD3 75 E8
Castleford WF10 125 B6
Hemsworth WF9 181 D6
Purston Jaglin WF7 145 C4
Shipley BD18 55 D5
Wetherby LS22 13 D7
Hawthorne Cl
Flockton WF4 157 D3
Gildersome LS27 97 D7
Lepton HD8 155 D3
Wakefield WF2 120 B3
Hawthorne Cres WF9 181 C6
Hawthorne Dr LS27 97 D7
Hawthorne Flats S63 194 D1
Hawthorne Gdns LS16 42 B5
Hawthorne Gr WF2 141 E7
Hawthorne Mount WF6 144 B7
Hawthorne Rise
Ackworth M T WF7 163 D5
Leeds LS14 62 C8
Hawthorne St
Bradford BD3 75 E8
Shafton S72 180 C3
Silsden BD20 5 D1
Hawthorne Terr
Huddersfield HD4 153 C4
Wakefield WF2 141 E7
Hawthorne View LS27 97 E7
Hawthorne Way
East Morton BD20 36 E8
Shafton S72 180 C3
Shelley HD8 173 F3
Hawthorn Gr
Ackworth M T WF7 163 F5
Burley in W LS29 21 F8
Pudsey LS13 57 D5
Rothwell LS26 100 F4
Silkstone S75 193 F1
Hawthorn La 6 LS7 204 A3
Hawthorn Mill 5 LS12 78 A4
Hawthorn Mount 3 LS7 204 A3
Hawthorn Pk LS14 62 A8
Hawthorn Pl 15 OL14 108 B6
Hawthorn Rd
Bacup OL13 106 A2
Leeds LS7 204 A3
Slaithwaite HD7 151 F1
Yeadon LS19 40 C7
Hawthorn St
Brighouse HX3 114 D8
4 Halifax HX1 202 C1
Hawthorns The
Glusburn BD20 16 C6
Lofthouse Gate WF1 121 D5
Ossett WF5 140 E3
Hawthorn Terr
Garforth LS25 82 C5
5 Halifax HX1 202 C1
Huddersfield HX1 154 B8
Ossett WF5 140 E3
Hawthorn Vale 7 LS7 204 A3
Hawthorn View
Baildon BD17 38 E3
5 Leeds LS7 204 A3
Hawthorn Way HX2 91 D7
Hawtop La WF4 177 F5
Haw View LS19 40 C8
Hayburn Gdns WF17 118 B5
Hayburn Rd WF17 118 A5
Haycliffe Ave BD7 74 A2
Haycliffe Dr BD7 73 F2
Haycliffe Gr BD7 74 A2
Haycliffe Hill Rd BD5 74 B3
Haycliffe La BD5, BD6 74 B2
Haycliffe Rd BD5 74 B3
Haycliffe Sch BD5 74 B2
Haycliffe Terr BD5 74 B3
Hayclose Mead BD6 94 A6
Hay Croft BD10 55 F8
Hayden St BD3 75 B6
Haydn's Terr LS28 57 E2
Haydn Ave WF3 121 E6
Haydn Cl LS27 98 A4
Haydn Ct 6 LS27 98 A4
Haydn Pl 22 BD13 72 E1
Hayfield Ave
Boston Spa LS23 30 C8
Huddersfield HD3 153 A7
Hayfield Cl
Baildon BD17 38 E4
Holmfirth HD9 189 D4
Normanton WF6 144 B8
Hayfields Cl BD22 34 E5
Hayfields The BD22 51 C8
Hayfield Terr LS12 209 C2
Hayfield Way WF7 163 D5
Haygill Nook BD23 1 E1
Hayhills La BD20 5 D4
Hayhills Rd BD20 5 E2
Hayleigh Ave 9 LS13 58 C3
Hayleigh Mount LS13 58 C3
Hayleigh St 8 LS13 58 C3
Hayleigh Terr 7 LS13 58 C3
Hayne La WF4 157 E5
Haynes St BD21 35 D6
Hays La HX2 91 C7
Hayson Cl WF12 118 F1
Haythorns Ave BD20 5 D1
Haythorns Mount BD20 5 D1
Hayton Dr LS22 13 F4
Hayton Wood View LS25 64 E8
Haywain The LS29 8 D3
Haywood Ave HD3 153 C7
Hazebrouck Dr BD17 38 B4
Hazel Ave
Dewsbury WF12 140 B7
Leeds LS14 62 C8
Hazel Bank WF2 141 E8
Hazel Beck BD16 54 A8
Hazel Cl
Birkenshaw BD11 96 A6
Dewsbury WF12 140 B7
Hazel Cres WF12 140 B7
Hazelcroft BD2 56 D4
Hazel Croft BD18 55 D7
Hazel Ct
Rothwell LS26 100 F4
Wakefield WF2 142 A8
Hazeldene BD13 92 D8
Hazeldene Cotts LS22 12 C5
Hazel Dr
Dewsbury WF12 140 B7
Halifax HX2 91 D7
Hazel Gdns WF10 125 D6
Hazel Gr
Bacup OL13 106 B3
Batley WF17 118 A4
Brighouse HX3 115 A7
Flockton WF4 157 D3
Huddersfield, Brackenhall HD2 136 B5
Huddersfield, Cowlersley HD7 152 F2
Pontefract WF8 125 E2
Sutton-in-C BD20 16 C5
Hazelgreave Hall Farm HX4 132 F3
Hazel Grove Rd BD20 16 C5
Hazelheads BD17 38 C5
Hazel Ho WF10 123 F5
Hazelhurst Ave 1 BD16 37 A1
Hazelhurst Brow BD9 54 D2
Hazelhurst Ct
Bradford BD3 75 C7
Bradford, Daisy Hill BD9 54 D2
Pudsey LS28 76 F7
Hazel Hurst Gr BD13 92 D7
Hazelhurst Rd BD9 54 D2
Hazel Hurst Rd BD13 92 D7
Hazelhurst Terr BD9 54 D2
Hazel La DN6 184 A2
Hazelmere Ave BD16 54 A8
Hazel Mount BD18 55 C7
Hazel Rd WF11 126 E2
Hazel Rise LS26 102 C1
Hazeltine Ct 2 WF6 123 C1
Hazel Wlk BD9 54 D2
Hazelwood Ave
Garforth LS25 83 A5
Keighley BD20 18 F1
Hazelwood Ct
Halifax HX1 203 B1
Lofthouse Gate WF1 121 D5
Hazelwood Gdns 1 WF9 181 E6
Hazelwood Rd
Bradford BD9 54 C3
Fitzwilliam WF9 163 B1
Lofthouse Gate WF1 121 D5
Hazelwood St OL14 108 B5
Hazledene Cres S72 180 D1
Hazledene Rd S72 180 D1
Headfield CE Jun Sch WF12 139 C5
Headfield La WF12 139 C5
Headfield Rd
Dewsbury WF12 139 D5
Huddersfield HD4 154 A3
Headfield View WF12 139 D4
Headingley Ave LS6 59 C5
Headingley Cres LS6 205 A4
Headingley Ct LS6 205 C4
Headingley Grounds (Cricket & Rugby League) LS6 205 A4
Headingley La LS6 205 B4
Headingley Mews WF1 121 B1
Headingley Mount LS6 59 C5
Headingley Rise LS6 205 C3
Headingley Sta LS5 59 B4
Headingley Terr LS6 205 C4
Headingley View LS6 205 A4
Headland Gr BD6 73 F1
Headland La WF12 139 F6
Headlands Ave WF5 140 C5
Headlands CE Jun & Inf Sch WF15 117 A4
Headlands Cl WF15 117 B3
Headlands Gr WF5 140 C5
Headlands La
Knottingley WF11 126 E4
Pontefract WF8 125 D1
Headlands Pk WF5 140 C5
Headlands Rd
Huddersfield HD1 154 A7
Liversedge WF15 117 A4
Ossett WF5 140 C5
Headlands St WF15 117 A3
Headlands The WF15 117 A3
Headlands Wlk WF5 140 C5
Headley Cotts LS24 48 A8
Headley La
Bramham LS23 30 E1
Thornton BD13 72 D5
Headrow Sh Ctr LS1 211 C4
Headrow The LS1 211 C4
Headwall Gn HD7 152 B3
Headway Bsns Ctr BD4 75 C2
Headway Bsns Pk WF2 142 B3
Heald Cl OL13 106 A8
Heald Ct HD9 188 D3
Healdfield Rd WF10 124 F8
Heald La OL13 106 A8
Healds Ave WF15 117 B4
Healds Rd WF13 118 A2
Heald St WF10 124 F8
Heald Terr HX4 133 A5
Healdwood Cl WF10 125 A8
Healdwood Rd WF10 125 A8
Healey Ave BD16 37 A2
Healey Cl WF17 117 F5
Healey Cres WF5 140 D3
Healey Croft La WF3 120 B7
Healey Dr WF5 140 D4
Healey Farm HD8 173 E4
Healey Green La HD5 155 F7
Healey Jun & Inf Sch WF17 117 F5
Healey La
Batley WF17 118 B5
10 Bingley BD16 37 A2
Dewsbury WF12 157 A7
Healey Lane Bsns Ctr WF17 117 F4
Healey Lane Mills Bsns Ctr WF17 118 A5
Healey Rd WF5 140 D3
Healey St WF17 117 F5
Healey View WF5 140 D4
Healey Wood Cres HD6 115 A1
Healey Wood Gdns HD6 136 B8
Healey Wood Gr HD6 136 B8
Healey Wood Rd HD6 115 B1
Heap La BD3 201 D4
Heap St
Bradford BD1 201 D3
Halifax HX3 92 C2
Hearter Montessori West Cliffe Sch BD20 18 C1
Heath Ave HX3 113 B4
Heath Cl
Dewsbury WF12 140 B8
Slaithwaite HD7 170 E7
Heathcliff BD22 51 B7
Heathcliffe Cl WF17 96 F3
Heathcote Ave LS14 45 F5
Heathcote Rise BD22 51 E8
Heath Cres
Leeds LS11 213 B3
Low Bradley BD20 4 C6
Heathcroft Bank LS11 213 B2
Heathcroft Cres LS11 213 B2
Heathcroft Dr LS11 213 B2
Heathcroft Lawn LS11 213 B2
Heathcroft Rise LS11 213 B2
Heathcroft Vale LS11 213 B2
Heathdale Ave HD2 135 F1
Heath Dr
Boston Spa LS23 30 B7
Low Bradley BD20 4 C6
Heather Ave HD9 170 E1
Heather Bank OL14 108 B1
Heather Bank Ave BD22 34 F4
Heather Bank Cl BD13 52 D5
Heather Cl
Lofthouse Gate WF1 121 D5
Ossett WF5 140 F3
South Kirkby WF9 182 D3
Heathercroft LS7 204 B2
Heather Croft WF4 144 C3
Heather Ct
Batley WF17 96 E2
Bingley BD16 37 A5
Huddersfield HD3 152 F8
Ilkley LS29 8 B3
Lofthouse Gate WF3 121 E5
Heatherdale Cl HX2 91 F1
Heatherdale Ct WF3 119 E8
Heatherdale Dr WF3 119 E8
Heatherdale Rd WF3 119 E8
Heather Dr HX2 91 A3
Heatherfield Cres HD1 153 D6
Heatherfield Rd HD1 153 D6
Heather Fold HD8 174 F1
Heather Gdns
Leeds LS13 77 E8
Scarcroft LS14 45 C7
Heather Gr
Bradford BD9 54 B3
Keighley BD21 35 A8
Leeds LS13 77 E8
Heathergrove Fold HD5 154 D7
Heatherlands Ave BD13 52 D2
Heather Pl BD13 72 B2
Heather Rd
Baildon BD17 38 D4
Meltham HD9 170 D1
Heather Rise LS29 21 F8
Heather Side BD17 38 B4
Heathers The WF4 144 C3
Heatherstones 3 HX3 113 B4
Heather Vale LS14 45 B7
Heather View
Bingley BD16 37 D5
Crofton WF4 144 C3
Elland HX5 135 B7
Ossett WF5 140 D5
Heathfield
Leeds LS16 42 B4
Mirfield WF14 137 F6
Heathfield Ave HX5 135 B7
Heathfield Cl
Bingley BD16 37 A4
East Ardsley WF3 119 F8
Heathfield Gr
Bradford BD7 73 E4
1 Halifax HX3 113 C4
Heathfield Grange 4 HX5 135 A7
Heathfield Ind Est HX5 135 A6
Heathfield La LS23 30 B8
Heathfield Mews HD7 152 E4
Heathfield Pl 2 HX3 113 C4
Heathfield Rd HD7 152 E4
Heathfield Rise HX6 132 C1
Heathfield Sch HX6 150 C8
Heathfield Sq 7 LS6 59 D6
Heathfield St HX5 135 A6
Heathfield Terr
Halifax HX3 113 C4
Leeds LS6 59 D6
Heathfield Wlk LS16 42 A5
Heath Gdns HX3 113 C4
Heath Gr
Batley WF17 118 F5
East Morton BD20 36 D8
Huddersfield HD4 153 E2
Leeds LS11 213 B3
Pudsey LS28 76 C6
Heath Hall HX1 203 B1
Heath Hall Ave BD4 75 B1
Heath Hill Rd HX2 91 A2
Heath House La HD7 152 B4
Heath House Mill HD7 152 C4
Heath La HX3 113 C4
Heath Lea HX1 203 B1
Heath Manor WF1 143 B4
Heathmoor Cl
Bradford BD10 56 A7
Halifax HX2 91 D6
Heathmoor Mount HX2 91 E6
Heathmoor Park Rd HX2 91 D6
Heathmoor Way HX2 91 D6
Heath Mount LS11 213 B3
Heath Mount Rd HD6 136 A8
Heathness Rd LS29 2 D1
Heath Park Ave HX1 203 B1
Heath Pk LS29 7 F3
Heath Pl LS11 213 B3
Heath Rd
Bradford BD3 56 B1
Dewsbury WF12 140 B8
Halifax HX1, HX3 203 B1
Huddersfield HD7 152 F1
Leeds LS11 213 B3
Slaithwaite HD7 170 E8
Heath Rise LS11 213 B2
Heath Royd HX3 113 C4
Heathroyde HX1 202 C3
Heath St
Bingley BD16 37 A3
Bradford BD3 75 C7
Halifax HX3 113 C4
Liversedge WF15 117 B2
Heath Terr BD3 75 C7
Heath View St HX1 203 B2
Heath Villas HX3 113 C4
Heath Wlk WF12 140 B8
Heathwood Dr HD7 152 C5
Heathy Ave HX2 92 A5
Heathy La HX2 92 A5
Heaton's Ct LS1 211 C3
Heaton Ave
Cleckheaton BD19 116 C7
Dewsbury WF12 139 E8
Keighley BD20 36 C7
Kirkheaton HD5 137 C1
Leeds LS12 209 C1
Heaton Avenue Fst Sch BD19 116 C7
Heaton Cl
Baildon BD17 38 B4
Bingley BD16 37 B4
Heaton Cres
Baildon BD17 38 B5
Bingley BD16 37 B4
Heaton Dr
Baildon BD17 38 B4
Bingley BD16 37 B4
Kirkheaton HD5 137 C2
Heaton Fold La HD1 153 D6
Heaton Gdns HD1 153 D6
Heaton Gr
Cleckheaton BD19 116 C7
Shipley, Heaton Grove BD9 55 B4
Shipley, Windhill BD18 55 C7
Heaton Grange WF17 118 E3
Heaton Hill BD6 93 E7
Heaton Moor Rd HD5 137 C1
Heaton Park Dr BD9 55 A3
Heaton Park Rd BD9 54 F3
Heaton Prim Sch BD9 54 D
Heaton Rd
Batley WF17 118 C
Bradford BD8, BD9 55 B
Huddersfield HD1 153 D
Heaton Royds La BD9 54 F
Heaton Royds Sch BD18 55 A
Heaton St Barnabas CE Prim Sch BD9 55 A
Heaton St
Ackworth M T WF7 163 E
Bradford BD4 201 D
4 Brighouse HD6 115 A
Cleckheaton BD19 116 D
Heatons Yd HD6 115 B
Heator La HD8 191 A
Hebble Brook Cl HX2 91 C
Hebble Ct HX2 91 D
Hebble Dean HX2 91 F
Hebble Dr HD9 189 A
Hebble End HX7 88 F
Hebble Gdns HX2 91 E
Hebble La
Halifax HX3 91 F
Meltham HD9 187 D
Hebble Mount HD9 170 E
Hebble Oval WF9 183 B
Hebble Row BD22 34 C
Hebble St
Dewsbury WF13 138 F
4 Huddersfield HD1 154 B
Hebble Vale Dr HX2 91 E
Hebble View HX3 91 E
Hebble Way WF9 183 B
Hebb View BD6 73 E
Hebden App LS14 62 B
Hebden Bridge Rd BD22 51 B
Hebden Bridge Sta HX7 89 B
Hebden Bridge Visitor & Canal Ctr★ HX7 89 A
Hebden Chase LS14 62 B
Hebden Cl LS14 62 B
Hebden Ct HD3 153 B
Hebden Gn LS14 62 C
Hebden Gr HX7 89 A
Hebden Path LS14 62 B
Hebden Pl LS14 62 B
Hebden Rd
Haworth BD22 51 D
Wakefield WF1 142 E
Hebden Royd CE Prim Sch HX7 88 E
Hebden Terr HX7 89 B
Hebden View HX7 89 B
Hebden Wlk LS14 62 C
Heber's Ghyll Dr LS29 7 E
Heber's Gr LS29 7 E
Heber's Mount LS29 7 E
Heber Cl BD20 17 F
Heber St BD21 35 B
Heckmondwike Gram Sch WF16 117 D
Heckmondwike Rd
Batley WF13 117 F
Dewsbury WF13 138 F
Hector Cl 7 BD6 74 C
Heddle Rise WF2 141 D
Heddon Cl BD5 201 B
Heddon Gr BD5 201 B
Heddon Pl LS6 59 E
Heddon St 8 LS6 59 E
Heddon Wlk BD5 201 B
Hedge Cl BD8 54 D
Hedge Side BD8 73 E
Hedge Top La HX3 93 B
Hedge Way BD8 54 E
Hedley Chase LS12 210 B
Hedley Cres WF1 121 B
Hedley Gdns LS12 210 B
Hedley Gn LS12 210 B
Hedley Rd WF2 160 A
Heidelberg Rd BD9 55 A
Height Gn HX6 112 B
Height La
Draughton BD23 1 D
Oxenhope BD22 51 D
Height Rd HX7 89 E
Heights HX6 132 E
Heights Bank LS12 77 F
Heights Cl LS12 77 E
Heights Ct WF15 116 B
Heights Dr
Leeds LS12 77 F
Linthwaite HD7 170 D
Heights E The LS12 77 E
Heights Garth LS12 77 E
Heights Gn LS12 77 E
Heights La
Batley WF16 117 E
Bingley BD16 37 B
Bradford BD9 54 D
Leeds LS12 77 F
Silsden BD20 5 B
Heights Par LS12 77 E
Heights The HD9 189 C
Heights Way LS12 77 F
Heights Wlk LS12 77 F
Heights W The LS12 77 E
Helena Ct LS25 102 F
Helena Pl LS25 102 F
Helena St LS25 102 F
Helena Way BD4 95 C
Helene Ct HD3 152 E
Helen Rose Ct BD18 38 E
Helen St
Huddersfield HD1 153 E
Shipley BD18 54 F
Helen Terr HD6 114 F

Hellewell's Row WF4 140 D1
Hellewell St 4 BD6 93 F7
Hell La WF1, WF4 143 E4
Hellwood La LS14 45 D7
Helme CE Jun & Inf Sch
HD9 170 E4
Helme La HD9 170 D3
Helme Pk HD9 170 D3
Helmet La HD9 170 D2
Helm La
Mirfield WF14 137 D5
Sowerby Bridge HX6 132 C8
Helmsley Ct LS10 99 C4
Helmsley Dr LS16 59 B7
Helmsley Rd
Boston Spa LS23 30 C7
Leeds LS16 59 B7
Wakefield WF2 142 F1
Helmsley St BD4 75 A4
Helston Cl LS10 99 A6
Helston Croft LS10 99 A5
Helston Garth LS10 99 A5
Helston Gn LS10 99 A5
Helston Gr HD9 171 E4
Helston Pl LS10 99 A5
Helston Rd
Middleton LS10 99 A5
Normanton WF6 123 B3
Helston Sq LS10 98 F6
Helston St LS10 98 F6
Helston Way LS10 99 A6
Helston Wlk LS10 99 A5
Helted Way HD5 154 E3
Hembrigg Gdns LS27 98 B2
Hembrigg Terr LS27 98 A2
Heming's Way WF9 183 B3
Hemingway Cl
Castleford WF10 125 D5
Leeds LS10 215 B3
Ryhill WF4 162 C1
Hemingway Garth LS10 215 B3
Hemingway Gn LS10 215 B3
Hemingway Rd BD10 56 D8
Hemishor Dr LS26 102 E8
Hemsby Gr 7 BD21 35 B4
Hemsby Rd WF10 124 C6
Hemsby St 6 BD21 35 B4
Hemsworth Arts & Com Coll
WF9 181 E7
Hemsworth La WF9 163 A5
Hemsworth Rd WF9 181 F4
Hemsworth Water Pk*
WF9 163 D1
Henacre Wood Ct BD13 92 E7
Henage St 10 BD13 72 D1
Henbury St LS7 207 A1
Henconner Ave LS7 60 C6
Henconner Cres LS7 60 C6
Henconner Dr LS7 60 C6
Henconner Garth LS7 60 C6
Henconner Gdns LS7 60 C6
Henconner Gr LS7 60 C6
Henconner La
Leeds, Chapel Allerton
LS7 60 C6
Leeds, Gamble Hill LS13 77 E8
Henconner Rd LS7 60 C6
Hendal La WF2 160 A5
Henderson Ave WF6 144 B8
Henderson Glen S71 179 A3
Henderson Pl 8 BD6 74 C1
Hendford Dr BD3 75 B8
Hen Holme La BD20 17 E7
Henley Ave
Bradford BD5 74 E2
Dewsbury WF12 139 E2
1 Leeds LS13 58 C2
Yeadon LS19 40 D3
Henley Cl LS19 40 D3
Henley Cres
Leeds LS13 58 C2
Yeadon LS19 40 D3
Henley Croft HD5 154 E6
Henley Ct BD5 74 F2
Henley Dr
Purston Jaglin WF7 145 D3
Yeadon LS19 40 C3
Henley Gr
Bradford BD5 74 E2
2 Leeds LS13 58 C2
Henley Hill LS19 40 C3
Henley Mount LS19 40 D3
Henley Pl LS13 58 C2
Henley Rd
Bradford BD5 74 F2
Dewsbury WF12 139 E2
Leeds LS13 58 C2
Henley St 3 LS13 58 C2
Henley Terr LS13 58 C2
Henley View
Leeds LS13 58 C2
Yeadon LS19 40 C3
Henrietta St 2 WF17 118 C5
Henry Ave
Havercroft WF4 180 C8
Leeds LS12 209 C1
Henry Cl S72 180 C3
Henry Frederik Ave HD4 171 C6
Henry Moore Ct WF10 125 B7
Henry Moore Inst* LS1 211 B4
Henry Moore Pl WF10 124 E7
Henry Pl S64 98 A4
Henry Ralph Ave HD4 153 C1
Henry St
Batley WF17 118 C2
Bradford BD14 73 C4
Brighouse HD6 115 A4
1 Halifax HX1 203 A2
Henry St *continued*
Huddersfield HD1 154 A6
Keighley BD21 35 C7
Thornton BD13 72 D6
Wakefield WF2 142 A6
Henry Terr LS19 39 F7
Henshaw Ave LS19 40 B6
Henshaw Cres LS19 40 B6
Henshaw La LS19 40 B6
Henshaw Mews LS19 40 B6
Henshaw Oval LS19 40 B7
Henshaw Rd OL14 108 B1
Henshaw Woods OL14 108 A2
Henson Gr WF10 125 B6
Heppenstall St HD4 154 B4
Hepton Ct LS9 208 B1
Hepton Dr HX7 88 F4
Heptonstall Jun & Inf Sch
HX7 88 F5
Heptonstall Mus* HX7 88 F5
Hepworth Ave LS27 98 B8
Hepworth Cl WF14 138 B6
Hepworth Cres
Holmfirth HD9 189 E3
Morley LS27 98 B8
Hepworth Dr WF14 138 C6
Hepworth Jun & Inf Sch
HD9 189 F1
Hepworth La WF14 138 B6
Hepworth Rd HD9 189 E3
Hepworths Bldgs HD2 136 D3
Hepworth St WF10 103 F1
Herbalist St LS12 210 B2
Herbert Pl BD3 75 E8
Herbert St
Bingley BD16 37 A3
Bradford, Clayton BD14 73 C3
Bradford, Holme Top BD5 74 D4
Castleford WF10 124 D7
Halifax HX1 202 B2
3 Shipley, Cottingley BD16 54 B6
2 Shipley, Saltaire BD18 37 F1
Herdwick View BD20 19 B1
Hereford Cl WF9 181 D8
Hereford St LS12 209 C4
Hereford Way BD4 75 A4
Heritage Ct HD9 170 D3
Heritage Rd WF17 118 C4
Heritage Way BD22 34 C2
Hermitage Mews HX1 203 C2
Hermitage Pk HD8 155 E2
Hermit St BD21 35 A2
Hermon Ave HX1 202 C2
Hermon Gr HX1 202 C2
Hermon Rd LS15 62 B1
Hermon St LS15 62 B1
Heron Cl
Dewsbury WF13 138 E6
Harden BD16 36 A1
Leeds LS17 43 F4
Queensbury BD13 72 C2
Steeton BD20 17 B6
Heron Ct 4 LS27 98 D4
Heron Dr WF2 160 C5
Heron Gr 5 LS17 43 F4
Herries Ct LS29 22 B4
Herriot Mews WF10 125 D5
Herriot Way WF1 121 B2
Herschel Rd BD8 73 D7
Hertford Chase LS15 81 C6
Hertford Cl LS15 81 D6
Hertford Croft LS15 81 D6
Hertford Fold LS15 81 C6
Hertford Lawn LS15 81 C6
Heseltine Cl WF6 123 A2
Heseltine La HX7 110 B4
Heshbon St BD4 75 C3
Hesketh Ave
East Ardsley WF3 119 D8
Leeds LS5 59 A5
Hesketh La WF3 119 D8
Hesketh Mount LS5 59 A5
Hesketh Pl
Brighouse HX3 115 A7
Leeds LS5 59 A5
Hesketh Rd LS5 59 A4
Hesketh Terr LS5 59 A4
Hesley Rd WF2 160 B5
Hessel Ct WF8 146 B8
Hessle Ave LS6 205 B3
Hessle Common La WF7 163 D7
Hessle La WF7 163 D8
Hessle Mount LS6 205 B3
Hessle Pl LS6 205 B3
Hessle Rd 7 LS6 205 B3
Hessle St 9 LS6 205 B3
Hessle Terr LS6 205 B3
Hessle View 10 LS6 205 B3
Hessle Wlk 8 LS6 205 B3
Heston Ho HX2 112 D5
Hetchell View LS17 28 D2
Hetton Dr BD3 75 D6
Hetton Rd LS8 208 B4
Heuthwaite Ave LS22 13 F4
Hever Gr HD5 155 A7
Hew Clews BD7 73 E3
Hewenden BD13 52 F5
Hewenden View BD13 52 D2
Hew Royd BD10 55 F8
Hexham Gn HD3 152 F5
Hey's Bldgs WF6 122 F4
Heybeck La WF3, WF12 119 C5
Heybeck Wlk BD4 75 F2
Hey Cliff Rd HD9 189 B5
Hey Cres HD9 170 D2
Heydon Cl LS6 42 F1
Heyford Ct BD2 55 D3
Heygate Cl BD17 38 D4
Heygate La
Baildon BD17 38 D4
Bramham LS23 30 F3
Hey Head La
Calderbrook OL15 129 B1
Todmorden OL14 108 D7
Hey La
Huddersfield, Lowerhouses
HD5 154 D3
Kirkburton HD9 172 B7
Ripponden HD3 151 B6
Heys Ave BD13 72 F6
Heys Cl WF11 127 A4
Heys Cres BD13 72 F6
Heys Gdns HD9 189 C8
Heysham Dr BD4 75 F3
Heys La
Halifax HX2 90 B6
Ripponden HX6 132 D1
Slaithwaite HD7 151 D2
Hey Slack La HD8 190 C2
Heys Rd HD9 189 C8
Hey St
Bradford BD7 74 D7
Brighouse HD6 115 B4
1 Todmorden OL14 108 C5
Heys The HD9 170 E4
Heywood Bottom HD8 192 A6
Heywood Cl HX3 93 A2
Heywood Ct HX3 93 A2
Heywood Pl HX1 203 A3
Heywood St 16 HX1 202 C3
Hick La WF17 118 D5
Hicks La LS26 102 D3
Hick St BD1 201 C3
Higgin Chamber HX2 111 C5
Higgin La HX3 113 E5
Higham & Dob La HX6 111 C3
Higham Way LS25 82 F8
High Ash BD18 55 E7
High Ash Ave
Clayton West HD8 176 A2
Leeds LS17 43 F5
High Ash Cl WF4 178 F7
High Ash Cres LS17 43 E5
High Ash Dr LS17 43 E5
High Ash Mount LS17 43 F5
High Ash Pk BD15 53 F1
High Bank BD20 4 C6
High Bank App LS15 81 D7
High Bank Cl
4 Addingham LS29 6 E8
Elland HX5 135 C7
Leeds LS15 81 D8
High Bank Fst Sch WF15 116 B5
High Bank Gate LS15 81 D7
High Bank Gdns LS15 81 E7
High Bank La BD18 54 E6
High Bank Pl LS15 81 D7
High Banks Cl BD20 18 F2
High Bank St LS28 57 D3
High Bank View LS15 81 D7
High Bank Way LS15 81 E7
Highbeck Pk BD20 19 B3
High Binns La BD22 51 D3
High Bradley La BD20 4 C7
Highbridge La HD8 175 C1
Highbridge Terr BD5 74 F1
High Brook Fall WF3 121 C7
High Brooms HD2 135 E1
Highburton CE Fst Sch
HD8 173 E8
Highbury Cl LS6 59 E6
High Bury Cl BD13 92 C8
Highbury La LS6 59 E6
Highbury Mount LS6 59 E6
Highbury Pl
Leeds LS6 59 E6
Pudsey LS13 77 A8
Highbury Rd
Bradford BD4 75 C6
Leeds LS6 59 E6
Highbury Sch HD6 135 E7
Highbury St LS6 59 E6
Highbury Terr
12 Dewsbury WF12 139 D8
Leeds LS6 59 E6
High Busy La
Bradford BD10 56 A8
Shipley BD18 55 F8
High Cl
Guiseley LS20 39 B8
Huddersfield HD5 154 E3
Kexbrough S75 177 D1
Ossett WF5 119 D1
Slaithwaite HD7 170 E8
Yeadon LS19 40 B3
High Clare Ct LS29 8 E3
High Cliffe LS4 59 C3
Highcliffe Ave HD2 135 F2
High Cliffe Cl 11 BD13 72 D6
Highcliffe Ct
Shelf HX3 93 B5
Wetherby LS22 13 F5
Highcliffe Dr HX2 112 D7
Highcliffe Ind Est LS27 97 E5
Highcliffe Rd
Batley WF17 118 C3
Morley LS27 97 F4
High Cliffe Terr LS22 13 E5
High Cote BD20 18 D2
High Court La LS2 212 A3
High Crags Prim Sch
BD18 55 C6
High Crest HD7 152 E2
Highcroft
Batley WF17 118 C3
Collingham LS22 29 A8
High Croft
4 Addingham LS29 6 F8
Halifax HX3 91 F3
Holmfirth HD9 188 E5
Queensbury BD13 72 E1
Highcroft Cl LS28 76 C8
Highcroft Cres HD5 154 F3
Highcroft Gdns BD21 35 F6
High Croft Rd OL14 108 C6
High Croft Way BD20 4 D1
High Cross La HX3 93 A7
High Ct
Heptonstall HX7 88 D6
Leeds LS2 212 A3
Highdale WF12 118 E2
Highdale Croft BD10 56 B8
Higher Ashenhurst OL14 108 A7
Higher Back La HX7 87 F4
Higher Brockwell HX6 112 A3
Higher Calderbrook
OL15 129 C1
Higher Calderbrook Rd
OL15 129 C2
Higher Change Villas
OL13 106 B4
Higher Coach Rd BD17 37 F2
Higher Downs BD8 73 D8
Higher Eastwood OL14 109 A8
Higher Grange Rd LS28 76 E8
Higher Hartley St BD20 16 B6
Higher Intake Rd BD2 56 C1
Higher Lodge St BD20 16 B6
Higher Park Royd Dr
HX6 132 E6
Higher Row BD21 35 D3
Higher Scholes BD22 33 F1
Higher School St 4 BD18 54 F8
Higherwood Cl BD21 35 E6
High Farm Fold WF9 164 E2
High Farm Mdw WF9 164 E2
Highfell Rise BD22 34 E5
High Fernley Ct 10 BD12 94 C4
High Fernley Prim Sch
BD12 94 C3
High Fernley Rd BD12 94 B3
Highfield
Boston Spa LS23 30 E8
Bradford BD4 75 D1
East Ardsley WF3 98 D1
Shelf HX3 93 C5
Highfield Ave
Bradford BD10 56 A7
Brighouse HD6 115 B8
Denby Dale HD8 191 A4
Elland HX4 134 B7
Leeds LS12 210 A1
Meltham HD9 170 D3
Pontefract, Myson Chair
WF8 126 A4
Pontefract WF8 146 C7
Shelf HX3 93 D7
Highfield Cl
Featherstone WF7 145 D8
Gildersome LS27 97 E7
Keighley BD20 19 D1
Leeds LS12 210 A1
Highfield Cres
Baildon BD17 38 C4
Bradford BD9 54 E4
7 Hebden Bridge HX7 89 A4
Kippax LS26 102 F5
Leeds LS12 210 A2
Meltham HD9 170 D3
Netherton WF4 157 F6
Pudsey LS28 76 D8
Rothwell LS26 101 C7
Highfield Ct
Castleford WF10 124 D6
Cullingworth BD13 52 D6
Leeds LS12 209 C1
Liversedge WF15 116 F2
Oakworth BD22 34 C2
Shepley HD8 190 E6
Highfield Ctr WF9 181 D6
Highfield Dr
Batley WF17 96 E2
Bradford BD9 54 E4
Garforth LS25 82 F5
Gildersome LS27 97 D7
Kippax LS26 102 F5
Liversedge FW15 116 E4
Luddenden HX2 111 E8
Wakefield WF2 141 E8
Yeadon LS19 40 C3
Highfield Garth LS12 210 A1
Highfield Gdns
Bradford BD9 54 D4
Dewsbury WF12 139 D3
Gildersome LS27 97 D7
Leeds LS12 209 C1
Highfield Gn
Kippax WF10 102 F6
Pudsey LS28 76 D8
Highfield Gr
Bradford BD10 56 A6
Halifax HX5 134 E8
Kippax WF10 102 F6
Highfield Grange WF4 141 A1
Highfield La
Barwick in E LS15 63 E5
Batley WF13 117 F4
Keighley BD21 35 B8
Lepton HD8 155 D5
Meltham HD9 170 C3
Newthorpe LS25 84 D5
Rothwell LS26 101 C7
8 Silsden BD20 5 E2
High Field La HX6 132 D6
Highfield Mews
1 Baildon BD17 38 C4
Garforth LS25 82 F5
Keighley BD20 19 D1
Highfield Mount
Dewsbury WF12 139 E1
Rothwell LS26 101 C6
Highfield Pl
7 Bradford BD8 55 C1
Halifax HX1 202 B2
Hemsworth WF9 181 C6
Kippax WF10 103 A6
Morley LS27 98 B3
Highfield Prim Sch LS17 43 E4
Highfield Rd
Aberford LS25 64 E8
Bradford BD2, BD10 56 B7
Brighouse HD6 135 E8
Cleckheaton BD19 116 C7
Elland HX5 134 F6
Hemsworth WF9 181 D6
Horbury WF4 141 A1
Keighley BD21 35 A8
Kirkburton HD8 173 E7
Leeds LS13 58 D2
Luddenden HX2 111 E8
Meltham HD9 170 D3
Netherton WF4 158 D5
Pontefract WF8 146 C6
Pudsey LS28 76 C8
Shipley BD9 55 C5
Slaithwaite HD7 151 F4
Highfield Rise
Ryhill WF4 162 D2
Wakefield WF2 141 E8
Highfields
Holmfirth HD9 188 D4
Huddersfield HD1 153 F7
Netherton WF4 158 D5
Ryhill WF4 162 D2
High Fields HX6 112 E4
Highfield Sch WF5 119 D1
Highfields Rd HD1 153 F7
Highfield St
Keighley BD21 35 B7
Leeds LS13 58 D2
Pudsey LS28 76 C8
Highfield Terr
Cleckheaton BD19 116 C7
Cullingworth BD13 52 D6
Dewsbury WF12 139 D3
Halifax HX1 202 B2
Pudsey LS28 76 C8
Queensbury BD13 92 D8
Ripponden HX6 132 E6
Shipley BD18 54 E8
Yeadon LS19 40 C3
Highfield View LS27 97 E7
Highfold LS19 40 A5
High Fold
Baildon BD17 38 C4
Keighley, East Morton BD20 19 D1
Keighley, Exley Head BD22 34 F5
Micklethwaite BD16 36 E8
High Fold La BD20 18 A2
Highgate
Bradford BD9 54 F4
Denholme BD13 71 E6
Glusburn BD20 16 C7
Highgate Ave HD8 155 F3
Highgate Cl BD13 73 C2
Highgate Cres HD8 155 E3
Highgate Dr HD8 155 F3
Highgate Gdns HX2 202 A4
Highgate Gr BD13 73 C2
Highgate La
Kirkheaton HD5 137 D1
Lepton HD8 155 E3
Highgate Rd
Bradford BD13 73 B2
11 Dewsbury WF12 139 D8
Highgate St WF17 118 F3
Highgate Terr 13 WF12 139 D8
High Gate Way S72 180 C2
Highgate Wlk HD8 155 F3
High Gn HD8 155 F2
High Green Dr BD20 5 D2
High Green Rd WF6 122 E3
Highgrove Ct WF6 122 F4
High Grove La HX3 113 E5
High Holly Garth BD21 35 D6
High House Ave BD2 56 A4
High House Edge HD7 170 C7
High House La
Halifax HX2 90 C4
Linthwaite HD7 170 C8
High House Mews 16 LS29 6 F8
High House Rd BD2 56 A4
High Hoyland La S75 193 B8
High Keep Fold WF4 159 F3
High La
Cowling BD22 32 A8
Halifax HX2 112 B8
Hebden Bridge HX7 110 D3
Holmfirth HD9 189 B3
Huddersfield HD4 154 C1
Sicklinghall HG3 12 A8
Highland Cl WF8 125 F3
Highlands
Burley in W LS29 21 E8
Leeds LS17 43 E5
Ossett WF5 140 C5
Highlands Ave HD5 154 F3
Highlands Cl
1 Bradford BD7 73 E3

Highlands Cl continued
Leeds LS10 . . . . **99** F8
Highlands Dr LS10 . . . . **99** F8
Highlands Gr
Bradford BD7. . . . . **73** E3
Leeds LS10 . . . . **99** F8
Highlands La HX2. . . . . . **91** F6
Highlands Pk HX2. . . . . . **91** F6
Highlands The WF15 . . **116** D5
Highlands Wlk LS10 . . . . **99** F8
Highland Ville HX3. . . . **114** D8
High Lea HD7. . . . . **168** F4
Highlea Cl LS19. . . . . **39** F5
High Lee Gn HX2. . . . . . **111** B6
Highlee La HX6, HX4. . . . **132** F7
High Lees Rd HX2. . . . . . **91** B5
High Level Way HX1. . . . **202** B4
Highley Hall Croft HD6 . **115** D3
Highley Pk HD6. . . . . . . **115** E2
High Malsis Farm BD20. . **16** A5
High Mdw BD20. . . . . . . **18** A1
High Mdws
Dewsbury WF12 . . . . . . **139** C1
Elland HX4. . . . . **134** C7
Walton WF2 . . . . **161** B6
Wilsden BD15 . . . . **53** C5
High Mill LS29 . . . . **3** A1
High Mill Bsns Pk 6
LS27 . . . . **98** A3
High Mill La LS29 . . . . **3** A1
Highmoor BD17. . . . . **38** A3
High Moor Ave LS17 . . . **43** E2
High Moor Cl LS17 . . . . . **43** E3
High Moor Cotts LS24 . . **31** E1
Highmoor Cres HD6. . . **115** D3
High Moor Cres LS17 . . **43** E3
High Moor Ct LS17. . . . . **43** E2
High Moor Dr LS17. . . . . **43** E3
High Moor Gr LS17. . . . . **43** E3
High Moor Grange LS16 . **24** D3
Highmoor La
Brighouse, Clifton HD6 . . **115** E4
Brighouse HD6. . . . . . . **115** F5
Cleckheaton HD6. . . . . . **116** A6
Highmoor Wlk BD17 . . . **38** A2
Highoak Garth BD22 . . . **34** C1
High Oxford St WF13 . . **124** C7
High Park Cres BD9. . . . **54** E3
High Park Dr BD9. . . . . . **54** E3
High Park Gr BD9. . . . . . **54** E3
High Pastures BD22. . . . **34** E5
High Peal Ct 12 BD13. . . **72** D1
High Poplars BD2. . . . . . **55** F4
High Rd WF12 . . . . **139** E7
High Ridge WF4 . . . . . . **158** E6
High Ridge Ave LS26 . . **100** E7
High Ridge Ct LS26 . . . **100** E6
High Ridge Pk LS26 . . . **100** E7
High Ridge Way LS16 . . **24** F2
Highroad Well La HX2. . **112** B7
Highroyd HD8 . . . . **155** F3
Highroyd Cres 1 HD5. . **154** D5
Highroyd La HD5. . . . . . **154** D6
High Royds Dr LS29 . . . . **22** B3
High Royds Hospl LS29. . **22** B2
High Spring Gardens La
BD20. . . . . **35** A8
High Spring Rd BD21. . . **35** F6
High St
Batley, Birstall WF17 . . . . **96** E1
Batley, Hanging Heaton
WF17 . . . . **118** F3
Batley WF16 . . . . **117** E4
Blackshaw Head HX7. . . . **88** A5
Boston Spa LS23 . . . . . . **30** D8
Bradford BD10. . . . . **56** B8
Bradford, Wibsey BD6 . . . **74** C1
Bramham LS23 . . . . **30** D2
Brighouse HD6. . . . . . . **115** B3
Brotherton WF11. . . . . . **105** C1
Castleford WF10 . . . . . . **124** C7
Clayton West HD8 . . . . . **175** F2
Cleckheaton BD19. . . . . **116** D8
Clifford LS23 . . . . **30** E5
Crigglestone WF4 . . . . . **159** E6
Crofton, Streethouse WF4,
WF7 . . . . **144** B5
Crofton WF4 . . . . **161** F8
Darton S75 . . . . **178** A2
Dewsbury, Daw Green WF12,
WF13 . . . . **139** B7
Dewsbury, Earlesheaton
WF12 . . . . **139** F7
Dewsbury, Overthorpe
WF12 . . . . **139** C1
Dewsbury, Overthorpe
WF12 . . . . **139** D1
Elland, Stainland HX4 . . . **133** F3
8 Elland, West Vale HX4 . **134** D7
Halifax HX1 . . . . **203** A2
Halifax, Luddenden HX2 . . **90** E1
Honley HD9 . . . . **171** A1
Horbury WF4 . . . . **141** A1
Huddersfield HD1 . . . . . **154** A5
Huddersfield, Paddock
HD1. . . . . **153** E5
Keighley BD21 . . . . **35** B7
Kippax LS25 . . . . **83** B1
Knottingley WF11 . . . . . **126** C5
Morley LS27 . . . . **98** A3
Normanton, Altofts WF6 . . **122** F4
Normanton WF6 . . . . . . **123** B2
Ossett WF5 . . . . **119** C1
Pudsey LS28 . . . . **57** D3
Queensbury BD13 . . . . . . **72** E1

High St continued
Royston S71. . . . . **179** B3
Shafton S72 . . . . **180** C2
Slaithwaite HD7. . . . . . **152** B5
South Elmsall WF9. . . . . **183** A3
South Hiendley S72 . . . . **180** E5
Steeton BD20. . . . . **17** C5
Sutton-in-C BD20. . . . . . **16** D4
Thornton BD13 . . . . **72** D6
Todmorden OL14 . . . . . **108** A3
Upton WF9. . . . . **183** B7
Wetherby LS22 . . . . **13** E5
Woolley WF4 . . . . **178** A2
Yeadon LS19 . . . . **40** C7
High Stones Rd HX7. . . **110** E3
High Street Ct HX2. . . . . **90** E1
High Street Pl BD10. . . . **56** B8
High Sunderland La HX3 . **92** D1
Highthorne Ave BD3 . . . **56** C1
Highthorne Ct LS17. . . . . **43** F4
Highthorne Dr LS17. . . . . **43** F4
Highthorne Gr
Leeds, Blackwood LS17 . . **44** A4
3 Leeds LS12. . . . . **209** A4
Highthorne Mount LS17 . **43** F4
Highthorne St LS12 . . . **209** A4
Highthorne View 6
LS12. . . . . **209** A4
Hightown Fst Sch WF15 . **116** C5
Hightown Ind Est WF10 . **124** B7
Hightown La HD9 . . . . . **189** A5
Hightown Rd WF16 . . . **116** D6
Hightown View WF15 . . **116** D5
High Trees La HX4 . . . . **133** E6
High View
Crigglestone WF4 . . . . . **159** E5
Royston S71. . . . . **179** B3
Highway LS20 . . . . **22** B1
High Ways LS14. . . . . **61** E1
High Weardley La LS17. . **26** A6
High Well Hill La S72 . . **180** C6
High Wheatley LS29. . . . . **8** E3
High Wicken Cl BD13. . . . **72** D6
High Wood LS29 . . . . **8** F3
Highwood Ave LS17 . . . **43** C3
Highwood Cres LS17 . . . **43** C3
High Wood Ct LS6 . . . . . **59** E5
Highwood Gr LS17 . . . . . **43** C2
High Wood La HD8. . . . . **174** B6
High Woodlands WF3 . . **120** C7
High Wood Rd WF17 . . . **97** A4
Higson Ct HD5. . . . . . . **155** A7
Higson Row HD8. . . . . . **175** F3
Hilberoyd Rd WF17 . . . **118** D5
Hilda St
Ossett WF5 . . . . **140** E4
Shipley BD9 . . . . **55** A4
Hill HD9. . . . . **188** F5
Hillam La LS25 . . . . **105** E5
Hillam Rd BD2. . . . . **55** D3
Hillam St BD5 . . . . **74** B3
Hillary Pl LS2. . . . . **206** B2
Hillary Rd BD18. . . . . . . **55** E7
Hillary St 2 WF13 . . . . **117** F3
Hillas Ct 4 HX3 . . . . . . **113** D3
Hillas Ind Est HX6. . . . . **112** D4
Hillbeck HX2 . . . . **91** F2
Hillbrook Rise LS29. . . . . . **7** F3
Hill Brow Cl BD15 . . . . . **54** A1
Hill Cl
Baildon BD17. . . . . **38** B2
Huddersfield HD3 . . . . . **134** F1
Pontefract WF8 . . . . . . **146** D7
Hill Clough BD22. . . . . . . **34** D7
Hill Clough Gr BD22. . . . **34** D7
Hillcote Dr BD5 . . . . **74** E4
Hillcourt Ave LS13 . . . . **58** C4
Hillcourt Croft LS13 . . . **58** C4
Hillcourt Dr LS13 . . . . . **58** C4
Hill Court Fold LS13. . . . **58** C4
Hillcourt Gr LS13 . . . . . **58** C4
Hill Court View LS13 . . . **58** B4
Hill Cres
Batley WF17 . . . . **97** A1
Burley in W LS29. . . . . . . **21** F7
Halifax HX3 . . . . **113** F5
Yeadon LS19 . . . . **40** C5
Hillcrest WF6. . . . . **122** E4
Hill Crest
Collingham LS22 . . . . . . **28** E8
Hebden Bridge HX7. . . . . **88** F3
Low Bradley BD20. . . . . . . **4** C6
Ripponden HX6 . . . . . . **132** C1
Ryhill WF4 . . . . **162** C1
Skellow DN6 . . . . **184** E1
1 Sowerby Bridge HX6 . . **112** B5
Swillington LS26 . . . . . . **82** A1
Hillcrest Ave
Batley WF17 . . . . **118** A5
Castleford WF10 . . . . . . **125** D6
Leeds LS7 . . . . **207** B4
Ossett WF5 . . . . **140** C8
Purston Jaglin WF7. . . . . **145** B5
Queensbury BD13 . . . . . . **92** F8
Silsden BD20. . . . . **5** E2
Hill Crest Ave
Denholme BD13. . . . . **52** E1
3 Sowerby Bridge HX6 . . **112** B5
Hillcrest Cl WF10 . . . . . **125** D7
Hill Crest Cl LS26 . . . . . **81** F1
Hillcrest Dr
Castleford WF10 . . . . . . **125** E6
Queensbury BD13 . . . . . . **92** F8
Hill Crest Dr BD13. . . . . **52** D1
Hillcrest Flats HD1 . . . . **153** F4
Hillcrest Mount
Brighouse BD19. . . . . . . **115** F7
Castleford WF10 . . . . . . **125** E6

Hillcrest Mount continued
Leeds LS16 . . . . **41** E4
Hill Crest Mount BD13. . . **52** D1
Hillcrest Pl LS7 . . . . **207** B4
Hillcrest Prim Sch LS7 . **207** B4
Hillcrest Rd
Castleford WF10 . . . . . . **125** E7
Queensbury BD13 . . . . . . **92** F8
Hill Crest Rd
Denholme BD13. . . . . **52** D1
Dewsbury WF12 . . . . . . **139** C5
Thornton BD13 . . . . **72** D7
Hillcrest Rise LS16. . . . . **41** E4
Hillcrest View LS7 . . . . **207** B4
Hill Crest View BD13 . . . **52** D1
Hillcroft WF8 . . . . **146** F5
Hill Croft
Ripponden HX6 . . . . . . **132** C1
Thornton BD13 . . . . **72** E7
Hillcroft Cl WF8 . . . . . . **147** D5
Hill Dr WF7. . . . . **164** A8
Hill End
Bradford BD7. . . . . **73** E3
Dewsbury WF12 . . . . . . **139** E4
Hill End Cl
Brighouse HX3. . . . . **94** A2
Leeds LS12 . . . . **77** F8
Hill End Cres LS12 . . . . . **77** F8
Hill End Gr BD7. . . . . **73** E3
Hill End La
Cullingworth BD13. . . . . **52** F8
Harden BD16 . . . . **36** A1
Queensbury BD13 . . . . . . **92** D8
Hill End Rd LS12 . . . . **77** F8
Hillesley Rd WF12. . . . . **119** A3
Hill Est WF9 . . . . **183** B7
Hillfold WF9 . . . . **183** B3
Hill Foot BD18 . . . . **54** E7
Hillfoot Ave LS28 . . . . . **76** B8
Hillfoot Cres LS28. . . . . **76** B8
Hillfoot Dr LS28. . . . . . . **76** B8
Hillfoot Rise LS28. . . . . **76** B8
Hillgarth
Dewsbury WF12 . . . . . . **139** D3
Knottingley WF11 . . . . . **126** E3
Hill Gr WF12 . . . . **134** F1
Hill Green Ct BD4 . . . . . **76** E2
Hill Grove Lea HD3. . . . **134** F1
Hill Gr S LS10. . . . . **99** F7
Hillhead Dr WF17 . . . . . **97** A1
Hill Ho WF7. . . . . **188** D2
Hill House Edge La BD22 . **70** B8
Hillhouse La HD1. . . . . . **154** B8
Hill House La
Holmfirth HD9. . . . . **188** E2
Oxenhope BD22. . . . . . . **51** C1
Hill House Rd HD9 . . . . **188** E2
Hillidge Rd LS10 . . . . . . **215** A4
Hillidge Sq LS10 . . . . . . **215** A4
Hillingdon Way LS17 . . . **43** B6
Hillings La
Guiseley LS20, LS29 . . . . **21** E3
Menston LS29 . . . . **21** E3
Hill La HD9 . . . . **188** E5
Hill Lands BD12. . . . . . . **94** C5
Hill Park Ave HX3 . . . . . **91** F1
Hill Park Mount HX6 . . **132** E6
Hill Pk WF14. . . . . **137** F2
Hill Pl OL14. . . . . **108** A3
Hill Primary Sch The
S63. . . . . **194** F1
Hill Rd
Castleford WF10 . . . . . . **124** F6
Wakefield WF2 . . . . **160** C4
Hill Rise WF17 . . . . **118** F4
Hill Rise Ave LS13. . . . . **58** C4
Hill Rise Gr LS13. . . . . . **58** C4
Hill Royd Cl HX2 . . . . . . **91** E7
Hillside
Byram WF11 . . . . **126** D7
Denby Dale HD8 . . . . . . **192** A6
Garforth LS25 . . . . **83** B6
Hillside Ave
Guiseley LS20 . . . . **22** D3
Huddersfield HD2 . . . . . **136** B2
Luddenden HX2 . . . . . . **111** D7
Oakworth BD22 . . . . **34** B2
Ripponden HX6 . . . . . . **132** E6
Hill Side Ave HD9 . . . . . **189** E2
Hillside Bldgs LS11 . . . . **214** A3
Hillside Cl
Addingham LS29 . . . . **6** E8
Wakefield WF2 . . . . **141** D3
Hillside Cres
10 Bacup OL13 . . . . **106** A7
Brierley S72. . . . . **181** A2
Huddersfield HD4 . . . . . **154** B2
Hillside Ct
Menston LS29 . . . . **21** F4
South Elmsall WF9. . . . . **183** A4
Hillside Gr
Brierley S72. . . . . **181** A2
Oakworth BD22 . . . . **34** B2
6 Pudsey LS28 . . . . **76** F7
Hillside Mount
Brierley S72. . . . . **181** A2
Pontefract WF8 . . . . . . **146** E8
Pudsey LS28 . . . . **77** A7
Hill Side Mount LS28. . . **57** E2
Hillside Rd
Ackworth M T WF7. . . . . **164** A6
Leeds LS7 . . . . **204** A3
Pontefract WF8 . . . . . . **146** E8
Shipley BD18 . . . . **55** D5
Hill Side Rd
Bingley BD16 . . . . **36** F3
Bradford BD3. . . . . **201** D3

Hillside Rise
Guiseley LS20 . . . . **22** D3
Liversedge WF15. . . . . . **117** A3
Hill Side Terr BD17 . . . . **38** C3
Hill Side Terr BD3 . . . . . **201** D4
Hillside View
Pudsey LS28 . . . . **77** A7
Slaithwaite HD7. . . . . . **152** E1
Sowerby Bridge HX6 . . . **112** A3
Hillside Works Ind Est
BD19. . . . . **95** D2
Hill St
Bradford, Bowling BD4 . . **75** B5
Bradford, Wibsey BD6. . . **74** A1
Cleckheaton BD19 . . . . . **116** C7
Halifax HX1 . . . . **203** A2
Haworth BD22 . . . . **51** C6
Holmfirth HD9. . . . . **189** E3
Leeds, Beeston Hill LS11. . **214** B3
Leeds, New Town LS9 . . . **207** B2
Leeds, New Town LS9 . . . **207** B2
Hillthorpe Cl LS10 . . . . . **99** C3
Hillthorpe Dr WF8 . . . . **165** A5
Hillthorpe Rd LS28. . . . . **76** E5
Hillthorpe Rise LS28 . . . **76** E5
Hillthorpe Sq 1 LS28. . **76** E5
Hillthorpe St 2 LS28. . . **76** E5
Hillthorpe Terr 3 LS28. . **76** E5
Hilltop S72 . . . . **180** F3
Hill Top
Brighouse HX3. . . . . **114** E7
Burley in W LS29. . . . . . . **9** E1
Castleford WF10 . . . . . . **123** F7
Cawthorne S75 . . . . **193** E5
Clayton West HD8 . . . . . **175** F2
Fitzwilliam WF9 . . . . . . **163** A3
Halifax HX2 . . . . **202** A1
Ilkley LS29 . . . . **8** A2
Knottingley WF11 . . . . . **126** F4
Queensbury BD13 . . . . . . **72** D2
Steeton BD20. . . . . **17** C5
Wakefield WF2 . . . . **160** C4
Hill Top Ave
Barnsley S71 . . . . **178** E1
Huddersfield HD2 . . . . . **135** B4
Leeds LS8 . . . . **207** C4
Hill Top Bank HD4 . . . . **171** C6
Hill Top CE Prim Sch
BD12. . . . . **94** C6
Hilltop Cl WF10 . . . . . . **104** A1
Hill Top Cl
East Ardsley WF3 . . . . . **119** E6
Fitzwilliam WF9 . . . . . . **163** A3
7 Leeds LS12. . . . . **77** F8
Notton WF4 . . . . **179** B6
Hill Top Cotts BD9 . . . . **54** E2
Hill Top Cres WF14. . . . **137** F1
Hill Top Croft HD4 . . . . **171** C6
Hill Top Ct
East Ardsley WF3 . . . . . **119** E6
Wakefield WF2 . . . . **160** C4
Hill Top Dr HD3 . . . . . . **153** A8
Hill Top Est
Batley WF16 . . . . **117** E4
South Kirkby WF9 . . . . . **181** F1
Hill Top Farm HD8 . . . . **173** E3
Hill Top Fold
Bradford BD12. . . . . **94** D6
Slaithwaite HD7. . . . . . **151** F1
Hill Top Gdns WF3 . . . . **119** E6
Hill Top Gn WF3 . . . . . . **119** D6
Hill Top Gr
Bradford BD15. . . . . **54** A1
East Ardsley WF3 . . . . . **119** E6
Hill Top La
Bradford BD15. . . . . **54** A1
Cragg Vale HX7 . . . . **110** B4
East Ardsley WF3 . . . . . **119** E6
Micklethwaite BD16. . . . **36** F8
Purston Jaglin WF4. . . . . **145** C1
Hill Top Mews WF11 . . . **126** F4
Hill Top Mount LS8 . . . **207** C4
Hill Top Pl
Leeds, Hyde Park LS6 . . . **205** C2
Leeds LS8 . . . . **207** C4
Hill Top Prim Sch WF3 . **119** E6
Hill Top Rd
Flockton WF4 . . . . **157** D3
Holmfirth HD9 . . . . **188** F1
Huddersfield, Grove Place
HD5. . . . . **154** D6
Huddersfield HD3 . . . . . **134** F1
Huddersfield, Paddock
HD1. . . . . **153** E5
Keighley BD21 . . . . **35** A5
Leeds LS12 . . . . **77** F8
Oakworth BD22 . . . . **34** B2
Slaithwaite HD7. . . . . . **152** A1
Thornton BD13 . . . . **72** C7
Wakefield WF2 . . . . **160** C4
Hill Top St LS6. . . . . **205** C2
Hill Top Terr HD8 . . . . . **175** F2
Hill Top View
East Ardsley WF3 . . . . . **119** D6
Holmfirth HD9 . . . . **199** B8
Normanton WF6 . . . . . . **144** A7
Hill Top Way BD22. . . . . **34** F7
Hill Top Wlk BD22. . . . . **34** F7
Hill Tree Pk HD4 . . . . . . **153** A1
Hillview OL15 . . . . **129** D1
Hill View
Halifax HX2 . . . . **91** F7
Mytholmroyd HX7 . . . . . **110** F8
Hill View Ave LS7 . . . . . **204** A3
Hillview Gdns HX3 . . . . . **93** A1
Hill View Mount LS7 . . . **204** A3
Hillview Rise BD4 . . . . . **75** E4
Hill View Terr 2 LS7. . . **204** A3

Hillway LS20 . . . . **39** C
Hillworth Village BD21 . . **35** B
Hilmian Way WF9 . . . . . **181** A
Hilton Ave BD18 . . . . . . **55** B
Hilton Cres BD17. . . . . . **38** C
Hilton Ct LS16 . . . . **24** A
Hilton Dr BD18. . . . . **55** B
Hilton Gr
Bradford BD7. . . . . **74** B
Leeds LS8 . . . . **204** C
Shipley BD18 . . . . **55** B
Hilton Grange LS16 . . . . **24** B
Hilton Mews LS16. . . . . . **24** A
Hilton Pl LS8 . . . . **207** C
Hilton Rd
Bradford BD7. . . . . **74** A
Leeds LS8 . . . . **207** C
Shipley BD18 . . . . **55** B
Hilton St 33 Hebden Bridge HX7 . . . **89** A
2 Leeds LS8. . . . . **207** C
Hilton Terr 3 LS8 . . . . . **207** C
Hinchcliffe Ave WF5 . . . **140** F
Hinchcliffe Mill Jun & Inf
Sch HD9 . . . . **188** C
Hinchcliffe St BD3 . . . . . **75** B
Hinchliffe Ave BD17. . . . **38** D
Hind's Chambers 4 HX1 **203** B
Hind Ct HD9 . . . . **170** C
Hindle Pl 2 LS27 . . . . . . **98** B
Hindley Rd WF15. . . . . . **117** A
Hindley Wlk BD7. . . . . . . **73** D
Hinds Cres WF9. . . . . . . **182** F
Hind St
6 Bradford BD8. . . . . . . **74** C
Bradford, Wyke BD12 . . . **94** C
Hinsley Ct LS6 . . . . **59** E
Hinton Cl WF8 . . . . **125** E
Hinton La WF11. . . . . . . **126** A
Hions Cl HD6 . . . . **136** A
Hipperholme Gram Sch
HX3. . . . . **114** C
Hipperholme & Lightcliffe
High Sch & Sports Coll
HX3. . . . . **114** F
Hipperholm & Lightcliffe
High Sch & Sports Coll
HX3. . . . . **115** A
Hipswell St BD3 . . . . **75** C
Hird Ave BD6 . . . . **94** C
Hird Rd BD12 . . . . **94** D
Hird St
Keighley BD21 . . . . **35** E
Leeds LS11 . . . . **214** A
Shipley BD17 . . . . **55** B
Hirst's Yd LS1 . . . . **211** C
Hirst Ave WF16 . . . . **117** D
Hirst Gr HX7 . . . . **89** B
Hirst La
Shepley HD8 . . . . **190** B
Shipley BD18 . . . . **54** E
Hirstlands Ave WF5 . . . **140** C
Hirstlands Dr WF5 . . . . **140** C
Hirst Lodge Ct BD2. . . . . **55** F
Hirst Mill Cres BD18. . . . **37** E
Hirst Rd
Dewsbury WF13 . . . . . . **118** C
Wakefield WF2 . . . . **141** D
Hirst St
Kippax WF10 . . . . **102** F
Mirfield WF14 . . . . **138** A
Todmorden OL14 . . . . . . **86** B
Hirst Wood Cres 1 BD18. **54** E
Hirst Wood Rd BD18 . . . . **54** E
Hive St BD22. . . . . **35** A
Hobart Bldgs HX7. . . . . . **89** D
Hobart Rd
Castleford WF10 . . . . . . **125** D
Dewsbury WF12 . . . . . . **118** F
Hobb End BD13 . . . . **72** C
Hobberley La LS17. . . . . . **44** F
Hobb Nook La LS21 . . . . **10** A
Hob Cote La BD22. . . . . . **34** A
Hob La
Haworth BD22 . . . . **50** C
Huddersfield HD4 . . . . . **153** B
Mytholmroyd HX2 . . . . . **111** A
Ripponden HX6 . . . . . . **132** C
Sowerby Bridge HX6 . . . **112** B
Hobson Fold 4 BD12 . . . **94** D
Hockney Rd BD8 . . . . **74** B
Hockney Rd Ind Est BD8. . **74** B
Hoctun Cl WF10 . . . . . . **124** E
Hodge La WF8 . . . . **166** E
Hodgewood La WF8. . . . **147** D
Hodgson Ave
Bradford BD3. . . . . **56** D
Leeds LS17 . . . . **44** A
Hodgson Cres LS17 . . . . **44** A
Hodgson Fold
Addingham LS29 . . . . **2** E
Bradford BD2. . . . . **55** F
Hodgson Ho 3 LS22 . . . . **13** F
Hodgson La BD11 . . . . . . **96** C
Hodgson Pl 6 LS27 . . . . **98** B
Hodgson St
Morley LS27. . . . . **98** C
Wakefield WF1 . . . . **216** A
Hodgson Terr WF12. . . . **139** D
Hodroyd Cl S72. . . . . . . **180** D
Hodroyd Cotts S72. . . . . **180** F
Hodroyd La S72. . . . . . . **180** D
Hoffman St HD3 . . . . . . **153** A
Hog Close La HD9. . . . . **200** C
Hogley La HD9 . . . . **188** C
Holays HD5. . . . . **154** E
Holbeck La LS11 . . . . . . **210** C
Holbeck Moor Rd LS11 . . **211** A

olbeck Twrs LS11 211 A1
olborn App LS6 206 A3
olborn Ct
Bradford BD12 94 C6
Leeds LS6 206 B3
olborn Gdns 4 LS6 206 A3
olborn Gn LS6 206 A3
olborn Gr LS6 206 A3
olborn St LS6 206 B3
olborn Terr LS6 206 B3
olborn Twrs LS6 206 B3
olborn View LS6 206 A3
olborn Wlk LS6 206 A3
olby Bsns Pk HX6 112 B3
olby Sq WF2 141 C4
olden Ing Way WF17 97 A4
olden La
Baildon BD17 38 D4
Silsden BD20 18 C6
olden Rd 1 BD6 74 B1
olden St BD22 34 F5
olderness Rd WF11 126 E4
olderness St 14 OL14 108 C5
oldforth Cl LS12 210 B3
oldforth Gdns LS12 210 B3
oldforth Gn LS12 210 B3
oldforth Pl LS12 210 B3
oldsworth Ct 6 BD19 116 D7
oldsworth Rd HX2, HX3 92 A6
oldsworth Sq BD2 56 D4
oldsworth St
Bradford BD1 201 C4
Cleckheaton BD19 116 D8
Shipley BD18 55 C6
oldsworth Terr HX1 203 C1
ole Bottom Rd OL14 108 B7
ole La BD20 5 B3
oles La WF11 126 E4
olgate Ave WF9 163 B3
olgate Cres WF9 181 C7
olgate Gdns WF9 181 C7
olgate Rd WF8 146 C5
olgate Terr WF9 163 B3
olgate View
Brierley S72 181 B3
Fitzwilliam WF9 163 B3
olker St
Bradford BD8 74 B8
Keighley BD21 35 C8
olland Pk BD9 54 E2
olland Rd LS25 83 C2
olland St WF17 118 D5
ollas La HX6 112 E2
ollerton La WF3 119 F7
ollies The LS21 24 D6
ollin Ave HD3 153 D7
ollinbank La WF16 117 E5
ollin Brigg La HD9 188 C2
ollin Close La BD2 55 E3
ollin Cres LS16 59 E7
ollin Ct LS6 59 D7
ollin Dr
Crigglestone WF4 159 E5
Leeds LS16 59 E7
ollin Edge HD8 192 A6
ollin Gate LS21 10 D2
ollingbourne Rd LS15 62 F2
ollin Gdns LS16 59 C7
ollingreave HD9 189 E7
ollin Greaves La HX3 92 D1
ollings Rd BD8 74 B8
ollings Sq
Bradford BD8 74 B8
Pudsey LS28 57 B7
ollings St
Bradford BD8 74 B8
Shipley BD16 54 B7
ollings Terr BD8 74 B8
ollings The LS26 102 B3
ollingthorpe Ave WF4 159 F3
ollingthorpe Ct WF4 159 F2
ollingthorpe Gr WF4 159 E3
ollingthorpe La WF4 159 E3
ollingthorpe Rd WF4 159 E2
ollingwell Hill BD13 72 E3
ollingwood Ave BD7 73 F4
ollingwood Ct BD7 73 E3
ollingwood Dr BD7 73 E4
ollingwood Gate LS29 7 F3
ollingwood La BD7 73 E3
ollingwood Mount BD7 73 E4
ollingwood Prim Sch
BD7 73 E3
ollingwood Rise LS29 7 F3
ollingworth La
Knottingley WF11 127 A4
Todmorden OL14 129 B8
ollin Hall HD7 152 C5
ollin Hall Dr LS29 7 E3
ollin Hall La
Huddersfield HD7 152 D5
Huddersfield, Scapegoat
HD7 152 C5
Kirkheaton WF14 137 D2
ollin Hall Rd BD18 54 E6
ollin Head BD17 38 F4
ollin Hill Ave LS8 61 C5
ollin Hill Dr LS8 61 C5
ollinhirst La WF4 158 F6
ollin House La
Clayton West HD8 193 A8
Holmfirth HD9 189 F5
ollinhurst WF10 102 F6
ollin La
Crigglestone WF4 159 D6
Leeds LS16 59 D7
Ripponden HX6 132 A3
Shipley BD18 55 D6
Hollin La *continued*
Sowerby Bridge HX6 112 C2
Wadsworth Moor HX2 90 B5
Hollin Mews LS16 59 D7
Hollin Mount LS16 59 D7
Hollin Park Ave LS8 61 D5
Hollin Park Cres LS8 61 D5
Hollin Park Ct LS28 57 A6
Hollin Park Dr LS28 57 A6
Hollin Park Mount LS8 61 D5
Hollin Park Par LS8 61 C5
Hollin Park Pl LS8 61 C5
Hollin Park Rd
Leeds LS8 61 D5
Pudsey LS28 57 A6
Hollin Park Terr LS8 61 D5
Hollin Park View LS8 61 C5
Hollin Rd
Leeds LS16 59 D7
Shipley BD18 55 C6
Hollin Rise BD18 55 C6
Hollinroyd Rd WF12 139 E8
Hollins
Hebden Bridge HX7 89 A4
Luddenden Foot HX2 111 C5
Hollins Ave WF13 117 F3
Hollins Bank HX6 112 B4
Hollins Bank La BD20 17 E4
Hollins Beck Cl LS25 103 A8
Hollins Cl BD20 17 F2
Hollins Cres 15 HX7 89 A3
Hollins Glen HD7 170 A8
Hollins Gr WF10 102 F6
Hollins Hey Rd HX4 134 D4
Hollins Hill BD17, LS20 39 B6
Hollins La
Halifax, Mixenden HX2 91 C5
Keighley BD20 17 F2
Luddenden Foot HX6 111 C5
Slaithwaite HD7 169 E6
Sowerby Bridge HX6 112 B5
Hollins Mdw OL14 108 A1
Hollins Mill La HX6 112 B4
Hollins Mount WF9 181 C7
Hollins Pk LS25 83 A1
Hollins Pl
Hebden Bridge HX7 89 A3
15 Walsden OL14 108 A1
Hollins Rd
2 Batley WF13 117 F2
Walsden OL14 108 A1
Hollins Row HD7 170 A8
Hollins St OL14 129 B8
Hollin St HX6 111 E1
Hollins Terr HX6 111 E1
Hollins The OL14 108 B6
Hollin Terr
Huddersfield HD3 153 C7
Shipley BD18 55 C6
Hollin View LS16 59 D7
Hollin Wood Cl BD18 54 E7
Hollinwood View BD16 36 D7
Hollis Pl LS3 205 C1
Hollowfield Croft BD12 95 B5
Hollowgate HD9 189 A5
Hollow The HD9 170 D2
Holly App WF5 140 D8
Holly Ave LS16 41 D3
Holly Bank
Ackworth M T WF7 163 E6
Elland HX5 134 E5
Garforth LS25 83 B6
Guiseley LS20 39 D8
Kirkheaton HD5 155 B8
2 Leeds LS6 59 D6
Sutton-in-C BD20 16 C5
Hollybank Ave
Batley WF17 118 C7
Denby Dale HD8 191 C6
Holly Bank Ct HD3 153 A7
Holly Bank Dr HX3 114 D8
Hollybank Gdns BD7 73 F3
Hollybank Gr BD7 73 E3
Holly Bank Ho 4 HD6 135 F8
Holly Bank Pk HD6 135 F8
Hollybank Rd BD7 73 F3
Holly Bank Rd
Brighouse HD6 135 F8
Huddersfield HD3 135 C1
Holly Bank Sch WF14 137 E8
Holly Bush Ct LS23 30 E7
Hollybush Gn LS22 29 C8
Hollybush Primary Sch
LS13 58 E3
Holly Cl
Crofton WF4 143 E1
Middleton LS10 99 B4
South Elmsall WF9 182 F2
Holly Cres
Crofton WF4 143 E1
East Ardsley WF3 120 E8
Ripponden HX6 132 C3
Hollycroft Ave S71 179 B3
Hollycroft Ct LS16 42 A3
Holly Ct
East Ardsley WF3 119 E6
1 Guiseley LS20 39 E8
Lofthouse Gate WF1 121 C5
Holly Dene WF5 140 D8
Holly Dr LS16 41 D3
Holly Farm S72 180 C3
Hollyfield Ave HD3 153 A7
Hollygarth Ct WF9 181 D7
Holly Gr
Batley WF17 118 B3
Brierley S72 181 A3
Halifax HX1 202 C2
Halifax, Wainstalls HX2 90 E4
Holly Gr *continued*
Huddersfield HD3 135 C1
Holly Hall La BD12 94 C4
Holly Ho 6 WF10 124 E7
Holly Mede WF5 140 D8
Hollynsmill HX4 134 D7
Hollyns Terr 6 HX4 134 C7
Holly Park Dr BD7 73 E4
Holly Park Gr BD7 73 E3
Holly Park Mills LS28 57 A6
Holly Pk LS18 40 F1
Holly Rd
Boston Spa LS23 30 B8
Huddersfield HD1 153 E4
Holly Royd HX6 132 D6
Hollyshaw Cres LS15 81 C8
Hollyshaw Gr LS15 81 C8
Hollyshaw La LS15 81 C8
Hollyshaw St LS15 81 C8
Hollyshaw Terr 4 LS15 81 C8
Hollyshaw Wlk LS15 62 C1
Holly St
Bradford BD6 73 D2
Hemsworth WF9 181 D7
Wakefield WF2 141 F7
Holly Terr HD1 154 B8
Holly Tree La LS15 81 E6
Holly View HX6 111 E1
Hollywell Gr LS12 209 B4
Hollywell La LS12 209 B4
Holman Ave LS25 82 F5
Holmcarr Ct 15 BD16 37 A3
Holmcliffe Ave HD4 153 F1
Holmclose HD9 188 C2
Holmdale Cres HD9 188 F8
Holmdene Dr WF14 138 A6
Holme's Terr HX2 202 A4
Holme Ave HD5 154 E5
Holmebank Mews HD9 172 C2
Holme Cl
Glusburn BD20 16 D6
Grange Moor WF4 156 E5
Holme Croft WF4 159 F7
Holme Ct HD9 189 E7
Holme Dr HX2 112 B6
Holme Farm Ct LS12 77 D3
Holme Farm La LS17, LS23 28 F3
Holme Field WF5 140 C7
Holmefield Rd
Glusburn BD20 16 D5
Huddersfield HD3 152 E6
Holmefield View BD4 75 F4
Holme Ghyll BD20 16 B6
Holme Gr LS29 21 F7
Holme House La
Halifax HX2 90 E4
Oakworth BD22 34 B5
Holme House Rd OL14 86 C1
Holme House St OL15 129 D1
Holme House View HX6 132 D2
Holme Ings LS29 7 C7
Holme Jun & Inf Sch
HD9 187 F1
Holme La
Bradford BD4 75 F1
Glusburn BD20 16 D6
Halton East BD23 1 D8
Holmfirth HD9 189 E7
Slaithwaite HD7 151 E1
Wakefield WF2 142 B3
Holme Leas Dr WF5 140 C7
Holme Mill La BD22 34 F6
Holme Mills Ind Est HD3 152 F4
Holme Pk LS29 21 F7
Holme Pl
Hebden Bridge HX7 89 A4
3 Huddersfield HD1 153 D7
Holme Rd HX2 112 B6
Holme Rise WF9 183 A2
Holmeside Cl HD4 171 F8
Holmes Rd HX6 112 C4
Holmes St
Bradford BD1 74 D8
Leeds LS11 211 C2
Holme St
Bradford BD5 74 D4
Brighouse HX3 115 A7
Hebden Bridge HX7 89 A3
Liversedge WF15 117 B4
Oxenhope BD22 51 C2
Todmorden OL14 107 E7
Holme Styes La HD9 199 A8
Holme Terr
Calderbrook OL15 129 D1
Mytholmroyd HX7 110 D7
Holme Top La BD5 74 D4
Holme Top St BD5 74 D4
Holme Valley Bsns Ctr
HD4 171 E8
Holme Valley Meml Hospl
HD9 189 A7
Holme View
Arthington LS21 25 C6
Ilkley LS29 8 A4
Holme View Ave HD9 188 D5
Holme View Dr HD9 188 D5
Holme View Pk HD9 188 E5
Holme Villas HD7 169 C6
Holme Way WF5 140 C7
Holme Well Rd LS10 99 E5
Holme Wood 14 BD4 75 E3
Holme Wood Rd
Bradford BD4 75 D3
Keighley BD22 34 F6
Holme Woods La HD9 197 F6
Holmfield HD8 175 F2
Holmfield Ave
Clayton West HD8 175 F2
Holmfield Ave *continued*
Wakefield WF2 142 B3
Holmfield Chase WF3 122 B6
Holmfield Cl
Clayton West HD8 175 F2
Pontefract WF8 125 F4
Holmfield Cotts LS26 102 E3
Holmfield Ct
Bradford BD1 201 A3
Pontefract WF8 125 F4
Holmfield Dr
Huddersfield HD7 152 F5
Leeds LS8 44 A1
Holmfield Gdns HX2 92 A5
Holmfield Gr WF2 142 B3
Holmfield Ind Est HX2 92 A7
Holmfield La
Castleford WF11, WF8 125 F5
Wakefield WF2 142 B3
Holmfield Rd HD8 175 F2
Holmfield St BD1 201 A3
Holmfield Terr HD8 175 F2
Holmfirth High Sch HD9 189 C8
Holmfirth Jun & Inf Sch
HD9 189 A4
Holmfirth Rd
Diggle OL3 185 D1
Holmfirth HD9 189 E7
Meltham HD9 170 E1
Shepley HD8 190 E6
Holmroyd Ave BD20 16 D6
Holmsley Ave WF9 182 A2
Holmsley Crest LS26 101 A6
Holmsley Field Ct LS26 101 C6
Holmsley Field La LS26 101 C6
Holmsley Garth LS26 101 B7
Holmsley Gr WF9 182 A2
Holmsley La
Rothwell LS26 101 B6
South Kirkby S72, WF9 181 E2
Holmsley Mount WF9 182 A2
Holmsley Wlk LS26 101 B6
Holmwood Ave LS6 59 E8
Holmwood Cl LS6 59 F8
Holmwood Cres LS6 59 F8
Holmwood Dr LS6 59 F8
Holmwood Gr LS6 59 F8
Holmwood Mount LS6 59 F8
Holmwood View LS6 59 E8
Holroyd Hill BD6 74 C1
Holroyd Mill La BD16 36 E8
Holroyd Sq HX4 133 F4
Holroyd St LS7 207 A2
Holsworthy Rd BD4 75 E3
Holt Ave
Huddersfield HD2 136 C4
Leeds LS16 42 C5
Holtby Gr HX3 115 A7
Holt Cl LS16 42 C4
Holt Cres LS16 41 F5
Holtdale App LS16 41 F5
Holtdale Ave LS16 41 F5
Holtdale Cl LS16 41 F5
Holtdale Croft LS16 41 F5
Holtdale Dr LS16 41 F5
Holtdale Fold LS16 41 F5
Holtdale Garth LS16 41 F5
Holtdale Gdns LS16 41 F5
Holtdale Gn LS16 41 F5
Holtdale Gr LS16 41 F5
Holtdale Lawn LS16 41 F5
Holtdale Pl LS16 41 F5
Holtdale Rd LS16 41 F5
Holtdale View LS16 41 F5
Holtdale Way LS16 41 F5
Holt Dr LS16 42 A5
Holt Farm Cl LS16 42 A5
Holt Farm Rise LS16 41 F5
Holt Garth LS16 42 A5
Holt Gdns
Bradford BD10 55 F8
Leeds LS16 42 C5
Holt Gn LS16 42 A5
Holt Head Rd HD7 170 B6
Holt La
Holmfirth HD9 188 F6
Leeds LS16 42 A5
Holt Lane Ct LS16 42 B4
Holt Park App LS16 42 A5
Holt Park Ave LS16 42 A5
Holt Park Cl LS16 42 A5
Holt Park District Ctr
LS16 41 F5
Holt Park Dr LS16 42 A5
Holt Park Gate LS16 42 A5
Holt Park Gdns LS16 42 A5
Holt Park Gn LS16 42 A5
Holt Park Gr LS16 41 F5
Holt Park Grange LS16 42 A5
Holt Park La LS16 42 A5
Holt Park Rd LS16 42 A5
Holt Park Rise LS16 42 A5
Holt Park Vale LS16 42 A5
Holt Park View LS16 41 F5
Holt Park Way LS16 42 A5
Holt Rd LS16 42 A5
Holt Rise LS16 42 A5
Holts La BD14 73 B5
Holt St OL15 129 D2
Holts Terr HX3 113 D4
Holt The BD18 55 C8
Holt Vale LS16 42 A5
Holt Way LS16 42 A5
Holt Wlk LS16 42 A5
Holybrook Ave BD10 56 D6
Holybrook Prim Sch
BD10 56 D6
Holycroft Prim Sch BD21 35 B6
Holycroft St BD21 35 B6
Holy Family RC Prim Sch
LS12 210 A3
Holy Family RC Sch The
BD20 18 B1
Holy Family & St Michaels
RC Prim Sch WF8 126 A1
Holy Name RC Prim Sch
LS16 42 A3
Holyoake Ave
Batley WF17 118 A5
Bingley BD16 36 F1
Linthwaite HD7 170 C8
Holyoake St OL14 86 A1
Holyoake Terr
Horbury WF4 140 E1
Slaithwaite HD7 152 D1
Holyrood Chase WF10 124 C7
Holyrood Cres WF6 122 F4
Holy Rood La LS25 104 E8
Holy Rosary & St Anne's RC
Prim Sch LS7 207 A3
Holy Spirit RC Prim Sch
WF16 117 D4
Holy Trinity CE Prim Sch
Halifax HX1 203 A2
Leeds LS16 41 D5
Ossett WF5 140 D6
Holy Trinity CE Senior Sch
HX2 92 A6
Holywell HD7 152 D1
Holywell Ash La BD8 55 D1
Holywell Dene WF10 125 A6
Holywell Gdns WF10 125 A6
Holywell Gr WF10 125 A6
Holywell Green Prim Sch
HX4 134 B4
Holywell Halt* BD23 1 B7
Holywell La
Castleford WF10 125 B6
Shadwell LS17 44 D5
Holywell Mount WF10 125 B6
Home Farm Cl BD6 73 D1
Home Farm Ct
Hooton Pagnell DN5 195 D5
West Bretton WF4 176 F7
Home Farm Mews LS29 22 A3
Home Farm Prim Sch
BD6 93 D8
Homefield Ave LS27 98 A2
Home Lea LS26 100 D7
Home Lea Dr LS26 100 D6
Homepaddock Ho LS22 13 F6
Homestead Dr WF2 141 F6
Homestead The WF16 117 E4
Homes The HD2 136 F3
Home View Terr BD8 55 B1
Honey Head La HD9 171 F3
Honey Hole Cl OL14 108 B4
Honey Hole Rd OL14 108 B4
Honey Holme La BB10 85 A7
Honey Pot View 5 BD22 51 C2
Honeysuckle Cl
Micklefield LS25 84 B5
Wakefield WF2 141 E7
Honeysuckle Dr WF12 139 D3
Honley Bsns Ctr HD9 172 A4
Honley CE Inf Sch HD9 171 F5
Honley CE Jun Sch HD9 171 F4
Honley High Sch & Coll
HD9 172 A5
Honley Rd HD4 172 D6
Honley Sq WF4 141 A1
Honley Sta HD9 172 B5
Honoria St HD1 136 A1
Hood St
Huddersfield HD4 171 F8
South Elmsall WF9 182 E1
Hoods The HD6 135 F7
Hoopoe Mews BD15 73 B7
Hooton Cres WF4 162 A1
Hooton Pagnell All Saints CE
Prim Sch DN5 195 C5
Hooton Rd DN5 195 F4
Hoowood La HD9 187 E3
Hopbine Ave BD5 74 E2
Hopbine Rd BD5 74 E2
Hope Ave
Bradford BD5 74 C2
Shipley BD18 55 D8
Hope Bldgs 11 OL14 108 C5
Hopefield Chase LS26 100 B4
Hopefield Cl LS26 100 B4
Hopefield Cres LS26 100 B4
Hopefield Ct
East Ardsley WF3 120 C7
Holmfirth HD9 199 B7
Rothwell LS26 100 B4
Hopefield Dr LS26 100 B4
Hopefield Gdns LS26 100 B4
Hopefield Gn LS26 100 B4
Hopefield Gr LS26 100 B4
Hopefield Mews LS26 100 B4
Hopefield Pl LS26 100 B4
Hopefield View LS26 100 B4
Hopefield Way
Bradford BD5 75 B1
Rothwell LS26 100 B4
Hopefield Wlk LS26 100 B4
Hope Hall St HX1 203 B2
Hope Hall Terr 7 HX1 203 B2
Hope Hill View BD16 54 A7
Hope La BD17 38 B3
Hope Pl BD21 35 B5
Hope Rd LS9 212 A4

Hope St W WF10 . . . 124 C7
Hopes Farm Mount [6] LS10 . . . 99 F7
Hopes Farm Rd [7] LS10 . . 99 F7
Hopes Farm View LS10 . . 100 A7
Hope St
Castleford WF10 . . . 104 C2
Darton S75 . . . 178 C1
Dewsbury WF13 . . . 118 C1
Halifax HX1 . . . 203 A3
Havercroft WF4 . . . 180 C8
[22] Hebden Bridge HX7 . . . 89 A3
Huddersfield HD3 . . . 153 B5
Morley LS27 . . . 98 A4
Normanton WF6 . . . 144 A8
Ossett WF5 . . . 140 F3
Shelf HX3 . . . 93 B4
Sowerby Bridge HX6 . . . 112 C3
Todmorden OL14 . . . 108 C5
Wakefield WF1 . . . 216 B3
Hope Street E [9] WF10 . . 124 D8
Hope Terr
Crofton WF4 . . . 143 F1
Slaithwaite HD7 . . . 152 D3
Hopetown Wlk WF6 . . . 123 C3
Hope View BD18 . . . 55 D7
Hopewell Pl [12] LS6 . . . 205 B2
Hopewell St WF17 . . . 118 B6
Hopewell Terr
[8] Horsforth LS18 . . . 58 B7
Kippax LS25 . . . 83 B1
Hopewell View LS10 . . . 99 D5
Hopewell Way WF4 . . . 159 E5
Hopkinson Dr BD4 . . . 95 C8
Hopkinson Rd HD2 . . . 136 B4
Hopkinsons Bldgs [4] HX3 91 F3
Hopkinson St [2] HX3 . . . 91 F3
Hopkin St BD4 . . . 75 E1
Hopps's Rd BD20 . . . 16 C7
Hops La HX3 . . . 91 D2
Hopton Ave
Bradford BD4 . . . 75 B1
Mirfield WF14 . . . 137 E2
Hopton Dr WF14 . . . 137 E2
Hopton Hall La WF14 . . . 137 F1
Hopton La WF14 . . . 137 F2
Hopton Mews LS12 . . . 209 B3
Hopton New Rd WF14 . . . 138 A3
Hopton Prim Sch WF14 . . . 137 F4
Hopwood Bank LS18 . . . 41 C2
Hopwood Cl LS18 . . . 41 C2
Hopwood Gr WF10 . . . 125 B7
Hopwood La HX1 . . . 202 C2
Hopwood Rd LS18 . . . 41 C2
Horace Waller VC Par WF12 . . . 119 A2
Horbury Bridge CE Jun & Inf Sch WF4 . . . 140 E1
Horbury Mews WF4 . . . 140 F2
Horbury Prim Sch WF4 . . 141 C1
Horbury Rd
Ossett WF5 . . . 140 E3
Wakefield WF2 . . . 141 E3
Horbury Sch WF4 . . . 141 C1
Horley Green La HX3 . . . 92 E2
Horley Green Rd HX3 . . . 113 E8
Hornbeam Ave WF2 . . . 142 A8
Hornbeam Cl BD15 . . . 53 F4
Hornbeam Gn [2] WF8 . . . 125 F1
Hornbeam Gr HX3 . . . 92 F4
Hornbeam Way LS14 . . . 62 C8
Hornby St HX1 . . . 202 B1
Hornby Terr HX1 . . . 202 B1
Horncastle St [2] BD19 . . . 116 E7
Horncastle View WF4 . . . 162 D2
Horn Cote La HD9 . . . 190 A6
Horncroft S75 . . . 193 F5
Horner Ave WF17 . . . 117 F6
Horner Cres WF17 . . . 117 F6
Horners Bldgs HX2 . . . 92 A5
Hornes La S75 . . . 178 C1
Horne St
Halifax HX1 . . . 203 A3
Wakefield WF2 . . . 142 C4
Horn La
Ingbirchworth S36 . . . 191 B1
Shepley HD9 . . . 190 A6
Silsden BD20 . . . 5 C4
Hornsea Dr BD15 . . . 53 C4
Horse Bank Dr HD4 . . . 153 E3
Horse Croft La HD8 . . . 174 B3
Horsefair LS22 . . . 13 E5
Horse Fair WF8 . . . 125 D1
Horsefair Ctr The LS22 . . . 13 F5
Horse Fair Flats [7] WF8 125 D1
Horsehold La HX7 . . . 88 E2
Horsehold Rd HX7 . . . 88 E2
Horse Pond La HD3 . . . 152 A7
Horse Race End WF1 . . . 143 C3
Horseshoe Ct BD15 . . . 53 B4
Horsfall St
Halifax HX1 . . . 202 C1
Morley LS27 . . . 97 F6
Todmorden OL14 . . . 108 E6
Horsforth Featherbank Inf Sch LS18 . . . 58 B7
Horsforth Newlaithes Jun Sch LS18 . . . 58 A6
Horsforth New Rd LS13 . . . 57 E6
Horsforth St Margaret's CE Primary Sch LS18 . . . 41 B1
Horsforth St Margaret's CE Prim Sch LS18 . . . 41 D1
Horsforth St Mary's RC Prim Sch LS18 . . . 41 C1
Horsforth Sch LS18 . . . 41 B1
Horsforth Sta LS18 . . . 41 C3
Horsforth Village Mus* LS18 . . . 58 B8
Horsham Ct BD22 . . . 34 E5
Horsham Rd [5] BD4 . . . 75 E2
Horsley Fold HD6 . . . 115 E2
Horsley St [5] BD6 . . . 74 C1
Horsman St BD4 . . . 75 E1
Horton Bank Ctry Pk* BD7, BD14 . . . 73 D3
Horton Cl LS13 . . . 57 F4
Horton Garth LS13 . . . 57 F4
Horton Grange Prim Sch BD7 . . . 74 B5
Horton Grange Rd BD7 . . . 74 B5
Horton Hall Cl BD5 . . . 74 D5
Horton Park Ave BD5, BD7 74 C5
Horton Park Prim Sch BD5 . . . 74 B4
Horton Pl HX2 . . . 91 F8
Horton Rise LS13 . . . 57 F4
Horton St
Batley WF16 . . . 117 D3
Halifax HX1 . . . 203 C2
Ossett WF5 . . . 140 C6
Horton Terr HX3 . . . 114 C8
Hospital La LS16 . . . 41 F3
Hospital Rd BD20 . . . 19 A1
Hostingley La WF12 . . . 140 B2
Hothfield Jun Sch BD20 . . . 5 D1
Hothfield St BD20 . . . 5 D1
Hough HX3 . . . 93 A1
Hough End Ave LS13 . . . 58 D1
Hough End Cl LS13 . . . 58 D1
Hough End Cres LS13 . . . 58 C1
Hough End Ct [1] LS13 . . . 58 D1
Hough End Garth LS13 . . . 58 C1
Hough End Gdns [2] LS13 . 58 D1
Hough End La LS13 . . . 58 C1
Hough Gr [16] LS13 . . . 58 C2
Hough La LS13 . . . 58 C2
Houghley Ave LS12 . . . 58 F2
Houghley Cl LS13 . . . 58 E2
Houghley Cres LS12 . . . 58 F3
Houghley La LS12, LS13 . . . 58 E1
Houghley Pl LS12 . . . 58 F2
Houghley Rd LS12 . . . 58 F2
Houghley Sq LS12 . . . 58 F2
Hough Side Cl LS28 . . . 77 B7
Hough Side La LS28 . . . 77 A7
Hough Side Rd LS28 . . . 77 A7
Hough Terr [17] LS13 . . . 58 C2
Houghton's Almshouses [1] HD5 . . . 154 F3
Houghton Ave WF11 . . . 126 B5
Houghton Pl BD1 . . . 201 A4
Houghton Rd S72 . . . 194 A1
Houghton St HD6 . . . 115 B3
Houghton Twrs [14] HX6 . . 112 B4
Hough Top LS13 . . . 77 B8
Hough Tree Rd LS13 . . . 77 C8
Hough Tree Terr LS13 . . . 77 C8
Hougomont BD13 . . . 72 C3
Houldsworth Ave WF16 . . 117 E7
Hoults La HX4 . . . 134 C8
Houndhill La WF7 . . . 145 F5
Hove Ct [3] WF16 . . . 117 D4
Hovingham Ave LS8 . . . 208 A4
Hovingham Gr LS8 . . . 208 A4
Hovingham Mount LS8 . . 208 A4
Hovingham Prim Sch LS8 . . . 208 A4
Hovingham Terr LS8 . . . 208 A4
Howard Ave
Huddersfield HD3 . . . 153 C7
Leeds LS15 . . . 80 F7
Howard CE Jun & Inf Sch WF7 . . . 164 B7
Howard Cres WF4 . . . 159 E6
Howard Ct LS15 . . . 80 F7
Howard Dr WF7 . . . 163 F4
Howard Pk BD19 . . . 116 E7
Howard Pl WF17 . . . 118 C3
Howard Rd HD3 . . . 153 C7
Howards Dean BD22 . . . 51 D8
Howard St
Batley WF17 . . . 118 C3
Bradford BD5 . . . 201 A2
Halifax HX1 . . . 202 C4
Ossett WF5 . . . 140 D7
Wakefield WF1 . . . 216 B3
Howard Villas BD19 . . . 116 E7
Howard Way
Calderbrook OL15 . . . 129 C1
Meltham HD9 . . . 170 E1
Howarth Ave BD2 . . . 56 A5
Howarth Cres BD2 . . . 56 A5
Howarth La HD1 . . . 153 E3
Howbeck Ave BD20 . . . 19 A1
Howbeck Dr BD20 . . . 36 A8
Howcans La HX3 . . . 92 B5
Howcroft Ct WF2 . . . 160 E7
Howcroft Gdns WF2 . . . 160 E7
Howden Ave
Keighley BD20 . . . 18 A2
Skellow DN6 . . . 184 E1
Howdenbrook HX3 . . . 93 E7
Howden Cl
Bradford BD4 . . . 75 F1
Darton S75 . . . 177 F1
Huddersfield HD4 . . . 152 F2
Howden Clough Ind Est WF17 . . . 97 B3
Howden Clough Rd LS27, WF17 . . . 97 D3
Howden Gdns LS6 . . . 205 B2
Howden Pl LS6 . . . 205 B2
Howden Rd BD20 . . . 5 F1
Howden Way WF1 . . . 142 E6
Howell La DN5 . . . 194 A4
Howes La HX3 . . . 92 F2
Howgate BD10 . . . 56 C8
Howgate Rd HD7 . . . 169 F8
Howgill Gn BD6 . . . 94 A6
Howlett Cross LS26 . . . 100 B4
Howley Mill La WF17 . . . 118 D7
Howley Park Cl LS27 . . . 97 F2
Howley Park Rd LS27 . . . 97 F2
Howley Park Rd E LS27 . . . 98 A1
Howley Park Terr LS27 . . . 97 F2
Howley Park Trad Est LS27 . . . 97 F2
Howley Park View LS27 . . 98 C1
Howley St WF17 . . . 118 D6
Howley Wlk WF17 . . . 118 E6
Howroyd's Yd WF5 . . . 119 C1
Howroyd La
Dewsbury WF12 . . . 156 E7
Ripponden HX4 . . . 133 B4
Howson Cl LS20 . . . 22 F1
Hoxton Mount LS11 . . . 213 C3
Hoxton St BD8 . . . 74 A8
Hoylake Ave HD2 . . . 135 F3
Hoyland Rd WF2 . . . 160 B5
Hoyland Terr WF9 . . . 182 A2
Hoyle Beck Cl HD7 . . . 152 D1
Hoyle Court Ave BD17 . . . 38 E3
Hoyle Court Dr BD17 . . . 38 E3
Hoyle Court Prim Sch BD17 . . . 38 E2
Hoyle Court Rd BD17 . . . 38 E3
Hoyle Fold BD22 . . . 34 F5
Hoyle Head Mills Ind Est WF12 . . . 139 F7
Hoyle House Fold HD7 . . 152 D1
Hoyle Ing HD7 . . . 152 D1
Hoyle Ing Rd BD13 . . . 72 F6
Hoyle Mill Rd WF9 . . . 163 D2
Hubberton Green Rd HX6 . . . 111 C2
Hubert St
Bradford BD3 . . . 75 B6
Halifax HX2 . . . 112 D7
Huddersfield HD3 . . . 134 E1
Huddersfield Gram Sch HD3 . . . 153 C6
Huddersfield New Coll HD3 . . . 152 F7
Huddersfield Obsy* HD4 170 F8
Huddersfield Rd
Batley WF17 . . . 117 E8
Bradford BD12 . . . 94 C4
Brighouse HD6 . . . 136 B7
Denshaw OL3 . . . 167 A4
Dewsbury, Ravensthorpe WF13 . . . 138 D4
Dewsbury, West Town WF13 . . . 139 B7
Halifax HX3 . . . 113 C4
Holmfirth HD9 . . . 189 A6
Holmfirth, New Mill HD9 . . 189 E7
Honley HD9 . . . 172 A5
Huddersfield HD3, HX5 . . . 135 A4
Ingbirchworth S36 . . . 191 E1
Kexbrough S75 . . . 177 C1
Kirkburton HD8 . . . 174 A4
Meltham HD4 . . . 171 A5
Skelmanthorpe HD8 . . . 174 D2
West Bretton S75, WF4 . . . 177 A6
Huddersfield Royal Infmy HD3 . . . 153 C8
Huddersfield Sta HD1 . . . 154 A6
Huddersfield Tech Coll
Huddersfield HD1 . . . 154 A6
Huddersfield, Salford HD4 153 F2
Huddersfield Tech Coll (Annexe) HD1 . . . 153 F7
Huddersfield Tech Coll (Brunel Ho) HD2 . . . 136 E2
Huddleston Ct
Dewsbury WF12 . . . 139 F8
Mirfield WF14 . . . 138 A4
Hud Hill HX3 . . . 93 B4
Hudroyd HD5 . . . 154 F3
Hudson's Terr [4] LS19 . . . 40 C7
Hudson Ave
Bradford BD7 . . . 74 B3
Notton WF4 . . . 179 B6
Hudson Cl
[1] Bradford BD7 . . . 74 B3
Wetherby LS22 . . . 13 E5
Hudson Cres BD7 . . . 74 B3
Hudson Croft HX4 . . . 150 F6
Hudson Gdns BD7 . . . 74 B4
Hudson Gr LS9 . . . 208 A1
Hudson Mews LS23 . . . 30 E7
Hudson Mill Rd HX7 . . . 88 C5
Hudson Pl LS9 . . . 208 B1
Hudson Rd LS9 . . . 208 A1
Hudson St
Bradford BD3 . . . 75 D7
Leeds LS9 . . . 208 A1
[2] Pudsey LS28 . . . 57 D1
Todmorden OL14 . . . 86 C1
Hudson The BD12 . . . 94 C3
Hudson View BD12 . . . 94 C3
Hudswell Rd LS10 . . . 215 A4
Hudswell St WF1 . . . 142 E3
Huggan Row [5] LS28 . . . 76 F7
Hughenden View LS27 . . . 98 A6
Hughendon Dr BD13 . . . 73 A6
Hughendon Wlk BD13 . . . 73 A6
Hugh Gaitskell Prim Sch LS11 . . . 213 C2
Hugh St WF10 . . . 124 D7
Hugill St BD13 . . . 72 D6
Hulbert Croft HD5 . . . 154 F4
Hulbert St BD16 . . . 37 A2
Hullenedge Gdns HX5 . . . 134 D6
Hullenedge La HX5 . . . 134 D6
Hullenedge Rd HX5 . . . 134 E6
Hullen Rd HX5 . . . 134 D6
Hullett Cl HX7 . . . 89 F1
Hullett Dr HX7 . . . 89 F1
Hull St LS27 . . . 98 B4
Hulme Sq WF10 . . . 104 D1
Hulme St [5] HX6 . . . 112 B3
Humber Cl
Castleford WF10 . . . 125 B8
Slaithwaite HD7 . . . 152 D1
Humber Pl WF4 . . . 141 A2
Humboldt St BD1 . . . 201 D3
Hume Crest [8] WF17 . . . 118 C5
Humley Rd WF2 . . . 160 B5
Hundhill La WF8 . . . 146 D2
Hungate La LS26 . . . 122 E8
Hungerford Rd HD3 . . . 153 D8
Hunger Hill
Halifax HX1 . . . 203 B2
Ilkley LS29 . . . 8 C7
Morley LS27 . . . 98 A3
Queensbury BD13 . . . 72 F1
Hunger Hills Ave LS18 . . . 41 A1
Hunger Hills Dr LS18 . . . 41 A1
Hunslet Bsns Pk
Leeds LS10 . . . 212 B1
Leeds LS10 . . . 215 B4
Hunslet Carr Prim Sch LS10 . . . 215 B2
Hunslet Green Ret Ctr LS10 . . . 215 A3
Hunslet Green Way LS10 215 A4
Hunslet Hall Rd LS11 . . . 214 B4
Hunslet Hall Sh Ctr LS11 214 B4
Hunslet La LS10 . . . 211 C2
Hunslet Moor Prim Sch LS11 . . . 214 C3
Hunslet Rd
Leeds LS10 . . . 211 C3
Leeds, Pottery Field LS10 . 212 A1
Hunslet St Joseph's RC Prim Sch LS10 . . . 215 B4
Hunslet St Mary's CE Prim Sch LS10 . . . 215 B3
Hunslet Trad Est LS10 . . . 215 C3
Hunston Ave HD3 . . . 153 B7
Hunsworth La BD19, BD4 . . 95 E4
Hunt Ct WF2 . . . 141 E6
Hunter Hill Rd HX2 . . . 91 A5
Hunterscombe Ct BD16 . . . 37 D5
Hunters Ct BD9 . . . 54 C4
Hunters Farm Glade WF9 . . . 163 B1
Hunters Gn BD13 . . . 52 D7
Hunters La OL14 . . . 107 F6
Hunters Mdw BD20 . . . 5 E2
Hunters Park Ave BD14 . . . 73 E5
Hunters Wlk LS22 . . . 13 E7
Huntingdon Ave HD2 . . . 136 F4
Huntingdon Rd HD6 . . . 115 C1
Huntington Cres LS16 . . . 59 C7
Huntock Pl HD6 . . . 114 F5
Huntsman's Cl HD4 . . . 171 D8
Huntsman's Way WF9 . . . 164 E2
Huntsman Fold WF2 . . . 141 D6
Huntsmans Cl
Bingley BD16 . . . 37 C5
Keighley BD20 . . . 35 A8
Hunt St
Castleford, Castleford Ings WF10 . . . 103 D1
Castleford WF10 . . . 124 B8
Huntwick Ave WF7 . . . 145 C4
Huntwick Cres WF7 . . . 145 B4
Huntwick Dr WF7 . . . 145 B4
Huntwick La
Purston Jaglin WF7 . . . 145 A5
West Hardwick WF7 . . . 144 F3
Huntwick Rd WF7 . . . 145 C4
Hunt Yd [3] BD7 . . . 74 A4
Hurst Knowle HD5 . . . 155 A4
Hurst La WF14 . . . 138 B4
Hurst Rd HX7 . . . 89 B4
Hurstville Ave BD4 . . . 95 F6
Hurstwood HD2 . . . 136 E4
Husler Gr LS7 . . . 207 A3
Husler Pl LS7 . . . 207 A3
Hustings The [3] WF15 . . . 117 A4
Hustler's Row LS6 . . . 59 D8
Hustlergate BD1 . . . 201 B3
Hustler St BD3 . . . 56 B1
Hutchinson's Pl LS5 . . . 59 A3
Hutchinson La [1] HD6 . . . 115 B2
Hutson St BD5 . . . 74 D4
Hutton Dr
Batley WF16 . . . 117 E4
South Elmsall WF9 . . . 183 A4
Hutton Rd BD5 . . . 74 C2
Hutton Terr
Bradford BD2 . . . 56 D5
Pudsey LS28 . . . 76 E7
Huxley Mount BD2 . . . 56 C5
Hydale Cl BD21 . . . 35 E5
Hydale Ct BD12 . . . 94 C6
Hyde Gr [4] BD21 . . . 35 D8
Hyde Park Cl LS6 . . . 205 C2
Hyde Park Cnr LS6 . . . 205 C3
Hyde Park Pl LS6 . . . 205 C3
Hyde Park Rd
Halifax HX1 . . . 202 C1
Leeds LS6 . . . 205 C2
Hyde Park St HX1 . . . 202 C1
Hyde Park Terr LS6 . . . 205 C3
Hyde Pk
Halifax HX1 . . . 202 C
Wakefield WF1 . . . 142 E
Hyde Pl LS2 . . . 206 A
Hyde St
Bradford BD10 . . . 39 B
Leeds LS2 . . . 206 A
Hyde Terr LS2 . . . 206 A
Hydro Cl LS29 . . . 8 F
Hyman Wlk WF9 . . . 183 A
Hyne Ave BD4 . . . 75 C
Hyrst Garth WF17 . . . 118 B
Hyrstlands Rd WF17 . . . 118 C
Hyrstmount Jun Sch WF17 . . . 118 C
Hyrst Wlk WF17 . . . 118 C

I

Ibbetson Cl [1] LS27 . . . 98 A
Ibbetson Croft [3] LS27 . . . 98 A
Ibbetson Ct LS27 . . . 98 A
Ibbetson Dr LS27 . . . 98 A
Ibbetson Mews [2] LS27 . . . 98 A
Ibbetson Oval LS27 . . . 98 A
Ibbetson Rd LS27 . . . 98 A
Ibbetson Rise LS27 . . . 98 A
Ibbotroyd Ave OL14 . . . 108 A
Ibbotson Flats [6] HD1 . . . 154 B
Ibbottson St WF1 . . . 142 F
Ida's The LS10 . . . 80 A
Ida & Robert Arthington Hospl LS16 . . . 41 F
Ida St
Bradford BD5 . . . 74 C
Leeds LS10 . . . 80 A
Iddesleigh St BD4 . . . 75 D
Idle CE Prim Sch BD10 . . . 39 B
Idlecroft Rd BD10 . . . 56 B
Idle Moor [1] BD10 . . . 55 E
Idle Rd BD2 . . . 56 B
Idlethorp Way BD10 . . . 56 C
Ilbert Ave BD4 . . . 75 C
Ilford St LS27 . . . 98 B
Ilkley Gram Sch LS29 . . . 8 C
Ilkley Hall Mews LS29 . . . 8 B
Ilkley Hall Pk LS29 . . . 8 B
Ilkley Rd
Addingham LS29 . . . 7 B
Burley in W LS29 . . . 9 D
Keighley BD20 . . . 19 C
Otley LS21 . . . 22 F
Ilkley Sta LS29 . . . 8 B
Illingworth Ave
Halifax HX2 . . . 91 E
Normanton WF6 . . . 122 E
Illingworth Cl
Halifax HX2 . . . 91 E
Yeadon LS19 . . . 40 C
Illingworth Cres HX2 . . . 91 E
Illingworth Dr HX2 . . . 91 E
Illingworth Gdns HX2 . . . 91 E
Illingworth Gr HX2 . . . 91 E
Illingworth Rd
Bradford BD12 . . . 94 F
Halifax HX2 . . . 91 E
Illingworth St WF5 . . . 140 D
Illingworth Villas [3] HX7 . 89 A
Illingworth Way HX2 . . . 91 E
Imex Spaces Bsns Pk BD6 74 C
Immaculate Heart of Mary RC Prim Sch LS17 . . . 43 D
Immanuel CE Com Coll BD10 . . . 39 C
Imperial Arc [23] HD1 . . . 154 A
Imperial Ave WF2 . . . 120 F
Imperial Rd HD1, HD3 . . . 153 D
Inchfield Rd OL14 . . . 129 A
Incline The HX3 . . . 113 E
Independent Ho WF16 . . . 117 E
Independent St BD5 . . . 74 C
Indus Cl WF16 . . . 117 E
Industrial Ave WF17 . . . 96 D
Industrial Rd HX6 . . . 112 B
Industrial St
Bacup OL13 . . . 106 A
Bingley BD16 . . . 36 F
Brighouse HD6 . . . 115 B
[13] Brighouse, Scholes BD19 . . . 115 F
Horbury WF4 . . . 159 C
Huddersfield HD4 . . . 154 A
Keighley BD22 . . . 35 A
Leeds LS9 . . . 207 C
Liversedge FW15 . . . 116 E
Todmorden OL14 . . . 108 C
Wakefield WF1 . . . 216 B
Industrial Terr
Halifax HX1 . . . 203 A
Huddersfield HD5 . . . 155 A
Industry St OL14 . . . 108 A
Infirmary Rd WF13 . . . 118 B
Infirmary St
Bradford BD1 . . . 201 A
Leeds LS1 . . . 211 B
Ingdale Dr HD9 . . . 189 B
Ing Field BD12 . . . 95 A
Ingfield Ave
Huddersfield HD5 . . . 154 D
Ossett WF5 . . . 140 E
Ingfield Terr
Slaithwaite HD7 . . . 152 A
Todmorden OL14 . . . 86 C
Ingham's Ave LS28 . . . 76 B
Ingham's View LS28 . . . 76 B
Ingham Cl
Halifax HX2 . . . 91 F

Ing–Jos 259

ngham Cl *continued*
Mirfield WF14 ... 138 C4
ngham Croft WF14 ... 138 C4
ngham Garth WF14 ... 138 C5
ngham La HX2 ... 71 E1
ngham Rd WF12 ... 139 D3
nghams Ct 23 HX3 ... 92 A1
ngham St LS10 ... 212 A1
nghams Terr LS28 ... 76 B8
ng Head HD7 ... 151 E1
ng Head Gdns HX3 ... 93 B4
ng Head La HD4 ... 173 A2
nghead Rd HD7 ... 151 D1
ng Head Terr HX3 ... 93 B4
ng La HD4 ... 154 A3
ngle Ave LS27 ... 97 F6
ngleborough Cl 10 BD4 ... 75 E3
ngleborough Dr LS27 ... 98 C3
nglebrough Sch WF8 ... 125 D1
ngleby Pl BD7 ... 74 A6
ngleby Rd BD7, BD8 ... 74 A7
ngleby St BD8 ... 74 A7
ngleby Way LS10 ... 99 E7
ngle Cres LS27 ... 98 A5
ngle Ct
Lepton HD8 ... 155 D4
Morley LS27 ... 97 F6
ngle Dene HX7 ... 88 D2
ngledew Cres LS8 ... 44 B2
ngledew Ct LS17 ... 43 D4
ngledew Dr LS8 ... 44 B2
ngle Gr LS27 ... 98 A5
ngle Row LS7 ... 204 A2
ngleton Cl 6 LS11 ... 214 B3
ngleton Dr LS15 ... 80 E7
ngleton Gr 11 LS11 ... 214 B3
ngleton Pl LS11 ... 214 B3
ngleton Rd HD4 ... 154 B2
ngleton St LS11 ... 214 B3
nglewood S75 ... 178 A1
nglewood App LS14 ... 62 B3
nglewood Ave HD2 ... 135 C1
nglewood Dr
Leeds LS14 ... 62 B3
Otley LS21 ... 22 F7
nglewood Pl LS14 ... 62 B3
nglewood Terr 8 LS6 ... 206 A4
ngram Cl LS11 ... 210 C1
ngram Cres
Knottingley WF11 ... 126 D3
Leeds LS11 ... 213 C4
ngram Ct 1 LS11 ... 211 A1
ngram Gdns LS11 ... 210 C1
ngram Par LS26 ... 100 E5
ngram Rd LS11 ... 210 C1
ngram Road Prim Sch
LS11 ... 210 C1
ngram Row LS11 ... 211 B2
ngram Sq 18 HX1 ... 202 C1
ngram St
Halifax HX1 ... 202 C1
Keighley BD21 ... 35 B3
Leeds LS11 ... 211 B2
ngram View LS11 ... 210 C1
ngrow La BD21, BD22 ... 35 A4
ngrow Prim Sch BD21 ... 35 A4
ngrow West Sta* BD21 ... 35 B4
ngs Ave LS20 ... 22 D2
ngsbeck Mews WF1 ... 216 B1
ngs Cl
Ryhill WF4 ... 162 C1
South Kirkby WF9 ... 182 D3
ngs Cres
Dewsbury WF12 ... 139 C2
Guiseley LS20 ... 22 C1
Leeds LS9 ... 80 B7
Liversedge WF15 ... 117 B4
ngs Croft HX3 ... 93 C6
ngs Ct LS20 ... 22 C1
ngs Dr
Low Bradley BD20 ... 4 C5
Mickletown LS26 ... 102 E3
ngs Holt WF9 ... 182 D4
ngs La
Castleford WF10 ... 103 F2
Cononley BD20 ... 4 A4
Dewsbury WF12 ... 139 C2
Guiseley LS20 ... 22 C2
Ledston WF10 ... 103 E4
Low Bradley BD20 ... 4 C5
Thorp Arch LS23 ... 31 A8
Wighill LS24 ... 31 F8
ngs Mere Ct WF11 ... 105 A4
ngs Mill WF5 ... 140 E6
ngs Mill Ave HD8 ... 175 F3
ngs Mill Dr HD8 ... 175 F2
ngs Mill Yd WF16 ... 117 D4
ngs Rd
Batley, Heckmondwike
WF16 ... 117 D4
Batley WF17 ... 118 A6
Dewsbury WF13 ... 118 E1
Fitzwilliam WF9 ... 163 B1
Huddersfield HD5 ... 155 A4
Leeds LS9 ... 80 B8
Liversedge WF15 ... 117 B5
Steeton BD20 ... 17 B7
Wakefield WF1 ... 216 B1
ngs Rise WF17 ... 118 B6
ng St BD3 ... 75 D7
ngs The
Brighouse HX3 ... 115 A6
Clayton West HD8 ... 175 F2
ngs View
Castleford WF10 ... 125 B8
Mickletown LS26 ... 102 E3
ngs Villa WF15 ... 117 C2

Ings Way
Bradford BD8 ... 73 E8
Ingbirchworth S36 ... 191 D1
Lepton HD8 ... 155 F3
Silsden BD20 ... 17 F8
Ings Way W HD8 ... 155 E3
Ingswell Ave WF4 ... 179 A7
Ingswell Dr WF4 ... 178 F7
Ings Wlk WF9 ... 182 D3
Ingwell Ct 3 WF1 ... 216 C2
Ingwell St WF1 ... 216 C2
Ingwell Terr BD19 ... 116 F7
Ingwood Par HX4 ... 134 C6
Inholmes La LS24 ... 15 C4
Inkerman Ct HD8 ... 192 A5
Inkerman St
6 Bacup OL13 ... 106 A2
Bradford BD2 ... 56 D4
Bradford, Cutler Heights
BD4 ... 75 D4
Inkerman Way HD8 ... 191 F5
Inkersley Rd BD1 ... 55 E1
Inmoor Rd BD4, BD11 ... 96 B7
Inner Hey HD7 ... 169 A4
Inner Ring Rd LS1, LS2 ... 206 C1
Innings The BD10 ... 56 A8
Institute Rd BD2 ... 56 C5
Institute St BD20 ... 16 C6
Intake HD7 ... 152 E5
Intake Cl WF3 ... 121 F5
Intake Gr BD2 ... 56 C2
Intake High Sch Arts Coll
LS13 ... 58 A3
Intake La
Batley WF17 ... 117 F8
Lofthouse Gate WF3 ... 121 F5
Meltham HD4 ... 170 F7
Middleton LS10 ... 99 C3
Ossett WF5 ... 140 E5
Pudsey LS13 ... 57 F3
Shepley HD8 ... 190 B4
Slaithwaite HD7 ... 169 F4
Steeton BD20 ... 17 B4
Thorner LS14 ... 45 D3
Woolley WF4 ... 177 E8
Yeadon LS19 ... 40 D3
Intake Mount LS10 ... 99 C4
Intake Rd
Bradford BD2 ... 56 C2
Pudsey LS28 ... 77 A8
Slaithwaite HD7 ... 151 C2
Intake Sq LS10 ... 99 C3
Intake Terr BD2 ... 56 C2
Intake The 3 LS25 ... 83 B1
Intake View LS10 ... 99 C3
Intercity Way LS13 ... 58 A1
Intermezzo Dr LS10 ... 80 B1
Invargarry Cl LS25 ... 83 B8
Inverness Rd LS25 ... 83 B7
Invertrees Ave LS19 ... 40 C4
Iona Pl 9 HX3 ... 92 B2
Iona St HX3 ... 92 C1
Iqbal Ct BD3 ... 75 D6
Iqra Prim Sch BD8 ... 55 C1
Ireland Bridge BD16 ... 36 E3
Ireland Cres LS16 ... 41 F3
Ireland St BD16 ... 36 E3
Ireland Terr BD16 ... 36 E3
Ireland Wood Prim Sch
LS16 ... 42 A4
Ireton St BD7 ... 74 B6
Iron Row LS29 ... 9 F1
Iron St BD19 ... 116 C7
Ironwood App LS14 ... 62 A3
Ironwood Cres LS14 ... 62 A3
Ironwood View LS14 ... 62 A4
Iron Works Pk BD4 ... 75 C5
Irving St HX1 ... 202 B1
Irving Terr BD14 ... 73 C3
Irvin Terr WF10 ... 124 C7
Irwell St BD4 ... 75 A5
Irwin App LS15 ... 80 F7
Irwin Ave WF1 ... 142 F7
Irwin Cres WF1 ... 142 E7
Irwin St LS28 ... 57 D2
Isaac St BD8 ... 74 B8
Islamia Girls High Sch
HD1 ... 153 E4
Islamic Acad BD5 ... 74 D3
Islamic Missionary Coll
BD7 ... 74 C6
Island Dr HD9 ... 172 C2
Island The WF11 ... 127 A5
Island View WF12 ... 139 B6
Islay Cl LS26 ... 100 F5
Isles St BD8 ... 73 F8
Ivanhoe Rd BD7 ... 74 B5
Ivegate
Bradford BD1 ... 201 B3
Yeadon LS19 ... 40 B7
Ive House La HX2 ... 111 E8
Iver Way BD18 ... 55 A7
Iveson App LS16 ... 41 F2
Iveson Cl LS16 ... 41 F2
Iveson Cres LS16 ... 41 F2
Iveson Ct LS16 ... 41 F2
Iveson Dr LS16 ... 41 F2
Iveson Garth LS16 ... 42 A2
Iveson Gdns LS16 ... 41 F2
Iveson Gn LS16 ... 41 F2
Iveson Gr LS16 ... 41 F2
Iveson Lawn LS16 ... 42 A2
Iveson Prim Sch LS16 ... 42 A2
Iveson Rd LS16 ... 41 F2
Iveson Rise LS16 ... 42 A2
Ives St BD17 ... 55 B8
Ivies The 6 LS28 ... 76 E7
Ivory St LS10 ... 211 C1

Ivy Ave LS9 ... 80 B8
Ivy Bank BD12 ... 94 C4
Ivy Bank Ct 1 BD17 ... 38 D2
Ivy Bank La BD22 ... 51 C6
Ivy Chase LS28 ... 77 B7
Ivy Cl
South Elmsall WF9 ... 182 F2
Wakefield WF1 ... 142 E8
Ivy Cotts S71 ... 179 D4
Ivy Cres
Brighouse HX3 ... 114 E7
Leeds LS9 ... 80 A7
10 Leeds LS9 ... 80 A8
Ivy Ct
Ilkley LS29 ... 8 B3
Leeds LS7 ... 204 A2
Ivy Farm Cl S71 ... 179 D1
Ivy Garth LS7 ... 204 A2
Ivy Gdns
Castleford WF10 ... 125 D5
Leeds LS13 ... 58 D4
Ivy Gr
Leeds LS9 ... 80 B8
Shipley BD18 ... 54 E7
Wakefield WF1 ... 142 E8
Ivy House Rd BD5 ... 74 E1
Ivy La
Boston Spa LS23 ... 30 C7
Bradford BD15 ... 54 A1
Halifax HX2 ... 91 D6
Wakefield WF1 ... 142 E8
Ivy Mount
Leeds LS9 ... 80 A8
Slaithwaite HD7 ... 151 F1
Ivy Pl
Glusburn BD20 ... 16 D7
Leeds LS13 ... 58 D4
Ivy Rd
Keighley BD21 ... 35 E6
Leeds LS9 ... 80 B8
Shipley BD18 ... 54 E7
Ivy St S
Halifax HX1 ... 202 C1
Keighley BD21 ... 35 B3
Ivy St
Brighouse HD6 ... 114 F3
Featherstone WF7 ... 145 D6
Halifax HX1 ... 202 C1
Huddersfield, Moldgreen HD4,
HD5 ... 154 C5
Huddersfield, Paddock
HD4 ... 153 C4
Keighley BD21 ... 35 B8
Leeds LS9 ... 80 A8
Ivy Terr
Bradford BD6 ... 94 B7
Bradford BD6 ... 94 B8
Brighouse HD6 ... 114 F3
Brighouse, Lydgate HX3 ... 114 E7
Calderbrook OL15 ... 129 D2
Keighley BD21 ... 35 F6
Low Bradley BD20 ... 4 C5
South Elmsall WF9 ... 183 A3
Ivy View 8 LS9 ... 80 A8
Ivy Wood Ct 7 BD7 ... 73 E3

J

Jacana Way BD6 ... 73 C1
Jacinth Ct HD2 ... 136 C2
Jack Bridge HX7 ... 88 A5
Jack Close Orch S71 ... 179 C4
Jackdaw Cl BD15 ... 73 B7
Jackdaw La LS23 ... 30 C8
Jack Field La BD20 ... 16 A4
Jack Hill HD2 ... 136 A1
Jackie Smart Ct LS7 ... 207 B3
Jackie Smart Rd 9 BD5 ... 74 E4
Jack La
Batley WF17 ... 118 D2
Leeds, Mint LS11 ... 211 B1
Leeds, Pottery Field LS10,
LS11 ... 212 A1
Jackman Dr LS18 ... 58 D7
Jack Royd HX3 ... 91 F2
Jackroyd La
Huddersfield HD4 ... 154 B2
Mirfield WF14 ... 137 E2
Jackson's La
Darrington WF8 ... 165 E7
Dewsbury WF13 ... 139 A1
Low Bradley BD20 ... 4 E5
Jackson Ave LS8 ... 204 C3
Jackson Hill La BD13 ... 92 F7
Jackson Ho 2 WF9 ... 181 D6
Jackson La HX4 ... 133 A5
Jackson Mdws HX4 ... 133 A5
Jackson Pl BD20 ... 16 D4
Jackson Rd LS7 ... 206 C3
Jackson St
Bradford BD3 ... 75 A6
Glusburn BD20 ... 16 D5
Jacks Way WF9 ... 183 C8
Jacky La BD22 ... 51 C6
Jacob's Row HD4 ... 153 F3
Jacob's Well BD1 ... 201 B2
Jacob's Well La WF1 ... 216 C3
Jacobs Croft BD14 ... 73 C4
Jacobs Ct WF4 ... 159 C8
Jacobs La BD22 ... 51 D8
Jacob St
Bradford BD5 ... 74 D4
Leeds LS2 ... 206 C1
Jacquard Ct BD19 ... 115 B7
Jacques Gr BD20 ... 5 F1
Jade Pl HD2 ... 136 C2
Jaggar La HD9 ... 171 F4

Jagger Green Dean HX4 ... 134 B3
Jagger Green La HX4 ... 134 C3
Jagger La
Emley HD8 ... 174 E7
Huddersfield HD5 ... 155 A8
Jail Rd WF17 ... 117 F5
Jail Yd LS26 ... 100 F5
Jakeman Cl WF3 ... 119 E8
Jakeman Ct WF3 ... 119 E8
Jakeman Dr WF3 ... 119 E8
James Ave
Leeds LS8 ... 204 C4
Steeton BD20 ... 17 A5
James Cl LS25 ... 83 A7
James Ct
1 Collingham LS22 ... 29 B8
Morley LS27 ... 98 C4
James Duggan Ave WF7 ... 145 D6
James Gate BD1 ... 201 B3
James Gibbs Cl WF7 ... 145 D6
James La HD4 ... 171 A6
James Mason Ct 1 HD1 ... 153 D7
James St E 8 BD21 ... 35 C6
James St
Batley WF17 ... 118 B4
Birkenshaw BD11 ... 96 A6
Bradford BD1 ... 201 B3
Bradford, Fairweather Green
BD15 ... 54 C1
Brighouse HD6 ... 115 A4
Castleford WF10 ... 103 D1
Dewsbury WF13 ... 118 B1
Elland, Holywell Green
HX4 ... 134 B4
Elland HX5 ... 135 A6
Glusburn BD20 ... 16 D7
Huddersfield HD7 ... 152 D4
Liversedge WF15 ... 117 B3
Mirfield WF14 ... 138 A7
Oakworth BD22 ... 34 B2
Slaithwaite HD7 ... 152 A1
South Hiendley S72 ... 180 F6
Thornton BD13 ... 72 D6
20 Todmorden OL14 ... 108 B6
Yeadon LS19 ... 40 B4
Jamie Ct BD10 ... 56 D6
Jane Gn HX2 ... 71 D2
Jane Hills BD17 ... 55 A8
Jane St
Denholme BD13 ... 52 D1
Shipley BD18 ... 54 F8
Janesway LS25 ... 82 F2
Janet St 5 BD22 ... 51 E8
Japonica Way BD3 ... 56 C1
Jaques Cl LS6 ... 59 B4
Jardine Ave WF7 ... 145 D6
Jardine Rd 10 BD16 ... 37 A3
Jarratt St E BD8 ... 55 B1
Jarratt St BD8 ... 55 B1
Jarrom Cl BD4 ... 75 D4
Jarvis Sq WF3 ... 100 A3
Jarvis Wlk WF3 ... 100 A3
Jasmine Gdns
Castleford WF10 ... 124 A5
Halifax HX1 ... 202 B2
Jasmin Terr BD8 ... 74 C8
Jason Terr WF17 ... 97 A2
Jasper St
Bradford BD10 ... 56 B8
Halifax HX1 ... 202 B3
Javelin Cl BD10 ... 56 B6
Jay House La HD6 ... 115 D5
Jay St BD22 ... 51 D6
Jean Ave LS15 ... 81 A7
Jebb La S75 ... 176 E3
Jenkin Dr WF4 ... 140 F1
Jenkin La WF4 ... 140 F1
Jenkin Rd WF4 ... 141 A1
Jenkinson Cl LS11 ... 211 A1
Jenkinson Lawn LS11 ... 211 A1
Jenkinsons Pl LS10 ... 99 D8
Jenkinson St WF17 ... 118 C2
Jenkyn La HD8 ... 190 D8
Jennetts Cres LS21 ... 22 F7
Jennings Cl BD20 ... 17 F8
Jennings Pl BD7 ... 74 A4
Jennings St 7 BD7 ... 74 A4
Jenny La
Baildon BD17 ... 38 D4
Mirfield WF14 ... 138 B7
Jensen Ave WF13 ... 117 F3
Jepson La HX5 ... 134 F6
Jeremy La WF16 ... 117 D4
Jer Gr BD7 ... 73 E2
Jer La BD7 ... 73 E2
Jermyn St BD1 ... 201 C3
Jerry Clay Dr WF2 ... 120 E2
Jerry Clay La WF2 ... 120 D2
Jerry Clay La Jun & Inf Sch
WF2 ... 120 E2
Jerry Fields Rd HX2 ... 111 D6
Jerry La
Silsden BD20 ... 6 F1
Sowerby Bridge HX6 ... 112 A3
Jersey Cl WF12 ... 118 F2
Jerusalem La HX2 ... 90 D4
Jerusalem Rd HD7 ... 170 B7
Jerusalem Sq HX3 ... 114 B4
Jervaulx Cl LS23 ... 30 C7
Jervaulx Cres BD8 ... 74 D8
Jerwood Hill Cl HX3 ... 92 D1
Jerwood Hill Rd HX3 ... 92 D1
Jesmond Ave
Bradford BD9 ... 54 F2
Royston S71 ... 179 C3
Jesmond Gr
Bradford BD9 ... 54 F2
Dewsbury WF13 ... 118 B1

Jessamine Ave LS11 ... 213 C2
Jessamine Pl BD20 ... 16 E6
Jessamine St WF13 ... 138 D5
Jesse St
Bradford BD5 ... 201 B1
Bradford, Fairweather Green
BD8 ... 73 D7
Jessop Ave HD5 ... 155 A3
Jessop Fold HD9 ... 171 F5
Jessop St
Castleford WF10 ... 124 D8
Wakefield WF2 ... 142 C4
Jester Pl BD13 ... 72 C2
Jewitt La LS22 ... 29 C7
Jew La BD22 ... 51 C1
Jilley Royd La HD2 ... 136 A4
Jill Kilner Dr LS29 ... 21 D8
Jill La WF14 ... 138 D8
Jim Allen La HX2 ... 90 C1
Jim La HD1 ... 153 D6
Jim Laker Pl BD18 ... 54 F7
Jinnah Ct BD8 ... 74 D8
Jinny Moor La LS26 ... 101 E8
Jin Whin Ct WF10 ... 124 A8
Jin-Whin Hill WF10 ... 124 A8
Jin-Whin Terr WF10 ... 124 A8
Joan Royd WF16 ... 117 D6
Joba Ave BD3 ... 75 B7
Joffre Ave WF10 ... 124 E6
John's Cres WF2 ... 120 E2
John Barker St OL14 ... 107 E8
John Booth Cl WF15 ... 116 F2
John Carr Ave WF4 ... 141 A2
John Charles Way LS12 ... 213 A4
John Eastwood Homes 13
OL14 ... 108 A1
John Escritt Rd BD16 ... 37 A2
John Gilmour Way LS29 ... 21 D8
John Haigh Rd HD7 ... 170 A8
John Hanson Ct BD13 ... 71 E6
John Jamieson Sch LS8 ... 61 C5
John Naylor La HX2 ... 111 E5
John Nelson Cl 9 WF17 ... 96 F1
Johnny La LS21 ... 23 A6
John O'Gaunts Wlk LS26 ... 100 F6
John Ormsby V C Way
WF12 ... 119 A2
John St W 4 HX6 ... 112 B4
Johns Ave WF3 ... 121 C6
Johns La HX5 ... 134 F4
John Smeaton Com High Sch
LS15 ... 62 E3
Johnson's Yd LS29 ... 9 F1
Johnson St
Bingley BD16 ... 36 F3
Bradford BD3 ... 75 D7
Mirfield WF14 ... 138 A3
Johnson Terr 1 LS27 ... 98 B4
John St
Baildon BD17 ... 38 C1
5 Batley, Birstall WF17 ... 96 E1
9 Batley, Heckmondwike
WF16 ... 117 D3
Bradford BD1 ... 201 B3
Bradford, Clayton BD14 ... 73 C4
Bradford, Tong Street BD4 ... 75 E1
Brighouse HD6 ... 115 A3
Castleford WF10 ... 124 C6
Cullingworth BD13 ... 52 D6
Denholme BD13 ... 52 D1
2 Dewsbury, Eastborough
WF12 ... 118 E1
Dewsbury, Ravensthorpe
WF13 ... 138 E5
Dewsbury WF13 ... 118 C2
Elland HX5 ... 134 F6
Elland, Lindwell HX4 ... 134 C7
Halifax HX1 ... 203 B3
Huddersfield HD3 ... 153 B4
Leeds LS6 ... 205 B3
Oakworth BD22 ... 34 D2
Shipley BD18 ... 55 A8
South Elmsall WF9 ... 182 F2
Thornton BD13 ... 72 D6
4 Todmorden OL14 ... 108 B5
Wakefield WF1 ... 216 C2
Yeadon LS19 ... 40 B4
Johnston St
Leeds LS6 ... 206 B4
Wakefield WF1 ... 216 C2
John Street Mkt BD1 ... 201 B3
John William St
3 Cleckheaton BD19 ... 116 D8
14 Elland HX5 ... 134 F6
Huddersfield HD1 ... 154 A6
Liversedge, Mill Bridge
WF15 ... 117 C4
1 Liversedge WF15 ... 117 B3
Jonathan Garth LS29 ... 6 E8
Jons Ave WF9 ... 182 A2
Jonscroft BD13 ... 92 D7
Jordan Rd LS13 ... 58 A2
Jordan Way BD3 ... 56 C1
Joseph Ave HX3 ... 93 A2
Joseph Crossley's Almhouses
HX1 ... 202 C2
Josephine Rd HD4 ... 153 A3
Joseph Priestley Coll,
Beeston Campus LS11 ... 214 C3
Joseph Priestly Coll LS27 ... 98 A4
Joseph Priestly Coll (Peel
Street Ctr) LS27 ... 98 B4
Joseph St
Bradford BD3 ... 201 D3
Bradford, Tong Street BD4 ... 75 E1

Joseph St continued
Leeds LS10 . . . . **215** B4
Joseph Stones Ho LS2 . **212** A4
Joseph Wright Ct BD10. . . **39** A1
Joshua St 13 OL14 . . . . . **108** B6
Jos La HD8 . . . . **190** E8
Jos Way HD8 . . . . **190** E8
Jowett's La BD20 . . . . **5** D3
Jowett House La BD10. . . **39** A2
Jowett Park Cres BD10. . . **39** A2
Jowett St BD1. . . . . **74** C7
Jowett Terr 6 LS27 . . . . **98** A2
Jowler HX2. . . . . **90** D5
Jubilee Ave
Lofthouse Gate WF1 . . . . . . **121** C4
Normanton WF6 . . . . **144** A8
Shelley HD8 . . . . **174** A2
Jubilee Bglws WF11 . . . . **126** E4
Jubilee Cl WF9 . . . . **181** F6
Jubilee Cotts WF4 . . . . . . **180** B8
Jubilee Cres
Birkenshaw BD11 . . . . **97** A7
Crofton WF4 . . . . **144** B3
Lofthouse Gate WF1 . . . . . . **121** C4
Jubilee Croft BD11. . . . . . **96** F7
Jubilee Ct WF3 . . . . **163** A4
Jubilee Dr 3 BD21. . . . . . **35** A5
Jubilee Gdns
11 Pontefract WF8 . . . . . **125** D1
Royston S71. . . . . **179** D4
Jubilee La HD4 . . . . **114** F2
Jubilee Mount HD6 . . . . . **114** F2
Jubilee Pl 6 LS27 . . . . . **98** B4
Jubilee Rd
Crofton WF4 . . . . **144** B3
Halifax HX3 . . . . **113** C2
Jubilee St N HX3. . . . . **92** A3
Jubilee St
Bradford BD8. . . . . **74** D8
Crigglestone WF4 . . . . **159** F3
Halifax HX3 . . . . **203** C2
7 Morley LS27 . . . . **98** B4
5 Morley LS27 . . . . **98** B4
11 Mytholmroyd HX7. . . . . **89** E1
Jubilee Terr
Ackworth M T WF7. . . . . . . **164** A8
4 Halifax HX3 . . . . **203** C2
5 Halifax HX3 . . . . **203** C2
Ripponden HX6 . . . . **132** E6
Jubilee Trees LS29 . . . . . . **21** C7
Jubilee Way
Grange Moor WF4 . . . . **156** E4
Pontefract WF8 . . . . **146** C8
Shipley BD18 . . . . **55** D8
Judy Haigh La WF12 . . . **157** D8
Judy La HD2 . . . . **136** B3
Julian Dr BD13 . . . . **73** C2
Julian St HD5. . . . . **154** E5
Julie Ave WF4 . . . . **159** E5
Jumb Beck Cl LS29. . . . . . **21** F8
Jumble Dyke 5 HD6 . . . **135** F8
Jumble Hole Rd OL14, HX7 **88** B1
Jumbles WF3 . . . . **100** C1
Jumbles La WF3 . . . . **100** C1
Jumble Wood HD8 . . . . . **155** D3
Jumples HX2 . . . . **91** D4
Jumples Cl HX2 . . . . **91** D4
Jumples Crag HX2 . . . . . . **91** D4
Jumples Ct HX2 . . . . **91** D4
Jumps La
Hebden Bridge HX7. . . . . . . **88** F1
Todmorden OL14 . . . . **107** E8
Jumps Rd OL14 . . . . **107** E8
Junction 1 Ret Pk LS11 . **213** A2
Junction 25 Bsns Pk
WF14. . . . . **137** F5
Junction Houses WF10. . **103** C1
Junction La WF5. . . . . . . **141** A4
Junction Rd
3 Dewsbury WF13. . . . . **139** B7
Shipley BD17 . . . . **55** C8
Junction Row 2 BD2 . . . **56** B4
Junction St LS10. . . . . . . **211** C2
Junction Terr 1 BD2 . . . **56** B4
June St 4 BD21 . . . . **35** C8
Juniper Ave LS26 . . . . . . **101** E6
Juniper Cl
Bradford BD8. . . . . **74** B8
Wakefield WF2 . . . . **141** E8
Juniper Gr HD4 . . . . **171** D6
Juniper Grove Mews
HD4 . . . . **171** D6
Juniper Pl LS9 . . . . **208** B1
Jupiter Cres BD2, BD10 . . **56** A5
Justin Way HD4. . . . . **153** A1

K

Kaffir Rd HD2. . . . . **153** D8
Karam Cl BD3 . . . . **75** C7
Karnac Rd LS8. . . . . **207** C4
Karon Dr WF4 . . . . **141** B1
Kateholm OL13 . . . . **106** A7
Katherine St 10 BD18. . . **54** F8
Katrina Gr WF7 . . . . **145** D4
Kaycell St BD4. . . . . **75** B2
Kay Cl LS27 . . . . **97** F2
Kaye's Fst Sch HD8 . . . . **175** F2
Kaye Hill BD13 . . . . **52** D6
Kaye La
Huddersfield HD5 . . . . **154** E2
Huddersfield, Linthwaite
HD7. . . . . **152** E3
Kaye St
Batley WF16 . . . . **117** D3

Kaye St continued
Dewsbury WF12 . . . . **139** D6
Kay St
Shipley BD18 . . . . **55** C5
Wakefield WF1 . . . . **216** C2
Kearsley Terr LS10 . . . . . **215** B2
Keasden Cl BD10. . . . . **39** A2
Keats Ave OL14 . . . . **108** D6
Keats Cl WF8 . . . . **125** D2
Keats Dr WF16. . . . . **117** E2
Keats Gr WF3 . . . . **121** E6
Keat St HD4 . . . . **153** E4
Kebble Cl BD18 . . . . **117** B7
Keble Garth LS25 . . . . . . **83** C2
Kebroyd Ave HX6 . . . . . . **132** E7
Kebroyd La HX6 . . . . **132** E7
Kebroyd Mount HX6 . . . . **132** E6
Kebs Rd OL14. . . . . **86** D3
Kedleston Rd LS8 . . . . . . **43** F3
Keeble Ho BD2 . . . . **56** D2
Keeldar Cl BD7 . . . . **74** B3
Keelham Dr LS19 . . . . **40** C4
Keelham La
Keighley BD20 . . . . **18** A2
Todmorden OL14 . . . . **87** D1
Keelham Pl BD13 . . . . . . **71** F5
Keelham Prim Sch BD13 . **71** F5
Keel Moorings LS13. . . . . **57** F5
Keenan Ave WF9. . . . . . . **182** E1
Keeper La
Birkenshaw BD4 . . . . **76** E2
Notton WF4 . . . . **178** D5
Keepers Fold BD10. . . . . . **39** B2
Keeton St LS9 . . . . **212** C4
Keighley Cl HX2 . . . . **91** E6
Keighley Coll BD21. . . . . . **35** D8
Keighley Coll (Harold Town
Bldg) BD21 . . . . **35** D8
Keighley Dr HX2 . . . . **91** E4
Keighley Ind Pk BD21 . . . **18** C1
Keighley Pl 6 LS28 . . . . **57** E2
Keighley Rd
Bingley BD16 . . . . **36** E5
Bradford BD8. . . . . **55** C3
Cullingworth BD13. . . . . . . **52** C7
Denholme BD13 . . . . **52** D2
Glusburn BD20 . . . . **16** E7
Halifax HX2 . . . . **71** D2
Halifax HX2 . . . . **91** E5
Harden BD16 . . . . **36** A2
Haworth BD22 . . . . **34** E3
Hebden Bridge HX7. . . . . . . **89** A4
Ilkley LS29. . . . . **7** F2
Low Bradley BD20 . . . . **4** B5
Oxenhope BD22. . . . . **51** D3
Silsden BD23 . . . . **17** D8
Skipton BD23 . . . . **4** A8
Steeton BD20. . . . . **17** E5
Wadsworth Moor HX7. . . . . **89** B8
Keighley Rd (Lidget)
BD22 . . . . **34** D2
Keighley Ret Pk BD21 . . . **18** C1
Keighley St Andrew's CE
First Sch BD22 . . . . **35** A7
Keighley & Worth Valley
Rlwy ★ BD21 . . . . **35** C5
Keilder Cres 6 BD6. . . . . **73** C2
Keir Hardie Cl WF16 . . . **117** C4
Kelburn Gr BD22. . . . . . . **34** B3
Kelcliffe Ave LS20 . . . . . **22** E1
Kelcliffe Gr LS20 . . . . **22** E1
Kelcliffe La LS20 . . . . **22** E2
Keldholme Cl LS13. . . . . . **57** F5
Keldholme Rd LS13 . . . . . **57** F5
Keldregate HD2. . . . . **136** E4
Kell Beck LS21. . . . . **10** F2
Kell Butts HX2. . . . . **90** F6
Kellett Ave LS12 . . . . **78** C4
Kellett Bldgs BD12 . . . . . **94** D5
Kellett Cres LS12 . . . . . . **78** C4
Kellett Dr LS12 . . . . **78** C4
Kellett Gr LS12 . . . . **78** C4
Kellett La LS12. . . . . **209** B1
Kellett Mount 2 LS12. . . **78** C4
Kellett Pl 3 LS12 . . . . . . **78** C4
Kellett Rd LS12 . . . . **209** B1
Kellett Terr 1 LS12 . . . . **78** C4
Kellett Wlk LS12. . . . . **78** C4
Kellingley Rd DN14,
WF11. . . . . **127** F4
Kell La
Halifax HX2 . . . . **90** E6
Northowram HX3. . . . . **92** F2
Kelloe St BD19. . . . . **95** D1
Kell St 6 BD16 . . . . **37** A3
Kellymoor Wlk 3 BD10 . . **56** A7
Kelmore Gr BD6 . . . . **93** E7
Kelmscott Ave LS15. . . . . **62** D3
Kelmscott Cres LS15 . . . . **62** D3
Kelmscott Garth LS15 . . . **62** E4
Kelmscott Gdns LS15. . . . **62** E3
Kelmscott Gr LS15 . . . . . . **62** D3
Kelmscott La LS15 . . . . . . **62** D3
Kelsall Ave LS6 . . . . **205** B2
Kelsall Gr LS6 . . . . **205** B2
Kelsall Pl LS6. . . . . **205** B2
Kelsall Rd LS6. . . . . **205** B2
Kelsall Terr LS6. . . . . . . **205** B2
Kelsey's St HX2 . . . . **202** A4
Kelsey St WF1 . . . . **202** B4
Kelso Ct LS3. . . . . **205** C1
Kelso Gdns LS2 . . . . **205** C1
Kelso Gr HD5 . . . . **155** A6
Kelso Ho 17 BD4 . . . . . . **75** E3
Kelso Hts LS6. . . . . **205** C1
Kelso Pl LS2. . . . . **205** C1
Kelso Rd LS2 . . . . **205** C2

Kelso St LS2. . . . . **205** C1
Kelstern Ho 5 BD4 . . . . **75** D5
Keltus Ave BD20 . . . . **16** D7
Kelvin Ave
Halifax HX2 . . . . **112** D6
Huddersfield HD5 . . . . . . **154** E6
Kelvin Cres HX2 . . . . **112** D6
Kelvin Ho BD4 . . . . **75** F3
Kelvin Rd HX5 . . . . **134** E6
Kelvin Way HD2. . . . . **56** C2
Kemp's Bridge WF2 . . . . **142** A6
Kemps Way HD9 . . . . **189** E3
Kempton Rd LS25 . . . . . . **83** A2
Kemsing Wlk LS15 . . . . . . **62** F2
Ken Churchill Dr WF4 . . . **141** A3
Kendal Bank LS3. . . . . . . **205** C1
Kendal Carr LS3 . . . . **206** A1
Kendal Cl
Castleford WF10 . . . . **125** E7
Leeds LS3 . . . . **205** C1
Kendal Croft WF10 . . . . . **125** E7
Kendal Dr
Castleford WF10 . . . . **125** D8
Crofton WF4 . . . . **143** C2
Leeds LS15 . . . . **80** E7
Kendal Garth WF10 . . . . . **125** E7
Kendal Gdns LS3 . . . . . . **125** E7
Kendal Gr LS3 . . . . **206** A1
Kendal La LS3 . . . . **206** A1
Kendall Ave BD18 . . . . . . **54** E8
Kendal Mellor Ct 11 BD21 **35** B7
Kendal Rd 2 LS3 . . . . . . **206** A1
Kendal Rise
Crofton WF4 . . . . **143** C2
Leeds LS15 . . . . **80** E7
Walton WF2 . . . . **161** A6
Kendal St BD21 . . . . **35** D6
Kendal Wlk LS3. . . . . **210** C4
Kendell St LS10 . . . . **211** C3
Kenilworth Ave LS27. . . . . **97** D6
Kenilworth Dr WF14. . . . . **137** F6
Kenilworth Dr HX3. . . . . . **115** A6
Kenilworth Gdns LS27. . . . **97** D7
Kenilworth Ho 5 BD15. . . **73** B8
Kenilworth Rd LS12 . . . . **209** C1
Kenilworth St BD4 . . . . . . **75** B4
Kenley Ave BD6 . . . . **74** A2
Kenley Mount BD6 . . . . . . **74** A2
Kenley Par BD6, BD7. . . . . **73** F2
Kenmore Ave BD19 . . . . . **116** C8
Kenmore Cl BD19 . . . . . . **116** C8
Kenmore Cres
Bradford BD6. . . . . **74** A2
Cleckheaton BD19 . . . . . . **116** C8
Kenmore Dr
Bradford BD6. . . . . **74** A2
Cleckheaton BD19 . . . . . . **116** C8
Kenmore Gr
Bradford BD6. . . . . **74** A2
Cleckheaton BD19 . . . . . . **116** C8
Kenmore Rd
Bradford BD6. . . . . **74** A2
Cleckheaton BD19 . . . . . . **116** C8
Lofthouse Gate WF2 . . . . . **120** F5
Kenmore View BD19 . . . . **116** C8
Kenmore Way BD19 . . . . **116** C8
Kenmore Wlk BD6 . . . . . . **74** A2
Kennedy Ave HD2. . . . . . **136** A5
Kennedy Cl WF12 . . . . . . **118** F3
Kennedy Ho 16 BD21 . . . **35** B4
Kennel La
Oxenhope BD22. . . . . **50** E2
Sowerby Bridge HX6 . . . . . **132** A8
Kennels La LS14. . . . . **46** B8
Kennerleigh Ave LS15. . . . **62** D1
Kennerleigh Cres LS15 . . . **62** D1
Kennerleigh Dr LS15 . . . . **62** D1
Kennerleigh Garth LS15 . . **62** D1
Kennerleigh Glen 2 LS15 **62** D1
Kennerleigh Gr LS15 . . . . **62** D1
Kennerleigh Rise 3 LS15. **62** D1
Kennerleigh Wlk
5 Bradford BD4. . . . . . . **75** F2
Leeds LS15 . . . . **62** C1
Kenneth St LS11 . . . . **210** C1
Kennet La LS25 . . . . **83** A4
Kennion St BD5. . . . . **74** D5
Kensington Ave LS14. . . . . **46** A4
Kensington Cl
Batley WF17 . . . . **118** B4
Halifax HX3 . . . . **113** A4
Kensington Ct
Leeds, Belle Isle LS10. . . . . . **99** F8
Leeds, Hyde Park LS6 . . . . **205** C3
Kensington Gdns
Castleford WF10 . . . . **124** C7
Elland HX5. . . . . **134** E6
2 Leeds LS10. . . . . **99** F8
Kensington Rd
Halifax HX3 . . . . **113** A3
Wakefield WF1 . . . . **216** A4
Kensington St
Bradford BD8. . . . . **55** A1
12 Keighley BD21. . . . . . **35** B6
Kensington Terr
Garforth LS25 . . . . **82** E7
Leeds LS6 . . . . **205** C3
Kensington Way 1 LS10 . **99** F7
Kenstone Cres BD10. . . . . **56** A7
Kent Ave
Pudsey LS28 . . . . **77** A7
Silsden BD20 . . . . **5** D1
Kent Cl
Pudsey LS28 . . . . **77** A7
Royston S71. . . . . **179** C4
Kent Cres LS28 . . . . **77** A7
Kent Dr LS28 . . . . **77** A7
Kentmere BD2. . . . . **55** F6

Kentmere App LS14 . . . . . **61** F5
Kentmere Ave
Brighouse BD12. . . . . **94** E1
Garforth LS25 . . . . **83** B6
Leeds LS14 . . . . **61** F7
Kentmere Cl LS14. . . . . . . **62** A5
Kentmere Cres LS14 . . . . . **61** F6
Kentmere Gate LS14 . . . . . **61** F7
Kentmere Gdns LS14. . . . . **61** F6
Kentmere Gn LS14 . . . . . . **61** F6
Kentmere Ho 4 BD4. . . . . **75** D5
Kentmere Rise LS14. . . . . . **62** A5
Kent Mews BD16. . . . . **37** B2
Kenton Dr WF4 . . . . **160** A8
Kenton Way BD4. . . . . **75** D4
Kent Rd
Bingley BD16 . . . . **37** B2
Pudsey LS28 . . . . **76** F6
Kent St
Bradford BD1. . . . . **201** B2
Halifax HX1 . . . . **203** A2
Kent Wlk 3 WF13. . . . . . **139** B8
Kenworthy Cl LS16. . . . . . **42** A5
Kenworthy Garth LS16 . . . **42** A5
Kenworthy Gate LS16 . . . . **42** A5
Kenworthy Gdns LS16. . . . **42** A5
Kenworthy La HX6 . . . . . **132** E6
Kenworthy Rise LS16. . . . . **42** A5
Kenworthy Vale LS16. . . . . **42** A5
Kenya Mount BD21. . . . . . **34** F8
Kenyon Bank HD8. . . . . . **191** F5
Kenyon La HX2 . . . . **112** D7
Kenyon St WF9 . . . . **183** A3
Kepler Gr LS8 . . . . **207** B2
Kepler Mount LS8. . . . . . **207** B2
Kepler Terr LS8. . . . . **207** B2
Keplestone Mews LS17. . . **43** E6
Kepstorn Cl LS5 . . . . **59** A5
Kepstorn Rd LS16. . . . . . . **59** B7
Kepstorn Rise 1 LS5. . . . **59** A5
Keren Gr WF2 . . . . **120** E2
Kerr Mackie Prim Sch
LS8 . . . . **61** A7
Kerry Garth LS18. . . . . . . **41** B1
Kerry Hill LS18. . . . . **41** C1
Kerry St LS18. . . . . **41** B1
Kershaw Ave WF10. . . . . **125** B7
Kershaw Cres HX2 . . . . . **111** D7
Kershaw Ct HX2 . . . . **111** D8
Kershaw Dr HX2 . . . . **111** D8
Kershaw La WF11 . . . . . . **126** E3
Kershaw Rd OL14 . . . . . . **108** A1
Kershaw St BD3 . . . . **75** D7
Kertland St WF12 . . . . . . **139** C7
Kester Rd WF17 . . . . **117** F5
Kesteven Cl BD4 . . . . **75** F2
Kesteven Ct 9 BD4 . . . . . **75** F2
Kesteven Rd BD4 . . . . **75** F2
Kestrel Bank HD4. . . . . . **171** E2
Kestrel Cl 4 LS17. . . . . . **43** F4
Kestrel Dr
Bradford BD2. . . . . **56** A4
Wakefield WF2 . . . . **160** D5
Kestrel Garth 2 LS27 . . . **98** D4
Kestrel Gr LS17 . . . . **43** F4
Kestrel Mews WF6 . . . . . **123** A1
Kestrel Mount BD2 . . . . . . **56** A4
Kestrel View
Cleckheaton BD19 . . . . **95** D1
Shelley HD8 . . . . **173** F3
Keswick Ave HD3 . . . . . . **135** A1
Keswick Cl
Halifax HX3 . . . . **113** A4
Todmorden OL14 . . . . **107** F7
Keswick Dr
Castleford WF10 . . . . **104** E2
Wakefield WF2 . . . . **141** E7
Keswick Grange LS17 . . . . **28** C5
Keswick La LS17 . . . . **28** C4
Keswick Rd S75. . . . . **178** A3
Keswick St BD4 . . . . **75** D5
Keswick View
Ackworth M T WF7. . . . . . . **163** D6
Bardsey LS17 . . . . **28** E5
Kettle La HD7. . . . . **169** B6
Kettlethorpe Hall Dr
WF2 . . . . **160** C6
Kettlethorpe High Sch
WF2. . . . . **160** C6
Kettlethorpe Rd WF2. . . . **160** C6
Kettlewell Dr BD5. . . . . . . **74** B3
Kew Hill HD3 . . . . **134** F3
Kew Hill Bottom HD3. . . . **134** F3
Key Hill La S72 . . . . **180** F3
Keys Ct LS11 . . . . **211** B2
Key Sike La OL14 . . . . . . **108** C5
Keystone Ave WF10 . . . . **124** E5
Khalaq Ct BD3 . . . . **75** B8
Khus Wlk BD21 . . . . **35** C4
Kidacre St LS10. . . . . . . **211** C1
Kiddal La LS15. . . . . **46** E3
Kidroyd HD5. . . . . **154** D4
Kidroyd La HD5. . . . . **154** E4
Kilburn Cl HD5. . . . . **154** D5
Kilburn La WF13 . . . . **118** C1
Kilburn Rd LS12. . . . . . . **209** C3
Kilby St WF1. . . . . **216** A3
Kildare Cres BD15 . . . . . . **54** A1
Kildare Terr LS12 . . . . . . **210** B2
Kildwick CE Prim Sch
BD20. . . . . **16** E8
Killingbeck Bridge LS14. . **61** E1
Killingbeck Dr LS14 . . . . . **61** E2
Killingbeck Ret Pk LS14. . **61** E2
Killinghall Ave BD2 . . . . . **56** B1
Killinghall Dr BD2. . . . . . . **56** B1
Killinghall Gr BD2. . . . . . . **56** B1
Killinghall Prim Sch BD3 . **56** C1

Killinghall Rd BD2, BD3 . . . **75** D7
Kiln Ave WF14. . . . . **137** F7
Kiln Bent Rd HD9 . . . . . . **198** A4
Kiln Brow HD7. . . . . **152** E4
Kilncroft HX4. . . . . **133** F7
Kiln Ct HD3. . . . . **134** E7
Kilner Bank HD5. . . . . . . **154** C4
Kilner Ho BD2 . . . . **56** D7
Kilner Rd BD6 . . . . **74** A4
Kilners Croft 14 LS29. . . . . **6** F1
Kiln Fold HD6. . . . . **115** D7
Kiln Hill HD7 . . . . **170** A4
Kiln Hill Ind Est HD7 . . . . **170** A4
Kiln Hill La BD20. . . . . **5** B1
Kilnhouse Bank La HD9 . . **188** B7
Kilnhurst Ave 13 OL14 . . **108** C7
Kilnhurst La OL14 . . . . . . **108** D7
Kilnhurst Mount OL14 . . . **108** D7
Kilnhurst Rd OL14. . . . . . **108** C7
Kiln La
10 Dewsbury WF13. . . . . **139** D7
Emley HD8 . . . . **175** F7
Wadsworth Moor HX7. . . . . **68** D3
Kilnsea Mount 13 BD4 . . . **75** E3
Kilnsey Fold BD20. . . . . **5** D3
Kilnsey Gr WF1 . . . . **142** E8
Kilnsey Hill WF17 . . . . . . **118** D3
Kilnsey Mews BD17 . . . . . **38** B4
Kilnsey Rd
Bradford BD3. . . . . **75** B6
Wakefield WF1 . . . . **142** E8
Kilnshaw La HX7. . . . . . . **109** F7
Kilpin Hill La WF13. . . . . . **117** F1
Kilroyd Ave BD19 . . . . **95** D3
Kilroyd Dr BD19. . . . . **95** E3
Kimberley Pl
Halifax HX3 . . . . **92** A4
Leeds LS9 . . . . **208** B3
Kimberley Rd LS9 . . . . . . **208** B3
Kimberley St
Bradford BD4. . . . . **75** C4
Brighouse HD6 . . . . **115** B3
Dewsbury WF12 . . . . **139** B5
Featherstone WF7 . . . . . . **145** C4
Halifax HX3 . . . . **92** A4
Ilkley LS29. . . . . **8** C1
Wakefield WF1 . . . . **142** C7
Kimberley View LS9. . . . . **208** B3
Kimberly Cl WF8. . . . . . . **165** B8
Kinara Cl BD21 . . . . **18** E1
Kinder Ave HD4. . . . . **152** F7
Kineholme Dr LS21 . . . . . **22** D7
Kineton Ave OL14. . . . . . **108** C6
King's Ave LS6 . . . . **205** B3
King's Bridge Rd HD4 . . . **154** B4
King's Cres WF8 . . . . **146** E3
King's Croft Gdns LS17. . . **43** D3
King's Ct 4 LS17. . . . . . . **43** C3
King's Dr
Batley WF17 . . . . **96** E1
Bradford BD2. . . . . **55** F8
King's Gate BD1 . . . . **55** E6
King's Mead WF8 . . . . . . **146** B3
King's Mill La HD4. . . . . . **154** B6
King's Mount
Knottingley WF11 . . . . . . **126** B3
Leeds LS17 . . . . **60** C7
King's Pl LS6 . . . . **205** A3
King's Rd
Bingley BD16 . . . . **36** E5
Bradford BD2. . . . . **55** F7
Cudworth S72. . . . . **180** C2
Ilkley LS29. . . . . **8** A4
Leeds LS6 . . . . **205** B3
King's Sq 4 LS6 . . . . **59** F4
King Alfred's Dr LS6 . . . . . **43** A3
King Alfred's Gn LS6. . . . . **43** A3
King Alfred's Way LS6. . . . **43** A3
King Alfred's Wlk LS6. . . . **43** A3
King Charles St LS1 . . . . **211** C4
King Charles Wlk 2 LS1 . **211** C4
King Cl LS17. . . . . **43** A4
King Cliffe Flats 4 HD1 . **154** A4
King Cliffe Rd HD1, HD2. . **136** A3
King Cross Rd HX1. . . . . . **202** C1
King Cross St HX1 . . . . . . **203** A4
King Dr LS17 . . . . **42** F7
King Edward Ave
Horsforth LS18. . . . . **41** C7
Kippax WF10 . . . . **102** F7
King Edward Cres LS18. . . **41** C7
King Edward Rd 2 BD13 . **72** D7
King Edward St
Dewsbury WF12 . . . . **139** B5
Halifax HX1 . . . . **203** B3
Hemsworth WF9 . . . . **181** E6
Leeds LS1 . . . . **211** C3
Normanton WF6 . . . . **123** A1
Sutton-in-C BD20. . . . . . . **16** D7
King Edward Terr
Burley in W LS29. . . . . **9** F7
1 Thornton BD13 . . . . . . **72** D6
King Edwin's Ct LS8. . . . . **61** A7
Kingfield LS20 . . . . **22** F7
Kingfisher Chase 18
HX6 . . . . **112** C7
Kingfisher Cl
Crigglestone WF4 . . . . **159** F7
8 Leeds LS17. . . . . **43** F7
Kingfisher Cres WF13 . . . **138** E3
Kingfisher Ct WF6 . . . . . . **123** A4
Kingfisher Gr
Bradford BD8. . . . . **73** C4
Huddersfield HD4 . . . . **171** E4
Wakefield WF2 . . . . **160** D2
Kingfisher La LS25 . . . . . . **64** F2
Kingfisher Mews LS27. . . . **98** C2
Kingfisher Reach LS22 . . . **13** B1

ngfishers The [9] BD20 ... 5 E1
ngfisher Way LS17 ... 43 F4
ng George Ave
Horsforth LS18 ... 41 C1
Leeds LS7 ... 204 A2
Morley LS27 ... 98 B6
ng George Croft LS27 ... 98 B5
ng George Gdns LS7 ... 204 A3
ng George Gr LS27 ... 98 B6
ng George Rd LS18 ... 41 C1
ng George St WF1 ... 121 B3
ng James's Sch HD4 ... 155 A2
ng La LS17 ... 43 B3
ng Royd La WF7 ... 163 C6
ngs Apartments HX1 ... 203 C3
ngs App LS13 ... 58 E2
ngs Ave
Castleford WF10 ... 125 A7
Ilkley LS29 ... 8 A4
Normanton WF6 ... 122 F5
ngsbury Pl HX1 ... 202 B3
ngs Chase LS26 ... 100 F6
ngs Cl
Ackworth M T WF7 ... 163 D5
Ilkley LS29 ... 7 E4
Ossett WF5 ... 140 C7
Otley LS21 ... 23 C7
Pontefract WF8 ... 146 C7
ngs Croft
Garforth LS25 ... 82 D6
Ossett WF5 ... 140 C8
South Kirkby WF9 ... 182 B3
ngs Ct
Batley WF17 ... 96 E1
Fitzwilliam WF9 ... 163 B1
Halifax HX1 ... 203 A2
Ilkley LS29 ... 8 A4
Skelmanthorpe HD8 ... 175 A2
Sutton-in-C BD20 ... 16 D4
ngsdale Ave
Birkenshaw BD11 ... 96 E6
Bradford BD2 ... 56 A3
ngsdale Cres BD2 ... 56 A3
ngsdale Ct LS14 ... 61 E6
ngsdale Dr BD2 ... 56 A3
ngsdale Gdns BD11 ... 96 E6
ngsdale Gr [1] BD2 ... 55 F3
ngs Dr
Bramhope LS16 ... 25 A1
Normanton WF6 ... 122 F5
ngsfield LS26 ... 100 B5
ngs Gr BD16 ... 37 A4
ngs Head Dr [2] WF14 ... 137 F6
ngs Head Rd WF14 ... 137 F6
ngsland Ct S71 ... 179 D4
ngsland Prim Sch WF3 ... 122 B6
ings Lea
Batley WF15 ... 117 C2
Halifax HX3 ... 113 B2
Ossett WF5 ... 140 C8
ingsley Ave
Birkenshaw BD11 ... 96 B4
Bradford BD2 ... 55 E3
Crofton WF4 ... 143 E2
Featherstone WF7 ... 145 D8
Huddersfield HD1 ... 153 E4
Knottingley WF11 ... 126 C5
Leeds LS16 ... 42 B5
Lofthouse Gate WF1 ... 121 B5
Sowerby Bridge HX6 ... 111 F3
Wakefield WF2 ... 160 D6
ingsley Cl
Birkenshaw BD11 ... 96 B4
Crofton WF4 ... 143 E2
Lofthouse Gate WF1 ... 121 B5
Wakefield WF2 ... 160 C6
ingsley Cres
Baildon BD17 ... 38 C2
Birkenshaw BD11 ... 96 B4
ingsley Croft BD20 ... 16 E7
ingsley Dr
Birkenshaw BD11 ... 96 B4
Castleford WF10 ... 125 D5
Leeds LS16 ... 42 B5
ingsley Garth WF1 ... 121 B5
ingsley Pl HX1 ... 202 C2
ingsley Rd LS16 ... 42 B5
ingsmark Freeway BD12, BD4 ... 94 F6
ings Mdw WF5 ... 140 C7
ingsmead
Leeds LS14 ... 62 A8
Ossett WF5 ... 140 C8
ings Mead LS26 ... 101 A6
ingsmead Dr LS14 ... 44 F1
ings Meadow Cl LS22 ... 13 D7
ings Meadow Dr LS22 ... 13 D7
ings Meadow Gr LS22 ... 13 D7
ings Meadow Mews LS22 ... 13 D7
ings Meadow View LS22 ... 13 D7
ingsmill Cl LS27 ... 97 F5
ings Paddock WF5 ... 140 C7
ings Rd
Bramhope LS16 ... 25 B1
Ilkley LS29 ... 7 F4
Normanton WF6 ... 122 E6
ings Sch The WF8 ... 146 C7
ing St
Batley WF16 ... 117 D4
Birkenshaw BD11 ... 96 F6
Bradford BD2 ... 56 C5
Brighouse HD6 ... 115 B2
Castleford WF10 ... 124 E5
Cleckheaton BD19 ... 116 E8
Cononley BD20 ... 4 A2
Elland HX5 ... 135 A6

King St *continued*
Fitzwilliam WF9 ... 163 B1
Halifax HX1 ... 203 C3
[11] Haworth BD22 ... 51 C6
Hebden Bridge, Mytholm HX7 ... 88 E3
Horbury WF4 ... 140 E1
Huddersfield HD1 ... 154 B6
Huddersfield, Oakes HD3 ... 153 C8
Keighley BD21 ... 35 B6
Leeds LS1 ... 211 B3
Mirfield WF14 ... 138 A4
Morley LS27 ... 98 A3
Mytholmroyd HX7 ... 110 E8
Normanton, Altofts WF6 ... 122 F4
Normanton WF6 ... 123 A1
Ossett WF5 ... 140 E4
Pontefract WF8 ... 146 C8
Pudsey LS28 ... 57 E1
Silsden BD20 ... 5 E1
Skelmanthorpe HD8 ... 175 A2
Sowerby Bridge HX6 ... 111 E3
Todmorden OL14 ... 108 D6
Wakefield WF1 ... 216 B2
Yeadon, Little London LS19 ... 40 A4
Yeadon LS19 ... 40 C7
Kingston Ave HD5 ... 154 E6
Kingston Cl
Halifax HX1 ... 202 B2
Wilsden BD15 ... 53 C5
Kingston Ct HX1 ... 202 B2
Kingston Dr
Halifax HX1 ... 202 B2
Normanton WF6 ... 123 D1
Kingston Gdns LS15 ... 62 B2
Kingston Gr BD10 ... 39 B1
Kingston Rd BD10 ... 39 B1
Kingston St HX1 ... 202 B2
Kingston Terr
Halifax HX1 ... 202 B2
Leeds LS2 ... 206 B2
Kings View
Halifax HX3 ... 114 A4
Pontefract WF8 ... 146 C7
Kingsway
Batley WF17 ... 96 E2
Bingley BD16 ... 37 A2
Birkenshaw BD11 ... 96 F6
Bradford BD2 ... 55 F6
Darton S75 ... 178 A1
[1] Dewsbury WF12 ... 139 D8
Garforth LS25 ... 82 D6
Keighley BD20 ... 19 A1
Leeds LS15 ... 81 C8
Lofthouse Gate WF3 ... 121 F2
Normanton WF6 ... 144 A8
Ossett WF5 ... 140 C6
Pontefract WF8 ... 125 D3
Kingsway Cl WF5 ... 140 C7
Kingsway Ct
Leeds LS17 ... 43 D1
Ossett WF5 ... 140 C7
Kingsway Dr LS29 ... 8 A4
Kingsway Garth LS25 ... 82 D6
Kingsway Ho [3] WF5 ... 140 D6
Kingswear Cl LS15 ... 62 D1
Kingswear Cres LS15 ... 62 D1
Kingswear Garth LS15 ... 62 D1
Kingswear Glen LS15 ... 62 D1
Kingswear Gr LS15 ... 62 D1
Kingswear Par LS15 ... 62 D1
Kingswear Rise [4] LS15 ... 62 D1
Kingswear View LS15 ... 62 D1
Kingswell Ave WF1 ... 121 C4
Kingswood Ave LS8 ... 44 A3
Kingswood Cres LS8 ... 43 F3
Kingswood Dr LS8 ... 43 F3
Kingswood Gdns LS8 ... 43 F3
Kingswood Gn HX3 ... 92 F1
Kingswood Gr LS8 ... 44 A3
Kingswood Pl [8] BD7 ... 74 A4
Kingswood St BD7 ... 74 A4
Kingswood Terr [9] BD7 ... 74 A4
Kinnaird Cl
Batley WF17 ... 118 F5
Halifax HX5 ... 134 F8
Kinsgate Ctr [13] HD1 ... 154 B6
Kinsley House Cres WF9 ... 163 A2
Kinsley Prim Sch WF9 ... 163 B2
Kinsley St WF9 ... 163 B1
Kipling Cl HD4 ... 153 D3
Kipling Ct BD10 ... 56 D7
Kipling Gr WF8 ... 125 D3
Kippax Ash Tree Prim Sch LS25 ... 83 B1
Kippax Greenfield Prim Sch LS25 ... 83 A2
Kippax Mount LS9 ... 212 C3
Kippax North Jun & Inf Sch LS25 ... 82 F4
Kippax Pl LS9 ... 212 C3
Kipping La BD13 ... 72 D6
Kipping Pl [6] BD13 ... 72 D6
Kirby Cote La HX7 ... 110 D3
Kirby Row HD5 ... 137 C1
Kirby St BD21 ... 18 D1
Kirk Beeston Cl LS11 ... 213 C2
Kirkbourne Gr BD17 ... 38 E2
Kirkbridge La HD9 ... 189 D7
Kirkbridge Way WF9 ... 182 F3
Kirkburn Pl BD7 ... 74 B6
Kirkburton CE Fst Sch HD8 ... 173 F6
Kirkburton Mid Sch HD8 ... 174 A7
Kirkby Ave LS25 ... 83 A5
Kirkby Cl WF9 ... 182 C3
Kirkby Garth LS14 ... 45 F6
Kirkbygate WF9 ... 181 E5

Kirkby La
Emley HD8, WF4 ... 175 B8
Sicklinghall LS22 ... 12 A5
Kirkby Leas HX1 ... 203 B2
Kirkby Rd WF9 ... 181 E6
Kirkcaldy Fold [12] WF6 ... 123 D1
Kirk Cl WF12 ... 140 B8
Kirkcroft BD13 ... 71 D8
Kirk Cross Cres S71 ... 179 C2
Kirkdale WF10 ... 125 C8
Kirkdale Ave LS12 ... 78 B4
Kirkdale Cres LS12 ... 78 B3
Kirkdale Dr
Crigglestone WF4 ... 159 D6
Leeds LS12 ... 78 B4
Kirkdale Gdns LS12 ... 78 B4
Kirkdale Gr LS12 ... 78 A4
Kirkdale Mount LS12 ... 78 B4
Kirkdale Terr LS12 ... 78 B3
Kirkdale View LS12 ... 78 B4
Kirkdale Way [5] BD4 ... 75 F1
Kirk Dr BD17 ... 38 D4
Kirkfield Ave LS14 ... 46 A6
Kirkfield Cl S75 ... 193 F4
Kirkfield Cres LS14 ... 46 A6
Kirkfield Dr LS15 ... 81 D7
Kirkfield Gdns LS15 ... 81 D7
Kirkfield La LS14 ... 46 A5
Kirkfields BD17 ... 38 E3
Kirkfield View LS15 ... 81 D7
Kirkfield Way S71 ... 179 C2
Kirkgate
Batley, Birstall WF17 ... 96 D1
Batley, Hanging Heaton WF17 ... 118 F3
Bradford BD1 ... 201 B3
Farnhill BD20 ... 16 E8
Huddersfield HD1 ... 154 B6
Leeds LS1, LS2 ... 211 C3
Leeds LS2 ... 212 A3
Otley LS21 ... 23 A7
Shipley BD18 ... 55 A8
Silsden BD20 ... 5 E1
Wakefield WF1 ... 216 C2
Kirkgate Arc LS21 ... 23 A7
Kirkgate Bsns Ctr WF1 ... 216 C1
Kirkgate Ctr BD1 ... 201 B3
Kirkgate La S72 ... 180 C6
Kirkgate Mkt LS2 ... 211 C4
Kirkham Ave WF2 ... 120 B3
Kirkhamgate Prim Sch WF2 ... 120 B2
Kirkham Rd BD7 ... 74 B5
Kirkham St LS13 ... 57 F5
Kirkhaw La WF11 ... 126 B6
Kirkheaton Prim Sch HD5 ... 137 B2
Kirk Hills LS14 ... 46 A5
Kirk La
Brighouse HX3 ... 114 C8
Yeadon LS19 ... 40 A7
Kirk La Mills LS19 ... 40 A7
Kirklands
Holmfirth HD9 ... 189 D7
Liversedge WF15 ... 117 A4
Thorner LS14 ... 45 F5
Kirklands Ave BD17 ... 38 E3
Kirklands Cl
Baildon BD17 ... 38 E2
Menston LS29 ... 22 A4
Yeadon LS19 ... 40 A8
Kirklands Ct BD17 ... 38 E3
Kirklands Gdns BD17 ... 38 E3
Kirklands La BD17 ... 38 E3
Kirklands Rd BD17 ... 38 E3
Kirklea HD8 ... 174 C3
Kirk Lea Cres HD3 ... 135 C1
Kirklees Cl LS28 ... 57 E4
Kirklees Croft LS28 ... 57 D4
Kirklees Dr LS28 ... 57 D4
Kirklees Garth LS28 ... 57 D4
Kirklees Light Rly* HD8 ... 174 D2
Kirklees Rd BD15 ... 73 B7
Kirklees Rise LS28 ... 57 D4
Kirkley Ave BD12 ... 94 C1
Kirkroyds Inf Sch HD9 ... 189 D7
Kirkroyds La HD9 ... 189 D7
Kirk Smeaton CE Prim Sch WF8 ... 166 D6
Kirkstall Abbey* LS5 ... 58 F4
Kirkstall Ave LS5 ... 58 F3
Kirkstall Design Ctr LS5 ... 59 A4
Kirkstall Gdns BD21 ... 35 C5
Kirkstall Gr BD8 ... 73 D7
Kirkstall Hill LS4, LS5 ... 59 B3
Kirkstall Ind Pk LS4 ... 205 A1
Kirkstall La LS5, LS6 ... 59 B4
Kirkstall Mount LS5 ... 58 F3
Kirkstall Rd LS4 ... 59 C2
Kirkstall St Stephen's CE Prim Sch LS6 ... 59 A4
Kirkstall Valley Prim Sch LS4 ... 59 C2
Kirkstone Ave HD5 ... 154 C6
Kirkstone Dr
Cleckheaton BD19 ... 117 B8
Halifax HX2 ... 112 C8
Kirkthorpe La WF1 ... 143 C6
Kirkwall Ave [3] LS9 ... 80 B7
Kirkwall Dr BD4 ... 75 E3
Kirkwood Ave LS16 ... 41 D4
Kirkwood Cl LS16 ... 41 D4
Kirkwood Cres LS16 ... 41 E5
Kirkwood Dr
Huddersfield HD3 ... 153 B8
Leeds LS16 ... 41 E5
Kirkwood Gdns LS16 ... 41 E5
Kirkwood Gn HD3 ... 153 B8

Kirkwood Gr
East Ardsley WF3 ... 119 F8
Leeds LS16 ... 41 D4
Kirkwood La LS16 ... 41 D5
Kirkwood Rise LS16 ... 41 E5
Kirkwood View LS16 ... 41 E5
Kirkwood Way LS16 ... 41 E5
Kismet Cl HX1 ... 202 C3
Kismet Gdns BD3 ... 75 C8
Kistvaen Gdns HD9 ... 170 C3
Kitchener Ave [1] LS9 ... 208 B1
Kitchener Gr LS9 ... 208 B2
Kitchener Mount [2] LS9 ... 208 B1
Kitchener Pl LS9 ... 208 B1
Kitchener St
Bradford BD12 ... 95 A5
Leeds LS9 ... 208 B1
[5] Rothwell LS26 ... 101 C6
Kitchen Fold HD7 ... 170 A8
Kitchenman Apartments HX1 ... 203 B1
Kite Mews BD8 ... 73 C7
Kit La BD20 ... 5 C6
Kitson Cl LS12 ... 209 C2
Kitson Gdns LS12 ... 209 C2
Kitson Hill Cres WF14 ... 137 F6
Kitson Hill Rd WF14 ... 137 F7
Kitson La HX6 ... 112 D1
Kitson Rd LS10 ... 212 A1
Kitson St
East Ardsley WF3 ... 98 D1
Leeds LS9 ... 212 C3
Shipley BD18 ... 55 C7
Kitson Wood Rd OL14 ... 107 E8
Kitty Fold [12] LS29 ... 6 F8
Kit Wood Cl BD4 ... 75 F2
Kliffen Pl HX3 ... 113 D4
Knaresborough Dr HD2 ... 136 A2
Knave Cl WF4 ... 141 D2
Knavesmire LS26 ... 100 B5
Knight's Fold BD7 ... 74 A4
Knightsbridge Ct
[18] Brighouse HD6 ... 115 A3
Halifax HX3 ... 113 C4
Knightsbridge Wlk BD4 ... 95 B8
Knights Cl LS15 ... 81 C8
Knights Croft LS22 ... 13 F7
Knightscroft Ave LS26 ... 100 E6
Knightscroft Dr LS26 ... 100 E6
Knightscroft Par WF9 ... 183 A2
Knightshill LS15 ... 81 D8
Knight St
Halifax HX1 ... 202 B2
Huddersfield HD1 ... 154 B7
Knightsway
Garforth LS25 ... 82 E6
Leeds LS15 ... 81 C8
Rothwell WF3 ... 100 B2
Wakefield WF2 ... 160 C6
Knoll Cl WF5 ... 140 E7
Knoll Gdns BD17 ... 38 B1
Knoll La HD9 ... 188 D8
Knoll Park Dr BD17 ... 38 B1
Knoll Pk WF3 ... 120 D7
Knoll The
Bramham LS23 ... 30 C3
Pudsey LS28 ... 57 A2
Knoll View [1] BD17 ... 38 B2
Knoll Wood Pk LS18 ... 58 D8
Knottingley CE Jun & Inf Sch WF11 ... 127 A4
Knottingley England Lane Jun & Inf Sch WF11 ... 126 F3
Knottingley High Sch & Sports Coll WF11 ... 127 A3
Knottingley Rd WF8, WF11 ... 126 B2
Knottingley Simpson's Lane Jun & Inf Sch WF11 ... 126 D3
Knottingley Sta WF11 ... 126 E4
Knott La
Steeton BD20 ... 16 F5
Yeadon LS19 ... 40 E1
Knotts Rd OL14 ... 107 D8
Knotty La HD8 ... 156 A3
Knowl Bank HD7 ... 152 E4
Knowle Ave
Huddersfield HD5 ... 154 E5
Leeds LS4 ... 205 A3
Knowle Gr [10] LS4 ... 205 A3
Knowle La
Bradford BD12 ... 94 D2
Meltham HD9 ... 171 A2
Knowle Mount LS4 ... 205 A3
Knowle Park Ave HD8 ... 190 F8
Knowle Pk Ind Est BD21 ... 35 B5
Knowle Pl [11] LS4 ... 205 A3
Knowler Cl WF15 ... 117 A5
Knowle Rd
Kirkheaton HD5 ... 155 C8
Leeds LS4 ... 205 A3
Slaithwaite HD7 ... 152 A1
Knowler Hill WF15 ... 117 A5
Knowler Way WF15 ... 117 A5
Knowles Ave BD4 ... 75 D2
Knowle Sch WF14 ... 138 A6
Knowles Croft [8] WF13 ... 117 F2
Knowles Hill [6] WF13 ... 117 F2
Knowles Hill Inf Sch WF13 ... 117 F2
Knowles Hill Rd WF13 ... 117 F1
Knowles La
Batley WF17 ... 118 B4
Bradford BD4 ... 75 D2
Cleckheaton BD19 ... 96 B2
Knowle Spring Rd [1] BD21 ... 35 B5

Knowles Rd
Batley WF17 ... 118 B4
Brighouse HD6 ... 136 B8
Knowles St
Bradford BD4 ... 75 C2
Denholme BD13 ... 71 D8
Knowles View BD4 ... 75 D2
Knowles Wlk WF9 ... 183 A4
Knowleswood Prim Sch BD4 ... 75 D3
Knowle Terr LS4 ... 205 A3
Knowle The HD8 ... 190 F8
Knowle Top Dr HX3 ... 114 E8
Knowle Top Rd HX3 ... 114 E8
Knowl Gr WF14 ... 138 A5
Knowl Rd
Holme HD9 ... 187 E4
Huddersfield HD7 ... 152 E4
Mirfield WF14 ... 138 A5
Knowl The [11] WF14 ... 137 F5
Knowl Top HX7 ... 88 C6
Knowlwood Rd OL14 ... 108 A3
Knowsley Ave [16] OL14 ... 108 A1
Knowsley St BD3 ... 75 A6
Knowsthorpe Cres LS9 ... 212 C1
Knowsthorpe Gate LS9 ... 80 B5
Knowsthorpe La
Leeds, Cross Green LS9 ... 80 A4
Leeds LS10, LS26 ... 80 E2
Knowsthorpe Rd LS9 ... 80 C4
Knowsthorpe Way LS9 ... 80 B4
Knox St LS13 ... 57 D5
Knutsford Gr BD4 ... 75 E2
Knutsford Mews [9] BD4 ... 75 E2
Komla Cl BD1 ... 201 C3
Krives La HD7 ... 169 E5
Kyffin Ave LS15 ... 80 E8
Kyffin Pl BD4 ... 75 E5

L

Laburnum Cl WF3 ... 120 C7
Laburnum Ct
Castleford WF10 ... 124 E6
Horbury WF4 ... 140 F1
Laburnum Dr BD17 ... 38 D4
Laburnum Gr
Brighouse HX3 ... 115 A6
Cleckheaton BD19 ... 96 A1
Haworth BD22 ... 51 E8
Horbury WF4 ... 140 F1
Huddersfield HD7 ... 152 F5
Skelmanthorpe HD8 ... 175 A1
Laburnum Pl
Bradford, Apperley Bridge BD10 ... 56 E8
Bradford, Clifton Villas BD8 ... 55 C1
Laburnum Rd
Batley WF13 ... 117 E2
[6] Shipley BD18 ... 55 D5
Wakefield WF1 ... 216 A3
Laburnum St
Bradford BD8 ... 55 C1
Pudsey LS28 ... 57 D1
Pudsey, Owlcotes Hill LS28 ... 76 C8
Laburnum Terr
Brighouse HX3 ... 94 A2
Huddersfield HD1 ... 154 B8
Laceby Cl BD10 ... 56 C8
Lacey St
Dewsbury WF13 ... 139 B8
Horbury WF4 ... 141 C2
Lacy Ave OL14 ... 108 A1
Lacy Gr LS22 ... 13 F4
Lacy St WF9 ... 181 C7
Lacy Way HX5 ... 135 A8
Ladbroke Gr BD4 ... 75 E1
Ladderbanks La BD17 ... 38 D4
Ladstone Park Cvn Site HX4, HX6 ... 133 A7
Ladstone Twrs [15] HX6 ... 112 B4
Lady Anne Bsns Pk WF17 ... 118 E6
Lady Ann Rd WF17 ... 118 E5
Lady Balk La WF8 ... 125 D3
Ladybeck Cl LS2 ... 212 A4
Ladybower Ave HD4 ... 152 F2
Lady Cl WF5 ... 140 C8
Lady Elizabeth Hastings CE Prim Sch WF10 ... 103 E6
Lady Elizabeth Hastings CE Sch LS23 ... 14 E1
Ladyfield [16] BD13 ... 72 D6
Lady Heton Ave WF14 ... 137 F6
Lady Heton Cl WF14 ... 137 E6
Lady Heton Dr WF14 ... 137 E6
Lady Heton Gr WF14 ... 137 E6
Lady House La HD4 ... 172 A8
Lady La
Bingley BD16 ... 37 A5
Huddersfield HD5 ... 155 A7
Leeds LS2 ... 212 A4
Wakefield WF2 ... 216 A1
Lady Lane Park Sch BD16 ... 37 A5
Lady Park Ave BD16 ... 37 A5
Lady Park Ct [2] LS17 ... 43 F4
Lady Pit La LS11 ... 214 B3
Ladyroyd Dr BD4 ... 95 E6
Ladysmith Cl WF7 ... 145 C6
Ladysmith Rd BD13 ... 92 C8
Ladywell Cl BD5 ... 74 E3
Ladywell La WF15 ... 116 B3
Ladywood Grange LS8 ... 61 D6
Ladywood Mead LS8 ... 61 D6

Lady Wood Rd LS8 . . . . 61 B6
Ladywood Terr HX1 . . . . . 202 C4
Ladywood Way WF13 . . . . 38 E4
Lafflands La WF4 . . . . 162 B1
Lairum Rise LS23 . . . . 30 D5
Laisterdyke BD4 . . . . 75 D6
Laisterdyke Bsns & Ent Coll
BD3 . . . . 75 D7
Laisteridge La BD5, BD7 . . 74 C5
Laith Cl LS16 . . . . 41 F3
Laithe Ave HD9 . . . . 188 C2
Laithe Bank Dr HD9 . . . . . 188 C2
Laithe Cl BD20 . . . . 5 E2
Laithe Croft WF17 . . . . . . 118 E5
Laithe Croft Rd WF17 . . . 118 E5
Laithe Field HX4 . . . . 133 D5
Laithe Gr BD6 . . . . 74 B1
Laithe Rd BD6 . . . . 74 B1
Laithes Chase WF2 . . . . . . 141 F7
Laithes Cl WF2 . . . . 141 F7
Laithes Cres WF2 . . . . 141 F7
Laithes Croft WF12 . . . . . . 139 E7
Laithes Ct WF2 . . . . 141 F7
Laithes Dr WF2 . . . . 141 D7
Laithes Fold WF2 . . . . 141 F7
Laithes View WF2 . . . . 141 D7
Laith Garth LS16 . . . . 41 F3
Laith Gdns LS16 . . . . 42 A3
Laith Gn LS16 . . . . 41 F3
Laith Rd LS16 . . . . 41 F3
Laith Staid La LS25 . . . . 65 F1
Laith Wlk LS16 . . . . 41 F3
Lakeland Cres LS17 . . . . . . 43 A6
Lakeland Ct LS15 . . . . 80 D6
Lakeland Dr LS17 . . . . 43 B6
Lakeland Way WF2 . . . . . . 161 A6
Lake Lock Dr WF3 . . . . 122 A6
Lake Lock Gr WF3 . . . . 122 A5
Lake Lock Rd WF3 . . . . 122 A5
Lake Row BD4 . . . . 75 B5
Lakeside
Keighley BD20 . . . . 19 E2
Marsden HD7 . . . . 169 A4
Lakeside Chase LS19 . . . . . 40 C4
Lakeside Cl LS29 . . . . 8 B5
Lakeside Ct
Huddersfield HD3 . . . . 153 B8
Leeds LS10 . . . . 215 A2
Normanton WF6 . . . . 123 D1
Lakeside Est WF4 . . . . 162 B2
Lakeside Gdns LS19 . . . . . . 40 C4
Lakeside Ind Est LS12 . . . . 77 F6
Lakeside Mdws WF8 . . . . 125 D3
Lakeside Pk WF6 . . . . 123 D1
Lakeside Rd LS12 . . . . 77 E6
Lakeside Terr LS19 . . . . 40 C4
Lakeside Units WF2 . . . . . 142 B2
Lakeside View LS19 . . . . . . 40 C4
Lakeside Wlk LS19 . . . . 40 C4
Lake St
Bradford BD4 . . . . 75 B5
[1] Keighley BD21 . . . . 18 E1
Leeds LS10 . . . . 215 A2
Lake Terr LS10 . . . . 215 A2
Lake View
Crigglestone WF2 . . . . 160 C4
Halifax HX3 . . . . 203 A4
Huddersfield HD4 . . . . 171 E8
Pontefract WF8 . . . . 125 C3
Lakeview Ct LS8 . . . . 61 C8
Lake Yd WF3 . . . . 122 A5
Lamb Cote Rd HD2 . . . . . . 136 D6
Lambecroft S71 . . . . 179 C1
Lambe Flatt S75 . . . . 177 C1
Lambert Ave LS8 . . . . 204 C2
Lambert Cl HX4 . . . . 134 D7
Lambert Dr LS8 . . . . 204 C2
Lambert Pl [5] BD2 . . . . 56 B2
Lamberts Arc [9] LS1 . . . . 211 C3
Lambert St [2] HX4 . . . . . . 134 D7
Lambert Terr LS18 . . . . 41 E1
Lamb Hall Rd HD3 . . . . . . 152 E8
Lamb Inn Rd WF11 . . . . . . 127 A4
Lambourne Ave BD10 . . . . 56 E5
Lambrigg Cres LS14 . . . . . . 62 A4
Lamb Springs La BD17 . . . 39 A5
Lambton Gr LS8 . . . . 207 C4
Lambton Pl LS8 . . . . 207 C4
Lambton St LS8 . . . . 207 C4
Lambton Terr LS8 . . . . 207 C4
Lambton View LS8 . . . . . . 207 C4
Lammas Ct LS14 . . . . 45 B7
Lamma Well Rd HD9 . . . . 189 A2
Lampards Cl BD15 . . . . 54 A2
Lamplands WF17 . . . . 118 D6
Lanark Dr LS18 . . . . 41 B4
Lanark Rise WF4 . . . . 162 A8
Lancaster Cl WF8 . . . . 146 D6
Lancaster Cres HD5 . . . . . 154 F4
Lancaster Ct [9] BD21 . . . . . 35 B5
Lancaster La HD9 . . . . 172 C1
Lancaster St
Castleford WF10 . . . . 104 D1
Thurnscoe S63 . . . . 194 E1
Lancastre Ave LS5 . . . . 58 F3
Lancastre Gr LS5 . . . . 58 F3
Lancelot Ct WF9 . . . . 183 A2
Lancet Rise WF3 . . . . 100 A3
Land's Bldgs WF5 . . . . . . 140 D7
Landemere Syke HX3 . . . . 93 A4
Landmark Ct LS11 . . . . . . 213 C3
Landor St BD21 . . . . 35 D8
Landown Ho [5] HX1 . . . . . 203 B3
Lands Beck Way WF15 . . . 116 F4
Landscove Ave BD4 . . . . . . 75 F2
Landsdown Ave WF9 . . . . 182 A1
Landseer Ave
East Ardsley WF3 . . . . 119 E8
Leeds LS13 . . . . 58 E3
Landseer Cl LS13 . . . . 58 D3
Landseer Cres LS13 . . . . . . 58 E3
Landseer Dr LS13 . . . . 58 E3
Landseer Gdns LS13 . . . . . 58 E3
Landseer Gn LS13 . . . . 58 D3
Landseer Gr LS13 . . . . 58 E3
Landseer Mount LS13 . . . . 58 E3
Landseer Rd LS13 . . . . 58 D3
Landseer Rise LS13 . . . . . . 58 D3
Landseer Terr LS13 . . . . . . 58 E3
Landseer View LS13 . . . . . . 58 E3
Landseer Way LS13 . . . . . . 58 D3
Landseer Wlk LS13 . . . . 58 D3
Lands Head La HX3 . . . . . . 93 A4
Landsholme Ct [15] BD4 . . . 75 F2
Lands La
Bradford BD10 . . . . 56 C5
Guiseley LS20 . . . . 22 E1
Leeds LS1 . . . . 211 C4
Landsmoor Gr BD16 . . . . . . 37 C5
Land St LS28 . . . . 57 D3
Lane Bottom
Blackshaw Head HX7 . . . . . 87 F4
Holmfirth HD9 . . . . 189 C7
Lane Cotts S71 . . . . 179 C3
Lane Court No 1 [6] HD6 . 115 B3
Lane Court No 2 [7] HD6 . 115 B3
Lane & Dowry Rd HD7 . . . 169 F7
Lane End
Baildon BD17 . . . . 38 C3
Harden BD16 . . . . 36 B1
Pudsey LS28 . . . . 76 F8
Thornton BD13 . . . . 72 D6
Lane End Croft LS17 . . . . . 42 F5
Lane End Ct LS17 . . . . 42 F5
Lane End Fold LS28 . . . . . . 76 F8
Lane End La [2] OL13 . . . . 106 A1
Lane End Mount LS28 . . . . 76 F8
Lane End Pl LS11 . . . . 211 B1
Lane End Rd OL13 . . . . . . 106 A1
Lane Ends
Halifax, Midgley HX2 . . . . . . 90 D1
Halifax, Wheatley HX2, HX3 91 E2
Lane Ends Cl
Bradford BD8 . . . . 73 F8
Fitzwilliam WF9 . . . . 163 A4
Lane Ends Gn HX3 . . . . . . 114 C8
Lane Ends La HX7 . . . . 89 C4
Lane Ends Terr HX3 . . . . . 114 C8
Lane Ends View WF3 . . . . 121 E5
Lane Fox Ct [7] LS19 . . . . . . 40 B7
Lane Hackings HD8 . . . . . 191 E7
Lane Hackings Gn HD8 . . 191 E7
Lane Head
Heptonstall HX7 . . . . 88 E5
Honley HD9 . . . . 171 F4
Ripponden HX6 . . . . 132 C6
Lane Head Cl S75 . . . . 178 A2
Lane Head La
Halifax HX2 . . . . 91 D8
Kirkburton HD8 . . . . 173 F6
Lane Head Rd
Cawthorne S75 . . . . 193 D3
Ripponden HX6 . . . . 132 C5
Shepley HD8 . . . . 190 E7
Lane Head Rise S75 . . . . . 178 A2
Lane House Gr HX2 . . . . . 111 E8
Lane Ings HD7 . . . . 169 A4
Laneside
Elland HX4 . . . . 134 A4
Kirkburton HD8 . . . . 174 A6
Morley LS27 . . . . 98 B7
Lane Side
Bacup OL13 . . . . 106 A4
Kirkheaton HD5 . . . . 155 C7
Queensbury BD13 . . . . 72 D3
Wilsden BD15 . . . . 53 C4
Laneside Cl LS27 . . . . 98 B7
Lane Side Cl BD12 . . . . 94 C4
Laneside Fold [11] LS27 . . . . 98 B7
Laneside Gdns LS27 . . . . . . 98 B7
Lane Side La HD5 . . . . 155 D7
Laneside St OL14 . . . . 108 A4
Lanes The LS28 . . . . 76 F8
Lane The
Leeds, Alwoodley LS17 . . . . 42 F5
Leeds LS9 . . . . 212 B3
Royston S71 . . . . 179 C4
Lane Top
Denholme BD13 . . . . 52 D2
Slaithwaite HD7 . . . . 152 E1
Langbar App LS14 . . . . 62 D6
Langbar Ave BD9 . . . . 54 D3
Langbar Cl LS14 . . . . 62 D5
Langbar Garth LS14 . . . . . . 62 D6
Langbar Gdns [1] LS14 . . . . 62 D5
Langbar Gn LS14 . . . . 62 D6
Langbar Gr LS14 . . . . 62 D5
Langbar Grange [9] LS14 . . 62 D5
Langbar Pl LS14 . . . . 62 D6
Langbar Rd
Ilkley LS29 . . . . 8 A6
Leeds LS14 . . . . 62 D5
Langbar Sq LS14 . . . . 62 D5
Langbar View LS14 . . . . 62 D6
Langcliff Cl S75 . . . . 178 A2
Langdale Ave
Bradford BD8 . . . . 73 E8
Brighouse BD12 . . . . 94 E1
Leeds LS6 . . . . 59 C4
Lofthouse Gate WF1 . . . . . 121 D5
Normanton WF6 . . . . 123 A4
Langdale Cl
Castleford WF10 . . . . 104 E2
Langdale Cl *continued*
Wetherby LS22 . . . . 13 D6
Langdale Cres HX2 . . . . 91 E1
Langdale Ct BD16 . . . . 37 A4
Langdale Dr
Ackworth M T WF7 . . . . . . 164 C7
Huddersfield HD5 . . . . 154 D7
Normanton WF6 . . . . 123 A4
[2] Queensbury BD13 . . . . . 72 D1
Wakefield WF2 . . . . 141 F6
Langdale Gdns LS6 . . . . 59 C4
Langdale Mews WF6 . . . . 123 A4
Langdale Mount WF2 . . . 161 A6
Langdale Rd
Batley WF12 . . . . 118 F2
Bradford BD10 . . . . 56 E4
Rothwell LS26 . . . . 101 B6
Langdales HX6 . . . . 112 A4
Langdale Sq WF2 . . . . 141 F6
Langdale St HX5 . . . . 134 F6
Langdale Terr LS6 . . . . 59 C4
Langford Cl LS29 . . . . 9 E1
Langford Ct LS29 . . . . 9 E1
Langford La LS29 . . . . 9 F1
Langford Mews LS29 . . . . . . 9 E1
Langford Rd LS29 . . . . 9 E1
Langford Ride LS29 . . . . 9 F1
Lang Kirk Cl BD20 . . . . 4 E1
Lang La BD2 . . . . 55 D5
Langlands Rd BD16 . . . . 54 A7
Langlea Terr HX3 . . . . 114 C8
Langley Ave
Bingley BD16 . . . . 37 A4
Bradford BD4 . . . . 75 C1
Leeds LS13 . . . . 58 A4
Langley Cl LS13 . . . . 58 A4
Langley Cres
Baildon BD17 . . . . 38 E3
Leeds LS13 . . . . 58 B4
Langley Garth LS13 . . . . . . 58 A4
Langley Gr BD16 . . . . 37 A4
Langley La
Baildon BD17 . . . . 38 E4
Clayton West HD8 . . . . 175 E2
Clayton West HD8 . . . . 175 E4
Langley Mount LS13 . . . . . 58 B4
Langley Pl LS13 . . . . 58 A4
Langley Rd
Bingley BD16 . . . . 37 A4
Leeds LS13 . . . . 58 B4
Langley Terr HD3 . . . . 153 A8
Langport Cl BD13 . . . . 72 F1
Langsett Croft HD2 . . . . . . 136 E5
Langsett Rd WF2 . . . . 160 B5
Langthorne Ct LS27 . . . . . . 98 C2
Langthwaite Grange Ind Est
WF9 . . . . 182 D2
Langthwaite La WF9 . . . . 182 E2
Langthwaite Rd WF9 . . . . 182 D2
Langton Ave BD4 . . . . 75 C1
Langton Cl BD19 . . . . 96 A2
Langton Gn LS12 . . . . 209 C1
Langton St HX6 . . . . 112 B5
Langtons Wharf LS2 . . . . 212 A3
Langwith Ave LS22 . . . . 29 A8
Langwith Ct [1] HX1 . . . . . 203 A1
Langwith Dr LS22 . . . . 28 E8
Langwith Mews [1] LS22 . . 29 A8
Langwith Terr LS22 . . . . 28 F8
Langwith Valley Rd LS22 . 28 E8
Lansdale Ct [14] BD4 . . . . . . 75 F2
Lansdown Ct [11] BD5 . . . . 74 E3
Lansdowne Ave WF10 . . . 124 F7
Lansdowne Cl
Baildon BD17 . . . . 38 F3
Batley WF17 . . . . 118 C6
Lansdowne Pl BD5 . . . . . . 201 A2
Lansdowne St LS12 . . . . . . 209 C2
Lanshaw Bank BD23 . . . . 3 B6
Lanshaw Cl LS10 . . . . 99 E6
Lanshaw Cres LS10 . . . . . . 99 E5
Lanshaw Pl LS10 . . . . 99 E6
Lanshaw Rd LS10 . . . . 99 E6
Lanshaw Terr LS10 . . . . 99 E6
Lanshaw View LS10 . . . . . . 99 E6
Lanshaw Wlk LS10 . . . . 99 E6
Lapage Prim Sch BD3 . . . . 75 C8
Lapage St BD3 . . . . 75 C7
Lapage Terr BD3 . . . . 75 C6
Lapwing Cl BD8 . . . . 73 B7
Larch Ave HD9 . . . . 189 C8
Larch Cl
Batley WF17 . . . . 97 A2
Halifax HX3 . . . . 91 E2
Kirkheaton HD5 . . . . 137 B1
Liversedge WF15 . . . . 117 C3
Normanton WF6 . . . . 144 B8
Oakworth BD22 . . . . 34 D2
Larch Ct WF10 . . . . 124 E6
Larch Dale HD2 . . . . 136 A4
Larch Dr BD6 . . . . 94 D7
Larchfield Rd LS10 . . . . . . 212 B1
Larchfield Way WF4 . . . . . 162 B1
Larch Gr BD16 . . . . 36 F5
Larch Hill BD6 . . . . 94 D7
Larch Hill Cres BD6 . . . . . . 94 D8
Larch La LS25 . . . . 83 B6
Larchmont BD14 . . . . 73 C4
Larch Rd HD1 . . . . 153 D5
Larch St BD21 . . . . 35 B4
Larchwood LS19 . . . . 40 C2
Larch Wood LS14 . . . . 45 C7
Larkfield Ave LS19 . . . . 40 C4
Larkfield Cres LS19 . . . . . . 40 C4
Larkfield Ct [13] HD6 . . . . 115 A3
Larkfield Dr LS19 . . . . 40 C4
Larkfield Mount LS19 . . . . 40 C4
Larkfield Rd
Pudsey LS28 . . . . 76 E8
Yeadon LS19 . . . . 40 C4
Larkfield Terr
Keighley BD21 . . . . 35 E6
Oakworth BD22 . . . . 34 D2
Lark Hill WF17 . . . . 118 A8
Lark Hill Ave BD19 . . . . . . 116 B6
Larkhill Cl LS8 . . . . 204 B4
Lark Hill Cl BD19 . . . . 116 B6
Lark Hill Dr BD19 . . . . 116 B6
Larkhill Gn LS8 . . . . 43 E1
Larkhill Rd LS8 . . . . 43 E1
Larkhill View LS8 . . . . 204 B4
Larkhill Way LS8 . . . . 43 E1
Larkhill Wlk LS8 . . . . 43 E1
Larks Hill WF8 . . . . 146 B6
Larks Hill Jun & Inf Sch
WF8 . . . . 146 B6
Larkspur Way WF2 . . . . . . 141 E7
Lark St
Bingley BD16 . . . . 36 F3
Haworth BD22 . . . . 51 D7
Keighley BD21 . . . . 35 B7
Oakworth BD22 . . . . 34 D2
Lark Vale BD16 . . . . 37 C4
Larwood Ave BD10 . . . . 56 E4
Lascelles Hall Rd HD5 . . . 155 C6
Lascelles Mount [4] LS8 . . 207 C3
Lascelles Pl [2] LS8 . . . . . . 207 C3
Lascelles Rd WF16 . . . . . . 117 E3
Lascelles Rd E LS8 . . . . . . 207 C3
Lascelles Rd W LS8 . . . . . 207 C3
Lascelles St LS8 . . . . 207 C3
Lascelles Terr LS8 . . . . . . 207 C3
Lascelles View [3] LS8 . . . 207 C3
Lastingham Gn BD6 . . . . . . 73 E1
Lastingham Rd LS13 . . . . . 57 F5
Last of the Summer Wine
Exhibition Mus The*
HD9 . . . . 189 A5
Latchmere Ave LS16 . . . . . 58 F8
Latchmere Cl LS16 . . . . 59 A8
Latchmere Crest [4] LS16 . 58 F8
Latchmere Cross [3] LS16 . 58 F8
Latchmere Dr LS16 . . . . 58 F8
Latchmere Gdns LS16 . . . . 59 A8
Latchmere Gn [5] LS16 . . . . 58 F8
Latchmere Rd LS16 . . . . . . 58 F8
Latchmere View LS16 . . . . 58 F8
Latchmere Wlk [4] LS16 . . . 59 A8
Latchmore Pk LS12 . . . . . 213 B4
Latchmore Rd LS12 . . . . . 213 B4
Latchmore Road Ind Est
LS12 . . . . 213 B4
Latham Ct BD19 . . . . 96 B2
Latham La BD19 . . . . 96 A2
Latham Lea BD19 . . . . 96 A2
Latimer St BD3 . . . . 75 D6
Launceston Dr BD4 . . . . . . 75 E2
Laund Rd
Huddersfield HD3 . . . . 134 E1
Slaithwaite HD7 . . . . 151 C3
Laura St
[8] Brighouse HD6 . . . . 115 A1
[5] Halifax HX3 . . . . 92 C1
Leeds LS12 . . . . 210 C2
Laureate Pl HX7 . . . . 89 F1
Laurel Bank
Brighouse BD12 . . . . 115 C8
East Keswick LS17 . . . . 28 C5
[21] Guiseley LS20 . . . . 22 E1
Halifax, Holdsworth HX2 . . . 92 A6
[11] Halifax HX1 . . . . 202 C1
Skelmanthorpe HD8 . . . . . 175 A2
Laurel Bank Cl HX2 . . . . . . 92 A6
Laurel Bank Ct LS6 . . . . 59 C4
Laurel Cl
East Keswick LS17 . . . . 28 C5
Elland HX5 . . . . 134 E6
Shelf HX3 . . . . 93 C6
Laurel Cres
Halifax HX2 . . . . 91 F3
Keighley BD21 . . . . 35 B8
Laurel Ct
Ossett WF5 . . . . 140 C6
Ryhill WF4 . . . . 162 B1
Laurel Dr WF17 . . . . 118 A7
Laurel Fold [9] LS12 . . . . . 209 C3
Laurel Gr
Batley WF17 . . . . 117 F7
Bingley BD16 . . . . 36 E5
Keighley BD21 . . . . 35 B8
[7] Leeds LS12 . . . . 209 C3
Silsden BD20 . . . . 5 D1
Laurel Hill Ave LS15 . . . . . . 81 D7
Laurel Hill Croft LS15 . . . . 81 D7
Laurel Hill Gdns LS15 . . . . 81 D7
Laurel Hill Gr LS15 . . . . 81 D7
Laurel Hill View LS15 . . . . 81 D7
Laurel Hill Way LS15 . . . . . 81 D6
Laurel Ho [4] WF10 . . . . . . 124 E7
Laurel Mount
Batley WF16 . . . . 117 D4
[14] Halifax HX1 . . . . 202 C1
Leeds LS7 . . . . 204 A1
Pudsey LS28 . . . . 76 E8
Laurel Pk BD15 . . . . 53 C4
Laurel Pl
Leeds LS12 . . . . 209 C3
Middleton LS10 . . . . 99 B3
Laurel St
Bradford BD3 . . . . 75 C6
Halifax HX1 . . . . 202 C1
[10] Leeds LS12 . . . . 209 C3
Laurels The
Bingley BD16 . . . . 37 B3
Dewsbury WF12 . . . . 139 F7
Laurels The *continued*
Leeds LS8 . . . . 204 C
Laurel Terr
Elland HX4 133
Leeds, Armley LS12 . . . . . 209 C
Leeds, Swarcliffe LS14 . . . . 62 D
Pudsey LS28 . . . . 76 E
Laurence Ct LS26 . . . . 101 C
Lauren Dr BD22 . . . . 35 A
Lavell Mews BD2 . . . . 56 C
Lavender Croft WF16 . . . . 117 E
Lavender Ct
Hemsworth WF9 . . . . 181 D
Huddersfield HD4 . . . . 171 D
[5] Shipley BD18 . . . . 55 D
Lavender Hill BD10 . . . . . . 56 C
Lavender Way WF9 . . . . . . 181 D
Lavender Wlk LS9 . . . . 212 C
Lavenham Pl DN6 . . . . 184 E
Laverack Field [6] BD12 . . . 94 C
Laverhills WF15 . . . . 116 D
Laverock Cres HD6 . . . . . . 114 F
Laverock La HD6 . . . . 114 F
Laverock Pl HD6 . . . . 114 F
Laverton Rd BD4 . . . . 75 B
Lavery Cl WF5 . . . . 140 D
Lavinia Terr BD14 . . . . 73 D
Law Cl LS22 . . . . 13 F
Lawcliffe Cres BD22 . . . . . . 51 D
Law Common Rd HD9 . . . 199 E
Lawefield Ave LS26 . . . . . 100 C
Lawefield Gr WF2 . . . . 142 A
Lawefield La WF2 . . . . 142 A
Lawkholme Cres [4] BD21 . 35 C
Lawkholme La BD21 . . . . . . 35 C
Law La HX3 . . . . 114 A
Lawler Cl HX3 . . . . 91 F
Lawn's La LS10 . . . . 215 B
Lawn Ave LS29 . . . . 9 F
Lawndale DN6 . . . . 184 F
Lawndale Fold S75 . . . . . . 177 F
Lawnhurst Mews WF13 . . 117 F
Lawn Rd LS29 . . . . 9 F
Lawns Ave LS12 . . . . 77 D
Lawns Cl
Gildersome LS12 . . . . 77 D
Normanton WF6 . . . . 122 E
Lawns Cres LS12 . . . . 77 D
Lawns Croft LS12 . . . . 77 D
Lawns Ct WF2 . . . . 120 E
Lawns Dene LS12 . . . . 77 D
Lawns Dr LS12 . . . . 77 D
Lawns Gn LS12 . . . . 77 D
Lawns Hall LS16 . . . . 42 B
Lawns Hall Cl LS16 . . . . 42 B
Lawns La
Gildersome LS12 . . . . 77 D
Lofthouse Gate WF2 . . . . . 120 E
Lawns Mount LS12 . . . . 77 D
Lawns Park Prim Sch
LS12 . . . . 77 E
Lawns Sq LS12 . . . . 77 D
Lawns Terr
East Ardsley WF3 . . . . 120 D
Gildersome LS12 . . . . 77 D
Lawns The
Batley WF16 . . . . 117 E
Halifax HX3 . . . . 113 B
Ilkley LS29 . . . . 8 A
Middlestown WF4 . . . . 158 A
Lawns View WF6 . . . . 122 E
Lawnswood Gdns LS16 . . . 42 B
Lawnswood Pk LS16 . . . . . 42 A
Lawnswood Rd BD21 . . . . . 35 A
Lawnswood Sch LS16 . . . . 59 B
Lawn Wlk LS29 . . . . 9 F
Lawrence Ave
Leeds LS8 . . . . 208 C
Pontefract WF8 . . . . 146 B
Lawrence Cres
Batley WF16 . . . . 117 D
Leeds LS8 . . . . 61 C
Lawrence Ct LS28 . . . . 76 D
Lawrence Dr BD7 . . . . 73 E
Lawrence Gdns LS8 . . . . . . 61 C
Lawrence Mews HD1 . . . . 153 E
Lawrence Rd
Halifax HX3 . . . . 113 B
Huddersfield HD1 . . . . 153 E
Leeds LS8 . . . . 208 C
Lawrence St [14] HX3 . . . . . 92 A
Lawrence Wlk LS8 . . . . 208 C
Law Slack Rd HD9 . . . . . . 199 D
Lawson Rd HD6 . . . . 115 B
Lawson St
Bradford BD3 . . . . 201 C
Leeds LS12 . . . . 209 B
Lawson Wood Ct [5] LS6 . . 42 F
Lawson Wood Dr LS6 . . . . . 42 F
Lawson Wood Drive
Apartments [4] LS6 . . . . . 42 F
Law St
Batley WF17 . . . . 117 F
Bradford BD4 . . . . 75 C
Cleckheaton BD19 . . . . . . 116 D
Todmorden, Cornholme
OL14 . . . . 86 B
Todmorden OL14 . . . . 129 B
Lawton St HD4 . . . . 154 A
Laycock La BD22 . . . . 34 C
Laycock Pl LS7 . . . . 207 A
Laycock Prim Sch BD22 . . 34 C
Lay Garth LS26 . . . . 100 E
Lay Garth Cl LS26 . . . . 100 E
Laygarth Dr HD5 . . . . 155 C
Lay Garth Fold WF3 . . . . . 100 D
Lay Garth Gdns LS26 . . . . 100 E
Lay Garth Gn LS26 . . . . . . 100 E

/ Garth Mead LS26 . . . . 100 E4
/ Garth Pl LS26 . . . . 100 E4
/ Garth Sq LS26 . . . . . . 100 E4
ythorpe Ct WF8 . . . . 147 A7
ythorp Terr BD20 . . . . . . 19 D1
yton Ave LS19 . . . . 40 E3
yton Cl LS19 . . . . 40 E2
yton Cres LS19 . . . . 40 D3
yton Dr LS19 . . . . 40 E3
yton La LS19 . . . . 40 E2
yton Mount LS19 . . . . 40 D3
yton Park Ave LS19 . . . . 40 E2
yton Park Cl LS19 . . . . . . 40 D3
yton Park Croft LS19 . . . 40 E2
yton Park Dr LS19 . . . . . 40 E2
yton Rd LS18, LS19 . . . . . 40 E3
yton Rise LS18 . . . . 40 F3
enby Dr LS22 . . . . 13 D6
enby Fold LS22 . . . . 13 D6
a Ave HX3 . . . . 113 C3
abank Ave LS25 . . . . 83 A5
ach Cres BD20 . . . . 18 E2
ach Rd BD20 . . . . 18 D2
ach Rise BD20 . . . . 18 E2
ach Way BD20 . . . . 18 E2
a Cl HD6 . . . . 115 A4
a Croft
lifford LS23 . . . . 30 D5
irfield WF14 . . . . 138 A6
tley LS21 . . . . 23 A7
a Ct BD7 . . . . 73 E2
adenhall St 10 HX1 . . . 202 B1
a Dr HD8 . . . . 190 F8
adwell La LS26, WF3 . . . 100 C4
a Farm Cres LS5 . . . . 58 F6
a Farm Dr LS5 . . . . 58 F6
a Farm Gr LS5 . . . . 58 F6
a Farm Mount LS5 . . . . . 58 F7
a Farm Pl LS5 . . . . 58 F6
a Farm Rd LS5 . . . . 58 F7
a Farm Row LS5 . . . . 58 F6
a Farm Wlk LS5 . . . . 58 F7
afield Ave
radford BD2 . . . . 56 C3
uddersfield HD3 . . . . 152 E6
afield Bank HD3 . . . . . . 152 E6
afield Cl
uddersfield HD2 . . . . 136 D4
eeds LS17 . . . . 43 B2
afield Cres BD2 . . . . 56 B3
afield Dr
radford BD2 . . . . 56 C4
eeds LS17 . . . . 43 B2
2 Pudsey LS28 . . . . 76 F5
afield Gr BD2 . . . . 56 C3
afield Grange LS17 . . . . 43 B2
afield Pl LS19 . . . . 39 F7
afield Terr BD2 . . . . 56 C3
afield Way BD2 . . . . 56 C3
afland St HX1 . . . . 202 C3
af St
astleford WF10 . . . . 124 C7
4 Haworth BD22 . . . . 51 E8
afsway BD6 . . . . 93 F6
a Head HD8 . . . . 190 E8
ah Pl LS12 . . . . 210 C2
ake St WF10 . . . . 124 E7
ak Hall Cres HD8 . . . . . 191 F6
ak Hall La HD8 . . . . 192 A6
a La
uddersfield HD4 . . . . 171 C6
urston Jaglin WF7 . . . . . . 145 E4
a Mill Park Cl LS19 . . . . 40 A7
a Mill Park Dr LS19 . . . . 40 A7
amington Dr BD10 . . . . . 56 C8
amington Rd LS29 . . . . . . 8 C5
amington St BD9 . . . . . . 55 B2
amington Terr
ewsbury WF12 . . . . 139 D6
Ilkley LS29 . . . . 8 C5
amside Wlk 8 BD4 . . . . 75 E2
a Park Cl LS10 . . . . 99 F7
a Park Croft LS10 . . . . . 100 A7
a Park Dr LS10 . . . . 99 F7
a Park Garth 5 LS10 . . . 99 F7
a Park Gdns 4 LS10 . . . 99 F7
a Park Gr LS10 . . . . 99 F7
a Park Vale LS10 . . . . . . 100 A7
a Rd WF17 . . . . 117 F8
a Rise HD9 . . . . 171 F3
aroyd St HD1 . . . . 154 B7
as Ave HD9 . . . . 188 F7
as Gdns HD9 . . . . 189 E4
aside Dr BD13 . . . . 72 D7
a Side Gdns HD3 . . . . . . 152 E7
asowe Ave LS10 . . . . . . 215 B2
asowe Cl LS10 . . . . 215 B2
asowe Ct 9 LS10 . . . . . 215 B2
asowe Garth LS10 . . . . 215 B2
asowe Gdns LS10 . . . . . 215 C2
asowe Rd LS10 . . . . 215 B2
a St
Huddersfield, Fartown
HD1 . . . . 136 A1
Huddersfield HD1 . . . . 154 A8
Huddersfield, Prince Royd
HD3 . . . . 135 C1
a Terr HD8 . . . . 175 A2
atham Ave WF7 . . . . . . 145 E4
atham Cres WF7 . . . . . . 145 F4
atham Dr WF7 . . . . 145 F4
atham Ho 3 LS22 . . . . . 13 E6
atham Park Rd WF7 . . 145 F4
a The LS25 . . . . 82 F5
ather Bank LS29 . . . . 9 E3
athley Ave LS29 . . . . 22 B4
athley Cres LS29 . . . . . . 22 B4
Leathley La
Menston LS29 . . . . 22 B4
Pool LS21 . . . . 24 B8
Leathley Rd
Leeds LS10 . . . . 212 A1
Menston LS29 . . . . 22 B4
Leathley St LS10 . . . . 212 A1
Leavens The BD10 . . . . . . 56 D8
Leaventhorpe Ave BD8 . . . 73 D7
Leaventhorpe Cl BD8 . . . . 73 D7
Leaventhorpe Gr BD13 . . . 73 C6
Leaventhorpe La BD13,
BD8 . . . . 73 C6
Leaventhorpe Way BD8 . . 73 D7
Leaverholme Cl BB10 . . . . 85 A7
Lea View WF17 . . . . 117 F8
Leavington Cl BD6 . . . . . . 94 B6
Leconfield Ct LS22 . . . . . . 13 C6
Leconfield Ho
Bradford BD10 . . . . 56 C7
15 Ilkley LS29 . . . . 8 B4
5 Wetherby LS22 . . . . 13 F6
Ledbury Ave LS10 . . . . 99 F4
Ledbury Cl 4 LS10 . . . . . . 99 F4
Ledbury Croft 3 LS10 . . . . 99 F4
Ledbury Dr LS10 . . . . 99 F4
Ledbury Gn 1 LS10 . . . . . . 99 F4
Ledbury Gr 2 LS10 . . . . . . 99 F4
Ledgard Bridge Mills Ind
Units WF14 . . . . 138 A3
Ledgard Dr WF4 . . . . 159 F7
Ledgard Way LS12 . . . . . . 209 C4
Ledgard Wharf 1 WF14 . 138 A3
Ledgate La LS25 . . . . 105 E4
Ledger La
Lofthouse Gate WF1 . . . . . 121 B4
Rothwell WF3 . . . . 100 C1
Ledger Lane Jun & Inf Sch
WF1 . . . . 121 B4
Ledger Pl WF1 . . . . 121 B4
Ledston Ave LS25 . . . . 83 A5
Ledston Luck Cotts LS25 . 83 E2
Ledston Luck Enterprise Pk
LS25 . . . . 83 D2
Ledston Luck Villas LS25 . 83 D2
Ledston Mill La
Ledston WF10 . . . . 103 E4
Ledston WF10 . . . . 103 E7
Lee Bank HX3 . . . . 92 B1
Lee Beck Gr WF3 . . . . 121 E8
Lee Bottom Rd OL14 . . . . 109 A5
Lee Bridge HX3 . . . . 203 A4
Lee Bridge Ind Est HX3 . . 203 A4
Lee Brig WF6 . . . . 122 F3
Lee Brigg Inf Sch WF6 . . . 122 E3
Leeches Hill HD3 . . . . 134 C1
Leech La BD13 . . . . 53 A8
Lee Cl BD15 . . . . 53 C6
Lee Clough Dr HX7 . . . . 89 F1
Lee Ct
Keighley BD21 . . . . 35 F6
10 Liversedge WF15 . . . . . 117 A5
Ossett WF5 . . . . 140 F4
Leeds 27 Ind Est LS27 . . . . 97 E5
Leeds Barnsdale Rd
WF10 . . . . 124 B6
Leeds Bradford International
Airport LS19 . . . . 40 E7
Leeds & Bradford Rd
LS13 . . . . 58 C4
Leeds Bsns Pk LS27 . . . . . . 97 E4
Leeds Cath* LS2 . . . . 211 B4
Leeds City Art Gal* LS1 . 211 B4
Leeds City Mus* LS1 . . . 211 B4
Leeds City Office Pk
LS11 . . . . 211 C2
Leeds College of Art &
Design LS2 . . . . 206 B1
Leeds College of Art &
Design (Jacob Kramer
Bldg) LS2 . . . . 206 B2
Leeds Coll of Bldg LS2 . . 207 A1
Leeds Coll of Music LS9 212 A4
Leeds Coll of Tech, Eastbank
Ctr LS9 . . . . 212 B3
Leeds Coll of Technology
LS2 . . . . 206 B1
Leeds Coll of Tech (South
Leeds Ctr) LS11 . . . . 99 B8
Leeds Dental Inst The
LS2 . . . . 206 A1
Leeds General Infmy
LS1 . . . . 206 B1
Leeds General Infmy,
Clarendon Wing LS2 . . 206 A1
Leeds Girls' High Sch
LS6 . . . . 205 C4
Leeds Gram Sch LS17 . . . . 43 F7
Leeds La LS15, LS26 . . . . . . 82 B4
Leeds Metropolitan Univ
Leeds, Headingley LS6 . . . . 59 B6
Leeds LS1 . . . . 206 B1
Leeds LS2 . . . . 206 C1
Leeds Met Univ LS16 . . . . . 42 E4
Leeds Nuffield Hospl The
LS3 . . . . 211 A4
Leeds Old Rd
Batley WF16 . . . . 117 D6
Bradford BD3 . . . . 75 E8
Leeds Rd
Barwick in E LS15 . . . . 63 B6
Batley WF17 . . . . 97 B2
Bradford, Bolton Outlanes
BD2 . . . . 56 B3
Bradford, Fagley BD2 . . . . . 56 C2
Bradford, Laisterdyke BD1,
BD3 . . . . 75 C6
Bradford, Thackley BD10 . . . 39 B2
Leeds Rd *continued*
Bramhope LS16, LS21 . . . . . 24 D4
Brighouse HX3 . . . . 114 E8
Castleford WF10 . . . . 124 D5
Collingham LS22 . . . . 29 A8
Dewsbury WF12 . . . . 118 E1
East Ardsley WF12 . . . . . . 119 B5
Guiseley LS20 . . . . 39 E8
Huddersfield HD2 . . . . 136 F2
Ilkley LS29 . . . . 8 D5
Kippax, Allerton Bywater
WF10 . . . . 103 A5
Kippax LS25 . . . . 83 A2
Liversedge WF16 . . . . 117 C5
Lofthouse Gate WF1 . . . . . 121 C5
Mickletown LS26 . . . . 102 B3
Northowram HX3 . . . . 114 A8
Ossett, Chickenley WF5 . . . 140 C8
Ossett, Gawthorpe WF5 . . 119 C1
Otley LS21 . . . . 23 D6
Rothwell LS26 . . . . 100 F7
Rothwell, Robin Hood LS26,
WF3 . . . . 100 B2
Shipley BD18 . . . . 55 D8
Wakefield WF1 . . . . 216 A4
Yeadon LS19 . . . . 40 D3
Leeds Rhinos Rugby League
FC LS6 . . . . 205 A4
Leeds Road Hospl BD3 . . . . 75 B7
Leeds Road Ret Pk HD1 . 154 C8
Leeds Sh Plaza LS1 . . . . . 211 C3
Leeds St BD21 . . . . 35 B7
Leeds Sta LS1 . . . . 211 B3
Leeds Valley Pk LS10 . . . . 100 B8
Lee Fair Ct WF3 . . . . 119 D6
Leefield Rd WF17 . . . . 117 E6
Leef St 8 HD5 . . . . 154 D6
Lee Gn WF14 . . . . 138 A6
Lee Head HD2 . . . . 153 F8
Leeke Ave WF4 . . . . 141 A2
Lee La
Ackworth M T WF7 . . . . 164 B8
Carlecotes S36 . . . . 200 F4
Darton S71 . . . . 178 E2
Halifax HX3 . . . . 92 D3
Horsforth LS18 . . . . 41 B2
Kirkburton HD8 . . . . 173 E6
Todmorden OL14 . . . . 108 F3
Wilsden BD16 . . . . 53 E6
Lee La E LS18 . . . . 41 B2
Lee La W LS18 . . . . 41 A2
Lee Mill Rd HX7 . . . . 89 A5
Lee Mills Ind Est HD9 . . . 189 D4
Leeming Ho 5 LS2 . . . . . . 211 C4
Leeming St BD1 . . . . 201 C4
Lee Moor La WF3 . . . . 121 E8
Lee Moor Rd WF3 . . . . 121 F6
Lee Mount Gdns 5 HX3 . . 92 A1
Lee Mount Prim Sch HX3 . 92 B1
Lee Mount Rd HX3 . . . . 92 A1
Lee Orchards LS23 . . . . 30 E8
Lee Rd WF13 . . . . 138 D5
Lee Royd 1 HX7 . . . . 88 F3
Lees Ave WF12 . . . . 139 C4
Lees Bank Ave BD22 . . . . . . 51 E8
Lees Bank Dr BD22 . . . . 51 E8
Lees Bank Hill BD22 . . . . . . 51 E8
Lees Bank Rd BD22 . . . . 51 E8
Lees Bldgs HX3 . . . . 114 C7
Lees Cl
Cullingworth BD13 . . . . 52 C6
Huddersfield HD5 . . . . 154 F7
Lees Cres WF4 . . . . 159 F7
Lees Dr WF12 . . . . 139 C4
Lees Hall Rd WF12 . . . . . . 139 C3
Lees Holm WF12 . . . . 139 C4
Lees House Rd WF12 . . . . 139 C5
Leeside Ave HD2 . . . . 136 C4
Leeside Com Prim Sch
WF16 . . . . 117 E6
Leeside Rd WF16 . . . . 117 E6
Lees La
Haworth BD22 . . . . 51 D8
Pudsey LS28 . . . . 57 D4
Lees Mill La HD7 . . . . 152 B1
Lees Moor Rd BD13 . . . . . . 52 C6
Lees Prim Sch BD22 . . . . . . 51 E8
Lees Rd 9 HX7 . . . . 89 A4
Lee St
Bradford BD1 . . . . 201 B2
Brighouse HD6 . . . . 115 A4
Dewsbury WF13 . . . . 138 E6
Liversedge WF15 . . . . 117 A5
3 Queensbury BD13 . . . . . . 92 D8
Wakefield WF1 . . . . 216 B2
Lees The BB10 . . . . 85 A7
Leesworth Ct 7 BD22 . . . . . 51 E8
Lee Terr BD12 . . . . 94 F5
Lee View
Bacup OL13 . . . . 106 A1
2 Hebden Bridge HX7 . . . . . 89 A4
Lee Way
Castleford WF10 . . . . 124 E5
Kirkburton HD8 . . . . 173 E7
Lee Wood Rd HX7 . . . . 88 F5
Legrams Ave BD7 . . . . 73 F5
Legrams La BD7 . . . . 74 A6
Legrams Mill La BD7 . . . . . 74 A6
Legrams St BD7 . . . . 74 C7
Legrams Terr BD7 . . . . 74 C7
Leicester Cl LS7 . . . . 206 B2
Leicester Gr LS7 . . . . 206 B2
Leicester Pl LS2 . . . . 206 B2
Leicester St BD4 . . . . 75 A4
Leicester Terr 9 HX3 . . . 113 B4
Leigh Ave WF3 . . . . 120 A8
Leigh Rd WF3 . . . . 120 A8
Leigh St
Ackworth M T WF7 . . . . 163 D5
Sowerby Bridge HX6 . . . . . 112 C5
Leighton Pl 1 LS1 . . . . . . 211 B4
Leighton St LS1 . . . . 211 A4
Leigh View WF3 . . . . 120 A8
Leisure Exchange The
BD1 . . . . 201 C2
Leisure La HD8 . . . . 175 E8
Leith Ct WF12 . . . . 139 E1
Leith Ho 15 BD4 . . . . 75 E3
Leith St BD21 . . . . 35 B8
Lemans Dr WF13 . . . . 117 F3
Le Marchant Ave HD3 . . . 153 C8
Le Mar View HX3 . . . . 113 E6
Lemington Ave HX1 . . . . . 202 C2
Lemon St
Bradford BD5 . . . . 74 C3
Halifax HX1 . . . . 202 B3
Lemon Tree Cl WF8 . . . . . 146 B6
Lenacre La WF4 . . . . 156 D1
Lendal Ho 2 BD4 . . . . 75 D5
Lenham Cl 1 LS27 . . . . 98 A2
Lennie St BD21 . . . . 35 B6
Lennon Dr BD8 . . . . 74 B8
Lennox Dr WF2 . . . . 141 D3
Lennox Gdns LS15 . . . . 81 C7
Lennox Rd
Leeds LS4 . . . . 205 A1
Todmorden, Cornholme
OL14 . . . . 86 A1
Todmorden, Portsmouth
OL14 . . . . 85 F1
Lenny Balk DN5, DN6 . . . . 195 E7
Lens Dr BD17 . . . . 38 C4
Lentilfield St HX3 . . . . 92 A2
Lentilfield Terr 6 HX3 . . . 92 A2
Lenton Dr LS11 . . . . 214 C2
Lenton Ho 2 BD4 . . . . 75 F2
Lenton Villas BD10 . . . . 39 B1
Leodis Ct LS11 . . . . 211 B2
Leodis Way LS10 . . . . 100 B8
Leonard's Pl 12 BD16 . . . . . 37 A2
Leonard St
Bingley BD16 . . . . 37 A2
Bradford BD12 . . . . 94 D3
Huddersfield HD2 . . . . 136 B1
Leopold Gdns LS7 . . . . 207 B3
Leopold Gr LS7 . . . . 207 A3
Leopold St
Leeds LS7 . . . . 207 B3
Ossett WF5 . . . . 141 A4
Lepton CE Jun & Inf Sch
HD8 . . . . 155 D3
Lepton La HD8 . . . . 174 A8
Lepton Pl LS27 . . . . 97 D7
Lesley Way HD4 . . . . 153 A1
Leslie Ave LS19 . . . . 40 C8
Leslie St HD2 . . . . 136 A1
Leslie Terr 5 LS6 . . . . 206 A3
Lesmere Gr BD7 . . . . 73 F2
Lessarna Ct BD4 . . . . 75 C5
Letchmire Rd WF10 . . . . . 103 C4
Leven Gdns LS22 . . . . 13 D7
Levens Bank LS15 . . . . 80 E6
Levens Cl LS15 . . . . 80 E6
Levens Garth LS15 . . . . 80 E6
Levens Pl LS15 . . . . 80 E6
Leventhorpe Cotts LS26 . 101 E8
Leventhorpe Ct 1 LS26 . . 101 C5
Leventhorpe Way LS26 . . 101 C5
Leveret Way WF17 . . . . 97 B1
Lever St
5 Bradford BD6 . . . . 74 A1
Todmorden OL14 . . . . 108 B5
Levita Gr BD4 . . . . 75 D4
Levita Pl
Bradford BD4 . . . . 75 E5
4 Leeds LS15 . . . . 80 F8
Lewes Fold 2 WF16 . . . . . 117 D4
Lewin Gr WF10 . . . . 125 D8
Lewis Bldgs LS29 . . . . 9 F1
Lewis Cl 19 BD13 . . . . 72 E1
Lewisham Ct LS27 . . . . 98 B4
Lewisham Gr LS27 . . . . 98 B4
Lewisham Rd HD7 . . . . 152 A1
Lewisham St LS27 . . . . 97 E3
Lewis St HX1 . . . . 203 A4
Lexington Cl BD4 . . . . 95 B8
Leybrook Croft WF9 . . . . . 181 E7
Leyburn Ave
Batley WF16 . . . . 117 E6
Brighouse HX3 . . . . 114 E8
Leyburne St BD8 . . . . 55 C1
Leyburn Gr
2 Bingley BD16 . . . . 37 A4
Shipley BD18 . . . . 55 A7
Leyburn Rd DN6 . . . . 184 F2
Leyden Rise BD15 . . . . 73 B8
Leyfield BD17 . . . . 38 B3
Leyfield Bank HD9 . . . . . . 189 C7
Ley Fleaks Rd BD10 . . . . . . 56 B7
Leygards La HD9 . . . . 170 C1
Ley La LS12 . . . . 210 A4
Leyland Croft HD2 . . . . . . 136 E6
Leyland Rd
Batley WF17 . . . . 96 E1
Castleford WF10 . . . . 125 D8
Leylands Ave BD9 . . . . 54 F3
Leylands Gr BD9 . . . . 54 F3
Leylands Ho BD21 . . . . 35 D6
Leylands La
Bradford BD9 . . . . 54 F3
Keighley BD21 . . . . 35 D6
Leylands Rd LS2 . . . . 207 A1
Leylands Terr BD9 . . . . 54 F3
Leymoor Rd HD7 . . . . 152 E5
Leys Cl BD10 . . . . 39 A1
Leysholme Cres LS12 . . . . 209 A2
Leysholme Dr LS12 . . . . . . 209 B2
Leysholme Terr LS12 . . . . 209 B2
Leysholme View LS12 . . . 209 B2
Leyside Dr BD15 . . . . 54 B1
Leys La
Boston Spa LS23 . . . . 14 C2
Emley HD8 . . . . 175 B6
Hampole DN6 . . . . 184 C2
Kirk Smeaton WF8 . . . . . . 166 C7
Knottingley WF11 . . . . 126 F1
Leys Rd WF8 . . . . 147 E6
Leys The WF9 . . . . 182 A1
Leyton Cres BD10 . . . . 56 B7
Leyton Dr BD10 . . . . 56 B7
Leyton Gr BD10 . . . . 56 B7
Leyton Terr BD10 . . . . 56 B7
Ley Top La BD15 . . . . 73 C8
Ley Top Prim Sch BD15 . . . 73 B8
Leywell Terr LS12 . . . . 209 A4
Libbey St 1 BD8 . . . . 55 C1
Library Cl HD8 . . . . 155 E3
Lichen Cl BD7 . . . . 74 A3
Lichfield Mount BD2 . . . . . 55 F4
Lichfield Rd WF12 . . . . 139 F8
Lickless Ave LS18 . . . . 41 D1
Lickless Dr LS18 . . . . 41 D1
Lickless Gdns LS18 . . . . 41 D1
Lickless Terr LS18 . . . . 41 D1
Lidgate Cl WF13 . . . . 118 C2
Lidgate Cres WF9 . . . . 182 E2
Lidgate Gdns WF13 . . . . . 118 C2
Lidgate La
Dewsbury WF13 . . . . 118 C2
Shafton S72 . . . . 180 B3
Lidget Ave BD7 . . . . 73 F5
Lidget Croft BD20 . . . . 4 C5
Lidget Green Prim Sch
BD7 . . . . 73 F6
Lidget Hill LS28 . . . . 76 E7
Lidget La WF4 . . . . 144 D1
Lidget Pl BD7 . . . . 74 A5
Lidget Rd BD20 . . . . 4 C5
Lidget St HD3 . . . . 135 B1
Lidgett Ave LS8 . . . . 204 C3
Lidgett Cres LS8 . . . . 204 C4
Lidgett Ct
Garforth LS25 . . . . 82 E6
Leeds LS8 . . . . 204 C4
Lidget Terr
Bradford BD14 . . . . 73 D4
Bradford, Scholemoor BD7 . 73 F5
Lidgett Gr LS8 . . . . 204 C3
Lidgett Hill LS8 . . . . 204 C3
Lidgett La
Garforth LS25 . . . . 82 E6
Leeds LS8 . . . . 204 C3
Skelmanthorpe HD8 . . . . . 174 F1
Lidgett Mount LS8 . . . . 43 F1
Lidgett Park Ave LS8 . . . . . 44 A1
Lidgett Park Ct LS8 . . . . . . 43 F1
Lidgett Park Gdns LS8 . . 204 C4
Lidgett Park Gr LS8 . . . . . 204 C4
Lidgett Park Mews LS8 . . . 44 A1
Lidgett Park Rd LS8 . . . . . . 44 A1
Lidgett Park View LS8 . . . . 43 F1
Lidgett Pl LS8 . . . . 204 C4
Lidgett Rise HD8 . . . . 174 F1
Lidgett Twrs LS8 . . . . 43 E1
Lidgett Way S71 . . . . 179 C5
Lidgett Wlk LS8 . . . . 204 C3
Lifton Pl LS2 . . . . 206 A2
Light Bank La BD20 . . . . 6 C3
Lightcliffe CE Prim Sch
HX3 . . . . 114 E8
Lightcliffe Prep Sch
HX3 . . . . 114 D7
Lightcliffe Rd
Brighouse HD6 . . . . 115 A4
Huddersfield HD4 . . . . 153 D4
Lightcliffe Royd La HX4 . 133 C6
Lightenfield La HD4 . . . . . 171 D7
Lightfoot Ave WF10 . . . . . 124 E6
Lightfoot Cl WF10 . . . . . . 124 D6
Lighthazles Chapel Rd
HX6 . . . . 132 A6
Lighthazles Rd HX6 . . . . . 132 B6
Lighthouse OL15 . . . . 129 C1
Lighthouse The 5 HD3 . . 153 D7
Light La WF2 . . . . 141 E8
Lightowler Cl 10 HX1 . . . . 202 C3
Lightowler Rd HX1 . . . . . . 202 C3
Lightowler St 10 BD6 . . . . . 74 C1
Lightridge Cl HD2 . . . . 136 A4
Lightridge Rd HD2 . . . . 135 F5
Light The LS1 . . . . 211 C4
Lilac Ave
Knottingley WF11 . . . . 126 E2
Wakefield WF2 . . . . 142 C3
Lilac Cl
Addingham LS29 . . . . 7 A8
Brighouse HD6 . . . . 115 C3
Lilac Ct HD2 . . . . 136 F3
Lilac Gr
Bradford BD4 . . . . 75 D6
Cleckheaton BD19 . . . . 96 A1
Shipley BD18 . . . . 55 D5
Lilac St HX3 . . . . 92 A1
Lilacs The
Guiseley LS20 . . . . 22 E1
Royston S71 . . . . 179 E4
Lilac Wlk HD7 . . . . 152 E5
Liley La
Kirkheaton WF14 . . . . 155 F8
Lepton WF14 . . . . 156 C6

Lilian St BD4 . . . . .75 C3
Lillands Ave HD6 . . . . . . .114 F2
Lillands La HD6 . . . . .114 F2
Lillands Terr HD6 . . . . . . .114 F2
Lilley St WF9 . . . . .181 D6
Lilley Terr WF9 . . . . .182 B2
Lilly La HX3 . . . . .203 C2
Lilly St HX6 . . . . .112 B3
Lily Croft BD8 . . . . .55 B1
Lilycroft Prim Sch BD9 . .55 B2
Lilycroft Rd BD9 . . . . .55 B2
Lilycroft Wlk BD9 . . . . . . .55 A2
Lilygarth WF11 . . . . .126 D5
Lily St
  Bradford BD8. . . . . .55 B1
  Todmorden OL14 . . . . . .107 E8
Lilythorne Ave BD10 . . . .56 C8
Lime Ave
  Hebden Bridge HX7 . . . . .88 F3
  Holmfirth HD9 . . . . .189 C8
  Todmorden OL14 . . . . . .108 A6
Lime Cl
  Addingham LS29 . . . . .6 D8
  Keighley BD20 . . . . .18 A1
Lime Cres
  South Elmsall WF9. . . . .182 E1
  Wakefield WF2 . . . . . . .142 F1
Lime Ct BD16 . . . . .36 E6
Lime Gr
  Barnsley S71 . . . . .179 C1
  Huddersfield HD7 . . . . .152 E5
  South Elmsall WF9. . . . .182 E1
  Yeadon LS19 . . . . .40 A4
Lime Pit La WF3 . . . . . . .121 F4
Limers Gate OL14 . . . . . .106 E4
Limes Ave
  Darton S75 . . . . .178 C2
  Halifax HX3 . . . . .113 C4
Limes Cl S75 . . . . .178 C2
Lime St
  Bingley BD16 . . . . .36 F3
  Bradford BD7. . . . . .74 B4
  Cleckheaton BD19 . . . . .116 C7
  Haworth BD22 . . . . .51 C6
  Huddersfield HD1 . . . . . .153 E4
  Keighley BD21 . . . . .35 B7
  Ossett WF5 . . . . .140 E4
  Todmorden OL14. . . . . .108 A6
Limestone Trail★ BB10 . .85 E6
Lime Tree Ave
  Batley WF17 . . . . .118 A4
  Boston Spa LS23 . . . . . .30 D8
  Elland HX5 . . . . .135 A4
  Leeds LS13 . . . . .43 E2
  Pontefract WF8 . . . . . . .146 B8
Lime Tree Cl LS26. . . . . .101 D7
Lime-Tree Cres LS25. . . . .83 C1
Lime Tree Ct WF9. . . . . .181 C6
Lime Tree Gdns LS23. . . .30 E7
Lime Tree Gr BD11. . . . . .96 A4
Limetrees WF8 . . . . .126 A4
Lime Tree Sq BD18. . . . . .54 D8
Lime Vale Way HD6 . . . . .73 E1
Limewood App LS14 . . . . .62 C4
Limewood Bsns Pk LS14. .62 B6
Limewood Ct LS14 . . . . . .62 A7
Limewood Rd LS14. . . . . .62 A6
Linburn Cl S71. . . . . .179 A4
Lincoln Ave
  Batley WF16 . . . . .117 D5
  Liversedge WF15. . . . . .116 F2
Lincoln Cl 11 BD8. . . . . . .55 C1
Lincoln Cres WF9 . . . . . .183 A4
Lincoln Ct
  Huddersfield HD5 . . . . . .155 A4
  3 Pudsey LS28 . . . . .57 D2
Lincoln Dr WF15 . . . . . . .117 A2
Lincoln Gr
  Huddersfield HD5 . . . . . .155 A4
  Liversedge WF15. . . . . .116 F2
Lincoln Green Ct LS9. . . .207 B1
Lincoln Green Rd LS9 . . .207 B1
Lincoln Rd
  Bradford BD8. . . . . .74 C8
  Dewsbury WF12 . . . . . . .118 F1
  Leeds LS9 . . . . .207 B1
Lincoln St
  Bradford BD15. . . . . .73 C8
  Castleford WF10 . . . . . .124 E8
  Huddersfield HD1 . . . . . .154 C6
  Todmorden OL14. . . . . . .86 B1
  Wakefield WF2 . . . . . . .142 A7
Lincoln Twrs LS9 . . . . . .207 B1
Lincoln Way 7 HX3 . . . . .92 E1
Lincoln Wlk LS25 . . . . . . .83 C2
Lincombe Bank LS8. . . . .204 B4
Lincombe Dr LS8 . . . . . . .204 B4
Lincombe Mount LS8 . . . .204 B4
Lincombe Rise LS8. . . . . .204 B4
Lincroft Ave HD5 . . . . . . .154 E5
Lincroft Cres LS13 . . . . . .58 E3
Lincs Wold WF15 . . . . . . .116 B4
Lindale Ave WF7 . . . . . . .164 C7
Lindale Cl LS10 . . . . .99 D7
Lindale Croft WF9 . . . . . .181 E6
Lindale Garth WF2 . . . . . .120 C2
Lindale Gr WF2 . . . . .120 D1
Lindale La WF2 . . . . .120 C2
Lindale Mount WF2 . . . . .120 D1
Linden Ave
  Bradford BD3. . . . . .75 E8
  Leeds LS14 . . . . .214 B3
  Todmorden OL14 . . . . . .108 A6
Linden Cl
  Bardsey LS17. . . . . .28 D4

Linden Cl continued
  Brighouse HD6 . . . . .115 C3
  Castleford WF10 . . . . . .125 D6
  Dewsbury WF12 . . . . . . .140 B7
  Knottingley WF11 . . . . . .126 C4
Linden Ct
  Leeds LS16 . . . . .59 D7
  Rothwell LS26 . . . . .100 B4
Linden Gdns 5 LS11 . . . .214 C3
Linden Gr LS11 . . . . .214 C3
Linden Mount LS11 . . . . .214 B3
Linden Pl
  13 Hebden Bridge HX7 . . . .89 A4
  3 Leeds LS11 . . . . .214 C3
  Sowerby Bridge HX6 . . . .112 C5
Linden Rd
  Elland HX5 . . . . .134 E6
  Halifax HX3 . . . . .113 C4
  Hebden Bridge HX7 . . . . .89 A4
  Huddersfield HD2 . . . . . .135 F1
  Leeds LS11 . . . . .214 B3
  Mytholmroyd HX7 . . . . . . .89 D1
Linden Rise BD21 . . . . . . .35 E5
Linden St LS11 . . . . .214 C3
Linden Terr
  Ackworth M T WF7 . . . . .163 D5
  Leeds LS11 . . . . .214 C3
  Pontefract WF8 . . . . . . .146 C8
Linden Way LS22 . . . . . . .13 D7
Lindholm Gdns 10 BD15. .73 B8
Lindisfarne Rd BD18 . . . . .54 F7
Lindley Ave HD3 . . . . . . .135 A2
Lindley CE Inf Sch HD3. .135 B1
Lindley Dr BD7 . . . . .73 F2
Lindley Jun Sch HD3. . . .135 B1
Lindley Lo HD3 . . . . .135 B1
Lindley Moor Rd HD3 . . .134 E2
Lindley Rd
  Bradford BD5. . . . . .74 D3
  Elland HX5 . . . . .134 F4
Lindley St HD3 . . . . .153 A5
Lindon St 18 BD22 . . . . . .51 C6
Lindrick Cl
  Cudworth S72 . . . . .180 C1
  6 Normanton WF6 . . . . . .123 D1
Lindrick Gr HX2 . . . . .91 F7
Lindrick Way HX2 . . . . . . .91 F7
Lindrick Wlk HX2 . . . . . . .91 F7
Lindsay Acre WF3 . . . . . .120 A8
Lindsay Ave WF2 . . . . . . .141 C5
Lindsay Rd LS25 . . . . . . .82 F6
Lindsey Cl S70 . . . . .207 B1
Lindsey Gdns LS9 . . . . . .207 B1
Lindsey Mount LS9. . . . . .207 B1
Lindsey Rd LS9 . . . . .207 B1
Lindwell Ave 6 HX4 . . . . .134 C7
Lindwell Gr 2 HX4. . . . . .134 C7
Lindwell Pl 1 HX4. . . . . .134 C7
Linefield Rd WF17 . . . . . .118 D5
Lineham Ct WF15 . . . . . .117 A2
Lineholme Ave OL14 . . . .107 E7
Linfit Fold HD7 . . . . .170 A8
Linfit La
  Kirkburton HD8 . . . . . . .174 B8
  Lepton HD8 . . . . .156 C1
  Slaithwaite HD7. . . . . . .170 B8
Linfoot Ct LS21 . . . . .22 F7
Lingamore Leys S63 . . . .194 D1
Lingards Rd HD7. . . . . . . .169 E7
Lingard St BD1 . . . . .201 C4
Lingards Terr HD7 . . . . . .169 C6
Ling Bob HX2 . . . . .112 D8
Ling Bob Croft HX2. . . . . .91 D1
Ling Bob Jun & Inf Sch
  HX2. . . . . .112 D8
Ling Croft LS23 . . . . .30 B8
Lingcroft Gn BD5 . . . . . . .75 A2
Lingdale Rd BD6. . . . . . . .94 B5
Lingfield App LS17 . . . . . .43 B3
Lingfield Bank LS17. . . . . .43 B3
Lingfield Cl LS17 . . . . .43 C3
Lingfield Cres
  11 Bradford BD13. . . . . . .73 C2
  Leeds LS17 . . . . .43 B3
Lingfield Dr
  Cullingworth BD22. . . . . .35 A1
  Leeds LS17 . . . . .43 C3
Lingfield Gate LS17 . . . . . .43 B3
Lingfield Gdns LS17 . . . . .43 B3
Lingfield Gn LS17 . . . . . . .43 B3
Lingfield Gr
  Leeds LS17 . . . . .43 C3
  Wilsden BD15 . . . . .53 D5
Lingfield Hill LS17 . . . . . .43 B3
Lingfield Mount LS17 . . . .43 C3
Lingfield Rd
  Leeds LS17 . . . . .43 C3
  Wilsden BD15 . . . . .53 C5
Lingfield Terr BD13. . . . . .73 C2
Lingfield View LS17 . . . . . .43 B3
Lingfield Wlk LS17 . . . . . .43 B3
Ling La LS14 . . . . .45 B7
Lingmell Cres 7 BD4 . . . . .75 F2
Ling Park App BD15. . . . . .53 C4
Ling Park Ave BD15. . . . . .53 C4
Ling Royd Ave HX2. . . . . .112 D8
Lings La DN6 . . . . .184 A8
Lingwell App 4 LS10 . . . . .99 C4
Lingwell Ave LS10. . . . . . .99 C5
Lingwell Chase WF3 . . . . .121 C6
Lingwell Cres LS10. . . . . .99 C5
Lingwell Ct
  Lofthouse Gate WF3 . . . .121 A5
  Middleton LS10 . . . . .99 C4
Lingwell Gate Cres WF1. .121 B5
Lingwell Gate Dr WF1 . . .121 B5

Lingwell Gate La
  East Ardsley WF3 . . . . . .120 F8
  Lofthouse Gate WF1 . . . .121 A6
  Middleton WF3 . . . . .99 F2
Lingwell Gdns 3 LS10 . . . .99 C4
Lingwell Gn 6 LS10. . . . . .99 C4
Lingwell Gr LS10. . . . . . . .99 C4
Lingwell Mews 7 LS10. . . .99 C4
Lingwell Nook La
  Lofthouse Gate, Lingwell Gate
    WF3 . . . . .121 A8
  Lofthouse Gate WF3 . . . .121 C6
Lingwell Park Ct LS10. . . .99 C5
Lingwell Rd LS10 . . . . . . .99 C4
Lingwell View 2 LS10. . . . .99 C4
Lingwell Wlk 5 LS10. . . . . .99 C4
Lingwood Ave BD8. . . . . .54 F1
Lingwood Cl HD9 . . . . . . .189 D7
Lingwood Rd BD8. . . . . . .73 F8
Lingwood Terr 1 BD8 . . . .73 F8
Link Rd
  Dewsbury WF12 . . . . . . .139 D7
  Huddersfield HD1 . . . . . .153 D6
  Wakefield WF1 . . . . .216 A4
Links Ave BD19 . . . . .95 D2
Links The
  Crigglestone WF4 . . . . . .159 E4
  Featherstone WF7. . . . . .124 D1
  Leeds LS11 . . . . .99 A7
Links View S75 . . . . .178 B2
Link The
  Pontefract WF8 . . . . . . .146 C6
  Swillington LS26 . . . . . . .81 F1
Linkway BD16 . . . . .54 A7
Linnburn Mews LS29. . . . . .8 B3
Linnet Cl BD8 . . . . .73 C7
Linnet Ct
  Mirfield WF14 . . . . .138 A8
  Morley LS27. . . . . .98 C8
Linnet Gr WF2 . . . . .160 D5
Linnet St BD21. . . . . .35 C8
Linnhe Ave BD6. . . . . .93 F6
Linshaws Rd HD9 . . . . . .198 E5
Linthwaite Ardron CE Jun &
  Inf Sch HD7 . . . . .152 E1
Linthwaite Bsns Ctr HD7 .152 D1
Linthwaite Clough Jun & Inf
  Sch HD7 . . . . .152 D1
Linton Ave
  Batley WF17 . . . . .118 A5
  Leeds LS17 . . . . .43 F4
  Silsden BD20 . . . . .5 E2
  Wetherby LS22 . . . . .13 D6
Linton Cl
  Leeds LS17 . . . . .43 E4
  Liversedge WF15 . . . . . .116 F5
Linton Comm LS22 . . . . . .13 A1
Linton Cres LS17. . . . . . . .43 F4
Linton Croft 3 LS16 . . . . .59 A8
Linton Dr LS17. . . . . .43 E4
Linton Gr
  Batley WF16 . . . . .117 E3
  Brighouse HD6 . . . . .135 E8
  Leeds LS17 . . . . .43 F4
Linton Hills Rd LS22. . . . . .13 C4
Linton La
  Linton LS22 . . . . .13 C4
  Spofforth LS22. . . . . .13 A7
Linton Mdws LS22 . . . . . . .13 C5
Linton Rd
  Collingham LS22 . . . . . . .13 B1
  Leeds LS17 . . . . .43 E4
  Wakefield WF1 . . . . .142 F6
  Wetherby LS22 . . . . .13 D5
Linton Rise
  Leeds LS17 . . . . .43 E4
  9 Normanton WF6 . . . . . .123 D1
Linton St
  Bradford BD4. . . . . .74 F4
  Keighley BD22 . . . . .34 F5
Linton View LS17 . . . . . . .43 E5
Lion Cott S75 . . . . .193 E4
Lion Ct LS29 . . . . .9 F1
Lion St BD22 . . . . .51 C7
Lion Ct LS12 . . . . .209 A3
Lionel St WF5 . . . . .140 E4
Lion St OL14 . . . . .108 A4
Liphill Bank Rd HD9. . . . .188 D4
Lippersley La LS29. . . . . . .6 B6
Lipscomb St HD3 . . . . . . .153 B5
Liquorice Way WF8 . . . . .146 C8
Lisbon Sq 6 LS1. . . . . . . .211 A4
Lisbon St LS1. . . . . .211 A4
Lisheen Ave WF10 . . . . . .124 C6
Lisheen Gr WF10. . . . . . . .124 C7
Lisker Ave LS21 . . . . .23 B7
Lisker Ct LS21 . . . . .23 B7
Lisker Dr LS21 . . . . .23 B7
Lismore Cl LS26 . . . . .100 F5
Lismore Rd BD20 . . . . . . .35 B8
Lissett Mews BD20 . . . . . .19 A1
Lister's Rd
  Halifax HX3 . . . . .113 E8
  Huddersfield HD2 . . . . . .136 B3
Lister Ave BD4. . . . . .75 B3
Lister Cl WF7 . . . . .145 C5
Lister Ct HX1 . . . . .203 B3
Listerdale WF15 . . . . .117 B5
Lister Gdns 1 BD8 . . . . . .55 C2
Lister Hill
  Horsforth LS18 . . . . .41 C2
  Sutton-in-C BD20. . . . . . .16 D4
Lister La
  Bradford BD2. . . . . .56 A3
  Halifax HX1 . . . . .202 C3

Lister Lane Sch BD2 . . . . .56 A3
Lister Rd WF7 . . . . .145 C5
Listers Ct LS29 . . . . .8 A4
Lister St
  Bradford, Dudley Hill BD4 . .75 C2
  Bradford, Tong Street BD4 . .75 E1
  Brighouse HD6 . . . . .115 A3
  Castleford WF10 . . . . . . .124 C8
  Halifax HX1 . . . . .203 B3
  Huddersfield HD5 . . . . . .154 C5
  Ilkley LS29 . . . . .8 A4
  Keighley BD21 . . . . .35 B6
Lister View BD8. . . . . .55 C1
Lister Ville BD15. . . . . . . .53 C5
Lister Wlk LS27 . . . . .97 F6
Listing Ave WF15 . . . . . . .117 B5
Listing Ct WF15 . . . . .117 B5
Listing Dr WF15. . . . . . . .117 B5
Listing La BD19, WF15 . . .117 B6
Litchfield Ct 12 BD5 . . . . .74 E3
Litell Royd WF7. . . . . . . .144 D5
Litherop La HD8 . . . . . . .176 C5
Litherop Rd S75 . . . . .176 D3
Little Baines St HX1. . . . .202 C3
Littlebeck Dr BD16. . . . . . .37 C3
Little Bradley HX4 . . . . . .134 C6
Little Brunswick St 6
  HD1 . . . . .154 A7
Little Cake HD9. . . . . . . .189 C2
Little Church La LS26 . . . .102 C2
Little Cote BD10 . . . . .39 A1
Little Cross St 1 BD5 . . . . .74 E2
Little Fountain St LS27 . . . .98 A3
Little Green La WF16. . . . .117 C5
Little Hallas HD8. . . . . . . .173 F6
Little Hemsworth WF9 . . .181 E6
Little Hew Royd 3 BD10 . . .38 F1
Littleholme St OL14 . . . . .108 A3
Little Horton Gn BD5. . . . .74 D5
Little Horton La
  Bradford BD5. . . . . .201 B2
  Bradford, Holme Top BD5 . .74 D4
Little John Cres WF2. . . . .141 E4
Little King St LS1 . . . . . . .211 B3
Little La
  Bradford BD9. . . . . .54 F1
  Holmfirth HD9 . . . . .188 F5
  Holmfirth, Wooldale HD9. .189 C6
  Ilkley LS29 . . . . .8 C4
  Keighley BD20 . . . . .19 E1
  7 Morley LS27. . . . . .98 C8
  Purston Jaglin WF7. . . . .145 E4
  South Elmsall WF9. . . . . .183 B3
  Upton WF9 . . . . .183 B7
  Wadsworth Moor HX7. . . .69 B6
Littlelands BD16 . . . . .54 A7
Little Lane Ct 8 LS27 . . . . .98 C8
Little Lepton HD8 . . . . . . .156 A2
Little London
  Linthwaite HD7 . . . . .170 C7
  Northowram HX3. . . . . . .92 F4
Little London Com Prim Sch
  LS7 . . . . .206 C2
Little Moor BD13. . . . . . . .73 A1
Littlemoor Cres LS28 . . . . .76 E5
Littlemoor Cres S LS28 . . .76 E5
Littlemoor Ct LS28 . . . . . .76 F6
Littlemoor Gdns
  Halifax HX2 . . . . .91 E6
  Pudsey LS28 . . . . .76 E5
Littlemoor Gr WF14 . . . . .137 F5
Littlemoor La LS14 . . . . . .45 F5
Little Moor Pl LS12. . . . . .209 B3
Littlemoor Rd
  Halifax HX2 . . . . .91 E6
  2 Mirfield WF14 . . . . . . .137 F5
  Pudsey LS28 . . . . .76 F6
Littlemoor View LS28 . . . . .76 F6
Little Neville St LS1 . . . . .211 B3
Little Pk BD10 . . . . .39 F1
Little Preston Hall
  Residential Pk LS26 . . . .82 B1
Little Queen St LS1 . . . . .211 A4
Little St BD22 . . . . .51 C7
Little Stubb HX7 . . . . .89 C1
Littlethorpe Hill WF15. . . .116 D1
Littlethorpe Rd WF15 . . . .116 D2
Littletown Jun & Inf Sch
  WF15 . . . . .117 A6
Littleway 11 LS17 . . . . . . .43 C1
Little Westfields S71. . . . .179 A4
Littlewood HX7 . . . . .110 C1
Littlewood Cl BD6. . . . . . .94 C7
Littlewood Croft HD4 . . . .154 A2
Little Wood Dr BD19 . . . . .95 D2
Little Woodhouse HD6 . . .115 A2
Little Woodhouse St
  LS2. . . . . .206 A1
Litton Croft WF1 . . . . . . .142 F7
Littondale Cl BD17 . . . . . .38 E4
Litton Rd BD22. . . . . .35 A6
Litton Way LS14 . . . . .62 B8
Litton Wlk S72 . . . . .180 C3
Liversedge Hall La WF15 .117 A3
Liversedge Row 5 BD7 . . .74 A3
Livingstone Cl BD2. . . . . . .55 F6
Livingstone Rd
  Bradford BD2. . . . . .55 F5
  Shipley BD2 . . . . .55 D4
Livingstone St N HX2. . . . .92 A5
Livingstone St 11 HX3. . . .92 A1
Livinia Gr LS7. . . . . .206 C2

Lloyds Dr BD12. . . . . .94 E1
Lloyd St OL14 . . . . .108 B1
Lobley St WF16. . . . . . . .117 E1
Locarno Ave BD9. . . . . . . .54 E1
Locherbie Gn BD15 . . . . . .54 E1
Lochy Rd BD6. . . . . .93 F8
Lockbridge Way HD3. . . . .153 E2
Lock La
  Castleford WF10 . . . . . .103 C1
  Normanton WF6 . . . . . . .122 F4
Lockside Rd LS10 . . . . . . .80 A4
Locksley Rd HD6. . . . . . . .115 D8
Lock St
  Dewsbury WF12 . . . . . . .139 D8
  Halifax HX3 . . . . .203 C3
  Todmorden OL14 . . . . . .108 A4
Locks The BD16. . . . . .36 F4
Lock View
  Bingley BD16 . . . . .36 F4
  Halifax HX5 . . . . .135 A4
Lock Way WF13. . . . . . . .138 E1
Lockwood's Yd 21 HD1. . .154 A4
Lockwood Ave WF14 . . . .138 E2
Lockwood Cl
  Huddersfield HD3 . . . . . .153 D1
  Leeds LS11 . . . . .214 B3
Lockwood Ct LS11 . . . . . .214 C2
Lockwood Pk LS11 . . . . . .214 C2
Lockwood Rd HD1 . . . . . .153 F4
Lockwood Scar HD4 . . . . .154 A1
Lockwood St
  Bradford, Brownroyd Hill
    BD6. . . . . .74 C7
  Bradford, Raw Nook BD12 . .94 B1
  5 Shipley BD18 . . . . .54 F8
Lockwood Sta HD1. . . . . .153 E4
Lockwood Way LS11 . . . . .214 C2
Lode Pit La BD16. . . . . . . .37 D2
Lodge Ave
  Castleford WF10 . . . . . .125 C7
  Elland HX5 . . . . .135 C4
Lodge Cl HD4. . . . . .153 E1
Lodge Dr
  Elland HX5 . . . . .135 C4
  Mirfield WF14 . . . . .138 C2
Lodge Farm Cl WF12. . . . .139 C2
Lodge Farm Gdns WF6 . . .122 F1
Lodge Gate BD13 . . . . . . .52 E3
Lodge Gate Cl BD13. . . . . .52 E3
Lodge Hill
  9 Addingham LS29 . . . . . . .6 E8
  Baildon BD17 . . . . .37 F2
Lodge Hill Cl LS12 . . . . . .77 E6
Lodge Hill Rd WF5 . . . . . .140 E3
Lodge Hill Wlk LS12. . . . . .77 E6
Lodge La
  Crofton WF4 . . . . .143 E1
  Leeds LS11 . . . . .214 A2
  Liversedge WF15 . . . . . .117 C4
  Wakefield WF2 . . . . .160 A5
Lodge Pl HX5 . . . . .135 C4
Lodge Rd
  Bradford BD10. . . . . .39 C3
  Pudsey LS28 . . . . .76 D2
Lodge Row 5 LS15 . . . . . .62 C2
Lodges Cl WF4. . . . . .162 C2
Lodge St
  Cullingworth BD13. . . . . . .52 D6
  Glusburn BD20 . . . . .16 E7
  Haworth BD22. . . . . .51 C6
  Hemsworth WF9 . . . . . . .181 C6
  Leeds LS2 . . . . .206 A1
  Skelmanthorpe HD8 . . . . .175 A1
Lodge Terr 13 LS11 . . . . .214 B3
Lodge The HD7 . . . . .152 E8
Lodore Ave BD2 . . . . .56 B1
Lodore Pl BD2 . . . . .56 B1
Lodore Rd BD2 . . . . .56 B1
Lofthouse Gate Prim Sch
  WF1 . . . . .121 C7
Lofthouse Pl LS2. . . . . . .206 B1
Lofthouse Terr LS2 . . . . . .206 C1
Loft St BD8 . . . . .73 F7
Logwood St HD1. . . . . . .154 A7
Loiner Ct LS9. . . . . .80 C7
Lombardi Ct WF5 . . . . . . .140 F7
Lombard St
  Halifax HX1 . . . . .202 C2
  Leeds LS15 . . . . .80 E7
  Yeadon LS19 . . . . .40 A4
Lombardy Cl HD9 . . . . . . .171 F7
Lombardy Garth WF2 . . . .142 A6
Lomond Ave LS18. . . . . . .41 B8
Londesboro Gr LS9 . . . . . .80 A3
Londesboro Terr LS9. . . . .80 A3
London La LS19. . . . . .40 A4
London Rd
  Slaithwaite HD7. . . . . . .152 A3
  Sowerby Bridge HX6 . . . .112 B1
  Todmorden OL14 . . . . . .109 C2
London Spring Rd HX6 . . .132 A2
London St LS19 . . . . .40 A4
Longacre WF10 . . . . .124 D8
Long Acre S71 . . . . .179 B5
Longacre La BD22. . . . . . .51 C3
Longacres BD22 . . . . .51 C3
Longbottom Ave
  Silsden BD20 . . . . .5 F1
  Sowerby Bridge HX6 . . . .111 E4
Longbottom Terr HX3 . . . .113 D3
Longbow Ave LS26. . . . . .102 C2
Longbow Cl HD2. . . . . . .136 C3
Longcauseway WF12 . . . .139 C2
Long Cl BD12. . . . . .94 E4
Long Cliffe Cl S72. . . . . . .180 C2
Longclose Ind Est LS9. . . .207 B3

ong Close La
Leeds LS9 212 C3
Shepley HD8 190 C7
South Elmsall WF9 183 C6
ong Crest WF8 146 E6
ongcroft
Huddersfield HD5 154 F2
Keighley BD21 35 C6
ong Croft S75 178 B1
ongcroft Link [3] BD1 74 D7
ongcroft Pl BD1 201 A3
ongcroft Rd LS29 8 E3
ong Croft St HD7 152 E4
ong Cswy
Blackshaw Head HX7 87 E4
Denholme BD13 71 C8
Dewsbury WF12 139 D3
Halton East BD23 1 D7
Leeds, Adel LS16 42 D3
Leeds LS9 212 C1
Lofthouse Gate WF3 121 F5
Ripponden HX6 131 F1
Todmorden OL14 108 F3
Wakefield WF1 216 C4
ong Cswy The
Holme Chapel BB10 85 D7
Mytholmroyd HX2 111 A6
ongdale Dr WF9 182 E4
ong Dam La WF4 162 B3
ongden Ave HD4 153 D2
ongdike Ct [7] LS25 83 B1
ongdike La LS25 103 C8
ongdon Ave HD8 155 E3
ongdon Wlk HD8 155 E3
ong Edge Low Rd HX6 111 B2
ong Edge Rd HX6 111 A3
ong Fallas Cres HD6 136 B8
ongfellow Ct [3] HX7 89 E1
ongfellow Gr WF3 121 E6
ongfield
Elland HX4 134 B4
Heptonstall HX7 88 F4
Longfield Ave
Huddersfield, Grove Place HD5 154 D7
Huddersfield, Leymoor HD7 152 E5
Northowram HX3 93 A1
[3] Pudsey LS28 76 F7
Longfield Cl
Huddersfield HD5 154 D7
Todmorden OL14 108 B4
Longfield Ct
Batley WF16 117 E4
Pudsey LS28 76 F7
Longfield Dr
Ackworth M T WF7 164 C7
Bradford BD4 75 C3
Darton S75 178 B1
Leeds LS13 81 A8
Pudsey LS13 57 F5
Longfield Garth LS13 57 F5
Longfield Gr
[2] Pudsey LS28 76 F7
Todmorden OL14 108 B4
Longfield La OL14 108 B3
Longfield Mount [1] LS28 76 F7
Longfield Rd
Batley WF16 117 D4
Pudsey LS28 76 E7
Todmorden OL14 108 B5
Longfield Rise OL14 108 B4
Longfield Terr
Northowram HX3 93 A1
Pudsey LS28 76 E7
Todmorden OL14 108 B4
Wakefield WF2 141 F7
Longfield Way OL14 108 B4
Longford Terr BD7 73 F5
Long Gate
Ripponden HX6 150 A8
Sutton-in-C BD20, BD22 33 B8
Long Grove Ave HD5 154 E6
Long Hey La OL14 108 C3
Long Heys HX4 134 C6
Long Hill Rd HD2 136 C4
Longhouse Dr BD13 71 D8
Longhouse La BD13 71 D8
Long House Rd HX2 91 C6
Long Ing HD9 188 D4
Long Ing Rd HD9 199 A7
Long La
Ackworth M T WF7 146 B1
Barwick in E LS15 63 E5
Bradford BD15 53 D1
Clayton West HD8 175 F3
Dewsbury WF12 139 F6
Flockton WF4 156 E1
Halifax, Bank Top HX3 113 F6
Halifax HX3 113 F6
Halifax, Wheatley HX2, HX3 91 E2
Harden BD16 36 A1
Hebden Bridge, Cragg Vale HX7 109 D3
Hebden Bridge HX7 88 E1
Honley HD9 172 A3
Huddersfield HD5 154 E7
Kirk Smeaton WF8 166 D3
Pontefract WF7, WF8 146 F7
Queensbury BD13 92 E7
Shepley HD8 190 E8
Shepley, Thunder Bridge HD8 173 E3
Shipley BD9 54 E5
Sowerby Bridge HX6 112 A2
Longlands Ave
Denholme BD13 52 D1
Slaithwaite HD7 151 E1
Longlands Bank HD9 189 B8
Longlands Cl WF5 140 E6
Longlands Dr BD22 51 D8
Longlands La LS22 12 D4
Longlands Rd
Batley WF13 118 A2
Ossett WF5 140 E6
Slaithwaite HD7 151 E1
Longlands St BD1 201 A3
Longlands Trad Est WF5 140 E6
Long Lee La BD21 35 E5
Long Lee Prim Sch BD21 35 E6
Longley Ct HD4 154 C3
Longley Edge La HD9 189 B1
Longley Edge Rd HD9 189 B1
Longley La
Holmfirth HD9 189 A1
Huddersfield HD4 154 D2
Sowerby Bridge HX6 111 F1
Longley Rd HD5 154 D4
Longley Sch HD5 154 C4
Long Lover La HX1, HX2 202 B4
Long Mdw WF7 146 A1
Long Mdws
Bradford BD2 55 E4
Bramhope LS16 24 E2
Burley in W LS29 9 F2
Garforth LS25 82 F5
Longmeadow HX4 133 A5
Long Meadow Ct LS25 83 A5
Long Meadow Gate LS25 82 F5
Long Moor La HD8 174 B1
Long Preston Chase BD10 56 D7
Long Reach HX2 91 A3
Long Riddings LS29 2 E1
Long Ridge HD6 136 A7
Long Row
Bradford BD12 94 D5
Crofton WF4 144 A5
Horsforth LS18 41 C2
Thornton BD13 72 C7
Long Row Ct [2] BD5 74 E3
Longroyd [1] BD10 55 F8
Longroyd Ave LS11 214 C3
Longroyd Cres
Leeds LS11 214 C3
Slaithwaite HD7 151 E1
Longroyd Cres N LS11 214 C3
Long Royd Dr BD17 38 E4
Longroyde Cl HD6 114 F1
Longroyde Gr HD6 135 F8
Longroyde Jun Sch HD6 114 F1
Longroyde Rd [3] HD6 115 A1
Longroyd Farm WF4 158 B7
Longroyd Gr LS11 214 C3
Longroyd La HD1 153 F5
Long Royd La HD8 191 B8
Longroyd Pl
Huddersfield HD1 153 E5
Leeds LS11 214 C3
Long Royd Rd HX6 111 C2
Longroyd St N LS11 214 C3
Longroyd St LS11 214 C3
Longroyd Terr LS11 214 C3
Longroyd View LS11 214 C3
Long Shaw La OL14 108 F4
Longside La BD7 74 C6
Longsight Rd S75 178 A1
Longsight Terr WF9 163 B1
Long St BD4 75 B5
Longstaff Ct HX7 88 E3
Long Thorpe La WF3 100 B1
Long Tongue Scrog La
Kirkheaton HD5 155 E7
Lepton HD5 155 F6
Long Wall HX5 134 E6
Longwood Ave BD16 36 E5
Longwood Cl
East Ardsley WF3 119 D8
Halifax HX3 113 B3
Leeds LS17 44 B5
Longwood Cres LS17 44 B5
Longwood Ct WF3 119 E8
Longwood Edge Rd HD3 152 E8
Longwood Fold WF3 119 E8
Longwood Garth WF3 119 E8
Longwood Gate HD3 152 F6
Longwood House Rd HD2 136 A3
Longwood Rd
East Ardsley WF3 119 E8
Huddersfield HD3 153 C5
Longwoods Wlk WF11 127 A5
Longwood Vale WF3 119 E8
Longwood View BD16 36 E5
Longwood Way LS17 44 B5
Longworth Rd WF9 181 D6
Lonk House La BD17 38 F4
Lonsbrough Ave WF16 117 D5
Lonsbrough Flats [7] HD1 154 B6
Lonsbrough Way WF9 183 A4
Lonsdale Ave [3] WF17 117 F7
Lonsdale Cl LS10 215 A1
Lonsdale Mdws LS23 30 D7
Lonsdale Rd WF1 216 A4
Lonsdale Rise WF3 119 E8
Lonsdale St BD3 75 B8
Lonsdale Terr [8] WF15 117 A4
Lord's Bldgs [7] LS27 98 A2
Lord's La HD6 115 B1
Lord La BD22 51 B8
Lordsfield Pl BD4 75 D1
Lord St
Batley WF13 117 F4
Dewsbury WF12 140 B7
Halifax HX1 203 B3
Lord St *continued*
[13] Haworth BD22 51 D7
Huddersfield HD1 154 B6
Keighley BD21 35 C7
Leeds LS12 210 C2
Slaithwaite HD7 151 F1
Sowerby Bridge HX6 112 C5
Wakefield WF1 142 F3
Walsden OL14 108 A1
Lord Terr LS12 210 C2
Loris St BD4 75 D1
Lorna Cotts WF8 125 D3
Lorne St
Bradford BD4 75 B3
[2] Haworth BD22 51 F8
Keighley BD21 35 E8
Lorry Bank LS7 206 C4
Loscoe Cl WF6 123 E3
Loscoe La
Featherstone WF6, WF7 124 A1
Normanton WF6 123 E2
Lothersdale Rd BD20 16 A7
Lotherton Hall* LS25 65 B5
Lotherton La
Aberford LS25 65 A6
Aberford LS25 65 B5
Lotherton Rd WF9 181 E7
Lotherton Way LS25 83 A8
Lot St BD22 51 D7
Loughrigg St BD5 74 E3
Loughrigg Wlk WF7 163 E6
Louisa St
Bradford BD10 56 B8
Castleford WF10 124 C8
Louis Ave BD5 74 C4
Louis Ct LS7 207 A3
Louis Gr LS7 207 B3
Louis Le Prince Ct LS8 207 C3
Louis St LS7 207 B3
Lound La DN5 195 F5
Lovaine Gr WF2 142 D1
Love La
Castleford WF10 124 C6
Halifax HX1 203 A1
Ossett WF5 140 C6
Pontefract WF8 146 B8
Rothwell LS26 100 E5
Wakefield WF2 216 A2
Love Lane Terr WF8 146 C8
Lovell Park Cl LS7 207 A1
Lovell Park Ct LS7 206 C1
Lovell Park Gate LS7 206 C1
Lovell Park Grange LS7 207 A1
Lovell Park Hill LS7 207 A1
Lovell Park Hts LS7 207 A1
Lovell Park Mews LS7 207 A1
Lovell Park Rd LS2, LS7 206 C1
Lovell Park Twrs LS7 206 C1
Lovell Park View LS7 207 A1
Lovell View WF4 162 A8
Low Ash Ave BD18 55 D7
Low Ash Cres BD18 55 D7
Low Ash Dr BD18 55 D7
Low Ash Gr BD18 55 D7
Low Ash Prim Sch BD18 55 D6
Low Ash Rd BD18 55 E7
Low Bank Dr BD22 34 B3
Low Bank La BD22 34 B2
Low Bank St LS28 57 D3
Low Beck LS29 8 D5
Low Cl
Bingley BD16 37 B2
Ilkley LS29 8 B5
Low Cliff Wlk WF16 117 E2
Low Close St LS2 206 A3
Low Comm
Huddersfield HD4 154 F1
Mickletown LS26 123 E8
Lowcroft LS22 29 A8
Low Croft S71 179 D3
Low Croft Ct LS16 24 E3
Low Cross Ct WF11 127 A5
Lowdale WF12 118 E2
Lowell Ave BD7 73 F5
Lowell Gr LS13 77 A8
Lowell Pl LS13 77 A8
Lower Ashgrove BD5 74 D6
Lower Back La HX7 87 F4
Lower Bank Ho HX4 133 D4
Lower Bankhouse LS28 76 D4
Lower Basinghall St LS1 211 B3
Lower Bentley Royd HX6 112 A4
Lower Bower La [1] WF13 117 F2
Lower Brig Royd HX6 132 E4
Lower Brockwell La HX6 111 F2
Lower Brunswick St LS2 207 A1
Lower Calderbrook OL15 129 C1
Lower Cambridge St WF10 124 E8
Lower Clay Pits HX1 202 B4
Lower Clifton St [11] HX6 112 C4
Lower Clyde St HX6 112 B3
Lower Collier Fold S75 193 F5
Lower Common La HD8 175 E1
Lower Constable Rd LS29 8 D3
Lower Copy BD15 54 B1
Lower Cross St
[1] Dewsbury WF13 118 C1
Halifax HX1 203 C3
Lower Crow Nest Dr HX3 115 B7
Lower Denby La HD8 192 B4
Lower Edge Rd HD6, HX5 135 D7
Lower Exley HX3 113 D1
Lower Ferney Lee OL14 108 A6
Lower Fields Prim Sch BD4 75 C4
Lower Finkil St HD6 114 F5
Lower Fitzwilliam St [4] HD1 154 B7
Lower Fleet BD13 72 D1
Lower Fold
Brighouse HD6 135 F6
Honley HD9 171 F5
Lower Gate HD3 153 C5
Lower George St
[5] Bradford BD6 74 B1
[5] Todmorden OL14 108 C5
Lower Globe St BD8 74 C8
Lower Gn [2] BD17 38 B2
Lower Grange HD2 136 E6
Lower Grange Cl BD8 73 C7
Lower Grattan Rd [6] BD1 74 D7
Lower Greave Rd HD9 188 B8
Lower Green Ave [11] BD19 115 F8
Lower Hagg HD9 172 B1
Lower Hall Cl WF15 116 F4
Lower Hall Cres HD5 155 C6
Lower Hall Dr WF15 116 F4
Lower Hall La WF15 116 F4
Lower Hall Mount WF15 116 F4
Lower Hall Rd HD5 155 C6
Lower Hathershelf HX2 111 A8
Lower Haughs HD7 152 B5
Lower Heights Farm BD21 35 C1
Lower Heights Rd BD13 72 C8
Lower Hey HD9 170 D3
Lower Holme
Baildon BD17 38 C1
Slaithwaite HD7 169 D8
Lower House Cl [2] BD10 55 F8
Lower House La HD8 156 B2
Lowerhouses HD7 152 E2
Lowerhouses CE Jun & Inf Sch HD5 154 D3
Lowerhouses La HD5 154 D3
Lowerhouses Rd HD3 153 B6
Lower Kipping La [10] BD13 72 D6
Lower Kirkgate
Bradford BD1 201 C3
Halifax HX1 203 C3
Lower La
Birkenshaw BD4 95 D5
Blackshaw Head HX7 87 E3
Bradford BD4 75 C4
Cleckheaton BD19 117 B7
Honley HD9 171 E4
Lower Laith Ave OL14 108 C5
Lower Langwith LS22 29 A8
Lower Lark Hill BD19 116 B7
Lower Maythorn La HD9 200 D8
Lower Mdws HD9 188 D5
Lower Mickletown LS26 102 F3
Lower Mill Bank Rd HX6 132 D7
Lower Mill Mews HD9 170 C2
Lower Newlands HD6 115 B1
Lower Northcroft WF9 183 A3
Lower Northfield La WF9 182 C3
Lower North St WF17 118 B4
Lower Oxford St WF10 124 D7
Lower Park Gn BD20 5 C1
Lower Park Royd Dr HX6 132 E6
Lower Peel St WF13 118 C1
Lower Pk HD4 172 A7
Lower Putting Mill HD8 192 B7
Lower Quarry Rd HD2, HD5 137 A6
Lower Range [9] HX3 92 C1
Lower Rayleigh St BD4 75 A5
Lower Rd HX4 150 F5
Lower Reins HD9 172 A6
Lower Rushton Rd BD3 75 E7
Lower Saltonstall HX2 90 D5
Lower Sandhills LS14 45 E3
Lower Scholes BD22 50 F8
Lower School St
Bradford BD12 94 C6
[3] Shipley BD18 54 F8
Lower Skircoat La HX3 113 C2
Lower Slack HX2 90 F6
Lower Slaids HD7 152 F1
Lower Smithy HX7 88 A5
Lower Station Rd WF6 123 A2
Lower Sunny Bank Ct HD9 170 C2
Lower Swift Pl HX6 132 B2
Lower Taythes La WF8 126 A1
Lower Tofts Rd LS28 76 E7
Lower Top of Hill HX4 150 F6
Lowertown BD22 51 C2
Lower Town End Rd HD9 189 C7
Lower Town Mills [11] BD22 51 C2
Lower Town St LS13 58 D2
Lower Viaduct St [2] HD1 154 B7
Lower Warrengate WF1 216 C2
Lower Wellgate [3] HX4 134 C7
Lower Wellhouse Rd HD7 152 D3
Lower Wellington Rd LS29 8 B4
Lower Westfield Rd [3] BD9 55 A1
Lower Wheat Royd HD5 154 F2
Lower Whitegate Rd HD4 154 B3
Lower Whiteshaw Mews BD13 52 D2
Lower Wormald HX6 131 F1
Lower Wortley Prim Sch LS12 78 B4
Lower Wortley Rd LS12 209 B1
Lower Wyke Gn BD12 115 B8
Lower Wyke La BD12 115 C8
Lower York Ct WF1 216 B3
Lower York St WF1 216 B3
Loweswater Ave BD6 93 F6
Loweswater Rd WF11 126 E2
Low Farm LS26 102 E8
Low Farm Gdns WF9 183 B7
Low Farm La WF7 164 A6
Lowfield Cl BD12 94 E5
Lowfield Cres
Hemsworth WF9 181 E7
Silsden BD20 17 F8
Lowfield La BD23 3 A4
Lowfield Rd
Dewsbury WF13 138 F8
Hemsworth WF9 181 F7
Low Fields Ave LS11 213 B4
Lowfields Bsns Pk HX5 135 A8
Lowfields Cl HX5 135 A8
Lowfields Rd LS11 213 B4
Low Fields Rd LS12 213 B4
Lowfields Way HX5 135 A8
Low Fields Way LS11 213 B4
Low Fold
Baildon BD17 38 C4
Bradford BD2 55 F2
Brighouse BD19 115 F8
Denby Dale HD8 191 E7
Denholme BD13 52 D2
Kirkburton HD4 172 F1
Kirkheaton HD5 155 B8
Leeds LS9 212 B2
Queensbury BD13 72 E2
Steeton BD20 17 D5
Yeadon LS19 40 B4
Low Fold Ct HD8 191 F3
Low Gate
Holmfirth HD9 189 B4
Kirkburton HD8 173 F6
South Elmsall WF9 183 A3
Low Gate La OL3 167 A1
Low Gn
Ackworth M T WF7 164 B7
[4] Bradford BD7 74 A3
Knottingley WF11 127 B4
Yeadon LS19 40 C3
Low Grange Cres LS10 215 B1
Low Grange View LS10 99 E8
Low Green Terr BD7 74 B3
Low Hall Cl LS29 22 A4
Low Hall Pl LS11 211 A2
Low Hall Rd
Menston LS29 22 B4
Yeadon LS18 57 E8
Low Hill BD17 38 C6
Low Hills La HD3 135 A1
Low Holland WF11 105 A4
Low House Dr BD20 17 E8
Low House Farm Ct [6] BD20 17 E8
Low House Fold WF15 116 F4
Low La
Batley WF17 96 E1
Bradford BD14 73 A5
Brighouse HD6 115 C6
Draughton BD23 1 E6
Halton East BD23 1 B8
Horsforth LS18 41 D1
Middlestown WF4 158 B8
Queensbury BD13 72 C3
Silsden BD20 5 C5
Silsden BD20 18 A6
Wadsworth Moor HX2 90 A7
Low Laithes HX6 112 A3
Lowlands Rd WF14 138 B4
Low Mill La
Addingham LS29 7 B8
Dewsbury WF13 138 E4
Keighley BD21 35 D7
Low Mill Rd WF5 140 C3
Low Mills Ind Est WF13 138 D4
Low Mills Rd LS12 78 B4
Low Moor Bsns Pk BD12 94 C6
Low Moor CE Prim Sch BD12 94 E6
Low Moor Cres WF4 159 F3
Low Moor Ind Est BD12 94 D6
Low Moor La WF4 159 E1
Low Moor Side LS12 77 D3
Low Moorside Cl LS12 77 E3
Low Moorside Ct LS12 77 D3
Low Moor Side La LS12 77 C2
Low Moor St BD12 94 D6
Low Moor Terr
Halifax HX2 112 D7
Leeds LS11 214 B2
Lowood La WF17 96 F3
Low Park Rd LS29, LS21 9 B5
Low Platt La HD3 151 B5
Low Rd
Dewsbury, Dewsbury Moor WF13 138 F8
Dewsbury, Earlsheaton WF12 139 E7
Dewsbury, Overthorpe WF13 139 C1
Huddersfield HD4 171 F8
Leeds LS10 215 B4

Low Road Prim Sch
LS10 . . . . **215** B3
Low Row S75 . . . . **177** E3
Lowry Rd WF3 . . . . **119** E8
Lowry View 6 BD21 . . . **35** C6
Low Shops La LS26 . . . . **100** C6
Low Spring Rd BD21 . . . . **35** F6
Low St
Brotherton WF11 . . . . . . **126** C7
Dewsbury WF13 . . . . **118** C1
East Ardsley WF3 . . . . **98** F1
Keighley BD21 . . . . **35** C7
Lowther Ave LS25 . . . . . . **82** E6
Lowther Cres LS26 . . . . **82** A2
Lowther Dr
Garforth LS25 . . . . **82** E6
Swillington LS26 . . . . **81** F2
Lowther Gr LS25 . . . . **82** E6
Lowther Rd LS25 . . . . . . **82** E6
Lowther St
Bradford BD2 . . . . **56** B2
Leeds LS8 . . . . **207** C4
Lowther Terr LS15 . . . . . **82** A6
Lowtown LS28 . . . . **76** F8
Low Town HD8 . . . . **173** F6
Lowtown Prim Sch LS28 . . **76** F7
Low Way
Bramham LS23 . . . . **30** D2
Clifford LS23 . . . . **30** D6
Low Well Rd 4 BD5 . . . **74** D3
Low Westwood HX7 . . **152** D2
Low Whitehouse Row
LS10 . . . . **212** A1
Low Wood BD15 . . . . **53** D4
Low Wood Ct BD20 . . . . . **18** B3
Low Wood Head BD20 . . . **18** D3
Low Wood Rise LS29 . . . . . **8** F3
Loxley Cl BD2 . . . . **56** D2
Loxley Gr LS22 . . . . **13** D8
Loxley St WF17 . . . . **118** A7
Lucas Ct LS6 . . . . **206** C3
Lucas Pl LS6 . . . . **206** A4
Lucas St LS6 . . . . **206** A4
Luck La HD1, HD3 . . . . . . **153** D6
Lucy Ave LS15 . . . . **80** E8
Lucy Hall Dr BD17 . . . . . . **37** F3
Lucy La HD8 . . . . **155** E5
Lucy St HX3 . . . . **203** C4
**Luddenden Dene CE Jun &
Inf Sch** HX2 . . . . **111** D8
Luddendenfoot Jun & Inf Sch
HX2 . . . . **111** E5
Luddenden La HX2 . . . . **111** D7
Luddendon Pl 3 BD13 . . **72** C2
Luddite Ho 8 WF15 . . . . **117** A5
Ludgate Hill LS2 . . . . . . **211** C4
Ludhill La HD4 . . . . **172** D5
Ludlam St BD5 . . . . **201** B1
Ludlow Ave LS25 . . . . **83** B7
Ludolf Dr LS17 . . . . **44** E4
Ludwell Cl WF12 . . . . . . **139** F1
Ludwood Cl HD9 . . . . . . **172** B5
Luis Ct BD17 . . . . **38** B4
Luke La HD9 . . . . **172** C1
Luke Rd BD5 . . . . **74** C4
Lulworth Ave LS15 . . . . . **81** D8
Lulworth Cl 1 LS15 . . . . **62** D1
Lulworth Cres LS15 . . . . . **62** D1
Lulworth Dr LS15 . . . . **81** D8
Lulworth Garth LS15 . . . . **81** D8
Lulworth Gr BD4 . . . . **75** D2
Lulworth View LS15 . . . . **81** D8
Lulworth Wlk LS15 . . . . . **62** D1
Lumb Bottom BD11 . . . . . **96** F7
Lumb Foot BD22 . . . . **50** E7
Lumbfoot Rd BD22 . . . . . **50** F7
Lumb Ghyll La LS29 . . . . . . **7** B6
Lumb Hall Way BD11 . . . . **96** F7
Lumb Hole Waterfall★
HX7 . . . . **69** A3
Lumb La
Bradford BD8 . . . . **74** D8
Halifax, Boothtown HX3 . . **92** B2
Halifax, Wainstalls HX2 . . . **90** F6
Huddersfield HD4 . . . . . . **172** D8
Liversedge WF15 . . . . . . **116** F2
Sowerby Bridge HX6 . . . . **132** C7
Lumb Rd HX7 . . . . **88** D5
Lumbrook HX3 . . . . **93** C2
Lumbrook Cl HX3 . . . . **93** C3
Lumb Terr HX2 . . . . **90** F6
Lumbutts La OL14 . . . . . **108** F4
Lumbutts Rd OL14 . . . . . **108** C3
Lumby Cl LS28 . . . . **76** F5
Lumby Garth LS17 . . . . . . **28** B6
Lumby La
East Keswick LS17 . . . . **28** B6
Pudsey LS28 . . . . **76** F6
Lumby Leys La LS25 . . . **105** A8
Lumby St BD10 . . . . **56** B8
Lumley Ave
Castleford WF10 . . . . **124** A7
Leeds LS4 . . . . **205** A3
Lumley Gr LS4 . . . . **205** A3
Lumley Hill WF10 . . . . . . **124** A7
Lumley Mount
Castleford WF10 . . . . **124** A6
Leeds LS4 . . . . **205** A3
Lumley Mount Bglws
WF10 . . . . **124** A6
Lumley Pl LS4 . . . . **205** A3
Lumley Rd
Batley WF12 . . . . **118** E2
Leeds LS4 . . . . **205** A3

Lumley St
Castleford WF10 . . . . **124** B7
Leeds LS4 . . . . **205** A3
Lumley Terr LS4 . . . . . . **205** A3
Lumley View LS4 . . . . . . **205** A3
Lumley Wlk LS4 . . . . **205** A3
Lunan Pl LS8 . . . . **207** C4
Lunan Terr LS8 . . . . **207** C4
Lund Dr WF16 . . . . **117** E3
Lund Hill La LS71 . . . . . **179** F5
Lund La BD22 . . . . **34** B6
Lund St
Bingley BD16 . . . . **36** F3
Bradford BD8 . . . . **73** E7
Keighley BD21 . . . . **35** C8
Lune St BD22 . . . . **51** F8
Lunnfields La LS75, WF11 **105** C4
Lupset Cres WF2 . . . . . . **141** E3
Lupton Ave LS9 . . . . **208** B1
Lupton St
Bradford BD8 . . . . **55** L1
Leeds LS10 . . . . **215** B3
Lustre St BD21 . . . . **35** A7
Luther Pl HD2 . . . . **153** E8
Luther St LS13 . . . . **57** E5
Luther Way BD2 . . . . **55** F3
Luton St
Halifax HX1 . . . . **202** B3
Huddersfield HD4 . . . . . . **152** F3
Keighley BD21 . . . . **35** B7
Luttrell Cl LS16 . . . . **42** A2
Luttrell Cres LS16 . . . . . . **42** A2
Luttrell Gdns LS16 . . . . . **42** A2
Luttrell Pl LS16 . . . . **42** A2
Luttrell Rd LS16 . . . . **42** A2
Lutyens The LS29 . . . . **7** F4
Luxor Ave LS8 . . . . **207** C4
Luxor Rd LS8 . . . . **207** C4
Luxor St LS8 . . . . **207** C4
Luxor View LS8 . . . . **207** C4
Lydbrook Pk HX3 . . . . . . **113** A1
Lyddon Terr LS2 . . . . . . **206** A2
Lydgate
Leeds LS9 . . . . **207** C1
Lepton HD8 . . . . **156** A3
Northowram HX3 . . . . **93** A3
Lydgate Cl HD9 . . . . **189** E6
Lydgate Dr
Bradford BD7 . . . . **73** F6
Holmfirth HD9 . . . . **189** E6
Lepton HD8 . . . . **156** A3
Lydgate Jun & Inf Sch
WF17 . . . . **118** F5
Lydgate Pk HX3 . . . . . . **114** E7
Lydgate Pl LS28 . . . . **57** A7
Lydgate Rd
Batley WF17 . . . . **118** F5
Shepley HD8 . . . . **190** E8
Lydgate Sch HD9 . . . . . **189** D7
Lydgate St LS28 . . . . **57** A7
Lydget Ct BD20 . . . . **18** A2
Lydgetts HD9 . . . . **188** B5
Lydia St LS2 . . . . **212** A4
Lyme Chase LS14 . . . . . . **61** F2
Lyme Terr BD4 . . . . **184** E1
Lymington Dr BD4 . . . . . . **75** E4
Lynch Ave 1 BD7 . . . . . . **73** F3
Lyncroft BD2 . . . . **55** F4
Lynda Gr WF5 . . . . **141** A4
Lyndale LS25 . . . . **103** A8
Lyndale Cres WF16 . . . . **117** E4
Lyndale Cvn Pk WF11 . . **126** C8
Lyndale Dr
Shipley BD18 . . . . **55** F7
Wakefield WF2 . . . . **120** E2
Lyndale Gr WF6 . . . . **123** C1
Lyndale Mews WF13 . . . **117** F3
Lyndale Rd BD16 . . . . **37** C5
Lyndean Gdns BD10 . . . . . **56** A7
Lynden Ave BD18 . . . . **55** E8
Lynden Ct BD6 . . . . **94** A7
Lyndhurst Ave HD6 . . . . **136** A7
Lyndhurst Cl LS15 . . . . . . **62** F7
Lyndhurst Cres LS15 . . . . **62** F7
Lyndhurst Gr BD15 . . . . . **53** C7
Lyndhurst Grove Rd HD6 **136** A7
Lyndhurst Rd
Barwick in E LS15 . . . . **62** F6
Brighouse HD6 . . . . **136** A8
Huddersfield HD3 . . . . . . **153** B8
Lyndhurst View LS15 . . . . **62** F6
Lyndon Ave
Bramham LS23 . . . . **30** C3
Garforth LS25 . . . . **82** E7
Lyndon Cl LS23 . . . . **30** C3
Lyndon Cres LS23 . . . . . . **30** C3
Lyndon Rd LS23 . . . . **30** C3
Lyndon Sq LS23 . . . . **30** C3
Lyndon Terr 1 BD16 . . . . **37** A3
Lyndon Way LS23 . . . . . . **30** C3
Lyndum Gr LS25 . . . . **83** A2
Lynfield Dr
Bradford BD9 . . . . **54** C3
Cleckheaton WF15 . . . . . **116** B5
Lynfield Mount BD18 . . . . **55** E8
Lynfield Mount Hosp BD9 **54** D2
Lynmoor Ct
Bradford BD10 . . . . **56** A7
Shipley BD10 . . . . **55** F7
Lynndale Ave
Glusburn BD20 . . . . **16** D7
Huddersfield HD2 . . . . . . **135** F1
Lynnfield Gdns LS15 . . . . **62** F6
Lynnwood Gdns LS28 . . . **76** C7
Lynsey Gdns BD4 . . . . **95** B7
Lynthorne Rd BD9 . . . . . . **55** C4

Lynton Ave
Boston Spa LS23 . . . . **30** D8
Bradford BD9 . . . . **54** F2
Huddersfield HD1 . . . . . . **153** F6
Middleton WF3 . . . . **99** E2
Lynton Dr
Bradford BD9 . . . . **54** F2
Keighley BD20 . . . . **18** F1
Shipley BD18 . . . . **55** A7
Lynton Gr
Bradford BD9 . . . . **54** F2
Halifax HX2 . . . . **71** F1
Lynton Terr 5 BD19 . . . **116** D8
Lynton Villas BD9 . . . . . . **54** F2
Lynwood Ave
Leeds LS12 . . . . **209** C1
Rothwell LS26 . . . . **101** D6
Shipley BD18 . . . . **55** E8
Lynwood Cl
Birkenshaw BD11 . . . . **96** B4
Featherstone WF7 . . . . . . **144** E4
Knottingley WF11 . . . . . . **127** A5
Lynwood Cres
Fitzwilliam WF9 . . . . **163** A4
Halifax HX1 . . . . **202** B1
Leeds LS12 . . . . **209** C1
Pontefract WF8 . . . . **146** D6
Rothwell LS26 . . . . **101** D6
Lynwood Ct BD22 . . . . . . **34** E5
Lynwood Dr
Barnsley S71 . . . . **179** C1
Wakefield WF2 . . . . **160** C6
Lynwood Garth LS12 . . . **209** C1
Lynwood Gr LS12 . . . . . . **78** C4
Lynwood Ho 13 BD4 . . . . **75** F2
Lynwood Mews 10 BD4 . . **75** F2
Lynwood Mount LS12 . . **209** C1
Lynwood Rise LS12 . . . . **209** C1
Lynwood View LS12 . . . **209** C1
Lyon Rd
Pontefract WF8 . . . . **146** D6
Steeton BD20 . . . . **16** F6
Lyon St
Queensbury BD13 . . . . . . **72** F1
Thornton BD13 . . . . **72** D7
Lysander Way BD16 . . . . . **54** B6
Lytham Cl WF6 . . . . **123** D1
Lytham Dr BD13 . . . . **73** B2
Lytham Gr LS12 . . . . **78** A4
Lytham Pl 15 LS12 . . . . . **78** A4
Lytham St HX1 . . . . **202** B3
Lytham Way HD3 . . . . . . **153** B8
Lytton Rd BD8 . . . . **73** F8
Lytton St
7 Halifax HX3 . . . . **92** C1
Leeds LS10 . . . . **215** A3

M

Mabel Royd BD7 . . . . **73** F5
Mabel St HX7 . . . . **89** E1
Mabgate LS9 . . . . **212** A4
Mabgate Gn LS9 . . . . . . **212** A4
Mabgate Mills Ind Ctr
LS9 . . . . **207** B1
MacAulay Rd HD2 . . . . . **135** F1
MacAulay St
25 Huddersfield HD1 . . . **154** A6
Leeds LS9 . . . . **207** B1
McBride Way LS22 . . . . . . **13** F5
McBurney Cl 2 HX3 . . . . . **92** B2
McClure Ho LS10 . . . . . . **212** A2
McCrea Apartments HX1 **203** B1
Macham St HD1 . . . . **153** F4
Mackenzie Ho LS10 . . . . **212** A2
Mackey Cres S72 . . . . . . **180** F3
Mackie Hill Cl WF4 . . . . . **159** D4
Mackie Hill Jun & Inf Sch
WF4 . . . . **159** D4
Mackingstone Dr BD22 . . . **34** B3
Mackingstone La BD22 . . . **34** B4
MacKinnon Ave WF2 . . . **123** C3
Mackintosh Ho 3 LS2 . . **207** A1
**Mackintosh Meml Homes
The** HX3 . . . . **113** A4
McLaren Ave WF9 . . . . . **183** D8
McLaren Fields 6 LS13 . . **58** C2
McMahon Dr BD13 . . . . . . **73** C2
McMillan Gdns BD10 . . . . **94** D7
Macturk Gr BD8 . . . . **55** A1
Maddocks St BD18 . . . . . . **55** A8
Madeley Rd WF4 . . . . . . **162** C1
Madeley Sq WF10 . . . . . **104** C1
Madgin La HD4 . . . . **171** A6
Madison Ave BD4 . . . . . . **75** E1
Madison Cl WF7 . . . . **163** D5
Madni Cl HX1 . . . . **203** A3
Madni Muslim Girls High Sch
WF12 . . . . **139** D6
Mafeking Ave LS11 . . . . **214** A1
Mafeking Gr LS11 . . . . . **214** A1
Mafeking Mount LS11 . . **214** A1
Mafeking Terr 1 BD18 . . . **55** D5
Mag Dale HD9 . . . . **171** F6
Magdalene Cl LS16 . . . . . **42** A3
Magdalene Fields WF6 . . **144** D8
Magdalene Rd WF2 . . . . **141** D5
Magdalen Rd HD9 . . . . . **187** C7
Magdalin Dr LS13 . . . . . . **58** A2
Magellan Ho LS10 . . . . . **212** A3
Magna Gr WF2 . . . . **142** E1
Magnolia Cl S72 . . . . **180** D2
Magnolia Dr BD15 . . . . . . **53** F4
Magnolia Ho 11 WF10 . . **124** A7
Magnolias WF17 . . . . **117** F7
Magpie Cl 1 BD6 . . . . **73** C1
Magpie La LS27 . . . . **98** C3

Maidstone St BD3 . . . . . . **75** C7
Maidwell Way BD6 . . . . . . **94** A6
Mail Cl LS15 . . . . **62** E3
Main Ave HD4 . . . . **152** F3
Main Gate HD9 . . . . **189** E2
Main Rd
Denholme BD13 . . . . **71** D8
East Morton BD20 . . . . **36** D8
Farnhill BD20 . . . . **16** E8
Steeton BD20 . . . . **16** F6
Mainspring Rd BD15 . . . . **53** C5
Main St
Aberford LS25 . . . . **64** E7
Addingham LS29 . . . . **6** F8
Badsworth WF9 . . . . **164** E2
Barwick in E, Arthursdale
LS15 . . . . **62** F6
Barwick in E LS15 . . . . **63** D7
Bingley BD16 . . . . **36** F3
2 Bradford, Carr House Gate
BD12 . . . . **94** C4
Bradford, Wesley Place
BD12 . . . . **94** E6
Burley in W LS29 . . . . **9** F1
Burton Salmon LS25 . . . . **105** E3
Collingham LS22 . . . . **29** B8
Cononley BD20 . . . . **4** A2
East Ardsley WF3 . . . . . . **120** D7
East Keswick LS17 . . . . . . **28** C5
Farnhill BD20 . . . . **4** D2
Garforth LS25 . . . . **82** E7
Glusburn BD20 . . . . **16** D6
Guiseley, Esholt BD17 . . . . **39** C5
Guiseley, Hawksworth LS20 **38** F8
Hampole DN6 . . . . **184** B1
Haworth BD22 . . . . **51** C7
Haworth, Stanbury BD22 . . **50** D7
Hillam LS25 . . . . **105** F8
Kippax WF10 . . . . **103** B4
Kirk Smeaton WF8 . . . . . **166** D6
Ledston WF10 . . . . **103** E6
Linton LS22 . . . . **13** C2
Low Bradley BD20 . . . . **4** C5
Menston LS29 . . . . **22** A4
Mickletown LS26 . . . . . . **102** D3
Newton Kyme LS24 . . . . . **31** E7
Pool LS21 . . . . **24** C7
Rothwell WF3 . . . . **100** D3
Shadwell LS17 . . . . **44** E4
Shipley BD16 . . . . **54** B6
Sicklinghall LS22 . . . . **12** C5
South Hiendley S72 . . . . . **180** D6
Sutton-in-C BD20 . . . . **16** D5
Thorner LS14 . . . . **45** F5
Upton WF9 . . . . **183** D8
Walton LS23 . . . . **15** A4
Wilsden BD15 . . . . **53** C5
Maister Pl BD22 . . . . **34** B3
Maitland Cl
Bradford BD15 . . . . **73** B7
Todmorden OL14 . . . . . . **129** A8
Maitland Pl LS11 . . . . . . **214** A4
Maitland St OL14 . . . . . . **129** A8
Maizebrook WF16 . . . . . . **117** F1
Maize St BD21 . . . . **35** A4
Majestic Way BD22 . . . . . **35** A4
Major St
Todmorden OL14 . . . . . . **108** C5
Wakefield WF2 . . . . **142** B3
Makin St WF2 . . . . **142** A5
Malais La BD20 . . . . **16** A5
Malden Rd 1 LS6 . . . . . . **42** F1
Malham Ave
Bradford BD9 . . . . **54** C3
Brighouse HD6 . . . . **135** E8
Malham Cl
Leeds LS14 . . . . **62** A4
Shafton S72 . . . . **180** C3
Malham Ct 7 BD20 . . . . . **17** E8
Malham Dr
Batley WF17 . . . . **118** A5
Liversedge WF15 . . . . . . **116** F1
Malham Rd
Brighouse HD6 . . . . **135** E7
Wakefield WF2 . . . . **142** F7
Malham Sq WF1 . . . . **142** F7
Malin Rd WF12 . . . . **118** F3
Mallard Ave WF2 . . . . . . **160** C5
Mallard Cl
Bradford BD10 . . . . **56** C5
Leeds LS10 . . . . **99** F7
Mallard Ct 1 BD8 . . . . . . **73** C7
Mallard Rd WF10 . . . . . . **124** C6
Mallards Cl WF16 . . . . . . **117** D3
Mallards The BD20 . . . . . . **5** E1
Mallard View BD22 . . . . . **51** C2
Mallard Way
3 Morley LS27 . . . . **98** D4
Slaithwaite HD7 . . . . **169** F8
Mallinson St WF13 . . . . . **118** A1
Mallory Cl BD7 . . . . **73** F2
Malmesbury Cl
Bradford BD4 . . . . **75** E1
Leeds LS12 . . . . **209** C2
Malmesbury Gr LS12 . . . **209** C2
Malmesbury Pl LS12 . . . **209** C2
Malmesbury St LS12 . . . **209** C2
Malmesbury Terr LS12 . . **209** C2
Malsis Cres BD21 . . . . **35** A6
Malsis Rd BD21 . . . . **35** B5
Maltby Ct LS15 . . . . **81** D7
Malthouse Cl LS14 . . . . . **45** C8
Malting Cl WF3 . . . . **100** B3
Malting Rise WF3 . . . . . . **100** B3
Maltings Ct LS11 . . . . . . **214** C4
Maltings Rd
Halifax HX2 . . . . **91** D2
Leeds LS11 . . . . **214** C4

Maltings The
Cleckheaton BD19 . . . . . . **116** C8
Leeds LS6 . . . . **205** B2
Mirfield WF14 . . . . **137** F5
Pontefract WF8 . . . . **125** D1
Rothwell WF3 . . . . **100** B3
Shepley HD8 . . . . **173** F1
Maltins The WF10 . . . . . **124** E8
Malt Kiln 8 BD14 . . . . . . **73** B4
Malt Kiln Croft WF2 . . . . **142** E1
Maltkiln Dr WF4 . . . . **176** F8
Maltkiln La
Castleford WF10 . . . . **124** E8
6 Kippax LS25 . . . . **83** B1
Malt Kiln La BD13 . . . . . . **72** C5
Malton Rd WF9 . . . . **183** D8
Malton St
Halifax, Woodlands HX3 . . **92** C4
8 Sowerby Bridge HX6 . . **112** B5
Malt Shovel Yd 1 BD10 . . **56** B8
Malt St BD22 . . . . **35** A4
Malvern Brow BD9 . . . . . . **54** D2
Malvern Cl WF10 . . . . . . **123** F5
Malvern Cres BD20 . . . . . **18** E3
Malvern Gr
Bradford BD9 . . . . **54** D1
Leeds LS11 . . . . **214** B4
Malvern Rd
Bradford BD9 . . . . **54** D2
Dewsbury WF12 . . . . **118** F1
Huddersfield HD4 . . . . . . **154** B4
Knottingley WF11 . . . . . . **126** E4
Leeds LS11 . . . . **214** A4
Malvern Rise
Huddersfield HD4 . . . . . . **154** B3
Leeds LS11 . . . . **214** A4
Malvern St LS11 . . . . . . **214** A4
Malvern View LS11 . . . . **214** A4
Manchester Rd
Bradford BD5 . . . . **74** D3
Huddersfield HD4 . . . . . . **153** C4
Marsden HD7 . . . . **168** B3
Manchester Rd Marsden
HD7 . . . . **168** E4
Manchester Rd (Slaithwaite)
HD7 . . . . **170** A8
**Manchester Road Clough
Head** HD7 . . . . **168** C4
**Manchester Road
(Linthwaite)** HD7 . . . . **152** D1
Manchester Sq 9 LS21 . . **23** A8
Mandale Gr BD6 . . . . **93** D8
Mandale Rd BD6 . . . . **73** C1
Mandarin Way LS10 . . . . . **99** F7
Mandela Cl LS7 . . . . **204** A1
Manderlay Gdns HD8 . . . **175** C7
Manderston Chase 8
LS13 . . . . **58** F2
Mandeville Cres BD6 . . . . **93** F8
Mangrill La LS14 . . . . **46** E6
Manitoba Pl LS7 . . . . **204** B2
Mankinholes Bank OL14 . **108** F3
Mankinholes Hall (YH)★
OL14 . . . . **109** A4
Manley Ct LS25 . . . . **82** F5
Manley Dr LS22 . . . . **13** C6
Manley Gr LS29 . . . . **8** D4
Manley Rd LS29 . . . . **8** E4
Manley Rise LS29 . . . . **8** D3
Manley St HD6 . . . . **115** A3
Mann's Bldgs WF17 . . . . . **97** B2
Mann's Ct BD1 . . . . **201** B3
Mannerley Gr BD19 . . . . **117** B6
Mannheim Rd BD9 . . . . . . **55** A2
Manningham Academic Inst
BD8 . . . . **55** D1
Manningham La BD1, BD8 . **55** D1
Mannville Gr BD22 . . . . . . **35** A6
Mannville Pl 15 BD22 . . . **35** A6
Mannville Rd BD22 . . . . . . **35** A6
Mannville St BD22 . . . . . . **35** A6
Mannville Terr BD7 . . . . . . **74** D6
Mannville Way 13 BD22 . . **35** A6
Mannville Wlk 14 BD22 . . **35** A6
Manor Ave
Leeds LS6 . . . . **205** B4
Ossett WF5 . . . . **140** F3
Manor Barn Stables LS21 . **23** A8
Manor Cl
Badsworth WF9 . . . . **164** E2
Birkenshaw BD11 . . . . **96** E7
Bradford BD8 . . . . **73** D8
Bramhope LS16 . . . . **24** D3
Halifax HX3 . . . . **113** B4
Kirk Smeaton WF8 . . . . . **166** D5
Notton WF4 . . . . **178** F7
Ossett WF5 . . . . **140** F3
Rothwell LS26 . . . . **100** E6
Todmorden OL14 . . . . . . **109** A4
Yeadon LS19 . . . . **40** B7
Manor Cres
Pool LS21 . . . . **24** C7
Rothwell LS26 . . . . **100** D5
Wakefield WF2 . . . . **141** E4
Walton WF2 . . . . **161** A4
Manor Crest WF4 . . . . . . **159** D5
Manorcroft WF6 . . . . **123** B2
Manor Croft
Hebden Bridge HX7 . . . . . **89** B3
Leeds LS15 . . . . **81** C7
Skelmanthorpe HD8 . . . . **175** A2
South Hiendley S72 . . . . . **180** D5
Manor Croft Gdns WF12 . **139** E8
Manor Ct
Aberford LS25 . . . . **64** E7
Fairburn WF11 . . . . **105** A4
Leeds LS11 . . . . **213** B1
Ossett WF5 . . . . **140** F3

Manor Ct *continued*
Otley LS21 23 A8
Royston S71 179 A3
Shadwell LS17 44 F4
[3] Shipley BD16 54 A7
Manordale Cl WF4 157 D3
Manor Dr
Crofton WF4 162 A7
Featherstone WF7 124 C1
Flockton WF4 157 D3
Halifax HX3 113 B4
Hebden Bridge HX7 89 B3
Leeds LS6 205 B4
Mirfield WF14 137 D7
Ossett WF5 140 F3
Royston S71 179 B3
Shipley BD16 54 B7
Skelmanthorpe HD8 175 A1
South Hiendley S72 180 D6
Manor Farm WF9 164 E2
Manor Farm Cl
Leeds LS10 99 D6
Shipley BD16 54 B6
Manor Farm Cres [11] LS27 98 C8
Manor Farm Ct
Crigglestone WF4 159 E4
Guiseley LS20 22 E1
Manor Farm Dr
Batley WF17 118 F5
Leeds LS10 99 D6
Morley LS27 98 C8
Manor Farm Est WF9 183 A3
Manor Farm Gdns LS10 99 C6
Manor Farm Gn LS10 99 C6
Manor Farm Gr LS10 99 C6
Manor Farm Rd
Crigglestone WF4 159 E4
Leeds LS10 99 D6
Manor Farm Rise LS10 99 D6
Manor Farm Way LS10 99 C5
Manor Farm Wlk LS10 99 D6
Manorfield LS11 213 C3
Manorfield Dr WF4 141 A2
Manorfield Inf Sch
WF17 118 A4
Manorfields Ave WF4 162 A8
Manorfields Ct WF4 162 A8
Manor Fold
Horsforth LS18 58 A8
Shipley BD16 54 B6
Manor Garth
Ledsham LS25 104 D8
Leeds LS15 81 C7
Walton WF2 161 A8
Manor Garth Rd
Dewsbury WF12 139 F7
Kippax LS25 83 B2
Manor Gdns
Batley WF12 119 A2
Cullingworth BD13 52 D5
Pool LS21 24 C7
Thorner LS14 46 A6
Manor Gr
Castleford WF10 124 E5
Keighley BD20 36 A8
Leeds LS7 204 A2
Ossett WF5 140 F3
Royston S71 179 B3
South Kirkby WF9 182 A1
Manor Grange HD8 190 D8
Manor Haigh Rd WF2 141 E4
Manor Heath Rd HX3 113 B4
Manor Ho [2] WF1 216 C2
Manor Hos HD9 170 F2
Manor House Bglws
WF11 126 F5
Manor House Croft LS16 42 D3
Manor House Cvn Site
WF4 157 D3
Manor House La LS17 43 F7
Manor House Mus & Art
Gall★ LS29 8 B4
Manor House Rd BD15 53 C6
Manor House St [5] LS28 76 E7
Manor La
Ossett WF5 140 F3
Shipley BD18 55 B7
Manorley La BD6 93 E6
Manor Mill La LS11 213 B1
Manor Occupation Rd
S71 179 B4
Manor Park Ave
Kippax WF10 103 B5
Pontefract WF8 125 F3
Manor Park Gdns BD19 96 B3
Manor Park Rise WF8 147 D4
Manor Park Way
Cleckheaton BD19 116 E6
Lepton HD8 155 D2
Manor Pk
Batley WF12 119 B3
Bradford BD8 73 D8
Darrington WF8 147 D5
Ledston WF10 103 E6
Mirfield WF14 137 C7
Oakworth BD22 34 C2
Scarcroft LS14 45 C7
Manor Pl [1] WF4 141 A1
Manor Rd
Batley WF17 118 F5
Beal DN14 127 F7
Clayton West HD8 176 A4
Dewsbury WF13 139 B7
Horbury WF4 141 A1
Horsforth LS18 58 A8
Huddersfield HD7 152 D4
Keighley BD20 18 A2
Kirkburton HD4 172 F6

Manor Rd *continued*
Leeds, Camp Field LS11 211 B2
Leeds, Green Side LS12 209 B1
Morley LS27 98 C8
Ossett WF5 140 F4
Rothwell LS26 100 D6
Shipley BD16 54 B7
Thurnscoe S63 194 C1
Wakefield WF2 141 F5
Walton WF2 161 A7
Manor Rise
Crigglestone WF4 159 E5
Huddersfield HD4 154 B4
Ilkley LS29 8 D4
Skelmanthorpe HD8 175 A1
Walton WF2 161 A8
Manor Row
Bradford BD1 201 B3
Bradford, Odsal BD12 94 C7
Manor Sq
Otley LS21 23 A8
[5] Yeadon LS19 40 B7
Manor St
[2] Bradford BD2 56 B3
Brighouse BD19 115 F6
Dewsbury WF12 139 D8
Huddersfield HD4 154 B4
Leeds LS7 207 A2
Otley LS21 23 A8
Manorstead HD8 175 A1
Manor Street Ind Est
LS7 207 B2
Manor Terr
Bradford BD2 56 B3
[4] Kippax LS25 83 B1
Leeds LS6 205 B4
[12] Yeadon LS19 40 B7
Manor The LS8 61 B6
Manor View
Castleford WF10 124 E5
Leeds LS6 205 B4
Pudsey LS28 76 E7
Shafton S72 180 C2
Upton WF9 183 A8
Manor Way
Batley WF17 118 A4
Sutton-in-C BD20 16 C4
Manscombe Rd BD15 54 C1
Manse Cres LS29 9 E1
Manse Dr HD4 153 A3
Mansel Mews BD4 75 E2
Manse Rd LS29 9 E1
Manse St BD3 75 C7
Manse Way BD20 16 D6
Mansfield Ave BD16 37 C5
Mansfield Ho [21] BD4 75 E3
Mansfield Pl LS6 59 D6
Mansfield Rd
Bradford BD8 55 C2
Burley in W LS29 9 E1
Mansion Gate LS7 204 B2
Mansion Gate Dr LS7 204 B2
Mansion Gate Mews LS7 204 B2
Mansion Gate Sq LS7 204 B2
Mansion Gdns HD4 153 F1
Mansion La
Halifax HX3 113 D4
Leeds LS8 44 B1
Mansion Terr [14] BD7 74 A4
Manston App LS15 62 C3
Manston Ave LS15 62 C3
Manston Cres LS15 62 C2
Manston Dr LS15 62 C3
Manston Gdns LS15 62 D3
Manston Gr LS15 62 C3
Manston La LS15 62 E2
Manston Prim Sch LS15 62 D3
Manston Rise LS15 62 C3
Manston Terr [5] LS15 62 D3
Manston Way LS15 62 C3
Mantra Ho Bsns Ctr [17]
BD21 35 B6
Manygates Ave WF1 142 D3
Manygates Cres WF1 142 D3
Manygates Ct WF1 142 D3
Manygates La WF1, WF2 142 D2
Manygates Pk WF1 142 D3
Manywells Brow BD13 52 C4
Manywells Brow Ind Est
BD13 52 D5
Manywells Cres BD13 52 D5
Manywells La BD13 52 B5
Maple Apartments WF1 216 C4
Maple Ave
Bradford BD3 75 E8
Huddersfield HD3, HD7 152 F5
Oakworth BD22 34 D2
Pontefract WF8 146 C5
Maple Cl
Castleford WF10 124 B5
Kirkheaton HD5 137 C1
Maple Croft
Huddersfield HD4 171 D6
Leeds, Farnley LS12 77 D5
Leeds, Moortown LS17 43 E3
Maple Ct
Leeds LS11 213 C2
Ossett WF5 140 E3
Maple Dr
Leeds LS12 77 D5
Pontefract WF8 146 D6
Wetherby LS22 13 E7
Maple Fold
Elland HX5 134 E5
Leeds LS12 77 D5
Maple Gdns LS17 28 E5
Maple Gr
Cleckheaton BD19 96 A1

Maple Gr *continued*
Gildersome LS12 77 D5
Huddersfield HD2 136 A5
Keighley BD20 18 A1
Normanton WF6 144 A7
Pontefract WF8 146 C5
Maple Pk LS12 213 B4
Maple Rd
Darton S75 178 A1
Dewsbury WF12 140 B7
Maple Rise LS26 100 F4
Maple St
[7] Halifax HX1 202 B1
Huddersfield HD5 154 C5
Todmorden OL14 129 A7
Wakefield WF2 141 F8
Maple Terr LS19 39 F7
Maple Way LS14 62 C8
Maple Wlk
Dewsbury WF12 140 B7
Knottingley WF11 126 E3
Maplin Ave HD3 134 F1
Maplin Dr [1] HD3 134 F1
Mapplewell Cres WF5 140 E5
Mapplewell Dr WF5 140 E5
Mapplewell Prim Sch
S75 178 C1
Marbridge Ct BD6 74 B2
Marchant St WF10 124 C8
Marchant Way LS27 78 C1
Marchbank Rd BD3 75 C8
March Cote La BD16 54 A6
Marchmont Cres LS25 102 F8
March St WF6 123 A1
Marchwood Gr BD14 73 D5
Marcia Cl BD10 56 C6
Marcus Way HD3 134 D1
Mardale Cres LS14 62 A3
Mardale Rd WF12 118 E2
Margaret's Ct [10] LS29 8 B4
Margaret Ave LS17 28 D4
Margaret Cl LS27 98 C6
Margaret Mcmillan Prim Sch
BD9 55 A2
Margaret St
Halifax HX1 203 A3
Keighley BD21 35 A8
Lofthouse Gate WF1 121 A4
Wakefield WF1 216 A3
Margate [2] LS26 101 C6
Margate Rd BD4 75 A4
Margate St HX6 112 A3
Margerison Cres LS29 8 E3
Margerison Rd LS29 8 E3
Margetson Rd BD11 97 A5
Margram Bsns Ctr HX1 203 A4
Marguerite Gdns WF9 183 D8
Marian Gr [9] LS11 214 B3
Marian Rd LS6 206 B3
Marian Terr LS6 206 B3
Maria St LS29 9 E2
Marie Cl HD5 155 C6
Marina Cres LS27 97 F3
Marina Gdns HX6 112 D4
Marina Terr HD7 152 E5
Mariner Ct LS14 62 C5
Marine Villa Rd WF11 126 F4
Marion Ave WF2 141 D8
Marion Cl WF9 182 C2
Marion Dr BD18 55 C7
Marion Gr WF2 141 D8
Marion St
Bingley BD16 37 A3
Bradford BD7 74 C7
Brighouse HD6 115 A3
Marizon Gr WF1 216 C3
Mark Bottoms La HD9 188 F6
Mark Cl BD10 56 C8
Market Ave [9] HD1 154 B6
Market Bsns Ctr The
HX1 202 C3
Market Cross [13] WF8 146 D8
Market Ct [5] BD13 72 E6
Market Pl
Batley, Birstall WF17 96 F1
Batley, Heckmondwike
WF16 117 D3
[6] Batley WF17 118 C5
[1] Cleckheaton BD19 116 E7
Dewsbury WF13 139 D8
Honley HD9 171 F4
Huddersfield HD1 154 A6
Keighley BD21 35 C7
Marsden HD7 168 F4
Meltham HD9 170 D2
Normanton WF6 123 A2
Ossett WF5 140 D5
[7] Otley LS21 23 A8
Pontefract WF8 146 D8
Pudsey LS28 76 E7
Slaithwaite HD7 169 F8
[4] Sowerby Bridge HX6 112 B3
Wetherby LS22 13 E5
Market St Arc [2] LS1 211 C3
Market Shops WF6 123 A2
Market Sq
[5] Batley WF17 118 C5
Shipley BD18 55 B7
Market St
Batley, Birstall WF17 96 E1
Batley, Heckmondwike
WF16 117 D3
Bingley BD16 36 F3
Bradford BD1 201 B3
[4] Bradford, Brownroyd Hill
BD6 74 C1
Brighouse HD6 115 B2
Cleckheaton BD19 116 E7

Market St *continued*
[3] Dewsbury WF13 139 D8
Featherstone WF7 145 C6
Halifax HX1 203 B3
Hebden Bridge HX7 89 A3
Hemsworth WF9 181 D7
Holmfirth HD9 189 A5
Huddersfield HD1 154 A6
Huddersfield, Milnsbridge
HD3 153 B5
Huddersfield, Paddock
HD1 153 E5
Keighley BD21 35 C7
Normanton WF6 123 A2
[8] Otley LS21 23 A8
Shipley BD18 55 B7
Steeton BD20 17 D5
Thornton BD13 72 E6
Todmorden OL14 108 A3
Wakefield WF1 216 B2
Market Wlk
[11] Holmfirth HD9 189 A5
Marsden HD7 168 F4
Markfield Ave BD12 94 C5
Markfield Cl BD12 94 C5
Markfield Cres BD12 94 D5
Markfield Dr BD12 94 C5
Markfield Ho [9] BD4 75 D5
Markham Ave
Leeds LS8 207 C4
Yeadon LS19 40 C5
Markham Cotts LS25 64 E8
Markham Cres LS19 40 C5
Markham Croft LS19 40 C5
Markham Mount HX1 202 A1
Markham St
Batley WF17 118 B4
Wakefield WF2 142 A6
Markington Mews LS10 99 C3
Markington Pl LS10 99 C3
Mark La
Leeds LS2 211 C4
Todmorden OL14 108 A7
Mark St
Bradford BD5 74 E3
Huddersfield HD1 153 E5
Liversedge WF15 117 B4
Wakefield WF1 142 C4
Marland Rd BD21 35 E8
Marlbeck Cl HD9 171 F3
Marlborough Ave
Byram WF11 126 D7
[7] Halifax HX3 113 B4
Marlborough Croft WF9 182 F4
Marlborough Ct
Menston LS29 22 B4
Scarcroft LS14 45 D8
Marlborough Gdns
Dewsbury WF13 118 B2
[17] Leeds LS2 206 B2
Marlborough Gr
[16] Hebden Bridge HX7 89 A3
Ilkley LS29 8 D3
[19] Leeds LS2 206 B2
Marlborough Grange [5]
LS1 211 A4
Marlborough Ho [9] HX5 134 F7
Marlborough Rd
Bradford, Cliffton Villas
BD8 55 C1
Bradford, Fourlands BD10 56 C8
Hebden Bridge HX7 89 A3
Huddersfield HD2 136 B5
Shipley BD18 55 A7
Marlborough Sq LS29 8 D3
Marlborough St
Keighley BD21 35 D8
Leeds LS1 211 A4
Ossett WF5 140 C5
Wakefield WF2 142 A6
Marlborough Terr HX7 89 A3
Marlborough Twrs [4]
LS1 211 A4
Marlborough Villas LS29 22 B4
Marlbro' Terr [5] WF13 118 B2
Marldon Rd HX3 93 A1
Marled Cl WF16 117 D5
Marley Cl BD8 73 E8
Marley Ct BD16 36 D7
Marley Gr LS11 213 C3
Marley La BD13, BD14 72 E3
Marley Mills Ind Est BD21 35 C6
Marley Pl LS11 213 C3
Marley Rd BD21 35 F8
Marley St
Bradford BD3 201 D3
Keighley BD21 35 C6
Leeds LS11 213 C3
Marley Terr LS11 213 C3
Marley View
Bingley BD16 36 D7
Leeds LS11 213 C3
Marling Rd HD2 135 B3
Marlo Rd WF12 119 A2
Marlott Rd BD18 55 E8
Marlow Cl HD5 154 F6
Marlowe Cl [3] LS28 76 F5
Marlowe Ct
Garforth LS25 82 F7
Guiseley LS20 22 D1
Marlow St BD21 35 E8
Marl Pit Hill WF8 146 A6
Marlpit La WF8 147 B5
Marmaville Ct WF14 138 C4
Marmion Ave BD8 73 C7
Marne Ave BD14 73 C3
Marne Cres BD10 56 B7
Marne Ct BD14 73 C3

Marquis Ave BD12 95 B5
Marriner's Dr BD9 55 B4
Marriner's Wlk BD21 35 C5
Marriner Rd BD21 35 C6
Marriot Gr WF2 142 F1
Marrtree Bsns Pk
Castleford WF10 124 E5
Silsden BD20 17 E8
Marsden Ave LS11 214 A2
Marsden Ct [3] LS28 57 D3
Marsden Gate HX4 151 E7
Marsden Gr LS11 214 A2
Marsden Inf Sch HD7 169 A4
Marsden Jun Sch HD7 169 A4
Marsden La
Marsden, Booth Naze
HD7 169 B7
Marsden HD7 169 A5
Marsden Meml Homes
LS28 57 D2
Marsden Mount LS11 214 A2
Marsden Pl LS11 214 A2
Marsden St HD8 175 A2
Marsden Sta HD7 168 F4
Marsden View LS11 214 A2
Marsett Way LS14 62 B8
Marsh
Honley HD9 171 F4
Pudsey LS28 76 C7
Marshall Ave
Crigglestone WF4 159 F3
Leeds LS15 62 D2
Marshall Cl [2] LS27 98 A4
Marshall Cres LS27 98 B2
Marshall Ct
Leeds LS11 211 A2
[15] Yeadon LS19 40 B7
Marshall Dr WF9 182 F3
Marshall Mews WF10 124 E8
Marshall Mill Ct HD8 175 E1
Marshall St
Keighley BD20 18 B1
Leeds, Cross Gates LS15 62 C2
Leeds LS11 211 B2
Lofthouse Gate WF3 121 F5
Mirfield WF14 138 A3
Morley LS27 98 B4
Yeadon LS19 40 B7
Marshall Terr LS15 62 C2
Marsham Gr HD3 153 C7
Marshaw Bridge HX7 110 C3
Marsh Croft WF11 126 C7
Marsh Ct LS28 76 C7
Marsh Delves HX3 113 F6
Marsh Delves La HX3 113 F6
Marsh End WF11 127 B5
Marshfield Pl BD5 74 D3
Marshfield Prim Sch BD5 74 C2
Marshfield St BD5 74 D3
Marsh Gdns HD9 171 F4
Marsh Gr BD5 74 C3
Marsh Grove Rd HD3 153 D8
Marsh Hall La HD4 172 F3
Marsh La
Birkenshaw BD11 96 A5
Blackshaw Head HX7 88 B3
Byram WF11 126 F6
Halifax HX3 113 F6
Knottingley WF11 127 B4
Leeds LS9 212 B4
Oxenhope BD22 51 B4
Shepley HD8 190 D7
Marsh Lea Gr WF9 181 F7
Marsh Mills Bsns Ctr [6]
HD3 153 D7
Marsh Platt La HD9 172 A5
Marsh Rd
Castleford WF10 124 A6
Holmfirth HD9 189 D3
Marsh Rise LS28 76 C7
Marsh St
Bradford BD5 74 D3
Cleckheaton BD19 116 E6
Leeds LS6 206 A3
Rothwell LS26 100 F5
Marsh Terr LS28 76 C7
Marsh Vale [3] LS6 206 A3
Marshway HX1 202 C4
Marsh Way WF1 216 C3
Marsland Ave WF1 216 C2
Marsland Ct BD19 95 D2
Marsland Pl
Bradford BD3 75 D7
[5] Wakefield WF1 216 C2
Marsland St WF1 216 C2
Marsland Terr WF1 216 C2
Marston Ave LS27 98 A3
Marston Cl BD13 72 F1
Marston Ct WF10 124 A6
Marston Mount LS9 207 B1
Marston Way LS22 13 C6
Marston Wlk WF6 122 E4
Marten Dr HD4 171 D7
Marten Gr HD4 171 E7
Marten Rd BD5 74 C3
Martin Bank Wood HD5 154 D5
Martin Cl LS27 98 C4
Martin Ct
Bradford BD6 73 C1
Leeds LS15 81 D8
Martindale Cl BD2 56 D3
Martindale Dr LS13 58 E1
Martin Frobisher Dr
WF6 122 F3

Martin Frobisher Inf Sch
WF6 . . . . **122** F4
Martingale Dr LS10 . . . . **99** D3
Martin Gr WF2. . . . . **160** E6
Martin Green La HX4 . . **134** A7
Martin St
Batley WF17 . . . . **96** E1
Brighouse HD6 . . . . **115** B3
Normanton WF6 . . . . . . **144** A8
Martin Terr LS4. . . . . **59** C2
Martlett Dr BD5. . . . . **74** F2
Marton Ave WF9 . . . . . . **181** C6
Marton Ct BD3. . . . . **75** D7
Marton Hts HX6 . . . . . . **112** A5
Marton St HX7 . . . . **89** A3
Mary's Way HX6 . . . . . . **112** A3
Maryfield Ave LS15 . . . . **62** A2
Maryfield Cl LS15 . . . . . **62** A2
Maryfield Cres LS15 . . . **62** B2
Maryfield Ct **5** LS15 . . . **62** B2
Maryfield Gdns
Leeds LS15 . . . . **62** A2
Ossett WF5 . . . . **140** F4
Maryfield Gn LS15 . . . . . **62** A2
Maryfield Mews LS15 . . **62** A2
Maryfield Vale **1** LS15 . . **62** A2
Marygate WF1 . . . . **216** B2
Maryland Ho LS6 . . . . . **205** C4
Mary Rose Ct WF7 . . . . **145** C4
Mary St
Bradford BD4. . . . . **75** C5
Bradford, Carr House Gate
   BD12. . . . . **94** C4
Brighouse HD6 . . . . . . **115** A4
Denholme BD13. . . . . . . **52** E1
East Ardsley WF3 . . . . **120** E8
Farnhill BD20. . . . . **4** D1
8 Oxenhope BD22 . . . . **51** C2
Pudsey LS28 . . . . **57** E4
Shipley BD18 . . . . **54** F8
5 Thornton BD13 . . . . . **72** D6
Mary Street Cvn Site BD4. **75** C5
Maryville Ave HD6 . . . . **114** E5
Masefield Ave BD9. . . . . **54** C3
Masefield St LS20. . . . . . **39** F8
Masham Gr LS12 . . . . . **210** A3
Masham Pl BD9. . . . . **54** F2
Masham St LS12 . . . . . **210** A3
Mason's Gn HX2 . . . . . . **91** E5
Mason Ct HD4 . . . . **153** B2
Masonic St HX1. . . . . . . **202** A2
Mason Sq **5** HX2 . . . . . **91** F3
Mason St HX7 . . . . **89** A3
Massey Fields BD22 . . . . **51** D8
Master La HX2. . . . . **112** F4
Matherville HD8 . . . . . . **175** A1
Matheson Ho BD3. . . . . **201** C4
Matlock St
9 Halifax HX3 . . . . **92** A1
Huddersfield HD4 . . . . **153** C4
Matrix Ct LS11. . . . . **214** B2
Matterdale Cl WF12. . . . **118** E2
Matterdale Rd WF12. . . **118** E2
Matthew Cl **3** BD20. . . . . **18** F1
Matthew Gr HD9. . . . . . **170** C2
Matthew La
Low Bradley BD20. . . . . . . **4** C5
Meltham HD9. . . . . **170** A2
Todmorden OL14 . . . . . **108** E7
Matty Marsden La WF4. . **140** E2
Maud Ave LS11 . . . . **214** B2
Maude Ave BD17. . . . . . . **38** C2
Maude Cres HX6 . . . . . . **111** E3
Maude La HX6 . . . . **132** D4
Maude St
Elland HX4. . . . . **134** D7
Halifax HX3 . . . . **92** A3
Leeds LS2 . . . . **212** A3
Maud Pl LS11 . . . . **214** B3
Maudsley St BD3. . . . . . . **75** B7
Maud St BD3 . . . . **75** B6
Maufe Way LS29 . . . . **8** B3
Maurice Ave HD6 . . . . . **114** F4
Mavis Ave
Dewsbury WF13 . . . . . . **139** A6
Leeds LS16 . . . . **41** E6
Mavis Gr LS16 . . . . **41** E6
Mavis La LS16 . . . . **41** E6
Mavis Rd WF13 . . . . . . **117** F3
Mavis St
Bradford BD3. . . . . **75** B7
Dewsbury WF13 . . . . . . **139** A6
Mawcroft Cl LS19 . . . . . **40** A5
Mawcroft Grange Dr LS19 **40** A5
Mawcroft Mews LS19 . . . **40** A5
Mawson Ct BD1. . . . . . . **201** B3
Mawson St **6** BD18 . . . . **54** F8
Maw St BD4 . . . . **201** C1
Maxwell Ave WF17 . . . . **118** C2
Maxwell Rd
Bradford BD6. . . . . **93** F8
Ilkley LS29. . . . . **8** D3
Maxwell St
Featherstone WF7 . . . . **145** C5
Morley LS27. . . . . **97** F3
May Ave
Morley LS27. . . . . **78** C1
Thornton BD13 . . . . **72** E6
Mayberry Dr S75. . . . . . **193** F1
Maybridge Ind Pk LS12 . **210** B4
Maybury Ave WF1. . . . . **160** A7
Maybush Ct WF1 . . . . . . **142** E3
Maybush Rd WF1 . . . . . **142** E3
May Ct LS27 . . . . **78** C1
Mayfair
Bradford BD5. . . . . **74** D4

Mayfair *continued*
Pontefract WF8 . . . . **125** D3
Mayfair Ave HX4 . . . . . . **133** F1
Mayfair Ct HX4 . . . . **142** A5
Mayfair Pl WF9 . . . . **181** D7
Mayfair Way BD4 . . . . . . **75** D5
Mayfield
Brighouse, Hipperholme
   HX3. . . . . **93** C1
Brighouse, Norwood Green
   HX3. . . . . **93** F2
Mayfield Ave
Bradford BD12. . . . . **94** D3
Brighouse HD6 . . . . . . **115** B8
Halifax HX1 . . . . **202** C2
Huddersfield HD5 . . . . **154** F6
Ilkley LS29. . . . . **8** D4
Mayfield Cl
Glusburn BD20 . . . . **16** C6
Ilkley LS29. . . . . **8** D4
Leeds LS11 . . . . **211** B1
Mayfield Ct WF5 . . . . . . **140** E3
Mayfield Dr
Halifax HX1 . . . . **202** C2
Keighley BD20 . . . . **36** C8
Mayfield Gdns
Halifax HX1 . . . . **202** C2
Ilkley LS29. . . . . **8** D5
Ossett WF5 . . . . **140** C8
Sowerby Bridge HX6 . . **112** D5
Mayfield Gr
Baildon BD17. . . . . **38** D3
Brighouse HD6 . . . . . . **115** B8
Halifax HX1 . . . . **202** C2
Huddersfield HD5 . . . . **154** F6
Wilsden BD15 . . . . **53** B6
Mayfield Mount HX1 . . . **202** C2
Mayfield Pl BD12 . . . . . . **94** C3
Mayfield Rd
Hebden Bridge HX7 . . . **89** A4
Ilkley LS29. . . . . **8** C4
Keighley BD20 . . . . **35** B8
Leeds LS15 . . . . **81** B8
Mayfield Rise
Bradford BD12. . . . . **94** D3
Ryhill WF4 . . . . **162** A1
Mayfield St **8** HX1 . . . . **202** C1
Mayfields Wlk WF9 . . . . **182** B1
Mayfield Terr
Bradford, Lane End BD14 . **73** C3
1 Bradford, Upper Wyke
   BD12. . . . . **94** D3
12 Cleckheaton BD19 . . **116** E7
Halifax HX1 . . . . **202** B3
Mayfield Terr S **9** HX1. . **202** C1
Mayfield View BD12. . . . . **94** D3
Maylea Dr LS21 . . . . **22** D6
Mayman Cl WF17 . . . . . **118** C5
Mayman La WF17 . . . . . **118** B5
Maynes Ct WF12 . . . . . . **139** D2
Mayo Ave BD5. . . . . **74** E2
Mayo Cl LS8 . . . . **61** D6
Mayo Cres BD5 . . . . **74** E1
Mayo Dr BD5 . . . . **74** E1
Mayo Gr BD5 . . . . **74** E1
Mayor's Walk Ave WF8 . **146** D7
Mayor's Wlk WF8 . . . . . **146** D7
Mayors Walk Cl WF8 . . . **146** D7
Mayors Wlk WF10. . . . . . **125** E7
Maypole Mews LS15 . . . **63** D8
Maypole Rd HD2 . . . . . . **136** C4
May St
Cleckheaton BD19 . . . . . **95** D1
Haworth BD22. . . . . **51** D6
Huddersfield HD4 . . . . **153** E4
Keighley BD21. . . . . **35** C8
Mayster Gr HD6. . . . . . . **135** F8
Mayster Rd HD6 . . . . . . **135** F7
Maythorne Ave WF17. . . **118** A4
Maythorne Cres BD14 . . . **73** D4
Maythorne Dr BD14 . . . . **73** E4
May Tree Cl BD14 . . . . . . **73** D5
Mayville Ave
Keighley BD20 . . . . **36** B8
Leeds LS6 . . . . **205** B3
Mayville Pl **5** LS6 . . . . **205** B3
Mayville Rd LS6. . . . . . . **205** B3
Mayville St **4** LS6 . . . . . **205** B3
Mayville Terr LS6. . . . . . **205** B3
Mazebrook BD19. . . . . . . **95** E2
Mazebrook Ave BD19. . . . **95** E2
Mazebrook Cres BD19. . . **95** E2
Mead Cl LS15. . . . . **81** E6
Meade The LS25. . . . . . . **82** F7
Mead Gr LS15. . . . . **81** E6
Meadow Bank
Ackworth M T WF7. . . . **146** A1
Dewsbury WF13 . . . . . . **138** F8
Holmfirth HD9 . . . . **189** C6
Ryhill WF4 . . . . **162** C1
Meadowbank Ave BD15 . **54** B1
Meadow Bank Cres
WF14. . . . . **137** E5
Meadow Bottom Rd
OL14 . . . . **108** B6
Meadow Brook Chase **6**
   WF6. . . . . **123** C1
Meadow Brook Cl WF6. . **123** C1
Meadowbrook Ct LS27 . . **97** E3
Meadow Brook Ct WF6. . **144** C8
Meadow Brook Gn **7**
   WF6. . . . . **123** C1
Meadow Cl
Bardsey LS17. . . . . **28** E6
Batley WF17 . . . . **97** A1
Boston Spa LS23 . . . . . . **30** C8
Cononley BD20 . . . . **4** A3

Meadow Cl *continued*
Harden BD16 . . . . **36** B1
Hemsworth WF9 . . . . . . **181** C6
Liversedge WF15. . . . . . **116** F1
Lofthouse Gate WF1 . . . **121** D5
Shelf HX3. . . . . **93** D6
Meadow Cres
Halifax HX3 . . . . **91** E2
Royston S71. . . . . **179** D3
Meadowcroft
Draughton BD23 . . . . **1** D6
Honley HD9 . . . . **171** E4
Meadow Croft
Birkenshaw, Drighlington
   BD11. . . . . **96** D6
East Keswick LS17. . . . . **28** C5
Hemsworth WF9 . . . . . . **181** E5
Huddersfield HD2 . . . . **136** F5
Keighley BD22 . . . . **34** E6
Leeds LS11 . . . . **211** B1
Lofthouse Gate WF1 . . . **121** C5
Menston LS29 . . . . **22** A4
Ripponden HX4 . . . . . . **133** B4
Shafton S72. . . . . **180** C3
Meadowcroft Cl
Bradford BD10. . . . . **55** F8
Lofthouse Gate WF1 . . . **121** D5
Meadowcroft Cres WF10 **125** A8
Meadowcroft Ct WF1 . . . **121** D5
Meadowcroft La HX6. . . **132** E5
Meadowcroft Mews
Castleford WF10 . . . . . . **125** A8
Leeds LS9 . . . . **212** B3
Meadowcroft Rd WF1 . . **121** D5
Meadowcroft Rise BD4. . **95** C8
Meadow Ct
Bradford BD15. . . . . **54** A4
Brighouse HD6 . . . . . . **115** E2
Castleford WF10 . . . . . . **125** D6
Ossett WF5 . . . . **140** C7
Royston S71. . . . . **179** D3
South Elmsall WF9. . . . **183** B3
Meadow Dr
Halifax HX3 . . . . **91** E2
Liversedge WF15. . . . . . **116** F1
Meadow End LS16 . . . . . **24** E2
Meadowfield Cl WF9 . . . **163** A3
Meadowfield Prim Sch
LS9 . . . . **80** D7
Meadowfield Rise WF3. . **122** B6
Meadowfields Cl WF4. . . **162** A8
Meadowfields Dr WF4 . . **162** A8
Meadowfields Rd WF4 . . **162** A8
Meadow Fold BD15 . . . . **53** D4
Meadow Garth
Bramhope LS16. . . . . . . **24** F1
Lofthouse Gate WF1 . . . **121** C5
Meadowgate WF5. . . . . . **140** C7
Meadowgate Croft WF3 . **100** B2
Meadowgate Dr WF3 . . . **100** B1
Meadowgate Vale WF3. . **100** B1
Meadow Gn HD7. . . . . . **170** D8
Meadowhurst Gdns LS28 . **76** D7
Meadow La
Cononley BD20 . . . . **4** A2
Dewsbury WF13 . . . . . . **118** C1
Halifax HX3 . . . . **91** E2
Leeds LS11 . . . . **211** C2
Liversedge WF15. . . . . . **116** F1
Slaithwaite HD7. . . . . . **151** F1
Wakefield WF2 . . . . **141** F7
Meadowlands BD19 . . . **94** E1
Meadow Lea BD20 . . . . . **16** C6
Meadow Park Cres LS28 . **57** B2
Meadow Park Dr LS28 . . **57** B2
Meadow Pk HD5 . . . . . . **137** B2
Meadow Rd
Bradford BD10. . . . . **56** E8
Castleford WF10 . . . . . . **124** B5
Garforth LS25 . . . . **83** A7
Leeds LS11 . . . . **211** B1
Royston S71. . . . . **179** D3
Meadow Rise WF9 . . . . . **181** C7
Meadowside BD17 . . . . . **38** E4
Meadow Side Rd WF3. . . **120** E8
Meadow St
Huddersfield HD1 . . . . . **153** D7
21 Todmorden OL14 . . . **108** B6
Meadows The
Askwith LS21 . . . . **10** A5
Bradford BD6. . . . . **74** C1
Denby Dale HD8 . . . . . **191** F5
Kippax WF10 . . . . **102** F6
Leeds LS16 . . . . **42** C3
Sowerby Bridge HX6 . . **112** A5
Meadow The
Normanton WF6 . . . . . . **144** A7
Scarcroft LS14. . . . . **45** D8
Meadow Vale
Lofthouse Gate WF1 . . . **121** D5
Netherton WF4 . . . . **158** D5
Meadow Valley LS17 . . . **43** B5
Meadow View
Barwick in E LS15 . . . . . **63** E8
Bradford BD12. . . . . **94** C1
Leeds LS6 . . . . **205** B3
Oakworth BD22 . . . . **34** D2
Ossett WF5 . . . . **140** C7
Skelmanthorpe HD8 . . . **175** B1
Meadow Way
Ackworth M T WF7. . . . **146** A1
Castleford WF10 . . . . . . **125** A8
East Ardsley WF3 . . . . **119** D7
Leeds LS17 . . . . **43** B5
Meadow Wlk
Badsworth WF9 . . . . . . **164** E3
Halifax HX3 . . . . **91** E2

Meadow Wlk *continued*
Leeds LS7 . . . . **204** B2
Mead Rd LS15 . . . . **81** E6
Mead St HD1 . . . . **136** A1
Meadstead Dr S71 . . . . **179** B3
Meadstead Fold S71 . . . **179** B3
Mead View BD4 . . . . **75** E3
Meadway
Bradford BD6. . . . . **93** F6
Featherstone WF7 . . . . **144** C5
Mead Way
Kirkburton HD8 . . . . . . **173** E7
Leeds LS15 . . . . **81** E6
Meagill Rise LS21. . . . . . **10** E2
Meal Hill HD7. . . . . **151** F2
Meal Hill La
Holmfirth HD9 . . . . **189** F3
Slaithwaite HD7. . . . . . **151** F2
Meal Hill Rd HD9 . . . . . **187** F1
Mean La
Haworth BD22. . . . . **50** D8
Meltham HD9. . . . . **170** E2
Meanwood CE Prim Sch
LS6 . . . . **59** E7
Meanwood Cl LS7. . . . . **206** B4
Meanwood Gr LS6 . . . . . **42** E1
Meanwood Hts LS7. . . . **206** A4
Meanwood Rd LS6, LS7 . **206** B4
Meanwood St LS7. . . . . **206** C2
Meanwood Twrs LS6. . . . **60** A8
Meanwood Valley Cl LS7 . **59** F6
Meanwood Valley Dr LS7. **59** F6
Meanwood Valley Gn LS7 . **59** F6
Meanwood Valley Gr 2
   LS7. . . . . **59** F6
Meanwood Valley Mount
LS7. . . . . **59** F6
Meanwood Valley Urban
Farm ★ LS7. . . . . **60** A5
Meanwood Valley Wlk
LS7. . . . . **59** F6
Mearclough Rd HX6. . . . **112** D4
Mearhouse Bank HD9 . . **189** E4
Mearhouse Terr HD9. . . **189** E4
Medeway LS28. . . . . **57** C2
Medhurst Ave LS25 . . . . **83** B2
Medley La HX3. . . . . **92** F4
Medley St WF10 . . . . . . **124** E7
Medlock Rd WF4. . . . . . **141** A1
Medway
Kirkheaton HD5 . . . . . . **137** B2
Queensbury BD13 . . . . . **92** F8
Medway Ave LS25 . . . . . **83** A5
Meeting House La HD7. . **152** A4
Meggison Gr BD5. . . . . . **74** C4
Meg La HD3 . . . . **153** B5
Megnaway **3** BD5 . . . . . **74** E4
Melba Rd BD5 . . . . **74** B3
Melbourne Ave WF2 . . . **120** F3
Melbourne Gr
Bradford BD3. . . . . **75** E8
Leeds LS13 . . . . **58** C2
Melbourne Mews WF2 . . **120** E4
Melbourne Pl BD5 . . . . . **201** A1
Melbourne Rd
Wakefield WF1 . . . . **142** A8
Walsden OL14 . . . . **108** A1
Melbourne St
22 Halifax HX3 . . . . **92** A1
31 Hebden Bridge HX7 . . **89** A3
Leeds LS2 . . . . **207** A1
4 Liversedge WF15 . . . . **117** B3
Melbourne Terr BD5 . . . **201** A1
Melbourne Villas WF9 . . **181** C6
Melcombe Wlk BD4 . . . . **75** E4
Melford Cl S75 . . . . **178** B1
Melford St BD4 . . . . **75** C2
Melilot Cl BD16 . . . . **37** B2
Mellor's Bldgs WF4 . . . . **156** D8
Mellor Brook HD7. . . . . **151** F4
Mellor La HD9 . . . . **188** B5
Mellor Mill La HX4 . . . . **134** B4
Mellor St
Halifax HX1 . . . . **202** C1
Todmorden OL14 . . . . . **107** E8
Mellor Terr HX1 . . . . . . **202** C1
Mellwood La WF9 . . . . . **182** F3
Melrose Cl HD5 . . . . **155** A6
Melrose Ct HX5 . . . . **134** E6
Melrose Dr LS29 . . . . **9** E2
Melrose Gr LS18 . . . . **58** E8
Melrose Pl
Horsforth LS18 . . . . **58** D8
Pudsey LS28 . . . . **76** D6
Melrose St
Bradford BD7. . . . . **74** A4
26 Halifax HX3 . . . . **92** A1
Melrose Terr
11 Bacup OL13 . . . . **106** A7
Elland HX5. . . . . **134** F6
Melrose Wlk LS18. . . . . . **58** E8
Meltham CE Prim Sch
HD9. . . . . **170** E1
Meltham Hall HD9 . . . . **170** F2
Meltham House La HD9 . **189** F4
Meltham Mills Ind Est
HD9. . . . . **170** E1
Meltham Mills Rd HD9 . . **170** F2
Meltham Moor Prim Sch
HD9. . . . . **170** C3
Meltham Rd
Honley HD9 . . . . **171** D2
Huddersfield HD1, HD4. . **153** F3
Marsden HD7. . . . . **169** C5
Melton Ave LS10 . . . . . . **99** F4

Melton Cl
Middleton LS10 . . . . **99** F4
South Elmsall WF9. . . . **183** A5
Melton Garth LS10. . . . . **99** F4
Melton Mews BD22 . . . . **51** D8
Melton Rd WF2 . . . . **160** A4
Melton St WF17 . . . . . . **118** B6
Melton Terr BD10. . . . . . **56** E4
Melton Way
Liversedge WF15. . . . . . **116** F1
Royston S71. . . . . **179** C5
Melville Cl LS6. . . . . **206** B3
Melville Gdns LS6. . . . . **206** B4
Melville Gr LS29 . . . . **8** E4
Melville Pl LS6. . . . . **206** B4
Melville Rd LS6 . . . . **206** B3
Melville St BD7 . . . . **74** C7
Memorial Dr LS6. . . . . . . **59** F7
Mendip Ave HD3 . . . . . **135** A1
Mendip Cl LS25 . . . . **82** F5
Mendip Rd WF12 . . . . . **118** F1
Mendip Way BD12 . . . . . **94** B6
Menin Dr BD17 . . . . **38** C5
Menston Dr LS29 . . . . . . **22** A3
Menstone St **7** BD8. . . . **74** C8
Menston Old La
Burley in W LS29 . . . . . . **21** F7
Menston LS29 . . . . **21** F7
Menston Prim Sch LS29 . **22** A4
Menston Sta LS29. . . . . **22** B5
Mercer Cl HD4. . . . . **171** C7
Merchants Ct
18 Bingley BD16 . . . . . . **37** A2
Bradford BD4. . . . . **75** A5
Merchants Ho **1** LS2. . . **207** A2
Merchants Quay LS9 . . . **212** A3
Mercia Way LS15 . . . . . . **62** E3
Mercury Row **4** LS21 . . . **23** A7
Merefield Way WF10 . . . **124** E5
Merewood Rd WF10. . . . **123** F7
Meriden Ave LS25. . . . . . **82** F5
Merlin Cl
Morley LS27. . . . . **98** C3
South Elmsall WF9. . . . **183** A2
Merlin Ct
Batley WF17 . . . . **118** A8
Huddersfield HD4 . . . . **171** E7
18 Keighley BD21 . . . . . . **35** B5
Merlin Gr BD8 . . . . **73** C7
Merlinwood Dr BD17 . . . **38** D4
Merlyn-Rees Ave LS27 . . **98** A4
Merlyn Rees Com High Sch
LS10 . . . . **99** E8
Merrall St BD22. . . . . . . **51** D8
Merrill Rd S63. . . . . **194** C1
Merrion Cres HX3. . . . . **113** E5
Merrion Ctr LS2 . . . . . . **206** C1
Merrion Pl LS2 . . . . **211** C4
Merrion St
Halifax HX3 . . . . **113** E5
Leeds LS1, LS2 . . . . . . **211** C4
Merrion Way LS2 . . . . . **206** C1
Merrivale Rd BD15 . . . . . **73** A3
Merry Bent La HX6. . . . . **132** A5
Merrybents St OL14 . . . **108** D5
Merrydale Rd BD4 . . . . . **95** A6
Mersey St **4** OL13 . . . . . **106** A1
Mertensia Ho LS9. . . . . **207** B1
Merton Ave LS28. . . . . . . **57** D2
Merton Cl LS25 . . . . **83** C2
Merton Dr LS28 . . . . **57** C2
Merton Fold **6** BD5. . . . . **74** E4
Merton Gdns LS28 . . . . . **57** C2
Merton Rd BD7 . . . . **74** D5
Merton St HD1. . . . . **154** A5
Merville Ave BD17 . . . . . **38** C5
Metcalfe St BD4 . . . . **75** B4
Methley Dr LS7 . . . . **204** A2
Methley Gr LS7. . . . . **60** C6
Methley La
Leeds LS7 . . . . **204** A2
Rothwell LS26 . . . . **101** E4
Methley Mount LS7 . . . **204** A2
Methley Park Hospl
LS26 . . . . **102** A3
Methley Pl LS7 . . . . **60** C6
Methley Prim Sch LS26. **102** D3
Methley Rd WF10 . . . . . **124** B8
Methley Road Ind Pk
WF10. . . . . **124** B8
Methley Terr LS7 . . . . . **204** A2
Methley View LS7. . . . . **204** A2
Methuen Oval **2** BD12 . . **94** C1
Metro Travel Intc BD1 . . **201** C2
Mettle Cote OL13. . . . . . **106** A1
Mews Ct WF7. . . . . **145** D5
Mews The
Leeds LS8 . . . . **61** C8
Normanton WF6 . . . . . . **123** B3
Mexborough Ave LS7 . . **207** A4
Mexborough Ct LS14. . . . **45** F5
Mexborough Dr LS7. . . . **207** A4
Mexborough Gr LS7 . . . **207** A4
Mexborough Ho **3** HX5 . **134** F7
Mexborough Pl LS7 . . . **207** A4
Mexborough Rd
Leeds LS7 . . . . **207** A4
Shipley BD2 . . . . **55** D5
Mexborough St LS7. . . . **207** A4
Meynell App LS11. . . . . . **211** A1
Meynell Ave LS26 . . . . . **100** C5
Meynell Ct LS15 . . . . **81** D7
Meynell Fold LS15 . . . . . **81** D6
Meynell Hts LS11 . . . . . **211** A1
Meynell La LS15 . . . . **81** D6
Meynell Mount LS26 . . . **100** F5
Meynell Rd LS15 . . . . . . **81** D6
Meynell Sq LS11 . . . . . . **211** A1

Meynell Wlk LS11 ... 211 A1
Meyrick Ave LS22 ... 14 A6
Miall St HX1 ... 202 C4
Michael Ave WF3 ... 121 E5
Mickle Ct WF10 ... 124 C7
Mickledore Cl [6] BD7 ... 73 E3
Mickledore Ridge BD7 ... 73 E3
Micklefield CE Prim Sch LS25 ... 84 A7
Micklefield Ct LS19 ... 40 B4
Micklefield La LS19 ... 40 B4
Micklefield Rd LS19 ... 40 B4
Micklegate WF8 ... 125 D1
Micklegate Sq [4] WF8 ... 125 D1
Micklemoss Dr BD13 ... 72 C2
Micklethwaite Dr BD13 ... 92 E8
Micklethwaite Gr LS22 ... 13 E4
Micklethwaite La BD16 ... 36 E7
Micklethwaite Mews LS22 13 E4
Micklethwaite Rd WF4 ... 159 F3
Micklethwaite Stables LS22 ... 13 E4
Micklethwaite Stps LS22 . 13 E4
Micklethwaite View LS22. 13 E4
Mickletown Rd LS26 ... 102 C3
Mickley St LS12 ... 210 A3
Middlebrook Cl BD8 ... 73 E7
Middlebrook Cres BD8 ... 73 D6
Middlebrook Dr BD8 ... 73 D7
Middlebrook Hill BD8 ... 73 D7
Middlebrook Rise BD8 ... 73 D7
Middlebrook View BD8 ... 73 E7
Middlebrook Way BD8 ... 73 E7
Middlebrook Wlk BD8 ... 73 E7
Middle Cl S75 ... 177 C1
Middlecliffe Dr S36 ... 200 D5
Middlecroft Cl LS10 ... 99 F8
Middlecroft Rd LS10 ... 99 F8
Middle Cross St LS12 ... 210 A3
Middle Dean St [1] HX4 ... 134 D6
Middlefield Ct BD20 ... 19 B1
Middlefield La WF8 ... 166 B4
Middle Field La WF4 ... 177 F6
Middlegate WF17 ... 96 E1
Middlegate Ct BD4 ... 95 B8
Middle Hall Cl WF15 ... 116 F4
Middleham Ct [11] BD4 ... 75 E3
Middleham Moor LS10 ... 99 D3
Middle La
Bradford BD14 ... 73 C5
Crofton WF4 ... 162 B7
Knottingley WF11 ... 127 A3
Linton LS22 ... 13 C2
Middlemoor LS14 ... 62 B8
Middlemost Cl HD2 ... 135 F1
Middle Oxford St WF10 ... 124 C7
Middle Rd
Dewsbury, Earlsheaton WF12 ... 139 E7
Dewsbury WF12, WF13 ... 139 B7
Leeds LS9 ... 80 D2
Middle St
Bradford BD1 ... 201 B3
Sowerby Bridge HX6 ... 111 E1
Middlestown Jun & Inf Sch WF4 ... 158 B7
Middlethorne Cl LS17 ... 44 B5
Middlethorne Ct LS17 ... 44 A5
Middlethorne Mews LS17. 44 B5
Middlethorne Rise LS17 .. 44 B5
Middleton Ave
Ilkley LS29 ... 8 B5
Leeds LS9 ... 207 C1
Rothwell LS26 ... 100 A5
Middleton Cl LS27 ... 98 C4
Middleton Cres LS11 ... 214 B2
Middleton Ct
Cleckheaton BD19 ... 116 F6
Liversedge WF15 ... 116 E4
Middleton District Ctr LS10 ... 99 D5
Middleton Gr
Leeds LS11 ... 214 B1
Morley LS27 ... 98 C4
Middleton La
Middleton WF3 ... 99 D3
Rothwell LS26 ... 100 A5
Middleton Park Ave LS10. 99 B4
Middleton Park Cir LS10 . 99 B5
Middleton Park Cres LS10 ... 99 C5
Middleton Park Ct LS10 .. 99 B4
Middleton Park Gn LS10.. 99 B4
Middleton Park Gr LS10.. 99 B4
Middleton Park Mount LS10 ... 99 B4
Middleton Park Pl LS10 .. 99 C4
Middleton Park Rd LS10.. 99 C5
Middleton Park Terr LS10 99 C4
Middleton Prim Sch LS10 99 B3
Middleton Rd
Ilkley LS29 ... 8 A4
Leeds LS10 ... 99 F8
Morley LS27 ... 98 C4
Middleton Rly* LS11 ... 214 C1
Middleton St Mary's CE Prim Sch LS10 ... 99 C5
Middleton St [5] BD8 ... 55 B1
Middleton Terr LS27 ... 98 C4
Middleton Way
Knottingley WF11 ... 126 F4
Leeds LS10 ... 99 F6
Middleway BD20 ... 5 F1
Middle Way BD21 ... 35 E7
Midge Hall Cl LS29 ... 9 E1
Midgeham Gr BD16 ... 36 A1
Midgehole La HX7 ... 89 A6
Midgehole Rd HX7 ... 89 A6
Midgeley Rd BD17 ... 38 A1
Midgley Almshouses [16] BD22 ... 51 E8
Midgley Chapel HX2 ... 90 B1
Midgley Gdns LS6 ... 206 A3
Midgley Pl LS6 ... 206 B3
Midgley Rd
Burley in W LS29 ... 9 E1
Mytholmroyd HX7 ... 89 F1
Midgley Rise WF8 ... 125 D3
Midgley Row BD4 ... 75 B1
Midgley Sch HX2 ... 90 C1
Midgley Terr LS6 ... 206 B3
Midland Cl LS10 ... 215 C3
Midland Cotts S71 ... 179 D7
Midland Garth LS10 ... 215 B3
Midland Hill BD16 ... 36 F3
Midland Mills LS11 ... 211 A2
Midland Mills Ind Est BD20 ... 16 E7
Midland Pas LS6 ... 205 C3
Midland Rd
Baildon BD17 ... 38 D2
Bradford BD8 ... 55 D1
Leeds, Hyde Park LS6 ... 205 C3
Leeds LS10 ... 215 B3
Pontefract WF8 ... 125 E1
Royston S71 ... 179 D4
Shipley BD9 ... 55 C5
Midland St
Huddersfield HD1 ... 154 B8
Rothwell LS26 ... 101 C6
Midland Terr
Bradford BD2 ... 55 E3
Keighley BD21 ... 35 C8
Shipley BD9 ... 55 C5
Mid Point BD3 ... 75 F8
Mid Point Bsns Pk BD3 ... 75 F8
Midway HD4 ... 171 A6
Midway Ave [1] BD16 ... 54 A7
Mid Yorkshire Nuffield Hosp LS18 ... 58 E8
Milan Rd LS8 ... 207 C3
Milan St LS8 ... 208 A3
Mildred St BD3 ... 56 A1
Mildred Sylvester Way WF6 ... 123 E2
Mile Cross Gdns HX1 ... 202 A2
Mile Cross Pl HX1 ... 202 A2
Mile Cross Rd HX1 ... 202 A2
Mile Cross Terr HX1 ... 202 A2
Mile End HD9 ... 170 D2
Miles Garth LS17 ... 28 F6
Miles Hill Ave LS7 ... 60 B6
Miles Hill Cres
Bradford BD4 ... 75 C1
Leeds LS7 ... 60 B6
Miles Hill Dr BD4 ... 75 C1
Miles Hill Gr LS7 ... 60 B6
Miles Hill Mount LS7 ... 60 A7
Miles Hill Pl LS7 ... 60 B7
Miles Hill Prim Sch LS7 .. 60 A7
Miles Hill Rd LS7 ... 60 B6
Miles Hill Sq LS7 ... 60 B6
Miles Hill St LS7 ... 60 B6
Miles Hill Terr LS7 ... 60 B6
Miles Hill View LS7 ... 60 B6
Milestone Ct LS28 ... 57 F2
Mile Thorn St HX1 ... 202 B3
Milford Gr BD19 ... 96 A3
Milford Pl
Bradford BD9 ... 55 A3
Leeds LS4 ... 205 A1
Milford St HD1 ... 154 A5
Milgate St S71 ... 179 D4
Millars Wlk WF9 ... 182 A1
Mill Ave HD5 ... 155 A7
Millbank
Pudsey LS28 ... 76 F6
Yeadon LS19 ... 40 B8
Mill Bank Cl HX6 ... 132 C7
Millbank Ct LS28 ... 76 F6
Millbank Fold LS28 ... 76 F6
Mill Bank Rd
Meltham HD9 ... 170 F1
Sowerby Bridge HX6 ... 132 D7
Mill Banks BD20 ... 5 E1
Millbank View LS28 ... 76 F6
Millbeck App LS27 ... 98 C4
Millbeck Cl BD8 ... 73 C6
Millbeck Dr BD16 ... 36 A1
Millbeck Gn LS22 ... 29 A8
Millbridge Jun & Inf Sch WF15 ... 117 B4
Millbrook Gdns WF13 ... 118 A3
Mill Carr Hill Rd BD12, BD4 ... 95 B5
Mill Chase Cl [3] WF2 ... 142 A6
Mill Chase Croft [1] WF2. 142 A6
Mill Chase Gdns [4] WF2. 142 A6
Mill Chase Rd [2] WF2 ... 142 A6
Mill Cl
Ackworth M T WF7 ... 164 A6
Meltham HD9 ... 170 D2
South Kirkby WF9 ... 182 A1
Mill Cotts WF7 ... 145 B5
Millcroft WF3 ... 121 E6
Mill Croft LS27 ... 97 D7
Millcroft Cl WF3 ... 121 E6
Millcroft Est LS21 ... 24 D7
Millcroft Rise WF3 ... 121 E6
Mill Ct [3] BD22 ... 51 C2
Mill Dam LS23 ... 30 E5
Mill Dam Jun & Inf Sch WF7 ... 164 A5
Mill Dam La WF8 ... 125 E2
Millenium Rd BD23 ... 4 A8
Millennia Pk WF2 ... 142 B3
Millennium Bsns Pk BD20 17 C6
Millennium Ct LS28 ... 76 F8
Millennium Dr LS11 ... 214 B1
Millennium Sq LS1 ... 206 B1
Millennium Way LS11 ... 214 B1
Miller Ave WF2 ... 142 D2
Miller Cl BD2 ... 55 E5
Miller Ct WF2 ... 160 B4
Miller Garth WF7 ... 164 A5
Millergate BD1 ... 201 B3
Miller Hill HD8 ... 192 A5
Miller Hill Bank HD8 ... 192 A5
Millers Croft
Ackworth M T WF7 ... 164 A6
Batley WF17 ... 97 B1
Royston S71 ... 179 C4
Millers Ct WF15 ... 117 B2
Millers Dale LS27 ... 97 F6
Millersdale Cl BD4 ... 95 A7
Mill Farm Dr WF2 ... 160 C4
Millfield Cl HD3 ... 153 C7
Millfield Cres WF8 ... 146 C6
Mill Field Ct [2] BD20 ... 5 E1
Mill Field Ends HX2 ... 111 C8
Millfield Rd WF4 ... 159 C8
Mill Field Rd BD16 ... 54 B7
Millfields
Ossett WF5 ... 140 C5
Silsden BD20 ... 5 D1
Millfold HD9 ... 188 C2
Mill Fold LS27 ... 97 D7
Mill Fold Way HX6 ... 132 E4
Mill Forest Way WF17 ... 118 F4
Mill Garth LS27 ... 97 D7
Millgarth Ct LS22 ... 29 B8
Millgarth St LS2 ... 212 A4
Millgate
Ackworth M T WF7 ... 164 A5
Bingley BD16 ... 36 F3
Elland HX5 ... 134 F7
Huddersfield HD4 ... 155 B2
Huddersfield, Yews Hill HD1 ... 153 E5
Mill Gn LS12 ... 210 C2
Mill Gr HD6 ... 114 F4
Mill Grath WF8 ... 146 C7
Mill Green Cl LS14 ... 62 C5
Mill Green Garth LS14 ... 62 C5
Mill Green Gdns LS14 ... 62 C5
Mill Green Pl LS14 ... 62 C4
Mill Green Rd LS14 ... 62 C5
Mill Green View LS14 ... 62 B5
Millhaven Mews [8] BD8 .. 55 D1
Mill Hey BD22 ... 51 D7
Mill Hill
Ackworth M T WF7 ... 164 A8
Haworth BD22 ... 51 C7
Leeds LS1 ... 211 C3
Normanton WF6 ... 123 A1
Pudsey LS28 ... 76 E5
Rothwell LS26 ... 100 E5
Mill Hill Ave WF8 ... 146 C6
Mill Hill Cl WF8 ... 147 D5
Mill Hill Gn LS26 ... 100 E5
Mill Hill La
Brighouse HD6 ... 114 F4
Liversedge HD6 ... 115 F1
Pontefract WF8 ... 146 C7
Mill Hill Rd WF8 ... 146 C7
Mill Hill Sq LS26 ... 100 E5
Mill Hill Top BD16 ... 53 B8
Mill House La HX6 ... 112 A2
Mill House Rise BD5 ... 75 B1
Milligan Ave BD2 ... 56 A5
Milligan Ct BD16 ... 36 A1
Milligans Pl BD20 ... 16 D7
Mill La
Ackworth M T WF7 ... 164 A6
Bacup OL13 ... 106 B3
Bardsey LS17 ... 28 E4
Batley, Hanging Heaton WF17 ... 118 E3
Batley, Howden Clough WF17 ... 97 B2
Birkenshaw BD11 ... 96 A6
Birkenshaw, Tong BD11 ... 77 A2
Bradford BD4, BD5 ... 201 C1
Bradford, Woodside BD6 ... 93 E6
Brighouse HD6 ... 115 B2
Castleford WF10 ... 103 D1
Cleckheaton BD19 ... 95 D3
[3] Collingham LS22 ... 29 B8
Darton S75 ... 177 E1
Dewsbury WF12 ... 140 A7
East Ardsley WF3 ... 120 E8
Elland HX4 ... 134 C4
Featherstone WF7 ... 144 D6
Flockton WF4 ... 157 D2
Gildersome LS27 ... 97 D7
Guiseley LS20 ... 38 D8
Halifax, Boothtown HX3 ... 92 B2
Halifax HX2 ... 91 D7
Huddersfield HD5 ... 137 B5
Leeds LS13 ... 58 A3
Low Bradley BD20 ... 4 C6
Mickletown LS26 ... 102 D3
Normanton WF6 ... 123 D4
Notton WF4 ... 178 D8
Oakworth BD22 ... 34 B2
Oakworth BD22 ... 34 C2
Otley LS21 ... 23 A8
Oxenhope BD22 ... 51 C3
Pontefract WF8 ... 125 F3
Pool LS21 ... 24 D7
Queensbury BD13 ... 72 C2
Ryhill WF4 ... 162 B1
Skellow DN6 ... 184 F2
South Elmsall WF9 ... 183 B4
Mill La *continued*
South Kirkby WF9 ... 182 A2
Steeton BD20 ... 17 C5
Thorp Arch LS23 ... 30 E8
Mill Lane Jun & Inf Sch WF17 ... 118 D3
Millmoor Cl BD9 ... 54 D2
Mill Moor Rd HD9 ... 170 C2
Mill Pit La LS26 ... 100 D7
Mill Pond Cl LS6 ... 59 E7
Mill Pond Gr LS6 ... 59 E7
Mill Pond La LS6 ... 59 E7
Mill Pond Sq LS6 ... 59 E7
Mill Race Fold HD9 ... 189 C8
Mill Rd WF13 ... 118 C2
Mill Row BD20 ... 16 F6
Mill Royd St HD6 ... 115 B2
Mill St E WF12 ... 139 D6
Mill St W WF12 ... 139 C7
Millshaw
Leeds LS11 ... 213 B1
Morley LS11 ... 213 A1
Mill Shaw La HD8, HD9 ... 190 B1
Millshaw Mount LS11 ... 98 E8
Millshaw Park Ave LS11 .. 98 D8
Millshaw Park Cl LS11 ... 98 D8
Millshaw Park Dr LS11 .. 213 A1
Millshaw Park La LS11 ... 98 D8
Millshaw Park Way LS11 213 A1
Millshaw Rd LS11 ... 98 E7
Millside S72 ... 180 C3
Millside Way HX3 ... 113 D3
Millside Wlk
Morley LS27 ... 98 C4
Shafton S72 ... 180 C3
Mill St
Batley WF17 ... 117 E8
Bradford BD1 ... 201 C3
Bradford, Wibsey BD6 ... 74 A1
Castleford WF10 ... 124 B7
Cullingworth BD13 ... 52 D6
Elland HX3 ... 113 A1
Glusburn BD20 ... 16 E6
Huddersfield HD4 ... 153 E4
Leeds LS9 ... 212 A3
Morley LS27 ... 98 A3
South Kirkby WF9 ... 182 A2
Sutton-in-C BD20 ... 16 E5
Mill Stables HD9 ... 170 F2
Millstone Cl WF7 ... 164 A5
Millstone Rise WF15 ... 117 B2
Mill Stram Dr HX2 ... 111 D7
Mill View
Burley in W LS29 ... 9 E2
Hemsworth WF9 ... 181 C6
Knottingley WF11 ... 126 B4
Ripponden HX6 ... 132 D4
[2] Shipley BD18 ... 55 A8
Wakefield WF2 ... 141 D7
Millward St WF4 ... 162 A1
Millwater Ave WF12 ... 139 B5
Millwood La OL14 ... 108 D5
Millwright LS2 ... 207 A1
Millwright Cl HD7 ... 168 E4
Millwright St LS2 ... 207 A1
Milne's Ave WF2 ... 141 F3
Milne Ct LS15 ... 81 D6
Milner's La WF8 ... 147 D4
Milner's Rd LS19 ... 39 F7
Milner Bank LS21 ... 22 D6
Milner Cl HX4 ... 134 C7
Milner Ct BD18 ... 54 E8
Milner Gdns LS9 ... 212 C2
Milner Ing BD12 ... 94 C5
Milner La
Elland HX4 ... 134 C7
Rothwell WF3 ... 100 A2
Thorner LS14 ... 45 F7
Milner Rd BD17 ... 38 B1
Milner Royd La HX6 ... 112 E3
Milner St
Halifax HX1 ... 203 A3
Huddersfield HD1 ... 153 E3
Ossett WF5 ... 119 C1
Milner Way WF5 ... 140 E6
Milnes Ct [4] BD6 ... 94 A8
Milnes Gr WF10 ... 125 B7
Milnes St LS12 ... 210 B2
Milne St BD7 ... 74 C7
Miln Rd HD1 ... 154 A8
Milnthorpe Cl LS23 ... 30 C3
Milnthorpe Cres WF2 ... 160 D7
Milnthorpe Dr WF2 ... 160 D8
Milnthorpe Garth LS23 ... 30 C3
Milnthorpe Gdns LS23 ... 30 C3
Milnthorpe Gn WF2 ... 160 D7
Milnthorpe La
Bramham LS23 ... 30 C3
Wakefield WF2 ... 142 D2
Milnthorpe Way LS23 ... 30 C3
Milroyd Cres WF17 ... 97 A2
Milshaw Park Trad Est LS11 ... 98 D8
Milton Ave
Liversedge WF15 ... 117 C3
Sowerby Bridge HX6 ... 112 B5
Milton Cl
Crigglestone WF4 ... 159 D6
Liversedge WF15 ... 117 C3
Milton Cres WF2 ... 141 C4
Milton Ct WF3 ... 121 F6
Milton Dr
Barwick in E LS15 ... 62 F7
Batley WF15 ... 117 C2
Fitzwilliam WF9 ... 163 B2
Milton Gdns WF15 ... 117 C2
Milton Gr WF13 ... 118 C2
Milton Pl
Halifax HX1 ... 203 A3
Ossett WF5 ... 140 D7
[17] Sowerby Bridge HX6 .. 112 B5
Milton Rd
Liversedge WF15 ... 117 C3
Wakefield WF2 ... 141 D4
Milton Sq WF16 ... 117 D4
Milton St
[1] Batley WF16 ... 117 D5
Bradford BD7 ... 74 C7
Castleford WF10 ... 124 C8
Denholme BD13 ... 71 E8
[20] Sowerby Bridge HX6 .. 112 B5
Wakefield WF2 ... 142 A5
Milton Terr
Cleckheaton BD19 ... 116 C8
Fitzwilliam WF9 ... 163 A4
[3] Halifax HX1 ... 203 A3
Leeds LS5 ... 59 A4
Yeadon LS19 ... 39 F7
Milton Wlk [10] WF13 ... 139 C8
Minden Cl WF8 ... 146 A7
Minden Way WF8 ... 146 A8
Minerva Ind Est LS26 ... 101 E7
Minerva St HD4 ... 152 F3
Mini Market [3] HD1 ... 154 C8
Minnie St
Haworth BD22 ... 51 C6
Keighley BD21 ... 35 B6
Minorca Mount BD13 ... 52 D1
Minstead Ave HD6 ... 135 D7
Minster Cl HX4 ... 134 B7
Minster Dr BD4 ... 75 D5
Minsthorpe Com Coll WF9 ... 183 A5
Minsthorpe La WF9 ... 182 E4
Minsthorpe Vale WF9 ... 182 F4
Mint St
Bradford BD2 ... 56 B2
Huddersfield HD1 ... 153 D7
Miramar HD2 ... 136 D5
Mirey Butt La WF11 ... 126 D3
Mirey La HX6 ... 111 C3
Mirfield Ave BD2 ... 56 A5
Mirfield Free Gram & Sixth Form The WF14 ... 137 F7
Mirfield Sta WF14 ... 138 A3
Miriam Lord Com Prim Sch BD8 ... 55 B1
Miry La
Barwick in E LS25 ... 46 F1
Cleckheaton WF15 ... 116 C5
Holmfirth, Netherthong HD9 ... 188 F8
Holmfirth, Thongsbridge HD9 ... 189 B8
Mytholmroyd HX7 ... 110 F6
Yeadon LS19 ... 40 B7
Mission St HD6 ... 115 C1
Mission View HD9 ... 188 F1
Mistal The BD10 ... 55 F8
Mistral Cl BD12 ... 94 C2
Mistral Gr WF15 ... 116 B5
Mistress La LS12 ... 209 C4
Mitcham Dr BD9 ... 55 A2
Mitchell Ave
[3] Dewsbury WF13 ... 118 B2
Huddersfield HD5 ... 155 B5
Mitchell Cl BD10 ... 39 C1
Mitchell La
Bradford BD10 ... 39 C1
Silsden BD20 ... 5 E1
Mitchell Sq
[7] Bradford BD5 ... 74 E4
[3] Silsden BD20 ... 5 E1
Mitchell St
Brighouse HD6 ... 115 A3
[6] Hebden Bridge HX7 ... 89 A2
Keighley BD21 ... 35 D8
Sowerby Bridge HX6 ... 112 C4
Todmorden OL14 ... 107 E8
Mitchell Terr BD16 ... 36 F2
Mitford Pl LS12 ... 210 A3
Mitford Rd LS12 ... 210 A3
Mitford Terr LS12 ... 210 A3
Mitford View LS12 ... 210 A3
Mitre Ct BD4 ... 75 D3
Mitre St
Dewsbury WF13 ... 139 A8
Huddersfield HD1 ... 153 E7
Mitton St
Bradford BD5 ... 74 C3
[2] Shipley BD16 ... 54 B6
Mixenden Cl HX2 ... 91 C5
Mixenden Com Prim Sch HX2 ... 91 B6
Mixenden Ct HX2 ... 91 D4
Mixenden La HX2 ... 91 D6
Mixenden Lane Ends HX2 91 B4
Mixenden Rd HX2 ... 91 C5
Mixenden Stones HX2 ... 91 C6
Moat Cres BD10 ... 56 C8
Moat End LS14 ... 45 F5
Moat Hill WF17 ... 97 A2
Moat Hill Farm Dr WF17 .. 97 A2
Moat House Sq LS23 ... 15 D1
Modder Ave LS12 ... 209 B3
Modder Pl LS12 ... 209 B3
Modd La HD9 ... 188 F4
Model Ave LS12 ... 210 A3
Model Rd LS12 ... 210 A3
Model Terr LS12 ... 210 A3
Moderna Bsns Pk HX7 .. 110 F8
Moderna Way HX7 ... 110 F8

Moffat Cl BD6 . . . . 93 F7
Moffatt Cl HX3 . . . . 91 F3
Moldgreen Com Prim Sch
HD5. . . . . .154 D5
Moles Head HD7 . . . . . .152 C6
Molly Hurst La WF4 . . . .177 F7
Mona's Terr 1 OL14 . . . .108 A1
Monarch Gate BD13. . . . 71 E6
Mona St
Slaithwaite HD7 . . . . . .151 F1
Wakefield WF2 . . . . . . .141 E6
Monckton Dr WF10 . . . .125 C6
Monckton Rd WF2 . . . . .142 B2
Monckton Road Ind Est
WF2. . . . . .142 A2
Mond Ave BD3. . . . . 56 D1
Monk Barn Cl 1 BD16. . . 37 A4
Monk Bridge Ave 11 LS6. . 59 F6
Monk Bridge Dr 6 LS6. . . 59 E6
Monk Bridge Gr 2 LS6. . . 59 E6
Monk Bridge Mount 10
LS6. . . . . 59 F6
Monk Bridge Pl 1 LS6. . . 59 E6
Monk Bridge Rd LS6. . . . 59 E6
Monk Bridge St LS6. . . . . 59 F6
Monk Bridge Terr LS6. . . 59 E6
Monkfield WF14 . . . . . . .137 E6
Monkhill Ave WF8 . . . . .125 D2
Monkhill Dr WF8. . . . . . .125 D2
Monkhill La WF8. . . . . . .125 D2
Monkhill Mount WF8. . . .125 D2
Monk Ings WF17 . . . . . . 96 D1
Monk Ings Ave WF17 . . . 96 C2
Monkmans Wharfe 7
BD20. . . . . .5 E1
Monk St
Bradford BD7. . . . . 74 C7
Wakefield WF1 . . . . . . .216 C4
Monkswood LS5 . . . . 58 F6
Monkswood Ave LS14 . . . 61 F8
Monkswood Bank LS14. . . 61 F8
Monkswood Cl LS14. . . . . 61 F8
Monkswood Dr LS14 . . . . 61 F8
Monkswood Gate 6 LS14 62 A8
Monkswood Gn LS14 . . . . 61 F8
Monkswood Hill LS14. . . . 61 F8
Monkswood Rise LS14 . . . 61 F8
Monkswood Wlk LS14. . . . 62 A8
Monkton Way S71 . . . . .179 C5
Monkwood Rd WF1 . . . .121 B5
Monson Ave LS28 . . . . . . 57 B6
Mons Rd OL14 . . . . .107 F7
Montagu Ave LS8 . . . . . . 61 C5
Montagu Cres LS8 . . . . . 61 C5
Montagu Ct LS8 . . . . 61 B6
Montagu Dr LS8 . . . . 61 B6
Montague Cres LS25 . . . . 83 A7
Montague Ct LS12 . . . . .209 A3
Montague Pl LS25 . . . . . 83 A7
Montague St
Bradford BD5. . . . . 74 C3
Sowerby Bridge HX6 . . . .112 A3
Wakefield WF1 . . . . . . .142 F2
Montagu Gdns LS8. . . . . 61 B5
Montagu Gr LS8 . . . . 61 C5
Montagu Pl LS8. . . . . 61 B5
Montagu Rd LS22 . . . . . . 14 A6
Montagu Rise LS8 . . . . .208 C4
Montagu View LS8. . . . . 61 B5
Montcalm Cres
Leeds LS10 . . . . .215 B2
Lofthouse Gate WF3 . . . .121 F3
Monterey Dr BD15 . . . . . 54 A4
Montfort Cl LS18. . . . . . . 41 B3
Montgomery Ave LS16 . . 59 C7
Mont Gr 1 BD5. . . . . 74 D3
Montpelier Terr 3 LS6. .206 A4
Montreal Ave LS7. . . . . .204 A2
Montreal St 10 OL14 . . . .108 A1
Montreal Terr LS13. . . . . 77 A8
Montrose Ave S75 . . . . .177 F1
Montrose Bldgs 5 HX7 . . 89 A4
Montrose Pl 2 BD13. . . . 72 C2
Montrose St BD2. . . . . . . 55 D4
Montrose Terr 4 HX7. . . 89 A4
Montserrat Rd BD4 . . . . . 75 F1
Monument Dr S72 . . . . .180 F2
Monument La WF8. . . . . .146 E7
Monument Mews WF8 . .146 E7
Moody St BD4 . . . . .201 C1
Moon Cl 12 WF17 . . . . . . 96 F1
Moor Allerton Ave LS17. . 43 E2
Moor Allerton Cres LS17 . 43 E2
Moor Allerton Ctr LS17. . 43 B2
Moor Allerton Dr LS17 . . 43 E2
Moor Allerton Gdns LS17. 43 D2
Moor Allerton Hall Prim Sch
LS8 . . . . 43 E1
Moor Allerton Way LS17. . 43 E2
Moor Ave
Clifford LS23 . . . . 30 D6
Leeds LS15 . . . . 80 F7
Lofthouse Gate WF3 . . . .121 E6
Moorbank Ct LS6 . . . . . . 59 E5
Moor Bottom
Cleckheaton BD19. . . . . .116 B7
Honley HD9 . . . . .171 D4
Moor Bottom La
Bingley BD16. . . . . 37 B3
Elland HX4. . . . . .134 A8
Halifax HX3 . . . . .113 A1
Keighley BD21. . . . . 35 B2
Sowerby Bridge HX2 . . . .111 A5
Moorbottom Rd HD1 . . .153 E4

Moor Bottom Rd
Halifax HX2 . . . . 91 F6
Ripponden HX4 . . . . . . .132 F5
Moorbrow HD9 . . . . . . .189 C2
Moor Cl
Huddersfield HD4 . . . . . .153 C1
Leeds LS10 . . . . .215 A2
Moor Close Ave BD13 . . . 92 C8
Moor Close Farm Mews 1
BD13. . . . . 92 C8
Moor Close La BD13. . . . 92 C8
Moor Close Par BD13. . . 72 D1
Moor Close Rd BD13. . . . 92 C8
Moorcock La HX7. . . . . . 87 C5
Moorcock Rd HX7 . . . . . 87 D5
Moor Cottage Cl HD4 . . .171 D7
Moor Cres LS11. . . . . . .214 C4
Moor Crescent Chase
LS11. . . . . .214 C4
Moor Crest Rd HD4 . . . .153 C3
Moorcrest Rise S75 . . . .178 B2
Moorcroft
Dewsbury WF13 . . . . . . .118 A1
Huddersfield HD7 . . . . . .152 D5
Ossett WF5 . . . . .140 D6
Moorcroft Ave
Bradford BD3. . . . . 56 D1
Haworth BD22. . . . . 34 E3
Moorcroft Avenues HD7 152 D5
Moorcroft Ct 1 WF5. . . .140 C6
Moorcroft Dr
Bradford BD4. . . . . 75 F1
Dewsbury WF13 . . . . . . .117 F1
Holmfirth HD9 . . . . .189 D7
Moorcroft Park Dr HD9 . 189 E7
Moorcroft Rd
Bradford BD4. . . . . 75 F1
Dewsbury WF13 . . . . . . .117 F1
Moorcroft Terr BD4. . . . . 95 F8
Moor Dr
Leeds LS6 . . . . 59 E6
Oakworth BD22 . . . . 34 C3
Otley LS21 . . . . 23 D8
Pudsey LS28 . . . . 76 F5
Moore Ave BD6, BD7 . . . 74 A2
Moor Edge BD16. . . . . . . 36 A2
Moor Edge High Side
BD16 . . . . 36 A2
Moorehouse Gr LS9. . . .207 B1
Moor End
Boston Spa LS23 . . . . . . 30 B8
Sowerby Bridge HX6 . . . .112 D2
Moor End Ave HX2 . . . . . 91 C1
Moorend CE Fst Sch
BD19. . . . . 95 C1
Moor End Gdns HX2. . . . 91 D1
Moor End La
Batley WF13 . . . . .117 F2
Sowerby Bridge HX6 . . . .112 D2
Moor End Rd
Halifax HX2 . . . . 91 B2
Halifax, Mixenden HX2 . . 91 B5
Huddersfield HD4 . . . . . .153 E3
Moor End Tech Coll
HD4. . . . . .153 D2
Moore St 5 BD21. . . . . . 35 C6
Moore View BD7 . . . . 73 F3
Moor Farm Gdns LS7. . . 60 C7
Moorfield
Birkenshaw BD11 . . . . . . 96 C4
Gildersome LS27 . . . . . . 97 C7
Wadsworth Moor HX7. . . 89 C5
Moorfield Ave
Bradford BD3. . . . . 56 D1
Brighouse BD19. . . . . . .115 E7
Leeds LS12 . . . . .209 A4
Menston LS29 . . . . 21 F4
Moorfield Bsns Pk LS19 . 40 D7
Moorfield Cl LS19. . . . . . 40 D6
Moorfield Cres
Hemsworth WF9 . . . . . . .181 C6
Leeds LS28 . . . . .209 A4
Pudsey LS28 . . . . 76 D6
Yeadon LS19 . . . . 40 D7
Moorfield Croft LS19. . . . 40 D6
Moorfield Ct
Grange Moor WF4. . . . . .156 E4
Yeadon LS19 . . . . 40 D6
Moorfield Dr
Baildon BD17. . . . . 38 C5
Oakworth BD22 . . . . 34 D3
Yeadon LS19 . . . . 40 D6
Moorfield Gdns LS28. . . . 76 D6
Moorfield Gr
Leeds LS12 . . . . .209 A4
Pudsey LS28 . . . . 76 D6
Moorfield Pl
Bradford BD10. . . . . 56 B8
Hemsworth WF9 . . . . . . .181 C6
Moorfield Rd
Huddersfield HD1 . . . . . .136 B1
Ilkley LS29. . . . . .8 F4
Leeds LS12 . . . . .209 A4
Shipley BD16 . . . . 54 A7
Yeadon LS19 . . . . 40 D7
Moor Field Rd HX4. . . . .133 A1
Moorfields LS13 . . . . 58 C3
Moorfields Sch LS29. . . . .8 D3
Moorfield St
Halifax HX1 . . . . .202 C1
Leeds, Hill Top LS12. . . .209 A4
Leeds, Woodhouse LS2 . .206 A3
Moorfield Terr LS19. . . . . 40 C7
Moorfield View WF15 . . .116 F1

Moorfield Way
Brighouse BD19, LS29. . .115 E7
Ilkley LS29. . . . . .8 F4
Moor Flatts Ave LS10. . . 99 C5
Moor Flatts Rd LS10. . . . 99 C5
Moor Fold HD9 . . . . . . .189 E7
Moorfoot La BD20 . . . . . .4 A3
Moorgarth Ave BD3. . . . 56 D1
Moorgate BD17 . . . . 38 C4
Moor Gate OL14 . . . . . .108 C3
Moorgate Ave
Bradford BD3. . . . . 56 D1
Kippax LS25. . . . . 83 A2
Moorgate Cl 1 LS25. . . . 83 A2
Moorgate Dr LS25 . . . . . 83 B2
Moorgate Flats HD9. . . .170 D2
Moorgate Rd LS25 . . . . . 83 A3
Moorgate Rise 2 LS25. . . 83 A2
Moorgate St 9 HX1 . . . .202 B1
Moor Gr
Lofthouse Gate WF3 . . . .121 E6
Pudsey LS28 . . . . 76 F5
Shelf HX3. . . . . 93 C7
Moor Grange LS19 . . . . . 40 C6
Moor Grange Ct 8 LS16. . 58 F8
Moor Grange Dr LS16 . . . 59 A8
Moor Grange Rise LS16 . 59 A8
Moor Grange View LS16. . 59 A8
Moorgreen Fold BD10. . . 56 A7
Moor Haven Ct LS17 . . . 43 A3
Moorhead Cl HD9. . . . . .170 D2
Moorhead Cres BD18. . . 54 E7
Moorhead La BD18. . . . . 54 E7
Moorhead Terr BD18. . . . 54 E7
Moorhen Bank LS12. . . . 77 D7
Moor Hey HX4 . . . . .133 F2
Moor Hey La
Elland, Elland Upper Edge HD2,
HX5. . . . . .135 C5
Elland, Sowood Green HX4 133 F2
Moor Hill Ct HX3. . . . . . .152 F8
Moor Hill Rd HD3 . . . . . .134 F1
Moorhouse Ave
Bradford BD2. . . . . 56 A5
Leeds LS11 . . . . .213 C1
Lofthouse Gate WF3 . . . .122 B6
Wakefield WF2 . . . . . . .142 A6
Moorhouse Cl
Lofthouse Gate WF3 . . . .122 B7
Normanton WF6 . . . . . . .123 C3
Oxenhope BD22. . . . . . . 51 C3
Moorhouse Cres WF2 . . .142 A6
Moorhouse Ct
Oxenhope BD22. . . . . . . 51 C3
South Elmsall WF9. . . . . .183 A1
Moor House Ct LS17 . . . 44 B4
Moorhouse Ct Mews
WF9. . . . . .183 A1
Moorhouse Dr BD11. . . . 95 F7
Moorhouse Gap DN6. . . .183 A1
Moorhouse Gr WF3 . . . .122 B7
Moorhouse La
Birkenshaw BD11 . . . . . . 96 A7
Hooton Pagnell WF9 . . . .183 D1
Oxenhope BD22. . . . . . . 51 C4
Ryhill WF4. . . . . .162 C4
Woolley S75. . . . . .177 C5
Moorhouse Terr
Halifax HX3 . . . . 92 B1
Lofthouse Gate WF3 . . . .122 B7
Moorhouse View
Lofthouse Gate WF3 . . . .122 B7
South Elmsall WF9. . . . . .183 B2
Moor House View HX7. . . 87 F4
Moorings The
Bradford BD10. . . . . 56 D8
Leeds, Alwoodley Gates
LS17. . . . . 43 E5
Leeds, Stourton LS10 . . . 80 B3
Moor Knoll Cl WF3. . . . .120 D8
Moor Knoll Dr WF3 . . . .120 D8
Moor Knoll La WF3. . . . .120 D8
Moor La
Addingham, Addingham Low
Moor LS29. . . . . .2 B1
Addingham LS29 . . . . . . .2 D1
Birkenshaw BD11 . . . . . . 96 C3
Burley in W LS29 . . . . . . 21 D7
Cleckheaton BD19 . . . . . . 96 B2
Clifton LS21. . . . . 10 C3
Collingham LS22 . . . . . . 29 F7
Darrington WF8. . . . . . . .147 A2
East Keswick LS17. . . . . . 28 A5
Guiseley LS20 . . . . 22 E2
Halifax HX2 . . . . 91 E4
Harewood LS17 . . . . 27 F6
Holmfirth HD9 . . . . .188 E8
Huddersfield HD4 . . . . . .171 D7
Kirkburton, Farnley Tyas
HD4. . . . . .172 F5
Kirkburton HD8 . . . . . . .173 F7
Marsden HD7. . . . . .169 E6
Menston LS29 . . . . 21 E4
Pontefract WF8 . . . . . . .146 E4
Steeton BD20. . . . . 17 A5
Stutton LS24 . . . . 48 F8
Thorp Arch LS23 . . . . . . 14 D5
Walsden OL14 . . . . .108 B3
Moorland Ave
Baildon BD17. . . . . 38 D5
Bingley BD16. . . . . 37 C5
Darton S75 . . . . .178 B2
Gildersome LS27 . . . . . . 97 C8
Guiseley LS20 . . . . 22 E1
Leeds LS6 . . . . .205 C2
Moorland Cl
Gildersome LS27 . . . . . . 97 C8
Halifax HX2 . . . . 91 E3

Moorland Cl continued
Leeds LS17 . . . . 43 D1
Slaithwaite HD7. . . . . . .170 E7
Moorland Cotts HX7 . . . .131 C8
Moorland Cres
Baildon BD17. . . . . 38 D4
Darton S75 . . . . .178 B2
Gildersome LS27 . . . . . . 97 B8
Guiseley LS20 . . . . 22 C2
Guiseley LS20 . . . . 22 E2
Leeds LS17 . . . . 43 C1
Menston LS29 . . . . 22 A5
Pudsey LS28 . . . . 57 A1
Moorland Dr
Birkenshaw BD11 . . . . . . 96 B6
Crigglestone WF4 . . . . . .159 F2
Guiseley LS20 . . . . 22 C2
Leeds LS17 . . . . 43 D1
Pudsey LS28 . . . . 57 A1
Moorland Gdns LS17 . . . 43 D1
Moorland Gr
Leeds LS17 . . . . 43 C2
Pudsey LS28 . . . . 76 A8
Moorland Ings LS17. . . . 43 C1
Moorland Leys 1 LS17. . . 43 C1
Moorland Mount BD19 . .116 B6
Moorland Pl
4 Bradford BD12. . . . . . 94 E5
Lofthouse Gate WF3 . . . .121 E8
Moorland Rd
Birkenshaw BD11 . . . . . . 96 E6
Bramhope LS16 . . . . 24 C2
Leeds LS6 . . . . .205 C2
Pudsey LS28 . . . . 57 A1
Moorland Rise
Leeds LS17 . . . . 43 C2
Meltham HD9 . . . . .170 D2
Moorlands
Holmfirth HD9 . . . . .189 C3
Ilkley LS29. . . . . .8 A2
Moorlands Ave
Birkenshaw BD11 . . . . . . 96 A4
Bradford BD3. . . . . 56 D1
5 Dewsbury WF13 . . . . .118 C1
Halifax HX2 . . . . 91 E3
Keighley BD22. . . . . 34 F4
1 Mirfield WF14. . . . . . .137 F6
Ossett WF5 . . . . .140 C8
Yeadon LS19 . . . . 40 D6
Moorlands Ave N WF13. . 118 B3
Moorlands Ave W WF13. . 118 B3
Moorlands Cres
Halifax HX2 . . . . 91 E3
Holmfirth HD9 . . . . .189 C3
Huddersfield HD3 . . . . . .134 D1
Moorlands Ct
3 Elland HX4. . . . . .134 B8
Wetherby LS22 . . . . 13 F5
Moorlands Dr
Halifax HX2 . . . . 91 E2
Yeadon LS19 . . . . 40 D6
Moorlands Ind Ctr BD19. . 95 D1
Moorlands Pl 1 HX1 . . . .203 A1
Moorlands Prim Sch
HD3. . . . . .134 D1
Moorlands Rd
Birkenshaw BD11 . . . . . . 96 A7
Dewsbury WF13 . . . . . . .139 B8
Elland HX4. . . . . .134 B8
Huddersfield HD3 . . . . . .134 D1
Moorlands Sch LS16 . . . . 42 D1
Moorlands Terr
6 Bacup OL13 . . . . . . .106 A1
Dewsbury WF13 . . . . . . .118 B1
Moorlands The
Bacup OL13 . . . . .106 A8
Boston Spa LS23 . . . . . . 30 C8
Leeds LS17 . . . . 43 E4
Wetherby LS22 . . . . 13 F5
Moorlands View
Clayton West HD8 . . . . . .176 A2
Halifax HX1 . . . . .203 A1
Wetherby LS22 . . . . 13 F5
Moorland Terr
Garforth LS25 . . . . 82 E6
Keighley BD22. . . . . 35 F6
Moorland View
Bradford BD12. . . . . 94 E5
Emley HD8. . . . . .175 A7
Leeds, Moortown LS17 . . 43 C2
Leeds, Whitecote LS13 . . 58 B4
Sowerby Bridge HX6 . . . .111 F3
Wilsden BD15 . . . . 53 D4
Moorland Wlk LS17. . . . . 43 C2
Moorlea BD17. . . . . 38 D3
Moorleigh Cl LS25. . . . . 83 B2
Moorleigh Dr LS25 . . . . . 83 B2
Moor Park Ave
Huddersfield HD4 . . . . . .153 C1
Leeds LS6 . . . . 59 D6
Moor Park Bsns Ctr
WF2 . . . . .142 A3
Moor Park Cl
Addingham LS29 . . . . . . .6 D8
Bradford BD3. . . . . 75 C8
Moor Park Cres LS29. . . . .6 D8
Moor Park Ct 5 WF12 . . .118 E1
Moor Park Dr
Addingham LS29 . . . . . . .6 D8
Bradford BD3. . . . . 75 D8
Leeds LS6 . . . . 59 D6
Moor Park Gdns LS6. . . .118 E1
Moor Park Gr 1 LS29. . . .6 E8
Moor Park Mount LS6. . . 59 E6
Moor Park Rd BD3 . . . . . 75 C8
Moor Park Villas LS6. . . . 59 E6

Moor Park Way LS29 . . . .6 E8
Moor Rd
Bramhope LS16 . . . . 24 D2
Calderbrook OL15 . . . . .129 C7
Featherstone WF7 . . . . . .145 D5
Ilkley LS29. . . . . .8 F4
Leeds, Far Headingley LS6. 59 D6
Leeds, Hunslet Carr LS10 214 C4
Leeds, Hunslet Moor LS10 214 C4
Lofthouse Gate WF3 . . . .121 E6
Menston LS29. . . . . 21 C7
Moor Rd Sta ★ LS10. . . .214 C4
Moor Royd
Halifax HX3 . . . . .113 A4
Honley HD9 . . . . .171 E3
Moorshutt Rd WF9 . . . . .181 C6
Moorside
Baildon BD17. . . . . 38 C5
Bradford BD9. . . . . 54 E4
Cleckheaton, Hartshead Moor
Side BD19. . . . . .116 A4
Cleckheaton, West End
BD19. . . . . .116 C7
Moor Side LS23. . . . . 30 B7
Moorside App BD11. . . . . 96 F5
Moorside Ave
Batley WF13 . . . . .117 F2
Birkenshaw BD11 . . . . . . 96 A7
Birkenshaw, Drighlington
BD11. . . . . 96 F5
Bradford BD2. . . . . 56 D2
Huddersfield HD4 . . . . . .153 C6
Steeton BD20. . . . . 17 A5
Moorside Cl
Birkenshaw BD11 . . . . . . 96 F5
Bradford BD2. . . . . 56 C3
Moor Side Cotts BD20. . . 19 B3
Moorside Cres
Bacup OL13 . . . . .106 A4
Batley WF13 . . . . .117 F2
Birkenshaw BD11 . . . . . . 96 F5
Crigglestone WF4 . . . . . .159 F2
Moorside Croft BD2. . . . . 56 C2
Moorside Ct LS29. . . . . . .8 C3
Moorside Dr
Birkenshaw BD11 . . . . . . 96 F5
Leeds LS13 . . . . 58 C4
Moorside Edge HD7. . . . .151 E3
Moorside End WF13. . . . .117 F2
Moorside Farm BD20. . . . 19 B3
Moorside Gdns
Birkenshaw BD11 . . . . . . 96 F5
Bradford BD2. . . . . 56 C4
Halifax HX3 . . . . 91 F4
Moorside Gn BD11 . . . . . 96 F6
Moorside La
Addingham LS29 . . . . . . .6 E4
Askwith LS21. . . . . 10 A7
Bradford BD3. . . . . 75 D7
Oxenhope BD22. . . . . . . 50 F5
Moor Side La HD7 . . . . .151 D3
Moorside Maltings LS11. .214 C4
Moorside Mews BD2 . . . . 56 C3
Moorside Mount BD11 . . . 96 F5
Moorside Paddock BD19 116 B6
Moorside Par BD11 . . . . . 96 F5
Moorside Pl
Batley WF13 . . . . .117 F2
Bradford BD3. . . . . 75 D7
Moorside Rd
Batley WF13 . . . . .117 F2
Birkenshaw BD11 . . . . . . 96 E5
Bradford, Bradford Moor
BD3. . . . . 75 D7
Bradford, Haigh Fold BD2. . 56 C3
Honley HD9 . . . . .171 E4
Kirkheaton HD5. . . . . . . .137 C1
Wilsden BD15 . . . . 53 C4
Moorside Rise BD19. . . . .116 B7
Moorside St
Bradford BD12. . . . . 94 B6
Leeds LS13 . . . . 58 C4
Moorside Terr
Birkenshaw BD11 . . . . . . 96 F5
Bradford BD2. . . . . 56 D2
Leeds LS13 . . . . 58 C4
Moorside Vale BD11 . . . . 96 F6
Moorside View BD11 . . . . 96 F5
Moorside Wlk BD11. . . . . 96 F5
Moor Smith Copse HX2. . 91 E7
Moors Sh Ctr The 4 LS29. .8 A4
Moor St
Oakworth BD22 . . . . 34 D3
9 Queensbury BD13 . . . 72 E1
Moor Stone Pl HX3 . . . . . 93 C5
Moor Terr BD2. . . . . 56 C1
Moorthorpe Ave BD3. . . . 56 D1
Moorthorpe Prim sch
WF9 . . . . .182 E3
Moorthorpe Sta WF9. . . .182 E3
Moortop BD11. . . . . 96 E6
Moor Top
Birkenshaw BD11 . . . . . . 96 D6
Gildersome LS12 . . . . . . 77 C1
Guiseley LS20 . . . . 22 E4
Mirfield WF14 . . . . .137 E6
Otley LS21. . . . . 22 E4
Moor Top Ave HD4. . . . .172 F2
Moor Top Dr WF3 . . . . . .181 D5
Moor Top Gdns HX2. . . . 91 E8
Moor Top La WF4. . . . . .156 D1
Moor Top Rd
Bradford BD12. . . . . 94 B6
Halifax HX2 . . . . .112 B8
Kirkheaton HD5. . . . . . . .137 C2
Moortown Corner Ho
LS17. . . . . 43 D2

Moortown Prim Sch LS17 **43** D2
Moor Valley Pk LS20 . . . . . **38** C7
Moorview LS26 . . . . **102** F3
Moor View
Bacup OL13 . . . .**106** A4
Batley WF16 . . . . **117** E2
Birkenshaw BD4 . . . .**96** A8
Crigglestone WF4 . . . .**159** F5
Flockton WF4 . . . .**157** C3
Leeds, Holbeck LS11 . . . . . .**211** A1
Leeds, Hyde Park LS6 . . . . .**205** C3
Meltham HD9 . . . .**170** C3
Mirfield WF14 . . . . **137** E6
Moorview Bsns Pk BD10. . **39** A2
Moor View Cl WF10 . . . . . . **124** F7
Moorview Cres BD16 . . . . . . **53** E6
Moorview Croft LS29 . . . . . **21** F5
Moorview Ct BD10 . . . . **39** A1
Moor View Ct BD20 . . . . . . **36** C7
Moorview Dr
Shipley BD18 . . . . **55** F7
Wilsden BD16 . . . . **53** E6
Moorview Gr BD21 . . . . **35** D5
Moor View Terr BD22 . . . . **50** D7
Moorville Ave BD3 . . . . **56** D1
Moorville Cl LS11 . . . . **214** B4
Moorville Ct LS11 . . . . **214** A4
Moorville Dr BD11 . . . . **96** A7
Moorville Gr LS11 . . . . **214** B4
Moorville Rd LS11 . . . . **214** B4
Moorway LS20 . . . . **39** C8
Moor Way BD22. . . . . **34** C3
Moorwell Pl BD2. . . . . **56** C4
Moravian Mus★ LS28 . . . . **76** E5
Moravian Pl BD5. . . . . **74** B2
Morefield Bank HD9 . . . . . **189** C8
More Pleasant HD3 . . . . . **151** F7
Moresby Rd BD6 . . . . **93** F6
Moresdale La LS14. . . . . . . **61** F3
Morlands Cl WF13 . . . . . . **117** F3
Morley Ave
Bradford BD3. . . . . **56** D1
Knottingley WF11 . . . . **127** A4
Morley Carr Rd BD12. . . . . **94** D5
Morley Fold HD8. . . . . **191** F5
Morley Hall La HX2 . . . . . **111** D6
Morley Hall Terr HX2. . . . **111** C6
Morley High Sch LS27. . . . **97** F3
Morley La HX3. . . . . **113** E3
Morley Newlands Prim Sch
LS27 . . . . **98** D5
Morley St BD7 . . . . **201** B2
Morley Sta LS27 . . . . **98** C5
Morley Victoria Prim Sch
LS27 . . . . **98** A5
Morley View HX3 . . . . **113** E3
Morningside
Bradford BD8. . . . . **55** B1
Denholme BD13. . . . . **52** E1
Morning St [11] BD21. . . . . **35** B4
Mornington Rd
Bingley BD16 . . . . **37** A3
Ilkley LS29 . . . . **8** C4
Mornington St BD21 . . . . . **35** B8
Mornington Villas BD8 . . **55** D1
Morpeth Pl LS9 . . . . **212** B3
Morpeth St
Bradford BD7. . . . . **74** C7
Queensbury BD13 . . . . **72** E1
Morrell Cres WF2. . . . . . . **120** F3
Morrell Ct BD4 . . . . **75** D3
Morris Ave LS5 . . . . **59** A5
Morris Cl WF9 . . . . **163** B2
Morris Gr LS5 . . . . **59** A5
Morris La LS5. . . . . **59** A5
Morris Mount LS5 . . . . **59** A4
Morrison St WF10. . . . . . . **124** E7
Morris Pl LS27. . . . . **97** F5
Morris View LS5 . . . . **59** A4
Morritt Ave LS15 . . . . **62** B1
Morritt Dr LS15 . . . . **80** F8
Morritt Gr LS15 . . . . **80** F8
Mortec Pk LS15. . . . . **62** E7
Mortimer Ave
Batley WF17 . . . . **117** F5
Bradford BD3. . . . . **56** D1
Mortimer Cl LS25 . . . . **82** E7
Mortimer Rise WF5 . . . . . **140** F6
Mortimer Row
Bradford BD3. . . . . **75** D7
Horbury WF4 . . . . **140** F1
Mortimer St
Batley WF17 . . . . **117** F5
Bradford BD8. . . . . **73** F8
Cleckheaton WF17 . . . . . . **116** D7
Mortimer Terr WF17 . . . . **117** F5
Morton Cres WF10 . . . . . . **124** F7
Morton Gn HD5 . . . . **155** A3
Morton Gr
Dewsbury WF12 . . . . **139** B3
East Morton BD20 . . . . **36** D8
Morton La
Bingley BD16 . . . . **36** D7
Keighley BD20 . . . . **36** D7
Morton Par WF2 . . . . **142** A6
Morton Rd BD4 . . . . **75** D5
Mortons Cl HX3. . . . . **113** E3
Morton Terr LS20 . . . . **22** D1
Morton Way HD3 . . . . **134** E1
Morton Wood Gr HD9 . . . **189** D3
Mortuary La LS12 . . . . **77** F8
Morvern Mdws WF9. . . . . **181** F7
Morwick Gr LS15. . . . . **62** F6
Morwick Terr LS14. . . . . . . **62** E8
Moselden La HX6 . . . . **150** D6
Moseley Pl LS6 . . . . **206** B3

Moseley Wood App LS16 . **41** D4
Moseley Wood Ave LS16. . **41** D6
Moseley Wood Bank LS16 **41** D5
Moseley Wood Cl LS16 . . . **41** D5
Moseley Wood Cres LS16. . **41** D5
Moseley Wood Croft LS16 **41** D4
Moseley Wood Dr LS16. . . **41** D5
Moseley Wood Gdns LS16 **41** D5
Moseley Wood Gn LS16 . . **41** D5
Moseley Wood Gr LS16 . . . **41** D5
Moseley Wood Rise LS16. . **41** D5
Moseley Wood View LS16 . **41** D6
Moseley Wood Way LS16 . **41** D6
Moseley Wood Wlk LS16 . **41** D5
Moser Ave BD2 . . . . **56** A5
Moser Cres BD2 . . . . **56** A5
Moss Bridge La LS13 . . . . . **57** F5
Moss Carr Ave BD21. . . . . . **35** F5
Moss Carr Gr BD21. . . . . . . **35** F5
Moss Carr Rd BD21 . . . . . . **35** F5
Mossdale BD9 . . . . **54** C3
Moss Dr HX2 . . . . **91** E6
Moss Edge Rd HD9. . . . . . **188** C1
Moss Edge View HD9. . . . **188** C2
Moss Gdns LS17 . . . . **43** A5
Moss Hall La HX7 . . . . **87** E4
Moss La
Halifax HX2 . . . . **91** E6
Hebden Bridge HX7 . . . . **89** A4
Moss Lea [4] LS27 . . . . **98** B7
Moss Rise
Holmfirth HD9 . . . .**188** E5
Leeds LS17 . . . . **43** A5
Moss Row BD15. . . . . **53** C6
Moss Side BD9 . . . . **54** E2
Moss St
Castleford WF10 . . . . **124** C8
Haworth BD22 . . . . **51** E8
Huddersfield HD4 . . . . **154** B4
Thornton BD13 . . . . **72** C7
Moss Syke LS14. . . . . **45** C8
Mosstree Cl BD13 . . . . **72** C2
Moss Valley LS17. . . . . **43** A5
Mossy Bank Cl BD13 . . . . . **72** E2
Mostyn Gr BD6 . . . . **94** A8
Mostyn Mount HX3. . . . . . **92** A3
Mostyn Wlk WF4. . . . . **159** F2
Motley La LS20 . . . . **22** E2
Moule Rise LS25 . . . . **64** B1
Moulson Cl BD6 . . . . **74** B1
Moulson Ct [1] BD4 . . . . . . **75** E3
Moulson Terr BD13 . . . . . . **71** D8
Moulton Chase WF9 . . . . **181** E7
Mountain Cres WF12. . . . **139** D2
Mountain Rd WF12. . . . . . **139** D2
Mountain View
Halifax HX2 . . . . **92** A6
Shipley BD18 . . . . **55** D6
Mountain Way HD5 . . . . . **155** C5
Mount Ave
Batley, Nunroyd WF16 . . . **117** E6
[3] Batley WF17. . . . . **118** D3
Bradford BD2. . . . . **56** C5
Halifax HX2 . . . . **112** C7
Hemsworth WF9 . . . . **181** D7
Huddersfield HD3 . . . . **134** D1
Wakefield WF2 . . . . **120** F3
Mountbatten Ave
Lofthouse Gate WF1 . . . . . **121** C5
Wakefield WF2 . . . . **160** E8
Mountbatten Cres WF1. . **121** C5
Mountbatten Ct [4] BD5. . **74** E2
Mountbatten Gdns HD3 . **153** B7
Mountbatten Gr WF1. . . . **121** D4
Mountcliffe View LS27 . . **98** B7
Mount Cres
Cleckheaton BD19 . . . . . . **116** D8
Halifax HX2 . . . . **112** C7
Holme Chapel BB10. . . . . . . **85** A8
Wakefield WF2 . . . . **141** F3
Mount Dr LS17. . . . . **43** B6
Mountfield Ave HD5. . . . . **155** B4
Mountfield Rd HD5 . . . . . **155** B5
Mountfields
Brighouse HX3. . . . . **114** E8
Leeds LS13 . . . . **205** C1
Mountfields Wlk WF9 . . . **182** B1
Mount Gdns
Cleckheaton BD19 . . . . . . **116** D8
Leeds LS17 . . . . **43** B6
Mount Gr BD2 . . . . **56** B5
Mountjoy Rd HD1. . . . . . . **153** F7
Mountjoy Sch HD1. . . . . . **153** F7
Mount Jun & Inf Sch The
WF2. . . . . **141** F3
Mount La
Brighouse HD6 . . . . **135** E6
Holme Chapel BB10. . . . . . . **85** A8
Todmorden OL14. . . . . **86** C3
Mountleigh Cl BD4. . . . . . . **95** A7
Mount Pellon HX2 . . . . . . **202** B4
Mount Pellon Jun & Inf Sch
HX1. . . . . **202** B4
Mount Pellon Rd HX2. . . . **202** A4
Mount Pisgah [6] LS21. . . . **23** A7
Mount Pisgah Terr [5]
LS21. **23** A7
Mount Pl BD18. . . . . **55** B8
Mount Pleasant
Ackworth M T WF7. . . . . . **163** F6
Addingham LS29 . . . . **6** F8
[1] Bradford BD6. . . . . **93** F7
Brighouse HD6 . . . . **135** E6
Castleford WF10 . . . . **124** F6
Denholme BD13. . . . . **71** D8
Dewsbury WF12 . . . . **139** E7
Emley HD8 . . . . **175** D7

Mount Pleasant *continued*
Glusburn BD20 . . . . **16** B6
Guiseley LS20 . . . . **22** E2
Horsforth LS18 . . . . **58** D8
Huddersfield HD1 . . . . **153** F3
Ilkley LS29 . . . . **8** C3
Keighley BD20 . . . . **36** C7
[8] Kippax LS25 . . . . **83** B1
Kirk Smeaton WF8 . . . . . . **166** F6
Leeds LS13 . . . . **58** B4
Menston LS29 . . . . **21** F4
Middleton LS10 . . . . **99** C5
Ripponden HX4 . . . . **132** F4
Sowerby Bridge HX6 . . . . . **111** D3
[18] Todmorden OL14 . . . . **108** B5
Mount Pleasant Ave
Halifax HX1 . . . . **203** A4
Leeds LS8 . . . . **204** C1
Mount Pleasant Ct [11]
LS28. **76** E8
Mount Pleasant Dr HX7 . . **89** F1
Mount Pleasant Gdns
[9] Kippax LS25 . . . . **83** B1
Leeds LS8 . . . . **204** C1
Mount Pleasant Jun & Inf
Sch HD1 . . . . **153** F3
Mount Pleasant La HD8 . **155** C4
Mount Pleasant Rd LS28. . **76** E8
Mount Pleasant St
Featherstone WF7. . . . . . . **145** D6
[1] Huddersfield HD5. . . . **154** D6
[3] Pudsey LS28. . . . . **76** E8
Queensbury BD13 . . . . **72** E1
Todmorden OL14. . . . . **86** A1
Mount Preston LS2 . . . . . **206** A1
Mount Preston St LS2. . . **206** A1
Mount Rd
Bradford, Eccleshill BD2 . . **56** B5
Bradford, Wibsey BD6. . . . . **74** A1
Huddersfield HD1 . . . . **153** D7
Lofthouse Gate WF3 . . . . . **121** F6
Marsden HD7. . . . . **168** D1
Mount Rise LS17 . . . . **43** B6
Mount Royd BD8. . . . . **55** C2
Mount St Mary's RC High Sch
LS9 . . . . **212** B3
Mount St W HX2 . . . . **202** A4
Mount Scar View HD9. . . **189** D4
Mount St
Batley WF17 . . . . **118** D3
Bradford, Bowling BD3, BD4 **75** B6
Bradford, Eccleshill BD2. . . **56** B5
Cleckheaton BD19 . . . . . . **116** D8
Halifax HX1 . . . . **203** B3
[6] Huddersfield, Milnsbridge
HD3. . . . . **153** A4
Huddersfield, Rashcliffe HD1,
HD4. . . . . **153** F7
Keighley BD21 . . . . **35** A7
Sowerby Bridge HX6 . . . . . **112** B4
[22] Todmorden OL14 . . . . **108** B6
Mount Tabor Rd HX2 . . . . **91** A4
Mount Tabor St LS28. . . . . **76** C7
Mount Terr
Batley WF17 . . . . **118** C3
Bradford BD2. . . . . **56** B5
Halifax HX2 . . . . **202** A4
[13] Sowerby Bridge HX6 . **112** B4
Mount The
Baildon BD17. . . . . **38** D2
Barwick in E LS15 . . . . **63** D6
Batley WF17 . . . . **96** E2
Castleford WF10 . . . . **125** C7
Kippax LS25 . . . . **83** A1
Leeds, Alwoodley LS17 . . . **43** B6
Leeds LS15 . . . . **62** B1
Normanton WF6 . . . . **123** B2
Pontefract WF8 . . . . **146** C8
Rothwell LS26 . . . . **100** F7
Todmorden OL14. . . . . **108** C6
Wakefield WF2 . . . . **141** F3
Wakefield, Wrenthorpe
WF2. . . . . **120** D1
Mount Vernon Rd LS19. . . **40** C4
Mount View
Halifax HX2 . . . . **91** A3
Morley LS27 . . . . **98** B7
Oakworth BD22 . . . . **34** B2
Queensbury BD13 . . . . **72** D1
Mount View Ct BD19 . . . . **116** C8
Mount View Rd HD9. . . . . **189** E2
Mount Wlk WF10 . . . . **124** D5
Mount Zion HD5 . . . . **154** C6
Mount Zion Ct OL14. . . . . . **86** A1
Mourning Field La WF8 . **165** D3
Mousehole La WF14. . . . . **138** C1
Moverley Flatts WF8 . . . . **146** E7
Mowat Ct WF15. . . . . **116** B6
Mowbray Chase LS26 . . . **101** B7
Mowbray Ct BD13. . . . . **52** C5
Mowbray Cres LS14 . . . . . . **62** A3
Mowbray St LS14. . . . . **62** A3
Moxon Cl WF8 . . . . **146** D6
Moxon Cl WF1. . . . . **121** B3
Moxon Pl WF2. . . . . **141** C5
Moxon Sq WF1 . . . . **216** C3
Moxon St WF1 . . . . **121** C4
Moxon Way WF1 . . . . **121** C4
Moynihan Cl LS8. . . . . **208** B4
Mozley Dr HX2 . . . . **91** F4
Mucky La WF5 . . . . **134** D4
Muddy La LS22 . . . . **13** B2
Muffit La BD19. . . . . **117** D8
Muff St BD4 . . . . **75** B6
Mug Mill La HX2 . . . . **157** E8
Mugup La HD9. . . . . **189** E1
Muir Ct LS6. . . . . **205** A4
Muirfield Ave WF7 . . . . . . **124** D1

Muirfield Cl S72 . . . . **180** C1
Muirfield Dr WF2 . . . . **142** A2
Muirfields The S75. . . . . . **178** A1
Muirhead Ct [6] BD4. . . . . . **75** E2
Muirhead Dr BD4 . . . . **75** E2
Muirhead Fold [7] BD4. . . . **75** E2
Muirlands The HD2 . . . . . **136** E5
Mulberry Ave
Leeds LS16 . . . . **42** D4
Ryhill WF4 . . . . **162** B1
Mulberry Chase LS21. . . . . **24** D6
Mulberry Ct BD4 . . . . **95** F8
Mulberry Garth
Leeds LS16 . . . . **42** E3
Thorp Arch LS23 . . . . **14** E1
Mulberry Gdns LS26. . . . . **102** A1
Mulberry Ho [12] WF10 . . **124** E7
Mulberry Pl WF4. . . . . **162** B1
Mulberry Rise LS16 . . . . . . **42** D4
Mulberry St
Huddersfield HD5 . . . . **154** C5
[15] Keighley BD21 . . . . . . **35** D8
Leeds LS10 . . . . **212** A1
Pudsey LS28 . . . . **76** E7
Mulberry Terr HD1. . . . . . **154** B8
Mulberry View LS16. . . . . . **42** D3
Mulberry Way HX3 . . . . . . **93** A4
Mulcture Hall Rd HX1 . . . **203** B2
Mulehouse La HD3. . . . . . **134** B1
Mulgrave St BD3. . . . . **75** B6
Mulhalls Mill [12] HX6 . . **112** C4
Mullins Ct LS9 . . . . **212** C3
Mullion Ave HD9 . . . . **171** E4
Mumford St BD5. . . . . **74** E3
Munby St BD8 . . . . **73** E7
Muncaster Rd LS25 . . . . . . **83** B8
Munster St BD4 . . . . **75** B3
Munton Cl BD6 . . . . **93** E6
Murdoch St BD21 . . . . **35** F8
Murdstone Cl [5] BD5. . . . . **74** E3
Murgatroyd St
Bradford BD5. . . . . **74** E2
Shipley BD17 . . . . **55** B8
Murray Rd HD2 . . . . **153** F8
Murray St [3] BD5 . . . . **74** C3
Murton Cl LS14 . . . . **62** A4
Murton Gr BD20 . . . . **17** D5
Museum Ct BD2 . . . . **56** C2
Museum St LS9 . . . . **207** C1
Musgrave Bank LS13 . . . . . **58** E2
Musgrave Ct WF2 . . . . **141** D4
Musgrave Dr BD2 . . . . **56** C2
Musgrave Gr [1] BD2 . . . . . **56** C2
Musgrave Mount
[2] Bradford BD2. . . . . **56** C2
Leeds LS13 . . . . **58** E2
Musgrave Rd BD2. . . . . **56** C2
Musgrave Rise LS13. . . . . . **58** E2
Musgrave St [2] WF17 . . . . **96** E1
Musgrave View LS13 . . . . . **58** E2
Musgrave St [2] WF17 . . . . **96** E1
Mushroom St LS9. . . . . . . **207** B1
Musselburgh St BD7 . . . . . **74** C7
Mutton La BD15. . . . . **53** D2
Myers Ave BD2 . . . . **56** A4
Myers Croft
Huddersfield HD5 . . . . **154** F6
Otley LS21. . . . . **23** A7
Myers La BD2. . . . . **56** A4
Myrtle Ave
Bingley BD16 . . . . **36** F2
Dewsbury WF13 . . . . **138** E5
Halifax HX2 . . . . **91** E4
Myrtle Cotts [8] OL13 . . . **106** A2
Myrtle Ct BD16 . . . . **36** F2
Myrtle Dr
Halifax HX2 . . . . **91** E4
Keighley BD22 . . . . **34** F1
Myrtle Gdns HX2. . . . . **91** E4
Myrtle Gr
Bingley BD16 . . . . **36** F2
Halifax HX2 . . . . **91** E4
[12] Queensbury BD13 . . . . **92** C8
Myrtle Park Prim Sch
BD16. . . . . **36** F2
Myrtle Pl
Bingley BD16 . . . . **36** F3
Halifax HX2 . . . . **91** E4
[11] Shipley BD18 . . . . **54** F8
Myrtle Rd
Dewsbury WF13 . . . . **138** E5
Elland HX5. . . . . **134** F6
Huddersfield HD7 . . . . **152** D4
Myrtle St
[12] Bingley BD16 . . . . **37** A3
Bradford BD3. . . . . **75** C6
[1] Huddersfield HD1. . . . **154** B7
Todmorden OL14. . . . . **108** B5
Myrtle View
Haworth BD22 . . . . **51** F8
Oakworth BD22 . . . . **34** D1
Myrtle Wlk BD16 . . . . **37** A3
Myson Ave WF8. . . . . **125** F4
Mytholm Bank HX7 . . . . . . **88** B3
Mytholm Cl HX7 . . . . **88** B3
Mytholm Ct HX7 . . . . **88** B3
Mytholmes La
Haworth BD22 . . . . **51** C8
Oakworth BD22 . . . . **34** D1
Mytholmes Terr BD22 . . . . **51** C8
Mytholm Mdws HX7 . . . . . **88** B3
Mytholmroyd Sta HX7. . . **110** E8

N

Nabbs La HD7 . . . . **151** F1
Nab Cres HD9 . . . . **170** C2
Nabcroft La HD4 . . . . **153** D3
Nabcroft Rise HD4 . . . . . . **153** D4
Nab End BD12. . . . . **94** D2
Nab End La HX4 . . . . **134** D7
Nab La
Batley WF17 . . . . **97** B2
Mirfield WF14 . . . . **137** F6
Shipley BD18 . . . . **54** D7
Nab The WF14 . . . . **137** E6
Naburn App LS14 . . . . **62** C8
Naburn Chase
Leeds LS14. . . . . **62** B7
Leeds LS14. . . . . **62** C7
Naburn Cl LS14. . . . . **62** C7
Naburn Ct LS14 . . . . **62** C8
Naburn Dr LS14. . . . . **62** B7
Naburn Fold LS14. . . . . **62** C7
Naburn Gdns LS14 . . . . **62** B7
Naburn Gn LS14 . . . . **62** B7
Naburn Pl LS14 . . . . **62** B8
Naburn Rd LS14. . . . . **62** B7
Naburn View LS14 . . . . **62** C7
Naburn Wlk LS14 . . . . **62** B7
Nab View BD20 . . . . **5** F3
Nab Water La BD22 . . . . . . **70** C6
Nab Wood Bank BD18. . . . **54** D7
Nab Wood Cl BD18. . . . . . . **54** E7
Nab Wood Cres BD18 . . . . **54** D7
Nab Wood Dr BD18 . . . . . . **54** D6
Nab Wood Gdns BD18. . . . **54** E7
Nab Wood Gr BD18 . . . . . . **54** D7
Nab Wood Mount BD18. . . **54** D7
Nab Wood Pl BD18 . . . . . . **54** D7
Nab Wood Rd BD18 . . . . . . **54** D6
Nab Wood Rise BD18. . . . . **54** D7
Nab Wood Sch BD16 . . . . . **54** C7
Nab Wood Terr BD18. . . . . **54** D7
Naden Cl [7] BD13. . . . . **73** C2
Naigh Moor Way S71. . . . **179** C5
Nairn Cl HD4 . . . . **153** C3
Nancroft Cres LS12 . . . . . **209** C3
Nancroft Mount LS12 . . . **209** C3
Nancroft Terr LS12. . . . . . **209** C4
Nanny Goat La LS25. . . . . . **82** D8
Nansen Ave [9] LS13 . . . . . **58** C2
Nansen Gr [10] LS13 . . . . . **58** C2
Nansen Mount [11] LS13 . . **58** C2
Nansen Pl LS13 . . . . **58** B2
Nansen St LS13 . . . . **58** A2
Nansen Terr LS13 . . . . **58** B2
Nansen View LS13 . . . . **58** B2
Naomi Rd HD4 . . . . **154** A2
Napier Ho OL14 . . . . **129** A8
Napier Rd
Bradford BD3. . . . . **75** D7
Elland HX5. . . . . **134** E6
Napier St
Bradford BD3. . . . . **75** D7
Keighley BD21 . . . . **35** D6
[2] Queensbury BD13 . . . . **72** F1
Napier Terr BD3 . . . . **75** D7
Naples St BD8 . . . . **55** B1
Napoleon Bsns Pk BD4. . . **75** B5
Nares St Upper BD21 . . . . **35** A3
Nares St
[9] Haworth BD22 . . . . **51** E8
Keighley BD21 . . . . **35** B7
Narrow Balk DN5 . . . . **195** E5
Narrowboat Wharf LS13 . . **57** F5
Narrow La BD16 . . . . **36** B1
Narrows The BD16 . . . . **36** B1
Naseby Garth LS9. . . . . . . **207** B1
Naseby Gdns [4] LS9. . . . **212** B4
Naseby Grange [3] LS9 . . **212** B4
Naseby Ho [1] BD4 . . . . **75** F1
Naseby Pl LS9 . . . . **212** B4
Naseby Rise BD13. . . . . **72** F1
Naseby Terr LS9 . . . . **212** B4
Naseby View LS9 . . . . **212** B4
Nashville Rd [4] BD22. . . . **35** A6
Nashville St [2] BD22. . . . . **35** A6
Nashville Terr [1] BD22 . . . **35** A6
Nassau Pl LS7 . . . . **207** B4
Nateby Rise WF3. . . . . **100** D3
Nathaniel Waterhouse
Homes HX1 . . . . **203** B2
Nathan La HX6. . . . . **132** C3
National Arts Education
Archive (Trust) Mus★
WF4 . . . . **176** E6
National Coal Mining Mus for
England★ WF4 . . . . **157** E6
National Mus of Photography,
Film & TV★ BD1 . . . . **201** B2
National Rd LS10 . . . . **215** B4
National Rd LS10 . . . . **215** B4
Natty Fields Cl HX2 . . . . . . **91** E7
Natty La HX2 . . . . **91** E7
Nature Way BD6 . . . . **93** E7
Navigation Cl HX5 . . . . . . **135** A8
Navigation Dr BD10 . . . . . . **56** E8
Navigation Gdns WF12 . . **139** B4
Navigation Rd
Castleford WF10 . . . . **103** D1
Dewsbury WF12 . . . . **139** B4
Halifax HX3 . . . . **203** C2
Navigation Rise HD3 . . . . **153** C4
Navigation Wlk LS10 . . . . **211** C3

Navvy La S71 179 D7
Naylor's Bldgs 5 BD19 115 F8
Naylor Ct WF13 118 D1
Naylor La HX2 90 C1
Naylors Ct FW15 116 F2
Naylors Garth LS6 59 F5
Naylor St
Dewsbury WF13 118 B2
Halifax HX1 202 B3
Ossett WF5 140 C8
Naze Rd OL14 107 F3
Naze View OL14 107 F3
Neale Rd 3 HD1 153 F3
Neale St 5 HX7 89 A2
Neal Pl LS10 212 A2
Neal St BD5 201 B2
Near Bank HD8 174 B2
Nearcliffe Rd BD9 55 A2
Near Crook BD17 38 F1
Near La HD9 170 E2
Neath Gdns LS9 61 D3
Necropolis Rd BD7 73 F5
Ned Hill Rd HX2 71 F3
Ned La
Bradford BD4 75 F4
Slaithwaite HD7 169 F8
Needles Inn La LS26 101 C7
Nell Gap Ave WF4 158 A7
Nell Gap Cres WF4 158 A6
Nell Gap La
Middlestown WF4 158 A6
Middlestown WF4 158 A7
Nelson Croft LS25 82 D5
Nelson Ct
14 Ilkley LS29 8 B4
Mickletown LS26 102 D3
Morley LS27 97 F2
Nelson Pl
1 Morley LS27 98 A5
Queensbury BD13 72 E1
Sowerby Bridge HX6 112 D4
Nelson Rd LS29 8 B4
Nelson St
Batley, Birstall WF17 96 F1
Batley WF17 118 A5
Bradford, Eastbrook BD5 201 B1
Bradford, Fairweather Green BD15 54 C1
Dewsbury WF13 139 C8
Haworth BD22 51 E8
Huddersfield HD1 153 F4
Liversedge WF15 117 B3
Normanton WF6 123 C3
3 Otley LS21 23 A7
8 Queensbury BD13 72 E1
South Hiendley S72 180 E5
Sowerby Bridge HX6 112 D4
Todmorden OL14 129 A8
Nene St BD5 74 C4
Nepshaw La LS27 97 F5
Nepshaw La N LS27 97 E5
Nepshaw La S LS27 97 D5
Neptune St LS9 212 A3
Neptune Way HD2 136 F3
Nesfield Cl LS10 99 F6
Nesfield Cres LS10 99 E6
Nesfield Garth LS10 99 E6
Nesfield Gdns LS10 99 E6
Nesfield Gn LS10 99 E6
Nesfield Rd
Ilkley LS29 7 F5
Leeds LS10 99 E6
Nesfield St BD1 201 B4
Nesfield View
Ilkley LS29 7 E4
Leeds LS10 99 F6
Nesfield Wlk LS10 99 E6
Nessfield Dr BD22 34 F5
Nessfield Gr BD22 34 F5
Nessfield Prim Sch BD22 34 F5
Nessfield Rd BD22 34 F5
Nest Est HX7 110 D8
Nestfield Cl WF8 125 D3
Nest La HX7 110 D8
Neston Way WF5 119 D1
Netherby St BD3 75 B7
Nether Cl HD5 154 E8
Nethercliffe Cres LS20 22 D2
Nethercliffe Rd LS20 22 D2
Nether Cres HD5 154 E8
Nethercroft WF17 118 E5
Netherdale Ct
Denby Dale HD8 192 D4
Wetherby LS22 14 A6
Netherend Rd HD7 151 F1
Netherfield Ave WF4 158 D5
Netherfield Cl
Castleford WF10 123 F5
Kirkburton HD8 173 F6
Yeadon LS19 40 B7
Netherfield Cres WF4 158 D5
Netherfield Croft S72 180 C2
Netherfield Ct LS20 22 D1
Netherfield Dr
Guiseley LS20 22 D2
Holmfirth HD9 189 A7
Netherfield Ind Pk WF13 138 E5
Netherfield Pl
Cleckheaton BD19 116 E7
Netherton WF4 158 D6
Netherfield Rd
Dewsbury WF13 138 E5
Guiseley LS20 22 D2
Netherfield Rise LS20 22 D1
Netherfield Terr 13 LS19 40 B7
Nether Hall Ave HD5 154 E8
Netherhall Rd BD17 38 D3
Netherhouses HD9 188 D5
Nether La HD9 187 C3
Netherlands Ave BD6 94 C7
Netherlands Avenue Sch BD6 94 D7
Netherlands Sq BD12 94 D7
Netherlea Dr HD9 188 F7
Netherleigh Prep Sch BD9 54 F2
Netherley Dr HD7 168 E2
Netherly Brow WF5 140 E3
Nether Moor Rd HD4 171 C8
Nether Moor View 19 BD16 37 A3
Netheroyd WF7 144 C5
Netheroyd Ct WF4 144 C4
Netheroyd Hill Rd HD2 136 A3
Netheroyd Pl WF4 144 B4
Nether St LS28 57 D4
Netherthong Prim Sch HD9 188 F8
Netherthong Rd HD9 187 F8
Netherton Fold HD4 171 C6
Netherton Hall Dr WF4 158 E6
Netherton Hall Gdns WF4 158 E6
Netherton Inf Sch HD4 171 D7
Netherton Jun & Inf Sch WF4 158 E6
Netherton La WF4 158 E7
Netherton Moor Rd HD4 171 E6
Netherwood BD13 71 D8
Netherwood Cl HD2 136 A3
Nettle Gr HX3 92 F1
Nettleton's Almshouses 3 HD5 154 F3
Nettleton Ave WF14 137 F5
Nettleton Chase WF5 119 C1
Nettleton Cl BD4 76 E2
Nettleton Ct LS15 81 D8
Nettleton Hill Rd HD7 152 B6
Nettleton Ho 1 WF9 181 D6
Nettleton Rd
Huddersfield HD5 155 A8
Mirfield WF14 137 F5
Nettleton St
Lofthouse Gate WF3 122 B6
Ossett WF5 140 C6
Nettleton Terr HD5 155 A8
Network Ctr WF7 145 A6
Neville App LS9 80 C6
Neville Ave
Bradford BD4 75 B1
Leeds LS9 80 C6
Neville Cl
Leeds LS9 80 C6
South Kirkby WF9 182 C3
Neville Cres LS9 80 D8
Neville Garth LS9 80 C6
Neville Gr
Huddersfield HD5 154 F4
Leeds LS9 80 C6
Swillington LS26 82 A2
Neville Mount LS9 80 C6
Neville Par LS9 80 C6
Neville Pl LS9 80 D7
Neville Rd
Bradford BD4 75 B4
Leeds LS9 80 D8
Leeds LS9, LS15 80 E7
Otley LS21 23 B7
Wakefield WF2 141 C5
Neville Row LS9 80 C6
Neville Sq LS9 80 D8
Neville St
Cleckheaton BD19 116 E7
14 Keighley BD21 35 D8
Leeds LS1 211 B3
Normanton WF6 123 B1
Wakefield WF1 142 F4
Neville Terr LS9 80 C6
Neville View LS9 80 C6
Neville Wlk LS9 80 C7
Nevill Gr BD9 54 D3
Nevins Rd WF13 138 D6
Nevison Ave WF8 125 E3
New Adel Ave LS16 42 A3
New Adel Gdns LS16 42 A3
New Adel La LS16 42 A3
Newall Ave LS21 10 F1
Newall Carr Rd
Clifton LS21 10 F6
Otley LS21 10 F2
Newall Cl
Menston LS29 22 B5
Otley LS21 10 F1
Newall Cres WF9 162 F3
Newall Hall Pk LS21 11 A1
Newall Mount LS21 22 F8
Newall St
Bradford BD5 74 D4
Todmorden OL14 129 A8
Newark Cl S75 178 B2
Newark Rd BD16 36 E5
Newark St BD4 75 B5
Newark Vale WF3 100 A3
New Augustus St BD1 201 C2
New Ave HD5 137 B1
New Bank HX3 203 B4
New Bank Rise BD4 75 D3
New Bank St LS27 98 B5
New Barton HX6 111 C2
New Bewerley Com Prim Sch The LS11 214 B4
New Biggin Hill WF2 160 C5
New Bond St HX1 203 A3
Newbridge Ind Est BD21 35 D7
Newbridge La BD23 1 D8
New Bridge Rd HD9 170 B2
New Briggate LS1, LS2 211 C4
New Brighton
Bradford BD12 95 A4
Denby Dale HD8 191 B3
Shipley BD16 54 C6
New Brook St LS29 8 B4
New Brunswick St
Halifax HX1 203 A3
Wakefield WF1 216 B1
Newburn Rd BD7 74 B5
Newbury Cl BD17 38 D4
Newbury Dr WF9 183 A5
Newbury Rd HD6 135 F7
Newbury Wlk HD5 137 C1
Newby Ct WF9 181 E7
Newby Garth LS17 44 B5
Newby Prim Sch BD5 74 D3
Newby Rd BD20 16 E8
Newby St BD20 16 D7
Newcastle Cl BD11 96 D5
Newcastle Farm Ct WF11 105 A4
Newcastle Ho BD1 201 C3
New Cl
Horsforth LS18 58 B8
Marsden HD7 151 C1
New Clayton Terr BD13 52 D5
New Close Ave BD20 5 E1
New Close La
Marsden HD7 151 C1
Norton DN6 184 E7
New Close Rd BD18 54 D7
New Clough Rd HX6 112 D1
New Coll Pontefract WF8 125 B1
Newcombe St HX5 135 A6
New Cote Cotts LS28 57 E3
New Craven Gate LS11 214 C4
New Cres LS18 58 B8
New Cross St
Bradford, Lower Woodlands BD12 95 B5
Bradford, West Bowling BD5 74 F3
New Dales La BD20 4 B7
New Delight HX7 69 A1
New England Rd BD21 35 C5
New Farmers Hill LS26 101 D7
Newfield Ave
Castleford WF10 124 E7
Normanton WF6 123 C1
Newfield Chase LS25 83 B5
Newfield Cl WF6 123 C1
Newfield Cres
Garforth LS25 83 B5
Normanton WF6 123 C1
Newfield Ct WF6 123 C2
Newfield Dr
Garforth LS25 83 B4
Menston LS29 22 A5
Newfield La LS25 104 D8
New Fold
Bradford BD6 93 E7
Holmfirth HD9 189 A5
Newforth Gr BD5 74 C2
Newgate
Mirfield WF14 138 A4
Pontefract WF8 146 C8
New Gate HD9 189 C1
Newgate La HD9 170 E2
Newgate St WF17 118 F3
New Grange View HX2 91 F8
New Grove Dr HD5 154 E7
New Hall App WF4 157 F4
Newhall Bank LS10 99 D5
Newhall Chase LS10 99 D6
Newhall Cl LS10 99 D6
New Hall Cl WF4 159 E4
Newhall Cres LS10 99 D6
Newhall Croft LS10 99 D7
Newhall Dr BD6 94 F8
Newhall Garth LS10 99 D5
Newhall Gate LS10 99 E7
Newhall Gdns LS10 99 D5
Newhall Gn LS10 99 D6
Newhall La WF14 138 B2
New Hall La WF4 157 F4
Newhall Mount
Bradford BD6 94 F8
Middleton LS10 99 D5
Newhall Park Prim Sch BD4 75 B1
Newhall Rd
Bradford BD4 75 B1
Leeds LS10 99 D6
New Hall Rd WF8 125 E3
New Hall Way WF4 157 F3
Newhall Wlk LS10 99 E6
Newhaven Bsns Ctr HD3 153 B5
New Hey Moor Hos HD8 173 F2
New Hey Rd
Bradford BD4 75 A4
Elland HD3 152 A8
Huddersfield HD2, HD6 135 D5
Huddersfield, Marsh HD2, HD3 153 C7
Huddersfield, Salendine Nook HD3 152 E8
Marsden HD3 150 D2
Slaithwaite HD2, HD3, HD6 151 D5
Newhill WF9 182 B1
New Ho HD7 169 F7
New Hold LS25 83 A8
Newhold Ind Est LS25 83 A8
New Holme Rd BD22 51 D6
New House La BD13 73 B1
Newhouse Pl 2 HD1 154 A7
New House Rd HD2 136 D4
Newill Cl BD5 75 A2
New Inn Ct 2 LS21 23 A7
New Inn St LS12 209 A3
New John St BD1 201 B3
New Kirkgate 4 BD18 55 B8
New La
Birkenshaw BD4 76 C2
Blackshaw Head HX7 88 D3
Bradford BD3, BD4 75 D6
Burton Salmon LS25 105 D3
Cleckheaton BD19 116 A6
Cragg Vale HX7 110 D4
Crigglestone WF4 159 E7
East Ardsley WF3 120 C8
Farnhill BD20 4 F2
Gildersome BD11, LS27 97 B8
Halifax, Copley HX3 113 B2
Halifax HX3 113 D4
Leeds LS11 211 B2
Marsden HD3 150 D4
Middleton LS10 99 B5
Pontefract WF8 125 D1
Skelmanthorpe HD8 175 B1
Slaithwaite HD7 152 A3
Slaithwaite, Scapegoat Hill HD7 152 B6
Sowerby Bridge HX2 111 B5
Upton WF9 183 A7
New Laithe HX4 133 B1
New Laithe Cl HD4 154 C2
New Laithe Hill HD4 154 C2
New Laithe La HD9 189 B5
New Laithe Rd
3 Bradford BD6 74 A1
Haworth BD22 49 E8
Huddersfield HD4 154 C2
Newlaithes Cres WF6 123 D2
Newlaithes Garth LS18 58 A6
Newlaithes Gdns LS18 58 B7
Newlaithes Rd LS18 58 B6
Newland Ave HD2 135 F1
Newland Cres WF4 159 E7
Newland Ct
Huddersfield HD2 135 F1
Wakefield WF1 142 E2
Newland La WF6 122 F1
Newland Rd HD5 155 B7
Newlands LS28 57 D2
Newlands Ave
Bradford BD3 56 D1
Clayton West HD8 175 F2
Northowram HX3 93 A3
Skellow DN6 184 F2
Sowerby Bridge HX6 111 E3
Yeadon LS19 40 A7
Newlands Cl HD6 115 B1
Newlands Cres
Morley LS27 98 E4
Northowram HX3 93 A3
Newlands Dr
Bingley BD16 36 E6
Glusburn BD20 16 D7
Lofthouse Gate WF3 121 E5
Morley LS27 98 D4
Northowram HX3 93 A3
Newlands Gate HX2 112 A7
Newlands Gr HX3 93 A3
Newlands La HD9 188 C5
Newlands Pl BD3 56 B1
Newlands Prim Sch WF6 144 A8
Newlands Rd HX2 112 B7
Newlands Rise LS19 40 A7
Newland St
Knottingley WF11 126 B5
Wakefield WF1 142 E2
Newlands The HX6 111 E2
Newlands View HX3 93 B3
Newlands Wlk WF3 121 E5
Newland View WF6 122 F3
New Lane Cres WF9 183 A7
New Lathe HX4 151 F8
Newlay Bridle Path 2 LS18 58 C7
Newlay Cl BD10 56 E7
Newlay Gr LS18 58 B6
Newlay La
Horsforth LS18 58 B7
Leeds LS13 58 C4
Newlay Lane Pl LS13 58 C4
Newlay Mount LS18 58 B6
Newlay Wood Ave LS18 58 C7
Newlay Wood Cl LS18 58 C7
Newlay Wood Cres LS18 58 C7
Newlay Wood Dr LS18 58 C7
Newlay Wood Fold 10 LS18 58 B7
Newlay Wood Gdns 3 LS18 58 C7
Newlay Wood Rd LS18 58 B7
Newlay Wood Rise LS18 58 C7
New Leeds LS13 58 B5
Newley Ave WF17 117 F8
New Line BD10 56 E7
New Longley HX6 112 A1
New Longley La HX6 112 A1
Newlyn WF17 118 A3
Newlyn Dr WF2 142 D2
Newlyn Rd BD20 19 A1
Newman Ave S71 179 C1
Newman St BD4 75 B2
New Market LS21 23 A7
Newmarket App LS9 80 B6
Newmarket Gn LS9 80 B6
Newmarket La
Leeds LS9 80 B6
Lofthouse Gate WF3 122 D8
New Market Pl BD1 201 B3
New Market St LS1 211 C3
Newmillerdam Ctry Pk* WF4 160 D2
New Mill La LS23 30 E5
New Mill Rd
Brockholes HD9 172 C3
Holmfirth HD9 189 B7
New North Par HD1 154 A6
New North Rd
Huddersfield HD1 153 F7
Liversedge WF16 117 C5
Slaithwaite HD7 152 A2
New Occupation La LS28 76 C6
New Otley Rd BD3 201 D4
New Park Ave LS28 57 E3
New Park Cl LS28 57 E3
New Park Croft LS28 57 E3
New Park Gr LS28 57 E3
New Park La WF2 141 B7
New Park Pl LS28 57 E3
New Park Rd BD13 72 D1
New Park St LS27 97 F3
New Park Vale LS28 57 E3
New Park View LS28 57 E2
New Park Way LS28 57 E3
New Park Wlk 7 LS28 57 D2
New Pepper Rd LS10 215 C3
New Popplewell La BD19 115 F8
Newport Ave LS13 58 A2
Newport Cres LS6 205 A3
Newport Gdns LS6 205 A3
Newport Mount LS6 205 A3
Newport Pl BD8 55 C1
Newport Rd
Bradford BD8 55 C1
Leeds LS6 205 A3
Newport St WF8 125 C1
Newport View LS6 205 A3
New Princess St LS11 211 B1
New Pudsey Sq LS28 57 C1
New Rd
Badsworth WF9 164 D2
Blackshaw Head HX7 87 F6
7 Bradford BD19 94 D2
Bramham LS23 30 D3
Castleford WF11 126 A5
Cawthorne S75 193 B5
Cragg Vale HX7 110 D1
Darton S75 178 B1
Denholme BD13 71 D8
Elland, Greetland HX4 134 B7
Elland, Old Lindley HX4 134 C2
Elland, Slack HD3 152 A8
Featherstone WF7 144 E7
Halifax HX1 203 B2
Halifax HX2 90 D1
Hebden Bridge, Hebble End HX7 88 F2
Hebden Bridge HX7 89 A3
Holmfirth HD9 189 A7
Horbury WF4 141 B1
Kirkheaton HD5 137 B2
Kirk Smeaton DN6 166 D8
Ledsham LS25 84 D2
Middlestown WF4 158 B7
Mytholmroyd HX7 110 E8
Penistone S36 192 E1
Purston Jaglin WF4 145 C1
Rothwell WF3 100 D3
Silsden BD20 5 E1
Todmorden, Mankinholes OL14 109 A5
Todmorden, Upper Eastwood OL14 108 F8
Woolley WF4 178 B6
Yeadon LS19 39 F7
New Rd E BD19 115 F8
New Road Prim Sch HX6 112 A3
New Road Side
Horsforth LS18 58 B7
Yeadon LS19 40 B4
New Road Sq HD6 135 E6
New Row
Badsworth WF9 164 E2
Bradford, Daisy Hill BD9 54 E2
Bradford, Wyke Common BD12 94 D2
Darrington WF8 147 C5
Elland HX4 134 C4
13 Holmfirth HD9 189 A5
Leeds LS15 81 E6
Micklefield LS25 84 A7
Pudsey LS28 57 A3
Shipley BD16 54 B8
Wakefield WF2 120 B2
Newroyd Rd BD5 74 E2
Newsam Ct LS15 81 A7
Newsam Dr LS15 80 E6
Newsam Green Rd LS26, LS26 81 E1
New Scarbro' Rd 1 LS13 58 D2
Newsholme La WF4 159 F7
Newsholme New Rd BD22 34 B4
Newsome Ave HD4 154 A2
Newsome High Sch & Sports Coll HD4 153 F1
Newsome Jun Sch HD4 154 A1
Newsome Rd HD4 154 B3
Newsome Rd S HD4 154 A1
Newsome St WF13 118 B1
New St
Ackworth M T WF7 163 F5

New St continued
Batley, Hanging Heaton WF17 118 E3
Batley WF17 118 C5
Bradford BD10 56 B8
Bradford, Bierley BD4 95 B8
Bradford, Lower Woodlands BD12 95 B5
Brighouse, Bailiff Bridge HD6 115 B7
Brighouse, Clifton HD6 115 D2
Castleford WF10 103 E1
Clayton West HD8 175 D1
Darton S75 178 B1
Denholme BD13 71 D8
Dewsbury WF12 139 F7
Elland HX4 133 F3
Fitzwilliam WF9 163 C1
Halifax, Pellon HX2 202 A4
Halifax, Southowram HX3 114 A4
14 Haworth BD22 51 C6
Honley HD9 171 F4
Horbury WF4 141 B1
Horsforth LS18 58 B8
Huddersfield HD1 154 A5
Huddersfield, Leymoor HD7 152 E4
Huddersfield, Milnsbridge HD3 153 A4
Huddersfield, Netherton HD4 171 C7
Huddersfield, Paddock HD1 153 E5
Kippax LS25 83 B1
Kirkheaton HD5 155 C8
Liversedge BD19 116 F6
Meltham HD9 170 D2
Micklethwaite BD16 36 E7
Oakworth BD22 34 D2
Ossett WF5 140 E5
Pudsey, Farsley LS28 57 D2
Pudsey LS28 76 E6
Royston S71 179 C3
Skelmanthorpe HD8 175 A2
Slaithwaite HD7 152 A1
South Elmsall WF9 182 E3
South Hiendley S72 180 D6
New Station St LS1 211 B3
Newstead Ave
Fitzwilliam WF9 163 A3
Halifax HX1 202 A3
Lofthouse Gate WF1 121 A5
Newstead Cres WF9 163 A4
Newstead Dr WF9 163 A3
Newstead Gdns HX1 202 A3
Newstead Gr
Fitzwilliam WF9 163 A3
Halifax HX1 202 A3
Newstead Heath HX1 202 A3
Newstead La WF4, WF9 162 F3
Newstead Mount WF9 163 A3
Newstead Pl HX1 202 A3
Newstead Rd
Barnsley S71 178 E1
Otley LS21 23 B7
Wakefield WF1 216 A3
New Stead Rise BD20 19 B1
Newstead Terr
Fitzwilliam WF9 163 A3
Halifax HX1 202 A3
Newstead View WF9 163 A3
New Street Cl LS28 76 E6
New Street Gdns LS28 76 E6
New Street Gr LS28 76 E6
New Sturton La LS25 83 B7
New Tanhouse 8 WF14 137 F5
New Temple Gate LS15 81 A7
New Toftshaw BD4 95 D8
Newton Ave WF1 121 B2
Newton Cl
Lofthouse Gate WF1 121 B1
Rothwell LS26 100 B4
Silsden BD20 5 D2
Newton Ct
Leeds LS8 61 C6
Lofthouse Gate WF1 121 B4
Rothwell LS26 100 B4
Newton Dr
Castleford WF10 125 B7
Holme Chapel BB10 85 A7
Lofthouse Gate WF1 121 C3
Newton Garth LS7 204 B1
Newton Gdns WF1 121 C1
Newton Gn WF1 121 B1
Newton Gr
Leeds LS7 207 B4
Todmorden OL14 107 F7
Newton Hill Jun & Inf Sch WF1 121 C2
Newton Hill Rd LS7 204 A1
Newton La
Fairburn WF10, WF11 104 C4
Ledston WF10 103 E4
Lofthouse Gate WF1 121 B4
Newton Lodge Cl LS7 60 C5
Newton Lodge Dr LS7 60 C5
Newton Par LS7 204 A1
Newton Park Ct LS7 204 B1
Newton Park Dr LS7 204 B1
Newton Park Mans LS7 204 A1
Newton Park View LS7 207 B4
Newton Pk HD6 114 F6
Newton Pl BD5 74 E4
Newton Rd LS7 204 B1
Newton Sq LS12 77 D3
Newton St
Bradford BD5 74 E3
9 Sowerby Bridge HX6 112 B4
Newton Terr LS7 60 C6
Newton View LS7 204 A1
Newton Villas LS7 60 C6
Newton Way BD17 38 C4
Newton Wlk LS7 207 B4
Newtown Ave S71 179 B4
New Town Cl BD21 35 B7
New Town Ct 15 BD21 35 A7
New Village Mews 15 LS27 98 C8
New Village Way LS27 98 C8
New Way
Batley WF17 118 C5
Guiseley LS20 22 C1
New Wellgate WF10 124 F6
New Wells WF1 216 B1
New Windsor Dr LS26 100 F6
New Wlk LS8 44 B1
New Works Rd BD12 94 D5
New York Cotts LS19 40 D2
New York La LS19 40 D2
New York Rd LS2, LS9 212 A4
New York St 1 LS2 212 A3
Nialls Ct BD10 39 B2
Nibshaw La BD19 117 A8
Nibshaw Rd BD19 117 A8
Nice Ave LS8 207 C4
Nice St LS8 208 A4
Nice View LS8 207 C4
Nicholas Cl BD7 73 F7
Nichol La HD9 190 A2
Nichols Cl LS22 13 C5
Nicholson Cl BD16 37 A6
Nicholson Ct LS8 61 A6
Nicholson St WF10 124 C7
Nichols Way LS22 13 C5
Nickleby Rd LS9 80 A8
Nicola Cl OL13 106 A7
Nicola Ct BD5 74 D4
Nicolsons Pl 1 BD20 5 E1
Nidd App LS22 13 D8
Nidd Ct 13 BD20 5 E1
Nidd Dr WF10 125 B8
Nidderdale Cl LS25 83 B5
Nidderdale Ho WF17 118 C3
Nidderdale Wlk BD17 38 E4
Nidd St BD3 75 B6
Nields Jun & Inf Sch HD7 169 F8
Nields Rd HD7 169 F8
Nightingale Crest WF2 141 C4
Nightingale St 5 BD21 35 D8
Nightingale Wlk BD16 37 C4
Nijinsky Way LS10 80 B1
Nile Cres BD22 34 F6
Nile Rd LS29 8 B4
Nile St
Haworth BD22 51 E8
Huddersfield HD1 153 F5
Keighley BD22 34 F6
Leeds LS2 212 A4
Nina Rd BD7 73 F3
Ninelands La LS25 83 A6
Ninelands Prim Sch LS25 83 A6
Ninelands Spur LS25 83 A6
Ninelands View LS25 83 A7
Ninevah La
Badsworth WF9 164 E3
Kippax WF10 102 F5
Nineveh Gdns LS11 211 A1
Nineveh Par LS11 211 A1
Nineveh Rd LS11 211 A1
Ninth Ave WF15 116 B5
Nippet La LS9 212 B4
Nixon Ave LS9 80 B7
Nixon Cl WF12 139 F1
Noble Ct HD4 171 D6
Noble St BD7 74 B5
Nog La BD9 55 A4
Nook Gdns LS15 62 F8
Nook Gn
Dewsbury WF12 139 D2
East Ardsley WF3 119 F7
Nooking The WF2 120 B3
Nook La
Sowerby Bridge HX6 131 F8
Wadsworth Moor HX7 89 D4
Nook Rd LS15 62 F8
Nooks The
Gildersome LS27 97 D6
Shepley HD8 190 E8
Nook The
Cleckheaton BD19 116 E8
Cullingworth BD13 52 D6
East Ardsley WF3 119 E6
Leeds LS17 43 D5
Nook View WF3 119 E6
Nook Wlk WF13 138 F8
Noon Cl WF3 121 E5
Nopper Rd HD4 170 F8
Nora Pl LS13 58 A3
Nora Rd LS13 58 A3
Nora Terr LS13 58 A3
Norbeck Dr BD22 51 E8
Norbury Rd BD10 56 E4
Norcliffe La HX3 114 A7
Norcroft Brow BD7 74 D6
Norcroft Ind Est BD7 74 C7
Norcroft La S75 193 F3
Norcroft St BD1, BD7 74 C7
Norcross Ave HD3 153 B7
Nordale Cl LS29 8 C5
Norfield HD2 136 A4
Norfolk Ave WF17 118 B3
Norfolk Cl
Brotherton WF11 126 C8
Calderbrook OL15 129 C1
Huddersfield HD1 153 F7
Norfolk Cl continued
Leeds LS7 204 A3
Rothwell LS26 101 D5
Norfolk Dr LS26 101 D5
Norfolk Gdns
Bradford BD1 201 B2
Leeds LS7 204 A3
Norfolk Gn LS7 204 A3
Norfolk Ho
Wakefield WF1 142 F3
4 Wetherby LS22 13 F6
Norfolk Mount LS7 204 A3
Norfolk Pl
Halifax HX1 202 C2
Leeds LS7 204 A3
Norfolk St
Batley WF17 118 B4
4 Bingley BD16 37 A3
8 Hebden Bridge HX7 89 A2
Norfolk Terr LS7 204 A3
Norfolk View LS7 204 A3
Norfolk Wlk
5 Dewsbury WF13 139 B8
Leeds LS7 204 A3
Norgarth Cl WF17 118 F5
Norham Gr BD12 94 D2
Norland CE Jun & Inf Sch HX6 112 D2
Norland Rd
Sowerby Bridge HX6 112 C3
Sowerby Bridge, Upper Greetland HX4, HX6 133 D8
Norland St BD7 73 F3
Norland Town Rd HX6 112 D2
Norland View
6 Halifax HX2 113 A4
Sowerby Bridge HX6 112 D4
Norman Ave
Bradford BD2 56 B5
4 Elland HX5 135 A6
Norman Cres BD2 56 B5
Norman Dr WF14 137 F6
Norman Gr
Bradford BD2 56 B5
Elland HX5 135 A6
Leeds LS5 59 A4
Norman La BD2 56 B5
Norman Mount
Bradford BD2 56 B5
Leeds LS5 59 A4
Norman Pl
7 Horbury WF4 141 B1
Leeds LS8 44 A2
Norman Rd
Denby Dale HD8 191 F5
Huddersfield HD2 136 A1
Mirfield WF14 137 F6
Norman Row LS5 59 A4
Norman St
Bingley BD16 37 A3
Elland HX5 135 A6
Halifax HX1 202 B1
15 Haworth BD22 51 D7
Leeds LS5 59 A4
Shipley BD18 55 D7
Normans Way WF2 142 F1
Norman Terr
Bradford BD2 56 B5
Elland HX5 135 A6
Leeds LS8 44 A2
Normanton All Saints CE Inf Sch WF6 123 B2
Normanton Common Prim Sch WF6 123 C4
Normanton Gr LS11 214 A4
Normanton Ind Est WF6 123 D3
Normanton Jun Sch WF6 123 B1
Normanton Pl LS11 214 A4
Normanton St
Horbury WF4 159 C8
Leeds LS11 214 A4
Normanton View WF6 144 B8
Norman View LS5 59 A4
Norquest Ind Pk WF17 97 A2
Norr Green Terr BD15 53 D6
Norridge Bottom 10 HD9 189 A5
Norris Cl HD5 155 A4
Norristhorpe Ave WF15 117 A2
Norristhorpe Jun & Inf Sch WF15 117 B2
Norristhorpe La WF15 117 B2
Nortech Cl LS7 207 A2
Northallerton Rd BD3 55 F1
Northampton St BD3 55 F1
North App LS24 48 A5
North Ave
Bradford BD8 55 D2
Castleford WF10 123 F7
Horbury WF4 141 C1
Otley LS21 23 A8
Pontefract WF8 146 B7
South Elmsall WF9 182 F2
Sutton-in-C BD20 16 D4
Wakefield WF1 216 B4
North Baileygate WF8 125 E1
North Bank Rd
Batley WF17 118 A6
6 Huddersfield HD2 135 F1
Shipley BD16 54 B5
North Beck Ho 13 BD21 35 B6
North Bridge HX1 203 B4
North Bridge St HX1 203 B4
North Broadgate La LS18 41 C1
Northbrook Croft 1 LS7 204 A3
Northbrook Pl LS7 204 A3
Northbrook St LS7 204 A3
North Brook St BD1 201 C4
North Byland HX2 91 E7
North Carr HD5 154 E7
North Carr Croft HD5 154 E7
North Cl
Featherstone WF7 124 C1
Leeds LS8 61 D6
Royston S71 179 C3
North Cliffe HX6 112 B3
North Cliffe Ave BD13 72 F6
North Cliffe Cl 7 BD13 72 E6
North Cliffe Dr BD13 72 E6
North Cliffe Gr 8 BD13 72 E6
North Cliffe La BD13 72 F6
Northcliffe Rd BD18 55 B6
Northcote WF5 119 C1
Northcote Cres LS11 214 B4
Northcote Dr LS11 214 B4
Northcote Fold LS22 13 B2
Northcote Gn LS11 214 B4
Northcote Rd BD2 56 B2
Northcote St LS28 57 D2
Northcote Terr BD2 56 B1
North Court Ind Est WF11 126 C5
North Cres WF9 183 B4
Northcroft
Shafton S72 180 C2
South Elmsall WF9 183 A3
Northcroft Ave WF9 183 A4
North Croft Gr LS29 8 A4
Northcroft Rise BD8 54 E1
North Cross Rd HD2 135 F2
North Ct LS2 211 C4
North Cut HD6 114 F2
Northdale Ave BD5 74 C2
Northdale Cres BD5 74 C2
Northdale Mount BD5 74 C2
Northdale Rd BD9 55 B5
North Dean Ave BD22 34 E7
North Dean Bsns Pk HX3 113 C1
North Dean Rd
Elland HX3 113 A1
Keighley BD22 34 F7
North Dean Wood (Nature Trail)* HX3 113 A1
North Dene Rd BD20 5 E2
North Dr
Bramhope LS16 24 F2
Huddersfield HD7 152 E4
North Edge HX3 93 C1
Northedge La HX3 93 D1
Northedge Mdw BD10 56 B6
Northedge Pk HX3 93 D1
Northern Cl BD7 73 F2
Northern Sch of Contemporary Dance LS7 207 A3
Northern St LS1 211 A3
North Farm Rd LS8, LS9 208 C3
North Featherstone Jun & Inf Sch WF7 145 E7
Northfield HX7 88 F5
Northfield Ave
Huddersfield HD1 153 E4
Knottingley WF11 126 F3
Ossett WF5 140 D6
Rothwell LS26 100 C4
South Kirkby WF9 182 C3
Wetherby LS22 13 E6
Northfield Cl 1 HX5 134 F6
Northfield Cres BD16 54 A7
Northfield Ct WF9 182 C3
Northfield Dr
Pontefract WF8 125 F1
South Kirkby WF9 182 C3
Northfield Gdns BD6 74 C1
Northfield Gr
Bradford BD6 74 C1
Huddersfield HD1 153 F3
Northfield Grange WF9 182 C3
Northfield La
Horbury WF4 141 C1
Kirkburton HD8 173 E8
South Kirkby WF9 182 C3
North Field La HD8 175 A2
Northfield Mews 1 LS22 13 E6
Northfield Pl
Bradford BD8 55 C1
Dewsbury WF13 118 C1
Rothwell LS26 100 B4
Wetherby LS22 13 E6
Northfield Prim Sch WF9 182 C3
Northfield Rd
Bradford BD6 74 B1
Crofton WF4 144 B3
Dewsbury WF13 118 B1
Knottingley WF11 126 F3
Ossett WF5 140 D7
North Field Rd DN5, DN6 195 D7
Northfields LS23 15 A3
Northfield St
Dewsbury WF13 118 C1
South Kirkby WF9 182 B3
Northfield Terr
Queensbury BD13 73 A1
Slaithwaite HD7 152 A2
North Fold 5 BD10 56 B8
Northgate
Baildon BD17 38 C4
Bradford BD1 201 B3
Cleckheaton BD19 116 D7
Dewsbury WF13 139 D8
Elland, Holywell Green HX4 134 B4
Elland HX5 134 F7
Northgate continued
Halifax HX1 203 B3
Heptonstall HX7 88 F5
Honley HD9 172 B6
Horbury WF4 141 A1
Huddersfield, Almondbury HD1, HD5 154 F3
Huddersfield HD1 154 B7
Liversedge WF16 117 C4
Pontefract WF8 125 D1
1 Rothwell LS26 101 C6
South Hiendley S72 180 E6
Wakefield WF1 216 B2
Wakefield WF1 216 B3
North Gate HD5, WF14 137 E3
Northgate Cl WF8 125 D1
Northgate Ho LS22 13 E5
Northgate La LS22 13 A3
Northgate Lo WF8 125 D1
Northgate Rise LS22 13 B2
Northgates LS22 13 E5
North Grange Mews LS6 205 C4
North Grange Mount LS6 59 F5
North Grange Rd LS6 205 C4
North Grove App LS22 13 E7
North Grove Ave LS22 13 E7
North Grove Cl LS8 61 D6
North Grove Cres LS22 13 E7
North Grove Ct LS22 13 E6
North Grove Dr
Leeds LS8 61 D6
Wetherby LS22 13 E7
North Grove Mount LS22 13 E6
North Grove Rd LS22 13 E7
North Grove Rise LS8 61 D6
North Grove Way LS22 13 F6
North Halifax Gram Sch The HX2 91 F6
North Hall Ave BD10 39 A2
North Hill LS14 45 D8
North Hill Cl LS8 61 C6
North Hill Ct LS6 59 F5
North Hill Dr HD5 155 C8
North Hill Rd LS6 205 C4
North Holme St BD1 201 B4
North Ives BD22 51 C4
North John St 3 BD13 72 E1
North King St WF17 118 D4
North La
Cawthorne S75 193 A2
Leeds, Headingley LS6 59 D5
Leeds, Oakwood LS8 61 C6
Rothwell LS26 101 C6
Slaithwaite HD7 151 D1
Northlands S71 179 C4
Northland View 12 WF8 125 D1
North Lane Ct HD8 175 C7
North Lane Gdns LS8 61 C6
North Lea 8 HX6 112 B4
Northlea Ave BD10 39 A1
Northleigh WF8 146 F2
North Lingwell Rd LS10 99 C5
North Lodge Fold WF13 117 F3
North Lodge La WF8 147 F4
North Mead LS16 24 F2
North Moor La HD5, WF14 137 C2
Northolme Ave LS16 59 B7
Northolme Cres LS16 59 B7
Northorpe Ct WF14 138 C6
Northorpe La WF14 138 C7
Northowram Gn HX3 93 A3
Northowram Prim Sch HX3 93 A3
North Par
Bradford, Allerton BD15 54 A2
Bradford BD1 201 B3
Burley in W LS29 9 E2
Halifax HX1 203 B3
Ilkley LS29 8 C4
Leeds LS16 59 A8
8 Morley LS27 98 B3
Otley LS21 23 A8
North Park Ave LS8 44 A1
North Park Gr LS8 44 A1
North Park Par LS8 204 C4
North Park Rd
Bradford BD9 55 B3
Leeds LS8 61 A8
North Park St WF13 118 A1
North Park Terr BD9 55 C2
North Parkway LS14 62 A6
North Pl
Mirfield WF14 138 A7
Sutton-in-C BD20 16 C5
North Point LS7 207 A1
North Queen St 1 BD21 35 C7
North Rd
Bradford BD6 74 B1
Dewsbury WF13 138 E6
Fairburn WF11 105 A4
Horsforth LS18 41 B3
Kirkburton HD8 173 E7
Leeds, Cross Gates LS15 62 C2
Royston S71 179 D4
Sutton-in-C BD20 16 C5
North Rise HD2 136 C2
North Road Terr WF1 216 A3
Northrop Cl 1 BD8 55 A1
North Row
Shepley HD8 190 D8
Sutton-in-C BD20 16 C5
North Royd
Brighouse HX3 93 C1
Ripponden HX4 133 B5

North Royds Wood S71.. **178** F1
North Selby HX2 .... **91** D7
Northside Ave BD7 ...... **74** A6
Northside Bsns Pk LS7. **207** A2
Northside Rd BD7...... **74** A6
Northside Ret Pk LS6 .. **59** F7
Northside Terr BD7 .... **73** F6
North St
  Addingham LS29 .... **7** A8
  Batley, Heckmondwike
    WF16 .... **117** D3
  Batley WF17 .... **118** B6
  Bradford BD1......... **201** C3
  Bradford, Oakenshaw BD12 **95** A4
  Bradford, Thackley BD10 .. **39** B2
  Castleford, New Fryston
    WF10 .... **104** C3
  Castleford WF10 ...... **124** C8
  Dewsbury WF13 ...... **118** C1
  Elland, Holywell Green
    HX4............. **134** B4
  4 Elland, West Vale HX4 **134** D7
  Glusburn BD20 .... **16** D7
  Haworth BD22......... **51** B7
  Huddersfield, Paddock
    HD1............. **153** D5
  Huddersfield, Rashcliffe
    HD1............. **153** E3
  Keighley BD21 .... **35** C7
  Leeds LS2, LS7 ...... **207** A1
  Mirfield WF14 .... **137** F4
  Normanton WF6 ...... **144** A8
  Otley LS21........... **23** A8
  8 Pudsey LS28....... **76** E8
  Silsden BD20 .... **5** E2
  South Kirkby WF9 .... **182** B3
  Sutton-in-C BD20 ...... **16** D5
  Wetherby LS22 .... **13** E5
  Yeadon LS19 .... **40** B4
Northstead WF13 ...... **138** D7
North Terr
  Batley WF17 .... **96** F1
  3 Leeds LS15........ **62** C2
  Yeadon LS19 .... **40** B7
Northumberland St **1**
  HD1.............. **154** B6
North Vale Ct BD19 .. **115** B7
North View
  Bradford BD15........ **54** A1
  Burley in W LS29....... **9** F1
  Dewsbury WF12 ...... **139** D6
  1 Elland HX4 .... **134** B4
  Knottingley WF11 .... **126** E4
  Leeds LS8 .... **61** D6
  Menston LS29 .... **22** A3
  Steeton BD20 .... **16** F6
  Sutton-in-C BD20 ...... **16** D5
  Wilsden BD15 .... **53** C5
North View Rd
  Birkenshaw BD4 ...... **96** A7
  Bradford BD3......... **55** F2
North View St
  Keighley BD20 .... **18** C1
  Pudsey LS28 .... **57** E2
North View Terr
  7 Dewsbury, Chapel Fold
    WF13 .... **117** F2
  2 Dewsbury WF13 .... **118** B2
  East Morton BD20 ..... **36** D8
  Haworth BD22 .... **51** C8
  5 Pudsey LS28...... **57** E2
Northway WF14 ...... **137** F7
North Way
  Huddersfield HD2 ...... **136** E4
  Leeds LS8 .... **61** D6
Northway Cres WF14 .. **137** F7
Northway Gdns WF14 .. **137** F7
Northwell Gate LS21 .. **10** E2
Northwest Bsns Pk LS6. **206** B3
North West Rd LS6... **206** B3
North Wing BD3 .... **201** C4
North Wlk
  Harden BD16........... **36** A1
  Hemsworth WF9 ...... **181** D8
Northwood Cl
  Pudsey LS28 .... **76** F5
  Rothwell LS26 .... **101** C7
Northwood Cres BD10... **56** C6
Northwood Falls LS26 .. **101** C7
Northwood Gdns LS15... **81** E7
Northwood Mount LS28 .. **76** F5
Northwood Pk
  Kirkburton HD8 ...... **173** E7
  Rothwell LS26 .... **101** C7
Northwood View LS28... **76** F5
Norton Cl
  Elland HX5 .... **134** F5
  Halifax HX2 .... **112** B7
Norton Dr HX2........ **112** B7
Norton Ho **3** BD4........ **75** D6
Norton & Kirk Smeaton Rd
  WF8 .... **166** E4
Norton Rd
  Leeds LS8 .... **44** A3
  Wakefield WF1 ...... **216** C3
Norton St
  Elland HX5 .... **134** F6
  Silsden BD20 .... **5** D1
  Wakefield WF1 ...... **142** E4
Norton Terr HD4 ...... **173** C2
Nortonthorpe Hall Sch
  HD8............... **175** D1
Nortonthorpe Ind Est
  HD8............... **175** D1
Norton Twr HX2 ...... **112** B7

Norton Way LS27 .... **98** A6
Norville Terr LS6 ...... **205** B4
Norwich Ave LS10...... **215** A2
Norwood
  Darrington WF8........ **147** A5
  Thorpe Audlin WF8.... **165** A4
Norwood Ave
  Birkenshaw BD11 ...... **96** B4
  Burley in W LS29........ **9** F1
  Shipley BD18 .... **55** B6
Norwood Bsns Pk BD12 .. **94** B2
Norwood Cl LS29 .... **9** F1
Norwood Cres
  Birkenshaw BD11 ...... **96** B4
  Pudsey LS28 .... **57** F2
Norwood Croft LS28 .... **57** F2
Norwood Dr
  Batley WF17 .... **117** F8
  Birkenshaw BD11 ...... **96** B4
  Brierley S72.......... **181** A3
Norwood Gr
  Birkenshaw BD11 ...... **96** B4
  Leeds LS6 .... **205** B3
Norwood Green Hill HX3 . **93** F2
Norwood Ho **6** BD4.... **75** D5
Norwood Mount LS6 .... **205** B3
Norwood Pk
  Huddersfield HD2 ...... **135** D1
  Ilkley LS29........... **7** F4
Norwood Pl
  Leeds LS6 .... **205** B3
  Shipley BD18 .... **55** B6
Norwood Rd
  Hemsworth WF9 ...... **181** D5
  Huddersfield HD2 ...... **135** C2
  Leeds LS6 .... **205** B3
  Shipley BD18 .... **55** B6
Norwood St
  Bradford BD5......... **74** D2
  Normanton WF6 ...... **123** D4
  Shipley BD18 .... **55** B6
Norwood Terr
  Brighouse HX3......... **94** A2
  Burley in W LS29........ **9** F1
  Leeds LS6 .... **205** B3
  Shipley BD18 .... **55** B6
Norwood View LS6...... **205** B3
Nostell Cl BD8 .... **74** D8
Nostell La WF4 .... **162** B2
Nostell Priory★ WF4 .... **162** E8
Noster Gr LS11 .... **213** C3
Noster Hill LS11 ...... **213** C3
Noster Pl LS11 .... **213** C3
Noster Rd LS11 .... **213** C3
Noster St LS11 .... **213** C3
Noster Terr LS11 ...... **214** A3
Noster View LS11 ...... **213** C3
Notre Dame RC Sixth Form
  Coll LS2............. **206** B3
Nottingham Cl WF3 .... **100** A3
Nottingham St BD3 .... **75** E7
Notton La WF4........ **179** B6
Nova La WF17 .... **96** D2
Nowell's Yd WF13...... **139** B8
Nowell App LS9........ **208** B1
Nowell Ave LS9........ **208** B1
Nowell Cl LS9 .... **208** B1
Nowell Cres LS9....... **208** B1
Nowell Ct LS9 .... **208** B1
Nowell End Row LS9.... **208** B1
Nowell Gdns LS9....... **208** B1
Nowell Gr LS9 .... **208** B1
Nowell La LS9 .... **208** B1
Nowell Mount LS9 ..... **208** B1
Nowell Par LS9 .... **208** B1
Nowell Pl
  Huddersfield HD5 ...... **154** E5
  Leeds LS9 .... **208** B1
Nowell St
  Dewsbury WF13 ...... **118** B1
  Leeds LS9 .... **208** B1
Nowell Terr LS9 .... **208** B1
Nowell View LS9....... **208** B1
Nowell Wlk LS9........ **208** B1
Nuffield Hospl HD2 .... **135** E1
Nunburnholme Wlk **2**
  BD10............... **56** C6
Nunbury Ho **8** BD4.... **75** D5
Nunington Ave **2** LS12.. **209** C4
Nunington St LS12 .... **210** A4
Nunington Terr **3** LS12. **209** C4
Nunington View **4** LS12.. **59** C1
Nunlea Royd HX3...... **115** A6
Nunn's Cl WF7......... **145** D4
Nunn's Croft WF7...... **145** D4
Nunn's Gn WF7........ **145** D4
Nunn's La WF7........ **145** D4
Nunnery La HD6....... **135** D7
Nunnery Way LS23 ..... **30** D5
Nunns Ave WF7....... **145** D3
Nunns Ct WF7........ **145** C3
Nunns View WF7...... **145** C3
Nunroyd WF16........ **117** D3
Nunroyd Ave
  Guiseley LS20 .... **39** F8
  Leeds LS17 .... **43** D1
Nunroyd Gr LS17....... **43** D1
Nunroyd Ho **1** BD4.... **75** D5
Nunroyd Lawn LS17..... **43** E1
Nunroyd Rd LS17...... **43** D1
Nunroyd St **4** LS17.... **43** D1
Nunroyd Terr **2** LS17.. **43** D1
Nunthorpe Rd LS13 .... **57** F5
Nurser La BD5 .... **74** D4
Nurser Pl BD5 .... **74** C4
Nursery Ave HX3...... **91** F3
Nursery Cl
  Baildon BD17......... **37** E2

Nursery Cl continued
  Halifax HX3 .... **91** F2
  Keighley BD20 .... **18** A3
  Leeds LS17 .... **43** C4
Nursery Garth LS22 .... **13** F6
Nursery Gr
  Dewsbury WF12 ...... **139** D4
  Halifax HX3 .... **91** F3
  Leeds LS17 .... **43** A4
Nursery La
  Addingham LS29 .... **7** A8
  Halifax HX3 .... **91** F3
  Leeds LS17 .... **43** C4
  Ripponden HX6 .... **132** B3
Nursery Lodge Ct HD5 .. **154** F7
Nursery Mount LS10 .... **215** B3
Nursery Mount Rd LS10 . **215** B2
Nursery Nook HX7 ...... **89** A4
Nursery Rd
  Bradford, Clayton BD14.... **73** B4
  Bradford, Pickles Hill BD7.. **73** F2
  Guiseley LS20 .... **22** D3
Nursery St
  Dewsbury WF12 ...... **139** C4
  Huddersfield HD2 ...... **136** A1
Nursery Way
  Boston Spa LS23 ...... **30** B8
  Clifford LS23 .... **30** D5
Nursery Wood Rd WF17 . **118** D3
Nussey Ave WF17 ...... **96** E2
Nutclough Rd HX7 ...... **89** B4
Nutfield St **12** OL14 .... **108** B6
Nuthatch Mews **2** BD6.. **73** C1
Nuttall Rd BD3......... **201** D4
Nuttall St **3** OL13...... **106** B3
Nutter La BD19, WF17.... **96** C2
Nutter Pl BD1......... **201** B3
Nutter St BD19........ **116** C7
Nutting Grove Terr LS12.. **77** E5
Nutwood Wlk BD6 ...... **93** F6

O

O'Cot La HD3......... **151** B4
O'Grady Sq **3** LS9 .... **212** C5
Oak Ave
  Bingley BD16......... **36** F2
  Bradford BD8......... **55** D2
  Burley in W LS29....... **21** F8
  Garforth LS25 .... **82** F7
  Huddersfield HD5 ...... **154** E5
  Huddersfield, Leymoor
    HD7............. **152** E5
  Lofthouse Gate WF3 ... **121** F4
  Meltham HD9.......... **170** C3
  Morley LS27.......... **98** B3
  Normanton WF6 ...... **144** A8
  Sowerby Bridge HX6 ... **112** B5
  Todmorden OL14 ...... **108** A7
Oak Bank
  16 Bingley BD16 ...... **37** A2
  Shipley BD18 .... **55** D5
Oakbank Ave BD22..... **34** F5
Oak Bank Broadway BD22 . **34** F5
Oak Bank Cres BD22 ... **34** F4
Oak Bank Ct BD22...... **34** F4
Oakbank Dr BD22....... **34** F5
Oakbank Gr BD22...... **34** F5
Oak Bank La BD22...... **34** F4
Oak Bank Mount BD22 .. **34** F4
Oakbank Rd LS29........ **8** A3
Oak Cl LS29 .... **21** F8
Oak Cres
  Garforth LS25 .... **82** F7
  Havercroft WF4 ...... **180** B8
  Leeds LS15 .... **80** F7
Oakdale BD16......... **37** A5
Oakdale Ave
  Bradford BD6......... **74** B1
  Shipley BD18 .... **55** D6
Oakdale Cl
  Bradford BD10........ **56** E3
  Halifax HX3 .... **92** A2
  Lofthouse Gate WF3 ... **121** B6
Oakdale Cres
  Bradford BD6......... **74** B1
  Huddersfield HD3 ...... **153** A8
Oakdale Dr
  Bradford BD10........ **56** E3
  Pool LS21............ **24** D6
  Shipley BD18 .... **55** E6
Oakdale Garth LS14 .... **45** B1
Oakdale Gr BD18....... **55** E6
Oakdale Mdw LS14..... **45** B1
Oakdale Pk LS21 .... **24** D6
Oakdale Rd
  Fitzwilliam WF9 ...... **163** B2
  Shipley BD18 .... **55** E6
Oakdale Terr BD6....... **74** B1
Oakdean HD2.......... **136** A4
Oakdene Cl LS28....... **76** F5
Oakdene Ct LS17....... **44** A4
Oakdene Dr
  Crofton WF4 .... **162** A8
  Leeds LS17 .... **44** A4
Oakdene Gdns LS17..... **44** A4
Oakdene Vale LS17..... **44** A4
Oakdene Way LS17..... **44** A4
Oak Dr
  Garforth LS25 .... **82** F7
  Slaithwaite HD7........ **152** D3
Oaken Bank Cres HD5... **154** D4
Oaken Cl OL13 .... **106** B3
Oakenclough Rd OL13.. **106** B3
Oakenshaw Ct BD12..... **94** C2

Oakenshaw La
  Bradford BD19........ **95** A3
  Crofton WF1, WF4 .... **143** A2
  Walton WF4, WF2 .... **161** A8
Oakenshaw St WF1 .... **142** F3
Oakes Ave HD9 .... **172** C2
Oakes Fold HD8 .... **156** A3
Oakes Gdns HX4....... **134** B4
Oakes La
  Brockholes HD9....... **172** D1
  Honley HD9 .... **172** C2
Oakes Rd HD3......... **153** B8
Oakes Rd S HD3....... **153** B7
Oakes St WF2......... **141** D6
Oakfield LS6.......... **205** B4
Oakfield Ave
  Bingley BD16......... **37** C2
  Rothwell LS26 .... **100** E6
Oakfield Cl
  Elland HX5 .... **134** E6
  Garforth LS25 .... **82** F6
  Menston LS29 .... **22** A6
Oakfield Cres WF11 .... **126** F3
Oakfield Ct S75....... **178** A1
Oakfield Dr
  Baildon BD17......... **38** D2
  Mirfield WF14 .... **137** F3
Oakfield Gr
  Bradford BD9......... **55** C2
  Skelmanthorpe HD8 ... **175** A1
Oakfield Park Sch WF7.. **164** A4
Oakfield Pk WF8....... **165** B4
Oakfield Rd
  Huddersfield HD2 ...... **135** E1
  Keighley BD21 .... **35** B4
Oakfield Terr
  Horsforth LS18........ **58** E8
  Shipley BD18 .... **55** D7
Oakford Terr LS16 ..... **41** F2
Oak Gr
  Garforth LS25 .... **83** A7
  Keighley BD21 .... **35** A4
  Morley LS27.......... **98** C3
Oakhall Pk BD13....... **72** E7
Oak Hall Pk WF4...... **159** C4
Oakham Garth LS9..... **80** C7
Oakham Mews **4** LS9... **80** B7
Oakhampton Ct LS8.... **61** C8
Oakham Way LS9...... **80** B7
Oakhead Terr BD20..... **16** D8
Oak Hill HX6.......... **132** E8
Oakhill Rd WF17....... **118** A7
Oak Ho
  9 Castleford WF10 .... **124** E7
  Leeds LS15 .... **80** E6
Oakhurst Ave **5** LS11... **214** A1
Oakhurst Gr LS11 ...... **213** C1
Oakhurst Mount LS11 ... **213** C1
Oakhurst Rd LS11...... **214** A1
Oakhurst St LS11 ...... **214** A1
Oak La
  Bradford BD9......... **55** C2
  4 Halifax HX1 ...... **202** C3
  Sowerby Bridge HX6 ... **132** E8
Oakland Crest WF4 .... **158** A7
Oakland Ct
  Batley WF17 .... **118** C6
  Kirkburton HD8 ...... **173** F7
Oakland Dr WF4 ...... **158** D5
Oakland Hill Est WF10... **125** F7
Oakland Hills **5** WF6 .. **123** C1
Oakland Rd
  Netherton WF4 .... **158** D5
  Wakefield WF1 ...... **142** E3
Oaklands
  Bradford BD10........ **56** A8
  Brighouse HD6 .... **114** F1
  Ilkley LS29........... **8** A3
  Rothwell WF3 .... **100** A3
  Shipley BD18 .... **54** D7
Oaklands Ave
  Leeds LS16 .... **42** D3
  Northowram HX3...... **93** B3
  Pudsey LS13 .... **57** E5
Oaklands Cl
  Holmfirth HD9 .... **189** A7
  Leeds LS16 .... **42** D3
Oaklands Croft WF2.... **161** B6
Oaklands Dr
  Batley WF17 .... **118** F5
  Huddersfield HD5 ...... **154** F5
  Leeds LS16 .... **42** D3
Oaklands Fold LS16..... **42** D3
Oaklands Gr
  Leeds LS16 .... **42** D3
  Pudsey LS13 .... **57** E5
Oaklands Rd LS13...... **57** E5
Oakland St BD20........ **5** D1
Oaklea Cl S75 .... **178** B2
Oaklea Gdns LS16...... **42** D3
Oaklea Hall Cl LS16 .... **42** D3
Oaklea Rd LS15........ **62** F6
Oak Leigh S75 .... **193** E4
Oakleigh Ave
  Bradford BD14........ **73** B3
  Halifax HX3 .... **113** C3
  Wakefield WF2 ...... **141** E5
Oakleigh Cl
  Bradford BD14........ **73** B4
  Crofton WF4 .... **144** C4
Oakleigh Gdns
  Bradford BD14........ **73** B3
  Mirfield WF14 .... **137** F3
Oakleigh Gr BD14...... **73** B3
Oakleigh Mews BD22.... **34** C2
Oakleigh Rd BD14...... **73** B4

Oakleigh Terr
  Bradford BD14.......... **73** B4
  8 Todmorden OL14 .... **86** B1
Oakleigh View BD17 .... **38** B3
Oakley Gr LS11 .... **214** C2
Oakley St WF3 .... **99** E1
Oakley Terr LS11....... **214** C2
Oakley View LS11 ..... **214** C2
Oakmont Cl **4** WF6 .... **123** C1
Oak Mount
  Bradford BD8......... **55** D2
  Todmorden OL14...... **108** B6
Oak Pl
  Baildon BD17......... **38** F4
  Garforth LS25 .... **82** E7
  Halifax HX1 .... **202** C3
  14 Sowerby Bridge HX6 . **112** B5
Oak Rd
  Garforth LS25 .... **82** E7
  Huddersfield HD2 ...... **137** A5
  Leeds, Halton LS15 .... **80** F7
  Leeds, New Wortley LS12 . **210** B3
  Leeds, Potternewton LS7 . **204** A1
  Morley LS27.......... **97** F3
  Shafton S72.......... **180** D2
Oak Ridge LS22........ **13** C5
Oakridge Ave LS29 ..... **22** B4
Oakridge Ct BD16...... **37** A4
Oak Rise
  Cleckheaton BD19...... **95** D2
  Pontefract WF8 ...... **125** E2
Oak Royd LS26........ **100** F4
Oakroyd Ave BD6 ...... **74** C1
Oakroyd Cl
  Birkenshaw BD11 ...... **96** A5
  Brighouse HD6 .... **115** B5
Oakroyd Ct HD8....... **174** A6
Oakroyd Dr
  Birkenshaw BD11 ...... **96** A4
  Brighouse HD6 .... **115** B5
Oakroyd Fold LS27 ..... **98** C8
Oakroyd Mount LS28 ... **76** E8
Oakroyd Rd
  12 Bradford, Brownroyd Oak
    BD6.............. **74** C1
  10 Bradford, Wibsey BD6 . **74** B1
Oakroyd Terr
  3 Baildon BD17 ...... **38** D2
  Bradford BD8......... **55** D2
  Morley LS27.......... **98** C8
  9 Pudsey LS28....... **76** E8
Oakroyd Villas BD8 .... **55** D2
Oak Scar La HD9....... **189** D3
Oaks Dr BD15......... **73** C8
Oaks Farm Cl S75 ..... **177** F1
Oaks Farm Dr S75 ..... **177** F1
Oaksfield LS26........ **102** D2
Oaks Fold BD5........ **74** E3
Oaks Green Mount HD6 . **135** F4
Oakshaw Ct BD4....... **75** A4
Oaks La
  Boston Spa LS23 ...... **30** D8
  Bradford BD15, BD8 .... **73** D8
Oaks Rd WF17........ **118** C4
Oak St
  5 Bacup OL13 ...... **106** A3
  Batley WF16 .... **117** D4
  Bradford BD14........ **73** B4
  Crofton WF4 .... **162** A7
  Elland HX5........... **134** F6
  Haworth BD22......... **51** D7
  15 Hebden Bridge HX7 .. **89** A4
  Lofthouse Gate WF1 ... **121** C4
  Morley LS27.......... **98** B7
  Oxenhope BD22........ **51** C3
  Pudsey LS28 .... **76** C8
  South Elmsall WF9..... **182** F1
  15 Sowerby Bridge HX6 . **112** B5
  Todmorden OL14...... **108** A4
Oaks The
  Crofton WF4 .. ·..... **144** B4
  Guiseley LS20 .... **22** E2
  Morley LS27.......... **98** B7
  Wilsden BD15 .... **53** B6
Oaks Wood Dr S75..... **178** A1
Oak Terr
  2 Elland HX4 .... **134** A4
  2 Halifax HX1 ...... **202** C3
  Huddersfield HD2 ...... **136** B2
  1 Leeds LS15....... **62** D3
  13 Sowerby Bridge HX6 . **112** B5
Oak Tree Ave
  Holmfirth HD9 .... **189** D3
  Lepton HD8 .... **155** D3
Oak Tree Bsns Pk LS14 .. **62** A7
Oak Tree Cl LS9........ **208** C3
Oak Tree Cres LS9 ..... **208** C3
Oak Tree Ct
  Leeds LS9 .... **208** C3
  Silsden BD20 .... **5** D2
Oak Tree Dr LS8....... **208** C3
Oak Tree Gr
  Hemsworth WF9 ...... **181** F6
  Leeds LS9 .... **208** C3
Oaktree La WF7........ **164** C5
Oak Tree Mdw WF2 .... **161** A4
Oak Tree Mount LS9 ... **208** C3
Oak Tree Pl LS9........ **208** C3
Oak Tree Rd HD8...... **155** D3
Oak Tree Terr HD8..... **155** D3
Oak Tree Wlk LS9...... **208** C3
Oakvale BD21 .... **35** B3
Oak View BD20.......... **5** E2
Oak View Terr **4** WF17.. **117** F8
Oak Villas
  Bradford BD8......... **55** D2
  Hebden Bridge HX7..... **88** D2

Oakville Rd HX7 . . . . 88 D2
Oakway BD11 . . . . 96 B4
Oakwell Ave
Batley WF17 . . . . 117 F6
Leeds, Gledhow LS8 . . . . . . 61 A6
Leeds LS12 . . . . 210 A3
Pontefract WF8 . . . . 146 C6
Oakwell Cl
Birkenshaw BD11 . . . . 97 A5
Bradford BD7 . . . . 74 B3
Fitzwilliam WF9 . . . . 163 A2
Oakwell Cres LS8 . . . . 61 A6
Oakwell Ct 4 LS13 . . . . . . 58 B3
Oakwell Dr LS8 . . . . 61 A6
Oakwell Gdns LS8 . . . . 61 A6
Oakwell Gr LS13 . . . . 58 C3
Oakwell Hall★ WF17 . . . . . 96 D3
Oakwell Hall Ctry Pk★
WF17 . . . . 96 D3
Oakwell Hall Visitor Ctr★
WF17 . . . . 96 C2
Oakwell Ind Pk WF17 . . . . . 97 A4
Oakwell Mount LS8 . . . . . . 61 A6
Oakwell Oval LS8 . . . . 61 A6
Oakwell Rd BD11 . . . . 97 A5
Oakwell Terr 2 LS28 . . . . . 57 D3
Oakwell Way WF17 . . . . . . 97 A3
Oakwood WF2 . . . . 141 D3
Oakwood Ave
Birkenshaw BD11 . . . . 96 A4
Leeds LS8 . . . . 61 B6
Royston S71 . . . . 179 C4
Shipley BD2 . . . . 55 D4
Wakefield WF2 . . . . 141 D6
Oakwood Boundary Rd
LS8 . . . . 61 B6
Oakwood Cl
Castleford WF10 . . . . 125 F6
Normanton WF6 . . . . 122 F4
Oakwood Cotts 4 WF5 . . 140 D5
Oakwood Cres S71 . . . . . . 179 B4
Oakwood Ct
Bradford BD8 . . . . 74 C8
Leeds LS8 . . . . 61 C6
Oakwood Dr
Bingley BD16 . . . . 37 A5
Hemsworth WF9 . . . . 181 E6
Leeds LS8 . . . . 61 B6
Normanton WF6 . . . . 122 F4
Rothwell LS26 . . . . 100 D7
Oakwood Garth LS8 . . . . . . 61 C6
Oakwood Gdns
Crigglestone WF4 . . . . 159 D6
Halifax HX2 . . . . 91 F4
Leeds LS8 . . . . 61 B6
Pudsey LS28 . . . . 76 E6
Oakwood Gn LS8 . . . . 61 C6
Oakwood Gr
Bradford BD8 . . . . 55 A1
Horbury WF4 . . . . 141 C2
Leeds LS8 . . . . 61 B6
Oakwood Grange LS8 . . . . 61 C6
Oakwood Grange La LS8 . 61 C6
Oakwood La LS8, LS9 . . . . 61 C5
Oakwood Mount LS8 . . . . . 61 B6
Oakwood Nook LS8 . . . . . . 61 B6
Oakwood Pk LS8 . . . . 61 C6
Oakwood Pl LS8 . . . . 61 B6
Oakwood Prim Sch LS8 . 208 C3
Oakwood Rd
Batley WF17 . . . . 118 E5
Royston S71 . . . . 179 B4
Oak Wood Rd LS22 . . . . . . 13 D7
Oakwood Rise LS8 . . . . 61 C6
Oakwood Terr LS28 . . . . . . 76 E6
Oakwood View LS8 . . . . . . 61 C6
Oakwood Wlk LS8 . . . . 61 C6
Oakworth Hall BD22 . . . . . 34 C2
Oakworth Prim Sch BD22 34 D2
Oakworth Rd BD21, BD22 . . 35 A6
Oakworth Sta★ BD22 . . . . . 34 D1
Oakworth Terr BD22 . . . . . 34 D2
Oasby Croft BD4 . . . . 75 E1
Oast House Croft WF3 . . . 100 B3
Oastler Ave HD1 . . . . 153 F6
Oastler Gr WF14 . . . . 138 A6
Oastler Pl BD12 . . . . 94 D6
Oastler Rd
Pudsey LS28 . . . . 57 B6
Shipley BD18 . . . . 54 F8
Oastler St WF13 . . . . 139 B8
Oates St WF13 . . . . 139 C8
Oatland Cl LS7 . . . . 206 C2
Oatland Ct LS7 . . . . 206 C2
Oatland Dr LS7 . . . . 206 C2
Oatland Gdns LS7 . . . . 207 A2
Oatland Gn LS7 . . . . 206 C2
Oatland Hts LS7 . . . . 207 A2
Oatland La LS7 . . . . 206 C2
Oatland Pl LS7 . . . . 206 C3
Oatland Rd LS7 . . . . 206 C2
Oatlands Dr LS21 . . . . 11 A1
Oatland Twrs LS7 . . . . 206 C2
Oats St BD22 . . . . 35 A4
Oban Cl WF3 . . . . 98 D1
Oban Pl 5 LS12 . . . . 209 B4
Oban St LS12 . . . . 209 B4
Oban Terr 6 LS12 . . . . . . 209 B4
Oberon Way 6 BD16 . . . . . . 54 B6
Occupation La
Aberford LS24 . . . . 47 D4
Batley WF13 . . . . 117 F3
Bramhope LS16 . . . . 24 B2
Dewsbury WF12 . . . . 140 B7
Halifax HX2 . . . . 91 F6
Holmfirth HD9 . . . . 189 E8
Honley HD9 . . . . 172 D1
Keighley BD22 . . . . 34 E4
Occupation La *continued*
Pudsey LS28 . . . . 76 C7
Occupation Rd
Huddersfield, Edgerton
HD3 . . . . 153 C8
Huddersfield, Newsome
HD4 . . . . 154 A2
Huddersfield, Sheepridge
HD2 . . . . 136 C3
Ochrewell Ave HD2 . . . . . 136 E3
Octagon Terr HX2 . . . . 112 E4
Odda La LS20 . . . . 21 E1
Oddfellows CHs WF7 . . . . 163 D5
Oddfellows Ho BD20 . . . . . . 4 A2
Oddfellows St
3 Brighouse HD6 . . . . 115 B4
Brighouse, Scholes BD19 . 115 F8
Mirfield WF14 . . . . 138 A5
Oddfellow St LS27 . . . . 98 A4
Oddfellows Villas HD5 . . 155 C8
Oddy's Fold LS6 . . . . 59 E8
Oddy Fold HX3 . . . . 92 B1
Oddy Pl
6 Bradford BD6 . . . . 74 B1
9 Leeds LS6 . . . . 59 D6
Oddy St BD4 . . . . 75 E1
Odsal Pl 9 BD6 . . . . 94 D8
Odsal Rd BD6 . . . . 94 D8
Office Village The WF5 . . 141 B6
Offley La WF4 . . . . 163 B6
Ogden Cres BD13 . . . . 52 D2
Ogden Ho BD4 . . . . 75 F3
Ogden La
7 Brighouse HD6 . . . . 135 F8
Denholme BD13 . . . . 52 D2
Halifax HX2 . . . . 71 D2
Ogden St HX6 . . . . 112 A3
Ogden View Cl HX2 . . . . . . 91 D7
Ogden Water Ctry Pk★
HX2 . . . . 71 C2
Ogden Water Visitor Ctr★
HX2 . . . . 71 C2
Ogilby Ct LS26 . . . . 101 B7
Ogilby Mews LS26 . . . . . . 101 B7
Old Allen Rd BD13 . . . . 53 B2
Old Appletree La BD15 . . . 54 A1
Old Arcade The 8 HX1 . . 203 B3
Old Bank
Halifax HX3 . . . . 203 C3
Ripponden HX6 . . . . 132 E4
Slaithwaite HD7 . . . . 169 F8
Old Bank Fold 13 HD5 . . . 154 D5
Old Bank Jun & Inf Sch
WF14 . . . . 138 A7
Old Bank Rd
Dewsbury WF12 . . . . 139 E8
Mirfield WF14 . . . . 138 A7
Old Bar La HD9 . . . . 200 B8
Old Barn Cl LS17 . . . . 43 A5
Old Bell Ct HX1 . . . . 203 B2
Old Boyne Hill Farm
WF4 . . . . 160 A3
Old Brandon La LS17 . . . . . . 44 E4
Old Bridge Rise LS29 . . . . . . 8 A5
Old Canal Rd BD1 . . . . 201 B4
Old Cawsey HX6 . . . . 112 C4
Old Chamber HX7 . . . . 89 A1
Old Church St 2 WF5 . . . 140 D5
Old Cl LS11 . . . . 98 D8
Old Cock Yd HX1 . . . . 203 B3
Old Corn Mill La BD7 . . . . . 74 A4
Old Corn Mill The BD20 . . 16 A6
Old Cross Stone Rd 17
OL14 . . . . 108 C5
Old Crown Rd WF2 . . . . . . 141 D3
Old Dalton La BD21 . . . . . . 35 D7
Old Earth HX5 . . . . 135 B7
Old Earth Prim Sch HX5 135 C7
Old Farm App LS16 . . . . 58 F8
Old Farm Cl LS16 . . . . 59 A8
Old Farm Cres BD4 . . . . 75 B3
Old Farm Cross LS16 . . . . . 59 A8
Old Farm Dr LS16 . . . . 59 A8
Old Farm Garth 2 LS16 . . 59 A8
Old Farm Par LS16 . . . . 59 A8
Old Farm Way WF9 . . . . . 183 B7
Old Farm Wlk 6 LS16 . . . . 58 F8
Old Farmyard The HD5 . . 137 C4
Oldfield HD9 . . . . 171 F1
Oldfield Ave LS12 . . . . . . 209 C2
Oldfield Cl
Micklefield LS25 . . . . 84 A7
Ossett WF5 . . . . 140 D8
Oldfield Ct LS7 . . . . 204 B2
Oldfield Gate BD22 . . . . . . 51 A7
Old Fieldhouse La HD2 . . 136 D1
Oldfield La
Batley WF16 . . . . 117 D3
Clayton West HD8 . . . . 175 F2
Collingham LS22 . . . . 13 E1
Haworth BD22 . . . . 51 A7
Haworth, Oldfield BD22 . . . . 50 C8
Leeds LS12 . . . . 210 A2
Oldfield Prim Sch BD22 . . 50 C8
Oldfield Rd HD9 . . . . 171 F1
Oldfield St
Halifax HX3 . . . . 92 A3
Huddersfield HD4 . . . . 153 E4
Leeds LS12 . . . . 209 C2
Old Fold 9 LS28 . . . . 57 D3
Old Forge Mews LS16 . . . . 24 D3
Old Garth Croft WF11 . . . 105 A4
Oldgate HD1 . . . . 154 B6
Old Gate
29 Hebden Bridge HX7 . . . . 89 A3
Holme HD9 . . . . 197 F7
Old Godley La HX3 . . . . 92 F1
Old Great North Rd
Brotherton WF11 . . . . 126 C8
Knottingley WF11 . . . . 126 C5
Old Ground HD7 . . . . 169 A8
Old Guy Rd BD13 . . . . 72 C1
Old Hall HX3 . . . . 113 D4
Old Hall Cl
Glusburn BD20 . . . . 16 B6
2 Haworth BD22 . . . . 51 C6
Old Hall Court Yd WF1 . . 143 A5
Old Hall La HD8 . . . . 175 E5
Old Hall Mews WF17 . . . . 118 C7
Old Hall Rd
Batley WF17 . . . . 118 C7
East Ardsley WF3 . . . . 119 F8
Glusburn BD20 . . . . 16 B6
Skellow DN6 . . . . 184 F2
Old Hall Way BD20 . . . . 16 B6
Oldham Rd HX6 . . . . 150 C6
Old Haworth La 6 LS19 . . . 40 B7
Old Hollings Hill LS20,
BD17 . . . . 39 C6
Old Joinery The BD20 . . . . 16 D7
Old La
Birkenshaw BD11 . . . . 96 B5
Bramhope LS16 . . . . 24 B3
Brighouse HD6 . . . . 115 B3
Cullingworth BD13 . . . . 52 D6
Gildersome BD11 . . . . 97 A8
Guiseley LS20 . . . . 38 E8
Halifax HX3 . . . . 92 B2
Halifax, Luddenden HX2 . . . 90 E1
Haworth BD22 . . . . 49 F7
Holme HD9 . . . . 187 C4
Huddersfield, Brackenhall
HD2 . . . . 136 D5
Huddersfield, Scapegoat Hill
HD7 . . . . 152 C5
Ilkley LS29 . . . . 8 D3
Leeds LS11 . . . . 213 C1
Marsden HD7 . . . . 169 D7
Nesfield LS29 . . . . 7 C7
Pool LS16 . . . . 23 F4
Todmorden OL14 . . . . 108 A3
Wadsworth Moor HX7 . . . . . 89 B8
Old Laithe La HX7 . . . . 89 C5
Old Lane Ct 2 HD6 . . . . . 115 B3
Old Langley La BD17 . . . . . 38 E4
Old Lee Bank HX3 . . . . 92 B1
Old Leeds Rd HD1 . . . . . . 154 B6
Old Lees Rd HX7 . . . . 89 A4
Old Lindley Rd HD3 . . . . . 134 D2
**Old Lodge Hill or Hardings
La** LS29 . . . . 7 F6
Old Main St BD16 . . . . 36 F3
Old Manse Croft BD22 . . . . 51 C3
Old Market HX1 . . . . 203 B3
Old Marsh
Pudsey LS28 . . . . 76 C7
7 Sowerby Bridge HX6 . . 112 B5
Old Meadows Rd OL13 . . 106 A5
Old Mill Bsns Pk LS10 . . . 215 C4
Old Mill Cl
Burley in W LS29 . . . . 9 F2
Hemsworth WF9 . . . . 181 C7
Old Mill Ct HD9 . . . . 189 F1
Old Mill Gr HX1 . . . . 202 A2
Old Mill La
Clifford LS23 . . . . 30 E5
Holmfirth HD9 . . . . 189 D8
Leeds LS10 . . . . 215 B4
Old Mill Rd BD18 . . . . 55 A8
Old Mill Ridge HX7 . . . . . . 89 C5
Old Mill The LS22 . . . . 13 E5
Old Mill View WF12 . . . . . 139 B5
Old Mill Yd WF5 . . . . 140 C3
Old Moll Rd HD4 . . . . 171 E5
Old Mount Farm WF4 . . . 178 A6
Old Mount Rd HD7 . . . . . . 168 E2
Old Oak Cl LS16 . . . . 59 A7
Old Oak Dr LS16 . . . . 59 A7
Old Oak Garth LS16 . . . . . . 58 F7
Old Oak Lawn LS16 . . . . 59 A7
Old Orchard The
Hemsworth WF9 . . . . 181 D7
Leeds LS13 . . . . 58 B4
Old Orch The LS21 . . . . 24 C7
Old Oxenhope La BD22 . . . 51 B4
Old Park Ct BD1 . . . . 201 D3
Old Park Rd
Bradford BD10 . . . . 56 C7
Leeds LS8 . . . . 61 A8
Old Police Sta LS9 . . . . . . 208 C1
Old Pool Bank LS21 . . . . . . 24 B5
Old Pool Rd LS21 . . . . 23 F8
Old Popplewell La BD19 . 115 E8
Old Power Way HX5 . . . . . 135 A8
Old Railway Goods Yd The
HD3 . . . . 153 A5
Old Rd
Bradford BD7 . . . . 73 E2
Denholme BD13 . . . . 71 D8
Holmfirth HD9 . . . . 188 D3
Morley LS27 . . . . 98 C8
Netherton WF4 . . . . 157 F6
Pudsey LS28 . . . . 57 D2
Thornton BD13 . . . . 73 A6
Wadsworth Moor HX7 . . . . . 69 A2
Old Riding La HX2 . . . . 90 F3
Old Robin 9 BD19 . . . . . . 116 D7
Oldroyd Cres LS11 . . . . . . 213 B2
Oldroyd Rd OL14 . . . . 108 E4
Oldroyd Way WF13 . . . . . 139 B8
Old Run Rd LS10 . . . . 215 A1
Old Run View LS10 . . . . 99 D8
Old Sawmill Cotts HX6 . . 132 C2
Old Sawmills The HX6 . . . 132 C2
Old School Ct WF10 . . . . . 124 C5
Old School Ho The
Bradford BD10 . . . . 39 F1
16 Morley LS27 . . . . 98 B4
Old School La HD5 . . . . . . 154 F3
Old School Lofts LS12 . . . 209 A4
Old School Mews
4 Morley LS27 . . . . 98 C8
Otley LS21 . . . . 23 B8
Old Schools Gdns 14 HX3 . 92 C1
Old School The WF14 . . . . 137 E6
Old School Way BD17 . . . . 38 C3
Old Shaw La HX7 . . . . 88 A4
Old Side Ct BD20 . . . . 19 E1
Old Souls Way BD16 . . . . . . 36 E6
Old South St HD1 . . . . 154 A6
Old St
Hampole DN6 . . . . 183 F1
Hooton Pagnell DN5 . . . . . 195 F7
Old Station Rd HX2 . . . . . 111 D7
Old Station Way LS29 . . . . . . 6 F8
Old Sunday School The
HX2 . . . . 112 B6
Old Town Hall Cotts HX7 . 89 B5
Old Town Mill La HX7 . . . . 89 B5
Old Town Prim Sch HX7 . . 89 C5
Old Turnpike HD9 . . . . 172 A4
Old Vicarage Cl 4 BD16 . . 54 B6
Old Village Sch The 13
BD14 . . . . 73 B4
Old Wakefield Rd 5
HD5 . . . . 154 D5
Old Water Mill The HX6 . 132 D7
Old Well Head HX1 . . . . . . 203 B2
Old Westgate WF13 . . . . . 139 C8
Old Whack House La LS19 39 F6
Old Wood La BD16, LS20 . . 21 B2
Old Woodyard The WF4 . 158 C2
Old Yew La HD9 . . . . 188 E2
Olicana Pk LS29 . . . . 8 A5
Olive Gr BD8 . . . . 73 E8
Olive Mount Ho LS13 . . . . . 58 F3
Olive Pl 23 BD13 . . . . 72 E1
Oliver Cl HX6 . . . . 112 B4
Oliver Ct BD11 . . . . 96 D5
Oliver Gdns WF14 . . . . . . 137 F7
Oliver Hill LS18 . . . . 58 C7
Oliver La HD7 . . . . 168 F4
Oliver Mdws HX5 . . . . 135 B7
Oliver Rd WF16 . . . . 117 E5
Olivers Mount WF8 . . . . . 146 E8
Oliver St BD4 . . . . 201 D1
Olive St HD1 . . . . 136 B1
Olive Terr
Bingley BD16 . . . . 37 A3
Marsden HD7 . . . . 169 C6
Olivia Ct 4 HX3 . . . . 92 B1
Ollerdale Ave BD15 . . . . . . 54 A3
Ollerdale Cl BD15 . . . . 54 A2
Ollerton Rd S71 . . . . 178 F1
Olney St HD7 . . . . 152 A1
Olrika Ct LS7 . . . . 207 A4
Olympic Pk 6 BD12 . . . . . . 94 E5
Omar St WF16 . . . . 117 C4
Onchan Dr OL13 . . . . 106 B1
One St BD1 . . . . 74 D7
Onslow Cres BD4 . . . . 75 B2
Ontario Pl LS7 . . . . 204 A2
Onward Bsns Pk WF7 . . . 163 D6
Onward Way WF9 . . . . 182 D1
Opal St BD22 . . . . 35 A4
Opus Point HX3 . . . . 113 C2
Orange St
Bradford BD3 . . . . 75 C6
Halifax HX1 . . . . 203 B3
Orange Terr HD1 . . . . 154 B8
Orange Tree Gr WF3 . . . . 120 C7
Orangewood HD9 . . . . 170 E5
Orchan Rd OL14 . . . . 107 F7
Orchard Ave WF3 . . . . 121 F5
Orchard Bsns Pk HX7 . . . 110 E8
Orchard Cl
Darton S75 . . . . 178 B1
East Ardsley WF3 . . . . 120 D6
Halifax HX2 . . . . 112 D6
Horbury WF4 . . . . 141 A2
Meltham HD9 . . . . 170 F1
Wakefield WF2 . . . . 120 F3
Orchard Croft
Batley WF17 . . . . 118 A3
Dewsbury WF12 . . . . 139 C5
Horbury WF4 . . . . 141 B1
2 Leeds LS15 . . . . 62 B2
Wakefield WF2 . . . . 120 E2
Walton WF2 . . . . 161 A7
Orchard Ct
Badsworth WF9 . . . . 164 E2
Bramham LS23 . . . . 30 D2
22 Guiseley LS20 . . . . 22 E1
Huddersfield HD3 . . . . 152 F6
Leeds LS6 . . . . 59 D7
Orchard Dr
Ackworth M T WF7 . . . . . . 164 A5
Crigglestone WF4 . . . . 159 F7
Fairburn WF11 . . . . 105 B5
Linton LS22 . . . . 13 B3
South Hiendley S72 . . . . . . 180 D6
Orchard Gate 1 LS21 . . . . . 23 A7
Orchard Gdns WF4 . . . . . . 159 F7
Orchard Gr
Bradford BD10 . . . . 56 D6
Castleford WF10 . . . . 124 A5
Menston LS29 . . . . 22 B4
Orchard Head Cres WF8 . 125 F4
Orchard Head Dr WF8 . . . 125 E4
Orchard Head La WF8 . . . 125 E4
Orchard La
Addingham LS29 . . . . 7 A8
Darrington WF8 . . . . 147 C5
Orchard La *continued*
3 Guiseley LS20 . . . . 22 E1
Orchard Lees HD5 . . . . . . 155 C8
Orchard Lo LS6 . . . . 205 C4
Orchard Mount LS15 . . . . . 62 C2
Orchard Pl HD9 . . . . 189 C6
Orchard Rd
Kirkheaton HD5 . . . . 155 C8
1 Leeds LS15 . . . . 62 B2
Wakefield WF2 . . . . 142 E1
Orchard Rise HX6 . . . . 111 F2
Orchard St W HD3 . . . . . . 153 A5
Orchard Sq LS15 . . . . 62 B2
Orchard St
Dewsbury WF12 . . . . 139 D6
Huddersfield HD4 . . . . 154 A4
5 Otley LS21 . . . . 23 B7
Orchards The
Ackworth M T WF7 . . . . . . 164 B7
Bingley BD16 . . . . 37 A5
3 Brighouse HD6 . . . . 135 F8
Cleckheaton BD19 . . . . 117 C8
Leeds LS15 . . . . 62 C2
Mickletown LS26 . . . . 102 C2
Orchard Terr
Cawthorne S75 . . . . 193 F4
Huddersfield HD4 . . . . 154 B4
Orchard The
Boston Spa LS23 . . . . 30 D8
Crofton WF4 . . . . 144 A1
Elland HX4 . . . . 133 F3
Featherstone WF7 . . . . 124 D1
Huddersfield HD7 . . . . 152 D4
Keighley BD21 . . . . 35 F7
12 Leeds LS15 . . . . 81 A8
Mirfield WF14 . . . . 138 B7
Normanton, Ashfield WF6 . 123 B2
Normanton WF6 . . . . 144 A8
Ossett WF5 . . . . 140 D5
Pontefract WF8 . . . . 146 F5
Wakefield WF2, WF4 . . . . . 120 F3
Orchard View
Brotherton WF11 . . . . 126 C8
Darrington WF8 . . . . 147 C5
Wetherby LS22 . . . . 13 E8
Orchard Way
Brighouse HD6 . . . . 115 A4
Guiseley LS20 . . . . 22 E1
Rothwell LS26 . . . . 100 F6
Orchard Wlk HX7 . . . . 89 F1
Orchid Cl 2 BD18 . . . . 55 D5
Orchid Crest WF9 . . . . 183 A8
Orchid Ct WF3 . . . . 100 B2
Orchid Gr HD4 . . . . 171 D6
Orchid View WF2 . . . . 141 E8
Oriental St 6 LS12 . . . . . . 209 C3
Orion Cres LS10 . . . . 99 E7
Orion Dr LS10 . . . . 99 E7
Orion Gdns LS10 . . . . 99 F7
Orion View LS10 . . . . 99 F7
Orion Wlk LS10 . . . . 99 F8
Orlando Cl WF14 . . . . 137 F7
Orleans St BD6 . . . . 93 F7
Ormonde Dr BD15 . . . . 73 A8
Ormonde Pl LS7 . . . . 206 C3
Ormond Rd BD6 . . . . 74 B1
Ormondroyd Ave BD6 . . . . 94 C8
Ormond St BD7 . . . . 74 A4
Orville Gdns LS6 . . . . 205 B4
Orwell Cl WF10 . . . . 125 C5
Osborne Ave WF4 . . . . 141 C2
Osborne Gr HX3 . . . . 114 D7
Osborne Pl
17 Hebden Bridge HX7 . . . . 89 A3
3 Todmorden OL14 . . . . . . 108 C5
Osborne St
Bradford BD5 . . . . 201 A1
Halifax HX1 . . . . 202 B4
13 Hebden Bridge HX7 . . . . 89 A3
15 Huddersfield HD5 . . . . . 154 D5
Osborne Terr WF17 . . . . . 118 C6
Osbourne Ct LS13 . . . . 58 D1
Osbourne Dr BD13 . . . . 72 E1
Osmond Ho 5 BD5 . . . . . . 201 B1
Osmondthorpe Cotts LS9 . 80 C7
Osmondthorpe La LS9 . . . . 80 C7
Osmondthorpe Terr 9
LS9 . . . . 80 B8
Osprey Cl
Leeds LS17 . . . . 43 F4
Wetherby LS22 . . . . 13 B1
Osprey Ct BD8 . . . . 73 C7
Osprey Dr HD4 . . . . 171 E7
Osprey Gr LS17 . . . . 43 F4
Osprey Mdw LS27 . . . . 98 D4
**Ossett Gawthorpe Jun & Inf
Sch** WF5 . . . . 119 C1
Ossett La WF12 . . . . 140 A6
Ossett Sch WF5 . . . . 140 D3
Osterley Gr BD10 . . . . 56 E5
Oswald Cl LS20 . . . . 22 D1
Oswald St BD18 . . . . 55 D7
Oswaldthorpe Ave BD3 . . . 56 D1
Otley La LS19 . . . . 40 B7
Otley Mount BD20 . . . . 19 E1
Otley Mus★ LS21 . . . . 23 A8
Otley Old Rd
East Carlton LS16 . . . . 24 B1
Leeds LS16 . . . . 41 F4
Otley Rd
Baildon BD17 . . . . 38 E2
Bingley BD16 . . . . 20 B1
Bingley, Eldwick Beck BD16 . 37 D6
Bradford BD3 . . . . 56 A1
Burley in W LS29 . . . . 22 B8

Otley Rd *continued*
Guiseley LS20 . . . . **22** D1
Harewood LS17 . . . . **26** C7
Keighley BD20 . . . . **19** F1
Leeds, Adel LS16 . . . . **42** C5
Leeds, Far Headingley LS6,
LS16 . . . . **59** D6
Menston LS29 . . . . **22** B5
Shipley BD17, BD18 . . . . **55** B7
Otley St
Halifax HX1 . . . . **202** B3
Keighley BD21 . . . . **35** B6
Ottawa Pl LS7 . . . . **204** A2
Otterburn Gdns LS16 . . . **42** B3
Otterburn St BD21 . . . . . **35** C8
Otter Lee La HX6 . . . . . **111** C1
Otters Holt WF4 . . . . . . **159** F7
Otterwood Bank LS22 . . **13** F7
Ottiwells Terr HD7 . . . . **168** F3
Ouchterlow Fold WF1 . . **121** C4
Ouchthorpe La WF1 . . . **121** C2
Oulton Dr LS26 . . . . **101** C3
Oulton La
Rothwell LS26 . . . . **100** F5
Rothwell, Woodlesford
LS26 . . . . **101** C6
Oulton Prim Sch LS26 . . **101** B6
Oulton Terr BD7 . . . . **74** C6
Ounsworth St BD7 . . . . . **75** B4
**Our Lady of Good Counsel
RC Prim Sch** LS14 . . . . **62** A6
**Our Lady of Lourdes RC Prim
Sch** HD2 . . . . **136** C4
**Our Lady of Victories RC
Prim Sch** BD21 . . . . . . **35** A7
**Our Lady & St Brendan's RC
Prim Sch** BD10 . . . . . . **56** D6
Ouse Dr LS22 . . . . **13** D8
Ouse St ■ BD22 . . . . . . **51** D7
Ouson Gdns S71 . . . . . . **179** C1
Outcote Bank HD1 . . . . . **154** A5
Outdoor Ind Est HD3 . . **153** B8
Outfield Cl WF16 . . . . . . **117** E4
Out Gang LS13 . . . . **58** D3
Outgang La LS13 . . . . **58** E3
Out La
Emley HD8 . . . . **175** C7
Holmfirth HD9 . . . . **188** F8
Outlands Rise BD10 . . . . **56** D8
Outside La BD22 . . . . **50** F2
Outwood Ave LS18 . . . . . **58** D7
**Outwood Grange Coll of
Tech** WF1 . . . . **121** A4
Outwood La LS18 . . . . . . **58** D7
Outwood Park Ct WF1 . . **121** B4
Outwood Sta WF3 . . . . . **121** A5
Outwood Wlk LS18 . . . . . **58** C7
Ouzel Dr BD6 . . . . **73** C1
Ouzelwell Cres WF12 . . . **139** B3
Ouzelwell La WF12 . . . . **139** A3
Ouzelwell Rd WF12 . . . . **139** B4
Ouzelwell Terr WF12 . . . **139** A4
Ouzlewell Gn WF3 . . . . **100** D2
Oval The
Baildon BD17 . . . . **38** B2
Beal DN14 . . . . **127** F5
Bingley BD16 . . . . **37** B2
Bradford BD8 . . . . **73** E8
Cleckheaton WF15 . . . . **116** C5
Garforth LS25 . . . . **83** A7
Guiseley LS20 . . . . **39** C8
Holmfirth HD9 . . . . **188** F7
Leeds, Hunslet LS10 . . . **215** B4
Leeds, The Oval LS14 . . . **61** F2
Lofthouse Gate WF1 . . . **121** C1
Notton WF4 . . . . **179** B6
Otley LS21 . . . . **10** F1
Rothwell LS26 . . . . **100** F5
Ovenden Ave HX3 . . . . . . **92** A1
Ovenden ■ HX3 . . . . **92** A1
Ovenden Cres HX3 . . . . . . **92** A2
Ovenden Gn HX3 . . . . **92** A2
Ovenden Rd HX3 . . . . **92** A2
Ovenden Road Terr ■
HX3 . . . . **92** A2
Ovenden Terr HX3 . . . . . . **92** A2
Ovenden Way HX3 . . . . . . **92** A1
Ovenden Wood Rd HX2 . . **91** D2
Overburn BD20 . . . . **16** D4
Overburn Rd BD20 . . . . . **16** D4
Overcroft The ■ WF4 . . **141** A1
Overdale HX6 . . . . **132** E7
Overdale Ave LS17 . . . . . **44** A5
Overdale Cl LS22 . . . . **13** D6
Overdale Dr BD10 . . . . . . **38** F1
Overdale Mount HX6 . . . **112** C5
Overdale Terr
Haworth BD22 . . . . **51** C7
■ Leeds LS15 . . . . **81** A8
Overend St ■ BD6 . . . . . . **74** A1
Overgreen Royd HX2 . . . . **91** A4
Overhall Pk WF14 . . . . . **138** B6
Overhall Rd WF14 . . . . . **138** B6
Over La LS19 . . . . **40** C3
Overland Cres BD10 . . . . . **56** D8
Overland Ind Est LS27 . . . **97** C5
Overmoor Fold ■ BD10 . . **56** A7
Overthorpe Ave WF12 . . **139** D1
Overthorpe CE Jun & Inf Sch
WF12 . . . . **139** C2
Overthorpe Rd WF12 . . . **139** D3
Overton Dr BD6 . . . . **73** E7
Overwood HX2 . . . . **202** A2
Ovington Dr BD4 . . . . **75** E2

Owen's Terr HD9 . . . . . . **171** E3
Owen Ct BD16 . . . . **37** A6
Owlar Bars Rd HD9 . . . . **170** C2
Owlcotes Ctr LS28 . . . . . . **57** D1
Owlcotes Dr LS28 . . . . **76** C8
Owlcotes Garth LS28 . . . . **76** B8
Owlcotes Gdns LS28 . . . . **76** C8
Owlcotes La LS28 . . . . . . **76** C8
Owlcotes Rd LS28 . . . . . . **76** B8
Owlcotes Terr LS28 . . . . . **76** C8
Owler La WF9 . . . . **164** F4
Owler Ings Rd HD6 . . . . **115** A2
Owler La WF17 . . . . **96** F3
Owler Mdws WF16 . . . . . **117** C5
Owler Park Rd LS29 . . . . . **7** F6
Owlers CI HD2 . . . . **136** F5
Owlers Wlk OL14 . . . . . . **107** F8
Owlet Garden BD18 . . . . . **55** C6
Owlet Hurst La WF15 . . . **117** B2
Owlet Rd BD18 . . . . **55** C7
Owlett Mead WF3 . . . . . . **99** E1
Owlett Mead Cl WF3 . . . . **99** E1
Owl La
Batley, Chidswell WF12 . . **119** A3
Ossett WF5 . . . . **119** B1
Owl Mews HD5 . . . . **155** C6
Owl Ridge LS27 . . . . **98** C3
Owl St ■ BD21 . . . . **35** D8
Oxenhope CE Prim Sch
BD22 . . . . **51** C3
Oxenhope Mus★ BD22 . . **51** C3
Oxenhope Sta★ BD22 . . . **51** C3
Oxfield Ct HD5 . . . . **155** A7
Oxford Ave LS20 . . . . **22** D1
Oxford Cl
Cleckheaton BD19 . . . . . **117** B8
Queensbury BD13 . . . . . . **92** C8
Oxford Court Gdns
WF10 . . . . **124** C7
Oxford Cres
Bradford BD14 . . . . **73** B4
Halifax HX3 . . . . **113** D4
Oxford Ct
■ Guiseley LS20 . . . . **22** E1
Halifax HX3 . . . . **113** D3
Oxford Dr
Cleckheaton BD19 . . . . . **117** B8
Kippax LS25 . . . . **83** A2
Oxford Grange BD19 . . . **117** C8
Oxford Ho ■ BD16 . . . . . **37** A3
Oxford La HX3 . . . . **113** E3
Oxford Pl
■ Baildon BD17 . . . . **38** E2
Bradford BD3 . . . . **201** C4
Huddersfield HD1 . . . . . **153** E3
Leeds LS1 . . . . **211** B4
Pudsey LS28 . . . . **57** E1
Oxford Rd
Batley WF17 . . . . **96** E1
Bradford BD2 . . . . **56** B2
Cleckheaton BD19 . . . . . . **96** B2
Dewsbury WF13 . . . . **118** B1
Guiseley LS20 . . . . **22** E1
Halifax HX1 . . . . **203** B2
Leeds LS7 . . . . **206** C3
■ Queensbury BD13 . . . . **92** C8
Wakefield WF1 . . . . **216** A4
Oxford Row LS1 . . . . **211** B4
Oxford St
Batley, Mount Pleasant
WF17 . . . . **118** A4
Bradford BD14 . . . . **73** B4
East Ardsley WF3 . . . . . . **120** E8
Featherstone WF7 . . . . . **145** C5
Guiseley LS20 . . . . **22** E1
Hebden Bridge HX7 . . . . . **88** F3
Huddersfield HD1 . . . . . **154** B7
Keighley BD21 . . . . **35** A6
Morley LS27 . . . . **97** F2
Normanton WF6 . . . . . . **123** C3
South Elmsall WF9 . . . . . **182** F2
Sowerby Bridge HX6 . . . **112** D4
Todmorden OL14 . . . . . **108** B5
Wakefield WF1 . . . . **142** E3
Oxford Terr
■ Baildon BD17 . . . . **38** E2
Batley WF17 . . . . **118** D4
Mytholmroyd HX7 . . . . . **110** F8
Oxford Villas ■ LS20 . . . **22** E1
Oxford Wlk BD19 . . . . . **117** B8
Ox Heys Mdws BD13 . . . . **73** A6
Ox Lee La HD9 . . . . **199** E8
Oxley Gdns BD12 . . . . **94** C7
Oxley Hall LS16 . . . . **59** C8
Oxley Rd HD2 . . . . **136** C4
Oxleys Sq HD3 . . . . **134** D1
Oxley St
Bradford BD8 . . . . **74** C8
Leeds LS9 . . . . **212** C3
Oxton Mount LS9 . . . . . **212** C4
Oxton Way LS9 . . . . **212** C4
Oyster Cl LS27 . . . . **98** C3
Oyster Park Inf Sch
WF10 . . . . **125** D8
Oyster Park Jun Sch
WF10 . . . . **125** D8

P

Pacaholme Rd WF2 . . . . **141** D8
Pack Fold HD7 . . . . **170** C8
Packhores Ct HD7 . . . . . **168** F4
Pack Horse Cl HD8 . . . . . **176** A4
Packington St BD13 . . . . . **72** C8
Pack Horse Ctr ■ HD1 . . **154** B6
Packington St BD13 . . . . . **72** C8
Padan St HX3 . . . . **113** D4
Pad Cote La BD22 . . . . . . **32** A8

Paddock BD9 . . . . **55** B4
Paddock Cl
Ackworth M T WF7 . . . . **163** D5
Birkenshaw BD11 . . . . . . **96** E5
Bradford BD12 . . . . **94** C1
Darton S75 . . . . **178** C1
Garforth LS25 . . . . **83** A6
Paddock Cvn Pk LS29 . . . . **3** A1
Paddock Dr BD11 . . . . . . **96** E5
Paddock Foot HD1 . . . . . **153** E5
Paddock Gn LS17 . . . . . . **28** C5
Paddock House La LS22 . . **12** B3
Paddock Jun & Inf Sch
HD1 . . . . **153** D5
Paddock La
Bingley BD16 . . . . **37** D6
Halifax HX2 . . . . **112** C8
Paddock Rd
Darton S75 . . . . **178** C1
Kirkburton HD8 . . . . . . **174** A7
Northowram HD8, S75 . . **92** E5
Paddocks The WF4 . . . . **157** C3
Paddock The
Baildon BD17 . . . . **38** F4
■ Brighouse BD19 . . . . **115** F8
Burton Salmon LS25 . . . **105** E3
Castleford WF10 . . . . . . **125** C6
Cullingworth BD13 . . . . . **52** D6
Dewsbury WF12 . . . . . . **139** F6
East Keswick LS17 . . . . . . **28** C5
Kirkheaton HD5 . . . . . . **155** C7
Knottingley WF11 . . . . . **126** F3
Leeds LS6 . . . . **59** F7
Normanton WF6 . . . . . . **123** B1
Rothwell LS26 . . . . **100** E5
Silsden BD20 . . . . **5** E1
Thorner LS14 . . . . **45** F5
Woolley WF4 . . . . **178** A7
Paddock View
Bardsey LS17 . . . . **28** D5
Castleford WF10 . . . . . . **125** B6
Paddy Bridge Rd HX7 . . . **89** D1
Padgett Way WF2 . . . . . **141** D7
Padgum ■ BD17 . . . . **38** C4
Padma Cl BD7 . . . . **74** B7
Padmans La LS23 . . . . **30** D8
Padstow Ave LS10 . . . . . . **99** A5
Padstow Gdns LS10 . . . . . **99** A5
Padstow Pl LS10 . . . . **99** A4
Page Hill HX2 . . . . **91** E2
Page St HD1 . . . . **154** B5
Paget Cres HD2 . . . . **135** D1
Paget St ■ BD21 . . . . **35** A7
Pagewood Ct BD10 . . . . . . **39** A1
Paigton Ct LS12, LS13 . . . **58** D1
Painthorpe La WF4 . . . . **159** E4
Painthorpe Terr WF4 . . . **159** E4
Paisley Gr ■ LS12 . . . . . **209** B4
Paisley Pl ■ LS12 . . . . . . **209** B4
Paisley St LS12 . . . . **209** B4
Paisley Terr ■ LS12 . . . . **209** B4
Paisley View ■ LS12 . . . **209** A4
Pakington St BD5 . . . . **74** D4
Palace House Rd HX7 . . . . **89** A2
Paleside La WF5 . . . . . . **140** D7
Palesides Ave WF5 . . . . . **140** D8
Palestine Rd ■ HX7 . . . . . **89** A4
Paley Rd BD4 . . . . **75** A4
Paley Terr BD4 . . . . **75** A4
Palin Ave BD3 . . . . **56** D1
Palma St OL14 . . . . **86** B1
Palm Cl BD6 . . . . **94** B8
Palmer's Ave WF9 . . . . . **183** B2
Palmer Rd BD3 . . . . **75** B8
Palmerston St ■ BD2 . . . . **56** B2
Palm St
Halifax HX3 . . . . **92** B2
Huddersfield HD4 . . . . . **154** B4
Pangbourne Rd S63 . . . . **194** C1
Pannal Ave WF1 . . . . . . **142** E8
Pannal St BD7 . . . . **74** A3
Panorama Dr LS29 . . . . **7** E3
Papyrus Villas LS24 . . . . . **31** C6
Parade The
Batley WF17 . . . . **118** A4
■ Bradford BD4 . . . . **75** E3
Bramhope LS16 . . . . **24** E3
Leeds LS9 . . . . **212** B3
Otley LS21 . . . . **10** E1
■ Shipley BD16 . . . . **54** A7
Yeadon LS19 . . . . **39** F6
Paradise Fields WF8 . . . **125** D1
Paradise Fold BD7 . . . . . . **73** E4
Paradise La
Halifax HX2 . . . . **112** B6
Stutton LS24 . . . . **48** B5
Paradise Pl LS18 . . . . **58** E8
Paradise Rd BD9 . . . . **54** F4
Paradise Sh Prec BD7 . . . **73** E4
Paradise St
Bradford BD1 . . . . **74** D7
Halifax HX1 . . . . **203** A2
Pudsey LS28 . . . . **57** D3
Paradise View BD15 . . . . **53** B6
Paragon Ave WF1 . . . . . **121** B2
Paragon Bsns Village
WF1 . . . . **121** B2
Paris HD9 . . . . **189** D3
Parish Ghyll Ct ■ LS29 . . . **8** A4
Parish Ghyll Dr LS29 . . . . . **7** F3
Parish Ghyll La LS29 . . . . . **7** F3
Parish Ghyll Rd LS29 . . . . . **8** A3
Parish Ghyll Wlk LS29 . . . **8** A3
Paris Mews HD9 . . . . . . **189** C2
Parison St WF10 . . . . . . **124** E5
Paris Rd HD9 . . . . **189** D4

Park Ave
Batley WF17 . . . . **118** D6
Bingley BD16 . . . . **36** F2
Birkenshaw BD11 . . . . . . **96** E6
Bradford BD10 . . . . **39** B2
Brierley S72 . . . . **181** B3
Castleford WF10 . . . . . . **124** F7
Clayton West HD8 . . . . . **175** F3
Crofton WF1 . . . . **143** D7
Darrington WF8 . . . . . . **147** C5
Dewsbury WF13 . . . . . . **139** B7
Elland HX5 . . . . **134** E6
Huddersfield HD1 . . . . . **153** F6
Keighley BD21 . . . . **35** B6
Kippax, Allerton Bywater
WF10 . . . . **103** C4
Kippax LS25 . . . . **83** C1
Leeds, Lady Wood LS8 . . . **61** C7
Leeds LS12 . . . . **209** B4
Leeds, Manston LS15 . . . **62** D2
Liversedge WF15 . . . . . . **117** A2
Lofthouse Gate, Outwood
WF1 . . . . **121** A4
Lofthouse Gate WF3 . . . **121** C6
Mirfield WF14 . . . . **138** B4
Morley LS27 . . . . **97** F3
Normanton WF6 . . . . . . **123** B2
Oakworth BD22 . . . . **34** D2
Pontefract WF8 . . . . **146** B8
■ Queensbury LS28 . . . . **76** E7
Royston S71 . . . . **179** D3
Shelley HD8 . . . . **173** F3
■ Shipley BD18 . . . . **55** A8
South Kirkby WF9 . . . . . **182** B2
Sutton-in-C BD20 . . . . . . **16** D5
Swillington LS26 . . . . **82** A1
Wakefield WF2 . . . . **142** B4
Yeadon, Larkfield LS19 . . **40** C4
Yeadon LS19 . . . . **40** A7
Park Bldgs LS21 . . . . **24** D7
Park Bottom BD12 . . . . . **94** C5
Park Cl
Batley WF17 . . . . **118** D3
Bingley BD16 . . . . **37** A4
Birkenshaw BD11 . . . . . . **96** E6
Brighouse HX3 . . . . **114** E7
Darrington WF8 . . . . . . **147** C5
Darton S75 . . . . **178** C1
Halifax HX2 . . . . **91** B2
Keighley BD21 . . . . **35** C5
Leeds LS13 . . . . **58** C3
Normanton WF6 . . . . . . **123** A1
Queensbury BD13 . . . . . . **72** D1
Ryhill WF4 . . . . **162** B1
Shelley HD8 . . . . **173** F3
Park Cliffe Rd BD2 . . . . . . **56** B2
Park Copse LS18 . . . . **41** A1
Park Cotts LS8 . . . . **44** B1
Park Cres
Addingham LS29 . . . . **7** A8
Bradford BD3 . . . . **56** A2
Castleford WF10 . . . . . . **125** C7
Gildersome LS27 . . . . **97** D6
Guiseley LS20 . . . . **39** C7
Halifax HX3 . . . . **92** A1
Leeds LS12 . . . . **209** B4
Rothwell LS26 . . . . **101** A6
Royston S71 . . . . **179** D3
Park Crest WF9 . . . . **181** D7
Parkcroft LS28 . . . . **57** D2
Park Cross St LS1 . . . . . . **211** B4
Park Ct
Bradford BD9 . . . . **55** C2
Featherstone WF7 . . . . . **124** D1
Ossett WF5 . . . . **140** F4
Pool LS21 . . . . **24** D6
Park Dale
Castleford WF10 . . . . . . **104** C1
Menston LS29 . . . . **22** A4
Parkdale Dr HX6 . . . . . . **132** E7
Park Dr
Batley WF17 . . . . **118** A7
Bingley BD16 . . . . **37** B5
Horsforth LS18 . . . . **58** A8
Huddersfield HD1 . . . . . **153** E7
Lofthouse Gate WF3 . . . **121** C7
Mirfield WF14 . . . . **138** B5
Shelley HD8 . . . . **173** F3
Shipley BD9 . . . . **55** B4
Sowerby Bridge HX6 . . . **112** D5
Sutton-in-C BD20 . . . . . . **16** D5
Park Drive Rd BD21 . . . . . **35** C5
Park Dr S HD1 . . . . **153** F6
Park Edge Cl LS8 . . . . **61** C7
Parker Ave WF6 . . . . **122** E4
Parker La WF14 . . . . **138** B5
Parker Rd
Dewsbury WF12 . . . . . . **139** C4
Horbury WF4 . . . . **141** C1
Parkers La BD20 . . . . **18** A3
Parker St
Batley WF16 . . . . **117** D4
East Ardsley WF3 . . . . . . **120** C7
Glusburn BD20 . . . . **16** D7
Park Est WF9 . . . . **182** C2
Park Farm HD8 . . . . **175** A4
Park Farm Gdns WF9 . . . **182** C5
Park Farm Ind Est LS11 . . **99** B8
Park Field LS29 . . . . **22** A4
Parkfield Ave
■ Elland HX5 . . . . **134** F6
Leeds LS11 . . . . **214** A3
Mirfield WF14 . . . . **138** C4

Parkfield Cl
Kippax LS25 . . . . **83** B3
Pudsey LS28 . . . . **76** E7
Parkfield Cres WF14 . . . . **138** C4
Parkfield Croft WF14 . . . **138** C4
Parkfield Ct LS14 . . . . . . **61** E3
Parkfield Dr
Boston Spa LS23 . . . . **30** C8
Ossett WF5 . . . . **141** A5
■ Queensbury BD13 . . . . **72** D1
Sowerby Bridge HX6 . . . **112** A2
Parkfield Gr LS11 . . . . . . **214** A3
Parkfield La
Featherstone WF7 . . . . . **124** C2
Sowerby Bridge HX6 . . . **112** D3
Parkfield Mount
Leeds LS11 . . . . **214** A3
Pudsey LS28 . . . . **76** E7
Parkfield Pl LS11 . . . . . . **214** A3
Parkfield Rd
Bradford BD8 . . . . **55** D2
Leeds LS11 . . . . **214** A3
Shipley BD18 . . . . **54** E8
Parkfield Row LS11 . . . . **214** A3
Park Fields HX2 . . . . **91** B2
Parkfield St LS11 . . . . . . **211** C1
Parkfield Terr
■ Pudsey LS28 . . . . **76** E7
Pudsey, Stanningley LS28 . . **57** E7
Parkfield View
Leeds LS11 . . . . **214** A3
Ossett WF5 . . . . **141** A5
Parkfield Way
Leeds LS14 . . . . **61** E3
Mirfield WF14 . . . . **138** B4
Parkgate
Huddersfield HD8 . . . . . **171** E7
South Kirkby WF9 . . . . . **182** B1
Park Gate BD1 . . . . **201** C3
Parkgate Ave WF1 . . . . . **142** E6
Park Gate Cl LS18 . . . . . . **58** B8
Park Gate Cres LS20 . . . . **39** C8
Park Gate Rd HD7 . . . . . **169** B6
Park Gdns
Byram WF11 . . . . **126** D8
Ossett WF5 . . . . **140** F4
Sowerby Bridge HX2 . . . **112** D5
Park Gn
Normanton WF6 . . . . . . **123** A1
Silsden BD20 . . . . **5** C2
Park Gr
Gildersome LS27 . . . . **97** D6
Halifax HX1 . . . . **202** B1
Horbury WF4 . . . . **140** F2
Horsforth LS18 . . . . **57** F8
Huddersfield HD1 . . . . . **153** C6
Keighley BD21 . . . . **35** C8
Mirfield WF14 . . . . **138** C4
■ Queensbury BD13 . . . . **72** D1
Shipley, Frizinghall BD9 . . **55** C4
Shipley, Moorhead BD18 . . **54** F8
Swillington LS26 . . . . . . **102** B8
Yeadon LS19 . . . . **40** A7
Park Grove Ct BD9 . . . . . **55** C4
Park Grove Rd WF2 . . . . **142** C5
Park Halt★ LS10 . . . . **99** D8
Parkhead HD8 . . . . **190** F5
Parkhead Cl
Bradford BD6 . . . . **94** A6
Royston S71 . . . . **179** A4
Park Head La
Holmfirth HD9 . . . . **188** E4
Shepley HD8 . . . . **190** F5
Park Hill
Huddersfield HD2 . . . . . **136** F6
Kexbrough S75 . . . . **177** B2
Park Hill Cl BD8 . . . . **54** D1
Parkhill Cres WF1 . . . . . **142** F6
Park Hill Dr BD8 . . . . **54** D1
Park Hill Gr WF1 . . . . . . **142** F6
Park Hill La WF1 . . . . . . **142** E6
Park Ho BD20 . . . . **17** C6
Park Holme LS7 . . . . **207** B4
Park House Cl BD12 . . . . . **94** B7
Park House Cres BD12 . . . **94** E7
Park House Ct S36 . . . . . **191** E1
Park House Dr WF12 . . . **139** D4
Park House Gr BD12 . . . . **94** E7
Park House Rd BD12 . . . . **94** E6
Park House Wlk BD12 . . . **94** E7
Parkin's Almshouses ■
HD5 . . . . **154** F3
Parkin Hall La HX6 . . . . **111** B1
Parkin La
Bradford BD10 . . . . **56** F8
Meltham HD9 . . . . **170** E2
Todmorden OL14 . . . . . **107** E5
Parkinson App LS25 . . . . **82** F8
Parkinson Cl WF1 . . . . . . **142** E6
Parkinson Fold LS29 . . . . . **7** A8
Parkinson La HX1 . . . . . **202** B2
**Parkinson Lane Com Prim
Sch** HX1 . . . . **202** C2
Parkinson Rd BD13 . . . . . **71** E8
Parkinson St BD5 . . . . **74** D4
Parkin Sq HD7 . . . . **152** B5
Parkin St WF15 . . . . **116** C5
Park Jun Sch WF10 . . . . **124** E7
Park La
Baildon BD17 . . . . **38** F4
Bradford, Holme Top BD5 . . **74** D4
Bradford, Park Lane BD14 . . **73** B4
Denby Dale HD8 . . . . . . **191** B5
Elland HX4 . . . . **133** F1
Emley HD8 . . . . **175** A4
Guiseley LS20 . . . . **39** C7
Halifax HX3 . . . . **113** C2
Huddersfield HD4 . . . . . **172** A1

Park La *continued*
Huddersfield, Town End HD7 ... 152 D4
Keighley BD21 ... 35 C5
Kippax, Allerton Bywater WF10 ... 103 C5
Kippax LS25 ... 103 C8
Ledsham LS25 ... 104 C8
Leeds LS1, LS3 ... 211 A4
Leeds, Roundhay LS8 ... 44 B2
Meltham HD9 ... 170 E2
Mickletown LS26 ... 102 A1
Mytholmroyd HX7 ... 110 C8
Pontefract WF7, WF8 ... 124 E1
Queensbury BD13 ... 72 F1
Rothwell LS26 ... 101 A6
Sicklinghall LS22 ... 12 B5
Sutton-in-C BD20 ... 16 D5
West Bretton WF4 ... 176 F7
Parkland Ave
Huddersfield HD3 ... 152 E6
Morley LS27 ... 97 E3
Parkland Cres LS6 ... 43 A1
Parkland Dr
Bradford BD10 ... 56 C7
Leeds LS6 ... 43 A1
Parkland Gdns LS6 ... 60 A8
Parkland Prim Sch BD10 . 56 D7
Parklands
Bingley BD16 ... 37 B5
Bramhope LS16 ... 24 D3
Castleford WF10 ... 124 E7
Holmfirth HD9 ... 188 E5
Ilkley LS29 ... 8 D4
Ossett WF5 ... 140 F4
Parklands Ave WF4 ... 140 E1
Parklands Cres
Bramhope LS16 ... 24 E3
Horbury WF4 ... 140 E1
Parklands Ct WF4 ... 140 E1
Parklands Dr
Horbury WF4 ... 140 E1
Sowerby Bridge HX6 ... 111 E1
Parklands Gate LS16 ... 24 E3
Parklands Girls High Sch LS14 ... 62 B4
Parklands Manor WF1 .. 216 C4
Parklands Prim Sch LS14. 62 B3
Parklands Wlk
Bramhope LS16 ... 24 E2
Shelley HD8 ... 173 F3
Parkland Terr LS6 ... 60 A8
Parkland View LS19 ... 40 B6
Park Lane Coll Horsforth Ctr LS18 ... 57 F7
Park Lane Coll, Leeds LS3 ... 211 A4
Park Lane E HD7 ... 152 D4
Park Lane Mews LS17 ... 44 B4
Park Lane W HD7 ... 152 D4
Park Lea
Huddersfield HD2 ... 136 F6
Middleton LS10 ... 99 C5
Parklee Ct BD21 ... 35 C6
Park Lo BD15 ... 53 C5
Park Lodge Cres WF1 ... 142 E6
Park Lodge Ct WF1 ... 142 E6
Park Lodge Gr WF1 ... 216 C2
Park Lodge La WF1 ... 142 F6
Park Lodge View HD8 ... 175 A1
Park Mead BD10 ... 39 B2
Parkmere Cl BD4 ... 95 B8
Park Mews LS21 ... 24 D6
Park Mill La WF5 ... 141 B8
Park Mill Way HD8 ... 175 F3
Park Mount
Leeds, Kirkstall LS5 ... 59 B4
Leeds LS12 ... 209 A4
Pool LS21 ... 24 B5
Park Mount Ave BD17 ... 38 E3
Park Nook HX3 ... 113 F2
Park Par
Dewsbury WF13 ... 139 B7
Leeds LS9 ... 80 A6
Morley LS27 ... 97 F3
Park Pl
Bradford BD10 ... 39 B2
Halifax HX1 ... 202 C2
Leeds LS1 ... 211 B4
Pontefract WF8 ... 146 B8
Park Pl E HX3 ... 114 E7
Park Pl W HX3 ... 114 E7
Park Rd
Batley, Bank Foot WF17 ... 118 D5
5 Batley WF16 ... 117 D4
Bingley BD16 ... 37 A4
Boston Spa LS23 ... 30 C8
Bradford BD5 ... 201 B1
Bradford, Greengates BD10 56 E6
Bradford, Odsal BD6 ... 94 C7
Bradford, Thackley BD10 ... 39 B2
Brierley S72 ... 181 B3
Castleford WF10 ... 125 A5
Clayton West HD8 ... 175 F3
Dewsbury, Earlsheaton WF12 ... 139 F7
Dewsbury, Ravensthorpe WF13 ... 138 F6
Dewsbury, Westborough WF13 ... 118 B1
Dewsbury WF12 ... 139 C6
Glusburn BD20 ... 16 C7
Guiseley LS20 ... 39 D8
Halifax HX1 ... 203 A2
Huddersfield, Lockwood HD4 ... 153 E4
Huddersfield, Milnsbridge HD4 ... 153 B4

Park Rd *continued*
Leeds, Colton LS15 ... 81 D6
Leeds LS12 ... 209 A4
Leeds, Whitecote LS13 ... 58 C3
Menston LS29 ... 22 A4
Pontefract WF8 ... 125 B2
Shipley BD18 ... 55 C7
Sowerby Bridge HX6 ... 112 D5
Todmorden OL14 ... 108 B6
Yeadon, Rawdon LS19 ... 40 B4
Yeadon, Shaw Lane LS19 ... 40 A7
Park Rd W HD4 ... 153 D4
Park Rise
Castleford WF10 ... 124 F7
Leeds LS13 ... 58 C4
Park Road Jun & Inf Sch WF17 ... 118 D5
Park Road Ret Pk WF8 .. 125 B2
Park Row
6 Brighouse HD6 ... 115 B2
Burley in W LS29 ... 9 F2
Leeds LS1 ... 211 B4
8 Otley LS21 ... 23 B8
Pudsey LS28 ... 57 E1
Sutton-in-C BD20 ... 16 D4
Park Row Ho LS1 ... 211 B4
Parkside
Barnsley S71 ... 179 D1
Bingley BD16 ... 37 B4
Cleckheaton BD19 ... 116 E7
10 Halifax HX3 ... 113 B4
Horsforth LS18 ... 58 A8
Middlestown WF4 ... 158 B6
Park Side
Cleckheaton BD19 ... 117 A7
Flockton WF4 ... 157 C3
Holmfirth HD9 ... 189 E4
Kirkheaton HD5 ... 137 C1
Parkside Ave
Leeds LS6 ... 59 F7
Queensbury BD13 ... 72 D1
Parkside Cl
Leeds LS6 ... 59 F8
Todmorden OL14 ... 86 B1
Parkside Cres LS6 ... 59 F8
Parkside Ct BD22 ... 51 E8
Parkside Dr BD9 ... 55 A3
Parkside Gdns LS6 ... 59 F7
Parkside Gn LS6 ... 59 F7
Parkside Gr
Bradford BD9 ... 55 A3
Leeds LS11 ... 214 A1
Parkside Ind Est LS11 ... 214 C2
Parkside La
Leeds LS11 ... 214 C2
Lofthouse Gate WF3 ... 121 E2
Parkside Mount LS11 ... 214 A1
Parkside Par LS11 ... 214 A1
Parkside Pl LS6 ... 59 F8
Parkside Rd
Bradford BD5 ... 74 E2
Leeds LS16, LS6 ... 59 E8
Pudsey LS28 ... 57 D2
Todmorden OL14 ... 86 B1
Parkside Row LS11 ... 214 A1
Parkside Sch BD13 ... 52 E6
Parkside Terr BD13 ... 52 E6
Parkside View LS6 ... 59 F8
Park Side Wlk LS28 ... 57 E2
Park Spring Gdns LS13 ... 58 B1
Park Spring Prim Sch LS13 ... 77 B8
Park Spring Rise LS13 ... 58 B1
Park Sq
1 Bradford BD6 ... 94 A8
Lofthouse Gate WF3 ... 121 C6
Northowram HX3 ... 93 A2
Ossett WF5 ... 140 F4
Pool LS21 ... 24 D6
Pudsey LS28 ... 76 E7
Park Sq E LS1 ... 211 B4
Park Sq N LS1 ... 211 B4
Park Sq S LS1 ... 211 B4
Park Sq W LS1 ... 211 B4
Park St
Batley, Brown Hill WF17 .. 117 E8
Batley, Nunroyd WF17 ... 117 D4
Brighouse HD6 ... 115 B2
Cleckheaton, Gomersall BD19 ... 117 C8
Cleckheaton, Hartshead Moor Side BD19 ... 116 B6
Dewsbury WF13 ... 118 D1
Glusburn BD20 ... 16 D6
Haworth BD22 ... 51 D7
Horbury WF4 ... 141 A1
Leeds, Gravelythorpe LS15 81 B8
Leeds, Hill Top LS12 ... 209 A4
Leeds LS1 ... 211 B4
Morley LS27 ... 98 C8
Ossett WF5 ... 140 F4
Shipley BD18 ... 55 A8
Slaithwaite HD7 ... 152 C6
Sowerby Bridge HX6 ... 112 D4
Wakefield WF1 ... 216 C1
Yeadon LS19 ... 40 A7
Parkstone HD2 ... 136 F6
Parkstone Ave LS16 ... 42 A1
Parkstone Dr BD10 ... 56 C5
Parkstone Gn LS16 ... 42 A1
Parkstone Gr LS16 ... 42 A1
Parkstone Mount LS16 ... 42 A1
Parkstone Pl LS16 ... 42 A1
Park Stone Rise HX3 ... 93 B5
Park Terr
Brighouse HX3 ... 114 D7
Halifax HX1 ... 202 C2
Keighley, Eastwood BD21 .. 35 D7

Park Terr *continued*
Keighley, Thwaites Brow BD21 ... 35 F6
Leeds LS6 ... 59 D6
Northowram HX3 ... 93 A1
6 Otley LS21 ... 23 B8
Pool LS21 ... 24 A5
5 Shipley BD18 ... 55 A8
South Elmsall WF9 ... 183 A2
Park The
Cawthorne S75 ... 193 E4
Halifax HX3 ... 114 A4
Park Top LS28 ... 57 E1
Park Top Cotts BD16 ... 37 B5
Park Top Row BD22 ... 51 C7
Park Towngate The HX3. 114 A4
Park View
Brierley S72 ... 181 B3
Castleford WF10 ... 125 B6
Cleckheaton BD19 ... 116 C7
Dewsbury, Thornhill WF12. 139 E2
Dewsbury WF12 ... 139 F8
Elland HX4 ... 152 A8
Fitzwilliam WF9 ... 163 B1
Halifax HX1 ... 202 C2
Halifax, Lydgate HX3 ... 114 E7
Holmfirth HD9 ... 189 A5
5 Kippax LS25 ... 83 B1
Leeds, Beeston Hill LS11 .. 214 A3
Leeds, Bramley LS13 ... 58 C3
Lofthouse Gate WF3 ... 121 C6
Marsden HD7 ... 169 A4
Mirfield WF14 ... 138 C4
Pudsey LS28 ... 76 E7
Royston S71 ... 179 D3
Shafton S72 ... 180 D2
South Kirkby WF9 ... 182 D3
Swillington LS26 ... 82 A1
Wakefield WF2 ... 141 E6
Yeadon LS19 ... 39 F7
Park View Ave
13 Haworth BD22 ... 51 E8
Leeds LS4 ... 205 A3
Northowram HX3 ... 93 A1
Yeadon LS19 ... 40 C4
Park View Cres LS8 ... 44 B2
Parkview Ct
Leeds LS8 ... 44 B2
Shipley BD18 ... 55 A7
Park View Gr LS4 ... 205 A3
Park View Rd
Bradford BD9 ... 55 B3
Darton S75 ... 178 D1
Leeds LS4 ... 205 A2
Park View Terr
Bradford BD9 ... 55 B3
Harden BD16 ... 36 B2
8 Leeds LS15 ... 81 A8
Yeadon LS19 ... 40 B4
Park Villa Ct LS8 ... 44 A1
Park Villas LS8 ... 44 A1
Park Villas Dr WF8 ... 125 B1
Parkville Pl LS13 ... 58 C3
Parkville Rd LS13 ... 58 C3
Park W LS26 ... 100 F5
Parkway
Bradford BD5 ... 74 F2
Crofton WF4 ... 143 F2
Gildersome LS27 ... 97 D6
Queensbury BD13 ... 72 D1
Steeton BD20 ... 17 B5
Steeton BD20 ... 17 C6
Park Way
Baildon BD17 ... 37 F1
Keighley BD21 ... 35 C5
Menston LS29 ... 22 A4
Pool LS21 ... 24 D7
Parkway Cl LS14 ... 61 E4
Parkway Ct LS14 ... 61 E3
Parkway Grange LS14 ... 61 E3
Parkways LS26 ... 101 B6
Parkways Ave LS26 ... 101 B5
Parkways Cl LS26 ... 101 B6
Parkways Ct LS26 ... 101 B6
Parkways Dr LS26 ... 101 B6
Parkways Garth LS26 ... 101 B5
Parkways Gr LS26 ... 101 B6
Parkway Twrs LS14 ... 61 E4
Parkway Vale
Leeds, Brooklands LS14 ... 61 F4
Leeds, Parklands LS14 ... 62 A4
Park Wlk WF4 ... 162 D1
Parkwood Ave LS8 ... 61 A7
Park Wood Ave LS11 ... 98 F8
Parkwood Cl
Leeds LS11 ... 98 F7
Shelley HD8 ... 173 F3
Park Wood Cres LS11 ... 98 F7
Parkwood Ct
Huddersfield HD7 ... 152 E6
Leeds LS8 ... 61 A8
Park Wood Dr LS11 ... 98 F8
Parkwood Gdns
Leeds LS8 ... 61 A7
Pudsey LS28 ... 57 A6
Parkwood Prim Sch BD21 35 D6
Parkwood Rd
Huddersfield HD3, HD7 ... 152 E6
Pudsey LS28 ... 57 B6
Shipley BD18 ... 54 F7
Park Wood Rd LS11 ... 98 F8
Parkwood Rise BD21 ... 35 C6
Parkwood St BD21 ... 35 E7
Parkwood View LS8 ... 61 A8
Parkwood Way LS8 ... 61 A7
Parliament Pl LS12 ... 210 A3
Parliament Rd LS12 ... 210 A3
Parliament St WF2 ... 216 A2

Parlington Ct LS15 ... 63 E7
Parlington Dr LS25 ... 64 E7
Parlington Ho LS25 ... 64 D7
Parlington La LS25 ... 64 C4
Parlington Mdw LS15 ... 63 E6
Parlington Villas LS25 ... 64 E7
Parma St BD5 ... 201 B1
Parnaby Ave LS10 ... 215 C1
Parnaby Rd LS10 ... 215 C1
Parnaby St LS10 ... 215 C1
Parnaby Terr LS10 ... 215 C1
Parratt Row BD3 ... 75 D7
Parrock La HX7 ... 89 B6
Parrott St BD4 ... 75 D1
Parry Cl BD16 ... 36 A1
Parry La BD4 ... 75 C5
Parsley Mews LS26 ... 102 C3
Parson's La LS29 ... 6 C8
Parsonage La HD6 ... 115 A2
Parsonage Rd
Bradford BD5 ... 74 E3
Bradford, Tyersal BD4 ... 75 D5
Mickletown LS26 ... 102 D3
Parsonage St S6 ... 92 D1
Parson La WF4 ... 178 A8
Parsons Gn LS22 ... 13 F5
Parsons Rd BD9 ... 55 A4
Parson St BD21 ... 35 D8
Partons Pl WF3 ... 121 C6
Partridge Cl 5 LS27 ... 98 D4
Partridge Cres WF12 ... 139 F1
Partridge Dr BD6 ... 73 C1
Paslew Ct BD20 ... 19 B1
Pasture Ave
Leeds LS7 ... 204 A3
Oakworth BD22 ... 34 C1
Pasture Cl BD14 ... 73 E4
Pasture Cres LS7 ... 204 A3
Pasture Dr WF10 ... 124 A6
Pasture Fold LS29 ... 9 E2
Pasture Gr LS7 ... 204 A3
Pasture La
Bradford BD14, BD7 ... 73 D4
Leeds LS7 ... 204 A3
Pasture Mount LS12 ... 209 B4
Pasture Par LS7 ... 204 A3
Pasture Pl LS7 ... 204 A3
Pasture Rd
Baildon BD17 ... 38 D2
Leeds LS8 ... 207 C4
Pasture Rise BD14 ... 73 D4
Pasture Side Terr E BD14. 73 D4
Pasture Side Terr W 7 BD14 ... 73 C4
Pasture St LS7 ... 204 A3
Pastures Way HD7 ... 152 D5
Pasture Terr LS7 ... 204 A3
Pasture View
Ackworth M T WF7 ... 163 D5
Leeds LS12 ... 209 B4
Pasture View Rd LS26 ... 100 E5
Pasture Way WF10 ... 124 A6
Pasture Wlk BD14 ... 73 C4
Patchett Sq BD13 ... 73 B1
Pateley Cres HD2 ... 136 A2
Patent St BD9 ... 55 B2
Paternoster La 10 BD7 ... 74 A4
Paterson Ave WF2 ... 142 A6
Patience La WF6 ... 122 F3
Patricia Gdns HX6 ... 112 A5
Patrick Gn LS26 ... 121 F8
Patterdale App LS22 ... 13 B5
Patterdale Dr HD5 ... 154 D6
Patterdale Rd WF12 ... 118 E2
Patterson Ct WF2 ... 120 F3
Pattie St BD20 ... 18 B1
Paulena Terr LS27 ... 98 B2
Pauline Terr WF10 ... 124 C7
Paul La
Kirkheaton HD5 ... 137 C4
Lepton HD8 ... 156 C2
Paul Row OL15 ... 129 D1
Pavement La HX2 ... 91 E8
Pavement St 15 BD19 ... 116 E7
Pavilion Bsns Pk LS12 ... 78 C4
Pavilion Cl
Brierley S72 ... 181 A3
Halifax HX1 ... 202 B3
Pudsey LS28 ... 57 E2
Pavilion Ct
Bradford BD4 ... 95 C8
Dewsbury WF12 ... 140 A6
Pavilion Gdns
Pudsey LS28 ... 57 E2
Rothwell LS26 ... 101 C6
Pavilion Mews LS6 ... 205 A3
Pavilion Way
Lofthouse Gate WF1 ... 121 C1
Meltham HD9 ... 170 E2
Pudsey LS28 ... 76 D7
Paw La BD13 ... 92 F7
Pawson St
Bradford BD4 ... 75 D6
East Ardsley WF3 ... 120 E8
Morley LS27 ... 97 F3
Rothwell LS26 ... 100 B2
Paxton Ct 6 LS13 ... 58 F2
Peabody St 6 HX3 ... 92 A1
Peace Hall Dr HD8 ... 155 C5
Peace St BD4 ... 75 C5
Peach Tree Cl WF8 ... 146 B6
Peach Wlk BD4 ... 75 B4
Peacock Ave WF2 ... 141 F7
Peacock Cl WF2 ... 141 F7
Peacock Ct LS19 ... 40 D6
Peacock Gn LS27 ... 98 D3
Peacock Gr WF2 ... 141 F7
Peacock La OL14 ... 129 B6

Peak Chase S72 ... 180 F2
Peak View WF13 ... 117 F2
Pearl St
Batley WF17 ... 118 A6
Keighley BD22 ... 35 A4
Pear Pl 3 OL14 ... 86 B1
Pearson's La WF12 ... 156 F7
Pearson Ave 14 LS6 ... 205 B3
Pearson Fold BD12 ... 94 F4
Pearson Gr LS6 ... 205 B3
Pearson La BD9 ... 54 D1
Pearson Rd 11 BD6 ... 94 D8
Pearson Rd W 4 BD6 ... 94 D8
Pearson Row 3 BD12 ... 94 D3
Pearsons Bldgs LS21 ... 23 B7
Pearson St
Bradford BD3 ... 75 C6
Cleckheaton, Hartshead Moor Side BD19 ... 116 A6
Cleckheaton, Marsh BD19. 116 E6
Leeds LS10 ... 212 A1
Normanton WF6 ... 123 A5
Pudsey LS28 ... 57 B7
Pearson Terr 16 LS6 ... 205 B3
Pear St
Halifax HX1 ... 202 B2
Huddersfield HD4 ... 153 E4
Keighley BD21 ... 35 A3
Oxenhope BD22 ... 51 C2
4 Todmorden OL14 ... 86 B1
Pear Tree Acre LS23 ... 14 E1
Pear Tree Cl WF8 ... 146 B6
Pear Tree Ct 4 BD20 ... 5 E2
Peartree Field La WF8 . 165 D5
Pear Tree Gdns LS15 ... 63 E6
Pear Tree La WF9 ... 181 D7
Pear Tree Mews HD4 ... 153 E4
Peartree Orch S71 ... 179 D5
Pear Tree Terr BD20 ... 4 C5
Peas Acre BD16 ... 36 E8
Peasborough View LS29.. 21 F8
Pease Cl WF8 ... 146 D6
Peasefold 13 LS25 ... 83 B1
Peasehill Cl LS19 ... 40 C4
Peasehill Pk LS19 ... 40 C4
Peaseland Ave BD19 ... 116 C7
Peaseland Cl BD19 ... 116 D7
Peaseland Rd BD19 ... 116 D7
Peaselands BD18 ... 55 A7
Peat Ponds HD3 ... 134 E1
Peckett Cl HD3 ... 153 C7
Pecket Well Coll HX7 ... 89 B7
Peckfield Bsns Pk LS25 .. 83 E6
Peckover Dr LS28 ... 76 A8
Peckover St BD1 ... 201 C3
Peebles Cl HD3 ... 135 B1
Peel Ave WF17 ... 118 C5
Peel Cl
Bradford BD4 ... 75 E6
Horbury WF4 ... 141 B1
Peel Cottage Rd OL14 ... 108 A1
Peel Cottage St 5 OL14. 108 A1
Peel Ct BD2 ... 56 A2
Peel Dr OL13 ... 106 B1
Peel Ho BD16 ... 37 B2
Peel Mills Bsns Ctr LS27 . 98 B4
Peel Park Dr BD2 ... 56 B2
Peel Park Terr BD2 ... 56 B2
Peel Park View BD3 ... 56 A1
Peel Pl LS29 ... 9 E2
Peel Row BD7 ... 74 A4
Peel Sq LS5 ... 59 A4
Peel St
Bingley BD16 ... 37 B3
Horbury WF4 ... 141 B1
5 Huddersfield HD1 ... 154 A5
Liversedge WF16 ... 117 C4
Marsden HD7 ... 168 F4
Morley LS27 ... 98 B4
Queensbury BD13 ... 72 F1
10 Sowerby Bridge HX6 ... 112 B4
Thornton BD13 ... 72 D6
Wilsden BD15 ... 53 C4
Peep Green Rd WF15 ... 116 C2
Pegholme Dr LS21 ... 22 D6
Pelham Ct
Bradford BD2 ... 56 B3
Middleton LS10 ... 99 D3
Pelham Pl LS7 ... 60 C7
Pelham Rd BD2 ... 56 B3
Pell Ct HD9 ... 189 C7
Pell La HD9 ... 189 C7
Pellon Ind Est HX1 ... 202 B4
Pellon La HX1 ... 202 C4
Pellon New Rd HX1, HX2. 202 B4
Pellon St OL14 ... 108 A2
Pellon Terr BD10 ... 39 B1
Pellon Wlk BD10 ... 39 B1
Pemberley Ct HX6 ... 132 C2
Pemberton Dr BD7 ... 74 D6
Pemberton Rd WF10 ... 125 B8
Pembridge Ct S71 ... 179 C4
Pembroke Cl LS27 ... 97 F5
Pembroke Ct HD4 ... 153 B2
Pembroke Dr
Morley LS27 ... 97 F5
5 Pudsey LS28 ... 76 E8
Pembroke Grange LS9 ... 61 D2
Pembroke Rd LS28 ... 76 E8
Pembroke Rise LS25 ... 83 C2
Pembroke St BD5 ... 74 E4
Pembroke Twrs LS9 ... 61 D3
Pembury Mount LS15 ... 62 F3
Penarth Ave WF9 ... 183 A7
Penarth Rd LS15 ... 62 B2

Penarth Terr WF9 182 F7
Penda's Dr LS15 62 D2
Penda's Gr LS15 62 D3
Penda's Way LS15 62 D3
Penda's Wlk LS15 62 D2
Pendennis Ave WF9 182 F4
Pendil Cl LS15 81 C8
Pendle Ave OL13 106 A3
Pendle Cl OL13 106 A2
Pendle Ct BD13 92 E7
Pendle Rd BD16 37 B3
Pendragon BD2 56 A3
Pendragon La BD2 56 B3
Pendragon Pl WF9 183 A2
Pendragon Terr LS20 39 D8
Penfield Gr BD14 73 C4
Penfield Rd BD11 96 F6
Pengarth BD16 37 C5
Penistone Hill Ctry Pk* BD22 51 A6
Penistone Mews BD22 51 C7
Penistone Rd
Denby Dale HD7, HD8, S36 191 C3
Holmfirth, Hade Edge HD9 199 D7
Kirkburton HD8 173 E5
Lepton HD8 155 C3
Shepley HD8, HD9 190 C6
Penlands Cres LS15 81 D7
Penlands Lawn LS15 81 D7
Penlands Wlk LS15 81 D7
Penlington Cl WF9 181 D5
Penn Cl BD2 56 B4
Penn Dr WF15 116 D6
Penn Gr WF15 116 D6
Pennine Camphill Com Coll WF4 160 A3
Pennine Cl
Darton S75 178 A2
Holmfirth HD9 188 D5
Queensbury BD13 92 D7
Wakefield WF2 141 E3
Pennine Cres HD3 152 E8
Pennine Dr HD8 175 D2
Pennine Edge S36 200 D6
Pennine Gdns HD7 152 D1
Pennine Gr OL14 108 C6
Pennine Ind Pk HX7 89 A4
Pennine Rd
Bacup OL13 106 A2
Dewsbury WF12 139 E8
Pennine Rise HD8 175 D2
Pennine View
Batley WF17 97 A2
Blackshaw Head HX7 87 F4
Darton S75 178 A2
Kirkheaton HD5 137 C2
Slaithwaite HD7 152 D1
Upton WF9 183 A8
Pennine Way
Clayton West HD8 175 D2
Hebden Bridge HX7 88 D1
Hemsworth WF9 181 F7
Heptonstall HX7 88 B6
Pennington Ct 14 LS6 206 A4
Pennington Gr 16 LS6 206 A4
Pennington La LS26 101 B2
Pennington Pl 1 LS6 206 A3
Pennington St LS6 206 A4
Pennington Terr
Bradford BD5 74 C4
15 Leeds LS6 206 A4
Pennithorne Ave BD17 38 C4
Penn St HX1 202 C4
Pennwell Croft 3 LS14 62 D5
Pennwell Dean LS14 62 D5
Pennwell Fold LS14 62 E5
Pennwell Garth LS14 62 D5
Pennwell Gate LS14 62 D5
Pennwell Gn LS14 62 D5
Pennwell Lawn LS14 62 E5
Pennyfield Cl LS6 42 F1
Penny Field Sch LS6 42 F1
Pennygate BD16 37 D6
Penny Hill Ctr The LS10 215 B4
Penny Hill Dr BD14 73 D4
Penny La HD5 155 B5
Penny Lane Way LS10 215 A4
Penny Spring HD5 154 E3
Pennythorne Ct LS19 40 A5
Pennythorne Dr LS19 40 A5
Penraevon Ind Est LS7 206 C3
Penraevon Ind Units LS7 206 C3
Penraevon St LS7 206 C3
Penrhyn Gdns HD4 153 C4
Penrith Cres WF10 104 E1
Penrith Gr LS12 209 C2
Penrose Beck Dr WF7 163 F5
Penrose Dr BD7 73 F3
Penrose Pl
Crigglestone WF2 159 F5
Northowram HX3 93 A2
Penryn Ave HD5 155 C8
Pentland Ave
Bradford BD14 73 C4
Knottingley WF11 126 E4
Pentland Cl BD22 35 A6
Pentland Dr LS25 82 F5
Pentland Gr WF2 141 E3
Pentland Inf Sch WF12 139 D5
Pentland Rd WF12 139 D6
Pentland Way 1 LS27 98 A3
Penuel Pl HX3 113 E3
Penzance Ct BD8 74 B8
Peplow Cl LS25 105 E3
Pepper Gdns LS13 58 E4
Pepper Hill HX3 93 A6
Pepper Hill Lea BD22 34 F2
Pepper Hills LS17 43 D4
Pepper La
Leeds LS10 215 C3
Leeds, Moorside LS13 58 D4
Pepper Rd LS10 215 C2
Pepper Royd St WF13 118 D1
Percival Ct HD3 152 F6
Percival St
Bradford BD3 201 D3
Huddersfield HD3 152 F6
Leeds LS2 206 B1
Percy St
Bingley BD16 37 A3
Huddersfield HD2 136 A1
Keighley BD21 35 C4
Leeds LS12 210 A2
Peregrine Ave LS27 98 D4
Peregrine Ct HD4 171 E7
Peregrine Way BD6 73 C1
Peridot Fold HD2 136 C2
Per La HX2 91 D8
Permain Ct HD4 154 B4
Perry Cl BD22 35 A4
Perseverance La 12 BD7 74 A4
Perseverance Mills
Bradford BD6 74 A1
6 Huddersfield HD4 153 F3
Perseverance Rd BD13 72 A3
Perseverance St
Baildon BD17 38 D4
Bradford BD12 94 C4
4 Castleford WF10 124 D8
Huddersfield HD4 154 A3
Pudsey LS28 76 C7
16 Sowerby Bridge HX6 112 B5
Perseverance Terr
Batley WF17 118 C3
Halifax HX1 202 C1
Rothwell LS26 100 E4
Perseverence St HD4 153 A3
Perth Ave BD2 55 E3
Perth Dr WF3 119 F8
Perth Mount LS18 41 B4
Peterborough Pl BD2 56 B3
Peterborough Rd BD2 56 B2
Peterborough Terr BD2 56 B3
Peterfoot Way S71 179 C1
Peter Hill WF17 118 D2
Peterhouse Dr LS21 23 C7
Peter La
Halifax HX2 112 B7
Morley LS27 98 D4
Peter Laycock Ind Est LS7 206 C3
Peter Row HX7 110 D4
Petersfield Ave LS10 99 E7
Petersfield Ho 1 BD4 75 F2
Petersgarth 5 BD18 54 E8
Peterson Rd WF1 216 C2
Pether Hill HX4 133 F3
Petrel Cl BD6 73 C1
Petrel Way LS27 98 C3
Petrie Cres LS13 57 D5
Petrie Gr BD3 75 E7
Petrie Rd BD3 75 E7
Petrie St LS13 57 D5
Petworth Croft 3 S71 179 B4
Peverell Cl 6 BD4 75 E3
Peveril Mount BD2 56 C3
Peversey Garth 3 BD10 56 C6
Pexwood Pl OL14 107 F3
Pexwood Rd OL14 107 F3
Pheasant Dr WF17 97 A3
Pheasant St BD21 35 D8
Philip's Gr WF3 121 C6
Philip's La WF8 147 C5
Philip Garth WF1 121 C5
Philippa Way LS12 78 C3
Philips Rd OL13 106 A7
Phillips Cl 1 LS18 41 C1
Phillips St WF10 124 B8
Phil May Ct LS12 210 B2
Phoebe La HX3 113 D4
Phoebe Lane Ind Est HX3 113 D4
Phoenix Ave
Emley HD8 175 D6
Garforth LS25 83 E6
Phoenix Cl LS14 62 A3
Phoenix Ct
Batley WF17 118 F5
Todmorden OL14 108 D6
Wakefield WF2 142 A6
Phoenix St
Brighouse HD6 115 B2
Todmorden OL14 108 D6
Phoenix Way BD4 75 E6
Picadilly Chambers BD1 201 B3
Piccadilly
Bradford BD1 201 B3
Wakefield WF2 216 A2
Pickard Bank LS6 59 F5
Pickard Ct LS15 81 C8
Pickard La BD20 5 E2
Pickard Way WF13 118 B1
Pickering Ave LS25 83 B8
Pickering Ct HD2 136 A1
Pickering Dr WF5 119 C1
Pickering La WF5 119 C1
Pickering Mount LS12 210 A4
Pickering St LS12 210 A4
Pickerings The BD13 92 E8
Pickersgill St WF5 140 C8
Picker St OL14 107 E8
Pickford Sq 3 HD3 153 A4
Pickford St HD3 153 A4
Pickhill Rd HD9 170 D3
Pickles Ct 19 OL14 108 B6
Picklesfield WF17 118 B2
Pickles Hill BD22 33 F1
Pickles La
Bradford BD7 73 F2
Skelmanthorpe HD8 175 B1
Pickles St
Batley WF17 118 B2
13 Keighley BD21 35 B5
Pickle Top HD7 151 E2
Pickthall Terr OL14 108 D5
Pickwood La HX6 112 E2
Picton St BD8 55 D1
Picton Way HD5 155 A7
Pictureville BD1 201 B2
Piece Hall HX1 203 C3
Piece Hall Yd BD1 201 B3
Piece Wood Rd LS16 41 D3
Pigeon Cote Cl LS14 62 A6
Pigeon Cote Rd LS14 62 A6
Piggott St HD6 115 A3
Pighill Top La HD7 151 F2
Pike End Rd HX6 150 C7
Pike Law La HD7 152 B5
Pike Law Rd HD7 152 B5
Pildacre Brow WF5 140 C6
Pildacre Croft WF5 140 C6
Pildacre Hill WF5 140 B6
Pildacre La WF5, WF12 140 B6
Pilden La WF3 120 C7
Pilgrim Ave WF13 138 F7
Pilgrim Cres WF13 138 F7
Pilgrim Dr WF13 138 F7
Pilgrim Way LS13 58 A2
Pilkington St WF2 142 C4
Pilling La HD8 175 C2
Pilling Top La HD8 174 C4
Pill White La LS21 11 F6
Pilmer Ct WF2 141 D4
Pilot St LS9 207 B1
Pincheon St WF1 216 C2
Pinder's Gr WF1 142 E8
Pinder Ave LS12 77 F4
Pinderfields General Hospl WF1 121 D1
Pinderfields Rd WF1 216 B3
Pinder Gr LS12 77 F4
Pinders Cres WF11 126 C5
Pinders Garth WF11 126 D5
Pinders Green Ct LS26 102 C1
Pinders Green Dr LS26 102 C1
Pinders Green Fold LS26 102 C1
Pinders Green Wlk LS26 123 C8
Pinders Sq WF1 216 C4
Pinder St LS12 77 F4
Pinder View LS12 77 F4
Pineapple Cotts WF1 143 E6
Pinebury Cl BD13 72 C1
Pinebury Dr BD13 72 D1
Pine Cl
Castleford WF10 124 E6
Wetherby LS22 13 E7
Pine Court Mews HD4 171 D6
Pine Croft BD20 18 A1
Pine Ct
Baildon BD17 38 B1
Huddersfield HD4 171 D6
2 Leeds LS2 212 A3
Pinedale BD16 36 F5
Pinefield Pl WF9 163 B2
Pine Gr WF17 118 B3
Pinehurst Ct HD3 135 B1
Pine Rd OL14 107 F7
Pines Gdns LS29 7 F3
Pine St
7 Bacup OL13 106 A1
Bradford BD1 201 C3
Halifax HX1 203 B2
Haworth BD22 51 C6
Huddersfield HD1 154 B7
South Elmsall WF9 182 E1
Pines The WF12 139 E6
Pine Tree Ave
Boston Spa LS23 30 E8
Pontefract WF8 146 B6
Pinewood Ave WF2 141 D6
Pinewood Cl LS29 8 A3
Pinewood Gdns HX4 134 B4
Pine Wood Gdns WF14 138 B5
Pinewood Pl WF11 126 E3
Pinfold 3 BD14 73 C4
Pinfold Cl
Dewsbury WF12 139 E2
Flockton WF4 157 C2
Knottingley WF11 126 C5
Mickletown LS26 102 D3
Mirfield WF14 138 B5
Ripponden HX4 133 A5
Pinfold Cross WF8 166 D5
Pinfold Ct LS15 81 B8
Pinfold Dr WF4 144 A1
Pinfold Gn HX6 111 E3
Pinfold Gr
Leeds LS15 81 A8
Wakefield WF2 142 E1
Pinfold Hill
Dewsbury WF13 139 B7
Leeds LS15 81 B8
Pinfold La
Brighouse HD6 135 D5
Flockton WF4 157 C2
Garforth LS25 82 F7
Kirk Smeaton WF8 166 D5
Leeds, Cookridge LS16 41 F7
Pinfold La *continued*
Leeds, Halton LS15 81 A8
Leeds, Moor Top LS12 209 B3
Lepton HD8 156 A3
Marsden HD3 151 C5
Mickletown LS26 102 E2
Mirfield WF14 138 C5
Royston S71 179 C2
Slaithwaite HD7 152 A4
Sowerby Bridge HX6 111 E4
Wakefield WF2 142 E1
Pinfold Mount LS15 81 B7
Pinfold Rd LS15 81 B7
Pinfold Rise LS25 64 E8
Pinfold Sq LS15 81 A8
Pingle Rise HD8 192 A7
Pin Hill La HX2 90 D1
Pink St BD22 51 C6
Pinnacle La HX7 109 E8
Pinnar Croft HX3 114 A4
Pinnar La HX3 113 F5
Pintail Ave BD6 73 C1
Pioneer Bsns Pk WF10 123 F4
Pioneer St
Dewsbury WF12 139 C4
Todmorden OL14 129 A7
Pioneer Way WF10 123 F4
Pipe & Nook La LS12 77 F7
Pipercroft BD6 93 E6
Piper Hill WF11 105 A4
Piper Ho 14 WF8 125 D1
Piper La LS21 22 F7
Pipers Cl WF2 120 D1
Piperwell Cl WF16 117 D5
Piper Well La HD8 190 E6
Pipit Mdw LS27 98 C3
Pippins App WF6 123 B3
Pippins Green Ave WF2 120 B2
Pirie Cl BD2 55 F3
Pitchstone Ct LS12 77 D7
Pitcliffe Way BD5 74 F4
Pitfall St LS1 211 C3
Pit Field Rd WF3 100 D2
Pit Hill HX3 203 C2
Pit La
Batley WF13 117 F2
Cleckheaton BD19 96 B2
Denholme BD13 52 C1
Micklefield LS25 83 F5
Mickletown LS26 102 D4
Queensbury BD13 72 C4
Pits La BD19 115 F6
Pitt Hill La HX4 133 D2
Pitt Row LS1 211 C3
Pitts St BD4 75 D4
Pitt St
Keighley BD21 35 D7
Liversedge WF15 117 B2
Todmorden OL14 108 D5
Pitt Street Bsns Ctr BD21 35 D7
Pitty Beck View BD15 73 B7
Place's Rd LS9 212 B3
Plaid Row LS9 212 B4
Plain La HX6 111 C2
Plains HD7 169 A5
Plains La
Halifax HX5 134 F8
Marsden HD7 169 A5
Plane Gn WF8 125 F1
Plane St
Huddersfield HD4 154 B3
Todmorden OL14 107 E7
Planet Earth Ctr* OL14 106 F4
Plane Tree Ave LS17 43 F4
Plane Tree Cl LS17 43 F4
Plane Tree Croft LS17 43 F4
Plane Tree Gdns LS17 43 F4
Plane Tree Gr LS19 40 D6
Plane Tree Nest HX2 202 A2
Plane Tree Nest La HX2 202 A1
Plane Tree Rd HX6 112 B5
Plane Tree Rise 3 LS17 43 F4
Plane Trees HX2 202 A4
Plane Trees Cl BD19 95 D3
Planetrees Rd BD4 75 C6
Planetrees St BD15 54 A1
Plane Tree View LS17 43 F4
Plantation Ave
Leeds, Blackwood LS17 44 A5
Leeds, Halton LS15 81 A7
Royston S71 179 D3
Plantation Dr HD4 154 A1
Plantation Fold BD22 34 F4
Plantation Gdns LS17 44 B5
Plantation Pl BD4 75 C4
Plantations The BD12 94 C6
Plantation Way BD17 38 D3
Platt Ct BD18 55 E8
Platt La HD7 152 A1
Platt Sq 7 BD19 116 D7
Playfair Rd LS10 215 A2
Playground LS12 77 D3
Playhouse Sq LS2 212 A4
Pleasance The LS26 82 A1
Pleasant Ct 2 LS6 206 A3
Pleasant Mount LS11 211 A1
Pleasant Pl
Bradford BD15 54 A1
Leeds LS11 211 A1
Pleasant Row 5 BD13 92 C8
Pleasant St
Bradford BD7 74 A4
Leeds LS11 211 A1
Sowerby Bridge HX6 112 C4
Pleasant Terr LS11 211 A1
Pleasant View
Denholme BD13 52 E1
Halifax HX2 90 C1
Pleasant View *continued*
Lofthouse Gate WF2 120 F7
19 Todmorden OL14 108 B5
Pledwick Cres WF2 160 D6
Pledwick Dr WF2 160 D5
Pledwick Gr WF2 160 C5
Pledwick La WF2 160 D5
Pledwick Rise WF2 160 D5
Plevna Terr BD16 36 F4
Plimsoll St
Bradford BD4 75 A4
Hemsworth WF9 181 D7
Ploughcroft La HX3 92 C3
Ploughmans Croft BD2 55 E4
Plover Dr WF17 117 F5
Plover Rd HD3 153 B8
Plover St
Bradford BD5 74 C3
Keighley BD21 35 C8
Plover Way LS27 98 D3
Plowmans Wlk LS19 39 F6
Plumpton Ave BD2 55 F6
Plumpton Cl BD2 56 A5
Plumpton Dr BD2 55 F6
Plumpton End BD2 56 A6
Plumpton Gdns BD2 55 F6
Plumpton Lea BD2 55 F6
Plumpton Mead BD2 55 F6
Plumpton Pk S72 180 C2
Plumpton Pl WF2 142 A6
Plumpton Rd WF2 142 A6
Plumpton St
Bradford BD8 74 A8
Wakefield WF2 142 A6
Plumpton Terr WF2 142 A5
Plumpton Wlk BD2 55 F6
Plum St
Halifax HX1 202 B2
Keighley BD21 35 A3
Plum Tree Cl WF8 146 B6
Plumtree Hill 2 LS29 6 F8
Plymouth Gr HX1 202 C4
Pochard Cl BD6 73 C1
Poet's Pl LS18 41 C2
Pog Hall HD7 170 C8
Pogson's Cotts LS14 62 C5
Pohlman St 4 HX1 202 B1
Point The WF2 141 F6
Pole Gate HD7 151 D4
Pole Gate Branch HD7 151 D4
Pole Rd BD22 33 F8
Police Flats 1 OL14 108 B5
Pollard's Fields WF11 126 B5
Pollard Ave
Bingley BD16 37 B5
Cleckheaton BD19 96 B1
Pollard Cl BD19 96 B1
Pollard La
Bradford BD2 56 B1
Leeds LS13 58 C5
Pudsey LS13 58 C5
Pollard St N HX3 203 C4
Pollard St S HD3 153 B4
Pollard St
Bradford BD4 201 C1
Huddersfield HD2 136 B2
Lofthouse Gate WF3 121 C6
1 Shipley BD16 54 B6
Todmorden OL14 107 E8
Pollard Way BD19 96 B1
Pollit Ave HX6 111 F3
Pollums La LS25, WF11 105 B6
Polperro Cl WF6 123 B3
Pomfret Ct WF8 147 A8
Pomfret Pl LS25 83 B8
Pond Cl HD4 153 F2
Ponden La BD22 50 A7
Ponderosa Cl LS8 207 C3
Pond Farm Dr HD6 114 E5
Pondfields Cl LS25 83 B2
Pondfields Crest LS25 83 B2
Pondfields Dr LS25 83 B2
Pondfields Pl LS25 83 B2
Pondfields Rise LS25 83 B2
Pond La HD8 156 A2
Pondon Cl WF9 181 E7
Pond St BD21 35 C8
Ponker La HD8 174 E1
Ponker Nook La HD8 174 F1
Ponsford Ho 7 BD4 75 D5
Pontefract Ave LS9 212 C3
Pontefract Baghill Sta WF8 146 E8
Pontefract Castle* WF8 125 E1
Pontefract General Infmy WF8 146 D8
Pontefract La
Leeds, Cross Green LS9, LS15 80 C5
Leeds, Newsam Green LS15 81 B3
Leeds, Richmond Hill LS9 212 C3
Pontefract Lane Cl LS9 212 C3
Pontefract Monkhill Sta WF8 125 E2
Pontefract Mus* WF8 146 D8
Pontefract Orchard Head Jun & Inf Sch WF8 125 E4
Pontefract Rd
Ackworth M T WF7 164 A8
Castleford WF10 124 E7
Crofton WF4 144 A2
Cudworth S72 180 C1
Featherstone WF7 145 E5
Hemsworth WF9 163 F2
Knottingley, Ferrybridge Hill WF11 126 D4
Knottingley WF8, WF11 126 B4
Leeds LS10, LS26 80 B2

Pontefract Rd continued
Normanton WF6 . . . . 123 D3
Pontefract St Giles CE Jun &
Inf Sch WF8 . . . . 125 D1
Pontefract St LS9 . . . . . . 212 C3
Pontefract Tanshelf Sta
WF8 . . . . 125 C1
Pontefract Terr 4 WF9 . 181 E6
Pontey Dr HD5 . . . . 155 E5
Pontey Farm Cvn Pk
HD9 . . . . 171 D3
Pontey Mount HD5 . . . . . 155 E5
Ponyfield Cl HD2 . . . . 135 E1
Pool Bank Cl LS21 . . . . . . 24 D7
Pool Bank Ct LS21 . . . . . . 24 D6
Pool Bank New Rd LS16,
LS21 . . . . 24 C5
Pool Ct BD3 . . . . 75 A7
Poole LS25 . . . . 105 E2
Poole Cres LS15 . . . . 62 E1
Poole La LS25 . . . . 105 E3
Poole Mount LS15 . . . . . . 62 E1
Poole Rd LS15 . . . . 62 E1
Poole Row LS25 . . . . 105 E3
Poole Sq LS15 . . . . 62 E1
Pool Hill La HD8 . . . . 192 D6
Pool in Wharfedale CE Prim
Sch LS21 . . . . 24 D7
Pool Rd
Otley LS21 . . . . 23 C8
Pool LS21 . . . . 24 B7
Pools La LS71 . . . . 179 E3
Pool Sq BD8 . . . . 74 D8
Pool St 4 BD21 . . . . 18 E1
Popeley Rd WF16 . . . . . . 117 C6
Popeley Rise BD19 . . . . . 117 C8
Pope St
Keighley BD21 . . . . 35 D8
Normanton WF6 . . . . 123 C5
Poplar Ave
Bradford BD7 . . . . 73 F2
Castleford WF10 . . . . 125 C7
Garforth LS25 . . . . 82 E6
Holmfirth HD9 . . . . 172 C1
Leeds LS15 . . . . 62 D2
Shafton S72 . . . . 180 C2
Shipley BD18 . . . . 55 C5
Sowerby Bridge HX6 . . . . 112 C5
Todmorden OL14 . . . . 108 A7
Wakefield WF2 . . . . 141 E5
Wetherby LS22 . . . . 13 E7
Poplar Bank HD8 . . . . . . 155 C3
Poplar Cl
Burley in W LS29 . . . . 21 F8
Leeds LS13 . . . . 77 F8
Poplar Cres
Halifax HX2 . . . . 91 F7
Morley LS27 . . . . 98 C1
Shipley BD18 . . . . 55 C5
Poplar Croft LS13 . . . . . . 77 E8
Poplar Ct LS13 . . . . 77 E8
Poplar Dr
Horsforth LS18 . . . . 57 F8
Keighley BD20 . . . . 36 C7
Normanton WF6 . . . . 123 A6
Shipley BD18 . . . . 55 C5
Poplar Garth LS13 . . . . . . 77 E8
Poplar Gate LS13 . . . . 77 E8
Poplar Gdns LS13 . . . . . . 77 E8
Poplar Gn
Leeds LS13 . . . . 77 E8
Pontefract WF8 . . . . 125 F1
Poplar Gr
Bradford BD7 . . . . 73 F2
Cleckheaton BD19 . . . . . . 116 C6
Harden BD16 . . . . 36 A1
Knottingley WF11 . . . . . . 126 E2
Pontefract WF8 . . . . 146 B8
Shipley BD18 . . . . 55 C5
Poplar Ho 3 WF10 . . . . . 124 E7
Poplar Mount LS13 . . . . . 77 E8
Poplar Rd
Bradford BD7 . . . . 74 A2
Shipley BD18 . . . . 55 C6
Poplar Rise
Leeds LS13 . . . . 58 E1
Skelmanthorpe HD8 . . . . 175 B1
Poplars Farm Prim Sch
BD2 . . . . 55 E4
Poplars Park Rd BD2 . . . . 55 E4
Poplar Sq 17 LS28 . . . . . . 57 D2
Poplar St
Halifax HX3 . . . . 203 B4
Huddersfield, Fartown
HD2 . . . . 136 A1
11 Huddersfield, Moldgreen
HD5 . . . . 154 D5
Lofthouse Gate WF3 . . . . 121 C6
Poplars The
Bramhope LS16 . . . . 24 F2
Guiseley LS20 . . . . 22 E2
Knottingley WF11 . . . . . . 127 B2
Leeds LS6 . . . . 205 B4
Lofthouse Gate WF3 . . . . 121 C8
Sutton-in-C BD20 . . . . 16 C4
Poplar Terr
Horbury WF4 . . . . 159 C8
17 Huddersfield HD5 . . . . 154 D5
14 Keighley BD21 . . . . 35 A7
Keighley, Crossflatts BD20 . 36 D7
Royston S71 . . . . 179 D4
South Elmsall WF9 . . . . . 183 A2
Poplar View
Bradford BD7 . . . . 73 E2
Brighouse HX3 . . . . 115 B6
Leeds LS13 . . . . 77 E8
Poplar Way LS13 . . . . 77 E8
Poplarwood Gdns BD10 . 56 E5

Popley Butts HD9 . . . . . . 170 D1
Popley Dr HD9 . . . . 170 D1
Popples HX2 . . . . 91 F7
Popples Dr HX2 . . . . 91 F7
Popples Side HX7 . . . . 88 D6
Poppleton Ct 1 WF3 . . . . 98 E1
Poppleton Dr WF3 . . . . . . 98 E1
Poppleton Rd WF3 . . . . . . 98 E1
Poppleton Rise WF3 . . . . 119 E8
Poppleton Way WF3 . . . . 119 E8
Popple Wells La HX2 . . . . 112 A7
Poppy Ct BD6 . . . . 93 F6
Poppyfield Ct 6 LS22 . . . . 13 F6
Poppy La WF3 . . . . 120 E8
Porchester Ho 6 HD5 . . . 154 D6
Portage Ave LS15 . . . . 80 F7
Portage Cres LS15 . . . . . . 80 F7
Portal Cres WF14 . . . . . . 138 A8
Portal Dr WF14 . . . . 138 A8
Porter Apartments 3
HX1 . . . . 203 A1
Portland Ave WF8 . . . . . . 125 B1
Portland Cl HD3 . . . . 153 C7
Portland Cres LS1 . . . . . . 206 B1
Portland Croft WF8 . . . . . 146 B8
Portland Ct BD21 . . . . 35 B6
Portland Gate
Leeds LS1 . . . . 206 B1
Wakefield WF1 . . . . 216 A3
Portland Ho
4 Bradford BD4 . . . . 75 D6
14 Elland HX5 . . . . 134 F7
Portland Pl
4 Bingley BD16 . . . . 37 A2
Halifax HX1 . . . . 203 B2
Upton WF9 . . . . 183 A7
Portland Rd
Halifax HX3 . . . . 203 C4
Leeds LS12 . . . . 209 C2
Portland St
Bradford BD5 . . . . 201 B2
Halifax HX1 . . . . 203 B3
Haworth BD22 . . . . 51 D7
Huddersfield HD1 . . . . . . 153 F6
Leeds LS11 . . . . 211 B4
Pudsey LS28 . . . . 77 A8
Wakefield WF1 . . . . 142 F3
Portland Way LS1 . . . . . . 206 B1
Portman Cl HX4 . . . . 133 F4
Portman St LS28 . . . . 57 B6
Portobello Ho 4 WF3 . . . 121 C6
Portobello Rd WF1, WF2 . 142 D3
Portree Dr BD6 . . . . 93 E8
Portsmouth Ave 5 BD3 . . 55 F1
Portwood St BD9 . . . . 54 D2
Post Hill Ct LS12 . . . . 77 D7
Post Office Rd
Bradford BD2 . . . . 56 C5
Featherstone WF7 . . . . . . 145 D5
Post Office Row HD8 . . . . 175 E2
Post Office St BD19 . . . . . 116 F6
Pothouse Rd BD6 . . . . 94 B8
Pot La BD12 . . . . 17 C6
Potovens Ct WF3 . . . . 121 C6
Potovens La
Lofthouse Gate WF1 . . . . 121 B5
Wakefield WF2 . . . . 120 F4
Potter Ave WF2 . . . . 141 E4
Potter Brow Rd BD17 . . . . 38 C7
Potter Cl BD12 . . . . 94 E5
Potternewton Ave LS7 . . . 60 B6
Potternewton Cres LS7 . . 60 B5
Potternewton Ct LS7 . . . . 60 C6
Potternewton Gdns LS7 . . 60 C6
Potternewton Gr LS7 . . . . 60 B6
Potternewton Hts LS7 . . . 60 C6
Potternewton La LS7 . . . . 60 B6
Potternewton Mansion Coll
of F Ed LS7 . . . . 204 B1
Potternewton Mount LS7 . 60 B6
Potternewton Prim Sch
LS7 . . . . 60 B5
Potternewton View LS7 . . 60 B6
Potters Croft WF8 . . . . . . 121 C6
Potters Gate HD8 . . . . . . 190 E1
Potters Wlk HD7 . . . . 152 E4
Potterton Cl LS15 . . . . 63 E8
Potterton Ct LS15 . . . . 63 E8
Potterton La LS15 . . . . 46 E2
Pottery La
Knottingley WF11 . . . . . . 126 D5
Rothwell LS26 . . . . 101 D7
Pottery Rd LS10 . . . . 215 A4
Pottery St
Castleford WF10 . . . . 124 B8
Huddersfield HD3 . . . . . . 152 E8
Potts' Terr WF6 . . . . 144 B8
Poulton Pl LS11 . . . . 214 C3
Poverty La HX6 . . . . 111 A1
Powell Ave BD5 . . . . 74 C4
Powell Rd
Bingley BD16 . . . . 37 B2
Shipley BD18 . . . . 55 D5
Powell St
Batley WF16 . . . . 117 E3
Castleford WF10 . . . . 124 D8
6 Halifax HX1 . . . . 203 B2
14 Halifax HX1 . . . . 203 B3
South Kirkby WF9 . . . . . . 182 B3
Powerhouse 1 Showcase
Theatre★ WF1 . . . . 216 A2
Poxton Gr WF9 . . . . 182 E1
Prail Cl WF8 . . . . 125 F1
Pratt La
Mirfield WF14 . . . . 138 A6
Shipley BD18 . . . . 55 C6
Preachers Mews 11 BD16 . 37 A3

Precinct The WF7 . . . . . . 145 C5
Premiere Pk LS29 . . . . 7 E3
Premier Way
Halifax HX5 . . . . 135 A8
Lofthouse Gate LS26 . . . . 121 F8
Preparatory Sch The BD9 . 54 E1
Prescott Ho HX1 . . . . 203 B2
Prescott Terr BD15 . . . . . . 54 B1
Preston La
Halifax HX2 . . . . 91 D2
Kippax LS26 . . . . 102 E7
Preston Par LS11 . . . . 214 A2
Preston Pl HX1 . . . . 202 C3
Preston St
Batley WF17 . . . . 118 C4
Bradford BD7 . . . . 74 C7
Dewsbury WF12 . . . . 139 E6
Preston Terr BD16 . . . . 36 E5
Preston View LS26 . . . . . . 82 B1
Prestwich Dr HD2 . . . . . . 135 F3
Prestwick Cl LS21 . . . . 22 C1
Prestwick Fold WF5 . . . . . 140 D7
Pretoria St
Castleford WF10 . . . . 124 E7
Featherstone WF7 . . . . . . 145 C4
Slaithwaite HD7 . . . . 151 F1
Wakefield WF1 . . . . 142 D3
Priest Bank Rd BD20 . . . . 16 E8
Priest Hill Gdns LS23 . . . . 13 D8
Priesthorpe Ave LS28 . . . . 57 B2
Priesthorpe Ct LS28 . . . . . 57 D4
Priesthorpe La LS28 . . . . . 57 D4
Priesthorpe Rd LS28 . . . . . 57 B4
Priesthorpe Sch LS28 . . . . 57 B2
Priest La HX6 . . . . 132 E4
Priestley Ave
Batley WF16 . . . . 117 D6
Bradford BD6 . . . . 94 C8
Priestley Cl LS28 . . . . 76 F8
Priestley Ct LS28 . . . . 76 F8
Priestley Dr LS28 . . . . 76 F8
Priestley Gdns
Liversedge WF16 . . . . . . 117 C5
Pudsey LS28 . . . . 76 F8
Priestley Gn HX3 . . . . 93 E1
Priestley Gr HD4 . . . . 153 F1
Priestley Hall BD16 . . . . . . 37 A5
Priestley Hill BD13 . . . . . . 92 C6
Priestley Pl HX6 . . . . 112 A3
Priestley Sq WF17 . . . . 96 E2
Priestley St
Bradford BD1 . . . . 201 C4
Thornton BD13 . . . . 72 D6
Priestley Terr 1 BD6 . . . . 74 C1
Priestley View LS28 . . . . . 76 F8
Priestley Wlk LS28 . . . . . . 76 F8
Priestman Cl BD8 . . . . 55 C1
Priestman St BD8 . . . . 55 C1
Priest Royd 4 S75 . . . . . . 178 A1
Priesthorpe Cl BD16 . . . . . 37 A4
Priesthorpe La BD16 . . . . . 37 A4
Priesthorpe Prim Sch
BD16 . . . . 37 A3
Priestthorpe Rd BD16 . . . . 37 A4
Priestwell St OL14 . . . . . . 108 C6
Primary Way BD2 . . . . 56 B1
Primitive St
8 Huddersfield HD1 . . . . 154 B6
Rothwell WF3 . . . . 100 D3
Primley Gdns LS17 . . . . . . 43 C4
Primley Park Ave LS17 . . . 43 D4
Primley Park Cl LS17 . . . . 43 C4
Primley Park Cres LS17 . . 43 C4
Primley Park Dr LS17 . . . . 43 C5
Primley Park Garth LS17 . 43 D5
Primley Park Gn LS17 . . . 43 D5
Primley Park Gr LS17 . . . 43 C4
Primley Park La LS17 . . . 43 C4
Primley Park Mount LS17 . 43 D4
Primley Park Rd LS17 . . . 43 C4
Primley Park Rise LS17 . . 43 D5
Primley Park View LS17 . 43 C4
Primley Park Way LS17 . . 43 D5
Primley Park Wlk LS17 . . . 43 D5
Primrose Ave
2 Leeds LS15 . . . . 81 A8
Swillington LS26 . . . . 82 B1
Primrose Bank BD16 . . . . . 37 B2
Primrose Cl
Leeds LS15 . . . . 81 A8
Pontefract WF8 . . . . 146 D7
Primrose Cres LS15 . . . . . . 62 A1
Primrose Ct
20 Guiseley LS20 . . . . 22 E1
Leeds LS17 . . . . 43 D5
Primrose Dene WF11 . . . . 126 D7
Primrose Dr
Bingley BD16 . . . . 37 C2
Castleford WF10 . . . . 125 C6
Leeds LS15 . . . . 81 A8
Primrose Garth 1 LS15 . . 80 F8
Primrose Gdns
Batley WF17 . . . . 118 E6
Leeds LS15 . . . . 62 A1
Primrose Gr
Huddersfield HD4 . . . . . . 154 A3
Keighley BD21 . . . . 35 E7
Leeds LS15 . . . . 62 A1
Primrose High Sch LS9 . . 207 B1
Primrose Hill
Batley WF17 . . . . 118 D5
Bradford BD7 . . . . 74 D5
Knottingley WF11 . . . . . . 127 A5
5 Pudsey LS28 . . . . 57 E1
Primrose Hill Cl LS26 . . . . 82 B1
Primrose Hill Dr LS26 . . . 102 B8

Primrose Hill Garth
LS26 . . . . 102 B8
Primrose Hill Gdns LS26 . 82 B1
Primrose Hill Gn LS26 . . 102 B8
Primrose Hill Gr LS26 . . . 82 B1
Primrose Hill High Sch
(Annexe) LS8 . . . . 207 B2
Primrose Hill Rd HD4 . . . 154 A4
Primrose Ho WF1 . . . . . . 216 C1
Primrose La
Bingley BD16 . . . . 37 C2
Boston Spa LS23 . . . . 30 C7
Crigglestone WF4 . . . . . . 159 D6
Kirkburton HD8 . . . . 173 D8
Leeds, Halton LS15 . . . . . . 81 A8
Leeds LS11 . . . . 214 C3
Liversedge WF15 . . . . . . 116 F5
Mirfield WF14 . . . . 138 C7
Shipley BD2 . . . . 55 D4
Primrose Lane Prim Sch
LS23 . . . . 30 D7
Primrose Rd LS15 . . . . 81 A8
Primrose Row BD17 . . . . . . 38 F4
Primrose St
2 Bradford BD8 . . . . 74 C8
Huddersfield HD4 . . . . . . 154 A4
Keighley BD21 . . . . 35 E7
Primrose Terr 38 HX7 . . . . 89 A3
Primrose Vale WF11 . . . . 127 A4
Primrose Way HX3 . . . . . . 93 D7
Primrose Wlk LS27 . . . . . . 98 C8
Prince's Ave LS8 . . . . 61 B7
Prince's Cres BD2 . . . . 55 E3
Prince's Ct 2 LS17 . . . . . . 43 C1
Prince's Gate HX3 . . . . . . 113 D4
Prince's St
Bradford BD6 . . . . 94 B8
4 Bradford, Buttershaw
BD6 . . . . 93 E7
Prince's Way BD1 . . . . 201 B2
Prince Albert Sq BD13 . . . 73 B2
Prince Edward Gr LS12 . . 78 A4
Prince Edward Rd LS12 . . 78 A4
Prince Henry's Gram Sch
(Language Coll) LS21 . . 11 A1
Prince Henry Rd LS21 . . . 11 A1
Princeroyd Way BD7 . . . . 74 A7
Princes Gate WF4 . . . . . . 141 D2
Princes Gr LS6 . . . . 59 D5
Princess Alexandra Wlk 7
HD1 . . . . 154 B6
Princess Apartments 7
HX1 . . . . 203 A1
Princess Ave
Dewsbury WF12 . . . . 140 A8
South Elmsall WF9 . . . . . 182 F2
Princess Cl WF12 . . . . 140 A8
Princess Cres WF12 . . . . . 140 A7
Princess Ct
Leeds LS17 . . . . 43 D3
Normanton WF6 . . . . 123 C1
Princess Fields LS15 . . . . . 81 D6
Princess Gdns 9 WF13 . . 139 B8
Princess Mary Ctr HX1 . . 202 C2
Princess of Wales Prec The
4 WF13 . . . . 139 C4
Princes Sq LS1 . . . . 211 B3
Princess Rd
Dewsbury WF12 . . . . 140 A7
Ilkley LS29 . . . . 8 A3
Princess St
Batley WF17 . . . . 118 C6
Brighouse HD6 . . . . 115 B2
Castleford WF10 . . . . 103 F1
Cudworth S72 . . . . 180 C1
Darton S75 . . . . 178 A1
Dewsbury WF12 . . . . 140 B8
3 Elland HX4 . . . . 134 D7
Halifax HX1 . . . . 203 B3
Hebden Bridge HX7 . . . . . 89 A4
3 Huddersfield HD1 . . . . 154 A5
Lofthouse Gate WF1 . . . . 121 B5
5 Mirfield WF14 . . . . 138 A4
Normanton WF6 . . . . 123 B2
Sowerby Bridge HX6 . . . . 112 C4
Wakefield WF1 . . . . 142 E2
Yeadon LS19 . . . . 40 A4
Princes St WF16 . . . . 117 C4
Prince St
Batley WF17 . . . . 118 C6
Bradford BD4 . . . . 75 C2
2 Dewsbury WF13 . . . . . 139 D8
Haworth BD22 . . . . 51 D7
Huddersfield HD4 . . . . . . 154 A4
Kippax WF10 . . . . 102 F7
Silsden BD20 . . . . 5 D1
Princeton Cl HX2 . . . . 91 E1
Princeville Prim Sch BD7 . 74 B6
Princeville Rd BD7 . . . . 74 B7
Princeville St BD7 . . . . 74 B6
Prince William Ct WF7 . . 145 C4
Prince Wood La HD2 . . . . 135 C2
Prior's La BD23 . . . . 1 E7
Priordale Rd WF7 . . . . . . 145 B4
Prior St BD21 . . . . 35 D8
Priory Bsns Pk WF9 . . . . . 163 B4
Priory Cl
8 Bingley BD16 . . . . 37 A4
Mirfield WF14 . . . . 137 E6
Normanton WF6 . . . . 122 F4
Ossett WF5 . . . . 140 D4
Wetherby LS22 . . . . 13 F6
Priory Croft WF5 . . . . 140 D5
Priory Ct
Bradford BD8 . . . . 74 D8
Cleckheaton, Birdacre BD19 96 A1
Huddersfield HD3 . . . . . . 135 B1

Priory Est WF9 . . . . 183 B3
Priory Gr BD16 . . . . 37 A4
Priory Grange WF4 . . . . . 162 A8
Priory Mews WF3 . . . . 121 F6
Priory Pl HD2 . . . . 136 F5
Priory Rd
Brighouse HD6 . . . . 115 C2
Ossett WF5 . . . . 140 D5
Purston Jaglin WF7 . . . . . 145 C4
Priory Ridge WF4 . . . . . . 162 A8
Priory Sq WF2 . . . . 161 A7
Priory Way WF14 . . . . . . 137 E6
Priory Wlk WF14 . . . . 137 E6
Privet Dr BD22 . . . . 34 D2
Privilege St LS12 . . . . 209 B3
Proctor St BD4 . . . . 75 D2
Prod La BD17 . . . . 37 E2
Progress Ave BD16 . . . . . . 36 A1
Prospect Ave
Halifax HX2 . . . . 112 E4
Leeds LS13 . . . . 58 C3
Normanton WF6 . . . . 123 B3
Pudsey LS28 . . . . 76 D8
Shipley BD18 . . . . 55 C7
Prospect Bank LS23 . . . . . 30 D3
Prospect Bsns Ctr HD1 . . 154 A5
Prospect Cl
Halifax HX2 . . . . 112 E4
Shipley BD18 . . . . 55 C7
Prospect Cotts
Kirkheaton HD5 . . . . 155 C8
South Elmsall WF9 . . . . . 182 E3
Prospect Cres
Keighley BD22 . . . . 34 E5
Leeds LS10 . . . . 215 A3
Prospect Ct
Halifax HX2 . . . . 112 E4
Pudsey LS28 . . . . 76 C8
Prospect Dr BD22 . . . . 34 E5
Prospect Gdns 4 LS15 . . . 81 B8
Prospect Gr
Pudsey LS28 . . . . 76 D8
Shipley BD18 . . . . 55 C7
Prospect La BD11 . . . . 96 E5
Prospect Mills BD13 . . . . . 72 E6
Prospect Mount
Keighley BD22 . . . . 34 E5
Shipley BD18 . . . . 55 C7
Prospect Pl
Bradford, Daisy Hill BD9 . . 54 F1
Bradford, Fagley BD2 . . . . 56 C2
Brighouse HX3 . . . . 94 A2
2 Brighouse, Waring Green
HD6 . . . . 115 A2
Elland HD3 . . . . 151 F8
Halifax HX2 . . . . 91 F3
Holmfirth HD9 . . . . 189 A4
Horsforth LS18 . . . . 58 B8
Leeds LS13 . . . . 58 C3
Ossett WF5 . . . . 140 E5
18 Queensbury BD13 . . . . 72 E1
Rothwell LS26 . . . . 100 F4
Rothwell, Town End WF3 . 100 B2
Prospect Rd
Batley WF16 . . . . 117 C5
Bingley BD16 . . . . 37 C5
Bradford BD3 . . . . 55 F1
Burley in W LS29 . . . . 21 F8
Cleckheaton BD19 . . . . . . 116 D7
Huddersfield HD3 . . . . . . 152 F6
Liversedge WF15 . . . . . . 116 D2
Ossett WF5 . . . . 140 D5
Prospect Row
Halifax HX2 . . . . 91 F3
Menston LS29 . . . . 21 C6
Prospect Sq
16 Pudsey LS28 . . . . 57 D2
Skelmanthorpe HD8 . . . . 175 A2
Prospect St
Batley WF17 . . . . 118 C6
Bradford BD4 . . . . 201 D1
Bradford, Bank Top BD10 . 56 C5
Bradford, Woodside BD6 . . 93 F7
11 Cleckheaton BD19 . . . 116 D8
Glusburn BD20 . . . . 16 D7
Halifax HX3 . . . . 203 C4
8 Haworth BD22 . . . . 51 C6
Horbury WF4 . . . . 159 C8
Huddersfield HD1 . . . . . . 154 A5
Keighley BD22 . . . . 34 F6
Pudsey, Farsley LS28 . . . . 57 D3
Pudsey LS28 . . . . 76 C8
Shipley BD18 . . . . 55 C7
Thornton BD13 . . . . 72 E6
Yeadon LS19 . . . . 40 C3
Prospect Terr
3 Batley WF13 . . . . 117 F2
Bradford BD15 . . . . 54 C1
Cleckheaton BD19 . . . . . . 116 D8
2 Horsforth LS18 . . . . . . 41 C1
Keighley BD20 . . . . 18 F2
Leeds, Bramley LS13 . . . . 58 C3
Liversedge WF15 . . . . . . 117 A4
Low Bradley BD20 . . . . . . 4 C6
Micklefield LS25 . . . . 84 A6
6 Pudsey, Farsley LS28 . . 57 D2
Pudsey, Rodley LS13 . . . . 57 E5
Rothwell LS26 . . . . 100 F4
South Kirkby WF9 . . . . . . 182 B2
Prospect View
Leeds LS13 . . . . 58 D3
Liversedge WF15 . . . . . . 116 C2
Queensbury BD13 . . . . . . 92 C8
Prospect Villas LS22 . . . . 13 E6
Prospect Way BD19 . . . . . 115 B6

Prospect Wlk BD18 . . . . 55 C7
Prosper St LS10 . . . . 215 B4
Providence Ave
　Baildon BD17 . . . . 38 C4
　Leeds LS6 . . . . 206 A4
Providence Bldgs HX3 . . 114 A4
Providence Chapel HX4 . 133 E3
Providence Cres BD22 . . . 34 C2
Providence Ct
　5 Morley LS27 . . . . 98 A5
　Oakworth BD22 . . . . 34 C2
Providence Gn WF8 . . . . . 125 E3
Providence Hill HX4 . . . . 133 E3
Providence La BD22 . . . . . 34 C1
Providence Pl
　5 Bradford BD12 . . . . 94 C4
　Brighouse HD6 . . . . 115 C1
　Garforth LS25 . . . . 82 E7
　Kippax WF10 . . . . 103 B3
　Leeds LS2 . . . . 206 C1
　Morley LS27 . . . . 97 D4
　4 Pudsey LS28 . . . . 57 E1
　Swillington LS15 . . . . . . 82 A6
Providence Rd LS6 . . . . . 206 A4
Providence Row
　Baildon BD17 . . . . 38 C4
　4 Bradford BD2 . . . . 56 B3
　Halifax HX2 . . . . 91 F3
　Keighley BD20 . . . . 19 E2
Providence St
　Batley WF17 . . . . 118 C5
　Bradford BD1 . . . . 201 A3
　Brighouse BD12 . . . . 94 E1
　2 Cleckheaton BD19 . . . 116 E8
　Dewsbury WF12 . . . . . . 139 F7
　18 Elland HX5 . . . . 134 F7
　Leeds LS9 . . . . 212 B3
　5 Pudsey LS28 . . . . 57 D2
　Todmorden OL14 . . . . . 129 A7
　Wakefield WF1 . . . . 216 B3
Providence Terr
　Leeds LS2 . . . . 206 A3
　Thornton BD13 . . . . 72 D6
Providential St WF4 . . . . 157 B2
Prune Park La BD15 . . . . . 53 F2
Pudding La OL14 . . . . 86 C2
Pudsey Bsns Ctr LS28 . . . 76 F7
Pudsey Grangefield Sch
　LS28 . . . . 76 E8
Pudsey Primrose Hill Prim
　Sch LS28 . . . . 57 D1
Pudsey Rd
　Leeds LS12, LS13 . . . . . 77 E7
　Pudsey LS28, S13 . . . . . 77 B7
　Todmorden OL14 . . . . . . 86 B2
Pudsey Tyersal Prim Sch
　BD4 . . . . 75 F6
Pudsey Waterloo Inf Sch
　LS28 . . . . 76 C7
Pudsey Waterloo Prim Sch
　LS28 . . . . 76 C7
Puffin Cl BD6 . . . . 73 C1
Pugneys Central Sta★
　WF2 . . . . 160 B8
Pugneys Ctry Pk★ WF2 . 160 B8
Pugneys Lakeside Sta★
　WF2 . . . . 160 A8
Pugneys Light Rly★ WF4 160 A8
Pugneys Rd WF2 . . . . 142 C2
Pule Green La HX3 . . . . . . 92 C3
Pullan Ave BD2 . . . . 56 C4
Pullan Dr BD2 . . . . 56 C4
Pullan Gr BD2 . . . . 56 C4
Pullan La BD17 . . . . 39 C5
Pullan St BD5 . . . . 74 D5
Pullman Ct LS27 . . . . 98 B5
Pulmans Pl HX3 . . . . 113 C2
Pumphouse La WF14 . . . 138 B6
Pump La
　Dewsbury WF13 . . . . . . 138 F8
　East Ardsley WF3 . . . . . 119 E5
　Kirkburton HD8 . . . . . . 174 C7
　West Hardwick WF4 . . . 163 A8
Pump St HD8 . . . . 191 B3
Punch Bowl Yd
　Brotherton WF11 . . . . . 126 C8
　Cleckheaton BD19 . . . . 116 C7
Pundles HX2 . . . . 91 E8
Purbeck Ct **1** BD4 . . . . . . 75 E2
Purbeck Gr LS25 . . . . 82 F6
Purcell Dr BD20 . . . . 5 D2
Purley Wlk BD6 . . . . 94 B8
Purlwell Ave WF17 . . . . . 118 B3
Purlwell Cres WF17 . . . . 118 B3
Purlwell Hall Rd WF17 . . 118 C4
Purlwell Inf Sch WF17 . . 118 B3
Purlwell La WF17 . . . . . . 118 C4
Purprise La HX7 . . . . 69 A1
Purston Ho **6** BD4 . . . . . . 75 F2
Purston Inf Sch WF7 . . . 145 D4
Purston La WF7 . . . . 145 F1
Purston Park Ct WF7 . . . 145 D4
Pussy La HD8 . . . . 174 A3
Putting Mill Wlk HD8 . . . 192 B6
Pye Nest Ave HX2 . . . . . . 202 A1
Pye Nest Ct WF15 . . . . . 116 D4
Pye Nest Dr HX2 . . . . 112 E4
Pye Nest Gdns HX2 . . . . 202 A1
Pye Nest Gr HX2 . . . . . . 202 A1
Pye Nest Rd HX2 . . . . . . 112 E4
Pye Nest Rise HX2 . . . . . 112 E4
Pyenot Ave BD19 . . . . . . 116 E6
Pyenot Dr BD19 . . . . 116 E6
Pyenot Gdns BD19 . . . . . 116 E6
Pyenot Hall La BD19 . . . 116 E6

Pymont Ct WF3 . . . . 100 C1
Pymont Dr LS26 . . . . 101 B7
Pymont Gr LS26 . . . . 101 B7
Pymroyd HD4 . . . . 153 B3
Pym St LS10 . . . . 212 A1
Pynate Rd WF17 . . . . 118 A6
Pyrah Fold **6** BD12 . . . . . 94 C4
Pyrah Rd BD12 . . . . 94 D7
Pyrah St
　Bradford BD12 . . . . 94 D4
　Dewsbury WF13 . . . . . . 118 C1

Q

QBM Bsns Pk WF17 . . . . . 96 F2
QF Ind Est BD4 . . . . 75 B4
Quail Ave BD6 . . . . 73 C1
Quail St BD21 . . . . 35 D8
Quaker Bottom HD8 . . . . 191 C3
Quaker Ho LS28 . . . . 206 A2
Quaker La
　Bradford BD5 . . . . 74 B3
　Cleckheaton BD19 . . . . 116 D6
　Cleckheaton, Hightown
　　WF15 . . . . 116 D5
　Huddersfield HD1 . . . . . 153 E5
Quakers La
　Ripponden HX6 . . . . . . 132 D3
　Yeadon LS19 . . . . 40 B5
Quarmby Croft HD3 . . . . 153 A7
Quarmby Fold HD3 . . . . . 153 A7
Quarmby Rd HD3 . . . . . . 153 B6
Quarrie Dene Ct LS7 . . . . 60 C6
Quarry Ave WF11 . . . . . . 127 A3
Quarry Bank Cl LS5 . . . . . 58 F6
Quarry Cl HD9 . . . . 172 C2
Quarry Cotts
　Horsforth LS18 . . . . 41 B1
　Steeton BD20 . . . . 17 D5
Quarry Ct
　Castleford WF10 . . . . . 124 D6
　Halifax HX3 . . . . 113 E7
　Huddersfield HD3 . . . . . 152 F7
Quarry Dene LS16 . . . . . . 59 D8
Quarry Dene Dr WF10 . . 125 B6
Quarry Dene Pk LS16 . . . 59 C8
Quarry Dr HD5 . . . . 155 C5
Quarry Farm Rd LS21 . . . 24 C5
Quarryfields WF14 . . . . . 138 B8
Quarryfield Terr WF3 . . . 120 D7
Quarry Gdns LS17 . . . . . . 43 A6
Quarry Hill
　Horbury WF4 . . . . 140 F1
　Huddersfield HD5 . . . . . 155 B4
　Rothwell LS26 . . . . 101 C6
　Sowerby Bridge HX6 . . . 112 B3
Quarry Hill Ind Est WF4 140 E1
Quarry Hill La LS22 . . . . . 13 E6
Quarry La
　10 Batley WF17 . . . . 96 F1
　East Ardsley WF12 . . . . 119 A6
　Huddersfield HD4 . . . . . 171 C7
　Kirkheaton HD5 . . . . . . 155 C5
　Morley LS27 . . . . 98 B2
　Upton WF9 . . . . 183 A8
Quarry Mount
　4 Holmfirth HD9 . . . . 189 A5
　Leeds LS6 . . . . 206 A4
　Ryhill WF4 . . . . 162 B1
　8 Yeadon LS19 . . . . 40 C7
Quarry Mount Pl **9** LS6 . 206 A4
Quarry Mount Prim Sch
　LS6 . . . . 206 A4
Quarry Mount St **6** LS6 . 206 A4
Quarry Mount Terr **10**
　LS6 . . . . 206 A4
Quarry Pl
　Bradford BD2 . . . . 56 B2
　Leeds LS6 . . . . 206 A3
　Mirfield WF14 . . . . 137 D6
Quarry Rd
　Cleckheaton BD19 . . . . 116 D7
　Cleckheaton, Gomersal
　　BD19 . . . . 117 B7
　Dewsbury WF13 . . . . . . 139 B7
　Halifax HX3 . . . . 91 C2
　Huddersfield HD4 . . . . . 153 B3
　Huddersfield, Marsh HD1 . 153 C6
　Liversedge WF15 . . . . . 117 A4
　Pool LS21 . . . . 24 B5
　Rothwell LS26 . . . . 101 D6
Quarryside Rd WF14 . . . 137 F5
Quarry St
　Ackworth M T WF7 . . . . 163 F5
　Keighley BD21 . . . . 35 D7
　Leeds LS6 . . . . 206 A4
　Shipley BD9 . . . . 55 A4
Quarry The
　Leeds LS17 . . . . 43 A6
　Wetherby LS22 . . . . . . 13 E6
Quarry View
　Ackworth M T WF7 . . . . 163 E5
　Dewsbury WF13 . . . . . . 117 F1
Quaver La BD15 . . . . 54 B1
Quay Cl BD6 . . . . 94 A8
Quayside BD17 . . . . 55 B8
Quayside The BD10 . . . . . 56 E8
Quay St HD1 . . . . 154 B6
Quays The LS1 . . . . 211 C3
Quba Ct **4** BD8 . . . . 55 C2
Quebec BD16 . . . . 54 B6
Quebec Ho **15** BD21 . . . . 35 B6
Quebec Rd HD3 . . . . 151 E5
Quebec St
　Bradford BD1 . . . . 201 B2
　Elland HX5 . . . . 135 A7
　Keighley BD21 . . . . 35 B6

Quebec St continued
　Leeds LS1 . . . . 211 B3
　Wakefield WF2 . . . . . . 216 A2
　9 Walsden OL14 . . . . . 108 A1
Queen's Arc LS1 . . . . . . 211 C4
Queen's Ave
　Bradford BD2 . . . . 55 F3
　Pontefract WF8 . . . . . . 146 A7
Queen's Cres
　Crofton WF4 . . . . 144 C4
　Ossett WF5 . . . . 140 D5
Queen's Ct
　Keighley BD16 . . . . 36 F3
　6 Leeds LS17 . . . . 43 C1
Queen's Dr
　Cudworth S72 . . . . 180 C1
　Ilkley LS29 . . . . 7 F3
　Ossett WF5 . . . . 141 A5
　Shafton S72 . . . . 180 B3
Queen's Drive La LS29 . . . 7 F3
Queen's Gate HX3 . . . . . 113 B4
Queen's Gdns
　Ilkley LS29 . . . . 8 A3
　Ossett WF5 . . . . 140 D5
Queen's Gr LS27 . . . . 97 F3
Queen's Park Dr WF10 . . 125 B8
Queen's Pl LS27 . . . . 98 B4
Queen's Prom LS27 . . . . . 98 A5
Queen's Rd
　Bingley BD16 . . . . 36 E6
　Boston Spa LS23 . . . . . 30 C8
　Bradford BD1, BD2, BD8 . 55 E2
　Brighouse HX3 . . . . 93 F2
　Cudworth S72 . . . . 180 C1
　Halifax HX1 . . . . 202 B3
　Huddersfield HD2 . . . . . 153 E8
　Ilkley LS29 . . . . 8 A3
　Keighley BD21 . . . . 35 B5
　Leeds LS6 . . . . 205 B2
　Morley LS27 . . . . 97 F3
　Pontefract WF8 . . . . . . 146 A7
Queen's Rise BD2 . . . . . . 55 F3
Queen's Sq WF8 . . . . 146 A7
Queen's Terr **6** WF5 . . . . 140 D5
Queen's Wlk
　Leeds LS6 . . . . 59 B6
　Ossett WF5 . . . . 140 F5
Queen Elizabeth Ct **18**
　BD22 . . . . 35 A6
Queen Elizabeth Dr WF6 144 B8
Queen Elizabeth Gdns
　HD1 . . . . 153 F6
Queen Elizabeth Gr WF1 142 E7
Queen Elizabeth Gram & Jun
　Gram Sch WF1 . . . . . . 216 B3
Queen Elizabeth Rd WF1 142 E7
Queen Elizabeth St **1** BD1 . 121 B4
Queen Margaret's Dr
　WF11 . . . . 126 D8
Queen Margarets Ave
　WF11 . . . . 126 D8
Queen Margarets Cl
　WF11 . . . . 126 D8
Queen's Ct LS1 . . . . 211 C3
Queen St S HD1 . . . . 154 B5
Queensbury Ave WF1 . . . 121 C5
Queensbury Ct WF6 . . . . 123 C1
Queensbury Rd HX3 . . . . 92 B5
Queensbury Sch BD13 . . . 92 E8
Queensbury Sq **6** BD13 . . 72 E1
Queens Cl
　Bingley BD16 . . . . 37 B2
　Leeds LS17 . . . . 60 C8
Queenscourt **3** LS27 . . . . 98 A4
Queens Ct
　Cleckheaton BD19 . . . . 96 B2
　8 Otley LS21 . . . . 23 A7
　10 Pudsey LS28 . . . . . . 76 E8
　Shipley BD18 . . . . 54 F8
Queens Dr
　Halifax HX3 . . . . 114 A4
　Pudsey LS28 . . . . 76 D8
　Rothwell WF3 . . . . 100 D3
　Wakefield WF2 . . . . . . 120 E1
Queens Dr Cl WF5 . . . . . 140 F5
Queensgate
　Bradford BD1 . . . . 201 B3
　Huddersfield HD1 . . . . . 154 B5
Queens Gr **2** BD15 . . . . . 35 B5
Queenshill App LS17 . . . . 43 C3
Queenshill Ave LS17 . . . . 43 C3
Queenshill Cl **2** LS17 . . . 43 C2
Queenshill Cres LS17 . . . 43 C3
Queenshill Ct **3** LS17 . . . 43 C2
Queenshill Dr LS17 . . . . . 43 C2
Queenshill Garth LS17 . . . 43 C2
Queenshill Gdns LS17 . . . 43 B2
Queenshill Lawn **1** LS17 . 43 C2
Queenshill Rd LS17 . . . . . 43 C2
Queenshill View LS17 . . . 43 C2
Queenshill Way LS17 . . . . 43 C2
Queenshill Wlk LS17 . . . . 43 C2
Queens Mead HX3 . . . . . . 93 A3
Queens Mill WF13 . . . . . 138 E6
Queens Mill Ind Est HD1 154 A4
Queens Mill Rd HD1,
　HD4 . . . . 154 A4
Queens Park Cl WF10 . . . 125 B8
Queens Pl
　Otley LS21 . . . . 23 A7
　Shipley BD18 . . . . 55 A4
Queen Sq LS2 . . . . 206 C1
Queen Square Ct LS2 . . . 206 B1
Queens Rd
　Castleford WF10 . . . . . 125 B8
　Shipley BD18 . . . . 54 F8
Queens Rd W HD4 . . . . . 153 B4
Queens Sq HD2 . . . . 136 D1

Queens Square Bsns Pk
　HD9 . . . . 172 A6
Queens St BD13 . . . . 52 D6
Queen St
　5 Baildon BD17 . . . . 38 C1
　Bingley BD16 . . . . 36 F3
　Bradford BD10 . . . . 56 D7
　3 Bradford, Buttershaw
　　BD6 . . . . 93 E7
　Castleford WF10 . . . . . 124 E8
　Cleckheaton BD19 . . . . 96 B2
　Dewsbury, Chickenley
　　WF12 . . . . 140 B7
　Dewsbury, Ravensthorpe
　　WF13 . . . . 138 E6
　East Ardsley WF3 . . . . . 120 D8
　Elland HX4 . . . . 134 C6
　7 Haworth BD22 . . . . . . 51 C6
　Horbury WF4 . . . . 141 A1
　Huddersfield HD1 . . . . . 154 B6
　Kippax LS26, WF10 . . . . 102 E6
　Leeds LS1 . . . . 211 A4
　Leeds, Stourton LS10 . . . 80 A2
　Liversedge WF16 . . . . . 117 C3
　Lofthouse Gate WF1 . . . 121 B4
　Mirfield WF14 . . . . 138 A4
　Morley LS27 . . . . 98 A5
　Mytholmroyd HX7 . . . . 110 E8
　Normanton WF6 . . . . . 123 A2
　Ossett WF5 . . . . 140 D5
　Pontefract WF8 . . . . . . 146 C8
　Rothwell WF3 . . . . 100 D3
　Silsden BD20 . . . . 5 E1
　Skelmanthorpe HD8 . . . 175 A2
　South Elmsall WF9 . . . . 182 F2
　Sowerby Bridge HX6 . . . 111 E3
　Steeton BD20 . . . . 17 C5
　Todmorden OL14 . . . . . 108 B5
　Wakefield WF1 . . . . . . 216 B3
　Wilsden BD15 . . . . 53 C4
　Yeadon LS19 . . . . 40 A4
Queens Terr
　Guiseley LS20 . . . . 22 D1
　3 Hebden Bridge HX7 . . 88 F3
　Otley LS21 . . . . 23 B7
Queensthorpe Ave LS13 . . 77 E8
Queensthorpe Cl LS13 . . . 77 E8
Queensthorpe Rise LS13 . 77 D8
Queensview LS14 . . . . . . 62 A5
Queensway
　Bingley BD16 . . . . 37 B2
　Garforth LS25 . . . . 82 D7
　Halifax HX1 . . . . 202 B4
　7 Keighley BD21 . . . . . . 35 C7
　Kirkburton HD8 . . . . . . 174 A5
　Leeds LS15 . . . . 81 C8
　Morley LS27 . . . . 98 A4
　Normanton WF6 . . . . . 144 A7
　Pontefract WF8 . . . . . . 125 F3
　Rothwell LS26 . . . . 100 E6
　Royston S71 . . . . 179 C4
　Yeadon LS19, LS20 . . . . 40 A8
Queensway Pl **1** WF8 . . 125 F3
Queensway Prim Sch
　LS19 . . . . 40 A8
Queenswood Cl LS6 . . . . . 59 A6
Queenswood Ct LS6 . . . . . 59 C4
Queenswood Dr LS6 . . . . . 59 A5
Queenswood Gdns LS6 . . . 59 C4
Queenswood Gn LS6 . . . . 59 A7
Queenswood Hts LS6 . . . . 59 C5
Queenswood Mount LS6 . . 59 B5
Queenswood Rd LS6 . . . . 59 B5
Queenswood Rise LS6 . . . 59 B4
Queen Tap Yd **24** HD4 . . 154 A6
Queen Terr **4** WF8 . . . . 146 B8
Queen Victoria Cres HX3 . 93 B3
Queen Victoria St LS1 . . . 211 C4
Quincy Cl BD2 . . . . 56 C4
Qureshi View **6** BD8 . . . . 55 C1

R

Raby Ave LS7 . . . . 207 A3
Raby Pk LS22 . . . . 13 D6
Raby St LS7 . . . . 207 A3
Racca Ave WF11 . . . . 127 B4
Racca Gn WF11 . . . . 127 A4
Race Moor La BD22 . . . . . 34 C3
Rachael St WF4 . . . . 140 F1
Racton St HD7 . . . . 151 F1
Radcliffe Ave BD2 . . . . . . 56 A5
Radcliffe Gdns LS28 . . . . 76 E6
Radcliffe Gr **2** LS28 . . . . 76 E6
Radcliffe La
　Halifax HX2 . . . . 90 C2
　Pudsey LS28 . . . . 76 E7
Radcliffe Pl WF1 . . . . . . 216 B2
Radcliffe Rd
　Huddersfield HD3 . . . . . 153 B4
　Slaithwaite HD7 . . . . . . 152 B2
　Wakefield WF2 . . . . . . 141 E4
Radcliffe St HD8 . . . . . . 174 F2
Radcliffe Terr **1** LS28 . . . 76 E6
Radfield Rd BD6 . . . . 74 E1
Radford Park Ave WF9 . . 182 B4
Radnor St
　Bradford BD3 . . . . 75 D7
　Leeds LS12 . . . . 210 B2
Radpoll Way BD6 . . . . 73 C1
Radwell Dr BD5 . . . . 201 B1
Raeburn Dr BD6 . . . . 94 A7
Rae St **3** BD8 . . . . 55 B6
Rae Ct WF3 . . . . 121 C5
Rae Rd BD18 . . . . 55 B6
Rafborn Ave HD3 . . . . . . 134 E1
Rafborn Gr HD3 . . . . 134 E1

Raglan Ave BD22 . . . . . . 34 F6
Raglan Cl WF10 . . . . 124 A8
Raglan Ct **8** HX1 . . . . . . 202 C3
Raglan Ind Est WF10 . . . 124 B8
Raglan Rd LS2, LS6 . . . . 206 A3
Raglan St
　Bradford BD3 . . . . 75 D7
　Halifax HX1 . . . . 202 C3
　Keighley BD22 . . . . 34 F6
　Queensbury BD13 . . . . . 72 F1
　7 Todmorden OL14 . . . 108 B5
Raglan Terr BD3 . . . . 75 E7
Ragley View HX7 . . . . 88 C4
Raikes La
　Batley WF17 . . . . 96 F2
　Birkenshaw, East Bierley
　　BD4 . . . . 95 E7
　Bradford BD4 . . . . 76 B2
Raikes Wood Dr BD4 . . . . 95 E7
Railes Cl HX2 . . . . 90 D1
Railes Cotts HX2 . . . . 90 D1
Railes La HX2 . . . . 90 D1
Railgate OL13 . . . . 106 C1
Railsfield Mount LS13 . . . 58 C2
Railsfield Rise LS13 . . . . . 58 C2
Railsfield Way LS13 . . . . . 58 C2
Railway Ave WF8 . . . . . . 125 C1
Railway Carriage Mus★
　BD21 . . . . 35 B4
Railway Cotts
　Bolton Abbey BD23 . . . . 2 C1
　Burton Salmon LS25 . . . 105 D4
　Dunford Bridge S36 . . . 199 F2
　Micklefield LS25 . . . . . . 84 A6
　South Elmsall WF9 . . . . 183 F1
Railway Ct HD8 . . . . 175 F3
Railway Rd
　Bradford BD10 . . . . 56 B8
　Ilkley LS29 . . . . 8 B4
　Leeds LS15 . . . . 62 C2
Railway St
　Bradford BD4 . . . . 75 C2
　2 Brighouse HD6 . . . . . 115 B1
　Cleckheaton BD19 . . . . 116 D7
　Dewsbury, Scout Hill
　　WF13 . . . . 139 A6
　Dewsbury WF12 . . . . . . 139 D7
　Huddersfield HD1 . . . . . 154 A6
　Keighley BD20 . . . . 18 C1
　Leeds LS9 . . . . 212 B3
　Liversedge WF16 . . . . . 117 C3
　Todmorden OL14 . . . . . 108 B6
Railway Terr
　1 Bradford BD21 . . . . . . 94 C5
　Brighouse HD6 . . . . 115 C2
　East Ardsley WF3 . . . . . 99 C1
　Elland HX3 . . . . 113 A2
　Featherstone WF7 . . . . 145 D5
　Fitzwilliam WF9 . . . . . . 163 A3
　Lofthouse Gate WF1 . . . 121 A5
　Normanton WF6 . . . . . 123 A2
Railway View
　Castleford WF10 . . . . . 124 B7
　Hebden Bridge HX7 . . . . 89 A2
　6 Walsden OL14 . . . . . 108 A1
Rainbow Mews BD6 . . . . . 93 F6
Raincliffe Gr LS9 . . . . 80 A8
Raincliffe Mount **10** LS9 . 80 A7
Raincliffe Rd LS9 . . . . 80 A7
Raincliffe St **13** LS9 . . . . 80 A8
Raincliffe Terr **11** LS9 . . . 80 A7
Raines Dr BD20 . . . . 4 C3
Rainsborough Ave WF11 126 C3
Raistrick Way BD18 . . . . . 55 D8
Rake HX7 . . . . 109 F8
Rake Bank HX2 . . . . 91 D3
Rake Head Barn La OL14 129 A8
Rake Head Rd HD9 . . . . . 197 E7
Rakehill Rd LS15 . . . . 63 D7
Raleigh Gdns OL15 . . . . . 129 C1
Raleigh St **5** HX1 . . . . . 202 B1
Ralph Thoresby High Sch
　LS16 . . . . 41 F4
Rampart Rd LS6 . . . . 206 A3
Ramsden Ave BD7 . . . . . . 73 E5
Ramsden Cl WF11 . . . . . . 126 D8
Ramsden Ct BD7 . . . . 74 A4
Ramsden La
　Holme HD9 . . . . 198 B2
　Todmorden OL14 . . . . . 128 F7
Ramsden Mill La HD7 . . . 152 E3
Ramsden Pl BD14 . . . . . . 73 B5
Ramsden Rd
　Calderbrook OL15 . . . . 128 C1
　Holme HD9 . . . . 198 C7
Ramsden St
　Castleford WF10 . . . . . 124 C5
　Halifax HX3 . . . . 91 F2
　Huddersfield HD1 . . . . . 154 A5
　Huddersfield, Leymoor
　　HD7 . . . . 152 E4
　Kippax LS25 . . . . 102 F8
　Todmorden OL14 . . . . . 129 A7
Ramsden Wood Rd OL14 129 A6
Ramsey Ave OL13 . . . . . . 106 A1
Ramsey Cres WF4 . . . . . 158 B7
Ramsey Ct WF4 . . . . 158 B7
Ramsey Rd WF4 . . . . 158 A7
Ramsey St BD5 . . . . 74 D3
Ramsey Terr **2** LS21 . . . . 23 B8
Ramsey View WF4 . . . . . 158 A7
Ramsgate WF3 . . . . 100 B3
Ramsgate Cres WF3 . . . . 100 B3
Ramsgate St HX1 . . . . . . 202 B3
Ramsgill Cl BD6 . . . . 93 E8
Ramshead App LS14 . . . . 62 A6
Ramshead Cl LS14 . . . . . 62 A2
Ramshead Cres LS14 . . . . 61 F7

Ramshead Dr LS14 62 A6
Ramshead Gdns LS14 61 F7
Ramshead Gr LS14 62 A6
Ramshead Hill LS14 62 A6
Ramshead Hts 1 LS14 62 A5
Ramshead Pl LS14 62 A6
Ramshead View LS14 62 A6
Randall Pl BD9 55 A3
Randall Well St BD7 201 A2
Randolph St
Bradford BD3 75 E8
Halifax HX3 203 B4
Leeds LS13 58 A2
Random Cl BD22 34 F5
Rand Pl BD7 74 C5
Rand St BD7 74 C5
Ranelagh Ave BD10 56 E5
Range Bank HX3 92 C1
Range Bank Top HX3 92 C1
Range Ct HX3 203 B4
Range Gdns HX3 92 C1
Range La HX3 92 C1
Range St HX3 92 C1
Ransdale Dr BD5 74 D3
Ransdale Gr BD5 74 D3
Ransdale Rd BD5 74 D3
Ranter's Fold WF4 141 A1
Raper View LS25 64 E8
Rapes Highway OL3 167 A5
Rashcliffe Hill Rd HD1 153 F4
Raspberry Pl BD20 16 D4
Rastrick Comm HD6 136 A8
Rastrick High Sch HD6 114 F1
Rastrick Prep Sch HD6 135 F8
Rathlin Rd WF12 118 F3
Rathmell Rd LS15 80 E7
Rathmell St BD5 74 D1
Ratten Row Rd HX6 111 C1
Rattle Row 5 HD9 189 A5
Raven Bank HX2 111 D6
Raven Cl WF7 124 A1
Raven La S72 180 A6
Raven Rd LS6 205 B4
Raven Royd S71 178 F1
Ravens Ave
Dewsbury WF13 139 A6
Huddersfield HD5 154 E5
Ravensbridge Ind Est
WF13 138 F6
Ravenscar Ave 6 LS8 61 A6
Ravenscar Mount 2 LS8 61 A6
Ravenscar Terr 3 LS8 61 A6
Ravenscar View LS8 61 A6
Ravenscar Wlk 4 LS8 61 A6
Ravenscliffe Ave BD10 56 E4
Ravenscliffe Cl HX3 113 C2
Ravenscliffe Fst Sch BD10 56 E4
Ravenscliffe High Sch
HX3 113 B2
Ravenscliffe Rd LS28 56 F6
Ravenscourt HD1 153 D5
Ravens Cres WF13 139 A6
Ravens Croft WF13 139 A6
Ravensdeane HD3 153 D8
Ravensfield Rd WF13 139 A6
Ravens Gr WF13 139 A6
Ravenshall Sch WF12 139 A4
Ravenshouse Rd WF13 138 F7
Ravensknowle Rd HD5 154 E5
Ravens Lodge Terr
WF13 139 A6
Ravensmead WF7 145 F5
Ravens Mount LS28 76 F7
Ravens St WF13 138 F6
Raven St
Bingley BD16 36 F3
Halifax HX1 202 B3
Huddersfield HD1 153 D5
Keighley BD21 35 B7
Ravensthorpe CE Jun Sch
WF13 138 E5
Ravensthorpe Ind Est
WF13 138 E5
Ravensthorpe Inf Sch
WF13 138 E6
Ravensthorpe Rd WF12 139 A4
Ravensthorpe Sta WF12 138 F4
Ravenstone Dr HX4 134 C6
Ravenstone Gdns BD20 16 E5
Ravensville BD20 16 E6
Ravens Way HD9 189 E4
Ravenswharfe Rd WF13 139 A6
Ravens Wlk WF13 139 A6
Ravensworth Cl LS15 62 F3
Ravensworth Way LS15 62 F3
Raven Terr BD8 73 C7
Rawden Hill LS21 25 F6
Rawdon Dr LS19 40 B3
Rawdon Hall Dr LS19 40 B3
Rawdon Littlemoor Prim Sch
LS19 40 B4
Rawdon Pk LS19 40 B5
Rawdon Rd
Haworth BD22 51 C7
Horsforth LS18 57 F8
Rawdon St Peter's CE Prim
Sch LS19 40 D3
Rawdon St BD22 35 A6
Raw End Rd HX2 112 A8
Rawfield La LS25, WF11 105 C6
Rawfolds Ave WF17 96 F2
Rawfolds Way BD19 116 F6
Rawgate Ave WF10 124 A7
Raw Hill 6 HD6 135 F8
Raw La
Halifax HX2 91 D5
Hebden Bridge HX7 89 D3
Raw Lane Bottom HX6 111 E3
Rawling St BD21 35 B5
Rawling Way LS6 60 A5
Raw Nook Rd HD3 152 E8
Rawroyds HX4 134 C5
Rawson Apartments
HX1 203 B1
Rawson Ave
Bradford BD3 75 D8
Halifax HX3 113 B3
Rawson Jun & Inf Sch
HX3 92 B2
Rawson Mkt BD1 201 B3
Rawson Pl
Bradford BD1 201 B3
Sowerby Bridge HX6 112 A3
Rawson Rd BD1 201 B3
Rawson St N HX3 92 B1
Rawson Sq
Bradford BD1 201 B3
Bradford, Thackley BD10 39 B1
Rawson St
Bradford BD12 94 D4
Halifax HX1 203 B3
Rawson Terr LS11 214 C3
Rawson Wood HX6 111 E2
Rawtenstall Bank HX7 88 E4
Rawthorpe Cres HD5 154 E8
Rawthorpe High Sch
HD5 154 E8
Rawthorpe Jun Sch HD5 154 D7
Rawthorpe La HD5 154 E7
Rawthorpe St James CE Inf
Sch HD5 154 E8
Rawthorpe Terr HD5 154 E8
Rayfield WF2 141 F5
Ray Gate
Holmfirth HD9 189 D8
Huddersfield HD3 152 D8
Wadsworth Moor HX2 89 F8
Raygill Cl LS17 44 B5
Raylands Cl LS10 99 F6
Raylands Ct LS10 99 F6
Raylands Fold LS10 99 F6
Raylands Garth LS10 99 F6
Raylands La LS10 99 F6
Raylands Pl LS10 99 F6
Raylands Rd LS10 99 F6
Raylands Way LS10 99 F6
Rayleigh St BD4 75 A4
Raymond Dr BD5 74 E2
Raymond St BD5 74 E2
Raynbron Cres BD5 74 F2
Raynel App LS16 42 A3
Raynel Cl LS16 42 A4
Raynel Dr LS16 42 A4
Raynel Garth LS16 42 A3
Raynel Gdns LS16 42 A4
Raynel Gn LS16 42 A3
Raynel Mount LS16 42 A4
Raynel Way LS16 41 F4
Rayner Ave
Batley WF16 117 D6
Bradford BD8 54 F1
Rayner Dr HD6 115 A4
Rayner Mount BD15 73 A8
Rayner Rd HD6 115 A4
Rayners Ave WF15 116 C4
Rayner St WF4 141 A1
Rayner Terr LS28 76 F8
Rayneville WF8 125 D3
Raynham Cres BD21 34 F8
Raynor Cl HD3 153 C7
Raynville App 1 LS13 58 E3
Raynville Ave LS13 58 E3
Raynville Cl LS13 58 E3
Raynville Cres LS12 58 F2
Raynville Ct 2 LS13 58 E3
Raynville Dene LS12 58 F3
Raynville Dr LS13 58 E3
Raynville Gdns 5 LS13 58 F2
Raynville Gn LS13 58 E3
Raynville Gr LS13 58 E3
Raynville Grange 3 LS13 58 E3
Raynville Mount LS13 58 E3
Raynville Pl 4 LS13 58 E3
Raynville Prim Sch LS13 58 E2
Raynville Rd LS12, LS13 58 E3
Raynville Rise LS13 58 E3
Raynville St LS13 58 E3
Raynville Terr LS13 58 E3
Raynville Way 7 LS13 58 F2
Raynville Wlk LS13 58 E2
Ray St HD1 154 B7
Ray Winfield Ind Est
WF7 163 E5
Raywood Cl LS19 40 A8
Reap Hirst Rd HD2 135 D2
Rear Rock Terr BD8 55 D1
Rebecca St BD1 74 D7
Recreation Ave 3 LS11 214 A4
Recreation Cres LS11 213 C4
Recreation Gr LS11 214 A4
Recreation La HX5 134 E6
Recreation Mount LS11 214 A4
Recreation Pl LS11 214 A4
Recreation Rd
Leeds LS11 213 C2
Sowerby Bridge HX6 112 C4
Recreation Row LS11 213 C4
Recreation St LS11 214 A4
Recreation Terr LS11 214 A4
Recreation View LS11 214 A4
Rectory Ave 2 WF10 124 D8
Rectory Cl
Barnsley S71 179 D1
Garforth LS25 82 F7
Marsden HD7 168 F4
Rectory Cres WF4 161 F8
Rectory Ct WF8 166 D6
Rectory Dr
Batley WF17 97 A1
Huddersfield HD5 155 B7
Rectory Garth WF9 181 D7
Rectory Gdn HD8 175 D7
Rectory La HD8 175 D8
Rectory Row 12 BD21 35 B7
Rectory St
3 Castleford WF10 124 D8
Leeds LS9 207 B1
Rectory View WF12 139 E3
Redbarn Cl LS10 99 C2
Redbeck Cotts LS19 57 E8
Red Beck Rd HX3 92 F1
Red Beck Vale BD18 55 A5
Red Brink La HX6 111 B2
Redburn Ave BD18 55 A5
Redburn Dr BD18 55 A5
Redburn Rd BD18 55 B5
Redcar La BD20 17 C2
Redcar Rd BD10 56 E6
Redcar St HX1 202 B3
Redcliffe Ave BD21 35 A7
Redcliffe Gr BD21 35 A7
Redcliffe St BD21 35 A7
Redcote La
Leeds LS4 59 C2
Leeds, Upper Armley LS12 59 B1
Red Deer Park La WF4,
WF12 156 E5
Red Delph Gdns 13 BD13 72 D1
Reddisher Rd HD7 168 E4
Red Doles Ind Est HD2 136 C1
Red Doles La HD2 136 C1
Red Doles Rd HD2 136 C2
Reddyshore Scout Gate
OL14 129 C5
Redesdale Gdns LS16 42 B3
Redfearn Ave WF16 117 D5
Red Hall App LS14 45 A1
Red Hall Ave
Leeds LS17 44 F1
Wakefield WF1 121 B2
Red Hall Chase LS14 45 A1
Redhall Cl LS11 213 B1
Redhall Cres LS11 213 B1
Red Hall Croft LS14 62 A8
Red Hall Ct
Leeds LS14 45 A1
Wakefield WF1 121 A2
Red Hall Dr LS14 45 A1
Red Hall Garth LS14 45 A1
Redhall Gate LS11 213 B1
Red Hall Gdns LS17 44 F1
Red Hall Gn LS14 45 A1
Red Hall La
Leeds LS14, LS17 45 A1
Wakefield WF1 121 A1
Red Hall Vale LS14 62 A8
Red Hall View LS14 45 A1
Red Hall Way LS14 45 A1
Red Hall Wlk LS14 45 A1
Redhill Ave
Castleford WF10 125 A6
East Ardsley WF3 119 E5
Redhill Chase WF10 125 A6
Redhill Cl
Bradford BD4 95 F7
East Ardsley WF3 119 E5
Redhill Cres WF3 119 E5
Redhill Dr
Castleford WF10 125 B7
East Ardsley WF3 119 E5
Redhill Gdns WF10 125 A7
Redhill Hts WF10 125 A6
Redhill Inf Sch WF10 125 C8
Redhill Jun Sch WF10 125 C8
Redhill Mount WF10 125 A7
Redhill Rd WF10 125 A7
Redhill View WF10 125 A6
Redhill Wlk WF10 125 A6
Red House Gdns LS29 22 A3
Redhouse La LS7 204 B3
Red House Mus The*
BD19 96 B1
Red La
Crofton WF1, WF4 143 E5
Featherstone WF7 144 E5
Meltham HD9 170 B2
Pudsey LS28 57 C3
Red Laithes Ct WF13 138 E6
Red Laithes La WF13 138 E6
Redland Cres WF9 163 B2
Redland Dr HD8 173 E7
Redland Gr S75 178 B2
Redlands Cl WF14 138 A7
Red Lees Rd BB10 85 A8
Red Lodge Cl LS8 61 D4
Redman Cl BD22 51 B7
Redman Garth BD22 51 B7
Redmayne Gr WF11 126 D3
Redmire Ct LS14 62 B4
Redmire Dr LS14 62 A4
Redmire St BD3 75 E7
Redmire View LS14 62 A4
Redruth Dr WF6 123 B3
Redshank Cl 3 BD6 73 C1
Redshaw Rd LS12 210 A2
Redthorne Way S72 180 C3
Red Vale BD19 96 B2
Redvers Cl LS16 42 A1
Redwald Dr LS20 22 D1
Redwing Cres HD3 152 F5
Redwing Dr BD6 73 C1
Redwing Pk WF14 138 A6
Redwood Ave
East Ardsley WF3 120 A8
Redwood Ave *continued*
Royston S71 179 C3
Redwood Cl
Keighley BD21 35 E5
Rothwell LS26 101 E6
Yeadon LS19 39 F7
Redwood Dr HD2 136 E5
Redwood Gr
Crofton WF4 144 C4
7 Huddersfield HD5 154 D6
Yeadon LS19 39 F7
Redwood Way LS19 39 F7
Reedling Dr LS27 98 C3
Reed Rd LS12 209 C2
Reedsdale Ave LS27 97 C7
Reedsdale Dr LS27 97 C7
Reedsdale Gdns LS27 97 C7
Reed St
Bacup OL13 106 A3
Huddersfield HD3 153 D7
Rees Way BD3 201 C4
Reeth Rd HD6 135 E8
Reevy Ave BD6 93 F8
Reevy Cres BD6 93 F8
Reevy Dr BD6 94 A8
Reevy Hill Prim Sch BD6 73 F1
Reevylands Dr BD6 94 A8
Reevy Park Ct 2 BD6 93 E8
Reevy Rd BD6 94 B8
Reevy Rd W BD6 93 E8
Reevy St BD6 74 A1
Reform St
Cleckheaton BD19 96 B1
4 Dewsbury WF13 118 A1
Regal Cl HX6 132 C1
Regal Ct WF12 139 E8
Regal Dr HX6 132 C1
Regal Par LS15 62 B2
Regency Ct
Bradford BD8 74 B8
Ilkley LS29 8 A3
Leeds LS6 205 B4
Regency Gdns WF3 120 A8
Regency Park Gr 4 LS28 76 E5
Regency Park Rd LS28 76 E5
Regency Rd 1 WF14 138 A4
Regency View BD3 56 A2
Regent Ave LS18 58 C7
Regent Cl
Brighouse HD6 135 E6
Horsforth LS18 58 C7
Regent Cres
Horsforth LS18 58 C7
South Hiendley S72 180 E5
Regent Ct
Halifax HX3 113 A4
10 Horsforth LS18 58 C7
Huddersfield HD1 153 E7
6 Ilkley LS29 8 A4
Leeds LS1 211 C3
Regent Ho 6 HX5 134 F7
Regent Mews WF17 118 F4
Regent Par 14 HX6 112 C4
Regent Park Ave LS6 205 C4
Regent Park Cross Ave
LS6 205 C4
Regent Park Terr LS6 205 C4
Regent Pl
Bradford BD10 39 A1
15 Hebden Bridge HX7 89 A4
12 Sowerby Bridge HX6 112 B5
Regent Rd
Horsforth LS18 58 B7
Huddersfield HD1 153 E7
Ilkley LS29 8 A4
Kirkheaton HD5 137 C2
Regents Pk WF1 142 E6
Regents Quay LS10 212 A3
Regent St
4 Bacup OL13 106 A2
Bradford BD10 56 D7
Bradford, Thackley BD10 39 A1
Castleford WF10 124 C7
Featherstone WF7 145 C5
Halifax HX1 203 A2
14 Haworth BD22 51 D7
Hebden Bridge HX7 89 A3
Hemsworth WF9 181 C7
Horbury WF4 140 F2
Leeds LS7 204 A3
Leeds, Mabgate LS2, LS7 207 A1
Liversedge WF16 117 C3
Mirfield WF14 138 A3
Normanton WF6 123 C4
Queensbury BD13 72 F1
South Elmsall WF9 182 E3
South Hiendley S72 180 E5
Wakefield WF1 142 E3
Walsden OL14 108 A1
Regent Terr
Leeds, Burley LS6 205 C2
Leeds LS7 204 A3
Regina Cres
Brierley S72 180 E2
Ryhill WF4 162 C1
Regina Dr LS7 204 A2
Regina Ho LS13 77 D8
Reginald Mount LS7 207 A4
Reginald Pl LS7 207 A4
Reginald Row LS7 207 A4
Reginald St
Bradford BD5 74 D3
Leeds LS7 207 A4
Reginald Terr LS7 207 A4
Reginald View LS7 207 A4
Reid Park Ave WF4 140 E1
Reighton Croft BD10 56 E6
Rein Ct LS25 64 E8
Rein Gdns WF3 119 C8
Rein Mews WF3 119 C8
Rein Rd
Horsforth LS18 58 C6
Morley LS27, WF3 98 C1
Reins Ave BD17 38 B1
Reins Rd HD6 135 E8
Rein St LS27 98 C1
Reins Terr HD9 172 A5
Rein The LS14 61 F6
Reinwood Ave
Huddersfield HD3 153 B7
Leeds LS8 61 E5
Reinwood Jun & Inf Schs
HD3 153 B7
Reinwood Rd HD3 153 B6
Rembrandt Ave WF3 119 F8
Renaissance Ct 14 LS27 98 C8
Renaissance Dr 13 LS27 98 C8
Renee Cl BD4 95 C8
Renfield Gr WF6 123 D3
Renshaw St BD10 39 B1
Renton Ave LS20 22 D1
Renton Dr LS20 39 D8
Renton Lea LS20 39 D8
Reservoir Pl
Dewsbury WF13 118 A1
4 Queensbury BD13 72 C2
Reservoir Rd
Batley WF17 117 F4
Halifax HX2 202 A4
Haworth BD22 50 F6
Reservoir Side Rd HD7 170 E6
Reservoir St WF13 118 A1
Reservoir View
Skelmanthorpe HD8 174 E2
Thornton BD13 72 D7
Restmore Ave LS20 22 D2
Retford Ho BD4 75 E1
Retford Pl BD7 74 C5
Reuben Goldberg La BD3 75 D8
Reuben St WF15 117 A5
Reva Cl BD16 37 B4
Reva Syke Rd BD14 73 B4
Revel Garth HD8 192 A5
Revie Rd LS11 213 C3
Reyden Mews LS12 209 C2
Reydon Wlk BD6 73 F1
Reyhill Gr BD5 201 B1
Reynolds Ave BD7 73 E5
Rhine St BD4 201 D1
Rhode's Hill La LS23 30 F3
Rhodes Ave WF16 117 D6
Rhodes Cres WF8 146 D6
Rhodes Gdns
Lofthouse Gate WF3 121 C6
9 Morley LS27 98 B3
Rhodes Ho 2 LS22 13 E6
Rhodesia Ave
Bradford BD15 73 C8
Halifax HX3 113 C3
Rhodesia St BD20 16 D6
Rhodes La LS23 30 C6
Rhodes Pl BD17 55 B8
Rhodes St
Castleford WF10 124 B7
Castleford WF10 124 C8
Halifax HX1 203 A3
Liversedge WF15 117 C4
Shipley BD18 55 A8
Rhodes Terr
Bradford BD2 56 B4
Leeds LS12 210 B2
Rhodesway BD8 73 D8
Rhodesway Sec Sch BD15 73 C8
Rhondda Pl HX1 202 A2
Rhum Cl BD6 93 F6
Rhyddings Ave WF7 163 F5
Rhyddings Dr WF7 163 F5
Rhyddings Gdns LS29 8 D4
Rhyl St WF7 145 D6
Rhylstone Mount BD7 73 F6
Ribble Ct 12 BD20 5 E1
Ribblesdale Ave LS25 83 B6
Ribble St BD21 35 E8
Ribbleton Gr BD3 201 D4
Ribstone St HX7 89 E1
Riccall Nook BD10 56 D6
Rice St 1 HD1 154 B5
Richard Gossop Ct LS29 9 E1
Richard Pl 4 HD6 115 A4
Richardshaw Dr LS28 57 E1
Richardshaw La LS28 76 E8
Richardshaw Rd LS28 57 F1
Richardson Ave BD6 94 C8
Richardson Cres LS9 80 C7
Richardson Rd LS9 80 C7
Richardson Sq 5 HD1 154 A6
Richardson St BD12 95 A4
Richard St
7 Bacup OL13 106 A7
Bradford BD3 201 D3
Brighouse HD6 115 A4
Wakefield WF1 216 B3
Richard Thorpe Ave
WF14 138 B5
Rich Gate HD9 189 B2
Richmond Ave
Huddersfield HD2 136 A2
Knottingley WF11 126 B5
Leeds LS6 205 B4
9 Pontefract WF8 125 D1
Sowerby Bridge HX6 111 F3
Richmond Cl
Halifax HX1 203 B4

Richmond Cl *continued*
Leeds LS13 58 A2
3 Morley LS27 98 A3
Rothwell LS26 100 F6
Richmond Croft LS9 212 C3
Richmond Ct
Crofton WF4 162 A8
Huddersfield HD4 152 F3
Ilkley LS29 8 C3
Leeds LS9 212 C3
10 Pontefract WF8 125 D1
Rothwell LS26 100 F6
Richmondfield Ave LS15 63 E6
Richmondfield Cl LS15 63 E6
Richmondfield Cres LS15 63 E6
Richmondfield Cross LS15 63 E6
Richmondfield Dr LS15 63 E6
Richmondfield Garth LS15 63 E7
Richmondfield Gr LS15 63 E6
Richmondfield La LS15 63 E6
Richmondfield Mount LS15 63 E6
Richmondfield Way LS15 63 E6
Richmondfield Wlk LS15 63 E6
Richmond Flats 7 HD1 154 B7
Richmond Garth WF5 140 F4
Richmond Gdns
Pudsey LS28 77 A7
Sowerby Bridge HX6 111 F3
Richmond Gr BD19 96 B2
Richmond Green St LS9 212 B3
Richmond Hill App LS9 212 B3
Richmond Hill Cl LS9 212 B3
Richmond Hill Prim Sch LS9 212 C2
Richmond Ho 28 BD16 37 A3
Richmond House Apartments 8 HX1 203 A1
Richmond House Sch LS16 59 C7
Richmond Lea WF14 138 A6
Richmond Mews BD18 54 F8
Richmond Mount LS6 205 B4
Richmond Park Ave WF15 117 A3
Richmond Pl
Ilkley LS29 8 C3
16 Shipley BD18 54 F8
Richmond Rd
Batley, Nunroyd WF16 117 E6
Batley WF17 118 D2
Bradford BD7 74 D6
Halifax HX1 203 A4
Leeds LS6 205 B4
Pudsey LS28 57 C2
17 Shipley BD18 54 F8
Upton WF9 183 A7
Wakefield WF1 216 A4
Richmond St
Castleford WF10 124 D7
Cleckheaton BD19 116 D7
Halifax HX1 203 A4
Keighley BD21 35 B8
Leeds LS9 212 B3
8 Todmorden OL14 108 C5
Richmond Terr
Guiseley LS20 22 D1
Otley LS21 22 F7
8 Pontefract WF8 125 D1
Pudsey LS28 77 A7
Richmond Way LS25 82 F5
Rickard St LS12 210 C2
Ridding Gate LS21 10 E1
Riddings Cl
Hemsworth WF9 181 D5
Huddersfield HD2 136 D3
Riddings Rd
Huddersfield HD2 136 D3
Ilkley LS29 8 B4
Riddings Rise HD2 136 E3
Riddlesden St 3 BD20 18 F1
Riddlesden View BD21 35 F7
Riddlesdon St Mary's CE Prim Sch BD20 18 E2
Rider Rd LS6 206 B4
Rider St LS9 212 B4
Ridge Ave WF4 158 A7
Ridge Bank OL14 108 B5
Ridge Cl
Guiseley LS20 39 C8
Huddersfield HD4 154 A3
Skelmanthorpe HD8 175 A1
Ridge Cres WF4 158 A6
Ridgedale Mount WF8 125 D4
Ridgefield St WF10 124 D7
Ridgefoot 2 OL14 108 B5
Ridge Gr LS7 60 A5
Ridge Hill HD6 114 E1
Ridge La BD20 5 C7
Ridge Lea HD6 114 F1
Ridge Mount LS6 206 A4
Ridgemount Rd BD20 18 E2
Ridge Mount Terr LS6 206 A4
Ridge Rd
Kippax LS25 83 D2
Leeds LS7 206 B4
Middlestown WF4 158 A6
Todmorden OL14 108 B5
Ridge St HD4 154 A3
Ridgestone Ave WF9 181 E7
Ridge Stps 20 OL14 108 B5
Ridge Terr LS6 59 E5
Ridge The LS22 13 C3
Ridge View
Elland HX5 135 C6
Pudsey LS13 77 C8
Ridge View Dr HD2 135 D2
Ridge View Gdns BD10 56 C7
Ridge View Rd HD6 115 A1
Ridgeway
Guiseley LS20 39 B8
Huddersfield HD5 154 E7
Queensbury BD13 92 F8
Shipley BD18 55 E6
Ridge Way
Leeds, Gipton Wood LS8 61 A5
Leeds, Gledhow LS8 204 C2
Ridgeway Cl
Huddersfield HD5 154 E7
Leeds LS8 204 C2
Ridgeway Cres S71 179 C1
Ridgeway Dr WF17 97 A1
Ridgeway Gdns HD6 114 E5
Ridgeway Mount BD22 34 F5
Ridgeway Sq WF11 126 F3
Ridgeways The HD7 170 D8
Ridgeway Terr 7 LS6 206 A4
Ridgeway The WF11 126 F3
Ridgewood Cl BD17 38 E3
Riding Head La HX2 90 E1
Riding Hill HX3 93 E6
Riding La HX2 91 D3
Ridings Bsns Pk HX1 202 B2
Ridings Cl WF3 121 B6
Ridings Croft BD5 75 B1
Ridings Ct WF3 121 B6
Ridings Fields HD9 172 C3
Ridings Gdns WF3 121 B6
Ridings La
Holmfirth HD9 189 C7
Huddersfield HD7 152 C4
Lofthouse Gate WF3 121 B6
Ridings Mews WF3 121 B6
Ridings Rd WF13 139 D8
Ridings Sch The HX3 91 F3
Ridings Sh Ctr WF1 216 B2
Riding St WF17 117 E6
Ridings The BD20 18 B3
Ridings Way
Bradford BD6 93 E8
Lofthouse Gate WF3 121 B6
Ridingwood Rise HD8 175 E2
Ridleys Fold LS29 6 F8
Rievaulx Ave BD8 74 C8
Rievaulx Cl LS23 30 C7
Rifle Fields HD1 153 F6
Rifle St HD1 154 B5
Rigg La WF7, WF8 164 E7
Rightox Rd HD9 172 C3
Rigton App LS9 212 B4
Rigton Bank LS17 28 E4
Rigton Cl LS9 212 C4
Rigton Dr LS9 212 B4
Rigton Gn
Bardsey LS17 28 E4
Leeds LS9 212 B4
Rigton Lawn LS9 212 B4
Rigton Mews LS9 212 B4
Rigton St BD5 74 D3
Riley La
Halifax HX2 91 F8
Kirkburton HD8 173 E6
Riley Pk HD8 173 F6
Riley St HD4 154 B4
Rillbank La LS3 205 C1
Rillbank St LS3 205 C2
Rill Ct WF9 181 D7
Rillington Mead BD10 56 D6
Rillside HD8 173 F1
Rills Mead LS21 23 A7
Rilston St BD7 74 B6
Rimswell Holt BD10 56 E6
Ringby La HX3 92 B4
Ringby Terr 1 HX3 92 C2
Ring Hay Rd BD4 76 A1
Ring O'Bells Yd 9 WF4 141 A1
Ring Rd LS15 62 C1
Ring Rd Adel LS16 42 D2
Ring Rd Beeston LS12 78 C3
Ring Rd Beeston Pk LS11 98 F7
Ring Rd Farsley LS28 57 C4
Ring Rd (Horsforth) LS18 58 E8
Ring Rd Low Wortley LS12 78 B4
Ring Rd Meanwood LS17 42 F2
Ring Rd Middleton LS10 99 F6
Ring Rd Moortown LS17 43 D3
Ring Rd Seacroft LS14 62 B6
Ring Rd Shadwell LS17 44 D2
Ring Rd Weetwood LS16 42 C1
Ring Rd West Pk LS16 42 A1
Ring Road Bramley LS13 77 C8
Ring Road Cross Gates LS15 62 C3
Ring Road Farnley LS12 77 E7
Ringstone HX4 133 A1
Ringstone Gr S72 181 B3
Ringway LS25 82 D6
Ringwood Ave LS14 62 A8
Ringwood Cres LS14 62 A8
Ringwood Ct WF1 121 D5
Ringwood Dr LS14 62 A8
Ringwood Edge HX5 134 D6
Ringwood Gdns LS14 62 A8
Ringwood Mount 1 LS14 62 A8
Ringwood Rd BD5 74 C3
Ringwood Way WF9 181 F7
Rink Par 7 WF17 118 D3
Rink St WF17 118 D3
Rink Terr 6 WF17 118 D3
Riparian Way BD20 16 E7
Ripley Cl WF6 123 D2
Ripley Close Ind Pk WF6 123 D2
Ripley Ct WF6 144 B8
Ripley Dr WF6 123 D3
Ripley La LS20 22 E2
Ripley Rd
Bradford BD4 74 F4
Liversedge WF15 116 F4
Ripley St
Bradford BD15 54 A2
Bradford, Ripleyville BD5 74 F4
Brighouse HX3 115 A7
Keighley BD20 18 F1
Ripley Terr HX2 111 D7
Ripon Ave HD2 136 B2
Ripon Ho
5 Elland HX5 134 F7
10 Pudsey LS28 57 D3
6 Sowerby Bridge HX6 112 C4
Ripon Rd WF12 118 F1
Ripon St HX1 202 A2
Ripon Terr HX3 92 B1
Ripponden Jun & Inf Sch HX6 132 E5
Ripponden New Bank HX6, HX4 132 E4
Ripponden Old Bank HX6 132 E4
Ripponden Old La HX6 132 B3
Risedale Ave WF17 97 B2
Risedale Cl WF17 97 B2
Rise La OL14 108 A5
Rise La Ho 22 OL14 108 B5
Rise The
Brierley S72 181 A2
Brotherton WF11 126 C8
Kippax LS25 83 A1
Leeds LS5 59 A5
Northowram HX3 93 A2
Pontefract WF8 146 E7
Rishworth Ave HD8 175 D6
Rishworth Bsns Complex HX6 132 D2
Rishworth Cl WF2 120 E2
Rishworth Hall Cl HX6 132 B1
Rishworthian Ct HX3 113 A1
Rishworth Mill La HX6 150 D8
Rishworth New Rd HX6 132 B1
Rishworth Pal HX6 150 D8
Rishworth Rd
Dewsbury WF12 139 D8
Ripponden HX4 133 A4
Rishworth Sch HX6 132 C2
Rishworth St
Dewsbury WF13 139 D8
Keighley BD22 34 F6
Wakefield WF1 216 B3
Rivadale View LS29 8 B5
Rivelin Rd WF10 124 C6
River Bank Ent Ctr WF13 139 A6
River Bank Way HX5 114 B1
Riverdale LS22 13 F4
Riverdale Ave WF3 121 F2
Riverdale Cl WF3 121 F2
Riverdale Cres WF3 121 F2
Riverdale Ct LS21 23 B8
Riverdale Dr WF3 121 F2
Riverdale Gdns
Boston Spa LS23 30 F7
Otley LS21 23 B8
Riverdale Rd
Lofthouse Gate WF3 121 F2
Otley LS21 23 A8
River Holme View HD9 172 C2
Riverine The HX6 112 D4
Rivermead WF2 142 D3
Rivermead Ct WF1 142 D3
River Mount 4 BD21 18 F1
River Pk HD9 171 F5
Riverside
Clayton West HD8 175 E3
Keighley BD21 35 E7
Wetherby LS22 13 E5
Riverside Ave LS21 11 B2
Riverside Bsns Pk LS29 8 D5
Riverside Cl LS21 11 B1
Riverside Cotts BD20 17 D8
Riverside Cres LS21 11 B1
Riverside Ct
Denby Dale HD8 192 A6
Featherstone WF7 145 C6
Halifax HX3 113 D3
Holmfirth HD9 188 C2
Huddersfield HD4 154 A4
Leeds LS1 211 C3
Shipley BD17 38 A1
Riverside Dr
Cleckheaton BD19 95 D1
Otley LS21 11 B2
Riverside Est BD17 55 B8
Riverside Ind Est
Dewsbury WF12 139 C7
Horbury WF4 158 E8
Riverside Jun Sch HX7 89 A3
Riverside Pk LS21 11 B1
Riverside The HD7 152 D2
Riverside Villas WF2 142 D2
Riverside Way
Dewsbury WF13 138 E4
Leeds LS1 211 A3
Riverside Wlk LS29 7 F5
River St
Brighouse HD6 115 C1
5 Haworth BD22 51 D7
8 Hebden Bridge HX7 88 F3
5 Keighley BD21 18 E1
Todmorden OL14 108 C5
River Valley View HD8 192 A6
River View
Boston Spa LS23 30 F7
Castleford WF10 124 B8
Ilkley LS29 8 E5
Mirfield WF14 137 D6
River Wlk BD16 36 F3
Riverwood Dr HX3 113 B2
Riviera Gdns LS7 60 C6
Rivock Ave
Keighley BD20 17 F3
Steeton BD20 17 D6
Rivock Gr BD20 17 F3
RM Grylls Mid Sch WF15 116 B4
Roach Grange Ave LS25 83 A3
Road End 4 HX4 134 C7
Roaine Dr HD9 189 B4
Roans Brae BD10 56 E6
Robb Ave LS11 214 A1
Robbins Terr WF7 145 D6
Robb St LS11 214 A1
Roberson Terr BD19 117 A8
Robert's St BD19 116 C7
Robert Ct WF15 116 F3
Robert La HD9 189 C7
Robert Ogden Sch The S63 194 B1
Robert St N 3 HX3 92 C2
Roberts Ave LS9 208 B1
Roberts Ct LS9 208 B2
Robertsgate WF3 100 B1
Robertshaw Ho 7 BD16 37 A2
Robertshaw Rd 11 HX7 88 F3
Robertson Ave HD6 136 A8
Roberts Pl LS9 208 C1
Roberts St
Goose Eye BD22 34 C6
Pudsey LS28 57 E1
4 Rothwell LS26 101 C6
Robert St
Bradford BD3 201 D2
9 Halifax HX3 92 A2
Haworth BD22 51 F8
Roberts Way WF2 142 F1
Roberttown CE Jun & Inf Sch WF15 116 E2
Roberttown Grange FW15 116 E2
Roberttown La WF15 116 F2
Robin's Ct BD12 95 A4
Robin's Gr LS26 100 F5
Robin Chase LS28 76 F7
Robin Cl
Bradford BD2 56 C4
Pontefract WF8 125 D3
Robin Dr
Bradford BD2 56 C4
Steeton BD20 17 B6
Robin Hill WF17 118 A8
Robin Hood Ave S71 179 D4
Robin Hood Cres WF2 141 D4
Robin Hood Gr HD2 136 C4
Robin Hood Hill HD4 171 F7
Robin Hood Prim Sch WF3 100 B2
Robin Hood Rd HD2 136 C4
Robin Hood St 1 WF10 124 E7
Robin Hood Way HD6 115 E2
Robinia Wlk WF2 142 A8
Robin La
Batley, Heckmondwike WF13 117 F3
Batley WF13 118 B2
Hemsworth WF9 181 A5
Pudsey LS28 76 E7
Royston S71 179 D4
Robin Rocks HD9 172 C2
Robin Royd Ave WF14 138 A8
Robin Royd Croft WF14 138 A8
Robin Royd Dr WF14 138 A8
Robin Royd Garth WF14 138 A8
Robin Royd Gr WF14 138 A8
Robin Royd La WF14 138 A8
Robinson Ct BD7 73 F6
Robinson La LS25 83 B1
Robinson St
Huddersfield HD1 154 C5
Kippax WF10 103 B4
5 Pontefract WF8 125 D1
Robin St
Bradford BD5 74 C4
Huddersfield HD1 153 D5
Robins The LS29 21 E8
Robin Wlk BD18 55 D6
Robinwood Ct LS8 44 A1
Robinwood Terr OL14 107 E8
Robson's Rd WF1 216 A2
Robson Cl WF8 146 D6
Robsons Dr HD5 154 D6
Rochdale Rd
Bacup OL13 106 A1
Elland HX4 134 B7
Ripponden HX6 131 C2
Slaithwaite HD7 151 F5
Sowerby Bridge, Pye Nest HX2, HX6 112 D5
Sowerby Bridge, Triangle HX6 111 F1
Todmorden, Knowl Wood OL14 108 A3
Todmorden OL14 129 B6
Rocheford Cl LS10 215 C3
Rocheford Ct LS10 215 C3
Rocheford Gdns LS10 215 C3
Rocheford Gr LS10 215 C3
Rocheford Wlk LS10 215 C3
Rochester Cl 3 OL13 106 A7
Rochester Ct WF4 141 C3
Rochester Dr WF4 141 C2
Rochester Gdns LS13 57 F4
Rochester Pl 5 HX5 134 F6
Rochester Rd WF17 96 F3
Rochester St
Bradford BD3 75 C7
Shipley BD18 55 C6
Rochester Terr LS6 205 A4
Rochester Wynd LS17 44 A4
Rockcliffe Ave BD17 38 C1
Rock Cliffe Mount HX2 111 D7
Rock Cotts HD9 189 E7
Rock Ct
Halifax HX3 92 A3
Morley LS27 98 B5
Rock Edge WF15 117 A5
Rockery Croft LS18 41 C2
Rockery Rd LS18 41 C2
Rockfield LS19 40 C7
Rockfield Terr 10 LS19 40 C7
Rock Fold HD7 152 D4
Rock Hill WF10 125 A6
Rockhill Cl WF17 96 F1
Rockhill La BD4 95 A7
Rock House Dr WF13 118 C2
Rockingham Cl LS15 62 F3
Rockingham La WF9 164 E4
Rockingham Rd LS15 62 F3
Rockingham St WF9 163 B3
Rockingham Way LS15 62 F3
Rock La
Leeds LS13 58 B4
Slaithwaite HD7 152 A3
Thornton BD13 72 C8
Rockland Cres BD7 73 E5
Rocklands Ave 2 BD17 38 C4
Rocklands Pl 3 BD17 38 C4
Rock Lea 5 BD13 72 F1
Rockley Cl HD5 154 E4
Rockley Dr WF2 160 B6
Rockley Grange Gdns LS25 82 D5
Rockley St WF13 139 D8
Rockliffe La OL13 106 A1
Rockliffe Rd OL13 106 A1
Rockmill Rd HD9 172 C2
Rock Nook OL15 129 D1
Rock Rd HD3 135 B2
Rocks La HX2 71 D1
Rocks Rd HX3 113 A4
Rock St
15 Brighouse HD6 115 A3
Huddersfield HD3 152 E7
Rocks View 3 HX2 113 A4
Rock Terr
Bradford BD8 55 D1
Brighouse HX3 114 D8
Castleford WF10 125 A6
Huddersfield HD3 135 B1
2 Leeds LS15 80 F8
Thornton BD13 72 D6
Walsden OL14 108 A2
Rock The HD7 152 E1
Rock View
Elland HX4 134 C4
Marsden HD7 168 F3
Rock Villas HD8 175 D1
Rockville Terr
15 Halifax HX1 202 C1
Yeadon LS19 40 C6
Rockwell La BD10 56 C6
Rockwood Cl
Darton S75 177 F1
Huddersfield HD2 136 E6
Rockwood Cres
Crigglestone WF4 159 D6
Pudsey LS28 57 A3
Rockwood Gr LS28 57 B3
Rockwood Hill Ct LS28 57 A2
Rockwood Rd LS28 57 A2
Rockwood Rise HD8 192 A7
Roderick St LS12 209 B3
Rodger La WF2 120 F2
Rodillian Sch WF3 100 B1
Rodin Ave BD8 73 D7
Rodley La
Emley HD8 175 D7
Leeds LS13 58 A4
Pudsey LS28, S13 57 D6
Rodney Yd WF1 216 B2
Rods Mills La LS27 98 B3
Rods View 4 LS27 98 B3
Roebuck La LS21 10 F4
Roebuck Meml Homes HD5 154 F6
Roebuck St WF17 96 F1
Roeburn Cl
Bradford BD6 73 E1
Darton S75 178 A2
Roedhelm Rd BD20 36 B8
Roe Ho BD17 38 B1
Roger Ct BD2 56 B2
Roger Dr WF2 142 D1
Roger Fold 1 LS25 83 B1
Roger Gate HX7 89 C1
Roger La HD4 154 C1
Rogers Ct WF3 121 F6
Rogerson Sq HD6 115 A3
Rogers Pl LS28 76 F8
Roils Head Rd HX2 112 C7
Rokeby Gdns
Bradford BD10 56 E6
Leeds LS6 59 C5
Roker La LS28 77 A5
Roman Ave
Huddersfield HD3 134 D1
Leeds LS8 44 A3
Romanby Shaw BD10 56 D6
Roman Cl HD3 134 D1

oman Cres LS8 44 B2
oman Dr
Huddersfield HD3 134 D1
Leeds LS8 44 B2
oman Gdns LS8 44 A2
oman Gr LS8 44 B2
oman Mount LS8 44 B2
oman Pl LS8 44 B2
oman Rd 5 WF17 117 F8
oman Rise WF8 146 C5
oman St S63 194 E1
oman Terr LS8 44 A2
oman View
Castleford WF10 125 B6
Leeds LS8 44 B2
ombald's View LS29 8 D5
ombalds Ave LS12 209 C4
ombalds Cres LS12 59 C1
ombalds Croft LS19 40 B7
ombalds Ct LS29 21 F4
ombalds Dr BD16 37 B3
ombalds Gr LS12 209 C4
ombalds La LS29 8 E3
ombalds Pl 1 LS12 59 C1
ombalds St LS12 59 C1
ombalds Terr LS12 209 C4
ombalds View
Leeds LS12 59 C1
Otley LS21 10 D2
omford Ave LS27 98 A3
omford Ct BD6 93 F6
omney Mount LS28 77 A5
omsey Cl HD3 134 F1
omsey Gdns BD4 75 E3
omsey Mews BD4 75 D3
omwood Cl WF9 163 B2
ona Croft LS26 101 A5
onald Dr BD7 74 A7
onaldsway Cl OL13 106 B1
on Lawton Cres LS29 21 D8
oo's Ct LS18 41 C1
oods La HD9 188 B3
ook's Nest Jun & Inf Sch
WF1 121 C4
ook's Nest Rd WF1 121 D4
ookeries Carleton Jun & Inf
Sch The WF8 146 E6
ookery La HX3 113 D3
ookery Pl HD6 115 B3
ookery The 13 LS29 6 F8
ookes Ave BD6 94 C8
ookes La HX3 94 A1
ookes View HX3 94 A2
ookhill Dr WF8 146 E7
ookhill Mount WF8 146 F7
ookhill Rd WF8 146 F7
ook La BD4 75 C2
ooks Ave BD19 116 C8
ooks Cl BD12 94 D1
ook St
Bingley BD16 36 F3
Huddersfield HD1 154 A7
ookwith Par BD10 56 E6
ookwood Ave
Kippax LS25 103 A8
Leeds LS9 80 D8
ookwood Cres LS9 80 C8
ookwood Croft LS9 80 C7
ookwood Gdns LS9 80 C8
ookwood Hill LS9 80 C8
ookwood Mount LS9 80 C8
ookwood Par LS9 80 C8
ookwood Pl LS9 80 C8
ookwood Rd LS9 80 C8
ookwood Sq LS9 80 D8
ookwood St LS9 80 C7
ookwood Terr LS9 80 C8
ookwood Vale LS9 80 C7
ookwood View LS9 80 C8
ooley Ave BD6 74 E1
ooley Banks HX6 111 E3
ooley Cl BD5 74 E1
ooley Cres BD6 94 E8
ooley Ct HX6 111 D3
ooley Hts HX6 111 D3
ooley La
Bradford BD4, BD5 75 B1
Sowerby Bridge HX6 111 D3
oomfield Ct 13 OL14 108 B5
oomfield Ho OL14 108 B5
oomfield St OL14 108 B5
ooms Fold LS27 98 A6
ooms La
Gildersome LS27 98 A8
Morley LS27 98 A6
ooms Way LS27 98 A7
oper Ave LS8 204 C4
opergate WF8 146 C8
opergate End WF8 146 C8
opergate Service Rd 4
WF8 146 C8
oper Gdns HX2 91 D4
oper Gn HX2 91 D4
oper Gr LS8 204 C4
oper La
Halifax HX2 91 F8
Queensbury BD13 72 B2
opers Arms Flats The
WF11 127 B4
oper St BD21 35 B7
opewalk WF11 127 A4
ope Wlk HX2 90 F7
ordin Hts HD2 136 C4
oscoe St LS7 207 A2
oseate Gn LS27 98 C3
ose Ave
Horsforth LS18 58 B7

Rose Ave *continued*
Huddersfield, Cowersley
HD4 152 F3
Huddersfield, Marsh HD3 153 C6
Upton WF9 183 A7
Rose Bank
5 Bradford BD8 55 C2
Burley in W LS29 21 E8
7 Otley LS21 23 A7
Rosebank Cres LS3 205 C2
Rosebank Gdns LS3 205 C1
Rosebank Ho LS6 205 C2
Rose Bank Pl BD8 73 E7
Rosebank Prim Sch LS3 205 C1
Rosebank Rd LS3 205 C1
Rose Bank Rd OL14 108 A5
Rosebank Row LS3 205 C1
Rosebank St WF17 118 B6
Roseberry St BD22 34 D2
Rosebery Ave
Halifax HX3 113 D4
Shipley BD18 55 C7
Rosebery Mount BD18 55 D7
Rosebery Rd BD8 55 C2
Rosebery St
Elland HX5 134 F6
3 Huddersfield HD2 135 F1
Pudsey LS28 76 C8
Todmorden OL14 86 C1
Rosebery Terr
Halifax HX1 202 C4
4 Pudsey LS28 57 F2
Rosebud Wlk LS8 207 B2
Rosechapel Cl BD6 93 F6
Rose Cl WF9 183 A7
Rosecliffe Mount LS13 58 C2
Rosecliffe Terr LS13 58 C2
Rose Croft LS17 28 C6
Rose Ct LS25 83 A7
Rose Ct (Leeds Girls High
Sch) LS6 205 C4
Rosedale LS26 100 F6
Rosedale Ave
Bradford BD15 53 F2
16 Huddersfield HD5 154 D5
Liversedge WF15 116 D2
Wakefield WF2 160 E8
Rosedale Bank LS10 215 A1
Rosedale Cl
Baildon BD17 38 A2
Normanton WF6 123 D1
Upton WF9 183 B7
Rosedale Ct
Birkenshaw BD4 95 E7
East Ardsley WF3 119 E6
Rosedale Dr WF3 119 E6
Rosedale Gdns
East Ardsley WF3 120 B8
Middleton LS10 215 A1
Rosedale Gn LS10 215 A1
Rosedale Ho WF13 118 C2
Rosedale Rise LS23 30 C7
Rosedale Wlk LS10 215 A1
Rose Farm App WF6 122 F4
Rose Farm Cl WF6 122 F5
Rose Farm Fold WF6 122 F5
Rose Farm Mdws WF6 122 F4
Rose Farm Rise WF6 122 F5
Rose Garth
Crofton WF4 143 F1
Menston LS29 21 C7
Rosegarth Ave HD9 189 C7
Rose Gr
17 Hebden Bridge HX7 89 A4
Mytholmroyd HX7 110 E8
Rothwell LS26 100 D6
Upton WF9 183 A7
Rose Grove La HX6 112 A5
Rose Heath HX2 91 D7
Rosehill Ave WF9 181 C6
Rosehill Cres BD12 94 C4
Rose Hill Dr HD2 135 D1
Rosehip Rise BD14 73 B3
Rose La WF9 163 D4
Roselee Cl HX3 113 E3
Rose Lynn Terr BD6 93 F7
Rosemary Ave LS12 210 A3
Rosemary Cl HD6 115 A1
Rosemary Gdns BD15 54 A1
Rosemary La
Brighouse HD6 115 A1
Halifax HX3 113 E3
Rose Mdws BD22 34 E5
Rosemont LS16 24 E3
Rosemont Ave
7 Leeds LS13 58 C2
4 Pudsey LS28 76 F8
Rosemont Dr LS28 76 F8
Rosemont Gr 8 LS13 58 C2
Rosemont La 2 BD17 38 D2
Rosemont Pl LS13 58 C2
Rosemont Rd LS13 58 C2
Rosemont St
Leeds LS13 58 C2
5 Pudsey LS28 76 F8
Rosemont Terr
Leeds LS13 58 C2
Pudsey LS28 76 F8
Rosemont View LS13 58 C2
Rosemont Wlk 6 LS13 58 C2
Rosemount OL13 106 A4
Rose Mount
Birkenshaw BD4 96 A8
Bradford BD2 56 A3
Huddersfield HD2 135 D1
Rosemount Ave HX5 135 A6
Rosemount Cl 2 BD21 35 B7
Rosemount Ct BD20 16 D4

Rosemount Dr WF6 123 D1
Rose Mount Pl LS12 210 A2
Rosemount Terr HX5 135 A6
Rosemount Wlk 1 BD21 35 B7
Rosendale Cl 5 OL13 106 B3
Rosendale Cres OL13 106 B3
Roseneath Pl LS12 210 A2
Roseneath St LS12 210 A2
Roseneath Terr LS12 210 A2
Rose Pl HX2 111 E5
Rose St
Bradford BD8 55 B1
Halifax HX1 202 B2
Haworth BD22 51 C6
Horsforth LS18 58 B8
Keighley BD21 35 F7
Todmorden OL14 108 B5
Rose Terr
11 Addingham LS29 6 F8
3 Halifax HX1 202 C3
2 Halifax, King Cross
HX2 113 A4
Horsforth LS18 58 A7
Huddersfield HD1 154 B8
Low Bradley BD20 4 C5
Rosetta Dr BD8 73 F8
Rosevale View HX6 112 C5
Rose Villas HX7 110 D8
Roseville Rd LS8 207 B2
Roseville St LS8 207 B2
Roseville Terr
Dewsbury WF12 139 F8
4 Leeds LS15 62 D3
Roseville Way LS8 207 B2
Rosewood Ave
Keighley BD20 18 F1
Kippax LS25 82 F3
Rosewood Ct
4 Leeds LS17 43 A3
Rothwell LS26 100 F7
Rosewood Gr BD4 75 D5
Rosewood Sq BD20 16 D4
Rosgill Dr LS14 62 A5
Rosgill Gn LS14 62 A5
Rosgill Wlk LS14 61 F5
Rosley Mount BD6 93 F6
Roslyn Ave HD4 171 C7
Roslyn Pl BD7 74 B6
Rossall Gr LS8 207 C4
Rossall Rd LS8 207 C4
Rossefield App LS13 58 D2
Rossefield Ave
Huddersfield HD2 135 E1
Leeds LS13 58 D2
Rossefield Chase LS13 58 D2
Rossefield Cl 3 LS13 58 D2
Rossefield Dr LS13 58 D2
Rossefield Gdns 8 LS13 58 D2
Rossefield Gn LS13 58 D2
Rossefield Gr LS13 58 D2
Rossefield Lawn LS13 58 D2
Rossefield Par LS13 58 D2
Rosse Field Pk BD9 55 B4
Rossefield Pl LS13 58 D2
Rossefield Rd BD9 55 A4
Rossefield Terr LS13 58 D2
Rossefield View LS13 58 D2
Rossefield Way LS13 58 C2
Rossefield Wlk 5 LS13 58 D2
Rossendale Pl 6 BD18 55 A7
Rossendale View OL14 109 A4
Rosse St
Bradford BD8 74 A8
Shipley BD18 55 B8
Rossett Bsns Pk LS13 58 B4
Rossett Ho BD3 201 C4
Ross Gr LS13 58 B4
Rossington Gr 4 LS8 207 B4
Rossington Pl 6 LS8 207 B4
Rossington Rd LS8 61 A5
Rossington St LS2 211 B4
Rossiter Dr WF11 126 D3
Rosslyn Ave WF7 163 F5
Rosslyn Cl WF7 163 F5
Rosslyn Ct
Ackworth M T WF7 163 F5
Dewsbury WF12 139 F7
Rosslyn Gr
Ackworth M T WF7 163 F5
Haworth BD22 51 C6
Rossmore Dr BD15 54 C1
Ross Terr LS13 58 A4
Rotcher HD7 169 E8
Rotcher La HD7 169 E8
Rotcher Rd HD9 189 A5
Rothbury Gdns LS16 42 B3
Rotherby Ct HX1 202 C4
Rother Garth WF9 183 B2
Rother Mews WF9 183 B2
Rothesay Terr BD7 74 C6
Rothwell CE Prim Sch
LS26 100 E6
Rothwell Dr HX1 203 A1
Rothwell Haigh Road Inf Sch
LS26 100 E6
Rothwell La LS26 101 B5
Rothwell Mount HX1 203 A1
Rothwell Prim Sch LS26 100 E4
Rothwell Rd HX1 203 A1
Rothwell St Mary's RC Prim
Sch LS26 100 F4
Rothwell St HD5 154 E6
Rough Hall La HX2 90 F5
Round Close Rd HD9 199 B6
Roundell Ave BD4 95 B8
Roundfield Pl BD13 72 D7
Roundhay Ave LS8 204 C1
Roundhay Cres LS8 204 C1

Roundhay Gdns LS8 204 C1
Roundhay Gr LS8 204 C1
Roundhay Hall Hospl LS8 61 A7
Roundhay Mount LS8 204 C1
Roundhay Park La LS17 44 B4
Roundhay Pk★ LS8 44 C1
Roundhay Pl LS8 204 C1
Roundhay Rd LS7, LS8 207 C3
Roundhay Sch Technology
Coll LS8 61 A7
Roundhay View LS8 204 C1
Roundhead Fold BD10 56 E8
Roundhill BD13 92 C8
Round Hill
Darton S75 178 A1
Halifax HX2 91 F6
Roundhill Ave BD16 54 B7
Round Hill Cl
Bradford BD14 73 B2
Halifax HX2 91 F6
Skelmanthorpe HD8 174 E2
Roundhill Jun Sch WF11 126 B5
Round Hill La HD5 137 B3
Roundhill Mount BD16 54 B7
Roundhill Pl BD1 201 A3
Round Hill Pl BD13 73 B2
Roundhill Rd WF10 124 D7
Roundhill St BD5 74 D4
Round Ings Rd HD3 152 A6
Round St
Bradford BD5 74 E3
Wakefield WF1 142 E4
Round Thorn Pl BD8 74 A8
Roundway HD9 172 A3
Roundway The LS27 97 F4
Roundwell Rd WF15 116 C5
Roundwood BD18 54 F7
Roundwood Ave
Baildon BD17 38 F3
Bradford BD10 56 E4
Round Wood Ave HD5 155 A6
Roundwood Cres WF2 141 C5
Roundwood Glen BD10 56 E6
Roundwood Ind Est WF5 141 B5
Roundwood Rd
Baildon BD17 38 E4
Ossett WF5 141 A4
Roundwood Rise WF2 141 D4
Roundwood View BD10 56 E6
Rouse Fold BD4 201 C1
Rouse Mill La WF17 118 D4
Rouse St 7 WF15 117 A4
Row HD7 169 C8
Rowan Ave
Bradford BD3 75 E7
Huddersfield HD4 171 D6
Normanton WF6 144 A7
Rowan Avenue Mews
HD4 171 D6
Rowanberry Cl BD2 56 B4
Rowan Cl
Batley WF17 97 A2
Knottingley WF11 126 E2
Pool LS21 24 E6
Rowan Ct
Bradford BD2 56 C1
Rothwell LS26 101 E6
Wakefield WF2 141 F8
Yeadon LS19 40 B5
Rowan Dr HD6 115 C3
Rowan Garth BD20 16 D6
Rowan Gn WF8 125 F1
Rowan La S72 180 E6
Rowan Pl LS25 83 B6
Rowan St BD20 18 A2
Rowans The
Baildon BD17 37 F3
Bramhope LS16 24 F2
Pudsey LS13 57 F3
Wetherby LS22 14 A6
Rowantree Ave BD17 38 B4
Rowantree Dr BD10 56 C6
Rowan Way HX3 93 A4
Rowanwood Gdns BD10 56 E5
Rowe Cl WF9 183 A4
Rowgate HD8 191 B6
Row Gate HD8 190 D6
Row La
Marsden HD7 169 C8
Sowerby Bridge HX6 111 D3
Rowland La HX7 89 C4
Rowland Pl LS11 214 B3
Rowland Rd LS11 214 B3
Rowlands Ave
Huddersfield HD5 154 F6
Upton WF9 183 A7
Rowland St S71 179 D4
Rowland Terr 6 LS11 214 C3
Rowlestone Rise BD10 56 E6
Rowley Croft WF9 183 A2
Rowley Ct
Lepton HD8 155 F3
South Elmsall WF9 183 A2
Rowley Dr
Ilkley LS29 8 F3
Lepton HD8 155 D3
Rowley La
Lepton HD8 155 E2
South Elmsall WF9 183 A2
Rowsley St 1 BD21 35 D7
Row St HD4 153 E4
Row The LS19 40 A4
Rowton Thorpe BD10 56 E6
Roxburghe Dale WF6 123 D1
Roxburgh Gr BD15 73 B8
Roxburgh Mews 4 LS13 58 F2
Roxby Cl LS9 207 B1
Roxby St BD5 74 D3

Roxholme Ave LS7 204 B1
Roxholme Gr LS7 204 B1
Roxholme Pl LS7 204 B1
Roxholme Rd LS7 204 B1
Roxholme Terr LS7 204 B1
Royal Acre HD7 152 B5
Royal Armouries Mus The★
LS10 212 A2
Royal Birkdale Way 7
WF6 123 D1
Royal Bsns Pk WF8 146 B8
Royal Cl
Bradford BD7 73 F3
Leeds LS10 215 A2
Royal Ct
Leeds LS10 215 A2
Pontefract WF8 146 B5
Royal Dr LS10 215 A2
Royal Gdns
Bradford BD9 54 D3
Leeds LS10 215 A2
Royal Gr LS10 215 A2
Royal Ind Pk HX1 203 A3
Royal Lofts The 2 HX6 112 B3
Royal London Ind Est The
LS11 213 C1
Royal Park Ave LS6 205 C3
Royal Park Gr LS6 205 C3
Royal Park Mount LS6 205 C3
Royal Park Rd LS6 205 C2
Royal Park Terr LS6 205 C3
Royal Park View LS6 205 C3
Royal Pl LS10 215 A2
Royal Terr
Boston Spa LS23 30 E8
Huddersfield HD3 153 A5
Royd Ave
Batley WF16 117 D6
Bingley BD16 37 C3
Darton S75 178 B1
Holmfirth HD9 189 E6
Huddersfield, Ainley Top
HD3 135 A3
Royd Cl BD20 16 D6
Royd Cotts OL14 108 B7
Royd Cres
Halifax HX1 202 B4
Mytholmroyd HX7 89 F1
Royd Croft HD3 153 B6
Roydfield St HD2 136 B2
Royd Head Farm WF5 140 C5
Roydhouse HD8 174 D5
Royd House Gr BD21 35 E5
Royd House La HD7 152 D1
Royd House Rd BD21 35 E5
Royd House Way BD21 35 E5
Royd House Wlk BD21 35 E5
Royd Ings Ave BD21 18 D1
Royd La
Halifax HX3 92 A3
Halifax, Illingworth HX2 91 E7
Holmfirth HD9 188 E2
Keighley BD20 18 B1
Ripponden HX6 132 D4
Todmorden OL14 108 B6
Roydlands St HX3 114 D7
Royd Mill Bsns Pk HD6 115 C2
Royd Moor La WF9 164 C1
Royd Moor Rd BD4 75 F1
Royd Mount
5 Halifax HX3 92 C2
Holmfirth HD9 189 A5
Roydon Gr BD9 55 A2
Royd Pl HX3 92 C2
Royd Rd
Meltham HD9 187 E8
Todmorden OL14 108 B7
Royd St Ave HD3 153 A5
Royds Ave
Birkenshaw BD11 96 B5
Brighouse HD6 115 B8
Castleford WF10 125 C8
Holmfirth HD9 189 D6
Huddersfield HD3 153 C5
Ossett WF5 140 C8
Slaithwaite HD7 152 D2
Royds Cl
Holmfirth HD9 189 D6
Leeds LS12 78 C4
Roydscliffe Dr BD9 54 F4
Roydscliffe Rd BD9 54 F4
Royds Cres HD6 115 B7
Royds Ct LS12 78 C4
Roydsdale Way BD4 95 A6
Royds Dr HD9 189 D6
Royds Edge HD9 170 E1
Royds Ent Pk BD6 73 E1
Royds Farm Rd LS12 78 C3
Royds Gr WF1 121 C5
Royds Hall Ave BD6 94 C8
Royds Hall High Sch
HD3 153 C6
Royds Hall La
Bradford BD12, BD6 94 B5
Bradford, Moor Top BD6 94 A7
Royds Hall Rd LS12 78 C4
Royds La
Leeds, Far Royds LS12 78 C4
Leeds LS12 78 C3
Rothwell LS26 101 A3
Royds Mount HD8 174 A7
Royds Park Cres BD12 94 D4
Royds Pk HD8 192 A6
Royds Sch Specialist
Language Coll LS26 101 B2

Royds St HD7 . . . . **168** F3
Royd St
Batley WF17 . . . . **118** E3
3 Bradford BD12 . . . . **94** C4
Huddersfield HD3 . . . . **153** A5
Keighley BD20 . . . . **18** B2
Slaithwaite HD7 . . . . **151** F1
Thornton BD13 . . . . **72** C6
Todmorden OL14 . . . . **108** A6
Wilsden BD15 . . . . **53** C5
Royds The
Clayton West HD8 . . . . **176** A3
Holmfirth HD9 . . . . **189** A5
Roydstone Rd BD3 . . . . **75** D8
Roydstone Terr BD3 . . . . **75** D8
Royds View HD7 . . . . **152** D1
Royd Terr
Hebden Bridge HX7 . . . . **89** A3
Huddersfield HD4 . . . . **171** E8
Royd The HX6 . . . . **132** D4
Royd View HX7 . . . . **89** E1
Royd Way BD21 . . . . **18** C1
Royd Well BD11 . . . . **96** B5
Royd Wells WF14 . . . . **138** A6
Royd Wood
Cleckheaton BD19 . . . . **116** D6
Oxenhope BD22 . . . . **51** D4
Roydwood Terr BD13 . . . . . . **52** D6
Roydwood Terr (Back)
BD13 . . . . **52** D6
Royle Fold WF16 . . . . **117** D4
Royles Cl WF9 . . . . **182** C2
Royles Head La HD3 . . . . . . **152** E6
Roy Rd BD6 . . . . **73** D1
Roy St OL14 . . . . **86** A1
Royston Cl WF3 . . . . **120** D6
Royston High Sch S71 . . . . . **179** B3
Royston Hill WF3 . . . . **120** D6
Royston La S71 . . . . **179** C2
Royston Meadstead Prim Sch
S71 . . . . **179** B3
Royston Parkside Prim Sch
S71 . . . . **179** C3
Royston Rd S72 . . . . **180** B1
Royston St John the Baptist
CE Prim Sch S71 . . . . **179** C3
Royston Summer Fields Prim
Sch S71 . . . . **179** A4
RSPB Fairburn Ings Visitor
Ctr ★ WF10 . . . . **104** C4
Ruby St
Batley WF17 . . . . **118** A7
Keighley BD22 . . . . **35** A4
Leeds LS9 . . . . **207** B1
Rudding Ave BD15 . . . . **54** A1
Rudding Cres BD15 . . . . **54** A1
Rudding Dr WF17 . . . . **117** F6
Rudding St HD4 . . . . **153** D4
Rudd La HX7 . . . . **110** A3
Rudd St **11** BD7 . . . . **74** A4
Rudgate
Newton Kyme LS24 . . . . **31** D4
Thorp Arch LS23, LS24 . . . . **15** D5
Rudgate Ct LS23 . . . . **15** C2
Rudgate HM Prison LS23 . . **15** A2
Rudgate Mews LS23 . . . . **15** A3
Rudgate Pk LS23 . . . . **15** A3
Ruffield Side BD12 . . . . **94** C5
Rufford Ave BD15 . . . . **40** C6
Rufford Bank LS19 . . . . **40** C6
Rufford Cl
Ryhill WF4 . . . . **162** A1
Yeadon LS19 . . . . **40** C6
Rufford Cres LS19 . . . . **40** C6
Rufford Ct HD3 . . . . **152** F5
Rufford Dr LS19 . . . . **40** C6
Rufford Gdns LS19 . . . . **40** B6
Rufford Park Prim Sch
LS19 . . . . **40** B6
Rufford Pl **2** HX3 . . . . . . **113** B4
Rufford Rd
Elland HX5 . . . . **134** F6
Halifax HX3 . . . . **113** B4
Huddersfield HD3 . . . . **152** F5
Rufford Ridge LS19 . . . . **40** C6
Rufford Rise LS19 . . . . **40** B6
Rufford St
Bradford BD3 . . . . **75** C7
Wakefield WF2 . . . . **141** F6
Rufford Villas **4** HX3 . . . . **113** B4
Rufus St
Bradford BD5 . . . . **74** B3
6 Keighley BD21 . . . . **35** C8
Rugby Ave HX3 . . . . **91** F3
Rugby Dr HX3 . . . . **91** F3
Rugby Gdns HX3 . . . . **91** F3
Rugby Mount HX3 . . . . **91** F3
Rugby Pl BD7 . . . . **74** B6
Rugby Terr HX3 . . . . **91** F3
Rumble Rd WF12 . . . . **118** F1
Rumbold Rd HD3 . . . . **153** D7
Rumple Croft LS21 . . . . **10** E2
Runnymede Ct BD10 . . . . **56** B7
Runswick Ave **1** LS11 . . . **210** C1
Runswick Gr BD5 . . . . **74** D1
Runswick Pl LS11 . . . . **211** A1
Runswick St
Bradford BD5 . . . . **74** D1
Leeds LS11 . . . . **211** A1
Runswick Terr
Bradford BD5 . . . . **74** D1
Leeds LS11 . . . . **211** A1
Runtlings WF5 . . . . **140** C5
Runtlings La WF5 . . . . **140** C4
Runtlings The WF5 . . . . **140** B5

Rupert Rd LS29 . . . . **8** A5
Rupert St
Haworth BD22 . . . . **51** F8
5 Keighley BD21 . . . . **35** C8
Ruscombe Pl S71 . . . . **179** C1
Rush Croft BD10 . . . . **38** F1
Rushcroft Terr BD17 . . . . . . **38** C3
Rushdene Ct BD12 . . . . **94** C1
Rushfield Vale HD8 . . . . **155** C4
Rushmoor Rd BD4 . . . . **75** D2
Rusholme Dr LS28 . . . . **57** C3
Rushton Ave BD3 . . . . **75** E8
Rushton Hill Cl HX2 . . . . **91** C1
Rushton Rd BD3 . . . . **75** E8
Rushton St
Halifax HX1 . . . . **202** B4
Pudsey LS28 . . . . **57** B6
Rushton Terr BD3 . . . . **75** E7
Rushworth Cl WF3 . . . . **121** E5
Rushworth St **18** HX3 . . . . . **92** A1
Ruskin Ave
Bradford BD9 . . . . **54** D3
Wakefield WF1 . . . . **121** A3
Ruskin Cl WF10 . . . . **125** B8
Ruskin Cres LS20 . . . . **39** F8
Ruskin Ct WF2 . . . . **120** F2
Ruskin Dr WF10 . . . . **125** B8
Ruskin Gr HD2 . . . . **136** D3
Ruskin Pl WF10 . . . . **125** B8
Ruskin St LS28 . . . . **57** C1
Ruskin Terr **24** HX3 . . . . . . **92** A1
Russel Ct LS17 . . . . **28** D3
Russell Ave
Crigglestone WF4 . . . . **159** F3
Queensbury BD13 . . . . **92** E8
Russell Cl
Batley, Heckmondwike
WF16 . . . . **117** E3
Batley WF17 . . . . **118** C5
Russell Gr BD11 . . . . **96** B5
Russell Hall La **15** BD13 . . **72** E1
Russell Hall Prim Sch
BD13 . . . . **72** E1
Russell Rd BD13 . . . . **92** D8
Russell St
Bradford BD5 . . . . **201** A1
Dewsbury WF13 . . . . **118** A1
Halifax HX1 . . . . **203** B3
Keighley BD21 . . . . **35** B7
Leeds LS1 . . . . **211** B4
Queensbury BD13 . . . . **72** E1
Shipley BD18 . . . . **55** C5
Todmorden OL14 . . . . **108** C5
Wakefield WF1 . . . . **142** C4
Russet Fold WF15 . . . . **117** A5
Russets The WF2 . . . . **160** E6
Russett Gr HD4 . . . . **154** C3
Russetts The HX3 . . . . **113** E8
Rustic Ave HX3 . . . . **114** A4
Rustless Cl BD19 . . . . **116** A6
Ruston Dr S71 . . . . **179** C4
Ruswarp Cres BD10 . . . . **56** D6
Ruth Ho BD3 . . . . **201** D3
Ruth St
15 Haworth BD22 . . . . **51** E8
Huddersfield HD4 . . . . **154** A2
Ruthven View LS8 . . . . **208** A3
Rutland Ave
Pontefract WF8 . . . . **146** D5
Wakefield WF2 . . . . **142** C2
Rutland Cl
Kippax LS25 . . . . **83** B2
6 Rothwell LS26 . . . . **101** D6
Rutland Ct **3** LS28 . . . . **76** E8
Rutland Dr
Crofton WF4 . . . . **143** C2
Kippax LS25 . . . . **83** B2
Rutland Ho **5** BD16 . . . . . . **37** A3
Rutland Ind Est WF1 . . . . . . **142** D4
Rutland Mount LS3 . . . . **210** C4
Rutland Rd
Batley WF17 . . . . **118** D6
Flockton WF4 . . . . **157** C3
Huddersfield HD3 . . . . **153** A5
Rutland St
Bradford BD4 . . . . **201** D1
7 Keighley BD21 . . . . **35** B5
Leeds LS3 . . . . **211** A4
Rutland Terr LS18 . . . . **210** C4
Rutland Wlk **7** WF13 . . . . . **139** B8
Ryan Gr BD22 . . . . **34** D8
Ryan Pl LS8 . . . . **208** A4
Ryan St BD5 . . . . **74** D3
Ryburn HX4 . . . . **133** D4
Ryburn Bldgs **3** HX6 . . . . . **112** B3
Ryburn Ct HX1 . . . . **202** B3
Ryburn Ho **6** HX1 . . . . **202** B3
Ryburn La HX6 . . . . **132** E5
Ryburn Pl WF2 . . . . **216** A1
Ryburn Rd HD3 . . . . **153** B7
Ryburn St HX6 . . . . **112** B3
Ryburn Terr
Halifax HX1 . . . . **202** B3
Ripponden HX6 . . . . **132** C1
Ryburn Valley High Sch
HX6 . . . . **111** E3
Ryburn View HX6 . . . . **132** C3
Rycroft Ave
Pudsey LS13 . . . . **58** B1
Shipley BD16 . . . . **54** A6
Rycroft Cl LS13 . . . . **58** B1
Rycroft Ct LS13 . . . . **58** B1
Rycroft Dr LS13 . . . . **58** B1
Rycroft Gdns LS13 . . . . **58** B1
Rycroft Gn LS13 . . . . **58** B1
Rycroft Pl LS13 . . . . **58** B1
Rycroft St BD18 . . . . **55** D5

Rycroft Twrs LS13 . . . . **58** A1
Rydal Ave
Baildon BD17 . . . . **37** E1
Garforth LS25 . . . . **82** F6
Shipley BD9 . . . . **55** C4
Rydal Cres
Morley LS27 . . . . **98** D5
Wakefield WF2 . . . . **141** E7
Rydal Dr
Huddersfield HD5 . . . . **154** D6
Morley LS27 . . . . **98** D5
Wakefield WF2 . . . . **141** E7
Rydale Ct
Cleckheaton WF15 . . . . **116** D4
Ossett WF5 . . . . **140** D4
Rydale Mews WF5 . . . . **140** D4
Rydal Gr WF15 . . . . **117** A1
Rydall Pl LS11 . . . . **210** C1
Rydall St LS11 . . . . **210** C1
Rydall Terr LS11 . . . . **210** C1
Rydal St
Castleford WF10 . . . . **125** D8
Keighley BD21 . . . . **35** A6
Ryder Cl WF8 . . . . **146** B8
Ryder Gdns LS8 . . . . **61** A7
Rydings Ave HD6 . . . . **115** A3
Rydings Cl **11** HD6 . . . . . . **115** A3
Rydings Dr HD6 . . . . **114** F3
Rydings Wlk HD6 . . . . **114** F3
Ryebank HD9 . . . . **189** B4
Ryebread WF10 . . . . **103** C1
Rye Close La HD9 . . . . **187** E4
Rye Croft HX2 . . . . **91** F6
Ryecroft Ave WF4 . . . . **162** C2
Ryecroft Cl WF1 . . . . **121** C5
Ryecroft Cres HX2 . . . . **91** D1
Ryecroft Dr HD3 . . . . **135** B1
Ryecroft Farm Cl S72 . . . . . **180** D7
Ryecroft La
Brighouse HD6 . . . . **136** C8
Halifax HX2 . . . . **91** D1
Holmfirth HD9 . . . . **189** C3
Ryecroft Prim Sch
Bradford BD4 . . . . **75** F2
Leeds LS11 . . . . **77** E6
Ryecroft Rd
Cullingworth BD21 . . . . **35** E1
Glusburn BD20 . . . . **16** B7
Harden BD16 . . . . **36** A1
Ryecroft St WF5 . . . . **140** C7
Ryecroft Terr HX2 . . . . **91** D1
Ryecroft Way BD20 . . . . **16** C6
Ryedale HD5 . . . . **137** B2
Ryedale Ave
Knottingley WF11 . . . . **126** E2
Leeds LS12 . . . . **78** B4
Ryedale Cl WF6 . . . . **123** A5
Ryedale Ct LS14 . . . . **61** F5
Ryedale Ho WF17 . . . . **118** C3
Ryedale Holt LS12 . . . . **209** C1
Ryedale Pk LS29 . . . . **8** D3
Ryedale Pl WF6 . . . . **123** A5
Ryedale Way
Bradford BD15 . . . . **54** A2
East Ardsley WF3 . . . . **119** E7
Ryefield Ave BD14 . . . . **73** B5
Rye Field La HX4 . . . . **150** F6
Rye Field La W HX4 . . . . . . **150** F6
Ryefields HD9 . . . . **189** D4
Ryefields Ave HD3 . . . . **153** A7
Ryefields Rd HD7 . . . . **152** E4
Ryefield Way BD20 . . . . **17** E8
Rye Garth LS22 . . . . **13** D8
Rye La HX2 . . . . **91** C1
Ryelands Gr BD9 . . . . **54** D4
Ryeland St BD20 . . . . **16** D7
Rye Pl LS14 . . . . **61** F1
Rye St BD21 . . . . **35** B4
Ryestone Dr HX6 . . . . **132** C2
Rye Way WF10 . . . . **125** B8
Ryhill Ind Est WF4 . . . . **162** B1
Ryhill Jun & Inf Sch
WF4 . . . . **162** B1
Ryhill Pits La WF4 . . . . **161** E1
Rylands Ho BD16 . . . . **37** B3
Rylands Mdw **17** BD22 . . . . **51** E8
Rylands Pk HX6 . . . . **132** C2
Rylstone Gdns BD3 . . . . **56** A1
Rylstone Gr WF1 . . . . **142** F8
Rylstone Rd BD17 . . . . **37** F2
Rylstone St **1** BD21 . . . . . . **35** E8
Rylston Gdns HX3 . . . . **113** B3
Ryndleside **4** HD3 . . . . . . **134** F1
Ryshworth Ave BD16 . . . . . . **36** D6
Ryshworth Bridge BD16 . . . . **36** D6
Ryshworth Cres BD16 . . . . . . **36** E7
Ryton Dale BD10 . . . . **56** E6

S

Sabine Fold WF4 . . . . **140** E1
Sable Crest BD2 . . . . **55** F4
Sackup La S75 . . . . **177** F1
Sackville App LS7 . . . . **206** C3
Sackville Rd BD20 . . . . **5** E2
Sackville St
Bradford BD1 . . . . **201** B3
Dewsbury WF13 . . . . **138** E6
14 Hebden Bridge HX7 . . **89** A4
Leeds LS7 . . . . **206** C3
Todmorden OL14 . . . . **108** C5
Sacred Heart RC Prim Sch
Hemsworth WF9 . . . . **181** D6
Leeds LS4 . . . . **59** B3
Sowerby Bridge HX6 . . . . . . **112** A3

Sacred Heart RC Prim Sch
The LS29 . . . . **8** D4
Saddler's La WF11 . . . . **105** C1
Saddlers Croft
Castleford WF10 . . . . **125** B6
1 Ilkley LS29 . . . . **8** A4
Saddlers Gr WF9 . . . . **54** E2
Saddlers Gr WF9 . . . . **164** E3
Saddler St **7** BD12 . . . . **94** C4
Saddleworth Rd
Elland HX4 . . . . **134** C7
Marsden HX4, HX6 . . . . **150** E5
Ripponden HX4, HX5 . . . . . **133** C5
Sadler Cl LS16 . . . . **42** C4
Sadler Copse LS16 . . . . **42** C4
Sadlers Wlk **7** LS22 . . . . . . **13** F6
Sadler Way LS16 . . . . **42** C4
Saffron Ct WF2 . . . . **141** E8
Saffron Dr BD15 . . . . **73** B8
Sagar La OL14 . . . . **86** D3
Sagar Pl LS6 . . . . **205** A4
Sagar St WF10 . . . . **124** D8
Sage St BD5 . . . . **74** C4
Sahara Ct BD8 . . . . **55** D2
St Abbs Cl BD6 . . . . **94** C7
St Abbs Dr BD6 . . . . **94** C7
St Abbs Fold BD6 . . . . **94** C7
St Abbs Gate BD6 . . . . **94** C7
St Abbs Way BD6 . . . . **94** C7
St Abbs Wlk BD6 . . . . **94** C7
St Aidan's CE Fst Sch
HD8 . . . . **175** A1
St Aidan's Rd BD17 . . . . **38** D2
St Aidans Sq BD16 . . . . **36** E6
St Aidans Rd LS26 . . . . **102** E8
St Aiden's Wlk WF5 . . . . . . **141** A4
St Alban's Ave
Halifax HX3 . . . . **113** C3
Huddersfield HX3 . . . . **135** A3
St Alban's Pl LS2 . . . . **206** C1
St Alban's Rd HX3 . . . . **113** C3
St Alban App LS9 . . . . **208** C1
St Alban Cl LS9 . . . . **208** C1
St Alban Cres LS9 . . . . **208** C1
St Alban Gr LS9 . . . . **208** C1
St Alban St LS9 . . . . **208** C1
St Alban Mount LS9 . . . . . . **208** C1
St Alban Rd LS9 . . . . **208** C1
St Albans Croft HX3 . . . . . . **113** D4
St Alban View LS9 . . . . **208** C1
St Andrew's CE Inf Sch
HD6 . . . . **115** A4
St Andrew's Cl
Morley LS27 . . . . **97** E3
Pudsey LS13 . . . . **57** E5
St Andrew's Cres BD12 . . . . **95** A4
St Andrew's Dr HD6 . . . . . . **115** A4
St Andrew's Gr LS27 . . . . . . **97** F3
St Andrew's Pl
Bradford BD7 . . . . **74** C6
Leeds LS3 . . . . **210** C4
St Andrew's Rd
Castleford WF10 . . . . **104** D1
Huddersfield HD1 . . . . **154** C7
St Andrew's St LS3 . . . . . . **210** C4
St Andrew's Terr BD20 . . . . **16** D7
St Andrew's Villas BD7 . . . . **74** C7
St Andrews CE Jun Sch
HD6 . . . . **115** A3
St Andrews Cl
Halifax HX2 . . . . **92** A5
1 Yeadon LS19 . . . . **40** C7
St Andrews Croft LS17 . . . . **43** B4
St Andrews Ct
Leeds LS3 . . . . **210** C4
Yeadon LS19 . . . . **40** B8
St Andrews Dr
Darton S75 . . . . **178** A1
Featherstone WF7 . . . . **124** D1
Kirkheaton WF5 . . . . **155** C8
Knottingley WF11 . . . . **126** C5
Leeds LS17 . . . . **43** C4
St Andrews Pl **15** WF6 . . . **123** D1
St Andrews Rd LS19 . . . . **40** C8
St Andrews Wlk LS17 . . . . . **43** C4
St Ann's Ave LS4 . . . . **205** A2
St Ann's Cl LS4 . . . . **59** C4
St Ann's Gdns LS4 . . . . **59** C3
St Ann's La LS4 . . . . **59** C3
St Ann's Mount LS4 . . . . . . **205** A3
St Ann's Pl HX1 . . . . **202** C4
St Ann's Rise LS4 . . . . **59** C3
St Ann's Sq LS4 . . . . **59** C4
St Ann's Tower Mews LS6 . **59** C4
St Ann's Way LS4 . . . . **59** C3
St Anne's Ave HD3 . . . . **135** A3
St Anne's Cl WF12 . . . . **139** D4
St Anne's Dr LS4 . . . . **59** C4
St Anne's Gn LS4 . . . . **59** C3
St Anne's Pl HX4 . . . . **133** E4
St Anne's RC Cath ★ LS2 . **211** B4
St Anne's RC Prim Sch
BD21 . . . . **35** B8
St Anne's Rd
Halifax HX3 . . . . **113** C2
Leeds LS6 . . . . **59** C5
St Anne's Sq
6 Holmfirth, Cliff HD9 . . **189** A5
Holmfirth, Netherthong
HD9 . . . . **188** F8
St Anne's St
Leeds LS2 . . . . **211** B4
Ryhill WF4 . . . . **162** B1
St Annes Terr BD17 . . . . **38** C3
St Annes Villas WF8 . . . . . . **125** E2
St Anns Sq HX6 . . . . **112** C4
St Anthony's Dr LS11 . . . . **213** C2

St Anthony's RC Prim Sch
Bradford BD14 . . . . **73** D5
Leeds LS11 . . . . **213** C2
Shipley BD18 . . . . **55** F8
St Anthony's Rd LS11 . . . . **213** B8
St Anthonys Gds BD18 . . . . **55** C6
St Anthonys Terr LS11 . . . **213** C2
St Augustine's CE Com Sch
BD3 . . . . **55** F8
St Augustine's CE Jun & Inf
Sch HX1 . . . . **202** C4
St Augustine's Terr
Bradford BD3 . . . . **56** A1
Halifax HX1 . . . . **202** C4
St Augustines RC Prim Sch
LS8 . . . . **208** B7
St Austin's RC Prim Sch
WF1 . . . . **216** C1
St Barnabas Rd
Cleckheaton WF15 . . . . **116** C5
Leeds LS11 . . . . **211** B2
St Bartholomew's CE Prim
Sch LS12 . . . . **209** C3
St Bartholomew's Cl
LS12 . . . . **209** C3
St Bartholomews Ct
WF2 . . . . **141** C2
St Bede's RC Gram Sch
BD9 . . . . **55** A3
St Benedict's RC Prim Sch
LS25 . . . . **82** F2
St Benedicts Chase LS13 . . **58** D1
St Benedicts Dr LS13 . . . . . **58** D1
St Benedicts Gdns LS13 . . . **58** D1
St Bernard's Ave WF8 . . . . **146** B4
St Bevan's Rd HX3 . . . . **113** C
St Blaise Ct BD5 . . . . **201** B3
St Blaise Sq BD1 . . . . **201** B3
St Blaise Way BD1 . . . . **201** B4
St Botolphs Cl WF11 . . . . . . **127** A4
St Catherine's Cres LS13 . . **58** D4
St Catherine's Dr LS13 . . . . **58** D4
St Catherine's Gn LS13 . . . . **58** D4
St Catherine's Hill LS13 . . **58** D4
St Catherine's Villas
WF1 . . . . **142** F7
St Catherine's Wlk LS8 . . . . **61** A4
St Catherines RC High Sch
HX2 . . . . **92** A4
St Catherine St WF1 . . . . **142** F7
St Cecila St LS2 . . . . **212** A4
St Chad's Ave
Brighouse HD6 . . . . **114** C
Leeds LS6 . . . . **59** D4
St Chad's CE Prim Sch
Brighouse HD6 . . . . **114** C
Leeds LS16 . . . . **59** B
St Chad's Ct LS6 . . . . **59** D
St Chad's Dr LS6 . . . . **59** C
St Chad's Gr LS6 . . . . **59** C
St Chad's Rd
Bradford BD8 . . . . **55** B
Leeds LS16 . . . . **59** D
St Chad's Rise LS6 . . . . **59** C
St Chad's View LS6 . . . . **59** C
St Chads Par **11** LS6 . . . . . . **59** D
St Christopher's Ave
LS26 . . . . **100** F
St Christopher's Wlk
WF1 . . . . **216** A
St Christopher Ho WF8 . . . **125** D
St Christophers Dr **6** LS29 . **6** F
St Clair Gn WF2 . . . . **141** D
St Clair Rd **7** LS21 . . . . . . **23** B
St Clair St WF1 . . . . **216** C
St Clairs Terr LS21 . . . . **23** B
St Clare's Ave BD2 . . . . **56** D
St Clare's RC Prim Sch
BD2 . . . . **56** D
St Clements Ave LS26 . . . . **100** E
St Clements Cl LS26 . . . . . . **100** D
St Clements Ct WF7 . . . . . . **163** E
St Clements Rise LS26 . . . . **100** D
St Columba's RC Prim Sch
BD4 . . . . **75** D
St Cuthbert's Ct WF7 . . . . . **146** A
St Cuthbert & the First
Martyrs RC Prim Sch
BD9 . . . . **55** A
St Cyprians Gdns LS9 . . . . **208** B
St David's Ct LS11 . . . . **211** B
St Davids Cl WF3 . . . . **100** b
St Davids Ct HX3 . . . . **92** B
St Davids Garth WF3 . . . . . **100** B
St Davids Rd
Otley LS21 . . . . **10** E
Rothwell WF3 . . . . **100** B
St Edmunds Cl WF10 . . . . **125** C
St Edward's RC Prim Sch
LS23 . . . . **30** D
St Edward's Terr LS23 . . . . . **30** D
St Edwards Cl WF11 . . . . . **126** E
St Elmo Gr **6** LS9 . . . . **80** A
St Eloi Ave BD17 . . . . **38** C
St Enoch's Rd BD5, BD6 . . **74** B
St Francis' RC Prim Sch
BD2 . . . . **56** A
St Francis Gdns HD2 . . . . **136** A
St Francis of Assisi RC Prim
Sch LS11 . . . . **214** B
St Francis Pl LS11 . . . . **211** B
St Francis RC Prim Sch
LS27 . . . . **97** F
St Gabriels Ct LS18 . . . . **41** B
St George's Apartments
HX6 . . . . **112** A
St George's Ave
Huddersfield HD3 . . . . **135** A

St George's Ave *continued*
Rothwell LS26 100 C7
St George's Cres LS26 100 C7
St George's Pl
Bradford BD5 201 B1
Bradford, Bowling BD5 75 B4
St George's Rd
Halifax HX3 92 A1
Holmfirth HD9 189 D4
Leeds LS1 206 B1
Wakefield WF2 141 D3
St George's Sq
Elland HD3 152 B8
27 Hebden Bridge HX7 89 A3
18 Huddersfield HD1 154 A6
St George's St
Bradford BD3 75 B6
28 Hebden Bridge HX7 89 A3
Huddersfield HD1 154 A6
St Georges Cres HX3 92 B1
St Georges Ct WF4 162 D2
St Georges Mews WF2 160 A5
St Georges Rd LS10 99 E5
St Georges Wlk WF2 160 C6
St Giles' View WF8 146 D7
St Giles Ave WF8 146 B8
St Giles Cl HD6 114 E5
St Giles Garth LS16 24 E3
St Giles Rd HX3 114 E7
St Gregory's RC Prim Sch LS14 62 D5
St Helen's Ave WF9 181 C7
St Helen's Dr LS25 83 F8
St Helen's Field HD4 155 A2
St Helen's Gate HD4 155 A2
St Helen's Gr WF2 142 F1
St Helen's La LS16 42 C3
St Helen's Pl 2 WF10 124 E7
St Helen's Way LS29 8 D4
St Helena Rd BD6 74 B1
St Helens Ave LS16 42 D3
St Helens CE Jun & Inf Sch WF9 181 C6
St Helens Cl LS16 42 D3
St Helens Croft LS16 42 C3
St Helens Gdns LS16 42 C3
St Helens Gr LS16 42 C3
St Helens St LS10 212 A1
St Helens Way LS16 42 D3
St Helier Gr BD17 38 D4
St Hilda's Ave 14 LS9 212 C2
St Hilda's Cres LS9 212 C2
St Hilda's Gr 15 LS9 212 C2
St Hilda's Mount 13 LS9 212 C2
St Hilda's Pl LS9 212 C2
St Hilda's Rd LS9 212 C2
St Hilda's Sch WF4 141 A2
St Hilda's Terr BD3 75 E8
St Hildas Cl S63 194 E1
St Ians Croft LS29 6 F7
St Ignatius RC Prim Sch WF5 140 E3
St Ive's Gdns HX3 113 C3
St Ive's Rd HX3 113 C3
St Ives Cl WF8 125 D3
St Ives Cres WF10 125 C5
St Ives Gr
Harden BD16 36 C2
Leeds LS12 209 A4
St Ives Mount LS12 209 A4
St Ives Pl BD16 36 C2
St Ives Rd BD16 36 C2
St James' Church Prim Sch BD15 73 B7
St James' Rd
Huddersfield HD1 153 D7
Ilkley LS29 8 A4
St James's Ct
Leeds LS8 207 B2
Wakefield WF2 142 B4
St James's Mews LS12 77 F8
St James's Mkt BD4 201 D2
St James's Pk WF1 142 E6
St James's Sq BD5 201 B1
St James's St LS22 13 E5
St James's Univ Hospl LS9 207 C2
St James's Univ Hospl Beckett Wing LS9 207 C1
St James's Univ Hospl The Becklin Ctr LS9 207 B1
St James App LS14 62 B4
St James Ave LS18 41 D1
St James Bsns Pk BD1 201 C2
St James CE Jun & Inf Sch WF4 159 F6
St James CE Prim Sch
Leeds LS15 62 D3
Wetherby LS22 13 F6
St James Cl LS12 77 F8
St James Cres LS28 76 B7
St James Ct
Brighouse HD6 115 B3
Halifax HX1 203 B3
Huddersfield HD4 155 A2
Ryhill WF4 162 C1
St James Dr LS18 41 D1
St James Pl BD17 38 F4
St James Quay LS10 212 A3
St James Rd
Baildon BD17 38 F4
Halifax HX1 203 B3
St James Rise WF2 141 C4
St James Sq HX3 93 A3
St James St
Batley, Heckmondwike WF16 117 D3
Batley WF17 118 C5
St James St *continued*
Halifax HX1 203 B3
St James Terr LS18 41 D1
St James Way
Crigglestone WF4 159 F6
Huddersfield HD5 154 E8
St James Wlk LS18 41 D1
St John's Ave
Batley WF17 118 A6
Huddersfield HD4 154 A2
Kirkheaton HD5 137 C1
Leeds LS6 205 C2
Ossett WF5 141 A5
12 Pudsey LS28 57 D3
Thorner LS14 45 F5
Wakefield WF1 216 A4
St John's CE Inf Sch WF13 139 A8
St John's CE Prim Sch
Brighouse HD6 115 E2
Leeds LS8 61 C6
Ripponden HX6 132 C1
St John's CE Prim Sch, Cliviger BB10 85 B6
St John's Chase WF1 216 A3
St John's Cl
Aberford LS25 47 E1
5 Hebden Bridge HX7 89 A3
Leeds LS6 205 C2
Ossett WF5 141 A5
Ripponden HX6 132 C1
St John's Cres
Bradford BD8 73 E8
Huddersfield HD1 154 A8
Normanton WF6 144 A7
Ossett WF5 141 A5
St John's Croft WF1 216 A4
St John's Cross
Cononley BD20 4 A2
Halifax HX2 91 F8
St John's Ct
4 Baildon BD17 38 E2
Keighley BD20 18 A2
Leeds LS7 207 A4
Lepton HD8 155 F3
Thorner LS14 45 F5
Wakefield WF1 216 A3
Yeadon LS19 40 A6
St John's Dr
Huddersfield HD1 154 A8
Yeadon LS19 40 A6
St John's Garth LS25 64 E8
St John's Gr
Leeds LS6 205 C2
Wakefield WF1 216 B4
St John's Ho 27 BD16 37 A3
St John's Hospital (Almshouses) LS25 104 D8
St John's La HX1 203 B2
St John's Mount WF1 216 A4
St John's N WF1 216 A3
St John's Pk LS29 21 F5
St John's Pl
Birkenshaw BD11 96 A6
7 Cleckheaton BD19 116 E7
Halifax HX1 203 B2
Leeds LS5 59 B4
St John's Prim Sch BD4 75 D1
St John's RC Sch for the Deaf LS23 30 D7
St John's Rd
Boston Spa LS23 30 D7
Huddersfield HD1 154 A8
Ilkley LS29 8 E4
Keighley BD20 18 A2
Kirkheaton HD5 137 C1
Leeds LS3 205 C1
Yeadon LS19 40 A6
St John's Sq WF1 216 A3
St John's St
Cononley BD20 4 A2
Horbury WF4 140 E1
Rothwell LS26 101 C5
Silsden BD20 5 E1
St John's Terr LS6 205 C2
St John's View
Batley WF17 118 A6
Boston Spa LS23 30 C7
St John's Way LS19 40 A6
St John's Wlk S71 179 D4
St John's Yd LS26 101 C5
St John Fisher RC High Sch WF13 118 B1
St John Par WF13 139 B7
St Johns Ave LS29 6 F8
St Johns CE Jun & Inf Sch, Golcar HD7 152 D5
St Johns Cl
Cleckheaton BD19 116 E7
Dewsbury WF13 139 B8
St Johns Ct HD9 188 F4
St Johns Ctr LS2 211 C4
St Johns Flats LS29 8 A3
St Johns Mews WF1 216 A3
St John St
Brighouse HD6 115 A1
Dewsbury WF13 139 B8
St Johns Way BD22 34 F6
St John The Baptist RC Prim Sch WF6 123 C2
St John The Evangelist RC Prim Sch BD6 73 E1
St John Wlk WF13 139 B8
St Joseph's Coll BD9 55 C3
St Joseph's Mount WF8 146 B7
St Joseph's RC Prim Sch
Batley WF13 118 A2
Bingley BD16 37 A3
St Joseph's RC Prim Sch *continued*
Bradford BD5 74 D4
Brighouse HD6 114 F5
Halifax HX3 203 C4
Huddersfield HD5 154 F6
Keighley BD21 35 B5
Pontefract WF8 146 C8
Pudsey LS28 76 F8
Todmorden OL14 108 B6
Wetherby LS22 13 E6
St Josephs Ct LS25 82 E7
St Josephs RC Prim Sch
Castleford WF10 124 E8
Otley LS21 23 A8
South Elmsall WF9 182 E3
St Jude's Pl BD1 201 A4
St Jude's St
Bradford BD8 74 D8
Halifax HX1 203 A1
St Julien's Mount S75 193 E4
St Julien's Way S75 193 E4
St Laurence's Cl BD2 55 E5
St Lawrence Cl LS28 76 D7
St Lawrence St LS7 204 A2
St Lawrence Terr LS28 76 E6
St Leonard's Ct 4 BD8 54 F1
St Leonard's Farm Pk* BD17 39 C5
St Leonard's Gr BD8 54 F1
St Leonard's Rd BD8 54 F1
St Leonards Cl LS29 6 F7
St Lucius's Cl HD4 172 E6
St Luke's CE Fst Sch BD19 116 B7
St Luke's Cl
Cleckheaton BD19 116 B7
Clifford LS23 30 D5
St Luke's Cres LS11 214 A4
St Luke's Gn LS11 214 A4
St Luke's Hospl
Bradford BD5 74 D4
Huddersfield HD4 153 C3
St Luke's Rd LS11 214 A4
St Luke's St LS11 214 A4
St Luke's Terr
Cleckheaton BD19 116 B7
East Morton BD20 36 D8
St Luke's View 4 LS11 214 A4
St Lukes CE Prim Sch BD2 56 D4
St Lukes Cl
Batley WF17 118 E4
Bradford BD5 201 B1
Middlestown WF4 158 B7
St Malachy's RC Prim Sch HX2 91 E3
St Margaret's Ave
Bradford BD4 75 D2
Horsforth LS18 41 B2
Leeds LS8 61 A6
Mickletown LS26 102 D3
St Margaret's Cl LS18 41 B2
St Margaret's Ct WF9 183 B6
St Margaret's Dr
Horsforth LS18 41 B2
Leeds LS8 61 A6
St Margaret's Gr LS8 61 A6
St Margaret's Pl BD7 74 B5
St Margaret's Rd
Bradford BD7 74 B6
Horsforth LS18 41 B2
Mickletown LS26 102 D3
St Margaret's Terr
Bradford BD7 74 B5
Ilkley LS29 8 B3
St Margaret's View LS8 61 A6
St Mark's Ave LS2 206 A2
St Mark's Flats LS2 206 A3
St Mark's Ho LS2 206 B3
St Mark's Pl LS22 94 C5
St Mark's Rd
Huddersfield HD3 153 A6
Leeds LS6 206 B3
St Mark's St
Leeds LS2 206 A3
Wakefield WF1 216 C4
St Mark's Terr LS22 94 C5
St Marks Ct HD8 190 E6
St Marks View HD3 153 A6
St Martin's Ave LS7 204 A1
St Martin's Cres LS7 204 A1
St Martin's Dr LS7 60 C6
St Martin's Gdns LS7 204 A1
St Martin's Gr
Castleford WF10 124 B6
Leeds LS7 204 A1
St Martin's Rd LS7 204 A1
St Martin's Terr LS7 204 A1
St Martin's View
7 Brighouse HD6 115 A3
Leeds LS7 204 A1
St Martins Ave
Bradford BD7 74 C7
Otley LS21 10 F2
St Martins Cl WF7 145 C4
St Martins Ct WF3 100 B2
St Martins Fold WF3 100 B2
St Mary's Ave
Batley WF17 118 B3
Bradford BD12 94 C2
Holmfirth HD9 188 F8
Mirfield WF14 138 C6
Swillington LS26 82 A1
St Mary's CE Jun & Inf Sch HX6 132 C7
St Mary's CE Prim Sch LS23 30 E7
St Mary's Cl
Bradford BD12 94 B2
East Ardsley WF3 119 D7
Garforth LS25 82 F6
Ilkley LS29 8 C4
Leeds LS12 210 A2
Leeds, Potternewton LS7 204 A1
South Elmsall WF9 183 A2
St Mary's Cres
Bradford BD12 94 B2
Holmfirth HD9 188 F8
St Mary's Ct
Kippax WF10 103 B4
Leeds LS7 204 A1
Meltham HD9 188 B8
St Mary's Dr BD12 94 C2
St Mary's Fold BD4 75 D5
St Mary's Garth LS17 28 B5
St Mary's Gdns 1 BD12 94 C2
St Mary's Hall LS9 212 B4
St Mary's Hospl LS12 77 F8
St Mary's Hts HX2 91 D5
St Mary's La
Kirkheaton HD5 155 C7
Leeds LS9 212 B4
St Mary's Mews HD9 171 F5
St Mary's Mount BD12 94 B2
St Mary's Park Ct 2 LS12 77 F8
St Mary's Park Gn 3 LS12 77 F8
St Mary's Pl
1 Castleford WF10 124 D8
Dewsbury WF12 139 D6
St Mary's RC Comp Sch LS29 22 C3
St Mary's RC Prim Sch
Bacup OL13 106 B2
Batley WF17 118 B6
Bradford BD1 201 C3
Halifax HX1 203 A2
St Mary's Rd
Bradford BD8, BD9 55 C2
Bradford, Swain Green BD4 75 D5
Holmfirth HD9 188 F8
Honley HD9 171 F5
Keighley BD20 18 F2
Leeds LS7 204 A1
Normanton WF6 122 F3
St Mary's Rise HD9 188 F8
St Mary's Sq
Bradford BD12 94 C2
Honley HD9 171 F5
Morley LS27 98 A4
St Mary's St
Boston Spa LS23 30 D8
Leeds LS9 212 A4
St Mary's Way HD9 188 F8
St Mary's Wlk
Micklefield LS25 83 F7
Micklefield LS25 84 A7
Mirfield WF14 138 C6
St Mary Magdalenes Cl 3 BD8 74 C8
St Marys Ave WF6 122 F4
St Marys Fold HD5 155 C8
St Marys Gate 12 HX5 134 F7
St Marys Park App LS12 77 F8
St Marys Park Cres LS12 77 F8
St Mary St HX1 203 A2
St Matthew's CE Prim Sch
Bradford BD5 74 E1
Leeds LS7 60 C7
St Matthew's Dr HX3 93 A3
St Matthew's Rd BD5 74 D1
St Matthew's St 2 LS11 211 A1
St Matthew's Wlk LS7 60 C8
St Matthew Rd WF13 139 B8
St Matthews Cl BD15 53 B4
St Matthews Ct HX3 93 A2
St Matthews Gr BD15 53 C4
St Matthews RC Prim Sch BD15 73 B8
St Matthias' Ct LS4 205 A2
St Matthias' Gr LS4 205 A2
St Matthias' St LS4 205 A2
St Matthias' Terr LS4 205 A2
St Mellion Ct 14 WF6 123 D1
St Michael's & All Angels CE Prim Sch HX3 93 D6
St Michael's CE Prim Sch WF2 141 E5
St Michael's Cl
Castleford WF10 124 D7
Dewsbury WF12 139 E1
Emley HD8 175 D7
Shipley BD16 54 B6
Wakefield WF2 142 A5
St Michael's Cres LS6 205 A4
St Michael's Gdns HD8 175 D7
St Michael's Gr LS6 205 A4
St Michael's Ho WF2 142 A5
St Michael's La LS6 205 A4
St Michael's Mount WF12 139 E1
St Michael's Rd
Bradford BD8 74 C8
Leeds LS6 205 A4
St Michael's Terr LS6 59 D5
St Michael's Villas LS6 205 A4
St Michael's Way LS29 21 F8
St Michael Ct LS13 58 D3
St Michaels Ave 1 WF8 146 B8
St Michaels Gn WF6 123 A1
St Michaels Way LS29 6 F7
St Nicholas RC Prim Sch LS9 61 D3
St Nicholas Rd LS29 8 A5
St Nicholas St WF10 124 D7
St Oswald's CE Prim Sch BD7 74 A4
St Oswald Ave WF9 146 B8
St Oswald Ct 2 WF9 181 E6
St Oswald Rd WF2 141 D5
St Oswalds CE Jun Sch LS20 39 E8
St Oswalds Garth LS20 22 F1
St Oswalds Pl WF5 140 E7
St Oswald St 5 WF10 124 D8
St Oswalds Terr LS20 22 E1
St Patrick's RC Prim Sch
Batley WF17 96 E2
Elland HX5 134 D6
Huddersfield HD2 153 E8
St Patrick RC Prim Sch LS9 80 A8
St Paul's Ave
Birkenshaw BD11 96 B5
Bradford BD6 94 B8
St Paul's CE Jun & Inf Sch WF2 141 E8
St Paul's CE Prim Sch BD6 94 B8
St Paul's Cl
3 Bradford BD8 55 C1
Upton WF9 183 D8
St Paul's Dr WF2 141 D8
St Paul's Gr
Bradford LS29 94 B8
Ilkley LS29 8 D4
St Paul's Pl LS1 211 B4
St Paul's RC Prim Sch LS17 43 A4
St Paul's Rd
Birkenshaw BD11 96 B5
Bradford, Manningham BD8 55 C2
Bradford, Wibsey Slack BD6 94 B8
Halifax HX1 202 B1
Keighley BD21 35 D6
Mirfield WF14 138 A4
Shipley BD18 55 A7
St Paul's St
Huddersfield HD1 154 B5
Leeds LS1 211 B4
1 Morley LS27 98 B3
St Paul's Terr 3 WF14 138 A4
St Paul's Wlk WF2 141 D8
St Paulinus Cl WF13 139 B8
St Paulinus RC Primary Sch WF13 139 A7
St Pauls Ct WF8 125 E3
St Pauls Rd HD5 155 B8
St Pauls Rise LS29 6 F8
St Peg Cl BD19 116 E7
St Peg La BD19 116 E7
St Peter's Ave
Rothwell LS26 100 F5
Sowerby Bridge HX6 111 F3
St Peter's CE Jun & Inf Sch WF17 96 E2
St Peter's CE Prim Sch
Leeds LS9 212 B4
Lofthouse Gate WF1 121 F5
St Peter's Cl
Batley WF17 96 D1
10 Mirfield WF14 137 F5
St Peter's Cres
Lofthouse Gate WF3 122 B6
Morley LS27 98 A6
St Peter's Ct
18 Keighley BD21 35 B6
Leeds LS13 58 D3
St Peter's Garth LS14 46 A6
St Peter's Gate
Thurnscoe S63 194 C1
Todmorden OL14 129 B8
St Peter's Gdns
Dewsbury WF12 139 F7
Leeds LS13 58 C3
St Peter's Gr WF4 141 B1
St Peter's Mount LS13 58 D2
St Peter's Par WF12 139 F7
St Peter's Pl LS9 212 A4
St Peter's RC Prim Sch BD3 75 B6
St Peter's Sq
Leeds LS9 212 A4
Sowerby Bridge HX6 111 E3
St Peter's St
2 Huddersfield HD1 154 B6
Leeds LS2 212 A4
St Peter's Way LS29 21 F4
St Peter & St Pauls RC Prim Sch LS19 39 F6
St Peters CE Jun Sch WF4 141 A1
St Peters Cres HD5 155 B8
St Peters Ct
Addingham LS29 6 F7
Horbury WF4 141 A1
Leeds LS11 214 C4
St Peters Gate WF5 140 D7
St Philip's Ave LS10 99 B5
St Philip's CE Prim Sch BD8 55 A1
St Philip's Cl
Burley in W LS29 9 F1
Dewsbury WF13 118 D1
St Philip's Dr LS29 21 F8
St Philip's RC Prim Sch LS10 99 B5
St Philip's Way LS29 21 F8
St Philips Cl LS10 99 B5
St Philips Ct HD3 135 B2

St Richards Rd LS21 10 F2
St Saviour's CE Jun Sch WF17 97 A1
Saint St 1 BD7 74 A4
St Stephen's CE Prim Sch BD5 74 E3
St Stephen's Ct
Leeds LS9 212 C4
Steeton BD20 17 C6
St Stephen's Rd
Bradford BD5 74 E3
Huddersfield HD1 153 F4
Leeds LS9 212 C4
Pudsey LS28 57 A7
Steeton BD20 17 C5
St Stephen's St HX3 113 A2
St Stephen's Terr BD5 74 D3
St Stephens Ct HX3 113 A2
St Swithins Ct WF3 121 F2
St Swithins Dr WF3 121 F2
St Swithins Gr WF3 121 F2
St Theresa's RC Prim Sch LS15 62 C4
St Thomas' Rd HD1 153 F5
St Thomas's Rd 2 BD1 74 D7
St Thomas's Terr WF8 125 F3
St Thomas a Beckett RC Coll WF2 142 E1
St Thomas CE Jun Sch WF7 145 C5
St Thomas Gdns HD2 136 F6
St Thomas Rd WF7 145 D5
St Thomas Row LS2 207 A1
St Urban's RC Prim Sch LS17 43 A1
St Vincent Rd LS28 76 F6
St Walburga's RC Prim Sch
Shipley BD18 54 F7
Shipley BD18 55 A7
St Wilfred's St LS28 57 B7
St Wilfrid's Ave
Leeds LS8 208 B3
Leeds LS8 208 B4
St Wilfrid's Cir LS8 208 B3
St Wilfrid's Cl BD7 73 F5
St Wilfrid's Cres
Bradford BD7 73 F5
Leeds LS8 208 B4
St Wilfrid's Dr LS8 208 A4
St Wilfrid's Garth LS8 208 B3
St Wilfrid's Gr LS8 208 B4
St Wilfrid's RC High Sch WF7 124 C1
St Wilfrid's Rd BD7 73 F5
St William's RC Prim Sch BD8 74 A7
St Winefride's RC Prim Sch BD6 94 B8
St Winifred's Cl HX2 91 D5
Salcombe Pl BD4 75 E2
Salem Pl
Garforth LS25 82 E7
Leeds LS10 211 C2
Salem St
Bradford BD1 201 B4
6 Hebden Bridge HX7 88 F3
Queensbury BD13 72 D1
Salendine Nook High Sch HD3 152 F7
Salford OL14 108 B4
Salford Way OL14 108 A4
Salisbury Ave
Baildon BD17 38 C3
Leeds LS12 209 C4
Salisbury Cl
Dewsbury WF12 139 F8
Normanton WF6 123 B3
Salisbury Ct LS18 41 D1
Salisbury Gr LS12 209 C4
Salisbury Ho 5 HX6 112 C4
Salisbury Mews
East Ardsley WF3 98 D1
Horsforth LS18 41 D1
Salisbury Pl
Halifax HX3 92 B1
Pudsey LS28 57 A7
Salisbury Rd
3 Bradford BD12 94 C6
Brighouse BD19 115 F8
Keighley BD22 35 A6
Leeds LS12 209 C4
Shipley BD9 55 C5
Salisbury St
Pudsey LS28 57 A6
Sowerby Bridge HX6 112 A3
Yeadon LS19 40 B4
Salisbury Terr
1 Halifax HX3 92 B1
Leeds LS12 209 C4
Salisbury View
Horsforth LS18 41 D1
Leeds LS12 209 C4
Salley St OL15 129 C2
Salmon Cres 4 LS18 41 C1
Sal Nook Cl BD12 94 E7
Sal Royd Rd BD12 94 E6
Saltaire
4 Haworth BD22 51 F8
Shipley BD18 54 E8
Saltaire Prim Sch BD18 54 F8
Saltaire Rd
Bingley BD16 37 D5
Shipley BD18 55 A8
Saltaire Sta BD18 37 F1
Saltburn Pl BD9 54 F2
Saltburn St HX1 202 B3
Salt Drake HX6 132 B8
Salterhebble Hill HX3 113 D3
Salterhebble Jun & Inf Sch HX3 113 D3
Salterhebble Terr 1 HX3 113 D3
Salterlee Prim Sch HX3 92 F2
Salter Oak Croft S71 179 C1
Salter Rake Gate OL14 129 B8
Salter Row 1 WF8 146 D8
Saltersgate Ave WF11 126 E4
Salters Gdn LS28 76 E7
Salter St WF17 118 B2
Salt Gram Sch BD17 37 F2
Salt Horn Cl BD12 94 F5
Saltonstall La HX2 90 D5
Salt Pie Alley WF2 216 A2
Salts Mill Art Gal* BD18 37 F1
Salts Mill Rd BD17 55 B8
Salt St
Bradford BD8 55 C1
Halifax HX1 202 C4
Samara Flats LS2 206 A2
Samara West Mount LS2 206 A1
Sampson St WF15 117 B4
Samuel Dr WF3 121 E5
Samuel St BD21 35 C7
Samuel Way BD18 55 D8
Sandacre Cl BD10 56 E3
Sandal & Agbrigg Sta WF1 142 E2
Sandal Ave WF2 142 E1
Sandal Bsns Ctr WF2 160 C7
Sandal Castle* WF2 142 D1
Sandal CE Jun Sch WF2 160 E8
Sandal Cliff WF2 142 E1
Sandale Wlk 5 BD6 93 F7
Sandal Grange Gdns WF2 160 F8
Sandal Hall Cl WF2 142 F1
Sandal Hall Mews WF2 142 E1
Sandall Cl LS25 83 B2
Sandall Magna HX3 93 E7
Sandal Park Ct WF1 142 D3
Sandal Prim Sch BD17 38 B3
Sandal Rise WF8 165 A5
Sandals Rd BD17 38 C3
Sandal St HX7 89 B3
Sandal Way WF17 96 F1
Sandbeck Ind Est LS22 13 F7
Sandbeck La LS22 14 B8
Sandbeck Pk LS22 13 F7
Sandbeck Way LS22 13 F7
Sandbed Ct LS15 62 D3
Sandbed La LS15 62 D3
Sandbed Lawns 3 LS15 62 D3
Sandbeds
Cullingworth BD13 52 C5
Honley HD9 171 F6
Sand Beds BD13 72 F1
Sandbeds Cres HX2 91 E1
Sandbeds Rd HX2 91 E1
Sandbeds Terr HX2 91 E1
Sandbeds Trad Est WF5 140 E7
Sandene Ave HD4 153 C2
Sandene Dr HD4 153 C2
Sanderling Ct 7 BD8 73 C7
Sanderling Garth 5 LS10 99 D5
Sanderling Way LS10 99 D5
Sanderson Ave
Bradford BD6 74 C1
Normanton WF6 123 A1
Sanderson La
Lofthouse Gate LS26 122 B8
Rothwell LS26 101 B1
Sanderson St WF1 216 C2
Sandfield Ave LS6 59 E6
Sandfield Garth LS6 59 E6
Sandfield Rd
Bacup OL13 106 A1
Bradford BD10 56 B6
Sandfield View LS6 59 E6
Sandford Pl LS5 59 A4
Sandford Rd
Bradford BD3 75 C7
Leeds LS5 59 B3
South Elmsall WF9 183 A5
Sandforth Ave HX3 92 C2
Sandgate Dr LS25 83 C2
Sandgate La
Kippax LS25 83 C1
Kippax LS25 83 D3
Sandgate Rise LS25 83 C2
Sandgate Terr LS25 83 C1
Sandgate Wlk 12 BD4 75 E2
Sandhall Ave HX2 112 D7
Sandhall Cres 5 HX2 112 D8
Sandhall Dr HX2 112 D7
Sandhall Gn HX2 112 D7
Sandhall La HX2 112 D7
Sandhill Cl WF8 125 D4
Sandhill Cres LS17 43 E4
Sandhill Ct LS17 43 D3
Sandhill Dr LS17 43 E4
Sandhill Fold BD10 56 A7
Sandhill Gr
Brierley S72 181 A1
Leeds LS17 43 E5
Sand Hill La LS17 43 D3
Sandhill Lawn WF8 146 C7
Sand Hill Lawns LS17 43 D3
Sandhill Mount
Bradford BD10 56 B6
Leeds LS17 43 E5
Sandhill Oval LS17 43 E5
Sandhill Rise WF8 125 D3
Sandholme Cres HX3 114 D7
Sandholme Dr
Bradford BD10 56 C6
Burley in W LS29 21 F8
Ossett WF5 140 D5
Sandholme Fold HX3 114 D7
Sandhurst Ave LS8 208 A3
Sandhurst Gr LS8 208 A3
Sandhurst Mount LS8 208 A4
Sandhurst Pl LS8 208 A3
Sandhurst Rd LS8 208 A3
Sandhurst St LS28 57 A7
Sandhurst Terr LS8 208 A3
Sandiford Cl LS15 62 D3
Sandiford Terr LS15 62 D3
Sandiway Bank WF12 139 D3
Sandleas Way LS15 62 F2
Sandlewood Cl LS11 211 A1
Sandlewood Cres LS6 42 F1
Sandlewood Ct 6 LS6 42 F1
Sandlewood Gn LS11 211 B1
Sandmead Cl
Bradford BD4 75 E3
Morley LS27 98 A6
Sandmead Croft LS27 98 A6
Sandmead Way 3 LS27 98 A6
Sandmoor Ave LS17 43 D6
Sandmoor Chase LS17 43 D5
Sandmoor Cl
Leeds LS17 43 D5
6 Thornton BD13 72 E6
Sandmoor Ct LS17 43 D5
Sandmoor Dr LS17 43 D5
Sandmoor Garth BD10 39 B1
Sandmoor Gdns HX3 93 B5
Sandmoor Gn LS17 43 C6
Sandmoor La LS17 43 D5
Sandmoor Mews LS17 43 D5
Sandon Gr LS10 215 B2
Sandon Mount LS10 215 B2
Sandon Pl LS10 215 B2
Sandown Ave
Crofton WF4 143 F1
Halifax HX2 91 E4
Sandown Rd HX2 91 E4
Sandpiper App LS27 98 C3
Sandpiper Ct WF4 159 D6
Sandpiper Mews
5 Bradford BD8 73 C7
Crigglestone WF4 159 D6
Sandpiper Rd WF4 159 D6
Sandringham App LS17 43 E3
Sandringham Ave
Knottingley WF11 126 C4
4 Pudsey LS28 76 E6
Sandringham Cl
Bradford BD14 73 D5
Morley LS27 98 C5
Pontefract WF8 146 C5
Sandringham Cres LS17 43 E3
Sandringham Ct
Bradford BD14 73 D5
Huddersfield HD2 136 E5
Leeds LS17 43 D4
Sandringham Dr LS17 43 D3
Sandringham Fold LS27 98 C5
Sandringham Gdns LS17 43 D3
Sandringham Gn LS17 43 E4
Sandringham Mount LS17 43 E3
Sandringham Rd
Bradford BD14 73 D5
Byram WF11 126 D7
Wetherby LS22 13 E6
Sandringham Way LS17 43 D3
Sandrock Rd WF8 125 E2
Sandsend Cl BD9 54 D3
Sands House La HD4 153 B1
Sandside Cl BD5 74 F2
Sands La
Dewsbury WF12 139 E7
Lepton HD5, HD8 155 F6
Mirfield WF14 138 D3
Sands Rd WF12 139 E6
Sand St
Haworth BD22 51 C6
Huddersfield HD1 154 B5
Keighley BD21 35 C8
Sandstone Cl HD9 171 F3
Sandstone Dr LS12 77 C7
Sandstone La HD4 153 B3
Sandway LS15 62 B2
Sandway Gdns LS15 62 B2
Sandway Gr LS15 62 B2
Sandwell St HD7 151 F1
Sandwich Cres HD2 135 F3
Sandyacres LS26 100 F6
Sandyacres Cres LS26 100 F6
Sandyacres Dr LS26 100 F6
Sandy Bank Ave LS26 100 F6
Sandy Banks BD16 53 B8
Sandy Beck BD15 54 A3
Sandybridge La S72 180 B4
Sandybridge Lane Ind Est S72 180 B3
Sandy Dyke La HX6 132 E8
Sandyfield Terr WF17 118 B6
Sandyfoot HX4 133 B4
Sandy Gate
Harewood LS17 26 E7
Hebden Bridge HX7 89 B4
Holmfirth HX7 189 C4
Keighley BD20 35 A8
Sandygate La WF9 181 C7
Sandy Gate La
Ackworth M T WF7 146 C3
Wadsworth Moor HX7 89 C4
Sandygate Terr BD4 75 D5
Sandy Gr LS26 100 F6
Sandy La
Huddersfield HD4 171 A7
Netherton WF4 158 C7
Sandylands
Glusburn BD20 16 D7
Huddersfield HD4 171 D6
Sandy Lane Prim Sch BD15 54 A4
Sandy Lobby LS21 24 C6
Sandymoor BD15 54 A4
Sandy Way 10 LS19 40 B7
Sandy Wlk
Bramhope LS16 24 F2
Wakefield WF1 216 A3
Sandywood Ct LS18 58 C7
Sandywood St BD21 35 C8
Sanford Ct 5 WF5 140 D5
Sangster Way BD5 75 A1
Sanquah Terr WF6 123 C3
Santa Monica Cres BD10 56 A7
Santa Monica Gr BD10 56 A7
Santa Monica Rd BD10 56 A7
Santingley La WF4 162 A6
Santorini LS12 211 A3
Sanworth St 2 OL14 108 C5
Sapgate La BD13 72 E6
Saplin St BD8 55 B1
Sapphire Ct WF17 118 A6
Sarah St WF3 120 D8
Sardinia St LS10 212 A1
Saunders Cl HD3 153 C7
Saunters Way WF6 123 A4
Savile Ave
Bradford BD10 56 C6
Emley HD8 175 D7
Leeds LS7 207 A4
Savile Bsns Ctr WF12 139 D7
Savile Cl HD6 115 D3
Savile Cres HX1 203 A2
Savile Ct WF14 138 A6
Savile Dr
Halifax HX1 203 A2
Horbury WF4 141 A2
Leeds LS7 207 A3
Savile Glen HX1 203 A2
Savile Gn HX1 203 B2
Savile Gr WF12 139 C7
Savile Ho 7 HX5 134 F7
Savile La HD6 115 D3
Savile Lea HX1 203 A2
Savile Mews WF12 139 C5
Savile Mount LS7 207 A3
Savile Par HX1 203 A1
Savile Park Gdns HX1 203 A1
Savile Park Mills HX1 202 C1
Savile Park Rd
Cleckheaton BD19 95 D3
Halifax HX1 203 A1
Savile Park St HX1 202 C1
Savile Park Terr 17 HX1 202 C1
Savile Pit La WF12 140 A8
Savile Pk
Halifax HX3 113 B4
Halifax, King Cross HX1 202 C1
Savile Pk Villas HX1 203 A1
Savile Pl
Leeds LS7 207 A3
Mirfield WF14 138 A7
Savile Prec WF10 124 C8
Savile Rd
Castleford WF10 124 C8
Dewsbury WF12 139 C6
Elland HX5 134 F6
Halifax HX1 203 A2
Hebden Bridge HX7 88 E3
Huddersfield HD3 153 C8
Leeds LS7 207 A3
Mickletown LS26 102 D3
Savile Royd HX1 203 A1
Savile Sq WF14 138 A5
Savile St
Batley WF17 118 D2
Cleckheaton BD19 95 D1
Emley HD8 175 D7
Huddersfield HD3 153 A5
Savile Terr HX1 202 C1
Savile Town CE Inf Sch WF12 139 D6
Savile Way HX5 135 A8
Savile Wlk
Brierley S72 181 B3
7 Dewsbury WF13 139 C8
Saville Cl WF3 100 C1
Saville Ct LS21 22 F7
Saville Gn LS9 212 C4
Saville Park Prim Sch HX1 202 C1
Saville Pk WF5 140 F4
Saville Rd HD8 175 A2
Saville St
Clayton West HD8 175 D1
Ossett WF5 140 F4
Wakefield WF1 216 B3
Savins Mill Way LS5 59 A4
Savoy Ct LS28 57 D1
Saw Hill HX6 132 E8
Sawley Cl WF1 142 E8
Sawley St BD21 35 B6
Saw Mill La LS29 7 A8
Saw Mill St LS11 211 B2
Saw Mill Yd LS11 211 B2
Sawood La BD22 70 F8
Sawrey Pl BD5 201 A2
Saw Yd WF1 216 B2
Sawyers Garth LS29 7 A8
Saxilby Rd BD20 19 B1
Saxon Ave WF9 181 F2
Saxon Cl
Emley HD8 175 C6
Upton WF9 183 E7
Saxon Ct
Bradford BD12 94 B3
Leeds LS17 43 B3
Saxondale Ct 1 WF4 141 B1
Saxon Gate LS17 43 B2
Saxon Gn LS17 43 A2
Saxon Gr
Leeds LS17 43 A2
South Kirkby WF9 182 A1
Saxon Mount
Leeds LS17 43 B3
South Kirkby WF9 181 F1
Saxon Rd LS17 43 A2
Saxon St
Bradford BD8 74 C8
Halifax HX1 202 B4
11 Walsden OL14 108 A1
Saxstead Rise LS12 209 C2
Saxton Ave BD6 73 F1
Saxton Ct LS25 82 F8
Saxton Gdns LS9 212 B3
Saxton Ho LS19 40 B6
Saxton La LS9 212 B3
Saxton Pl HD5 155 A4
Saxton St WF15 117 C5
Sayers Cl LS5 59 B4
Sayle Ave BD4 75 B1
Sayner La LS10 212 B1
Sayner Rd LS10 212 A2
Scafell Ct WF12 118 E2
Scaitcliffe View OL14 107 F7
Scala Ct LS10 212 A1
Scalebor Park Cl LS29 21 E8
Scalebor Sq LS29 21 D8
Scale Hill HD2 136 A2
Scaley St BD3 75 D7
Scaly Gate
Shepley, Barnside HD9 190 A2
Shepley HD9 190 A5
Scammonden Rd HX4 133 B3
Scapegoat Hill Jun & Inf Sch HD7 152 B6
Scape View HD7 152 E4
Scarboro Mdws WF14 138 A5
Scarborough Gr 3 BD18 55 A7
Scarborough La WF3 98 D1
Scarborough Rd
Otley LS21 22 F7
Shipley BD18 55 A7
Scarborough St
Dewsbury WF12 139 D6
East Ardsley WF3 119 D8
Scarborough Terr WF12 139 D6
Scar Bottom Cotts HX7 110 E8
Scar Bottom La HX4 133 F7
Scarbro' Junc LS13 58 D1
Scarbro Terr HX5 134 F6
Scarcroft Ct LS14 45 D8
Scarcroft Grange LS14 45 C6
Scar End Cl OL13 106 A8
Scar Fold HD9 189 A5
Scargill Cl LS9 207 C1
Scargill Grange LS9 212 C4
Scar Gr HD4 153 F2
Scar Head Rd HX6 112 B3
Scar Hill Cotts HX4 133 E4
Scar Hole La HD8, HD9 190 A3
Scarhouse La HD7 152 E4
Scar La HD3, HD7 152 F4
Scarlet Hts BD13 72 F1
Scarr Bottom Rd HX2 112 F4
Scarr End La
Batley WF13 117 F2
Dewsbury WF12 139 F5
Scarr End View WF13 117 F2
Scarr Green Cl HD9 170 E2
Scarsdale La LS17 28 E6
Scarsdale Ridge LS17 28 E6
Scarth Ave LS9 208 A2
Scarth Terr WF3 122 B6
Scar Top HD7 152 E4
Scar Top Cotts BD22 50 B7
Scar Top La HD4 171 D6
Scar Top Rd BD22 50 A7
Scarwood Cl 8 BD16 37 A4
Scarwood Terr 7 HD3 153 A4
Scatcherd Gr LS27 97 F4
Scatcherd La LS27 97 F4
Scatcherd Park Ave LS27 98 A5
Scatcherds Bldgs LS27 98 B6
Scawthorpe Cl WF8 125 F1
Sceptone Gr S72 180 C3
Schofield Ct 4 LS27 98 A4
Schofield La HD5 154 D6
Schofield Pl OL15 129 D2
Schofield St
Calderbrook OL15 129 D2
13 Todmorden OL14 108 B6
Scholars Way BD20 18 F2
Scholars Wlk BD2 56 B3
Scholebrooke Ct BD4 75 E1
Scholebrook La BD4 76 C4
Scholemoor Ave BD7 73 E5
Scholemoor La BD7 73 E5
Scholemoor Rd BD7 73 F5
Scholes (Elmet) Prim Sch LS15 62 F6
Scholes Fst Sch BD19 115 E8
Scholes Jun & Inf Sch HD9 189 D3
Scholes La
Barwick in E LS15 62 E8
Brighouse BD19 115 F7
Elland HX4 113 A1
Haworth BD22 33 F1

Scholes Moor Rd HD9 . . 189 C2
Scholes Rd
Castleford WF10 . . . . 104 D1
Holmfirth HD2, HD7, WF10 189 E3
Huddersfield HD2 . . . . . . 136 A2
Scholes St BD5 . . . . 74 D2
Scholey Ave HD6 . . . . . . 136 A8
Scholey Head La BB10 . . 85 A8
Scholey Rd HD6 . . . . . . 136 A8
Schoolaboards La **3**
WF8 . . . . 146 F8
School Ave WF13 . . . . . . 117 F1
School Cl
Crofton WF4 . . . . 144 B4
Gildersome LS12 . . . . . . 77 D3
Halifax HX2 . . . . 91 F7
Ripponden HX6 . . . . 132 E4
School Cote Brow HX3 . . 92 B6
School Cote Terr HX3 . . . 92 B6
School Cres
Dewsbury WF13 . . . . 117 F1
Halifax HX2 . . . . 91 F7
Wakefield WF2 . . . . 141 D4
School Croft
Brotherton WF11 . . . . . . 126 C8
Rothwell LS26 . . . . 100 E6
School Ct WF6 . . . . 123 D3
School Dr WF11 . . . . 126 C5
School Farm La WF7 . . . 164 A7
School Fold BD12 . . . . . . 94 B6
Schoolgate LS15 . . . . . . 63 E7
School Gn
Bramhope LS16 . . . . 24 E2
Brighouse HD6 . . . . 136 A8
Thornton BD13 . . . . 73 A6
School Gr WF13 . . . . 117 F1
School Green Ave BD13 . 72 C8
School Gn Ave BD13 . . . 72 B8
School Hill
Crigglestone WF2 . . . . . . 160 B4
Huddersfield HD4 . . . . . . 171 A7
Kirkburton HD8 . . . . 173 F6
School House Fold BD20 . 18 F2
School La
Aberford LS25 . . . . 64 E7
Addingham LS29 . . . . 2 E1
8 Bradford BD6 . . . . . . 74 B1
Castleford WF10 . . . . 124 F6
Collingham LS22 . . . . . . 29 B8
Denby Dale HD8 . . . . . . 192 A6
Dewsbury WF13 . . . . 117 F1
East Keswick LS17 . . . . . 28 C5
Emley HD8 . . . . 175 D7
Halifax, Illingworth HX2 . 91 F7
Halifax, Southowram HX3 114 A3
Harewood LS17 . . . . 44 C8
Horbury WF4 . . . . 141 A1
Huddersfield HD4 . . . . . . 171 F4
Huddersfield, Hill Side
HD5 . . . . 155 B7
Huddersfield, Paddock
HD1 . . . . 153 E5
Leeds, Chapel Allerton LS7 . 60 B7
Leeds, Halton LS15 . . . . . 81 A8
Leeds, Meanwood LS6 . . . 59 E6
Leeds, Whitkirk Lane End
LS15 . . . . 81 E7
Liversedge WF15 . . . . . . 116 C2
Marsden HD7 . . . . 169 C6
Ryhill WF4 . . . . 162 B1
Slaithwaite HD7 . . . . 152 B6
Thorp Arch LS23 . . . . 14 F4
12 Todmorden OL14 . . . 108 B5
Wakefield WF2 . . . . 120 E2
Walton WF2 . . . . 161 A7
School Land La HX7 . . . . 87 F6
School Mews LS22 . . . . 209 C3
School Pl **16** BD12 . . . . 94 C4
School Rd
Keighley BD22 . . . . 34 F7
Pontefract WF8 . . . . 146 F7
Slaithwaite HD7 . . . . 152 B6
Wakefield WF2 . . . . 141 D4
Wetherby LS22 . . . . 13 F6
School Ridge BD13 . . . . . 72 C8
School St W HD3 . . . . . . 153 B8
School Sq BD3 . . . . 75 D7
School St
7 Batley WF17 . . . . . . 96 F1
Bradford BD1 . . . . 201 B3
Bradford, Bierley BD4 . . . 95 B8
Bradford, Clayton BD14 . . 73 B4
Bradford, Dudley Hill BD4 . 75 C3
Bradford, Oakenshaw BD12 95 A4
Bradford, Odsal BD12 . . . 94 C6
Castleford, Castleford Ings
WF10 . . . . 103 E1
Castleford WF10 . . . . . . 124 C8
Cleckheaton BD19 . . . . . 116 B7
Cullingworth BD13 . . . . . 52 D6
Darton S75 . . . . 177 E1
Denholme BD13 . . . . 52 E1
Denholme BD13 . . . . 71 E8
Dewsbury, Chickenley
WF12 . . . . 140 B8
Dewsbury, Ravensthorpe
WF13 . . . . 138 E5
Dewsbury WF13 . . . . 139 D8
East Ardsley WF12 . . . . . 119 D5
Elland HX4 . . . . 134 B7
Halifax HX1 . . . . 203 C2
14 Hebden Bridge HX7 . 89 A3
Holmfirth HD9 . . . . 189 A5
Honley HD9 . . . . 171 F5
Huddersfield HD5 . . . . . . 154 D1
Keighley BD20 . . . . 18 A2
Liversedge, Norristhorpe
WF15 . . . . 117 B2
Liversedge WF15 . . . . . . 116 F2

School St continued
, Mapplewell S75 . . . . . . 178 C1
Morley, Churwell LS27 . . . 98 C8
Morley, City LS27 . . . . . . 98 B4
Ossett WF5 . . . . 119 C1
Pudsey, Farsley LS28 . . . . 57 D3
Pudsey LS28 . . . . 76 D6
Shipley BD16 . . . . 54 B7
Steeton BD20 . . . . 17 C5
Thurnscoe S63 . . . . 194 D1
Upton WF9 . . . . 183 D8
Wilsden BD15 . . . . 53 C5
School Terr
Clayton West HD8 . . . . . 175 F2
Fairburn WF11 . . . . 105 A4
Garforth LS25 . . . . 83 A8
Shelley HD8 . . . . 174 A3
School View LS6 . . . . . . 205 B3
School Wlk BD22 . . . . . . 34 F7
School Yard View **17** HX3. 92 C1
School Yd 141 B1
Schreiber Bsns Pk WF1 . 142 D4
Scissett CE Fst Sch HD8 175 D2
Scissett Mid Sch HD8 . . 175 D2
Sconce La BD16, BD17 . . 38 B7
Scopsley Gn WF12 . . . . . 156 E8
Scopsley La WF12 . . . . . 156 E8
Scorcher Hills La DN6. . . 184 C5
Score Croft HD8 . . . . . . 175 A2
Score Hill HX3 . . . . 93 A4
Scoresby St BD1 . . . . . . 201 C3
Scotchman Cl LS27 . . . . 97 F2
Scotchman La LS27 . . . . 97 E1
Scotchman Rd BD9 . . . . 55 A2
Scotch Park Trad Est
LS12 . . . . 210 A4
Scotgate Rd HD9 . . . . . 171 E4
Scotland HX2 . . . . 90 C2
Scotland Cl LS18 . . . . . . 41 B4
Scotland La LS18 . . . . . . 41 B5
Scotland Mill La LS16 . . 42 F1
Scotland St WF17 . . . . . 96 C2
Scotland Way LS18 . . . . 41 A4
Scotland Wood Rd LS17. . 42 F2
Scott's Almshouses LS10 215 C1
Scott's Cotts HD8 . . . . . 175 F3
Scott Ave WF16 . . . . . . 117 D6
Scott Cl
Sutton-in-C BD20 . . . . . . 16 D5
Swillington LS26 . . . . . . 82 A1
Scott Dr WF4 . . . . 162 A8
Scott Gn LS27 . . . . 97 B8
Scott Green Cres LS27 . . 97 C8
Scott Green Dr LS27 . . . 97 C8
Scott Green Gr LS27 . . . 97 C8
Scott Green Mount LS27. . 97 B8
Scott Green View LS27 . . 97 C8
Scott Hall Ave LS7 . . . . . 206 C4
Scott Hall Cres LS7 . . . . 60 B6
Scott Hall Dr LS7 . . . . . . 206 C4
Scott Hall Gn LS7 . . . . . 60 C5
Scott Hall Gr LS7 . . . . . . 60 C5
Scott Hall Pl LS7 . . . . . . 60 C5
Scott Hall Rd LS7, LS17 . . 60 B6
Scott Hall Row LS7 . . . . 207 A4
Scott Hall Sq LS7 . . . . . 60 C5
Scott Hall St LS7 . . . . . . 206 C4
Scott Hall Terr LS7 . . . . 60 C5
Scott Hall Way LS7 . . . . 60 C6
Scott Hall Wlk LS7 . . . . . 206 C4
Scott Hill HD8 . . . . 175 F3
Scott Ho OL14 . . . . 129 A8
Scott La
Cleckheaton BD19 . . . . . 116 E8
Cleckheaton, Gomersal
BD19 . . . . 96 B1
Keighley BD20 . . . . 18 E2
Morley LS27 . . . . 97 E3
Wetherby LS22 . . . . 13 E5
Scott La W BD20 . . . . . . 18 E2
Scott Mews LS22 . . . . . . 13 E5
Scotts Hill Cl LS14 . . . . . 45 F5
Scott St
3 Bradford BD6 . . . . . . 94 D8
Keighley BD21 . . . . 35 C7
Pudsey LS28 . . . . 76 F6
Todmorden OL14 . . . . . . 129 A8
Scott Vale HD2 . . . . 136 D3
Scott Wood La
Leeds, Buslingthorpe
LS7 . . . . 206 C4
Leeds, Scott Hall LS7 . . . 60 B5
Scotty Bank **7** HD6 . . . 115 A2
Scotty Croft La HD6 . . . . 115 A1
Scout Bottom La HX7 . . . 110 F8
Scout Cl HX7 . . . . 110 F8
Scout Hill Rd WF13 . . . . 139 A6
Scout Hill Terr **2** WF13 . 139 A6
Scout Hill View **1** WF13. 139 A6
Scout La HD7 . . . . 151 B1
Scout Rd HX7 . . . . 110 F8
Scout Road Prim Sch
HX7 . . . . 110 F8
Scrapers Gate OL14 . . . . 108 B8
Scrapers La OL14 . . . . . . 108 B8
Sculptor Pl **14** HD6. . . . 115 A3
SDH Ind Est HX6. . . . . . 112 B3
Seacroft Ave LS14 . . . . . 62 B5
Seacroft Cres LS14 . . . . 62 B5
Seacroft Gate LS14. . . . . 62 B5
Seacroft Grange Prim Sch
LS14 . . . . 61 F3
Seacroft Ind Est LS14 . . 62 A1
Seacroft Ind Est LS14 . . 62 B7
Seaforth Ave LS9 . . . . . . 208 A3
Seaforth Gr LS9. . . . . . . 208 A3
Seaforth Mount LS9. . . . 208 A3
Seaforth Pl LS9 . . . . 208 A3

Seaforth Rd LS9 . . . . . . 208 B3
Seaforth Terr LS9. . . . . . 208 A3
Seagrave Rd HD4 . . . . . 153 C3
Seaton St BD3 . . . . 75 B7
Seckar La WF4 . . . . 178 B8
Secker St WF2 . . . . 142 B3
Second Ave
Bardsey LS17 . . . . 28 E5
Bradford BD3 . . . . 56 C1
Cleckheaton WF15 . . . . . 116 B4
Fitzwilliam WF9 . . . . 163 A4
6 Halifax HX3 . . . . 113 B4
Horbury WF4 . . . . 140 F1
Huddersfield, Dalton HD5 . 154 F7
Huddersfield HD7 . . . . . . 152 D4
2 Keighley BD21 . . . . . . 35 B6
Kirkheaton HD5 . . . . 137 C1
Leeds LS12 . . . . 210 B3
Lofthouse Gate WF1 . . . . 121 B2
Rothwell LS26 . . . . 100 F7
South Kirkby WF9 . . . . . 181 F1
Upton WF9 . . . . 183 A8
Wetherby LS22 . . . . 13 F5
Yeadon LS19 . . . . 40 C5
Second St BD12. . . . . . . 94 E6
Sedan St **5** HX1 . . . . . . 203 B2
Sedbergh Cl LS15 . . . . . 80 D7
Sedbergh Dr LS29. . . . . . 8 C3
Sedbergh Pk LS29 . . . . . 8 B3
Sedburgh Rd HX3 . . . . . 203 C1
Sedgegarth LS14. . . . . . 45 F6
Sedge Gr BD22 . . . . 51 C8
Sedgewick St **3** WF17 . 96 E1
Sedgfield Terr **1** BD1. . . 74 D7
Sedgwick Cl BD8 . . . . . . 74 B8
Seed Croft
Halifax HX2 . . . . 91 C6
Steeton BD20 . . . . 17 C5
Seed Row BD4 . . . . 95 B8
Seed St BD12 . . . . 94 D6
Seemore Ctr WF5 . . . . . 140 D6
Sefton Ave
Brighouse HD6 . . . . 114 F5
Leeds LS11 . . . . 214 A3
Sefton Cres HD6 . . . . . . 114 F5
Sefton Ct **3** LS6 . . . . . . 59 D6
Sefton Dr
Brighouse HD6 . . . . 114 F5
Ilkley LS29. . . . . 8 B3
Sefton Gr BD2 . . . . 56 B3
Sefton Ho **19** BD4 . . . . . 75 E3
Sefton La HD9 . . . . 170 D2
Sefton Pl
1 Bradford BD2. . . . . . 56 B3
Keighley BD21 . . . . 35 C8
Sefton Rise WF12 . . . . . 139 D4
Sefton St
Halifax HX1 . . . . 202 C4
Keighley BD21 . . . . 35 C8
Leeds LS11 . . . . 214 B3
Sefton Terr
Halifax HX1 . . . . 202 C4
Leeds LS11 . . . . 214 A3
Selborne Gr
Bradford BD9 . . . . 55 B2
Keighley BD21 . . . . 35 B5
Selborne Mount BD9 . . . 55 C2
Selborne Terr
Bradford BD9 . . . . 55 B2
Shipley BD18 . . . . 55 B6
Selborne Villas BD9. . . . 55 B3
Selbourne Ave WF12 . . . 139 C5
Selbourne Dr WF12 . . . . 139 C5
Selbourne Rd WF12 . . . . 139 C5
Selbourne Villas BD14. . . 73 C3
Selby LS9 . . . . 91 D6
Selby Ave LS9 . . . . 80 E8
Selby Rd
Garforth LS25 . . . . 83 C4
Leeds, Austhorpe LS15 . . . 81 E7
Leeds, Halton LS9, LS15 . . 80 E8
Leeds, Whitkirk LS15 . . . . 81 C8
Micklefield LS25 . . . . . . 84 B4
Swillington LS15, LS25 . . 82 B6
Selby St WF1 . . . . 216 C3
Seldon St BD5 . . . . 74 B3
Selene Cl BD19 . . . . 96 C2
Sellars Fold **4** BD7 . . . . 74 A4
Sellerdale Ave BD12 . . . 94 D1
Sellerdale Dr BD12. . . . . 94 D2
Sellerdale Rise BD12. . . . 94 D1
Sellerdale Way BD12 . . . 94 D1
Selso Rd WF12. . . . . 118 F1
Seminary St LS2 . . . . . . 206 A1
Semon Ave BD2 . . . . . . 55 F5
Senior St
Dewsbury WF13 . . . . 139 B7
Huddersfield HD5 . . . . . . 154 E5
Senior Way BD5 . . . . . . 201 B2
Sentry HD9 . . . . 171 F5
Sergeantson St **14** HD1. . 154 A6
Serpentine Rd BD19. . . . 116 D7
Servia Dr LS7 . . . . 206 C3
Servia Gdns LS7 . . . . . . 206 C3
Servia Hill LS6, LS7 . . . . 206 B3
Servia Rd LS7 . . . . 206 B3
Service Rd LS9 . . . . 80 C3
Sessions House Yd WF8. 125 C1
Seven Acres BD13. . . . . . 71 D8
Seven Hills Prim Sch
LS27 . . . . 98 B4
Sevenoaks Mead BD15 . . 54 B1
Seventh Ave
Cleckheaton WF15. . . . . . 116 B5
Rothwell LS26 . . . . 101 A7
Severn Rd
Bradford BD2. . . . . 56 A3

Severn Rd continued
Leeds LS10 . . . . 215 C3
Severn Way LS10 . . . . . . 215 C3
Sewage Works Rd LS9 . . 80 C3
Sewell Rd BD3 . . . . 75 B6
Sewerbridge La WF7 . . . 145 A8
Seymour St
Bradford BD3. . . . . 75 A6
Wakefield WF2 . . . . 142 C4
Seymour Wlk HD9 . . . . . 170 E2
Shackleton St OL14 . . . . 86 C1
Shackleton Terr BD16. . . 36 A1
Shade Prim Sch OL14 . . 108 A3
Shade St OL14 . . . . 108 A3
Shadwell La
Leeds, Moortown LS17 . . . 43 D2
Leeds, Slaid Hill LS17 . . . 44 B5
Shadwell Park Ave LS17 . 44 C5
Shadwell Park Cl LS17. . . 44 C5
Shadwell Park Ct LS17 . . 44 C4
Shadwell Park Dr LS17. . . 44 C4
Shadwell Park Gdns LS17 44 C5
Shadwell Park Gr LS17 . . 44 C4
Shadwell Prim Sch LS17 . 44 F4
Shadwell Wlk LS17. . . . . 43 E3
Shady La BD20. . . . . 4 A3
Shaftesbury Ave
Beal DN14 . . . . 127 F5
Bradford BD9. . . . . 54 D1
Brighouse HD6 . . . . 136 B7
Leeds LS8 . . . . 44 A2
Shipley BD18 . . . . 55 C7
Shaftesbury Ct BD9 . . . . 54 D1
Shaftesbury Rd LS8 . . . . 44 A2
Shafton Hall Dr S72. . . . 180 B3
Shafton La LS11 . . . . . . 210 C1
Shafton Pl LS11 . . . . . . 210 C1
Shafton Prim Sch S72. . . 180 C2
Shafton St LS11 . . . . . . 211 A1
Shafton View LS11 . . . . 210 C1
Shakespeare App LS9 . . 207 C1
Shakespeare Ave
Normanton WF6 . . . . . . 144 A7
Todmorden OL14 . . . . . . 108 D6
Shakespeare Bldgs HD1 . 153 D6
Shakespeare Cl
Bradford BD3. . . . . 75 A8
Calderbrook OL15 . . . . . 129 C1
Guiseley LS20 . . . . 39 F8
Leeds LS9 . . . . 207 C1
Shakespeare Cres WF10 125 D5
Shakespeare Ct LS9 . . . 207 C1
Shakespeare Gdns LS9 . 207 C1
Shakespeare Grange
LS9. . . . . 207 C1
Shakespeare Lawn LS9. . 207 C1
Shakespeare Rd LS20 . . 39 F8
Shakespeare St
Halifax HX1 . . . . 203 B2
Leeds LS9 . . . . 207 C2
Shakespeare Twrs LS9 . . 207 C1
Shakespear Prim Sch LS6 59 F6
Shalimar St HX1 . . . . . . 202 B3
Shambles The
11 Huddersfield HD1. . . 154 B6
Wetherby LS22 . . . . 13 E5
Shancara Ct **3** WF3. . . . 98 E1
Shann Ave BD18 . . . . . . 34 F8
Shann Cres BD21 . . . . . . 34 F8
Shann La BD20 . . . . 17 F1
Shannon Cl
Brighouse HD6 . . . . 135 E7
Ilkley LS29. . . . . 7 F3
Shannon Dr HD3 . . . . . . 134 D1
Shannon Rd
Brighouse HD6 . . . . 135 E7
Leeds LS9 . . . . 212 B4
Shannon St LS9 . . . . . . 212 B4
Shann St BD2. . . . . 55 D4
Shapla Cl BD22 . . . . 35 A6
Sharehill HD7 . . . . 152 C3
Share Hill HD7 . . . . 152 C3
Sharket Head Cl BD13. . . 72 E1
Sharlston Com Sch WF4. 134 B4
Sharnaley Ct WF8 . . . . . 147 A8
Sharneyford Prim Sch
OL13 . . . . 106 C5
Sharon Cotts WF5 . . . . . 140 D7
Sharp Ave BD6. . . . . 94 C8
Sharpe St
Batley WF17 . . . . 117 D3
Bradford BD5. . . . . 201 B2
Sharp House Rd LS10 . . 99 F4
Sharp La
Huddersfield HD4, HD5 . . 154 F2
Middleton LS10, WF3. . . . 99 F4
Sharp Lane Prim Sch
LS10 . . . . 99 E5
Sharp Mews LS6 . . . . . . 59 F5
Sharp Row LS28 . . . . . . 76 E6
Sharp Royd HD5 . . . . . . 155 A4
Sharp St
11 Bradford BD6 . . . . . 74 C1
Dewsbury WF13 . . . . 118 D1
Shaw's Terr HD7 . . . . . . 168 F4
Shaw Ave WF6. . . . . 123 C2
Shaw Barn Croft LS22 . . 13 C5
Shaw Barn La LS22. . . . . 13 C5
Shaw Booth La HX2 . . . . 90 F4
Shaw Bsns Pk HD1. . . . . 154 C6
Shaw Cl
Elland HX4 . . . . 134 C4
Garforth LS25 . . . . 83 A5
Guiseley LS20 . . . . 39 F8
Normanton WF6 . . . . . . 123 C2
South Elmsall WF9. . . . . 183 A4
Shaw Croft Hill HX7 . . . 89 B7

Shawcross Bsns Pk
WF12 . . . . 119 A2
Shaw Cross Inf Sch
WF12 . . . . 119 A3
Shawfield Ave HD9. . . . . 188 D4
Shaw Fields HD7 . . . . . . 169 C8
Shaw Fields La HD7 . . . . 169 C8
Shaw Fold WF2 . . . . 142 E1
Shaw Gate HD7 . . . . 169 F6
Shaw Gr HD9 . . . . 171 E4
Shaw Hill HX1 . . . . 203 B1
Shaw Hill La HX3 . . . . . . 203 C1
Shaw House Sch 55 A3
Shaw La
Barnsley, Carlton S71 . . . 179 E1
Darton S75 . . . . 178 C2
Elland, Holywell Green
HX4 . . . . 134 C3
Elland HX5 . . . . 135 C3
Guiseley LS20 . . . . 22 F1
Halifax HX3 . . . . 203 C1
Holmfirth HD9 . . . . 188 D4
Huddersfield HD7 . . . . . . 153 B4
Keighley BD21 . . . . 35 D3
Leeds LS6 . . . . 59 D6
Marsden HD7 . . . . 169 A8
Oxenhope BD22. . . . . . . 51 B2
Ripponden HX6 . . . . 132 C2
Shelf HX3. . . . . 92 F6
Slaithwaite HD7. . . . . . . 152 C3
Sowerby Bridge HX6 . . . 112 C1
Todmorden OL14 . . . . . . 86 C3
Shaw Lea Gdns LS20. . . . 22 F1
Shaw Leys LS19. . . . . . . 40 A8
Shaw Lo HX1 . . . . 203 C1
Shawmount HX2 . . . . . . 111 E8
Shaw Rise WF6 . . . . 123 C2
Shaw Royd LS19 . . . . . . 40 A8
Shaw Royd Ct LS19. . . . . 40 A8
Shaws La
Barwick in E LS15 . . . . . . 63 C6
Sowerby Bridge HX6 . . . 111 A2
Shaw St
5 Bradford BD12. . . . . . 94 B6
Cleckheaton BD19 . . . . . 116 B7
Elland HX4 . . . . 134 C4
Mirfield WF14 . . . . 138 A5
Shaw Villas LS20. . . . . . 22 F1
Shaw Wood Ave OL14 . . . 109 A6
Shay Cl BD9 . . . . 54 F4
Shay Cres BD9 . . . . 54 E4
Shay Ct
Bradford BD9. . . . . 54 F4
Crofton WF4 . . . . 143 E1
Leeds LS6 . . . . 206 B3
Shay Dr BD9 . . . . 54 E4
Shayfield La WF3 . . . . . . 100 D3
Shay Fold BD9 . . . . 54 E4
Shay Gap Rd BD22 . . . . 34 C7
Shay Gate BD15. . . . . . . 53 E4
Shay Gr BD9 . . . . 54 F4
Shay Grange BD9 . . . . . 54 E5
Shay La
Bradford BD9. . . . . 54 F4
Crofton WF4 . . . . 143 E1
Halifax HX2, HX3. . . . . . . 92 A4
Holme HD9 . . . . 187 E3
Walton WF2 . . . . 161 C2
Wilsden BD15 . . . . 53 D4
Shay Lane Prim Sch
WF4 . . . . 143 E1
Shay St LS6. . . . . 206 B3
Shay Syke HX1. . . . . 203 C1
Shay The (Halifax Town FC &
Blue Sox RLFC) HX1 . . 203 B1
Sheaf St LS10. . . . . 212 A2
Shearbridge Pl BD7 . . . . 74 C6
Shearbridge Rd BD7 . . . 74 C6
Shearbridge Terr BD7. . . 74 C6
Shearburn WF5 . . . . 140 D8
Sheardale HD9 . . . . 171 E4
Shearing Cross Gdns **1**
HD1 . . . . 154 B8
Shearing Path LS29 . . . . .2 C7
Shed St BD21 . . . . 35 C7
Sheep Hill La BD13. . . . . 73 B2
Sheepridge Gr HD2 . . . . 136 C3
Sheepridge Rd HD2. . . . 136 C3
Sheepscar Gr LS7. . . . . . 207 A1
Sheepscar Row LS7. . . . 207 A3
Sheepscar St N LS7. . . . 207 A3
Sheepscar St S LS7. . . . 207 A1
Sheepscar Way LS7. . . . 207 A3
Sheepwalk La
Castleford WF10 . . . . . . 125 D6
Upton WF9. . . . . 183 D8
Sheerien Cl S71 . . . . 178 E1
Sheffield Rd HD9 . . . . . . 189 E3
Sheila Terr HD9 . . . . 117 C3
Shelby Grange **1** BD10. . 56 C6
Sheldon Ridge BD4 . . . . 95 B7
Sheldrake Ave BD8 . . . . 73 C7
Sheldrake Rd WF10 . . . . 124 D6
Shelf Hall La HX3 . . . . . . 93 C8
Shelf Jun & Inf Sch HX3. . 93 A5
Shelf Moor HX3 . . . . 93 C7
Shelf Moor Rd HX3 . . . . 93 C7
Shelf Rd HX7 . . . . 88 F3
Shelldrake Dr LS10. . . . . 99 D5
Shelley Ave WF16 . . . . . 117 E2
Shelley Cl LS26 . . . . 101 C3
Shelley Coll HD8. . . . . . . 174 E2
Shelley Cres LS26. . . . . . 101 C3
Shelley Ct
6 Bingley BD16 . . . . . . 37 A4

Shelley Ct *continued*
Horbury WF4 141 C2
Shelley Dr WF11 126 B4
Shelley Fst Sch HD8 174 A3
Shelley Gr BD8 73 E8
Shelley La HD8 174 A5
Shelley Sta* HD8 174 B1
Shelley Wlk WF3 121 E6
Shelley Woodhouse La
HD8 174 D1
Shell La LS28 57 B5
Shelton Ct BD13 52 E1
Shepcote Cl LS16 41 F3
Shepcote Cres LS16 41 F3
Shepherd's Gr LS7 207 B4
Shepherd's La LS7, LS8 207 C4
Shepherd's Pl LS8 207 C4
Shepherds Croft BD22 51 D8
Shepherds Gr HD2 136 E3
Shepherd St 1 BD7 74 B4
Shepherds Thorn La
HD2 136 C6
Shepley Bridge WF14 138 D4
Shepley Fst Sch HD8 190 E8
Shepley Mount WF14 138 B7
Shepley Rd HD4 173 C2
Shepley St WF1 142 E7
Shepley Sta HD8 173 F1
Shepstye Rd WF4 141 A1
Shepton Ho 8 BD5 201 B1
Sherborne Dr BD22 34 E5
Sherborne Rd
Bradford BD7 74 D6
Bradford, Thackley BD10 39 B1
Sherbourne Dr LS6 42 E1
Sherbrooke Ave LS15 80 F7
Sherburn App LS14 62 C6
Sherburn Cl
Birkenshaw BD11 96 B6
Leeds LS14 62 C6
Skellow DN6 184 E2
Sherburn Ct LS14 62 C6
Sherburn Gr BD11 96 B6
Sherburn Pl LS14 62 C6
Sherburn Rd
Brighouse HD6 135 E8
Leeds LS14 62 C6
Sherburn Rd N LS14 62 B7
Sherburn Row LS14 62 C6
Sherburn Sq LS14 62 C6
Sherburn Wlk LS14 62 C6
Sheridan Cl LS28 76 F6
Sheridan Ct LS28 76 F6
Sheridan Ho LS27 97 C6
Sheridan St
Bradford BD4 75 B4
Lofthouse Gate WF1 121 C5
Sheridan Way LS28 76 F6
Sheriff La BD16 37 D4
Sherwell Gr BD15 54 C1
Sherwell Rise BD15 54 C1
Sherwood Ave
Cleckheaton BD19 117 B8
Huddersfield HD2 136 F5
Sherwood Cl
Batley WF13 117 F3
Bingley BD16 37 C5
Cleckheaton BD19 117 B8
Sherwood Dr
Crigglestone WF2 159 F5
Huddersfield HD4 171 C7
Skellow DN6 184 E2
Sherwood Gdns WF3 100 B2
Sherwood Gn WF3 100 A3
Sherwood Gr
Shipley BD18 54 E8
Wakefield WF2 141 E4
Sherwood Ho 3 BD4 75 D5
Sherwood Ind Est WF3 100 B3
Sherwood Pl BD2 56 B2
Sherwood Rd HD6 115 C2
Sherwood Way S72 180 A1
Shetcliffe La BD4 95 C8
Shetcliffe Rd BD4 95 B8
Shetland Cl BD2 55 F4
Shibden Dr WF17 117 F6
Shibden Garth HX3 114 A8
Shibden Grange Dr HX3 92 F1
Shibden Hall* HX3 113 F8
Shibden Hall Croft HX3 114 A8
Shibden Hall Rd
Brighouse HX3 114 A8
Halifax HX3 113 F8
Shibden Head Ct BD13 92 C7
Shibden Head La BD13 92 D7
Shibden Head Prim Sch
BD13 92 D8
Shibden View BD13 92 D7
Shiela Henry Dr BD6 73 C1
Shield Cl LS15 62 E3
Shield Hall La HX6 111 C4
Shill Bank Ave WF14 138 D6
Shill Bank La WF14 138 C6
Shillbank View WF14 138 C6
Shillinghill La WF8 126 C2
Shilling St WF1 216 C4
Shinwell Dr WF9 183 D8
Shipley Airedale Rd BD1,
BD3 201 C3
Shipley CE Prim Sch
BD18 55 B6
Shipley Coll BD18 55 A8
Shipley College (Mill Bldg)
BD18 37 F1
Shipley Fields Rd BD18 55 C5
Shipley Glen Cable
Tramway* BD17 37 F2
Shipley Hospl BD18 55 A7
Shipley Sta BD18 55 C7
Ship St HD6 115 B2
Shipton Mews LS27 98 B3
Ship Yd WF1 216 C1
Shire Cl
Bradford BD6 93 F7
Morley LS27 98 B2
Shire Ct LS27 98 B1
Shire Gr LS27 98 B1
Shire Oak Prim Sch LS6 59 E5
Shire Oak Rd LS6 59 E5
Shire Oak St LS6 59 D5
Shire Rd LS27 98 B1
Shires Bsns Pk BD7 74 A5
Shires Ct LS23 30 E8
Shires Fold 4 HD3 153 D7
Shires Gr WF3 121 F5
Shires Hill 4 HD1 153 E5
Shirley Ave
Batley WF17 96 E2
Bradford BD12 94 C1
Cleckheaton BD19 117 B8
Shirley Cl 10 LS21 23 B7
Shirley Cres BD12 94 C1
Shirley Dr LS13 58 C4
Shirley Gr
Brighouse HX3 115 A7
Cleckheaton BD19 117 B8
Shirley Manor Gdns BD12 94 B1
Shirley Manor Prim Sch
BD12 94 C1
Shirley Mount BD19 117 B8
Shirley Par BD19 117 A8
Shirley Pl
Bradford BD12 94 C1
Cleckheaton BD19 117 B8
Shirley Rd
Bradford, Shearbridge
BD7 74 B6
Bradford, Tong Street BD4 75 D1
Cleckheaton BD19 117 B8
Shirley Sq BD19 117 B8
Shirley St
Denholme BD13 52 E1
3 Haworth BD22 51 B7
Shipley BD18 54 F8
Shirley Terr BD19 117 B8
Shirley Wlk BD19 117 B8
Shoebridge Ave BD20 16 F6
Shoebroad La OL14 108 B4
Shoe Market 4 WF8 146 D8
Sholebroke Ave LS7 207 A4
Sholebroke Ct LS7 207 A4
Sholebroke Mount LS7 206 C4
Sholebroke Pl LS7 207 A4
Sholebroke St LS7 207 A4
Sholebroke Terr LS7 204 A1
Sholebroke View LS7 207 A4
Shone Ct LS27 98 B2
Shop La
Kirkheaton HD5 155 C8
Lofthouse Gate WF3 121 B8
Shore End La HX2 90 A7
Shore Gn OL14 86 C2
Shoreham Rd LS12 209 C2
Shore New Rd OL14 86 B1
Short Cl BD12 94 B5
Short La LS7 60 C7
Short Row BD12 94 D6
Short St
Dewsbury WF12 140 A7
Featherstone WF7 145 C5
5 Todmorden OL14 108 B5
Shortway
Pudsey LS28 57 A1
Thornton BD13 73 A6
Shortwood La DN5 194 B4
Shrike Cl BD6 73 C1
Shroggs Rd HX1, HX3 202 C4
Shroggs St HX1 202 C4
Shroggs The BD20 17 C5
Shroggs Vue Terr HX1 202 C4
Shuttle Eye Way WF4 156 E4
Shuttle Fold BD22 51 D8
Shuttleworth La BD8 73 E8
Shuttocks Cl LS25 83 A3
Shuttocks Fold LS25 83 B3
Shutts La HX3 93 E2
Shutt The WF4 159 B8
Sickleholme Ct HD2 136 E5
Sickle St BD19 116 E8
Sicklinghall Com Prim Sch
LS22 12 B5
Sicklinghall Rd LS22 13 B5
Siddal Gr HX3 113 D4
Siddal La HX3 113 E3
Siddall St LS11 211 B2
Siddal New Rd HX3 203 C1
Siddal Prim Sch HX3 113 E3
Siddal St HX3 113 E3
Siddal Top La HX3 113 E3
Siddal View HX3 113 E4
Siddon Dr HD5 155 A3
Side Copse LS21 23 B8
Side La HD3 152 F6
Sides Rd WF8 146 D6
Sidings Cl BD2 55 D3
Sidings The
Dewsbury WF12 139 C6
Guiseley LS20 22 D1
Shipley BD18 55 C8
Sidney St LS2 211 C4
Siegen Cl LS27 98 A4
Sigget La OL14 107 F6
Sigott St HD3 152 F6
Sike Cl
Holmfirth HD9 189 D5
Kexbrough S75 177 D1
Sike La
Holmfirth HD9 189 D5
Walton WF2 161 B5
Sikes Cl HD5 154 F4
Silcoates Ave WF2 120 E1
Silcoates Ct WF2 141 E8
Silcoates Dr WF2 120 E1
Silcoates La WF2 120 E1
Silcoates Sch WF2 120 E1
Silcoates St WF2 142 A7
Silk Mill App LS16 41 E2
Silk Mill Ave LS16 41 E3
Silk Mill Bank LS16 41 D2
Silk Mill Cl LS16 41 D3
Silk Mill Dr
Keighley BD20 19 E1
Leeds LS16 41 E2
Silk Mill Gdns LS16 41 D2
Silk Mill Gn LS16 41 E2
Silk Mill Mews LS16 41 F2
Silk Mill Rd LS16 41 D2
Silk Mill Way LS16 41 E2
Silk St BD9 55 A2
Silkstone Cl LS25 64 B1
Silkstone Cres WF2 160 C6
Silkstone Crest WF6 122 F4
Silkstone Ct
5 Leeds LS15 62 C1
Normanton WF6 122 F4
Silkstone La S75 193 F3
Silkstone Rd BD3 75 B8
Silkstone Sq WF10 103 C4
Silkstone Way LS15 62 C1
Silsbridge St 4 BD1 74 D7
Silsden House Gdns BD20 5 C2
Silsden Rd
Addingham LS29 6 C7
Keighley BD20 18 E4
Low Bradley BD20 4 D5
Silson La BD17 38 E4
Silver Birch HD9 172 C3
Silver Birch Ave BD12 94 D2
Silver Birch Cl BD12 94 D2
Silver Birch Dr BD12 94 D2
Silver Birch Gr BD12 94 D2
Silver Court Ind Est HD5 154 C5
Silver Ct LS28 57 F1
Silverdale Ave
Guiseley LS20 39 E8
Keighley BD20 18 E1
Leeds LS17 44 B5
Silverdale Cl LS20 39 E7
Silverdale Cres LS20 39 E8
Silverdale Dr LS20 39 E7
Silverdale Gr LS20 39 D8
Silverdale Grange LS20 39 E7
Silverdale Mount LS20 39 E7
Silverdale Rd
Bradford BD5 74 E2
Guiseley LS20 39 D8
Silverdale Terr HX4 134 A6
Silverhill Ave BD3 56 D1
Silverhill Dr BD3 56 D1
Silverhill Rd BD3 56 C1
Silver Ho LS2 206 C1
Silver La LS19 40 B7
Silver Mill Cotts LS21 23 B6
Silver Mill Hill LS21 23 B6
Silver Royd Ave LS12 77 F6
Silver Royd Bsns Pk LS12 77 F7
Silver Royd Cl LS12 77 F6
Silver Royd Dr LS12 77 F6
Silver Royd Garth LS12 77 F6
Silver Royd Gr LS12 77 F6
Silver Royd Hill LS12 77 F6
Silver Royd Pl LS12 77 F6
Silver Royd Rd LS12 77 F6
Silver Royd St LS12 77 F6
Silver Royd Terr LS12 77 F6
Silver St E HD5 154 C5
Silver St W HD5 154 C5
Silver St
3 Bradford BD8 55 B1
Fairburn WF11 105 A4
Halifax HX1 203 B3
Heptonstall HX7 88 F5
Huddersfield HD5 154 C6
Leeds LS11 211 A2
Lofthouse Gate WF1 121 B3
Todmorden OL14 129 A7
Wakefield WF1 216 B2
Silvertrees LS16 24 D3
Silverwood Ave HX2 91 C1
Silverwood Way WF9 163 B2
Silverwood Wlk HX2 91 C1
Silwood Dr BD2 56 C3
Simeon St OL14 129 A8
Simes St BD1 201 A3
Simm Carr La HX3 92 D4
Simmonds La HX1 203 C1
Simmons Ct LS9 212 C2
Simmons Way LS8 208 B4
Simms Dene BD15 54 A4
Simon Cl BD4 75 F2
Simon Fold BD12 94 C2
Simon Green Rd HD7 152 B3
Simon Marks Ct LS12 209 C1
Simpson Apartments 6
HX1 203 A1
Simpson Gr
Bradford BD10 39 C1
Leeds LS12 210 A3
Simpson Rd
Mytholmroyd HX7 110 D8
South Elmsall WF9 183 B4
Simpsons Fold E 17
LS10 211 C3
Simpsons Fold W 18
LS10 211 C3
Simpsons La WF11 126 D3
Simpson St
East Ardsley WF3 120 E8
6 Halifax HX3 92 B2
Keighley BD21 35 A7
Sim Royd La HD8 192 D4
Sinclair Garth WF2 160 E8
Sinclair Rd BD2 55 F5
Sinden Mews BD10 39 B2
Sinderhill Ct HX3 93 A4
Singleton St BD1 55 E1
Sion Hill HX3 113 E3
Sir Francis Crossley's
Almhouses HX1 203 A3
Sir George Martin Dr
LS16 42 D4
Sir Isaac Holden Pl BD7 74 C7
Sir Karl Cohen Sq LS12 209 B3
Sir Wilfred Pl 3 BD10 56 B8
Siskin Ct LS27 98 B3
Siskin Dr BD6 73 C1
Sisley La OL14 109 A4
Sissons Ave LS10 99 B4
Sissons Cres LS10 99 B3
Sissons Dr LS10 99 B4
Sissons Gn LS10 99 B4
Sissons Gr LS10 99 B4
Sissons La LS10 99 B4
Sissons Mount LS10 99 A3
Sissons Pl LS10 99 B4
Sissons Rd LS10 99 A3
Sissons Row LS10 99 B4
Sissons St LS10 99 B4
Sissons Terr LS10 99 B3
Sissons View LS10 99 B3
Sitka Cl S71 179 B2
Siward St WF9 163 A4
Sixrood La DN6 184 F5
Sixth Ave
Bradford BD3 56 C1
Cleckheaton WF15 116 B5
Rothwell LS26 101 A6
Sizers Ct LS19 40 A5
Skelbrooke Dr WF8 146 D5
Skelda Rise LS29 8 B3
Skellow Dr 6 BD4 75 F1
Skellow Hall Gdns DN6 184 F1
Skellow Rd DN6 184 F1
Skelmanthorpe Bsns Pk
HD8 175 A2
Skelmanthorpe Fst Sch
HD8 175 B2
Skelmanthorpe Sta*
HD8 175 A3
Skelton Ave
Darton S75 178 B1
Leeds LS9 80 B8
Skelton Cres
Huddersfield HD4 153 B3
Leeds LS9 80 B8
Skelton Grange Rd LS10 80 B2
Skelton Mount LS9 80 B8
Skelton Pl LS9 80 B8
Skelton Rd LS9 80 B8
Skeltons La LS14 45 C1
Skelton St LS9 80 B8
Skelton Terr LS9 80 B8
Skelton Wlk BD10 56 D7
Skelwith App LS14 62 A2
Skelwith Wlk LS14 62 A2
Skinner La
Bradford BD8 55 C2
Leeds LS7 207 A1
Pontefract WF8 125 D2
Skinner St LS1 211 A4
Skippon Terr LS14 45 F6
Skipton Ave HD2 136 B2
Skipton Rd
Addingham LS29 2 D1
Farnhill BD20 4 C1
Glusburn BD20 16 E6
Ilkley LS29 7 E4
Keighley BD20 18 B2
Kildwick BD20 16 D8
Low Bradley BD20 4 B6
Silsden BD20 5 C2
Steeton BD20 17 B5
Skipton Rise LS25 83 B7
Skipton St WF17 118 C2
Skircoat Gn HX3 113 C2
Skircoat Green Rd HX3 113 C3
Skircoat Lo HX3 113 B2
Skircoat Moor Cl HX3 113 A4
Skircoat Moor Rd HX3 113 A4
Skircoat Rd HX1 203 B1
Skirden Ct HX2 91 E7
Skirrow St BD16 54 B6
Skopos Motor Mus*
WF17 118 D4
Skye Croft S71 179 C5
Skye Rd BD9 55 A3
Skye View LS26 100 F5
Skylark Ave BD6 73 C1
Slack HD3 152 A7
Slack Bottom HX7 88 E6
Slack Bottom Rd BD6 94 A8
Slack End BD6 93 F7
Slack House La HX7 89 B7
Slack La
Crofton WF4 144 A1
Elland HD3 152 A8
Halifax HX2 90 B4
Holmfirth HD9 189 B4
Oakworth BD22 34 B3
Slack La *continued*
Ripponden, Barkisland
HX4 133 A
Ripponden HX6 131 F
South Hiendley S72 180 B
Wakefield WF2 160 C
Slacks La
Marsden HD7 169 A
Slaithwaite HD7 169 E
Slack Top HX7 88 D
Slack Top La HD8, HD9 190 C
Sladdin Row BD13 92 C
Slade Cl LS23 30 D
Slade Ho BD2 56 D
Slade La
Brighouse HD6 135 F
Keighley BD20 18 E
Sladen Bridge BD22 50 F
Sladen St 6 BD21 35 A
Slades La HD9 170 E
Slades Rd HD7 152 B
Slade Wlk WF17 96 F
Slaid Hill Ct LS17 44 B
Slaids HD7 152 F
Slaithwaite Ave WF12 139 C
Slaithwaite CE Jun & Inf Sch
HD7 169 E
Slaithwaite Cl WF12 139 C
Slaithwaite Gate HD7 152 A
Slaithwaite Rd
Dewsbury WF12 139 D
Meltham HD7, HD9 170 B
Slaithwaite Sta HD7 151 F
Slant Gate
Huddersfield HD7 152 E
Kirkburton HD8 173 E
Slant La OL14 108 D
Slate Quarry La BD16 37 B
Slater Ave HX7 89 A
Slater Bank 18 HX7 89 A
Slater Ing La HX7 88 C
Slaters Rd LS28 57 E
Slates La LS29 8 B
Slaymaker La BD22 34 C
Slead Ave HD6 114 F
Slead Cres HD6 114 F
Slead Ct HD6 114 F
Slead Gr HD6 114 F
Slead Royd HD6 114 F
Slead View HD6 114 F
Sledbrook Cres S36 200 C
Sledgate La HD7 169 E
Sledge Gate HD3 151 A
Sledmere Croft LS14 62 C
Sledmere Garth LS14 62 C
Sledmere Gn LS14 62 C
Sledmere La LS14 62 C
Sledmere Pl LS14 62 C
Sledmere Sq LS14 62 C
Sleep Hill La
Hampole DN6 184 B
South Elmsall DN6 183 F
Sleights La LS17 27 B
Sleningford Gr BD18 54 E
Sleningford Rd
Bingley BD16 36 E
Shipley BD18 54 E
Sleningford Rise BD16 36 F
Sleningford Terr BD16 36 E
Slicer's Yd BD16 36 F
Slingsby Cl BD10 56 D
Slipper La WF14 137 E
Slippery Ford La BD22 33 C
Slippy La HX2 91 C
Slutwell La WF8 146 D
Smalewell Cl LS28 76 D
Smalewell Dr LS28 76 C
Smalewell Gdns LS28 76 C
Smalewell Gn LS28 76 D
Smalewell Rd LS28 76 C
Smalldrink La BD20 16 D
Small La
Cawthorne S75 193 B
Huddersfield HD7 152 D
Small Lees Rd HX6 132 D
Smallpage 21 BD13 72 E
Small Page Fold 7 BD13 72 E
Smallpage Yd WF1 216 B
Small Shaw La HX7 69 A
Smallwood Gdns WF12 119 A
Smallwood Rd
Batley, Chidswell WF12 119 A
Batley, Chidswell WF12 119 A
Smawell La WF4 179 B
Smawthorne Ave WF10 124 D
Smawthorne Gr WF10 124 D
Smawthorne Henry Moore
Prim Sch WF10 124 D
Smawthorne La WF10 124 D
Smeatley's La WF8 166 E
Smeaton App LS15 62 E
Smeaton Gr LS26 82 A
Smeaton Rd WF9 183 E
Smiddles La BD5 74 D
Smiddy Hill LS23 15 A
Smirthwaite St WF1 216 B
Smirthwaite View WF6 123 A
Smith's Terr HX3 92 A
Smith Ave BD6 94 C
Smith Cotts WF10 104 C
Smith Cres HD6 135 E
Smitherd's St BD21 35 C
Smithfield Ave HX3 114 C
Smith House Ave HD6 115 A
Smith House Cres HD6 115 A
Smith House Gr HD6 115 A
Smith House La HX3 115 A
Smithies Cl HX4 133 A

mithies Hill Ind Est
WF17 . . . . 117 F8
mithies La
Batley WF17 . . . . 96 E1
Liversedge FW16 . . . . . . 117 D2
mithies Moor Cl WF17 . 117 F7
mithies Moor Cres
WF17 . . . . 117 F8
mithies Moor La WF17 . 117 F7
mithies Moor Rise
WF17 . . . . 117 F8
mith La
Bradford BD9 . . . . 54 F2
Ripponden HX6 . . . . 132 B4
mith Rd
Bradford BD7 . . . . 74 B3
Dewsbury WF13 . . . . 117 F1
miths Ave HD3 . . . . 153 D7
mithson Ave WF10 . . . . 125 C6
mithson St LS26 . . . . . . 100 F4
mith St
Bradford BD7 . . . . 74 D7
Bradford, Bierley BD4 . . . 95 B8
Castleford, Castleford Ings
WF10 . . . . 103 F1
Castleford, New Fryston
WF10 . . . . 104 C2
Keighley BD21 . . . . 35 A8
Liversedge WF15 . . . . . . 117 B3
Shipley BD16 . . . . 54 B6
mithville BD21 . . . . 18 F1
mith Way WF10 . . . . . . 140 E7
mithwell La HX7 . . . . . . 88 E5
mith Wlk WF9 . . . . 183 A4
mithy Carr La HD6 . . . . 115 A4
mithy Cl
Crofton WF4 . . . . 161 F8
Skelmanthorpe HD8 . . . . 175 A1
mithy Clough La HX6 . . 132 B3
mithy Ct 5 LS22 . . . . . . 29 B8
mithy Fold BD13 . . . . . . 73 C2
mithy Greaves LS29 . . . . 7 C7
mithy Hill
Bradford BD6 . . . . 74 C1
Denby Dale HD8 . . . . . . 191 F3
Denholme BD13 . . . . 71 E6
Keighley BD22 . . . . 34 F4
mithy La
Bardsey LS17 . . . . 28 C2
Burley in W LS29 . . . . . . 21 E8
Denton LS29 . . . . 9 B7
East Ardsley WF3 . . . . . 119 F8
Heptonstall HX7 . . . . 88 A4
Holmfirth HD9 . . . . 188 C2
Huddersfield HD5 . . . . . 154 C5
Leeds LS16 . . . . 41 E6
Netherton WF4 . . . . 157 F6
Ripponden HX6 . . . . 150 D7
Skelmanthorpe HD8 . . . . 175 A1
Wilsden BD15 . . . . 53 C6
mithy Mills La LS16 . . . . 42 D2
mithy Nook OL15 . . . . . 129 C1
mithy Par WF12 . . . . . . 139 F1
mithy Pl HD9 . . . . 172 B3
mithy Place La HD9 . . . 172 B2
mithy St HX1 . . . . 203 C3
mithy Wlk WF12 . . . . . 139 F1
myth St WF1 . . . . 216 A2
nail La HX7 . . . . 110 B8
naith Wood Dr LS19 . . . 40 C1
naith Wood Mews LS19 . 40 C1
nape Dr BD7 . . . . 73 C2
napes Fold HD5 . . . . . . 154 F4
nape St BD21 . . . . 35 C4
napethorpe Cres WF2 . 141 D3
napethorpe Gate WF2 . 141 C4
napethorpe Prim Sch
WF2 . . . . 141 D4
napethorpe Rd WF2 . . . 141 D4
naygill Ind Est BD23 . . . . 4 A8
nelsins La BD19 . . . . 95 C1
nelsins Rd BD19 . . . . 95 C1
nittle Rd HD9 . . . . 199 B6
nowden App LS13 . . . . . 58 D2
nowden Cl LS13 . . . . 58 D2
nowden Cres LS13 . . . . . 58 D2
nowden Fold LS13 . . . . . 58 D2
nowden Gdns LS13 . . . . 58 E2
nowden Gn LS13 . . . . . . 58 D2
nowden La LS13 . . . . . . 58 D2
nowden Lawn LS13 . . . . 58 D2
nowden Rd BD18 . . . . . . 55 D7
nowden Royd LS13 . . . . 58 D3
nowden St BD1 . . . . 201 B4
nowdens Wlk BD14 . . . . 73 D4
nowden Vale LS13 . . . . . 58 D2
nowden Way LS13 . . . . . 58 D3
nowden Wlk 7 LS13 . . . 58 D2
nowdon Ave WF11 . . . . 126 C4
nowdon St WF17 . . . . . 118 B4
nowdrop Mews 8 BD15. 73 D4
now Hill Cl WF1 . . . . . . 121 A1
now Hill Rise WF1 . . . . 121 A1
now Hill View WF1 . . . 216 A4
nug La HD9 . . . . 190 A1
nydale Ave WF6 . . . . . . 123 C1
nydale Cl WF6 . . . . 123 C1
nydale Ct WF6 . . . . 123 C1
nydale Gr WF6 . . . . 123 C1
nydale Rd WF6 . . . . 123 C1
oaper House La HX3 . . . 93 D1
oaper La BD6 . . . . 93 D8
od House Dn HX3 . . . . . 92 A3
oho Gr WF2 . . . . 142 A6
oho St
Bradford BD1 . . . . 201 A3
Halifax HX1 . . . . 202 B3
olid HD4 . . . . 153 F2

Solomon Hill HX2 . . . . . . 90 D1
Solway Rd WF17 . . . . . . 118 F5
Somerdale Cl LS13 . . . . . 58 D1
Somerdale Gdns LS13 . . . 58 D1
Somerdale Gr LS13 . . . . . 58 D1
Somerdale Wlk LS13 . . . . 58 D1
Somerset Ave
Baildon BD17 . . . . 38 B4
Brighouse HD6 . . . . 136 B7
Somerset Cres HD5 . . . . 154 C5
Somerset Ct WF11 . . . . . 126 F4
Somerset Rd
Huddersfield HD5 . . . . . 154 D4
Pudsey LS28 . . . . 76 D8
Somers Pl 3 LS1 . . . . . . 211 B4
Somers St LS1 . . . . 211 A4
Somerton Dr BD4 . . . . . . 75 E2
Somerville Ave
Bradford BD6 . . . . 94 B7
Leeds LS14 . . . . 61 F2
Somerville Dr LS14 . . . . . 61 F2
Somerville Gn LS14 . . . . . 61 F2
Somerville Gr LS14 . . . . . 61 F3
Somerville Mount 2
LS14 . . . . 62 A2
Somerville Pk BD6 . . . . . 94 B7
Somerville Terr LS23 . . . . 23 C8
Somerville View LS14 . . . 61 F2
Sommerville Mews LS28 . 57 C1
Sonning Rd BD15 . . . . . . 73 B8
Soothill Hall WF17 . . . . 118 E4
Soothill La
Batley WF17 . . . . 118 E5
East Ardsley WF17 . . . . . 119 A5
Sorbus Way HD8 . . . . . . 155 E3
Sorrel Cl WF8 . . . . 146 D7
Sorrell Way BD17 . . . . . . 38 F4
Sorrin Cl BD10 . . . . 56 A7
Sotheron Croft WF8 . . . 147 C5
Soureby Cross Way BD4 . 95 F7
Sourhall Cotts OL14 . . . 107 D6
Sourhall Ct OL14 . . . . . . 107 D6
Sourhall Rd OL14 . . . . . 107 C5
South Accommodation Rd
LS10, LS9 . . . . 212 B1
Southampton St 4 BD3 . 55 F1
South App
Bramham LS24 . . . . 47 C6
Stutton LS25 . . . . 48 A3
South Ave
Castleford WF10 . . . . . . 123 F7
Horbury WF4 . . . . 141 C1
Huddersfield, Cowlersley
HD4 . . . . 152 F3
Huddersfield, Sheepridge
HD2 . . . . 136 B2
Pontefract WF8 . . . . 146 B7
South Elmsall WF9 . . . . 182 F2
South Baileygate WF8 . . 125 E1
South Bank
East Keswick LS17 . . . . . 28 C6
3 Queensbury BD13 . . . . 72 F1
South Bank Rd WF17 . . 118 A6
South Brook Terr BD7 . . 201 A2
South Carr WF2 . . . . 90 D1
South Cl
Guiseley LS20 . . . . 39 B8
Royston S71 . . . . 179 C2
South Cliffe
Halifax HX3 . . . . 113 E6
Thornton BD13 . . . . 72 E6
Southcliffe Dr BD17 . . . . 38 C1
Southcliffe Way BD17 . . . 38 C1
South Clough Head HX2 . 112 A8
Southcote Pl 6 BD10 . . . 56 B8
Southcote St 14 LS28 . . 57 D2
South Craven St BD20 . . . 16 D6
South Cres WF9 . . . . . . 183 B4
South Croft
Denby Dale HD8 . . . . . . 191 F3
Shafton S72 . . . . 180 C3
South Croft Ave BD11 . . 96 A6
South Croft Dr BD11 . . . 96 A7
South Croft Gate BD11 . 96 A6
South Crosland CE Jun Sch
HD4 . . . . 171 D7
South Cross Rd HD2 . . . 135 F2
Southdale CE Jun Sch
WF5 . . . . 140 E4
Southdale Gdns WF5 . . . 140 E5
Southdale Rd WF5 . . . . 140 E5
Southdene HD5 . . . . 154 E5
Southdown Cl BD9 . . . . . 54 E2
Southdown Ct BD9 . . . . . 54 E2
Southdown Rd BD17 . . . . 38 B1
South Dr
Guiseley LS20 . . . . 39 B8
Pudsey LS28 . . . . 57 D2
Royston S71 . . . . 179 C2
Wakefield WF2 . . . . 142 E1
South Edge
Keighley BD20 . . . . 35 A8
Shipley BD18 . . . . 54 F7
Southedge Cl HX3 . . . . . 114 C7
South Edge Terr HX3 . . . 114 C7
South End Ave LS13 . . . . 58 E1
South End Ct LS13 . . . . . 58 E2
South End Gr LS13 . . . . . 58 E1
South End Mount 2 LS13 58 E1
South End Terr 1 LS13 . . 58 E1
Southern Rd HD4 . . . . . 153 A3
South Farm Cres LS9 . . 208 C2
South Farm Rd LS9 . . . . 61 D2
Southfield
Bramhope LS16 . . . . 24 F2
Heptonstall HX7 . . . . 88 F4

Southfield Ave
Bradford BD6 . . . . 94 C8
Keighley BD20 . . . . 19 A2
Leeds LS17 . . . . 43 E2
Purston Jaglin WF7 . . . . 145 B4
Southfield Cl
Horbury WF4 . . . . 141 B1
Wakefield WF2 . . . . 120 E1
Southfield Ct HD8 . . . . . 173 F7
Southfield Dr
Keighley BD20 . . . . 19 A2
Leeds LS17 . . . . 43 E2
Southfield Fold WF4 . . . 159 B8
Southfield Ho 8 LS29 . . . . 6 F8
Southfield La
Addingham LS29 . . . . 6 F8
Bradford BD5, BD7 . . . . . 74 B3
Keighley WF4 . . . . 159 B8
Southfield Mount
Keighley BD20 . . . . 18 F2
Leeds LS12 . . . . 209 C3
Middleton LS10 . . . . 215 B1
Southfield Rd
Addingham LS29 . . . . 6 F8
Bingley BD16 . . . . 37 A1
Bradford BD5 . . . . 74 C2
Burley in W LS29 . . . . 9 E1
Crofton WF4 . . . . 144 B3
Huddersfield HD5 . . . . . 155 A4
Knottingley WF11 . . . . . 126 F3
Southfield Sq BD8 . . . . . . 55 C1
Southfield St LS12 . . . . . 209 C3
Southfields View WF4 . . 158 D5
Southfield Terr
Addingham LS29 . . . . 6 F8
Birkenshaw BD11 . . . . . . 96 A6
Brighouse HX3 . . . . 93 C1
Southfield Way BD20 . . . 19 A2
Southgate
Bradford BD1 . . . . 201 B3
16 Dewsbury WF13 . . . . 139 C8
Elland HX5 . . . . 134 F6
Guiseley LS20 . . . . 39 B7
Halifax HX1 . . . . 203 B3
Honley HD9 . . . . 171 F4
Huddersfield HD1 . . . . . 154 B6
Pontefract WF8 . . . . 146 D8
Rothwell LS26 . . . . 101 C6
Shafton S72 . . . . 180 D2
South Hiendley S72 . . . . 180 E6
Wakefield WF1 . . . . 216 B2
Southgate Ho HX1 . . . . 203 B2
South Gr
Brighouse HD6 . . . . 114 E5
Shipley BD18 . . . . 54 F7
South Hawksworth St 3
LS29 . . . . 8 B4
South Hiendley Jun & Inf Sch
S72 . . . . 180 D6
South Hill Cl LS10 . . . . . . 99 F7
South Hill Croft 3 LS10 . 99 F7
South Hill Dr BD10 . . . . . 37 C2
South Hill Gdns LS10 . . . 99 F7
South Hill Gr LS10 . . . . . 99 F7
South Hill Rise LS10 . . . . 99 F7
South Hill Way LS10 . . . . 99 F7
South La
Cawthorne S75 . . . . 193 C1
Elland, Blackley HX5 . . . 134 F4
Elland HX5 . . . . 134 F4
Holmfirth HD9 . . . . 189 A5
Netherton WF4 . . . . 158 D4
Shelf HX3 . . . . 93 C7
Southlands
Baildon BD17 . . . . 38 B1
Halifax HX2 . . . . 71 F1
Horsforth LS18 . . . . 41 B1
Kirkheaton HD5 . . . . 137 B1
Southlands Ave
Bingley BD16 . . . . 37 A1
Bradford BD13 . . . . 73 C6
Keighley BD20 . . . . 19 A1
Leeds LS17 . . . . 60 C8
Yeadon LS19 . . . . 40 E2
Southlands Cl
Badsworth WF9 . . . . 164 E2
7 Leeds LS17 . . . . 43 C1
Southlands Cres LS17 . . . 60 C8
Southlands Dr
Huddersfield HD2 . . . . . 136 A3
Keighley BD20 . . . . 19 A1
Leeds LS17 . . . . 60 C8
Southlands Gr
Bingley BD16 . . . . 37 A1
Bradford BD13 . . . . 73 B6
Keighley BD20 . . . . 19 A1
Southlands Gr W BD20 . . 19 A2
Southlands Mount BD20 . 19 A1
Southlands Rd BD20 . . . . 19 A1
South Lane Gdns HX5 . . 134 F5
Southlea Ave BD22 . . . . . 34 E2
Southlea Cl BD12 . . . . . . 95 A5
South Lee LS18 . . . . 41 B1
South Leeds Bsns Pk
LS10 . . . . 215 A4
South Leeds High Sch
LS11 . . . . 213 C4
South Leeds Stad LS11 . . 99 C8
Southleigh Ave LS11 . . . . 99 A8
Southleigh Cres LS11 . . . 99 A8
Southleigh Croft LS11 . . . 99 B8
Southleigh Dr LS11 . . . . . 99 A8
Southleigh Garth LS11 . . 99 B8
Southleigh Gdns LS11 . . . 99 A8
Southleigh Gr LS11 . . . . . 99 A8
Southleigh Grange LS11 . 99 B8
Southleigh Rd LS11 . . . . . 99 A8
Southleigh View LS11 . . . 99 A8

South Mead LS16 . . . . . . 24 F2
Southmere Ave BD7 . . . . 74 A3
Southmere Cres BD7 . . . 74 A3
Southmere Dr BD7 . . . . . 73 F3
Southmere Gr 3 BD7 . . . 74 A3
Southmere Oval BD7 . . . 73 F3
Southmere Prim Sch BD7 74 A3
Southmere Rd BD7 . . . . . 74 A3
Southmere Terr BD7 . . . . 74 A3
Southmoor La WF11 . . . 127 D3
Southmoor Rd S72, WF9 181 D3
South Mount LS17 . . . . . 28 B6
South Nelson St LS27 . . . 98 A5
Southolme Cl LS5 . . . . . . 59 A6
South Ossett Inf Sch
WF5 . . . . 140 E4
Southowram Bank HX3 . 113 E6
South Par
4 Bradford BD8 . . . . 55 D1
Cleckheaton BD19 . . . . . 116 C7
Elland HX5 . . . . 134 F5
Elland, Stainland HX4 . . . 133 F3
Halifax HX1 . . . . 203 C2
Ilkley LS29 . . . . 8 A4
Leeds, Headingley LS6 . . 59 D5
Leeds LS1 . . . . 211 B4
Morley, City LS27 . . . . . . 98 A4
7 Morley, Town End LS27. 98 B3
Ossett WF5 . . . . 141 A4
8 Otley LS21 . . . . 23 B7
Pudsey LS28 . . . . 76 E6
Wakefield WF1 . . . . 216 B2
South Parade Cl LS28 . . . 76 D6
South Parade Inf Sch
WF5 . . . . 140 F4
South Parade Jun Sch
WF5 . . . . 140 F4
South Park Terr LS28 . . . 76 F4
South Parkway LS14 . . . . 62 A4
South Park Way WF2 . . . 120 F4
South Parkway App LS14,
LS9 . . . . 61 E3
South Pl 13 LS27 . . . . . . 98 B4
South Queen St LS27 . . . 98 B3
South Rd
Cullingworth BD13 . . . . . 52 D5
Leeds LS9 . . . . 80 C3
Shipley BD9 . . . . 55 C4
South Ridge LS25 . . . . . . 83 A1
South Royd HD5 . . . . . . 155 A4
South Royde Ave HX3 . . 113 C4
Southroyd Pk LS28 . . . . . 76 F4
Southroyd Prim Sch LS28 76 E6
Southroyd Rise LS28 . . . . 76 E5
South Selby HX2 . . . . 91 D6
South Sq BD13 . . . . 72 D6
South St
Bacup OL13 . . . . 106 A3
Bradford, Little Horton BD5 74 C3
Bradford, Oakenshaw BD12 95 A4
Brighouse HD6 . . . . 115 A3
Denholme BD13 . . . . 71 D8
Dewsbury, Savile Town
WF12 . . . . 139 D6
Dewsbury WF13 . . . . . . 139 C8
East Morton BD20 . . . . . 36 D8
Elland HX4 . . . . 134 B4
Halifax HX1 . . . . 203 A2
Hemsworth WF9 . . . . . . 181 E6
Holmfirth HD9 . . . . 189 C6
Huddersfield, Netherton
HD4 . . . . 171 D6
Huddersfield, Paddock
HD1 . . . . 153 D5
Keighley, Knowle Park BD21 35 B5
6 Liversedge WF15 . . . . 117 B4
2 Mirfield WF14 . . . . 138 A3
Morley LS27 . . . . 98 B4
Normanton WF6 . . . . . . 144 A7
Ossett WF5 . . . . 140 D4
Ryhill WF4 . . . . 162 D1
Thornton BD13 . . . . 72 D7
Wakefield WF2 . . . . 216 C1
Yeadon LS19 . . . . 40 B4
South Terr
Dewsbury WF12 . . . . . . 139 E6
Ossett WF5 . . . . 140 E3
South View
1 Batley WF17 . . . . 96 F1
Bradford BD10 . . . . 56 D7
Castleford, New Fryston
WF10 . . . . 104 C2
Castleford WF10 . . . . . . 124 E5
Clifford LS23 . . . . 30 D5
Collingham LS22 . . . . 28 F8
Crigglestone WF4 . . . . . 159 D4
Dewsbury WF12 . . . . . . 139 D6
East Ardsley WF12 . . . . 119 D5
Farnhill BD20 . . . . 4 D1
Featherstone WF7 . . . . . 145 D6
Glusburn BD20 . . . . 16 D6
7 Guiseley LS20 . . . . 22 E1
Halifax, Snydal HX3 . . . . 113 E4
Halifax, Southowram HX3 114 A4
Haworth BD22 . . . . 51 C7
Horsforth LS18 . . . . 58 C7
Huddersfield HD1 . . . . . 153 D5
Keighley BD20 . . . . 19 C1
4 Leeds LS15 . . . . 62 C2
Menston LS29 . . . . 22 A3
Pudsey, Crimbles LS28 . . 76 F8
Pudsey LS28 . . . . 57 C1
Rothwell LS26 . . . . 100 D6
Shipley BD9 . . . . 55 C4
Slaithwaite HD7 . . . . . . 152 B6
Sowerby Bridge HX2 . . . 111 F5
Wetherby LS22 . . . . 13 E8

Smi–Spa 289

South View continued
Yeadon LS19 . . . . 39 F7
Southview Bsns Pk LS19 . 39 E7
South View Cl
Birkenshaw BD4 . . . . 95 E7
Yeadon LS19 . . . . 39 F7
South View Cres LS19 . . . 39 F7
South View Ct HX3 . . . . 114 D6
South View Dr BD4 . . . . . 95 F7
South View Gdns WF8 . . 147 A8
South View Gr BD19 . . . 117 B7
South View Rd
Birkenshaw BD4 . . . . 95 E7
Middleton LS10 . . . . 215 B1
9 Yeadon LS19 . . . . 40 B7
South View St OL14 . . . . 86 C1
South View Terr
Baildon BD17 . . . . 38 C4
Dewsbury, Ravensthorpe
WF13 . . . . 138 E6
4 Dewsbury WF13 . . . . . 118 B2
Grange Moor WF4 . . . . . 156 E4
Halifax HX1 . . . . 202 B4
1 Otley LS21 . . . . 23 B7
Silsden BD20 . . . . 5 D1
Yeadon LS19 . . . . 40 C6
Southwaite Cl LS14 . . . . . 61 F4
Southwaite Garth LS14 . . 61 F4
Southwaite La LS14 . . . . . 61 F4
Southwaite Lawn LS14 . . 61 F4
Southwaite Pl LS14 . . . . . 61 F4
Southway
Bingley BD16 . . . . 37 C5
Burley in W LS29 . . . . 9 C3
Guiseley LS20 . . . . 39 B8
Horsforth LS18 . . . . 41 A3
Huddersfield HD3 . . . . . 135 C1
Ilkley LS29 . . . . 8 D3
Mirfield WF14 . . . . 137 F7
South Way
Birkenshaw BD4 . . . . 95 E7
Shipley BD18 . . . . 54 D7
Southwell Ave HD3 . . . . 153 B7
Southwell La WF4 . . . . . 159 A8
South Wlk BD16 . . . . 36 A1
Southwood Ave HD9 . . . 172 B5
Southwood Cl LS14 . . . . . 62 C4
Southwood Cres LS14 . . . 62 C4
Southwood Gate LS14 . . . 62 C4
Southwood Rd LS15 . . . . 62 C4
Sovereign's Way WF12 . . 139 B3
Sovereign Bsns Ctr 5
HD4 . . . . 153 F3
Sovereign Bsns Pk LS10 212 A2
Sovereign Cl WF17 . . . . . 96 F1
Sovereign Ct LS17 . . . . . 43 E6
Sovereign Gdns WF6 . . . 123 A2
Sovereign Ind Est HD8 . 190 F6
Sovereign Pk BD17 . . . . . 38 E4
Sovereign St
Halifax HX1 . . . . 203 A3
Leeds LS1 . . . . 211 B3
Sowden's Yd 10 LS6 . . . . 59 D6
Sowden Bldgs BD2 . . . . . 56 B2
Sowden Grange 15 BD13 . 72 D6
Sowden La HX3 . . . . 93 F3
Sowden Rd BD9 . . . . 54 D3
Sowden St BD7 . . . . 74 B3
Sowerby Bridge High Sch
HX6 . . . . 112 C5
Sowerby Bridge Sta HX6 112 C3
Sowerby Croft HX6 . . . . 112 C2
Sowerby Croft La HX6 . . 112 C2
Sowerby Gn HX6 . . . . . . 111 D3
Sowerby La HX2 . . . . . . 111 C6
Sowerby New Rd HX6 . . 111 F3
Sowerby St HX6 . . . . . . 112 B3
Sowerby Village CE Prim Sch
HX6 . . . . 111 E3
Sowgate La WF8, WF11 . 126 B3
Sowood Ave WF5 . . . . . 140 E3
Sowood Ct WF5 . . . . . . 140 F3
Sowood Fold HX4 . . . . . 133 F1
Sowood Gdns WF5 . . . . 140 F3
Sowood Grange WF5 . . . 140 F3
Sowood La
Flockton WF12 . . . . 157 B6
Ossett WF5 . . . . 140 E3
Sowood St LS4 . . . . 59 C2
Sowood View WF5 . . . . 140 F3
Soyland Town HX6 . . . . 132 D5
Soyland Town Rd HX6 . . 132 D6
Spa Bottom HD8 . . . . . 155 C5
Spa Croft Rd WF5 . . . . . 141 A4
Spa Ctyd HD8 . . . . 155 C4
Spa Fields HD7 . . . . 152 B1
Spa Fields Ind Est HD7. 152 B1
Spa Fold WF3 . . . . 121 F4
Spa Gr WF2 . . . . 141 E3
Spa Green La HX6 . . . . . 132 C3
Spa Hill WF17 . . . . 118 D5
Spaines Rd HD2 . . . . . . 136 A1
Spa La
Bingley BD16 . . . . 37 A5
Boston Spa LS23 . . . . . . 30 E7
Ossett WF5 . . . . 141 A4
Slaithwaite HD7 . . . . . . 152 B1
Spalding Twrs LS9 . . . . . 207 B1
Spa Mews LS23 . . . . 30 E7
Spandola Ct BD22 . . . . . 34 F8
Sparable La WF1 . . . . . . 142 E3
Spark House La HX3 . . . 112 C3
Spark La S75 . . . . 178 C1
Sparks Rd HD3 . . . . 153 B7
Spark St HD3 . . . . 152 F7

Sparrow Rise HD9 . . . . **170** D2
Sparrow Wharfe LS2 . . **211** C3
Spartal La LS25 . . . . **103** E8
Spartan Rd BD12 . . . . **94** D5
Sparth La HD9 . . . . **188** B4
Spa St
Batley WF17 . . . . **118** D5
Ossett WF5 . . . . **141** B4
Spa Terr
Boston Spa LS23 . . . . **30** E7
Lepton HD8 . . . . **155** C5
Spawd Bone La WF11 . . **126** E3
Spa Well Gr S72 . . . . **181** A3
Speak Cl WF1 . . . . **142** F8
Speakers Ct WF13 . . . . . **139** B8
Spear Fir LS17 . . . . **28** A2
Spearhead Way **14** BD21 . . **35** C8
Speedwell Mount **6** LS6 **206** B3
Speedwell Rd WF10 . . . **123** E5
Speedwell St
Huddersfield HD1 . . . . . . **153** D5
7 Leeds LS6 . . . . **206** B3
Speeton Ave BD7 . . . . **73** E2
Speeton Rd BD7 . . . . **73** D2
Spen App LS16 . . . . **58** F7
Spen Bank
Cleckheaton BD19 . . . . . . **116** F7
Leeds LS16 . . . . **59** A7
Spenborough Ind Est
WF15 . . . . **117** C3
Spence La LS12 . . . . **210** C2
Spenceley St
Leeds LS2 . . . . **206** A2
Leeds LS2 . . . . **206** A3
Spencer Ave
Bradford BD7 . . . . **74** A5
Morley LS27 . . . . **98** A2
Silsden BD20 . . . . **5** E2
Spencer Cl BD20 . . . . **16** E7
Spencer Croft S75 . . . . . **193** F5
Spencer La HX7 . . . . **89** A1
Spencer Mount LS8 . . . . **207** B3
Spencer Pl LS7 . . . . **207** B3
Spencer Rd BD7 . . . . **74** A5
Spencer St
2 Keighley BD21 . . . . **35** A7
7 Keighley BD21 . . . . **35** B7
4 Mirfield WF14 . . . . . . **138** A3
Skelmanthorpe HD8 . . . **175** A2
Sutton-in-A BD20 . . . . . . **16** D5
Spencer Terr HD2 . . . . . . **136** D3
Spen Cl BD4 . . . . **95** B7
Spen Common La LS24 . . **47** F6
Spen Cres LS16 . . . . **58** F7
Spen Dr LS16 . . . . **59** A8
Spenfield Ct WF15 . . . . . **117** A2
Spen Gdns LS16 . . . . **59** B8
Spen Gn LS16 . . . . **58** F7
Spen La
Cleckheaton BD19 . . . . . . **117** A8
Leeds, Ireland Wood LS16 . . **42** A1
Leeds LS16, LS5, LS6 . . . **59** A7
Spen Lawn LS16 . . . . **58** F7
Spen Mews LS16 . . . . **59** A7
Spennithorne Ave LS16 . . **42** A2
Spennithorne Dr LS16 . . **42** B1
Spennithorne Rd DN6 . . **184** F2
Spen Rd LS16 . . . . **59** B8
Spenser Rd LS20 . . . . **39** F8
Spenser Rise LS20 . . . . . **39** F8
Spens Ho LS2 . . . . **206** B1
Spenslea Gr LS27 . . . . . . **98** A2
Spen Trad Est BD19 . . . . **95** D1
Spen Vale St WF16 . . . . . **117** D2
Spen Valley Ind Pk BD19. . **116** F6
Spen Valley Rd WF13 . . . **138** F6
Spen Valley Sports Coll
WF15 . . . . **117** A3
Spen View WF16 . . . . **117** F1
Spen View La BD4 . . . . . . **95** B7
Spen Wlk LS16 . . . . **58** F7
Spibey Cres LS26 . . . . . **100** D7
Spibey La LS26 . . . . **100** D7
Spicer House La S36 . . . **191** A1
Spicer St BD5 . . . . **74** C3
Spiers Garth BD6 . . . . **74** D1
Spindle St HX2 . . . . **92** A5
Spindles The **3** LS10. . . . **99** D8
Spinkfield Rd HD2 . . . . . **153** F8
Spink Ho **2** WF8. . . . . . **125** D1
Spink La WF8 . . . . **125** D1
Spink Pl BD8 . . . . **74** D8
Spinks Gdns LS14 . . . . . . **62** B4
Spink St BD8 . . . . **74** D8
Spink Well La WF3 . . . . . . **98** F1
Spinkwell Rd **4** WF13 . . **118** C1
Spinners Ave WF1 . . . . . **121** C1
Spinners Chase LS28 . . . **76** E7
Spinners Cl HX1 . . . . **202** B4
Spinners Hollow HX6 . . **132** D3
Spinners Way
Brighouse BD19 . . . . **115** F8
1 Haworth BD22 . . . . **51** F8
Mirfield WF14 . . . . **138** A3
Spinneyfield HD2 . . . . . . **136** A3
Spinneyfield Ct LS9 . . . . **212** B3
Spinney Rise BD4 . . . . **75** F1
Spinney The
Brighouse HD6 . . . . **115** A5
Draughton BD23 . . . . **1** D5
Hebden Bridge HX7 . . . . . **89** B2
Keighley BD20 . . . . **36** D7
Leeds LS9 . . . . **212** B3
Leeds, Moortown LS17 . . . **43** E2
Wakefield WF2 . . . . **160** E7

Spinney The *continued*
Wetherby LS22 . . . . **13** D6
Yeadon LS19 . . . . **40** A2
Spinning Mill Ct BD18. . . **54** E8
Spinning Mill The BD22 . . **51** C8
Spion Kop LS14 . . . . **45** F5
Spire Ct
Huddersfield HD1 . . . . . . **153** E7
Huddersfield, Marsh HD3 . **153** D7
Spitalgap La WF8 . . . . . . **147** C6
Spittal Hardwick La
WF10 . . . . **125** C5
Spittlerush La WF8 . . . . . **166** F4
Spofforth Hill LS22. . . . . . **13** D6
Spofforth Wlk LS25 . . . . . **83** B7
Spout Fold WF2 . . . . **141** D6
Spout Hill HD6 . . . . **135** E6
Spout House La HD6 . . . **114** E6
Spring Ave
Gildersome LS27 . . . . **97** C8
Keighley BD21 . . . . **35** E6
Springbank
Garforth LS25 . . . . **82** C6
Yeadon LS19 . . . . **40** A3
Spring Bank
Batley WF15 . . . . **117** C2
Cullingworth BD13 . . . . . . **52** D5
Halifax HX2 . . . . **90** E1
Kirkburton HD8 . . . . **173** E7
5 Leeds LS5 . . . . **59** A4
Pontefract WF8 . . . . **146** D7
Springbank Ave
Gildersome LS27 . . . . **97** C7
Pudsey LS28 . . . . **57** E3
Springbank Cl LS28 . . . . . **57** E3
Springbank Cres
Garforth LS25 . . . . **82** C6
Gildersome LS27 . . . . **97** C8
Huddersfield HD2 . . . . . . **136** D1
Springbank Croft HD9. . . **188** D4
Springbank Dr LS28 . . . . . **57** E4
Spring Bank Dr WF15 . . . **117** B2
Springbank Gr LS28 . . . . . **57** E3
Spring Bank Ind Est HX6 **112** B2
Springbank Mews WF3. . **121** A6
Spring Bank Pl BD8 . . . . . **55** D2
Spring Bank Prim Sch
LS6 . . . . **205** B4
Springbank Rd
Gildersome LS27 . . . . **97** C8
Huddersfield HD2 . . . . . . **136** D1
Pudsey LS28 . . . . **57** E3
Springbank Rise LS28 . . . **57** E3
Spring Bank Terr **10** LS20. **22** E1
Spring Bottom OL14 . . . **128** F7
Spring Cl
Bingley BD16 . . . . **37** B2
Fitzwilliam WF9 . . . . **163** B2
Garforth, East Garforth
LS25 . . . . **83** A8
Garforth LS25 . . . . **83** B6
Keighley BD21 . . . . **35** E6
Morley LS27 . . . . **98** A7
Springcliffe BD8 . . . . **55** B1
Springcliffe St BD8 . . . . . **55** B1
Spring Close Ave LS9 . . **212** C2
Spring Close Gdns LS9 . **212** C2
Spring Close St LS9 . . . . **212** C2
Spring Close Wlk LS9 . . **212** C2
Spring Dale HD9 . . . . . . **171** F5
Springdale Ave HD1 . . . . **153** F4
Springdale Cres BD10 . . . **56** C7
Springdale St HD1 . . . . . **153** F4
Spring Dr BD21 . . . . **35** E6
Spring Edge HX1 . . . . . . **113** A4
Spring Edge N HX1 . . . . . **202** C1
Spring Edge S HX1 . . . . . **202** C1
Spring Edge W HX1 . . . . **202** B1
Spring End Rd WF4 . . . . **141** B3
Spring Farm WF4 . . . . . . **179** A6
Spring Farm La BD16. . . . **36** A1
Spring Farm Mews BD15 . **53** C2
Springfield
Boston Spa LS23 . . . . **30** D8
Brighouse, Hipperholme
HX3. . . . . **114** C8
Clifford LS23 . . . . **30** D5
Elland BD3 . . . . **152** B8
Queensbury BD13 . . . . . . **72** D1
Sowerby Bridge HX6 . . . . **112** A3
Springfield Ave
Bacup OL13 . . . . **106** A3
Batley WF17 . . . . **118** B5
Bradford BD7 . . . . **73** F5
Clayton West HD8 . . . . . . **175** E2
Hemsworth WF9 . . . . **181** E6
Honley HD9 . . . . **171** F3
Ilkley LS29 . . . . **8** C4
Morley LS27 . . . . **98** A6
Pontefract WF8 . . . . **125** F1
Slaithwaite HD7 . . . . **169** E7
Springfield Cl
Clayton West HD8 . . . . . . **175** E2
Horsforth LS18 . . . . **41** E1
Leeds LS10 . . . . **80** A2
Springfield Cres
Morley LS27 . . . . **98** A6
Norton WF8 . . . . **166** E5
Springfield Ct
Keighley BD20 . . . . **35** A8
Leeds LS17 . . . . **44** A4
Normanton WF6 . . . . **144** B8
Yeadon LS19 . . . . **40** B8
Springfield Dr
Cleckheaton WF15. . . . . . **116** C5
Denby Dale HD8 . . . . **191** A4

Springfield Gdns
Horsforth LS18 . . . . **41** D1
Keighley BD20 . . . . **35** A8
Pudsey LS28 . . . . **76** F6
Springfield Gn LS10 . . . . **215** B2
Springfield Gr
Bingley BD16 . . . . **36** F3
Brighouse HD6 . . . . **115** A5
Springfield Grange WF2 **141** D6
Springfield Ho **3** BD19. . **116** E7
Springfield La
Birkenshaw BD4 . . . . **76** F2
Cleckheaton FW15. . . . . . **116** E5
Kirkburton HD8 . . . . **173** E7
Morley LS27 . . . . **98** A6
Springfield Mills HD8 . . **191** F5
Springfield Mount
Addingham LS29 . . . . **2** F1
Horsforth LS18 . . . . **41** D1
Leeds, Armley LS12 . . . . **209** A4
Leeds, Woodhouse LS2 . . **206** A1
South Elmsall WF9 . . . . . **182** E1
Springfield Pk WF14 . . . . **138** B5
Springfield Pl
Bradford BD1 . . . . **201** A4
Bradford, Springfield BD10 . **56** B6
Garforth LS25 . . . . **82** C6
Guiseley LS20 . . . . **22** E1
Leeds LS10 . . . . **215** B2
Otley LS21 . . . . **22** F7
Springfield Rd
Baildon BD17 . . . . **38** B4
Elland HX5 . . . . **135** B7
Guiseley LS20 . . . . **22** E1
Keighley BD20 . . . . **35** A8
Morley LS27 . . . . **98** A6
Springfield Rise
Horsforth LS18 . . . . **41** D1
Rothwell LS26 . . . . **100** F4
Springfields
Castleford WF10 . . . . **124** E8
Knottingley WF11 . . . . . . **127** B3
Springfields Ave WF11 . . **127** B4
Springfield St
Bradford BD8 . . . . **74** C8
Rothwell LS26 . . . . **100** F4
Thornton BD13 . . . . **72** E6
Springfield Terr
Bradford BD8 . . . . **74** C8
Brighouse BD20 . . . . **94** F1
Brighouse, Hipperholme
HX3 . . . . **114** C8
Cleckheaton WF15. . . . . . **116** C5
Cragg Vale HX7 . . . . **110** C3
Cullingworth BD13 . . . . . . **52** E5
Dewsbury WF13 . . . . **118** C1
Elland HD3 . . . . **134** B1
Emley HD8 . . . . **175** A7
Guiseley LS20 . . . . **39** E8
Halifax HX2 . . . . **90** C1
Pudsey LS28 . . . . **76** F7
4 Pudsey, Stanningley
LS28 . . . . **57** D1
Springfield View WF1 . . **145** A8
Springfield Wlk LS18. . . . **41** D1
Spring Gardens La BD20 . **18** A1
Spring Gardens Mount
BD20 . . . . **18** B1
Spring Gardens Rd BD9 . . **55** A3
Spring Garden St BD13 . . **72** E1
Spring Gdns
12 Bacup OL13 . . . . **106** A3
Batley WF17 . . . . **118** B5
Birkenshaw BD11 . . . . **96** F6
Bradford BD1 . . . . **201** B4
Brighouse HX3. . . . . **93** F2
Burley in W LS29 . . . . **9** F1
Harewood LS17 . . . . **27** A7
Holmfirth HD9 . . . . **188** E5
Morley LS27 . . . . **98** C7
Silsden BD20 . . . . **5** D1
Sowerby Bridge HX6 . . . . **112** A5
Spring Gr
Barnsley S71 . . . . **179** D1
Clayton West HD8 . . . . . . **175** E2
Halifax HX1 . . . . **202** A3
Hebden Bridge HX7 . . . . . **89** A4
Spring Grove Cotts HX4 . **150** F7
Spring Grove Jun & Inf Sch
HD1. . . . . **153** F5
Spring Grove St HD1 . . . **154** A5
Spring Grove Terr **18**
LS6. . . . . **205** B2
Spring Grove View **15**
LS6. . . . . **205** B2
Spring Grove Wlk **13**
LS6. . . . . **205** B2
Spring Hall Cl HX3 . . . . . **93** B5
Spring Hall Ct HX1. . . . . **202** A4
Spring Hall Dr HX2 . . . . . **202** A3
Spring Hall Gdns HX2 . . **202** A3
Spring Hall Gr HX2 . . . . . **202** A3
Spring Hall La HX1. . . . . **202** A3
Spring Hall Pl HX1 . . . . . **202** A3
Springhead BD22 . . . . **51** C8
Spring Head
Halifax HX2 . . . . **91** E1
Shelf HX3. . . . . **93** C5
Spring Head La HD7 . . . . **168** F5
Springhead Mills BD22. . **51** C8
Springhead Rd
Rothwell LS26 . . . . **101** A6
Thornton BD13 . . . . **72** F6
Spring Head Rd
Haworth BD22 . . . . **51** C8
Thornton BD13 . . . . **72** E6
Spring Head Terr BD13. . . **72** C8

Spring Hill
Baildon BD17 . . . . **37** F3
Leeds, Adel East Moor LS16 **42** E4
Leeds, Buslingthorpe LS7 . **206** C4
Shipley BD18 . . . . **55** E7
Wilsden BD15 . . . . **53** C5
Springhill Ave WF4 . . . . . **162** A8
Springhill Cl WF1 . . . . . . **121** A5
Springhill Dr WF4. . . . . . . **144** A1
Springhill Gr WF4. . . . . . . **144** A1
Springhill Mount WF4. . . **162** A8
Springhill Pl BD15 . . . . . . **53** C5
Springhills WF1 . . . . **121** A5
Springhill Terr **4** LS6. . . . **59** E6
Spring Holes La BD13 . . . **72** D7
Springhouses HD8 . . . . . **191** F5
Springhurst Rd BD18. . . . **55** A7
Spring La
Baildon BD16 . . . . **37** D6
Barnsley S71 . . . . **179** D1
Batley WF17 . . . . **118** B7
Crofton WF4 . . . . **162** B7
Elland HX4 . . . . **134** A7
Holmfirth, Hinchcliffe Mill
HD9. . . . . **188** D2
Holmfirth, New Mill HD9 . **189** E5
Holmfirth, Upperthong
HD9. . . . . **188** E4
Wetherby LS22 . . . . **14** C5
Springlodge Pl **5** BD8 . . **55** D1
Springmead Dr LS25 . . . . **82** F6
Spring Mill Fold HX2. . . . . **90** F8
Spring Mill La WF5. . . . . . **140** F6
Spring Mill St BD5 . . . . . . **74** E4
Spring Mount BD21 . . . . . **35** E5
Spring Park Rd BD15 . . . . **53** C6
Spring Pl
Bradford BD7 . . . . **74** C5
Keighley BD21 . . . . **35** E5
Spring Ram Bsns Pk
S75 . . . . **177** D1
Spring Rd LS6 . . . . **205** B4
Spring Rise
Draughton BD23 . . . . **1** D5
Keighley BD21 . . . . **35** E6
Spring Row
Harden BD16 . . . . **36** B1
Keighley BD21 . . . . **35** B6
Oxenhope BD22. . . . . **51** E1
17 Queensbury BD13 . . . . **72** E1
Springroyd Terr BD8. . . . . **73** F8
Spring Side Rise HD7 . . . **152** D5
Springs La
Ilkley LS29. . . . . **8** C4
Thorp Arch LS23 . . . . **14** F6
Springs Rd
Guiseley LS19, LS20 . . . . **39** E6
Holme HD9 . . . . **187** B4
Spring St
Bradford, Sandy Lane
BD15 . . . . **54** A3
Bradford, Springfield BD10 . **56** B6
Brighouse HD6 . . . . **115** A2
Dewsbury WF13 . . . . **118** C1
3 Haworth BD22 . . . . **51** F8
7 Huddersfield HD1. . . . . **154** A6
Keighley BD21 . . . . **35** C8
Liversedge WF15. . . . . . . **117** B4
Marsden HD7. . . . . **168** F3
Ripponden HX6 . . . . **132** D4
Slaithwaite HD7. . . . . **169** F8
Todmorden OL14. . . . . . . **86** C1
Springs The WF1 . . . . . . **216** B2
Springstone Ave
Hemsworth WF9 . . . . **181** E7
Ossett WF5 . . . . **140** D7
Springwood Ave BD18. . . **55** A7
Springwood Pl BD18 . . . . **55** A7
Springwood Rd BD18. . . . **55** A7
Spring Terr
Halifax HX3 . . . . **203** C4
Halifax, Wainstalls HX2. . . **90** F8
Keighley BD21 . . . . **35** B6
Ripponden HX4 . . . . **133** E3
South Elmsall WF9 . . . . . **182** F2
Sowerby Bridge HX6 . . . . **112** C2
Springvale Cl WF4 . . . . . **144** C3
Springvale Rd WF9 . . . . . **182** C3
Springvale Rise WF9 . . . **181** D8
Spring Valley LS28 . . . . . . **57** E1
Spring Valley Ave LS13. . . **58** C1
Spring Valley Cl
Leeds LS13 . . . . **58** C1
5 Liversedge WF15 . . . . **117** A5
Spring Valley Cres LS13 . **58** C1
Spring Valley Croft LS13 . **58** C1
Spring Valley Ct LS13. . . . **58** C1
Spring Valley Dr LS13. . . . **58** C1
Spring Valley Sq **3**
WF15 . . . . **117** A5
Spring Valley St **4**
WF15 . . . . **117** A5
Spring Valley View LS13. . **58** C1
Spring Valley Wlk LS13. . . **58** C1
Spring View
Gildersome LS27 . . . . **97** C8
Holme Chapel BB10 . . . . . **85** A8
Luddenden Foot HX2 . . . **111** D6
Ossett WF5 . . . . **140** F6
Thornton BD13 . . . . **72** C8
Spring Villas
Mytholmroyd HX7 . . . . . . **89** F1
5 Todmorden OL14 . . . . . **86** B1
Springville Gdns WF9 . . **183** B7
Springville Terr BD10 . . . . **56** B7
Spring Way BD21 . . . . **35** E6
Springwell Ave LS26 . . . . **82** A1

Springwell Cl
Batley WF15 . . . . **117** C
4 Yeadon LS19 . . . . **40** C
Springwell Ct
East Ardsley WF3 . . . . **98** E
Hemsworth WF9 . . . . **181** E
Leeds LS12 . . . . **210** C
Springwell Dr BD5 . . . . . **74** E
Springwell Rd
Leeds LS12 . . . . **210** C
Ossett WF5 . . . . **140** E
Swillington LS26 . . . . **82** A
Spring Wells BD22 . . . . . . **34** C
Springwell St LS12 . . . . . **210** C
Springwell Terr
Bradford BD6 . . . . **74** A
3 Yeadon LS19 . . . . **40** C
Springwell View
4 Batley WF17 . . . . **96** F
Leeds LS12 . . . . **211** A
Springwood Ave
Bradford BD5 . . . . **74** F
Huddersfield HD1 . . . . . . **153** F
Spring Wood Ave HX3. . . **113** B
Springwood Bsns Pk
HX4. . . . . **134** C
Springwood Com Prim Sch
BD8. . . . . **74** C
Springwood Ct LS8 . . . . . **61** B
Spring Wood Dr HX3. . . . **113** B
Springwood Gdns
Halifax HX3 . . . . **113** B
Leeds LS8 . . . . **61** B
Spring Wood Gdns BD5 . . **74** F
Springwood Gr LS8 . . . . . **61** B
Springwood Hall Cl HD1. **153** C
Springwood Hall Gdns
HD1 . . . . **153** F
Springwood Mews LS8. . . **61** C
Springwood Rd
Holmfirth HD9 . . . . **189** C
Leeds LS8 . . . . **61** C
Yeadon LS19 . . . . **40** A
Springwood Sq **6** HD1. . **154** A
Springwood St **10** HD1. . **154** A
Springwood Terr BD2 . . . **55** E
Sprinkwell Cl BD3 . . . . . . **55** F
Spruce Ave S71 . . . . **179** E
Spruce Ct WF2 . . . . **142** A
Spruce Dr
Huddersfield HD4 . . . . . . **171** D
Northowram HX3. . . . . **93** A
Spruce Drive Mews HD4 . **171** D
Spruce Hts HD6. . . . . **115** A
Spruce St **16** BD21 . . . . . . **35** D
Spruce Wlk OL14 . . . . . . **129** A
Sprutts La HX7 . . . . **89** B
Spry La S63 . . . . **194** B
Spur Dr LS15 . . . . **62** E
Spurr Gr WF2. . . . . **161** B
Spurrier's Ave WF11 . . . . **126** C
Spurr St WF17 . . . . **118** D
Square
Halifax HX1 . . . . **203** B
Northowram HX3. . . . . **93** A
Square Chapel ★ HX1. . . **203** C
Square Hill HD5 . . . . **155** B
Square Rd
Halifax HX1 . . . . **203** C
Todmorden OL14. . . . . . . **129** A
Square St BD4 . . . . **75** A
Square The
Batley WF17 . . . . **117** F
Boston Spa LS23 . . . . **30** E
2 Bradford BD8. . . . . **73** C
Castleford WF10 . . . . **125** C
Farnley LS21 . . . . **11** D
Harewood LS17 . . . . **27** A
Keighley BD20 . . . . **19** D
Kippax LS25 . . . . **83** A
Knottingley WF11 . . . . . . **126** C
Mytholmroyd HX7 . . . . . . **89** D
Shepley HD8 . . . . **190** E
Square View OL14 . . . . . **129** B
Squire Gn BD8. . . . . **54** F
Squire La BD8, BD9. . . . . **54** F
Squirrel Cl WF13. . . . . . . **118** A
Squirrel Ct HD2. . . . . **135** C
Squirrel Ditch HD4. . . . . **154** C
Squirrel End WF13 . . . . . **118** A
Squirrel Hall Dr WF13 . . **117** F
Squirrel La BD13. . . . . **72** B
Squirrels Drey WF4 . . . . **159** F
Squirrel Way LS17 . . . . . . **43** F
Squirrel Wlk WF13 . . . . . **118** A
Stable Ct
Pudsey LS28 . . . . **57** E
Slaithwaite HD7. . . . . **152** A
Stable Fold BD12 . . . . **94** D
Stableford Gdns HD2. . . . **135** D
Stableford Manor HD7 . . **152** E
Stable Mews BD16 . . . . . . **53** E
Stablers Wlk WF6. . . . . . . **123** A
Stables La LS23 . . . . **30** E
Stables The
4 Otley LS21 . . . . **23** A
Walton WF2 . . . . **161** A
Stackgarth HD6. . . . . **136** A
Stackhills Rd OL14. . . . . . **108** C
Stacks La HX7 . . . . **110** F
Stadium Rd BD6 . . . . **94** D
Stadium Way
Huddersfield HD1 . . . . . . **154** C
Leeds LS11 . . . . **213** B
South Elmsall WF9 . . . . . **183** B
Stafford Ave HX3 . . . . . . **113** C
Stafford Hill La HD5. . . . **155** C
Stafford Par HX3 . . . . . . **113** C

Stafford Pl HX3 113 C4
Stafford Rd HX3 113 C3
Stafford Sq HX3 113 D3
Stafford St
Bradford BD4 75 B4
Castleford WF10 124 C8
Leeds LS10 215 B4
Morley LS27 97 F2
Stafford Terr WF2 141 F6
Stainbeck Ave LS7 59 F6
Stainbeck Cnr LS7 60 C7
Stainbeck Gdns
Bradford BD6 93 D8
Leeds LS7 60 B7
Stainbeck La LS7 60 B7
Stainbeck Rd
Leeds, Chapel Allerton LS7 60 C8
Leeds LS7 60 A7
Stainbeck Wlk LS7 60 B7
Stainburn Ave
Castleford WF10 125 A5
Leeds LS17 43 E1
Stainburn Cres LS17 43 E1
Stainburn Dr LS17 43 D1
Stainburn Gdns LS17 43 E1
Stainburn Ho 5 LS17 43 D1
Stainburn Mount LS17 204 B4
Stainburn Par 6 LS17 43 D1
Stainburn Rd LS17 204 A4
Stainburn Terr LS17 204 A4
Stainburn View LS17 43 E1
Staincliffe CE Jun Sch WF17 118 A3
Staincliffe Cl 10 WF13 118 A1
Staincliffe Cres 4 WF13 117 F2
Staincliffe Ct BD20 5 D1
Staincliffe Hall Rd WF17 118 A4
Staincliffe Rd WF13 118 A1
Staincliffe View WF13 117 F2
Staincross Comm S75 178 B2
Stainecross Ave HD4 153 C2
Staines Croft HD5 154 E6
Stainland Dean HX4 133 D2
Stainland Rd
Elland HX4 134 C6
Elland, Sowood Green HD3 152 A8
Halifax HX4 113 D1
Ripponden HX4 133 B4
Stainmore Cl LS14 62 A3
Stainmore Pl LS14 62 A3
Stainton Cl BD6 93 E8
Stainton La LS26, WF3 100 D3
Staircase La LS16, LS21 24 D5
Stairfoot Cl LS16 42 D5
Stair Foot La LS16 42 E5
Stairfoot View LS16 42 D5
Stairfoot Wlk LS16 42 D5
Staithe Ave LS10 99 D5
Staithe Cl LS10 99 D5
Staithe Gdns 2 LS10 99 D5
Staithgate La BD6 94 D7
Stake La HX7 110 E7
Stake Lane Bank HD9 189 C4
Stakes Fold WF16 117 E4
Stallabrass St 5 BD8 74 C8
Stalley Royd La HD9 189 F3
Stamford Ave WF10 124 A6
Stamford St BD4 75 B5
Stamford Way S75 178 B2
Stammergate La LS22 13 C2
Stamp Hill Cl LS29 6 D8
Stanacre Pl BD3 201 C4
Stanage La HX3 93 C7
Stanally St OL14 107 E8
Stanbury Village Sch BD22 50 D6
Stancliffe Way HD5 137 B1
Standale Ave LS28 76 D8
Standale Cres LS28 76 D8
Standale Rise LS28 76 D8
Standard Dr HD4 153 B2
Standard Ind Est BD2 56 C3
Standbridge Cl WF2 160 A5
Stand Bridge Garth WF4 159 F5
Standbridge La
Wakefield, Kettlethorpe WF2 160 B6
Wakefield, Stand Bridge WF2 160 C7
Standbridge Prim Sch WF2 160 A5
Standiforth La HD5 154 F6
Standiforth Pl HD5 154 F6
Standiforth Rd HD5 154 D6
Standish Cres WF9 182 C4
Stanhall Ave 3 LS28 57 D1
Stanhope Ave
Cawthorne S75 193 F5
Horsforth LS18 41 C2
Stanhope Cl LS18 41 C2
Stanhope Dr LS18 58 C8
Stanhope Gdns WF3 99 E1
Stanhope Gr WF3 99 E1
Stanhope Rd WF3 99 E1
Stanhope St HD8 175 D1
Stanier Ho LS18 41 C3
Stanks App LS14 62 D4
Stanks Ave LS14 62 D4
Stanks Cl LS14 62 E4
Stanks Cross LS14 62 E4
Stanks Dr LS14 62 D5
Stanks Garth LS14 62 E4
Stanks Gdns LS14 62 D5
Stanks Gn LS14 62 E4
Stanks Gr LS14 62 D4
Stanks La N LS14 62 C5
Stanks La S LS14 62 D4
Stanks Par LS14 62 D4
Stanks Rd LS14 62 D4
Stanks Rise LS14 62 E5
Stanks Way LS14 62 D4
Stanleigh Croft 37 HX7 89 A3
Stanley Ave LS9 207 C2
Stanley Cotts WF6 123 A2
Stanley Cryer Ct 6 OL14 108 D6
Stanley Ct HX1 202 B3
Stanley Dr LS8 44 B2
Stanley Gr LS20 39 E8
Stanley Grove Prim Sch WF3 121 F3
Stanley La
Elland HX4 134 A3
Liversedge WF15 117 A5
Lofthouse Gate WF1 121 D4
Stanley Marsh Nature Reserve* WF3 121 E4
Stanley Mills Bsns Pk HD3 152 F4
Stanley Pl
Batley WF17 118 D5
Huddersfield HD7 152 D4
Leeds LS9 208 A2
Stanley Rd
Halifax HX1 202 B1
Huddersfield, Ainley Top HD3 135 A3
Huddersfield HD3 135 C1
Keighley BD22 35 A4
Leeds, Chapeltown LS7 207 A3
Leeds LS9 208 A2
Liversedge WF15 117 A2
Shipley BD2 55 D4
Wakefield WF1 216 C3
Stanley St N HX2 92 A5
Stanley St W 1 HX6 112 B3
Stanley St
Bingley BD16 37 A3
Bradford, Greengates BD10 56 D7
Bradford, Idle BD10 56 B8
Brighouse HD6 115 B3
Castleford WF10 124 E8
Cleckheaton BD19 116 D8
Featherstone WF7 145 D7
Haworth BD22 51 E8
Holmfirth HD9 188 D2
Huddersfield HD1 153 E3
Keighley BD21 35 B8
Shipley BD18 55 C5
16 Sowerby Bridge HX6 112 C4
Wakefield WF1 216 C2
Stanley Terr
Batley WF17 118 D6
Leeds, Armley LS12 209 C3
Leeds LS9 208 A2
Stanley View LS12 209 C3
Stanmoor Dr WF3 121 E6
Stanmore Ave LS4 59 C3
Stanmore Cres LS4 59 C3
Stanmore Gr LS4 59 C3
Stanmore Hill LS4 205 A3
Stanmore Mount LS4 59 C3
Stanmore Pl
Bradford BD7 74 A5
Leeds LS4 59 C3
Stanmore Rd LS4 59 C3
Stanmore St LS4 59 C3
Stanmore Terr LS4 59 C3
Stanmore View LS4 59 C3
Stannard Well Dr WF4 141 B2
Stannard Well La WF4 141 C2
Stannary HX4 134 A4
Stannary Pl HX1 203 A4
Stannery End La HX7 110 F7
Stanningley Ave HX2 91 C5
Stanningley By-Pass
Leeds LS13 58 D1
Pudsey LS13 58 B1
Stanningley Ct 7 LS28 57 F2
Stanningley Dr HX2 91 C5
Stanningley Field Cl LS13 58 A1
Stanningley Gn HX2 91 C6
Stanningley Gr 7 WF16 117 D3
Stanningley Prim Sch LS28 57 E2
Stanningley Rd
Halifax HX2 91 C5
Leeds LS12, LS13 58 D1
Pudsey LS28 57 F2
Stansfield Cl
Castleford WF10 125 B8
Halifax HX1 202 C3
Stansfield Ct HX6 112 B3
Stansfield Dr WF10 125 C8
Stansfield Grange HX6 111 E1
Stansfield Hall OL15 129 C1
Stansfield Hall Rd OL14 108 C6
Stansfield Mill La HX6 111 F1
Stansfield Pl BD10 39 B1
Stansfield Rd
Castleford WF10 125 B8
Todmorden OL14 108 B5
Stansfield St 14 OL14 108 B6
Stansfield Terr 6 OL14 86 B1
Stan Valley WF8 166 E6
Stanwell Ave HD2 135 D1
Stanwick Ho BD2 55 D4
Stapleton Ho BD2 55 D4
Stapper Gn BD15 53 B6
Starbeck Rd WF1 142 E8
Starkey La BD20 4 E1
Starkie St BD21 35 B6
Starling Ho 4 WF9 181 D6
Star St BD5 74 C3
Star Terr HD6 135 E7
Starting Post BD10 55 F7
Starwort Cl WF8 146 D7
Station App
Burley in W LS29 21 E8
Honley HD9 172 B5
Todmorden OL14 108 B5
Station Ave LS13 58 C2
Station Cl LS25 82 F7
Station Cotts
Kippax LS25 102 F8
Newton Kyme LS24 31 C6
West Hardwick WF4 162 D5
Station Cres LS12 209 B3
Station Ct
Clayton West HD8 175 F3
Garforth LS25 82 F8
Leeds LS15 62 C1
Lepton HD8 155 C3
Station Fields LS25 82 F7
Station Gdns LS22 13 D5
Station Gr
Glusburn BD20 16 D7
12 Leeds LS13 58 C2
Station Ind Pk HX2 111 D7
Station La
Birkenshaw BD11 96 B6
2 Collingham LS22 29 B8
East Ardsley, Thorpe on the Hill WF3 99 D1
East Ardsley, Tingley WF3 98 E1
East Ardsley WF3 98 E2
Featherstone WF7 145 C5
Huddersfield HD4 171 F8
Huddersfield, Wellhouse HD7 152 D3
Liversedge WF16 117 D3
Pontefract WF8 146 E8
Rothwell LS26 101 D7
Shepley HD8 173 F1
Thorner LS14 45 F6
Station Mount LS13 58 C2
Station Par
Leeds LS5 59 B4
Todmorden OL14 85 F1
Station Pl LS13 58 C2
Station Plaza 8 LS29 8 B4
Station Rd
Ackworth M T WF7 164 C7
Arthington LS21 24 F6
Baildon BD17 38 D3
Barwick in E LS15 62 F6
Batley WF17 118 D4
Birkenshaw BD11 96 E6
Bradford BD1 55 E2
Bradford, Clayton BD14 73 C4
5 Bradford, Raw Nook BD12 94 E5
Bradford, Wyke BD12 94 B2
Brighouse HD6 115 C2
Brighouse, Hipperholme HX3 114 C7
Burley in W LS29 9 E1
Castleford WF10 124 D8
Cleckheaton BD19 116 E8
Cullingworth BD13 52 D6
Darton S75 177 E1
Denholme BD13 71 E8
Dewsbury, Earlsheaton WF12 139 F6
Dewsbury WF12 139 C5
Elland HX4 134 C4
Garforth LS25 82 F8
Glusburn BD20 16 D7
Guiseley, Esholt BD17 39 C6
Guiseley LS20 22 D1
Halifax, Holmfield HX3 92 A5
Haworth BD22 51 D7
Hebden Bridge HX7 89 B2
Hemsworth WF9 181 E7
Holmfirth HD9 189 A5
Honley HD9 172 A5
Horsforth LS18 41 C3
Huddersfield, Bradley HD2 137 A5
Huddersfield HD4 171 C6
Huddersfield, Wellhouse HD7 152 E3
Ilkley LS29 8 B4
Kippax WF10 103 C4
Kirkburton HD4 173 C2
Knottingley WF11 126 C5
Leeds, Carr Crofts LS12 209 B3
Leeds, Cross Gates LS15 62 C2
Lepton HD8 155 D3
Liversedge WF16 117 D3
Luddenden Foot HX2 111 D7
Marsden HD7 168 F4
Meltham HD9 170 F2
Menston LS29 22 B4
Mickletown LS26 102 C3
Mirfield WF14 138 A4
Morley LS27 98 B5
Normanton WF6 122 F3
Oakworth BD22 34 D1
Ossett WF5 140 E4
Otley LS21 23 A7
Oxenhope BD22 51 C2
Queensbury BD13 72 F2
Royston S71 179 B4
Ryhill WF4 162 A1
Shepley HD8 190 E8
Shipley BD18 55 B7
Skelmanthorpe HD8 175 A2
Slaithwaite HD7 152 A1
South Elmsall WF9 183 A3
Sowerby Bridge HX6 112 C3
Steeton BD20 17 D6
Todmorden OL14 86 C1
Wilsden BD13 53 A4
Station Road Ind Est LS25 102 F7
Station St
Huddersfield HD1 154 A6
Meltham HD9 170 D2
Pudsey LS28 76 D6
Wakefield WF1 142 E2
Station Terr
Kippax WF10 103 C4
Leeds LS13 58 C2
Royston S71 179 E4
Skelmanthorpe HD8 175 A2
Station View
Leeds LS15 62 C1
Oxenhope BD22 51 C3
Steeton BD20 17 D5
Station Way LS12 209 B3
Station Works Ind Pk BD21 35 E7
Station Yd WF17 118 D5
Staups La
Blackshaw Head OL14 88 A2
Northowram HX3 92 F1
Staveley Ct
Bingley BD16 36 F4
Shipley BD18 54 D8
Staveley Dr BD18 54 D7
Staveley Gr BD22 35 A3
Staveley Rd
4 Bingley BD16 37 A4
Bradford BD7 74 B6
Keighley BD22 35 A4
Shipley BD18 54 D8
Staveley Way BD22 35 A4
Stavely Mews 5 BD16 37 A4
Staverton Gr BD13 72 E7
Staverton St HX2 202 A3
Staybrite Ave BD16 54 A7
Staygate Gn BD6 74 E1
Staynton Cres HD2 136 F5
Stead's Yd LS18 41 C2
Stead Gate HD8 174 D2
Stead Hill Way BD17 38 F1
Steadings Way BD22 34 E5
Stead La
Ilkley LS29 21 B8
Kirkheaton HD5 155 B8
Ripponden HX6 132 C2
Thorner LS14 45 F5
Steadman St BD3 75 B6
Steadman Terr BD3 75 B6
Stead Rd BD4 95 E8
Stead St
Halifax HX1 203 A3
Shipley BD17 55 B8
Steanard La WF14 138 C3
Steander LS9 212 A3
Steed Court Bsns Pk WF9 183 C8
Steele La HX4 133 C1
Steel Terr LS26 100 F5
Steep La HX6 111 B4
Steeplands HD2 136 F6
Steeple Ave WF4 156 E4
Steeple Cl LS27 98 B1
Steeple View HD7 152 D4
Steep Riding HD9 172 C3
Steerforth Cl 7 BD5 74 E3
Steeton Gr BD20 17 C6
Steeton Hall Gdns BD20 17 D6
Steeton Prim Sch BD20 17 D5
Steeton & Silsden Sta BD20 17 D6
Stella Gdns WF8 125 F2
Stell Hill BD22 34 D5
Stephen Cl HX3 93 A1
Stephen Cres BD2 55 E3
Stephen Rd BD6 73 F2
Stephen Row HX3 93 A2
Stephenson Cl WF12 118 E1
Stephenson Dr LS12 77 E3
Stephenson Rd BD15 53 D2
Stephenson St 2 BD7 74 B3
Stephensons Way LS29 8 B4
Stephenson Way LS12 77 D3
Stephen St 10 HX7 89 A3
Stepping Stones
Keighley BD20 19 E1
Ripponden HX6 132 D3
Steps Ind Pk HD9 172 A6
Steps La HX6 112 C5
Steps The HX6 112 C5
Sterling Ct WF3 98 E2
Sterling Ind Pk WF10 124 F5
Sterling Way WF3 98 D2
Stevenson Ave WF10 125 C5
Stewart Cl
Bradford BD2 56 C5
Leeds LS15 81 C7
Stewart St BD22 51 E8
Sticker La BD4 75 C4
Stile Common Inf Sch HD4 154 B3
Stile Common Jun Sch HD4 154 A3
Stile Common Rd HD4 154 B3
Stile Hill Way LS15 81 E6
Stile Moor Rise OL14 108 A7
Stile Rd OL14 108 A7
Stile Terr HX6 111 E1
Stillington Ho BD2 55 D4
Stillwell Dr WF2 160 E8
Stillwell Garth WF2 160 E8
Stillwell Gr WF2 160 E8
Stirley Hill HD4 172 B7
Stirling Cres
Bradford BD4 75 E3
Horsforth LS18 41 B4
Stirling Rd LS29 9 D1
Stirling St
Halifax HX1 203 A2
Silsden BD20 5 E2
Stirling Way LS25 83 B7
Stirrup Gr BD2 55 F4
Stirton St 3 BD5 74 D3
Stithy St WF5 140 C8
Stockeld La LS22 12 D6
Stockeld Pk* LS22 12 E7
Stockeld Rd LS29 8 A4
Stockeld Way LS29 8 A5
Stockerhead La HD7 170 A8
Stockheld La LS15 45 F1
Stock Hey La OL14 109 C6
Stockhill Fold BD10 56 D7
Stockhill Rd BD10 56 D7
Stockhill St WF13 139 A8
Stockingate WF9 182 B2
Stockingate Mill Jun Sch WF9 182 A1
Stockinger La LS29 6 F8
Stocking La
Aberford LS25 65 A7
Knottingley WF11 127 C4
Stock La HX2 112 C7
Stocks App LS14 62 B4
Stocks Ave HX7 110 D8
Stocksbank Dr WF14 137 D6
Stocks Bank Rd WF14 137 E6
Stocks Cres HX7 110 D8
Stocks Dr
Mytholmroyd HX7 110 D8
Shepley HD8 190 E8
Stocksfield View BD13 73 B1
Stocks Gdns HX7 110 D8
Stocks Hill
Leeds, Armley LS12 209 C4
Leeds, Holbeck LS11 211 A1
Leeds LS13 58 D3
Menston LS29 21 F4
Stocks Hill Cl
Barnsley S71 179 C1
Keighley BD20 19 D1
Stockshill Garth LS29 21 F4
Stocks La
Batley WF17 118 C5
Bradford BD13 73 B1
Halifax HX2 90 E2
Kirkburton HD4 173 B1
Mytholmroyd HX7 110 D8
Sowerby Bridge HX6 111 E3
Stocks Lane Prim Sch BD13 73 B1
Stocksmoor Rd WF4 158 C2
Stocks Moor Rd HD4 173 B2
Stocksmoor Sta HD4 173 C2
Stocks Rd LS14 62 C4
Stocks Rise LS14 62 B4
Stocks St LS7 206 C3
Stocks Way HD8 190 D8
Stocks Wlk HD5 154 F3
Stockwell Ct BD19 115 F8
Stockwell Dr WF17 118 D6
Stockwell Hill HD4 171 F8
Stockwell Vale HD4 171 F8
Stod Fold HX2 91 C8
Stogden Hill BD13 73 B1
Stone Acre Ct 3 BD5 74 E2
Stone Acre Hts HD9 170 F1
Stone Arches BD5 74 E4
Stonebridge 9 BD10 56 B8
Stonebridge App LS12 77 E6
Stonebridge Ave LS12 77 F6
Stonebridge Gr LS12 77 E6
Stonebridge La LS12 77 E6
Stonebridge Wlk HD8 173 F1
Stone Brig Gn LS26 100 D4
Stone Brig La LS26 100 D4
Stonechat Rise LS27 98 C4
Stone Cliffe 1 HX3 113 A4
Stonecliffe Bank LS12 77 E6
Stonecliffe Cl LS12 77 E6
Stonecliffe Cres LS12 77 E6
Stonecliffe Dr
Leeds LS12 77 E6
Middlestown WF4 158 B7
Stonecliffe Garth LS12 77 E6
Stonecliffe Gdns LS12 77 E6
Stonecliffe Gn LS12 77 E6
Stonecliffe Gr LS12 77 E6
Stonecliffe Lawn LS12 77 E6
Stonecliffe Mount LS12 77 E6
Stonecliffe Pl LS12 77 E6
Stonecliffe Terr LS12 77 E6
Stonecliffe View LS12 77 E6
Stonecliffe Way LS12 77 E5
Stonecliffe Wlk LS12 77 E5
Stonecroft
Bradford BD2 56 C4
Lofthouse Gate WF3 121 E5
Stone Croft Ct LS26 101 C5
Stonecroft Gdns HD8 190 F8
Stonecroft Mount HX6 112 C6
Stone Crop Dr WF10 124 A5
Stone Ct
East Morton BD20 36 D8
South Hiendley S72 180 E5
Stone Dale Cl LS21 24 E6
Stonedene Ct WF16 117 E3
Stone Dene Pk LS22 13 F6
Stonefield LS14 45 D8
Stonefield Ave HD4 153 B3
Stonefield Cl BD2 56 B5
Stonefield Pl WF17 96 F1

Stonefield Rd HD4 153 B3
Stonefield St
Cleckheaton BD19 116 A6
Dewsbury WF13 118 C1
Stonefield Terr LS27 98 C8
Stonefleece Ct HD9 171 F3
Stone Fold HD9 171 F4
Stonegate
Bingley BD16 37 A5
Leeds LS7 206 C3
Ossett WF5 140 F3
Stonegate App LS7 59 F6
Stonegate Chase LS7 59 F7
Stonegate Cl LS17 43 D3
Stonegate Cres LS7 60 A7
Stone Gate Ct HD4 153 E2
Stonegate Dr
Leeds LS7 60 A7
Pontefract WF8 146 C6
Stonegate Edge LS7 60 A7
Stonegate Farm Cl LS7 59 F7
Stonegate Gdns LS7 59 F7
Stonegate Gn LS7 59 F6
Stonegate Gr LS7 60 A7
Stonegate La
Ackworth M T WF7 163 E5
Leeds LS7 59 F7
Stonegate Mews LS7 59 F6
Stonegate Pl LS7 59 F6
Stonegate Rd
Bradford BD10 56 C6
Leeds LS17 43 C2
Stonegate View LS7 59 F7
Stonegate Wlk LS7 60 A6
Stone Gr BD20 17 C6
Stone Hall Rd BD2 56 B4
Stonehaven Ct BD21 35 E5
Stone Hill BD16 37 B5
Stonehouse Dr BD13 92 C8
Stone House Fold BD22 34 B2
Stonehurst LS14 62 D4
Stonehurst Rd 2 WF14 138 A6
Stonehyrst Ave WF13 118 D1
Stone La BD22 51 B2
Stonelea
Birkenshaw BD4 96 A8
Ripponden HX4 133 A5
Stonelea Ct
Leeds, Far Headingley LS6 59 D5
Leeds LS7 60 A7
Stonelea Dr HD6 135 F7
Stone Lea Gr WF9 183 A2
Stoneleigh 4 BD13 72 F1
Stoneleigh Ave LS17 43 F4
Stoneleigh Cl LS17 43 F4
Stoneleigh Ct
Bradford BD19 94 E1
Leeds LS17 43 F4
Shelley HD8 174 A2
Stoneleigh Garth LS8 43 F3
Stoneleigh Gr WF5 140 D5
Stoneleigh La LS17 43 F3
Stoneleigh Mews HD2 135 D1
Stoneleigh Way LS17 43 F3
Stonely Dr OL14 129 A7
Stone Mill App LS6 59 E7
Stone Mill Ct LS6 59 E7
Stone Mill Way LS6 59 E7
Stone Pits La LS27 97 D5
Stoneroyd WF4 156 E5
Stoneroyd Farm WF4 157 D3
Stones Bank HX6 132 C2
Stones Dr HX6 132 B2
Stones La
Huddersfield HD7 152 D3
Linthwaite HD7 170 C8
Todmorden OL14 107 E4
Stones Rd OL14 107 F4
Stone St
Baildon BD17 38 E2
Bradford BD1 201 B3
Bradford, Sandy Lane BD15 54 A3
Cleckheaton BD19 116 C7
4 Haworth BD22 51 C6
Queensbury BD13 72 C2
Stone Stay Fold 2 LS29 6 E8
Stones Terr OL14 108 A2
Stone Terr BD16 36 B2
Stone Wood La HD4, HD8 173 D1
Stoney Bank La HD9 189 D8
Stoney Bank Rd HD9 189 D8
Stoney Bank St WF13 139 A6
Stoney Battery HX3 203 B4
Stoney Battery Rd HD1 153 D4
Stoneybrook Cl WF4 176 F8
Stoney Butts La HX4 133 B5
Stoneycroft 3 LS18 58 B8
Stoney Croft
Cleckheaton BD19 117 B7
Yeadon LS19 40 C4
Stoneycroft La BD20 18 B2
Stoney Croft La HX4 133 B5
Stoney Cross St HD4 153 F2
Stoney Ford La HD5 137 B1
Stoney Garth WF4 159 F3
Stoney Hill HD6 115 A2
Stoneyhurst Sq BD4 75 E3
Stoneyhurst Way 2 BD4 75 E3
Stoney La
Batley WF17 118 D6
Brighouse HX3 115 A6
Crigglestone WF4 159 F2
Halifax HX3 92 A3
Stoney La *continued*
Horsforth LS18 58 B8
Huddersfield, Blue Bell Hill HD4 153 F2
Huddersfield, Longwood HD3 152 F6
Lofthouse Gate WF2 120 D5
Menston LS29 21 D6
Mirfield WF14 138 D7
Shadwell LS14, LS17 45 B5
Stoney Ridge Ave BD9 54 B4
Stoney Ridge Hospl BD16 54 C5
Stoney Ridge Rd BD16 54 C5
Stoney Rise LS18 58 B8
Stoney Rock Ct LS9 207 C1
Stoney Rock Gr LS9 207 C1
Stoney Rock La LS9 207 C1
Stoney Royd S71 178 F1
Stoney Royd La OL14 107 F7
Stoney Royd Terr HX3 113 D4
Stoneys Fold BD15 53 B6
Stoney St BD20 18 B2
Stoneythorpe 2 LS18 58 B8
Stony Gate HD9 188 E2
Stony La
Blackshaw Head HX7 88 D2
Bradford, Eccleshill BD2 56 C5
Bradford, Sandy Lane BD15 53 F2
Brighouse HX3 114 C4
Elland HX4 134 A8
Honley HD9 171 F3
Ripponden HX6 132 D5
Todmorden OL14 86 E2
Stony Royd LS28 57 C3
Stony Royd La HX7 110 A4
Stony Royd Terr HD7 170 C8
Stoodley Cl OL14 109 A5
Stoodley Glen OL14 109 A7
Stoodley Grange OL14 109 B5
Stoodley La OL14 109 B7
Stoodley Pike Mon★ OL14 109 C5
Stoodley Terr HX2 202 A1
Stoodley View HX7 89 B4
Stopford Ave WF2 160 E8
Stopford Garth WF2 160 E8
Storey Pl LS14 61 E1
Storie Cres WF2 141 E4
Storiths Ct 7 LS29 6 F8
Storiths La BD23 3 B8
Stormer Hill La HX6 112 D1
Storr Hill BD12 94 D4
Storrs Hill Rd WF4, WF5 140 E2
Storth Ave HD4 152 F3
Storthes Hall La HD8 173 C6
Storth Pl HD2 135 F1
Storths Rd HD2 135 F1
Story Stones BD16 37 D5
Stotfold Rd DN5 194 E3
Stott Hill BD1 201 C3
Stott Rd LS6 205 B3
Stott St LS12 210 A3
Stott Terr BD2 56 D4
Stourton Rd LS29 7 F5
Stowe Gr LS9 80 C8
Stowell Mill St BD5 74 D4
Stows of Sowerby (Craft Centre)★ HX6 111 C4
Stradbroke Way LS12 209 C2
Stradmore Rd BD13 71 E8
Strafford Way BD10 56 E8
Straightacres La BD10 56 D5
Straight La
Addingham LS29 6 D5
Halifax HX2 91 D5
Hampole DN6 184 B4
Straits 7 BD17 38 C4
Stralau St WF17 118 C6
Strand BD16 54 B6
Strands Ct WF4 158 E6
Strangford Ct BD10 56 D8
Stranglands La WF11 126 B5
Stratford Ave LS11 214 A3
Stratford Cl HD7 152 E5
Stratford Rd BD7 74 B5
Stratford St LS11 214 B3
Stratford Terr LS11 214 B3
Strathallan Dr BD17 38 D3
Stratheden Rd WF2 142 A7
Strathmore Ave LS9 208 A2
Strathmore Cl BD2 56 B3
Strathmore Dr
Baildon BD17 38 B4
Leeds LS8 208 A3
Strathmore Gdns WF9 183 B4
Strathmore Rd LS29 8 E4
Strathmore St LS9 208 B2
Strathmore Terr LS8 208 A3
Strathmore View LS9 208 A2
Stratton Cl HD6 115 B1
Stratton Pk HD6 115 B1
Stratton Rd HD6 115 C1
Stratton View BD4 75 E4
Stratton Wlk BD15 73 A8
Stratus Cl WF7 163 F4
Strawberry Ave
Garforth LS25 82 E6
Liversedge WF15 117 A3
Strawberry Bank WF15 117 A4
Strawberry Fields 8 BD21 35 C8
Strawberry Gdns S71 179 D4
Strawberry La LS12 209 C3
Strawberry Rd LS12 209 C3
Strawberry Sq 2 WF16 117 D3
Strawberry St
Keighley BD21 35 C8
Silsden BD20 5 D1
Straw View BD10 55 F8
Stray The BD10 56 A6
Stream Head Rd BD13 53 B2
Streamside LS6 59 E6
Streamside Fold HX7 110 E8
Street 1 LS23 31 A8
Street 2 LS23 31 B8
Street 3 LS23 15 B1
Street 5 LS23 15 B2
Street 6 LS23 15 B3
Street 7 LS23 15 C2
Street 8 LS23 15 D2
Street Furlong La WF8 147 B7
Street Head La BD22 50 E8
Streethouse Sta WF7 144 D5
Street La
Gildersome LS27 97 C6
Hooton Pagnell DN5 195 F3
Keighley BD20 19 C2
Leeds LS17 43 E2
Street The LS29 6 D8
Strensall Gn 6 BD6 93 E8
Stretch Gate HD8 173 F1
Stretchgate La HX2 202 A4
Stretton Ave LS6 42 E1
Stretton Cl WF7 124 A1
Strickland Ave LS17 45 A4
Strickland Cl LS17 44 F4
Strickland Cres LS17 44 F4
Strickland Rd WF9 183 D8
Strike La HD8 174 F3
Strikes La BD20 16 E3
Strines Moor Rd HD9 199 C8
Strines St OL14 129 A7
Stringer's Yd 11 WF4 141 A1
Stringer Cl BD4 95 C8
Stringer House La HD8 175 A7
Stringer La 5 WF4 141 B1
Strone The BD10 39 F1
Strong Close Gr BD21 35 E7
Strong Close Rd BD21 35 E7
Strong Close Way BD21 35 E7
Stuart Ct 1 BD5 74 E4
Stuart Gr
Normanton WF6 123 A4
Slaithwaite HD7 170 A8
Stuart Pl HD2 136 F5
Stuart Rd WF8 125 C1
Stuart St
Castleford WF10 124 E8
Pontefract WF8 125 C1
Stubbin Fold HD9 188 C3
Stubbing Brink HX7 88 E3
Stubbing Dr HX7 88 E3
Stubbing Holme Rd HX7 88 F3
Stubbing La
Elland HX4 133 E5
Sowerby Bridge HX6 132 E8
Stubbings Cl HX7 110 E8
Stubbings Inf Sch HX7 89 A3
Stubbings Rd BD17 37 F2
Stubbings St HX7 110 E8
Stubbing Way BD18 55 C6
Stubbin La
Denby Dale HD8 192 B6
Holmfirth HD9 188 C3
Stubbin Rd HD7 169 B5
Stubbins HX6 132 E8
Stubbs La WF3 120 E7
Stubham Rise LS29 8 A5
Stubley Farm Rd WF16 117 D6
Stubley Holme OL14 86 A1
Stubley La OL14 86 B1
Stubley Rd WF16 117 C6
Stubley St WF1 216 A2
Stubs Beck La BD19 95 D2
Studdley Cres BD16 37 B3
Studfold View LS14 62 A2
Studio Rd LS3 205 B1
Studleigh Terr HD6 114 E5
Studley Ave BD6 94 B7
Studley Cl BD20 19 D1
Studley Rd BD3 55 F2
Stumpcross Cl WF8 125 F3
Stumpcross Ct WF8 125 F3
Stumpcross La WF8 125 F3
Stumpcross Mdws WF8 125 F2
Stumpcross Way WF8 125 F3
Stunsteds Rd BD19 116 D8
Sturges Gr BD2 56 B1
Sturton Ave LS25 83 A7
Sturton Gr HX2 91 E6
Sturton Grange La LS25 83 C7
Sturton La
Garforth LS25 83 A8
Halifax HX2 91 E7
Stutely Gr HD2 136 E5
Styebank La LS26 100 F6
Styes La HX6 111 D4
Sty La BD16 36 F6
Styveton Way BD20 17 B6
Suddards Fold 13 BD7 74 A4
Sude Hill HD9 189 F6
Sude Hill Terr HD9 189 F6
Sudforth La DN14 127 F5
Suffield Cl LS27 97 B8
Suffield Cres LS27 97 B8
Suffield Dr LS27 97 B8
Suffield Rd LS27 97 B8
Suffolk Ave WF17 118 B3
Suffolk Cl WF5 140 C4
Suffolk Ct LS19 40 B7
Suffolk Ho WF1 142 F3
Suffolk Pl BD2 55 F4
Suffolk Rise HD2 136 C4
Suffolk St WF17 118 B4
Sufton St HD2 135 F1
Sugar Hill LS29 6 F8
Sugar Hill Cl LS26 101 C3
Sugar La
Dewsbury WF12 139 E8
Wakefield WF1 142 E3
Sugar Well App LS7 60 A5
Sugarwell Ct LS7 206 B4
Sugar Well Mount LS7 60 A5
Sugar Well Rd LS7 60 A5
Sugden's Almshouses BD22 34 E3
Sugden Cl HD6 136 A8
Sugden Pl 6 BD6 93 E7
Sugden St
Bradford BD12 94 F4
Bradford, Lister Hills BD1 74 C7
Sugdens Terr HD6 135 D7
Sulby Gr BD10 56 E7
Sullivan Cl HD4 153 D3
Sullivan Gr WF9 182 B1
Summerbank Cl BD11 96 F7
Summerbridge Cl WF17 118 A6
Summerbridge Cres
Bradford BD10 56 D5
Cleckheaton BD19 96 C2
Summerbridge Dr BD10 56 D5
Summerdale BD19 96 B2
Summerfield Ave
Brighouse HD6 115 B6
Leeds LS13 58 A3
Summerfield Cl
Baildon BD17 38 B3
Byram WF11 126 E8
Summerfield Ct HX2 92 A5
Summerfield Dr
Baildon BD17 38 B3
Byram WF11 126 E8
Leeds LS13 58 A3
Summerfield Gdns LS13 58 A3
Summerfield Gn
Baildon BD17 38 B3
Leeds LS13 58 A3
Summerfield Gr
Baildon BD17 38 B3
Lepton HD8 155 D2
Summerfield Pk BD17 38 B3
Summerfield Pl LS13 58 A3
Summerfield Prim Sch LS13 57 F3
Summerfield Rd
Bradford BD10 56 C6
Leeds LS13 58 A3
Todmorden OL14 108 D5
Summerfield Rd W OL14 108 C5
Summerfield Wlk LS13 58 A3
Summer Ford Croft S36 191 D1
Summergate Pl HX1 202 B2
Summergate St HX1 202 B2
Summer Hall Ing BD12 94 C4
Summerhill Ave BD20 17 D6
Summerhill Dr BD20 17 D6
Summerhill Gdns LS8 44 B2
Summerhill Gr LS25 82 D6
Summerhill La BD20 17 D6
Summerhill Pl LS8 44 B3
Summerhill Rd
Garforth LS25 82 D6
Mickletown LS26 102 D2
Summer Hill St BD7 74 A5
Summer La
Emley HD8 175 D6
Royston S71 179 B4
Summerlands Gr BD5 75 A2
Summerland Terr HX6 112 D4
Summer Lea BD10 56 A8
Summerley Ct BD10 56 B7
Summer Mdw WF8 146 C7
Summer Rd S71 179 B4
Summerscale St HX1 202 C4
Summerseat Pl BD7 74 C5
Summersgill Sq LS18 58 B8
Summer St
Halifax HX1 202 B1
Huddersfield, Netherton HD4 171 D7
Huddersfield, Rashcliffe HD1, HD4 153 F4
Summervale HD9 189 A6
Summer View S71 179 B3
Summerville Rd
Bradford BD7 74 C6
Pudsey LS28 57 C2
Summit St BD21 35 B8
Sunbeam Ave LS11 214 B3
Sunbeam Gr 7 LS11 214 B3
Sunbeam Pl LS11 214 B3
Sunbeam Terr LS11 214 B3
Sun Bldgs HX2 90 F5
Sunbridge Rd BD1 74 D7
Sunbury Gr HD5 154 E6
Sun Ct WF7 145 C8
Sunderland Ct 6 HD6 115 A3
Sunderland Rd
Bradford BD9 55 C2
Low Bradley BD20 4 D5
Sunderland St
5 Halifax HX1 203 A3
Haworth BD22 51 F8
Keighley BD21 35 B6
Sundown Ave BD7 73 E4
Sun Field LS28 57 D1
Sunfield Cl LS28 57 D2
Sunfield Dr LS28 57 D2
Sunfield Gdns LS28 57 D2
Sunfield Pl LS28 57 D2
Sunfield Terr 11 BD19 116 E7
Sun Fold HX1 203 C2
Sun Hill Dr BD17 37 E3
Sunhurst Cl BD22 34 C2
Sunhurst Dr BD22 34 C2
Sun La
Burley in W LS29 9 E2
Haworth BD22 50 E7
Wakefield WF1 216 C2
Sunningdale
Bradford BD8 73 D8
Micklefield LS25 83 F8
Sunningdale Ave
Darton S75 178 A1
Leeds LS17 43 A4
Sunningdale Cl LS17 43 A4
Sunningdale Cres BD13 52 E5
Sunningdale Croft HD2 135 F3
Sunningdale Dr
Cudworth S72 180 C1
Leeds LS17 43 A4
Sunningdale Gn LS17 43 A4
Sunningdale Rd HD4 153 D3
Sunningdales 11 WF6 123 D1
Sunningdale Way LS17 43 A4
Sunningdale Wlk LS17 43 A4
Sunny Ave
South Elmsall WF9 183 B2
Upton WF9 183 A7
Sunnybank
Denby Dale HD8 191 F5
Micklefield LS25 84 B6
Sunny Bank
Bradford, Daisy Hill BD9 54 D2
Bradford, Upper Common BD12 94 E4
Fitzwilliam WF9 163 A3
Huddersfield HD4 171 A7
Knottingley WF11 127 A4
Leeds LS8 204 C1
Morley LS27 98 C8
Mytholmroyd HX7 89 F1
Normanton WF6 144 B7
Queensbury BD13 72 F1
Ryhill WF4 162 A1
5 Shipley BD18 55 B7
Sunnybank Ave 5 LS18 58 B7
Sunny Bank Ave
Bradford BD5 74 D1
Mirfield WF14 138 A8
Pudsey BD3 56 F1
Sunnybank Cl BD19 115 F7
Sunnybank Cres
Elland HX4 134 B7
Yeadon LS19 40 D7
Sunnybank Ct LS19 40 D7
Sunnybank Dr
Elland HX4 134 B7
Sowerby Bridge HX6 112 C4
Sunny Bank Dr WF14 137 F8
Sunny Bank Gr
Bradford BD3 56 F1
Leeds LS8 204 C1
Mirfield WF14 138 A7
Sunnybank Grange 1 HD6 115 A2
Sunnybank La HX4 134 B7
Sunny Bank La
Batley WF17 118 D7
Bradford BD3 56 F1
Brighouse HX3 114 B6
Cragg Vale HX7 110 C4
Sunny Bank Par WF14 137 F8
Sunnybank Rd
Elland HX4 134 B7
7 Horsforth LS18 58 B7
Huddersfield HD3 153 D8
Sunny Bank Rd
Batley WF17 118 D6
Bradford BD5 74 D1
Brighouse HD6 115 A2
Glusburn BD20 16 C6
Halifax HX2 91 C5
Meltham HD9 170 C2
Mirfield WF14 138 A8
Slaithwaite HD7 152 B3
Wadsworth Moor HX7 69 A3
Sunnybank St
Ossett WF5 140 D5
Sowerby Bridge HX6 112 C4
Sunnybank Terr HD6 115 A3
Sunny Bank Terr
4 Halifax HX3 92 C1
9 Todmorden OL14 86 B1
Sunnybank View HD3 152 F6
Sunny Bank View LS8 204 C1
Sunnybank Villas BD20 16 C6
Sunny Bank Wlk WF14 138 A7
Sunnybank Woods WF17 118 D6
Sunny Brae Cres BD16 37 B2
Sunny Brow HD4 171 F8
Sunny Brow La BD9 54 D2
Sunnycliffe BD20 36 D8
Sunny Dale BD13 52 D2
Sunnydale Ave 3 HD6 136 A8
Sunnydale Cres LS21 22 D6
Sunnydale Croft WF5 140 E4
Sunnydale Gr BD21 35 F6
Sunnydale Pk
Keighley BD20 19 E1
Ossett WF5 140 E5
Sunnydale Rd WF5 140 F5
Sunnydale Ridge LS21 22 D6
Sunnydale Terr WF5 140 E5
Sunnydene LS14 61 F1
Sunnyfield WF3 120 C7
Sunnyfield Ave BB10 85 A8
Sunnyfield Dr WF9 163 A3
Sunny Gr 5 LS27 98 C8
Sunny Heys Rd HD9 170 D3
Sunny Heys W HD9 170 D2

unny Hill WF2 120 E1
unnyhill Ave HD5 137 B2
unny Hill Ave BD21 34 F5
unny Hill Cl WF2 120 E2
unnyhill Cres WF2 120 D1
unnyhill Croft WF2 120 E2
unny Hill Gr BD21 34 F5
unny Hill House Sch WF2 120 E1
unnylea HD7 169 A4
unnymead HD8 175 E2
unny Mead HD5 155 A6
unny Mount
  Brighouse HX3 114 C7
  Harden BD16 36 B1
  Keighley BD21 35 B8
  Keighley, Braithwaite BD22 34 E8
  Keighley, Crossflatts BD20 36 C7
unnymount Terr 5 WF17 96 F1
unnyridge Ave LS28 76 B8
unny Royd BD20 4 C5
unnyside
  Batley WF16 117 D3
  Brighouse HD6 136 D8
  Elland HX4 134 A1
  Halifax HX3 114 E7
  Huddersfield HD2 153 E8
  Todmorden OL14 108 A5
unnyside Ave
  East Ardsley WF3 119 D8
  Liversedge WF15 116 F2
unnyside La BD3 55 F1
unnyside Rd LS13 58 B1
unny Side St 1 HX3 92 C1
unnyvale Gdns HX3 114 C6
unnyvale Mount WF9 182 E3
unny View WF3 120 C6
unnyview Ave LS11 213 C3
unny View Cres HD2 136 D3
unnyview Gdns LS11 213 C3
unnyview Terr LS11 213 C3
unny View Terr 11 BD13 92 C8
unrise Ct LS27 97 C7
unroyd Ave WF4 141 B2
unroyd Hill WF4 141 B2
unset Ave LS6 59 E8
unset Dr
  Ilkley LS29 8 D5
  6 Leeds LS6 59 E7
Sunset Hilltop LS6 59 E8
Sunset Mount 5 LS6 59 E7
unset Rd LS6 59 E7
unset Rise LS6 59 E8
unset Terr LS29 8 E5
unset View LS6 59 E8
unshine Ct BD6 93 F6
unshine Mills LS12 209 A3
un Side HD8 190 F5
un St
  Bradford BD1 201 C4
  Haworth BD22 51 C6
  Keighley BD21 35 C6
  Keighley, East Morton BD20 19 E1
  Pudsey LS28 57 E1
  Steeton BD20 17 A5
  Yeadon LS19 40 C7
Sun Terr OL14 86 B1
Sun Vale Ave OL14 129 B7
Sun Way HX3 113 F5
Sunways WF14 137 F7
Sun Wood Ave HX3 93 B4
Sun Wood Terr HX3 93 B4
Surat Rd HD7 151 F2
Suresnes Rd BD21 35 B7
Surgery St BD22 51 D6
Surrey Gr
  Bradford BD5 74 E4
  Pudsey LS28 76 E8
Surrey Rd 4 LS28 76 E8
Surrey St
  Batley WF17 118 D5
  Halifax HX1 202 A2
  Keighley BD21 35 E8
  Todmorden OL14 108 B6
Sussex App LS10 215 C3
Sussex Ave
  Horsforth LS18 41 C3
  Leeds LS10 215 C3
Sussex Cl WF9 181 D8
Sussex Cres WF10 125 E8
Sussex Gdns LS10 215 C3
Sussex Gn LS10 215 C3
Sussex Pl LS10 215 C3
Sussex St
  Batley WF17 118 D5
  Keighley BD21 35 E8
  Leeds LS9 212 B3
Sussex Wlk 2 WF13 139 B8
Sutcliffe Pl 6 BD6 94 D8
Sutcliffe St HX2 202 A4
Sutcliffe Wood La HX3 114 C6
Sutherland Ave LS8 44 A2
Sutherland Cres LS8 44 A2
Sutherland Dr HD4 153 C2
Sutherland Mount LS9 208 A2
Sutherland Rd
  Brighouse HX3 114 E8
  Leeds LS9 208 A2
Sutherland St LS12 210 B2
Sutherland Terr LS9 208 A2
Sutton App LS14 61 E1
Sutton Ave
  Bradford BD2 56 A4
  Huddersfield HD5 155 A7
Sutton Cres
  Bradford BD4 75 E5
  Leeds LS14 61 E1
Sutton Ct BD16 36 F2
Sutton Dr
  Cullingworth BD13 52 D5
  Huddersfield HD5 155 A8
Sutton Fields BD20 16 C6
Sutton Gr
  Bradford BD4 75 E5
  2 Morley LS27 98 A3
Sutton-in-Craven CE Prim Sch BD20 16 D5
Sutton-in-Craven Com Prim Sch BD20 16 D5
Sutton La
  Byram WF11 126 E7
  Sutton-in-C BD20 16 E5
Sutton Rd BD4 75 E5
Sutton St LS12 210 C2
Suzanne Cres WF9 182 E3
Swaine Hill Cres LS19 40 A7
Swaine Hill St LS19 40 A7
Swaine Hill Terr LS19 40 A7
Swain House Cres BD2 56 A5
Swain House Prim Sch BD2 56 A5
Swain House Rd BD2 56 A5
Swain Mount BD2 56 A5
Swale App 13 WF6 123 D1
Swale Cres LS25 83 B6
Swale Ct 4 BD20 17 E8
Swaledale Ho WF17 118 C3
Swale Dr WF10 125 B8
Swale Rise LS22 13 D8
Swales' Yd 2 WF8 146 C8
Swales Moor Rd HX3 92 C4
Swallow Ave LS12 209 A2
Swallow Cl
  7 Leeds LS17 43 F4
  Pool LS21 24 D6
Swallow Cres LS12 209 A2
Swallow Dr
  Leeds LS17 44 A4
  Pool LS21 24 D6
Swallow Fold BD8 73 C7
Swallow Garth WF2 160 D5
Swallow Gr HD4 171 E6
Swallow Hill WF17 118 A8
Swallow La HD7 152 C5
Swallow Mount LS12 209 A2
Swallow St
  1 Huddersfield HD1 154 A5
  7 Keighley BD21 35 D8
  Liversedge WF16 117 D3
Swallow Vale LS27 98 D4
Swan Ave BD16 37 C4
Swan Bank Ct HD9 189 A4
Swan Bank La
  Halifax HX3 203 C1
  Holmfirth HD9 189 A4
Swan Ct HD1 153 E3
Swan Fold HX7 88 F5
Swan Hill BD9 55 C4
Swanhill La WF8 146 D7
Swan La
  Elland HD3 134 B1
  Huddersfield HD1 153 E3
Swan St
  Bradford BD5 201 B2
  Leeds LS1 211 C4
Swarcliffe App LS14 62 C4
Swarcliffe Ave LS14 62 D5
Swarcliffe Bank LS14 62 C5
Swarcliffe Dr LS14 62 C4
Swarcliffe Dr E LS14 62 D4
Swarcliffe Gn LS14 62 D4
Swarcliffe Par LS14 62 C4
Swarcliffe Prim Sch LS15 62 C5
Swarcliffe Rd LS14 62 C5
Swardale Gn LS14 62 C4
Swardale Rd LS14 62 C4
Swarland Gr BD5 201 B1
Swartha La BD20 6 A2
Swastika Stone* LS29 7 D2
Sweep La HD9 189 B3
Sweet Oak HX6 132 E8
Sweet St W LS11 211 A2
Sweet St LS11 211 B2
Swift's Fold HD9 171 F5
Swift Dr BD6 73 D1
Swift Pl HX6 132 B2
Swift Way WF2 160 D5
Swillington Ho WF8 125 D2
Swillington La LS15, LS26 82 A4
Swillington Prim Sch LS26 82 A2
Swincar Ave LS19 40 B7
Swincliffe Cl BD19 96 A4
Swincliffe Cres BD19 96 B3
Swincroft WF5 140 E5
Swindon Rd WF13 139 C8
Swinegate LS1 211 C3
Swine La
  Keighley BD20 36 B8
  West Hardwick WF4 162 D5
Swine Market La HX7 110 A3
Swine Mkt HX1 203 B3
Swineshead La OL14 108 B3
Swineshead Rd OL14 108 A3
Swinnow Ave LS13 58 A1
Swinnow Cl LS13 58 A1
Swinnow Cres LS28 58 A2
Swinnow Dr LS13 58 A1
Swinnow Garth LS13 58 A1
Swinnow Gdns LS13 58 A1
Swinnow Gn LS28 77 A8
Swinnow Gr LS13 58 A1
Swinnow La
  Leeds LS13 58 A1
  Pudsey LS13 77 B8
Swinnow Prim Sch LS13 77 A8
Swinnow Rd LS13 58 B1
Swinnow View LS13 58 A1
Swinnow Wlk LS13 58 A1
Swinton Pl BD7 74 B5
Swinton Terr HX1 202 B1
Swires Rd
  Bradford BD2 56 C1
  Halifax HX1 203 A2
Swires Terr HX1 203 A2
Swiss St WF10 103 E1
Swithen's La LS26 100 F4
Swithen's St LS26 100 F4
Swithenbank Ave WF5 140 D8
Swithenbank St WF5 119 C1
Swithen Hill S75 177 B3
Swithens Ct LS26 100 F4
Swithens Dr LS26 100 E4
Swithens St LS26 100 E4
Sycamore Ave
  Bingley BD16 36 F2
  Bradford BD7 73 F6
  Huddersfield HD3, HD7 152 F5
  Kippax LS25 82 F2
  Knottingley WF11 126 D3
  Leeds, Halton LS15 81 A8
  Leeds, Potternewton LS8 204 C1
  Meltham HD9 170 D1
  Todmorden OL14 108 A7
  Wakefield, Brag Lane End WF2 120 F3
  Wakefield, Flanshaw WF2 141 F7
Sycamore Chase LS28 76 F7
Sycamore Cl
  Batley WF12 118 F2
  Bradford BD3 201 D4
  Bramhope LS16 24 F1
  Knottingley WF11 126 D2
  Leeds LS6 206 A4
  Leeds, Meanwood LS6 59 F7
  Lepton HD8 155 F3
Sycamore Copse WF2 141 F5
Sycamore Croft LS11 214 B3
Sycamore Ct
  Bradford BD3 201 D4
  Huddersfield HD3 152 F5
  Ilkley LS29 8 A5
  Kirkburton HD8 173 F7
  Leeds LS8 61 C6
  Pontefract WF8 125 E2
Sycamore Dr
  Addingham LS29 7 A8
  Brighouse HX3 115 A6
  Cleckheaton BD19 116 B7
  Elland HX5 134 D6
  Royston S71 179 A3
Sycamore Fold
  Leeds LS11 214 B3
  Pool LS21 24 D6
Sycamore Gn
  Denby Dale HD8 191 E7
  Pontefract WF8 125 F1
Sycamore Gr
  Normanton WF6 144 A8
  Steeton BD20 16 F5
  Wakefield WF2 141 F7
Sycamore Grange HD7 152 E5
Sycamore Ho 5 WF10 124 E7
Sycamore Ind Est WF16 117 D2
Sycamore La
  Holmfirth HD9 189 D7
  West Bretton WF4 176 F8
Sycamore Rd WF9 181 C6
Sycamore Rise HD9 189 D7
Sycamore Row LS13 58 A4
Sycamore St WF1 142 E4
Sycamores The
  Bramhope LS16 24 F1
  Dewsbury WF13 118 B2
  Guiseley LS20 22 E2
  Halifax, Illingworth HX2 91 E6
  Halifax, King Cross HX2 112 F4
  Horbury WF4 141 C1
Sycamore Terr
  Honley HD9 171 E3
  Horbury WF4 159 C8
Sycamore View
  Brighouse HD6 114 F3
  Keighley BD22 34 F6
Sycamore Way
  Batley WF17 96 F1
  Featherstone WF7 145 D6
Sycamore Wlk
  Pudsey LS28 57 D2
  Thurnscoe S63 194 D1
Sydenham Pl BD3 56 A2
Sydenham Rd LS11 210 C2
Sydenham St LS11 210 C2
Sydney Gdns OL15 129 C1
Sydney St
  13 Bingley BD16 37 A3
  Liversedge WF15 117 B3
  Pudsey LS28 57 D2
  Rothwell LS26 101 D6
Syke Ave
  Dewsbury WF12 139 F8
  East Ardsley WF3 119 D7
Syke Cl WF3 119 C7
Syke Fold BD19 116 D7
Syke Gdns WF3 119 D7
Syke Gn LS14 45 C8
Syke Gr WF12 139 F8
Syke House La HX4 133 F7
Syke Ing Cl WF12 140 A7
Syke Ing Terr WF12 140 A7
Syke La
  Brighouse HX3 93 E1
  Dewsbury WF12 139 F7
Syke La *continued*
  Halifax HX2 71 E2
  Queensbury BD13 92 F7
  Scarcroft LS14 45 B8
  Sowerby Bridge HX6 112 B3
Syke Rd
  Dewsbury WF12 139 F8
  East Ardsley WF3 119 D7
  Wetherby LS22 14 A5
Sykes Ave
  Batley WF16 117 E5
  Mirfield WF14 138 C6
Sykes Cl
  Ackworth M T WF7 163 D5
  Batley WF17 118 E6
Sykes Fold BD22 51 E1
Sykes Gate HX7 131 C7
Sykes Head BD22 34 D3
Syke Side BD20 18 B2
Sykes La
  Batley WF12 119 A4
  Bradford BD12 95 A4
  Oakworth BD22 34 D2
  Silsden BD20 5 E1
Sykes Rd WF17 118 E6
Sykes St
  7 Castleford WF10 124 D8
  Cleckheaton BD19 116 D7
Syke St WF12 139 F7
Sykes Wlk WF17 118 E6
Syke Terr WF3 119 C7
Syke View WF12 139 F8
Sylhet Cl BD1 74 D8
Sylvan Ave BD13 92 D8
Sylvan Ridge HD2 136 C4
Sylvester Ave WF6 144 A7
Symons St WF2 216 A1
Syringa Ave BD15 54 A4
Syringa St HD1 153 D7

T

Tabbs Ct BD19 94 F1
Tabbs La BD19 94 F1
Tadcaster Gram Sch LS24 31 D2
Tadman St WF1 142 C4
Tagore Ct BD3 75 D6
Tainton Pk LS12 210 B2
Talbot Ave
  Huddersfield HD3 135 C1
  Leeds, Burley LS4 59 C3
  Leeds, Lidgett Park LS17, LS8 43 F2
Talbot Cres LS8 43 F2
Talbot Ct
  Leeds LS8 43 F1
  Normanton WF6 123 A2
Talbot & Falcon Yd WF1 216 B2
Talbot Fold LS8 43 F1
Talbot Gdns LS8 43 F2
Talbot Gr LS8 43 F2
Talbot Ho 2 HX5 134 F6
Talbot Mount LS4 59 C3
Talbot Prim Sch LS8 43 F2
Talbot Rd LS8 43 F1
Talbot Rise LS17 43 F2
Talbot Row WF17 118 D5
Talbot St
  Batley WF17 118 C4
  Bradford BD7 74 C7
  4 Keighley BD21 35 A7
  Normanton WF6 123 A2
Talbot Terr
  Leeds LS4 59 C3
  Rothwell LS26 100 E4
Talbot View
  Leeds LS4 59 C3
  1 Mirfield WF14 138 A6
Talbot Yd LS26 102 E3
Tallow Mews HD8 175 A1
Tall Trees LS17 43 C3
Tall Trees Dr WF7 145 D8
Tamar St BD5 74 C4
Tammy Hall St 1 WF1 216 B2
Tamworth St BD4 75 E6
Tandem Ind Est HD5 155 B6
Tandem Way HD5 155 B6
Tandy Trad Est The LS12 205 A1
Tanfield Cl S71 179 A4
Tanfield Dr LS29 9 E2
Tanfield Rd HD1 153 F8
Tanglewood LS11 99 A7
Tanglewood Ct 2 BD6 74 A1
Tan House Ct BD4 95 B7
Tanhouse Hill
  Brighouse HX3 114 C7
  Horsforth LS18 58 E8
Tanhouse La WF14 156 B7
Tan House La
  Ackworth M T WF7 164 B7
  Shelf HX3 93 A5
  Wilsden BD15 53 B6
Tan House Pk HX3 114 C7
Tanhouse St WF13 138 F6
Tan La BD4 95 B6
Tannerbrook Cl BD14 73 D4
Tanner Hill Rd BD7 73 E3
Tanners HD7 169 F7
Tanner St WF15 116 B5
Tannery Ct
  Bradford BD10 56 D8
  Mirfield WF14 137 E6
  Pudsey LS28 76 F7
Tannery Sq LS6 59 E7
Tannett Gn BD5 74 F2
Tan Pit Cl DN5 194 D4
Tan Pit La DN5 194 D4
Tanpits 18 HX7 89 A3
Tanshelf Dr WF8 146 C8
Tanshelf Ind Est WF8 125 C1
Tansy End BD22 51 E2
Tanton Cres BD14 73 D4
Tanton Wlk BD14 73 D4
Tanyard Ave HD3 153 A7
Tanyard Croft S72 181 A3
Tanyard Fold WF4 160 A3
Tanyard Rd
  Huddersfield, Milnsbridge HD3 153 B4
  Huddersfield, Quarmby HD3 153 A7
Tarn Cl WF10 104 E1
Tarn Ct
  Ilkley LS29 8 C3
  Keighley BD20 34 F8
  Lofthouse Gate WF1 121 B3
Tarnhill Mews BD5 74 E4
Tarn Hows Wlk WF7 163 F6
Tarn La
  Laycock BD20, BD22 34 B8
  Scarcroft LS17 44 E7
Tarn Rd WF7 145 E4
Tarnside Dr LS14 62 A3
Tarn View Rd LS19 40 D7
Tatefield Gr LS25 83 A1
Tatefield Pl LS25 83 A1
Tateley Cl WF5 119 D1
Tateley La WF5 119 C1
Tate Naylor St WF13 118 B2
Tatham Way LS8 61 C6
Tatton St WF1 142 F3
Taunton Ho 7 BD5 201 B1
Taunton St BD18 55 A8
Taverngate LS20 38 E8
Tavern St WF1 216 C2
Tavistock Cl LS12 210 A2
Tavistock Mews LS12 210 A2
Tavistock Pk LS12 210 A2
Tavistock Way
  Crigglestone WF2 160 A5
  Leeds LS12 210 A2
Tavora St WF1 216 B3
Tawny Beck LS13 77 C8
Tawny Cl
  Bradford BD4 75 E1
  1 Morley LS27 98 D4
Tay Ct BD2 56 D5
Taylor's Bldgs HD4 154 A2
Taylor Ave BD20 5 D1
Taylor Cl WF5 140 F4
Taylor Cres WF5 140 F4
Taylor Dr WF5 140 F4
Taylor Gr LS26 102 E3
Taylor Hall La WF14 137 F8
Taylor Hill S75 193 E4
Taylor Hill Rd HD4 153 E1
Taylor La
  Barwick in E LS15 63 B5
  Halifax BD13 72 A3
  Slaithwaite HD7 152 B5
Taylor Rd 10 BD6 94 D8
Taylors Cl LS14 62 B4
Taylor St
  Batley WF17 118 C4
  Cleckheaton BD19 116 C7
  Huddersfield HD7 152 E4
Taylor Wood Cotts WF4 163 B6
Tealbeck App LS21 23 B7
Tealbeck Ho 2 LS21 23 B7
Tealby Cl LS16 41 E2
Teal Cl WF10 124 D6
Teal Ct BD20 17 B6
Teal Dr LS27 98 D4
Teale Ct LS7 204 B2
Teale Dr LS7 204 B2
Teal Ho BD20 17 A6
Teall's Croft WF5 140 E7
Teall Ct WF5 141 A5
Teall St
  Ossett WF5 141 A5
  Wakefield WF1 216 B2
Teal Mews
  Middleton LS10 99 D5
  Steeton BD20 17 A6
Teapot Cnr DN5 194 D4
Teasdale St BD4 75 B3
Teasel Cl
  Bradford BD12 95 A4
  Cleckheaton WF15 116 C5
Technology Dr WF17 118 E4
Teddington Ave HD5 154 F6
Tees Cl WF10 125 B8
Teesdale Pl WF11 126 E2
Tees St BD5 74 C3
Telephone Pl LS9 207 A1
Telford Cl
  Castleford WF10 124 B7
  Leeds LS10 215 B2
  Silsden BD20 17 F8
Telford Ct BD7 74 B6
Telford Gdns 2 LS10 215 B2
Telford Pl LS10 215 B2
Telford St 7 LS10 215 B2
Telford Terr LS10 215 B2
Telford Way WF2 120 F5
Telford Wlk 3 LS10 215 B2
Telscombe Dr BD4 75 D2
Temperance Field BD12 94 D3
Temperance Fields BD19 115 F8
Temperance St 1 LS28 57 E1

Tempest Gn 13 BD6 . . . . . . **74** C1
Tempest Pl LS11 . . . . **214** A3
Tempest Rd
  Leeds LS11 . . . . **214** B2
  South Kirkby WF9 . . . . **182** C4
Templar's Way BD8 . . . . . . **73** E8
Templar Dr HD5 . . . . **154** D5
Templar Gdns LS22 . . . . . . **13** F7
Templar La
  Leeds, Quarry Hill LS2 . . **212** A4
  Leeds, Swarcliffe LS15 . . . **62** D4
Templar Pl LS2 . . . . **212** A4
Templars Cl HX4 . . . . . . **134** A7
Templar St
  Leeds LS2 . . . . **212** A4
  Wakefield WF1 . . . . **142** F3
Templars Way LS25 . . . . **82** F6
Temple Ave
  Leeds LS15 . . . . **81** A6
  Rothwell LS26 . . . . **100** F7
Temple Cl
  16 Huddersfield HD1 . . . **154** A6
  Leeds LS15 . . . . **81** A6
Temple Cres LS11 . . . . . . **214** A3
Temple Ct
  Leeds LS15 . . . . **80** F7
  Rothwell LS26 . . . . **100** F7
Temple Gate LS15 . . . . . . **81** B7
Templegate Ave LS15 . . . **81** B6
Templegate Cl LS15 . . . . . **81** B6
Templegate Cres LS15 . . . **81** B6
Temple Gate Dr LS15 . . . **81** A7
Templegate Gn LS15 . . . . **81** B7
Templegate Rd LS15 . . . . **81** B6
Templegate Rise LS15 . . . **81** A6
Templegate View LS15 . . . **81** B6
Templegate Way LS15 . . . **81** B6
Templegate Wlk LS15 . . . . **81** B7
Temple Gdns WF6 . . . . . . **122** F4
Temple Gn LS26 . . . . **101** A7
Temple Gr LS15 . . . . **81** A7
Temple La
  Calderbrook OL15 . . . . **129** D1
  Leeds LS15 . . . . **81** B7
Temple Lawn LS26 . . . . **101** A7
Temple Lea LS15 . . . . **81** B7
Temple Mews WF10 . . . . **124** C7
Temple Moor High Sch
  Science Coll LS15 . . . . . . **81** A5
Templenewsam Ctry Pk★
  LS15 . . . . **81** A5
Templenewsam Halton Prim
  Sch LS15 . . . . **81** A8
Temple Newsam Ho★
  LS15 . . . . **81** B5
Templenewsam Rd LS15 . . **81** A5
Templenewsam View
  LS15 . . . . **80** F6
Temple Park Cl LS15 . . . . . **81** A7
Temple Park Gdns LS15 . . **81** A7
Temple Park Gn LS15 . . . . **81** A7
Temple Rd WF13 . . . . **139** A7
Temple Rhydding Dr
  BD17 . . . . **38** C2
Temple Rise LS15 . . . . **81** A6
Temple Row
  9 Keighley BD21 . . . . **35** B7
  Leeds LS15 . . . . **81** E6
Temple Row Cl LS15 . . . . . **81** E6
Templer Terr LS27 . . . . . . **98** B2
Temple St
  Bradford BD9 . . . . **55** B2
  Castleford WF10 . . . . **124** C7
  Huddersfield HD3 . . . . . . **135** B1
  10 Keighley BD21 . . . . **35** B7
Templestowe Cres LS15 . . **62** C1
Templestowe Dr 3 LS15 . **81** C8
Templestowe Gdns 5
  LS15 . . . . **81** B8
Templestowe Hill 1 LS15 **62** B1
Temple View
  Leeds LS9 . . . . **212** C2
  Rothwell WF3 . . . . **100** C1
Temple View Gr LS9 . . . . **80** A7
Temple View Pl LS9 . . . . **212** C3
Temple View Rd LS9 . . . . **212** C3
Temple View Terr LS9 . . . **212** C2
Temple Vue 8 LS6 . . . . . **59** D6
Temple Wlk LS15 . . . . **81** B8
Tenbury Fold BD4 . . . . **75** E3
Tenby Terr HX1 . . . . **202** B4
Ten Lands La WF4 . . . . . **180** A7
Tennants Ct WF11 . . . . . . **127** A4
Tennis Ave BD4 . . . . **75** E1
Tennis Way BD17 . . . . **38** A1
Tennyson Ave
  Lofthouse Gate WF3 . . . . **121** E6
  Sowerby Bridge HX6 . . . . **113** F3
  Todmorden OL14 . . . . . . **108** D6
Tennyson Cl
  Knottingley WF11 . . . . . . **126** B4
  Pudsey LS28 . . . . **76** F6
Tennyson Pl
  Bradford BD3 . . . . **75** B8
  Brighouse HX3 . . . . **114** C8
  4 Cleckheaton BD19 . . . **116** D8
Tennyson Rd BD6 . . . . **94** B8
Tennyson St
  Guiseley LS20 . . . . **39** F8
  12 Halifax HX3 . . . . **92** A1
  6 Keighley BD21 . . . . **35** B5
  Morley LS27 . . . . **98** B4
  11 Pudsey, Farsley LS28 . . **57** D2
  Pudsey LS28 . . . . **76** F6
Tennyson Terr LS27 . . . . . **98** B4

Tennyson Way WF8 . . . . . **125** D2
Ten Row HD8 . . . . **191** A4
Tenter Cl
  Batley WF17 . . . . **118** C6
  Skelmanthorpe HD8 . . . . **175** A2
Tenter Croft 5 BD17 . . . . **38** C4
Tentercroft Ct WF13 . . . . **118** D1
Tenterden Way LS15 . . . . **62** F2
Tenterfield Rd WF5 . . . . **140** E5
Tenterfield Rise HX3 . . . . **93** A1
Tenterfields
  Bradford BD10 . . . . **56** E8
  Luddenden Foot HX2 . . . **111** E5
Tenter Fields WF12 . . . . **139** B6
Tenterfields Bsns Pk
  HX2 . . . . **111** E5
Tenterfield Terr OL14 . . . **108** E6
Tenter Hill
  Bradford BD14 . . . . **73** B4
  Bramham LS23 . . . . **30** C2
  Holmfirth HD9 . . . . **189** F4
Tenter Hill La HD4 . . . . . **136** D4
Tenter Hill Rd HD9 . . . . . **189** D7
Tenter House CH HD8 . . . **192** B5
Tenters Cl WF11 . . . . **126** D5
Tenters Gr HD2 . . . . **136** C3
Tenth Ave WF15 . . . . **116** C5
Ternhill Gr BD5 . . . . **201** B1
Tern Pk LS22 . . . . **13** B1
Tern St BD5 . . . . **74** C3
Terrace Gdns HX3 . . . . **92** B1
Terrace The
  Boston Spa LS23 . . . . **30** E7
  Honley HD9 . . . . **171** E3
  Pudsey LS28 . . . . **76** E4
Terracotta Dr BD15 . . . . . . **73** A8
Terrington Crest BD14 . . . **73** D4
Terry Lug Cotts LS23 . . . . **29** E1
Terry Rd 2 BD12 . . . . **94** E5
Tetley Dr BD11 . . . . **96** B4
Tetley La HX3 . . . . **93** A2
Tetley Pl BD2 . . . . **55** F3
Tetley St BD1 . . . . **201** A3
Teville Ct BD4 . . . . **75** A4
Tewit Cl HX2 . . . . **91** F7
Tewit Gdns HX2 . . . . **91** F7
Tewit Gn HX2 . . . . **91** F7
Tewit Hall Gdns HX2 . . . . **91** F6
Tewit Hall Rd BD3 . . . . . . **75** C8
Tewit La HX2 . . . . **91** F7
Tewitt Cl BD20 . . . . **17** B6
Tewitt La
  Bingley BD16 . . . . **37** B6
  Wilsden BD13 . . . . **53** A2
Tew St WF2 . . . . **142** C4
Texas St LS27 . . . . **98** B2
Thackeray Gr HD4 . . . . . **153** D3
Thackeray Rd BD10 . . . . . **56** D4
Thackeray Wlk WF11 . . . **126** B4
Thacker Gate Rd HX6 . . . **111** B4
Thackley Ave BD18 . . . . . . **39** A2
Thackley Ct BD18 . . . . **55** C8
Thackley Old Rd BD18 . . . **55** D8
Thackley Prim Sch BD10 . **39** B1
Thackley Rd BD10 . . . . **39** A2
Thackley View BD10 . . . . . **39** A2
Thackray Ave WF16 . . . . **117** E5
Thackray La WF8 . . . . . . **125** E1
Thackray Medical Mus★
  LS8 . . . . **207** C2
Thackray St
  Halifax HX2 . . . . **112** D7
  Morley LS27 . . . . **98** A3
Thames Dr LS25 . . . . **83** B6
Thanes Cl HD2 . . . . **135** E1
Thanet Garth 2 BD20 . . . . **17** E8
Thane Way LS15 . . . . **62** E3
Thatchers Way BD19 . . . . **96** B1
Theaker La LS12 . . . . **209** B4
Theakston Mead BD14 . . . **73** C4
Thealby Cl LS9 . . . . **212** B4
Thealby Lawn LS9 . . . . . **207** B1
Thealby Pl 1 LS9 . . . . . . **212** B4
Thearne Gn BD14 . . . . **73** D4
Theatre Royal & Opera Ho★
  WF1 . . . . **216** A2
Theatre Wlk 1 LS1 . . . . . **211** C4
Theodore St LS11 . . . . . . **214** A2
Thewlis La HD4 . . . . **153** B1
Thick Hollins HD9 . . . . . **170** F1
Thick Hollins Dr HD9 . . . **170** F1
Thick Hollins Rd
  Holmfirth HD9 . . . . **188** A7
  Meltham HD9 . . . . **187** F8
Third Ave
  Bradford BD3 . . . . **56** C1
  Cleckheaton WF15 . . . . . **116** B5
  Halifax HX3 . . . . **113** B4
  Huddersfield HD7 . . . . . . **152** D4
  1 Keighley BD21 . . . . **35** B6
  Kirkheaton HD5 . . . . **137** C1
  Leeds LS12 . . . . **210** A2
  Lofthouse Gate WF1 . . . . **121** C2
  Rothwell LS26 . . . . **101** C4
  Upton WF9 . . . . **183** A8
  Wetherby LS22 . . . . **13** F5
Third St 2 BD12 . . . . **94** E6
Thirkhill Ct 4 BD5 . . . . . . **74** E4
Thirkleby Royd BD14 . . . . **73** C4
Thirlmere Ave
  Brighouse BD12 . . . . **94** E1
  Elland HX5 . . . . **135** B7
Thirlmere Cl LS11 . . . . **98** E8
Thirlmere Dr
  Castleford WF10 . . . . **125** D7
  East Ardsley WF3 . . . . . . **120** A8
  Wetherby LS22 . . . . **13** B6

Thirlmere Gdns
  6 Bradford BD2 . . . . **56** B2
  Leeds LS11 . . . . **98** E8
Thirlmere Gr BD17 . . . . . . **37** E1
Thirlmere Pl WF11 . . . . . **126** E2
Thirlmere Rd
  Batley WF12 . . . . **118** F2
  Wakefield WF2 . . . . **141** E6
Thirsk Cl HD2 . . . . **136** B2
Thirsk Dr LS25 . . . . **83** A2
Thirsk Gr LS10 . . . . **99** D3
Thirsk Grange BD14 . . . . . **73** D4
Thirsk Row LS1 . . . . **211** B3
Thirstin Gdns HD4 . . . . . **171** F5
Thirstin Rd HD4 . . . . **171** F5
Thirteenth Ave WF15 . . . **116** B5
Thistle Bottom HX7 . . . . . **88** D2
Thistle Cl HD2 . . . . **135** E2
Thistle Dr WF9 . . . . **182** F7
Thistle Hill HD8 . . . . **155** C5
Thistle Hill Ave HD5 . . . . **155** C5
Thistle Hill Cl WF7 . . . . . **144** D5
Thistle Hill Dr WF7 . . . . . **144** D5
Thistle St HD1 . . . . **154** B8
Thistle Way LS27 . . . . **97** C5
Thistlewood Rd WF1 . . . . **121** E5
Thomas Ct BD6 . . . . **74** C1
Thomas Danby Coll LS7 . . **207** A2
Thomas Fold BD2 . . . . **56** B2
Thomas St S HX1 . . . . . . **202** C2
Thomas St W HX1 . . . . . **202** C1
Thomas St
  Batley, Heckmondwike
    WF16 . . . . **117** D3
  Batley WF17 . . . . **118** B6
  Brighouse HD6 . . . . **115** A1
  Castleford WF10 . . . . **103** E1
  Elland, Holywell Green
    HX4 . . . . **134** B4
  Elland HX5 . . . . **135** A6
  Glusburn BD20 . . . . **16** D7
  Halifax HX1 . . . . **203** B3
  Haworth BD22 . . . . **51** D6
  Hemsworth WF9 . . . . **181** E6
  Huddersfield, Lindley HD3 . **135** B1
  Huddersfield, Yews Hill
    HD1 . . . . **153** E4
  Leeds LS6 . . . . **206** A3
  9 Liversedge WF15 . . . . . **117** A4
  Todmorden OL14 . . . . . . **106** C1
Thomas Way WF9 . . . . . **183** A4
Thompson's Yd WF1 . . . . **216** A2
Thompson Ave
  Bradford BD2 . . . . **55** F5
  Castleford WF10 . . . . **125** E6
Thompson Cl HX3 . . . . . . **114** C7
Thompson Dr WF2 . . . . . **120** F3
Thompson Gn BD17 . . . . . **38** A2
Thompson La BD17 . . . . . . **38** A1
Thompson St
  Normanton WF6 . . . . **123** A2
  Shipley BD18 . . . . **55** A8
Thong La HD9 . . . . **189** A8
Thoresby Dr BD19 . . . . . **117** B8
Thoresby Gr BD7 . . . . **73** E3
Thoresby Pl LS2 . . . . **206** B1
Thorgrow Cl HD8 . . . . . . **155** C4
Thornaby Dr BD14 . . . . . . **73** C4
Thornacre Cres BD18 . . . . **55** E7
Thornacre Rd BD18 . . . . . . **55** E7
Thorn Ave
  Bradford BD9 . . . . **54** D4
  Dewsbury WF12 . . . . **139** C2
Thorn Bank OL13 . . . . . . **106** A2
Thornbank Ave BD22 . . . . **34** F4
Thornber Gr BD20 . . . . **5** E2
Thornberry Dr WF15 . . . . **116** B5
Thornbridge Mews 3
  BD2 . . . . **56** B4
Thornbury Ave
  Bradford BD3 . . . . **75** D8
  Leeds LS16 . . . . **59** C7
Thornbury Cres BD3 . . . . . **75** D8
Thornbury Dr BD3 . . . . . . **75** D8
Thornbury Gr BD3 . . . . . . **75** D8
Thornbury Pk WF2 . . . . . **141** F4
Thornbury Prim Sch BD3 . **75** E7
Thornbury Rd
  Bradford BD3 . . . . **75** D7
  Wakefield WF2 . . . . **141** F4
Thornbury St BD3 . . . . **75** D7
Thorn Cl BD18 . . . . **55** E6
Thorncliff HD8 . . . . **174** B7
Thorncliffe Est WF17 . . . **118** A3
Thorncliffe House Flats 1
  HD3 . . . . **135** B1
Thorncliffe La HD8 . . . . . **175** D7
Thorncliffe Park Ind Est 10
  BD8 . . . . **55** D1
Thorncliffe Rd
  Batley WF17 . . . . **118** B3
  Bradford BD8 . . . . **55** D1
  Keighley BD22 . . . . **34** F6
Thorncliffe St HD3 . . . . . **135** B1
Thorncliff Green Rd
  HD8 . . . . **174** C7
Thorncliff La HD8 . . . . . . **174** C7
Thorn Cres
  7 Bacup OL13 . . . . **106** A2
  Leeds LS8 . . . . **208** B3
Thorncroft Rd BD6 . . . . . . **74** A1
Thorn Cross LS8 . . . . **208** C4
Thorndale Rise BD2 . . . . . . **55** F4
Thorndene Way BD4 . . . . . **96** A7
Thorn Dr
  Bacup OL13 . . . . **106** A2
  Bradford BD9 . . . . **54** D4
  Leeds LS8 . . . . **208** B3

Thorn Dr continued
  Queensbury BD13 . . . . **92** C7
Thorne Cl
  Normanton WF6 . . . . **123** C1
  Pudsey LS28 . . . . **76** B8
Thorne End Rd S75 . . . . . **178** B2
Thornefield Cres WF3 . . . **119** D8
Thorne Gr LS26 . . . . **101** A6
Thorner CE Primary Sch
  LS14 . . . . **46** A6
Thorne Rd HD1 . . . . **153** E4
Thorner La
  Bardsey LS23 . . . . **29** D2
  Barwick in E LS14 . . . . **45** E1
  Scarcroft LS14 . . . . **45** E8
Thorner Rd
  Bardsey LS23 . . . . **29** E1
  Barwick in E LS14 . . . . **46** D8
  Bramham LS23 . . . . **30** B2
Thornes Farm App LS9 . . **80** D5
Thornes Farm Way LS9 . . **80** D5
Thornes Fold WF2 . . . . . **155** F3
Thornes Ind Est WF1 . . . **142** C4
Thornes Lane Wharf
  WF1 . . . . **142** D4
Thornes Moor Ave WF2 . . **142** A3
Thornes Moor Cl WF2 . . . **142** A3
Thornes Moor Dr WF2 . . . **142** A3
Thornes Moor Rd WF2 . . . **142** A3
Thornes Office Pk WF2 . . **142** B3
Thornes Park Ct WF2 . . . **142** B3
Thornes Pk
  Brighouse HD6 . . . . **115** A1
  Shipley BD18 . . . . **55** D5
Thorne St 1 HX4 . . . . . . **134** A4
Thornes Wharf Workshops
  WF1 . . . . **142** D4
Thorneycroft Rd BD20 . . . **19** B1
Thorney La HX2 . . . . **90** D2
Thornfield
  Bingley BD16 . . . . **36** E4
  Dewsbury WF12 . . . . **139** D6
  Haworth BD22 . . . . **51** D6
Thornfield Ave
  Bradford BD6 . . . . **94** D8
  Huddersfield HD4 . . . . . . **153** E3
  Pudsey LS28 . . . . **57** C3
Thornfield Cl BD19 . . . . . **116** C6
Thornfield Ct 4 LS15 . . . . **62** B2
Thornfield Dr 3 LS15 . . . . **62** B2
Thornfield Hall 4 BD13 . . **72** E6
Thornfield Mews 4
  Leeds LS15 . . . . **62** B2
  Micklethwaite BD16 . . . . . **36** E7
Thornfield Mount WF17 . . **97** A1
Thornfield Pl BD2 . . . . **56** C3
Thornfield Rd
  Huddersfield HD4 . . . . . . **153** E3
  Leeds LS16 . . . . **59** B8
Thornfield Rise 2 HX4 . . **134** B7
Thornfield St 1 HX4 . . . . **134** B7
Thornfield Terr BD15 . . . . **53** B4
Thornfield Way LS15 . . . . **62** B2
Thorn Garth
  Cleckheaton BD19 . . . . . . **116** C6
  Keighley BD20 . . . . **18** A1
Thorngate BD13 . . . . **52** F1
Thorn Gdns OL13 . . . . . . **106** A2
Thorn Gr
  Bradford BD9 . . . . **54** D4
  Leeds LS8 . . . . **208** B3
Thorn Hill HX4 . . . . **133** F2
Thornhill Ave
  Haworth BD22 . . . . **34** E3
  Huddersfield HD3 . . . . . . **153** C7
  Shipley BD18 . . . . **55** D5
Thornhill Bridge La HD6 . **115** A3
Thornhill Cl
  Middlestown WF4 . . . . . . **158** B7
  Pudsey LS28 . . . . **57** B7
  Walton WF2 . . . . **161** A6
Thorn Hill Cl HX4 . . . . . . **133** F2
Thornhill Croft
  Leeds LS12 . . . . **209** B2
  Walton WF2 . . . . **161** A7
Thornhill Ct LS12 . . . . . . **209** C2
Thornhill Dr
  Pudsey LS28 . . . . **57** B8
  Shipley BD18 . . . . **55** D5
  Walton WF2 . . . . **161** A7
Thornhill Gr
  Pudsey LS28 . . . . **57** B7
  Shipley BD18 . . . . **55** D5
  Steeton BD20 . . . . **17** B6
Thornhill Hey HX4 . . . . . **133** F2
Thornhill Ho BD3 . . . . **75** E8
Thornhill Jun & Inf Sch
  WF12 . . . . **139** E1
Thornhill Lees CE Inf Sch
  WF12 . . . . **139** C4
Thornhill Park Ave
  WF12 . . . . **139** D4
Thornhill Pl
  Bradford BD3 . . . . **75** E8
  1 Brighouse HD6 . . . . . . **115** A1
  Leeds LS12 . . . . **209** B2
Thornhill Rd
  Brighouse HD6 . . . . **115** A1
  Castleford WF10 . . . . **124** E6
  Dewsbury, West Town WF12,
    WF13 . . . . **139** B7
  Dewsbury WF12 . . . . **139** C5
  Huddersfield, Edgerton
    HD3 . . . . **153** D8
  Huddersfield HD3 . . . . . . **153** A6
  Leeds LS12 . . . . **209** C2

Thorn Dr continued
  Middlestown WF4 . . . . . . **158** A5
  Steeton BD20 . . . . **17** B
Thornhills Beck La HD6 . **115** B
Thornhills La HD6 . . . . . **115** C
Thornhill St
  Dewsbury WF12 . . . . **139** C
  Leeds LS12 . . . . **209** B
  Pudsey LS28 . . . . **57** B
  Wakefield WF1 . . . . **216** B
Thornhill Street Bglws
  WF1 . . . . **216** B
Thornhill Terr BD3 . . . . . . **75** D
Thornie View WF12 . . . . **139** C
Thorn La
  Bradford BD9 . . . . **54** D
  Leeds LS8 . . . . **204** C
Thornlea Cl LS19 . . . . **39** F
Thornleigh WF12 . . . . . . **139** D
Thornleigh Ave WF2 . . . . **142** C
Thornleigh Cres WF2 . . . **142** C
Thornleigh Croft WF2 . . . **142** C
Thornleigh Dr
  Liversedge WF15 . . . . . . **117** B
  Wakefield WF2 . . . . **142** C
Thornleigh Garth WF2 . . **142** C
Thornleigh Gdns LS9 . . . **212** C
Thornleigh Gr
  1 Leeds LS9 . . . . **212** C
  Wakefield WF2 . . . . **142** C
Thornleigh Mount 3
  LS9 . . . . **212** C
Thornleigh Rd
  Huddersfield HD4 . . . . . . **153** C
  Wakefield WF2 . . . . **142** C
Thornleigh St 4 LS9 . . . . **212** C
Thornleigh View 2 LS9 . **212** C
Thornmead Rd BD17 . . . . . **38** D
Thorn Mount LS8 . . . . . . **208** C
Thorn Park Sch for Deaf
  Children BD9 . . . . **54** D
Thorn Pl 18 OL14 . . . . . . **108** C
Thorn Rd WF12 . . . . **139** C
Thorn Royd Dr BD4 . . . . . **75** F
Thornsgill Ave BD4 . . . . . **75** C
Thorn St
  Bacup OL13 . . . . **106** A
  Batley WF17 . . . . **96** E
  Bradford BD8 . . . . **55** A
  3 Haworth BD22 . . . . **51** E
Thorn Terr LS8 . . . . **208** C
Thornton's Arc LS1 . . . . . **211** C
Thornton Ave LS12 . . . . . **209** A
Thornton Cl
  Batley WF17 . . . . **96** F
  Hemsworth WF9 . . . . **181** D
Thornton Ct
  11 Bradford BD8 . . . . **73** F
  Upton WF9 . . . . **183** D
Thornton Gdns LS12 . . . . **209** A
Thornton Gr LS12 . . . . . . **209** A
Thornton Gram Sch BD13 **73** B
Thornton Hall Farm BD13 **72** F
Thornton La BD5 . . . . **74** C
Thornton Lodge Hall
  HD1 . . . . **153** E
Thornton Lodge Rd HD1 . **153** F
Thornton Moor Rd BD13,
  BD22 . . . . **71** B
Thornton Old Rd BD8 . . . . **73** C
Thornton Prim Sch BD13 . **72** C
Thornton Rd
  Bradford BD13, BD8 . . . . . **73** C
  Brighouse HD6 . . . . **135** E
  Denholme BD13 . . . . **71** F
  Dewsbury WF12 . . . . **139** C
  Thornton BD13 . . . . **72** C
Thorntons Dale LS18 . . . . **58** B
Thornton Sq 8 HD6 . . . . **115** A
Thornton St
  Bradford BD1 . . . . **74** C
  Burley in W LS29 . . . . **9** E
  Cleckheaton, Hartshead Moor
    Side BD19 . . . . **116** A
  Cleckheaton, Marsh BD19 . **116** F
  Dewsbury WF13 . . . . **139** B
  Halifax HX1 . . . . **202** B
Thornton Terr 2 HX1 . . . **202** B
Thornton View Rd BD14 . . **73** C
Thorntonville BD19 . . . . . **116** F
Thorntree Ave WF4 . . . . **143** E
Thorntree Cl WF8 . . . . . . **147** D
Thorntree Ct WF4 . . . . . . **143** E
Thorn Tree St HX1 . . . . . **202** B
Thorn View
  Elland HX5 . . . . **135** A
  Halifax, Luddenden HX2 . . **90** A
  6 Halifax, Woodlands HX3 . **92** C
  Leeds LS8 . . . . **208** C
  Mytholmroyd HX7 . . . . . . **110** D
Thornville 5 LS27 . . . . . . **98** B
Thornville Ave 8 LS6 . . . **205** B
Thornville Cres 11 LS6 . . **205** B
Thornville Ct
  Bradford BD8 . . . . **55** D
  Leeds LS6 . . . . **205** B
Thornville Gr 6 LS6 . . . . **205** B
Thornville Mount
  3 Dewsbury WF13 . . . . . **139** A
  5 Leeds LS6 . . . . **205** B
Thornville Pl
  Dewsbury WF13 . . . . **139** A
  Leeds LS6 . . . . **205** B
Thornville Rd LS6 . . . . . . **205** B
Thornville Row LS6 . . . . . **205** B
Thornville St
  Dewsbury WF13 . . . . **139** A
  Leeds LS6 . . . . **205** B

hornville Terr
  Dewsbury WF13 . . . . 139 B6
7 Leeds LS6 . . . . 205 B2
hornville View WF13 . . . . 205 B2
horn Wlk LS8 . . . . 208 C3
hornwood Cl S63 . . . . . . 194 C1
hornwood Rd S63 . . . . . . 194 D1
horold Ho **5** BD10 . . . . . . 56 C7
horp Arch HM Prison
LS23 . . . . 15 A2
horp Arch Mill LS23 . . . . 30 E8
horp Arch Trad Est LS23 . 15 B2
horp Ave HD9 . . . . 189 B4
horpe Ave BD13 . . . . . . 73 A6
horpe Cl LS20 . . . . 39 B8
horpe Cres LS10 . . . . . . 99 C3
horpe Ct LS10 . . . . 99 C3
horpe Dr LS20 . . . . 22 C1
horpe Garth LS10 . . . . . . 99 B3
horpe Gate Est WF9 . . . . 165 A4
horpe Gdns LS10 . . . . . . 99 C3
horpe Gr
  Middleton LS10 . . . . 99 C4
  Thornton BD13 . . . . 73 A6
horpe Green Dr HD7 . . . . 152 E6
horpe La
  East Ardsley WF3 . . . . . . 98 F1
  Guiseley LS20 . . . . 22 B1
  Huddersfield HD5 . . . . . . 155 A4
  Middleton LS10, WF3 . . . . 99 A2
  Thorpe Audlin WF8 . . . . . 165 A4
horpe Lower La WF3 . . . . 100 A3
horpe Mill Ct HX6 . . . . . . 132 F8
horpe Mount LS10 . . . . . . 99 B3
horpe Pk LS15 . . . . 81 F7
horpe Pl HX6 . . . . 111 C2
Thorpe Prim Sch
  Bradford BD10 . . . . 56 B8
  Middleton WF3 . . . . 99 E2
horpe Rd
  East Ardsley WF3 . . . . . . 120 C7
  Middleton LS10 . . . . 99 C4
  Pudsey LS28 . . . . 76 E8
  Thornton BD13 . . . . 73 A6
horpes Ave HD8 . . . . . . 192 A7
horpes Cres HD8 . . . . . . 175 A1
horpe Sq LS10 . . . . 99 D4
horpe St
  Halifax HX3 . . . . 92 B2
  Keighley BD21 . . . . 35 C8
  Leeds LS15 . . . . 81 A8
  Middleton LS10 . . . . 99 C3
horpe Terr HX2 . . . . 90 E1
horpe View
  Middleton LS10 . . . . 99 C3
  Ossett WF5 . . . . 140 D8
  Wakefield WF2 . . . . 141 F6
horp Garth BD10 . . . . . . 56 B8
horp Ho **1** LS27 . . . . . . 98 A4
horverton Dr BD4 . . . . . . 95 E8
horverton Gr BD4 . . . . . . 95 E8
hreadneedle Ct HX1 . . . . 202 B1
hreadneedle St HD1 . . . . 154 A6
hreap Croft HX2 . . . . . . 91 F6
hree Lane Ends WF10 . . 124 A8
Three Lane Ends Bsns Ctr
WF10 . . . . 124 A8
Three Lane Ends Com Prim
Sch WF10 . . . . 124 A8
Three Nooked Mews
BD10 . . . . 56 B8
hree Nooks La S72 . . . . 180 B1
hree Sisters Sq **1** HD1 . 154 A8
hreshfield BD17 . . . . . . 38 C3
hreshfield Cres BD11 . . . 96 A6
hrice Fold BD9 . . . . 55 F8
hrift Way BD16 . . . . 36 F2
hrostle Ave LS10 . . . . . . 99 B3
hrostle Bank HX1 . . . . . 202 B1
hrostle Crest WF7 . . . . . 145 A8
hrostle Dr LS10 . . . . 99 B3
Throstle Farm Jun & Inf Sch
WF11 . . . . 126 F2
hrostle Hill LS10 . . . . . . 99 B3
hrostle La LS10 . . . . 99 C3
hrostle Mount
  Middleton LS10 . . . . 99 B3
  Sowerby Bridge HX2 . . . . 111 F5
Throstle Nest
  Batley WF17 . . . . 118 A4
  Mytholmroyd HX7 . . . . . 110 D8
hrostle Nest Cl LS21 . . . 10 D2
hrostle Nest Rd BD20 . . . 5 D2
Throstle Nest View **4**
LS18 . . . . 58 C7
hrostle Par LS10 . . . . . . 99 B3
hrostle Pl LS10 . . . . 99 B3
Throstle Rd
  Middleton, Belle Isle LS10 . 99 E5
  Middleton LS10 . . . . 99 B3
Throstle Row
  Knottingley WF11 . . . . . . 126 E2
  Middleton LS10 . . . . 99 B3
hrostle Sq LS10 . . . . 99 B3
Throstle St
  Middleton LS10 . . . . 99 B3
  Todmorden OL14 . . . . . . 129 B6
hrostle Terr LS10 . . . . . . 99 C3
hrostle View LS10 . . . . . . 99 B3
hrostle Wlk LS10 . . . . . . 99 B3
hroxenby Way BD14 . . . . 73 C4
hrum Hall Cl HX1 . . . . . 202 B3
hrum Hall La HX1 . . . . . 202 B3
Thrum Hall Ind Pk HX2 . . 202 A4
hrush Hill Rd **6** HX7 . . . 89 E1

Thrush St BD21 . . . . 35 D8
Thryberg St BD3 . . . . . . 75 A7
Thunder Bridge La HD8 . 173 D4
Thunderhead Ridge
WF10 . . . . 124 E5
Thunderton La HX6 . . . . 111 C2
Thurgory Gate HD8 . . . . 155 E3
Thurgory La HD8 . . . . . 155 E4
Thurlestone Ct BD20 . . . . 36 B8
Thurley Dr BD4 . . . . 75 B2
Thurley Rd BD4 . . . . 75 B2
Thurnscoe La S72 . . . . . 194 A1
Thurnscoe Rd BD1 . . . . 201 A4
Thurrish La HX7 . . . . . . 69 B6
Thursby St BD3 . . . . 75 B7
Thurstonland Bank Rd
HD9 . . . . 172 D1
Thurstonland Endowed Fst
Sch HD4 . . . . 172 F2
Thurstonland Rd HD4 . . 172 E5
Thwaite Gate LS10 . . . . 215 C3
Thwaite La LS10 . . . . . . 80 A3
Thwaite Mills Industrial
Mus ★ LS10 . . . . 80 B3
Thwaites Ave LS29 . . . . . 8 C5
Thwaites Bridge BD21 . . 35 F7
Thwaites Brow Rd BD21 . 35 F6
Thwaites La BD21 . . . . . . 35 E7
Tibgarth LS22 . . . . 13 B3
Tichborne Rd **4** BD5 . . . 74 E3
Tichborne Rd W BD5 . . . 74 E3
Tichborne St FW15 . . . . 116 E4
Tichbourne St WF17 . . . 117 F4
Tickhill St BD3 . . . . 75 B6
Tiding Field La HD7 . . . . 151 D2
Tidswell St WF16 . . . . . 117 E4
Tilbury Ave **8** LS11 . . . . 213 C4
Tilbury Gr **6** LS11 . . . . 213 C4
Tilbury Mount LS11 . . . . 213 C4
Tilbury Par **7** LS11 . . . . 213 C4
Tilbury Rd LS11 . . . . . . 213 C4
Tilbury Row LS11 . . . . . 213 C4
Tilbury Terr LS11 . . . . . 213 C4
Tilbury View **9** LS11 . . . 213 C4
Tile La LS16 . . . . 42 D3
Tile St BD8 . . . . 55 B1
Tile Terr HD6 . . . . 115 A1
Tiley Sq **5** BD5 . . . . 74 E4
Till Carr La HX3 . . . . . . 115 A8
Tillotson's Ct BD20 . . . . . 4 A2
Tillotson Ave HX6 . . . . . 112 A3
Tillotsons Bldgs HX2 . . . 111 D7
Tillotson St BD20 . . . . . . 5 D2
Timbercliffe OL15 . . . . . 129 D1
Timber St
  3 Elland HX5 . . . . 134 F6
  4 Keighley BD21 . . . . . . 35 E8
Timberwood HD8 . . . . . 173 D4
Timble Dr BD16 . . . . 37 B4
Tim La BD22 . . . . 34 B1
Timmey La HX6 . . . . . . 112 A5
Timothy La WF17 . . . . . 118 D7
Tinderley Gr HD5 . . . . . 154 F4
Tingley Ave WF3 . . . . . . 98 F8
Tingley Comm LS27, WF3 . 98 C1
Tingley Cres WF3 . . . . . . 98 C1
Tinker La
  Lepton HD8 . . . . 156 B2
  Meltham HD9 . . . . 170 D1
Tinkingfield La LS24 . . . . 15 C8
Tinkler Stile BD10 . . . . . 55 F8
Tinsel Rd WF12 . . . . . . 118 F1
Tinshill Ave LS16 . . . . . . 41 E3
Tinshill Cl LS16 . . . . 41 E3
Tinshill Cres LS16 . . . . . 41 E4
Tinshill Dr LS16 . . . . 41 E4
Tinshill Garth LS16 . . . . 41 E4
Tinshill Gr LS16 . . . . 41 E4
Tinshill La LS16 . . . . 41 E4
Tinshill Mount LS16 . . . . 41 E4
Tinshill Rd LS16 . . . . 41 D4
Tinshill View LS16 . . . . . 41 E4
Tinshill Wlk LS16 . . . . . . 41 E5
Tinsworth Rd WF2 . . . . 160 A4
Tintagel Ct WF6 . . . . . . 123 B3
Tintern Ave
  Bradford BD8 . . . . 73 D7
  Huddersfield HD3 . . . . . . 152 F5
Tippaty La WF11 . . . . . . 127 A7
Tipping La HD8 . . . . . . 175 D7
Tipsey Ct S75 . . . . 178 D1
Tisma Dr BD4 . . . . 95 C8
Titan District Ctr BD12 . . 94 C2
Titania Cl **7** BD16 . . . . . 54 B6
Tithe Barn Fold LS15 . . . 63 D7
Tithe Barn La LS17 . . . . 28 C2
Tithe Barn Rd WF11 . . . 127 A4
Tithe Barn St
  Dewsbury WF13 . . . . . . 139 D8
  Horbury WF4 . . . . 141 A1
Tithe Barn View HD6 . . . 136 C8
Tithefields HD8 . . . . . . 155 C4
Tithe House Way HD2 . . 136 E6
Titus Cl HD8 . . . . 174 D6
Titus St BD18 . . . . 54 F8
Tiverton Wlk **4** BD4 . . . . 75 E2
Tivoli Pl
  Bradford BD5 . . . . 74 C4
  Ilkley LS29 . . . . 8 C3
Tivy Dale S75 . . . . 193 E4
Tivy Dale Cl S75 . . . . . . 193 E4
Tivy Dale Dr S75 . . . . . . 193 E4
Toby La BD7 . . . . 74 A5
Toby Wood La HD8 . . . . 191 D5
Todd Terr **2** BD7 . . . . . . 74 B4
Todley Hall Farm BD22 . . 34 A6
Todley Hall Rd BD22 . . . 34 A6

Todmorden CE Jun & Inf Sch
OL14 . . . . 108 A5
Todmorden Com Coll
OL14 . . . . 108 B5
Todmorden High Sch
OL14 . . . . 107 F6
Todmorden Old Rd OL13 106 B5
Todmorden Rd
  Bacup OL13 . . . . 106 B4
  Calderbrook OL15 . . . . . 129 D2
Todmorden Sta OL14 . . 108 A5
Todwell La BD5 . . . . 74 C3
Tofrek Terr BD4 . . . . . . 172 F6
Tofts Ave BD12 . . . . 94 C2
Tofts Grove Gdns HD6 . 135 F7
Tofts Grove Pl HD6 . . . . 135 F7
Toftshaw Fold BD4 . . . . . 95 D8
Toftshaw La BD4 . . . . . . 95 E8
Toftshaw New Rd BD4 . . 95 D8
Tofts House Cl LS28 . . . . 76 E7
Tofts Rd
  Cleckheaton BD19 . . . . . 116 D7
  Pudsey LS28 . . . . 76 D7
Toft St LS12 . . . . 210 A2
Toll Bar La WF2 . . . . . . 120 D1
Toll Bar Rd WF10 . . . . . 123 F7
Toller Dr BD9 . . . . 54 E3
Toller Gr BD9 . . . . 54 F3
Toller La BD8, BD9 . . . . . 55 A1
Toller Pk BD9 . . . . 54 F3
Tollgate Cl S72 . . . . 180 C1
Tollgate Ct BD8 . . . . 55 A1
Tolson's Yd **12** HD5 . . . 154 D5
Tolson Cres HD5 . . . . . . 154 E7
Tolson Grange HD5 . . . . 154 F5
Tolson Mus ★ HD5 . . . . 154 E6
Tolson St
  Dewsbury WF13 . . . . . . 118 C1
  Ossett WF5 . . . . 140 B8
Tolworth Fold **1** BD15 . . 73 B8
Tomahawk Trail WF10 . . 124 F5
Tombridge Cres WF9 . . . 163 B1
Tom Dando Cl WF6 . . . . 123 E2
Tom La HD4 . . . . 153 B3
Tomling Cote La BD20 . . . 18 B8
Tomlinson's Yd HD1 . . . 154 B6
Tom Wood Ash La WF9 . 183 E2
Tonbridge Cl BD6 . . . . . . 93 F8
Tong App LS12 . . . . 77 D6
Tong Dr LS12 . . . . 77 D7
Tong Gate LS12 . . . . . . 77 D7
Tong Gn LS12 . . . . 77 D6
Tong Hall Bsns Ctr BD4 . 76 D2
Tong La
  Bacup OL13 . . . . 106 B2
  Birkenshaw BD4 . . . . 76 E2
Tong Park St BD17 . . . . . 38 F5
Tong Rd LS12 . . . . 77 C6
Tong Sch BD4 . . . . 96 A8
Tong St
  Birkenshaw BD4 . . . . 95 F8
  Bradford BD4 . . . . 75 D1
Tongue La LS6 . . . . 42 F1
Tong Way LS12 . . . . 77 D7
Tong Wlk LS12 . . . . 77 D7
Tony Miller App BD17 . . . 55 C8
Tootal St WF1 . . . . 216 C1
Toothill Ave HD6 . . . . . 136 A4
Toothill Bank HD6 . . . . 136 A4
Toothill La HD6 . . . . . . 136 A4
Toot Hill La WF10 . . . . . 111 B2
Toothill La S HD6 . . . . . 135 F6
Topaz Cl HD2 . . . . 136 C2
Topcliffe Ave LS27 . . . . . 98 C4
Topcliffe Cl WF3 . . . . . . 98 C2
Topcliffe Ct **1** LS27 . . . . 98 C4
Topcliffe Fold LS27 . . . . . 98 C2
Topcliffe Gn **7** LS27 . . . 98 C4
Topcliffe Gr LS27 . . . . . . 98 C2
Topcliffe La
  Morley, Tingley Common
  LS27 . . . . 98 D2
  Morley, Topcliffe LS27 . . . 98 C2
Topcliffe Mead **6** LS27 . 98 C4
Topcliffe Mews **8** LS27 . 98 C4
Top Fold WF11 . . . . 105 A4
Top Headlands WF5 . . . 140 C5
Top House Ct WF8 . . . . 166 D6
Top House Farm Mews
WF11 . . . . 105 A4
Top La
  Clayton DN5 . . . . 194 B5
  West Bretton WF4 . . . . . 158 D1
Top Land Country Bsns Pk
HX7 . . . . 110 E8
Top Mdw WF14 . . . . . . 137 F2
Top Moor Side LS11 . . . 211 A1
Top O' Th' Bank HD9 . . . 172 E1
Top o' Th' Close Rd
OL14 . . . . 129 C6
Top o' Th' Hill Rd OL14 . 108 A1
Top o' th' Moor HD4 . . . 173 C2
Top o' The Hill HD7 . . . 169 E7
Top of Carr **1** WF17 . . . 118 B2
Top of the Hill HD9 . . . . 172 E1
Top Orch WF4 . . . . 162 B1
Top Rd HD8 . . . . 191 E7
Top Row
  Darton S75 . . . . 177 E5
  Huddersfield HD4 . . . . . . 171 E8
Top St
  Hemsworth WF9 . . . . . . 181 C7
  Todmorden OL14 . . . . . . 128 F7
Top Stone Cl LS25 . . . . 105 E3
Tor Ave BD12 . . . . 94 C1
Torcote Cres HD2 . . . . . 136 C5

Tordoff Ave BD7 . . . . . . 73 E5
Tordoff Gn **4** BD6 . . . . . 94 B8
Tordoff Pl LS5 . . . . 59 A4
Tordoff Rd **5** BD12 . . . . 94 E6
Tordoff Terr LS5 . . . . . . 59 A4
Tornwood Cl BD22 . . . . . 34 C2
Toronto Pl LS7 . . . . 204 A2
Torre Cl LS9 . . . . 80 A8
Torre Cres
  Bradford BD6 . . . . 73 D1
  Leeds LS9 . . . . 80 B8
Torre Dr LS9 . . . . 208 A1
Torre Gdns LS9 . . . . . . 212 C4
Torre Gn LS9 . . . . 212 C4
Torre Gr
  Bradford BD6 . . . . 73 D1
  Leeds LS9 . . . . 208 A1
Torre Hill LS9 . . . . 208 B1
Torre La LS9 . . . . 80 B8
Torre Mount LS9 . . . . . 208 A1
Torre Pl LS9 . . . . 80 A8
Torre Rd
  Bradford BD6 . . . . 73 D1
  Leeds LS9 . . . . 80 A8
Torre Sq LS9 . . . . 208 B1
Torre View LS9 . . . . 208 B1
Torre Wlk LS9 . . . . 208 B1
Torridon Cres BD6 . . . . . 93 E6
Torridon Rd WF12 . . . . 118 E2
Tor View HD9 . . . . 172 C2
Totties La HD9 . . . . 189 D5
Toulston La LS23 . . . . . . 30 F2
Tower Ave WF9 . . . . . . 183 A8
Tower Bldgs **1** WF16 . . 117 D3
Tower Cswy OL14 . . . . . 107 B7
Tower Dr The LS21 . . . . . 24 E6
Tower Gdns HX2 . . . . . 112 F4
Tower Gr LS12 . . . . 209 A4
Tower Hill HX6 . . . . 112 B4
Tower House St LS2 . . . 206 C1
Tower La
  Leeds, Hill Top LS12 . . . 209 A4
  Leeds LS12 . . . . 77 F8
Tower Mews LS12 . . . . 209 A4
Tower Pl **6** LS12 . . . . . . 77 F8
Tower Rd BD18 . . . . 54 E8
Towers Cl WF4 . . . . 162 A8
Towers La WF4 . . . . . . 144 B1
Towers Paddock WF9 . . 125 A7
Towers Sq LS6 . . . . 60 A8
Tower St
  Bradford BD2 . . . . 56 B2
  Todmorden OL14 . . . . . . 86 A1
Towers Way LS6 . . . . . . 60 A8
Tower View HX2 . . . . . . 202 A1
Towlerton La WF2 . . . . 120 E2
Town Ave HD1 . . . . 154 C8
Town Cl LS18 . . . . 41 B1
Townclose View LS25 . . 102 F8
Town Cres HD1 . . . . . . 154 C8
Town End
  Bradford BD7 . . . . 74 A4
  Garforth LS25 . . . . 82 E8
  Gildersome LS27 . . . . . . 97 D7
  Huddersfield, Almondbury
  HD5 . . . . 154 F4
  Huddersfield, Town End
  HD7 . . . . 152 D4
  Ossett WF5 . . . . 140 D5
Town End Ave
  Ackworth M T WF7 . . . . 164 C7
  Holmfirth HD9 . . . . 189 C6
Town End Cl
  Glusburn BD20 . . . . 16 D6
  Leeds LS13 . . . . 58 E1
Town End Cres HD9 . . . 189 C7
Town End La HD8 . . . . . 156 A3
Town End Mews BD20 . . 16 C6
Townend Pl BD20 . . . . . . 16 C6
Townend Rd LS12 . . . . . 209 B1
Town End Rd
  Bradford BD14 . . . . 73 B5
  Holmfirth HD9 . . . . 189 C7
Town End View HD9 . . . 189 B6
Townfield BD15 . . . . 53 C5
Townfield La HX7 . . . . . . 88 F5
Town Fields Rd HX5 . . . 134 E6
Townfield View HX7 . . . . 88 F5
Townfold WF5 . . . . 140 E6
Towngate
  8 Baildon BD17 . . . . . . 38 C4
  Brighouse, Clifton HD6 . . 115 E2
  Brighouse, Hipperholme
  HX3 . . . . 114 C8
  Darton S75 . . . . 178 B1
  Heptonstall HX7 . . . . 88 F5
  Holmfirth HD9 . . . . 189 A5
  Huddersfield HD4 . . . . . . 154 A2
  Keighley BD21 . . . . 35 C7
  Mirfield WF14 . . . . 138 B6
  Ossett WF5 . . . . 140 F6
  Shipley BD18 . . . . 55 D7
Town Gate
  2 Bradford BD10 . . . . . . 56 B8
  Bradford, Wyke BD12 . . . 94 C3
  Brighouse BD19 . . . . 115 F8
  4 Guiseley LS20 . . . . . . 22 E1
  Hebden Bridge HX2 . . . . 90 B1
  Holmfirth, Hepworth HD9 . 189 D7
  Holmfirth, Netherthong
  HD9 . . . . 188 F8
  Holmfirth, Upperthong
  HD9 . . . . 188 D5
  Kirkburton HD8 . . . . 173 E8
  Lepton HD8 . . . . 156 A4
  Marsden HD7 . . . . 168 F4
  Northowram HX3 . . . . . . 93 A2
  Pudsey LS28 . . . . 57 B6

Town Gate continued
  Sowerby Bridge HX6 . . . . 111 E3
Towngate Ave HD6 . . . . 115 D3
Town Gate Cl LS20 . . . . 22 E1
Towngate Gr WF14 . . . . 138 B5
Towngate Ho **1** HX5 . . . 134 F7
Towngate Mews **1** S75 . 178 B1
Towngate Prim Sch WF5 140 F6
Towngate Rd WF17 . . . 118 A5
Town Gn LS12 . . . . 139 E7
Town Hall Bldgs **2** HX5 . 135 A6
Town Hall St E **2** HX1 . . 203 B3
Town Hall Sq **4** LS19 . . . 40 B7
Town Hall St
  4 Elland HX5 . . . . 134 F6
  1 Holmfirth HD9 . . . . . . 189 A5
  Keighley BD21 . . . . 35 C7
  4 Mirfield WF14 . . . . . . 138 A4
  Sowerby Bridge HX6 . . . . 112 B4
Town Hall Way WF12 . . 139 D8
Town Head HD9 . . . . . . 171 F5
Town Head Fold LS29 . . . 6 E8
Town Hill LS23 . . . . 30 D2
Town Hill St BD6 . . . . . . 54 B6
Town Ing Mills HX4 . . . . 133 F3
Town Ing Way HX4 . . . . 133 F3
Town La BD10 . . . . 39 B1
Townley Ave HX3 . . . . . 114 A4
Townley Rd WF2 . . . . . 141 D4
Town Moor HD4 . . . . . . 172 F2
Town Pl HD1 . . . . 154 C8
Town Rd HD5 . . . . 137 C1
Towns Head Trad Ctr LS29 . 6 E8
Town Sq LS18 . . . . 41 B1
Town St
  Batley WF17 . . . . 118 C2
  Birkenshaw BD11 . . . . . . 96 A6
  Dewsbury WF12 . . . . . . 139 F7
  Gildersome LS27 . . . . . . 97 D7
  Guiseley LS20 . . . . 22 E1
  Hemsworth WF9 . . . . . . 181 C7
  Horsforth LS18 . . . . 41 B1
  Leeds, Beeston LS11 . . . 213 B2
  Leeds LS7 . . . . 204 A3
  Leeds, Moor Top LS12 . . . 209 B3
  Middleton LS10 . . . . 99 C5
  Pudsey, Farsley LS28 . . . 57 D3
  Pudsey, Rodley LS13 . . . . 57 F5
  Pudsey, Stanningley LS28 . 57 E2
  Rothwell WF3 . . . . 100 D2
  Yeadon LS19 . . . . 40 B7
  Yeadon, Rawdon LS19 . . . 40 D3
Town Street Mews LS7 . 204 A3
Town Street Wlk **8** LS7 . 204 A3
Town Terr HD1 . . . . 154 C8
Town The WF12 . . . . . . 139 D2
Town Top HD5 . . . . 137 C1
Town Wells Dr LS28 . . . . 57 B6
Towton Dr WF10 . . . . . 124 A6
Track Mount WF17 . . . . 118 B2
Track Rd WF17 . . . . 118 B3
Trackside BD12 . . . . 94 F5
Trafalgar Ct HD2 . . . . . 136 B4
Trafalgar Gdns LS27 . . . 98 A3
Trafalgar Rd
  Dewsbury WF13 . . . . . . 118 B1
  Ilkley LS29 . . . . 8 B4
Trafalgar Sq **2** HX1 . . . 202 C1
Trafalgar St
  Batley WF17 . . . . 118 A4
  Bradford BD1 . . . . 201 B4
  3 Halifax HX1 . . . . 202 C1
  Leeds LS2 . . . . 212 A4
Trafford Ave LS9 . . . . . 208 B5
Trafford Gr LS9 . . . . 208 B3
Trafford Terr LS9 . . . . . 208 B5
Tramways BD12 . . . . 94 F5
Tranbeck Rd LS20 . . . . . 22 B1
Tranfield Ave LS20 . . . . 22 C1
Tranfield Cl LS20 . . . . . . 22 C1
Tranfield Ct LS20 . . . . . . 22 C1
Tranfield Gdns LS20 . . . 22 C1
Tranmere Ct LS20 . . . . . 22 C1
Tranmere Dr LS20 . . . . . 22 C1
Tranmere Par LS20 . . . . 22 C1
Tranmere Park Prim Sch
LS20 . . . . 39 C8
Tranquility LS15 . . . . . . 62 C2
Tranquility Ave LS15 . . . 62 C2
Tranquility Ct **2** LS15 . . 62 C2
Tranquility Wlk **1** LS15 . 62 C2
Transperience Way BD4 . 94 F6
Transvaal Terr WF17 . . . 118 B7
Tranter Gr BD4 . . . . 75 E5
Tranter Pl LS15 . . . . 80 C4
Travis Ho LS14 . . . . 129 A7
Travis Lacey Terr **8**
WF13 . . . . 139 B8
Tray Royd HX2 . . . . 90 C2
Treadwell Mills BD1 . . . 201 C3
Treasurers Ho WF8 . . . . 125 D2
Tredgold Ave LS16 . . . . 24 F2
Tredgold Cl LS16 . . . . . 24 E2
Tredgold Cres LS16 . . . . 24 E3
Tredgold Garth LS16 . . . 24 E3
Treefield Ind Est LS27 . . 97 D6
Tree La HX2 . . . . 90 F5
Trees St **5** BD8 . . . . 55 C1
Tree Tops Ct LS8 . . . . . . 61 C7
Tree Top View BD13 . . . 72 C2
Trelawn Ave LS6 . . . . . . 59 D5
Trelawn Cres **12** LS6 . . . 59 D5
Trelawn Pl LS6 . . . . 59 D5
Trelawn St LS6 . . . . 59 D5
Trelawn Terr LS6 . . . . . . 59 D5

Tremont Gdns LS10 ....215 B2
Trenam Park Dr BD10 ....39 A2
Trenance Dr BD18 ....54 F7
Trenance Gdns HX4 .....134 A7
Trenholme Ave BD6 ....94 B6
Trenic Cres LS6 ....205 A3
Trenic Dr LS6 ....205 A3
Trent Ave
  Garforth LS25 ....83 B6
  Normanton WF6 ....123 A4
Trent Bridge Way WF1 ..121 C1
Trentham Ave 2 LS11 ..214 B2
Trentham Gr 7 LS11 ....214 B2
Trentham Pl 9 LS11 .....214 B2
Trentham Row 6 LS11 ..214 B2
Trentham St LS11 ....214 B2
Trentham Terr 20 LS11 ..214 B2
Trenton Dr BD8 ....55 C1
Trenton Rd WF17 ....118 F3
Trent Rd LS9 ....208 A1
Trent St LS11 ....211 B1
Trescoe Ave LS13 ....58 E1
Tresham Ct WF12 ....118 F2
Trevelyan Sq LS1 ....211 C3
Trevelyan St
  Brighouse HD6 ....115 A5
  9 Huddersfield HD5 ..154 D5
Trevor Foster Way BD5 ..74 F2
Trevor Terr WF2 ....120 E6
Triangle Bsns Pk WF17 ..97 A3
Triangle CE Prim Sch
  HX6 ....111 E1
Triangle The 2 HD1 ....153 E5
Triath Ct WF17 ....117 E6
Trilby St WF1 ....216 C3
Trimmingham La HX2 ...202 A2
Trimmingham Rd HX2 ...202 A2
Trimmingham Villas
  HX2 ....202 A2
Trinity & All Saints' Coll
  LS18 ....41 A3
Trinity All Saints CE Prim
  Sch BD8 ....37 A2
Trinity Bsns Ctr WF1 ....216 C1
Trinity Bsns Pk WF2 .....216 B1
Trinity Church Gate
  WF1 ....216 C2
Trinity Cl HX2 ....92 A6
Trinity Ct
  Honley HD9 ....171 F4
  South Elmsall WF9 .....183 A3
Trinity Dr HD8 ....191 F5
Trinity Gr 2 HD6 ....115 A4
Trinity Ho
  Dewsbury WF13 ....118 C2
  1 Wakefield WF1 ......216 C2
Trinity One LS9 ....212 A3
Trinity Pl
  Bingley BD16 ....37 A2
  Halifax HX1 ....203 B2
Trinity Rd
  Bradford BD5 ....74 D5
  Halifax HX1 ....203 B2
Trinity Rise LS21 ....23 B7
Trinity St
  Batley WF17 ....118 C2
  Halifax HX1 ....203 B2
  Hebden Bridge HX7 ....88 F3
  Huddersfield HD1 ....153 F7
  12 Keighley BD21 ......35 C8
  Leeds LS1 ....211 C4
  Mirfield WF14 ....138 A4
  Pontefract WF8 ....125 D1
  Wakefield WF1 ....142 F3
Trinity Street Arc LS1 ...211 C3
Trinity View
  Bradford BD12 ....94 E7
  Halifax HX3 ....203 C2
  Ossett WF5 ....140 D7
Trinity Wlk
  Bradford BD12 ....94 E7
  South Elmsall WF9 .....183 A4
Trip Garth LS22 ....13 B2
Trip La LS22 ....13 A2
Tripping Gn HX2 ....71 D1
Tristram Ave BD5 ....75 A2
Tristram Ctr The LS12 ...213 B4
Triumph Cl LS11, LS12 ..211 A4
Troon Cl WF6 ....123 D1
Troon Dr HD2 ....135 F3
Troon Way WF2 ....142 A2
Trooper La HX3 ....113 E5
Trooper Terr HX3 ....203 C1
Tropical World ★ LS8 ....44 B1
Trough La
  Cullingworth BD13 .....52 A3
  South Elmsall WF9 .....183 A3
Troughton Pl LS28 ....76 F5
Troughton St LS28 ....76 F5
Trough Well La WF2 ....120 E3
Troutbeck Ave BD17 .....37 E1
Troydale Gdns LS28 ......77 B5
Troydale Gr LS28 ....77 B5
Troydale La LS28 ....77 B5
Troy Hill
  Horsforth LS18 ....41 C2
  Morley LS27 ....98 A5
Troy Rd
  Horsforth LS18 ....41 C2
  Morley LS27 ....98 A5
Troy Rise LS27 ....98 B5
Trueman Ave WF16 ......117 E5
Trueman Ct BD12 ....94 E6
Trueman Way WF9 ....183 A4
Truncliffe BD5 ....74 D1

Truncliffe Ho BD5 ....74 D1
Trundles La WF11 ....127 B4
Truro Dr WF6 ....123 B3
Truro St LS12 ....209 C4
Truro Wlk WF6 ....123 B3
Trust Fold LS25 ....105 E3
Tubby La HD2 ....136 B1
Tudor Barn Ct BD18 .....55 D7
Tudor Cl
  Pontefract WF8 ....146 C5
  Pudsey LS28 ....57 C2
Tudor Croft HD2 ....136 F5
Tudor Ct
  18 Bradford BD5 ....201 B1
  South Elmsall WF9 .....182 F3
Tudor Gdns LS11 ....213 B2
Tudor Ho 5 WF1 ....216 B2
Tudor Lawns
  Leeds LS8 ....61 C7
  Lofthouse Gate WF2 ...120 E5
Tudor St
  Bradford BD5 ....74 D4
  Slaithwaite HD7 ....170 A8
Tudor Way WF12 ....139 B3
Tuel La HX6 ....112 B4
Tuel Lane Inf Sch HX6 ..112 B4
Tufton St BD20 ....5 E1
Tuke Gr WF1 ....216 C4
Tulip Ret Pk LS10 ....215 A3
Tulip St
  Haworth BD22 ....51 C5
  Leeds LS10 ....215 A3
Tulyar Ct BD16 ....37 B3
Tumbling Cl WF5 ....140 E6
Tumbling Hill WF8 ....147 A5
Tumbling Hill St BD7 ....74 D6
Tun La S72 ....180 D7
Tunnacliffe Rd HD4 ......154 B3
Tunnel St
  Denholme BD13 ....71 D8
  Huddersfield HD4 ....171 C7
Tunnicliffe Pl BD20 ......5 D1
Tunstall Gn 7 BD4 ....75 E3
Tunstall Rd LS11 ....214 C3
Tunwell La BD2 ....56 C4
Tunwell St BD2 ....56 C4
Tup La WF4 ....180 C8
Turbary Ave 2 LS28 .....57 E2
Turbid La HD4 ....171 A6
Turbury La HX4 ....133 E8
Turf Ct BD13 ....52 C5
Turf La BD13 ....52 C5
Turgate La HX6 ....111 A1
Turkey Hill LS28 ....76 F6
Turley Cote La HX4 ......134 C2
Turlow Ct LS9 ....212 A3
Turnberry Ave LS17 .....43 B4
Turnberry Cl
  East Ardsley WF3 ....119 D8
  Leeds LS17 ....43 B4
Turnberry Ct
  Keighley BD20 ....18 A3
  1 Normanton WF6 .....123 D1
Turnberry Dr
  East Ardsley WF3 ....119 D8
  Leeds LS17 ....43 B4
Turnberry Fold LS17 ....43 B4
Turnberry Gdns WF3 ....119 D8
Turnberry Gr
  Cudworth S72 ....180 C2
  Leeds LS17 ....43 B4
Turnberry Park Rd LS27 ..97 D4
Turnberry Pl LS17 ....43 B4
Turnberry Rise LS17 .....43 B4
Turnberry View LS17 ....43 B4
Turnbridge Rd HD1 ......154 C6
Turnbull Ct LS8 ....61 D5
Turner's La 1 HX3 ....92 B2
Turner Ave
  Batley WF17 ....118 C5
  Bradford BD7 ....73 F5
Turner Ave N HX2 ....91 D5
Turner Ave S HX2 ....91 E4
Turner Cl
  East Ardsley WF3 ....119 E8
  4 Ossett WF5 ....140 D6
Turner Cres LS21 ....11 B1
Turner Dr WF3 ....119 E8
Turner La
  Addingham LS29 ....6 C6
  Addingham LS29 ....6 D8
  Halifax HX3 ....92 D1
Turner Pl
  Bradford BD7 ....74 B5
  Halifax HX2 ....91 E5
Turner St 5 LS28 ....57 D3
Turners Yd LS28 ....57 D3
Turner View HX2 ....91 E4
Turner Way WF2 ....216 B1
Turney St HX3 ....92 A2
Turnip La WF12 ....139 D2
Turnkey Pk LS12 ....78 C4
Turn o The Nook WF5 ...140 C6
Turnpike Cl BD11 ....96 A4
Turnpike St 2 HX5 ....135 A7
Turnshaw Rd
  Haworth BD22 ....33 F2
  Kirkburton HD8 ....174 A6
Turnshaws Ave HD8 .....174 A7
Turnshaws Cl HD8 ....174 A7
Turnsteads Ave BD19 ...116 B8
Turnsteads Cl BD19 ......116 C8
Turnsteads Cres BD19 ..116 C8
Turnsteads Dr BD19 .....116 C8
Turnsteads Mount BD19 ..116 C8
Turnstone Ct 3 LS10 ....99 D5
Turnways The LS6 ....59 C4
Turret Hall Rd HX7 ....88 C2

Turret Royd Rd HX7 .....88 D2
Turton Gn LS27 ....97 D7
Turton St WF1 ....216 C2
Turton Vale LS27 ....97 D6
Turver's La WF11 ....127 F3
Turvin Cotts HX7 ....110 C1
Turvin Rd OL15 ....130 D2
Tuscany Way WF6 ....123 B6
Twain Cres WF10 ....125 C6
Tweedale Gdns WF13 ...139 B8
Tweedale St 1 WF13 ....139 B8
Tweed Cl WF17 ....97 A1
Tweedy St BD15 ....53 C5
Twelfth Ave WF15 ....116 B5
Twickenham Ct BD8 .....145 D2
Twill Cl WF2 ....141 D7
Twist Clough HX7 ....110 D4
Twitch Hill WF4 ....141 B1
Twivey St WF10 ....124 C7
Two Gates
  Holmfirth HD9 ....188 E3
  Slaithwaite HD7 ....151 E1
Two Gates Way S72 .....180 C2
Two Laws Rd BD22 ......49 D8
Tyas Gr LS9 ....80 B7
Tyas La HD7 ....151 B2
Tyburn La HD8 ....175 C6
Tyersal Ave BD4 ....75 F6
Tyersal Cl BD4 ....75 F6
Tyersal Cres BD4 ....75 F6
Tyersal Ct BD4 ....75 F6
Tyersal Dr BD4 ....75 F6
Tyersal Garth BD4 ....75 F6
Tyersal Gn BD4 ....75 F6
Tyersal Gr BD4 ....75 F6
Tyersal La
  Bradford BD4 ....75 E4
  Pudsey BD4, LS28 .....76 A5
Tyersal Pk BD4 ....75 F6
Tyersal Rd BD4 ....75 F6
Tyersal Terr BD4 ....75 F6
Tyersal View BD4 ....75 F6
Tyersal Wlk BD4 ....75 F6
Tyhme Ct BD15 ....73 B8
Tyler Cl WF6 ....123 E2
Tyndale Ave WF4 ....141 C2
Tyndale Wlk WF16 ....117 E5
Tynedale Ct LS7 ....60 A6
Tyne St
  Bradford BD3 ....201 C4
  18 Haworth BD22 ......51 D7
  Keighley BD21 ....35 D7
Tynwald Cl LS17 ....43 A2
Tynwald Dr LS17 ....43 A2
Tynwald Gdns LS17 ......43 A2
Tynwald Gn LS17 ....43 A3
Tynwald Hill LS17 ....43 A2
Tynwald Ho 8 BD4 ....75 F2
Tynwald Mount LS17 ....43 A2
Tynwald Rd LS17 ....43 A2
Tynwald Wlk LS17 ....43 A3
Tyrls The BD1 ....201 B2
Tyrrell Ct WF2 ....141 D7
Tyrrel St BD1 ....201 B3
Tyson St
  Bradford BD1 ....201 A4
  Halifax HX1 ....202 A2

U

Ullswater Ave WF12 ....118 E3
Ullswater Cl
  Batley WF12 ....118 E2
  Elland HX5 ....135 B7
Ullswater Cres
  Leeds LS15 ....80 E7
  Rothwell LS26 ....101 C6
Ullswater Dr
  Bradford BD6 ....93 F6
  Wetherby LS22 ....13 C6
Ullswater Rd WF12 ......118 E3
Ullswater Rise LS22 .....13 C5
Una Pl HD2 ....153 E8
Underbank Ave HX7 .....88 C1
Underbank End Rd HD9 ..189 B3
Underbank Old Rd HD9 ..189 B4
Undercliffe La BD3 ....56 A1
Undercliffe Old Rd BD2 ..56 B1
Undercliffe Pl HX3 ....114 B7
Undercliffe Prim Sch BD2 ..56 B2
Undercliffe Rd BD2 ......56 B3
Undercliffe Rise LS29 ...8 E2
Undercliffe St BD3 ....56 B1
Undercliffe Terr HX2 ....112 F4
Underwood Dr LS19 .....40 C1
Underwood Ho BD3 .....201 C4
Union Cross Yd HX1 .....203 B3
Union Ct LS21 ....22 F7
Union Gr WF15 ....117 B3
Union House La BD13 ...73 C2
Union La HX2 ....71 D1
Union Pl LS11 ....211 B2
Union Rd
  Bradford BD12 ....94 C7
  Bradford, Great Horton BD7 ..74 B5
  Liversedge WF15 ....117 B3
Union St S OL14 ....108 B5
Union Sq WF1 ....216 C2
Union St
  2 Baildon BD17 ....38 E2
  Batley WF17 ....96 F1
  Dewsbury WF13 ....139 D8
  6 Elland HX4 ....134 D7
  Halifax HX1 ....203 B2
  Hemsworth WF9 ....181 E6
  6 Huddersfield HD1 ...154 B7
  Huddersfield, Oakes HD3 ..153 B8

Union St continued
  Leeds LS2 ....212 A4
  Liversedge WF16 ......117 C3
  Micklethwaite BD16 ...36 E7
  Mirfield WF13 ....138 E5
  1 Morley LS27 ....98 C8
  Ossett WF5 ....140 D6
  Otley LS21 ....22 F7
  11 Queensbury BD13 ..72 E1
  Slaithwaite HD7 ....151 F1
  Sowerby Bridge, Triangle
    HX6 ....111 E1
  Sowerby Bridge, Willow Field
    HX6 ....112 C4
  Wakefield WF1 ....216 B3
Union Terr LS7 ....60 C6
Union Yd BD10 ....56 B8
United Bsns Pk LS12 ....213 B4
Unity Cl LS6 ....206 B4
Unity Ct WF13 ....139 B8
Unity Hall Ct WF3 ....119 F7
Unity St N BD16 ....36 F2
Unity St S BD16 ....36 F2
Unity St
  Hebden Bridge HX7 ....89 A4
  Keighley BD20 ....18 F2
  Rothwell WF3 ....100 D3
  Todmorden OL14 ....129 A8
Unity Terr HX1 ....202 A2
University Rd LS2 ....206 A2
University St WF10 ......124 D7
Univ of Bradford
  Bradford, Little Horton Green
    BD5 ....74 C5
  Bradford, Shearbridge BD7 ..74 D6
Univ of Bradford Sch of
  Management BD9 ....55 B4
Univ of Huddersfield
  HD1 ....154 B5
Univ of Leeds LS2 ....206 A2
Univ of Leeds (Headley Hall
  Farm) LS24 ....48 B7
Unna Way HD1 ....154 A7
Unwin Pl BD9 ....54 E2
Upcroft Ct 5 BD13 ......72 C2
Upland Cres LS8 ....61 A5
Upland Gdns LS8 ....208 A4
Upland Gr LS8 ....61 A5
Upland Rd LS8 ....208 A4
Uplands
  Huddersfield HD2 ......135 E1
  Keighley BD20 ....18 A1
Uplands Ave BD13 ....73 B2
Uplands Cl BD13 ....73 B2
Uplands Cres BD13 ......73 B2
Uplands Dr WF14 ....138 A6
Uplands Gr BD13 ....73 B2
Uplands The WF8 ....146 C7
Upper Abbots Royd Cvn Site
  HX4 ....133 A6
Upper Accommodation Rd
  LS9 ....212 B3
Upper Ada St 8 BD18 ..54 F8
Upper Addison St BD4 ..201 C1
Upper Allerton La BD13 ..72 E8
Upper Ash Gr WF3 ......183 B3
Upper Ashley La 1 BD17 ..55 B8
Upper Bank End Rd HD9 ..189 B4
Upper Bank Hey Bottom
  HX6 ....132 E3
Upper Barker St 4 HX7 ..88 B3
Upper Basinghall St LS1 ..211 B4
Upper Batley La WF17 ..118 B8
Upper Batley Low La
  WF17 ....118 C8
Upper Battye St WF16 ..117 A4
Upper Bell Croft HX3 ...114 A4
Upper Bell Hall HX1 .....202 C1
Upper Birks HX7 ....110 D5
Upper Bolton Brow HX6 ..112 D4
Upper Bonegate HD6 ...115 B3
Upper Brig Royd HX6 ...132 E4
Upper Brockholes HX2 ..91 D8
Upper Brow Rd HD1 .....153 D5
Upper Butts BD19 ....116 D7
Upper Calton St BD21 ..35 B5
Upper Camroyd St WF13 ..118 D1
Upper Carr La LS28 .....57 A6
Upper Carr St WF15 ....117 A5
Upper Castle St BD5 ....74 F4
Upper Chelsea St BD21 ..35 B5
Upper Clough Rd HD7 ..170 D7
Upper Commercial St
  WF17 ....118 C5
Upper Common La HD8 ..192 B6
Upper Croft Rd WF17 ...118 B4
Upper Cross St 2 WF13 ..118 C1
Upper Ellistones Ct HX4 ..134 A7
Upper Exley HX3 ....113 E1
Upper Fawth Cl BD13 ...73 A1
Upper Ferndown Gn
  BD15 ....54 A1
Upperfield Dr HD7 ....152 C4
Upper Field House La
  HX6 ....111 D2
Upper Field La S75 .....176 E1
Upper Fold HD9 ....171 F4
Upper Fountain St HX6 ..112 B4
Upper Fyfe La BD17 .....38 E3
Upper Gate HD9 ....189 E2
Upper George St
  Batley WF16 ....117 D4
  4 Bradford BD6 ....74 B1
  3 Huddersfield HD1 ...154 A6
Upper George Yd 9
  HX1 ....203 B3
Upper Gn
  5 Baildon BD17 ....38 B2

Upper Gn continued
  1 Bradford BD7 ....74 A3
Upper Grange Ave 9
  BD15 ....73 B8
Upper Green Ave
  10 Brighouse BD19 ....115 F8
  East Ardsley WF3 ......119 C9
Upper Green Cl WF3 ....119 E7
Upper Green Dr WF3 ...119 D7
Upper Green La HD6 ....114 B5
Upper Green Way WF3 ..119 D7
Upper Hagg HD9 ....172 B2
Upper Hagg Rd HD9 .....172 B2
Upper Hall Fold HX4 .....133 B4
Upper Hall View HX3 ....93 A3
Upper Hatfield Pl WF4 ..162 D2
Upper Haughs HD7 ......152 C5
Upper Haugh Shaw 10
  HX1 ....202 C1
Upperhead Row 11 HD1 ..154 A6
Upper Heaton La HD5 ...137 B2
Upper Heights Rd BD13 ..72 C8
Upper Hird St BD21 .....35 A5
Upper Hirst HD3 ....152 D8
Upper Holme HD7 ....169 D8
Upper House Fold HD8 ..191 F5
Upper House La WF15 ..116 C4
Upper House Rd HD9 ....199 C8
Upper House St BD4 ....75 B5
Upper Hoyle Ing BD13 ..72 F7
Upper Kirkgate HX1 .....203 C3
Upper La
  Cleckheaton BD19 .....117 C7
  Emley HD8 ....175 D6
  Netherton WF4 ....158 A4
  Northowram HX3 ....92 F3
  Todmorden OL14 ....87 D1
Upper Langwith LS22 ...28 E8
Upper Lombard St LS19 ..40 A4
Upper Lumb La HX7 .....110 C4
Upper Lunns Ct S71 .....179 E3
Upper Marsh HX3 ....113 F5
Upper Marsh La BD22 ...51 A5
Upper Martin Gn HX4 ...134 A7
Upper Mary St 9 BD18 ..54 F8
Upper Maythorne La
  HD9 ....200 D8
Upper Mdws
  Holmfirth HD9 ....188 D5
  Queensbury BD13 .....92 E8
Upper Millergate BD1 ...201 B3
Upper Mill Row BD20 ...19 E2
Upper Mills View HD9 ..170 C2
Uppermoor LS28 ....76 D7
Uppermoor Cl LS28 .....76 D6
Upper Mosscar St BD3 ..201 D3
Upper Mount HD9 ....170 F1
Upper Mount St
  Batley WF17 ....118 C3
  Huddersfield HD1 ......153 F4
Upper Nidd St BD3 ......75 D8
Upper Norcroft S75 .....193 F3
Upper North St WF17 ...118 B4
Upper Parish Ghyll La LS29 ..7 F3
Upper Park Gate BD1 ...201 C3
Upper Peel St 1 WF13 ..118 D1
Upper Piccadilly BD1 ...201 B3
Upper Quarry Rd HD2 ..137 A2
Upper Raglan St 17
  OL14 ....108 B6
Upper Range HX3 ....92 C1
Upper Rd WF17 ....118 B2
Upper Reins HD9 ....172 A5
Upper Rushton Rd BD3 ..56 D1
Upper School St BD20 ..17 C5
Upper Seymour St BD3 ..75 B7
Upper South St WF13 ..118 C1
Upper Station Rd WF17 ..118 B4
Upper Sunny Bank Mews
  HD9 ....170 C2
Upper Sutherland Rd
  HX3 ....114 E8
Upper Swain Royd Mews
  BD15 ....53 E4
Upperthong Jun & Inf Sch
  HD9 ....188 B5
Upperthong La HD9 .....188 E5
Upper Town BD22 ....51 C2
Upper Town St LS13 ....58 C3
Upper Warrengate WF1 ..216 C2
Upper Washer La HX2 ..202 B1
Upper Wellhouse Rd
  HD7 ....152 C2
Upper Westlock Ave LS9 ..208 A1
Upper West Scausby HX2 ..91 F8
Upper West St WF17 ....118 C5
Upper Whitley Jun & Inf Sch
  WF4 ....156 C5
Upper Willow Hall HX2 ..112 D6
Upper Woodlands Rd
  BD8 ....55 A1
Upper Woodview Pl 16
  LS11 ....214 B2
Upper Wortley Ct LS12 ..209 B3
Upper Wortley Dr LS12 ..209 B3
Upper Wortley Rd LS12 ..209 B3
Upper York St WF1 ......216 B3
Upton Prim Sch WF9 ....183 C8
Upton St WF17 ....118 B6
Upwood La BD20 ....19 D2
Upwood Pk BD22 ....51 E3
Urban Terr WF4 ....156 E5
Ure Cres BD8 ....74 D8
Ure Gr LS22 ....13 D8
Usher St BD4 ....201 D1
Usher Street Prim Sch
  BD4 ....201 D1

Uttley St 7 HX3 92 B2

V

Vale Ave
Knottingley WF11 126 D4
Leeds LS8 44 A3
Vale Bower HX7 110 D8
Vale Cl HD5 154 F3
Vale Cres WF11 126 D4
Vale Crest WF11 126 D4
Vale Gr
Queensbury BD13 72 F1
Silsden BD20 5 D1
Vale Head Gr WF11 126 D4
Vale Head Mount WF11 126 D4
Vale Jun & Inf Sch The WF11 126 D4
Vale Mill La BD22 34 D1
Valentine Ct BD13 72 E7
Valentine Mews WF3 121 C8
Vale Rd WF9 163 B1
Vale St
Bacup OL13 106 A3
Brighouse HD6 115 A3
2 Keighley BD21 18 E1
Todmorden OL14 108 B5
Valestone Ave WF9 181 E7
Vale Terr
Knottingley WF11 126 D5
Mytholmroyd HX7 110 D8
Oakworth BD22 34 D1
Vale The
Collingham LS22 29 A8
Leeds LS6 59 F5
Vale View
Ackworth M T WF7 164 B7
Silsden BD20 5 D1
Valley Ave
Brighouse HX3 115 A8
South Elmsall WF9 183 B3
Valley Bsns Pk HX2 92 A5
Valley Cl LS17 43 A5
Valley Cres WF2 120 F2
Valley Ct
Bradford BD1 55 E1
Castleford WF10 124 A5
Leeds LS17 204 A4
Liversedge WF15 117 B5
Valley Dr
Dewsbury WF12 139 E1
Ilkley LS29 8 E4
Kippax LS26 102 E8
Leeds LS15 62 B1
Wakefield WF2 120 F2
Valley Farm Rd LS10 80 A1
Valley Farm Way LS10 80 A1
Valley Fold BD13 92 E8
Valley Gdns
Darrington WF8 147 E4
Leeds LS7 60 C8
Valley Gn LS28 76 F6
Valley Gr
Halifax HX2 91 F7
Pudsey LS28 76 F6
Valley Head HD2 135 C2
Valley Hts BD13 52 E1
Valley Mills Ind Est BD10 56 E8
Valley Mount
Kippax LS25 83 A2
Pudsey LS13 77 A8
Valley Par BD8 55 D1
Valley Parade Football Gd BD8 55 D1
Valley Pl BD1 55 E1
Valley Rd
Bradford BD1 201 B4
Cleckheaton BD19 116 E8
Darrington WF8 147 E4
Darton S75 178 A1
Dewsbury WF12 139 F1
4 Hebden Bridge HX7 89 A3
Ilkley LS29 8 D5
Keighley BD21 35 F7
Kippax LS25 83 A2
Leeds LS13 58 C5
Liversedge WF15 117 B4
Morley LS27 98 C5
Ossett WF5 140 D4
5 Pontefract WF8 146 D8
Pudsey LS28 76 F6
Shipley BD18 55 C6
Valley Rd Bsns Pk WF15 117 A4
Valley Ridge
Kippax, Kippax Common LS25 82 F3
Kippax LS25 82 F2
Valley Rise LS13 58 C5
Valley Sq LS28 76 F6
Valley St WF9 182 F2
Valley Terr LS17 43 F3
Valley The LS17 43 A5
Valley View
Baildon BD17 38 B1
Glusburn BD20 16 C7
Halifax HX5 134 F8
Halifax, Illingworth HX2 91 F7
Harden BD16 36 A1
Heptonstall HX7 88 F4
South Elmsall WF9 183 B3
Valley View Cl BD22 34 E3
Valley View Gdns 12 BD22 51 E8
Valley View Gr BD2 56 A2
Valley View Rd
Heptonstall HX7 88 F4
Ossett WF5 140 D4
Valley Way HX2 91 F7
Vancouver Pl LS7 204 B2
Vantage Point LS27 97 F1
Varley Rd HD7 169 F7
Varley St LS28 57 D1
Vassali Ho LS1 211 C3
Vaughan St
Bradford BD1 74 D7
1 Halifax HX1 202 B1
Vegal Cres HX3 91 F2
Velocity E LS11 211 B2
Velocity N LS11 211 B2
Velocity S LS11 211 B2
Velocity W LS11 211 B2
Venn St HD1 154 B6
Ventnor Cl
Cleckheaton BD19 96 B2
Ossett WF5 140 D5
Ventnor Dr WF5 140 D5
Ventnor St BD3 75 A7
Ventnor Terr HX3 113 B4
Ventnor Way WF5 140 D5
Vento Cl BD6 94 B8
Venture St OL13 106 A3
Verdun Rd BD6 94 A8
Vere Sq BD5 74 E4
Verity Spur LS9 80 E8
Verity St BD4 95 F7
Verity View LS9 61 E1
Vermont Cl HD7 152 C5
Vermont St LS13 58 A2
Verner St WF7 145 C4
Vernon Ave HD1 153 F7
Vernon Cl HD1 153 F7
Vernon Ct BD20 35 B8
Vernon Pl
Bradford BD2 56 B2
Pudsey LS28 57 E1
Queensbury BD13 92 C7
Todmorden OL14 108 A3
Wakefield WF2 142 B3
Vernon Rd
Leeds LS1 206 B1
Liversedge WF15 117 C4
Vernon St
Haworth BD22 51 F8
Leeds LS2 206 B1
Todmorden OL14 108 A3
Vesper Cl LS5 58 F6
Vesper Court Dr LS5 58 E6
Vesper Ct LS5 58 E6
Vesper Gate Cres LS5 58 F6
Vesper Gate Dr LS5 58 E5
Vesper Gate Mount LS5 58 F6
Vesper Gdns LS5 58 F5
Vesper Gr 2 LS5 59 A4
Vesper La LS5 58 F5
Vesper Mount LS5 59 A4
Vesper Pl 4 LS5 59 A4
Vesper Rd LS5 58 E6
Vesper Rise LS5 58 E6
Vesper Terr 3 LS5 59 A4
Vesper Way LS5 58 E6
Vesper Wlk LS5 58 E6
Vestry St BD4 75 B3
Viaduct Rd LS4 205 A1
Viaduct St
Huddersfield HD1 154 A7
Pudsey LS28 57 D1
Slaithwaite HD7 152 A1
Vicarage Ave
Gildersome LS27 97 C6
Leeds LS5 59 B4
Vicarage Cl
Bradford BD12 94 C2
Lofthouse Gate WF1 121 C5
South Kirkby WF9 182 C3
Vicarage Ct BD19 116 D8
Vicarage Dr
Meltham HD9 170 D1
Pudsey LS28 76 D7
Vicarage Gdns
Birkenshaw BD11 96 A5
Brighouse HD6 135 F8
Featherstone WF7 145 D8
Otley LS21 23 A7
Vicarage La
Bramham LS23 30 D3
Featherstone WF7 145 D5
Royston S71 179 C3
Vicarage Mdw WF14 138 C5
Vicarage Mdws HD9 189 B4
Vicarage Pl LS5 59 B4
Vicarage Rd
Dewsbury, Savile Town WF12 139 C5
Dewsbury WF12 139 D8
Huddersfield HD3 153 B6
Leeds LS6 205 C2
Shipley BD18 55 E8
Vicarage St N WF1 216 C3
Vicarage St S WF1 216 C2
Vicarage St LS5 59 B4
Vicarage Terr
Batley WF17 118 A7
Leeds LS5 59 B4
Vicarage View LS5 59 B4
Vicar La
Bradford BD1 201 C2
Leeds LS1, LS2 211 C4
Ossett WF5 140 E3
Vicar Park Dr HX2 112 B8
Vicar Park Rd HX2 112 B8
Vicars Rd LS8 207 C4
Vicar St 11 WF15 117 A5
Vicars Terr
Kippax WF10 103 B4
Leeds LS8 207 C4
Vickerman Cres HD4 153 F1
Vickerman St HX1 202 B2
Vickers Ave
Leeds LS5 58 F3
South Elmsall WF9 182 E1
Vickersdale LS28 57 E2
Vickers St
Castleford WF10 124 D7
Morley LS27 97 F2
Morley LS27 97 F3
Victor Dr LS20 39 E8
Victoria App WF1 121 B3
Victoria Ave
Batley WF17 118 C4
Bradford BD2 56 D4
Brighouse HD6 115 C3
Cleckheaton BD19 116 D7
Elland HX5 134 E6
Halifax HX1 202 B2
Haworth BD22 51 C8
Horsforth LS18 58 A7
Ilkley LS29 7 F4
7 Keighley BD21 35 C8
Leeds LS9 80 B7
Menston LS29 22 A5
Morley LS27 98 A5
Rothwell LS26 100 E4
Shipley BD18 54 F8
Sowerby Bridge HX6 112 C5
Wakefield WF2 142 A6
Yeadon LS19 40 D8
Victoria Bldgs HX7 110 C2
Victoria Chase HX3 115 B8
Victoria Cl
Horsforth LS18 58 A7
Huddersfield HD4 171 F8
Ilkley LS29 8 A4
Kippax WF10 103 B4
Yeadon LS19 40 D7
Victoria Cotts LS25 105 D4
Victoria Cres
Dewsbury WF13 118 A2
Elland HX5 134 F6
Horsforth LS18 58 A7
Pudsey LS28 76 C7
Victoria Ct
Batley WF17 96 F1
Castleford WF10 124 D6
Keighley BD21 35 B8
Leeds LS14 62 D4
6 Morley LS27 98 A5
2 Pudsey LS28 57 F2
18 Shipley BD18 54 F8
Upton WF9 183 A7
Victoria Dr
Bradford BD2 56 D4
Dewsbury WF12 139 C4
Horsforth LS18 58 A7
Ilkley LS29 7 F4
Morley LS27 98 B6
Northowram HX3 93 B3
Victoria Gdns
Horsforth LS18 58 B7
Ilkley LS29 7 F4
Pudsey LS28 76 C7
Victoria Gr
Horsforth LS18 58 A6
Ilkley LS29 7 F4
Leeds LS9 80 B8
Pudsey LS28 76 C7
Wakefield WF2 141 D3
Victoria Grange Dr LS27 98 A5
Victoria Grange Way 4 LS27 98 A5
Victoria Ho
6 Leeds, Headingley LS5 59 A4
Leeds LS1 211 B4
Victoria Ind Est BD2 56 C4
Victoria Ind Pk LS14 62 B8
Victoria Jun Sch LS26 100 D6
Victoria La
Huddersfield HD1 154 B6
Huddersfield, Town End HD7 152 C4
Victoria Mews
Horsforth LS18 58 A7
15 Keighley BD21 35 B7
7 Morley LS27 98 A5
Victoria Mills
Batley WF17 118 B6
Holmfirth HD9 188 E4
Victoria Mount LS18 58 A7
Victoria Park Ave LS13, LS5 58 F3
Victoria Park Gr LS13, LS5 58 E3
Victoria Park St 9 BD21 35 D8
Victoria Park View BD21 35 D8
Victoria Pk
Halifax HX1 202 C3
Shipley BD18 54 F7
Victoria Pl
Boston Spa LS23 30 D4
Brighouse HD6 115 B1
Castleford WF10 124 E8
Halifax HX1 202 B3
Honley HD9 171 F4
Huddersfield HD4 153 A1
6 Huddersfield, Moldgreen HD5 154 D5
Leeds LS11 211 B2
7 Mirfield WF14 137 F5
Yeadon LS19 40 A7
Victoria Prim Sch
Keighley BD21 35 A7
Leeds LS9 80 B8
Victoria Quarter LS1 211 C4
Victoria Rd
Bradford BD2, BD10 56 C5
Bradford, Wibsey Slack BD6 94 A8
Victoria Rd *continued*
Brighouse, Bailiff Bridge HD6 115 B7
Brighouse, Hipperholme HX3 114 D7
Burley in W LS29 9 E2
Cleckheaton BD19 117 C8
Dewsbury, Thornhill Lees WF12 139 C4
Dewsbury WF13 118 C1
Elland HX5 134 E6
Glusburn BD20 16 D6
Guiseley LS20 39 D8
Halifax HX1 202 C3
Haworth BD22 51 D7
Hebden Bridge HX7 89 A4
Huddersfield HD1 153 F4
Ilkley LS29 7 F4
Keighley BD21 35 B5
Leeds, Camp Field LS11 211 B2
Leeds, Hyde Park LS6 205 B3
Leeds, Kirkstall LS5 59 A4
Leeds, Whinmoor LS14 62 B7
Liversedge WF15 117 A3
Meltham HD9 170 D2
Morley LS27 98 A6
Oakworth BD22 34 D2
Pudsey, Farsley LS28 57 D2
Pudsey LS28 76 C7
Rothwell LS26 100 D6
Royston S71 179 D4
Shipley BD18 54 F8
Sowerby Bridge HX6 112 B3
Todmorden OL14 108 B6
Victoria Rise LS28 76 C7
Victoria Sh Ctr BD8 74 A8
Victoria Spring Bsns Pk WF15 117 B4
Victoria Springs HD9 188 E4
Victoria Sq
12 Holmfirth HD9 189 A5
Leeds LS1 211 B4
Ripponden HX6 132 D4
Victoria St
Ackworth M T WF7 163 D5
3 Baildon BD17 38 C1
Batley, Birstall WF17 96 F1
Batley, Carlinghow WF17 118 B6
Batley, Nunroyd WF16 117 D4
Bradford BD1 201 A4
11 Bradford, Clayton BD14 73 B4
Bradford, Fagley BD2 56 D2
Bradford, Sandy Lane BD15 54 A3
Bradford, Thackley BD10 39 B2
Brighouse, Clifton HD6 115 C2
Brighouse HD6 115 B1
Castleford WF10 124 B8
Clayton West HD8 175 E2
Cleckheaton BD19 116 D8
Cullingworth BD13 52 E6
Dewsbury WF13 138 E6
Elland HX4 134 D7
Featherstone WF7 145 D5
Halifax HX1 203 B3
Hemsworth WF9 181 E6
Holmfirth HD9 189 A5
Horbury WF4 140 F1
Huddersfield, Deighton HD2 136 E3
Huddersfield, Folly Hall HD1 154 A4
Huddersfield HD3 153 C8
Huddersfield, Moldgreen HD5 154 D5
Kippax WF10 103 B4
Leeds, Chapel Allerton LS7 204 A3
Leeds LS2 205 C1
Leeds, Pottery Field LS10 212 A2
Lofthouse Gate WF1 121 B4
Marsden HD7 168 F4
Micklethwaite BD16 36 E7
Morley, Churwell LS27 98 C7
Morley, Morley Hole LS27 97 F5
Oakworth BD22 34 D2
Pontefract WF8 125 D3
Pudsey LS28 57 B6
Queensbury BD13 72 F1
Shipley BD17 55 B8
Sowerby Bridge HX6 112 B3
Sutton-in-C BD20 16 D5
Todmorden OL14 86 C1
Wakefield WF2 142 A7
Wetherby LS22 13 F5
Wilsden BD15 53 C4
Victoria Terr
10 Addingham LS29 6 F8
Brighouse HX3 114 D7
Clayton West HD8 175 F2
1 Guiseley LS20 22 E1
Halifax HX1 202 C2
4 Halifax, King Cross HX2 113 A4
Horbury WF4 140 E1
5 Keighley BD21 35 D7
4 Leeds, Far Headingley LS6 59 D6
7 Leeds, Headingley LS5 59 A4
Leeds LS3 205 C1
Low Bradley BD20 4 C5
Luddenden Foot HX2 111 E5
1 Pudsey LS28 57 F2
Shipley BD18 37 F1
Todmorden OL14 109 A7
Yeadon LS19 40 D7
Victoria Theatre The★ HX1 203 B3
Victoria Way WF1 121 B3
Victoria Wlk
Horsforth LS18 58 A7
3 Leeds LS1 211 C4
Victor Rd
Bradford BD9 55 B2
South Kirkby WF9 182 C2
Victor St
Batley WF17 118 D5
Bradford BD9 55 B2
Bradford, Bradford Moor BD3 75 E7
Castleford WF10 124 C5
South Elmsall WF9 182 F2
Victor Terr
Bradford BD9 55 B2
Halifax HX1 202 C4
Victory Ave HD3 153 C5
Victory La WF3 122 A2
Victory Rd LS29 8 B4
Vienna Ct 12 LS27 98 C8
View Croft Rd BD17 55 C8
Viewlands HD2 136 B4
Viewlands Cres LS29 22 D5
Viewlands Mount LS29 22 D5
Viewlands Rise LS29 22 D5
View Rd BD20 35 A8
View Row BD15 73 C8
View St HD5 154 D5
Views The S75 178 B1
View The
Leeds, Alwoodley Park LS17 43 A6
Leeds LS8 61 A8
Vignola Terr BD14 73 C5
Viking Ave HD8 175 D6
Viking Rd WF8 146 E8
Villa Cl WF7 164 B8
Villa Gdns WF17 118 D3
Village Ave LS4 205 A3
Village Gdns LS15 81 D6
Village Mews BD15 53 C5
Village Pl LS4 205 A2
Village Rd LS16 25 F1
Village St The LS4 205 A2
Village St HX3 94 A2
Village Terr LS4 205 A3
Village The
Kirkburton, Farnley Tyas HD4 172 F6
Kirkburton, Thurstonland HD4 172 F1
Thorp Arch LS23 14 E1
Villa Gr BD16 37 A4
Villa Mount BD12 94 C1
Villa Rd BD16 37 A4
Villa St HX6 112 C4
Villier Ct BD15 54 B1
Vincent Ave BD20 17 A5
Vincent St
Bradford BD1 201 A3
Halifax HX1 202 B2
Vine Ave BD19 116 C8
Vine Cl HD6 115 D2
Vine Cres BD19 116 D8
Vine Ct
Brighouse HD6 115 D2
2 Guiseley LS20 39 E8
Vine Garth HD6 115 D3
Vine Gr HD6 115 D2
Vine Ind Est HD6 114 F3
Vine Pl 5 BD2 56 B3
Vinery Ave LS9 80 A8
Vinery Cl HD8 175 F2
Vinery Gr 3 LS9 80 A8
Vinery Mount LS9 80 A7
Vinery Pl LS9 80 A7
Vinery Rd LS4 205 A2
Vinery St 4 LS9 80 A8
Vinery Terr LS9 80 A7
Vinery View LS9 80 A7
Vine St
Bradford BD7 74 B4
Cleckheaton BD19 116 D8
Huddersfield HD1 154 C8
Vine Terr
Halifax HX1 203 A2
3 Thornton BD13 72 D6
Vine Terr E BD8 73 E8
Vine Terr W BD8 73 E7
Vineyard HD7 152 D5
Vint Rise BD10 56 A8
Violet St N HX1 202 C4
Violet St
Halifax HX1 202 C3
Haworth BD22 51 C6
Violet Terr 2 HX6 112 C4
Virginia Cl WF2 121 A6
Virginia Ct WF2 121 A6
Virginia Dr WF2 121 A6
Virginia Gdns WF2 121 A6
Virginia Rd HD3 153 C7
Virginia St BD14 73 C3
Virginia Terr
4 Bradford BD14 73 C4
Thorner LS14 45 F5
Vissett Cl WF9 181 B6
Vissitt La WF9 181 B6
Vista Ct HD7 152 F4
Vivian Pl BD7 74 A3
Vivien Rd BD8 73 C8
Vollan's Ct LS14 62 A5
Vulcan Cl WF13 139 C8
Vulcan Gdns WF13 139 C8
Vulcan Rd WF13 139 C8

Vulcan St
Bradford BD4............**75** D1
Brighouse HD6..........**115** C1
12 Walsden OL14....**108** A1

W

Waarburton HD8........**175** D6
Waddington St **1** BD21 ..**35** C6
Wade House Ave HX3 ...**93** C6
Wade House Rd HX3 ....**93** C6
Wade La LS2 ....**211** C4
Wade St
Bradford BD1...........**201** B2
Halifax HX1 ....**203** C3
Pudsey LS28 ....**57** D3
Wadhouse La WF4 ......**160** A8
Wadlands Cl LS28.......**57** D4
Wadlands Dr LS28 ......**57** C4
Wadlands Gr LS28 ......**57** C4
Wadlands Rise LS28.....**57** C3
Wadman Rd HD9........**189** D3
Wadsworth Ave OL14....**108** A4
Wadsworth Ct HX1.......**202** C4
Wadsworth La HX7......**89** C3
Wadsworth St HX1.......**202** B4
Waggon La WF9 ....**183** C8
Wagon La BD16.........**37** A1
Wagtail Cl BD6 ....**73** C1
Wain Brow HD4.........**171** F8
Waincliffe Cres LS11 ....**213** C1
Waincliffe Dr LS11 ......**98** F8
Waincliffe Garth LS11 ...**213** C1
Waincliffe Ho **5** BD4 ...**75** D6
Waincliffe Mount LS11 ...**98** F8
Waincliffe Pl LS11 ......**213** C1
Waincliffe Sq LS11 .....**213** C1
Waincliffe Terr LS11 ....**98** F8
Wain Cl HD4............**171** F8
Waindale Cl HX2........**91** A3
Waindale Cres HX2 .....**91** A3
Waindike Cl WF6 ....**123** C3
Waindyke Way WF6.....**123** D2
Wainfleet Ho BD3.......**75** E8
Waingate Pk HD7 ......**152** D1
Wainhouse Rd HX1 .....**202** B1
Wainhouse Terr HX2....**202** B1
Wainman Sq 2 BD12 ..**94** C3
Wainman St
Baildon BD17............**38** D4
1 Bradford BD12........**94** C3
Halifax HX1 ....**202** B3
2 Shipley BD17........**55** B8
Wain Pk HD4...........**171** F8
Wainscott Cl HX7.......**89** B6
Wainsgate La HX7 .....**89** B6
Wainsgate HX7 ....**89** B6
Wainstalls HX2 ....**90** F5
Wainstalls Jun & Inf Sch
  HX2...................**90** F5
Wainstalls La HX2.......**90** F5
Wainstalls Lodge La HX2.**90** E5
Wainstalls Rd HX2 .....**90** F5
Waites Croft WF2.......**120** B2
Waite St WF2...........**141** E6
Waites Terr LS21 ....**23** B7
Wakefield 41 Bsns Pk
  WF2..................**120** F4
Wakefield 41 Ind Pk
  WF2..................**120** F5
Wakefield Ave LS14.....**61** F1
Wakefield Castle Grove Inf
  Sch WF2 ....**142** E2
Wakefield City Farm★
  WF4..................**159** D2
Wakefield City High Sch
  WF1..................**142** F7
Wakefield Coll
  Wakefield, Thornes Park
    WF2................**142** A4
  Wakefield WF1 ......**216** A3
Wakefield Coll (Whitwood
  Ctr) WF10...........**124** A6
Wakefield Commercial Pk
  WF4..................**158** E8
Wakefield Cres WF12 ...**139** F8
Wakefield Europort WF6 **123** B6
Wakefield Gate HX3.....**112** F4
Wakefield Girls High Sch
  WF1..................**216** A3
Wakefield Greenhill Jun &
  Inf Sch WF1..........**216** A3
Wakefield Heath View Com
  Prim Sch WF1 ....**142** E7
Wakefield Hendal Prim Sch
  WF2..................**160** B5
Wakefield Independent Sch
  WF4..................**162** F6
Wakefield Kirkgate Sta
  WF1..................**216** C1
Wakefield Lawefield Prim
  Sch WF2.............**142** A5
Wakefield Meth Jun & Inf
  Sch WF2.............**142** C3
Wakefield Mus★ WF1 ..**216** B2
Wakefield Old Rd 6
  WF12.................**139** D8
Wakefield Pinders Prim Sch
  WF1..................**216** C1
Wakefield Rd
  Ackworth M T WF7.....**163** E5
  Birkenshaw BD11......**97** A5
  Bradford BD4..........**75** B4

Wakefield Rd continued
  Brighouse, Clifton HD6 ...**115** D1
  4 Brighouse HD6.......**115** B2
  Brighouse, Lydgate HD6,
    HX3.................**114** E7
  Clayton West HD8 ....**175** E2
  Darton S75 ....**178** C2
  Denby Dale HD8 ......**192** B7
  Dewsbury WF12 ......**139** E8
  Featherstone WF7.....**145** B5
  Fitzwilliam WF9.......**163** B2
  Flockton WF4.........**157** C4
  Garforth LS25, LS26 ...**82** C4
  Gildersome LS27 ......**97** D5
  Halifax HX3 ....**113** B2
  Horbury WF4..........**141** C2
  Huddersfield HD1, HD5..**154** D5
  Leeds LS10 ....**215** C2
  Lepton HD8 ....**155** D3
  Liversedge HD6, WF14 ..**137** A7
  Liversedge, Mill Bridge
    WF15...............**117** B4
  Ossett WF5 ....**140** F7
  Pontefract WF8 ......**146** B7
  Rothwell LS26 ....**100** B6
  Rothwell, Royds Green
    LS26...............**101** C2
  Wakefield WF5, WF2...**141** B6
Wakefield St John's CE Jun
  & Inf Sch WF1........**216** A4
Wakefield St Mary's CE Prim
  Sch WF1.............**216** C2
Wakefield Sandal Magna Jun
  & Inf Sch WF1........**142** E2
Wakefield Tutorial Prep Sch
  LS27.................**98** A4
Wakefield Westgate Sta
  WF2..................**216** A2
Walden Dr BD9.........**54** C3
Walden Howe Cl WF7 ..**145** C8
Walden St WF10........**124** D7
Waldorf Way WF2......**216** B1
Walesby Ct LS16.......**41** E2
Walford Ave LS9.......**80** A8
Walford Gr LS9.........**80** A8
Walford Mount LS9.....**80** A8
Walford Rd LS9........**80** A8
Walford Terr LS9.......**80** A8
Walker's La
  Leeds LS12 ....**78** C4
  Silsden BD20 ....**5** D7
Walker's Pl BD20 ......**17** E8
Walker's Rd LS6 ....**59** F5
Walker's Terr WF1......**216** A2
Walker Ave
  Bradford BD7..........**73** C4
  Wakefield WF2 ....**141** F7
Walker Cl BD20 ....**16** B6
Walker Dr BD8.........**74** B8
Walkergate
  Otley LS21 ....**23** A8
  Pontefract WF8 ......**125** E1
Walker Gn WF12.......**139** E2
Walker La
  Horbury WF4..........**141** B1
  Sowerby Bridge HX7...**112** D4
  Wadsworth Moor HX7...**89** C5
Walker Pl
  7 Morley LS27 ....**98** B7
  Shipley BD18 ....**55** C8
Walker Rd
  Bradford BD12........**94** F4
  Horsforth LS18 ....**41** B1
  Menston LS29 ....**21** F4
Walkers Gn LS12.......**78** C4
Walkers Mount
  Batley WF17 ....**118** C3
  Leeds LS6 ....**59** F5
Walkers Row LS19......**40** A7
Walker St
  Bradford BD4..........**95** B8
  3 Brighouse BD19....**115** F8
  Cleckheaton BD19.....**116** D8
  Dewsbury, Earlsheaton
    WF12...............**139** F6
  Dewsbury, Ravensthorpe
    WF13...............**138** D3
  Dewsbury, Thornhill Lees
    WF12...............**139** D3
Walker Terr
  Bradford BD4..........**75** B4
  Cullingworth BD13......**52** D5
Walker Wood BD17.....**37** F2
Walkin House Farm HD9 **188** E3
Walkley Ave WF16......**117** D3
Walkley Gr 10 WF16....**117** D3
Walkley La WF16.......**117** D2
Walkley Terr WF16.....**117** E2
Walkley Villas WF16 ...**117** E2
Walk The
  Keighley BD21 ....**35** C6
  Pudsey LS28 ....**57** C2
Wallace Gdns WF3.....**121** B6
Wallace St HX1 ....**202** B2
Wallbank Dr BD18......**55** C6
Walled Gdn The WF4...**178** A7
Waller Clough Rd HD7 ..**151** F4
Wallingford Mount BD15 .**73** B7
Wallis St
  Bradford, Brown Royd
    BD8................**74** A7
  Bradford, Green Side BD8..**73** F7
  Sowerby Bridge HX6 ...**112** B4
Wall Nook HD8 ....**190** D6
Wall Nook La HD8 .....**190** D6
Wallroyds HD8.........**191** F5
Wall St BD22 ....**34** F6
Walmer Gr LS28 ....**76** F5

Walmer Villas BD8 .....**55** D1
Walmsley Dr WF9.......**183** B7
Walmsley Rd LS6 ......**205** B3
Walnut Ave
  Dewsbury WF12 ......**140** B7
  Wakefield WF2 ....**141** F7
Walnut Bsns Pk HX1 ...**202** C3
Walnut Cl
  Dewsbury WF12 ......**140** A6
  Leeds LS14 ....**62** C8
Walnut Cres
  Dewsbury WF12 ......**140** A6
  Wakefield WF2 ....**141** F7
Walnut Dr
  Dewsbury WF12 ......**140** B7
  Normanton WF6 ......**144** A7
  Pontefract WF8 ......**146** C6
Walnut Gr WF12 ....**140** B7
Walnut Pl WF12........**140** A7
Walnut Rd WF12.......**140** B7
Walnut St
  Bradford BD3..........**75** C6
  Halifax HX1 ....**202** C3
  13 Keighley BD21 .....**35** B4
  South Elmsall WF9.....**182** F1
Walpole Rd HD4 ....**153** D3
Walsden CE Inf Sch
  OL14.................**108** B1
Walsden Est OL14......**129** B7
Walsden Jun Sch OL14..**108** A1
Walsden Sta OL14......**108** A1
Walsh's Sq 19 HX1 .....**202** C1
Walsham Dr HD3 ....**134** F1
Walshaw La HX7.......**68** C3
Walshaw St 2 BD7 ....**74** A4
Walsh La
  Bingley BD16..........**37** A7
  Gildersome LS12 ......**77** D2
Walsh St HX1..........**202** B3
Walter Clough La HX3...**114** C5
Walter Cres LS9 ....**212** C3
Walter St
  Bradford BD10........**56** B8
  Leeds LS4 ....**205** A1
  Shipley BD2..........**55** D4
Waltham Dr DN6........**184** E2
Waltin Rd HD9.........**188** F1
Walton Chase LS23 ....**14** F3
Walton Cl OL13 ....**106** A1
Walton Croft HD5......**154** E6
Walton Dr BD11........**96** F5
Walton Fold 2 OL14....**108** D6
Walton Garth BD11 ....**96** F5
Walton Grove Inf Sch
  WF2..................**161** B6
Walton Jun Sch WF2...**161** A7
Walton La
  Brighouse BD19.......**115** F6
  Wakefield WF2 ....**160** F8
Walton Locks WF2......**161** B7
Walton Rd
  Thorp Arch LS23 .....**15** A3
  Upton WF9...........**183** D8
  Wetherby LS22, LS23 ...**14** C4
Walton St
  Bradford BD4..........**201** C1
  Glusburn BD20 ....**16** D5
  Leeds, Holbeck LS11 ...**211** B2
  Leeds, Hunslet LS10 ...**215** B4
  Sowerby Bridge HX6 ...**112** B4
Walton Station La WF2..**160** F7
Walton View WF4.......**161** F8
Walt Royd HX2.........**91** D3
Waltroyd Rd BD19......**116** C7
Wansford Cl
  Bradford BD4..........**75** E2
  Leeds LS15 ....**81** E8
Wanstead Cres BD15....**73** B8
Wapping Nick La HX4 ..**134** E3
Wapping Rd BD3........**201** C4
Warburton Pl 9 BD6....**74** C1
Warcock La OL13 ......**106** B3
Ward's End HX1 ....**203** B2
Ward Bank Rd HD9.....**189** A4
Ward Ct HD6 ....**135** F7
Ward Fall WF4.........**159** F3
Ward La
  Lofthouse Gate WF3 ...**122** A2
  Middleton LS10 ....**215** A1
Wardle Cres BD22 .....**34** F8
Wardman St BD20 .....**18** E1
Ward Place La HD9 ....**188** F3
Wards Hill WF17 ....**118** C5
Wards Hill Ct 11 WF17..**118** C5
Ward Sq 26 HD1 ......**154** A6
Ward St
  Bradford BD7..........**74** A3
  Dewsbury WF13 ......**118** D1
  4 Keighley BD21 .....**35** B6
  Leeds LS10 ....**212** A1
Wareham Cnr 2 BD4 ...**75** E2
Warehouse Hill Rd HD7 .**169** A4
Warehouse St WF17.....**118** D4
Warhurst Rd HX5 ......**135** A8
Waring Way WF12 .....**118** E1
Warkworth Terr 13 OL13 **106** A3
Warland End Gate OL14 .**129** C5
Warlbeck LS29.........**7** F4
Warley Ave BD3 ....**75** D8
Warley Dene HX2 ......**112** B6
Warley Dr BD3.........**75** D8
Warley Edge HX2 ......**112** C7
Warley Edge La HX2 ...**112** B7
Warley Gr
  Bradford BD3.........**75** D8
  Halifax HX2 ....**112** D7
Warley Rd HX1, HX2 ...**202** A2

Warley Road Prim Sch
  HX1..................**202** A2
Warley St HX1 ....**202** C2
Warley Town La HX2 ...**112** A6
Warley Town Sch HX2 ..**112** B6
Warley View
  Halifax HX2 ....**112** D7
  Leeds LS13 ....**58** B4
Warley Wood Ave HX2 ..**111** F5
Warley Wood La HX2...**111** F5
Warmfield La WF1......**143** E7
Warmfield View WF1....**142** F7
Warm La LS19 ....**40** A5
Warmleigh Cvn Pk BD13..**72** B1
Warneford Ave WF5....**140** D7
Warneford Rd HD4.....**153** A3
Warneford Rise HD4 ...**153** A3
Warneford Sq HX1.....**202** B1
Warnford Gr BD4.......**75** D3
Warrel's Ave 4 LS13 ...**58** C3
Warrel's Ct LS13 ......**58** C2
Warrel's Gr LS13 ......**58** C2
Warrel's Mount LS13 ...**58** C2
Warrel's Pl LS13 ......**58** C3
Warrel's Row 4 LS13 ..**58** C2
Warrel's St LS13 ......**58** C2
Warrel's Terr 19 LS13 ..**58** C2
Warren Ave
  Bingley BD16.........**37** B5
  Knottingley WF11 .....**126** D3
  Wakefield WF2 ....**142** D2
Warren Cl
  Liversedge WF15......**117** B2
  Royston S71..........**179** D5
Warren Ct WF1 ....**216** C2
Warren Dr
  Bingley BD16.........**37** B4
  Featherstone WF7.....**145** A8
Warrenfield Ct HD2.....**136** D3
Warren Ho WF1........**216** B2
Warren House La
  East Carlton LS19 ....**23** D1
  Huddersfield HD3 .....**135** A3
Warren La
  Arthington LS21.......**25** A7
  Bingley BD16.........**37** B4
  Bramham S24 ....**31** B1
  Darton S75 ....**178** B4
Warren Park Cl HD6 ...**114** E5
Warren Pk HD6 ....**114** E6
Warren Rd WF2........**145** B6
Warrenside BD22.......**136** E4
Warrens La
  Birkenshaw WF17 ....**96** D5
  Cleckheaton WF17.....**96** D3
Warren St WF12 ....**139** D6
Warren Terr BD16 .....**37** C3
Warrenton Pl BD7 .....**74** A5
Warren Wlk S71 ....**179** D5
Warrington Terr HD7 ...**168** E4
Warsop Rd S71 ....**178** E1
Warton Ave BD4 ......**75** B1
Warwick Ave HD7......**152** E5
Warwick Cl
  Bradford BD4..........**75** B4
  1 Halifax HX3 ....**113** B4
Warwick Ct **1** LS18 ....**58** C7
Warwick Dr BD4 ....**75** B2
Warwick Rd
  Batley WF17 ....**118** D3
  Bradford BD4..........**75** B4
Warwick Road Jun & Inf Sch
  WF17.................**118** C3
Warwick St WF1 ....**142** F3
Waryn Ho 4 BD10 .....**56** C7
Wasdale Cres WF2.....**141** E7
Wasdale Rd WF2.......**141** E7
Washburn Ct
  10 Silsden BD20 .....**5** E1
  Wetherby LS22 ....**13** D8
Washburn Dr BD20.....**16** C7
Washer La HX2 ....**112** E4
Washer Lane Ind Est
  HX2..................**112** F4
Washfold Rd HX7 ......**131** B7
Washington Pl LS13....**77** A8
Washington St
  Bradford BD8..........**54** F1
  20 Halifax HX3 ....**92** A1
  Leeds LS12 ....**210** B4
  Pudsey LS13 ....**77** A8
Washington Terr LS13...**77** A8
Washpit New Rd WF9 ..**189** B3
Wasp Nest Rd HD1.....**136** B1
Waste La
  Huddersfield HD5 .....**154** E4
  Mirfield, Lower Hopton
    WF14...............**138** A3
  Mirfield WF14 ....**137** F3
  Wadsworth Moor HX7...**69** A5
Waste The WF14.......**137** F3
Wastwater Dr BD6 .....**93** F6
Watchit Hole La WF8...**165** C4
Watchley La DN5.......**195** B3
Watercock St BD4 .....**201** D1
Watercroft HD5........**154** F3
Waterfall Cotts HD7....**168** D5
Waterfall Fold WF8 ....**125** E3
Waterfront Mews BD10..**56** B9
Watergate
  Brighouse HX3.........**114** C7
  Huddersfield HD1 .....**154** B6
  Mickletown LS26 .....**102** B1
  Pontefract WF8 ......**125** C1
Watergate Rd WF12....**139** B7
Water Gn HX6 ....**132** A6
Water Green La HX6 ...**132** A6

Water Hill HX6.........**112** A5
Water Hill La HX6, HX2..**112** A5
Waterhouse Ct LS10 ...**215** B5
Waterhouse Dr WF3 ...**120** B7
Waterhouse Gr WF2 ...**142** A6
Waterhouse St
  Halifax HX1 ....**203** B1
  3 Keighley BD21 .....**35** A4
  8 Keighley BD21 .....**35** B4
Watering Mdw LS27....**98** D4
Watering Trough Cotts
  WF7..................**164** A6
Water La
  Bradford BD1..........**74** D7
  Darrington WF8.......**146** D2
  Dewsbury, Scout Hill
    WF12...............**139** B6
  Halifax HX1, HX3......**203** C2
  Keighley BD21 ....**35** B4
  Kirk Smeaton WF8.....**166** E6
  Leeds, Camp Field LS11 .**211** A2
  Leeds, Gamble Hill LS12 .**77** D7
  Leeds LS11 ....**211** C3
  Lofthouse Gate WF3 ...**121** F4
  Netherton WF4 ....**158** D8
  Pontefract WF8 ......**125** F3
  Pudsey LS28 ....**57** D3
  Shelley HD8 ....**174** A3
  South Kirkby WF9 ....**181** F4
  Woolley WF4 ....**178** A8
  Yeadon LS18 ....**40** F1
Water Lane Cl WF4 ....**158** D8
Water Lily Rd BD9 .....**55** A2
Waterloo Apartments 19
  LS10.................**211** C4
Waterloo Bank HX7 ....**89** B6
Waterloo Cl WF10......**123** F5
Waterloo Cres
  Bradford BD10........**56** F8
  Leeds LS13 ....**58** D4
Waterloo Fold 2 BD12..**94** D2
Waterloo Gr LS28......**76** B7
Waterloo La LS13 .....**58** D3
Waterloo Mills 6 BD20..**5** D1
Waterloo Mount LS28...**76** B8
Waterloo Rd
  Bingley BD16.........**36** F3
  Brighouse HD6 ......**115** A3
  Huddersfield HD5 ....**155** B6
  Pudsey LS28 ....**76** B7
Waterloo Rise HD5.....**155** A6
Waterloo St
  Leeds LS10 ....**211** C3
  Wakefield WF1 ......**142** D4
Waterloo Terr HX6.....**112** C6
Waterloo Way LS13 ...**58** D3
Water Mill Ct
  Goose Eye BD22 .....**34** B6
  Holmfirth HD9........**189** E6
Water Row HD9........**189** E6
Water Royd Ave WF14..**138** A6
Water Royd Cres WF14 .**138** A6
Water Royd Dr WF14 ...**138** A6
Water Royd La WF14 ...**138** A6
Waterside
  Bingley BD16.........**36** D5
  Fairburn WF11.........**105** A4
  Halifax HX3 ....**203** C2
  Holmfirth HD9........**188** D2
  Huddersfield HD1 .....**153** F5
  Huddersfield, Salford HD1 **153** F2
  Oxenhope BD22.......**51** C2
  Silsden BD20 ....**17** F8
  Slaithwaite HD7.......**152** A1
Waterside Ct LS13......**57** F5
Waterside Fold HX7.....**89** A4
Waterside Ind Pk LS10 ..**80** B2
Water Side La HD9......**188** D2
Waterside Mdws LS25...**64** F2
Waterside Mill BD22 ...**51** E1
Waterside Rd
  Bradford BD8..........**74** A8
  Leeds LS10 ....**80** B3
Waterside The HD9 ....**172** C1
Waterside Units WF2...**142** B2
Waterside Wlk WF14 ...**137** D5
Watersole La LS23 .....**14** B4
Waters Rd HD7 ....**168** C5
Water St
  Brighouse HD6 ......**115** B3
  Clayton West HD8 ....**175** D1
  Holmfirth HD9........**188** D3
  Huddersfield HD1 .....**153** F5
  2 Huddersfield, Rashcliffe HD1,
    HD4................**153** F3
  Sowerby Bridge HX6...**112** B3
  Todmorden OL14......**108** B5
Water Stalls Rd HX6, HX7 **110** F2
Waterstone Ct WF13...**117** F4
Waterton Cl
  South Kirkby WF9 ....**182** D3
  Walton WF2 ....**161** A6
Waterton Gr WF2.......**141** F5
Waterton Jun & Inf Sch
  WF2..................**141** D4
Waterton Rd WF2......**141** E4
Water View WF10......**103** D1
Waterwheel La BD22...**34** C2
Waterwheel Rise HD4...**153** D3
Waterwood Cl WF3.....**119** F7
Waterworks Rd WF17...**117** F4
Watery La HD9.........**197** F8
Watford Ave HX3 ......**93** F3
Watkin Ave BD13 ......**72** F6
Watkinson Ave HX2....**91** F4
Watkinson Bglws HX2...**91** E3
Watkinson Dr HX2......**91** F4
Watkinson Rd HX2.....**91** F4

Watling Rd WF10 104 E1
Watmough St 2 BD7 74 A3
Watroyd La HD7 152 B2
Watson's La LS24 31 D5
Watson Ave WF12 140 B8
Watson Cl BD22 51 C2
Watson Cres WF1 142 E7
Watson Mill La HX6 112 B2
Watson Rd LS14 61 F1
Watson St
Morley LS27 97 F3
Normanton WF6 123 A2
Wattlesyke LS22 29 E8
Watts St BD14 73 B4
Watt St BD4 75 D6
Watty Hall Ave BD6 74 A2
Watty Hall La BD6 74 B2
Watty Hall Rd BD6 74 A2
Watty La OL14 107 F3
Watty Terr OL14 107 F3
Wauchope St WF2 216 A1
Wauds Gates BD17 38 C1
Waulkmill Cl WF9 183 A7
Wavell Garth WF2 160 F7
Wavell Gr WF2 160 F7
Waveney Rd LS12 209 C1
Waverley Ave
Bradford BD7 74 B5
Keighley BD20 36 B8
Waverley Cres HX3 114 C7
Waverley Garth LS11 214 B4
Waverley Pl BD7 74 B5
Waverley Rd
Bradford BD7 74 B5
Elland HX5 134 F5
Huddersfield HD1 153 F7
Waverley St
Dewsbury WF12 139 C7
Slaithwaite HD7 151 F1
Waverley Terr
Bradford BD7 74 B5
Brighouse HX3 114 C7
Huddersfield HD1 153 D7
Waverton Gn BD6 93 F7
Wavertree Park Gdns 12
BD12 94 C4
Wayland App LS16 42 D4
Wayland Cl LS16 42 D4
Wayland Croft LS16 42 D4
Wayland Ct LS16 42 D4
Wayland Dr LS16 42 D4
Wayne Cl WF17 118 C6
Wayside Ave LS14 28 D1
Wayside Cres
Bardsey LS14 28 D1
Bradford BD2 56 B5
Wayside Ct BD20 18 A2
Wayside Mount LS14 28 D1
Weardale Cl BD4 75 C1
Weardley La LS17 26 B6
Weatherall Pl DN6 184 F2
Weatherhead Pl BD20 5 F1
Weatherhill Cres HD3 135 A2
Weather Hill La
Cragg Vale HX7 110 E4
Holme HD9 198 E8
Weatherhill Rd HD3 135 A2
Weatherhouse Terr HX2 91 D1
Weaver Cotts BD22 51 C3
Weaver Ct 8 BD10 56 B8
Weaver Gdns LS27 98 D3
Weavers Brook HX2 91 E3
Weavers Chase WF2 141 D7
Weavers Cotts 1 BD22 51 C2
Weavers Croft
Bradford BD10 39 B2
Cleckheaton BD19 116 F6
Pudsey LS28 76 F6
Weavers Ct
Batley WF16 117 E4
Leeds LS12 209 B3
Meltham HD9 170 F2
1 Pudsey LS28 76 F5
Sowerby Bridge HX6 112 C6
Weavers Grange LS20 22 E2
Weavers Hill BD22 51 C6
Weavers La BD13 52 D6
Weavers Rd WF8 125 E1
Weavers Row LS28 76 F6
Weaver St LS4 205 A1
Weavers Wlk
Denby Dale HD8 192 B7
3 Silsden BD20 5 E2
Weaverthorpe Rd BD4 75 E1
Weaverthorpe Ret Pk
BD4 75 E1
Weaving La WF12 139 B6
Weaving Shed The 19
HX6 112 C4
Webb's Terr HX3 203 C4
Webb Dr BD2 56 A2
Weber Ct BD3 75 C7
Webster Hill WF13 139 C8
Webster Pl
Bradford BD3 75 B7
Normanton WF6 123 A2
Webster Row LS12 209 B2
Webster St
Bradford BD3 75 B7
4 Dewsbury WF13 139 C8
Webton Ct LS7 204 A3
Wedgemoor Cl 14 BD12 94 C4
Wedgewood Ct LS8 44 A1
Wedgewood Dr LS8 44 A1
Wedgewood Gr LS8 44 A1
Wedgewood Sch BD4 75 F2
Weeland Ave WF4 144 B3
Weeland Cres WF4 144 C4
Weeland Ct WF11 127 A4
Weeland Dr WF4 144 C3
Weeland Rd
Beal DN14 127 D4
Crofton WF4 144 C3
Knottingley WF11 127 D4
Weetlands Cl LS25 83 B2
Weetshaw Cl S72 180 C1
Weetshaw La S72 180 B1
Weetwood Ave LS16 59 D7
Weetwood Cres LS16 59 D8
Weetwood Ct LS16 59 C8
Weetwood Grange Gr
LS16 59 B8
Weetwood House Ct LS16 59 B8
Weetwood La LS16 59 D7
Weetwood Mill La LS16 59 D8
Weetwood Park Dr LS16 59 B8
Weetwood Prim Sch LS16 59 D7
Weetwood Rd
Bradford BD8 74 A8
Leeds LS16 59 B8
Weetwood Wlk LS16 59 C8
Weetworth Ave WF10 124 F6
Weetworth Pk WF10 124 E6
Weir Bottom OL13 106 A7
Weir La OL13 106 A7
Weir Side HD7 168 F4
Weir St OL14 108 A3
Weir View WF10 103 D1
Welbeck Dr BD7 73 E4
Welbeck La WF1 143 A8
Welbeck Rd
Batley WF17 96 F2
Leeds LS9 80 A7
Welbeck Rise BD7 73 E4
Welbeck St
Castleford WF10 124 D8
Wakefield WF1 142 D3
Welburn Ave
Brighouse HX3 114 D7
Leeds LS16 59 B7
Welburn Cl WF2 142 F1
Welburn Dr LS16 59 B7
Welburn Gr LS16 59 B7
Welburn Mount BD6 93 E8
Welbury Dr BD8 55 C2
Weldon Ct BD4 75 E4
Weldon Dr HD3 152 A8
Welfare Ave LS15 63 E7
Welham Wlk BD3 56 A1
Welhouse Ct LS8 61 A5
Welland Dr LS25 83 B6
Wellands Gn BD19 116 B7
Wellands La BD19 116 A7
Wellands Terr BD3 75 C7
Well Bank Rd BD4 75 D3
Well Cl
Addingham LS29 2 E1
Kippax LS26 102 E8
Yeadon LS19 40 C3
Well Close Rise LS7 206 C2
Well Close St HD6 115 B3
Wellcroft LS21 23 B7
Well Croft BD18 55 B7
Wellcroft Gdns HX3 114 C8
Wellcroft Gr WF3 119 F7
Wellcroft Ho ST1 179 C3
Weller Cl 6 BD5 74 E3
Wellesley Gn WF2 141 E7
Wellesley Ho 1 BD4 75 D6
Wellesley St BD1 201 C3
Wellfield Ave WF4 156 E5
Wellfield Bank HD4 153 D2
Wellfield Cl
Grange Moor WF4 156 E5
Huddersfield HD7 152 E2
Wellfield Gdns
Queensbury BD13 72 D3
Royston S71 179 D5
Wellfield La LS29 9 E2
Wellfield Rd HD3 153 C7
Wellfield Terr
Gildersome LS27 97 C7
Todmorden OL14 108 B4
Well Fold BD10 56 B8
Wellgarth
Bradford BD6 93 F7
Halifax HX1 203 A1
Well Garth LS15 62 C2
Well Garth Bank LS13 58 B4
Well Garth Mount LS15 62 C2
Wellgarth Rd WF7 145 E4
Well Garth View LS13 58 C4
Wellgate
Castleford WF10 124 F6
Darton S75 178 B1
Elland HX4 134 C8
3 Ossett WF5 140 D5
Slaithwaite HD7 152 B3
Wellgate Prim Sch S75 178 B1
Well Gr
Brighouse HD6 114 F5
Huddersfield HD2 136 C3
Well Green La HD6 114 F5
Wellhead Cl LS16 24 E4
Well Head Dr HX1 203 B2
Well Head La
Halifax HX1 203 B2
Sowerby Bridge HX6 111 C3
Wellhead Mews WF4 159 F4
Well Heads BD13 72 A6
Well Hill
Honley HD9 171 F4
Otley LS21 22 F7
Yeadon LS19 40 B7
Well Hill Gr S71 179 C4
Wellholme HD6 115 B3
Well Holme Mead LS12 77 E3
Wellhouse WF14 138 B7
Wellhouse Ave WF14 138 B7
Well House Ave LS8 61 A5
Wellhouse Cl WF14 138 A7
Wellhouse Court Mews
WF14 138 B6
Well House Cres LS8 61 A5
Well House Dr LS8 61 A5
Well House Gdns LS8 61 A5
Wellhouse Gn HD7 152 D3
Wellhouse Jun & Inf Sch
HD7 152 D3
Wellhouse La
Huddersfield HD5 137 A1
Mirfield WF14 138 B7
Well House Rd LS8 61 A5
Well Houses HD9 188 F2
Well Ings Cl HD8 173 F1
Wellington Arc 7 HD6 115 B2
Wellington Bridge St
Leeds LS12 210 C4
Leeds LS12 211 A3
Wellington Bsns Ctr
HX5 135 A7
Wellington Cres BD18 55 A7
Wellington Ct
Birkenshaw BD11 96 A6
Halifax HX2 202 A4
1 Shipley BD18 55 A7
Wellington Garth 3 LS13 58 D4
Wellington Gdns LS13 58 D4
Wellington Gr
3 Bradford BD2 56 B2
Leeds LS13 58 D4
Pudsey LS28 76 C7
Wellington Hill LS14 45 A3
Wellington Mount LS13 58 D4
Wellington Pl
Bradford BD2 56 C3
2 Halifax HX1 203 C2
Knottingley WF11 126 D4
Leeds LS1 211 A3
Wellington Prim Sch BD2 56 B3
Wellington Rd
Bradford BD2 56 B3
Dewsbury WF13 139 C8
Ilkley LS29 8 B4
Keighley BD21 35 C7
Leeds LS12, LS3 210 C3
Leeds, New Wortley LS12,
LS3 210 B2
Todmorden OL14 108 B6
Wilsden BD15 53 C4
Wellington Rd E 11
WF13 139 C8
Wellington Rd Ind Est
LS12 210 C3
Wellington St S HX1 203 C2
Wellington St W HX1 203 A2
Wellington St
Batley WF17 118 C4
Bingley BD16 36 F3
Bradford BD1 201 C3
8 Bradford, Haigh Fold
BD2 56 B3
Bradford, Idle BD10 56 B7
Bradford, Lower Grange
BD15 54 C1
Bradford, Swain Green BD4 75 D6
Castleford WF10 124 B8
12 Dewsbury WF13 139 C8
Huddersfield HD3 153 B8
Leeds LS1 211 A3
3 Liversedge WF15 117 B3
Morley LS27 98 A4
Queensbury BD13 72 F1
Wakefield WF2 141 E7
Wilsden BD15 53 C4
Wellington Terr
Leeds LS13 58 D4
Marsden HD7 169 A4
Wellington Wlk 9 WF13 139 C8
Well La
Batley WF17 118 D5
Brighouse HD6 115 E2
Dewsbury WF13 138 F8
Guiseley LS20 22 E1
Halifax HX1 203 C3
Holmfirth HD9 189 B4
Kippax LS25 83 A1
Leeds LS7 204 A3
Todmorden OL14 108 B5
Yeadon LS19 40 B7
Yeadon, Rawdon LS19 40 C3
Well Royd Ave HX2 112 C7
Well Royd Cl HX2 112 D7
Wells Croft LS6 59 E7
Wells Ct
Halifax HX3 92 B1
Ilkley LS29 8 B3
Ossett WF5 140 C5
Yeadon LS19 40 B7
Wells Gr 13 LS20 22 E1
Wells Green Gdns HD9 188 F7
Wells Ho 10 HX6 112 C4
Wells Mount
Denby Dale HD8 191 A6
14 Guiseley LS20 22 E1
Wells Prom LS29 8 B3
Wells Rd
Dewsbury WF12 139 E2
Guiseley LS20 22 E1
Ilkley LS29 8 B3
Well St
Bradford BD1 201 C3
Denholme BD13 71 D8
3 Dewsbury WF12 118 E1
Well St *continued*
3 Elland HX4 134 B4
12 Guiseley LS20 22 E1
Huddersfield HD1 153 F5
Keighley BD21 35 B7
Liversedge WF15 117 A5
Pudsey LS28 57 D3
Sutton-in-C BD20 16 E5
Todmorden OL14 108 B4
Wilsden BD15 53 C5
Wells Terr
Brighouse HX3 94 A2
11 Guiseley LS20 22 E1
Wells The
Halifax, Highroad Well
HX2 112 D7
Halifax, Pye Nest HX2 202 A1
Wellstone Ave LS13 77 B8
Wellstone Dr LS13 58 B1
Wellstone Garth LS13 77 C8
Wellstone Gdns LS13 77 B8
Wellstone Gn LS13 58 B1
Wellstone Rd LS13 77 B8
Wellstone Rise LS13 77 B8
Wellstone Way LS13 77 B8
Wells Wlk LS29 8 B3
Wellthorne Ave S36 191 E1
Wellthorne La S36 191 D1
Well View 9 LS20 22 E1
Welton Gr LS6 205 B3
Welton Mount LS6 205 B3
Welton Pl LS6 205 B3
Welton Rd LS6 205 B3
Welwyn Ave
Batley WF17 117 F6
Shipley BD18 55 F7
Welwyn Dr
Baildon BD17 38 C2
Shipley BD18 55 F7
Welwyn Rd WF12 118 F3
Wembly Ave BD13 72 F6
Wenborough La BD4 75 F3
Wendel Ave LS15 63 D7
Wendron Cl WF15 116 F1
Wendron Way BD10 56 B7
Wenlock St BD3 201 D2
Wenning St BD21 35 E8
Wensley Ave
Leeds LS7 60 C7
Shipley BD18 55 A7
Wensley Bank BD13 72 C6
Wensley Bank Terr BD13 72 C6
Wensley Bank W BD13 72 C6
Wensley Cres LS7 60 C7
Wensleydale Ave LS12 58 F2
Wensleydale Cl 2 LS12 58 F2
Wensleydale Cres LS12 58 F2
Wensleydale Ct LS7 60 C7
Wensleydale Dr LS12 58 F2
Wensleydale Ho WF13 118 C2
Wensleydale Mews 1
LS12 58 F2
Wensleydale Par 2
WF17 117 F8
Wensleydale Rd BD3 75 E7
Wensleydale Rise
Baildon BD17 38 E4
3 Leeds LS12 58 F2
Wensleydale Way BD20 19 B1
Wensley Dr
Leeds LS7 60 C7
Pontefract WF8 146 E6
Wensley Gdns LS7 60 B8
Wensley Gn LS7 60 B7
Wensley Gr
Brighouse HD6 135 E8
Leeds LS7 60 C7
Wensley Lawn LS10 99 C4
Wensley Rd LS7 60 B8
Wensley St E 6 WF4 141 A1
Wensley St 5 WF4 141 A1
Wensley View LS7 60 C7
Went Ave WF7 145 C3
Wentbridge La WF8 165 C6
Wentbridge Rd WF7 145 E4
Wentcliffe Rd WF11 126 B4
Went Croft WF8 146 D5
Wentdale WF8 166 E6
Went-Dale Rd WF8 146 D5
Went Edge Rd
Kirk Smeaton WF8 165 F6
Thorpe Audlin WF8 165 E6
Went Fold WF8 146 D5
Went Garth WF8 146 D5
Went Gr WF7 145 C3
Went Hill Cl WF7 164 A8
Went La
Purston Jaglin WF4 145 D2
West Hardwick WF4 163 C7
Wentvale Ct WF8 165 D7
Went View WF8 165 A5
Wentwell Rd WF7 144 D5
Wentworth Ave
Emley HD8 175 C6
Leeds LS17 43 C4
Wentworth Cl
Menston LS29 22 A4
Woolley WF4 177 F7
Wentworth Cres LS17 43 C4
Wentworth Ct
Brighouse HD6 135 F7
Leeds LS17 43 C4
Wentworth Dr
Crofton WF4 162 A8
Emley HD8 175 C6
Halifax HX2 91 F7
South Kirkby WF9 182 C3
Wentworth Gate LS22 13 B6
Wentworth Gr HX2 91 F7
Wentworth Park Rise
WF8 147 D5
Wentworth Rd WF7 145 B4
Wentworth St
Huddersfield HD1 153 F7
Wakefield WF1 216 A3
Wentworth Terr
Fitzwilliam WF9 163 B3
Wakefield WF1 216 A3
Yeadon LS19 40 D3
Wentworth Way
Leeds LS17 43 C4
Wakefield WF2 142 E1
Wepener Mount LS9 208 B1
Wepener Pl LS9 208 B1
Werner Ct WF10 124 E5
Wesleyan Terr BD4 75 C3
Wesley App LS11 213 C2
Wesley Ave
Bradford BD12 94 E7
Holmfirth HD9 188 F8
4 Leeds LS12 209 C3
Wesley Ave S 3 BD12 94 E6
Wesley Cl
Batley WF17 96 E1
Leeds LS11 213 C3
Wesley Croft LS11 213 C3
Wesley Ct
3 Halifax HX1 203 B3
Leeds, Beeston LS11 213 C2
Leeds, Woodhouse LS6 206 A3
Ossett WF5 140 C6
Yeadon LS19 39 F7
Wesley Dr BD12 94 E7
Wesley Garth LS11 213 C3
Wesley Gn LS11 213 C2
Wesley Gr BD10 39 C1
Wesley Hall Ct WF3 121 F2
Wesley Ho LS11 213 C2
Wesley Pl
Bradford BD12 94 E6
Dewsbury WF13 139 C8
Keighley BD21 35 B3
5 Leeds, Armley LS12 209 C3
Leeds LS9 212 B3
Purston Jaglin WF7 145 D4
Silsden BD20 5 E1
Sowerby Bridge HX6 111 D3
Wesley Rd
Leeds LS12 209 C3
Pudsey LS28 57 C2
Wesley Row 13 LS28 76 E8
Wesley Sq 7 LS28 76 E7
Wesley St
Castleford, Cutsyke
WF10 124 C5
Castleford WF10 124 D8
Cleckheaton BD19 116 D8
Dewsbury WF13 139 C8
Leeds LS11 213 C3
Morley LS27 98 A4
Ossett WF5 140 D6
5 Otley LS21 23 A8
Pudsey, Farsley LS28 57 D3
Pudsey, Rodley LS13 57 F5
Pudsey, Stanningley LS28 57 D1
South Elmsall WF9 182 E2
Wakefield WF1 142 E3
Wesley Terr
1 Bacup OL13 106 A7
Denby Dale HD8 191 F6
Leeds LS13 58 D3
Pudsey LS28 76 E8
Pudsey, Rodley LS13 57 F5
Wesley View
6 Pudsey LS28 76 E8
Pudsey, Rodley LS13 57 F5
Wessen Ct HD7 168 F4
Wessenden Head Rd
HD9 170 D1
Wessenden Rd HD7 169 A1
West Acre Dr WF17 118 E5
Westacres HD6 136 B8
West Acres WF11 126 D7
West Ave
Baildon BD17 38 C3
Boston Spa LS23 14 C1
Bradford BD15 53 F3
Brighouse HX3 115 A7
Halifax HX3 113 B4
Honley HD9 171 F4
Horbury WF4 141 C1
Huddersfield HD3 135 C1
Leeds LS8 61 C8
Pontefract WF8 146 A8
Royston S71 179 D4
South Elmsall WF9 183 B4
West Bank
Batley WF17 118 B6
Bradford BD9 54 F4
Halifax HX2 91 D4
Keighley BD22 34 F8
West Bank Cl BD22 34 F8
West Bank Gr BD20 18 E2
West Bank Rd BD20 18 D2
West Bank Rise BD22 34 F8
Westborough Dr HX2 112 D7
Westborough High Sch
WF13 139 A8
Westbourne Ave
Garforth LS25 82 D6
Leeds LS11 214 B3
1 Pontefract WF8 146 C7

Westbourne Cl
Otley LS21 22 E7
Wakefield WF2 160 C6
Westbourne Cres
Garforth LS25 82 D6
Halifax HX3 113 D3
Pontefract WF8 146 B7
Westbourne Dr
Garforth LS25 82 D6
Guiseley LS20 22 C1
Menston LS29 22 A5
Westbourne Gdns LS25 82 D6
Westbourne Gr
Garforth LS25 82 D6
Halifax HX3 113 D3
Otley LS21 22 E7
Westbourne Mount
[13] Leeds LS11 214 B3
[2] Pontefract WF8 146 C7
Westbourne Pl
[12] Leeds LS11 214 B3
Pudsey LS28 57 D1
Westbourne Prim Sch BD8 55 B2
Westbourne Rd
Bradford BD8 55 B2
Huddersfield HD1 153 D7
Pontefract WF8 146 C7
Westbourne St LS11 214 B3
Westbourne Terr
Garforth LS25 82 D6
Halifax HX3 113 D3
[20] Queensbury BD13 72 E1
West Bretton Jun & Inf Sch WF4 176 F8
Westbrook Cl LS18 41 B2
Westbrook Ct HX1 203 A4
Westbrook Dr HD5 155 B6
Westbrook La LS18 41 B2
Westbrook Lane Prim Sch LS18 41 B3
Westbrook St BD7 74 D6
Westbrook Terr WF17 118 B6
Westburn Ave BD22 34 F5
Westburn Cres BD22 34 F5
Westburn Gr BD22 34 F5
Westburn Pl BD19 116 C8
Westburn Way BD22 34 F5
Westbury Cl BD4 75 D5
Westbury Gr LS10 215 C2
Westbury Mount LS10 215 C1
Westbury Pl HX1 202 A2
Westbury Pl N LS10 215 C2
Westbury Pl S LS10 215 C1
Westbury Rd BD6 73 D1
Westbury St
Bradford BD4 75 D5
Elland HX5 135 A7
Middleton LS10 215 C1
Westbury Terr
Halifax HX1 202 A2
Middleton LS10 215 C1
West Busk La LS21 22 D6
West Byland HX2 91 D7
West Carr La HD3 150 D2
West Chevin Rd
Menston LS29 22 E5
Otley LS21 22 E5
West Cl
Huddersfield HD2 136 B2
Normanton WF6 123 A3
Pontefract WF8 146 E5
Westcliffe Ave BD17 38 B3
Westcliffe Dr HX2 112 D7
Westcliffe Mews [3] BD18 55 B7
Westcliffe Rd
Cleckheaton BD19 116 C7
Shipley BD18 55 B7
Westcliffe Rise BD19 116 C7
Westcombe Ave LS8 44 A2
Westcombe Ct [13] BD12 94 C4
West Cote Dr BD10 38 F1
Westcroft HD9 171 E4
West Croft
[5] Addingham LS29 6 F8
Bradford BD12 94 C2
Sutton-in-C BD20 16 D4
Westcroft Ave HX3 93 B4
Westcroft Dr WF5 119 C1
Westcroft Rd
Bradford BD7 74 A4
Hemsworth WF9 181 D7
West Ct
[6] Leeds LS13 58 C1
Leeds, Roundhay LS8 61 C8
West Dale LS23 14 C1
Westdale Dr LS28 76 D8
Westdale Gdns LS28 76 D8
Westdale Gr LS28 76 D8
Westdale Mews LS28 76 D8
Westdale Rd LS28 76 D8
Westdale Rise LS28 76 D8
West Dene
Leeds LS17 43 F6
Silsden BD20 5 E2
West Dr
Oxenhope BD22 51 C3
Pontefract WF8 146 E7
West End
Boston Spa LS23 14 C1
Cleckheaton BD19 116 C8
Gildersome LS27 97 C7
Gildersome, New Farnley LS12 77 D3
Hebden Bridge HX7 89 A3

West End *continued*
Holmfirth HD9 188 F8
Queensbury BD13 92 D8
West End App LS27 97 E3
West End Ave
Featherstone WF7 145 A8
Holmfirth HD9 189 C6
Royston S71 179 A3
West End Cl LS18 40 F1
West End Cres S71 179 A3
West End Dr
Cleckheaton BD19 116 C6
Horsforth LS18 41 A1
West End Est LS27 97 E3
West End Gr LS18 40 F1
West End La LS18 40 F2
West End Mid Sch BD19 116 C7
West End Prim Sch
Hemsworth WF9 181 C7
Horsforth LS18 40 F1
West End Rd
Halifax HX1 202 A2
Huddersfield HD7 152 C4
Pudsey LS28 57 B6
West End Rise LS18 40 F1
Westend St BD1 74 D7
West End Terr
Bradford BD2 56 B5
Guiseley LS20 22 C1
[4] Mytholmroyd HX7 89 E1
[1] Shipley BD18 55 A8
Westercroft HX3 93 B3
Westercroft Garth [4] BD13 92 C8
Westercroft La HX3 93 B3
Westercroft View HX3 93 B3
Westerley Cl HD8 174 A3
Westerley Cres BD20 5 C1
Westerley La HD8 174 A3
Westerly Croft LS12 209 C4
Westerly Rise LS12 209 C4
Westerly Way HD8 174 A3
Westerman Cl WF7 145 D6
Westerman St WF1 142 E3
Western Ave
Batley WF17 97 A1
Keighley BD20 18 D3
Pontefract WF8 125 F1
Western Ct WF8 125 F1
Western Gales Way WF6 123 D1
Western Gr LS12 209 B1
Western Ho [3] HX3 92 B2
Western Mount LS12 209 B1
Western Pl BD13 73 B1
Western Rd
Huddersfield HD4 153 A4
Leeds LS12 209 B1
Western St LS12 209 B1
Western Way
Bradford BD6 94 A7
Bradford, Buttershaw BD6 93 F7
Westerton Cl WF3 120 B8
Westerton Ct BD12 95 B5
Westerton Prim Sch WF3 119 D7
Westerton Rd WF3 119 E7
Westerton Wlk WF3 120 B8
West Farm Ave LS10 99 B5
Westfell Cl BD22 34 F6
Westfell Rd BD22 34 F6
Westfell Way BD22 34 F6
Westfield
Brighouse HX3 114 D7
Pudsey LS28 57 D1
Thornton BD13 73 A6
Wadsworth Moor HX7 89 C5
West Field
Sowerby Bridge HX6 112 C2
Thorner LS14 45 E4
Westfield Ave
Brighouse HX3 114 D7
Castleford WF10 124 C5
Dewsbury WF12 140 A8
Huddersfield HD3 153 B7
Kippax, Allerton Bywater WF10 103 A5
Kippax LS25 83 A1
Knottingley WF11 126 F3
[5] Leeds LS12 77 F8
Meltham HD9 170 C3
Pontefract WF8 146 C6
Skelmanthorpe HD8 174 F1
Yeadon LS19 39 F6
Westfield Bglws
[3] South Elmsall WF9 182 F2
South Elmsall WF9 183 A2
Westfield Bldgs LS27 98 C1
Westfield Cl
Batley WF16 117 C5
Normanton WF6 123 A1
Rothwell LS26 100 C4
Yeadon LS19 39 F6
Westfield Cotts WF8 146 C5
Westfield Cres
Bradford BD2 56 B1
Keighley BD20 18 F2
Leeds LS3 205 C1
Ossett WF5 140 C5
Ryhill WF4 162 A1
Shipley BD18 55 E6
Thurnscoe S63 194 C1
Wakefield WF2 120 B2
Westfield Ct
Horbury WF4 140 F2
Huddersfield HD5 154 D6
Leeds, Burley Lawn LS3 205 C1
Leeds, Town End LS12 209 B1
Mirfield WF14 138 A5

Westfield Ct *continued*
Rothwell LS26 100 C4
Westfield Dr
Brighouse HX3 114 D7
Keighley BD20 18 F1
Ossett WF5 140 C5
Skelmanthorpe HD8 174 F1
Yeadon LS19 39 F6
Westfield Farm WF5 140 C6
Westfield Gdns
Brighouse HX3 114 D7
Kippax LS25 82 F2
Westfield Gr
Ackworth M T WF7 164 C8
Bradford BD10 56 A8
Castleford WF10 124 C5
Dewsbury WF13 138 F8
Ingbirchworth S36 191 D1
Kippax WF10 103 A5
Shipley BD18 55 E6
Wakefield WF1 216 B4
Yeadon LS19 39 F6
Westfield Ind Est LS19 40 A7
Westfield La
Bradford BD10 56 A8
Brighouse BD12, BD19 94 D1
Darrington WF8 147 C3
Emley HD8 174 F8
Kippax LS25 83 A1
Norton WF8 166 F3
Shipley BD18 55 F7
South Elmsall WF9 182 F2
South Milford LS25 84 F2
Thorner LS14 45 E4
West Field La HD9 189 C6
Westfield Mount LS19 39 F6
Westfield Oval LS19 39 E6
Westfield Pk WF1 216 B4
Westfield Pl
Brighouse BD19 94 E1
Halifax HX1 202 C2
Morley LS27 98 A4
Wakefield WF2 120 B2
Westfield Rd
Batley WF16 117 D5
Bradford BD9 55 A2
Bradford, Clayton BD14 73 B4
Hemsworth WF9 181 D7
Horbury WF4 140 F2
Keighley BD20 18 F1
Knottingley WF11 126 F3
Leeds LS3 205 C1
Morley LS27 98 A4
Rothwell LS26, WF3 100 C3
Wakefield WF1 216 B4
Westfields
Castleford WF10 124 C5
Royston S71 179 A4
Westfields Ave WF14 138 B5
Westfields Rd WF14 138 A5
Westfield St
Batley WF16 117 C5
Halifax HX1 203 A2
Ossett WF5 140 C5
Westfield Terr
Baildon BD17 38 C4
Bradford BD2 56 B1
[2] Bradford, Clayton BD14 73 B4
Halifax HX1 202 C4
[4] Horbury WF4 141 A1
Kippax WF10 103 A5
Leeds, Chapel Allerton LS7 60 C7
Leeds LS3 205 C1
[2] Mytholmroyd HX7 89 E1
Wakefield WF1 216 B4
Westfield View WF1 216 B4
Westfield Villas WF4 140 F1
West Garforth Jun Sch LS25 82 E6
Westgarth LS22 13 B3
West Garth Mews BD17 38 B2
Westgate
Baildon BD17 38 C4
Bradford BD1 74 D7
Bradford, Eccleshill BD2 56 C4
Brighouse HD6 115 E2
Cleckheaton BD19 116 D7
Dewsbury WF13 139 D8
Elland HX5 134 F7
Elland, Stainland HX4 133 F3
Guiseley LS20 39 B8
Halifax HX1 203 B3
Hemsworth WF9 181 C6
Honley HD9 171 F4
Huddersfield, Almondbury HD5 154 F2
Huddersfield HD1 154 A6
Leeds LS1 211 A4
Liversedge WF16 117 C4
Meltham HD9 170 D2
Otley LS21 22 F7
Shipley BD18 55 B8
Wakefield WF1, WF2 216 B2
Wetherby LS22 13 E5
West Gate HD9 188 F1
Westgate Cl WF3 121 C8
Westgate Ct WF3 121 C8
Westgate End WF2 142 A5
Westgate Gr WF3 121 C8
Westgate Hill St BD4 96 B8
Westgate Ho
Halifax HX1 203 B3
Pudsey LS28 76 C8
Westgate La WF3 121 C8
Westgate Mkt HX1 203 B3
Westgate Prim Sch LS21 22 F7
Westgate Ret & L Pk WF2 216 A1

Westgate Terr
Birkenshaw BD4 96 A8
[14] Dewsbury WF13 139 C8
West Gr
[11] Baildon BD17 38 C4
Royston S71 179 A4
West Grange Cl LS10 215 A1
West Grange Dr LS10 215 A1
West Grange Fold LS10 215 A1
West Grange Garth LS10 215 A1
West Grange Gdns LS10 215 A1
West Grange Gn LS10 215 A1
West Grange Rd LS10 215 A1
West Grange Wlk LS10 215 A1
West Grove Ave HD5 154 D6
Westgrove Bldgs [17] HX6 112 B4
Westgrove Ct BD19 116 C8
West Grove St [10] LS28 57 D1
West Grove Terr HX1 203 A3
West Hall La LS29 3 A1
Westhill Ave BD13 52 E5
West Hill Ave LS7 60 C7
West Hill St HX1 203 A3
West Hill Terr LS7 60 C7
West Ho [2] HX5 134 F7
Westholme Rd HX1 202 B2
Westholme St BD1 201 A2
West Ings Cl WF11 127 B5
West Ings Cres WF11 127 B5
West Ings Ct WF11 127 B5
West Ings La WF11 127 B5
West Ings Mews WF11 127 B5
West Ings Way WF11 127 B5
West La
Askwith LS21 9 E5
Baildon BD17 38 B3
Boston Spa LS23 14 C1
Cleckheaton BD19 96 B1
Crofton WF4 144 B2
Halifax HX3 113 F3
Haworth BD22 51 B7
Keighley BD21, BD22 35 A7
Low Bradley BD20 4 C5
Sutton-in-C BD20 16 C4
Thornton BD13 72 D6
West Laithe HX7 88 F4
Westland Cl BD20 16 E6
Westland Ct LS11 99 B8
Westland Rd LS11 214 B1
Westlands Dr BD15 54 C1
Westlands Gr BD15 54 C1
Westland Sq LS11 99 B8
Westlea WF7 145 E1
Westlea Ave BD20 18 F1
West Lea Cl LS17 43 B1
West Lea Cres
East Ardsley WF3 119 D7
Yeadon LS19 39 F6
West Lea Dr
East Ardsley WF3 119 D6
Leeds LS17 43 B1
West Lea Garth LS17 43 B1
West Lea Gdns LS17 43 B1
West Lea Gr LS19 39 F6
West Leeds High Sch LS12 209 A3
West Leeds St BD21 35 A7
Westleigh [3] BD16 37 A4
Westleigh Cl BD17 38 A2
Westleigh Dr BD17 38 A2
Westleigh Rd BD17 38 A2
Westleigh Way BD17 38 A2
West Ley HD9 171 E4
West Lo LS29 21 E8
Westlock Ave LS9 208 A1
West Lodge Cres HD2 135 B4
West Lodge Gdns LS7 60 C6
Westmead LS28 57 A1
West Mead WF10 125 A7
Westminster Ave BD14 73 A4
Westminster CE Prim Sch BD3 55 F1
Westminster Cl LS13 57 F4
Westminster Cres
Bradford BD14 73 A4
Leeds LS15 80 E7
Westminster Croft LS13 57 F4
Westminster Dr
Bradford BD14 73 A4
Pudsey LS13 57 F4
Westminster Gdns BD14 73 A4
Westminster Pl [1] BD3 55 F1
Westminster Rd
Bradford BD3 55 F1
Brighouse HX3 114 D6
Westminster Terr [2] BD3 55 F1
Westmoor Ave BD17 38 B4
Westmoor Cl BD17 38 B4
Westmoor Jun Sch WF13 117 F1
West Moorlands Ave WF13 118 B1
Westmoor Pl [5] LS13 58 B3
Westmoor Rd LS13 58 B3
West Moor Rd WF9 163 A2
Westmoor Rise LS13 58 B3
Westmoor St LS13 58 B3
West Moor View HD9 171 E4
Westmoreland Mount [1] LS13 58 D4
Westmorland Ho [4] WF1 216 B2
Westmorland St WF1 216 B2
West Mount Pl HX1 202 C4
West Mount St
Leeds LS11 214 A3
[11] Pontefract WF8 146 C8

West Oaks Com Specl Sch LS23 30 E7
Westoff La S72 180 D7
Weston Ave BD13 92 D8
Weston Cres LS21 10 F1
Weston Dr LS21 10 E1
Weston La LS21 10 E1
Weston Moor Rd LS21 10 D8
Weston Park View LS21 10 D1
Weston Rd LS29 8 B4
Weston Ridge LS21 10 E1
Weston St BD22 34 F5
Weston Vale Rd BD13 92 D8
Westover Ave [6] LS13 58 C3
Westover Cl LS13 58 D3
Westover Gdns LS28 76 C7
Westover Gn LS13 58 C3
Westover Gr [3] LS13 58 C3
Westover Mount [10] LS13 58 C3
Westover Rd LS13 58 C3
Westover St [2] LS13 58 C3
Westover Terr [1] LS13 58 C3
Westover View [5] LS13 58 C3
West Par
Guiseley LS20 22 E1
Halifax HX1 203 A2
Ilkley LS29 8 C4
Leeds LS16 59 A8
Rothwell LS26 100 F5
Sowerby Bridge HX6 112 D4
Wakefield WF1 216 B2
West Parade Flats [2] HX1 203 A2
West Parade St WF1 216 B1
West Park Ave LS8 44 B3
West Park Chase LS8 44 A3
West Park Cl LS8 44 A3
West Park Cres LS8 44 B2
West Park Dr
Darrington WF8 147 D2
Leeds LS16 59 A8
West Park Dr E LS8 44 B3
West Park Drive W LS8 43 F3
West Park Gdns LS8 44 B2
West Park Gr
Batley WF17 118 A5
Leeds LS8 44 B2
West Park Pl LS8 44 B2
West Park Rd
Batley WF17 117 F4
Bradford BD8 73 F8
Leeds LS8 44 B2
West Park St
[8] Brighouse HD6 115 B2
Dewsbury WF13 118 B1
West Park Terr
Batley WF17 118 A5
[8] Bradford BD8 73 F8
West Pasture Cl LS18 40 F1
West Pinfold S71 179 C2
West Pk
Guiseley LS20 22 C2
Pudsey LS28 76 D7
West Pl HD5 154 D6
Westray LS12 211 A3
West Rd LS9 80 C3
West Rd N LS9 80 D3
Westridge Dr HD4 153 C1
Westroyd
Clifton LS21 11 A3
Pudsey LS28 76 C6
West Royd
Halifax HX3 114 C8
Wilsden BD15 53 C4
Westroyd Ave
Cleckheaton BD19 95 D2
Pudsey LS28 76 C6
West Royd Ave
Bradford BD2 56 B4
Halifax HX1 202 C2
Mirfield WF14 138 A6
Shipley BD18 55 E8
West Royd Cl
Halifax HX1 202 C1
Shipley BD18 55 D8
Westroyd Cres LS28 76 C6
West Royd Cres BD18 55 E8
West Royd Dr
[3] Mirfield WF14 138 A6
Shipley BD18 55 E8
Westroyd Gdns LS28 76 C6
West Royd Gr
Mirfield WF14 138 A6
Shipley BD18 55 E8
West Royd Mount BD18 55 E8
West Royd Pk WF14 138 A6
West Royd Rd BD18 55 E8
West Royd Terr BD18 55 E8
West Royd Villas [1] HX1 202 C1
West Royd Wlk BD18 55 E8
West Scausby Pk HX2 91 E7
West Shaw La BD22 51 A3
West Side Ret Pk LS20 39 F7
West Slaithwaite Rd HD7 169 C7
West St
Baildon BD17 38 C4
Batley, Lower Soothill WF17 118 E5
Batley WF17 118 D5
Birkenshaw BD11 96 E5
Bradford BD2 56 B3
Bradford, Eastbrook BD1 201 C2
Brighouse, Bailiff Bridge HD6 115 B7
[2] Brighouse, Waring Green HD6 115 A3
Castleford WF10 124 C8

West St *continued*
Cleckheaton BD19 116 D7
Cleckheaton, Gomersal BD19 96 B1
Dewsbury WF12 139 C7
Elland HX4 134 B4
Halifax HX1 202 C3
Hemsworth WF9 181 C7
Huddersfield HD3 135 B1
Ilkley LS29 8 B4
Leeds LS3 210 C4
Morley LS27 98 B3
Normanton WF6 123 A2
Pudsey LS28 76 E8
Royston S71 179 D4
Ryhill WF4 162 C1
Shelf HX3 93 B4
South Elmsall WF9 183 B4
South Hiendley S72 180 E5
South Kirkby WF9 182 A2
Sowerby Bridge HX6 112 B3
Todmorden OL14 108 A6
Wakefield WF2 141 F5
West Terrace St 9 LS28 57 D1
West Vale
Dewsbury WF12 139 B6
Leeds LS12 210 B1
Westvale Mews LS13 58 E1
West Vale Prim Sch HX4 134 D7
West View
Ackworth M T WF7 163 D5
Arthington LS21 24 F6
Batley WF17 118 B2
Bradford BD4 75 A4
Brighouse BD19 94 F1
Crigglestone WF4 159 E4
Crofton WF1 143 C3
Draughton BD23 1 D5
Elland HX4 134 A4
Halifax, Boothtown HX3 92 B2
Halifax HX1 202 B2
Hebden Bridge HX7 88 E4
Holme Chapel BB10 85 A8
Huddersfield HD1 153 D5
Ilkley LS29 8 B3
Kippax LS25 83 B2
Leeds LS11 214 A4
Micklefield LS25 84 B6
Mytholmroyd HX7 110 D7
Normanton WF6 122 F5
Otley LS21 23 B8
19 Pudsey LS28 57 D2
Rothwell LS26 101 C5
Silsden BD20 5 E2
Wakefield WF2 120 B2
Yeadon LS19 39 F7
Westview Ave BD20 35 B8
West View Ave
Burley in W LS29 9 E1
Castleford WF10 125 A7
Halifax HX2 202 A3
Shipley BD18 55 E7
Westview Cl BD20 4 C5
West View Cl BD18 55 E7
West View Cres HX2 202 A3
Westview Ct BD20 35 A8
West View Ct LS19 39 F7
West View Dr HX2 202 A3
Westview Gr BD20 35 A8
West View Ho 9 BD16 37 A2
West View Rd
Burley in W LS29 9 E1
Halifax HX3 92 B2
West View Rise HD1 153 D5
West View St 8 BD22 51 F8
West View Terr
Halifax, Bradshaw HX2 71 F1
Halifax, Pellon HX2 202 A4
Westview Way BD20 35 B8
West Villa Rd LS20 22 E1
Westville Ave LS29 8 A4
Westville Cl LS29 8 A4
Westville House Prep Sch LS29 8 D7
Westville Rd LS29 8 A4
Westville Way BD13 72 D6
Westward Croft HD3 135 C2
Westward Ho
Halifax HX3 92 A4
16 Queensbury BD13 72 E1
Westway
Batley WF17 118 F3
Bingley BD16 37 B5
Bradford BD9 54 C2
Garforth LS25 82 D6
Guiseley LS20 39 B8
Keighley BD20 17 F1
Mirfield WF14 137 F7
Pudsey LS28 57 C3
West Way
Leeds LS1 211 A4
Shipley BD18 54 D7
Westways WF2 120 F2
Westways Cl WF2 120 F2
Westways Dr LS8 61 C7
Westways Rise WF2 120 F2
West Wells Cres WF5 140 C5
West Wells Rd WF5 140 D5
Westwinds WF7 145 F1
West Winds LS29 21 E5
Westwinn Garth LS14 45 C1
Westwinn View LS14 45 C1
Westwood Ave
Bradford BD2 56 B5
Honley HD9 172 C5
Westwood Cl
Featherstone WF7 145 D7
Westwood Cl *continued*
Morley LS27 98 B6
Westwood Cotts LS23 30 E5
Westwood Cres BD16 54 A8
Westwood Ct
Huddersfield HD4 155 A3
Middleton LS10 99 A5
Westwood Dr LS29 7 F2
Westwood Edge Rd HD7 152 A3
Westwood Fold HD7 152 B2
Westwood Gr BD2 56 B5
Westwood Park Community Hosp BD6 73 C1
Westwood Prim Sch LS11 99 A4
Westwood Rd
Castleford WF10 124 B5
Ossett WF5 140 F5
West Wood Rd LS10 98 F4
Westwood Rise
Ilkley LS29 7 F2
Morley LS27 98 B6
Westwood Side LS27 98 B7
Westwood St HD5 137 A6
Westwood Way LS23 30 D8
Westy Bank Croft BD20 17 C2
West Yorkshire Ind Est BD4 95 E8
West Yorkshire Playhouse The* LS2 212 A4
West Yorkshire Pol HQ WF1 216 B3
West Yorkshire Ret Pk WF17 97 A4
Wetherby Bsns Pk LS22 13 F6
Wetherby Gr 8 LS4 59 C2
Wetherby Grange LS22 14 A2
Wetherby High Sch LS22 13 F5
Wetherby Pl LS4 205 A2
Wetherby Race Course LS22 14 B6
Wetherby Rd
Bardsey LS17 28 E4
Bramham LS23 30 C3
Kirk Deighton LS22 13 E8
Leeds LS8 61 D7
Scarcroft LS14, LS17 45 C6
Sicklinghall LS22 12 D5
Thorp Arch LS23 14 F4
Wetherby LS22 13 D3
Wetherby Terr 6 LS4 59 C2
Wetherhill St WF17 118 B5
Wetherill Terr 4 WF13 117 F3
Wetlands Rd HD9 170 E1
Wetton Ct BD3 75 D7
Weydale Ave HD3 153 A8
Weyhill Dr BD15 73 B8
Weymouth Ave
Bradford BD15 73 A8
Huddersfield HD3 153 B7
Weymouth St HX1 203 B3
Whack House Cl LS19 40 A6
Whack House La LS19 40 A7
Whalley La BD13 52 E2
Whams Rd S36 200 F2
Wharf Cl WF12 139 D7
Wharfe Bank LS22 28 E8
Wharfebank Bsns Ctr LS21 22 E7
Wharfe Cl LS16 42 D4
Wharfe Cres LS21 24 D7
Wharfe Ct 11 BD20 5 E1
Wharfedale Ave LS7 206 B4
Wharfedale Bsns Pk BD4 75 E1
Wharfedale Cres
Garforth LS25 82 F6
Skelmanthorpe HD8 175 B1
Wharfedale Ct
Leeds LS14 61 F5
Otley LS21 23 A8
Pool LS21 24 D7
Wharfedale Dr
Ilkley LS29 8 C4
Normanton WF6 123 A4
Wharfedale Gdns BD17 38 E4
Wharfedale General Hospl LS21 10 F2
Wharfedale Gr LS7 206 B4
Wharfedale Ho WF17 118 C3
Wharfedale Lawns LS22 13 E5
Wharfedale Mews 2 LS21 23 A8
Wharfedale Mount
Leeds LS7 206 B4
Shelf HX3 93 B5
Wharfedale Pl LS7 206 B4
Wharfedale Rd BD4 95 A7
Wharfedale Rise
Bradford BD9 54 C2
East Ardsley WF3 119 D7
Wharfedale St LS7 206 B4
Wharfedale Terr LS22 13 B1
Wharfedale View
3 Addingham LS29 6 E8
Leeds LS7 206 B4
Menston LS29 22 A4
Wharfe Gr LS22 13 D5
Wharfe Grange LS22 13 D5
Wharfe Pk LS29 7 A8
Wharfe Rein LS22 28 E8
Wharfeside La LS29 8 C5
Wharfe St 3 LS21 23 B8
Wharfe View
Pool LS21 24 C7
Wetherby LS22 13 D5
Wharfe View Rd LS29 8 B4
Wharfe Way WF10 125 B8
Wharf St
Bradford BD1 201 C4
Wharf St *continued*
Brighouse HD6 115 B2
Dewsbury WF12 139 D7
Leeds LS2 212 A3
Shipley BD17 55 B8
Sowerby Bridge HX6 112 C4
14 Walsden OL14 108 A1
Wharncliffe Cres BD2 56 D4
Wharncliffe Dr BD2 56 D4
Wharncliffe Gr
Bradford BD2 56 D4
Shipley BD18 55 B6
Wharncliffe Rd
Shipley BD18 55 B6
Wakefield WF2 160 A4
Whartons Prim Sch The LS21 11 A2
Wharton Sq BD13 73 B1
Wharton St 4 WF15 117 B4
Whartons The LS21 11 A2
Wharton Terr 3 WF16 117 D3
Wheat Cl
Dewsbury WF13 138 F8
Holmfirth HD9 188 B1
Wheatcroft WF10 125 B7
Wheatcroft Ave WF17 118 C4
Wheater Ho WF1 216 B2
Wheater Rd BD7 74 A5
Wheat Field Ave HD3 153 A8
Wheatfield Ct LS28 76 D6
Wheathead Cres BD22 34 E5
Wheat Head Dr BD22 34 F5
Wheathead La BD22 34 E5
Wheathouse Rd HD2 135 F1
Wheathouse Terr 5 HD2 135 F1
Wheatings The WF5 140 F5
Wheatlands
Ilkley LS29 8 C4
Pudsey LS28 57 C2
Wheatlands Ave
Bradford BD9 54 E2
Glusburn BD20 16 C7
Wheatlands Cres BD9 54 E2
Wheatlands Dr
Bradford BD9 54 E2
Liversedge WF15 116 F2
Wheatlands Garth BD20 16 C7
Wheatlands Gr BD9 54 E2
Wheatlands La BD20 16 C7
Wheatlands Sq BD9 54 E2
Wheatley Ave
Ilkley LS29 8 E4
Normanton WF6 123 B1
Wheatley City HX3 92 E2
Wheatley Cl 3 HX3 92 A1
Wheatley Ct HX2 91 D4
Wheatley Dr WF14 138 A3
Wheatley Gdns LS29 8 E3
Wheatley Gr LS29 8 F3
Wheatley Hill La HD8 192 E8
Wheatley La LS29 8 F4
Wheatley Lane Ends HX2 91 E2
Wheatley Rd
Halifax HX3 91 F2
Ilkley LS29 8 C3
Wheatley Rise
Darton S75 178 B2
Ilkley LS29 8 E3
Wheaton Ave LS15 81 B8
Wheaton Ct 9 LS15 81 A8
Wheatroyd Cres WF5 140 D3
Wheatroyd La HD5 154 E2
Wheat St BD22 35 A4
Wheel Race BD13 52 F1
Wheelwright Ave LS12 209 A1
Wheelwright Cl LS12 209 A1
Wheelwright Dr WF13 118 B2
Wheelwright St 13 WF13 139 C8
Wheldale Ct WF10 104 B1
Wheldale La WF10 104 E2
Wheldon Inf Sch WF10 124 E8
Wheldon Rd WF10 104 B2
Whernside Mount BD7 73 E2
Whernside Way HX2 91 A3
Wherwell Rd HD6 136 C8
Whetley Cl BD8 74 C8
Whetley Gr BD8 55 A1
Whetley Hill BD8 74 C8
Whetley La BD8 74 A8
Whetley Prim Sch BD8 74 A8
Whetley Terr 1 BD8 74 C8
Whewell St 4 WF17 96 E1
Whiddon Croft LS29 21 F5
Whimbrel Cl 4 BD8 73 C7
Whimbrel Mews LS27 98 C3
Whinbeck Ave WF6 123 C1
Whinberry Pl 1 WF17 96 F3
Whinbrook Cres 5 LS17 43 C1
Whinbrook Ct 3 LS17 43 C1
Whinbrook Gdns LS17 43 C1
Whinbrook Gr LS17 43 C1
Whin Cl WF9 181 D5
Whincop Ave WF10 124 A7
Whincover Bank LS12 77 F5
Whincover Cl LS12 77 F5
Whincover Cross LS12 77 F5
Whincover Dr LS12 77 E5
Whincover Gdns LS12 77 F5
Whincover Gr LS12 77 F5
Whincover Grange LS12 77 F5
Whincover Hill LS12 77 F5
Whincover Mount LS12 77 F5
Whincover Rd LS12 77 F5
Whincover View LS12 77 F5
Whincup Gdns 4 LS10 215 B2
Whinfield
Ilkley LS29 7 E3
Whinfield *continued*
Leeds LS16 42 B4
Whinfield Ave BD22 34 E7
Whinfield Cl BD22 34 F8
Whinfield Dr BD22 34 E8
Whinfield Pl WF5 141 B4
Whingate LS12 209 A3
Whingate Ave LS12 209 A3
Whingate Bsns Pk LS12 209 B3
Whingate Cl LS12 209 A3
Whingate Ct LS12 209 B3
Whingate Gn LS12 209 A3
Whingate Gr LS12 209 A3
Whingate Prim Sch LS12 209 A3
Whingate Rd LS12 209 A3
Whin Gdns S63 194 D1
Whingrove Ave HD9 170 D1
Whin Knoll Ave BD21 34 F8
Whinmoor Cl S75 193 F1
Whinmoor Cres LS14 45 A1
Whinmoor Ct
Leeds LS14 45 A1
Silkstone S75 193 F1
Whinmoor Dr
Clayton West HD8 176 A4
Silkstone S75 193 F1
Whinmoor Gdns LS14 45 A1
Whinmoor St Paul's CE Prim Sch LS14 62 A8
Whinmoor View S75 193 F1
Whinmoor Way
Leeds LS14 62 C6
Silkstone S75 193 F1
Whinmore Gdns BD19 117 C7
Whin Mount WF6 144 C8
Whinney Brow BD10 55 F8
Whinney Cl WF7 144 D5
Whinney Field HX3 113 C4
Whinney Hill Pk HD6 115 B5
Whinney La WF7 144 D5
Whinney Moor Ave WF2 141 E4
Whinney Royd La HX3 93 A5
Whinn Moor La LS17 44 F3
Whinside Cres S63 194 C1
Whins La
Sicklinghall LS22, HG3 12 C8
Thorp Arch LS23 14 F1
Whin St BD21 35 A7
Whins The BD21 35 A2
Whin View Ct WF4 162 C1
Whin Wood Grange LS14 62 B8
Whirlaw Ave OL14 108 A7
Whirlaw La OL14 108 B8
Whiskers La HX3 92 E4
Whisperwood Cl WF1 121 D5
Whisperwood Rd WF1 121 D5
Whistler Dr WF10 124 F4
Whitacre Cl HD2 136 E3
Whitacre St HD2 136 E3
Whitaker Ave BD2 56 C3
Whitaker Cl BD2 56 C3
Whitaker House Apartments 9 HX1 203 A1
Whitaker St
Batley WF17 118 D4
Pudsey LS28 57 D2
Whitaker Wlk 4 BD22 51 C2
Whitburn Way 7 BD15 73 B8
Whitby Ave HD2 136 B2
Whitby Cres WF12 139 F8
Whitby Ct HD8 174 A1
Whitby Rd BD8 55 A1
Whitby Terr BD8 55 A1
Whitcliffe Mount Coll BD19 116 B8
Whitcliffe Rd BD19 116 D8
Whitcliffe Road Fst Sch BD19 116 D8
Whitcliffe Sq BD19 116 D8
White's Bldgs WF5 140 D7
White's Rd WF1 216 C2
White's Row WF4 140 D1
White's Terr 6 BD8 55 B1
White's View BD8 74 B8
White Abbey BD20 16 B6
White Abbey Rd BD8 74 C8
Whiteacre St HD2 136 F3
White Apron St WF9 182 B2
Whitebeam Gn 1 WF8 125 F1
Whitebeam La 6 LS10 99 D8
Whitebeam Pk HD2 135 D2
Whitebeam Wlk BD2 56 B5
White Birch Terr HX3 91 F2
Whitebridge Ave LS9 80 E8
Whitebridge Prim Sch LS15 80 E7
Whitebridge Spur LS9 61 E1
Whitebridge View LS9 61 E1
White Castle Ct BD13 72 B2
Whitechapel Cl LS8 61 C6
Whitechapel Gr BD19 95 A1
Whitechapel Mid Sch BD19 116 C8
Whitechapel Rd
Brighouse BD19 116 A8
Cleckheaton BD19 116 C8
Whitechapel Way LS8 61 B6
Whitecliffe Cres LS26 82 A2
Whitecliffe Dr LS26 82 A2
Whitecliffe Rise LS26 82 A2
Whitecote Gdns LS13 58 B4
Whitecote Hill LS13 58 B4
Whitecote La
Leeds LS13 58 B4
South Milford LS25 84 F4
Whitecote Prim Sch LS13 58 D4
Whitecote Rise LS13 58 B4
White Cross
Guiseley LS20 22 C2
Huddersfield HD2 136 E5
White Cross Gdns S72 180 D6
White Cross Rd WF12 118 E2
White Ct WF4 162 A8
White Field La HX7 110 C8
Whitefield Pl BD8 74 A8
Whitegate
East Keswick LS17 28 C6
Halifax HX3 113 D4
White Gate
Halifax HX2 91 D7
Honley HD9 171 F5
Whitegate Dr HX3 113 D4
Whitegate Hill WF8 164 E8
Whitegate La WF8 164 E8
Whitegate Rd
Halifax HX3 113 D4
Huddersfield HD4 154 B4
White Gate Rd HD9 188 D1
Whitegates Cl WF1 121 A1
Whitegates Gr HD8 155 D2
Whitegate Terr HX3 113 D4
Whitegate Top HX3 113 E5
White Gr LS8 61 A8
Whitehall Ave
Bradford BD12 94 C1
Mirfield WF14 138 A7
Wakefield WF1 121 A1
Whitehall Cres WF1 121 A1
Whitehall Croft LS26 100 F5
Whitehall Cross LS12 78 A4
Whitehall Ct 2 WF4 141 B1
Whitehall Gr
Birkenshaw BD11 96 B5
Birkenshaw, Drighlington BD11 96 D6
Whitehall Pl LS12 210 C2
Whitehall Quay LS1 211 B3
Whitehall Rd
Birkenshaw BD11 96 E6
Bradford BD12 94 C1
Cleckheaton BD19 95 D2
Gildersome LS12 77 D2
Leeds LS1, LS12 211 A3
Linthwaite HD7 170 C8
Whitehall Rd E BD11 96 B5
Whitehall Rd W
Birkenshaw BD11 96 A4
Cleckheaton BD19 95 E3
Whitehall Rise WF1 142 A8
Whitehall St
Brighouse HX3 114 D8
Wakefield WF2 141 F5
Whitehall Trad Est LS12 77 F4
Whitehall Waterfront LS1 211 A3
Whitehall Way WF13 139 D8
White Hart Dr HD4 154 A2
White Hart Fold
Ripponden HX6 132 C3
South Elmsall WF9 183 B6
10 Todmorden OL14 108 B5
Whitehaven Cl BD6 93 F7
Whitehead's Terr 1 HX1 202 B3
Whitehead Gr BD2 56 C1
Whitehead La
Huddersfield HD4 154 A3
Meltham HD4, HD7 170 F6
Whitehead Pl BD2 56 C1
Whitehead St BD3 75 B6
White Hill HD7 169 C7
Whitehill Cres HX2 91 E6
Whitehill Dr HX2 91 E6
Whitehill Gn HX2 91 F6
Whitehill Prim Sch HX2 91 E6
Whitehill Rd
Halifax HX2 91 E6
Haworth BD22 33 D5
White Holme Dr LS21 24 E6
Whitehorn Rd WF10 124 F4
White Horse Cl WF17 97 B2
White Horse Fold WF10 103 E6
White Horse Yd WF1 216 B2
White Hos HX7 89 D1
Whitehouse Ave LS26 102 D8
White House Bglws WF2 142 B3
Whitehouse Cres LS26 102 E8
Whitehouse Dr LS26 102 D8
Whitehouse La
Swillington LS26 82 C2
Yeadon LS19 40 F8
Whitehouse St LS10 212 A1
White House Visitor Ctr* LS21 23 A6
White La
Bradford BD6 74 D1
Haworth BD22 33 F3
Hooton Pagnell DN5 195 E4
White Laith Ave LS14 62 B8
White Laith Ct 3 LS14 62 B8
White Laithe App
Leeds LS14 45 B1
Leeds LS14 62 B8
White Laithe Cl LS14 62 B8
White Laithe Croft LS14 62 B8
White Laithe Garth 2 LS14 62 B8
White Laithe Gdns LS14 62 C8
White Laithe Gn LS14 62 C8
White Laithe Gr LS14 62 C8
White Laithe Rd LS14 62 B8
White Laithe Wlk LS14 62 C8

White Laith Prim Sch LS14 . . . 62 C7
Whitelands 1 LS28 . . . 76 F8
White Lands LS19 . . . 40 A4
Whitelands Cres BD17 . . . 38 D3
Whitelands Rd BD17 . . . 38 D3
White Lane Top 1 BD6 . . 94 D8
White Lee HX7 . . . 89 F1
White Lee Cl WF16 . . . 117 E6
White Lee Croft HX7 . . . 89 F1
White Lee Gdns HX7 . . . 89 F1
White Lee Rd WF16 . . . 117 E6
White Lee Side WF16 . . . 117 E6
White Lee Terr HX7 . . . 110 F8
Whiteley Ave HX6 . . . 111 F3
White Ley Bank HD9 . . . 190 A7
Whiteley Croft LS21 . . . 23 A7
Whiteley Croft Garth LS21 22 F7
Whiteley Croft Rd LS21 . . . 23 A7
Whiteley Croft Rise LS21 . 23 A7
Whiteley Croft Yd LS21 . . . 23 A7
White Ley Rd WF8 . . . 166 E1
Whiteley St
Featherstone WF7 . . . 145 C5
Halifax HX1 . . . 203 A2
Huddersfield HD3 . . . 153 B4
Whiteley Terr HX6 . . . 132 C2
White Lo LS8 . . . 208 A4
Whitelock St LS7 . . . 207 A1
Whitemoor Way BD13 . . . 71 E6
White Moss Cl WF7 . . . 163 F6
Whiteplatts St 16 OL14 . . 108 B6
White Rose Ave
Garforth LS25 . . . 83 A8
Huddersfield HD5 . . . 154 F6
White Rose Ct WF2 . . . 141 E5
White Rose Ctr LS11 . . . 99 E7
White Rose Mead LS25 . . . 83 A7
White Rose Way LS25 . . . 83 A7
White Slack Gate OL14 . . 129 A6
White St 7 LS26 . . . 101 C6
Whitestone Cres LS19 . . . 40 B7
Whitestone Dr BD20 . . . 19 D1
Whitestone La 2 HD1 . . . 154 B8
Whitestones HD4 . . . 173 B2
White Walls La HD9 . . . 187 F3
Whiteways BD2 . . . 55 E3
White Wells Gdns HD9 . . 189 D3
White Wells Rd HD9 . . . 189 D3
White Wells Visitor Ctr* LS29 . . . 8 B2
Whitewood Cl S71 . . . 179 B3
Whitfield Ave LS10 . . . 215 B4
Whitfield Gdns LS10 . . . 215 B4
Whitfield Pl LS10 . . . 215 B4
Whitfield Sq LS10 . . . 215 B4
Whitfield St
9 Cleckheaton BD19 . . . 116 D8
Leeds LS8 . . . 207 C3
Whitfield Way LS10 . . . 215 B4
Whitham Cl LS23 . . . 30 D8
Whitkirk Cl LS15 . . . 81 E8
Whitkirk La LS15 . . . 81 D8
Whitkirk Prim Sch LS15 . . 81 C7
Whitlam St BD18 . . . 54 F8
Whitley Dr HX2 . . . 92 A6
Whitley Gdns LS8 . . . 207 B3
Whitley Grange Hospl WF12 . . . 138 F1
Whitley La HX3 . . . 114 A5
Whitley Pl WF10 . . . 103 B4
Whitley Rd
Dewsbury WF12 . . . 139 B1
Keighley BD21 . . . 35 A5
Whitley Common HD9, S36 200 E7
Whitley Spring Cres WF5 . . . 140 F6
Whitley Spring Rd WF5 . . 140 F6
Whitley St
Bingley BD16 . . . 36 F3
Bradford BD3 . . . 201 D3
Whitley Way WF4 . . . 156 E5
Whitteron Cl HD3 . . . 135 B1
Whittle Cres BD14 . . . 73 B5
Whitton Croft Rd 18 LS29 . . 8 B4
Whitty La HX2 . . . 112 B6
Whitwell Ave HX5 . . . 135 B7
Whitwell Dr
Elland HX5 . . . 135 B7
Featherstone WF7 . . . 144 D5
Whitwell Gr HX5 . . . 135 B7
Whitwell Green La HX5 . . 135 B6
Whitwell Main WF7 . . . 144 D5
Whitwell St BD4 . . . 201 D1
Whitwood Common La WF10 . . . 123 E5
Whitwood Ent Pk WF6 . . 123 F5
Whitwood Freight Ctr WF10 . . . 123 D5
Whitwood La
Brighouse HD6 . . . 115 D7
Castleford WF10 . . . 123 E6
Whitwood Terr WF10 . . . 123 E5
Whitworth Rd 1 WF13 . . 139 B7
Whitworth Terr HX1 . . . 203 B1
Wholestone Gate HD7 . . . 152 B5
Whyment Cl LS27 . . . 78 C1
Whytecote End BD12 . . . 94 C4
Wibsey Bank BD6 . . . 74 D1
Wibsey Park Ave BD6 . . . 94 A8
Wibsey Prim Sch BD6 . . . 74 B1
Wicken Cl BD10 . . . 56 C6
Wicken La BD13 . . . 72 D7
Wicket LS28 . . . 57 B7
Wicket Dr WF1 . . . 121 C1
Wickets Cl BD6 . . . 94 D8
Wickets The
Batley WF17 . . . 118 B2
4 Bradford BD2 . . . 56 C2
Leeds LS6 . . . 59 F7
Leeds, Whitkirk Lane End LS15 . . . 81 E7
Wakefield WF2 . . . 160 E8
Wickham Ave
Boston Spa LS23 . . . 30 C8
Bradford BD6 . . . 94 C8
Wickham Cl LS23 . . . 30 C8
Wickham St
Brighouse BD19 . . . 94 F1
Leeds LS11 . . . 214 A3
Wicking La HX6 . . . 132 A8
Wickins La HD9 . . . 188 D6
Wickleden Gate HD9 . . . 189 D3
Widdop Cl 8 BD13 . . . 73 C2
Widdop Rd HX7 . . . 88 D6
Wide La
Morley, Bantam Grove LS27 . . . 98 D4
Morley LS27 . . . 98 C3
Oakworth BD22 . . . 34 B3
Widow's Row LS25 . . . 64 E6
Wigan St BD1 . . . 74 D7
Wigeon App LS27 . . . 98 C4
Wiggan La HD2 . . . 136 D4
Wiggin Cross HD7 . . . 152 E1
Wighill La LS23 . . . 15 D2
Wighill St BD20 . . . 16 D5
Wightman St BD3 . . . 56 A1
Wignall St BD20 . . . 18 B2
Wigton Chase LS17 . . . 44 A5
Wigton Gate LS17 . . . 43 E6
Wigton Gn LS17 . . . 43 F6
Wigton Gr LS17 . . . 43 E6
Wigton La LS17 . . . 43 F6
Wigton Moor Prim Sch LS17 . . . 43 F5
Wigton Park Cl LS17 . . . 43 F6
Wike La
Bardsey LS17 . . . 28 B3
Harewood LS17 . . . 27 C2
Wike Ridge Ave LS17 . . . 44 B6
Wike Ridge Cl LS17 . . . 44 A6
Wike Ridge Ct LS17 . . . 44 B6
Wike Ridge Fold LS17 . . . 44 A6
Wike Ridge Gr LS17 . . . 44 B5
Wike Ridge La LS17 . . . 44 C7
Wike Ridge Mews LS17 . . . 44 B5
Wike Ridge Mount LS17 . . 44 B5
Wike Ridge View LS17 . . 44 A5
Wilberlee HD7 . . . 151 D2
Wilberlee Jun & Inf Sch HD7 . . . 151 D2
Wilby St BD19 . . . 116 D7
Wilcock La BD20 . . . 4 F5
Wilcroft Terr HX7 . . . 89 B8
Wild's Yd WF1 . . . 216 C1
Wilday Cl BD16 . . . 36 E6
Wildfell Mews BD13 . . . 72 E6
Wild Gr LS28 . . . 76 A7
Wild Heather Cl BD13 . . . 52 C5
Wildspur Gr HD9 . . . 189 E4
Wildspur Mills HD9 . . . 189 E5
Wild Wood Rise OL14 . . . 86 C1
Wilford Rd S71 . . . 178 E1
Wilfred Ave LS15 . . . 81 B8
Wilfred St
Bradford BD14 . . . 73 D4
2 Leeds LS15 . . . 81 B8
Wilfrid Terr LS12 . . . 78 A4
Wilkinson Fold 9 BD12 . . 94 C3
Wilkinson Ho OL14 . . . 107 E8
Wilkinson Terr BD7 . . . 73 F6
Wilkinson Way LS21 . . . 10 E1
Wilkin St BD21 . . . 35 B7
Willan's Rd WF13 . . . 118 C1
Willans Ave LS26 . . . 100 E7
Willerton Cl WF12 . . . 119 B3
Willgutter La BD22 . . . 33 F1
William Ave 2 LS15 . . . 80 E8
William Fison Ride LS29 . . 21 D8
William Foster Way LS29 . 21 D8
William Henry Smith Sch HD6 . . . 135 E8
William Henry St
1 Brighouse HD6 . . . 115 A3
2 Shipley BD18 . . . 54 F8
William Hey Ct LS9 . . . 208 B2
William Horsfall St HD4 . 153 C3
William Prince Gr WF1 . . 142 E4
William Rise LS15 . . . 80 E8
William Royd La WF16 . . 117 E5
Williams Ct 13 LS28 . . . 57 D3
Williams Dr BD20 . . . 17 B5
Williamson St HX1 . . . 202 C4
Williams Rd BD20 . . . 17 B5
William St
Batley WF13 . . . 117 F3
Bradford BD1, BD5 . . . 201 B2
Bradford, Buttershaw BD6 . 93 F7
Bradford, Swain Green BD4 75 D5
Bradford, Tong Street BD4 . 75 D1
10 Brighouse HD6 . . . 115 A1
Castleford, New Fryston WF10 . . . 104 C2
Castleford WF10 . . . 103 D1
Denholme BD13 . . . 52 D1
Dewsbury, Ravensthorpe WF13 . . . 138 E5
Dewsbury WF12 . . . 139 E8
Elland HX4 . . . 134 D6
3 Huddersfield HD1 . . . 154 B7
Huddersfield, Paddock Brow HD4 . . . 153 C4
William St *continued*
Leeds LS6 . . . 205 B3
2 Liversedge WF15 . . . 117 B4
Morley LS27 . . . 98 C8
Pudsey LS28 . . . 57 F2
8 Pudsey, Stanningley LS28 . . . 57 D1
Wakefield WF1 . . . 216 C1
William View LS15 . . . 80 E8
Willis St LS9 . . . 212 B3
Willoughby Terr LS11 . . . 210 C1
Willow App LS4 . . . 205 B1
Willow Ave
Bradford BD2 . . . 56 A6
Clifford LS23 . . . 30 D6
Leeds LS4 . . . 205 B1
Willow Bank
Halifax HX1 . . . 202 C1
Huddersfield HD2 . . . 135 F2
Luddenden Foot HX2 . . . 111 D6
Todmorden OL14 . . . 108 B6
Willow Bank Cl BD15 . . . 73 B7
Willow Bank Dr WF8 . . . 125 E3
Willowbank Gr HD5 . . . 137 B1
Willow Beck WF4 . . . 179 A6
Willowbridge Cl WF10 . . 124 A5
Willowbridge La WF10 . . 124 A6
Willowbridge Rd WF8 . . . 166 F5
Willowbridge Way WF10 123 F5
Willowbrook DN6 . . . 184 F2
Willow Cl
Bradford BD6 . . . 94 C7
Burley in W LS29 . . . 9 E1
Cleckheaton BD19 . . . 117 B7
Guiseley LS20 . . . 22 E1
Halifax HX2 . . . 112 D6
Leeds LS4 . . . 205 B1
Skelmanthorpe HD8 . . . 175 A1
Willow Clough HX6 . . . 132 D2
Willow Cres
Bradford BD2 . . . 56 A6
Clifford LS23 . . . 30 D6
Leeds LS15 . . . 80 F7
Normanton WF6 . . . 144 A8
Sowerby Bridge HX6 . . . 112 C5
Willow Croft
Cleckheaton BD19 . . . 116 C7
Menston LS29 . . . 22 A4
Willow Ct
Batley WF17 . . . 118 C6
Castleford WF10 . . . 124 E6
Featherstone WF7 . . . 124 C1
Pool LS21 . . . 24 D6
Wakefield WF2 . . . 141 D7
Willow Dene Ave HX2 . . . 112 D5
Willowdene La WF8 . . . 125 D3
Willow Dr
Bradford BD6 . . . 94 C7
Halifax HX2 . . . 112 D6
Havercroft WF4 . . . 180 B8
Hemsworth WF9 . . . 181 D5
Wakefield WF1 . . . 142 E3
Willow Field HD8 . . . 156 A3
Willowfield Ave HX2 . . . 112 D5
Willowfield Cl HX2 . . . 112 D6
Willowfield Cres
Bradford BD2 . . . 56 A6
Halifax HX2 . . . 112 D6
Willowfield Dr HX2 . . . 112 D5
Willowfield Rd HX2 . . . 112 D6
Willowfield St BD7 . . . 74 B6
Willowfield Terr HX2 . . . 202 A1
Willowfield View HX2 . . . 112 D6
Willow Fold WF2 . . . 141 F7
Willow Garth
Crigglestone WF4 . . . 159 F6
Featherstone WF7 . . . 124 C1
Leeds LS4 . . . 205 B1
South Elmsall WF9 . . . 183 B2
Willow Garth Ave
Glusburn BD20 . . . 16 D7
Leeds LS14 . . . 62 B8
Willowgarth Cl WF4 . . . 180 A8
Willow Garth Cl LS14 . . . 62 B8
Willowgarth High Sch S72 . . . 181 A1
Willow Gdns
Bradford BD2 . . . 56 A6
Castleford WF10 . . . 125 D5
Guiseley LS20 . . . 22 E1
Halifax HX2 . . . 202 A1
Wakefield WF2 . . . 141 D7
Willow Glade LS23 . . . 30 D5
Willow Gn WF1 . . . 121 B3
Willow Gr
Bradford BD2 . . . 56 A6
Clifford LS23 . . . 30 D6
Huddersfield HD7 . . . 152 E5
Keighley BD21 . . . 35 A3
Kippax LS25 . . . 82 F3
Ossett WF5 . . . 140 E3
Wakefield WF1 . . . 142 E3
Willow Hall Dr HX6 . . . 112 D5
Willow Hall Fold HX6 . . . 112 D5
Willow Hall La HX6 . . . 112 D5
Willow Hos HX6 . . . 112 D5
Willow La
Castleford WF10 . . . 125 F7
Clifford LS23 . . . 30 D5
Crofton WF1 . . . 143 D7
Featherstone WF7 . . . 124 C1
Huddersfield HD1 . . . 154 A8
Wakefield WF2 . . . 141 D7
Willow La E
Featherstone WF7 . . . 124 C1
Huddersfield HD1 . . . 154 B8
Willow Mews WF2 . . . 141 F6
Willowmore Fold WF7 . . 145 C6
Willow Mount WF2 . . . 141 F7
Willow Park Dr HX3 . . . 93 D6
Willow Park Jun Sch WF8 . . . 146 F8
Willow Pk
Lofthouse Gate WF1 . . . 121 B2
Pontefract WF8 . . . 146 F8
Willow Rd
Batley WF17 . . . 118 E4
Castleford WF10 . . . 124 D6
Knottingley WF11 . . . 127 A5
Leeds LS4 . . . 205 B1
Pudsey LS28 . . . 57 D2
Thurnscoe S63 . . . 194 D1
Wakefield WF2 . . . 141 D7
Willow Rise HX2 . . . 112 D6
Willow Sq 3 LS26 . . . 101 C5
Willow St
Bradford BD8 . . . 74 A8
Cleckheaton BD19 . . . 95 D1
Halifax HX1 . . . 202 C2
Sowerby Bridge HX6 . . . 112 D4
Willows The
Baildon BD17 . . . 37 E2
Crigglestone WF4 . . . 159 F5
Halifax HX2 . . . 91 E7
Harden BD16 . . . 36 B1
Horbury WF4 . . . 141 A1
8 Leeds LS17 . . . 43 C2
Willow Terr
Batley WF17 . . . 118 E4
Sowerby Bridge HX6 . . . 112 C5
Willow Terrace Rd LS1 . . 206 B1
Willow Tree Cl BD21 . . . 35 D5
Willow Tree Gdns
Bingley BD16 . . . 37 C5
Burley in W LS29 . . . 9 F2
Willow Vale LS22 . . . 13 E7
Willow View
Sowerby Bridge HX6 . . . 112 C5
Wakefield WF2 . . . 141 F7
Willow Villas BD2 . . . 56 A6
Willow Way BD20 . . . 16 C4
Willow Well Rd LS15 . . . 80 F8
Willow Wlk
Fitzwilliam WF9 . . . 163 B2
Liversedge WF15 . . . 117 A3
Wills Gill LS20 . . . 22 F1
Willwood Ave HD3 . . . 153 B7
Wilman Dr WF5 . . . 140 C6
Wilman Hill 3 BD6 . . . 74 B1
Wilman Post WF5 . . . 140 C6
Wilmar Dr HD3 . . . 134 E1
Wilmer Dr
Shipley, Frizinghall BD18 . . . 55 A5
Shipley, Heaton Grove BD9 . 55 A4
Wilmer Rd BD9 . . . 55 A3
Wilmington Gr LS7 . . . 206 C2
Wilmington St LS7 . . . 207 A2
Wilmington Terr LS7 . . . 206 C2
Wilmot Rd LS29 . . . 8 C4
Wilmur Mount HX2 . . . 111 E6
Wilsden Hill Rd BD15 . . . 53 B5
Wilsden Old Rd BD16 . . . 36 B1
Wilsden Prim Sch BD15 . . 53 C5
Wilsden Rd
Bradford BD15 . . . 53 F3
Harden BD16 . . . 36 B1
Wilshaw Mill Rd HD9 . . . 188 B7
Wilshaw Rd HD9 . . . 188 B8
Wilson's Row LS26 . . . 102 F3
Wilson Ave
Mirfield WF14 . . . 137 F5
Ossett WF5 . . . 141 A4
Steeton BD20 . . . 17 B6
Wilson Cl OL14 . . . 108 A8
Wilson Ct WF1 . . . 121 C4
Wilson Dr WF1 . . . 121 B4
Wilson Fold BD12 . . . 94 D5
Wilson Gdns 5 HD3 . . . 153 A4
Wilson Rd
Bingley BD16 . . . 36 F4
Bradford BD12 . . . 94 E4
Halifax HX1 . . . 202 B1
Mirfield WF14 . . . 137 F5
Wilson St
Bradford BD8 . . . 55 C1
Castleford WF10 . . . 124 C8
Featherstone WF7 . . . 145 C5
Glusburn BD20 . . . 16 D7
Pontefract WF8 . . . 125 D1
Sutton-in-C BD20 . . . 16 E5
Wilsons Yd 6 LS28 . . . 57 D1
Wilson Terr WF14 . . . 137 F5
Wilson Wood St WF17 . . . 118 C2
Wilton Ave HD2 . . . 136 E5
Wilton Gr LS6 . . . 59 E6
Wilton Ind Ct WF17 . . . 117 F8
Wilton Rd LS29 . . . 8 A3
Wilton St
Bradford BD5 . . . 201 B2
Brighouse HD6 . . . 114 F3
Dewsbury WF12 . . . 139 D7
Wilton Terr BD19 . . . 116 D7
Wimborne Dr
Bradford BD15 . . . 54 C1
Keighley BD21 . . . 34 F8
Winbrooke Terr BD6 . . . 74 A1
Winburg Rd BD7 . . . 74 A5
Winchester Bsns Pk BD4 . 75 D4
Winchester Cl WF2 . . . 120 D1
Winchester Gdns BD4 . . . 75 D5
Winchester Ho
3 Huddersfield HD5 . . . 154 D6
8 Sowerby Bridge HX6 . . 112 C4
Winchester St LS12 . . . 210 A3
Winchester Way WF9 . . . 183 A4
Winden Cl
Crigglestone WF4 . . . 159 D
Lofthouse Gate WF3 . . . 121 C
Winden Gr WF3 . . . 121 B
Windermere Ave LS29 . . . 22 A
Windermere Dr
Garforth LS25 . . . 82 F
Knottingley WF11 . . . 126 E
Leeds LS17 . . . 42 F6
Windermere Rd
Bacup OL13 . . . 106 A
Baildon BD17 . . . 37 F
Batley WF12 . . . 118 E2
Bradford BD7 . . . 73 E
Castleford WF10 . . . 125 D
Meltham HD9 . . . 170 E
Wakefield WF2 . . . 141 F
Windermere Rise BD19 . . 115 B6
Windermere Terr 3 BD7 . 73 E
Winders Dale 2 LS27 . . . 98 A6
Windgate BD20 . . . 17 F8
Windhill Ave S75 . . . 178 A
Windhill CE Prim Sch BD18 . . . 55 D7
Windhill Cres
Darton S75 . . . 178 A3
Wakefield WF1 . . . 142 E8
Windhill Ct WF1 . . . 142 F8
Windhill Dr S75 . . . 178 A3
Windhill La S75 . . . 178 A3
Windhill Mount S75 . . . 178 A3
Windhill Old Rd BD10 . . . 38 F1
Windhill Rd WF1 . . . 142 F8
Windhill View WF1 . . . 216 C4
Winding Rd HX1 . . . 203 C3
Winding Rise BD19 . . . 115 B7
Winding Way LS17 . . . 43 B5
Windle Edge S36 . . . 199 D1
Windle La BD20 . . . 4 A2
Windle Royd La HX2 . . . 112 C7
Windmill App LS10 . . . 99 E8
Windmill Ave S72 . . . 181 A1
Windmill Chase LS26 . . . 100 E4
Windmill Cl LS10 . . . 99 E7
Windmill Cotts LS15 . . . 81 F6
Windmill Cres
Northowram HX3 . . . 93 A2
Skelmanthorpe HD8 . . . 175 B1
Windmill Ct
Leeds, Blue Hill LS12 . . . 209 A2
Leeds, Whinmoor LS14 . . . 62 B6
Windmill Dr HX3 . . . 93 A2
Windmill Field Rd LS26 . . 100 E4
Windmill Fold 1 LS19 . . . 40 C6
Windmill Gdns LS15 . . . 81 D7
Windmill Gn LS26 . . . 100 E4
Windmill Gr BD19 . . . 117 B6
Windmill Hill
Bradford BD6 . . . 74 A1
Northowram HX3 . . . 93 A2
Pudsey LS28 . . . 76 C6
Windmill Hill La
Emley HD8 . . . 174 F8
Flockton WF4 . . . 156 F1
Windmill La
Batley WF17 . . . 97 A1
Bradford BD6 . . . 74 C1
Guiseley LS20 . . . 22 D4
Rothwell LS26 . . . 100 E4
Shepley HD8 . . . 190 D3
Yeadon LS19 . . . 40 C6
Windmill Pl 2 LS19 . . . 40 C6
Windmill Prim Sch LS10 . . 99 E8
Windmill Rd
Bramham LS23 . . . 30 E4
Leeds LS10 . . . 99 E8
Windmill Rise
Aberford LS25 . . . 64 E6
Leeds LS12 . . . 209 A2
Windmill Terr HD4 . . . 171 F8
Windmill View HD9 . . . 189 C2
Windross Cl WF6 . . . 123 A4
Windsor Ave
Ackworth M T WF7 . . . 164 C7
Leeds LS15 . . . 81 B8
Silsden BD20 . . . 5 D1
Windsor Cl
Batley WF12 . . . 119 B2
Kippax LS25 . . . 83 A2
Normanton WF6 . . . 123 C1
Windsor Cres
Halifax HX2 . . . 91 E1
Oakworth BD22 . . . 34 B2
Rothwell LS26 . . . 100 E6
Wakefield WF1 . . . 121 A1
Windsor Ct
Batley WF12 . . . 119 A2
12 Bradford BD5 . . . 201 B1
4 Leeds LS13 . . . 58 D1
Leeds, Moor Allerton LS17 . 43 E2
5 Morley LS27 . . . 98 A4
2 Shipley BD18 . . . 55 B7
Windsor Dr
Huddersfield HD5 . . . 155 A6
Knottingley WF11 . . . 126 B5
Liversedge WF15 . . . 117 B2
Skelmanthorpe HD8 . . . 175 B1
Windsor Gdns WF12 . . . 119 B2
Windsor Gn LS25 . . . 83 B7
Windsor Gr
Oakworth BD22 . . . 34 B2
Thornton BD13 . . . 72 D6
Windsor Mount LS15 . . . 81 B8
Windsor Oval WF3 . . . 119 D5
Windsor Pl
6 Hebden Bridge HX7 . . . 89 A4
Huddersfield HD2 . . . 136 E5

Windsor Rd
Batley, Chidswell WF17 ... 119 B2
Batley, Copley Hill WF17 ... 97 B2
Hebden Bridge HX7 ...... 89 A4
Hemsworth WF9 .... 181 F6
Huddersfield HD4 .... 152 F3
Oakworth BD22 .... 34 B2
Shipley BD18 .... 55 B7
Todmorden OL14 .... 108 A6
Wakefield WF2 .... 120 F1
Windsor Rise WF8 ...... 146 B5
Windsor St
Bradford BD4 .... 201 D1
Halifax HX1 .... 203 B2
South Elmsall WF9 .... 183 A2
Windsor Terr LS27 ...... 97 D7
Windsor View
Batley WF12 .... 119 B2
1 Hebden Bridge HX7 ... 89 A4
Windsor Wlk
Batley WF17 .... 97 B2
Brighouse HX3 .... 115 A6
Windy Bank La
Cleckheaton WF15 .... 116 B4
Queensbury BD13 .... 92 B6
Windy Gr BD15 .... 53 D4
Windy Harbour La OL14 .. 87 B1
Windyridge St WF4 ..... 140 F2
Wine St LS1 .... 211 B4
Wine Tavern La HX6 .... 111 B3
Wine Tavern Rd HX6 .... 111 B3
Winfield Dr
Birkenshaw BD4 .... 95 E6
Huddersfield HD3 .... 152 F8
Winfield Gr 4 LS2 ..... 206 B2
Winfield Pl 1 LS2 ..... 206 B2
Winfield Terr 2 LS2 .... 206 B2
Wingate Ave BD22 ...... 34 F6
Wingate Croft WF2 ..... 160 F8
Wingate Gr WF2 .... 160 F8
Wingate Way BD22 ...... 34 F6
Winget Ave HD4 .... 152 F3
Wingfield Ct BD16 ...... 37 A4
Wingfield Mount BD3 .... 75 B8
Wingfield St BD3 .... 75 B8
Winmarith St S71 .... 179 B3
Winney Bank La HD9 .... 189 C5
Winnipeg Pl LS7 .... 204 A2
Winnow La LS23 .... 30 B7
Winrose App LS10 ...... 99 E7
Winrose Ave LS10 ...... 215 A1
Winrose Cl BD12 .... 94 C4
Winrose Cres LS10 ..... 99 E8
Winrose Dr LS10 .... 99 D8
Winrose Garth LS10 .... 99 E8
Winrose Gr LS10 .... 99 E8
Winrose Hill LS10 ...... 215 B1
Winscar Ave 4 BD13 .... 73 C2
Winsford Dr HD5 .... 155 B7
Winslow Rd BD10 .... 56 E4
Winstanley Terr LS6 .... 205 B3
Winston Ave BD20 ...... 16 E7
Winston Gdns 2 LS6 .... 59 C5
Winston Mount LS6 ..... 59 C5
Winston Terr BD7 ...... 74 A5
Winter's Cotts HX7 ..... 88 C2
Winter's La HX7 .... 88 C2
Winter Ave S71 .... 179 C5
Winterbourne Ave LS27 . 98 B6
Winterburn La HX2 ..... 112 A6
Winterburn St 1 BD21 .. 35 C8
Winterbutlee Gr 18 OL14 108 A1
Winterbutlee Rd OL14 ... 108 A1
Winter Ct BD15 .... 54 A3
Winter Hill
Elland HD3 .... 152 A7
Halifax HX3 .... 114 A3
Slaithwaite HD7 .... 170 B7
Winterneb HX2 .... 111 E5
Wintersett Cl WF4 ...... 162 A1
Wintersett La WF4 ...... 162 A5
Winter St HX1 .... 202 B1
Winterton Dr BD12 ..... 94 C5
Winthorpe Ave WF3 .... 99 D2
Winthorpe Cres WF3 .... 99 D2
Winthorpe St LS6 ...... 59 F6
Winthorpe View WF3 ... 99 E2
Winton Gn 3 BD6 ...... 94 B6
Winton Mill 22 HX6 .... 112 C4
Winton St HD1 .... 153 E3
Wintoun St LS7 .... 207 A1
Wirefield Rd 8 BD22 ... 35 A4
Wiston Dr WF8 .... 125 E3
Wistons La HX5 .... 135 A7
Witchfield Ct HX3 ...... 93 D6
Witchfield Hill HX3 ..... 93 D6
Witham Rd BD18 .... 54 E8
Witham Way LS25 ...... 83 B6
Withens Ct S75 .... 178 A1
Withens End La HX4 .... 150 E7
Withens Hill Croft HX2 . 91 D7
Withens La
Hebden Bridge HX7 ...... 109 F3
Ripponden HX4 .... 150 F8
Withens New Rd
Halifax HX2 .... 71 B2
Hebden Bridge HX7 ...... 109 E3
Withens Rd
Batley WF17 .... 96 E2
Halifax HX2 .... 91 A4
Withinfield Ct HX3 ..... 114 A4
Withinfields HX3 .... 114 A4
Withinfields Prim Sch
HX3 .... 114 A5
Withins Cl BD5 .... 74 B3
Withyside HD8 .... 192 A6
Witmore St WF9 .... 183 A3
Witton St WF1 .... 216 C3

Woburn Dr HD5 .... 155 B6
Woburn Terr 1 BD14 ... 73 B4
Woburn Way WF6 ...... 123 D1
Wold BD13 .... 72 D6
Wolfstones Rd HD9 ..... 188 D6
Wolley Ave LS12 .... 77 D3
Wolley Ct LS12 .... 77 D3
Wolley Dr LS12 .... 77 D3
Wolley Gdns LS12 ...... 77 D3
Wolseley Rd LS4 .... 205 A2
Wolseley St BD14 ...... 73 C5
Wolseley Terr 1 HX1 ... 202 C3
Wolsey Ave 2 WF8 .... 146 B8
Wolston Cl BD4 .... 75 E2
Womersley Ct LS28 ..... 76 D6
Womersley Pl 4 LS28 ... 76 D6
Womersley Rd WF11 .... 127 B2
Womersley St 1 HX1 ... 202 B3
Wonder St WF1 .... 216 C1
Wood's Row LS28 ...... 57 C1
Woodacre Cres LS17 .... 28 C3
Woodacre Gn LS17 ..... 28 C4
Woodacre La LS17 ..... 28 C4
Woodale Ave BD9 ...... 54 D3
Woodalls Bldgs WF11 ... 127 A4
Wood Ave WF16 .... 117 D5
Wood Bank Sch HX2 ... 111 E8
Woodbine Ave 5 WF8 .. 146 C8
Woodbine Gr BD10 ..... 56 B7
Woodbine Pl
Hebden Bridge HX7 ...... 88 E3
Mytholmroyd HX7 .... 110 F8
Woodbine Rd HD1 ...... 136 B1
Woodbine St
Bradford BD1 .... 201 D3
6 Halifax HX1 .... 202 C1
Ossett WF5 .... 140 D7
Woodbine Terr
Bradford BD6 .... 56 B7
Clayton West HD8 .... 175 F3
7 Halifax HX1 .... 202 C1
9 Horsforth LS18 .... 58 C7
Leeds, Bramley LS13 .... 58 E2
Leeds, Headingley LS6 .. 59 E6
Todmorden OL14 .... 86 B1
Wood Bottom La HD6 .. 114 E4
Wood Bottom Rd HD4 .. 171 C5
Woodbourne LS8 .... 61 C7
Woodbourne Ave LS17 .. 43 C5
Woodbridge Ave LS25 .. 83 B8
Woodbridge Cl
Leeds LS6 .... 59 B5
Wakefield WF1 .... 142 E6
Woodbridge Cres LS6 .. 59 A6
Woodbridge Fold LS6 ... 59 A5
Woodbridge Garth LS6 . 59 A5
Woodbridge Gdns LS6 .. 59 A5
Woodbridge Gn LS6 .... 59 B5
Woodbridge Lawn LS6 .. 59 A5
Woodbridge Pl LS6 ..... 59 A5
Woodbridge Rd LS6 .... 59 A5
Woodbridge Vale LS6 ... 59 B5
Woodbrook Ave HX2 ... 91 C5
Woodbrook Cl HX2 ..... 91 C5
Woodbrook Pl HX2 ..... 91 C5
Woodbrook Rd HX2 .... 91 C5
Woodburn Ave WF12 ... 139 F6
Woodbury Rd BD8 ..... 55 B2
Woodchurch View HD9 . 189 B8
Wood Cl
Baildon BD17 .... 38 B2
Fitzwilliam WF9 .... 163 A2
Leeds LS7 .... 60 C7
Low Bradley BD20 ...... 4 C5
Normanton WF6 .... 122 E3
Rothwell LS26 .... 100 D6
Wood Close Bottom
HD7 .... 170 C8
Woodcock St WF1 ...... 142 D4
Woodcock Way WF1 .... 183 A4
Woodcot Ave BD17 ..... 38 D2
Wood Cote Fold BD22 .. 34 B6
Wood Cres LS26 .... 100 D6
Woodcroft WF2 .... 142 E1
Wood Croft
Brighouse HD6 .... 114 F1
Sowerby Bridge HX4 .... 114 F1
Woodcroft Grange HX2 . 112 D6
Woodcross LS27 .... 98 A6
Woodcross End LS27 ... 98 A7
Woodcross Fold LS27 ... 98 A7
Woodcross Garth LS27 . 98 A7
Woodcross Gdns LS27 .. 98 A6
Wood Dr LS26 .... 100 C6
Woodedge Ave HD5 .... 155 A6
Woodend WF10 .... 102 F6
Wood End
4 Huddersfield HD4 .... 153 F3
Shepley HD8 .... 190 C8
Wood End Cl HX3 ...... 113 B3
Wood End Cotts WF14 . 137 F4
Woodend Cres WF10 ... 102 F5
Wood End Cres BD18 .. 55 D8
Woodend Ct BD5 ...... 74 F2
Wood End La
Ripponden HX4 .... 133 D6
Shepley HD8 .... 190 C7
Woodend Rd WF14 ..... 137 F4
Wood End Rd HD4 ..... 171 E8
Woodeson Ct LS13 ..... 57 F5
Woodeson Lea LS13 .... 57 F5
Wood Farm La HD9 .... 172 C2
Woodfield Ave
Batley WF17 .... 118 A4
Elland HX4 .... 134 B7
Woodfield Cl BD10 ..... 56 D8
Woodfield Ct HD2 ...... 153 F8

Woodfield Dr
Elland HX4 .... 134 C6
Low Bradley BD20 ...... 4 C5
Woodfield Pk WF2 ..... 161 A6
Woodfield Rd
Cullingworth BD13 ...... 52 E7
Norton DN6 .... 184 E8
Woodfield St OL14 ..... 108 A6
Woodfield Terr LS28 .... 76 F6
Woodford Ave HX3 ..... 113 D4
Woodford Cl BD15 ..... 73 A8
Woodford Dr HD5 ...... 155 B7
Woodgarth Gdns BD4 .. 75 F3
Wood Gn WF10 .... 123 F5
Wood Gr
Leeds LS12 .... 77 D7
Ossett WF5 .... 140 D8
Woodhall Ave
Bradford BD3 .... 56 E1
Leeds LS8 .... 58 E6
Woodhall Cl
Crigglestone WF4 .... 159 F6
Middlestown WF4 .... 158 A6
Pudsey LS28 .... 57 A2
Woodhall Cres HX3 ..... 113 A3
Woodhall Croft LS28 ... 57 A2
Woodhall Ct
Leeds LS15 .... 81 D6
Pudsey LS28 .... 57 A5
Woodhall Dr
Ackworth M T WF7 ...... 163 F6
Batley WF17 .... 118 A4
Leeds LS5 .... 58 E6
Woodhall Gr LS26 ...... 102 D3
Woodhall La LS28 ...... 57 A2
Woodhall Park Ave LS28 57 B2
Woodhall Park Cres E
LS28 .... 57 B1
Woodhall Park Cres W
LS28 .... 57 A1
Woodhall Park Croft LS28 57 B1
Woodhall Park Dr LS28 . 57 B1
Woodhall Park Garth LS28 57 A2
Woodhall Park Mount
LS28 .... 57 A2
Woodhall Pl BD3 .... 56 E1
Woodhall Rd
Bradford BD2, BD3, LS28 56 E2
Pudsey, Calverley LS28 .. 57 A5
Woodhall Terr BD3 ..... 56 E1
Woodhall View BD3 .... 56 F1
Woodhead Cl
Huddersfield HD2 .... 136 C3
2 Ossett WF5 .... 140 D6
Woodhead La
Brighouse HD6 .... 115 E2
Gildersome LS27 .... 97 C7
Woodhead Rd
Batley WF17 .... 97 B4
Bradford BD7 .... 74 B6
Brockholes HD9 .... 172 B3
Holmfirth, Hinchcliffe Mill
HD9 .... 188 D3
Huddersfield HD4 .... 153 E2
Woodhead St
14 Cleckheaton BD19 ... 116 E7
Halifax HX2 .... 202 A4
Wood Hey La HX7 ...... 89 B1
Wood Hill LS26 .... 100 D6
Wood Hill Cres LS16 .... 41 C3
Wood Hill Ct LS16 ...... 41 D4
Wood Hill Garth LS16 .. 41 D4
Wood Hill Gdns LS16 ... 41 D4
Wood Hill Gr LS16 ..... 41 D4
Wood Hill Rd LS16 ..... 41 D4
Woodhill Rise HD10 .... 56 E8
Wood Hill Rise LS16 .... 41 D4
Woodhill View LS22 .... 13 E6
Woodhouse Ave
Huddersfield HD2 .... 136 C2
Keighley BD21 .... 35 C5
Woodhouse Cl
East Ardsley WF3 .... 120 B6
Keighley BD21 .... 35 C5
Woodhouse Cliff LS6 ... 206 A4
Woodhouse Cotts HD3 . 151 D5
Woodhouse Cres WF6 .. 144 B8
Woodhouse Dr BD21 ... 35 C5
Woodhouse Flats LS2 ... 206 A2
Woodhouse Gdns HD6 .. 136 C8
Woodhouse Gr
Huddersfield HD2 .... 136 C2
Keighley BD21 .... 35 C5
Todmorden OL14 .... 108 D5
Woodhouse Grove Sch
BD10 .... 39 F1
Woodhouse Hall Rd HD2 136 C2
Woodhouse Hill HD2 .... 136 C2
Woodhouse Hill Ave
LS10 .... 215 B2
Woodhouse Hill Gr 8
LS10 .... 215 B2
Woodhouse Hill Pl LS10 215 B2
Woodhouse Hill Rd LS10 215 B2
Woodhouse Hill Terr 5
LS10 .... 215 B2
Woodhouse La
Brighouse HD6 .... 136 B8
East Ardsley WF3 .... 120 B5
Emley HD8 .... 176 A7
Halifax HX3 .... 113 A3
Holmfirth HD9 .... 188 D1
Woolley WF4, S75 ...... 178 B5
Woodhouse Mill OL14 .. 108 E5
Woodhouse Mount WF6 144 A8

Woodhouse Prim Sch
HD6 .... 136 B8
Woodhouse Rd
Keighley BD21 .... 35 C4
Todmorden OL14 .... 108 E6
Wakefield WF1 .... 142 F7
Woodhouse Sq 7 LS3 .. 206 A1
Woodhouse St LS6 ..... 206 A3
Woodhouse Terr 12 BD6 94 D8
Woodhouse Way HX3 .. 35 C5
Woodhouse Wlk BD21 . 35 C5
Woodkirk Ave WF3 .... 119 D8
Woodkirk Gdns WF12 .. 119 B6
Woodkirk Gr
Bradford BD12 .... 94 C1
East Ardsley WF3 .... 119 D8
Woodkirk High Specialist
Science Sch WF3 ..... 119 C8
Woodkirk Int Freight
Terminal WF12 .... 119 B6
Wood La
Bardsey LS14 .... 28 E3
Barnsley S71 .... 179 C1
Barwick in E LS15 ..... 62 E6
Batley WF17 .... 118 D3
Bradford BD2 .... 55 F5
Brighouse, Hipperholme
HX3 .... 114 B8
Brighouse HX3 .... 114 D2
Castleford WF10 .... 123 F5
Crigglestone WF4 ...... 160 B3
Darton S71 .... 178 E2
Denby Dale HD8 .... 191 E6
Dewsbury WF13 .... 118 D1
Gildersome LS12 .... 77 E2
Halifax HX2 .... 91 E2
Holmfirth HD9 .... 189 A6
Horsforth LS18 .... 58 C8
Huddersfield HD4 ...... 154 C3
Kippax LS26 .... 102 E7
Kirkburton HD8 .... 173 C4
Kirkheaton WF14 ...... 137 E4
Leeds, Chapel Allerton LS7 60 C7
Leeds, Far Headingley LS6 59 E5
Leeds, Farnley LS12 .... 77 D7
Leeds, New Blackpool LS12 78 A3
Leeds, Whitecote LS13 . 58 C4
Netherton WF4, WF12 .. 157 E7
Northowram HX3 .... 93 B1
Pudsey LS28 .... 57 B7
Rothwell LS26 .... 100 D6
Slaithwaite HD7 .... 169 F5
Sowerby Bridge HX6 ... 111 E4
Thorp Arch LS23 ...... 14 E3
Wadsworth Moor HX2 .. 90 B5
Woodland Ave
Crofton WF1 .... 143 C7
Swillington LS26 .... 82 A1
Woodland Cl
Bradford BD9 .... 54 C4
Crigglestone WF4 ...... 159 F2
Leeds LS15 .... 81 C8
Woodland Cres
Rothwell LS26 .... 100 D6
Shipley BD9 .... 54 C4
Swillington LS26 .... 82 A1
Woodland Croft
Horsforth LS18 .... 41 C2
Thorp Arch LS23 ...... 15 A3
Woodland Ct
Bingley BD16 .... 36 E5
Leeds LS8 .... 61 A5
Thorp Arch LS23 ...... 14 F3
Woodland Dell HX7 .... 88 C2
Woodland Dr
Brighouse HD6 .... 114 F1
Leeds LS7 .... 204 A3
Sowerby Bridge HX2 ... 112 D5
Swillington LS26 ...... 81 F1
Thorp Arch LS23 ...... 14 F3
Wakefield WF2 .... 160 B6
Woodland Gr
Ackworth M T WF7 ..... 146 A1
Dewsbury WF13 .... 138 F8
Leeds LS7 .... 207 B4
Shipley BD9 .... 54 C5
Swillington LS26 ...... 82 A1
Woodland Hall HX7 .... 88 A4
Woodland Hill LS15 .... 81 B8
Woodland La LS7 ...... 204 A3
Woodland Mdws HD8 .. 173 F7
Woodland Mews LS7 ... 207 B4
Woodland Mount 1 LS7 207 B4
Woodland Park Rd LS6 . 59 E5
Woodland Pk LS26 ..... 101 C5
Woodland Rd
Huddersfield HD2 ...... 136 F2
Leeds LS15 .... 81 B8
Wakefield WF2 .... 141 D5
Woodland Rise
Huddersfield HD2 ...... 135 F1
Leeds LS15 .... 81 C8
Wakefield WF2 .... 141 D6
Woodlands
Crofton WF4 .... 143 F1
East Ardsley WF3 ...... 120 C7
Horbury WF4 .... 141 C6
Ilkley LS29 .... 8 D4
Leeds LS17 .... 43 E2
Ossett WF5 .... 140 D7
Sowerby Bridge HX6 ... 111 F2
Woodlands Ave
Bradford BD13 .... 73 B1
Castleford WF10 .... 125 C4
Cleckheaton BD19 ...... 96 A1
Halifax HX3 .... 92 C1
Holmfirth HD9 .... 189 C8
Lepton HD8 .... 155 E3

Woodlands Ave continued
Pudsey LS28 .... 57 C1
Todmorden OL14 .... 108 B6
Woodlands CE Prim Sch
BD12 .... 95 A4
Woodlands Cl
Denby Dale HD8 .... 192 A6
East Ardsley WF3 ...... 120 C7
Huddersfield HD2 ...... 137 A6
Ilkley LS29 .... 7 E4
Pudsey BD10 .... 39 F1
Scarcroft LS14 .... 45 C8
Woodlands Cres
Cleckheaton BD19 ...... 96 A1
Hemsworth WF9 .... 181 E8
Woodlands Croft LS25 . 103 B8
Woodlands Ct
8 Bradford BD8 .... 74 C8
Kippax LS25 .... 103 B8
Leeds LS16 .... 42 B1
Woodlands Dr
Cleckheaton BD19 ...... 96 A1
East Ardsley WF3 ...... 120 C7
Garforth LS25 .... 83 B6
Lepton HD8 .... 155 E2
Morley LS27 .... 97 F6
Pudsey BD10 .... 39 F1
Skelmanthorpe HD8 .... 175 B1
Yeadon LS19 .... 40 C2
Woodlands End HD8 ... 155 E3
Woodlands Fold BD11 . 96 B5
Woodlands Glade BD17 37 F2
Woodlands Gr
Baildon BD17 .... 37 F2
Bradford BD13 .... 73 B1
Halifax HX3 .... 92 C1
Ilkley LS29 .... 7 E4
Kippax LS25 .... 103 C8
Pudsey LS28 .... 57 C1
Shipley BD16 .... 54 B7
Woodlands La WF13 ... 138 F8
Woodlands Mount WF2 92 C2
Woodlands Park Gr LS28 76 D5
Woodlands Park Rd LS28 76 D5
Woodlands Pk
Bradford BD19 .... 95 B3
Scarcroft LS14 .... 45 C8
Woodlands Prim Sch
LS9 .... 208 B3
Woodlands Sq
Brighouse HD6 .... 115 C1
1 Leeds LS12 .... 77 F8
Woodlands Rd
Batley WF17 .... 118 A8
Bingley BD16 .... 37 C4
2 Bradford BD8 .... 55 A1
Bradford, Little Moor BD13 73 A1
Cleckheaton BD19 ..... 96 A1
Halifax HX5 .... 134 F8
Halifax, Woodlands HX3 92 C1
Lepton HD8 .... 155 E3
Woodlands Rd E HD8 .. 155 D3
Woodlands Rise
Haworth BD22 .... 51 C6
Ilkley LS29 .... 7 E4
Woodlands St BD8 ..... 74 C8
Woodlands Terr
Bradford BD8 .... 55 A1
Bradford, Lower Woodlands
BD12 .... 95 B5
Pudsey LS28 .... 57 C1
Woodlands The
Hebden Bridge HX7 .... 89 A2
Meltham HD9 .... 170 E1
Pontefract WF8 .... 146 E6
Woodlands View
8 Halifax HX3 .... 92 C1
Kippax LS25 .... 103 C8
Leeds LS17 .... 44 A3
Scarcroft LS14 .... 45 C7
Woodlands Way HD8 .. 155 E2
Woodland Terr LS7 .... 60 A7
Woodland View
Blackshaw Head HX7 ... 88 C2
Crofton WF1 .... 143 C4
East Ardsley WF3 ...... 119 D6
Leeds LS7 .... 204 A3
Pontefract WF8 .... 146 E6
Wakefield WF2 .... 57 A7
Wood Lane Ct LS6 .... 59 E5
Woodlark Cl BD6 ...... 73 D1
Woodlea
Boston Spa LS23 ...... 30 D8
6 South Elmsall WF9 ... 182 F2
Wood Lea
Byram WF11 .... 126 D8
Todmorden OL14 ...... 107 E8
Woodlea App
9 Leeds LS6 .... 42 F1
Yeadon LS19 .... 39 F6
Woodlea Ave
Huddersfield HD3 ...... 153 C6
Leeds LS6 .... 42 F1
Woodlea Chase LS6 .... 59 F8
Woodlea Croft 10 LS6 . 42 F1
Woodlea Ct
Leeds, Blackwood LS17 . 44 B4
Leeds, Meanwood LS6 .. 59 F8
Woodlea Dr
Leeds LS6 .... 42 F1
Yeadon LS19 .... 39 F5
Woodlea Fold LS6 ..... 42 F1
Woodlea Garth LS6 .... 42 F1
Woodlea Gate LS6 ..... 59 F8

Woodlea Gdns LS6 42 F1
Woodlea Gn LS6 42 F1
Woodlea Gr
[1] Leeds, Beeston LS11 213 C3
Leeds, Meanwood LS6 59 F8
Yeadon LS19 39 F6
Woodlea Holt [7] LS6 42 F1
Woodlea La LS6 42 F1
Woodlea Lawn [8] LS6 42 F1
Woodlea Mount
Leeds LS11 214 A3
Yeadon LS19 39 F6
Woodlea Pk LS6 59 F8
Woodlea Pl
Leeds, Beeston Hill LS11 214 A3
Leeds, Meanwood LS6 42 F1
Woodlea Rd LS19 39 F5
Woodlea Sq LS6 59 F8
Woodlea St LS11 213 C3
Woodlea View
Leeds LS6 59 F8
Yeadon LS19 39 F5
Woodleigh HX7 88 E3
Woodleigh Ave
Bradford BD5 74 E1
Garforth LS25 82 E7
Woodleigh Cres WF7 163 F6
Woodleigh Gr HD4 153 C1
Woodleigh Hall Mews
LS19 40 E1
Woodlesford Cres HX2 91 B2
Woodlesford Prim Sch
LS26 101 D7
Woodlesford Sta LS26 101 D7
Woodliffe Cres LS7 60 C7
Woodliffe Ct LS7 60 C7
Woodliffe Dr LS7 60 C7
Woodlock Cl HD2 136 C4
Woodman Ave
Elland HX5 134 F5
Huddersfield HD2 137 A5
Woodman Ct BD6 93 E6
Woodman St LS15 81 A8
Woodmoor Cl WF4 159 E4
Woodmoor Dr WF4 159 E4
Woodmoor Rd WF2 160 B5
Wood Moor Rd WF9 181 F7
Woodmoor Rise WF4 159 E5
Wood Mount
Netherton WF4 157 F6
Rothwell LS26 100 C6
Wood Nook HD8 191 F6
Woodnook Cl LS16 41 D2
Woodnook Dr LS16 41 D3
Woodnook Garth LS16 41 D3
Wood Nook La
Honley HD9 171 C2
Sowerby Bridge HX6 112 C5
Woodnook Rd LS16 41 D3
Wood Nook Terr LS28 57 C1
Wood Park View S71 178 F1
Woodpecker Cl BD15 73 B7
Woodpecker Rd LS29 9 E2
Wood Pit La HD9 189 F3
Wood Pl BD8 74 C8
Wood Rd
Bradford BD5 74 E4
Shipley BD9 55 C4
Wood Row LS26 102 B3
Woodrow Cres LS26 102 A3
Woodrow Dr BD12 94 E6
Woodroyd
Huddersfield HD7 152 C5
Sowerby Bridge HX2 111 F5
Woodroyd Ave
Barnsley S71 179 C1
Bradford BD5 74 F2
Honley HD9 172 B5
Woodroyd Cl S71 179 C1
Woodroyd Cres HX6 112 A5
Woodroyd Dr HX3 91 F2
Woodroyd Gdns
Ilkley LS29 8 F3
Sowerby Bridge HX2 111 F5
Wood Royd Hill La HD9 200 B8
Woodroyd Rd
Bradford BD5 74 E3
Bradford, Marshfields BD5 74 E2
Woodroyd Terr BD5 74 F2
Wood St N HX3 92 B2
Woods Ave HD7 169 B4
Woodside
Castleford WF10 125 C8
Denby Dale HD8 192 A6
Keighley BD20 18 A1
Mickletown LS26 102 A3
Normanton WF6 123 A1
Shipley BD18 55 D8
Wakefield WF2 120 E2
Wood Side HX4 133 D5
Woodside Ave
Crofton WF4 144 C3
Leeds, Burley LS4 59 C2
Leeds LS6 59 F7
Shipley, Cottingley BD16 53 F7
[2] Shipley, Saltaire BD18 54 E8
Wakefield WF2 120 E2
Woodside Cl LS27 98 A6
Woodside Cotts [1] HD3 153 A4
Woodside Cres
Batley WF17 118 A4
Crofton WF4 144 C4
Halifax HX3 92 B1
Shipley BD16 53 F7
Woodside Ct
Cullingworth BD13 52 D6
Horsforth LS18 58 E8
Ilkley LS29 8 A6
Leeds LS16 41 F1
Woodside Dr
Morley LS27 98 A7
Shipley BD16 53 F7
Wakefield WF2 120 E2
Woodside Gdns [6] LS27 98 A7
Woodside Gr
Elland HX4 134 D6
Halifax HX3 92 C1
Kippax WF10 102 F6
Woodside Hill Cl LS18 58 E8
Woodside La
Huddersfield HD2 136 B4
[7] Morley LS27 98 A7
Woodside Lawn LS12 77 D7
Woodside Lo HD8 173 B6
Woodside Mews LS6 59 F7
Woodside Mount HX3 203 A4
Woodside Park Ave LS18 58 D8
Woodside Park Dr LS18 58 D8
Woodside Pl
Halifax HX3 92 B1
Leeds LS4 59 C2
Woodside Prim Sch BD6 94 A6
Woodside Rd
Boston Spa LS23 30 B7
Bradford BD12 94 C4
Halifax HX3 203 A4
Huddersfield HD4 153 D2
Silsden BD20 5 C1
Woodside St WF10 102 F6
Woodside Terr
[6] Elland HX4 134 D6
Halifax HX3 92 C1
[7] Leeds LS4 59 C2
Woodside Veiw HD4 152 F3
Woodside View
Elland HX4 134 D6
Halifax HX3 92 B1
Holmfirth HD9 188 E4
Leeds LS4 59 C2
Lofthouse Gate WF3 121 B8
Shipley BD16 54 A7
Woodsley Gn LS6 205 C2
Woodsley Rd
Bradford BD10 56 A6
Leeds LS2, LS3, LS6 205 C2
Woodsley Terr LS2 206 A1
Woods Mews LS29 8 C4
Woods Mount HD7 169 B4
Woodsome Ave WF14 137 E6
Woodsome Dr
Lepton HD8 155 D2
Mirfield WF14 137 F6
Woodsome Est WF17 118 B4
Woodsome Hall La HD8 173 C8
Woodsome Lees La HD8 173 D7
Woodsome Pk HD8 155 D2
Woodsome Rd HD4, HD8 155 B2
Wood Sq HX3 92 B2
Wood St
[4] Baildon BD17 38 C1
Batley WF17 118 C5
Bradford BD15 54 C1
Bradford, Lister Hills BD8 74 C8
Brighouse HD6 115 B2
Castleford WF10 124 C8
Clayton West HD8 175 D1
Cleckheaton BD19 116 C7
Crofton WF4 144 B3
Dewsbury WF13 118 D1
East Ardsley WF3 120 D8
Elland HX5 135 A6
[5] Haworth BD22 51 C6
Horsforth LS18 41 C2
Huddersfield HD1 154 A6
Huddersfield, Longwood
HD3 153 A5
Huddersfield, Moldgreen
HD5 154 D6
Keighley BD21 35 C6
Morley LS27 97 F5
Ossett WF5 140 D8
Skelmanthorpe HD8 174 F2
Slaithwaite HD7 151 F1
South Hiendley S72 180 F6
Steeton BD20 17 C5
[5] Todmorden OL14 108 B6
Wakefield WF1 216 B2
Woods Terr HD7 169 B4
Woodstock Cl LS16 42 D3
Woodstock Cres HD3 153 B8
Woodstock Wlk BD5 201 B1
Wood Terr HD4 154 A3
Woodthorne Croft LS17 44 A4
Woodthorpe BD13 71 D8
Woodthorpe Cl WF2 160 E7
Woodthorpe Dr WF2 160 E7
Woodthorpe Gdns WF2 160 D6
Woodthorpe Glades
WF2 160 E7
Woodthorpe La WF2 160 E6
Woodthorpe Manor WF2 160 E6
Woodthorpe Park Dr
WF2 160 E7
Woodthorpe Terr HD1 153 F5
Wood Top
Brighouse HD6 114 E5
Hebden Bridge HX7 89 B1
Marsden HD7 168 F3
[3] Shipley BD18 55 D8
Wood Top Rd HX7 89 B2
Woodvale Cl BD4 75 E5
Woodvale Cres BD16 37 A5
Woodvale Gr BD7 73 E5
Wood Vale Office Pk
HD6 115 B4
Woodvale Rd HD6 115 B3
Woodvale Terr LS18 58 D7
Woodvale Way BD7 73 E5
Woodview
Birkenshaw BD11 96 D7
Bradford BD8 55 D3
Wood View
Baildon BD17 38 A2
Castleford WF10 124 A8
Denholme BD13 52 C3
Huddersfield HD2 135 D1
Ilkley LS29 8 D5
Morley LS27 98 C8
Woodview Ave BD17 38 F4
Wood View Ave WF10 124 A7
Wood View Bglws WF10 124 A7
Woodview Cl LS18 41 C2
Wood View Cl WF10 124 A7
Wood View Cres WF10 124 A7
Woodview Ct LS14 62 D5
Wood View Dr BD2 56 D2
Woodview Gr LS11 214 B2
Wood View Gr HD6 114 F4
Woodview Mews LS14 62 D5
Woodview Mount LS11 214 B2
Woodview Pl LS11 214 B2
Woodview Rd
Keighley BD22 34 F4
Leeds LS11 214 B2
Woodview St LS11 214 B2
Woodview Terr
Bradford BD8 55 D3
[8] Keighley BD21 35 B4
Leeds LS11 214 B2
Wood View Terr LS27 98 D8
Wood Villas HX7 88 C1
Woodville Ave
Horsforth LS18 58 D8
Huddersfield HD7 152 E4
Woodville Cres LS18 58 D8
Woodville Ct
Leeds LS8 44 B1
Wakefield WF2 142 C2
Woodville Gr
[9] Haworth BD22 51 F8
Horsforth LS18 58 D8
Middleton LS10 215 B1
Woodville Mount LS10 215 B1
Woodville Pl
Bradford BD9 54 F4
Horsforth LS18 58 E8
Huddersfield HD2 136 E6
Woodville Rd
Dewsbury WF12 139 D8
Keighley BD20 35 B8
Woodville Sq LS10 215 B1
Woodville St
[25] Halifax HX3 92 A1
Horsforth LS18 58 E8
[2] Shipley BD18 55 D8
Woodville Terr
Bradford BD5 201 A1
[10] Haworth BD22 51 F8
Horsforth LS18 58 D8
[1] Shipley BD18 55 D8
Wood Vine St LS28 57 C1
Woodward Ct WF14 138 B7
Woodway
Horsforth LS18 58 C7
Shipley BD16 53 F7
Woodway Dr LS18 58 C7
Wood Wlk S71 179 C5
Woodworth Gr BD21 35 B3
Wood Yard Cotts WF1 161 B8
Woolcomb Ct BD9 55 B2
Woolcombers Hall [6]
BD18 55 B7
Woolcroft Dr HD9 189 C6
Wooldale Cliff Rd HD9 189 B5
Wooldale Jun Sch HD9 189 D6
Wooldale Rd HD9 189 C6
Wooler Ave LS11 214 A2
Wooler Dr LS11 214 A2
Wooler Gr LS11 214 A2
Wooler Pl LS11 213 C2
Wooler Rd LS11 213 C2
Wooler St LS11 213 C2
Woolford Way WF3 121 D6
Wool Gate BD16 54 B7
Woolgreaves Ave WF2 160 D6
Woolgreaves Cl WF2 160 D6
Woolgreaves Croft WF2 160 D6
Woolgreaves Dr WF2 160 D7
Woolgreaves Garth WF2 160 D6
Wooller Rd BD12 94 D5
Woolley Colliery Rd S75 177 E2
Woolley Edge La WF4 177 E6
Woolley Hall Gdns WF4 178 A7
Woolley Low Moor La
WF4 159 D2
Woolley Park Gdns WF4 178 A7
Woolley View WF4 159 F2
Woollin Ave WF3 119 E6
Woollin Cres WF3 119 E6
Woolmarket [6] WF8 146 D8
Woolpack's Yd WF1 216 A2
Woolpack HX1 203 B3
Wool Pl HD8 175 B1
Woolrow La HD6 115 C6
Wool Row La HD8 174 C5
Wool Royd HD7 151 C2
Woolshops HX1 203 B3
Wool St WF16 117 D3
Woolstocks La S75 193 E3
Wootton St BD5 74 E4
Worcester Ave LS10 99 F4
Worcester Cl WF3 99 C1
Worcester Dr LS10 99 F4
Worcester Gr HD4 154 B3
Worcester Pl BD4 75 A4
Worden Gr BD7 73 E4
Wordsworth App WF8 125 D2
Wordsworth Ct LS26 101 C3
Wordsworth Dr
Knottingley WF11 126 B4
Rothwell LS26 101 C3
Wordsworth Gr WF3 121 F5
Wordsworth Way BD16 37 A5
Workhouse La
Elland HX4 134 D6
Halifax HX2 112 A7
World's End LS19 40 C7
World End View BD13 72 C7
Wormald Row LS2 211 C4
Wormalds Bldgs [3] HD1 154 A8
Wormald St
Dewsbury WF13 139 C8
Huddersfield HD5 154 F3
Liversedge WF15 117 C3
Wormalds View WF12 139 B6
Worrall Rd WF2 160 A4
Worrall St LS27 97 F3
Worsley Pl DN6 184 F2
Worsnop Bldgs [15] BD12 94 C4
Worsnop St BD12 94 D6
Worstead Rd BD22 51 F8
Worsted Cl HX1 202 B4
Worth Ave BD21 18 E1
Worth Bridge Rd BD21 35 E8
Worth Enterprise Pk
BD21 35 F7
Worthing Head Cl [2]
BD12 94 D3
Worthinghead Prim Sch
BD12 94 D3
Worthing Head Rd BD12 94 D3
Worthing St BD12 94 D3
Worthington Ct [10] BD8 74 C8
Worthington St BD8 74 C8
Worth Valley Prim Sch
BD22 35 A3
Worthville Cl BD21 35 C5
Worth Way BD21 35 C6
Wortley Bsns Pk LS12 209 B3
Wortley High Sch LS12 209 A2
Wortley Hts LS12 210 A2
Wortley La LS12 210 C2
Wortley Moor La LS12 209 B2
Wortley Moor Rd LS12 209 A3
Wortley Pk LS12 210 B2
Wortley Pl WF9 181 C7
Wortley Rd LS12 209 B3
Wortley St BD16 37 B3
Wortley Twrs LS12 210 B2
Worts Hill La HD3 151 B4
Worts Hill Side HD7 151 C4
Wrangbrook La WF9 183 D7
Wrangbrook Rd WF9 183 D8
Wrangthorn Ave LS6 205 C3
Wrangthorn Pl LS6 205 C3
Wrangthorn Terr LS6 205 C3
Wray's Bldgs WF4 141 A1
Wrelton Cl S71 179 B3
Wren Ave BD7 73 E5
Wrenbeck Ave LS21 11 B2
Wrenbeck Cl LS21 11 B2
Wrenbeck Dr LS21 11 B2
Wrenbury Ave LS16 41 D5
Wrenbury Cres LS16 41 E5
Wrenbury Gr LS16 41 E5
Wren Croft WF8 125 D3
Wren Dr LS27 98 D3
Wren Garth WF4 160 D5
Wren Hill WF17 118 A8
Wren Nest Rd HX6 132 A4
Wren St
[17] Haworth BD22 51 D7
Huddersfield HD1 153 D5
Keighley BD21 35 C8
Wrenthorpe La
Wakefield WF2 120 D1
Wakefield, Wrenthorpe
WF2 120 E1
Wrenthorpe Prim Sch
WF2 120 F2
Wrenthorpe Rd WF2 120 E2
Wrexhall Rd WF12 118 E2
Wrexham Rd LS29 9 D2
Wright Ave BD22 34 D3
Wright St
[9] Bacup OL13 106 A7
Oakworth BD22 34 D2
Sutton-in-C BD20 16 D5
Wrigley HX2 91 E6
Wrigley Ave BD4 75 B1
Wrigley Ct HD4 171 D5
Wrigley Hill HX2 91 E5
Wroe Cres BD12 94 C3
Wroe Pl BD12 94 C3
Wroe St WF13 117 F1
Wroe Terr BD12 94 C3
Wrose Ave
Bradford BD2 56 A5
Shipley BD18 55 D6
Wrose Brow Rd BD18 55 D8
Wrosecliffe Gr BD10 55 F8
Wrose Dr BD18 55 D6
Wrose Gr BD18 55 D6
Wrose Hill Pl BD2 55 D5
Wrose Mount BD18 55 E6
Wrose Rd
Bradford BD2 56 A6
Shipley BD18 55 E6
Wrose View
Baildon BD17 38 C3
Shipley BD18 55 D6
Wycliffe CE Prim Sch
BD18 55 A8
Wycliffe Cl LS13 57 D5
Wycliffe Dr LS17 43 D2
Wycliffe Gdns BD18 55 A8
Wycliffe Rd
Pudsey LS13 57 D5
Shipley BD18 55 A8
Wycliffe St WF5 140 D7
Wycoller Rd BD12 94 C4
Wycombe Gn BD4 75 E3
Wykebeck Ave LS9 80 D7
Wykebeck Cres LS9 80 D8
Wykebeck Gdns LS9 80 D8
Wykebeck Gr LS9 80 D8
Wykebeck Mount LS9 80 D8
Wykebeck Pl LS9 80 E8
Wykebeck Prim Sch LS9 61 D2
Wykebeck Rd LS9 80 D8
Wykebeck Sq LS9 80 D8
Wykebeck St LS9 80 D8
Wykebeck Terr LS9 80 D8
Wykebeck Valley Rd LS9 61 D2
Wykebeck View LS9 80 D8
Wyke Bottoms BD12 94 F4
Wyke Cres BD12 94 D2
Wyke La BD12 94 E3
Wykelea Cl BD12 94 D3
Wyke Manor Com Coll
BD12 94 C3
Wyke Manor Sch BD12 94 D3
Wyke Old La HD6 115 B7
Wyncliffe Ct [7] LS17 43 C2
Wyncliffe Gdns LS17 43 D2
Wyncroft Gr LS16 24 F2
Wyncroft Rise BD18 55 D5
Wyndham Ave BD2 55 F3
Wyndy Ridge BD13 72 C7
Wynford Ave LS16 42 B1
Wynford Dr WF9 183 A3
Wynford Gr LS16 42 B1
Wynford Mount LS16 42 A1
Wynford Rise LS16 42 B1
Wynford Terr LS16 42 A1
Wynford Way BD12 94 E7
Wynmore Ave LS16 24 F2
Wynmore Cres LS16 24 F2
Wynmore Dr
Bramhope LS16 24 F2
Huddersfield HD3 134 F1
Wynne St BD1 74 D8
Wynthorpe Rd WF4 141 B1
Wynyard Dr LS27 97 F4
Wyre Cl BD6 73 E1
Wytehill Chase HX3 93 A3
Wyther Dr LS5 59 A3
Wyther Gn LS5 59 A3
Wyther La LS5 58 F3
Wyther Lane Ind Est LS5 58 F3
Wyther Park Ave LS12 58 F1
Wyther Park Cl [1] LS12 58 F1
Wyther Park Cres LS12 58 F2
Wyther Park Gr LS12 58 F2
Wyther Park Hill LS12 58 F2
Wyther Park Mount LS12 58 F1
Wyther Park Pl LS12 58 F2
Wyther Park Rd LS12 58 F1
Wyther Park Sq LS12 58 E1
Wyther Park St LS12 58 F1
Wyther Park Terr LS12 58 F1
Wyther Park View LS12 58 F2
Wyvern Ave HD3 153 C6
Wyvern Cl
Batley WF17 118 C6
Bradford BD7 73 F5
Wyverne Rd HD7 152 E4
Wyvern Pl HX2 202 A4
Wyvern Terr HX2 202 A4
Wyvil Cres LS29 8 E5
Wyvil Rd LS29 8 E5

Y

Yarborough Croft HX3 93 A4
Yard Four [1] WF17 117 F8
Yardley Way BD12 94 E6
Yard No 4 WF16 117 F4
Yarn Ct BD19 115 B7
Yarn St LS10 215 B4
Yarwood Gr [2] BD7 73 E3
Yate La BD22 51 C3
Yates Flat BD18 55 D6
Yates La HD3 153 B4
Yeadon Airport Ind Est
LS19 23 F1
Yeadon Dr HX3 114 A4
Yeadon Ho BD20 16 C5
Yeadon Moor Rd
Yeadon LS19 40 E6
Yeadon LS19 41 A8
Yeadon Westfield Inf Sch
LS19 39 F6
Yeadon Westfield Jun Sch
LS19 39 F6
Ye Farre Cl [3] HD6 115 A4
Yeoman Ct [5] BD6 73 C2
Yewbank Cl LS29 8 A4
Yewbank Terr LS29 8 A4
Yew Ct [4] LS29 8 A4
Yewdall Rd LS13 57 E5
Yewdall Way BD10 56 C6
Yew Gr HD4 152 F3
Yew Green Ave HD4 153 E3
Yew Green Rd HD4 153 E3

Yew La LS25 . . . . **83** B6
Yew Pk HD6 . . . . **114** E5
Yews Gn BD13 . . . . **72** E3
Yews Hill Rd HD1, HD4 . . **153** E4
Yews Mount HD1 . . . . **153** F4
Yew St HD2 . . . . **136** A1
Yew Tree HD7 . . . . **169** F7
Yew Tree Ave BD8 . . . . **54** D1
Yew Tree Cl
  Low Bradley BD20 . . . . **4** C6
  Shipley BD18 . . . . **55** D6
Yew Tree Cres BD8 . . . . . . **54** E1
Yew Tree Ct
  3 Leeds LS17 . . . . **43** A3
  6 Liversedge WF15 . . . . . **117** A5
  Todmorden OL14 . . . . . . **129** A8
Yew Tree Dr LS26 . . . . **101** E6
Yew Tree Gr BD8 . . . . **54** E1
Yew Tree La
  Bradford BD13 . . . . **72** E8
  Holmfirth HD9 . . . . **188** C3
  Huddersfield HD4, HD7 . . **152** F3
  Leeds LS15 . . . . **81** E6
  Slaithwaite HD7 . . . . **169** F7
Yew Tree Rd
  Huddersfield HD2, HD3 . . . **135** B3
  Shepley HD8 . . . . **173** F1

Yew Trees HX3 . . . . **114** A4
Yew Trees Ave HX3 . . . . . . **93** A3
Yew Trees Croft HX2 . . . . . **90** C1
Yew Tree St WF1 . . . . **142** E4
Yew Tree Wlk WF11 . . . . . **126** E2
York Ave HD2 . . . . **136** A2
York Cl WF9 . . . . **183** A4
York Cres **5** BD16 . . . . **37** A2
York Ct WF17 . . . . **118** C6
York Dr
  Batley, Bank Foot WF17 . . . **118** D6
  Batley, Nunroyd WF16 . . . . **117** D6
York Gate LS21 . . . . **23** C4
York Gate Gdn LS16 . . . . . **42** D5
York Gr Batley WF17 . . . . . **118** D6
  4 Mirfield WF14 . . . . **137** F5
York Ho Bradford BD10 . . . . **56** C7
  4 Elland HX5 . . . . **134** F7
  2 Pudsey LS28 . . . . **57** D2
  7 Sowerby Bridge HX6 . . **112** C4
York Pl
  Ackworth M T WF7 . . . . . . **164** B7
  8 Cleckheaton BD19 . . . . **116** D8
  Leeds LS1 . . . . **211** B4
  15 Todmorden OL14 . . . . . **108** B5
  Wetherby LS22 . . . . **13** F6

York Rd
  Batley WF17 . . . . **118** C6
  Burley in W LS29 . . . . **9** F1
  Dewsbury WF12 . . . . **139** F8
  Leeds, Killingbeck LS14, LS9 **61** E1
  Leeds LS9 . . . . **212** C4
  Leeds, Whinmoor LS14,
    LS15 . . . . **62** C6
  5 Mirfield WF14 . . . . **137** F5
  Wetherby LS22 . . . . **14** D7
York Road Ind Est LS22 . . . **13** F6
Yorkshire County Cricket
  Club LS6 . . . . **205** A4
Yorkshire Cricket Sch
  LS6 . . . . **205** A4
Yorkshire Martyrs RC Coll
  BD4 . . . . **96** A8
Yorkshire Mill Village
  WF17 . . . . **118** D5
Yorkshire Produce Ctr
  LS9 . . . . **80** A6
Yorkshire Sculpture Pk★
  WF4 . . . . **176** E7
Yorkshire Television
Studios
  LS3 . . . . **205** B1
Yorkshire Way BD7 . . . . . . **74** B3

York St
  Bingley BD16 . . . . **37** A2
  Bradford BD8 . . . . **73** E7
  Brighouse HD6 . . . . **115** A1
  Castleford WF10 . . . . **124** E8
  Glusburn BD20 . . . . **16** D7
  Halifax HX1 . . . . **203** A2
  2 Hebden Bridge HX7 . . . **89** A2
  Hemsworth WF9 . . . . **181** E5
  Leeds LS9 . . . . **212** A3
  Normanton WF6 . . . . **122** F3
  Queensbury BD13 . . . . **72** E1
  Thurnscoe S63 . . . . **194** F1
  Todmorden OL14 . . . . **108** B6
Yorkstone HD4 . . . . **153** B3
York Terr HX3 . . . . **92** B1
York Villas WF6 . . . . **123** B2
Young's Ct LS25 . . . . **64** E6
Young St BD8 . . . . **73** F8
Young Street Ind Est BD8 . **73** F8
Yvette Ct **15** BD21 . . . . **35** B4

Z

Zakaria Muslim Girls High
  Sch WF17 . . . . **118** D4

Zealand St BD4 . . . . **75** D4
Zermatt Gr LS7 . . . . **60** C6
Zermatt Mount LS7 . . . . . . **60** C6
Zermatt St LS7 . . . . **204** A2
Zermatt Terr LS7 . . . . **204** A2
Zetland Pl LS8 . . . . **207** C3
Zetland St
  12 Huddersfield HD1 . . . . **154** B6
  Wakefield WF1 . . . . **216** B2
Zion Cl HD3 . . . . **135** B1

Addresses

Name and Address	Telephone	Page	Grid reference

Name and Address	Telephone	Page	Grid reference

Addresses

Name and Address	Telephone	Page	Grid reference

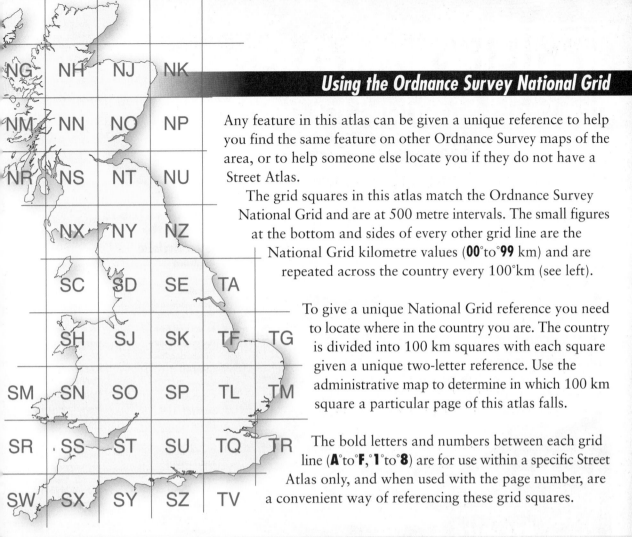

Using the Ordnance Survey National Grid

Any feature in this atlas can be given a unique reference to help you find the same feature on other Ordnance Survey maps of the area, or to help someone else locate you if they do not have a Street Atlas.

The grid squares in this atlas match the Ordnance Survey National Grid and are at 500 metre intervals. The small figures at the bottom and sides of every other grid line are the National Grid kilometre values (**00** to **99** km) and are repeated across the country every 100 km (see left).

To give a unique National Grid reference you need to locate where in the country you are. The country is divided into 100 km squares with each square given a unique two-letter reference. Use the administrative map to determine in which 100 km square a particular page of this atlas falls.

The bold letters and numbers between each grid line (**A** to **F**, **1** to **8**) are for use within a specific Street Atlas only, and when used with the page number, are a convenient way of referencing these grid squares.

Example   The railway bridge over DARLEY GREEN RD in grid square B1

Step 1: Identify the two-letter reference, in this example the page is in **SP**

Step 2: Identify the 1 km square in which the railway bridge falls. Use the figures in the southwest corner of this square: Eastings **17**, Northings **74**. This gives a unique reference: **SP 17 74**, accurate to 1 km.

Step 3: To give a more precise reference accurate to 100 m you need to estimate how many tenths along and how many tenths up this 1 km square the feature is (to help with this the 1 km square is divided into four 500 m squares). This makes the bridge about **8** tenths along and about **1** tenth up from the southwest corner.

This gives a unique reference: **SP 178 741**, accurate to 100 m.

Eastings (read from left to right along the bottom) come before Northings (read from bottom to top). If you have trouble remembering say to yourself Along the hall, THEN up the stairs !

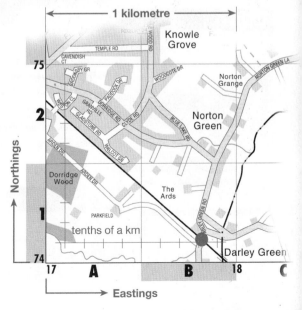

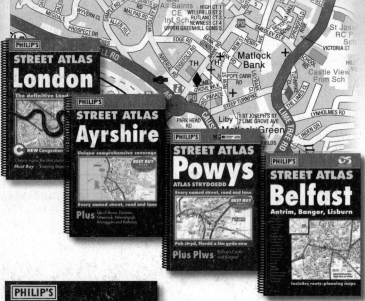